**RUGBY FOOTBALL UNION**

YEARBOOK 2009-10

EDITOR & STATISTICIAN
STEPHEN MCCORMACK

Telephone: 07711 287355
Fax: 0161 926 8900
E mail: stephen.mccormack@btinternet.com

Published in 2009 by Rugby Football Union

Copyright © Rugby Football Union

ISBN 978-1-904626-56-5

All rights reserved.
No part of this publication may be reproduced in any form or by any means – graphic, electronic or mechanical, including photocopying, recording, taping or information storage and retrieval systems – without the prior permission in writing of the publishers.

The Authors have asserted their right under the Copyright, Designs and Patent Act, 1998, to be identified as the authors of the work.

Rugby Football Union, Rugby Road, Twickenham, TW1 1DS
Tel: 0871 222 2120 Fax: 020 8892 9816
Email: communityrugbyinfo@rfu.com   Web: rfu.com

1

CONTENTS

Editorial	5
Acknowledgements	6
Review of the Season including Roll of Honour	8
RFU Information for Clubs	11
NCA Officers & Executive Members	20
Fixture Exchange Secretaries	21
RFUW	22
RFU Contacts List	23
Club Index	814
Guinness Premiership	33
The Championship	127
National Division One	221
National Division Two North	321
National Division Two South	369
Northern Division	417
Midlands Division	497
London & South East Division	581
South West Division	681
Premiership Players	771

FOREWORD

BY FRANCIS BARON
CHIEF EXECUTIVE

RUGBY FOOTBALL UNION

The RFU Yearbook for 2009/10 will be invaluable throughout the season and comes thoroughly recommended.

Whether you need directions to an opposition club, contact and website details or want to read a review of 2008/09 and how a team has fared it will provide all the details.

This publication has become a bible for the sport and I very much hope that it helps everyone to enjoy another great season of rugby.

powered by uSwitch.com

Earn £££s for your club.

Ever wanted that new kit but never had the cash? Couldn't get the funds for that new scrum machine? Here's your club's chance, thanks to the RFU's new partnership with uSwitch.com. For each club member, friend or colleague who switches to a cheaper home energy supplier, your club earns money. Brilliant.

IT'S UNLIMITED
For every switch made, your club earns commission.

EVERYONE WINS
Switching can save you hundreds of £££s. You save, your club gets paid.

IT'S SEASON-LONG
The quicker you start, the quicker your club starts earning.

IT'S NOT JUST ENERGY
There's car insurance, credit cards and loads more, so get switching.

No catch, just a switch.

To find out more, go to
www.uSwitch.com/rfu

conversion zone
TRY_CONVERT_REWARD

EDITORIAL

The global recession, the worst since the 1930s, has required a general tightening of belts in the sports world and rugby union is no exception, with corporate hospitality sales down in line with the rest of the sport and leisure industry. However, public sales remain resilient and with careful financial management and cost cutting, the RFU is endeavouring to maintain last year's level of funding for the community game.

Rugby union remains the fastest growing sport in the country and, with some 686,000 playing, England is the world's largest rugby playing nation. The aim in the Union's third Strategic Plan is for all clubs in full membership to have one new team BY 2016 and to continue to attract new players, both men and women to the game, building on the Go Play and Play On campaigns.

The success of the national team is always important in driving up numbers. England went into the Investec Challenge autumn internationals with Martin Johnson at the helm, having been appointed England Team Manager in the summer. A win against the Pacific Islanders was followed by disappointing losses to South Africa and New Zealand. However, by the start of the RBS 6 Nations much work had been done and England finished the tournament as top points scorers, with their best result since 2003 and second to Grand Slam winning Ireland.

In the IRB Junior World Championsips in June England U20s reached the final before going down to the Junior All Blacks after putting in some fine performances which augurs particularly well for the future.

As this publication went to press, England's bid to host the 2015 Rugby World Cup had been recommended by Rugby World Cup Ltd and ratification was awaited from the IRB Council. The RFU is confident that England could host the kind of tournament to benefit world rugby and leave a lasting legacy for the global game. The government considered it "an outstanding bid" and agreed a support package to bring the Rugby World Cup to the birthplace of the game.

The new eight-year agreement between the RFU and Premier Rugby is already delivering benefit and the Guinness Premiership season saw some great matches before capacity crowds. Leicester Tigers were the top side in England, winning the Premiership and then going on to win the Championship final at Twickenham, beating London Irish, and reaching the Heineken Cup Final before going down narrowly to Leinster in the final. It is the second time the Tigers have won the end of season playoffs with their first back in 2006/07 and they have now reached the final in five consecutive seasons, whilst in the Heineken Cup they reached their fifth final and were runners up for the third time.

Dean Richards and his Harlequins side finished second in the Premiership, their highest ever finish, and reached the quarter final of the Heineken Cup after topping their Pool with an impressive double of French giants Stade Francais.

With French clubs attracting English players like Jonny Wilkinson and Riki Flutey all who wish to be selected to play for England squads must ensure that their clubs across the channel sign up to release required in the Elite Player Squads agreement. So far the signs are that this will not be an issue for the squads selected from 1 July 2009.

In the National Leagues, Leeds Tykes again bounced straight back into the Premiership as they did two seasons ago and will be working to stay at the top level, while London Scottish, continue their climb up the league pyramid and are now in National One with a sixth promotion in nine seasons.

Barnes, Shelford, Hull and Westoe will be playing in the National leagues for the first time in their history, so good luck to them and everyone else running out onto pitches up and down the country and those organising the teams and clubs during the coming season.

Stephen McCormack

Editor

Stephen.mccormack@btinternet.com

ACKNOWLEDGEMENTS

It is that time of the year again when I say thank you as we finish the seventh edition of the RFU Yearbook. Technology plays a big part in our lives nowadays and no more than in the production of the RFU Yearbook. The team at ANIX, who host our database, have again saved us many hours and for this we are very grateful, can't even imagine now how we did it all in the past. Andy Rouse has been as supportive as ever on the technical side in delivering the expertise to help extract the data from the database and has done so with a smile on his face despite us trying his patience.

The most important thank you goes to all those who have supplied the information to us this season. As last year, detail for the Premiership to Level Six has been provided by clubs and all information from Levels 7-12 and non league has been taken from RugbyFirst (information taken from RugbyFirst as at 8th July). This year we have at the same time asked that all clubs continue to update their RugbyFirst detail to ensure that the RFU can keep in contact with the correct personnel over the season. We would like to thank everyone for their patience to make sure we got there in the end and got the information as near perfect as possible.

Remember that some of the information we have taken out of the RFU Yearbook in recent seasons is available on the RFU website www.rfu.com through the results section and the Community Club pages. Comprehensive coverage is available on the RFU website right down to Level Five with statistics on all matches including team line ups and scorers.

A big thank you goes to Jessica Mills at the RFU who has taken a hands on approach and been there for us at every turn, thanks also to Aileen Smith who is new to the RFU. We have worked very closely with Felicity Hogben, RugbyFirst Data Administrator at the RFU to make sure any detail sent to us by clubs has also been updated on RugbyFirst to ensure detail is as up to date and accurate as possible.

The most important thanks goes to all those who have supplied information to us over the last few months as we look to make sure the RFU Yearbook lands on your doorstep before the first competitive match of the 2009/10 season.

Specials thanks this year goes to Duncan Wood (Gloucester), Charlotte Wellington (Bromsgrove), Ben Mottram (Worcester Warriors), Steve Cohen (Old Patesians), Brian Norman (Hull Ionians) and John Shotton (Tynedale).

Just remember we are only as good as the information we are given so if your information is not correct it may because we were given the wrong information or in some cases no information at all. Please remember putting together a publication of this size in such a short time with strict deadlines means some errors will appear and for those we apologise. We would appreciate if you could let us know about them.

Stephen McCormack
Editor
Telephone: 07711 287355
Fax: 0161 926 8900
E mail: stephen.mccormack@btinternet.com

Thanks to the many people who have helped us put this 2009/10 Yearbook together.

Premiership - Bath: Kate Oram, Gloucester: Duncan Wood. Harlequins: Helen Bayes. Leeds Tykes: Phil Daly. Leicester Tigers: Gary Sherrard. London Irish: Patrick Lennon. London Wasps: Laura Brown. Newcastle: Mark Smith. Northampton: Chris Wearmouth. Sale: Dave Swanton. Saracens: Mike Hartnett. Worcester: Ben Mottram.

Championship - Bedford Blues: Andrew Irvine & Debra Rayer. Birmingham Solihull: Trish Smith & Jo Kilby. Bristol: Nicola Locke. Cornish Pirates: Phil Westren. Coventry: John Butler & Joanne Davies. Doncaster: Martin Haythorne & John Lowe. Exeter Chiefs: Carolinr Moore. London Welsh: Damian Dolan. Moseley: Dave Bettis. Nottingham: Annie Bowden. Plymouth Albion: Louise Kessell. Rotherham: Allan Mchale.

National One - Blackheath: Fran Cotton. Blaydon: Jim Huxley. Cambridge: Mal Schofield, Chris Fell. Cinderford: Rob Horgan. Esher: Dave Page. Launceston: Sarah Goodwin. London Scottish: Buffy Mair. Manchester: Jenni Deakin. Newbury: David Smith. Nuneaton: Maggie Mander & John Green. Otley: Ronnie Franks. Redruth: David Penberthy. Sedgley Park: Mark Mold. Stourbridge: Huw Jenkins. Tynedale: John Shotton. Wharfedale: Chris Ellwood.

National Two North - Bradford & Bingley: Nick Patterson. Broadstreet: Richard Skene & Charlie McGinty. Caldy: Roger Flahsman. Fylde: Allan Foster. Harrogate: Stuart Young & Bill Barrack. Huddersfield: Ian Cleave. Hull: Dominic Ward. Hull Ionians: Brian Norman. Kendal: John Hutton. Leicester Lions: Sophie Balfe. Loughborough Students: Alan Buzza. Macclesfield: Bev Roberts. Preston Grasshoppers: Ken Moore. Rugby Lions: Linda Dainty. Westoe: John Wells. Waterloo: Andrea Davies.

National Two South - Barking: Andy Pudney, Barnes: David Doonan. Bridgwater & Albion: Tony Pomeroy. Canterbury: David Haigh. Clifton: Brian Jordan. Dings Crusaders: Steve Lloyd. Ealing: Les O'Gorman & David Steene. Henley Hawks: Noel Armstead. Lydney: David Kent. Mounts Bay: Arthur Edwards. Richmond: Andrew Gordon & Andy Quigley. Rosslyn Park: Bob Jackson. Shelford: Tony Roberts. Southend: Neil Harding. Westcombe Park: John Ward Turner. Worthing: David Hinchliffe.

National Three North - Beverley: Dave Holmes. Birkenhead Park: Pete Greville. Chester: Mike Dangerfield. Cleckheaton: Ian Philip Johnson. Darlington Mowden Park: Kevin Robinson. Middlesbrough: Don Brydon. Morley: Dennis Elam. Penrith: . Rochdale: Tim Taylor. Rossendale: Alec Graham. Sheffield Tigers: Alick Bish. Stockport: Richard Hope & Gillian Stone. West Hartlepool: David Picken. West Park St Helens: Ian Worsley.

National Three Midlands - Ampthill: Warren Kay. Bedford Athletic: Jeremy Tyrell. Bromsgrove: Charlotte Wellington. Hereford: Guy Griffiths. Hinckley: John Skelton. Kenilworth: Willie Whitesmith. Kettering - Pater May. Longton: Richard Bailey. Luctonians: Huw Davies & Simon Green Price. Luton: Rob Thomas. Malvern: Bill Pomeroy & Peter Woods. Newport Salop: David Rees. Peterborough: Paul Gardner. South Leicester: Brian Kirkpatrick.

National Three London - Basingstoke: Sue Byatt. Bishop's Stortford: Julia Rontree. Bracknell: Peter Hickin. Diss; Sue English. Dorking: Mark Thornberry. Havant: Roger Boydell. Haywards Heath: James Melody. Hertford: Tony Edlin & John Atkinson. Jersey: Alison O'Haire & Bill Dempsey. North Walsham: Tony Marcantoni. Old Albanians: Robin Farrar. Portsmouth: Catherine Whapham. Sutton & Epsom: Nick Harris. Tring: Deric Newman.

National Three South West - Bournemouth: John Hardcastle. Barnstaple: Trevor Edwards. Chinnor: Bob Mitchell. Chippenham: Darren McMillan. Cleve: Roy Price. Coney Hill: . Exmouth: Chris Parks. Maidenhead: Geoff Cowan. Oxford Harlequins: Keith Latham. Old Patesians: Steve Cohen. Reading: Craig Hunter. Redingensians: George Nattriss. Taunton: Oli Massingham. Weston: Jack Russell.

REVIEW OF THE SEASON
BY ROB WILDMAN

Up until Pretoria it was a season of smiles for the Irish. The national team won a Grand Slam (the first since 1948), Leinster lifted the Heineken Cup and the A team gained a Churchill Cup success over England Saxons in steamy Denver. But the overriding memory of 2008-09 will be the unforgettable showdown between South Africa and the British and Irish Lions at Loftus Versfeld.

The Second Test had an abundance of great skills, a dramatic finish and a rich streak of rawness that makes spectators want more and more. The Irish played a major role in the Lions challenge but instead of a late drop goal to win the Slam, this time the Lions suffered a match-winning, series-deciding penalty goal through his late charge on Fourie du Preez. Morne Steyn supplied the kick to end South Africa's 12 years of hurt since losing the 1997 series.

For courage and commitment, the Lions had no peers in 2008-09. Somehow after the disappointment of the first two Tests, they picked themselves up to win the final game in Johannesburg. It was another memorable match to complete a series which highlighted the drawing power of the Lions.

The top-class rugby calendar has become an ultra professional programme yet the Lions showed that tradition remains firmly part of the sport. Three months after Wales and Ireland had gone toe-to-toe at the Millennium Stadium the same players were uniting to form a touring team that quashed any thoughts that it was on the road to extinction. For that collective resolve, British and Irish rugby supporters should applaud the management skills of Ian McGeechan and Gerald Davies plus the heroic contributions from a squad led by Paul O'Connell.

For McGeechan the Lions provided the high point of 2008-09 after his personal disappointment of leaving Wasps as Director of Rugby. The 2007-08 Guinness Premiership champions slipped to seventh and missed out on qualification for the Heineken Cup. The sport's gossip columns had pointed to a change some weeks before Wasps announced that New Zealander Tony Hanks was taking over.

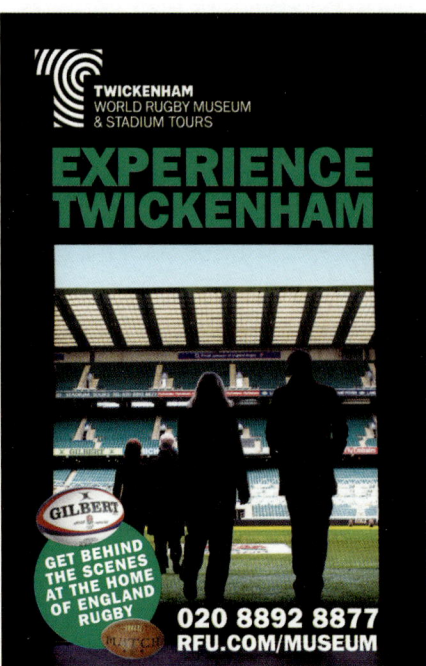

There was no doubting the most successful coach of 2008-09. That honour went to Ireland's Declan Kidney. Some questioned his wisdom in jumping from Munster, the 2008 Heineken Cup champions, to be in charge of a national squad that had failed to win a big prize under the careful guidance of Eddie O'Sullivan.

Kidney proved to be an adept master at squeezing the best out of the old guard plus bringing in younger blood led by Jamie Heaslip, Stephen Ferris and Luke Fitzgerald. The Six Nations fixtures also helped Ireland through early home games against France and England at Croke Park.

By the time Ireland arrived in Cardiff, the team had become consumed by the demands of a sporting-mad nation to win a first Grand Slam since the days of Jack Kyle. For ferocity, the match at the Millennium Stadium almost matched the Lions and the Boks in Pretoria. Who would have thought O'Connell and Mike Phillips would be on the same side some three months later?

Ireland finished a season of smiles via Leinster's Heineken Cup triumph over Leicester at Murrayfield and a success in the Churchill Cup where the A team beat the England Saxons, 49-22. Instead of watching the Lions, Kidney was directing operations in Denver to look at his future talent.

England had mounted a much closer challenge to Ireland

ROLL OF HONOUR
2008-09

Guinness Championship	Leicester Tigers
Guinness Premiership	Leicester Tigers
Heineken Cup	Leinster
European Challenge Cup	Northampton Saints
EDF Energy Cup	Cardiff
National One	Leeds Carnegie
National Two	Birmingham Solihull
National Three North	Nuneaton
National Three South	London Scottish
EDF Energy National Trophy	Moseley
North One	Westoe
London One	Shelford
Midlands One	Broadstreet
South West One	Clifton
National League Play offs	Hull
	Barnes
EDF Energy Intermediate Cup	Hartpury College
EDF Energy Senior Vase	Cullompton
EDF Energy Junior Vase	Brighton

in the RBS Six Nations Championship. Martin Johnson's team finished runners up after finishing the tournament by beating France (34-10) and Scotland (26-12). If they had found their stride earlier then they might have beaten Ireland in Dublin instead of losing 14-13.

Johnson finished his first season in charge having won five from 11 games. It was a difficult campaign not helped by the demanding schedule of the autumn in which England took on Australia, South Africa and New Zealand over three weeks. It was a harsh baptism for the World Cup-winning captain-turned-manager.

The Tri Nation teams each recorded a victory at Twickenham to leave England on the back foot. England clearly struggled and a glut of yellow cards, including four in the defeat by New Zealand, did not help.

By the end of the season, though, Johnson felt that his England team had turned the corner. Second place in the Six Nations was better than forecasted at the start of the campaign when Ireland, Wales and France looked superior.

Johnson pointed to the emergence of new faces in full-back Delon Armitage and hooker Dylan Hartley who were involved in every game. However, there were some eyebrows raised over the decision to pick Andy Goode ahead of Danny Cipriani for the games at the end of the season was one surprising call..

That said, Goode had finished England's top scorer in the Six Nations (60 points), having been recalled to the squad at the start of the championship. He emerged as the No 1 choice after injury to Toby Flood and finished by starting the two end-of-season games against Argentina which brought one win at Old Trafford and a defeat in the Andean city of Salta.

Meanwhile, Cipriani finished his season on the subs bench in Denver having lost out to Northampton's Stephen Myler (pictured below celebrating victory in the semi-final of the European Challenge Cup) for the starting berth against Ireland. At one stage, the Lions were keen to call up Cipriani for duty once Tom Shanklin had been ruled out only for a question mark over his fitness to block the move.

It was another ex-Leicester player who stole the coaching awards on the domestic front in England. Richard Cockerill started the season at Welford Road as assistant to South African Heyneke Meyer who had taken over following the dismissal of Marcelo Loffreda in May 2008.

Cockerill was elevated into the No 1 position once Meyer decided that he needed to return to South Africa for

domestic reasons. It was widely looked upon as a short-term decision, but the former England hooker promptly changed Leiester's fortunes by guiding his team from fifth position at Christmas to finish the season champions of the Guinness Premiership.

As Leicester found form in putting together a sequence of 12 wins in 13 games to collect the Premiership prize, there were some notable declines in the Premiership. Wasps never clambered out of the bottom half while Gloucester, top at the end of January, had slipped to sixth by May.

The fall off in form brought a shake up in the coaching staff and the end of Dean Ryan's tenure in favour of assistant Bryan Redpath. The turnover of players highlighted the unstable nature of Kingsholm. Olly Barkley returned to Bath and was followed to the exit door by other notable names including Ryan Lamb, Iain Balshaw, Anthony Allen and Carlos Nieto.

For once, the relegation issue in the Premiership was settled early after Bristol had fallen seven points behind Newcastle, the 11th-placed team, by the end of January. Again, failure brought a change in coaching staff, Richard Hill taking the blame for the decline of a team who had finished third in 2006-07 following promotion from National League One.

Leeds know all about a yo-yo existence between the Premiership and National League One. By outstaying Exeter, the Headingley club gained a third chance in the top flight since 2001.

Exeter and Bristol will clash in a new 12-team Championship that starts in September 2009. The ramifications of the new competition meant four teams had to be relegated from the existing National League One as part of a revamp for the whole competitive system.

A new play-off system will be launched next April in an attempt to increase competition and interest.
If the teams find half the resolve and energy of the Lions then the new competition will serve English rugby well

The Third RFU Strategic Plan 2008/09 - 2015/16

The Rugby Football Union's third Strategic Plan for 2008/09 - 2015/16 sets out the strategic objectives and policies for the administration and development of the game in England.
It is being made available on rfu.com as a downloadable pdf and the RFU will be holding a series of roadshows as well as producing an Executive Summary. All Council members have published hard copies of the full Strategic Plan.

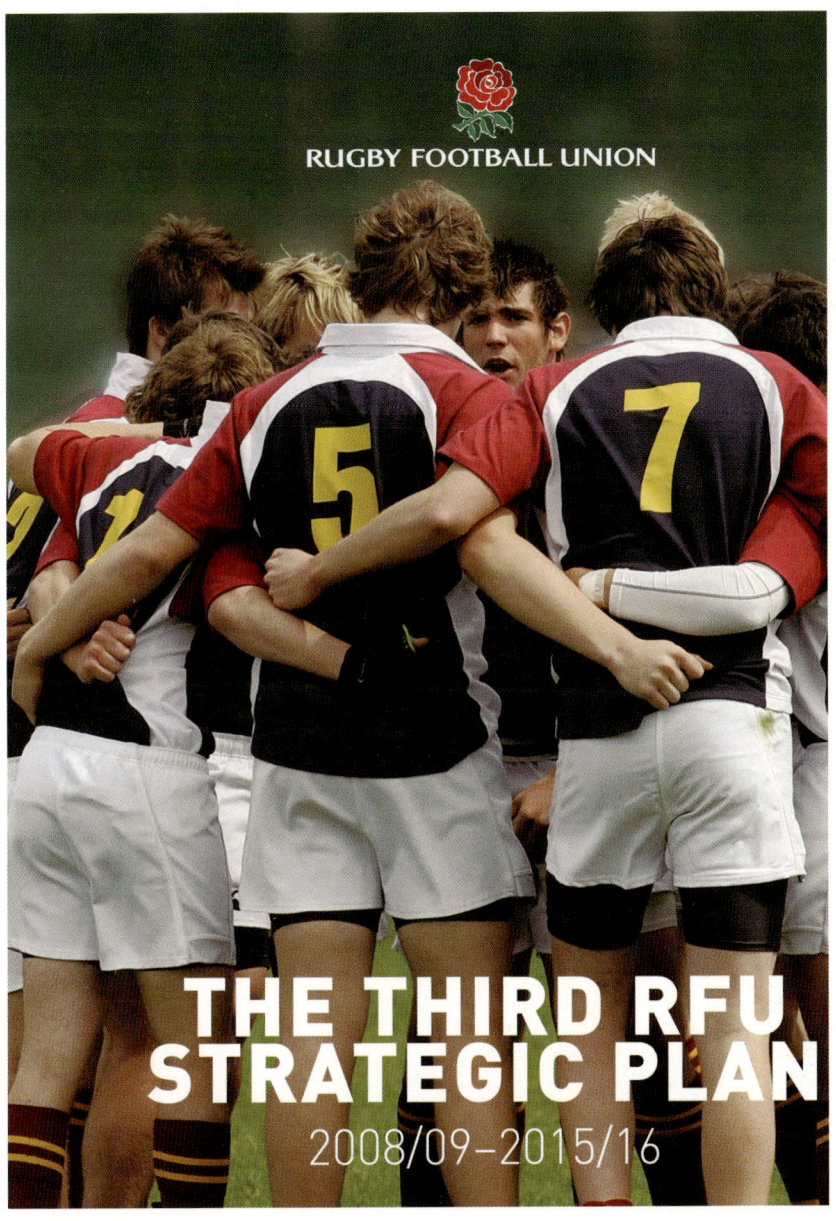

THIS IS RUGBY - Rugby Core Values

Rugby is a game for all shapes and sizes. As a result, a complete cross section of the community is involved in rugby union in England, with over $2^{1/4}$ million players, 1,900 rugby clubs, 3,100 schools, 37,000 referees, 57,000 coaches and some 40,000 volunteers involved.

All share a common purpose, and core values, which are captured here by the Rugby Football Union, the governing body of the sport in England, based on an extensive dialogue with the whole game.

Teamwork   Discipline   Respect   Sportsmanship   Enjoyment

Teamwork
Teamwork is essential to our sport.
- We play selflessly: working for the team, not for ourselves alone, both on and off the field.
- We speak out if our team or sport is threatened by inappropriate words or actions.
- We take pride in our team, rely on one another and understand that each player has a part to play.
- We welcome all new team members and include all because working as a team enriches our lives.

Discipline
Strong discipline underpins our sport.
- We ensure that our sport is one of controlled physical endeavour and that we are honest and fair.
- We obey the 'Laws of the Game' which ensure an inclusive and exciting global game.
- We support our disciplinary system, which protects our sport and upholds its values.
- We observe the sport's Laws and regulations and report serious breaches.

Respect
Respect forms the basis of our sport.
- We hold in high esteem our sport, its values and traditions and earn the respect of others by the way we behave.
- We respect our match officials and accept their decisions.
- We respect opposition players and supporters.
- We value our coaches and those who run our clubs and treat clubhouses with consideration.

Sportsmanship
Sportsmanship is the foundation rugby union is built upon
- We uphold the rugby tradition of camaraderie with team mates and opposition.
- We observe fair play both on and off the pitch and are generous in victory and dignified in defeat.
- We play to win but not at all costs and recognise both endeavour and achievement.
- We ensure that the wellbeing and development of individual players is central to all rugby activity.

Enjoyment
Enjoyment is the reason we play and support rugby union.
- We encourage players to enjoy training and playing.
- We use our sport to adopt a healthy lifestyle and build life skills.
- We safeguard our young players and help them have fun.
- We enjoy being part of a team and part of the rugby family because it enhances confidence and self esteem.

Helplines for clubs

The RFU has two helplines set up for clubs who may need financial or legal advice.

The Club Financial Support line is available to clubs who may be experiencing financial pressures and provides access to a network of volunteers with experience of club finances. Open Monday - Friday from 9a.m. to 7p.m. on 01782 610315, the line is managed by Malcolm Duncan, the former Council member for Staffordshire who has significant experience in club finances.

The RFU Legal Helpline (0844 5618177) provides immediate access to free independent legal advice on all aspects of rugby operations and management and is open Monday - Friday (excluding Bank Holidays) from 9a.m. to 7p.m.

Make the Most of RugbyFirst

This season sees the biggest upgrade of RugbyFirst, the RFU's whole game online administration system, since its launch in October 2006, with changes to both the database and applications helping to support rugby in England at all levels.

A total database rebuild improves efficiency and the Criminal Records Bureau (CRB) and Welfare administration system has been redesigned. A new administration system for all RFU employees enables them to give more support at grass roots level and there is now the ability to link clubs and universities to more than one CB. Email logging has been improved and an awards section added to display coaching, refereeing, first aid or volunteering awards attained.
RugbyFirst began as a tool for competitions and player registrations. Clubs can now register their own players, list their officers and use the team builder facility to select players and contact them via email. More graphics mean that clubs can give their sites an individual look, with headers, rolling banners and pictures.
Says Project Manager Paul Chorley, "Through RugbyFirst, clubs can have their own distinctive site, easily check which members have coaching or refereeing qualifications and, importantly, easily see who is CRB cleared. All clubs are on the system and that is linked to such important requirements as funding and international ticket allocation.
"Feedback suggests that satisfaction levels are at an all time high, which is pleasing. The RFU is very much committed to this facility and it does have a high priority, with both the RFU Chief Executive and Finance Director on the 20-member RugbyFirst Project Board."
If you have any questions please contact The RugbyFirst Helpdesk at rugbyfirstsupport@therfu.com between 11 am and 7.30pm on Monday, Wednesday, Friday & Saturday
RugbyFirst home page   http://www.rfu.com/clubs

Grand Draw
Help Your Club to Cash In!

 The RFU Grand Draw can help your club or school raise valuable cash towards new kit, the club tour or to make the clubhouse warmer. Last year's top prize was £10,000 with another 46 great prizes for individuals as well as two special club draws. We expect the 2009/10 prize lists to be just as exciting. In 2008/9 680 clubs and schools raised almost £400,000 of which they received 90 per cent as a donation to their funds.
Packs for the Grand Draw will be issued during October. For further information contact grand.draw@therfu.com or call 0560 169 2548.

President's XV Recognition Awards

Since launching in 2006, the President's XV Recognition Awards have distributed over £30,000 of prize money to clubs to reward innovation and excellence in the grassroots game. Newly inaugurated RFU President, John Owen, will launch this season's awards in November, with brand new categories that clubs across the country can nominate themselves for; from fundraising and developing new coaches and referees to reaching out to the local community. For more information on the programme, categories and how to apply, visit www.rfu.com/volunteer

vRUGBY

vRugby aims to creat new opportunities for young people aged 16-25 to volunteer in rugby union. Teams of young volunteers will take part in short-term 'bite size projects' that give them the opportunity to get involved at their local rugby clubs using one of four themes:

vRugbyFun - plan, organise and deliver a fun rugby event for others to take part in healthy exercise and attract people to your club

vRugbyLife - use rugby's ethos to run a session to educate young people about healthy lifestyles and raise your profile within the local area

vRugbyCash - raise money for a project of your choice to benefit your rugby club

vRugbyForce - make improvements to your clubs facilities with a mini makeover

Use vRugby to kick-start your club project with the help of young people who are either existing club members or completely new to your club.

For more information go to www.rfu.com/vRugby

Leadership Academy

The RFU's Leadership Academy is a very successful programme to develop rugby leaders of the future, with a personalised training programme for all delegates to help them develop the skills and confidence needed to lead rugby in the 21st century.

Individuals working voluntarily at the grassroots level of the game and identified as potential leaders are nominated by clubs, CBs, Referee Societies and other organisations affiliated to the RFU.
Full details of the programme can be found at www.rfu.com/clubs/leaders

Volunteers Week 2010

This annual celebration of volunteering across the UK will run from 1 - 7 June 2010. It is an excellent platform for rugby to reward, encourage and recruit volunteers. Please visit www.volunteersweek.org.uk for more information.

THE RFU INJURED PLAYERS FOUNDATION

Serious injuries are very rare in rugby union* but they are devastating for players and their families.

The Rugby Football Union has, with trustees from the former rugby charity SPIRE, set up the RFU Injured Players Foundation to help those catastrophically injured both at the time of their injury and into the future.

The Foundation helps and supports players from all levels of the game who suffer injuries which may cause permanent and severe disability.

There are currently 132 former players who need ongoing help and support, their injuries stretching back to the 1960s. The Injured Players Foundation is there for them and for anyone who suffers a catastrophic injury in the future.

In addition to supporting the injured players after the event, the Foundation is working with experts in the field and the other Unions to ensure that wherever possible these injuries are prevented; that where injuries occur they have appropriate immediate injury management; and that the necessary specialist trauma care can be readily accessed.

Says 52-year-old solicitor Peter Chadwick, seriously injured playing for his local team at the age of 25 and a wheelchair user ever since, "I've had help from SPIRE over the years, with equipment and adaptations, but what I really want to know is that when I am 72 and struggling there will be financial support and help there. This new RFU Injured Players Foundation can only be good news. We need to minimise injuries but will always need to help those few who are seriously injured playing rugby."

Visit www.rfuipf.org.uk
to discover more and see how you can help.

*The risk of suffering a catastrophic injury while playing rugby in England is 0.8 per 100,000 people per annum and lower than other sports globally in the following order: American football (1.0 person per 100,000 people per annum), swimming (1.8), rugby league (2.0), skiing (2.5), ice hockey (4.0), gymnastics (8.2), and horse riding (29.7) - Dr Colin Fuller, Centre for Sports Medicine, University of Nottingham: 'Catastrophic Injuries in Rugby Union: An assessment of risk' (July 2007)

The Welfare of Young People in Rugby Union

The RFU's safeguarding team have a range of resources, courses and guidance to help clubs ensure they provide a safe, child-friendly environment. For more information on all aspects of safeguarding young people visit the RUSafe website; it provides help for players, parents, coaches, welfare officers and club managers alike, visit http://clubs.rfu.com/Clubs/portals/RUSafe/

The team are responsible for the processing of ISA and CRB forms on behalf of all rugby clubs, helping to ensure that appropriate adults are involved with young players. Guidance on these background checks can also be found on the above site. The RFU continues to do what is necessary to ensure the suitability of those working with young people and to safeguard children involved in rugby union working with the appropriate statutory agencies.

Equity in Rugby Union

The RFU's equity team, based in the Community Rugby Department work across all regions in England delivering more rugby opportunities for those currently under represented in the game, these include:

- Women and girls (in conjunction with the RFUW)
- People from Black and Ethnic Minority groups
- People with disabilities
- People from socially deprived backgrounds
  (e.g. inner city areas, low-income groups, those in the criminal justice system, etc)

Disability rugby in particular is a growing area for playing, coaching, refereeing and volunteering) the RUAble website has more information. The RFU already supports GB Wheelchair Rugby and England Deaf Rugby and is developing structures for other forms of disability to get involved - http://clubs.rfu.com/Clubs/portals/RUAble/

Club Educational Links

The RFU provide a supportive and accredited club structure with strong joint programmes between the School Sports Partnership and local club networks. Templates and guidance for schools, colleges and universities and partner clubs to discuss and formulate their links are available from www.rfu.com

Clubs and Schools working together

There are now 429 School Sport Partnerships, which includes 10,000 schools, offering rugby to their pupils. These partnerships are working with 472 Mini and Youth Seal of Approval accredited clubs to provide playing and leadership opportunities for young people. The links between schools and clubs have been formalised through over 950 written agreements and there have been some fantastic examples of clubs and schools working together.

North Dorset RFC has strong links with local schools and is a partner to other sports clubs in the community. They have 'Link Agreements' with five local schools, three secondary and two primary schools, with 'Link Students' appointed. Representatives of the club attend 'Sports Award Days' and present prizes provided by the club supporting and promoting rugby across all age groups, boys and girls. The club hosts referee courses for the teachers and supplies coaches for out of school hours learning sessions. Grounds, facilities and referees are provided for inter school matches and the club hosts five major competitions and festivals for local schools.

They have helped older students to develop their skills and achieve sports related qualifications. They also work with local youth groups, hold Open Days and work with the Youth Development Leaders, particularly with 'Special Needs' groups.

Links like these are replicated across the country and for more information go to www.rfu.com or e-mail community@therfu.com

Seal of Approval

What is Seal of Approval?
Community Rugby introduced the Mini and Youth Seal of Approval accreditation programme in 2002 It recognises the effort and achievement of clubs that reach, maintain and improve on the required Seal of Approval standard and show they are committed to the provision of a quality rugby union experience for their young players.
Community Rugby has worked with Sport England to integrate the Mini and Youth Seal of Approval accreditation with the Sport England Clubmark scheme and any club awarded the Community Rugby Mini and Youth Seal of Approval will also have achieved Clubmark accreditation.
In 2009 Whole Club Seal of Approval was introduced to build on the success of the Mini and Youth version to ensure that good practice is spread throughout the whole club.

The award
The Seal of Approval and the Sport England Clubmark accreditation scheme are based upon a three year rolling award system in which a club will be assessed on its continuing ability to provide a safe and effective club environment.

Further information
All clubs that have, or are planning to have, a mini and youth section should be working towards Mini and Youth Seal of Approval accreditation by 2011. If you are interested in Whole Club Seal of Approval or if you believe your club has the desire to provide a quality assured rugby experience for its young players, please contact your local Rugby Development Officer or go to www.rfu.com for more details

Rugby Ready / Goodyear Partnership

IRB Rugby Ready, developed by the International Rugby Board and run in England by the RFU, under the banner of Start Coaching Rugby Ready, in association with Goodyear and Sport England, supports coaches, referees and players by providing best practice models for physical conditioning, technique, injury prevention and injury management.

The Start Coaching Rugby Ready programme consists of a three-hour workshop and online resource covering specific technical aspects of the game, injury prevention and injury management and is aimed at all those responsible for the well being of rugby players, no matter what their age or experience.

The initiative was developed by the IRB in consultation with RFU Coach Development Manager, Will Feebery.

Since 1st September 2008 everyone applying for an RFU Level One coaching award has had to complete an online Rugby Ready assessment. From September 2009 attendance at a Rugby Ready course will be a condition of entry on to a Level One course. This is to ensure that all coaches are fully aware of the safety implications of coaching the game.

For further information go to www.rfu.com/coach

Coach Licensing

The Governments UK Coaching Framework calls on each National Governing Body (NGB) to 'Set out and implement the steps needed to establish coaching as a professionally regulated vocation, recognising volunteer, paid part-time and paid full-time roles. As a first step NGBs might conduct a feasibility study on the licensing and registration of coaches'.

The RFU's Coach Licensing Scheme pilot is up and running and being well received within the Midlands East region, thanks to the support and cooperation of clubs and the three Constituent Bodies, (Notts, Lincs & Derbys, Leicestershire and East Midlands) within the region.

This scheme is underpinned by a range of Continuous Professional Development courses, further detail of which can be found following.

To find out further details on Coach Licensing go to rfu.com/coach

Continuous Professional Development Courses for Coaches

Fourteen new Continuous Personal Development [CPD] courses for coaches have been created this year; these programmes have been designed to support coaches within their specific coaching roles, e.g. Ruck/Maul for coaches of Mini/Midi players or Defence Play for coaches of adult players.

The courses are designed to run for $2^{1/2}$ hours and primarily delivered at local level within clubs, or clusters of clubs/schools by trained Coach Developers. Club Coaching coordinators are being provided with the support to identify which courses are most suitable for their coaches.

For more information on these courses please go to rfu.com/coach

RFU Referee Department Awards

Referees can undertake the **Entry Level Referee Award (ELRA)**, a two stage introductory award for new or inexperienced referees. The course comprises significant practical activity and covers areas such as game management, communication, materiality and contextual judgement. The mini midi course is now available on a CD Rom and can be undertaken as part of the ELRA.

Referees may also attend **Referee Education Evenings (REEs)**, at which they will undertake modules of the **Continuous Referee Development Award (CRDA)**, including Scrum, Tackle/Ruck and Understanding the Game. The REEs last approximately 2 hours and are designed to equip referees with skills in specific areas of the game.

For further information on Referee Department Awards, please visit www.rfu.com/referee

Rugby Union Proficiency Awards
For Clubs, Schools, Colleges and Universities

The Rugby Union Proficiency Awards are an important tool to help players, teachers and coaches assess rugby union skills. They are designed to be an enjoyable method by which players can identify their strong skills and the skills that they need to develop; they can also assess their fitness for rugby union. Each Award contains a series of tests suitable for each age banding in the game from U7 to adult. Certificates are available for each award at bronze, silver and gold level.
The pack is supported by a DVD.

For further details and to find out where to purchase a pack go to www.rfu.com

FIXTURE EXCHANGE SECRETARIES 2009-10

Bath & District Combination
Gerry Wheeler, 28 Priddy Close, Frome, Somerset, BA11 2XZ
Tel: 01373 469688 (H) 07813 996627 (M)
Email: geraldwheeler@btinternet.com

Bristol & District Combination
Alan Stanton   Email: alan@bristolcombination.co.uk
07980 156441 (M) (6.30pm-9pm midweek, Sat 10.30am-2pm, not available Sundays)
www.bristolcombination.co.uk

Cornwall
M Gee, Foxglove Cottage, 70 Halsetown, St Ives, Cornwall, TR36 3LZ   Tel/fax: 01736 797777
07713 325354 (M)   Email: secretary@swrugby.co.uk
Website: www.cornwall-rfu.org.uk

Cumbria
W G Anderson, 18 Hensingham Road, Whitehaven, Cumbria, CA28 8PS
Tel: 01946 692844 (H) 07840 671816 (M)

Devon
Paul Harris, 15 Blagdon Close, Crediton, Devon, EX17 1EL
Tel: 07545 994498 (M)
Email: paul@blagdon15.eclipse.co.uk

Dorset and Wiltshire
Mr & Mrs D Foyle, 12 Powys Close, Dorchester, Dorset, DT1 2RG   Tel: 01305 266144 (H)
Email: dickmave@dfoyle.fsnet.co.uk

East Midlands (plus National Leagues)
Mrs L May, 107 Pytchley Road, Kettering, Northants, NN15 6NA
Tel: 01536 310770 (H) Tue-Fri 6-10pm, Sat 8.30am-11.30am

Hampshire
A Mott, Little Chilla, New Road, Landford, Salisbury, Wiltshire SP5 2AZ   Tel: 08456 443422 (H)
Email: andrew@hantsfix.info
Website: www.hantsfix.info

Hertfordshire
P J Braddock, 43 Winstre Road, Borehamwood, Herts, WD6 5DR   Tel: 020 8207 6373 (H/B/F)
Email: fixture.exchange@talk21.com

Kent
R Sykes, 232 Reculver Road, Belting, Herne Bay, Kent, CT6 6QB   Tel: 01227 374246.   Evenings only (From 7.30pm onwards)
Email: bobchris@hotmail.com

Manchester and District
Vic Thomas, 5 Portree Close, off Cambell Road, Winton, Eccles, Manchester, M30 8LX
Tel: 0161 788 7540 (H)   07515 956811 (M)
Email: vicshe@supanet.com
Anne Clarke
Tel: 01942 207771 (H) contact from 6pm on Thursdays until the end of the week;   07920 161540 (M)

Merseyside and District
Mr Neil Speakes, 93 Talbot Street, Whitchurch, Shropshire, SY13 1PJ   Tel: 01948 665573 (H)
Email: neilspeakes@btinternet.com

Middlesex
P J Braddock, 43 Winstre Road, Borehamwood, Herts, WD6 5DR   Tel: 020 8207 6373 (H/B/F)
Email: fixture.exchange@talk21.com

The Midlands (National & Divisional Leagues)
The Fixtures Pool at www.fixturespool.com
Men on Saturdays,
women, juniors and minis on Sundays. 24/7 service
Roger & Karyl Rees, 2 Wain Close, Alcester, Warwickshire B49 6LA
Telephone back-up service on 01789 400082 Mon-Sat 9am-9pm. Registered clubs only

North East
D A Thompson, 12 Aldsworth Close, Springwell, Gateshead, Tyne & Wear, NE9 7PG
Tel: 0191 416 9839 (H)   07778 809125 (M)
Email: dat_rugby@hotmail.com

North Gloucestershire
Derek Howell, 40 Fox Elms Road, Gloucester, GL4 0BS
Tel: 01452 410585   Email: howzatglos@hotmail.com

Plymouth and District Combination
Sam Smale, 1 Colwill Walk, Mainstone, Plymouth, Devon PL6 8XF   Tel: 01752 219521

Sussex
Ken Nichols, 189 St Helens Road, Hastings, East Sussex, TN34 2EA   Tel: 01424 423614 (H)
07903 322782 (M)   Email: kenskars@freezone.co.uk

Yorkshire
S Corns, 83 Chapel Street, Wath-upon-Dearne, Rotherham, S63 7RJ   Tel: 01709 874911 (H)
07889 370839 (M)   Email: s.corns@barnsley.org

NATIONAL CLUBS ASSOCIATION

www.ncarugby.org

Officers and Executive Committee for 2009-10

Chairman and RFU Representative
Norman Robertson
3 Crabtree Close
Hagley
Stourbridge
West Midlands DY9 0PU
Tel: (H) 01562 886011
Mobile: 07802 226767
email njr90@hotmail.com

Secretary
Ivor Horscroft
The Firs
South Tehidy
Camborne
Cornwall TR14 0HU
Tel 01209 612244
Mobile 07850 720406
Fax 0870 0510711
email ivor@silver.demon.co.uk

Treasurer
Peter Thompson
6 Ryecroft, Pedmore
Stourbridge, West Mids. DY9 9EH
Tel (H) 01384 373800
Fax: (H) 01384 443800
Tel: (B) 0121 428 4000
Fax: (B) 0121 428 3000
Fax: (B) 0121 428 3991 (Conf)
Mobile: 07836 562221
email: (H)
petera.thompson@blueyonder.co.uk
(B) ceo@thompsonandbryan.com

EXECUTIVE COMMITTEE

North

Michael Harrison
Old Hall Farm
Threshfield
Skipton
North Yorkshire BD23 5Pl
Tel: 01756 7522777
Fax: 01756 7522777
email: chrisharri@msn.com

Bill Barrack
15 Eastgate Close
Bramhope
Leeds
Yorkshire LS16 9AR
Tel: (H) 0113 284254
Mobile: 07887 824020
email: bill.barrack@talktalk.net

Midlands

Maggie Mander-Howells
Homeland, Weddington Road
Caldecoate, Nuneaton
Warwickshire CV10 0TS
Tel: (H) 02476 381803
Fax: 02476 383925
Mobile: 07808 734054
email: margaret.mander@btopenworld.com

Mal Malik
105, Bilton Road
Rugby
Warwickshire CV22 7AS
Tel: 01788 560067
Fax: 01788 33488
Mobile 07836 710530
email: mal@malmalik.com

London & South East

Dave Page
10 Oldbury Close
Frimley
Surrey GU16 6XT
Mobile: 07973 488142
email: davidpage532@btinternet.com

Robin Taylor
24 Pinchbeck Road
Green Street Green
Orpington, Kent BR6 6DR
Tel 01689 855052
Mobile 07774 212029
Fax 01689 600717
email rit@waitrose.com

South West

Major Tony Randell
Langdon,
Werrington,
Launceston,
Cornwall PL15 8NK
Tel: 01566 785407
email: ranfellangdon@aol.com

Mr. Tony Pomeroy
Hafod-y-Gan, Newton Road
North Petherton, Somerset TA6 6SN
Tel: 01278 662181
Fax: 01278 662178
Mobile: 07976 518773
email: pomeroyhome@aol.com

The forthcoming season is a crucial year for England Women, with their defence of the RBS 6 Nations but also the 2010 IRB Women's Rugby World Cup.

Women's rugby ultimate tournament will be staged in London in August and September and England, runners-up in 2006, will this year be hoping to go one better and lay their hand on world rugby's ultimate prize.

They head into the new season in fine form having lifted the RBS 6 Nations crown for an impressive fourth time, something that has never been achieved before in women's rugby. Only Wales stood in their way of securing the grand slam beating England 16-15 in the dying minutes of the match. England were also crowned the IRB Women's World Cup 7s Plate Champions in March, seeing off Canada 12-0 in the final.

England's World Cup campaign builds some serious momentum in November when they take on reigning World Champions New Zealand in three tests. Most noticeably they'll be taking on the mighty Black Ferns in an Investec Challenge Double Header, alongside England men and the All Blacks, at Twickenham Stadium on November 21st.

England Head Coach Gary Street said: "Winning the Six Nations for a fourth time was a marvellous achievement, but I'm now focusing on the year ahead and the Rugby World Cup. We won the Six Nations because the championship was built on team effort and morale. We have a really close knit management and coaching team, and that rubs off on our playing squad. Graham Smith (assistant coach) has been a real force in our togetherness and teamwork and certainly a crucial element to our latest success. We certainly hope that success can be carried forward into 2010."

RFU CONTACTS

(0871 Numbers - Calls to this number are charged at 10 pence per minute from a BT landline. Calls from mobile and other networks may vary.)

Chief Executive's Office
Francis Baron OBE	Chief Executive	020 8831 6682
Claudia Brightman	PA to the Chief Executive	020 8831 6551
Jo Walkley	(Maternity Cover for PA to the Chief Executive)	020 8831 6551
Sam Dimmock	Secretarial Assistant	020 8831 6532
		Fax 020 8892 6993

Legal - RFU Secretary
Karena Vleck	Company Secretary & Legal Officer	020 8831 6703
Karen Neale	Legal Officer	020 8831 6648
Stephanie Cameron	PA to Company Sec. & Legal Officer	020 8831 6506
		Fax 020 8891 3814

Discipline
Bruce Reece-Russel	Disciplinary Manager	020 8831 6667
Brenda Parkinson	Assistant to Disciplinary Manager	020 8831 6702
Liam McTiernan	Technical Assistant	020 8831 6547
		Fax 020 8892 9816

Council Services
Maureen Brewer	Matches Administrator	020 8831 6679
Sandie Le Good	Meetings Administrator	020 8831 6573
Amy Andreas	Administrative Assistant (on Maternity Leave)	020 8831 6715

Business Operations
Paul Vaughan	Business Operations Director	020 8831 6603
Caroline Quinney	PA to Business Operations Director	020 8831 6615
Neil Armit	Business Development Manager	020 8831 6737
Lawson Hill	Corporate Sales Manager	020 8831 8743
	Undergraduate Marketing Executive	020 8831 6707
Carol Griffin	General Manager – ERSC	020 8831 6567
Vicky Cheevers	Marketing & Communications Mgr	020 8831 6738

Sponsorship
Jenny Simms	Sponsorship Account Director	020 8831 6623
Sarah Lemerle	Sponsorship Account Manager	020 8831 6526
Rob Porteous	Sponsorship Account Manager	020 8831 6729
Georgie Simmons	Sponsorship Account Executive	020 8831 6686
		Fax 020 8891 6993

Retail Operations
Andy Ward	Head of Retail	020 8831 6507
Jane Barron	Licensing & Marketing Manager	020 8831 6685
Emma Eggs	Buying & Product Development Executive	020 8831 6617
Jane Cowell	Retail & Licensing Admin Assistant	020 8831 7445
		Fax 020 8891 3254

The Rugby Store
RFU Direct		0871 2222003
South Stand Store		020 8831 6733
York Street Store	17 -19 York Street, Twickenham	020 8892 9250
Wendy Pocock	Retail Operations Manager	020 8831 6600

The Museum Of Rugby
Michael Rowe	Museum Curator	020 8892 8877
Lindsay Simmons	Tours Manager	020 8892 8877
Anna Renton	Collections Officer	020 8892 8877
Phil McGowan	Museum Officer	020 8892 8877
Amy Rolph	Tours Officer	020 8838 8877

RFU CONTACTS

(0871 Numbers - Calls to this number are charged at 10 pence per minute from a BT landline. Calls from mobile and other networks may vary.)

Communications

Peter Thomas	Corporate Communications and Public Affairs Director	020 8831 6791/ 07803 204543
Richard Prescott	England Teams Media Director	020 8831 6513/ 07711 259179
Patricia Mowbray	Corporate Publications Manager	020 8831 6514
Dave Barton	National Media Manager	07736 517 610
Nicki Drinkwater	Media Manager	020 8831 6626/ 07764 660187
Jessica Chambers	Press Officer	020 8831 6563/ 07702 779 462
Fraser Cullen	Community Relations Manager	020 8831 6533 07730 814 164
Simon Mills	Community Rugby Media Manager	07702 661 214/ 020 8831 6760
Paul Bolton	Midlands Regional Press Officer	07966 102 495
Tony Simpson	Northern Regional Press Officer	07764 336 708
Julia Hutton	South West Regional Press Officer	07971 474 557
Hugh Godwin	London & South East Press Officer	07968 392 688
Lucie Bonsey	Communications Secretary and Administrator	020 8831 6582 07894 789703

Community Rugby

Andrew Scoular	Director of Community Rugby	020 8831 6710
Erin Kirby	PA to Director of Community Rugby	020 8831 7470
Adele Steer	Assist. Sec. to Director of Community Rugby	020 8831 7466
Andy Lees	National Clubs Development Manager	07740 565066
Paula Hanson	Community Rugby Administrator - CB & Club	020 8831 7992 Fax 020 8831 7442

Coaching Development

Gary Henderson	Head of Coaching Development	07740 565067
Des Diamond	Coaching Development Manager	07860 812194
Will Feebery	Coaching Development Manager	07740 565058
Gary Townsend	Coaching Development Manager	07738 029111
John Lawn	Coach Development Officer – Yorkshire & NE	07738 029109
Nick Scott	Coach Development Officer – Midlands East	07738 029112
Ian Thompson	Coach Development Officer – North West & Cumbria	07738 029110
Ian Bletcher	Coach Development Officer - Midlands West	07764 699642
Jon Bates	Coach Development Officer - London South	07764 336709
Tony Robinson	Coach Development Officer – London North	07894 783339
Gavin Williams	Coach Development Officer - Southern Region	07764 960391
Alan Hubbleday	Coach Development Officer – South West Region	07764 960374
Linda Fell	Coaching Administration Manager	020 8831 6711
Stephen Hornsby	Multi-Media Technician	020 8831 7443
Nevil Jeffery	Coaching Resources Officer	020 8831 7443
Matt Knight	Coaching Administrator	020 8831 7499
Judy Weavers	Secretary	020 8831 6509

Regional Rugby Development Managers (RRDMs)

Matthew Carter	RRDM North East & Yorkshire	07740 565 068
Dave Southern	RRDM North West	07740 565 059
Steve Peters	RRDM Midlands West	07764 960 411
Jeff Mapp	RRDM Midlands East	07740 565 063

Rob Drinkwater	RRDM London North	07734 856 766
Peter Macaulay	RRDM London South	07764 336 700
Clive Cashell	RRDM South	07764 960 383
Andy Blackmore	RRDM South West	07764 960 392

Referee Department

Richard Glynne-Jones	Referee Manager	07736 722 324
Dave Broadwell	Referee Development Manager - SE	07802 435 745
Steve Harland	Referee Development Manager - SW	07738 029 107
Paul Renton	Referee Development Manager - North	07739 300 438
Alan Biggs	Referee Development Manager – Midlands	07894 783 372
Paul Freestone	Referee Development Officer - Midlands	07738 029262
Ed Turnill	Referee Development Officer - South East	07894 783373
Nigel Cowley	Referee Development Officer - South West	07894 783 378
Will Halford	Referee Development Officer – North	07894 790340
Andy Melrose	Training and Education Officer	07710 465 230
Steve Leyshon	Panel Development Manager	07738 029 108
Steve Savage	Panel Development Officer	07734 985 977
Bobbie Haynes	Appointments & Administration Team Leader	020 8831 6752
Nida Ahmad	Development Team Administrator	020 8831 6751
Juliet Smith	Referee Department Administrator	020 8831 6753
Lindsay Piper	Awards & Products Administrator	020 8831 6637

Schools and Youth Department

Mark Saltmarsh	National Schools Development Manager	07740 565 061
Elisa Blackborough	Administration Manager - Schools Dev.	020 8831 6755
Hayley Mintern	Administrator – Schools Dev.	020 8831 6756
Peter Bath	National Students Dev. Manager	07764 960 397
Charley Cullender	Administrator - Students	020 8831 6757
		Fax 020 8831 7442

Medical

Mike England	Community Rugby Medical Director	07921 891380
Karen Hood	Community Rugby Medical Manager	020 8831 7451
Bethan Palmer	Sports Injury Administrator	0208 831 7999
Tim Bonnett	Client Service Executive	0208 831 7999
Dave Philips	Injured Player Welfare Officer	07894 489716

Equity, Inclusion and Safeguarding

Nic Scott	Equity, Inclusion & Safeguarding Manager	07764 960403
Ann Hutchins	Safeguarding Executive	020 8831 7479
Annie Davis	Safeguarding Adviser	020 8831 7479
Chris Rawlings	Safeguarding Compliance Officer	020 8831 7454
Alexis Holding	Equity and Safeguarding Administrator	020 8831 7987
		Fax 020 8892 4446

Volunteer

Carole Thelwall-Jones	CB Volunteer Manager	07734 856792
Vacant	Volunteer Executive South West	
Carly Jackson	Volunteer Executive South East	07872 672478
Alex Thompson	Volunteer Executive Midlands	07894 489756
Mike Hart	Volunteer Executive North	07894 489755
		Fax 020 8831 7442

RFU CONTACTS

(0871 Numbers - Calls to this number are charged at 10 pence per minute from a BT landline. Calls from mobile and other networks may vary.)

Elite Rugby Department
Rob Andrew   Elite Rugby Director   020 8831 6505

England
Martin Johnson	England Team Manager	020 8831 6777
John Wells	England Forwards Coach	020 8831 6777
Brian Smith	England Attack Coach	020 8831 6777
Mike Ford	England Defence Coach	020 8831 6777

Elite Player Development
Stuart Lancaster	Head of Elite Player Development	020 8831 6705
John Elliott	Elite Player Development Manager	020 8831 6581

Elite Coach Development
Kevin Bowring	Head of Elite Coach Development	020 8831 6705
Nigel Redman	Elite Coach Development Manager	020 8831 6705
Jon Callard	National Academy Coach	020 8831 6777
John Fletcher	National Academy Coach	020 8831 6581
Martin Haag	National Academy Coach	020 8831 6581
Simon Hardy	National Academy Coach	020 8831 6705
Mark Mapletoft	National Academy Coach	020 8831 6581
Ben Ryan	National Academy Coach	020 8831 6620
Peter Walton	National Academy Coach	020 8831 6581

Elite Referees
Ed Morrison	Elite Referee Manager	020 8831 6734
Brian Campsall	Elite Referee Development Manager	020 8831 6734
Tony Spreadbury	Elite Referee Development Manager	020 8831 6734
Wayne Barnes	Full Time Referee	020 8831 6734
Rob Debney	Full Time Referee	020 8831 6734
JP Doyle	Full Time Referee	020 8831 6734
Greg Garner	Full Time Referee	020 8831 6734
David Pearson	Full Time Referee	020 8831 6734
Andrew Small	Full Time Referee	020 8831 6734
Chris White	Full Time Referee	020 8831 6734

Elite Rugby Services
Nathan Martin	General Manager, Elite Rugby	020 8831 6777
Rob Burgess	England Team Operations Manager	020 8831 6726
Sarah Butterworth	PA to Elite Rugby Director	020 8831 6505
Katie Daniel	Elite Player & Elite Coach Development Administrator	020 8831 6705
Charlotte Gibbons	England Player Administration Manager (U18 and U20)	020 8831 6581
Nadine Keating	Elite Player Administration Manager (Saxons and Sevens)	020 8831 6620
Lisa Packham	PA to England Team Manager and General Manager, Elite Rugby	020 8831 6777
Hazel Penfold	PA to Heads of Sports Science & Medicine	020 8831 6765
Kate Saddler	Elite Referees Administrator	020 8831 6734
Dave Tennison	England Kit Technician	020 8831 6590

Sports Science & Medicine
Roy Headey	Head of Sports Science & Medicine	020 8831 6765
Dr Simon Kemp	Head of Sports Medicine	020 8831 6765
Calvin Morriss	England Fitness Coach	020 8831 6765
Paul Stridgeon	Assistant England Fitness Coach	020 8831 6765
Simon Worsnop	National Academy Head of Fitness	020 8831 6765
Neil Taylor	Strength & Power Coach	020 8831 6765
Barney Kenny	Head of Physiotherapy	020 8831 6531
Phil Pask	Physiotherapist	020 8831 6765

Paul Frawley	England Masseur	020 8831 6765
Steph Brennan	Physiotherapist	020 8831 6765
Matt Lovell	Nutritionist	020 8831 6765
Ruth Hibbins-Butler	Business Systems & Data Manager	020 8831 6534
John Hall	Head of Data Analysis (PGIR)	01225 510114
Tony Ashton	Performance Analyst (PGIR)	01225 510114
Becky Cancea	Performance Analyst (PGIR)	01225 510114
Michael Hughes	Performance Analyst (PGIR)	01225 510114

Finance Department

Nick Eastwood	Finance Director	0208 831 6529
Karen Mackay	PA to Finance Director	0208 831 6518
Sarah Abdelghafar	Sales Ledger Accountant	0208 831 6522
Natasha Barker	Payables Accountant p/t	0208 831 6759
Sue Bates	Credit Controller	0208 831 6714
Keith Campbell	Management Accountant	0208 831 6684
Laura Carney	Accounts Assistant	0208 831 6552
Marcus Deering	Group Accountant	020 8831 6717
Jonny Heap	Senior Management Accountant	020 8831 6730
Aoife Hogan	Management Accountant	020 8831 7467
Elizabeth Humphrey	Internal Auditor p/t	020 8831 6631
David Ingmire	Tax Consultant p/t	0208 831 6631
Tricia Lewis	Group Systems Accountant	020 8831 6524
John Moulson	Head of Finance	0208 831 6537
Sandra Negreira	Club Accountant	020 8831 6538
Carmen Romay	Accounts Assistant	020 8831 6517
Michael Rootes	Match Accountant	0208 831 6556
		Fax 020 8892 7159

Planning, Funding & Resources.

Nick Bunting	Head of Public Affairs & Planning, Funding & Resources	020 8831 7453
Natalie Anderson	PA to Head of Public Affairs & Planning, Funding & Resources	020 8831 6772
Simon Winman	Head of Funding & Facilities	07740 162 436
Ross Baxter	Funding & Facilities Manager –Midlands	07764 960 405
Rick Bruin	Funding & Facilities Manager –South East	07738 029 211
Ted Mitchell	Funding & Facilities Manager - North	07738 029 212
Dave Stubley	Funding & Facilities Manager – South West	07736 722 387
Fran Thornber	Rugby Football Foundation Administrator	020 8831 7985
Jessica Mills	Administration & Resources Manager	020 8831 6769
Aileen Smith	Publications & Resources Administrator	020 8831 6762
Katharine Bessent	Kit & Resources Administrator	020 8831 6773
Kate Saunders	Digital Media Manager	020 8831 6712
James Burke	Website Project Manager	020 8831 6687
Justin Gough	Digital Media Project Manager	020 8831 6779
Annabel Gibson	Digital Media Content Co-Ordinator	020 8831 7601
Tom Hines	Web Editor	020 8831 6774
Carol Cooper	Management Information Executive	020 8831 6770
Felicity Hogben	Rugby First Data Administrator	020 8831 7440
		Fax 020 8892 8204

Human Resources

Ian King	Head of Human Resources	020 8831 6643
Helen Gates	HR Partner	020 8831 6673
Hannah Binns	HR Partner	020 8831 6739
Lynn Graco	HR Secretary / Administrator	020 8831 6758
Jenny Lane	Pay & Benefits Manager	020 8831 6638
Diane Keaveney	Senior Payroll Officer	020 8831 6719
Donna Friary	Payroll Administrator	020 8831 6639
Helen Ormond	Payroll Administrator	020 8831 6646
Marie Sefton	Learning & Development Manager	020 8831 6677
		Fax 020 8831 6640

RFU CONTACTS

(0871 Numbers - Calls to this number are charged at 10 pence per minute from a BT landline. Calls from mobile and other networks may vary.)

Office Services

Alisha Bird	Services Executive	020 8831 6570
Beryl Brister	Office Services Assistant	020 8831 6545
Sandra Dunn	Office Services Assistant	020 8831 6699
Jenny Cutler	Receptionist	020 8831 6527
Lauren Wall	Receptionist	020 8831 6527
Richard Marlow	Driver / Fleet Services Assistant	020 8831 6699 / 07921 891277 Fax 020 8892 9816

IT

Rob Mackmurdie	Head of IT	020 8831 6720
Zoe Fitzpatrick	Secretary to Head of IT	020 8831 6584
Lynda Eastwood	IT Administrator	020 8831 6671
George Vaughan	Project Manager	020 8831 6630
Mike Morris	Network Manager	020 8831 6693
Katharine Lewis	Helpdesk Analyst	020 8831 6767
Stuart Wright	IT Support	020 8831 7956
Rob Nelson	IT Support	020 8831 6553
Paul May	IT Support	020 8831 6697
Adrian Toerien	IT Support	020 8831 6595
Paul Chorley	Rugbyfirst Development Manager	020 8831 6647
Matthew Lord	Project Manager	0208 831 7602
Max Burton	Training Officer (Rugbyfirst)	0208 831 6793
Mario Rajakone	Web Project Manger	020 8831 6502
Junior Carimber	SQL Developer	020 8831 6502
RugbyFirst Helpdesk		0870 999 2003 Fax 020 8831 6660

RFUW

Rosie Williams	Managing Director	020 8831 7481
Nicola Ponsford	MBE Head of Performance	07976 056571
David Rose	Head of Development	07702 626266
Susan Allen	Head of Support Services	020 8831 6607
Helen Williams	Finance Manager	020 8831 6695
Richard Tamplin	Comms & Database Co-ordinator	020 8831 6761
Rachel Carter	Logistics Co-ordinator	020 8831 6606
Vanessa Gray	Administrator	020 8831 7996
Kelly Rainey	Player Development Support Officer	020 8831 7468
Gemma Ryan	Development Support Officer	0208 831 6788
Holly Hart	Resource & Volunteer Support Officer	0208 831 7482
Julia Hutton	Media Officer	07971 474557
Gary Street	England Coach	07813 915 453
Graham Smith	England Assistant Coach	07855 300 084
Tom Stokes	Player Development Manager	07971 950 551
James Fisher	WRDM London North & South	07809 512738
Jo Hawley	WRDM South West	07841 367392
Vicki Putson	WRDM North	07841 367391
Claire Antcliffe	WRDM Midlands	07841 367447
Clare Cooper	WRDM South Region	07779 266060
Keeley Fathers	Competitions Officer	07779 231970
Laura Jane Adams	Club & Coach Officer (E. Midlands)	07912 540942
Maggie Alphonsi	Club & Coach Officer (London)	07912 540943
Barry Maddocks	Club & Coach Officer (South West)	07912 540946

Kevin Moggridge	Club & Coach Officer (South West)	07912 540950
Simon Burgess	Club & Coach Officer (South East)	07912 540944
Mark Harper	Club & Coach Officer (North West)	07912 540945
Andy Paton	Club & Coach Officer (W. Midlands)	07841 367446
Gordon Piper	Club & Coach Officer (Yorkshire)	07912 540947
Andrew Skipper	Club & Coach Officer (East)	07912 540948

Stadium

Richard Knight	Stadium Director	020 8831 6560
Ellie Harris	Stadium Events and Operations Executive	020 8831 7493
Keith Kent	Head Groundsman	020 8831 7490
		Fax 020 8892 5533

Technical & Facilities

Neil Theuma	Head of Technical & Facilities	020 88316520
Krysia Budgen	Facilities Administrator	020 8831 6519
Kieron Woods	Manager Technical & Facilities	020 8831 6521
Kieran Ballinger	Ground Foreman	020 8831 7496
Workshop		020 8831 6536
Dressing Room		020 8831 6539

Safety & Security

Nigel Cox	Stadium Operations Manager	020 8831 7455
Ken Taylor	Safety & Event Manager	020 8831 6692
Stuart Doyle	Security Operations Supervisor	020 8831 7462
Clive Griffiths	Security Operations Supervisor	020 8831 6528
Jacqui Parry	Stadium Staffing Co-ordinator	020 8831 6515
Jim Burton	Security Officer	020 8831 6589
Gareth Bennett	Security Officer	020 8831 6589
Danny Brown	Security Officer	020 8831 6589
Roland Hill	Security Officer	020 8831 6589
Steven Ewens	Security Officer	020 8831 6589
Andrew Tucker	Security Officer	020 8831 6589
Alex Dunn	Security Officer	020 8831 6589
Jamie Higginson	Security Officer	020 8831 6589
Kevin Anthony	Security Officer	020 8831 6589
GATE F		020 8831 6589
GATE D		020 8744 1863
24 Emergency Number		020 8831 6589/6544
		Fax 020 8892 5533

Ticket Office

Patricia Murphy	Ticket Office Manager	0871 222 2017
Phil Scholey	Asst Ticket Office & Debenture Manager	0871 222 2017
Lisa Prior	Asst Ticket Office & Systems Manager	0871 222 2017
Barry Aherne	Group Sales Manager	0871 222 2017
Stephanie Harris	Assistant Debenture Officer	0871 222 2017
Steve Furze	Ticket Officer	0871 222 2017
Helen Street	Ticket Officer	0871 222 2017
Sue Backhurst	Ticket Office Administrator	0871 222 2017
Julie Cannon	Ticket Office Administrator	0871 222 2017
Linda Cook	Ticket Office Administrator	0871 222 2017
Hannah Collins	Ticket Office Administrator	0871 222 2017
Carol Holden	Ticket Office Administrator	0871 222 2017
Laura Hudson	Ticket Office Administrator	0871 222 2017
Alison Morris	Ticket Office Administrator	0871 222 2017
Ben Saunders	Ticket Office Administrator	0871 222 2017
		Email: tickets@rfu.com
		Fax 020 8831 6670

RFU CONTACTS

(0871 Numbers - Calls to this number are charged at 10 pence per minute from a BT landline. Calls from mobile and other networks may vary.)

Tournaments & Competitions

Terry Burwell	Tournaments & Competitions Director	020 8831 6669
Helen Beale	PA to Tournaments & Competitions Director	020 8831 6503
Pam Cartwright	International Tours and Sevens Manager	020 8831 6636
Penny Craig	Teams Administrator	020 8831 6749
Megan Higham	Teams Administrator	020 8831 6778
Tracy Fox-Young	Events & Tournaments Manager	020 8831 6672
Jo Tyler	Events & Tournaments Executive	020 8831 7498
Jennie Smith	Tournaments & Competitions Secretary	020 8831 6688
Andrew Rogers	Regulations Manager	020 8831 6644
Nicky Cook	Rugby Operations Administrator	020 8831 7993
Chris Burns	Competitions Manager	020 8831 6641
Tom Brewis	Competitions Administrator	020 8831 6501
Tom Price	Database Assistant	0208 831 6784
Gavin Dovey	Anti Doping Officer	020 8831 7441
Thomas Cleary	Anti Doping Assistant	0208 831 7471
Billy Clark	Age Grade Competitions Manager	020 8831 6681
Sarah Bailey	Competitions Assistant	020 8831 6775
Beverley Collier	Leisure Rugby Administrator	020 8831 6510
Dan Brown	Leisure Rugby Project Manager	07764 960 393
Dave Fotherby	Event Co-ordinator	07894 783 347
		Fax 020 8892 4446

Twickenham Experience Limited

Hotline Number		0870 143 2400
Chris Morris	Managing Director	020 8831 7975
Natalie Bell	Sales Manager	020 8831 7971
Holly Hammill	Financial Controller	020 8831 7973
Matt Smith	Operations Manager	020 8831 7477
Rob Brumell	Event Manager	020 8831 7983
Sharon Moy-Taylor	Retail Operations Manager	020 8831 7972
Sarah Leatherland	Event Administration Manager	020 8831 7497
Gemma Lane	Match day Sales Executive	020 8831 7977
Linda Uttley	Sales Executive	020 8831 7988
Anna Fowler	Sales Executive	020 8831 7981
David Roohan	Sales Executive	020 8831 6780
Marianne Parkin	Accounts Assistant	020 8831 7978
David Finch	Accounts Assistant	020 8831 7974
Michelle Sanbar	Location Accountant	020 8831 7495
Penny Pottinger	Event Manager	020 8831 7980
Hazel Duckworth	Assistant Event Manager	020 8831 7456
Oliver Wright	Assistant Event Manager	020 8831 7487
Holly Bee	Event Manager	020 8831 7456
Laura Stones	Event Co-ordinator	020 8831 7984
Maeve Fitzmaurice	Event Co-ordinator	020 8831 7979
Janine Nottage	Sales Executive	020 8831 7986
Ryan Matthee	Head Chef	020 8831 6649
Nikki Mcendoo	Staffing Manager	020 8831 7492
Jo Griffiths	Staffing Officer	020 8831 7494
John Snarey	BOH Manager	020 8891 3821
Justin Latter	Assistant BOH Manager	020 8891 3821
Pete Snarey	Cellar Logistics	020 8831 7487
Scott Jones	Cellar Hospitality Supervisor	020 8831 6652
Stephanie Aldridge	Kitchen Administrator	020 8831 6649
		Fax 0870 143 2401

Highlights Floodlighting Ltd

Specialist Floodlighting Installation Contractors

THE LEADING NAME IN THE FLOODLIGHTING INDUSTRY

Our fully trained installation teams have expertise in all fields of the floodlighting industry.

Our services include design and build schemes for all applications of indoor and outdoor floodlighting for the Sports Industry.

Service and Maintenance Contracts undertaken. All Civil works undertaken i.e. cable trenching and foundations. All electrical works carried out to NICEIC Regulations.

We offer a comprehensive Architectural Design and Build program for Non League clubs as well as structural testing on existing columns and towers for insurance purposes and the Health and Safety Executive.

Newbury House, One London Road, Luton, Beds. LU1 3UE
Contact Name Mark Peckham
tel: 01582 730729 fax: 01582 726558 mob: 07885 672722
web: www.highlights.co.uk email: mail@highlights.co.uk

Guinness Premiership – Summer Transfers

Bath - IN: Olly Barclay (Fly half – Gloucester), Nicky Little (Fly Half - Padova), Matt Carraro (Centre/wing – New South Wales), Julian Salvi (Back row – ACT), Ben Skirving (Back row – Saracens), Luke Watson (Back row – Western Province), Chris Cracknell (Back row – Exeter Chiefs)
OUT: Laurence Ovens (Prop – Newcastle), Michael Lipman (Back row), Alex Crockett (Centre), Andrew Higgins (Winger) Justin Harrison (Lock – released), James Scaysbrook (Back row – Exeter Chiefs)

Gloucester - IN: Pierre Capdevielle (Prop – Brive), Darren Daidiuk (Hooker – Cornish Pirates), Rupert Harden (Prop – Tynedale), Dave Attwood (Lock – Bristol), Tom Voyce (Wing – London Wasps), Nicky Robinson (Centre – Cardiff), Seru Rabeni (Centre – Leicester Tigers), Eliota Fuimaono- Sapolu (Fly half- Bath)
OUT: Olly Barkley (Fly half – Bath), Anthony Allen (Centre – Leicester Tigers)

Harlequins - IN: Rory Clegg (Fly half – Newcastle Falcons), James Johnson (Prop), Karl Dickson (Scrum half – Bedford Blues), Gonzalo Camacho (Centre), John Andress (Prop – Exeter Chiefs), Lewis Stevenson (Lock – Exeter Chiefs), Josh Drauniniu (Winger – Exeter Chiefs)
OUT: Andy Gomersall (Scrum Half – released), Mike Ross (Prop – released), De Wet Barry (Centre – released), Chris Malone (Fly half – released), Alex Rogers (Prop – released), Mickey Pointing (Hooker – released), Peter bracken (Prop – released), James Englis (lock – released), Charlie Amesbury (Winger - Newcastle Falcons), Phil Davies (Back row – released), James Brooks (Prop – released), Tom Sargaent (Back row – released)

Leeds Carnegie - IN: Ceiron Thomas (Fly half – Llanelli), Alfie Tooala (Back row – Bristol), Henry Fa'afili (Winger – Biarritz), Marco Wentzel (Lock – Leicester Tigers), Gareth Hardy (Prop- New South Wales)
OUT: Tom Biggs (Wing – Newcastle Falcons), Rob Vickerman (Centre – Newcastle Falcons)

Leicester Tigers - IN: Anthony Allen (Centre – Gloucester), Geoff Parling (Back row- Newcastle), James Grindal (Scrum half – Newcastle).   OUT: Julien Dupuy (Scrum half – Stade Francais), Marco Wentzel (Lock – Leeds Carnegie), Tom Varndell (Winger – London Wasps)

London Irish - IN: Andy Perry (Lock – Newcastle), Andy Buist (Lock – Newcastle), James Tideswell (Prop – Plymouth A.)
OUT: James Hudson (Lock – Newcastle Falcons), James Bailey (Winger – Lyon)

London Wasps - IN: David Lemi (Winger – Bristol), Ben Jacobs (Centre – Saracens), Warren Fury (Scrum half – London Irish), Chris Whitehead (Hooker – Coventry), Tom Varndell (Winger – Leicester Tigers), Dan Ward Smith (Back row – Bristol), Steve Kefu (Centre – Castres)
OUT: Tom Voyce (Wing – Gloucester), Josh Lewsey (Wing – retired), James Haskell (Back row – Stade Francais), Tom Palmer (Lock – Stade Francais), Riki Flutey (Centre – Brive), Rafael Ibanez (Hooker – retired)

Newcastle Falcons - IN: Chris Micklewood (Utility Back – Brive), Laurence Ovens (Prop – Bath), Gcobani Bobo (centre - Western Stormers), Rob Vickerman (Centre – Leeds Carnegie), Jimmy Gopperth (Fly Half – Wellington), Filipo Levi (Lock - Ospreys), Josh Afu (Flanker – Doncaster), Charlie Amesbury (Winger – Harlequins) , Tom Biggs (Winger – Leeds Carnegie), Alex Walker (Hooker – Saracens), James Hudson (Lock – London Irish)
OUT: Tom May (Centre -), Jonny Wilkinson (Fly Half – Toulon), Geoff Parling (Lock – Leicetser Tigers), Phil Dowson (No 8 – Northampton Saints), David Wilson (Prop – Bath), Andy Buist (Lock – London Irish) James Grindal (Scrum half – Leicester Tigers), Andy Long (Hooker)

Northampton Saints - IN: Phil Dowson (No 8 – Newcastle), Shane Geraghty (Fly half – London Irish), Santiago Gonzalez Bonorino (Prop – Leicester Tigers), Brian Mujati (Prop – Western Province), Dan Vickerman (Lock -)
OUT: Tom Smith (Prop - Retired), Matt Lord (Lock – retired), Barry Stewart (Prop – retired), Ben Lewitt (Back row – released), Neil Starling (Released), Will Harries (Wing – released), Phil Hoy (Released)

Sale Sharks - IN: Ben Cohen (Winger – Brive), Dave Seymour (Back row – Saracens), Sisa Koyamaibole (Back row – Toulon), David Bishop (Centre Ospreys), Jack Forster (Prop – Gloucester), Gavin Kerr (Prop), Mahonri Schwalger (Hooker), Marika Vakacegu (Full back).   OUT: Sebastian Chabel (Lock – Racing Metro), Juan Martin Fernandez Lobbe (Back row – Toulon), Luke McAllister (Fly half - returns to New Zealand)

Saracens - IN: Derek Hoogaard (Fly half – Leicester Tigers), Mouritz Botha (Lock – Bedford Blues), Ernst Joubert (Back row – Lions), Schalk Brits (Hooker – Western Stormers), Frik Venter (Prop – Natal Sharks), Rhys Gill (Prop – Cardiff)
OUT: Dave Seymour (Back row – Sale Sharks), Alex Walker (Hooker – Newcastle Falcons)

Worcester Warriors - IN: Adam Black (Prop – Gwent Dragons)
OUT: Hal Luscombe (Centre – retired), Darren Morris (Prop – released), Chris Horsman (Prop – retired)

2008-2009 SEASON	Review & Statistics	34-43

2009-10 CLUBS

Bath Rugby	44
Gloucester	50
Harlequins	56
Leeds Carnegie	62
Leicester Tigers	68
London Irish	74
London Wasps	80
Newcastle Falcons	86
Northampton Saints	92
Sale Sharks	98
Saracens	104
Worcester Warriors	110

RECORDS SECTION
(currently PREMIERSHIP, previously Division 1)

| Roll of Honour | | 116 |
| Year by Year Records | | 118 |

ALL-TIME RECORDS

Various All Time Records		120
Most Tries	in a Match	122
Most Points	in a Match	123
	in a Season	124
Team & Individual Records		125

FIXTURES 2009-10	Bath	Gloucester	Harlequins	Leeds carnegie	Leicester Tigers	London Irish	London Wasps	Newcastle Falcons	Northampton saints	Sale Sharks	Saracens	Worcester Warriors
Bath		27/12	27/03	08/05	26/09	28/11	12/09	24/10	09/01	17/04	31/10	20/02
Gloucester	05/09		13/02	27/03	21/11	24/04	24/10	05/12	19/09	27/02	03/04	02/01
Harlequins	03/10	28/11		09/01	12/09	31/10	26/12	03/04	20/02	08/05	19/09	06/03
Leeds	02/01	04/10	06/12		14/02	20/09	28/02	06/09	04/04	22/11	07/03	25/04
Leicester Tigers	03/04	20/02	24/04	28/11		06/03	09/01	19/09	31/10	26/12	08/05	03/10
London Irish	14/02	13/09	28/02	18/04	25/10		27/09	22/11	08/05	28/03	27/12	05/12
London Wasps	24/04	07/03	05/09	01/11	04/02	04/04		03/01	04/10	14/02	21/02	20/09
Newcastle Falcons	07/03	10/01	25/09	27/12	18/04	19/02	08/05		27/11	13/09	04/10	01/11
Northampton	05/12	17/04	21/11	26/09	27/02	02/01	27/03	13/02		24/10	24/04	05/09
Sale Sharks	18/09	30/10	01/01	19/02	04/09	02/10	27/11	23/04	05/03		08/01	02/04
Saracens	28/02	27/09	18/04	25/10	01/01	05/09	22/11	28/03	12/09	05/12		14/02
Worcester	21/11	08/05	24/10	11/09	27/03	09/01	17/04	26/02	26/12	26/09	27/11	

2008-09 LEAGUE TABLE

		P	W	D	L	F	A	PD	4T	<7	Pts
									Bonus Pts		
1	Leicester Tigers	22	15	1	6	582	401	181	5	4	71
2	Harlequins	22	14	1	7	516	387	129	5	3	66
3	London Irish	22	12	1	9	551	386	165	7	9	66
4	Bath	22	13	2	7	539	438	101	4	5	65
5	Sale Sharks	22	13	0	9	447	410	37	5	5	61
6	Gloucester	22	12	0	10	435	448	-13	5	4	57
7	London Wasps	22	11	0	11	431	416	15	2	7	53
8	Northampton Saints	22	10	1	11	443	434	9	2	5	49
9	Saracens	22	9	0	13	437	447	-10	3	8	47
10	Newcastle Falcons	22	9	1	12	362	456	-94	2	4	44
11	Worcester	22	7	2	13	348	530	-182		2	34
12	Bristol	22	2	1	19	299	637	-338	1	6	17

2008-09 RESULTS MATRIX

	Bath	Bristol	Gloucester	Harlequins	Leicester Tigers	London Irish	London Wasps	Newcastle	Northampton	Sale	Saracens	Worcester
Bath		45-8	17-21	3-16	25-21	20-20	22-14	36-25	25-14	24-20	33-18	37-19
Bristol	20-33		10-29	14-17	17-23	13-18	18-36	3-35	14-13	6-9	16-23	37-18
Gloucester	36-27	39-10		24-20	8-20	23-21	24-22	39-23	33-10	24-17	22-16	6-13
Harlequins	21-14	31-13	14-9		26-26	27-28	32-10	31-12	27-6	38-20	21-15	60-14
Leicester Tigers	24-22	73-3	24-10	27-14		24-22	19-28	20-3	29-19	37-31	46-16	38-5
London Irish	16-20	38-21	42-12	9-14	28-31		26-14	48-8	32-27	28-6	27-14	38-17
London Wasps	23-27	21-19	34-3	24-18	36-29	21-16		12-6	9-5	12-13	33-24	10-11
Newcastle Falcons	14-15	17-3	10-7	24-16	14-10	8-24	17-23		32-22	9-14	13-9	16-16
Northampton Saints	28-28	30-8	40-22	23-13	17-13	21-17	24-20	13-19		38-3	20-15	21-13
Sale Sharks	23-16	32-13	23-9	28-6	27-13	14-8	31-3	25-32	24-18		18-15	9-17
Saracens	20-16	37-13	21-25	21-24	13-16	16-13	19-14	44-14	26-12	24-23		23-6
Worcester	17-34	20-20	14-10	23-30	17-19	15-32	13-12	26-11	12-22	20-37	22-8	

2008-09 LEADING SCORERS

MOST POINTS

			T	C	P	DG
239	Glen Jackson	Saracens	1	18	62	4
212	Butch James	Bath	2	35	44	-
187	Charlie Hodgson	Sale Sharks	5	24	34	4
158	Stephen Myler	Northampton Saints	-	19	38	2
146	Danny Cipriani	London Wasps	1	12	38	1
144	Peter Hewat	London Irish	3	18	30	1
130	Nick Evans	Harlequins	2	12	31	1
127	Olly Barkley	Gloucester	1	7	36	-
126	Toby Flood	Leicester Tigers	4	14	26	-
112	Tom May	Newcastle Falcons	5	15	18	1
104	Willie Walker	Gloucester	2	8	22	4
104	Willie Walker	Worcester	2	8	22	4
88	Julian Dupuy	Leicester Tigers	2	15	16	-
84	David Walder	London Wasps	-	6	24	-
81	Ed Barnes	Bristol	-	15	17	-
75	Chris Malone	Harlequins	1	14	13	1
68	Ryan Lamb	Gloucester	1	12	11	2
64	Bruce Reihana	Northampton Saints	4	4	12	-

MOST TRIES

			First Half	Second Half	Home	Away
10	Joe Maddock	Bath	6	4	6	4
10	Ugo Monye	Harlequins	5	5	5	5
9	Mark Cueto	Sale Sharks	6	3	4	5
9	Paul Diggin	Northampton Saints	8	1	8	1
9	David Lemi	Bristol	4	5	4	5
7	Iain Balshaw	Gloucester	5	2	6	1
7	Lee Robinson	Bristol	2	5	3	4
7	Olly Morgan	Gloucester	6	1	5	2
7	Mike Brown	Harlequins	4	3	4	3
7	Adam Thompstone	London Irish	2	5	3	4
6	Scott Hamilton	Leicester Tigers	4	2	4	2
6	Sailosi Tagicakibau	London Irish	3	3	3	3
6	Steffon Armitage	London Irish	4	2	4	2
6	Danny Care	Harlequins	2	4	4	2
6	Johne Murphy	Leicester Tigers	2	4	3	3
6	Daniel Williams	Newcastle Falcons	4	2	3	3

MOST PENALTIES
62 Glen Jackson Saracens

MOST CONVERSIONS
35 Butch James Bath

MOST DROP GOALS
4 Charlie Hodgson (Sale); Glen Jackson (Saracens); Willie Walker (Gloucester/Worcester)

TRIES FOR
By Position

	TOTAL	BACKS	FORWARDS	Full Backs	Wing	Center	Half Backs	Front Row	Second Row	Back Row	Penalty Tries
Bath	57	35	22	7	15	7	6	7	3	12	1
Bristol	32	24	8	2	15	4	3	2	1	5	1
Gloucester	42	32	10	8	14	6	4	1	2	7	1
Harlequins	57	36	21	8	15	5	8	9	1	11	3
Leicester Tigers	61	47	14	9	11	17	10	5	3	6	1
London Irish	63	37	26	5	18	9	5	4	3	19	1
London Wasps	31	21	10	0	9	7	5	4	1	5	2
Newcastle Falcons	38	23	15	0	15	3	5	3	3	9	0
Northampton Saints	41	29	12	5	16	7	1	5	2	5	0
Sale Sharks	43	25	18	6	8	5	6	3	5	10	1
Saracens	37	25	12	1	15	5	4	5	2	5	1
Worcester	29	18	11	4	5	7	2	4	2	5	1
Totals :	531	352	179	55	156	82	59	52	28	99	13

TRIES AGAINST
By Position

	TOTAL	BACKS	FORWARDS	Full Backs	Wing	Center	Half Backs	Front Row	Second Row	Back Row	Penalty Tries
Bath	47	32	15	3	16	9	4	6	1	8	1
Bristol	75	48	27	11	13	15	9	7	7	13	2
Gloucester	43	31	12	4	17	4	6	5	1	6	1
Harlequins	33	26	7	2	9	7	8	1	1	5	3
Leicester Tigers	40	23	17	7	10	5	1	6	3	8	0
London Irish	35	20	15	3	5	5	7	5	3	7	1
London Wasps	41	29	12	6	14	5	4	2	0	10	1
Newcastle Falcons	43	28	15	6	12	6	4	3	2	10	0
Northampton Saints	38	23	15	2	11	4	6	5	4	6	2
Sale Sharks	36	22	14	2	14	5	1	4	0	10	0
Saracens	37	29	8	4	14	9	2	2	4	2	1
Worcester	63	41	22	5	21	8	7	6	2	14	1
Totals :	531	352	179	55	156	82	59	52	28	99	13

KICKING STRIKE RATE

		Conversions		Penalties		TOTAL	
S/R%	(Minimum 20 attempts)	Att	Suc	Att	Suc	Att	Suc
69.57	Glen Jackson (Saracens)	32	18	83	62	115	80
69.30	Butch James (Bath)	48	35	66	44	114	79
65.52	Stephen Myler (Northampton Saints)	26	19	61	38	87	57
77.33	Charlie Hodgson (Sale Sharks)	34	24	41	34	75	58
64.86	Peter Hewat (London Irish)	33	18	41	30	74	48
70.42	Danny Cipriani (London Wasps)	16	12	55	38	71	50
65.15	Olly Barkley (Gloucester)	16	7	50	36	66	43
71.67	Nick Evans (Harlequins)	15	12	45	31	60	43
71.43	Toby Flood (Leicester Tigers)	18	14	38	26	56	40
61.54	Ed Barnes (Bristol)	22	15	30	17	52	32
64.71	Tom May (Newcastle Falcons)	21	15	30	18	51	33
58.70	Chris Malone (Harlequins)	25	14	21	13	46	27
68.18	Willie Walker (Gloucester & Worcester)	12	8	32	22	44	30
77.50	Julian Dupuy (Leicester Tigers)	18	15	22	16	40	31
81.08	David Walder (London Wasps)	8	6	29	24	37	30
63.89	Ryan Lamb (Gloucester)	17	12	19	11	36	23
67.86	Luke McAlister (Sale Sharks)	6	5	22	14	28	19
57.14	Bruce Reihana (Northampton Saints)	6	4	22	12	28	16
68.00	Rory Clegg (Newcastle Falcons)	9	5	16	12	25	17
64.00	Adrian Jarvis (Bristol)	7	7	18	9	25	16
65.22	Tom Homer (London Irish)	9	4	14	11	23	15
47.83	Waisea Luveniyali (Harlequins)	15	10	8	1	23	11
57.14	Shane Geraghty (London Irish)	11	5	10	7	21	12
80.00	Sam Vesty (Leicester Tigers)	14	11	6	5	20	16
80.00	Derick Hougaard (Leicester Tigers)	9	7	11	9	20	16
70.00	Matthew Jones (Worcester)	5	3	15	11	20	14

DISCIPLINE RECORD

	SIN BIN			Sin Bin Violent Conduct			Breakdown Professional Foul			RED		
	Total	H	A	Total	H	A	Total	H	A	Total	H	A
Bath	-			6	3	3	6	3	3	1	0	1
Bristol	1	0	1	9	3	6	10	3	7	-		
Gloucester	1	0	1	11	6	5	12	6	6	-		
Harlequins	-			10	2	8	10	2	8	-		
Leicester Tigers	-			8	2	6	8	2	6	1	1	0
London Irish	2	0	2	8	5	3	10	5	5	1	1	0
London Wasps	-			7	5	2	7	5	2	-		
Newcastle Falcons	1	1	0	9	3	6	10	4	6	-		
Northampton Saints	-			8	2	6	8	2	6	-		
Sale Sharks	1	0	1	12	5	7	13	5	8	-		
Saracens	1	1	0	8	0	8	9	1	8	-		
Worcester	-			13	4	9	13	4	9	-		
TOTAL	7	2	5	109	40	69	114	41	73	3	2	1

PREMIERSHIP

37

2008-09 REVIEW

Leicester Tigers
- Leicester Tigers were top of the table at the end of the regular season and went on to win the Guinness Championship at Twickenham with a narrow win over London Irish
- It was the second Guinness Championship for the Tigers following on form 2006/07
- The Tigers finished top of the table for the 8th time since the introduction of League rugby back in 1987/88
- Leicester Tigers were top points scorers and had the third best defensive record in the Premiership
- Matt Smith, Ben Kay and Aaron Mauger started the most matches, 18, with Kay coming on in three more for 21 appearances out of 22
- Fly half Toby Flood in his first season at the club was top scorer with 126 points from 11 starts which French scrum half Julian Dupuy next with 88 points in his debut season
- In the try scoring stakes wingers Johne Murphy and Scott Hamilton led the way with six each which is the lowest total to top the Tigers try scoring list since 2004/05
- Against the other top four sides they picked up four wins and a draw with just one defeat, 25-21 away at Bath
- Had 10 different Nationalities play for them during the season with England leading the way with 25 and New Zealand next with five
- They used 36 different starters during the season which was the sixth highest total in the Premiership
- Were the second highest try scorers with 62 two behind London Irish, and had the best record for tries in the final quarter with 26
- They also had the best record for tries by backs with 47, 10 more than anyone else
- The Tigers were fifth in the list for tries conceded with 40 but only conceded eight in the last quarter of matches which was the second lowest total in the division
- They conceded 23 tries in the first half and only the bottom two Bristol and Worcester conceded more
- The Tigers had two teenagers score tries, scrum half Ben Youngs and back rower Dan Hemingway
- At the other end of the scale they had two of the oldest try scorers in the Premiership, Mefin Davies & Julian White

Harlequins
- They finished second which is their best ever finish in the Premiership having finished third four times and improved four places on last season
- Finished the season as the fourth highest scorers and had the second best defensive record
- Quins had 10 different Nationalities play during the season, there were 23 English players and Ireland was the next highest with three
- Prop Ceri Jones and flanker Chris Robshaw both started 21 out of the 22 matches and Robshaw came on as a replacement in the other match, Jones has now stated 43 out of Quins last 44 Premiership matches over the last two seasons
- New Zealand International fly half Nick Evans was the leading scorer with 130 points
- Former New Zealand International Andrew Mehrtens was the last Kiwi before Evans to top score for Quins with 189 in 2005/06
- England wing Ugo Monye was the top try scorer with 10 tries the most by a Quins player in the Premiership since Dan Luger scored 11 back in 1998/99, for Monye is was a one try improvement from his previous best set back in 2003/04
- Quins had 32 different players start which was the third fewest, just one more than Bath and Northampton Saints
- They only had three players 21 or under start during the season which was the joint lowest number in the Premiership, but at the other end of the scale they only had eight players over 30 which was the lowest figure in the Premiership
- Quins were the joint top scorers in the first half of matches with 27 tries in the opening 40 minutes
- They only conceded three tries in the opening 20 minutes of matches which was the lowest figure in the division
- The Quins front row contributed nine tries which was the most by any front row in the Premiership and only one opposition front rower scored against them
- In matches against the other top four sides they, won three lost two and drew once, and did the double over Bath
- Quins conceded three penalty tries which was the most in the league

London Irish
- Finished third in the regular season but got to Twickenham for the Championship final before losing to Leicester
- They improved four places on the previous season and equalled their best ever finish in the top flight which dates back to 2005/06
- Had the amazing record of picking up a losing bonus point in all nine of their defeats which was two more than any other side
- Irish also picked up the most try bonus points, seven, two more than any other side
- They had the best defensive record in the division and the second best scoring record
- The Irish struggled in matches against the other top four sides with just one win and a draw to go with four defeats
- No 8 Chris Hala'uifa was the only ever present starting all 22 league matches but was replaced in 11 of them
- Australian full back Peter Hewat was top scorer with 144 points for the second season running but this time with 59 points more in 16 starts
- In the try scoring stakes winger Adam Thompstone led the way with seven tries in 10 starts, which is the most since Topsy Ojo two seasons ago
- The Irish had 33 different starters which was the fourth fewest in the Premiership
- The Irish had the fewest players 30 or over play during the season with just eight
- Tom Homer was the second youngest player to appear in the Premiership during the season aged 18 years 236 days
- At the other end of the scale they had the oldest player in the Premiership, Mike Catt aged 37 years 220 days
- The Irish had the joint best record for tries conceded, just 36 including just 20 on the road which was the fewest in the division
- The Irish had the best record for fewest tries conceded in the last quarter of matches, just seven
- The Irish back row contributed 19 of the clubs 64 tries which was the highest figure in the Premiership, seven more than any other side and with 18 their wingers were the most prolific in the Premiership
- They only conceded five tries to opposition wingers during the season which was easily the lowest

Bath
- Bath finished in fourth place a one place drop on the previous season as they finished in the top four for the fourth time in the last six seasons
- South African World Cup winner Butch James started the most matches for Bath, 20, one more than Australian second row Justin Harrison but Harrison came on in two further matches so taking part in 21 out of 22.
- But it was prop Duncan Bell who played in all 22 matches starting 16 and coming on as a replacement in the other six matches
- James also top scored with 212 points which is the most points by a Bath player since Olly Barkley scored 219 back in 2003/04
- In the try scoring stakes New Zealander Joe Maddock leading the way with 10 tries, which was double the number he scored two seasons ago when he also topped the clubs try scoring list, and he scored twice as many tries as anyone else during the season
- In his four seasons at the club Maddock has scored 23 tries in 80 appearances, including 70 starts
- In matches against the other top four sides they picked up two wins, a draw and three defeats
- Bath had just 31 starters which was the joint lowest figure along with Northampton Saints but only had three players 21 or under which was the lowest total in the Premiership
- They scored 58 tries including 27 in the first half which was the highest total in the Premiership
- Bath had the best record for tries in the opening quarter with 17 three more than any other side
- Although they finished fourth they had the 10th worst defensive record with 48 tries conceded, only the bottom two conceded more
- The Bath front row contributed seven tries - the second most by any front row in the Premiership after Quins
- 16 of the 48 tries they conceded were scored by the opposition's wingers - the third highest in the Premiership

2008-09 REVIEW

Sale Sharks
- Sale Sharks finish fifth for a second successive season as they again miss out on the Play offs
- The Sharks had 36 different starters, only four sides used more
- Charlie Hodgson was the only Sharks ever present and was replaced just twice, he also started the most matches last season and has started 42 of his sides last 44 matches
- Hodgson finished as the leading scorer for the fifth successive season and for the seventh time in eight seasons
- During the season Hodgson passed 1500 Premiership points and moved his all time club records for conversions, penalties and drop goals to 203, 295 and 28 respectively in his 128 appearances, including 124 starts
- Also during the season he passed 2200 points for the Sharks in all competitions
- In matches against the top four they had a good record with four wins and four defeats, with the wins all coming at Edgeley Park
- They had 24 English players with Wales the next best represented country with six players
- Sale's James Gaskell at 18 years 178 days was the youngest player to appear in the Premiership
- Full back/wing Mark Cueto topped the try scoring list for the Sharks with nine tries as he topped the try scoring list for the fourth time in eight seasons and for the first time since 2005/06 – he went against the trend with six of his nine tries coming in the first half and five of them on the road
- He has now scored 64 tries and is within 11 of Steven Henley's all time record for the club from 128 appearances including 124 starts
- He has now scored 91 tries for Sale in all competitions
- They had the joint meanest defence along with Quins and London Irish with just 36 tries conceded including just 11 at home and 11 in the first half which are both the lowest in the division
- Sale's second row has scored five tries which is the most by any second row in the Premiership

Gloucester
- After finishing top of the table in the regular season for the last two seasons the Cherry and Whites were down in sixth place, their lowest position since 2004/05 when they also finished sixth
- They did collect five try bonus points which was the second most in the division
- Olly Barkley, in his first and only season at the club, topped scored with 127 points, the lowest total to top the clubs points scoring list in the last 11 seasons
- In the try scoring stakes backs Olly Morgan and Iain Balshaw led the way with seven tries to finished joint top try scorers for the club for the first time, both were prolific in the first half of matches with Morgan scoring six and Balshaw five in the opening 40 minutes
- Gloucester were the only Premiership side to have scored more tries in the first half than in the second, 24 to 19
- They did only manage 10 tries in the final quarter which was the second lowest total in the Premiership
- They conceded 12 tries in the opening 20 minutes of matches', only Bristol and Northampton Saints conceded more
- Second row Alex Brown started the most matches 19, two more than any other player and also came on as a replacement in two other matches
- Prop Nick Wood took part in all 22 matches starting 17 and coming on as a replacement in the other five
- Winger/centre James Simpson Daniel extended his all time club try scoring record to 44 with four in nine appearances during the season; his 44 tries coming in 118 matches including 104 starts over nine seasons at the club
- In eight matches against the top four sides they have four wins and four defeats including doing the double over Bath - Leicester Tigers were the only side to do the double over them
- They had 12 sin bins during the season with centre Anthony Allen the only player to pick up two
- Five of the 12 were awarded by Wayne Barnes in three matches
- Only used players from seven different countries, England led with 26 and next on the list was Scotland with five
- Gloucester had 38 different players start during the season which was the second most in the Premiership along with Saracens and one behind Worcester
- They only managed one try through their front row which was the lowest total in the Premiership
- They did only give up six tries to the opposition back row which was the second lowest total in the division
- In winger Charlie Sharples they had one of only eight teenagers to score in the Premiership

London Wasps
- Terrible season for London Wasps as they drop down to seventh in the league table, their lowest finish since 2001/02 when they were also seventh
- They did though pick up seven losing bonus points which was the third highest, after London Irish's nine, in their 11 defeats and Saracens with eight
- They did though only manage two try bonus points only the bottom two picked up fewer
- Out of favour England International Danny Cipriani led the scoring charts for the second successive season with 146 points down on his 188 the previous season
- Leading try scorer was centre Riki Flutey with just four which is the lowest total to top the Wasps try scoring list in over a decade, he finished one clear of scrum half Joe Simpson who ended the season playing for the England Saxons in the Churchill Cup
- Simpson aged 20 years and 134 days was the youngest player to appear for the club during the Premiership season
- Second row Simon Shaw aged 36 years 236 days was the oldest player to appear for the club in the Premiership just under two years older than French hooker Raphael Ibanez
- Wasps managed just 33 tries which was the joint second lowest number in the Premiership and were dreadful starters with just five tries in the opening quarter
- Only five of their tries were scored by their back row which was the joint lowest number in the Premiership but they did concede 10 tries to opposition back rows which was the third highest total in the division
- Winger Tom Voyce started the most matches, 21 out of 22, one more than utility back Josh Lewsey in his final season of professional rugby
- Lewsey only managed two tries and fell two short of Kenny Logan's club record of 48 leagues tries, Lewsey finished with 46 in his 11 year career at the club, and in total scored 53 league tries with seven for Bristol in two seasons
- In the forwards it was prop Tim Payne who started the most 16, one more than Simon Shaw
- In matches against the top four sides in the Premiership they did well with four wins and four defeats including doing the double over Champions Leicester Tigers whilst Bath did the double over them
- Only used players from six countries, England led the way with 30 and next was Ireland with five
- They fielded nine players 21 or under which was the second most in the division after Worcester Warriors

Northampton Saints
- On their return to the Premiership the Saints were eighth in the league table which is the best since they were sixth in 2005/06
- Having picked up 23 try bonus points in National One last season they were to manage just two on their return to the Premiership
- Fly half Stephen Myler finished the season as top scorer with 158 points in his first season of top flight rugby
- In the try scoring stakes winger Paul Diggin led the way with nine, one behind leaders Joe Maddock and Ugo Monye, it was the best by a Saints player in the Premiership since Bruce Reihana managed 13 in 2003/04, eight of his tries came in the first half, against the trend, and eight at home, with the trend
- Ex Scottish International Prop Tom Smith was at 37 years and 176 days the second oldest player to play in this season's competition, 46 days younger than Mike Catt
- At the other end of the scale second row Courtney Lawes was their youngest player at 19 years 343 days, 125 days older than hooker Joe Gray
- Irish centre James Downey started the most matches, 20 but prop Soane Tonga'uiha took part in all 22 matches starting 16 and coming on as a replacement in the other six and his one try coming against Bath
- In their eight matches against the top four sides they managed three wins and a draw and they were all at home
- They had seven different Nationalities play for them during the season, 20 were English and the next biggest representation was form Ireland and Scotland with five each
- Only five of their tries came from their back row which was the joint lowest total in the Premiership
- Had the fifth best defensive record in terms of tries conceded 40, the same as Champions Leicester Tigers
- They had just 31 starters which was the joint lowest number in the Premiership and had just five other players who played as replacements only, 20 of them were English
- Had the joint third best home record in the division after Leicester Tigers and Harlequins with nine wins and a draw to go with just one defeat and surprisingly that was at the hands of the Falcons

2008-09 REVIEW

Saracens
- Saracens finished a disappointing ninth a drop of a place on the previous season
- They did though pick up eight losing bonus points in their 13 defeats and it could have been so different
- Fly half Glen Jackson was the leading scorer in the division with 239 points, 27 more than Bath's Butch James
- It was a fifth successive season Jackson has finished leading scorer for the club and the third time he has passed 200 points with his second best ever points tally. His total included a club record 62 penalty goals which beat the old record of 58 which was shared by Michael Lynagh and Gavin Johnson
- Jackson took his Sarries all time career total to 1005 which included extending his records for conversions and penalty goals to 123 and 223 respectively and he passed 00 points in just 93 matches including 87 starts
- In all competitions during the season Jackson scored 359 points including 105 in the European Challenge Cup
- In the try scoring two players led the way with a disappointing total of just four tries, wing Noah Cato and wing/centre Rod Penney with three of Cato's four coming on the road
- Jackson started most matches, 21 missing just the one, five more than any other player
- In matches against the top four they managed just two wins to go with six defeats with both Leicester Tigers and Quins doing the double over them
- Had players from 11 different nationalities play during the season, England led the way with 26 and next on the list was South Africa with five
- They had 38 different players start matches during the season which was the joint second most and in total had 44 players with six more playing as replacements only, Worcester were the only side to use more, 46
- Had the most players 30 or over 18, three more than Bristol
- They did have the fourth best defensive record in terms of tries conceded just 38
- 15 of Sarries tries were scored by their wingers, the second highest in the Premiership after Northampton Saints
- Only conceded two tries to the opposition back row - the lowest in the Premiership, & three less than anyone else
- Former New Zealand international scrum half Justin Marshall was the oldest player to play for the club during the season aged 35 years 263 days

Newcastle Falcons
- The Falcons finished 10th a one place improvement on the previous season with 10 points more and you have to go back to 2001/02 for their last top half of the table finish
- Centre/fly half Tom May ended as leading scorer for the first time ever with 112 points which is the most by a Falcons players since Matt Burke scored 147 in 2005/06
- May also scored five tries which was good enough for second place in the try scoring list behind wing Danny Williams and four of the six came in the first half of matches
- In matches against the top four sides they managed two wins, against the top two at home Leicester Tigers and Harlequins; in only one of the six defeats did they manage a losing bonus point
- No 8 Phil Dowson was the only man to start all 22 matches for the Falcons and was only replaced twice all season
- May was just behind him with 21 starts four more than anyone else
- Adam Balding was subbed in all 17 of his starts during the season which must be some sort of record for a non front row player
- They only had four different Nationalities play during the season 31 Englishmen, the most by any Premiership side, whilst next on the list with five was New Zealand, followed by two Scotsman and a South African
- The Falcons had just 35 different starters which was the fifth lowest in the Premiership
- They only had seven players over 30 play which was the lowest total in the Premiership
- Prop Joe McDonnell was the oldest Falcon during the season at 35 years and 213 days
- The Falcons were the only side to score more tries on the road than at home, 23 to 15, the 15 was the lowest total for any side at home whilst the 23 was the third highest of any side on the road
- They are also the third highest scorers in the opening quarter of matches with 11 tries but in the second quarter they had the worst record in the Premiership with just five tries
- They only conceded 12 tries at home in 11 matches only Sale Sharks with 11 conceded fewer

Worcester Warriors
- Worcester Warriors dropped a place in the table to 11th this season but were some 17 points ahead of bottom of the table Bristol to equal their worst finish in the Premiership in five seasons
- They were the only side not to pick up a try bonus point and only managed two losing bonus points in 13 defeats
- It was the first time in five seasons in the Premiership they have conceded over 500 points
- Willie Walker, who joined on loan from Gloucester during the season, top scored with 74 points - 27 more than Matt Jones managed
- In the try scoring stakes it was former Australian International Chris Latham who led the way with just four tries
- Last season's leading try scorer Miles Benjamin only managed one try this season from 13 starts compared to nine tries last season
- New Zealander Greg Rawlinson played the most matches 20, 19 starts and one match as a replacement, one more than centre Dale Rasmussen
- Two other players played 20 matches hooker Aleki Lutui and back row man Netani Telei both with 15 starts and five matches as a replacement
- In matches against the top four they lost all eight and only in the two home defeats against the top two did they take a losing bonus point, their only two in their 13 defeats bizarrely
- They used 39 different starters which was the most in the division and had seven more as replacements only
- Had eight different Nationalities turn out during the season, England led with 29 players followed by Wales with six
- Did the double over both Gloucester and London Wasps during the season
- They were the lowest try scorers in the division with 30 and only managed seven in the last 20 minutes of matches which was three fewer than anyone else
- Worcester with 14 conceded more tries to opposition back rowers than any other side

Bristol
- After a four season stay in the Premiership Bristol are relegated back into the second tier of English rugby under its new guise of the 'Championship' slipping three places on last season
- They managed just two wins and finished 17 points adrift of second bottom Worcester Warriors, all this after finishing third three seasons ago and qualifying for the Heineken Cup
- They only managed 299 points all season and shipped 637 defensively
- They managed just the one try bonus point but did pick up six losing bonus points
- Fly half Ed Barnes led the way with 81 points which was 14 fewer than Jason Strange managed last season
- In the try scoring stakes Samoan International David Lemi was the top scorer with nine tries for the third time in four seasons with his second best ever total, this was two more than his opposite wing Lee Robinson
- Lemi was third highest scorer in the Premiership and in four seasons at the club has an impressive 33 tries in 67 matches including 64 starts and is one of the Bristol all time record of 34 held by Sean Marsden
- They used 36 different starters and had six other players play as replacements only
- 25 of their players were English and in total they had players from 10 different countries play during the season
- No 8 Dan Ward Smith started 20 of the 22 matches and came on as a replacement in the other two
- David Lemi was next with 19 starts and one match as a replacement whilst Barnes started 18 and came on three times to play in all but one of their 22 league matches
- They lost all eight matches against the top four and managed three losing bonus points along the way
- Conceded 77 tries 13 more than anyone else including 50 on the road
- Only eight of their tries were scored by forwards which was the lowest total in the Premiership
- They conceded 11 tries to opposition full backs which was the highest in the division

BATH

Founded: 1865
Colours:
Blue with black and white
Change colours:
White with black & blue
Website: www.bathrugby.com

KEY PERSONNEL

Chairman	Andrew Brownsword
Chief Executive	Bob Calleja
Commercial Director	Tim Davies
Finance Director	Mark Wilson
Head Coach	Steve Meehan
Team Manager	Dave Guyan
Media Manager	Kate Oram

CONTACT DETAILS
Bath Rugby,
11 Argyle Street, Bath BA2 4BQ
Tel: 01225 325200 (Office)   Fax: 01225 325201
email: info@bathrugby.com

GROUND DETAILS
Ground Address
The Recreation Ground, Bath. BA2 6PW.

Capacity: 10,600 (9,980 + 520 in boxes +100 in suite)
Covered Seating: 2,000
Open Seating: 6,350
Terracing: 1,630

Directions: M4 Junction 18, Bath 10 miles south. Follow signs to Bath City Centre and then signs to the Recreation Ground.

Nearest BR Station: Bath Spa
From station walk up Manvers St. towards centre of town. Turn right into North Parade & left down steps.

Car Parking: None on ground, unlimited 'Park & Ride'.

Admission
Matchdays:
Adult £20-£34; OAP/student/u18 £16-£34; Youth £10-£34
Season Tickets: New member: Adult £225-£455;
           OAP/student/u18 £160-£420; Youth £80-£420
Ticket Office: 0871 721 1865

Club Shop: 1 Argyle Street, Bath BA2 4BA
Open Mon to Sat 9.00-5.30pm, Sunday 10.00-4.00pm
Contact Jackie Povey Tel: 01225 311950.

Clubhouse: Open on Match days
           Bars and food kiosks open 2 $^{1/4}$ hours before kick-off.
Contact Dean Quintin   Email: dean.quintin@bathrugby.com
Telephone: 01225 469230

PROGRAMME
Size: 245 x 170mm   Pages: 84
Price: £3
Editor: Kate Oram
Advertising: Peter Francomb at Green Park Publishing. peter@greenparkpublishing.co.uk

REVIEW OF THE SEASON 2008-09

The 2008-09 season was full of highs and lows for Bath Rugby. Not only had they begun the term with the loss of star players Steve Borthwick, Olly Barkley and Zak Feaunati, but they also had to suffer the continued uncertainty of their position on The Rec.

Thankfully, what this club certainly does not lack is stoicism and from a questionable beginning the team were quick to make their mark on both the Guinness Premiership and the European stage, reaching the semi-finals and quarter finals respectively. In bitter irony, Bath Rugby lost to Leicester Tigers in both matches and that was the high price they paid for beating the Tigers in heart-stopping fashion in November. Few fans will forget the moment when Butch James chipped a kick on the wing to Alex Crockett before the fly half rushed over the line for the match clinching try – it was the stuff of dreams -and from that Bath continued to display last minute victories that helped make the West Country side one of the most exciting teams to watch all season.

Since that November afternoon, the try-scorer James was laid off with an ACL injury, star player and firm favourite Matt Stevens had his rugby career curtailed after his shock admission, Danny Grewcock spent most of the season wearing a boot and to just pour more acid into the wound, Michael Lipman received a hamstring injury that prevented him from joining the fray in the knock out stages

But, this is Bath Rugby. Nothing has made the group of players from the sleepy city by the River Avon more determined and, ultimately, more united.

Tempering the daunting events, Bath were finally been able to announce that the prodigal son, Olly Barkley shall be returning back to The Rec on a two-year contract, Ben Skirving and Davey Wilson join at the start of the season, Ryan Davis is now fighting fit and playing with spirit and Lee Mears was named in the Lions squad. All these factors typify why Bath Rugby is not only a successful club, but a desired one also.

45

BATH'S SEASON - 2008-09

Date	H/A	Opponents	Result & Score	Att.	15	14	13	12	11
GUINNESS PREMIERSHIP									
07-09	A	Bristol	W 33-20	11021	Abendanon	Maddock/t	Cheeseman/t	Fuimaono Sapolu	Banahan
13-09	H	Gloucester	L 17-21	10600	Abendanon/t	Maddock/t	Cheeseman(a/c)	Fuimaono Sapolu	Banahan
20-09	A	London Irish	W 20-16	8221	Abendanon	Maddock	Crockett	Fuimaono Sapolu	Cuthbert/3p
27-09	H	Worcester	W 37-19	10600	Abendanon/t	Maddock/t	Crockett	Berne/t	Cuthbert
01-10	N	London Wasps	W 27-23	9052	Abendanon	Maddock/t	Crockett	Berne	Cuthbert
15-11	H	Leicester Tigers	W 25-21	10600	Maddock	Higgins	Crockett	Berne	Banahan
22-11	A	Northampton Saints	D 28-28	13473	Cuthbert/t	Higgins	Crockett	Fuimaono Sapolu	Banahan
30-11	A	Harlequins	L 14-21	12178	Abendanon	Stephenson	Cheeseman	Hape	Banahan
20-12	H	Sale Sharks	W 24-20	10600	Abendanon	Maddock	Crockett	Fuimaono Sapolu	Banahan/t
27-12	H	Northampton Saints	W 25-14	10600	Cuthbert	Maddock	Crockett	Hape	Banahan/t
04-01	A	Leicester Tigers	L 22-24	17498	Abendanon	Maddock/t	Crockett	Hape	Higgins
14-02	A	Worcester	W 34-17	10096	Maddock/t	Stephenson	Hape	Fuimaono Sapolu	Higgins/3t
21-02	H	London Irish	D 20-20	10600	Maddock/t	Higgins	Crockett	Fuimaono Sapolu	Banahan/t
28-02	A	Gloucester	L 27-36	16121	Maddock	Higgins/t	Crockett	Fuimaono Sapolu	Banahan
07-03	H	Bristol*	W 45-8	10600	Maddock/2t	Higgins	Crockett/2t	Hape	Banahan
15-03	A	Saracens	L 16-20	8092	Abendanon	Maddock	Crockett/t	Berne	Banahan
21-03	H	Newcastle Falcons	W 36-25	10600	Abendanon	Maddock/t	Crockett	Berne/tc	Banahan
27-03	A	Sale Sharks	L 16-23	9808	Abendanon	Stephenson	Cheeseman	Hape	Higgins
01-04	H	London Wasps	W 22-14	10600	Abendanon	Maddock	Crockett	Hape	Banahan
04-04	H	Harlequins	L 3-16	10600	Abendanon	Maddock	Crockett	Hape	Banahan
19-04	A	Newcastle Falcons	W 15-14	7804	Maddock	Higgins	Cheeseman	Hape/t	Banahan
25-04	H	Saracens	W 33-18	10600	Abendanon	Higgins/t	Cheeseman	Hape	Banahan/t
HEINEKEN CUP									
12-10	N	Toulouse	L 16-18	31885	Abendanon/t	Maddock	Crockett	Berne	Banahan
19-10	H	Gwent Dragons	W 13-9	10600	Abendanon	Maddock	Crockett	Berne	Banahan(f/t)
07-12	H	Glasgow Caledonians	W 35-31	10600	Abendanon	Stephenson/2t	Cheeseman(a/t)	Fuimaono Sapolu	Banahan
14-12	N	Glasgow Caledonians	W 25-19	3306	Abendanon	Maddock/t	Berne/t	Fuimaono Sapolu	Banahan/2t
18-01	N	Gwent Dragons	W 15-12	6108	Abendanon	Maddock/t	Crockett	Fuimaono Sapolu	Banahan
25-01	H	Toulouse	D 3-3	10600	Abendanon	Maddock	Crockett	Berne	Banahan
Q.F. 11-04	N	Leicester Tigers	L 15-20	26100	Abendanon	Maddock/t	Crockett(a/t)	Hape	Banahan
EDF ENERGY CUP									
04-10	H	Leicester Tigers	L 15-19	10600	Kydd/cp	Stephenson	Hape	Cheeseman	Higgins/2t
24-10	A	Sale Sharks	W 24-21	7655	Cuthbert/3cp	Crane	Cheeseman	Hape/t	Stephenson/t
31-10	A	Cardiff	L 18-24	10139	Cuthbert/p	Maddock/tp	Crockett	Hape	Higgins/t
GUINNESS CHAMPIONSHIP									
S.F. 09-05	N	Leicester Tigers	L 10-24	18850	Abendanon	Maddock	Crockett	Hape	Banahan

SCORING BREAKDOWN

WHEN	Total	First Half	Second Half	1/4	2/4	3/4	4/4
the POINTS were scored	539	289	250	154	135	118	132
the POINTS were conceded	438	220	218	90	130	83	135
the TRIES were scored	58	27	31	17	10	14	17
the TRIES were conceded	48	22	26	8	14	6	20

HOW	Total	Pen. Try	Backs	Forwards	F Back	Wing	Centre	H Back	F Row	Lock	B Row
the TRIES were scored	58	1	35	22	7	15	7	6	7	3	12
the TRIES were conceded	48	1	32	15	3	16	9	4	6	1	8

KEY: *after opponents name indicates a penalty try.
Brackets after a player's name indicates he was replaced. eg (a) means he was replaced by replacement code "a" and so on.
/ after a player or replacement name is followed by any scores he made - eg /t, /c, /p, /dg or any combination of these

PREMIERSHIP

10	9	1	2	3	4	5	6	7	8
James/3c4p	Claassens	Barnes	Mears	Stevens	Harrison	Short	Hooper	Scayesbrook	Faamatuainu/t
James	Claassens	Flatman	Mears	Stevens	Harrison	Short	Hooper	Lipman/t	Faamatuainu
James/t2p	Claassens	Barnes	Mears	Bell	Harrison	Short	Hooper	Lipman	Scayesbrook
James/3c2p	Claassens	Flatman	Mears	Stevens(b/t)	Harrison	Short	Hooper	Lipman/t	Faamatuainu
James/2cp	Claassens/t	Barnes	Dixon/t	Stevens/t	Harrison	Short	Hooper	Lipman	Faamatuainu
James/t2c2p	Bemand	Barnes	Dixon/t	Bell	Harrison	Grewcock	Short	Faamatuainu	Browne/t
James/2c3p	Bemand	Barnes	Dixon	Bell	Harrison	Grewcock	Short	Faamatuainu/t	Browne/t
James/3p	Claassens	Flatman	Dixon	Bell	Harrison	Short	Hooper	Faamatuainu	Browne/t
James/c4p	Claassens	Barnes	Mears	Stevens	Harrison	Short	Faamatuainu	Lipman	Browne/t
James/2c2p	Claassens/2t	Flatman	Mears	Stevens	Hooper	Short	Beattie	Lipman	Faamatuainu
James/2cp	Bemand	Barnes	Dixon/t	Bell	Hooper/t	Short	Beattie	Scayesbrook	Browne
James/4c2p	Claassens	Flatman	Dixon	Bell	Harrison	Hooper	Beattie	Scayesbrook	Browne
James/cp	Claassens	Browne	Lipman	Beattie	Hooper/t	Harrison	Bell	Dixon	Flatman
James/3c2p	Claassens	Barnes	Hawkins/2t	Bell	Harrison	Short	Beattie	Scayesbrook	Browne
James/6cp	Bemand	Barnes	Hawkins	Bell	Hooper	Short	Beattie	Scayesbrook	Faamatuainu(c/t)
James/c3p	Bemand	Flatman	Hawkins	Bell	Harrison	Short	Hooper	Scayesbrook	Browne
James/2c5p	Bemand	Flatman	Hawkins	Bell	Harrison	Hooper	Beattie/t	Lipman	Browne
Davis/3p(d/c)	Bemand	Barnes	Hawkins	Bell	Harrison	Hooper	Faamatuainu/t	Lipman	Browne
James/c5p	Bemand	Flatman	Mears	Bell	Harrison	Short	Beattie	Lipman	Faamatuainu/t
James/p	Bemand	Barnes	Mears	Bell	Harrison	Hooper	Beattie	Scayesbrook	Faamatuainu
James(e/cp)	Claassens/t	Flatman	Mears	Bell	Harrison	Short	Beattie	Lipman	Hooper
Davis/3c4p	Claassens	Flatman	Mears	Bell	Harrison	Short/t	Beattie	Lipman	Hooper
James/2p	Claassens/t	Flatman	Mears	Stevens	Harrison	Short	Hooper	Lipman	Faamatuainu
James/c2p	Claassens	Flatman	Mears	Stevens	Harrison	Short	Hooper	Lipman	Faamatuainu
James/3c3p	Claassens	Flatman	Dixon	Stevens	Hooper	Short	Beattie/t	Lipman	Browne
James/cp	Claassens	Barnes	Dixon	Stevens	Harrison	Grewcock	Beattie	Lipman	Browne
James/cp	Claassens	Flatman	Mears	Stevens	Harrison	Hooper/t	Beattie	Scayesbrook	Browne
James/p	Claassens	Barnes	Mears	Bell	Harrison	Hooper	Beattie	Lipman	Browne
James/cp	Claassens	Flatman	Mears	Bell	Harrison	Short	Beattie	Lipman	Faamatuainu
Fuimaono Sapolu	Bemand	Flatman	Hawkins	Ion	Harrison	Hobson	Ovens	Scayesbrook	Jackson
Fuimaono Sapolu	Bemand	Barnes	Hawkins	Bell	Harrison	Hooper/t	Ovens	Lipman	Browne
Berne/c	Bemand	Flatman	Dixon	Bell	Short	Grewcock	Beattie	Scayesbrook	Browne
Davis	Claassens/t	Flatman	Mears	Bell	Harrison	Short	Beattie	Scayesbrook	Hooper/t

REPLACEMENTS

a- S Berne   b- D Bell   c- D Browne   d- J Cuthbert
e- R Davis   f- A Higgins

LEAGUE APPEARANCES

20	Butch James
19	Justin Harrison (2)
18	Joe Maddock
17	Stuart Hooper (4), Peter Short (3)

LEAGUE POINTS SCORERS

Pts	Player	T	C	P	DG
212	Butch James	2	35	44	-
50	Joe Maddock	10	-	-	-
32	Ryan Davis	-	4	8	-
25	Daniel Browne	5	-	-	-
25	Andrew Higgins	5	-	-	-

NUMBER OF PLAYERS USED

31 plus 5 as a replacement only

47

BATH STATISTICS

LEAGUE

TEAM RECORDS

MOST POINTS
Scored at Home: 84 v Sale 26.4.97
Scored Away: 68 v Rotherham 14.4.01
Conceded at Home: 40 v Wasps 14.9.96
Conceded Away: 68 v Gloucester 04.05.02

MOST TRIES
Scored in a match: 14
v Bedford 13.1.90 & v Sale 26.4.97
Conceded in a match: 7 v London Irish 17.4.99

BIGGEST MARGINS
Home Win: 77pts - 84-7 v Sale 26.4.97
Away Win: 56pts - 68-12 v Rotherham 14.4.01
Home Defeat: 18pts
11-29 v 30.03.02 & 9-27 v Leicester 09.03.02
Away Defeat: 56pts - 12-68 v Gloucester 04.05.02

MOST CONSECUTIVE
Victories: 15
Defeats: 6 (2)

INDIVIDUAL RECORDS

MOST APPEARANCES
by a forward: 157 (9) Martin Haag
by a back: 142 (5) Adedayo Adebayo

MOST CONSECUTIVE
Appearances: 50 Tony Swift 9.9.89-25.9.93
Matches scoring Tries: 6 Andy Nicol, Adedayo Adebayo
Matches scoring points: 15 Jon Callard

MATCH RECORDS

Most Points
27 Olly Barkley v Rotherham 11.10.03 (H)

Most Tries
4 Jeremy Guscott v Bedford 13.1.90 (H)
   Tony Swift v Bedford 13.1.90 (H)
   Jeremy Guscott v Lon. Scot 15.5.99 (H)

Most Conversions
10 Stuart Barnes v Bedford 13.1.90 (H)

Most Penalties
7 Olly Barkley v London Irish 1.9.02 (A)
   v Gloucester 7.4.07 (H)

Most Drop Goals
2 Iain Balshaw v Lon Irish 10.04.02 (A)
   Chris Malone v Lon Irish 24.04.05

SEASON RECORDS

Most Points	294	MikeCatt	98-99
Most Tries	16	Adedayo Adebayo	96-97
Most Conversions	51	Jon Callard	96-97
Most Penalties	53	Mike Catt	99-99
Most Drop Goals	9	Chris Malone	04-05

CAREER RECORDS

Most Points	1177	Jon Callard	89-00
Most Tries	67	Jeremy Guscott	85-99
Most Conversions	186	Jon Callard	89-00
Most Penalties	261	Ollie Barkley	00-08
Most Drop Goals	22	Chris Malone	04-07

LAST TEN SEASONS

	Division	P	W	D	L	F	A	P.D.	Pts	Pos	Most Points	Most Tries
99-00	P1	22	15	2	5	690	425	265	43	2	184 Jon Preston	15 Iain Balshaw
00-01	P1	22	14	0	8	680	430	250	70	3	172 Jon Preston	9 Tom Voyce
01-02	P	22	7	0	15	311	524	-213	28	11	129 Olly Barkley	2 by 5 players
02-03	P	22	7	2	13	385	490	-105	36	11	155 Olly Barkley	6 Simon Danielle
03-04	P	22	18	0	4	508	311	197	79	1	219 Olly Barkley	6 Isaac Feau'nati
04-05	P	22	12	0	8	407	366	41	58	4	133 Chris Malone	4 Matt Tindalli
05-06	P	22	9	1	12	441	494	-53	46	9	130 Chris Malone	4 Chris Malone
06-07	P	22	8	2	12	428	492	-64	45	8	185 Olly Barkley	5 Joe Maddock
07-08	P	22	15	0	7	526	387	139	69	3	173 Olly Barkley	10 Mike Banahan
08-09	P	22	13	2	7	539	441	98	65	4	212 Butch James	10 Joe Maddock

RFU SENIOR CUP

OVERALL PLAYING RECORD

	P	W	O	L	F	A	Pts Diff
Home	36	24	0	12	841	390	451
Away	41	31	0	10	727	482	245
Neutral	11	10	0	1	236	137	99
TOTAL	88	65	0	23	1804	1009	795

TEAM RECORDS

Highest Score: 82 v Oxford 88/89
Biggest Winning Margin: 73 (82-9) v Oxford 88/89
Highest Score Against: 39 v Leicester 96/97
Biggest Losing Margin: 24 (27-3) v Wilmslow 73/74

SEASON BY SEASON

Season	Result	Season	Result	Season	Result	Season	Result	Season	Result
71-72	1R	78-79	1R	85-86	Winners	92-93	3R	99-00	4R
72-73	1R	79-80	QF	86-87	Winners	93-94	Winners	00-01	4R
73-74	2R	80-81	4R	87-88	QF	94-95	Winners	01-02	6R
74-75	QF	81-82	3R	88-89	Winners	95-96	Winners	02-03	QF
75-76	1R	82-83	DNQ	89-90	Winners	96-97	6R	03-04	QF
76-77	1R	83-84	Winners	90-91	3R	97-98	5R	04-05	Runners-up
77-78	1R	84-85	Winners	91-92	Winners	98-99	4R		

Anglo-Welsh Cup

05-06	SF
06-07	Gp
07-08	Gp
08-09	GP

Premiership Championship

02-03	-
03-04	R-Up
04-05	-
05-06	-
06-07	-

07-08	S.F.
08-09	S.F.

EUROPEAN COMPETITIONS

TEAM RECORDS

Highest Score
75 v L Aquila 03/04

Biggest Winning Margin
64 Pts 75-11 v L Aquila 03/04

Highest Score Against
38 v Saracens 00/01
38 v Montferrand 03/04

Biggest Losing Margin
22 Pts 31-9 v Munster 2000/01

INDIVIDUAL RECORDS

Most Points in a match
33 Mike Catt v B Treviso 96/97

Most Tries in a match
4 Mike Catt v B Treviso 96/97

Most Conversions in a match
10 Oliver Barkley v L Aquila 03/04

Most Penalties in a match
6 Jon Callard v Toulouse 99/00
6 Jon Preston v Castres 00/01

Most Drop Goals in a match
1 by 4 players - Mike Catt, Matt Perry, Chris Malone (3), Ollie Barkley

CAREER RECORDS

Most Appearances:
54 Steve Borthwick
48: Ollie Barkley (4)
45 (2) Danny Grewcock
37: Matt Perry
36 (7) David Banres

Most Points:
575 Ollie Barkley
216 Jonathan Callard
118 Matt Perry
97 Jon Preston
91 Butch James

Most Tries:
14 Olly Barkley,
10 Mike Catt,
9: Tom Voyce

SEASON BY SEASON

Season		Result
1996-97	C	QF
1997-98	C	Winners
1998-99	-	D N Play
1999-00	C	Gp Stage
2000-01	C	Gp Stage
2001-02	C	Gp Stage
2002-03	S	Runners-up
2003-04	S	SF
2004-05	C	Gp Stage
2005-06	C	SF
2006-07	S	Runners-up
2007-08	CC	Winners
2008-09	C	QF

OVERALL PLAYING RECORD

	P	W	D	L	F	A	Pts Diff
Home	42	38	1	3	1320	612	708
Away	43	26	0	17	1039	825	214
Neutral	3	2	0	1	59	56	3
Total	88	66	1	21	2418	1493	925

49

GLOUCESTER RUGBY

GLOUCESTER RUGBY

Founded: 1873

Website: www.gloucesterrugby.co.uk

Colours: Cherry and white

Change colours: Blue and white

KEY PERSONNEL

Managing Director: Ken Nottage

Chairman: Tom Walkinshaw

Treasurer: Pete Darnborough

Team Secretary: Adrienne Eley Tel 01452 702121
email:Adrienneeley@gloucesterrugby.co.uk

Director of Rugby: Dean Ryan

Rugby Manager: Alex Hennessy Tel 07894 489737
email: alexhennessy@gloucesterrugby.co.uk

Media Manager: Duncan Wood Tel 07833 795745
email: duncanwood@gloucesterrugby.co.uk

Commercial Secretary: Mandy Isom 07970 869997

CONTACT DETAILS

Gloucester Rugby, Kingsholm Stadium, Kingsholm Road, Gloucester GL1 3AX
Tel: 0871 871 8781   Fax: 01452 383321   email: admin@gloucesterrugby.co.uk

GROUND DETAILS

Address:
Kingsholm Stadium, Kingsholm Rd., Gloucester. GL1 3AX.
Tel: 0871 871 8781

Capacity: 16,267
Covered Seating: 10,333   Terrace: 5,967

Directions:

Park & Ride: Our Park and Ride facility runs every 20 minutes for two hours before and after each home Guinness Premiership fixture. Supporter's vehicles can be securely parked at the British Energy overspill car park at Barnwood which is signposted around the city with yellow AA road signs. Swanbrook Bus Company provide the shuttle service at £1 for adults and .50p for all concessions. More than 600 cars can use this facility into Kingsholm and it is easy for all supporters with excellent access from junction 11A of M5.

By Road: M5 Junct 11a – follow signs to city centre. Detailed instructions and maps available on the website.

By Rail: Gloucester station is only a 10 minute walk.

By Bus: The bus station is also centrally located and only 10 minutes walk.

Club House: Open matchdays. Available for function hire, contact sales team on 01452 300951

South Stand – Kingsholm Business Centre. Fully catered banqueting and conference facilities. Contact Sales team on 01452 872269.

Club Shop: Open weekdays 10am until 4pm and Saturdays 9am until 4pm. Matchday opening hours vary according to kick off time

PROGRAMME

Size: A5   Pages: 76   Price: £3
Editor: Duncan Wood
Advertising:
Contact Dunwoody Publishing 01635 35599

Admission Prices

South Stand (Covered Seating), Gold £43, Silver: Adult £37, Concession £28, Junior £20, Bronze: Adult £26, Concession £22, Junior £13

East Stand (Covered Seating), Adult £26, Concession £22, Junior £13

The Shed (Covered Unallocated Standing), Adult £22, Concession £18, Junior £12

The West Terrace (Unallocated Standing), Adult £23, Concession £19, Junior £11

(L-R) - **Back row**: Iain Balshaw, James Forrester, Adam Eustace, Alex Brown, Will James, Peter Buxton, Marco Bortolami
3rd row: Matthew Watkins, David Young, Olly Morgan, Carlos Nieto, Lesley Vainikolo, Andrew Hazell, Jack Adams, Olly Barkley
2nd row: Akapusi Qera, Ross McMillan, Charlie Sharples, Henry Trinder, Nick Wood, Dan Williams, Alasdair Strokosch, Gareth Delve, Alasdair Dickinson, Olivier Azam, James Simpson-Daniel
Front row: Jack Forster, Mark Foster, Andy Titterrell, Rory Lawson, Dave Lewis, Mike Tindall, Ryan Lamb, Willie Walker, Luke Narraway, Anthony Allen

REVIEW OF THE SEASON 2008-09

2008-9 was a season that promised so much for Gloucester Rugby but, in the space of 7 days, unravelled as three defeats left the club empty handed.

Heading into the final stretch, Gloucester were all set for possibly the most successful campaign in the club's history with the team riding high in the Guinness Premiership table and finalists in the EDF Energy Cup.

However, a combination of injuries and a punishing fixture schedule in the final week of the season saw defeat to the Cardiff Blues in the Twickenham showpiece followed by two Guinness Premiership defeats and Gloucester missed out on the end of season playoffs having topped the table for long periods.

It was a disappointing finale for Dean Ryan's men who had entered the season with high hopes. New signings such as Olly Barkley, Apo Satala and Matthew Watkins boosted the previous season's squad whilst the most capped All Black prop of all time, Greg Somerville, was confirmed as an Autumn arrival.

And, after a disappointing home defeat to Leicester Tigers to get the competitive season underway, the team started to find their form with some notable scalps being taken at Kingsholm in particular.

Lesley Vainikolo was in fine form on the wing, terrorising opposing defences with 8 tries before the end of the calendar year. However, the big winger was ruled out for the season in early January and the club slipped out of the Heineken Cup later in the month.

Gloucester's home form kept them in the chase for Guinness Premiership honours as spring passed but, a lack of wins on their travels would prove to be their ultimate undoing as victory at Bristol on December 27th would prove to be their final away league win of the season.

A brutal injury list caught up with the squad as the campaign approached its finale and Ryan was forced to play several players three times in the final week.

2008-9 will go down as "what might have been" and everyone at Kingsholm will be looking to bounce back next season.

GLOUCESTER RUGBY

GLOUCESTER'S SEASON - 2008-09

Date	H/A	Opponents	Result & Score	Att.	15	14	13	12	11
GUINNESS PREMIERSHIP									
07-09	H	Leicester Tigers	L 8-20	13180	Morgan/t	Simpson-Daniel	Tindall	Allen	Vainikolo
13-09	A	Bath	W 21-17	10600	Morgan	Simpson-Daniel	Watkins	Tindall	Vainikolo
20-09	H	Harlequins	W 24-20	12216	Morgan/t	Watkins	Tindall	Barkley/p	Vainikolo
26-09	A	Sale Sharks	L 9-23	9019	Balshaw	Simpson-Daniel	Watkins	Barkley/3p	Vainikolo
30-09	H	Newcastle Falcons	W 39-23	12861	Morgan	Balshaw/3t	Watkins	Tindall	Simpson-Dan
16-11	A	Saracens	W 25-21	8535	Morgan/t	Balshaw	Tindall	Allen/t	Vainikolo/t
21-11	H	Bristol	W 39-10	15297	Morgan/t	Balshaw	Tindall	Allen	Watkins
29-11	H	Northampton Saints	W 33-10	13494	Balshaw/t	Watkins	Tindall	Allen(a/t)	Vainikolo/t
20-12	A	London Irish	L 12-42	12706	Morgan(b/p)	Foster	Watkins	Tindall	Vainikolo
27-12	A	Bristol	W 29-10	11845	Morgan/t	Watkins	Tindall/2t	Barkley/c	Vainikolo/t
03-01	H	Saracens	W 22-16	16500	Morgan/t	Watkins	Tindall	Barkley/c5p	Vainikolo
11-01	A	Newcastle Falcons	L 7-10	5026	Morgan	Watkins	Tindall	Barkley/c	Foster
31-01	H	London Irish	W 23-21	13974	Walker	Balshaw/t	Trinder	Allen	Simpson-Dan
14-02	H	Sale Sharks	W 24-17		Balshaw	Foster/t	Watkins	Barkley/c3p	Simpson-Dan
21-02	A	Harlequins	L 9-14	12636	Balshaw	Sharples	Trinder	Barkley/3p	Simpson-Dan
28-02	H	Bath	W 36-27	16121	Morgan	Balshaw	Simpson-Daniel/2t(ac/3p)Allen		Sharples/t
07-03	A	Leicester Tigers	L 10-24	17498	Morgan	Balshaw/t	Trinder	Barkley/cp	Sharples
14-03	H	London Wasps	W 24-22	15294	Morgan/t	Balshaw/t	Allen	Barkley/3p	Sharples
22-03	A	Worcester*	L 10-14	12024	Morgan	Balshaw	Watkins	Allen	Sharples
04-04	A	Northampton Saints	L 22-40	13426	Morgan	Foster/t	Watkins	Allen(a/p)	Sharples
21-04	H	Worcester	L 6-13	14035	Morgan	Watkins	Simpson-Daniel	Barkley/2p	Foster
25-04	N	London Wasps	L 3-34	10000	Morgan	Sharples	Trinder	Barkley/p	Foster
HEINEKEN CUP									
11-10	H	Biarritz	W 22-10	11723	Morgan	Balshaw	Tindall	Barkley/c4p	Simpson-Dan
19-10	N	Cardiff	L 24-37	27140	Morgan/t	Balshaw/2t	Tindall	Barkley/3cp	Simpson-Dan
06-12	A	Calvisano*	W 40-17	3500	Morgan	Foster/t	Watkins(e/t)	Barkley/5c	Vainikolo
13-12	H	Calvisano	W 48-5	13970	Morgan	Foster/t	Watkins/2t	Tindall	Vainikolo/2t
18-01	H	Cardiff	L 12-16	14916	Walker	Balshaw	Watkins	Barkley/4p	Simpson-Dan
23-01	A	Biarritz	L 10-24	7000	Morgan	Balshaw	Watkins	Barkley/cp	Simpson-Dan
EDF ENERGY CUP									
04-10	H	London Wasps	W 24-19	7864	Walker/tc3p	Foster	Adams	Tindall	Vainikolo/t
25-10	H	Gwent Dragons	W 25-20	8057	Balshaw/t	Foster	Tindall	Barkley/cp	Vainikolo/2t
02-11	A	Newcastle Falcons	W 11-10	3614	Walker	Balshaw	Barkley/2p	Tindall	Vainikolo
S.F. 28-03	N	Ospreys	W 17-0		Morgan	Balshaw/t	Tindall	Allen	Simpson-Dan
Final 18-04	N	Cardiff*	L 12-50	54899	Morgan	Watkins	Simpson-Daniel	Allen	Foster/t

SCORING BREAKDOWN

WHEN	Total	First Half	Second Half	1/4	2/4	3/4	4/4
the POINTS were scored	435	235	200	84	151	107	93
the POINTS were conceded	448	251	197	116	135	60	137
the TRIES were scored	43	24	19	8	16	9	10
the TRIES were conceded	44	22	22	12	10	6	16

HOW	Total	Pen. Try	Backs	Forwards	F Back	Wing	Centre	H Back	F Row	Lock	B Row
the TRIES were scored	43	1	32	10	8	14	6	4	1	2	7
the TRIES were conceded	44	1	31	12	4	17	4	6	5	1	6

KEY: * after opponents name indicates a penalty try.
Brackets after a player's name indicates he was replaced. eg (a) means he was replaced by replacement code "a" and so on.
/ after a player or replacement name is followed by any scores he made - eg /t, /c, /p, /dg or any combination of these

PREMIERSHIP

10	9	1	2	3	4	5	6	7	8
Lamb/p	Lawson	Wood	Titterell	Nieto	James	Bortolami	Buxton	Strokosch	Narraway
Walker/tc2pdg	Cooper	Wood	Azam	Nieto	James	Brown	Buxton	Hazell	Narraway/t
Walker/c2pdg	Cooper	Wood	Azam	Nieto	James	Brown	Strokosch/t	Hazell	Narraway
Lamb	Lawson	Dickinson	Azam	Young	Bortolami	Brown	Buxton	Hazell	Narraway
Barkley/c4p	Cooper	Wood	Lawson	Dickinson	Brown	Bortolami	Buxton	Strokosch	Narraway
Lamb/2c2p	Lewis	Wood	Azam	Forster	James	Brown	Buxton	Satala	Strokosch
Lamb/t4cpdg	Lewis	Wood	Azam	Forster	James	Brown/t	Buxton/2t	Satala	Narraway
Lamb/2c3p	Lewis	Wood	Azam	Nieto	James	Bortolami	Buxton	Strokosch	Narraway/t
Lamb/3p	Cooper	Wood	Lawson	Somerville	Bortolami	Brown	Buxton	Strokosch	Narraway
Lamb/2cp	Lawson	Wood	Azam	Nieto	James	Brown	Strokosch	Satala	Narraway
Lamb	Lewis	Wood	Azam	Nieto	Eustace	Brown	Strokosch	Satala	Narraway
Walker	Lawson/t	Dickinson	Titterell	Nieto	Bortolami	Brown	Strokosch	Satala	Narraway
Barkley/6p	Lawson	Dickinson	Azam	Somerville	Eustace	Brown	Strokosch	Satala	Delve
Spencer(c/dg)	Lawson	Wood	Azam	Somerville	James	Brown	Satala/t	Hazell	Delve
Spencer	Lawson	Wood	Titterell	Somerville	Bortolami	Brown	Narraway	Hazell	Delve
Spencer/cp	Lawson/t	Wood	Azam	Somerville	Eustace	Brown	Satala	Hazell	Delve
Spencer	Lawson	Wood	Azam	Somerville	Eustace	Brown	Narraway	Hazell	Delve
Spencer	Lawson	Wood	Azam	Somerville	James	Brown	Narraway	Hazell	Delve(d/t)
Spencer/cp	Lawson	Wood	Azam	Somerville	James	Brown	Satala	Qera	Narraway
Lamb/2c	Lawson	Wood/t	Azam	Somerville	James/t	Brown	Strokosch	Qera	Delve
Spencer	Cooper	Dickinson	Lawson	Nieto	Eustace	Brown	Narraway	Qera	Delve
Spencer	Lawson	Dickinson	Lawson	Somerville	Eustace	Bortolami	Narraway	Satala	Delve
Lamb/p	Cooper	Dickinson	Azam	Nieto	Bortolami	Brown	Buxton	Strokosch	Narraway
Lamb	Cooper	Dickinson	Azam	Nieto	Bortolami	Brown	Buxton	Strokosch	Narraway
Lamb/t	Lawson	Dickinson	Lawson	Nieto	James	Bortolami/t	Buxton	Strokosch	Narraway/t
Lamb/6c2p	Cooper	Dickinson	Titterell	Nieto	Eustace	Bortolami	Buxton	Satala	Narraway/t
Lamb	Cooper	Dickinson	Azam	Nieto	Bortolami	Brown	Strokosch	Satala	Narraway
Walker	Cooper	Dickinson	Azam	Nieto	James	Brown	Strokosch	Satala	Narraway
Lamb/dg	Lawson	Dickinson	Azam	Young	Bortolami	Brown	Satala	Hazell	Strokosch
Walker	Lawson	Dickinson	Lawson/t	Nieto	Eustace	Bortolami	Buxton	Hazell	Strokosch
Lamb	Cooper	Wood	Titterell	Nieto	Eustace	Brown	Buxton	Hazell(f/t)	Strokosch
Lamb/3pdg	Lawson	Dickinson	Azam	Somerville	James	Brown	Strokosch	Hazell	Delve
Lamb(a/c)	Lawson	Wood	Azam	Somerville	Brown	James	Narraway	Qera	Delve

REPLACEMENTS

a- O Barkley b- W Walker c- R Lamb d- A Qera
e- M Tindall f- A Satala

LEAGUE APPEARANCES

19 Alex Brown (2)
17 Olly Morgan, Luke Narraway, Nick Wood (5)
15 Olivier Azam (6)

LEAGUE POINTS SCORERS

Pts	Player	T	C	P	DG
127	Olly Barkley	1	7	36	-
68	Ryan Lamb	1	12	11	2
35	Olly Morgan	7	-	-	-
35	Iain Balshaw	7	-	-	-
30	Willie Walker	1	2	5	2

NUMBER OF PLAYERS USED

38 plus 1 as a replacement only

GLOUCESTER STATISTICS
LEAGUE

TEAM RECORDS

MOST POINTS
Scored at Home: 68 v Bath 04.05.02
Scored Away: 50 v Leeds 12.05.02
Conceded at Home: 45 v Bath 21.9.96
Conceded Away: 75 v Harlequins 31.8.96

MOST TRIES
Scored in a match: 11 v Sale 16.4.88
Conceded in a match: 11
v Harlequins 31.8.96
v Bath 30.4.97

BIGGEST MARGINS
Home Win: 56pts - 68-12 v Bath 04.05.02
Away Win: 46pts - 49-3 v Orrell 16.11.96
Home Defeat: 24pts - 11-35 v Northampton 11.3.00
Away Defeat: 56pts - 19-75 v Harlequins 31.8.96

MOST CONSECUTIVE
Victories: 8
Defeats: 7

INDIVIDUAL RECORDS

MOST APPEARANCES
by a forward: 137 Rob Fidler
by a back: 140(11) Terry Fanolua

MOST CONSECUTIVE
Appearances: 47 Dave Sims 11.4.92-25.3.95
Matches scoring Tries: 4 Phillipe St Andre
Matches scoring points: 48 Mark Mapletoft

MATCH RECORDS

Most Points
28   Simon Mannix   v Northampton 16.5.99 (H)

Most Tries
5   Lesley Vainikolo   v Leeds 16.9.07 (A)

Most Conversions
7   Simon Mannix   v Bedford 16.5.00 (H)
    Ludovic Mercier   v Bath 4.5.02 (H)

Most Penalties
9   Simon Mannix   v Harlequins 23.9.00 (H)

Most Drop Goals
3   Ludovic Mercier   v Sale 22.09.01 (A)

SEASON RECORDS

Most Points	334	Ludovic Mercier	01-02
Most Tries	9	Elton Moncrieff	99-00
		Chris Catling	99-00
		Junior Paramore	01-02
		James Simpson-Daniel	01-02, 03-04, 07-08
		Jake Boer	02-03
		Lesley Vainikolo	07-08
Most Conversions	42	Ludovic Mercier	01-02 & 02-03
Most Penalties	49	Ludovic Mercier	05-06
Most Drop Goals	12	Ludovic Mercier	01-02

CAREER RECORDS

Most Points	848	Mark Mapletoft	94-99
Most Tries	40	James Simpson-Daniel	00-08
Most Conversions	122	Ludovic Mercier	01-03/05-07
Most Penalties	183	Mark Mapletoft	94-99
Most Drop Goals	16	Ludovic Mercier	01-03/05-06

LAST TEN SEASONS

	Division	P	W	D	L	F	A	P.D.	Pts	Pos	Most Points	Most Tries
99-00	P1	22	15	0	7	628	490	138	40	3	282 Simon Mannix	9 C Catling & E Moncrieff
00-01	P1	22	10	0	12	473	526	-53	48	7	187 Simon Mannix	6 Jason Little
01-02	P	22	14	0	8	692	485	207	68	3	334 Ludovic Mercier	9 Junior Paramore & James Simpson-Daniel
02-03	P	22	17	2	3	617	396	221	82	1	255 Ludovic Mercier	9 Jake Boer
03-04	P	22	14	0	8	493	409	84	63	4	206 Henry Paul	9 James Simpson Daniel
04-05	P	22	10	1	11	407	487	-80	47	6	136 Henry Paul	6 Terry Fanolua / Marcel Garvey
05-06	P	22	11	1	10	483	385	98	59	5	213 Ludovic Mercier	6 James Simpson Daniel
06-07	P	22	15	2	5	531	404	127	71	1	159 Willie Walker	5 James Forrester, James Bailey
07-08	P	22	15	0	7	551	377	174	74	1	152 Ryan Lamb	9 James Simpson Daniel & Lesley Vainikolo
08-09	P	22	12	0	10	435	448	-13	57	6	127 Olly Barkley	7 Olly Morgan, Iain Balshaw

RFU SENIOR CUP

OVERALL PLAYING RECORD

	P	W	O	L	F	A	Pts Diff
Home	46	32	0	14	1110	469	641
Away	45	31	0	14	764	573	191
Neutral	6	4	1	1	97	102	-5
TOTAL	97	67	1	29	1971	1144	827

TEAM RECORDS

Highest Score: 87 v Exeter 85/86 (H)
Biggest Winning Margin: 84Pts (87-3) v Exeter 85/86 (H)
Highest Score Against: 35 v Wasps 98/99 (A)
Biggest Losing Margin: 19 Pts v Northampton 97/98 (A)

SEASON BY SEASON

71-72	Winners	78-79	1R	85-86	QF	92-93	3R	99-00	QF
72-73	2R	79-80	QF	86-87	QF	93-94	QF	00-01	5R
73-74	2R	80-81	QF	87-88	4R	94-95	4R	01-02	QF
74-75	2R	81-82	Shared	88-89	SF	95-96	SF	02-03	Winners
75-76	2R	82-83	3R	89-90	Runners-up	96-97	SF	03-04	6R
76-77	QF	83-84	DNQ	90-91	4R	97-98	5R	04-05	SF
77-78	Winners	84-85	SF	91-92	SF	98-99	SF		

Anglo-Welsh Cup

05-06	Gp Stage
06-07	Gp Stage
07-08	Gp Stage
08-09	S.F.

Premiership Championship

02-03	R-Up	07-08	S.F.
03-04	-	08-09	-
04-05	-		
05-06	-		
06-07	R-Up		

EUROPEAN COMPETITIONS

TEAM RECORDS

Highest Score
106 v Bucharest 29.10.05

Biggest Winning Margin
103 (106-3) v Bucharest 29. 10.05

Highest Score Against
62 v Swansea 96/97

Biggest Losing Margin
50 (62-12) v Swansea 96/97

INDIVIDUAL RECORDS

Most Points in a match
34 Mark Mapletoft v Ebbw Vale 96/97

Most Tries in a match
5 Daren O'Leary v Gran Palma Rugby 5.1.02
Tom Beim v Viadana 15.10.00

Most Conversions in a match
12 Henry Paul v Gran Palma Rugby 5.1.02

Most Penalties in a match
6 Ludovic Mercier v Ebbw Vale 01/02

Most Drop Goals in a match
2 Ludovic Mercier v La Rochelle 01/02

CAREER RECORDS

Most Appearances
43: Terry Fanolua (3)
40: James Simpson Daniel (2)
37: Phil Vickery (1)
30: Alex Brown (2)
28: Mark Cornwall (12)

Most Points
297: Ludovic Mercier
237: Henry Paul
165: James Simpson Daniel

Most Tries
33: James Simpson Daniel
17: James Forrester
12: Terry Fanolua

SEASON BY SEASON

1996-97	S	Gp Stage
1997-98	S	Q.F.
1998-99	-	D N Play
1999-00	S	Gp Stage
2000-01	C	S.F.
2001-02	S	S.F.
2002-03	C	Gp Stage
2003-04	C	Q.F.
2004-05	C	Gp Stage
2005-06	CC	Winners
2006-07	C	Gp Stage
2007-08	C	Q.F.
2008-09	C	Gp Stage

OVERALL PLAYING RECORD

	P	W	D	L	F	A	Pts Diff
Home	42	35	1	6	1576	619	957
Away	36	19	1	19	929	861	68
Neutral	3	1	0	2	78	81	-3
Total	81	57	2	28	2786	1561	1022

HARLEQUIN F.C.

HARLEQUINS

Founded: 1866

Nickname: Quins

Colours: Magenta, sky blue, chocolate brown, French grey, black and green

Change colours: White, light blue, magenta, green and black

Website: www.quins.co.uk

KEY PERSONNEL

President: Bob Hiller

Chairman: Charles Jillings

Chief Executive: Mark Evans

Director of Rugby: Dean Richards

Team Manager & Fixture Secretary: Don Shaw
Richardson Evans Sports Pavilion, Roehampton Vale, London SW15 3PQ
Tel: 020 8780 6422 Fax: 0870 132 6422 email: dons@quins.co.uk

Press and PR Manager: Sarah Butler
Tel: 020 8410 6045 / 07990 571807 Fax: 020 8410 6001 email: sarahb@quins.co.uk

Sales Manager: Julian Gent
Tel: 020 8410 6060 email: juliang@quins.co.uk

Sponsorship Manager: Laura Oakes
Tel: 020 8973 2671 email: laura.oakes@expsports.co.uk

Head of Community: Richard Varney
Tel: 020 8410 6031 email: richv@quins.co.uk

Ticket Manager: Jon Salinger
Tel: 020 8410 6043 email: jons@quins.co.uk

GROUND DETAILS

Twickenham Stoop Stadium, Langhorn Drive, Twickenham TW2 7SX
Tel: 0208 410 6000   Fax: 0208 410 6001
e-mail: mail@quins.co.uk

Capacity: 12,638 - all covered seating

Directions:
By Car: M25, M3, A316 – the ground is next to Richmond upon Thames Tertiary College and opposite Twickenham Stadium.
By Train: Out of the station and turn right before going left at the lights. Take the first left into Court Way and the first left again into Craneford Way. Follow this road all way to the end where the stadium is located.

Nearest BR Station: Twickenham.   **Car Parking**: Yes

Admission:
Matchday: Adults: £17 - £40, Concessions: £20 - £23, Under 16's: £7-£10
Season: Adults: £185 - £580, Under 16's: £70 - £115

Club Shop:
Open Mon. - Sat. 10-4.
Contact Angela Langley
Tel: 0208 410 6051 email: angelal@quins.co.uk

Clubhouse:
Open Matchdays from 1pm
Food and drink available matchdays from 1pm
Functions: Available 7 days a week.
Contact Zoe Westlake – 020 8410 6053 / zoew@quins.co.uk

PROGRAMME

Size: 165 x 240mm
Pages: 80   Price: £3
Editor: Sarah Butler

Advertising Rates
Contact Sarah Butler 020 8410 6045
sarahb@quins.co.uk

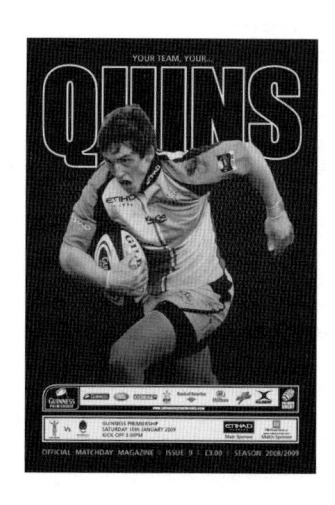

Harlequins squad 2008/09

REVIEW OF THE SEASON 2008-09

Harlequin FC enjoyed one of their best seasons on record in 2008/09, finishing second in the Guinness Premiership and reaching the quarter finals of the Heineken Cup.

The Guinness Premiership season saw Quins continue their fantastic come-back since returning to the top flight in 2006, with wins against every other Premiership team (including away wins at Bath and London Irish, and home wins against Gloucester, Wasps and Northampton) apart from Leicester Tigers, the eventual Guinness Premiership winners.

After finishing second in the league, Quins secured a home play-off draw against old rivals London Irish. A tense game saw Quins end the season with a surprising 0-17 home defeat, allowing London Irish to progress through to the final at Twickenham.

After finishing the 2007/08 Heineken Cup season winless, Quins were determined to make an impression on the European competition, and with wins over Scarlets and Ulster in the early rounds, the London side were well on their way.

Back to back games against French giants, Stade Francais, was always going to be a tough ask for the young London side, but Dean Richards' men proved more than up to the task, winning both games in dramatic style. A fine defensive effort saw the team steal the win at the Stade de France, becoming only the second side after Munster to do so.

The return fixture at the Twickenham Stoop saw the two sides battle out another tense match, in horrendous conditions. The game was tied at full-time, but with the last play of the game (all 29 phases of it!) fly-half, Nick Evans, scored a vital drop-goal, which sealed the win for the home side.

After qualifying for the quarter finals with a home game, Quins drew Leinster. A tense battle saw full-back, Mike Brown, score the only try of the game, but Leinster (the eventual Heineken Cup winners) proved too strong, and the game finished 5-6.

Despite the lack of silverware, the 2008/09 season will go down in Quins history for many reasons, but there is the feeling that this is only the beginning for Richards' young side.

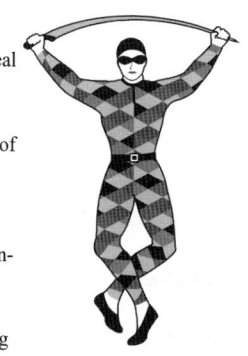

HARLEQUINS

QUINS' SEASON - 2008-09

PREMIERSHIP

Date	H/A	Opponents	Result & Score	Att.	15	14	13	12	11
GUINNESS PREMIERSHIP									
06-09	N	Saracens	W 24-21	52000	Brown	Strettle/t	Tiesi	Turner-Hall	Monye/t
13-09	H	Bristol	W 31-13	9497	Brown/t	Strettle	Tiesi/t	Turner-Hall/t	Monye
20-09	A	Gloucester	L 20-24	12216	Brown/t	Strettle	Tiesi	Turner-Hall	Monye
27-09	H	London Irish	L 27-28	11007	Brown	Strettle	Tiesi	Turner-Hall	Monye/t
02-10	A	Worcester	W 30-23	9222	Brown/t	Strettle	Tiesi/t	Turner-Hall	Monye/2t
16-11	H	London Wasps	W 32-10	12638	Evans/tc4p	Williams	Masson	Turner-Hall	Amesbury
22-11	A	Leicester Tigers	L 14-27	17432	Brown	Williams	Masson	Turner-Hall	Amesbury
30-11	H	Bath	W 21-14	12178	Brown	Stegmann	Barry	Turner-Hall/t	Williams
20-12	A	Northampton Saints	L 13-23	13349	Brown	Stegmann	Barry	Turner-Hall	Monye/t
27-12	H	Leicester Tigers	D 26-26	50000	Brown/t	Williams	Barry	Turner-Hall	Monye/t
04-01	N	London Wasps*	L 18-24	10000	Brown	Williams	Tiesi	Turner-Hall(d/p)	Monye
31-01	H	Northampton Saints*	W 27-6	12332	Brown	Williams	Barry	Turner-Hall	Strettle
14-02	A	London Irish	W 14-9	12321	Brown	Williams	Tiesi	Turner-Hall	Monye
21-02	H	Gloucester	W 14-9	12636	Brown	Strettle	Tiesi	Turner-Hall	Williams/t
01-03	A	Bristol	W 17-14	5005	Brown	Strettle/t	Tiesi	Turner-Hall	Williams(f/t)
07-03	H	Saracens	W 21-15	12638	Brown	Strettle	Tiesi	Turner-Hall	Monye
15-03	A	Newcastle Falcons	L 16-24	7705	Brown/t	Strettle	Tiesi	Turner-Hall	Williams
22-03	H	Sale Sharks	W 38-20	11592	Brown	Stegmann/t	Strettle	Barry/t	Williams
01-04	A	Worcester	W 60-14	10446	Brown/t	Williams/t	Tiesi	Turner-Hall	Monye/2t
04-04	H	Bath*	W 16-3	10600	Brown	Strettle	Tiesi	Barry	Monye
17-04	A	Sale Sharks	L 6-28	9579	Williams	Strettle	Tiesi	Barry	Stegmann
25-04	H	Newcastle Falcons	W 31-12	12638	Brown/t	Williams	Tiesi	Turner-Hall	Monye/t
HEINEKEN CUP									
11-10	A	Llanelli	W 29-22	8236	Brown	Amesbury	Tiesi	Turner-Hall	Monye/t
18-10	H	Ulster*	W 42-21	12638	Brown/t	Williams/2t	Monye	Turner-Hall/t	Amesbury
06-12	N	Stade Francais	W 15-10	76569	Brown	Williams/t	Tiesi	Turner-Hall/t	Monye
13-12	H	Stade Francais	W 19-17	12638	Brown	Williams	Tiesi	Turner-Hall/t	Monye
17-01	A	Ulster*	L 10-21	8861	Brown	Williams	Tiesi	Turner-Hall	Amesbury
24-01	H	Llanelli	W 29-24	11083	Evans/3cp	Williams/t	Tiesi	Turner-Hall	Monye
Q.F. 12-04	H	Leinster	L 5-6	12638	Brown/t	Strettle	Tiesi	Turner-Hall	Monye
EDF ENERGY CUP									
05-10	N	Ospreys	L 23-24	8057	Williams	Taione	Barry/t	Masson	Amesbury
25-10	H	London Irish	L 17-32	11173	Williams	Stegmann	Masson	Taione	Amesbury/t
02-11	A	Worcester	W 27-14	8113	Brown/t	Williams	Masson	Turner-Hall	Stegmann/t
GUINNESS CHAMPIONSHIP									
S.F. 09-05	H	London Irish	L 0-17	12638	Brown	Williams	Tiesi	Turner-Hall	Monye

SCORING BREAKDOWN

WHEN			Total	First Half	Second Half		1/4	2/4	3/4	4/4
the POINTS were scored			516	278	238		147	131	87	151
the POINTS were conceded			387	189	198		76	113	97	101
the TRIES were scored			60	27	33		14	13	12	21
the TRIES were conceded			36	14	22		3	11	10	12

HOW	Total	Pen. Try	Backs	Forwards	F Back	Wing	Centre	H Back	F Row	Lock	B Row
the TRIES were scored	60	3	36	21	8	15	5	8	9	1	11
the TRIES were conceded	36	3	26	7	2	9	7	8	1	1	5

58

KEY: * after opponents name indicates a penalty try.
Brackets after a player's name indicates he was replaced. eg (a) means he was replaced by replacement code "a" and so on.
/ after a player or replacement name is followed by any scores he made - eg /t, /c, /p, /dg or any combination of these

10	9	1	2	3	4	5	6	7	8
Evans/c3pdg	Care	Jones	Fuga	Ross	Kohn	Robson	Robshaw	Skinner	Easter
Luveniyali/3c	Care/t	Jones	Fuga	Ross	Kohn	Robson	Robshaw	Skinner	Easter(a/t)
Malone/tcp	Care/t	Jones	Fuga	Ross	Kohn	Robson	Robshaw	Skinner	Easter
Malone/2c2p(b/c)	Care/t	Jones	Botha	Ross	Kohn	Evans	Easter	Skinner	Guest/t
Malone/2c2p	Care	Jones	Botha	Ross	Kohn	Evans	Robshaw	Skinner	Guest
Malone/dg	Gomersall	Jones	Botha	Ross	Kohn	Evans	Robshaw/t	Skinner	Guest/t
Evans/3p	Poluleuligaga	Jones	Botha(c/t)	Ross	Kohn	Evans	Robshaw	McMillen	Guest
Evans/c3p	Gomersall	Jones/t	Fuga	Ross	Percival	Evans	Robshaw	Skinner	Guest
Evans/c2p	Gomersall	Jones	Fuga	Ross	Percival	Evans	Robshaw	Skinner	Easter
Evans/2c4p	Care	Jones	Fuga	Ross	Percival	Robson	Robshaw	Skinner	Easter
Evans/cp	Care/t	Croall	Brooker	Ross	Percival	Robson	Robshaw	Skinner	Easter
Evans/3c2p	Gomersall	Jones	Botha/t	Ross	Kohn(e/t)	Robson	Robshaw	Skinner	Guest
Evans/3p	Gomersall	Jones/t	Botha	Lambert	Kohn	Robson	Robshaw	Skinner	Guest
Evans/tc(d/c)	Gomersall	Jones	Botha	Ross	Kohn	Robson	Robshaw	Skinner	Guest
Malone/c	Gomersall	Jones	Botha/t	Ross	Kohn	Robson	Robshaw	Skinner	Guest
Evans/c3p	Care/t	Jones/t	Botha	Ross	Kohn	Robson	Robshaw	Skinner	Guest
Evans/3p(d/c)	Gomersall	Jones	Botha	Ross	Kohn	Robson	Robshaw	Skinner	Guest
Malone/3c4p	Gomersall	Jones	Botha/t	Lambert	Percival	Evans	Robshaw	Skinner	Guest/t
Malone/2c(b/3c)	Care/t	Jones	Fuga/t	Ross	Kohn	Evans	Robshaw/t	Skinner(g/3t)	Guest
Malone/c3p	Care	Jones	Botha	Ross	Percival	Robson	Robshaw	McMillen	Easter
Luveniyali/p	Gomersall/p	Jones	Botha	Ross	Percival	Robson	Robshaw	Skinner	Easter
Luveniyali/3c	Care	Jones	Fuga/t	Ross	Percival	Robson	Robshaw	Skinner	Easter/2t
Malone/2c5p	Care/t	Jones	Botha	Ross	Kohn	Evans	Robshaw	Skinner	Guest
Malone/3c2p	Care/t	Jones	Botha	Ross	Kohn	Evans	Robshaw	Skinner	Easter
Evans/cp	Care	Jones	Fuga	Ross	Percival	Evans	Robshaw	Skinner	Easter
Evans/c3pdg	Care	Jones	Fuga	Ross	Percival	Evans	Robshaw	Skinner	Easter
Evans/cp	Care	Jones	Brooker	Ross	Percival	Robson	Robshaw	Skinner	Easter
Malone	Care	Jones	Fuga	Ross	Percival/t	Robson/t	Robshaw/t	Skinner	Easter
Evans	Care	Jones	Botha	Ross	Percival	Robson	Robshaw	Skinner	Easter
Luveniyali/2c3p	Gomersall	Croall	Fuga/t	Lambert	Percival	Robson	Robshaw	McMillen	Davies
Jewell/c	Williams	Croall	Brooker	Lambert	Percival	Robson/t	Davies	McMillen/t	Guest
Malone/2c2p(h/c)	Gomersall	Jones	Botha	Ross	Kohn	Evans	Robshaw/t	Skinner	Davies
Evans	Care	Jones	Fuga	Ross	Percival	Robson	Robshaw	Skinner	Easter

REPLACEMENTS

a- T Guest   b- W Luveniyali   c- C Brooker   d- C Malone
e- J Evans   f- U Monye   g- N Easter   h- N Evans

LEAGUE APPEARANCES

21 Ceri Jones (1), Chris Robshaw (1)
20 Mike Ross, Will Skinner, Mike Brown
19 Jordan Turner Hall (2)

LEAGUE POINTS SCORERS

Pts	Player	T	C	P	DG
130	Nick Evans	2	12	31	1
75	Chris malone	1	14	13	1
50	Ugo Monye	10	-	-	-
35	Mike Brown	7	-	-	-
30	Danny Care	6	-	-	-
25	Nick Easter	5	-	-	-

NUMBER OF PLAYERS USED

32 plus 4 as a replacement only

HARLEQUINS' STATISTICS

LEAGUE

TEAM RECORDS

MOST POINTS
Scored at Home: 89 v Orrell 5.10.96
Scored Away: 91 v West Hartlepool 23.3.96
Conceded at Home: 57 v Wasps 17.9.94
Conceded Away: 77 v Bath 29.4.00

MOST TRIES
Scored in a match: 14 v W. Hartlepool 23.3.96
Conceded in a match: 10 v Bath 29.4.00

BIGGEST MARGINS
Home Win: 71pts - 89-18 v Orrell 5.10.96
Away Win: 70pts - 91-21 v W. Hartlepool 23.3.96
Home Defeat: 49pts - 5-54 v Leicester 6.5.00
Away Defeat: 58pts - 19-77 v Bath 29.4.00

MOST CONSECUTIVE
Victories: 19 (3.9.05 - 25.02.06)
Defeats: 8

INDIVIDUAL RECORDS

MOST APPEARANCES
by a forward: 173 (10) Jason Leonard
by a back: 124(5) Daren O'Leary

MOST CONSECUTIVE
Appearances: 42 Andy Mullins 16.11.91-30.4.94
Matches scoring Tries: 5 Daren O'Leary
Matches scoring points: 21 John Schuster

MATCH RECORDS

Most Points
28 John Schuster v Bath 21.11.98 (H)

Most Tries
5 Ugo Monye v Exeter 22.10.05 (H)

Most Conversions
9 Paul Challinor v W Hartlepool 23.3.96 (A)

Most Penalties
7 David Pears v Rosslyn P 7.12.91 (A)
Paul Burke v Wasps 22.9.01 (H)
Paul Burke v Lon Irish 1.9.01 (H)

Most Drop Goals
3 David Pears v Wasps 16.9.95 (H)

SEASON RECORDS

Most Points	331	John Schuster	98-99
Most Tries	18	Simon Keogh	05-06
Most Conversions	36	John Schuster	98-99
Most Penalties	77	John Schuster	98-99
Most Drop Goals	7	David Pears	95-96

CAREER RECORDS

Most Points	807	Paul Burke	00-04
Most Tries	65	Daren O'Leary	93-01
Most Conversions	69	Paul Burke	00-04
Most Penalties	167	Paul Burke	00-04
Most Drop Goals	16	Paul Burke	00-04

LAST TEN SEASONS

	Division	P	W	D	L	F	A	P.D.	Pts	Pos	Most Points	Most Tries
99-00	P1	22	7	0	15	441	687	-246	28	10	84 Rob Liley	7 Brandon Daniel
00-01	P1	22	7	0	15	440	538	-98	38	11	133 Paul Burke	7 Will Greenwood
01-02	P	22	5	3	14	434	507	-73	35	9	258 Paul Burke	4 Nick Greenstock & Matt Moore
02-03	P	22	9	0	13	461	560	-99	44	7	188 Paul Burke	6 Will Greenwood & Matt Moore
03-04	P	22	10	2	10	502	449	53	54	6	134 Andrew Dunne	9 Ugo Monye
04-05	P	22	6	1	15	416	459	-43	38	12r	186 Jeremy Staunton	5 Simon Keogh
05-06	N1	26	25	0	1	1001	337	664	121	1p	189 AndrewMehrtens	18 Simon Keogh
06-07	P	22	10	0	12	503	438	65	51	7	181 Adrain Jarvis	9 Mike Brown
07-08	P	22	12	0	10	480	440	40	63	6	115 Adrain Jarvis	5 Tom Williams
08-09	P	22	14	1	7	519	387	132	66	2	130 Nick Evans	10 Ugo Monye

RFU SENIOR CUP

OVERALL PLAYING RECORD

	P	W	O	L	F	A	Pts Diff
Home	50	37	0	13	1220	627	593
Away	40	26	0	14	787	610	177
Neutral	5	2	0	3	108	103	5
TOTAL	95	65	0	30	2115	1340	775

TEAM RECORDS

Highest Score: 88 v Thurrock 99/00
Biggest Winning Margin: 88 (88-0) v Thurrock
Highest Score Against: 45 v London Welsh 72/73
Biggest Losing Margin: 33
(45-12) v London Welsh 72/73

SEASON BY SEASON

Season	Result	Season	Result	Season	Result	Season	Result	Season	Result
71-72	QF	78-79	2R	85-86	QF	92-93	Runners up	99-00	QF
72-73	1R	79-80	SF	86-87	4R	93-94	SF	00-01	Runners up
73-74	1R	80-81	3R	87-88	Winners	94-95	SF	01-02	SF
74-75	DNQ	81-82	QF	88-89	SF	95-96	QF	02-03	QF
75-76	DNQ	82-83	QF	89-90	3R	96-97	SF	03-04	6R
76-77	1R	83-84	SF	90-91	Winners	97-98	4R	04-05	6R
77-78	SF	84-85	QF	91-92	Runners up	98-99	QF		

Anglo-Welsh Cup

05-06	N.A.
06-07	Gp Stage
07-08	Gp Stage
08-09	Gp Stage

National Trophy

05-06	Winners
06-07	N.A.
07-08	N.A.
08-09	N.A.

Premiership Championship

02-03	-
03-04	-
04-05	-
05-06	N.A.
06-07	-
07-08	-
08-09	S.F.

EUROPEAN COMPETITIONS

TEAM RECORDS

Highest Score
73 v Caerphilly 02/03

Biggest Winning Margin
60 (63-3) v El Salvador 03/04

Highest Score Against
51 v Toulouse 97/98 & Munster 01/02

Biggest Losing Margin
41 (51-10) v Toulouse 97/98

INDIVIDUAL RECORDS

Most Points in a match
27 Paul Burke v Narbonne 00-01

Most Tries in a match
3 Jim Staples v Caledonia 96/97
Jamie Williams Neath 96/97

Most Conversions in a match
9 Nathan Williams v Caerphilly 02/03

Most Penalties in a match
7 Thierry Lacroix v Bourgoin 97/98

Most Drop Goals in a match
2 Gareth Rees v Cardiff 99/00

CAREER RECORDS

Most Appearances
32: Jason Leonard (4)
22: Daren O'Leary (2)
21: Keith Wood
20: Pat Sanderson (4), B Davison (8)

Most Points
200: Paul Burke
100: Adrian Jarvis
91: Thierry Lacroix

Most Tries
11: Jamie Williams, Daren O'Leary
9: Will Greenwood
5: Keith Wood, George Harder

SEASON BY SEASON

1996-97	C	Q.F.
1997-98	C	Q.F.
1998-99	-	-
1999-00	C	Gp Stage
2000-01	S	Winners
2001-02	C	Gp Stage
2002-03	S	2nd Rd
2003-04	S	Winners
2004-05	C	Gp Stage
2005-06	-	-
2006-07	CC	Gp Stage
2007-08	C	Gp Stage
2008-09	C	Q.F.

OVERALL PLAYING RECORD

	P	W	D	L	F	A	Pts Diff
Home	30	19	1	10	841	611	230
Away	32	14	1	176	728	755	-27
Neutral	3	3	0	0	86	71	15
Total	65	36	2	27	1655	1437	218

LEEDS CARNEGIE

KEY PERSONNEL

Chairman Paul Caddick
Chief Executive Gary Hetherington
Director of Rugby Andy Key

Leeds Rugby Academy, Clarence Fields, Bridge Rd., Kirkstall, Leeds LS5 3BW
Tel: 0113 239 9190 Fax: 0113 239 9199

Founded: 1991
Colours: Navy blue & amber
Change colours: White, green & purple
Web site: www.leedscarnegie.com

Head Coach Neil Back
Club Administrator

Mike Bidgood   Leeds Rugby Ltd
St. Michael's Lane, Leeds LS6 3BR
Tel: 0113 203 3202, Fax: 08444 248 6652
Mobile: 07710 342054
email: mike.bidgood@leedsrugby.com

Media Manager Phil Daly

Leeds Rugby Ltd - as above
Tel: 0113 203 3281, Fax: 08444 248 6652
Mobile: 07885 995330
email: phil.daly@leedsrugby.com

GROUND DETAILS

Address: Headingley Carnegie Stadium, St Michaels Lane, Headingley, Leeds. LS6 3BR
Tel: 08444 248 6651 Fax: 08444 248 6652 Ticket Hotline: 0871 423 1315
email: info@leedsrugby.com

Capacity: 22,000   Seated: 7,000   Covered 18,000

Directions: Take M621 - Leave at J2, signposted Headingley Stadium. Follow the A643 (A58) Wetherby road - at the next r'about take the City Centre/Wetherby A58 exit. Almost immediately, bear left to Ilkley (A65) and the airport. At the lights (TGI Friday is on the left), turn left into Kirkstall Road A65. Straight on for about .75 mile (Yorkshire TV on the right). There is a sign at the traffc lights showing "Headingley 1.5 miles." Stay in the right-hand lane. Turn right and go up the hill to another set of traffc lights at the crossroads. Carry straight on up Cardigan Road (Co-op is on the left). After the pedestrian lights and bus stop turn left into St Michael's Lane, signposted Headingley Stadium. The Ground is on your right

For directions to Leeds Rugby Academy go to:
www.leedscarnegie.com
and click on the section named 'How to find us'.

Nearest BR Station:
Headingley or Burley are both 5 mins walk.

Car Parking: Limited at ground on matchdays.

Club Shop: Open 9-5 Mon-Fri, Sat 9-4.
Tel 0113 203 3228
Range available online at www.leedscarnegie.com

ADMISSION

Matchday	Adult	OAP/Student	Junior
Ground	£17	£10	£5
Paddock seat	£20	£13	£8
Main & Carnegie Stands	£22	£15	£10

Season	Adult	OAP/Student	Junior
Ground	£187	£110	£10
Paddock seat	£220	£143	£15
Main & Carnegie Stands	£242	£165	£20

PROGRAMME

Size: 160 x 160 mm   Pages: 60   Price: £2.50
Editor: Phil Daly
Advertising Rates: On application, call 0113 203 3222

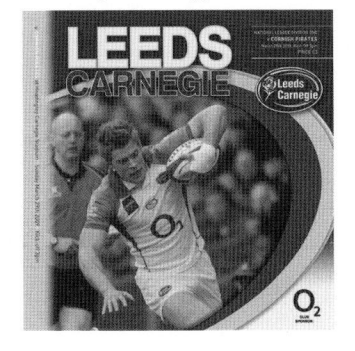

Back Row: John Carey (Team Manager), Scott Barrow, Hendre Fourie, Jon Pendlebury, Rhys Oakley, Danny Paul, Kearnan Myall, Phil Murphy, Erik Lund, Tom Denton, Lee Blackett, Scott Armstrong, Andy Boyde, Jon Goodridge, , Giles Lindsay (Head of Analysis)
Middle Row: Steve Carter (Head Conditioner), Jonny Hepworth, Alberto Di Bernardo, Rob Vickerman, Richard Welding, Tom McGee, Fosi Pala'amo, Phil Nilsen, Peter Bucknall, Peter Wackett, Adam Hopcroft, James Brooks, Joe Bedford, Dan White, Paris Payne (Head Physiotherapist)
Front Row: Daryl Powell (Assistant Backs & Skills Coach), Tom Biggs, Vili Ma'asi, Leigh Hinton, Rob Rawlinson (Club Captain), Andy Key (Director of Rugby), Mike MacDonald (captain), Neil Back (Head Coach), Jon Dunbar, Scott Mathie, Calum Clark, Jason Strange, Simon Middleton (Defence & Skills Coach)
Additional head and shoulders: Steve Nance; Steve Depledge; Adam Greendale; Luther Burrell.

REVIEW OF THE SEASON 2008-09

Leeds Carnegie book their return to the Guinness Premiership with 26 wins out fo 28 games in National Division One.

The club will go into the new season in the top flight with renewed optimism following a close season that has seen Andy Key and Neil Back strengthen their squad and the club return to the ownership of Leeds Rugby Limited under the Chairmanship of Paul Caddick after two years under the management of Leeds Met University.

Following the departure of previous Director of Rugby Stuart Lancaster, the club appointed Andy Key as Director of Rugby and Neil Back MBE as Head Coach in the summer of 2008 and the pair have transformed the club in their first season.

Full back Leigh Hinton finished as top try scorer with 11 tries taking him to third in the all time list for the club.

South African back rower Hendre Fourie was named as the club's Player of the Year whilst England U20 captain Calum Clark was named Young Player of the Year for the second season running.

The season saw the departure of three stalwarts of the club with England Sevens internationals Tom Biggs and Ro Vickerman moving to Newcastle and former Powergen Cup winner Jon Dunbar leaving Headingley Carnegie after five years in Yorkshire.

The club continues to produce quality players through their impressive Academy structure under the leadership of Manager Diccon Edwards. The U19 side claimed victory in the Yorkshire Cup by beating Beverley in the Final having already disposed of three other senior sides on the way to the Final. The link up with Prince Henrys Grammar School is also reaping rewards and builds on the innovative and holistic approach the club has to youth development.

The only disappointment in a season of fantastic achievements came with defeat to Moseley in the EDF Energy National Trophy Final at Twickenham however with the consolation of their place once again secured in the elite of English rugby, Leeds Carnegie can look forward to a bright future.

LEEDS'S CHAMPIONSHIP SEASON - 2008-09

NATIONAL ONE

Date	H/A	Opponents	Result & Score	Att.	15	14	13	12	11
31-08	H	Nottingham	W 34-19	3703	Hinton	Armstrong	Hepworth/t	Barrow	Biggs/t
06-09	A	Exeter	W 14-13	5693	Hinton	Welding/t	Hepworth	Barrow	Biggs
14-09	H	Otley	W 58-14	4112	Welding/t	Armstrong/2t	Vickerman/2t	Brooks	Biggs
21-09	A	Rotherham	W 41-24	2021	Hinton	Welding(a/2t)	Hepworth	Barrow	Biggs
28-09	H	Manchester	W 57-0	3092	Goodridge	Armstrong	Vickerman	Paul	Wackett/2t
04-10	A	London Welsh*	W 38-0	1449	Hinton/tc	Welding	Hepworth	Barrow/t	Biggs(c/t)
11-10	A	Sedgley Park*	W 52-7	886	Hinton/2t6c	Welding	Hepworth	Barrow	Armstrong/t
19-10	H	Coventry	W 57-5	2972	Hinton	Welding/2t	Hepworth/2t	Paul	Biggs/3t
25-10	A	Esher	W 52-8	1124	Goodridge/t	Armstrong(d/2t)	Vickerman	Paul/t	Blackett
01-11	H	Doncaster	W 28-13	3415	Hinton/2t	Welding	Hepworth	Barrow	Biggs
09-11	H	Bedford	W 19-8	3051	Hinton	Welding	Hepworth	Barrow/t	Biggs/t
16-11	A	Cornish Pirates	W 25-23	3853	Hinton	Welding/t	Vickerman	Paul	Biggs/t
23-11	H	Moseley	W 53-20	2203	Goodridge/4t	Welding	Hepworth	Paul	Blackett/t
29-11	A	Newbury*	W 89-12	316	Goodridge/t(f/2c)	Hinton/2t	Hepworth/t	Barrow	Blackett/4t
07-12	H	Plymouth Albion	W 49-18	2528	Goodridge	Hinton/t	Hepworth/t	Barrow/t	Blackett
14-12	A	Nottingham	W 19-12	2663	Hinton	Welding	Hepworth/t	Barrow	Blackett
20-12	H	Exeter*	W 18-16	5463	Hinton	Blackett(h/t)	Hepworth	Barrow	Goodridge
26-12	A	Otley	W 66-10	2610	Goodridge	Armstrong/t	Vickerman/2t	Paul(i/t)	Biggs/2t
04-01	H	Rotherham	W 28-3	3271	Hinton/t	Goodridge	Vickerman	Barrow/t	Biggs
25-01	A	London Welsh	W 35-10	2471	Hinton/t	Welding	Hepworth/t	Barrow	Biggs
01-02	H	Sedgley Park	W 66-0	2029	Goodridge/t	Blackett	Hepworth/2t	Paul	Armstrong/2t
14-02	A	Coventry	W 15-11	1600	Hinton	Blackett/t	Hepworth	Barrow	Welding
22-02	H	Esher	W 47-21	2945	Goodridge/t	Blackett/t	Biggs	Barrow	Armstrong
07-03	A	Doncaster	L 12-27	2203	Hinton/t	Welding/t	Hepworth	Barrow	Blackett
14-03	H	Bedford	L 24-27	2955	Hinton	Welding	Hepworth	Barrow	Blackett/t
29-03	H	Cornish Pirates	W 33-9	3806	Hinton/t	Welding	Hepworth	Paul(i/t)	Blackett/t
04-04	A	Moseley	W 31-26	832	Hinton	Goodridge/t	Hepworth	Barrow	Blackett
08-04	H	Manchester	W 104-0	1781	Goodridge	Armstrong/3t	Vickerman/2t	Paul	Biggs/4t
12-04	H	Newbury*	W 57-14	3564	Hinton/t	Welding	Hepworth/t	Barrow(b/2t)	Blackett/t
25-04	A	Plymouth Albion	W 17-6	4998	Goodridge	Welding	Vickerman/t	Paul	Biggs

EDF ENERGY NATIONAL TROPHY

	Date	H/A	Opponents	Result & Score	Att.	15	14	13	12	11
4	17-01	A	Dings Crusaders	W 59-0		Goodridge/t	Blackett	Vickerman/2t	Brooks/tc	Welding
5	08-02	H	Coventry	W 52-0		Goodridge/t	Blackett	Hepworth/t(d/t)	Paul/c	Welding/2t
Q.F.	28-02	A	Birmingham Solihull	W 26-24		Hinton/t	Welding	Blackett	Paul	Goodridge
S.F.	22-03	A	Nottingham	W 14-13		Hinton	Blackett	Vickerman/t	Paul	Biggs
Final	18-04	N	Moseley	L 18-23	10000	Hinton	Blackett	Vickerman	Barrow	Goodridge

SCORING BREAKDOWN

WHEN	Total	First Half	Second Half	1/4	2/4	3/4	4/4
the POINTS were scored	1238	621	617	298	323	249	260
the POINTS were conceded	376	158	218	65	93	110	108
the TRIES were scored	176	84	92	40	44	45	47
the TRIES were conceded	39	12	27	5	7	13	14

HOW	Total	Pen. Try	Backs	Forwards	F Back	Wing	Centre	H Back	F Row	Lock	B Row
the TRIES were scored	176	5	110	61	19	48	28	15	18	8	35
the TRIES were conceded	39	-	31	8	3	11	12	5	2	3	3

KEY: * after opponents name indicates a penalty try.
Brackets after a player's name indicates he was replaced. eg (a) means he was replaced by replacement code "a" and so on.
/ after a player or replacement name is followed by any scores he made - eg /t, /c, /p, /dg or any combination of these

10	9	1	2	3	4	5	6	7	8
Di Bernardo/4c2p	Bedford	McDonald	Ma'asi	McGee	Murphy	Pendlebury	Paul	Fourie/t	Oakley/t
Di Bernardo/2c	Mathie	McDonald	Ma'asi/t	Palaamo	Murphy	Pendlebury	Paul	Fourie	Oakley
Di Bernardo/t6c2p	Mathie	Palaamo	Rawlinson	Bucknall	Lund	Pendlebury	Boyde	Fourie/2t	Oakley
Di Bernardo/t4cp	Bedford	McDonald/t	Rawlinson	McGee	Murphy	Pendlebury	Dunbar	Fourie/2t	Oakley
Di Bernardo/3c(b/t3c)	Bedford	McDonald/2t	Nilsen	Bucknall	Lund/t	Myall	Dunbar/2t	Fourie/t	Oakley
Di Bernardo/4cp	Mathie	McDonald	Rawlinson	Palaamo	Murphy	Pendlebury	Dunbar	Fourie/t	Oakley
Brooks/t	Mathie	McDonald	Rawlinson	McGee	Lund	Pendlebury/t	Myall/t	Clarke	Paul/t
Di Bernardo/6c	Bedford	Palaamo	Rawlinson	McGee	Murphy	Myall	Paul/t	Fourie/t	Oakley
Strange/t6c	Mathie/t	McDonald/t	Nilsen	McGee	Lund	Pendlebury	Dunbar/t	Clarke	Oakley
Strange/2c3p	Bedford	McDonald	Rawlinson/t	McGee	Murphy	Pendlebury	Myall	Fourie	Oakley
Strange/2c	Mathie	Palaamo	Rawlinson	McGee	Murphy	Pendlebury	Myall	Clarke/t	Oakley
Di Bernardo/2c2p	Mathie	Palaamo	Rawlinson	Gomez	Lund	Myall/t	Clarke	Fourie	Oakley
Di Bernardo/2t5cp	Bedford(e/t)	Palaamo	Nilsen	Gomez	Lund	Pendlebury	Paul	Clarke	Oakley
Di Bernardo/10c	Bedford/t	Palaamo	Nilsen/t	Bucknall	Murphy/t	Pendlebury	Paul	Fourie	Oakley(g/t)
Strange/4c2p	Bedford/t	McGee	Rawlinson	Bucknall	Murphy	Myall	Clarke	Fourie/t(g/t)	Oakley/t
Strange/c4p	Bedford	McDonald	Rawlinson	Bucknall	Lund	Pendlebury	Myall	Fourie	Oakley
Strange/c2p	Bedford	McDonald	Rawlinson	Bucknall	Murphy	Pendlebury	Clarke	Fourie	Oakley
Brooks/2t8c	Mathie	McGee	Nilsen	Bucknall	Lund	Myall/t	Boyde/t	Clarke	Paul
Strange/4c	Mathie	McDonald/t	Nilsen	McGee	Murphy	Pendlebury	Myall	Clarke/t	Oakley
Di Bernardo/3c3p	Bedford	McDonald	Rawlinson(j/t)	McGee	Murphy	Pendlebury(k/t)	Myall	Fourie	Oakley
Brooks/t8c	Mathie	McGee(l/t, g/t))	Rawlinson	Bucknall	Lund	Pendlebury(m/t)	Paul	Rowan	Oakley
Di Bernardo/cp	Bedford	McDonald	Rawlinson	McGee	Murphy	Pendlebury	Myall	Rowan/t	Oakley
Strange/5c(n/t)	Bedford	McDonald/2t	Rawlinson	McGee/t	Murphy	Pendlebury	Myall	Clarke/t	Dunbar/t
Di Bernardo/c	Bedford	McGee	Rawlinson	Gomez	Murphy	Pendlebury	Myall	Rowan	Oakley
Di Bernardo/c4p	Bedford	McDonald	Ma'asi	Gomez	Murphy	Pendlebury	Myall	Boyde	Oakley
Di Bernardo/2c3p	Bedford	McDonald	Rawlinson	McGee	Lund	Pendlebury	Dunbar	Clarke	Oakley(k/t)
Di Bernardo/4cp	Mathie	McDonald	Ma'asi	Gomez	Murphy	Pendlebury/t	Dunbar	Clarke	Oakley/2t
Strange/12c	Bedford(p/t)	Palaamo(o/t)	Nilsen/t	McGee	Lund	Denton	Boyde/t	Davidson/t	Paul/2t
Di Bernardo/6c	Mathie	McDonald	Ma'asi	Gomez	Murphy	Pendlebury/t	Dunbar/t	Clarke	Oakley(k/t)
Strange/c	Mathie	Palaamo/t	Nilsen(j/t)	McGee	Lund	Murphy	Clarke	Fourie	Paul
Di Bernardo/6c(t/t)	Mathie/t	McGee	Nilsen	Bucknall	Lund	Myall	Boyde/2t	Rowan/t	Dunbar
Di Bernardo/5c	Mathie	McGee/t	Nilsen	Bucknall	Lund	Myall	Boyde/t	Rowan	Oakley/t
Strange/c(r/2c)	Mathie	Hopcroft/t	Ma'asi	Swainston/t	Lund	Myall(s/t)	Boyde	Rowan	Dunbar
Strange/2p(r/c)	Bedford	McGee	Rawlinson	Gomez	Lund	Pendlebury	Myall	Davidson	Oakley
Di Bernardo/c2p	Bedford	McDonald/t	Rawlinson	Gomez	Lund	Pendlebury	Clarke	Fourie(q/t)	Oakley

REPLACEMENTS

a - S Armstrong   b - J Brooks   c - J Goodridge   d - L Hinton
e - S Mathie   f - J Strange g - A Boyde   h - T Biggs
i - S Barrow   j - V Ma#asi   k - D Paul   l - J Gomez   m - P Murphy   n - H Paul
o - M McDonald   p - D White   q - K Myall   r - A Di Bernardo   s - S Freer   t - J Hepworth

LEAGUE APPEARANCES

25   Rhys Oakley (1)
23   Jonathan Pendlebury (4),
21   John Hepworth, Leigh Hinton (4)
19   Phil Murphy (5), M McDonald (4)

NUMBER OF PLAYERS USED

35 plus 6 as a replacement only

LEAGUE POINTS SCORERS

Pts	Player	T	C	P	DG
211	Alberto Di Bernardo	4	64	21	-
118	Jason Strange	1	40	11	-
89	Leigh Hinton	15	7	-	-
73	James Brooks	7	19	-	-
65	Tom Biggs	13	-	-	-

LEEDS STATISTICS

LEAGUE

TEAM RECORDS

MOST POINTS
Scored at Home: 84 v Walsall 1.3.97
Scored Away: 84 v Clifton 12.4.97
Conceded at Home: 50 v Gloucester 12.05.02
Conceded Away: 64 v London Wasps 18.11.01

MOST TRIES
Scored in a match: 14
v Redruth 9.1.96 (H) & v Walsall 1.3.97 (H)
Conceded in a match: 8 v Gloucester 1.12.01 (H)

BIGGEST MARGINS
Home Win: 81pts - 84-3 v Walsall 1.3.97
Away Win: 75pts - 84-9 v Clifton 12.4.97
Home Defeat: 33pts - 17-50 v Gloucester 12.5.02
Away Defeat: 50pts - 14-64 v London Wasps 18.11.01

MOST CONSECUTIVE
Victories: 23 (31.8.08 - 22.2.09)
Defeats: 10 (21.10.07 - 09.03.08)

INDIVIDUAL RECORDS

MOST APPEARANCES
by a forward: 163 (4) Mike Shelley
by a back: 75 (10) Craig Emmerson

MOST CONSECUTIVE
Appearances: 65 Sateki Tuipulotu 7.9.96 - 3.1.99
Matches scoring Tries: 7 Simon Middleton
Matches scoring points: 46 Sateki Tuipulotu

MATCH RECORDS

Most Points
31 Braam van Straaten v Lon Irish 8.9.02 (H)

Most Tries
5 Simon Middleton v Otley 24.1.98 (H)

Most Conversions
9 Gerry Ainscough v Clifton 7.12.96 (H)

Most Penalties
9 Braam van Straaten v Lon Irish 8.9.02 (H)

Most Drop Goals
2 Dan Eddie v Broughton Park 19.2.94 (H)
   Colin Stephens v Exeter 9.9.95 (H)
              v Lon Welsh 19.10.96 (H)

SEASON RECORDS

Most Points	337	Richard Le Bas	00-01
Most Tries	19	Graham Mackay	00-01
Most Conversions	72	Richard LeBas	00-01
Most Penalties	68	Braam van Straaten	02-03
Most Drop Goals	5	Colin Stephens	96-97
		Gordon Ross	02-03

CAREER RECORDS

Most Points	769	Sateki Tuipulotu	96-99
Most Tries	39	Tom Biggs	04-09
Most Conversions	135	Sateki Tuipulotu	96-99
Most Penalties	118	Sateki Tuipulotu	96-99
Most Drop Goals	13	Colin Stephens	96-99

LAST TEN SEASONS

	Division	P	W	D	L	F	A	P.D.	Pts	Pos	Most Points		Most Tries	
99-00	P2	26	22	0	4	794	269	525	44	2	190	Jon Benson	14	Matt Oliver
00-01	N1	26	24	0	2	1032	407	625	116	1p	337	Richard Le Bas	19	Graham Mackay
01-02	P	22	6	0	16	406	654	-248	28	12	132	Braam van Straatan	12	Dan Scarborough
02-03	P	22	12	2	8	478	435	43	58	5	252	Braam van Straatan	8	Dan Scarborough
03-04	P	22	7	1	14	449	588	-139	37	11	128	Gordon Ross	7	Dan Scarborough
04-05	P	22	9	0	13	380	431	-51	43	8	161	Gordon Ross	6	Andre Snyman
05-06	P	22	5	0	17	363	573	-210	28	12r	102	Gordon Ross	8	Tom Biggs
06-07	N1	30	24	2	4	960	474	486	123	1p	302	Leigh Hinton	15	Richard Welding
07-08	P	22	2	1	19	336	732	-396	12	12r	127	Alberto Di Bernardo	7	Tom Biggs
08-09	N1	30	28	0	2	1236	376	860	133	1p	211	Alberto Di Bernardo	15	Leigh Hinton

RFU SENIOR CUP

OVERALL PLAYING RECORD

	P	W	O	L	F	A	Pts Diff
Home	14	10	0	4	493	180	313
Away	14	6	0	8	302	385	-83
Neutral	1	1	0	0	20	12	8
TOTAL	29	17	0	12	815	577	238

TEAM RECORDS

Highest Score: 100 v Morley 21.10.00
Biggest Winning Margin: 100 (100-0) v Morley 21.10.00
Highest Score Against: 73 v Northampton 4.11.00
Biggest Losing Margin: 49 (49-0) v Leicester 30.02.99

SEASON BY SEASON

71-72	1R / DNQ	78-79	DNQ / DNQ	85-86	3R / DNQ	92-93	2R	99-00	4R
72-73	DNQ / DNQ	79-80	DNQ / DNQ	86-87	DNQ / DNQ	93-94	2R	00-01	4R
73-74	1R / 1R	80-81	DNQ / 3R	87-88	3R / DNQ	94-95	2R	01-02	QF
74-75	DNQ / DNQ	81-82	DNQ / 2R	88-89	2R / DNQ	95-96	5R	02-03	6R
75-76	1R / QF	82-83	DNQ / DNQ	89-90	4R / 1R	96-97	5R	03-04	SF
76-77	DNQ / DNQ	83-84	3R / DNQ	90-91	2R / 1R	97-98	2R	04-05	Winners
77-78	DNQ / DNQ	84-85	3R / DNQ	91-92	2R / 1R	98-99	5R		

From 71-72 until 91-92 the figure on the left shows **Headingley RFC** and that on the right **Roundhay RFC**

Anglo-Welsh Cup

05-06	Gp Stage
06-07	N.A.
07-08	Gp Stage
08-09	N.A.

National Trophy

05-06	N.A.
06-07	5th Rd
07-08	N.A.
08-09	R-up

Premiership Championship

02-03	-
03-04	-
04-05	-
05-06	-
06-07	N.A.
07-08	-
08-09	N.A.

EUROPEAN COMPETITIONS

TEAM RECORDS

Highest Score
121 v Valladolid 5.12.04
Biggest Winning Margin
121 (121-0) v Valladolid 5.12.04
Highest Score Against
43 v Worcester 2.04.05
Biggest Losing Margin
31 (41-10) v Parma 29.09.01

INDIVIDUAL RECORDS

Most Points in a match
26 Gordon Ross v Valladolid 5.12.04 (H)
Most Tries in a match
3 by five player - Jamie Mayer, Chris Hall, Tim Stimpson, Jordan Crane, Mark McMillan
Most Conversions in a match
13 Gordon Ross v Valladolid 5.12.04 (H)
Most Penalties in a match
4 Braam van Straatan v Pontypridd 02/03 (H)
Most Drop Goals in a match
1 Dan Parks v Beziers 7.10.01 (H)

CAREER RECORDS

Most Appearances
16: Gordon Ross (2),Tom Palmer (6)
14: Andre Snyman
12: Danny Scarborough, Tristan Davies, Stuart Hooper (3) & Phil Murphy
Most Points
160: Gordon Ross
69: Tim Stimpson
67: Alberto de Bernardo
45: Jon Benson
Most Tries
8: Tim Stimpson
5: Jamie Mayer, Chris Hall, Dan Scarbrough, Andre Snyman

SEASON BY SEASON

1996-97	-	N.A.
1997-98	-	N.A.
1998-99	-	N.A.
1999-00	-	N.A.
2000-01	-	N.A.
2001-02	S	Gp Stage
2002-03	S	2nd Rd
2003-04	C	Gp Stage
2004-05	S	S.F.
2005-06	C	Gp Stage
2006-07	-	N.A.
2007-08	CC	Q.F.
2008-09	-	N.A.

OVERALL PLAYING RECORD

	P	W	D	L	F	A	Pts Diff
Home	18	13	1	4	660	304	356
Away	18	4	1	13	350	443	-93
Neutral	-	-	-	-	-	-	-
Total	36	17	2	17	1010	747	263

67

LEICESTER TIGERS

KEY PERSONNEL

Chairman	Peter Tom CBE
Chief Executive	Peter Wheeler
Managing Director	David Clayton
Company Secretary	Mary Ford
Fixture Sec. & League Contact	Jo Hollis Leicester Tigers, Aylestone Road, Leicester. LE2 7TR Tel: 0116 217 1326 Fax: 0116 217 8339 email: jo.hollis@tigers.co.uk
Head Coach	Richard Cockerill

Founded: 1880
Nickname: Tigers
Colours: Green, red and white
Change colours: Pale blue
Website: www.leicestertigers.com

GROUND DETAILS

Address: Aylestone Road, Leicester. LE2 7TR
Tel: 08701 283430   **Fax:** 0116 285 4766
Capacity: 24,000
Seated: 19,500   **Covered:** 17,500

Directions:
From M1 (North and South) and M69 (East)
Exit the motorway at Junction 21 (M1). Follow the signs for the city centre via Narborough Road (A5460). After 3 miles, at the crossroad junction with Upperton Road, turn right. Continue over the River Soar, onto Walnut Street, and follow the signs to the city centre. The stadium is 1/2 mile ahead.
From A6 (South): Follow the signs for the city centre, coming in via London Road. At the main set of lights opposite the entrance to the railway station (on the right), turn left onto the Waterloo Way. Continue over the next set of traffic lights onto Tigers Way. The stadium is immediately in front of you.

Nearest BR Station: Leicester (London Road).

Car Parking: There are several car parks within close proximity. Euro Park on the cinema and supermarket complex is a short two minutes walk away. NCP car park on Welford Road is a five minute walk away. NCP on East Street in the city centre is a 10 minute walk away.

ADMISSION
Matchday: Juniors from £8; Concessions from £18; Adults from £20; Family from £48.
Season Tickets: Juniors from £100; Concessions from £220; Adults from £255; Family from £610.

Club Shop: Mon – Sat: 9am-4.45pm. Matchdays open until 6pm (on 3pm kick off). Manager - Sara Watson, 0116 2171 267.
City centre Shop: Mon – Sat: 9am-5.30pm, Sun-10am-4.30pm. Manager, Andy Martin, 0116 2559 664

Clubhouse: Reception open 8am – 6pm
Food available at outlets around the ground on matchdays
Conference & Events: 0116 2171 278
Facilities Manager: Jack Russell 0116 2171 255

CONTACT DETAILS

Leicester Tigers,
Aylestone Road, Leicester LE2 7TR
Tel: 0844 856 1880
Fax: 0116 285 4766
e-mail: tigers@tigers.co.uk

PROGRAMME

Size: 240mm x 170mm (B5)
Pages: 92   Price: £3
Editor: Gary Sherrard
Advertising: Contact sales on 0116 2171 287

L-R - Back row: Tom Youngs, Julien Dupuy, Matt Smith, Johne Murphy, Ben Pienaar, Greig Tonks, Ben Woods, Ben Herring, Greg Sammons, Ben Youngs, Sam Vesty, Derick Hougaard.   **Middle row:** Matt O'Connor, Paul Burke, Dan Cole, Brett Deacon, Ayoola Erinle, Jordan Crane, Tom Varndell, Richard Blaze, Marco Wentzel, Louis Deacon, Tom Croft, Seru Rabeni, Marcos Ayerza, Santiago Bonorino, Martin Castrogiovanni, Boris Stankovich, Richard Cockerill
Front row: Alesana Tuilagi, Mefin Davies, Dan Hipkiss, Ben Kay, Harry Ellis, Geordan Murphy, Martin Corry, Heyneke Meyer, Aaron Mauger, Lewis Moody, Benjamin Kayser, George Chuter, Julian White, Toby Flood.

REVIEW OF THE SEASON 2008-09

The 2008/09 season ended with a record eighth league championship for Leicester Tigers and a fifth appearance in the final of Europe's Heineken Cup.

Losing just once in the last three months of league action, the silverware was hoisted by Martin Corry, in his last season before retirement, and stand-in skipper Geordan Murphy after a 10-9 win over London Irish in the final.

The consistency in the last third of the season was remarkable enough, even without considering a change of head coach and the unavailability of some key men due to injury or suspension.

But it spoke volumes for the approach of new head coach Richard Cockerill, his assistants Matt O'Connor and Paul Burke, and the players.

Under Heyneke Meyer, Tigers had got the term off to a flying start with just one defeat in the opening eight fixtures in league and cup. But Meyer returned to South Africa at Christmas on compassionate grounds and Cockerill picked up the baton.

After qualifying for the knockout stages of the Heineken Cup by topping a group featuring Ospreys and Perpignan, Tigers blazed a trail to the top of the Guinness Premiership - and stayed there.

Aaron Mauger's influence increased by the week, Ben Kay and Julian White led a powerful pack, Julien Dupuy and Scott Hamilton made a mark and Sam Vesty experienced a rebirth.

In successive weekends from the end of April, Tigers put 73 points on Bristol to seal top spot in the league, beat Cardiff Blues in European semi-final shoot-out, toppled Bath in the Guinness Premiership play-off and pipped Irish in the final to be crowned English champions.

Leinster denied the Double when they came out on top of a titanic tussle in the Heineken Cup Final, but it was a season to remember as Tigers also heralded a new era with the start of redevelopment of their Welford Road home.

TIGERS' SEASON - 2008-09

GUINNESS PREMIERSHIP

Date	H/A	Opponents	Result & Score	Att.	15	14	13	12	11
07-09	A	Gloucester	W 20-8	13180	G Murphy/t	Varndell	Smith	Hipkiss	Tuilagi
13-09	H	London Irish	W 24-22	16553	G Murphy/t	Varndell	Hipkiss	Mauger	Smith
20-09	A	Worcester	W 19-17	10846	G Murphy	Varndell	Smith	Mauger	J Murphy
26-09	H	London Wasps	L 19-28	17498	G Murphy	Varndell	Smith	Mauger/t	J Murphy
01-10	H	Northampton Saints	W 29-19	17498	G Murphy	J Murphy/t	Hipkiss/t	Mauger	Smith
15-11	A	Bath	L 21-25	10600	G Murphy	J Murphy/t	Hipkiss	Mauger	Smith
22-11	H	Harlequins	W 27-14	17432	Hamilton	J Murphy/t	Hipkiss	Mauger	Smith/t
28-11	A	Sale Sharks	L 13-27	9586	G Murphy	J Murphy	Rabeni	Mauger/t	Smith
20-12	H	Newcastle Falcons	W 20-3	17240	G Murphy/t	Hamilton	Smith	Mauger/t	J Murphy
27-12	A	Harlequins	D 26-26	50000	Hamilton	J Murphy/t	Hipkiss	Mauger	Smith
04-01	H	Bath	W 24-22	17498	G Murphy	J Murphy	Hipkiss	Mauger	Smith
10-01	A	Northampton Saints	L 13-17	13582	G Murphy	J Murphy	Rabeni	Mauger	Smith
15-02	N	London Wasps	L 29-36	9581	Hamilton/t	Smith	Rabeni(c/t)	Mauger	Tuilagi
21-02	H	Worcester	W 38-5	17081	G Murphy	Hamilton	Smith/t	Mauger	Tuilagi/t
01-03	A	London Irish	W 31-28	12154	Hamilton	J Murphy	Smith/2t	Mauger	Tuilagi
07-03	H	Gloucester	W 24-10	17498	G Murphy/dg	Hamilton	Smith	Mauger	Tuilagi
13-03	A	Bristol	W 23-17	6037	Hamilton	Smith	Hipkiss/t	Mauger	Tuilagi
21-03	H	Saracens*	W 46-16	16328	Hamilton/2t	J Murphy	Hipkiss/t(f/t)	Mauger	Tuilagi
27-03	A	Newcastle Falcons	L 10-14	7614	G Murphy	Hamilton	Erinle	Mauger	Tuilagi
04-04	H	Sale Sharks	W 37-31	17418	G Murphy	Hamilton/2t	Hipkiss/t	Vesty/tc	Tuilagi/t
19-04	A	Saracens	W 16-13	11275	G Murphy	Hamilton/t	Erinle/t	Hipkiss	J Murphy
25-04	H	Bristol	W 73-3	18816	G Murphy/2t2c	Smith	Hipkiss/t(f/t)	Vesty/t3c	J Murphy/t(e/t)

HEINEKEN CUP

12-10	H	Ospreys	W 12-6	17498	G Murphy	J Murphy	Hipkiss	Mauger	Smith
18-10	A	Benetton Treviso*	W 60-16	7000	G Murphy/t	J Murphy/3t	Hipkiss	Mauger	Smith
06-12	H	Perpignan	W 38-27	17371	G Murphy	Hamilton	Hipkiss	Mauger/t	Smith/t
14-12	A	Perpignan	L 20-26	14466	G Murphy	Hamilton/t	Hipkiss	Mauger	Smith
17-01	H	Benetton Treviso*	W 52-0	16746	G Murphy/t(c/2t)	Hamilton/2t	Rabeni	Mauger/2t	Smith/t
24-01	N	Ospreys	L 9-15	18285	G Murphy	Hamilton	Rabeni	Flood	Smith
Q.F. 11-04	N	Bath	W 20-15	26100	G Murphy	Hamilton	Hipkiss	Erinle	Tuilagi
S.F. 03-05	N	Cardiff	D 26-26	44212	G Murphy/t	Hamilton/t	Hipkiss	Vesty	J Murphy
Final 23-05	N	Leinster	L 16-19	66856	G Murphy	Hamilton	Erinle	Hipkiss	Tuilagi

EDF ENERGY CUP

04-10	A	Bath	W 19-15	10600	Vesty	Varndell	Erinle	Youngs	Tuilagi
25-10	A	Cardiff	L 9-23	9815	J Murphy	Raven	Hipkiss	Flood	Smith
31-10	H	Sale Sharks*	W 30-20	16550	Smith	Murphy	Rabeni	Youngs/t	Varndell

GUINNESS CHAMPIONSHIP

S.F. 09-05	N	Bath	W 24-10	18850	G Murphy	Hamilton	Hipkiss/t	Erinle	J Murphy
Final 16-05	N	London Irish	W 10-9	81601	G Murphy	Hamilton	Erinle	Hipkiss	J Murphy

SCORING BREAKDOWN

WHEN	Total	First Half	Second Half	1/4	2/4	3/4	4/4
the POINTS were scored	582	259	323	120	139	117	206
the POINTS were conceded	401	231	170	115	116	95	75
the TRIES were scored	62	24	38	10	14	12	26
the TRIES were conceded	40	23	17	11	12	9	8

HOW	Total	Pen. Try	Backs	Forwards	F Back	Wing	Centre	H Back	F Row	Lock	B Row
the TRIES were scored	62	1	47	14	9	11	17	10	5	3	6
the TRIES were conceded	40	-	23	17	7	10	5	1	6	3	8

KEY: * after opponents name indicates a penalty try.
Brackets after a player's name indicates he was replaced. eg (a) means he was replaced by replacement code "a" and so on.
/ after a player or replacement name is followed by any scores he made - eg /t, /c, /p, /dg or any combination of these

PREMIERSHIP

10	9	1	2	3	4	5	6	7	8
Flood/tc2p	Ellis(A/c)	Ayerza	Chuter	White	Blaze	Kay	Croft	Herring	Crane
Flood/3cp	Ellis	Ayerza	Chuter	White	Blaze	Kay	Croft/t	Herring/t	Crane
Flood/4p	Dupuy/tc	Ayerza	Kayser	White	Corry	Kay	Croft	Herring	Crane
Flood/c4p	Dupuy	Ayerza	Kayser	Cole	Corry	Wentzel	Croft	Woods	Crane
Flood/tc4p	Ellis	Stankovich	Kayser	White	Corry	Wentzel	Croft	Herring	Crane
Hougaard/c3p	Dupuy	Stankovich	Chuter(b/t)	Cole	Blaze	Wentzel	Corry	Moody	Crane
Hougaard/t3c2p	Dupuy	Stankovich	Chuter	Cole	Wentzel	Kay	Corry	Moody	Deacon
Hougaard	Dupuy/c2p	Ayerza	Chuter	Cole	Corry	Kay	Deacon	Moody	Crane
Flood/2c2p	Dupuy	Stankovich	Chuter	White	Wentzel	Kay	Newby	Moody	Deacon
Flood/2c4p	Dupuy	Stankovich	Kayser	White	Corry	Wentzel	Croft/t	Moody	Crane
Hougaard/c3pdg	Dupuy	Stankovich	Kayser	White	Corry	Kay	Croft/2t	Moody	Newby
Flood/tc2p	Dupuy	Stankovich	Chuter	White	Wentzel	Kay	Croft	Herring	Deacon
Vesty/tc	Dupuy/2cp	Stankovich	Chuter	Cole	Deacon	Kay	Newby	Woods	Crane/t
Vesty/t3c	Dupuy/2cp(i/t)	Ayerza/t	Kayser	Castrogiovanni	Deacon	Kay	Newby	Woods	Crane
Vesty	Dupuy/2c4p	Ayerza/t	Davies	Cole	Deacon	Kay	Newby	Woods	Crane
Vesty	Dupuy/7p	Ayerza	Kayser	White	Deacon	Kay	Croft	Woods	Pienaar
Vesty/c3p	Dupuy/c	Ayerza	Davies	Cole/t	Deacon	Kay	Wentzel	Woods	Pienaar
Vesty/2c(h/2cp)	Dupuy/cp	Ayerza	Chuter	Cole	Deacon/t	Kay	Woods	Herring	Pienaar
Flood/cp	Ellis	Stankovich	Chuter	Castrogiovanni	Deacon(g/t)	Kay	Croft	Woods	Corry
Flood/2c2p	Ellis	Ayerza	Chuter	White	Deacon	Kay	Croft	Woods	Pienaar
Vesty/2p	Ellis	Ayerza	Chuter	Castrogiovanni	Croft	Kay	Newby	Woods	Crane
Flood/t	Dupuy/t4c	Stankovich	Kayser	White/t	Croft	Kay(d/t)	Newby	Moody	Crane
Flood/4p	Ellis	Ayerza	Kayser	White	Corry	Kay	Croft	Woods	Crane
Flood/2t3cp(/3c)	Ellis	Ayerza	Kayser	White	Wentzel	Kay	Corry	Croft	Crane/2t
Flood/t3c4p	Ellis	Ayerza	Kayser	White	Corry	Kay	Croft	Moody	Crane/t
Flood/2c2p	Dupuy	Ayerza	Kayser	White	Corry	Kay	Croft/t	Moody	Crane
Flood/6c	Youngs	Castrogiovanni	Chuter	White	Wentzel	Kay	Croft	Woods	Crane
Hougaard/3p	Dupuy	Stankovich	Kayser	White	Corry	Wentzel	Croft	Woods	Crane
Vesty/5p	Ellis(a/t)	Ayerza	Chuter	Castrogiovanni	Deacon	Kay	Croft	Woods	Pienaar
Flood	Dupuy/2c4p	Ayerza	Chuter	Castrogiovanni	Croft	Kay	Newby	Woods	Crane
Vesty	Dupey/c3p	Ayerza	Chuter	Castrogiovanni	Croft	Kay	Newby	Woods/t	Crane
Hougaard/c3pdg	Youngs/t	Stankovich	Davies	Cole	Raven	Kay	Hemingway	Pearson	Deacon
Hougaard/3p	Ellis	Stankovich	Chuter	White	Blaze	Wentzel	Corry	Croft	Crane
Hougaard/2c3p	Dupuy	Stankovich	Kayser	Cole	Blaze	Kay	Deacon	Moody	Newby/c
Vesty/t	Dupuy/3cp	Ayerza	Chuter	Castrogiovanni	Croft	Kay	Newby	Woods(j/t)	Crane
Vesty	Dupuy/cp	Ayerza	Chuter	White	Croft	Kay	Newby	Woods	Crane/t

REPLACEMENTS

a- J Dupey   b- M Davies   c- J Murphy   d- B Woods
e- A Erinle   f- T Varndell g- D Hemingway h- D Hougaard
i- B Youngs   j- L Moody

LEAGUE APPEARANCES

18 Aaron Mauger, Matt Smith, Ben Kay (3)
16 Julian Dupuy (4), Geordan Murphy
14 Johne Murphy (4)

NUMBER OF PLAYERS USED

36 plus 5 as a replacement only

LEAGUE POINTS SCORERS

Pts	Player	T	C	P	DG
126	Toby Flood	4	14	26	-
88	Julian Dupuy	2	15	16	-
57	Sam Vesty	4	11	5	-
49	Derick Hougaard	1	7	9	1
32	Geordan Murphy	5	2	-	1

LEICESTER STATISTICS

LEAGUE

TEAM RECORDS

MOST POINTS
Scored at Home: 83 v Newcastle 19.02.05
Scored Away: 55 v London Irish 17.5.98
Conceded at Home: 31 v Harlequins 26.11.89
Conceded Away: 47 v Bath 12.4.97

MOST TRIES
Scored in a match: 12 v W Hartlepool 16.5.99
Conceded in a match: 7 v Bath 11.1.92

BIGGEST MARGINS
Home Win: 73pts - 83-10 v Newcastle 19.02.05
Away Win: 49pts - 54-9 v Harlequins 6.5.00
Home Defeat: 17pts - 15-32 v Northampton 25.10.03
Away Defeat: 38pts - 9-47 v Bath 12.4.97

MOST CONSECUTIVE
Victories: 13
Defeats: 5 (4.10.03 - 1.11.03)

INDIVIDUAL RECORDS

MOST APPEARANCES
by a forward: 196 (5) Darren Garforth
by a back: 146(15) Leon Lloyd

MOST CONSECUTIVE
Appearances: 32 Darren Garforth 28.3.92-3.4.94
Matches scoring Tries: 4 Geordan Murphy, Nnamdi Ezulike
Matches scoring points: 24 John Liley

MATCH RECORDS

Most Points
32 Tim Stimpson v Newcastle 21.9.02 (H)

Most Tries
4 Rory Underwood v Newcastle 12.3.94 (H)
   Geordan Murphy v Saracens 24.2.01 (H)

Most Conversions
11 Andy Goode v Newcastle 19.02.05 (H)

Most Penalties
8 John Liley v Bristol 28.10.95 (H)
   Tim Stimpson v Gloucester 2.12.00(H)
   Andy Goode v Sale 28.1.06 (H)

Most Drop Goals
3 Jez Harris v Wasps 23.11.91 (H)
                v Bath 15.4.95 (H)

SEASON RECORDS

Most Points	321	Tim Stimpson	99-00
Most Tries	16	Neil Back	98-99
Most Conversions	52	Tim Stimpson	99-00
Most Penalties	64	John Liley	95-96
Most Drop Goals	13	Jez Harris	94-95

CAREER RECORDS

Most Points	1180	Tim Stimpson	98-04
Most Tries	73	Neil Back	91-05
Most Conversions	149	Tim Stimpson	98-04
Most Penalties	257	Tim Stimpson	98-04
Most Drop Goals	37	Jez Harris	87-95

LAST TEN SEASONS

	Division	P	W	D	L	F	A	P.D.	Pts	Pos	Most Points		Most Tries
99-00	P1	22	18	1	3	687	425	262	51	1	321 Tim Stimpson	10	Dave Lougheed
00-01	P1	22	18	1	3	571	346	225	82	1	260 Tim Stimpson	8	Geordan Murphy / Neil Back
01-02	P	22	18	0	4	658	349	309	83	1	212 Tim Stimpson	9	Geordan Murphy / Steve Booth
02-03	P	22	12	0	10	448	396	52	55	6	161 Tim Stimpson	5	Geordan Murphy / JoshKronfeld
03-04	P	22	11	3	8	537	430	107	55	5	148 Andy Goode	6	Austin Healey
04-05	P	22	15	3	4	665	323	342	78	1	259 Andy Goode	4	By six players
05-06	P	22	14	3	5	518	415	103	68	2	200 Andy Goode	14	Tom Varndell
06-07	P	22	14	1	7	569	456	113	*71	2	144 Andy Goode	9	Tom Varndell
07-08	P	22	13	0	9	539	428	111	64	4	185 Andy Goode	13	Tom Varndell
08-09	P	22	15	1	6	582	401	181	71	1	126 Toby Flood	6	Scott Hamilton, Johne Murphy

RFU SENIOR CUP

OVERALL PLAYING RECORD

	P	W	O	L	F	A	Pts Diff
Home	40	33	1	6	1211	446	765
Away	55	40	0	15	1119	625	494
Neutral	12	5	0	7	174	174	0
TOTAL	107	78	1	28	2504	1245	1259

Other detail: Home Bye 4th rd 99-00

TEAM RECORDS

Highest Score: 83 v Otley 00/01
Biggest Winning Margin: 76 (76-0) v Exeter 92/93
Highest Score Against: 47 v London Irish 99/00
Biggest Losing Margin: 40 (47-7) v Lon. Irish 99/00

SEASON BY SEASON

71-72	1R		78-79	Winners		85-86	SF		92-93	Winners		99-00	5R
72-73	QF		79-80	Winners		86-87	SF		93-94	R-up		00-01	SF
73-74	1R		80-81	Winners		87-88	4R		94-95	SF		01-02	QF
74-75	DNQ		81-82	SF		88-89	R-up		95-96	R-up		02-03	SF
75-76	1R		82-83	R-up		89-90	QF		96-97	Winners		03-04	6R
76-77	2R		83-84	3R		90-91	4R		97-98	5R		04-05	6R
77-78	R-up		84-85	QF		91-92	SF		98-99	SF			

Anglo-Welsh Cup

05-06	SF
06-07	Winners
07-08	Runners-up
08-09	Gp Stage

Premiership Championship

02-03	-
03-04	-
04-05	R-up
05-06	R-up
06-07	Winners

07-08	R-up
08-09	Winners

EUROPEAN COMPETITIONS

TEAM RECORDS

Highest Score
90 v Glasgow 97/98

Biggest Winning Margin
71 (90-19) v Glasgow 97/98

Highest Score Against
38 v Stade Francais 99/00

Biggest Losing Margin
33 (33-0) v Ulster 03/04

INDIVIDUAL RECORDS

Most Points in a match
35 Joel Stransky v Glasgow 1.11.97

Most Tries in a match
4 Michael Horak v Glasgow 1.11.97
Tom Varndell v Clermont Auvergne 20.1.06

Most Conversions in a match
10 Joel Stransky v Glasgow 1.11.97

Most Penalties in a match
7 Tim Stimpson v Perpignan 01/02

Most Drop Goals in a match
2 Andy Goode v Pau 00/01

CAREER RECORDS

Most Appearances
66: Martin Corry (3),
62: Geordan Murphy (1)
54: Ben Kay (9)
51: Graham Rowntree (8)
49: Martin Johnson (2)

Most Points
406: Andy Goode
363: Tim Stimpson
142: Geordan Murphy
106: Joel Stransky

Most Tries
21: Geordan Murphy,
19: Leon Lloyd
16: Neil Back

SEASON BY SEASON

1996-97	C	Runners-up
1997-98	C	Q-F
1998-99	-	D N Play
1999-00	C	Gp Stage
2000-01	C	Winners
2001-02	C	Winners
2002-03	C	QF
2003-04	C	Gp Stage
2004-05	C	S-F
2005-06	C	Q-F
2006-07	C	Runners-up
2007-08	C	Gp Stage
2008-09	C	??

OVERALL PLAYING RECORD

	P	W	D	L	F	A	Pts Diff
Home	45	38	0	7	1498	647	851
Away	37	19	2	16	829	742	87
Neutral	9	5	0	4	163	178	-15
Total	91	62	2	27	2500	1567	923

LONDON IRISH

Founded: 1898
Nickname: The Exiles
Colours:
Green & blue shirts, white shorts
Change colours:
White & green shirts, white shorts
Website: www.london-irish.com

KEY PERSONNEL

Chairman	Andrew Coppel CBE
Chief Executive	Andy Martin
Director of Finance	Paul Gunn
Head Coach	Toby Booth
Rugby Manager	Kieran McCarthy
Rugby Media Manager	Paddy Lennon

CONTACT DETAILS

London Irish, The Avenue, Sunbury on Thames, Middx. TW16 5EQ
Tel: 01932 783034   Fax: 01932 784462
email: info@london-irish.com

GROUND DETAILS

Address: Madejski Stadium, J11, M4, Reading, Berkshire RG2 0FL
Tel: 0118 968 1100   email: info@readingfc.co.uk
Capacity: 24,100 - all covered seating
Directions: The stadium is located off the A33, one mile north of Junction 11 on the M4.
Nearest BR Station: Reading Central, shuttle bus service on matchdays.
Car Parking   4,000 cars at the stadium
Admission   Matchdays: From £23 in advance in the South Stand (cheaper if purchased in advance)
Season Tickets: From £240 in South Stand
Megastore   Open 9-5 weekdays, Matchdays 12-6pm.
Clubhouse   The Avenue, Sunbury-on-Thames. Open for matches at Sunbury & special events.
Available for private function hire. Contact Terry Long   07989 540 809
Programme: Size: Super A5   Price: £3   Pages: 84   Editor: Paddy Lennon
Advertising Rates Contact: James Durbin (01932 750 102)

REVIEW OF THE SEASON 2008-09

London Irish's season got off to the best possible start with an opening day win over London Wasps, the current Guinness Premiership Champions, at Twickenham Stadium. A combination of ferocious defence, understanding of the ELVs and sound execution of the game plan resulted in an important victory.

The players displayed great mental strength in putting themselves into a position to win the subsequent league matches against Leicester Tigers and Bath Rugby, only to fall at the last hurdle. At Welford Road they lost by the narrowest of margins, 17-16. The following Saturday, although Irish pushed Bath to the limit, the team had to be satisfied with a losing bonus point.

The club earned nine valuable league points from two remarkable performances against Harlequins and Sale Sharks respectively. After trailing 20-8 at half-time against old rivals Harlequins, the Exiles produced an exceptional second half of rugby, scoring 20 points, to win by 28-27. Four days later, Irish hosted Sale Sharks at Madejski Stadium and ended the early league leaders unbeaten run by outscoring them by four tries to none.

The opening EDF Energy Cup fixture of the season was away to Worcester who took their chances and emerged comfortable winners by 22-5. Irish set new club records for the number of points scored and the biggest winning margin in any match it has played in the professional era in defeating Rugby Rovigo by 78-3 in the opening round of the European Challenge Cup. That was followed up with an away win over Connacht in Galway.

A return visit to the Stoop in the EDF Energy Cup was a reprise of the match four weeks earlier, thanks to another dramatic second half turnaround. That set up a match with the Ospreys, the cup holders. In a thrilling contest at Madejski Stadium, the Exiles beat the Welsh team but were unable to deny them a crucial bonus point that saw them progress.

An important away win over Newcastle Falcons was followed by a competitive and compelling, action-packed 80 minutes against Saracens in Reading. Irish outscored the 'Men in Black' by three tries to one. The first of the season's visits to the West Country was to Bristol on 30th November and brought a narrow 18-13 win.

December had back-to-back home and away wins over US Dax in the European Challenge Cup before a crucial Premiership match with Gloucester on 20th December. Irish's 42-12 win saw them take over top place in the Premiership table for the first time since October 1999. The important Christmas and New Year period brought a home win over Newcastle and bonus point losses to Saracens and Sale. That was enough for the Exiles to return to the top of the Premiership table going into the New Year.

Another two Challenge Cup victories over Connacht and Rugby Rovigo in January earned the club a home quarter-final against Bourgoin.

Kingsholm continued to be a difficult arena for the Exiles on 31st January when the Cherry-and-Whites won narrowly. The following weekend London Irish had to play 60 minutes of the home match against Harlequins with 14 men and lost by four points.

Two exceptional second half performances against Bath (away) and Leicester Tigers (home) in late February/early March resulted in a draw and a three point loss respectively, however four precious league points were earned that saw the club holding on to third place in the Premiership.

The consistently good form of London Irish in the first half of the season resulted in record call-ups to national squads for the Six Nations. Club captain Bob Casey was with the Ireland squad and Delon Armitage, Steffon Armitage, Shane Geraghty, Nick Kennedy and Paul Hodgson were with the England EPS. That combined with injuries to five key players tested the depth of the squad to the full during February and March.

The annual visit to Adam's Park for the last of the regular season's "local derby" fixtures resulted in a 21-16 loss to London Wasps. That was followed by a run of three home matches in the Premiership against Worcester Warriors, Northampton Saints and Bristol Rugby respectively. Playing in front of home support, including a 21,295 attendance at the St. Patrick's celebration match with Saints, encouraged the team to three home wins that saw the Exiles move back into third place in the Premiership. A disappointing performance against Bourgoin in the quarter-final of the European Challenge Cup on 9th April resulted in a 32-30 defeat.

Six points from the two final matches, both away, of the regular Premiership season, a losing bonus point at Northampton and five points from the win at Worcester, saw the Exiles finish the regular season in third place in the table and so qualify for the end of season play-offs for only the second time.

The play-off formula whereby first plays fourth and second is at home to third meant that London Irish faced the short trip down the A316 to the Twickenham Stoop for the third time this season. Harlequins had finished the league campaign in good form and were favourites to take the semi-final. On Saturday 9th May however they faced a confident Exiles who kept the home team scoreless until half-time. In the second half A Delon Armitage penalty started the scoring, that was followed by tries from James Hudson and Mike Catt, both converted by Armitage, for a 17-0 scoreline that saw Irish through to their first Guinness Premiership Final.

A capacity crowd of 81,601 filled Twickenham Stadium for the Exiles' first Guinness Premiership Final on 14th May. The opposition were the mighty Leicester Tigers who had finished top of the table at the end of the regular season. Irish held the Tigers to a 3-3 score at half-time although they were unlucky not to lead at the interval as they had the East Midlands team under severe pressure in the final minutes of the half.

A Delon Armitage penalty gave Irish the lead in the 48th minute. Intense pressure by Leicester was finally rewarded when Jordan Crane crashed over for a try in the 61st minute, Julian Dupuy added the extras. A second Armitage penalty in the 71st minute reduced the lead to one point and set up an exciting finale. The Tigers held out to deny Irish a first Championship crown.

The end of season record shows an impressive outcome: Guinness Premiership finalists, third place in league at end of regular season; European Challenge Cup quarter-finalists; Heineken Cup qualification for 2009-10 with more player involved in international teams than ever before.

IRISH'S SEASON - 2008-09

Date	H/A	Opponents	Result & Score	Att.	15	14	13	12	11
GUINNESS PREMIERSHIP									
06-09	N	London Wasps	W 26-14	52000	Hewat/2c4p	Ojo	D Armitage	Mapusua	Tagicakibau
13-09	A	Leicester Tigers	L 22-24	16553	Hewat/2c	Ojo	D Armitage/t	Mapusua/t	Tagicakibau
20-09	H	Bath	L 16-20	8221	Hewat/p	Ojo	D Armitage(h/t)	Mapusua	Tagicakibau
27-09	A	Harlequins	W 28-27	11007	Hewat/t2c3p	Ojo	D Armitage/2t	Mapusua	Tagicakibau
01-10	H	Sale Sharks	W 28-6	7453	D Armitage	Ojo	Seveali'i	Mapusua	Tagicakibau/t
16-11	A	Newcastle Falcons	W 24-8	5009	Hewat/3cp	Ojo	Seveali'i	Geraghty	Bailey
23-11	H	Saracens	W 27-14	8954	Hewat/4p	Ojo	Seveali'i	Geraghty	Homer/2t
30-11	A	Bristol	W 18-13	6225	Hewat/c2p	Ojo	Seveali'i	Mapusua	Tagicakibau
20-12	H	Gloucester	W 42-12	12706	D Armitage/t	Ojo	Seveali'i	Mapusua	Tagicakibau
27-12	A	Saracens	L 13-16	16082	Hewat/2p	Ojo	Seveali'i	Mapusua	Tagicakibau
03-01	H	Newcastle Falcons	W 48-8	10978	Hewat/t4cp(k/t)	Ojo/t	Seveali'i	Mapusua/t	Homer
09-01	A	Sale Sharks	L 8-14	9430	Hewat	Ojo/t	Seveali'i	Mapusua	Homer
31-01	A	Gloucester	L 21-23	13974	D Armitage	Ojo/t	Seveali'i	Mapusua	Thompstone/*
14-02	H	Harlequins	L 9-14	12321	Hewat/2p	Ojo	Seveali'i	Mapusua	Thompstone
21-02	A	Bath	D 20-20	10600	Homer	Ojo/t	Seveali'i	Mapusua/t	Thompstone/*
01-03	H	Leicester Tigers	L 28-31	12154	Homer(l/t)	Ojo	Seveali'i	Mapusua/t	Thompstone
08-03	N	London Wasps	L 16-21	9525	Geraghty/c3p	Thompstone/t	Seveali'i	Mapusua	Tagicakibau
15-03	H	Worcester	W 38-17	8434	Homer/2c3p	Thompstone	Seveali'i	Mapusua	Tagicakibau
22-03	H	Northampton Saints*	W 32-27	21295	Homer/2c6p	Thompstone/t	Seveali'i	Mapusua	Tagicakibau
04-04	H	Bristol	W 38-21	11262	Homer/2p	Thompstone/2t	D Armitage/c	Mapusua	Tagicakibau
18-04	A	Northampton Saints	L 17-21	13405	Ojo	Thompstone	D Armitage/4p	Mapusua	Tagicakibau/t
25-04	A	Worcester	W 32-15	11241	Armitage/2cp	Thompstone/t	Richards	Mapusua	Tagicakibau/t
EUROPEAN CHALLENGE CUP									
11-10	H	Rovigo	W 78-3	5857	D Armitage/2tc	Ojo/t	Seveali'i/2t	Mapusua/t(d/t)	Tagicakibau
17-10	A	Connacht	W 27-10	4186	D Armitage	Ojo/2t	Seveali'i/t	Mapusua/t	Tagicakibau
05-12	A	Dax	W 38-0	4335	Hewat/4c	Ojo	Seveali'i	Mapusua	Tagicakibau/2
11-12	H	Dax	W 59-7	6004	D Armitage/t	Ojo/t	Seveali'i/2t	Gower	Shabbo
17-01	H	Connacht	W 75-5	8795	Hewat/5t	Ojo/2t	Mapusua	Geraghty/10c	Bailey/t
24-01	N	Rovigo	W 23-9	1200	D Armitage	Thompstone/t	Seveali'i	Gower	Bailey(g/t)
Q.F. 09-04	H	Bourgoin	L 30-32	6455	D Armitage/c5p	Ojo	Mapusua/t	Gower	Tagicakibau
EDF ENERGY CUP									
05-10	A	Worcester	L 5-22	7433	Bailey	De Vedia	Shabbo	Geraghty	Thompstone
25-10	A	Harlequins	W 32-17	11173	Hewat/2tc	Bailey/t	Shabbo	Gower	Thompstone/*
02-11	H	Ospreys	W 23-19	9293	Hewat/2c3p	Ojo	Seveali'i	Mapusua/t	Tagicakibau/t
GUINNESS CHAMPIONSHIP									
S.F. 09-05	A	Harlequins	W 17-0	12638	Hewat	Thompstone	D Armitage/2cp	Mapusua	Tagicakibau
Final 16-05	N	Leicester Tigers	L 9-10	81601	Hewat/dg	Thompstone	D Armitage/2p	Mapusua	Tagicakibau

SCORING BREAKDOWN

WHEN	Total	First Half	Second Half	1/4	2/4	3/4	4/4
the POINTS were scored	551	250	301	115	135	123	178
the POINTS were conceded	386	229	157	113	116	90	67
the TRIES were scored	64	26	38	11	15	15	23
the TRIES were conceded	36	20	16	12	8	9	7

HOW	Total	Pen. Try	Backs	Forwards	F Back	Wing	Centre	H Back	F Row	Lock	B Row
the TRIES were scored	64	1	37	26	5	18	9	5	4	3	19
the TRIES were conceded	36	1	20	15	3	5	5	7	5	3	7

KEY: * after opponents name indicates a penalty try.
Brackets after a player's name indicates he was replaced. eg (a) means he was replaced by replacement code "a" and so on.
/ after a player or replacement name is followed by any scores he made - eg /t, /c, /p, /dg or any combination of these

PREMIERSHIP

10	9	1	2	3	4	5	6	7	8
Catt	Hodgson	Corbisiero	Coetzee	Rautenbach	Johnson	Kennedy	Thorpe/t	S Armitage	Hala'ufia/t
Hickey/p	Hodgson	Laa'aetoa	Coetzee	Rautenbach	Rouse	Johnson	Thorpe	S Armitage/t	Hala'ufia
Hickey/p	Richards	Corbisiero/t	Paice	Rautenbach	Kennedy	Johnson	Thorpe	S Armitage	Hala'ufia
Hickey	Richards	Corbisiero	Paice	Rautenbach	Kennedy	Johnson	Thorpe	S Armitage	Hala'ufia
Hewat/tcpdg	Hodgson	Corbisiero/t	Coetzee	Laa'aetoa	Kennedy	Casey	Thorpe/t	S Armitage	Hala'ufia
Catt	Hodgson	Dermody	Paice	Rautenbach	Kennedy	Roche	Thorpe/t	Danagher/t	Hala'ufia(i/t)
Catt	Hodgson	Dermody	Paice	Rautenbach	Kennedy	Roche	Thorpe/t	S Armitage	Hala'ufia
Geraghty/t	Hodgson	Dermody	Paice	Laa'aetoa	Roche	Casey	Danagher	S Armitage	Hala'ufia
Hewat/2c6p	Hodgson/t	Dermody	Paice	Laa'aetoa	Hudson	Casey	Thorpe(j/t)	S Armitage	Hala'ufia
Geraghty/c	Hodgson	Dermody	Paice	Laa'aetoa	Hudson	Casey	Danagher/t	S Armitage	Hala'ufia
Geraghty/c	Hodgson	Corbisiero/t	Paice	Laa'aetoa	Hudson	Casey	Danagher/t	S Armitage/t	Hala'ufia
Geraghty/p	Hodgson	Dermody	Coetzee	Laa'aetoa	Hudson	Casey	Danagher	S Armitage	Hala'ufia
Hewat/c3p	Hodgson	Dermody	Paice	Laa'aetoa	Kennedy	Casey	Thorpe	Danagher	Hala'ufia
Catt	Lalanne/p	Dermody	Paice	Laa'aetoa	Johnson	Hudson	Thorpe	S Armitage	Hala'ufia
Geraghty/cp	Hodgson	Dermody	Buckland	Corbisiero	Hudson	Casey	Thorpe	S Armitage	Hala'ufia
Geraghty/c2p	Hodgson	Dermody	Buckland	Laa'aetoa	Hudson	Johnson	Thorpe	S Armitage/2t	Hala'ufia
Catt	Hodgson	Dermody	Buckland	Laa'aetoa	Hudson	Johnson	Danagher	S Armitage	Hala'ufia
Catt	Hodgson	Dermody/t	Coetzee	Skuse	Hudson/t	Johnson	Thorpe/t	Danagher	Hala'ufia/t
Catt	Hodgson	Dermody	Coetzee	Skuse	Hudson	Johnson	Danagher	S Armitage	Hala'ufia
Catt	Hodgson/t	Dermody	Paice	Skuse	Kennedy/2t	Hudson	Danagher	S Armitage/t	Hala'ufia
Hewat	Hodgson	Dermody	Paice	Skuse	Kennedy	Hudson	Thorpe	S Armitage	Hala'ufia
Hewat	Hodgson/t	Dermody	Coetzee	Skuse	Kennedy	Casey	Danagher/t	S Armitage	Hala'ufia/t
Hewat/8c	Hodgson/t(c/2t)	Corbisiero	Coetzee	Laa'aetoa	Kennedy	Casey	Thorpe	S Armitage	Hala'ufia/t
Hewat/2cp	Hodgson	Corbisiero	Buckland	Laa'aetoa	Kennedy	Casey	Thorpe	S Armitage	Hala'ufia
Geraghty/t	Hodgson(e/2t)	Corbisiero	Paice	Laa'aetoa	Roche	Casey/t	Danagher	S Armitage	Hala'ufia
Hewat/t8cp	Lalanne(f/2t)	Murphy	Buckland	Corbisiero	Hudson/t	Casey	Roche	Danagher	Thorpe
Catt	Hodgson	Dermody	Paice	Skuse	Hudson/t	Casey	Thorpe	S Armitage/t	Hala'ufia/t
Geraghty/c2p	Lalanne	Laa'aetoa	Buckland	Skuse	Hudson	Johnson	Roche/t	Danagher	Thorpe
Hewat	Richards	Murphy	Coetzee	Laa'aetoa	Kennedy/dg	Hudson	Roche	S Armitage/t	Thorpe
Hickey	Richards/t	Murphy	Buckland	Rautenbach	Johnson	Casey	Fisher	Danagher	Thorpe
Geraghty/p(b/c)	Parker	Dermody	Buckland	Rautenbach	Johnson	Hudson	Danagher	S Armitage	Fisher
Geraghty	Hodgson	Dermody	Paice	Rautenbach	Hudson	Casey	Thorpe	S Armitage	Hala'ufia
Catt/t	Hodgson	Dermody	Coetzee	Skuse	Kennedy(a/t)	Casey	Danagher	S Armitage	Hala'ufia
Catt	Hodgson	Dermody	Coetzee	Skuse	Hudson	Casey	Danagher	S Armitage	Hala'ufia

REPLACEMENTS

a- J Hudson   b- E Hickey   c- P Richards   d- S Geraghty
e- A Lalanne   f- W Fury   g- D Shabbo   h- E Seveali'i
i- S Armitage   j- D Danagher   k- M Catt   l- S Tagicakibau

LEAGUE APPEARANCES

22 Chris Hala'uifa
20 Seilala Mapusua
19 Steffon Armitage (2), Paul Hodgson (2)
17 Topst Ojo (2)

NUMBER OF PLAYERS USED
33 plus 3 as a replacement only

LEAGUE POINTS SCORERS

Pts	Player	T	C	P	DG
144	Peter Hewat	3	18	30	1
51	Tom Homer	2	4	11	-
41	Delon Armitage	4	3	5	-
36	Shane Geraghty	1	5	7	-
35	Adam Thompson	7	-	-	-

LONDON IRISH STATISTICS

LEAGUE

TEAM RECORDS

MOST POINTS
Scored at Home: 62 v Harlequins 25.4.98
Scored Away: 56 v London Wasps 30.4.06
Conceded at Home: 65 v Northampton 9.9.95
Conceded Away: 66 v Harlequins 14.9.96

MOST TRIES
Scored in a match: 9 v London Wasps 30.4.06 (A)
Conceded in a match: 11 v Harlequins 14.9.96 (A)

BIGGEST MARGINS
Home Win: 48pts
62-14 v Harlequins 25.4.98 & 56-8 v Newcastle 2.10.99
Away Win: 42pts - 55-13 v Saracens 22.11.01
Home Defeat: 48pts - 16-64 v Bath 11.3.00
Away Defeat: 59pts - 7-66 v Harlequins 14.9.96

MOST CONSECUTIVE
Victories: 8
Defeats: 7

INDIVIDUAL RECORDS

MOST APPEARANCES
by a forward: 145 (10) Kieron Dawson
by a back: 174(5) Justin Bishop

MOST CONSECUTIVE
Appearances: 29 Rob Henderson
Matches scoring Tries: 4 Rob Saunders:
Matches scoring points: 24 Michael Corcoran

MATCH RECORDS

Most Points
32   Niall Woods   v Harlequins 25.4.98 (H)

Most Tries
4   Niall Woods   v Northampton 5.1.99 (A)

Most Conversions
8   Niall Woods   v Harlequins 25.4.98 (H)

Most Penalties
8   Jarod Cunningham   v Bristol 10.9.90 (H)

Most Drop Goals
3   Mark Mapletoft v Northampton 27.12.04

SEASON RECORDS

Most Points	343	Barry Everitt	01-02
Most Tries	12	Niall Woods	98-99
Most Conversions	46	Jarrod Cunningham	99-00
Most Penalties	83	Barry Everitt	01-02
Most Drop Goals	8	Barry Everitt	01-02

CAREER RECORDS

Most Points	1236	Barry Everitt	00-07
Most Tries	55	Conor O'Shea	95-01
Most Conversions	95	Barry Everitt	00-07
Most Penalties	312	Barry Everitt	00-07
Most Drop Goals	25	Barry Everitt	00-07

LAST TEN SEASONS

	Division	P	W	D	L	F	A	P.D.	Pts	Pos	Most Points		Most Tries	
99-00	P1	22	9	1	12	613	616	-3	25	8	324	Jarod Cunningham	10	Conor O'Shea
00-01	P1	22	10	1	11	476	576	-100	45	8	182	Barry Everitt	8	Paul Sackey
01-02	P	22	11	3	8	574	465	109	57	4	343	Barry Everitt	6	Paul Sackey, Justin Bishop
02-03	P	22	8	1	13	432	485	-53	40	9	238	Barry Everitt	8	Paul Sackey
03-04	P	22	10	1	11	424	456	-32	49	8	145	Mark Mapletoft	8	Paul Sackey
04-05	P	22	8	0	14	378	421	-43	40	10	145	Barry Everitt	6	Scott Staniforth
05-06	P	22	14	0	8	493	454	39	66	3	112	Riki Flutey	8	Delon Armitage
06-07	P	22	12	0	10	398	407	-9	53	6	83	Shane Geraghty	8	Topsy Ojo
07-08	P	22	13	0	9	433	382	51	59	7	85	Peter Hewat	6	Sailosi Tagicakibau
08-09	P	22	12	1	9	557	390	167	66	3	144	Peter Hewat	7	Adam Thompstone

PREMIERSHIP

RFU SENIOR CUP

OVERALL PLAYING RECORD

	P	W	O	L	F	A	Pts Diff
Home	30	18	0	12	506	424	82
Away	37	22	0	15	666	635	31
Neutral	4	1	0	3	75	90	-15
TOTAL	71	41	0	30	1247	1149	98

TEAM RECORDS

Highest Score: 57 v Exeter 00/01
Biggest Winning Margin: 45 (57-12) v Exeter 00/01
Highest Score Against: 46
v Nottingham 90/91 & Leicester 95/96
Biggest Losing Margin: 36 (46-10) v Nottingham 90/91

SEASON BY SEASON

71-72	1R	78-79	2R	85-86	1R	92-93	3R	99-00	SF
72-73	DNQ	79-80	Runners up	86-87	3R	93-94	5R	00-01	QF
73-74	DNQ	80-81	4R	87-88	3R	94-95	5R	01-02	Winners
74-75	2R	81-82	3R	88-89	4R	95-96	SF	02-03	SF
75-76	2R	82-83	3R	89-90	2R	96-97	5R	03-04	QF
76-77	1R	83-84	4R	90-91	QF	97-98	QF	04-05	SF
77-78	1R	84-85	DNQ	91-92	3R	98-99	QF		

Anglo-Welsh Cup

05-06	Gp Stage
06-07	Gp Stage
07-08	Gp Stage
08-09	Gp Stage

Premiership Championship

02-03	-	07-08	-
03-04	-	08-09	R-up
04-05	-		
05-06	SF		
06-07	-		

EUROPEAN COMPETITIONS

TEAM RECORDS

Highest Score
78 v Rovigo 11.10.08

Biggest Winning Margin
75 (78-3) v Rovigo 11.10.08

Highest Score Against
63 v Swansea 96/97

Biggest Losing Margin
26 (32-6) v Begles 96/97

INDIVIDUAL RECORDS

Most Points in a match
26 By three players

Most Tries in a match
5 Peter Hewat v Connacht 17.01.09

Most Conversions in a match
9 Jarrod Cunningham v Valladolid 01/02

Most Penalties in a match
7 By two players
Barry Everitt (x2), Jarrod Cunningham

Most Drop Goals in a match
2 Barry Everitt v Toulouse 02/03

CAREER RECORDS

Most Appearances
43: Justin Bishop (1)
35 Declan Danagher (7)
31: Neal Hatley, Bob Casey (2)
24: Ryan Strudwick (4)

Most Points
378: Barry Everitt
175: Peter Hewat
139: Jarrod Cunningham
113: Mark Mapletoft

Most Tries
13: Conor O'Shea
12: Topsi Ojo
11: Justin Bishop

SEASON BY SEASON

1996-97	S	Gp Stage
1997-98	S	Gp Stage
1998-99	-	-
1999-00	S	S.F.
2000-01	S	Gp Stage
2001-02	S	S.F.
2002-03	C	Gp Stage
2003-04	S	2nd Rd
2004-05	CC	2nd Rd
2005-06	CC	R-Up
2006-07	C	Gp Stage
2007-08	C	S.F.
2008-09	CC	Q.F.

OVERALL PLAYING RECORD

	P	W	D	L	F	A	Pts Diff
Home	37	29	1	7	1398	626	772
Away	38	20	0	18	1015	855	160
Neutral	2	-	-	2	61	69	-8
Total	68	41	1	26	2364	1550	864

LONDON WASPS

Founded:
1867
Nickname:
Wasps
Colours:
Black and gold
Change colours:
White
Website:
www.wasps.co.uk

KEY PERSONNEL

Club Owner	Steve Hayes
Executive Chairman	Mark Rigby
Chief Executive	Tony Copsey
Director of Rugby	Tony Hanks
Financial Director	Peter Wear
Commercial Director	Peter Scrivener
Head of Sponsorship	Gareth Lloyd
1XV Manager	Kevin Harman Tel: 020 8993 8298 email kevin.harman@wasps.co.uk
Community Rugby Manager	Dave Larham
Operations Manager	JP Robinson
Merchandise Manager	Fiona Stockley
Media Contact	Communications Executive, Laura Brown Tel: 020 8896 4878 email laura.brown@wasps.co.uk

CONTACT DETAILS

London Wasps Training Ground, Twyford Ave., Acton, London W3 9QA
Tel: 0208 993 8298   Fax: 0208 993 2621

GROUND DETAILS

Address: Adams Park,
Hillbottom Road, High Wycombe, Bucks. HP12 4HJ
Ticket Hotline: 0844 225 2990
Capacity: 10,516   Seated: 8,300
Car Parking: Limited space at the stadium. London Wasps recommend supporters make use of the park and ride operating from just off J4 of the M40 before and after home games or the train and ride service from High Wycombe Train Station.
Nearest BR Station: High Wycombe, Chiltern Lines from Marylebone. Shuttle buses operate between the train and bus stations and Adams Park stadium before and after home games
Admission
Matchday: Adults from £15 - £45, concessions from £8 - £15.
Season: Adults from £185-£540, concessions from £95-£160.
Directions: From the M40, exit at Junction 4 and take the exit for A4010 (John Hall Way). Follow this road crossing 3 mini roundabouts until the road becomes New Road. Keep on New Road until next mini roundabout take left turn onto Lane End Road. Cross next mini roundabout onto Hillbottom Road, this will take you on to Adams Park.
Clubhouse: Gates open approximately three hours before kick-off. Supporters are advised to check the website for details prior to each game. Food available at several outlets around the ground at home games. Various hospitality packages are available, for further details contact Alistair Beynon on 020 8896 4874
Club Shop: London Wasps Club shop located in the Eden Shopping Centre is open Monday – Friday 9am – 5.30pm, telephone: 01494 443 085. The Club Shop located at Adams Park is open on matchdays from gates open until 1 Hour after final whistle, telephone: 01494 455 757. Internet Mail Order, Monday – Friday 10am – 4pm, telephone: 08704287910.

PROGRAMME

Size: 165 x 240mm (B5)   Pages: 84
Price: £3   Editor: Laura Brown
Advertising Alistair Beynon on 020 8896 4874

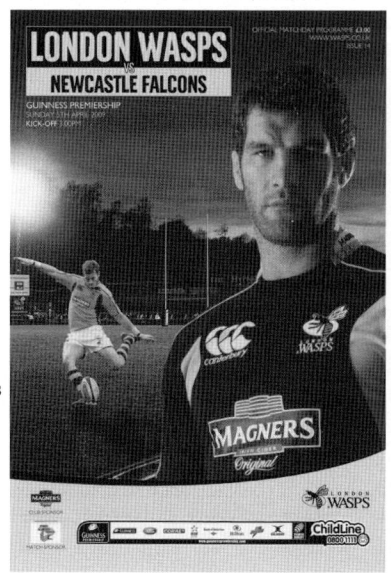

REVIEW OF THE SEASON 2008-09

London Wasps has a disastrous season by their standards over recent years finishing the season trophy less for the first time since 2001/02 and with James Haskell, Riki Flutey and Tom Palmer all off to play in France this coming season Wasps could find themselves in a transitional period.

In the Guinness Premiership they were down in seventh place their joint second worst season ever having finished ninth once back in 1997/98. They went out of the Pool stages of the Heineken Cup for the second season running when finishing second to Leinster, and in fact have failed to get out of the Pool stage of the Heineken Cup four times in the last five years, the only time they did they went on to win the competition. In the EDF Cup they were second in their Pool managing two wins in three matches after losing their opener to Gloucester.

In the Guinness Premiership they got off to a poor start with three straight defeats and after breaking their duck with a win at Welford Road of all places went onto lose their next three matches for a six defeats and one win start to the season, and in four of those defeats they took a losing bonus point. They then found some form and won five out of six to climb the table including another win over Leicester Tigers to complete the double over the eventual Champions. They then suffered another dip in form with four defeats in six matches before finishing the season showing some form with three straight wins including a 34-3 win over Gloucester on the final day of the season. After losing their opening three matches at Adams Park they went eight unbeaten till the end of the season.

In the Heineken Cup they started with a home win over Castres but a week later suffered one of their worst ever defeats in Europe when going down 41-11 at Leinster. They did the double over Edinburgh before Christmas and made it four in a row beating Leinster at Adams Park. They went to Castres knowing they had to win to have a chance of going through to the knockout stage but they could get the win and went down 21-15 with the French side snatching a win with a 75th minute converted try.

In the EDF Cup they went out to fellow Premiership side Gloucester who narrowly beat them in their opening Pool match, they went on to beat Newcastle Falcons and Gwent Dragons but with Gloucester winning all three of their matches they progressed to the semi finals.

WASPS' SEASON - 2008-09

PREMIERSHIP

Date	H/A	Opponents	Result & Score	Att.	15	14	13	12	11
GUINNESS PREMIERSHIP									
06-09	N	London Irish	L 14-26	52000	van Gisbergen/c	Sackey	Waldouck	Lewsey(a/c)	Voyce
14-09	N	Worcester	L 10-11	7668	Lewsey	Sackey/t	Waldouck	Flutey	Voyce
20-09	A	Northampton Saints	L 20-24	13021	Lewsey	Sackey	Waldouck/t	Flutey	Voyce
26-09	A	Leicester Tigers	W 28-19	17498	Voyce	Sackey	Waldouck	Flutey	Lewsey
01-10	N	Bath	L 23-27	9052	Voyce	Sackey	Waldouck	Flutey/t	Lewsey
16-11	A	Harlequins	L 10-32	12638	van Gisbergen/c	Lawlor	Lewsey	Mitchell	Voyce
23-11	N	Sale Sharks	L 12-13	8367	Mitchell	Bishay	Lewsey	van Gisbergen	Voyce
28-11	N	Newcastle Falcons	W 23-17	5489	Mitchell	Bishay	Lewsey	van Gisbergen	Voyce
20-12	N	Saracens	W 33-24	9324	Mitchell(e/3cp)	Sackey/t	Hoadley/t	Lewsey/t	Voyce
26-12	A	Sale Sharks	L 3-31	10841	Mitchell	Bishay	Lewsey	Flutey	Voyce
04-01	N	Harlequins*	W 24-18	10000	van Gisbergen	Bishay/t	Waldouck	Flutey	Voyce
15-02	N	Leicester Tigers	W 36-29	9581	van Gisbergen	Bishay/t	Waldouck	Lewsey	Voyce
22-02	N	Northampton Saints	W 9-5	10000	van Gisbergen	Bishay	Waldouck	Lewsey	Voyce
28-02	A	Worcester	L 12-13	9543	van Gisbergen	Mitchell	Waldouck	Lewsey	Voyce
08-03	N	London Irish*	W 21-16	9525	van Gisbergen	Mitchell	Waldouck	Lewsey	Voyce
14-03	A	Gloucester	L 22-24	15294	van Gisbergen	Mitchell/t	Waldouck	Lewsey(e/c5p)	Voyce
22-03	N	Bristol	W 21-19	8498	van Gisbergen	Mitchell/t	Waldouck	Lewsey	Voyce
29-03	A	Saracens	L 14-19	16257	van Gisbergen	Lewsey	Waldouck	Flutey	Voyce/t
01-04	A	Bath	L 14-22	10600	van Gisbergen(a/p)	Mitchell	Waldouck	Flutey/t	Voyce
05-04	N	Newcastle Falcons	W 12-6	9740	van Gisbergen	Mitchell	Waldouck	Lewsey	Voyce
19-04	N	Bristol	W 36-18	6508	van Gisbergen	Sackey	Waldouck	Flutey	Lewsey/t
25-04	N	Gloucester	W 34-3	10000	Mitchell	Voyce/t	Waldouck	Flutey/2t	Lewsey
HEINEKEN CUP									
12-10	N	Castres	W 25-11	8800	Staunton	Sackey/t	Lewsey/t	Flutey	Voyce/t
18-10	N	Leinster	L 11-41	18500	Staunton/t	Sackey	Lewsey	Flutey	Voyce
05-12	N	Edinburgh Reivers	W 25-16	7711	van Gisbergen	Sackey	Waldouck	Flutey	Lewsey
14-12	N	Edinburgh Reivers	W 19-11	7596	van Gisbergen	Sackey	Waldouck	Lewsey	Voyce
17-01	N	Leinster	W 19-12	33282	van Gisbergen	Sackey	Waldouck	Flutey	Lewsey
25-01	A	Castres	L 15-21	7233	van Gisbergen	Sackey	Waldouck/t	Flutey	Lewsey
EDF ENERGY CUP									
04-10	A	Gloucester	L 19-24	7864	Mitchell	Odejobi	Hoadley	Waldouck(e/p)	Voyce
24-10	A	Newcastle Falcons	W 26-13	5202	van Gisbergen	Sackey/t	Lewsey	Staunton	Voyce/t
02-11	N	Gwent Dragons	W 21-10	7980	van Gisbergen	Lewsey/t	Hoadley	Staunton	Voyce

SCORING BREAKDOWN

WHEN	Total	First Half	Second Half	1/4	2/4	3/4	4/4
the POINTS were scored	431	236	195	117	119	87	108
the POINTS were conceded	416	215	201	111	104	83	118
the TRIES were scored	33	13	20	5	8	8	12
the TRIES were conceded	42	20	22	10	10	9	13

HOW	Total	Pen. Try	Backs	Forwards	F Back	Wing	Centre	H Back	F Row	Lock	B Row
the TRIES were scored	33	2	21	10	0	9	7	5	4	1	5
the TRIES were conceded	42	1	29	12	6	14	5	4	2	-	10

KEY: * after opponents name indicates a penalty try.
Brackets after a player's name indicates he was replaced. eg (a) means he was replaced by replacement code "a" and so on.
/ after a player or replacement name is followed by any scores he made - eg /t, /c, /p, /dg or any combination of these

PREMIERSHIP

10	9	1	2	3	4	5	6	7	8
Flutey	Redden/t	Payne	Ibanez	Barnard	Shaw	Birkett	Worsley	Rees/t	Haskell
Walder/cp	Redden	Payne	Ibanez	Vickery	Shaw	Palmer	Worsley	Rees	Haskell
Walder/5p	Redden	Payne	Ward	Vickery	Birkett	Palmer	Worsley	Haskell	Hart
Staunton/c5p2dg	Robinson	Vickery	Webber	Barnard(b/t)	Birkett	Palmer	Worsley	Rees	Hart
Cipriani/c3p(a/c)	Redden	Payne	Ibanez	Vickery	Shaw	Palmer	Worsley	Rees/t	Hart
Staunton/p	Robinson(c/t)	Payne	Webber	Barnard	Skivington	Birkett	Hart	Betsen	Worsley
Walder/4p	Robinson	French	Ibanez	Barnard	Skivington	Birkett	Leo	Betsen	Worsley
Walder/6p	Redden	French	Webber	Barnard(d/t)	Skivington	Birkett	Leo	Betsen	Worsley
Cipriani/3p	Redden	Payne	Webber	Vickery	Shaw	Palmer	Worsley	Rees	Haskell
Walder/p	Simpson	French	Ward	Payne	Shaw	Birkett	Worsley	Betsen	Ellis
Cipriani/c3p(e/p)	Redden	French	Webber	Vickery	Shaw	Skivington	Leo	Betsen	Haskell
Cipriani/3c5p	Robinson	Payne	Ward	Barnard	Shaw	Skivington	Leo	Betsen/t	Hart/t
Cipriani/3p	Robinson	Payne	Webber	Barnard	Shaw	Skivington	Birkett	Betsen	Hart
Cipriani/4p	Redden	Holford	Ward	French	Shaw	Skivington	Birkett	Betsen	Hart
Cipriani/c3p	Robinson	Payne	Webber	Barnard/t	Shaw	Skivington	Betsen	Rees	Hart
Cipriani	Redden	Beech	Webber	Payne	Birkett	Skivington	Betsen	Rees	Hart
Cipriani/3p(e/c)	Redden	Payne	Webber	Baker(d/t)	Birkett	Skivington	Betsen	Rees	Hart
Cipriani/3p	Simpson	Beech	Webber	Barnard	Shaw	Skivington	Haskell	Rees	Leo
Cipriani/2p	Simpson	French	Ward	Payne	Shaw	Birkett	Worsley	Betsen	Hart
Cipriani/3pdg	Robinson	Payne	Webber	Baker	Shaw	Skivington	Haskell	Rees	Hart
Cipriani/t4cp	Simpson/2t	Payne	Webber	Barnard	Shaw	Skivington	Betsen/t	Rees	Worsley
Cipriani/2c2p(a/2c)	Simpson	Payne	Webber	Vickery	Shaw/t	Skivington	Worsley	Betsen	Hart
Cipriani/2c2p	Redden	Payne	Ibanez	Vickery	Shaw	Palmer	Haskell	Rees	Worsley
Cipriani/2p	Redden	Payne	Ibanez	Vickery	Shaw	Palmer	Haskell	Rees	Worsley
Cipriani/c6p	Redden	Payne	Webber	Vickery	Skivington	Birkett	Betsen	Rees/t	Haskell
Walder/tc4p	Redden	Payne	Webber	Vickery	Shaw	Birkett	Betsen	Rees	Haskell
Cipriani/c3p(e/p)	Redden	Payne	Webber	Vickery	Shaw	Birkett	Worsley	Betsen/t	Haskell
Cipriani/tcp	Redden	Payne	Webber	Vickery	Shaw	Birkett	Worsley	Betsen	Haskell
Staunton/2p	Robinson/t	French	Webber	Holford	Shaw	Birkett	Haskell/t	Betsen	Worsley
Cipriani/3c	Robinson(c/t)	Payne	Webber	Barnard	Birkett	Palmer	Haskell	Rees/t	Worsley
Walder/c3p	Robinson	Payne	Webber	Barnard(b/t)	Leo	Birkett	Hart	Betsen	Worsley

REPLACEMENTS

a- J Staunton   b- D Varley   c- J Simpson   d- C Beech
e- D Walder

LEAGUE APPEARANCES

21	Tom Voyce
20	Josh Lewsey
17	Dominic Waldouck
16	Tim Payne (1)

LEAGUE POINTS SCORERS

Pts	Player	T	C	P	DG
146	Danny Cipriani	1	12	38	1
84	David Walder	-	6	24	-
37	Jeremy Staunton	-	6	24	-
20	Riki Flutey	4	-	-	-
15	Joe Simpson	3	-	-	-

NUMBER OF PLAYERS USED

37 plus 2 as a replacement only

LONDON WASPS STATISTICS

LEAGUE

TEAM RECORDS

MOST POINTS
Scored at Home: 65 v Orrell 22.3.97
Scored Away: 57 v Harlequins 17.9.94
Conceded at Home: 56 v London Irish 30.4.06
Conceded Away: 45 v London Irish 17.5.00; v Leics 9.9.01

MOST TRIES
Scored in a match: 9
v Coventry 13.4.88 (H); v Bedford 12.3.90 (A);
v Liverpool St H 20.4.91; v Orrell 2.3.97 (H) &
v Bedford 26.3.00 (H)
Conceded in a match: 9
v London Irish 30.4.06

BIGGEST MARGINS
Home Win: 57pts - 62-5 v Orrell 22.3.97
Away Win: 31pts - 57-26 v Harlequins 17.9.94
Home Defeat: 31pts - 3-34 v Harlequins 9.3.96
17-48 v Leicester 8.5.04
Away Defeat: 32pts - 6-38 v Leicester 12.10.93

MOST CONSECUTIVE
Victories: 11 (21.11.03 - 18.4.04)
Defeats: 6

INDIVIDUAL RECORDS

MOST APPEARANCES
by a forward: 231 (15) Lawrence Dallaglio 96-08
by a back: 173 (11) Alex King 96-07

MOST CONSECUTIVE
Appearances: 36 Richard Kinsey 29.2.92-30.4.94
Matches scoring Tries: 4 Kenny Logan
Matches scoring points: 25 Gareth Rees

MATCH RECORDS

Most Points
29   Alex King   v Leeds Tykes 18.11.01 (H)
Most Tries
5   Kenny Logan   v Orrell 22.3.97 (H)
Most Conversions
8   Alex King   v Bedford 26.3.00 (H)
Most Penalties
9   Alex King   v Newcastle 11.11.01 (H)
Most Drop Goals
2   Jon Ufton   v Saracens 23.9.95 (H)
     Rob Andrew   v Sale 30.9.95 (A)
     Guy Gregory   v Leicester 6.4.96 (A)
     Alex King   v Bath 6.4.03 (H)

SEASON RECORDS

Most Points	291	Gareth Rees 96-97
Most Tries	11	Kenny Logan 96-97
		Paul Sampson 00-01
Most Conversions	47	Kenny Logan 00-01
Most Penalties	62	Gareth Rees 96-97
Most Drop Goals	9	Alex King 01-02

CAREER RECORDS

Most Points	1000	Alex King	96-07
Most Tries	48	Kenny Logan	96-04
Most Conversions	135	Alex King	96-07
Most Penalties	176	Alex King	96-07
Most Drop Goals	34	Alex King	96-07

LAST TEN SEASONS

	Division	P	W	D	L	F	A	P.D.	Pts	Pos	Most Points	Most Tries
99-00	P1	22	11	1	10	640	661	-21	31	7	136 Kenny Logan	9 Josh Lewsey
00-01	P1	22	16	0	6	663	428	235	74	2	282 Kenny Logan	11 Paul Sampson
01-02	P	22	12	0	10	519	507	12	54	7	183 Alex King	6 Fraser Waters
02-03	P	22	13	2	7	553	460	93	67	2	246 Alex King	10 Josh Lewsey
03-04	P	22	16	0	6	575	406	169	73	2	211 Mark Van Gisbergen	7 Tom Voyce
04-05	P	22	15	1	6	561	442	119	73	2	179 Mark van Gisbergen	11 Tom Voyce
05-06	P	22	12	3	7	527	447	80	64	4	199 Mark van Gisbergen	10 Tom Voyce
06-07	P	22	12	1	9	504	431	73	61	5	84 Mark van Gisbergen	8 Paul Sackey
07-08	P	22	14	2	6	599	459	140	70	2	188 Danny Cipriani	8 Tom Voyce
08-09	P	22	11	0	11	431	416	15	54	7	146 Danny Cipriani	4 Riki Flutey

RFU SENIOR CUP

OVERALL PLAYING RECORD

	P	W	O	L	F	A	Pts Diff
Home	34	23	1	10	742	416	326
Away	37	23	1	13	796	458	338
Neutral	7	3	0	4	167	201	-34
TOTAL	78	49	2	27	1705	1075	630

Other - Home Bye 4th Rd 99-00; Away Disq. 6th Rd 04-05

TEAM RECORDS

Highest Score: 84 v Rugby Lions 96/97
Biggest Winning Margin: 76 (84-8) v Rugby Lions 96/97
Highest Score Against: 48 v Saracens 97/98
Biggest Losing Margin: 36 (43-7) v Leicester 78/79

SEASON BY SEASON

71-72	DNQ	78-79	SF	85-86	Runners up	92-93	SF	99-00	Winners
72-73	DNQ	79-80	1R	86-87	Runners up	93-94	4R	00-01	4R
73-74	DNQ	80-81	3R	87-88	SF	94-95	Runners up	01-02	6R
74-75	1R	81-82	3R	88-89	QF	95-96	QF	02-03	6R
75-76	1R	82-83	4R	89-90	3R	96-97	6R	03-04	QF
76-77	DNQ	83-84	QF	90-91	QF	97-98	Runners up	04-05	6R
77-78	1R	84-85	4R	91-92	4R	98-99	Winners		

Anglo-Welsh Cup

05-06	Winners
06-07	Gp Stage
07-08	S.F.
08-09	Gp Stage

Premiership Championship

02-03	Winners	07-08	Winners
03-04	Winners	08-09	-
04-05	Winners		
05-06	SF		
06-07	-		

EUROPEAN COMPETITIONS

TEAM RECORDS

Highest Score
77-17 v Toulouse 96/97

Biggest Winning Margin
71 Pts 71-0 v Benetton Treviso 16.12.06

Highest Score Against
54-28 v Swansea 00/01

Biggest Losing Margin
31 Pts 0-31 v Stade Francais 00/01

INDIVIDUAL RECORDS

Most Points in a match
27 Jon Ufton v Toulouse 96/97

Most Tries in a match
4 Kenny Logan v Calvisano 03/04

Most Conversions in a match
8 Mark van Gisbergen v B Treviso 16.12.06

Most Penalties in a match
8 Gareth Rees v Cardiff 96/97
Mark van Gisbergen v Leicester 5.12.04

Most Drop Goals in a match
2 Alex King v Biarritz 24.10.04

CAREER RECORDS

Most Appearances
62: Simon Shaw (3)
60 (1): Lawrence Dallaglio
55: Alex King (3)
50: Joe Worsley (4), Josh Lewsey (3)

Most Points:
391: Alex King
277: Kenny Logan
208: Mark Van Gisbergen

Most Tries:
19: Kenny Logan
18: Josh Lewsey

SEASON BY SEASON

1996-97	C	Gp Stage
1997-98	C	Q.F.
1998-99	-	-
1999-00	C	Q.F.
2000-01	C	Gp Stage
2001-02	C	Gp Stage
2002-03	S	Winners
2003-04	C	Winners
2004-05	C	Gp Stage
2005-06	C	Gp Stage
2006-07	C	Winners
2007-08	C	Gp Stage
2008-09	C	Gp Stage

OVERALL PLAYING RECORD

	P	W	D	L	F	A	Pts Diff
Home	39	32	1	6	1300	601	699
Away	38	19	0	19	967	905	62
Neutral	4	4	-	-	137	91	46
Total	81	55	1	25	2404	1597	807

NEWCASTLE FALCONS

NEWCASTLE FALCONS

Founded: 1877
Nickname: Falcons
Colours:
(Home) Black with white trim
(Away) White with black trim
Web site:
www.newcastle-falcons.co.uk

KEY PERSONNEL

Chairman:	Dave Thompson	
Director of Rugby	Steve Bates	
Assistant Coaches	Alan Tait, Stuart Grimes, Ian Peel	
Media Manager	Mark Smith	0191 214 2866
Business Development Manager	Anna Humphreys	0191 214 2808
Community Manager	Melanie Magee	0191 214 2804
Stadium Manager	David Culling	0191 214 2803

CONTACT DETAILS

Newcastle Falcons, Kingston Park, Brunton Road,
Newcastle upon Tyne NE13 8AF
Main reception   Tel: 0191 214 5588
Tickets   Tel: 0871 226 60 60

GROUND DETAILS

Address: Kingston Park Stadium, Brunton Road, Kenton Bank Foot, Newcastle upon Tyne NE13 8AF
Tel: 0191 214 5588 (Main reception)
Ticket hotline: 0871 226 6060

Capacity: 10,200
Seated: 4,000
Covered: 7,000

Directions: From the A1 Western by-pass, take the turning for Newcastle Airport and then follow signs for Kingston Park which is approx 1 mile from the A1.
If travelling by air take any Metro from the airport. Kingston Park is only a few stops away.

Nearest BR Station: Newcastle Central - take Metro marked to the airport which stops at Kingston Park station

Car Parking:
Approx 500 spaces on site @ £8, + 200 at nearby school

Admission: Matchday: £15 - £40
Season: From £118 for adults & £34 for juniors

Club Shop: 10am until 5pm Mon to Sat and home matchdays.
Contact Alison Leigh, 0191 214 2830

Clubhouse: Hiding Place Sports Bar open noon until midnight every day. Food and drink available. Hiding Place Lounge Bar also available. Due Dieci Pizzeria Ristorante open every day. Numerous match-day bars and catering outlets also available. Extensive conference and banqueting facilities available

PROGRAMME

Size: A5   Pages: 76   Price: £3
Editor: Mark Smith
Advertising:
Green Park Publishing: 0117 977 9188

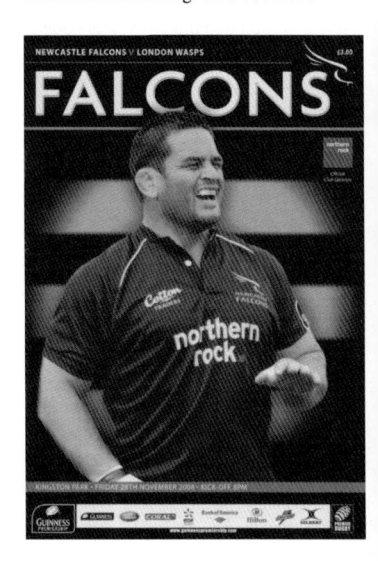

L-R - Back row: John Stokoe, Mark Wilkinson, Hall Charlton, John Rudd, Rob Miller, Spencer Davey, Rory Clegg, Sean Tomes, Tom Dillon, Tim Swinson, Danny Williams, Rob Vickers, Ross Batty, Ian Peel, Mark Laycock.
Middle row: Ian Smith, Alan Tait, Andy Ramshaw, Bob Morton, Stuart Grimes, Jon Golding, David Wilson, Ed Williamson, Andy Buist, Ross Beattie, Eni Gesinde, Andy Perry, Mark Sorenson, Carl Hayman, Russell Winter, Rob Bowen, Marten Brewer, Barrie Graham, Steve Bates.
Front row: Brent Wilson, Tom May, Joe McDonnell, Matt Thompson, Adam Balding, Ollie Phillips, Steve Jones, Jamie Noon, Phil Dowson, Andy Long, Geoff Parling, Alex Tait, Joe Shaw, James Grindal, Tim Visser, Micky Ward, Jonny Wilkinson.

REVIEW OF THE SEASON 2008-09

Newcastle Falcons started the season with stability in mind, with Steve Bates installed as the club's permanent director of rugby after a successful spell as caretaker.

Further international quality was added to the coaching ranks with the arrivals of Scotland duo Alan Tait and Stuart Grimes as assistant coaches, complementing a staff which already contained ex-Newcastle prop Ian Peel.

On the recruitment front the Falcons had a fairly low-key summer of 2008, with England Saxons No.8 Adam Balding, Doncaster centre Spencer Davey and England rugby league international Danny Williams the only recruits - but Williams went on to shine with nine tries in his 17 union starts.

The squad was further bolstered in November with the arrival of Tongan centre Tane Tu'ipulotu, who went on to become a mainstay of the backline with 22 consecutive starts.

Early home wins over Northampton and Bristol got the Falcons off to a flyer, but with injuries to key men hitting hard, it was a February renaissance which really sparked the season into life, as a thumping victory at relegation rivals Bristol was followed up with a further five consecutive victories to ease fears of the drop.

In Europe there was to be another Challenge Cup quarter-final as they came through a pool containing El Salvador, Brive and Overmach Parma, bowing out at the quarter-final stage to Saracens.

A tenth place Guinness Premiership finish was their ultimate reward for a resurgence which included victories over Leicester, Northampton and Gloucester, but with improvement very much in mind, it was a heavily-changed playing squad which lined up for the start of the 09/10 campaign.

NEWCASTLE FALCONS

NEWCASTLE'S SEASON - 2008-09

Date	H/A	Opponents	Result & Score	Att.	15	14	13	12	11
GUINNESS PREMIERSHIP									
07-09	H	Sale Sharks	L 9-14	5224	Tait	May	Noon	Davey	Rudd
14-09	H	Northampton Saints	W 32-22	4620	Tait	Phillips/t	Noon	Davey	Rudd
21-09	A	Saracens	L 14-44	8139	Tait	May/t	Noon	Davey	Rudd
26-09	H	Bristol	W 17-3	6056	Jones	Visser	Noon	May	Rudd/t
30-09	A	Gloucester	L 23-39	12861	Jones	Phillips	Noon	May/t	Visser
16-11	H	London Irish	L 8-24	5009	Jones	Williams	May	Tuipulotu	Rudd
21-11	A	Worcester	L 11-26	10162	Jones	Williams/t	May	Tuipulotu	Rudd
28-11	H	London Wasps	L 17-23	5489	Jones	Williams/t	May/t	Tuipulotu	Rudd
20-12	A	Leicester Tigers	L 3-20	17240	May	Visser	Davey	Tuipulotu	Rudd
27-12	H	Worcester	D 16-16	7108	May	Visser	Noon	Tuipulotu	Rudd
03-01	A	London Irish	L 8-48	10978	May	Visser/t	Noon	Tuipulotu	Rudd
11-01	H	Gloucester	W 10-7	5026	May/p	Williams/t	Noon	Tuipulotu	Visser
13-02	N	Bristol	W 35-3	8108	Tait	Williams	Noon	Tuipulotu	Rudd
20-02	H	Saracens	W 13-9	6204	Tait	Williams	Noon	Tuipulotu	Rudd/t
28-02	A	Northampton Saints	W 19-13	12908	Tait	Williams/t	Noon	Tuipulotu	Rudd
08-03	A	Sale Sharks	W 32-25	8427	Tait	Williams/t(e/t)	Noon	Tuipulotu	Visser
15-03	H	Harlequins	W 24-16	7705	Tait	Fenby	Noon	Tuipulotu	Visser/t
21-03	A	Bath	L 25-36	10600	Tait	Visser/t	Noon	Tuipulotu	Fenby/t
27-03	H	Leicester Tigers	W 14-10	7614	Tait	Visser	Noon	Tuipulotu/t	Rudd
05-04	N	London Wasps	L 6-12	9740	Tait	Visser	Noon	Tuipulotu	Rudd
19-04	H	Bath	L 14-15	7804	Tait	Williams/t	Noon	Tuipulotu	Rudd
25-04	A	Harlequins	L 12-31	12638	Tait	Williams	May/c	Tuipulotu	Rudd
EUROPEAN CHALLENGE CUP									
11-10	H	Dulciora El Salvador*	W 68-0	3789	Jones/t	Williams	Noon/t	May/t	Visser/t
16-10	N	Brive	L 24-36	6953	Jones	Visser/t	Noon	May	Rudd
06-12	N	Parma	W 20-14	1400	Jones(i/t)	Williams/t	Noon	Tuipulotu	May
14-12	H	Parma	W 21-16	3902	May	Visser	Noon/t	Tuipulotu	Rudd
17-01	H	Brive	L 9-10	4514	Jones	Williams	Noon	Tuipulotu	Visser
25-01	N	Dulciora El Salvador	W 43-14	2328	May	Williams/t	Noon	Tuipulotu	Tait
Q.F. 12-04	A	Saracens	L 13-32	7711	Tait	Williams/t	Noon	Tuipulotu	Rudd
EDF ENERGY CUP									
03-10	A	Gwent Dragons*	L 14-25	4683	Jones	Phillips/t	Dillon	Davey	Williams
24-10	H	London Wasps	L 13-26	5202	Jones	Phillips	Noon	May	Rudd
02-11	H	Gloucester	L 10-11	3614	Jones	Williams	May	Davey	Rudd

SCORING BREAKDOWN

WHEN	Total	First Half	Second Half	1/4	2/4	3/4	4/4
the POINTS were scored	362	171	191	108	63	102	89
the POINTS were conceded	456	251	205	124	127	81	124
the TRIES were scored	38	16	22	11	5	12	10
the TRIES were conceded	43	17	26	7	10	9	17

HOW	Total	Pen. Try	Backs	Forwards	F Back	Wing	Centre	H Back	F Row	Lock	B Row
the TRIES were scored	38	-	23	15	-	15	3	5	3	3	9
the TRIES were conceded	43	-	28	15	6	12	6	4	3	2	10

KEY: * after opponents name indicates a penalty try.
Brackets after a player's name indicates he was replaced. eg (a) means he was replaced by replacement code "a" and so on.
/ after a player or replacement name is followed by any scores he made - eg /t, /c, /p, /dg or any combination of these

PREMIERSHIP

10	9	1	2	3	4	5	6	7	8
Clegg/3p	Grindal	McDonnell	Long	Hayman	Buist	Sorenson	Balding	Wilson	Dowson
Wilkinson/2c5pdg	Grindal	McDonnell	Long	Hayman	Sorenson	Buist/t	Balding	Williamson	Dowson
Wilkinson/t2c	Grindal	Ward	Long	Hayman	Perry	Sorenson	Balding	Williamson	Dowson
Wilkinson/2cp	Grindal	McDonnell	Thompson	Hayman	Perry	Sorenson	Balding/t	Williamson	Dowson
Wilkinson/p(a/cp)	Charlton	Ward	Thompson/t	Hayman	Perry	Sorenson	Balding	Williamson	Dowson/t
Clegg/p	Charlton	Golding	Long	Ward	Swinson	Sorenson	Williamson	Wilson/t	Dowson
Clegg/2p	Charlton	Golding	Thompson	Wilson	Parling	Sorenson	Swinson	Wilson	Dowson
Clegg/2cp	Grindal	Golding	Thompson	Wilson	Parling	Sorenson	Williamson	Wilson	Dowson
Miller(b/p)	Charlton	Golding	Thompson	Wilson	Swinson	Sorenson	Williamson	Wilson	Dowson
Clegg/c3p	Young	Golding	Thompson	Wilson	Swinson	Sorenson	Balding	Wilson	Dowson/t
Clegg/p	Grindal	Ward	Thompson	Hayman	Parling	Sorenson	Dowson	Wilson	Balding
Clegg/c	Young	Wilson	Vickers	Hayman	Swinson	Parling	Dowson	Williamson	Balding
May/3c3p	Young	Wilson	Vickers	Hayman	Swinson	Parling/t(d/t)	Dowson	Williamson/t	Balding(c/t)
May/c2p	Young	Wilson	Vickers	Hayman	Swinson	Parling	Dowson	Williamson	Balding
May/t2c	Young	Golding/t	Vickers	Hayman	Swinson	Parling	Dowson	Wilson	Balding
May/3c2p	Young	Golding/t	Vickers	Hayman	Swinson	Sorenson	Dowson	Wilson/t	Balding
May/tc4p	Young	Golding	Vickers	Hayman	Swinson	Sorenson	Dowson	Wilson	Balding
May/2c2p	Young	Golding	Vickers	Hayman	Swinson	Parling	Dowson	Wilson/t	Balding
May/2pdg	Charlton	Golding	Thompson	Hayman	Parling	Sorenson	Swinson	Wilson	Dowson
May/2p	Young	Ward	Vickers	Hayman	Parling	Sorenson	Dowson	Wilson	Balding
May/2c	Young/t	Ward	Vickers	Wilson	Swinson	Sorenson	Winter	Dowson	Balding
Miller	Young(f/t)	Ward	Thompson	Wilson	Swinson	Sorenson	Winter	Dowson	Balding
Clegg/9c	Charlton	McDonnell	Thompson(k/t)	Hayman	Swinson/t	Sorenson	Beattie	Williamson/t	Dowson/2t
Clegg/t3cp	Charlton	McDonnell	Long	Hayman	Perry	Sorenson	Balding(j/t)	Williamson	Dowson
Miller/2c2p	Charlton	Golding	Thompson	Wilson	Swinson	Sorenson	Balding	Wilson	Dowson
Miller/t3c	Young/t	Ward	Thompson	Wilson	Swinson	Sorenson	Williamson	Wilson	Balding
May/3p	Young	Wilson	Vickers	Hayman	Swinson	Sorenson	Dowson	Wilson	Balding
Clegg/4c	Young/t	Golding/t	Vickers/t(h/t)	Wilson	Swinson/t	Perry	Dowson/t	Williamson	Balding
May/p	Young	Wilson	Thompson	Hayman	Parling	Sorenson	Dowson/t	Wilson	Balding
Clegg/2c	Young	Golding	Vickers	Ward	Tomes	Swinson	Beattie	Welch	Winter
Clegg/c2p	Grindal	McDonnell	Long	Hayman	Perry	Sorenson	Balding	Wilson	Winter(g/t)
Miller/c(a/p)	Charlton	Golding/t	Vickers	Ward	Swinson	Sorenson	Williamson	Wilson	Dowson

REPLACEMENTS

a- R Clegg b- S Jones c- B Wilson d- A Perry
e- A Fenby f- H Charlton g- R Vickers h- M Thompson
i- J Rudd j- O Phillips k- A Long

LEAGUE APPEARANCES

22	Phil Dowson
21	Tom May
17	Adam Balding, Jamie Noon, John Rudd, Mark Sorenson (3), Tane Tuipulotu

LEAGUE POINTS SCORERS

Pts	Player	T	C	P	DG
112	Tom May	5	15	18	1
46	Rory Clegg	-	5	12	-
41	Jonny Wilkinson	1	6	7	1
30	Danny Williams	6	-	-	-
20	Brent Wilson	4	-	-	-
15	Tim Visser	3	-	-	-

NUMBER OF PLAYERS USED

34 plus 3 as a replacement only

NEWCASTLE STATISTICS

LEAGUE

TEAM RECORDS

MOST POINTS
Scored at Home: 156 v Rugby 5.10.96
Scored Away: 75 v Moseley 19.10.96
Conceded at Home: 52 v Northampton 21.10.95
Conceded Away: 83 v Leicester 19.2.05

MOST TRIES
Scored in a match: 24 v Rugby 5.10.96 (H)
Conceded in a match: 11 v Leicester 19.2.05 (A)

BIGGEST MARGINS
Home Win: 151pts - 156-5 v Rugby 5.10.96
Away Win: 66pts - 75-9 v Moseley 19.10.96
Home Defeat: 43pts - 9-52 v Northampton 21.10.95
Away Defeat: 73pts - 10-83 v Leicester 19.2.05

MOST CONSECUTIVE
Victories: 6 (x2)
Defeats: 12

INDIVIDUAL RECORDS

MOST APPEARANCES
by a forward: 164 (7) Richard Arnold
by a back: 189 (4) Tom May

MOST CONSECUTIVE
Appearances: 44 Neil Frankland 13.1.90-2.10.93
Matches scoring Tries: 8 Gary Armstrong
Matches scoring points: 22 Rob Andrew

MATCH RECORDS

Most Points
36 Rob Andrew v Rugby 5.10.96 (H)

Most Tries
5 Pat Lam v Rotherham 4.5.97 (H)

Most Conversions
18 Rob Andrew v Rugby 5.10.96 (H)

Most Penalties
8 Jonny Wilkinson v 1.9.02 (H)

Most Drop Goals
2 David Johnson v Bedford 5.12.87 (A)
   Jonny Wilkinson v Harlequins 16.3.02 (H)
   David Walder v Northampton 17.9.05 (A)

SEASON RECORDS

Most Points	306	Jonny Wilkinson	98-99
Most Tries	23	John Bentley	96-97
Most Conversions	95	Rob Andrew	96-97
Most Penalties	53	Jonny Wilkinson	98-99
Most Drop Goals	4	David Johnson	87-88
		Jonny Wilkinson	02-03
		David Walder	03-04/05-06

CAREER RECORDS

Most Points	1484	Jonny Wilkinson	97-09
Most Tries	60	Gary Armstrong	95-02
Most Conversions	196	Jonny Wilkinson	97-09
Most Penalties	302	Jonny Wilkinson	97-09
Most Drop Goals	22	Jonny Wilkinson	97-09

LAST TEN SEASONS

	Division	P	W	D	L	F	A	P.D.	Pts	Pos	Most Points		Most Tries	
99-00	P1	22	6	2	14	377	630	-253	19	9	163	Jonny Wilkinson	3	Four players
00-01	P1	22	11	0	11	554	568	-14	57	6	198	Jonny Wilkinson	7	Michael Stephenson & Gary Armstrong
01-02	P	22	12	1	9	490	458	32	56	6	215	Jonny Wilkinson	8	Michael Stephenson
02-03	P	22	8	0	14	388	545	-157	40	10	205	Jonny Wilkinson	7	Jamie Noon
03-04	P	22	7	2	13	497	525	-28	45	9	185	David Walder	12	Tom May
04-05	P	22	9	2	11	475	596	-121	47	7	150	Jonny Wilkinson	7	Michael Stephenson
05-06	P	22	9	1	12	416	433	-17	47	7	147	Matt Burke	9	Matt Burke
06-07	P	22	9	0	13	435	528	-93	44	9	89	Toby Flood	6	Jamie Noon
07-08	P	22	7	0	15	333	542	-209	34	11	85	Jonny Wilkinson	7	Tom May
08-09	P	22	9	1	12	362	456	-94	44	10	112	Tom May	6	Danny Williams

RFU SENIOR CUP

OVERALL PLAYING RECORD

	P	W	O	L	F	A	Pts Diff
Home	39	28	0	11	859	492	367
Away	43	26	0	17	721	582	139
Neutral	7	5	0	2	188	161	27
TOTAL	89	59	0	30	1768	1235	533

TEAM RECORDS

Highest Score: 53 v Bridgwater 93/94
v Pertemps Bees 03/04
Biggest Winning Margin: 52 (52-0) v Ruislip 91/92
Highest Score Against: 58 v Wasps 94/95
Biggest Losing Margin: 46 (12-58) v Wasps 94/95

SEASON BY SEASON

71-72	1R	78-79	SF	85-86	3R	92-93	QF	99-00	5R
72-73	1R	79-80	QF	86-87	4R	93-94	5R	00-01	Winners
73-74	2R	80-81	Runners up	87-88	4R	94-95	4R	01-02	SF
74-75	QF	81-82	QF	88-89	3R	95-96	5R	02-03	6R
75-76	Winners	82-83	3R	89-90	4R	96-97	QF	03-04	Winners
76-77	Winners	83-84	3R	90-91	4R	97-98	QF	04-05	6R
77-78	2r	84-85	3R	91-92	QF	98-99	Runners up		

Anglo-Welsh Cup

05-06	Gp Stage
06-07	Gp Stage
07-08	Gp Stage
08-09	Gp Stage

Premiership Championship

02-03	-	07-08	-
03-04	-	08-09	-
04-05	-		
05-06	-		
06-07	-		

EUROPEAN COMPETITIONS

TEAM RECORDS

Highest Score
99 v Cross Keys 00/01

Biggest Winning Margin
97 (97-0) v Duc El Salvador 20.1.08

Highest Score Against
53 v Newport 01/02

Biggest Losing Margin
40 (8-47) v Stade Francais 2.4.05

INDIVIDUAL RECORDS

Most Points in a match
31 David Walder v L'Aquila 10.12.05

Most Tries in a match
4 Ollie Phillips v Duc El Salvador 20.1.08

Most Conversions in a match
12 David Walder v Cross Keys 00/01

Most Penalties in a match
7 Jonny Wilkinson 99/00

Most Drop Goals in a match
1 by Jonny Wilkinson (2),
David Walder (2) &
Tom May (3)

CAREER RECORDS

Most Appearances
58: Jamie Noon
50: Tom May (4)
40: Micky Ward (8)

Most Points
394: Jonny Wilkinson
227: David Walder
116: Matt Burke
102: Tim Stimpson

Most Tries
17: Jamie Noon
14: Tom May
12: Michael Stephenson

SEASON BY SEASON

1996-97	-	DNQ
1997-98	S	S.F.
1998-99	-	-
1999-00	S	Q.F.
2000-01	S	S.F.
2001-02	C	Gp Stage
2002-03	S	Q.F.
2003-04	S	2nd Rd
2004-05	C	Q.F.
2005-06	CC	S.F.
2006-07	CC	Q.F.
2007-08	CC	S.F.
2008-09	CC	Q.F.

OVERALL PLAYING RECORD

	P	W	D	L	F	A	Pts Diff
Home	37	33	0	4	1525	484	841
Away	37	19	0	18	920	781	139
Neutral	2	0	0	2	20	65	-45
Total	76	52	0	24	2465	1330	935

NORTHAMPTON SAINTS

KEY PERSONNEL

Chairman	Keith Barwell
Chief Executive	Allan Robson
Director of Rugby	Jim Mallinder
Team Manager	Lennie Newman
Rugby Administrator	Ann Oldfield
Marketing Manager	Brian Facer	01604 599131
Communications Manager	Chris Wearmouth	01604 599125
Commercial Manager	Andrew Kendrick	01604 599137
Head of Community	Sian Haynes	01604 599113
Stadium Manager	Melvyn Payne	01604 599153

Founded: 1880
Nickname: Saints
Colours: Black, green & gold
Change colours: White
Web site: www.northamptonsaints.co.uk

CONTACT DETAILS

Northampton Saints
Franklin's Gardens, Weedon Road, Northampton NN5 5BG
Tel: 01604 751543 (Swbd)
01604 581000 (Ticket Office)
Fax: 01604 599110 (Commercial) 01604 599100 (Playing)

GROUND DETAILS

Address:
Franklin's Gardens, Weedon Road, Northampton NN5 5BG
Capacity: 13,600
Seated: 12,100
Covered: 13,600

Directions:
From North - Come off J16 of M1, follow signs to Northampton and town centre. after 3 roundabouts proceed down hill (Weedon Road) and ground is on the right.
From South - Come off J15a of M1 follow signs to Sixfields. Turn right at TGI Fridays and follow Walter Tull Way into Edgar Mobbs Way. Ground car parking is on the left.

Nearest Railway Station: Northampton
Car Parking: Follow directions as above.

Admission:	Season	Matchday
Adults	£260-£520	£22-£46
Concessions	£155-£520	£13-£46
Juniors	£145-£520	£13-£46

Club Shop:
11am-5pm Mon-Wed; 11am-7pm Thurs; 9am-5pm Fri; 9am-5pm Matchday Saturdays & 9am-12noon Non-matchday Saturdays
Tel:01604 599111

Clubhouse:
Open noon to close on match days with carvery, restaurant, snack bars and vans, as well as VIP hospitality.
Conferences and banqueting catered.
Contact Trish Popiel 01604 751543

PROGRAMME
Size: A5   Pages: 76
Price: £3
Editor: Chris Wearmouth
Advertising Andrew Kendrick 01604 751543

REVIEW OF THE SEASON 2008-09

It was always going to be tough for the Saints to top their memorable, unbeaten run through National League One. But on a balmy May evening at the Twickenham Stoop they managed to do just that by beating Bourgoin to lift the first piece of major silverware in nine years.

That European Challenge Cup success brings Heineken Cup rugby back to Franklin's Gardens this coming season, and it was just reward for a campaign in which the Saints looked well at home in the Guinness Premiership and in Europe.

An opening day success against Worcester at the Gardens set the tone for the season, with only Newcastle (win) and Bath (draw) taking points off the Saints on their home turf. One top-four team after another left Northampton with their tale between their legs, including the Guinness Premiership champions Leicester – much to the delight of the black, green and gold faithful.

Away from home it was a different tale. After being in contention at places like Newcastle, Leicester and Saracens, the Saints had to wait until the trip to Bristol in November for their first league point on the road, and the game at Worcester in March 2009 for their first win. No doubt this will be an area highlighted for improvement by Jim Mallinder and his coaches.

Saints also had a promising run in the EDF Energy Cup, reaching the semi-finals, where they were narrowly beaten 11-5 by eventual winners Cardiff.

But it was in Europe where the Saints excelled, coming through the toughest pool in the Challenge Cup with 29 points from a possible 30 – not bad when the opponents included Montpellier, Toulon and Bristol! Home knock-out games against Connacht and Saracens set up the final against Bourgoin and a piece of silverware for the trophy cabinet.

SAINTS' SEASON - 2008-09

PREMIERSHIP

Date	H/A	Opponents	Result & Score	Att.	15	14	13	12	11
\multicolumn{10}{l}{**GUINNESS PREMIERSHIP**}
07-09	H	Worcester	W 21-13	13094	Reihana/c3p	Ashton	Clarke/t	Downey	Lamont
14-09	A	Newcastle Falcons	L 22-32	4620	Reihana/c4p	Ashton	Clarke	Downey	Lamont/t
20-09	H	London Wasps	W 24-20	13021	Reihana/t2cp	Ashton/t	Ansbro	Downey(j/c)	Lamont/t
27-09	A	Saracens	L 12-26	7409	Myler/3pdg	Reihana	Ansbro	Downey	Lamont
01-10	A	Leicester Tigers	L 19-29	17498	Myler/c4p	Ashton	Ansbro	Mayor	Reihana
16-11	A	Bristol	L 13-14	6310	Foden	Ashton	Mayor	Downey/t	Reihana
22-11	H	Bath	D 28-28	13473	Myler/2c2pdg	Ashton	Reihana	Downey	Diggin/t
29-11	A	Gloucester	L 10-33	13494	Myler/cp	Ashton	Reihana	Downey	Diggin
20-12	H	Harlequins	W 23-13	13349	Reihana	Diggin	Clarke/t	Downey/t	Lamont
27-12	A	Bath	L 14-25	10600	Reihana	Diggin	Clarke	Downey	Lamont
03-01	H	Bristol	W 30-8	13090	Foden/t	Diggin/t	Clarke/t	Downey	Lamont
10-01	A	Leicester Tigers	W 17-13	13582	Foden/t	Diggin/2t	Clarke	Downey	Lamont
31-01	A	Harlequins	L 6-27	12332	Reihana	Diggin	Clarke	Downey	Lamont
14-02	H	Saracens	W 20-15	13153	Foden	Diggin	Clarke	Downey	Reihana/t
22-02	N	London Wasps	L 5-9	10000	Foden/t	Diggin	Clarke	Downey	Reihana
28-02	H	Newcastle Falcons	L 13-19	12908	Reihana	Ashton	Mayor	Downey	Diggin/t
07-03	A	Worcester	W 22-12	10319	Foden	Diggin/t	Clarke(k/t)	Downey	Reihana
14-03	H	Sale Sharks	W 38-3	13250	Foden/t	Diggin/t	Ansbro	Downey/t	Reihana
22-03	A	London Irish	L 27-32	21295	Foden	Reihana/t4p	Ansbro	Downey	Lamont
04-04	H	Gloucester	W 40-22	13426	Foden	Diggin/2t	Ansbro	Downey	Reihana/t
18-04	H	London Irish	W 21-17	13405	Foden	Diggin	Ansbro	Downey	Reihana
25-04	A	Sale Sharks	L 18-24	9724	Ashton	Diggin	Ansbro	Clarke	Lamont/t
\multicolumn{10}{l}{**EUROPEAN CHALLENGE CUP**}
09-10	N	Toulon	W 56-3	9000	Reihana	Ashton/t	Ansbro/2t	Downey(f/t)	Lamont/t
18-10	H	Montpellier*	W 51-7	12179	Reihana	Ashton/t	Ansbro/t	Downey)f/t)	Lamont
06-12	H	Bristol	W 66-3	12607	Reihana/t	Ashton/3t	Mayor	Downey(e/t)	Diggin/2t
14-12	N	Bristol	W 25-21	5220	Ashton	Diggin	Clarke/t	Mayor/t	Lamont
15-01	N	Montpellier	W 28-24	6952	Reihana	Ashton(c/t)	Clarke	Mayor/t	Diggin
24-01	H	Toulon	W 52-11	12059	Reihana	Ashton/2t	Clarke	Downey	Lamont
Q.F. 11-04	H	Connacht	W 43-13	9119	Foden	Diggin	Ansbro/t	Downey(a/t)	Reihana/t
S.F. 01-05	H	Saracens	W 16-13	11073	Foden	Diggin	Clarke	Downey	Reihana/t
Final 22.05	N	Bourgoin	W 15-3	9260	Foden	Diggin	Clarke	Downey	Reihana
\multicolumn{10}{l}{**EDF ENERGY CUP**}
04-10	H	Bristol	W 30-17	11301	Diggin/t	Ashton/t	Mayor/t	Mordt	Lamont
26-10	A	Saracens	L 19-33	6984	Foden/t	Ashton	Mayor	Mordt	Diggin
01-11	H	Llanelli	W 33-20	12042	Reihana/t	Ashton/2t	Mayor	Downey	Lamont/t
S.F. 28-03	N	Cardiff	L 5-11		Foden	Diggin	Ansbro/t	Downey	Reihana

SCORING BREAKDOWN

WHEN	Total	First Half	Second Half	1/4	2/4	3/4	4/4
the POINTS were scored	443	233	210	96	137	93	117
the POINTS were conceded	434	219	215	135	84	82	133
the TRIES were scored	41	20	21	8	12	7	14
the TRIES were conceded	40	19	21	13	6	8	13

HOW	Total	Pen. Try	Backs	Forwards	F Back	Wing	Centre	H Back	F Row	Lock	B Row
the TRIES were scored	41	-	29	12	5	16	7	1	5	2	5
the TRIES were conceded	40	2	23	15	2	11	4	6	5	4	6

KEY: * after opponents name indicates a penalty try.
Brackets after a player's name indicates he was replaced. eg (a) means he was replaced by replacement code "a" and so on.
/ after a player or replacement name is followed by any scores he made - eg /t, /c, /p, /dg or any combination of these

PREMIERSHIP

10	9	1	2	3	4	5	6	7	8
Spencer	Dickson	Tonga'uiha	Shields(j/t)	Murray	Fernandez Lobbe	Day	Best	Gray	Wilson
Spencer/p	Dickson	Tonga'uiha	Hartley	Murray	Fernandez Lobbe	Day	Best	Gray	Wilson
Spencer	Dickson	Tonga'uiha	Hartley	Murray	Fernandez Lobbe	Day	Best	Gray	Wilson
Spencer	Dickson	Tonga'uiha	Hartley	Murray	Fernandez Lobbe	Day	Hopley	Gray	Wilson
Spencer	Foden	Smith	Hartley	Murray/t	Lord	Day	Hopley	Gray	Wilson
Myler/c2p	Dickson	Smith	Shields	Stewart	Fernandez Lobbe	Day	Hopley	Easter	Wilson
Spencer	Foden	Smith	J Gray	Stewart(g/t)	Fernandez Lobbe	Kruger	Hopley	Easter/t	Wilson
Spencer	Foden	Smith	J Gray/t	Murray	Fernandez Lobbe	Day	Easter	Gray	Wilson
Myler/2c3p	Dickson	Tonga'uiha	Hartley	Murray	Fernandez Lobbe	Day	Easter	Gray	Wilson
Myler/3p	Dickson	Tonga'uiha	Hartley	Murray	Fernandez Lobbe	Kruger/t	Easter	Gray	Wilson
Myler/3c3p	Dickson	Tonga'uiha	Hartley	Murray	Fernandez Lobbe	Kruger	Easter	Gray	Wilson
Myler/c	Dickson	Smith	Hartley	Murray	Fernandez Lobbe	Kruger	Easter	Gray	Hopley
Myler/2p	Dickson	Tonga'uiha	Shields	Stewart	Fernandez Lobbe	Kruger	Easter	Gray	Hopley
Myler/5p	Dickson	Tonga'uiha	Sharman	Stewart	Fernandez Lobbe	Kruger	Easter	Best	Wilson
Myler	Dickson	Tonga'uiha	Hartley	Murray	Lawes	Kruger	Easter	Best	Wilson
Myler/cp(b/t)	Dickson	Tonga'uiha	Sharman	Stewart	Day	Kruger	Lawes	Best	Wilson
Everitt/2cp	Dickson	Smith	Hartley	Murray	Lawes	Kruger	Best	Gray/t	Wilson
Everitt/c4p(i/2c)	Dickson	Tonga'uiha	Sharman	Stewart	Fernandez Lobbe	Kruger	Lawes	Best	Wilson/t
Everitt/cp	Dickson	Tonga'uiha	Sharman	Stewart	Lawes	Kruger	Easter	Best	Wilson/t
Myler/2c4p(b/2c)	Dickson	Tonga'uiha	Hartley/t	Murray	Lawes	Kruger	Best	Gray	Wilson
Myler/c3p	Dickson/t	Tonga'uiha	Hartley	Murray	Lawes	Kruger/t	Best	Gray	Wilson
Myler/c2p	Foden	Tonga'uiha	Sharman	Stewart	Fernandez Lobbe	Lawes	Best/t	Gray	Easter
Myler/5c3p(b/c)	Foden/t(h/t)	Smith	Hartley	Murray	Fernandez Lobbe	Lawes	Hopley	Gray	Wilson
Myler/5c3p	Foden	Smith(g/t)	Hartley	Murray	Fernandez Lobbe	Lawes	Hopley	Gray/t	Wilson
Myler/5c (d/3c)	Dickson	Tonga'uiha	Hartley	Murray	Fernandez Lobbe	Day	Easter/2t	Gray	Wilson/t
Myler/cp	Foden/2t	Tonga'uiha	Hartley	Stewart	Day	Rae	Easter	Gray	Hopley
Myler/t2c3p	Foden	Tonga'uiha	Hartley	Stewart	Day	Kruger	Easter	Gray	Hopley
Myler/t5cp(b/2c)	Foden	Tonga'uiha/2t	Shields	Murray	Fernandez Lobbe	Kruger	Lawes	Gray	Easter/2t
Myler/c6p(b/p)	Dickson	Tonga'uiha	Hartley	Murray	Fernandez Lobbe	Kruger	Best/t	Gray	Wilson
Myler/c2pdg	Dickson	Tonga'uiha	Hartley	Murray	Fernandez Lobbe	Kruger	Best	Gray	Easter
Myler/5p	Dickson	Tonga'uiha	Hartley	Murray	Fernandez Lobbe	Kruger	Best	Gray	Easher
Everitt/2c2p	Dickson/t	Tonga'uiha	Shields	Stewart	Lord	Rae	Lawes	Lewitt	Milligan
Myler/3p	Dickson	Tonga'uiha	Shields	Stewart	Lord	Day	Lawes	Lewitt/t	Wilson
Myler/2c3p	Foden	Smith	Shields	Murray	Fernandez Lobbe	Lawes	Hopley	Gray	Wilson
Myler	Dickson	Smith	Hartley	Murray	Fernandez Lobbe	Kruger	Best	Gray	Wilson

REPLACEMENTS
a- C Mayor b- B Everitt c- S Lamont d- C Spencer
e- J Clarke f- P Diggin g- S Tonga'uiha h- L Dickson
i- S Myler j- D Hartley k- J Ansbro

LEAGUE APPEARANCES

- 20 James Downey
- 19 Bruce Reihana (2), Roger Wilson
- 18 Lee Dickson (3)
- 16 Soane Tonga'uiha (6), Stephen Myler (4),

NUMBER OF PLAYERS USED
31 plus 5 as a replacement only

LEAGUE POINTS SCORERS

Pts	Player	T	C	P	DG
158	Stephen Myler	-	19	38	2
64	Bruce Reihana	4	4	12	-
45	Paul Diggin	9	-	-	-
33	Barry Everitt	-	6	7	-
20	Ben Foden	4	-	-	-

NORTHAMPTON STATISTICS
LEAGUE

TEAM RECORDS

MOST POINTS
Scored at Home: 96 v Sedgley Park 26.1.08
Scored Away: 69 v Waterloo 28.10.95
Conceded at Home: 50 v Lon. Scottish 3.10.87
Conceded Away: 60 v Orrell 27.10.90

MOST TRIES
Scored in a match: 14 - v Sedgley Park 26.1.08
Conceded in a match: 11 v Orrell 27.10.90

BIGGEST MARGINS
Home Win: 93pts - 96-3 v Sedgley Park 26.1.08
Away Win: 66pts - 69-3 v Waterloo 28.10.95
Home Defeat: 47pts - 3-50 v Lon. Scottish 3.10.87
Away Defeat: 60pts - 0-60 v Orrell 27.10.90

MOST CONSECUTIVE
Victories: 30
Defeats: 9 - 18.9.04 - 28.11.04

INDIVIDUAL RECORDS

MOST APPEARANCES
by a forward: 146 (36) John Phillips
by a back: 144 (8) Matt Dawson

MOST CONSECUTIVE
Appearances: 31 Frank Packman
Matches scoring Tries: 4 Ian Hunter
Matches scoring points: 18 Paul Grayson

MATCH RECORDS

Most Points
36 Bruce Reihana v Sedgley Park 26.1.08 (H)

Most Tries
6 Chris Ashton v Launceston v 26.4.08 (H)

Most Conversions
13 Buce Reihana v Sedgley Park 26.1.08 (H)

Most Penalties
7 Paul Grayson v Richmond 21.2.98 (H)
v Leicester 29.4.00 (A)

Most Drop Goals
3 John Steele v Wasps 23.3.91 (A)

SEASON RECORDS

Most Points	262	Bruce Reihana	07-08
Most Tries	39	Chris Ashton	07-08
Most Conversions	76	Paul Grayson	95-96
Most Penalties	58	Paul Grayson	95-96
Most Drop Goals	4	Paul Grayson	96-97

CAREER RECORDS

Most Points	1899	Paul Grayson	93-04
Most Tries	51	Ben Cohen	96-07
Most Conversions	257	Paul Grayson	93-04
Most Penalties	418	Paul Grayson	93-04
Most Drop Goals	18	Paul Grayson	93-04

LAST TEN SEASONS

	Division	P	W	D	L	F	A	P.D.	Pts	Pos	Most Points	Most Tries
98-99	P1	26	19	0	7	754	556	198	38	2	156 Paul Grayson	14 Pat Lam
99-00	P1	22	13	0	9	551	480	71	35	5	99 Ali Hepher	6 Ben Cohen
00-01	P1	22	13	0	9	518	43	55	59	4	219 Paul Grayson	9 Ben Cohen
01-02	P	22	12	1	9	506	426	80	56	5	238 Paul Grayson	8 Ben Cohen
02-03	P	22	13	0	9	512	376	136	62	3	211 Paul Grayson	6 Ben Cohen
03-04	P	22	15	1	6	574	416	158	70	3	234 Shane Drahm	13 Bruce Reihana
04-05	P	22	8	0	14	410	473	-63	40	11	180 Shane Drahm	3 By five players
05-06	P	22	10	1	11	464	488	-24	53	6	206 Bruce Reihana	7 Ben Cohen
06-07	P	22	6	1	15	342	499	-157	33	12r	66 Carlos Spencer, Bruce Reihana	8 Mark Robinson
07-08	N1	30	30	0	0	1321	343	978	143	1p	262 Bruce Reihana	39 Chris Ashton
08-09	P	22	10	1	11	443	434	9	49	8	158 Stephen Myler	9 Paul Diggin

RFU SENIOR CUP

OVERALL PLAYING RECORD

	P	W	O	L	F	A	Pts Diff
Home	39	27	0	12	940	456	484
Away	36	19	0	17	658	636	22
Neutral	6	2	0	4	127	162	-35
TOTAL	81	48	0	33	1725	1254	471

TEAM RECORDS

Highest Score: 118 v Nuneaton 99/00 (H)
Biggest Winning Margin: 115 Pts - 118-3 v Nuneaton 99/00 (H)
Highest Score Against: 44 v Orrell 02/03 (A)
Biggest Losing Margin: 31 Pts - 7-38 v London Irish 01/02 (N)

SEASON BY SEASON

71-72	1R	78-79	1R	85-86	4R	92-93	SF	99-00 Runners up
72-73	1R	79-80	1R	86-87	DNQ	93-94	5R	00-01 QF
73-74	QF	80-81	1R	87-88	3R	94-95	QF	01-02 Runners up
74-75	1R	81-82	4R	88-89	3R	95-96	4R	02-03 Runners up
75-76	QF	82-83	2R	89-90	SF	96-97	QF	03-04 6R
76-77	2R	83-84	4R	90-91	Runners up	97-98	SF	04-05 QF
77-78	QF	84-85	3R	91-92	4R	98-99	5R		

Anglo-Welsh Cup

05-06	Gp Stage
06-07	Gp Stage
07-08	N.A.
08-09	S.F.

National Trophy

05-06	N.A.
06-07	N.A.
07-08	Winners
08-09	N.A.

Premiership Championship

02-03	S.F.	07-08	N.A.
03-04	S.F.	08-09	-
04-05	-		
05-06	-		
06-07	-		

EUROPEAN COMPETITIONS

TEAM RECORDS

Highest Score
68 v Parma 9.12.06

Biggest Winning Margin
59 Pts - v Toulon 66-7 96/97

Highest Score Against
50 v Montferrand 01/02

Biggest Losing Margin
33 Pts 50-17 v Montferrand 01/02

INDIVIDUAL RECORDS

Most Points in a match
29 Ali Hepher v Neath 99/00

Most Tries in a match
3 Harvey Thorneycroft v Orrell 96/97
Ben Cohen v Viadana 22.10.05

Most Conversions in a match
8 Paul Grayson v Nice 97-98

Most Penalties in a match
7 Paul Grayson v Toulon 96/97

CAREER RECORDS

Most Appearances:
57: Ben Cohen
41: Steve Thompson (4)
33: Paul Grayson (3)
30: Budge Pountney

Most Points
383: Paul Grayson
155: Ben Cohen
135: Stephen Myler
123: Matt Dawson

Most Tries
31: Ben Cohen
11: Bruce Reihana
10: Matt Dawson
7: Nick Beal, Chris Ashton

SEASON BY SEASON

1996-97	S	Q.F.
1997-98	S	Gp Stage
1998-99	-	D N Play
1999-00	C	Winners
2000-01	C	Gp Stage
2001-02	C	Gp Stage
2002-03	C	Q.F.
2003-04	C	Gp Stage
2004-05	C	Q.F.
2005-06	CC	Q.F.
2006-07	CC	S.F.
2007-08	-	N.A.
2008-09	CC	Winners

OVERALL PLAYING RECORD

	P	W	D	L	F	A	Pts Diff
Home	37	29	0	8	1118	548	590
Away	36	18	0	18	883	712	171
Neutral	4	2	0	2	64	96	-32
Total	77	49	0	28	2070	1353	729

SALE SHARKS

Founded: 1861
Nickname: Sharks
Colours:
Blue and white
Change colours:
All white
Web site: www.salesharks.co.uk

KEY PERSONNEL

Chairman	Brian Kennedy
Chief Executive	James Jennings
Media, PR & Supporter Liaison	Dave Swanton, c/o Sale Sharks Tel: 0161 286 8915 Fax: 0161 286 8900 email: dave.swanton@salesharks.co.uk
Commercial Manager	Nathan Bombrys c/o Sale Sharks Tel: 0161 286 8888 Fax: 0161 286 8900
Director of Rugby	Kingsley Jones
Head Coach	Jason Robinson
Corporate Hospitality	Julie Loynd & Colin McKevitt
Conference Centre GM	Blair Glen
Community	Jonny Acheson, john.acheson@salesharks.com
Supporters Club	Anne Blakeney chairman@salesupporters.co.uk
Ticketing	John Mann

CONTACT DETAILS

Sale Sharks RUFC, Edgeley Park, Hardcastle Road, Stockport, Cheshire SK3 9DD
Tel 0161-286-8888   Fax 0161-286-8900   email: dave.swanton@salesharks.co.uk

GROUND DETAILS

Address:
Edgeley Park, Hardcastle Rd., Stockport, Cheshire SK3 9DD
Tel/Fax 0161-286-8888
email: dave.swanton@salesharks.co.uk

Capacity: 10,872
　　　　Seated: 10,812   Covered: 9,372

How to get there: For full details see website www.salesharks.com/findus
By Car: Stockport is easy to reach via the M60 motorway, which passes directly through the centre of the town (J1/J2). It is also easily accessible via the M62 (Liverpool to Yorkshire), M61/M6 (North), and the M56/M6 (Midlands/South). The A6 across the Peak District is also a viable route between Derby, Nottingham East Midlands and East Anglia
By Bus: Stockport is well connected by an extensive local bus service. Numbers 11, 368, 369 pass Edgeley Park directly
Nearest BR Station: Stockport, 10 minutes walk
Airport: Manchester International Airport is about 20 minutes away by taxi

Car Parking: None at ground.

Admission: Season Tickets - Adult prices from £199
　　　　　　Matchday Adult prices from £16 if booked in advance - phone 08444 994994 for full details.

Club Shop:
Monday to Friday 1pm - 5.30pm. Contact Manager, Lisa Robinson.

PROGRAMME

Size: B3   Pages: 88   Price: £2.50
Editor: Dave Swanton
Advertising: Please phone Julie Loynd

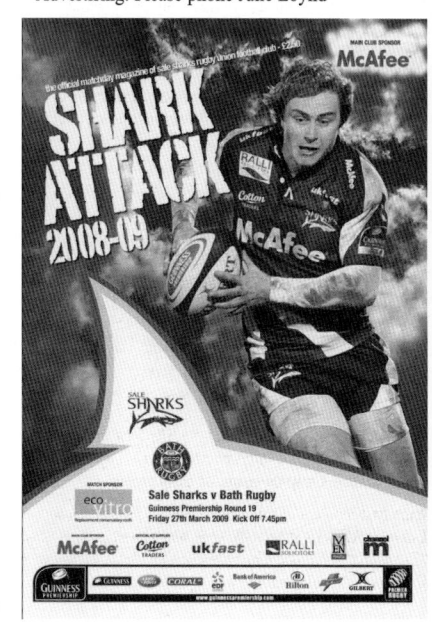

REVIEW OF THE SEASON 2008-09

Sale Sharks ended fifth in the Guinness Premiership for the second successive season, in their view a disappointment, but they had several interesting experiences on the way. The club broke a defensive record, gave twelve players their debuts, sizzled in France, were swept aside in Munster and bade, "Au revoir" to their Director of Rugby plus several members of the playing staff, who have headed across the Channel this Summer.

In their first four Premiership fixtures, the Sharks created a record by winning all four and not conceding a try, whilst scoring just three themselves. At Newcastle, they overcame a 16-year-old record of defeats, scoring their only try through fly half Charlie Hodgson in a 14-9 win. The Sharks managed two second half tries (and still none against) when Gloucester were beaten 23-9 at Edgeley Park. Then came October 1st and defeat at London Irish (6-28) which not only smashed the unbeaten record but dented a few reputations.

An EDF encounter at home to Cardiff Blues saw a predominantly young team including eight players making their debut: the Welsh side snatched it (18-17) near the end. Focus was diverted to France the following week, with an opening Heineken Cup encounter at ASM Clermont Auvergne. A four-try blitz in an outstanding 32-15 victory was the Sharks' finest hour on foreign soil. Munster arrived, showing all their 'big game' experience to leave Stockport with a crafty 24-16 win under their belts. It was back to EDF business, and another 'mixed' side with two more debut boys. Despite a brace of tries from Chris Bell, Bath took the spoils 24-21, but the Sharks went mighty close near the end. Glory was within the young team's grasp at Leicester in the final EDF game, pulling back level before conceding late points. Two further debuts there, making it the round dozen in the competition. The following weekend saw a return to Guinness Premiership action, and a disappointing home defeat (9-17) to Worcester Warriors. The squad's spirit was never in question, and this was verified when the Sharks snatched victory at Wasps (13-12) with four minutes to go in atrocious conditions, then denied the Tigers any reward against a ten-change side. The Sharks lost a tough battle in the final minute at Bath just before Christmas before recording convincing home wins against Wasps (31-3) and London Irish (14-8). They then joined the list of teams to suffer at the hands of the Munster machine, conceding six tries in a widely-publicised defeat. The side recovered against Clermont Auvergne, completing their Heineken Pool fixtures in second spot, and followed up with a convincing bonus point victory at Worcester, with Kingsley Jones in full charge for the first time – against one of his former clubs. A 17-24 defeat followed at Gloucester (where Jones was club captain), Bristol were beaten, then followed four successive defeats as the injuries mounted up. The visit of Bath to Edgeley Park heralded the return of the club's international force, and the team duly obliged 23-16. Much depended on a daunting trip to Leicester. Despite facing fourteen men for most of the game, the Sharks couldn't overcome the Tigers, who later went on to emulate the Sharks' feat of 2006 and become Guinness Premiership champions after topping the table. Home wins against Quins and Saints, with four-try bonus points, were an absolute 'must' and the side duly obliged. They went into their final game reliant on others to 'slip up' but they didn't, and the team, now directed by Kingsley Jones, ended up one place short of the play offs but safely qualified for the Heineken Cup. They were left to rue the weakness of their squad during the international windows. 'If only' was the phrase applicable to those defeats against Worcester and Newcastle at home, and the lack of bonus points during the cautious early victories.

Nine first-teamers left the club at the end of the season, the most sadly missed likely to be skipper Juan Martin Fernandez Lobbe. Luke McAlister's stay at the club was ended prematurely by injury, whilst to the others, it's a case of, "Merci beaucoup" and "Bonne chance". The club is left with plenty of class within the ranks: Sheridan, Roberts, Peel, Hodgson and Cueto to name but five internationals, and plenty of promising youngsters waiting for their chance to shine.

SHARKS' SEASON - 2008-09

PREMIERSHIP

Date	H/A	Opponents	Result & Score	Att.	15	14	13	12	11	10
GUINNESS PREMIERSHIP										
07-09	A	Newcastle Falcons	W 14-9	5224	Tait	Cueto	McAlister/3p	Thomas	Doherty	Hodgson/t
12-09	H	Saracens	W 18-15	8321	Tait	Lamont	McAlister/3p	Bell	Doherty	Hodgson/2pd
19-09	A	Bristol	W 9-6	8111	Tait	Cueto	McAlister/3p	Thomas	Lamont	Hodgson
26-09	H	Gloucester	W 23-9	9019	Lamont	Tait	McAlister/c2p	Thomas/cp	Doherty/t	Hodgson
01-10	A	London Irish	L 6-28	7453	Tait	Cueto	Bell	McAlister	Doherty	Hodgson/2p
14-11	H	Worcester	L 9-17	7602	Tait	Cueto	Keil	Bell	Doherty	Hodgson/3p
23-11	N	London Wasps	W 13-12	8367	MacLeod	Cueto/t	McAlister	Bell	Doherty	Hodgson/c2p
28-11	H	Leicester Tigers	W 27-13	9586	Lamont/t	Cueto/t	Tait	McAlister/3c2p	Doherty	Hodgson
20-12	A	Bath	L 20-24	10600	Cueto/2t	Bell	Tuilagi	McAlister/tcp	Doherty	Hodgson
26-12	H	London Wasps	W 31-3	10841	Cueto/t	Bell	Tuilagi	McAlister	Doherty	Hodgson/t4cp
09-01	H	London Irish	W 14-8	9430	Cueto/t	Bell	Tuilagi	McAlister	Doherty	Hodgson/2pd
31-01	A	Worcester	W 37-20	10387	MacLeod	Bell/t	Tait	Thomas	Ripol/t	Hodgson/4c2
14-02	A	Gloucester	L 17-24		MacLeod	Bell	McAlister	Thomas/t	Ripol	Hodgson/t2cp
20-02	H	Bristol	W 32-13	8605	MacLeod/t	Bell	Tait	Keil	Ripol	Hodgson/3c2
01-03	A	Saracens	L 23-24	8311	MacLeod	Bell	Keil	Thomas/tc2p	Doherty	Hodgson
08-03	H	Newcastle Falcons	L 25-32	8427	MacLeod	Bell	Tait	Thomas	Ripol	Hodgson/c6p
14-03	A	Northampton Saints	L 3-38	13250	Lamont	Kuadey	Keil	Bell	Doherty	Hodgson/dg
22-03	A	Harlequins	L 20-38	11592	MacLeod	Lamont	McAlister	Keil	Doherty	Hodgson/t5p
27-03	H	Bath	W 23-16	9808	MacLeod	Cueto/t	Tait	Thomas	Ripol	Hodgson/tc2p
04-04	A	Leicester Tigers	L 31-37	17418	MacLeod	Cueto/2t	Tait	Keil	Ripol	Hodgson/2c4
17-04	H	Harlequins*	W 28-6	9579	MacLeod	Doherty	Tait	Tuilagi(c/t)	Ripol	Hodgson/4c
25-04	H	Northampton Saints	W 24-18	9724	MacLeod	Cueto	Tait/t	Tuilagi	Ripol	Hodgson/2c
HEINEKEN CUP										
11-10	A	Clermont Auvergne	W 32-15	15681	Lamont	Cueto/t	McAlister/t3cpdg	Thomas(c/t)	Doherty/t	Wigglesworth
19-10	H	Munster	L 16-24	10928	Lamont	Cueto	McAlister/c3p	Keil	Doherty	Wigglesworth
05-12	H	Montauban	W 36-6	6926	Lamont	Cueto	Tuilagi/t	McAlister	Doherty	Hodgson/4cp
13-12	N	Montauban	L 12-16		Tait	Cueto	Tuilagi	McAlister	Doherty	Hodgson/4p
16-01	A	Munster	L 14-37	26000	Cueto	Bell	Tuilagi	McAlister/2p	Doherty	Hodgson/tp
24-01	H	Clermont Auvergne	W 26-17	7466	MacLeod	Cueto	Tait	Thomas	Ripol/t	McAlister/c3p
EDF ENERGY CUP										
04-10	H	Cardiff	L 17-18	7485	MacLeod/4p	Kuadey	Keil/t	Tuilagi	Ripol	Wigglesworth
24-10	H	Bath	L 21-24	7655	MacLeod	Cueto	Tuilagi	Bell/2t	Royle	Hodgson/c3p
31-10	A	Leicester Tigers	L 20-30	16550	Doherty	Kuadey	Keil	Bell/2t	Styles	MacLeod/2c2

SCORING BREAKDOWN

WHEN			Total	First Half	Second Half		1/4	2/4	3/4	4/4
the POINTS were scored			447	229	218		106	123	115	103
the POINTS were conceded			410	193	217		84	109	100	117
the TRIES were scored			44	20	24		10	10	10	14
the TRIES were conceded			36	11	25		5	6	12	13

HOW	Total	Pen. Try	Backs	Forwards	F Back	Wing	Centre	H Back	F Row	Lock	B Row
the TRIES were scored	44	1	25	18	6	8	5	6	3	5	10
the TRIES were conceded	36	-	22	14	2	14	5	1	4	-	10

KEY: * after opponents name indicates a penalty try.
Brackets after a player's name indicates he was replaced. eg (a) means he was replaced by replacement code "a" and so on.
/ after a player or replacement name is followed by any scores he made - eg /t, /c, /p, /dg or any combination of these

9	1	2	3	4	5	6	7	8
Peel	Faure	Briggs	Roberts	Jones	Schofield	Abraham	Fernandez Lobbe	Chabal
Wigglesworth	Sheridan	Bruno	Roberts	Cox	Cockbain	Jones	Abraham	Chabal
Peel	Sheridan	Bruno	Roberts	Jones	Schofield	Ormsby	Abraham	Chabal
Wigglesworth	Faure	Bruno	Turner	Cox	Cockbain	Ormsby	Abraham	Chabal/t
Peel	Sheridan	Briggs	Turner	Schofield	Cox	Ormsby	Fernandez Lobbe	Chabal
Wigglesworth	O'Donnell	Briggs	Turner	Schofield	Cockbain	Ormsby	Abraham	Fearns
Wigglesworth	Roberts	Jones	Turner	Schofield	White	Tait	Briggs	Fearns
Wigglesworth	Faure	Jones	Roberts	Chabal	Schofield/t	White	Briggs	Fernandez Lobbe
Peel	Sheridan	Briggs	Turner	Chabal	Schofield	White	Abraham	Fernandez Lobbe
Wigglesworth	Faure	Jones	Roberts	Chabal	Schofield	White	Briggs	Fernandez Lobbe/2t
Peel	Faure	Jones	Roberts	Chabal	Schofield	Jones	Briggs	Fernandez Lobbe
Peel	Faure	Bruno	Roberts	Chabal	Schofield	Jones/t	Briggs/t	Fernandez Lobbe
Wigglesworth	Roberts	Bruno	Turner	Schofield	Cox	Jones	Abraham	Fernandez Lobbe
Peel	Faure	Bruno(a/t)	Roberts/t	Chabal	Schofield	Jones	Abraham	Fernandez Lobbe/t
Wigglesworth	Faure	Briggs	Roberts	Schofield/2t	Cockbain	Jones	Abraham	Fernandez Lobbe
Peel	Roberts	Jones	Turner	Schofield	Cox	White	Briggs/t	Fernandez Lobbe
Leck	O'Donnell	Briggs	Roberts	Schofield	Cockbain	Jones	Fearns	Fernandez Lobbe
Cliff	O'Donnell	Bruno	Roberts	Jones	Cockbain	Fearns	Briggs	Fernandez Lobbe
Wigglesworth	Sheridan	Bruno	Roberts	Jones	Cockbain	White	Briggs	Fernandez Lobbe/t
Peel	Sheridan	Bruno	Roberts	Jones	Cockbain	White	Briggs/t	Fernandez Lobbe
Peel(b/t)	Sheridan	Bruno	Roberts	Chabal/t	Schofield	White	Briggs	Fernandez Lobbe
Wigglesworth	Faure	Bruno	Roberts/t	Chabal	Schofield/t(d/t)	Jones	Briggs	Fernandez Lobbe/t
Peel	Faure	Briggs	Roberts	Jones	Ormsby	Abraham	Fernandez Lobbe	Chabal
Peel	Faure	Briggs	Roberts	Chabal	Cockbain(e/t)	Jones	Abraham	Fernandez Lobbe
Peel	Faure	Jones(d/t)	Roberts/t	Chabal	Schofield	Fearns	Briggs	Fernandez Lobbe/2t
Wigglesworth	Sheridan	Jones	Roberts	Chabal	Schofield	Abraham	Briggs	Fernandez Lobbe
Wigglesworth	Faure	Jones	Roberts	Chabal	Schofield	Jones	Briggs	Fernandez Lobbe
Peel/t	Sheridan	Bruno	Turner	Jones	Cockbain	Fearns	Abraham	Tait/t
Leck	Faure	Jones	Halsall	Jones	Cockbain	White	Tait	Fearns
Leck	O'Donnell	Jones	Halsall	Schofield	Cockbain	White	Tait	Fearns
Peel	O'Donnell	Jones	Turner	Schofield	White	Hills	Fernandez Lobbe	Fearns

REPLACEMENTS a- N Briggs   b- R Wigglesworth   c- R Keil
d- D Tait   e- D Schofield

LEAGUE APPEARANCES

22 Charlie Hodgson
18 Eifion Roberts (2)
17 Neil Briggs (5), Juan Martin Fernandez Lobbe, Dean Schofield (3)

NUMBER OF PLAYERS USED

36 plus 4 as a replacement only

LEAGUE POINTS SCORERS

Pts	Player	T	C	P	DG
187	Charlie Hodgson	5	24	34	4
57	Luke McAlister	1	5	14	-
45	Mark Cueto	9	-	-	-
25	JM Fernandez Lobbe	5	-	-	-
23	Lee Thomas	2	2	3	-
20	Dean Schofield	4	-	-	-

SALE STATISTICS

LEAGUE

TEAM RECORDS

MOST POINTS
Scored at Home: 88 v Otley 12.2.94
Scored Away: 50 v Bedfordl 14.5.00
Conceded at Home: 58 v Saracens 29.10.99
Conceded Away: 84 v Bath 26.4.97

MOST TRIES
Scored in a match: 14 v Otley 12.2.94 (H)
Conceded in a match:
12 - v Harlequins 23.4.88 (A) & v Bath 24.4.97 (A)

BIGGEST MARGINS
Home Win: 79pts - 88-9 v Otley 12.2.94
Away Win: 32pts - 40-8 v Orrell 18.1.97
Home Defeat: 46pts - 12-58 v Saracens 29.10.99
Away Defeat: 77pts - 7-84 v Bath 26.4.97

MOST CONSECUTIVE
Victories: 7
Defeats: 11

INDIVIDUAL RECORDS

MOST APPEARANCES
by a forward: 149 (15) Dave Baldwin
by a back: 169 (2) Jim Mallinder

MOST CONSECUTIVE
Appearances: 39 Phillip Stansfield 22.10.88-14.3.92
Matches scoring Tries: 8 Simon Verbickas
Matches scoring points: 18 Shane Howarth

MATCH RECORDS

Most Points
27 Simon Mannix v Northampton 9.3.97 (H)
   Charlie Hodgson v Leeds 25.11.01 (A)

Most Tries
5 Simon Verbickas v Otley 12.2.94 (H)

Most Conversions
9 Paul Turner v Otley 12.2.94 (H)

Most Penalties
7 Simon Mannix v Northampton 9.3.97 (H)
   Shane Howarth v Wasps 18.4.98 (H)
   Nicky Little v Bath 19.8.00 (H)

Most Drop Goals
2 David Pears, Paul Tuner (3 times),
   Charlie Hodgson (5 times), Lee Thomas

SEASON RECORDS

Most Points	273	Charlie Hodgson	01-02
Most Tries	16	Simon Verbickas	93-94
Most Conversions	44	Charlie Hodgson	01-02
Most Penalties	49	Charlie Hodgson	05-06
Most Drop Goals	9	Charlie Hodgson	07-08

CAREER RECORDS

Most Points	1510	Charlie Hodgson	00-09
Most Tries	75	Steven Hanley	98-05
Most Conversions	203	Charlie Hodgson	00-09
Most Penalties	295	Charlie Hodgson	00-09
Most Drop Goals	28	Charlie Hodgson	00-09

LAST TEN SEASONS

	Division	P	W	D	L	F	A	P.D.	Pts	Pos	Most Points		Most Tries	
99-00	P1	22	7	0	15	381	633	-252	18	11	101	Nicky Little	6	Steven Hanley
00-01	P1	22	8	1	13	561	622	-61	43	10	163	Nicky Little	10	Steven Hanley
01-02	P	22	14	1	7	589	517	72	69	2	273	Charlie Hodgson	13	Mark Cueto
02-03	P	22	12	2	8	558	470	88	62	4	141	Charlie Hodgson	14	Steven Hanley
03-04	P	22	9	3	10	510	472	38	53	7	131	Braan van Straaten	13	Steven Hanley
04-05	P	22	13	0	9	513	442	71	60	3	195	Charlie Hodgson	10	Mark Cueto
05-06	P	22	16	1	5	573	444	129	74	1	208	Charlie Hodgson	5	Mark Cueto
06-07	P	22	8	1	13	414	500	-86	42	10	80	Charlie Hodgson	6	Chris Bell
07-08	P	22	14	0	8	481	374	107	63	5	201	Charlie Hodgson	8	Ben Foden
08-09	P	22	13	0	9	451	416	35	*60	5	187	Charlie Hodgson	9	Mark Cueto

RFU SENIOR CUP

OVERALL PLAYING RECORD

	P	W	O	L	F	A	Pts Diff
Home	37	23	0	14	876	621	255
Away	40	24	0	16	651	525	126
Neutral	2	0	0	2	36	46	-10
TOTAL	79	47	0	32	1563	1192	371

TEAM RECORDS

Highest Score: 59 v Waterloo 00/01 (H)
Biggest Winning Margin: 57 (57-0) v Orrell 96/97 (A)
Highest Score Against: 47 v Northampton 98/99 (H)
Biggest Losing Margin: 36 (0-36) v Orrell 91/92 (H)

SEASON BY SEASON

71-72	DNQ	78-79	1R	85-86	3R	92-93	3R	99-00	5R
72-73	SF	79-80	DNQ	86-87	3R	93-94	QF	00-01	SF
73-74	QF	80-81	QF	87-88	QF	94-95	QF	01-02	6R
74-75	2R	81-82	QF	88-89	2R	95-96	4R	02-03	6R
75-76	SF	82-83	4R	89-90	4R	96-97	Runners up	03-04	Runners up
76-77	1R	83-84	3R	90-91	3R	97-98	SF	04-05	QF
77-78	1R	84-85	QF	91-92	4R	98-99	4R		

Anglo-Welsh Cup

05-06	Gp Stage
06-07	Q.F.
07-08	Gp Stage
08-09	Gp Stage

Premiership Championship

02-03	-	07-08	-
03-04	-	08-09	-
04-05	S.F.		
05-06	Winners		
06-07	-		

EUROPEAN COMPETITIONS

TEAM RECORDS

Highest Score
93-0 v Roma 01/02

Biggest Winning Margin
93 (93-0) v Roma 01/02

Highest Score Against
53 v Pau 99/00

Biggest Losing Margin
35 (44-9) v Agen 00/01

INDIVIDUAL RECORDS

Most Points in a match
24 Charlie Hodgson
v Caerphilly 00/01 & v Connacht 04/05

Most Tries in a match
3 by five players: John Fowler, Matt Moore,
Apollo Perelini, Mark Cueto & Chris Mayor.

Most Conversions in a match
7 Simon Mannix & Charlie Hodgson

Most Penalties in a match
7 Nikki Little v Agen 00/01

Most Drop Goals in a match
1 on a number of occasions

CAREER RECORDS

Most Appearances
43: Mark Cueto
38: Charlie Hodgson (5)
36: Dean Schofield (8)
33 Chris Jones (10), 33: Steven Hanley (2)
29: Jason Robinson

Most Points
489: Charlie Hodgson
154: Nikki Little
105: Mark Cueto
83: Shane Howarth

Most Tries
21: Mark Cueto
16: Steven Hanley

SEASON BY SEASON

1996-97	S	Gp Stage
1997-98	S	Gp Stage
1998-99	-	D N Play
1999-00	S	Gp Stage
2000-01	S	Gp Stage
2001-02	S	Winners
2002-03	C	Gp Stage
2003-04	C	Gp Stage
2004-05	CC	Winners
2005-06	C	Q.F.
2006-07	C	Gp Stage
2007-08	CC	S.F.
2008-09	C	Gp Stage

OVERALL PLAYING RECORD

	P	W	D	L	F	A	Pts Diff
Home	43	34	0	9	1431	662	769
Away	42	18	1	23	933	951	-18
Neutral	3	3	-	-	80	52	28
Total	88	55	1	32	2444	1605	779

SARACENS

KEY PERSONNEL

Chairman	Nigel Wray
Chief Executive	Edward Griffiths
Director of Rugby	Brendan Venter
Rugby Manager	Mike Hynard
Communication Manager	Mike Hartwell
Operations Manager	Stuart Parker

Founded: 1876

Nickname: Sarries / Men in black

Colours: Black with red trim, black shorts & socks

Change colours: Red shirts, white shorts & socks

Web site: www.saracens.com

CONTACT DETAILS

Saracens Limited,
Woollam Playing Fields, 160 Harpenden Road, St Albans AL3 6BB
Tel: 01727 792800   Fax: 01727 792801

GROUND DETAILS

Address:
Vicarage Road Stadium, Vicarage Road, Watford. WD1 8ER

Capacity: 18,214 - all covered seating
(Reduced due to redevelopment works)

Ground Directions:
From north: Exit M1 at junction 5 and take third exit and follow signs to Watford Town Centre. Join the ring road in the middle lane, moving into the left lane after the second set of lights and follow the signs to the Hospital and West Watford. Follow the mini one-way system around the pedestrian precinct, continuing straight up Vicarage Road where you will see the stadium on your left hand side. Parking is available at the Watford General Hospital

Nearest BR Station: Watford Junction, Watford High Street

Car Parking: No

Admission: (all covered seating)
Matchday – From £15 in advance.

Season - Adults from £99, Children from £49

Club Shop:
Matchdays at Vicarage Road Stadium

PROGRAMME

Size: 17 x 24cm - B5
Pages: 84
Price: £3
Editor: Mike Hartwell

REVIEW OF THE SEASON 2008-09

Saracens started the season with a narrow 24-21 defeat to Harlequins in the London Double Header at Twickenham. Tries from Adam Powell and Neil de Kock made it a close-fought contest, but a late penalty separated the two sides.

In Round 2 of the Premiership, Saracens raced into a 9-0 lead at Sale Sharks but the home side fought back on a night dominated by the kickers and a Charlie Hodgson drop goal with the last kick of the game won the match.

Round 3 was a different story as Saracens, playing at Vicarage Road for the first time in the 2008/09 season, ran in five second half tries to beat Newcastle Falcons 44-14. Kameli Ratuvou, Kevin Sorrell, Hugh Vyvyan, Rodd Penney and Gordon Ross all crossed the whitewash to make it a bonus point win for the home team.

A 26-12 win over Northampton Saints followed with Michael Owen and Rodd Penney crossing the line in the win and when Sarries beat Bristol at the Memorial Ground in Round 5, it took the North London club to fifth in the Premiership heading into the break for the EDF Energy Cup and Europe. Defeats to London Irish and Gloucester in the Premiership were sandwiched between home wins over Worcester, London Irish and Bristol.

A narrow defeat at home to Llanelli Scarlets was disappointing but the highlight was the display of the younger Saracens players on display when no fewer than six made their debuts. Sarries followed that up with victories against Northampton Saints and Bristol in the competition, but it wasn't enough to make the semi-finals of the competition for the second year running.

In the European Challenge Cup, six wins from their pool matches saw Saracens secure a home quarter-final in the competition against Newcastle Falcons which ended in a comfortable victory for the home side. But a 16-13 defeat in the semi-finals against Northampton Saints ended hopes of a final appearance.

An injury crisis at scrum half saw the club move to sign Justin Marshall and he quickly settled into life with Saracens having been one of the instrumental players in the club's win over Sale Sharks in early March this following narrow defeats to Northampton Saints and Newcastle Falcons. Marshall has also starred in the club's 19-14 win over Wasps – picking up the Man of the Match Award – and he was instrumental in the fightback from 16-0 down to beat Bath 20-16.

However, the club ended the campaign with defeats at home against Leicester Tigers – only their second defeat at Vicarage Road all season – and on their travels to Bath to finish ninth in the Guinness Premiership.

SARACENS' SEASON - 2008-09

Date	H/A	Opponents	Result & Score	Att.	15	14	13	12	11
GUINNESS PREMIERSHIP									
06-09	N	Harlequins	L 21-24	52000	Scarbrough	Leonelli Morey	Sorrell	Powell/t	Ratuvou
12-09	A	Sale Sharks	L 15-18	8321	Haughton	Penney	Sorrell	Powell	Ratuvou
21-09	H	Newcastle Falcons	W 44-14	8139	Haughton	Penney/t	Sorrell/t	Powell	Ratuvou/t
27-09	H	Northampton Saints	W 26-12	7409	Haughton	Penney/t	Sorrell	Powell	Ratuvou
01-10	A	Bristol	W 23-16	7215	Haughton	Penney	Sorrell	Powell	Ratuvou/t
16-11	H	Gloucester*	L 21-25	8535	Goode	Sorrell	Powell	Farrell	Cato
23-11	A	London Irish	L 14-27	8954	Goode	Penney	Powell	Farrell	Cato
30-11	H	Worcester	W 23-6	6059	Goode	Ratuvou/t	Powell	Farrell(d/t)	Cato
20-12	N	London Wasps	L 24-33	9324	Goode	Ratuvou	Sorrell	Farrell	Cato/2t
27-12	H	London Irish	W 16-13	16082	Goode	Ratuvou	Sorrell	Powell	Cato
03-01	A	Gloucester	L 16-22	16500	Goode	Ratuvou	Sorrell	Farrell	Haughton/t
11-01	H	Bristol	W 37-13	5881	Wyles	Haughton	Sorrell	Barritt/t	Cato
14-02	A	Northampton Saints	L 15-20	13153	Goode	Haughton	Sorrell	Farrell	Cato
20-02	A	Newcastle Falcons	L 9-13	6204	Goode	Haughton	Powell	Barritt	Ratuvou
01-03	H	Sale Sharks	W 24-23	8311	Goode	Haughton	Ratuvou	Powell	Cato/t
07-03	A	Harlequins	L 15-21	12638	Goode	Haughton/t	Ratuvou	Powell	Cato
15-03	H	Bath	W 20-16	8092	Goode	Haughton	Ratuvou	Barritt	Penney/2t
21-03	A	Leicester Tigers	L 16-46	16328	Wyles/t	Haughton	Powell	Barritt	Penney
29-03	H	London Wasps	W 19-14	16257	Wyles	Leonelli Morey/t	Ratuvou	Barritt	Penney
04-04	A	Worcester	L 8-22	10118	Wyles	Haughton	Jacobs	Farrell	Penney
19-04	H	Leicester Tigers	L 13-16	11275	Goode	Wyles	Leonelli Morey/t	Barritt	Penney
25-04	A	Bath	L 18-33	10600	Goode	Wyles/t	Powell	Farrell	Cato/t
EUROPEAN CHALLENGE CUP									
12-10	H	Mont de Marsan**	W 53-3	5893	Wyles/t	Cato/t	Sorrell	Farrell	Ratuvou
18-10	N	Viadana	W 35-12	4175	Wyles	Penney	Sorrell	Farrell	Ratuvou/t
06-12	N	Bayonne	W 16-6	6000	Goode	Ratuvou	Powell	Farrell	Cato
14-12	N	Bayonne	W 36-0	5635	Goode	Ratuvou/t	Sorrell	Powell	Cato/t
18-01	H	Viadana	W 36-19	6146	Wyles	Haughton	Ratuvou/t	Powell/t	Cato
23-01	A	Mont de Marsan	W 24-3	1800	Goode	Cato	Sorrell	Farrell/t	Penney
Q.F. 12-04	H	Newcastle Falcons	W 32-13	7711	Goode	Wyles	Powell	Barritt/t	Penney
S.F. 01-05	A	Northampton Saints	L 13-16	11073	Wyles	Penney/t	Leonelli Morey	Barritt	Cato
EDF ENERGY CUP									
05-10	H	Llanelli	L 17-26	6068	Scarbrough	Thrower	Leonelli Morey/t	Goode	Cato/t
26-10	H	Northampton Saints	W 33-19	6984	Goode	Leonelli Morey	Powell	Farrell	Cato/t
01-11	A	Bristol	W 24-22	5025	Goode/t	Thrower	Powell	Farrell	Cato/t

SCORING BREAKDOWN

WHEN	Total	First Half	Second Half	1/4	2/4	3/4	4/4
the POINTS were scored	437	221	216	106	115	88	128
the POINTS were conceded	447	201	246	88	113	118	128
the TRIES were scored	38	15	23	8	7	8	15
the TRIES were conceded	38	16	22	8	8	9	13

HOW	Total	Pen. Try	Backs	Forwards	F Back	Wing	Centre	H Back	F Row	Lock	B Row
the TRIES were scored	38	1	25	12	1	15	5	4	5	2	5
the TRIES were conceded	38	1	29	8	4	14	9	2	2	4	2

KEY: * after opponents name indicates a penalty try.
Brackets after a player's name indicates he was replaced. eg (a) means he was replaced by replacement code "a" and so on.
/ after a player or replacement name is followed by any scores he made - eg /t, /c, /p, /dg or any combination of these

PREMIERSHIP

10	9	1	2	3	4	5	6	7	8
Jackson/c3p	de Koch/t	Lloyd	Cairns	Johnson	Borthwick	Vyvyan	Jack	Seymour	Owen
Jackson/5p	de Koch	Aguero	Ongaro	Johnson	Borthwick	Vyvyan	Jack	Saull	Owen
Jackson/c4pdg(b/tc)	de Koch	Aguero	Ongaro	Johnson	Borthwick	Vyvyan/t	Jack	Saull	Owen
Jackson/2c3p(b/p)	de Koch	Aguero	Ongaro	Johnson	Borthwick	Vyvyan	Jack	Saull	Owen/t
Jackson/5pdg	de Koch	Aguero	Ongaro	Johnson	Borthwick	Vyvyan	Skirving	Saull	Owen
Jackson/c3p	de Koch	Lloyd	Cairns	Visagie	Chesney	Vyvyan	Skirving/t	Saull	Owen
Jackson/3p	de Koch	Lloyd	Cairns	Visagie	Ryder	Vyvyan	Skirving	van Heerden/t	Owen
Jackson/tc2p	de Koch	Aguero	Ongaro	Visagie	Owen	Vyvyan	van Heerden	Saull	Skirving
Jackson/c4p	de Koch	Aguero	Ongaro	Johnson	Borthwick	Jack	Skirving	van Heerden	Owen
Jackson/c3p	Raulini/t	Lloyd	Ongaro	Johnson	Borthwick	Jack	van Heerden	Saull	Owen
Jackson/c3p	de Koch	Aguero	Ongaro	Mercey	Vyvyan	Jack	Skirving	van Heerden	Owen
Jackson/3c3p(b/c)	de Koch	Aguero/t	Ongaro	Johnson	Borthwick/t	Jack	van Heerden	Saull	Skirving/t
Jackson/4pdg	Marchon	Lloyd	Cairns	Johnson	Vyvyan	Ryder	van Heerden	Saull	Skirving
Jackson/3p	Marshall	Lloyd	Cairns	Johnson	Ryder	Vyvyan	van Heerden	Saull	Skirving
Jackson/c3pdg	Marshall	Lloyd/t	Cairns	Johnson	Jack	Vyvyan	van Heerden	Saull	Skirving
Jackson/cp	Marshall	Aguero	Cairns	Mercey	Jack	Vyvyan	van Heerden/t	Seymour	Skirving
Jackson	Marshall	Visagie	Walker/t	Mercey(e/t)	Ryder	Chesney	Jack	van Heerden	Skirving
Jackson/c2p	Marshall/dg	Mercey	Walker	Visagie	Ryder	Vyvyan	van Heerden	Seymour	Skirving
Jackson/c4p	Marshall	Aguero	Ongaro	Johnson	Ryder	Borthwick	Jack	van Heerden	Skirving
Ross/p	Marshall	Aguero	Ongaro(f/t)	Johnson	Borthwick	Ryder	Jack	Melck	Skirving
Jackson/c2p	de Koch	Aguero	Ongaro	Mercey	Vyvyan	Chesney	Jack	Seymour	Melck
Jackson/c2p	de Koch	Mercey	Walker	Johnson	Borthwick	Vyvyan	Jack	Saull	Skirving
Jackson/5c2p(b/c)	de Koch/t	Aguero	Ongaro	Johnson	Borthwick	Vyvyan	Jack	Saull/t(c/t)	Owen
Jackson/c7p(b/c)	de Koch/t	Aguero	Ongaro	Johnson	Borthwick	Vyvyan	Jack	Saull	Owen
Jackson/c3p	de Koch(a/t)	Aguero	Ongaro	Johnson	Borthwick	Jack	van Heerden	Saull	Owen
Ross/2c4p	de Koch/t	Aguero	Ongaro	Johnson	Borthwick	Jack/t	Skirving	van Heerden	Owen
Jackson/t3c5p	Raulini	Aguero	Ongaro	Johnson	Borthwick	Jack	van Heerden	Saull	Skirving
Ross/3cp	Wilson	Aguero/t	Ongaro	Johnson	Borthwick	Chesney	Seymour	Saull	Barrell/t
Jackson/2c5pdg	de Koch	Aguero	Ongaro	Johnson/t	Borthwick	Chesney	Jack	Seymour	Skirving
Jackson/c2p	de Koch	Aguero	Ongaro	Johnson	Borthwick	Ryder	Jack	Saull	Skirving
Ross/2cp	Raulini	Lloyd	Cairns	Mercey	Chesney	Spencer	Barrell	Saull	Skirving
Ross/c6pdg	Raulini/t	Lloyd	Cairns	Visagie	Borthwick	Chesney	Barrell	Saull	Skirving
Jackson/c4p	Raulini	Lloyd	Cairns	Visagie	Ryder	Vyvyan	Skirving	Saull	Owen

REPLACEMENTS
a- J Raulini
b- G Ross
c- B Skiving
d- B Barritt
e- D Barrell
f- A Walker

LEAGUE APPEARANCES
21 Glen Jackson
16 Ben Skiving (5), Hugh Vyvyan (2)
15 Chris Jack

LEAGUE POINTS SCORERS

Pts	Player	T	C	P	DG
239	Glen Jackson	1	18	62	4
20	Noah Cato	4	-	-	-
20	Rod Penney	4	-	-	-
15	Gordon Ross	1	2	2	-
15	Kameli Ratuvou	3	-	-	-

NUMBER OF PLAYERS USED
38 plus 6 as a replacement only

107

SARACENS STATISTICS

LEAGUE

TEAM RECORDS

MOST POINTS
Scored at Home: 56 v Sale 12.3.00
Scored Away: 58 v Sale 29.10.99
Conceded at Home: 49 v Bath 27.4.91
Conceded Away: 66 v Bath 03.5.08

MOST TRIES
Scored in a match:
9 - v Gosforth 22.4.89 & v Bedford 16.04.00
Conceded in a match: 9 v Sale 18.9.93, Bath 3.5.08

BIGGEST MARGINS
Home Win: 49pts - 55-6 v Newcastle 17.10.99
Away Win: 46pts - 58-12 v Sale 29.10.99
Home Defeat: 43pts - 6-49 v Bath 27.4.91
Away Defeat: 49pts - 3-52 v Sale 18.9.93

MOST CONSECUTIVE
Victories: 17
Defeats: 7

INDIVIDUAL RECORDS

MOST APPEARANCES
by a forward: 165(2) Tony Diprose
by a back: 151 Kevin Sorrell

MOST CONSECUTIVE
Appearances: 68 Brian Davies
Matches scoring Tries: 6 Dave McLagen:
Matches scoring points: 20 Michael Lynagh/Thierry Lacroix

MATCH RECORDS

Most Points
30 Ryan Constable v Bedford 16.4.00 (A)

Most Tries
6 Ryan Constable v Bedford 16.4.00 (A)

Most Conversions
6 Gavin Johnson v Lon Scot 26.9.98 (A)
Thierry Lacroix v Newcastle 17.10.99 (H)
v Sale 29.10.99 (A)
v Bedford 16.4.00 (A)

Most Penalties
9 Thierry Lacroix v Wasps 27.11.99 (H)
Luke Smith v Gloucester 8.9.01 (H)

Most Drop Goals
2 By 3 players - Andy Lee (3 times),
Ben Rudling, Gareth Hughes

SEASON RECORDS

Most Points	318	Gavin Johnson	98-99
Most Tries	12	Brandon Daniel	98-99
		Ryan Constable	99-00
Most Conversions	52	Gavin Johnson	98-99
Most Penalties	62	Glen Jackson	08-09
Most Drop Goals	6	Andy Lee	94-95
		Andy Goode	02-03

CAREER RECORDS

Most Points	905	Glen Jackson	04-09
Most Tries	31	Thomas Castaignede	00-08
Most Conversions	123	Glen Jackson	04-09
Most Penalties	223	Glen Jackson	04-09
Most Drop Goals	16	Andy Lee	89-95

LAST TEN SEASONS

	Division	P	W	D	L	F	A	P.D.	Pts	Pos	Most Points	Most Tries
99-00	P1	22	14	0	8	729	514	215	37	4	280 Thierry Lacroix	12 Ryan Constable
00-01	P1	22	12	0	10	589	501	88	58	5	133 T Castaignede	6 Dan Luger
01-02	P	22	7	0	15	425	671	-246	34	10	194 Luke Smith	4 Tim Horan
02-03	P	22	8	0	14	499	589	-90	42	8	204 Andy Goode	6 Richard Haughton
03-04	P	22	8	1	13	397	543	-146	39	10	115 Andy Goode	7 R Haughton, T Castaignede
04-05	P	22	12	2	8	384	428	-44	57	5	77 Glen Jackson	4 R Haughton, Ben Johnston
05-06	P	22	8	1	13	433	483	-50	46	10	238 Glen Jackson	7 Danny Scarbrough
06-07	P	22	12	2	8	539	399	140	63	4	272 Glen Jackson	7 Kameli Ratuvou
07-08	P	22	11	0	11	533	525	8	52	8	179 Glen Jackson	7 Adam Powell
08-09	P	22	9	0	13	437	447	-10	47	9	239 Glen Jackson	4 Noah Cato, Rod Penney

RFU SENIOR CUP

OVERALL PLAYING RECORD

	P	W	O	L	F	A	Pts Diff
Home	29	20	0	9	548	379	169
Away	37	16	0	21	726	629	97
Neutral	1	1	0	0	48	18	30
TOTAL	67	37	0	30	1322	1026	296

TEAM RECORDS

Highest Score: 76 v Morley 98/99
Biggest Winning Margin: 68 (76-8) v Morley 98/99
Highest Score Against: 51 v Gloucester 02/03 (A)
Biggest Losing Margin: 31 (51-20) v Gloucester 02/03 (A)

SEASON BY SEASON

71-72	2R	78-79	DNQ	85-86	4R	92-93	4R	99-00	5R
72-73	1R	79-80	DNQ	86-87	3R	93-94	QF	00-01	QF
73-74	2R	80-81	3R	87-88	4R	94-95	4R	01-02	QF
74-75	DNQ	81-82	2R	88-89	3R	95-96	5R	02-03	QF
75-76	1R	82-83	3R	89-90	4R	96-97	QF	03-04	QF
76-77	SF	83-84	1R	90-91	4R	97-98	Winners	04-05	QF
77-78	1R	84-85	4R	91-92	4R	98-99	QF		

Anglo-Welsh Cup

05-06	Gp Stage
06-07	Gp Stage
07-08	S.F.
08-09	Gp Stage

Premiership Championship

02-03	-	07-08	-
03-04	-	08-09	-
04-05	-		
05-06	-		
06-07	S.F.		

EUROPEAN COMPETITIONS

TEAM RECORDS

Highest Score
151 v Dinamo Bucharest 02/03
Biggest Winning Margin
151 (151-0) Dinamo Bucharest 02/03
Highest Score Against
43 v Biarritz 05/06
Biggest Losing Margin
30 (13-43) v Biarritz 05-06

INDIVIDUAL RECORDS

Most Points in a match
31 Jannie de Beer v Bologna
Most Tries in a match
4 Darragh O'Mahony v Bologna
Most Conversions in a match
13 Jannie de Beer v Bologna
Most Penalties in a match
7 Glen Jackson v Viadana 18.10.08
Most Drop Goals in a match
1 Thomas Castaignede (2),
Nicky Little, Glen Jackson (2)

CAREER RECORDS

Most Appearances
53: Kevin Sorrell (1)
42 Kris Chesney (3)
35: Richard Hill
28: Glen Jackson (1)
27: Darragh O'Mahony
Most Points
410 Glen Jackson
175: Thomas Castaignede
117: Niki Little
95: Darragh O'Mahony
Most Tries
20: Richard Haughton
19: Darragh O'Mahony
14: Ben Johnston, Matt Cairns
12: Tom Shanklin

SEASON BY SEASON

1996-97	S	DNP
1997-98	S	Gp Stage
1998-99	C	DNP
1999-00	C	Gp Stage
2000-01	C	Gp Stage
2001-02	C	Q.F.
2002-03	S	S.F.
2003-04	S	Q.F.
2004-05	CC	Q.F.
2005-06	C	Gp Stage
2006-07	CC	S.F.
2007-08	C	S.F.
2008-09	CC	S.F.

OVERALL PLAYING RECORD

	P	W	D	L	F	A	Pts Diff
Home	40	35	0	5	1766	646	1120
Away	35	21	1	13	921	650	234
Neutral	-	-	-	-	-	-	-
Total	75	56	1	18	2687	1333	1354

WORCESTER WARRIORS

KEY PERSONNEL

Tel. & Fax: + 01905   all email addresses are : @warriors.co.uk

Chairman & Chief Executive	Cecil Duckworth OBE
Company Secretary	Louise Brook Tel: + 459300; Fax: + 459302; email: louise.brook@
General Manager	Charlie Little Tel: + 459355; Fax: + 459302 email: charlie.little@
Stadium Manager / Matchday Safety Officer	Shaun Roberts Tel: + 459324; Fax: + 459352 email: shaun.roberts@
Director of Rugby	Mike Ruddock
Team Manager	Alun Carter Tel: + 459359; Fax: + 459311 email: alun.carter@
Commercial Director	Kathy Leather Tel: + 459326; Fax: + 459333 email: kathy.leather@
Sixways Events	Bryan Ryan Tel: + 459307; Fax: + 459333 email: bryan.ryan@
Financial Controller	Jamie Evans Tel: + 459344; Fax: + 459302 email: jamie.evans@
Media & PR Manager	Ben Mottram Tel: + 459340; Fax: + 459352 email: media@
Marketing	Lydia Pearson Tel: + 459340; Fax: + 459352 email: lydia.pearson@
Box Office Manager	Maxine James Tel: + 454183; Fax: + 459352 email: tickets@
Community Manager	Tom Ryder Tel: + 459317; Fax: + 459352 email: tom.ryder@

Founded: 1871
Nickname: 'Warriors'
Colours:
Navy blue, white and gold (Home)
Change colours:
Red, white and gold (Away)
Website: www.warriors.co.uk

GROUND DETAILS

Address:
Worcester Warriors, Sixways Stadium, Warriors Way, Worcester. WR3 8ZE
Tel: 01905 454183   Fax: 01905 459352   email: rugby@warriors.co.uk

Capacity: 12,024
Seated capacity: 11,455   Covered capacity: 11,455

Directions:
Leave M5 junction 6, follow A4538 to Droitwich, Sixways is on your left 200 metres after joining this road..

Car Parking: Season ticket holders only on site matchdays.
Off site parking & 'park & ride' available

Nearest BR Station: Worcester Foregate Street. Rugby Special bus service outside station every 10 mins.

Admission:
Matchday: Adults £21-£38; Junior £11-£38 * cheaper if purchased in advance
Season: Adults £210-£420; Juniors £125-£420
Contact Warriors Box Office for more information

Club Shop: Tel: 01905 454747

CONTACT DETAILS

c/o Worcester Warriors,
Sixways, Warriors Way,
Worcester. WR3 8ZE
Tel: 01905 454183
Fax: 01905 459333
email: rugby@warriors.co.uk

PROGRAMME

Size: B5
Pages: 84
Price: £3
Editor: Ben Mottram
Advertising: Kathy Leather 01905 459326

REVIEW OF THE SEASON 2008-09

Worcester Warriors suffered a series of injuries and misfortunes during the 2008/09 season that robbed the club of a chance to climb the Guinness Premiership table.

Guinness Premiership safety was secured after an impressive run of form in the latter stages of a season when Director of Rugby Mike Ruddock admitted he was never able to select his strongest side.

Despite long term injuries to star performers, such as Chris Latham, Marcel Garvey, Miles Benjamin, Chris Horsman, Sam Tuitupou, Chris Pennell, Matthew Jones and summer signing Hal Luscombe, many results have shown the potential at Sixways Stadium.

The double was secured over then champions London Wasps and away success at Sale Sharks underlined the wealth of talent at the club. Warriors also made the semi-final of the European Challenge Cup before Bourgoin proved to strong in France.

The club was twice been forced to dig into the transfer market for loan deals, with Irish ace Eoghan Hickey appearing for Warriors before Willie Walker stepped into the fly half role. Walker produced several invaluable match winning performances for the club including the dream derby day double over Gloucester – his summer switch to Worcester was soon confirmed.

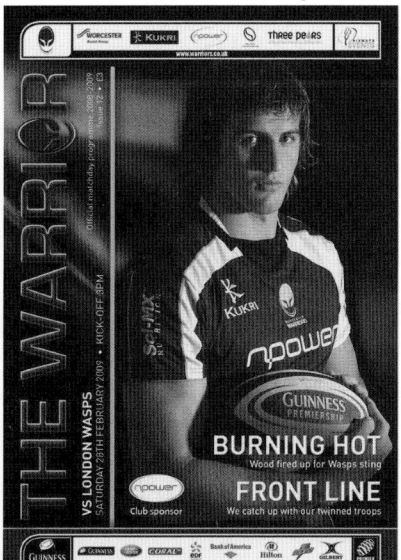

Other arrivals to the club include Olivier Sourgens and Adam Black and Ruddock believes the lessons of 2008/09 have been learnt as Warriors look to kick on and finally achieve the rich potential that so many believe exists at the club.

"It was an up-and-down season — but what has shown is the character of the team," said Ruddock. "We know we can deliver when our backs are against the wall. That has been a defining value of this team over the years to try and avoid relegation.

"We avoided relegation by a country mile, we got wins and did the double over Wasps and Gloucester, the first time we have ever done that as a club. We know we are capable of doing things. We have blooded 16 players this year who have either been on academy contracts or still are.

"That will make us stronger in the longer term so that when we get the likes of Latham and Tuitupou back, we will be in far better shape to launch a much stronger challenge up the league."

WORCESTER'S SEASON - 2008-09

GUINNESS PREMIERSHIP

Date	H/A	Opponents	Result & Score	Att.	15	14	13	12	11
07-09	A	Northampton Saints	L 13-21	13094	Latham	Gear	Rasmussen	Tuitupou	Benjamin
14-09	N	London Wasps	W 11-10	7668	Latham	Pennell	Rasmussen	Tuitupou/t	Benjamin
20-09	H	Leicester Tigers	L 17-19	10846	Latham	Pennell	Rasmussen	Tuitupou	Benjamin
27-09	A	Bath	L 19-37	10600	Latham	Pennell/tp	Rasmussen	Tuitupou	Benjamin
02-10	H	Harlequins	L 23-30	9222	Latham	Fellows	Rasmussen	Tuitupou	Benjamin/t
14-11	A	Sale Sharks	W 17-9	7602	Latham	Pennell	Rasmussen	Tuitupou	Benjamin
21-11	H	Newcastle Falcons	W 26-11	10162	Latham/t	Pennell/p	Rasmussen	Tuitupou/t	Benjamin
30-11	A	Saracens	L 6-23	6059	Pennell/2p	Gear	Rasmussen	Tuitupou	Benjamin
20-12	H	Bristol*	D 20-20	10015	Latham/t	Gear	Rasmussen	Tuitupou	Pennell
27-12	A	Newcastle Falcons	D 16-16	7108	Latham	Gear	Rasmussen	Tuitupou	Pennell
31-01	H	Sale Sharks	L 20-37	10387	Latham/t	Gear	Luscombe	Rasmussen	Garvey/t
14-02	H	Bath	L 17-34	10096	Latham/t	Gear	Rasmussen	Crichton/t	Garvey
21-02	A	Leicester Tigers	L 5-38	17081	Walker	Gear	Rasmussen	Crichton	Garvey
28-02	H	London Wasps	W 13-12	9543	Gear	Garvey	Luscombe	Grove/t	Benjamin
07-03	H	Northampton Saints	L 12-22	10319	Latham	Gear	Rasmussen	Grove	Garvey
15-03	A	London Irish	L 17-38	8434	Latham	Gear	Luscombe	Rasmussen	Garvey
22-03	H	Gloucester	W 14-10	12024	Latham	Garvey/t	Gear	Rasmussen	Benjamin
29-03	A	Bristol	L 18-37	5403	Walker/c2p	Garvey	Grove	Rasmussen/t	Benjamin
01-04	A	Harlequins	L 14-60	10446	Crichton/c	Penn	Luscombe	King	Fellows/t
04-04	H	Saracens	W 22-8	10118	Walker/c3pdg	Garvey	Grove/t	Rasmussen	Benjamin
21-04	A	Gloucester	W 13-6	14035	Walker/c2p	Garvey	Grove	Rasmussen	Gear
25-04	H	London Irish	L 15-32	11241	Crichton	Fellows	Gear(c/t)	Grove	Benjamin

EUROPEAN CHALLENGE CUP

11-10	A	Padova	W 55-6	2200	Latham/3tc	Gear/t	Grove/2t	Tuitupou/t	Fellows/t
19-10	A	Bucuresti*	W 53-17	1300	Crichton	Gear/2t	Grove	Tuipulotu/t	Benjamin
05-12	A	Bourgoin	L 14-29		Fellows	Gear	Rasmussen	Grove/t	Benjamin
13-12	H	Bourgoin	W 27-6	7791	Hickey	Gear	Rasmussen	Tuitupou/t	Fellows
17-01	H	Bucuresti*	W 38-19	7323	Latham/t(h/2c)	Gear/t	Luscombe	Rasmussen	Pennell
24-01	H	Padova**	W 68-17	7523	Latham(a/c)	Gear/t	Luscombe	Rasmussen/t	Fellows/t
Q.F. 11-04	H	Brive	W 29-18	4323	Gear	Garvey/2t	Grove/t	Rasmussen	Benjamin
S.F. 02-05	A	Bourgoin	L 11-22		Gear	Fellows	Grove	Rasmussen	Benjamin/t

EDF ENERGY CUP

05-10	A	London Irish	W 22-5	7433	Latham(a/t)	Fellows	Grove	Tuitupou	Benjamin/2t
26-10	N	Ospreys	L 22-37	7025	Latham	Pennell	Grove	Tuitupou/t	Fellows
02-11	H	Harlequins	L 14-27	8113	Latham	Gear	Grove	Tuitupou	Pennell

SCORING BREAKDOWN

WHEN	Total	First Half	Second Half	1/4	2/4	3/4	4/4
the POINTS were scored	348	177	171	57	120	97	74
the POINTS were conceded	530	252	278	118	134	113	165
the TRIES were scored	30	13	17	4	9	10	7
the TRIES were conceded	64	27	37	12	15	13	24

HOW	Total	Pen. Try	Backs	Forwards	F Back	Wing	Centre	H Back	F Row	Lock	B Row
the TRIES were scored	30	1	18	11	4	5	7	2	4	2	5
the TRIES were conceded	64	1	41	22	5	21	8	7	6	2	14

KEY: * after opponents name indicates a penalty try.
Brackets after a player's name indicates he was replaced. eg (a) means he was replaced by replacement code "a" and so on.
/ after a player or replacement name is followed by any scores he made - eg /t, /c, /p, /dg or any combination of these

PREMIERSHIP

10	9	1	2	3	4	5	6	7	8
Jones/c2p	M Powell	Mullan	Lutui/t	Taumoepeau	Rawlinson	Gillies	Talei	Wood	Horstmann
Jones/p(a/p)	R Powell	Mullan	Lutui	Horsman	Rawlinson	Bowley	Wood	Collins	Talei
Crichton/2cp	R Powell	Mullan/t	Lutui	Horsman	Rawlinson	Bowley	Wood	Collins	Talei/t
Crichton/c3p	R Powell	Mullan	Lutui	Taumoepeau	Rawlinson	Gillies	Horstmann	Wood	Talei
Jones/t2c2pdg	R Powell	Mullan	Lutui	Taumoepeau	Rawlinson	Gillies	Horstmann	Wood	Talei
Jones/4p	R Powell	Mullan	Fortey	Taumoepeau	Rawlinson	Gillies	Talei/t	Sanderson	Horstmann
Jones/p(a/2c2p)	M Powell	Mullan	Fortey	Taumoepeau	Rawlinson	Gillies	Talei	Sanderson	Horstmann
Crichton	M Powell	Mullan	Lutui	Taumoepeau	Rawlinson	Gillies	Talei	Sanderson	Horstmann
Hickey/2c2p	M Powell	Mullan	Lutui	Taumoepeau	Rawlinson	Gillies	Talei	Sanderson	Horstmann
Hickey/c3p	R Powell	Mullan	Lutui	Horsman	Rawlinson	Gillies	Talei	Sanderson/t	Horstmann
Carlisle/2c2p	R Powell	Mullan	Lutui	Taumoepeau	Rawlinson	Bowley	Talei	Sanderson	Horstmann
Carlisle/2c(b/p)	R Powell	Mullan	Lutui	Taumoepeau	Rawlinson	Bowley	Wood	Sanderson	Horstmann
Carlisle	M Powell	Morris	Fortey	Taumoepeau	Bowley/t	Gillies	Wood	Sanderson	Horstmann
Walker/cpdg	M Powell	Mullan	Lutui	Taumoepeau	Rawlinson	Bowley	Wood	Sanderson	Horstmann
Walker/4p	M Powell	Mullan	Lutui	Taumoepeau	Rawlinson	Bowley	Talei	Sanderson	Horstmann
Walker/t2cp	R Powell	Mullan	Lutui	Morris	Rawlinson/t	Bowley	Talei	Sanderson	Horstmann
Walker/3p	R Powell	Mullan	Fortey	Black	Rawlinson	Bowley	Collins	Sanderson	Horstmann
Jones	R Powell	Mullan	Fortey	Morris	Rawlinson	Bowley	Wood	Sanderson	Horstmann/t
Carlisle/c	M Powell	Gilding	Fortey	Ruwers/t	Lyons	Gillies	Collins	Abbott	Wood
Jones/p	R Powell	Black	Lutui	Morris	Rawlinson	Bowley	Wood	Sanderson	Horsman
Jones	R Powell	Black	Lutui	Morris	Rawlinson	Kitchener	Wood	Sanderson	Talei/t
Carlisle/cp	M Powell	Black	Fortey/t	Morris	Kitchener	Bowley	Wood	Collins	Talei
Jones/4c	M Powell	Morris	Fortey	Taumoepeau	Kitchener	Gillies	Wood	Collins	Talei(e/t)
Jones/4c2p(h/t2c)	R Powell/t	Mullan	Lutui	Taumoepeau	Rawlinson	Gilllies/t	Wood	Cox	Talei
Carlisle/2c	M Powell	Mullan	Lutui/t	Horsman	Rawlinson	Gillies	Talei	Sanderson	Horstmann
Carlisle/c5p	M Powell	Morris	Fortey(f/t)	Taumoepeau	Bowley	Gillies	Talei	Sanderson	Horstmann
Hickey/2c	R Powell/t(g/2t)	Mullan	Fortey	Taumoepeau	Rawlinson	Gillies	Talei	Sanderson	Horstmann
Carlisle/t8c	M Powell	Mullan	Lutui	Taumoepeau	Rawlinson(i/2t)	Bowley/t	Cox	Sanderson	Horstmann/t
Jones/3cp	R Powell	Black	Lutui	Morris	Rawlinson	Bowley	Wood	Sanderson/t	Horstmann
Carlisle/2p	R Powell	Black	Lutui	Morris	Rawlinson	Kitchener	Wood	Sanderson	Talei
Jones/c	Jones	Morris	Fortey	Horsman	Kitchener/t	Gillies	Cox	Abbott	Talei
Jones/c5p	R Powell	Mullan	Lutui	Taumoepeau	Rawlinson	Gillies	Cox	Abbott	Talei
Jones/2c	M Powell	Mullan	Lutui	Taumoepeau	Rawlinson	Kitchener	Cox	Abbott/t(d/t)	Talei

REPLACEMENTS

a- L Crichton   b- W Walker   c- G Crook   d- P Sanderson
e- G Rawlinson f- A Lutui   g- M Powell h- J Carlisle
i- G Kitchener

LEAGUE APPEARANCES

19   Dale Rasmusen, Greg Rawlinbson (1)
17   Matt Mullan (1)
16   Kai Horstmann (2)

NUMBER OF PLAYERS USED

38 plus 8 as a replacement only

LEAGUE POINTS SCORERS

Pts	Player	T	C	P	DG
74	Willie Walker	1	6	17	2
47	Matthew Jones	1	3	11	1
38	Loki Crichton	-	6	3	-
21	Joe Carlisle	-	6	3	-
21	Eoghan Hickey	-	3	5	-
20	Chris Latham	4	-	-	-

WORCESTER STATISTICS

LEAGUE

TEAM RECORDS

MOST POINTS
Scored at Home: 78
v Liverpool St Helens 21.3.98 & v Waterloo 20.11.99
Scored Away: 84 v Wakefield 16.10.99
Conceded at Home: 48 v Sale Sharks 11.2.06
Conceded Away: 60 v Harlequins 01.04.09

MOST TRIES
Scored in a match: 13 v Wakefield 16.10.99 (A)
Conceded in a match: 10 v v Harlequins 01.04.09 (H)

BIGGEST MARGINS
Home Win: 68pts - 78-10 v Waterloo 20.11.99
Away Win: 69pts - 84-15 v Wakefield 16.10.99
Home Defeat: 27pts - 11-38 v Leicester Tigers 13.11.04
Away Defeat: 54pts - 3-57 v Sale Sharks 24.9.04

MOST CONSECUTIVE
Victories: 28 (19.4.03 - 24.4.04)
Defeats: 8 (2.9.06 - 17.11.06)

INDIVIDUAL RECORDS

MOST APPEARANCES
by a forward: 180(13) Tony Windo
by a back: 94(7) Nick Baxter

MOST CONSECUTIVE
Appearances: 24 Duncan Hughes
Matches scoring Tries: 9 Nick Baxter
Matches scoring points: 17 Tim Smith

MATCH RECORDS

Most Points
31 Sateki Tuipulotu — v Henley 20.1.01

Most Tries
6 Nick Baxter — v Otley 21.2.98 (A)

Most Conversions
9 Richard LeBas — v Liverpool St H 21.3.98(H)
  Tony Yapp — v Waterloo 20.11.99 (H)
  Tommy Hayes — v Bristol 3.4.04 (H)

Most Penalties
5 Tim Smith — v Leeds 27.12.97 (A)
  James Brown — 2 times 04/05, 06/07
  Shane Drahm — 3 times 05/06

Most Drop Goals
2 James Brown — v Leeds 4.2.05 (A)
               v Newcastle 10.4.05 (A)
  Shane Drahm — v Lon Irish 11.9.05 (A)

SEASON RECORDS

Most Points	349	Sateki Tuipulotu	00-01
Most Tries	29	Nick Baxter	97-98
Most Conversions	98	Tommy Hayes	03-04
Most Penalties	52	Shane Drahm	05-06
Most Drop Goals	5	James Brown	04-05

CAREER RECORDS

Most Points	507	Shane Drahm	05-08
Most Tries	88	Nick Baxter	95-01
Most Conversions	107	Tommy Hayes	03-05
Most Penalties	108	Shane Drahm	05-08
Most Drop Goals	9	Shane Drahm	05-08

LAST TEN SEASONS

	Division	P	W	D	L	F	A	P.D.	Pts	Pos	Most Points	Most Tries
99-00	P2	26	19	0	7	865	450	415	38	3	229 Tony Yapp	13 Nick Baxter
00-01	N1	26	23	1	2	844	387	457	112	2	349 Sateki Tuipulotu	17 Sateki Tuipulotu
01-02	N1	26	23	0	3	941	364	577	108	2	125 Chris Garrard	25 Chris Garrard
02-03	N1	26	23	0	3	1185	431	754	114	2	126 Duncan Roke	26 Duncan Roke
03-04	N1	26	26	0	0	1119	340	779	125	1p	303 Tommy Hayes	19 Daren O'Leary
04-05	P	22	9	0	13	365	493	-128	42	9	113 James Brown	5 Ben Hinshelwood
05-06	P	22	9	1	12	451	494	-43	47	8	233 Shane Drahm	6 Aisea Havili
06-07	P	22	6	1	15	346	459	-113	34	11	156 Shane Drahm	3 By three players
07-08	P	22	6	2	14	387	472	-85	36	10	118 Shane Drahm	9 Miles Benjamin
08-09	P	22	7	2	13	348	530	-182	34	11	74 Willie Walker	4 Chris Latham

RFU SENIOR CUP

OVERALL PLAYING RECORD

	P	W	O	L	F	A	Pts Diff
Home	14	9	0	5	379	197	182
Away	18	11	0	7	525	318	207
Neutral	0	0	0	0	0	0	0
TOTAL	32	20	0	12	904	515	389

TEAM RECORDS

Highest Score: 76 v Tynedale 00/01
Biggest Winning Margin: 68 (73-5) v Bracknell (A) 02/03
Highest Score Against: 42 v Saracens 00/01
Biggest Losing Margin: 29 (42-13) v Saracens 00/01

SEASON BY SEASON

71-72	DNQ	78-79	DNQ	85-86	DNQ	92-93	2R	99-00	4R
72-73	DNQ	79-80	DNQ	86-87	DNQ	93-94	DNQ	00-01	5R
73-74	DNQ	80-81	DNQ	87-88	DNQ	94-95	DNQ	01-02	5R
74-75	DNQ	81-82	DNQ	88-89	DNQ	95-96	4R	02-03	6R
75-76	DNQ	82-83	2R	89-90	DNQ	96-97	2R	03-04	5R
76-77	DNQ	83-84	DNQ	90-91	DNQ	97-98	5R	04-05	6R
77-78	DNQ	84-85	DNQ	91-92	DNQ	98-99	4R		

Anglo-Welsh Cup

05-06	Gp Stage
06-07	Gp Stage
07-08	Gp Stage
08-09	Gp Stage

Premiership Championship

02-03	NA
03-04	NA
04-05	-
05-06	-
06-07	-

07-08	-
08-09	-

EUROPEAN COMPETITIONS

TEAM RECORDS

Highest Score
67 v Rovigo 04/05

Biggest Winning Margin
53pts (67-14) v Rovigo 04/05

Highest Score Against
40 v Brive 04/05

Biggest Losing Margin
30pts (10-40) v Brive 04/05

INDIVIDUAL RECORDS

Most Points in a match
21 Shane Drahm, v Montauban 17.11.07

Most Tries in a match
3 Uche Odouza v Rovigo 11.12.04
Aisea Havili v Northampton 01.4.26

Most Conversions in a match
6 Shane Drahm v Gran Parma 15.12.07

Most Penalties in a match
3 Shane Drahm v Connacht (x2), Bath

Most Drop Goals in a match
1 Shane Drahm v Gloucester, Montauban

CAREER RECORDS

Most Appearances
24: Pat Sanderson (1)
22: Thinus Delport (3)
21: Craig Gillies (4)
17 Shane Drahm (3), Drew Hickey (5)

Most Points
211: Shane Drahm
60: Rico Gear
59: James Brown
57: Thinus Delport
51: Tommy Hayes

Most Tries
12: Rico Gear
11: Thinus Delport
9: Pat Sanderson
6: Shane Drahm

SEASON BY SEASON

1996-97	NA	
1997-98	NA	
1998-99	NA	
1999-00	NA	
2000-01	NA	
2001-02	NA	
2002-03	NA	
2003-04	NA	
2004-05	S	Runners-up
2005-06	CC	S.F.
2006-07	CC	Gp Stage
2007-08	CC	Runners-up
2008-09	CC	S.F.

OVERALL PLAYING RECORD

	P	W	D	L	F	A	Pts Diff
Home	19	18	-	1	723	275	648
Away	18	11	1	6	512	348	164
Neutral	2	-	-	2	26	47	-21
Total	39	29	1	9	1261	670	591

RECORDS SECTION
DIVISION ONE
(CURRENTLY PREMIERSHIP)

DIVISION ONE

ROLL OF HONOUR

	CHAMPIONS	Runners-up	Nos of Clubs/Games	Leading Points Scorer
1987-88	Leicester	Wasps	12/11	126 Dusty Hare (Leicester)
1988-89	Bath	Gloucester	12/11	103 Rob Andrew (Wasps)
1989-90	Wasps	Gloucester	12/11	126 John Liley (Leicester)
1990-91	Bath	Wasps	13/12	126 Rob Andrew (Wasps)
1991-92	Bath	Orrell	13/12	125 John Liley (Leicester)
1992-93	Bath	Wasps	13/12	122 Jonathan Webb (Bath)
1993-94	Bath	Leicester	10/18	202 Jez Harris (Leicester)
1994-95	Leicester	Bath	10/18	196 Mark Tainton (Bristol)
1995-96	Bath	Leicester	10/18	272 John Liley (Leicester)
1996-97	Wasps	Bath	12/22	291 Gareth Rees (Wasps)
1997-98	Newcastle	Saracens	12/22	279 Michael Lynagh (Saracens)
1998-99	Leicester	Northampton	14/26	331 John Schuster (Harlequins)
99-2000	Leicester	Bath	12/22	324 Jarod Cunningham (London Irish)
2000-01	Leicester	London Wasps	12/22	282 Kenny Logan (Wasps)
2001-02	Leicester	Sale	12/22	343 Barry Everitt (London Irish)
2002-03	Gloucester	London Wasps	12/22	255 Ludovic Mercier (Gloucester)
2003-04	Bath	London Wasps	12/22	266 Andy Goode (Leicester/Saracens)
2004-05	Leicester	London Wasps	12/22	259 Andy Goode (Leicester)
2005-06	Sale	Leicester	12/22	244 Jason Strange (Bristol)
2006-07	Gloucester	Leicester	12/22	272 Glen Jackson (Saracens)
2007-08	Gloucester	London Wasps	12/22	201 Charlie Hodgson (Sale)
2008-09	Leicester	Harlequins	12/22	239 Glen Jackson (Saracens)

RELEGATED CLUBS
87-88 - Coventry, Manchester Sale
88-89 - Waterloo, Liverpool St. Helens
89-90 - Bedford
90-91 - Moseley, Liverpool St. Helens
91-92 - Nottingham, Rosslyn Park
92-93 - Saracens, London Scottish, West Hartlepool, Rugby
93-94 - Lon. Irish, Newcastle Gosforth
94-95 - Northampton
95-96 -
96-97 - Orrell, West Hartlepool
97-98 - Bristol (via Play-off)
98-99 - West Hartlepool
99-00 - Bedford
00-01 - Rotherham
01-02 -
02-03 - Bristol
03-04 - Rotherham
04-05 - Harlequins
05-06 - Leeds
06-07 - Northampton
07-08 - Leeds
08-09 - Bristol

LEICESTER TIGERS - GUINNESS CHAMPIONS 2009

		MOST TRIES		MOST PENALTIES		MOST CONVERSIONS
87-88	11	Andrew Harriman (Harlequins)	31	Dusty Hare (Leicester)	15	Dusty Hare (Leicester)
88-89	10	Jeremy Guscott (Bath)	25	Dusty Hare (Leicester)	13	Rob Andrew (Wasps) & Stuart Barnes (Bath)
89-90	10	Tony Swift (Bath)	24	David Pears (Harlequins)	29	Stuart Barnes (Bath)
90-91	9	Andrew Harriman (Harlequins)	26	Rob Andrew (Wasps)	21	Martin Street (Orrell)
91-92	9	Rory Underwood (Leicester)	28	John Steele (Northampton)	19	John Liley (Leicester)
92-93	7	Stuart Barnes (Bath)	31	Michael Corcoran (Lon Irish)	19	Jonathan Webb (Bath)
93-94	11	Daren O'Leary (Harlequins)	41	Jez Harris (Leicester)	25	Jonathan Callard (Bath)
94-95	8	Paul Holford (Gloucester)	56	Mark Tainton (Bristol)	19	Rob Andrew (Wasps)
95-96	14	Daren O'Leary (Harlequins)	64	John Liley (Leicester)	43	Jonathan Callard (Bath)
96-97	16	Adebayo Adedayo (Bath)	62	Gareth Rees (Wasps)	51	Jonathan Callard (Bath)
97-98	17	Domonic Chapman (Rich)	58	Mark Mapletoft (GLoucester)	44	Rob Andrew (Newcastle)
98-99	16	Neil Back (Leicester)	77	John Schuster (Harlequins)	52	Gavin Johnson (Saracens)
99-00	15	Ian Balshaw (Bath)	66	Jarod Cunningham (Lon Irish)	52	Tim Stimpson (Leicester)
00-01	11	Paul Sampson (Wasps)	58	Paul Grayson (Northampton)	47	Kenny Logan (Wasps)
01-02	13	Mark Cueto (Sale)	83	Barry Everitt (London Irish)	48	Ludovic Mercier (Gloucester)
02-03	14	Steven Hanley (Sale)	68	Braam van Straatan (Leeds)	42	Ludovic Mercier (Gloucester)
03-04	13	Steven Hanley (Sale) Bruce Reihana (Northampton)	50	Ollie Barklay (Bath)	43	Andy Goode (Leicester/Saracens)
04-05	11	Tom Voyce (London Wasps)	46	Shane Drahm (Northampton)	50	Andy Goode (Leicester)
05-06	14	Tom Varndell (Leicester)	65	Jason Strange (Bristol)	32	by three players
06-07	11	David Lemi (Bristol)	57	Glen Jackson (Saracens)	35	Glen Jackson (Saracens)
07-08	13	Tom Varndell (Leicester)	42	Charlie Hodgson (Sale)	37	Danny Cipriani (London Wasps)
08-09	10	Joe Maddock (Bath) & Ugo Moyne (Harlequins)	62	Glen Jackson (Saracens)	35	Butch James (Bath)

DIVISION ONE

Constitution	12 87-88	12 88-89	12 89-90	13 90-91	13 91-92	13 92-93	10 93-94	10 94-95	10 95-96	12 96-97
Bath	4	1	3	1	1	1	1	2	1	2
Bedford			12							
Bristol	9	7	9	11	10	6	4	6	6	9
Coventry	11r									
Gloucester	5	2	2	6	4	5	8	7	8	6
Harlequins	3	8	7	3	8	8	6	8	3	3
Leeds										
Leicester	1	6	5	4	6	3	2	1	2	4
Liverpool St Helens		12r		13r						
London Irish					9	7	9r			10
London Scottish					10r					
Moseley	7	10	11	12r						
Newcastle							10r			
Northampton				9	3	4	5	10r		8
Nottingham	8	4	6	8	12r					
Orrell	6	5	8	5	2	9	7	5	7	12r
Richmond										
Rosslyn Park		9	10	7	13r					
Rotherham										
Rugby					11	13r				
Sale	12r							4	5	5
Saracens			4	10	5	11r			9	7
Wasps	2	3	1	2	7	2	3	3	4	1
Waterloo	10	11r								
West Hartlepool						12r		9	10	11r
Worcester										

Premiership Championship

From 2002-03 until 2004-05 the top three teams in the final league standings played for this trophy. 2nd placed played 3rd placed in a semi-final with the winner playing the 1st placed team.

In 2005-06 this changed to the top four teams,
with 1st v 4th and 2nd v 3rd in the semi-finals - home advantage given to 1st & 2nd.

YEAR BY YEAR RECORDS

12 97-98	14 98-99	12 99-00	12 00-01	12 01-02	12 02-03	12 03-04	12 04-05	12 05-06	12 06-07	12 07-08	12 08-09
3	6	2	3	11	11	1	4	9	8	3	4
	13	12r									
12r		6	9	8	12r			11	3	9	12r
7	10	3	7	3	1	4	6	5	1	1	6
10	4	10	11	9	7	6	12r		7	6	2
				12	5	11	8	12r		12r	
4	1	1	1	1	6	5	1	2	2	4	1
11	7	8	8	4	9	8	10	3	6	7	3
	12										
1	8	9	6	6	10	9	7	7	9	11	10
8	2	5	4	5	3	3	11	6	12r		8
5	9										
			12r			12r					
6	11	11	10	2	4	7	3	1	10	5	5
2	3	4	5	10	8	10	5	10	4	8	9
9	5	7	2	7	2	2	2	4	5	2	7
	14r										
						9	8	11	10	11	

		Winner			**Winner**
	2002-03	London Wasps		2007-08	London Wasps
	2003-04	London Wasps		2008-09	Leicester Tigers
	2004-05	London Wasps			
	2005-06	Sale Sharks			
	2006-07	Leicester Tigers			

PREMIERSHIP

119

DIVISION ONE
ALL TIME RECORDS

SEASON RECORDS

MOST POINTS

EVOLUTION OF RECORD

126	Dusty Hare	Leicester	1987-88
202	Jez Harris	Leicester	1993-94
272	John Liley	Leicester	1996-97
291	Gareth Rees	Wasps	1996-97
331	John Schuster	Harlequins	1998-99
343	Barry Everitt	London Irish	2001-02

The ALL-TIME RECORDS can be found overleaf.

MOST TRIES

EVOLUTION OF RECORD

11	Andrew Harriman	Harlequins	1987-88
14	Daren O'Leary	Harlequins	1995-96
16	Adedayo Adebayo	Bath	1996-97
17	Domonic Chapman	Richmond	1997-98

ALL-TIME RECORDS

17	Domonic Chapman	Richmond	1997-98
16	Adedayo Adebayo	Bath	1996-97
16	Neil Back	Leicester	1998-99
15	Daren O'Leary	Harlequins	1996-97
15	Iain Balshaw	Bath	1999-00
14	Daren O'Leary	Harlequins	1995-96
14	Tom Beim	Sale	1997-98
14	Steven Hanley	Sale	2002-03
14	Tom Varndell	Leicester Tigers	2005-06
13	Steven John	West Hartlepool	1996-97
13	Tom Beim	Sale	1996-97
13	Gary Armstrong	Newcastle	1997-98
13	Mark Cueto	Sale Sharks	2001-02
13	Tom Varndell	Leicester Tigers	2007-08

MOST DROP GOALS

EVOLUTION OF RECORD

ALL-TIME RECORDS

MOST CONVERSIONS

EVOLUTION OF RECORD

15	Dusty Hare	Leicester	1987-88
29	Stuart Barnes	Bath	1989-90
43	Jonathon Callard	Bath	1995-96
51	Jonathon Callard	Bath	1996-97
52	Gavin Johnson	Saracens	1998-99

ALL-TIME RECORDS

52	Gavin Johnson	Saracens	1998-99
52	Tim Stimpson	Leicester	1999-00
51	Jonathon Callard	Bath	1996-97
51	Jonny Wilkinson	Newcastle	1998-99
50	Mike Catt	Bath	1998-99
50	Andy Goode	Leicester Tigers	2004-05
48	Ludovic Mercier	Gloucester	2001-02
47	Thierry Lacroix	Saracens	1999-00
47	Kenny Logan	London Wasps	2000-01
46	Jarod Cunningham	London Irish	1999-00
45	Gareth Rees	Wasps	1996-97
44	Rob Andrew	Newcastle	1997-98
44	Charlie Hodgson	Sale	2001-02

MOST PENALTIES

EVOLUTION OF RECORD

31	Dusty Hare	Leicester	1987-88
41	Jez Harris	Leicester	1993-94
56	Mark Tainton	Bristol	1994-95
64	John Liley	Leicester	1995-96
77	John Schuster	Harlequins	1998-99
83	Barry Everitt	London Irish	2001-02

ALL-TIME RECORDS

83	Barry Everitt	London Irish	2001-02
77	John Schuster	Harlequins	1998-99
68	Braam van Straatan	Leeds Tykes	2002-03
66	Jarod Cunningham	Lon Irish	1999-00
65	Jason Strange	Bristol	2005-06
64	John Liley	Leicester	1995-96
64	Ludovic Mercier	Gloucester	2001-02
63	T Stimpson	Leicester	1999-00
62	Gareth Rees	Wasps	1996-97
62	Simon Mannix	Gloucester	1999-00
62	Paul Burke	Harlequins	2001-02
62	Glen Jackson	Saracens	2008-09

120

ALL TIME RECORDS

MATCH RECORDS

MOST PENALTIES

EVOLUTION OF RECORD
6	Dusty Hare	Leicester v Rosslyn P.	19.11.88
7	David Pears	Quins v Rosslyn P.	07.12.91
8	John Liley	Leicester v Bristol	28.10.95
9	Thierry Lacroix	Saracens v Wasps	07.11.99

ALL-TIME RECORDS
9	Thierry Lacroix	Saracens v Wasps	07.11.99
9	Simon Mannix	Gloucester v Harlequins	23.09.00
9	Luke Smith	Saracens v Gloucester	08.09.01
9	Alex King	Wasps v Newcastle	11.11.01
9	Braam Van Straatan	Leeds v London Irish	08.09.02
8	John Liley	Leicester v Bristol	28.10.95
8	Jarrod Cunningham	London Irish v Bristol	10.09.00
8	Tim Stimpson	Leicester v Gloucester	02.12.00
8	Barry Everitt	London Irish v Bath	10.04.02
8	Jonny Wilkinson	Newcastle v Lon Wasps	01.09.02
8	Andy Goode	Leicester v Sale	28.01.06
7	David Pears	Quins v Rosslyn P.	07.12.91
7	Jez Harris	Leicester v Bristol	11.12.93
7	Rob Andrew	Wasps v Orrell	11.12.93
7	Jez Harris	Leicester v Gloucester	29.01.94
7	Mark Tainton	Bristol v Leicester	05.11.94
7	John Liley	Leicester v Bath	07.09.96
7	Simon Mannix	Sale v Northampton	08.03.97
7	Paul Grayson	N'hampton v Richmond	08.03.97
7	Shane Howarth	Sale v Wasps	18.04.98
7	Joel Stransky	Leicester v Lon Irish	31.02.99
7	Steven Vile	W Hart'pool v Richmond	17.04.99
7	Tim Stimpson	Leicester v Newcastle	02.05.99
7	Tim Stimpson	Leicester v Gloucester	08.04.00
7	Paul Grayson	Northampton v Leicester	29.04.00
7	Nicky Little	Sale v Bath	19.08.00
7	Tim Stimpson	Leicester v Lon. Wasps	18.11.00
7	Barry Everitt	Lon. Irish v Harlequins	19.11.00
7	Kevin Sorrell	Saracens v Harlequins	17.12.00
7	Barry Everitt	London Irish v Bristol	24.02.01
7	Paul Burke	Harlequins v Lon Irish	01.09.01
7	Barry Everitt	Lon Irish v Leeds	09.09.01
7	Paul Burke	Harlequins v Wasps	22.09.01
7	Alex King	Wasps v Leicester	31.03.02
7	Barry Everitt	Lon Irish v Newcastle	08.05.02
7	Oliver Barkley	Bath v London Irish	01.09.02
7	Felipe Contepomi	Bristol v London Wasps	08.09.02
7	Tim Stimpson	Leicester v Newcastle	21.09.02
7	Glen Jackson	Saracens v Northampton	05.11.05
7	Charlie Hodgson	Sale v Bristol	08.01.06
7	Andy Goode	Leicester v Lon Irish	08.01.06
7	Matt Burke	Newcastle v Leicester	24.02.06
7	Barry Everitt	London Irish v Newcastle	22.09.06
7	Olly Barkley	Bath v Gloucester	07.04.07
7	Jason Strange	Bristol v Worcester	03.05.08

DIVISION ONE — PREMIERSHIP

MOST POINTS

EVOLUTION OF RECORD
21	Ian Aitchison	Waterloo v Sale	02.01.88
23	Jamie Salmon	Quins v Waterloo	27.02.88
24	Dusty Hare	Leicester v Rosslyn P.	19.11.88
26	John Liley	Leicester v Bedford	23.09.89
27	David Pears	Quins v Bedford	14.10.89
28	Martin Strett	Orrell v Rosslyn P.	21.03.92
31	John Liley	Leicester v Rosslyn P.	21.03.92
32	Niall Woods	Lon. Irish v Harlequins	25.04.98
32	Tim Stimpson	Leicester v Newcastle	21.09.02

The ALL-TIME RECORDS can be found overleaf.

MOST TRIES

EVOLUTION OF RECORD
3	Peter Shillingford	Moseley v Wasps	05.02.88
4	Gary Hartley	Nottingham v Bedford	18.11.89
5	Kenny Logan	Wasps v Orrell	22.03.97
6	Ryan Constable	Saracens v Bedford	16.04.00

The ALL-TIME RECORDS can be found overleaf.

MOST DROP GOALS

ALL-TIME RECORD
3	John Steele	Northampton v Wasps	23.09.91
3	Jez Harris	Leicester v Wasps	23.11.91
3	Jez Harris	Leicester v Bath	15.04.95
3	Matthew McCarthy	Orrell v W. Hartlepool	07.12.96
3	Mark Mapletoft	Lon Irish v Northampton	27.12.04

MOST CONVERSIONS

EVOLUTION OF RECORD
10	Stuart Barnes	Bath v Bedford	13.01.90
13	Rich Butland	Richmond v Bedford	17.05.99

ALL-TIME RECORDS
13	Rich Butland	Richmond v Bedford	17.05.99
11	Andy Goode	Leicester v Newcastle	19.02.05
10	Stuart Barnes	Bath v Bedford	13.01.90
10	Andy Goode	Leicester v Rotherham	01.05.04
9	Paul Challinor	Quins v W. Hartlepool	23.03.96
9	Olly Barkley	Bath v Saracens	03.05.08
8	Martin Strett	Orrell v Rosslyn P.	28.04.90
8	Will Carling	Quins v Orrell	05.10.96
8	Mike Catt	Bath v Sale	26.04.97
8	Niall Woods	Lon. Irish v Harlequins	25.04.98
8	Mike Catt	Bath v London Scottish	16.05.99
8	Alex King	Wasps v Bedford	26.03.00

121

ALL TIME RECORDS
DIVISION ONE
MOST TRIES IN A MATCH

6	Ryan Constable	Saracens v Bedford	16.04.00
5	Kenny Logan	Wasps v Orrel	22.03.97
	Lesley Vainkolo	Leeds Carnegie v Gloucester	16.09.07
4	Gary Hartley	Nottingham v Bedford	18.11.89
	Tony Swift	Bath v Bedford	13.01.90
	Jeremy Guscott	Bath v Bedford	13.01.90
	Paul Hamer	Orrell v Rugby	13.03.93
	Tony Underwood	Leicester v Newcastle Gosforth	12.03.94
	Daren O'Leary	Harlequins v Gloucester	31.08.96
	Tom Beim	Sale v Bristol	09.11.97
	Niall Woods	London Irish v Northampton	05.01.99
	Elton Moncrieff	Gloucester v Bedford	06.05.00
	Geordan Murphy	Leicester v Saracens	24.02.01
	Tom May	Newcastle Falcons v Rotherham	09.11.03
	Sean Lamont	Northampton v Saracens	18.02.06
	Edward Thrower	London Wasps v Bath	12.11.06

3 TRIES IN A MATCH

Peter Shillingford, Moseley v Wasps, 05.02.88; Mark Charles, Leicester v Sale, 26.03.88; Andrew Harriman, Harlequins v Nottingham, 01.04.88; Simon Smith, Wasps v Coventry, 13.04.88; Andrew Harriman, Harlequins v Sale , 23.04.88. Jeremy Guscott, Bath v Moseley, 12.11.88; Mark Bailey, Wasps v Moseley, 19.11.88. John Liley, Leicester v Bedford, 23.09.89; Mike Wedderburn, Harlequins v Bedford, 14.10.89; Mark Bailey, Wasps v Gloucester, 14.10.89; Derrick Morgan, Gloucester v Rosslyn Park, 11.11.89; Jonathan Callard, Bath v Bedford, 13.01.90; Chris Gerard, Leicester v Moseley, 13.01.90; Paul Manley, Orrell v Rosslyn Park, 31.03.90. Dewi Morris, Orrell v Liverpool St H, 13.10.90; Dewi Morris, Orrell v Northampton, 27.10.90; Rory Underwood, Leicester v Northampton, 21.01.91; Andrew Harriman, Harlequins v Bristol, 30.03.91; Will Carling, Harlequins v Bristol, 30.03.91; Graham Childs , Wasps v Liverpool StH, 20.04.91; Rob Andrew, Wasps v Bristol, 27.04.91; Rory Underwood, Leicester v Moseley, 27.04.91. Steve Hackney, Leicester v Lon. Irish, 04.01.92; Tony Swift, Bath v Leicester, 11.01.92; Rory Underwood, Leicester v Rosslyn Park, 21.03.92; Mike Lloyd, Bristol v Rugby, 28.03.92; Martin Pepper, Nottingham v Rosslyn Park, 04.04.92; Chris Oti, Wasps v Bristol, 25.04.92. Stuart Barnes, Bath v W. Hartlepool, 27.03.93; Derek Eves, Bristol v Rugby, 22.03.93. Ian Wynn, Orrell v Wasps, 30.04.94. Simon Morris, Gloucester v W. Hartlepool, 17.09.94; Damian Hopley, Wasps v Sale , 15.10.94. Jeremy Guscott, Bath v Bristol, 14.10.95; Graeme Smith, Orrell v Wasps, 28.10.95; Rob Kitchen, Harlequins v Bristol, 06.01.96; Graeme Smith, Orrell v Saracens, 13.01.96; Aadel Kardooni, Leicester v W. Hartlepool, 17.02.96; Spencer Bromley, Harlequins v Sale, 30.03.96; Aadel Kardooni, Leicester v Sale , 17.04.96. Michael Corcoran, Harlequins v Lon. Irish, 14.09.96; Adedayo Adebayo, Bath v Lon. Irish, 05.10.96; Huw Harries, Harlequins v Orrell, 05.10.96; Mike Lloyd, Gloucester v W. Hartlepool, 18.01.97; Jonathan Sleightholme, Bath v Northampton, 19.01.97; Jonathan Sleightholme, Bath v Lon. Irish, 08.03.97; Domonic Chapman, Richmond v Bristol, 10.04.98; Justin Bishop, Lon. Irish v Harlequins, Harlequins v W. Hartlepool, 22.03.97; Tom Beim, Sale v W. Hartlepool, 05.04.97; Andy Nicol, Bath v Gloucester, 30.04.97; Richard Wallace, Saracens v Lon. Irish, 30.04.97. David Rees, Sale v Bristol, 09.11.97; Gary Armstrong, Newcastle v Bristol, 27.12.97; Jim Naylor, Newcastle v Lon. Irish, 11.01.98; Eric Peters, Bath v Gloucester, 11.02.98; Richard Wallace, Saracens v Bristol, 14.02.98; Harvey Thorneycroft, Northampton v Bristol, 14.03.98; Will Greenwood, Leicester v Richmond, 28.03.98; Domonic Chapman, Richmond v Bristol, 10.04.98; Justin Bishop, Lon. Irish v Harlequins, 25.04.98. Chris Catling, Gloucester v Newcastle, 17.10.98; Darragh O'Mahoney, Bedford v Richmond, 31.10.98; Tony Underwood, Saracens v Saracens, 31.10.98; Pat Lam, Northampton v Sale, 2.1.99; Tony Diprose, Saracens v W. Hartlepool, 13.2.99; Iain Balshaw, Bath v Saracens, 28.3.99; Richard Todd, London Irish v Bath, 17.4.99; Gary Armstrong, Newcastle v Richmond, 21.4.99; Darragh O'Mahoney, Bedford v W. Hartlepool, 2.5.99; Brian Cusack, Richmond v Bedford, 16.5.99; Mel Deane, Richmond v Bedford, 16.5.99; Neil Back, Leicester v W. Hartlepool, 16.5.99. Shaun Berne, Bath v Gloucester, 9.10.99; Josh Lewsey, Wasps v Bedford, 23.3.00; Darragh O'Mahoney, Saracens v Harlequins, 24.4.00; Rob Henderson, Wasps v Sale, 30.4.00; Neil Back, Leicester v Bath, 21.5.00. Frank Schisano, Bristol v Rotherham, 02.09.00; Rob Henderson, London Wasps v Gloucester, 17.09.00; Dan Luger, Saracens v Rotherham, 24.09.00; Steve Hanley, Sale v Harlequins, 02.12.00; Kenny Logan, London Wasps v Rotherham, 01.04.01; Rob Thirlby, Bath v Rotherham, 14.03.01; Tom Voyce, Bath v Rotherham, 14.04.01 ; Mike Catt, Bath v London Irish, 14.03.01. James Daniel-Simpson, Gloucester v Bath, 04.05.02; Neil Back, Leicester v Leeds, 19.04.02; Martin Shaw, Sale v Bristol, 13.04.02. Marcel Garvey, Gloucester v Bristol, 21.09.02; Brendon Daniel, Bristol v Newcastle 01.12.02; Simon Shaw, London Wasps v Saracens, 16.03.03; James Forrester, Gloucester v Bristol, 16.03.03. George Chuter, Leicester v Rotherham, 01.05.04; Mark Cueto, Sale v Newcastle, 23.04.04; Steve Hanley, Sale v Gloucester, 26.03.04; Fraser Waters, Sale v Wasps, 10.10.03; Tom May, Newcastle v Gloucester. 05.10.03; Ugo Monye, Rotherham v Harlequins, 20.09.03 Chris Jones, Sale v Worcester, 24.9.04; Tom Varndell, Leicester v Worcester, 13.11.04; Matthew Burke, Newcastle v Leeds, 14.11.04; Tom Voyce, London Wasps v Northampton, 20.2.05; Tom Varndell, Leicester v Wasps, 22.04.06; Tom Voyce, Wasps v London Irish, 30.04.05; Anthony Elliott, Newcastle v Leeds, 6.05.06; David Strettle, Harlequins v Newcastle, 01.01.07; Matt Banahan, Bath v Leeds, 22.02.07; Tom Varndell, Harlequins v Leicester, 06.01.08; Francisco Leonelli Morey, Saracens v Leeds, 30.03.08; Tom Cheeseman, Worcester v Bath, 19.04.08; Akapusi Qera, Gloucester v Leeds, 19.04.08; Francisco Leonelli Morey, Saracens v London Wasps, 20.04.08; Tom Voyce, Leeds v London Wasps, 10.05.08

2008-09
3 TRIES IN A MATCH

Iain Balshaw	Gloucester v Newcastle Falcons	30.09.08	
Andrew Higgins	Worcester v Bath		14.02.09
Nick Easter	Harlequins v Worcester		01.04.09

DIVISION ONE　　　　　　　　　　　ALL TIME RECORDS
MOST POINTS IN A MATCH

32	Niall Woods	London Irish v Harlequins	25.04.98
	Tim Stimpson	Leicester Tigers v Newcastle	21.09.02
31	John Liley	Leicester v Rosslyn Park	21.03.92
	David Walder	Newcastle v Saracens	26.11.00
	Tim Stimpson	Leicester v Saracens	24.02.01
	Felipe Contepomi	Bristol v Northampton	16.04.01
	Braam van Straatan	Leeds v London Irish	08.09.02
	Olly Barkley	Bath v Saracens	03.05.08
30	Steven Vile	West Hartlepool v Richmond	17.04.99
	Ryan Constable	Saracens v Bedford	16.04.00
	Felipe Contepomi	Bristol v London Wasps	08.02.03
	Andy Goode	Leicester Tigers v Rotherham	01.05.04
29	Thomas Castaignede	Saracens v Rotherham	24.09.00
	Kenny Logan	London Wasps v Sale	14.04.01
	Jonny Wilkinson	Newcastle v London Wasps	23.09.00
	Alex King	London Wasps v Leeds Tykes	18.11.01
	Contepomi, Felipe	Bristol v Leeds Tykes	23.09.01
	Luke Smith	Saracens v Gloucester	08.09.01
28	Martin Strett	Orrell v Rosslyn Park	28.04.90
	John Liley	Leicester v Bristol	28.10.95
	Gavin Johnson	Saracens v London Scottish	26.09.98
	John Schuster	Harlequins v Bath	21.11.98
	Steven Vile	West Hartlepool v Gloucester	14.03.99
	Simon Mannix	Gloucester v Northampton	16.05.99
	Kenny Logan	London Wasps v Rotherham	01.04.01
	Paul Burke	Harlequins v Saracens	16.11.01
	Tim Stimpson	Leicester Tigers v Bath	22.09.01
	Andy Goode	Leicester Tigers v London Wasps	08.05.04
	Andy Goode	Leicester v Newcastle	19.02.05
27	David Pears	Harlequins v Bedford	14.10.89
	Mark Mapletoft	Gloucester v Leicester	01.02.98
	Niall Woods	London Irish v Northampton	05.01.99
	Thierry Lacroix	Saracens v Wasps	07.11.99
	Simon Mannix	Gloucester v Harlequins	23.09.00
	Jarrod Cunningham	London Irish v Bristol	10.09.00
	Alex King	London Wasps v Leicester Tigers	31.03.02
	Charles Hodgson	Leeds Tykes v Sale	25.11.01
	Alex King	London Wasps v Newcastle Falcons	11.11.01
	Barry Everitt	London Irish v Leeds Tykes	09.09.01
	Oliver Barklay	Bath v Rotherham	11.10.03
	Andy Goode	Leicester Tigers v Sale	28.01.06

26

John Liley, Leicester v Bedford, 23.09.89;
Paul Grayson, Northampton v Bristol, 02.10.93;
Andy Lee, Saracens v West Hartlepool, 14.10.95;
Rob Liley, Leicester v London Irish, 31.10.96;
Simon Mannix, Sale v Northampton, 09.03.97;
Paul Grayson, Northampton v London Irish, 13.12.97;
Kenny Logan, Wasps v London Irish, 19.09.98;
Rich Butland, Richmond v Bedford, 16.05.99;
Thierry Lacroix, Saracens v Leicester, 05.12.99;
Jonny Wilkinson, Newcastle v Gloucester, 30.04.00;
Niki Little, Sale v Bristol, 06.09.00;
Andy Goode, Saracens v Northampton, 28.09.02

Stuart Barnes, Bath v West Hartlepool, 27.03.93;
Mark Tainton, Bristol v Leicester, 05.12.94;
Paul Challinor, Harlequins v West Hartlepool, 23.03.96;
John Stabler, West Hartlepool v London Irish, 28.12.96;
Mike Catt, Bath v Sale, 26.04.97;
Thierry Lacroix, Harlequins v Wasps, 13.12.97;
Mike Catt, Bath v London Scottish, 15.05.99;
Jarrod Cunningham, London Irish v Newcastle, 02.10.00;
Kenny Logan, Wasps v Saracens, 13.02.00;
Tim Stimpson, Leicester v Gloucester, 02.12.01;
Barry Everitt, London Irish v Bath, 10.04.02;
Charlie Hodgson. Sale v Bristol, 08.01.06

ALL TIME RECORDS

DIVISION ONE

MOST POINTS IN A SEASON

Points	Player	Club	Season	Tries	Cons.	Pens.	D.G.
343	Barry Everitt	London Irish	2001-02	2	30	83	8
334	Ludovic Mercier	Gloucester	2001-02	2	48	64	12
331	John Schuster	Harlequins	1998-99	5	36	77	1
324	Jarrod Cunningham	London Irish	99-2000	6	46	66	
321	Tim Stimpson	Leicester	99-2000	5	52	63	1
318	Gavin Johnson	Saracens	1998-99	8	52	58	
306	Jonny Wilkinson	Newcastle	1998-99	9	51	53	
294	Mike Catt	Bath	1998-99	7	50	53	
291	Gareth Rees	Wasps	1996-97	3	45	62	
282	Simon Mannix	Gloucester	99-2000	3	36	62	3
282	Kenny Logan	London Wasps	2000-01	10	47	46	-
280	Thierry Lacroix	Saracens	99-2000	3	47	55	2
279	Michael Lynagh	Saracens	1997-98	5	37	58	2
275	Mark Mapletoft	Gloucester	1997-98	5	35	58	2
273	Charles Hodgson	Sale	2001-02	7	44	48	2
272	John Liley	Leicester	1995-96	5	26	64	1
272	Glen Jackson	Saracens	2006-07	5	35	57	2
269	Mark Mapletoft	Gloucester	1996-97	6	25	58	5
266	Andy Goode	Leicester Tigers/Saracens	2003-04	6	43	46	4
263	Kenny Logan	Wasps	1998-99	8	35	51	
260	Tim Stimpson	Leicester	2000-01	7	27	57	-
259	Andy Goode	Leicester Tigers	2004-05	3	50	42	6
258	Paul Burke	Harlequins	2001-02	3	21	62	5
255	Ludovic Mercier	Gloucester	2002-03	6	42	45	2
253	Joel Stransky	Leicester	1997-98	5	39	47	3
253	Gareth Rees	Wasps	1997-98	1	34	57	3
252	Braam van Straatan	Leeds Tykes	2002-03	-	24	68	-
246	Shane Howarth	Sale	1998-99	9	42	37	
246	Alex King	London Wasps	2002-03	1	35	52	5
244	Jason Strange	Bristol	2005-06	1	22	65	-
240	Steven Vile	W Hartlepool	1998-99	5	28	52	1
239	Glen Jackson	Saracens	2008-09	1	81	62	4
238	Paul Grayson	Northampton	2001-02	1	31	55	2
238	Barry Everitt	London Irish	2002-03	3	17	56	7
238	Glen Jackson	Saracens	2005-06	3	32	51	2
237	Niall Woods	London Irish	1997-98	8	34	43	
236	Jonathan Callard	Bath	1995-96	3	43	45	
234	Shane Drahm	Northampton Saints	2003-04	5	37	45	
233	Shane Drahm	Worcester	2005-06	3	25	52	4
226	Rob Andrew	Newcastle	1997-98	6	44	35	1
224	Jonathan Callard	Bath	1996-97	4	51	34	
224	Shane Howarth	Sale	1997-98	4	39	41	1
221	Felipe Contepomi	Bristol	2001-02	9	25	40	2
219	Paul Grayson	Northampton	2000-01	1	20	58	-
219	Oliver Barklay	Bath	2003-04	5	22	50	
215	Niall Woods	London Irish	1998-99	12	25	35	
215	Jonny Wilkinson	Newcastle	2001-02	2	32	44	3
213	Ludovic Mercier	Gloucester	2005-06	2	25	49	2
212	Tim Stimpson	Leicester	2001-02	5	29	43	-
212	Butch James	Bath	2008-09	2	35	44	-

124

DIVISION ONE   ALL TIME RECORDS

TEAM RECORDS

Highest score:	**106**	Bedford 12 Richmond 106. 16.5.99
Highest aggregate:	**118**	As above
Highest score by a losing side:	**41**	London Irish 52 W Hartlepool 41. 28.12.96
Highest scoring draw:	**38**	Bath 38 v Sale 38 27.4.96
Most consecutive wins:	**17**	Bath 1993-94 through 1994-95
Most consecutive defeats:	**22**	Rotherham 2003-04
Most points for in a season:	**863**	Bath 1996-97
Least points for in a season:	**70**	Bedford 1989-90
Most points against in a season:	**1007**	West Hartlepool 1998-99
Least points against in a season:	**95**	Orrell 1991-92
Most tries for in a season:	**116**	Bath 1996-97
Most tries against in a season:	**134**	W Hartlepool 1998-99
Least tries for in a season:	**8**	Waterloo 1988-89
Least tries against in a season:	**6**	Bath 1988-89, Wasps 1992-93
Most conversions for in a season:	**77**	Bath 1996-97
Most conversions against in a season:	**69**	Orrell 1996-97
Most penalties for in a season:	**87**	Harlequins 1998-99
Most penalties against in a season:	**73**	Sale 1998-99
Least penalties for in a season:	**7**	Bedford 1989-90
Least penalties against in a season:	**11**	Harlequins 1987-88
Most drop goals for in a season:	**13**	Leicester 1994-95 & Harlequins 1995-96
Most drop goals against in a season:	**8**	Wasps 1993-94 & 1995-96

INDIVIDUAL RECORDS

Most points in a season:	**343**	Barry Everitt (London Irish) 2001-02
Most tries in a season:	**17**	Dominic Chapman (Richmond) 1997-98
Most conversions in a season:	**52**	Gavin Johnson (Saracens) 1998-99 & Tim Stimpson (Leicester) 1990-00
Most penalties in a season:	**83**	Barry Everitt (London Irish) 2001-02
Most drop goals in a season:	**13**	Jez Harris (Leicester) 1994-95
Most points in a match:	**32**	Niall Woods, *London Irish* v Harlequins 25.4.98
		Tim Stimpson, *Leicester* v Newcastle 21.09.02
Most tries in a match:	**6**	Ryan Constable, Bedford v *Saracens* 16.4.00
Most conversions in a match:	**13**	Rich Butland, Bedford v *Richmond* 16.5.99
Most penalties in a match:	**9**	Thierry Lacroix, *Saracens* v Wasps 7.11.99
		Simon Mannix, *Glocester* v Harlequins 23.09.00
		Luke Smith, *Saracens* v Gloucester 8.9.01
		Alex King, *London Wasps* v Newcastle 11.11.01
		Braam van Straatan, *Leeds Tykes* v Lon Irish 28.9.02
Most drop goals in a match:	**3**	John Steele, *Northampton* v Wasps 23.3.91
		Jez Harris, *Leicester* v Wasps 23.11.91
		David Pears, *Harlequins* v Wasps 16.9.95
		Matthew McCarthy, *Orrell* v W Hartlepool 7.12.96

125

Support the RFU Injured Players Foundation

RFU Injured Players Foundation

The Foundation helps and supports players from all levels of the game who suffer injuries whilst playing rugby which may cause permanent and severe disability.

Injury prevention

The RFU Injured Players Foundation works with a number of partners to produce preventative or promotional resources that could help to reduce rugby related injuries as well as inform future law changes.

We have a number of current research projects including:

- Investigation of the cause of injuries within youth community and academy rugby to determine if the occurrence and severity is comparable between different ages and also levels of participation.

- A detailed injury surveillance system has been set up to collect injury data from across the community game. This will enable us to monitor trends in injury over time at all levels of the game. The 09/10 season will collect data from 40 clubs and the numbers of teams involved will increase year on year.

- We are supporting a masters research project investigating the awareness of concussion and the guidelines available for the management of this injury. This will inform us if more promotional and educational work is required to ensure players, coaches, schools and clubs are fully aware of the signs, symptoms and necessary practice involved with concussion injuries.

- We are also working with the IRB and other National Governing Bodies to examine catastrophic injuries which occur in Rugby Union throughout the world. By sharing information and resources we can get a much clearer picture of how and why these injuries happen and investigate ways to reduce their occurrence.

**Visit www.rfuipf.org.uk
to discover more and see how you can help**

CHAMPIONSHIP

2008-2009 SEASON   Review & Statistics   128-137

2009-10 CLUBS

Club	Page
Bedford Blues	138
Birmingham Solihull	144
Bristol	150
Coventry	156
Doncaster	162
Exeter	168
London Welsh	174
Moseley	180
Nottingham	186
Penzance Newlyn	192
Plymouth Albion	198
Rotherham Titans	204

RECORDS SECTION
currently Championship
(previously National 1 & Division 2)

Roll of Honour	210
Year by Year Records	212

ALL-TIME RECORDS

All Time Records		214
Most Tries	in a Match	216
Most Points	in a Match	217
	in a Season	218
Team & Individual Records		219

FIXTURES 2009-10

	Bedford	Birmingham	Bristol	Coventry	Doncaster	Exeter	London Welsh	Moseley	Nottingham	Penzance	Plymouth Alb.	Rotherham
Bedford		10/10	26/09	12/09	20/02	31/10	26/12	14/11	16/01	30/01	12/12	09/01
Birmingham & Solihull	02/01		12/09	14/11	30/01	17/10	12/12	31/10	19/12	16/01	20/02	03/10
Bristol	19/12	05/12		31/10	16/01	03/10	05/09	17/10	14/11	02/01	30/01	19/09
Coventry	04/12	05/02	22/01		01/01	18/09	06/11	02/10	16/10	18/12	23/10	04/09
Doncaster	05/09	07/11	24/10	10/10		05/12	23/01	19/12	03/10	19/09	09/01	06/02
Exeter	23/01	09/01	26/12	12/12	12/09		10/10	20/02	30/01	14/11	26/09	24/10
London Welsh	03/10	19/09	20/02	30/01	31/10	02/01		16/01	05/12	17/10	14/11	19/12
Moseley	06/02	23/01	09/01	26/12	26/09	05/09	24/10		19/09	05/12	10/10	07/11
Nottingham	24/10	26/09	06/02	09/01	26/12	07/11	12/09	12/12		06/09	23/01	10/10
Penzance/Newlyn	07/11	24/10	10/10	26/09	12/12	06/02	09/01	12/09	05/09		26/12	23/01
Plymouth Albion	19/09	05/09	07/11	16/01	17/10	19/12	06/02	02/01	31/10	03/10		05/12
Rotherham Titans	17/10	26/12	12/12	20/02	14/11	16/01	26/09	30/01	02/01	31/10	12/09	

2008-09 LEAGUE TABLE

		P	W	D	L	F	A	PD	Bonus Pts 4T	<7	Pts
1	Leeds Carnegie	30	28	0	2	1238	376	862	20	1	133
2	Exeter	30	23	2	5	1077	453	624	20	3	119
3	Bedford	30	23	0	7	892	472	420	17	2	111
4	Nottingham	30	22	0	8	973	499	474	16	4	106
5	Doncaster	30	21	2	7	895	571	324	14	3	105
6	London Welsh	30	19	0	11	788	611	177	11	6	91
7	Cornish Pirates	30	16	1	13	743	578	165	11	5	82
8	Moseley	30	13	0	17	814	782	32	13	8	73
9	Coventry	30	14	0	16	639	712	-73	11	5	72
10	Rotherham	30	15	1	14	794	775	19	9	3	70
11	Plymouth Albion	30	13	2	15	607	669	-62	7	3	66
12	Esher	30	12	1	17	676	830	-154	9	2	61
13	Sedgley Park	30	6	0	24	458	1206	-748	6	4	34
14	Newbury	30	4	2	24	419	1047	-628	2	5	27
15	Otley	30	3	1	26	418	1118	-700	3	6	21
16	Manchester	30	2	0	28	433	1165	-732	4	5	17

2007-08 RESULTS MATRIX

	Bedford	Cornish Pirates	Coventry	Doncaster	Esher	Exeter	Leeds carnegie	London Welsh	Manchester	Moseley	Newbury	Nottingham	Otley	Plymouth	Rotherham	Sedgley Park
Bedford		6-26	23-9	42-20	50-8	23-26	27-24	32-33	62-0	17-15	53-12	23-16	37-12	37-9	32-18	53-7
Cornish Pirates	5-6		32-14	23-33	7-16	23-32	23-25	8-10	25-10	19-15	48-5	20-31	55-13	30-14	27-32	56-14
Coventry	3-26	16-0		26-20	33-8	35-28	11-15	36-30	29-18	27-10	31-7	22-37	48-3	6-7	31-32	29-24
Doncaster	50-21	24-24	34-22		50-25	29-34	27-12	26-13	52-10	41-17	37-9	25-14	36-15	28-23	28-22	42-5
Esher	13-18	3-19	27-18	10-23		8-46	8-52	21-32	36-19	23-17	49-18	3-25	48-16	31-28	32-59	76-10
Exeter	40-21	38-7	45-8	9-9	12-12		13-14	10-3	40-5	70-10	44-5	29-18	80-17	29-0	76-21	71-5
Leeds Carnegie	19-8	33-9	57-5	28-13	47-21	18-16		35-10	57-0	53-20	57-14	34-19	58-14	49-19	28-3	66-0
London Welsh	23-32	23-38	21-23	31-16	43-19	16-21	0-38		57-10	50-37	40-12	30-36	39-25	22-9	27-17	60-0
Manchester	5-25	6-12	24-41	23-39	28-40	19-26	0-104	14-19		21-50	35-17	23-49	14-15	5-31	35-54	35-51
Moseley	23-26	26-37	34-12	12-19	22-13	32-24	26-31	9-15	48-7		36-9	24-26	36-26	50-32	43-21	51-17
Newbury	0-34	10-39	14-10	17-50	8-14	20-37	12-89	9-20	26-6	12-30		16-23	26-20	19-11	21-23	27-30
Nottingham	15-7	23-19	55-0	18-9	36-14	14-15	12-19	30-24	57-8	44-17	48-3		95-5	43-19	33-13	32-24
Otley	17-23	25-31	13-32	16-27	12-18	0-69	10-66	6-9	29-18	0-20	12-12	3-43		16-31	7-39	14-7
Plymouth Albion	14-31	20-12	13-5	21-18	36-14	14-41	6-17	24-25	47-6	26-17	17-17	26-25	23-15		20-33	31-7
Rotherham	10-33	28-34	28-27	26-29	19-40	35-21	24-41	7-20	15-13	47-23	62-5	20-6	42-13	10-10		22-0
Sedgley Park	0-64	27-35	27-30	3-41	27-26	12-35	7-52	11-43	12-16	17-44	42-37	5-50	36-29	11-27	20-12	

2008-09 LEADING SCORERS

MOST POINTS

			T	C	P	DG
298	Jamie Lennard	Doncaster	5	57	46	7
261	David Jackson	Nottingham	18	51	23	-
228	Gareth Steenson	Exeter	3	60	31	-
224	Neil Hallett	Esher	3	55	33	-
216	James Pritchard	Bedford	4	53	30	-
211	Alberto Di Bernardo	Leeds Carnegie	4	64	21	-
180	Mark Harris	London Welsh	7	32	24	3
178	Rhys Jones	Cornish Pirates	3	26	32	5
176	Tim Taylor	Nottingham	11	32	19	-
173	Michael Whitehead	Rotherham	7	27	27	1
158	Aled Thomas	London Welsh	5	29	23	2
158	William Twelvetrees	Bedford	18	16	12	-
143	Kieran Hallett	Plymouth Albion	2	23	27	2
135	Tristan Roberts	Moseley	6	30	15	-
134	Myles Dorrian	Coventry	7	21	18	1
130	Phil Jones	Sedgley Park	7	28	13	-
127	Richard Vasey	Moseley	1	28	18	4
121	Tom Barlow	Rotherham	1	28	20	-
121	Gareth Wynne	Manchester	3	11	28	-
118	Jason Strange	Leeds Carnegie	1	40	11	-
104	Tom Rhodes	Otley	-	13	26	-

MOST TRIES

			First Half	Second Half	Home	Away Sub
18	David Jackson	Nottingham	6	12	11	7
18	William Twelvetrees	Bedford	9	9	10	8
17	James Rodwell	Moseley	7	10	12	5
16	Sean Marsden	Exeter	10	6	10	6
16	Jon Feeley	Rotherham	6	10	6	10
16	Matthew Jess	Exeter	4	12	10	6
16	Douglas Flockhart	Esher	7	9	7	9
15	Leigh Hinton	Leeds Carnegie	7	8	7	8
15	Eric Claasans	Rotherham	10	5	7	8
15	Paul McKenzie	Exeter	7	8	10	5
14	Paul Sampson	London Welsh	7	7	8	6
14	Ian Davey	Bedford	7	7	9	5
14	Peter Swatkins	Sedgley Park	8	6	8	6
14	Jack Cobden	Nottingham	10	4	9	5
13	Wes Davies	Doncaster	4	9	10	3
13	Tom Biggs	Leeds Carnegie	5	8	6	7
13	Karl Dickson	Bedford	6	7	6	7
13	Marika Vakacegu	Cornish Pirates	5	8	9	4
13	Josh Drauniniu	Exeter	5	8	6	7
12	George Lowe	Esher	7	5	4	8

MOST PENALTIES
46 Jamie Lennard Doncaster

MOST CONVERSIONS
64 Alberto di Bernardo Leeds Carnegie

MOST DROP GOALS
7 Jamie Lennard Doncaster

TRIES FOR
By Position

	TOTAL	BACKS	FORWARDS	Full Backs	Wing	Center	Half Backs	Front Row	Second Row	Back Row	Penalty Tries
Bedford	123	88	35	7	42	17	22	6	10	19	0
Cornish Pirates	93	65	28	14	29	7	15	7	4	17	2
Coventry	83	51	32	3	17	14	17	9	4	19	0
Doncaster	102	58	44	7	24	15	12	10	6	28	7
Esher	85	62	23	6	26	21	9	8	4	11	1
Exeter	150	101	49	21	46	22	12	19	9	21	2
Leeds Carnegie	171	110	61	19	48	28	15	18	8	35	5
London Welsh	89	59	30	15	23	12	9	10	5	15	8
Manchester	48	33	15	6	9	11	7	6	4	5	2
Moseley	97	59	38	1	33	19	6	7	9	22	8
Newbury	48	30	18	3	12	6	9	6	3	9	0
Nottingham	127	82	45	21	30	15	16	14	11	20	3
Otley	46	30	16	5	13	8	4	4	5	7	1
Plymouth Albion	64	42	22	8	14	14	6	10	1	11	3
Rotherham	96	65	31	9	31	15	10	4	5	22	4
Sedgley Park	64	50	14	4	24	11	11	2	4	8	0
Totals :	1486	985	501	149	421	235	180	140	92	269	46

TRIES AGAINST
By Position

	TOTAL	BACKS	FORWARDS	Full Backs	Wing	Center	Half Backs	Front Row	Second Row	Back Row	Penalty Tries
Bedford	50	37	13	5	16	9	7	4	2	7	1
Cornish Pirates	57	39	18	9	17	6	7	5	3	10	7
Coventry	91	70	21	10	34	17	9	5	7	9	3
Doncaster	65	48	17	7	20	6	15	5	1	11	1
Esher	107	72	35	12	29	16	15	15	4	16	4
Exeter	52	38	14	4	19	9	6	4	4	6	1
Leeds Carnegie	39	31	8	3	11	12	5	2	3	3	0
London Welsh	69	45	24	9	21	9	6	6	4	14	2
Manchester	170	109	61	13	47	33	16	15	6	40	1
Moseley	102	78	24	11	30	15	22	5	9	10	2
Newbury	138	91	47	12	42	20	17	14	6	27	8
Nottingham	54	40	14	9	14	11	6	4	3	7	0
Otley	149	89	60	13	37	28	11	16	13	31	5
Plymouth Albion	83	43	40	8	16	12	7	9	8	23	2
Rotherham	95	57	38	10	25	11	11	10	1	27	2
Sedgley Park	165	98	67	14	43	21	20	21	18	28	7
Totals :	1486	985	501	149	421	235	180	140	92	269	46

KICKING STRIKE RATE

		Conversions		Penalties		TOTAL	
S/R%	(Minimum 20 attempts)	Att	Suc	Att	Suc	Att	Suc
80.77	Alex Davies (Plymouth Albion)	12	9	14	12	26	21
76.47	Tom Rhodes (Otley)	19	13	32	26	51	39
76.12	Jason Strange (Leeds Carnegie)	54	40	13	11	67	51
76.00	James Brooks (Leeds Carnegie)	25	19	0	0	25	19
75.89	Alberto Di Bernardo (Leeds Carnegie)	84	64	28	21	112	85
75.00	Adam Greendale (Otley)	12	9	8	6	20	15
72.97	Michael Whitehead (Rotherham)	36	27	38	27	74	54
72.58	Tristan Roberts (Moseley)	41	30	21	15	62	45
72.46	Kieran Hallett (Plymouth Albion)	32	23	37	27	69	50
72.34	Ross Laidlaw (Plymouth Albion)	23	17	24	17	47	34
72.00	Ben Stevenson (Newbury)	29	18	21	18	50	36
71.54	Neil Hallett (Esher)	76	55	47	33	123	88
70.83	Matt Riley (Sedgley Park)	12	8	12	9	24	17
70.59	Tom Barlow (Rotherham)	40	28	28	20	68	48
70.55	Jamie Lennard (Doncaster)	83	57	63	46	146	103
70.27	Aled Thomas (London Welsh)	41	29	33	23	74	52
69.64	Myles Dorrian (Coventry)	30	21	26	18	56	39
68.92	Tim Taylor (Nottingham)	47	32	27	19	74	51
68.42	Gareth Steenson (Exeter)	89	60	44	31	133	91
67.89	David Jackson (Nottingham)	72	51	37	23	109	74
67.47	Mark Harris (London Welsh)	45	32	38	24	83	56
66.67	Danny Gray (Exeter)	56	37	7	5	63	42
66.67	Oliver Thomas (Moseley)	16	10	20	14	36	24
66.67	Tom Eaton (Manchester)	12	6	9	8	21	14
66.40	James Pritchard (Bedford)	89	53	36	30	125	83
65.00	Joseph Knowles (Manchester)	9	5	11	8	20	13
64.79	Richard Vasey (Moseley)	44	28	27	18	71	46
62.96	Jonathan West (Rotherham)	22	13	5	4	27	17
60.00	Gareth Griffiths (Newbury)	18	10	32	20	50	30
60.00	Douglas Sanft (Cornish Pirates)	9	7	11	5	20	12
59.09	Gareth Wynne (Manchester)	23	11	43	28	66	39
58.59	Rhys Jones (Cornish Pirates)	48	26	51	32	99	58
58.49	Ronnie McLean (Coventry)	35	19	18	12	53	31
57.75	Phil Jones (Sedgley Park)	46	28	25	13	71	41
56.00	William Twelvetrees (Bedford)	31	16	19	12	50	28
55.56	James Moore (Cornish Pirates)	20	11	7	4	27	15
55.32	Alistair Warnock (Doncaster)	27	13	20	13	47	26

DISCIPLINE RECORD

	SIN BIN			Sin Bin Breakdown								
				Violent Conduct			Professional Foul			RED		
	Total	H	A	Total	H	A	Total	H	A	Total	H	A
Bedford	2	1	1	18	7	11	20	8	12	-		
Cornish Pirates	1	0	1	15	6	9	16	6	10	2	2	0
Coventry	1	0	1	11	2	9	12	2	10	1	1	0
Doncaster	3	1	2	14	3	11	17	4	13	1	0	1
Esher	-			14	4	10	14	4	10	-		
Exeter	1	0	1	12	4	8	13	4	9	1	0	1
Leeds Carnegie	3	2	1	6	3	3	9	5	4	-		
London Welsh	1	0	1	10	2	8	11	2	9	-		
Manchester	4	2	2	12	6	6	16	8	8	-		
Moseley	3	2	1	19	9	10	22	11	11	-		
Newbury	3	3	0	20	9	11	23	12	11	-		
Nottingham	6	2	4	9	4	5	15	6	9	-		
Otley	3	1	2	17	5	12	20	6	14	-		
Plymouth Albion	2	2	0	9	3	6	11	5	6	-		
Rotherham	7	4	3	9	6	3	16	10	6	1	1	0
Sedgley Park	2	1	1	10	5	5	12	6	6	-		
	42	21	21	204	78	126	241	96	145	6	4	2

2008-09 REVIEW

- Leeds Carnegie take the National One title for the second time in three seasons winning by some 14 points. They were also the highest points scorers and had the best defensive record
- Moseley took the most losing bonus points - eight from their 17 defeats
- Sedgley Park conceded the most points, 1206, which is the most ever conceded in this league, although the previous record of 1178 was set by Moseley in only a 26 match season, 2002/03
- Top points scorer was Doncaster's Jamie Lennard with 298 - only good enough for 16th on the all time list
- Lennard dropped seven goals during the season which was one off the division record set by Guy Gregory for Nottingham back in 1992/93
- The top try scorers with 18 were Nottingham's David Jackson and Bedford Blues Will Twelvetrees. This is the lowest total to top the division since Dean Lax scored 18 for Rotherham back in the 1999/00 season
- The two sides promoted from National Two, Otley and Manchester, finished in the bottom two
- Leeds Carnegie kicked a record 130 conversions during the season - 11 more than Newcastle back in the 1996/97 season
- Only two players started all 30 matches during the season, Arthur Brenton, Plymouth Albion second row, and Doug Flockhart, Esher back
- Eight other players started 29 matches and three of them came on in the other match, Nick Flynn, Manchester, Tim Taylor, Nottingham, and Brad Hunt, Rotherham
- Leeds Carnegie wing Tom Biggs was the only player to run in two hat tricks during the season
- The only prop to score a hat trick during the season was the Exeter Chiefs' Chris Budgen whilst in the second row Moseley's Ali Muldowney was the only one to cross the line three times in a match
- Two players had the unwelcome distinction to be on the bench in 27 of their sides 30 matches, hooker Stuart Pearl (Coventry), and prop Tom Mantell (Manchester)
- Five players were sin binned four times and Otley provided two of them, Dan Hyde and Michael McCormish
- The most by a back was three by two players Martin Nutt (Newbury) and Keni Fisilau (Plymouth Albion)
- Rotherham Titans and Bedford Blues used the least number of starters during the season with just 29, and they only used three other players who only appeared as replacements

Leeds Carnegie

- Leeds Carnegie win promotion back to the Premiership at the first attempt just like they did three seasons ago after a five year stint in the top league in English rugby
- With 28 wins and just two defeats they finish with 10 points more than when they won the title three years ago
- They took 20 try bonus points which was the same as the Chiefs
- Argentine fly half Alberto Di Bernardo was again the top points scorer with 211 which was an improvement on last season's 127
- He kicked 64 conversions which was the most in the division but eight short of the club record set by Richard LeBas back in 2000/01
- They also had another player reach 100 points, Jason Strange with 118 which included 40 conversions
- In the try scoring stakes full back Leigh Hinton led the way with 15 which the same as Richard Welding scored when they last won the National One title three seasons ago when he finish top try scorer
- Hinton has now scored 426 points for the club in three seasons in 64 starts and three matches as a replacement
- Hinton holds the unique record off having scored 300 points in a season for three different clubs, Orrell, Bedford Blues and Leeds Carnegie
- Just behind Hinton was winger Tom Biggs with 13, Biggs had been their top try scorer in their last two Premiership campaigns when they were relegated with seven and eight tries respectively
- Biggs is now the all time top try scorer for Leeds Carnegie in league rugby with 39 tries passing the previous record of 29 set by Sateki Tuipulotu, his tries have come from 73 starts and 10 matches as a replacement

Exeter Chiefs

- Exeter Chiefs were again runners up in National One some 14 points behind the Champions and have been runners up in three of the last five seasons
- They collected 20 try bonus points which was the same as Champions Leeds Carnegie and three losing bonus points in their five defeats
- They topped 1000 league points in a season for the first time finishing with 1077 which beat their previous best of 940 back in 2002/03
- Gareth Steenson led the scoring with 228 in his first season at the club, which the third highest total in the division he has now had three different clubs in three seasons and has notched up 779 points from 67 starts and 17 matches as a replacement playing for Rotherham, Cornish Pirates and Exeter Chiefs
- The battle to finish leading try scorer was a close one with three players battling it out and in the end two of them, Sean Marsden and Matthew Jess, finished joint top with 16, one more than Paul McKenzie – last season Jess was leading scorer for Launceston with 17 in this division
- All time leading scorer Tony Yapp ended up playing late in the season and added 20 points to his points tally moving on to 1526
- No 8 Richard Baxter made the most starts with 27, whilst Flanker Tom Johnson and fly half Steenson played in 27 matches
- Prop Chris Budgen was the only player in his position to score a hat trick of tries during the season

Bedford Blues

- Bedford Blues finished in third place some points behind runners up Exeter Chiefs and improved three places on last season and their best finish since being runners up in the 2005/06 season
- Canadian International full back James Pritchard topped the points scoring list for a third successive season and the fifth time in eight years with his 216 points and took his all time Bedford record to 1306 and his League total to 1566 having also scored points for Northampton Saints and Plymouth Albion and averages over 10 points a game with 144 appearances including 139 starts
- He took Andy Finnie's record for career penalties moving onto 205 two more than Finnie's old record
- In the try scoring stakes fly half William Twelvetrees led the way with 18 which also the joint most in the division, and was a new Bedford Blues record for a season, one more than Ben Whetstone scored in 1996/97
- Twelvetrees started most matches, 28 two more than flanker Gregor Gillanders Gillanders did though come on in the other four matches and took part in all 30 league matches
- In matches against the other top four sides they managed two wins and slipped to four defeats, but one of the wins was against the Champions, Leeds Carnegie
- Their 64-0 away win at Sedgley Park was their record biggest away win beating their 60 point win at Fylde back in December 1997
- They finished the season with 10 successive wins after losing at Exeter Chiefs in early January

Nottingham

- They dropped from third last season to fourth this season collecting 10 points less than last season
- They did though score over 150 points more and had a better defensive record
- Full back/wing David Jackson led the way with both points and tries with 261 and 18 respectively
- In the league only Doncaster's Jamie Lennard scored more points than Jackson, and he finished joint top try scorer with Bedford's William Twelvetrees
- Jackson moved passed 600 league points for the club and finished the season with 622 and that is second on the all time list behind Richard Southam's 651
- Jackson is now the all time leading try scorer for the club in the league with 59, 10 more than Richard Lloyd's record
- Fly half Tim Taylor was also in the top ten points scorers in the division with 176 which included a club record 29 points in a match in the home win over Otley and was made up of a try nine conversions and two penalty goals and was four points more than the previous record held by Guy Gregory going back to 1993
- The nine conversions equalled the club record held by Gregory
- They set a new club record for highest score and biggest win with the 95-5 win over Otley in early March
- Had a nine match winning run early season which was a new club record beating the previous record by one

133

2008-09 REVIEW

Doncaster Knights
- Doncaster dropped a place from last season to fifth although with 105 points they had seven more than last season scoring over 100 points more but conceding 20 more
- Jamie Lennard top scored for the club, and the division, with 298 points after his move from Rotherham Titans, just failing to become the third Knights player to score 300 points in a league season after the Liley brothers
- In the try scoring stakes winger Wes Brown led the way with 13 tries which was the same as Donovan van Vuuren scored last season but way off the club record of 25
- Davies took his tally to 30 tries in 66 starts over the last three seasons
- Prop Ngazu Tau took his club record for appearances to 127 plus 18 as a replacement
- Second row Glen Kenworthy started the most matches, 29 and came on as a replacement in the other and has started 58 of the clubs last 60 league matches
- Winger van Vuuren set a new club record for appearances by a back as he moved onto 95, five more than the previous record held by Chris Conway
- In matches against the top four sides they did well with three wins and a draw to go with four defeats

London Welsh
- The Welsh finished in sixth place their best finish since they were fifth in the 2002/03 season and improved one place on last season
- They took six losing bonus points in their 11 defeats which was the second most in the division
- Full back Mark Harris topped scored with 180 points, 22 more than Aled Thomas
- Full back/wing Paul Sampson was top try scorer for the Welsh for the second successive season with 14, three more than he managed last season, it was the best return since Matt Vines scored 17 back in 2000/01 for the club
- In matches against the top four sides in the division they managed just one win and seven defeats with the win coming at Bedford Blues
- They did well on the road and had the fourth best record away from home with 10 wins and five defeats, which was one win more than they managed at Old Deer Park
- Sampson started the most matches for the Welsh with 29 out of 30, three more than any other player, back rower Tom Brown and prop Paul Doran Jones

Cornish Pirates
- The Pirates dropped two places to seventh in the table which was their worst finish in the division since they were 10th six seasons ago in their first season in National One
- They finished nine points behind sixth placed London Welsh and nine points clear of eighth placed Moseley
- Rhys Jones topped scored with 178 points including a division high five drop goals in his first full season of league rugby having previously played for Sale Sharks and Cardiff Blues
- He dropped three goals in the match against Plymouth Albion which was a club record with no Pirates player scoring more than one in a match previously and his five for the season was also a club record
- Full back Marika Vakacegu was the leading try scorer with 13 tries two more than winger Brian Tuohy
- Second row Ben Gulliver started the most matches 28 and came off the bench in the other two to appear in all 30 league games, the only player to do so
- In matches against the top four they were beaten seven times and their only win was away at Bedford 26-6
- Struggled at home and ended the season with a losing record, seven wins and eight defeats whilst on the road they had the fifth best record with nine wins and a draw to go with five defeats

Moseley
- Moseley finished eighth in the table a two place improvement on last season, their best finish in the division since they were seventh back in 1999/00
- They took 13 try bonus points which was the sixth highest in the division
- They also took the most losing bonus points in the division, eight in their 17 defeats
- Their 814 points was their highest ever in a league season
- Tristan Roberts top scored for the club with 135 which was eight more than Richard Vasey
- Ollie Thomas extends his all time club record to 1084 points and improved his record for conversions and penalties to 165 and 218 respectively
- Centre Andy Reay started most matches, 28, one more than prop Nathan Williams who took part in 28 matches coming on as a replacement in another game

134

Moseley cont.
- But it was scrum half Gareth Taylor who took part in the most matches starting 24 and coming on in five more for a total of 29 appearances
- Back Andy Binns increased his club record for appearances to 247 plus 12 as a replacement
- Second row Richard Stott extended his club record for appearances by a forward to 157 plus 25 as a replacement
- In the try scoring No 8 James Rodwell led the way with 17 which was only one off finishing leading scorer in the division and they came in just 21 starts
- Wing Nathan Bressington took his all time club record for tries to 60 with nine more
- Second row Ali Muldowney scored five tries and they were all away from home
- Set a new record for most points in a home league match with 51 against Sedgley Park in mid March which was one better than the previous best
- They also set a new record for points in an away match when beating Manchester 50-21, a four point improvement on their previous best
- They equalled their biggest ever away win in the Manchester game of 29 points which they had previously achieved away at Wakefield back in 1997

Coventry
- Coventry finished in ninth place for the second season running but with nine more points than last season
- They collected five losing bonus points which was the four highest number in the division
- Fly half Myles Dorrian topped the scoring list for the first time with 132 which is the lowest total to top the scoring for the club in four seasons
- No 8 Laurie McGlone topped the try scoring list with 11 which is the highest total for seven years, since Kurt Johnson scored 14 back in the 2002/03 season
- Hooker Chris Whitehead and No 8 Laurie McGlone led the way with 28 starts and Whitehead came on in the other two league matches and McGlone one
- Prop Rob Dugard started 25 matches and came on in the other five of Coventry's league games
- Winger Kurt Johnson passed the 100 try mark for Coventry with his two during the season and is now on 101
- Johnson started six matches to take his record for appearances by a back to 197 starts and 13 as a replacement
- Veteran hooker Dave Addleton made an appearances form the bench during the season to add to his all time appearance record, 216 starts and 36 appearances from the bench
- Hooker Stuart Pearl sat on the bench 27 times coming on in 23 of those matches
- In matches against the top four sides they managed just the one win to go with seven defeats with the win coming at home to Exeter Chiefs

Rotherham
- The Titans were 10th a one place improvement on the previous season taking 12 more points from five more wins although they did pick up fewer try bonus points
- Michael Whitehead top scored with 178 points and it is the third time in four seasons he has finished top scorer for the Titans with 85 points more than last season
- That took Whitehead passed the 400 mark for the Titans in his four seasons at the club and he finished on 419
- In the try scoring stakes winger Jon Feeley led the way with 16 tries to top the try scoring list for a second season, one ahead of Errie Claassens, his 15 tries took him to 38 for the club
- Feeley scored 10 of his 16 tries on the road whilst Claassens scored 10 of his 15 in the first half of matches; both these figures were against the trend
- Two players started 29 of the clubs 30 league matches, centre Brad Hunt and Whitehead with Hunt coming on in the match he did not start in
- Hooker Nigel Conroy started 23 matches and came on in the other seven matches
- They scored 100 tries during the season and scored more away from home than at Clifton Lane, Otley were the only other side to score more tries away from home
- They set a new record for points conceded away from home, 76 at Exeter Chiefs, one more than the previous record against Leicester Tigers when they were in the Premiership
- The 11 tries they conceded in this defeat equalled the club record which had happened twice before against Newcastle and Northampton Saints

135

2008-09 REVIEW

Plymouth Albion
- Albion finished 11th which was three places down on last season and their worst ever finish in the division which was previously 9th in 2002/03 their first season in the division
- Ended the season with seven straight defeats and although they finished two places lower in the table they actually got more points, 66 to 64
- Kieran Hallett top scored with 143 points with last year's leading scorer Ross Laidlaw chipping in with 90 points
- In the try scoring list only six tries was enough to finish leading try scorer with centre Matthew Hopper and wing Justin Mensah Coker joint top
- Second row Arthur Brenton was the only man to start all 30 matches for Albion
- They only conceded 85 tries during the season, which was fewer than Coventry, Rotherham and Moseley who all finished above them in the table
- Centre Keni Fisilau was sin binned three times which was joint sixth on the list and Albion only picked up 11 all season which was the second lowest number after Champions Leeds Carnegie
- Fisilau has now started 143 matches for Albion in the league which is second amongst backs playing for the club

Esher
- Esher again finished 12th in their second season of National One rugby but with five sides relegated because of the new 'Championship' they were one of them
- They conceded fewer points and scored nearly 200 points more and picked up 12 more points, 61 to 49
- They only managed two losing bonus points in 17 defeats which was the lowest total in the division
- Neil Hallett scored 224 points which was the four highest in the division as he finished top of the Esher scoring charts for a fifth season
- He has now scored 1242 points in the league for Esher and during the season he passed 1500 league points having also scored points for Bracknell and Rosslyn Park
- Winger/full back Douglas Flockhart was the leading try scorer with 16, 4th best in the division, to top the Esher try scoring list for a second season and a five try improvement on last season
- Flockhart was also the only player to start all 30 league matches for the club which follows on form last season when he played all but one match for Esher
- Four tries behind Flockhart was England under 29 centre George Lowe who scored his 12 tries form just 16 starts

Sedgley Park
- Park finished 13th and with five relegated are back down a division after five years in National One
- They were a place higher than last season but picked up 10 points fewer, 44 to 34
- They conceded 1206 points which was the most in the division and the most they have ever conceded in a season
- Only picked up 12 sin binnings during the season which was the fourth lowest figure in the division
- Phil Jones top scored for Park with 130 points for the fourth straight season but he failed to reach the 200 point mark for the first time as he took his park all time points record to 848 in four seasons, in total he has scored 1611 league points with Orrell and Rotherham as well
- He extended his all time record for conversions and penalty goals to 140 and 139 respectively
- Second row Glen Townson was the only Park ever present playing every minute of every match never being replaced whilst Matt Riley was one start behind him
- In the try scoring wing Peter Swatkins in his first season of senior rugby led the way with 14 tries in 28 starts
- They suffered their biggest ever home defeat when beaten 64-0 v Bedford Blues and it was also the most points they have conceded in a home league match
- Suffered a club record 12 consecutive defeats between the 13th December till the 4th April before ending the run with a home win over Otley

Newbury
- Newbury finished 14th in the table a drop of a place on the previous season but with five sides relegated their four season stay in the second tier of English rugby has come to an end
- They only managed two try bonus points all season which was the lowest in the division and were the second lowest scorers in the division by a point from Otley but Otley played a game fewer
- Ben Stevenson finished top scorer for Newbury with 95 points, one more than Gareth Griffiths
- Suffered their worst ever defeat when beaten at home by Champions Leeds Carnegie going down 89-12 and also conceded a record 13 tries, one more than their previous worst
- Wing John Hylton had the most starts 24 but fly half Gareth Griffiths started 23 and came on in six more to make 29 appearances in total
- They only had four players start 20 or more league matches which was the lowest in the division

Otley
- Otley were 15th in the table and were relegated back after just one season in National One. This is the second time this has happened in three seasons
- Tom Rhodes top scored with 104 points in his first season at the club
- Winger Peter Wackett was the leading try scorer with seven tries the lowest total to top the try scoring list at the club since Mark Kirkby back in 2001/02
- Scrum half Dave McCormack started the most games 25 and with two appearances from the bench played in 27 matches which was also the most, two more than prop Ryan Wederell
- They lost a club record 12 consecutive matches at the start of the season before eventually winning narrowly away at Manchester in November

Manchester
- Manchester on their return to National One finished bottom four points behind Otley with just two wins all season in their 30 matches
- Gareth Wynne top scored for Manchester with 121 points. This is the third consecutive season he has been top scorer but with his lowest total to date
- Wynne has now scored 554 points for the club in the league second only to all time leading scorer Steve Swindells who holds the club record with 1410 points
- In the try scoring centre Andre Wilson led the way with seven tries the lowest number to top the try scoring list since Isaac Richmond scored six in 2003/04, Wilson took his Manchester career total to 40 tries as he passed 100 league appearances for the club
- Prop Nick Flynn started the most matches, 29 out of 30 and took his all time record for appearances to 168 plus 13 matches as a replacement
- Second row Ed Norris appeared in all 30 matches starting 28 and coming on in the other two as a replacement
- Scrum half Will Runciman also took part in all 30 matches starting 21 and coming on as a replacement in the other nine matches
- Suffered their worst ever defeat when losing 104-0 in their home match against Champions Leeds Carnegie but the match was played at Headingley midweek
- They conceded a record 16 tries, three more than the previous record which was set against Exeter Chiefs in February 2004
- Suffered a club record 16 straight defeats from the start of the season till just before Christmas when they were 16-12 away day winners at local rivals Sedgley Park, their previous worst run was a 12 match losing run back in 2003/04

BEDFORD BLUES

BEDFORD BLUES

Founded: 1886
Nickname: The Blues
Colours:
Oxford and Cambridge blue.
Change colours:
Cambridge and Oxford blue.

Website: www.bedfordrugby.co.uk

KEY PERSONNEL

President	Gareth Davies
Chairman	Geoff Irvine
Company Secretary	Alan Buchanan
Commercial Manager	Andy Irvine
Rugby Administrator incl Media Liaison Fixture Secretary League Contact	Debra Rayer Tel: 01234 321888 Fax: 01234 347511 email: debra@bedfordrugby.co.uk
Director of Rugby	Mike Rayer
Commercial Consultant	Ted Carroll
Events Manager	Melissa White

CONTACT DETAILS

Bedford Blues Ltd, Goldington Road, Beford MK40 3NF
Tel: 0871 871 1886
Fax: 01234 347511
e-mail: info@bedford.rugby.co.uk

GROUND DETAILS

Address:
Goldington Road, Bedford. MK40 3NF.
Tel: 0871 871 1886   Fax: 01234 347511
e-mail: info@bedford.rugby.co.uk
Capacity: 4,684
Seated: 1200 (covered 800)

Directions:
From M1 - J13 onto A421. On edge of Bedford join Southern relief road, signed Cambridge. At r'about at end of relief road, turn left to Bedford Town Centre. Ground approx. 4 miles on right.
From A1 - Join A421 just south of St. Neots. After 8 miles this road takes you on to Goldington Road, into Bedford and ground is on the right.

Nearest BR Station: Bedford, Midland Road - 1 mile from ground.
Car Parking: For hospitality & officials only at ground, but plenty around the ground.

Match-day admission
Stand: £20 Adult, Student £16, Under 16 £16
Ground: Adult £16, Student £12, Under 16 £2
Adults Advance & online: Stand £16, Ground £12a

Club Shop:
Open matchdays and online @ www.bedfordrugby.co.uk

Clubhouse:
Thursday 1830 – 2300
Lunches available on 1st XV match days
Hospitality available on match days in Marquee, £23-50 per person
Functions contact Debra Rayer as above

PROGRAMME

Size: A5   Pages: 32
Price: £2.00
Editor: Ted Carroll
Advertising rates contact: Ted Carroll

REVIEW OF THE SEASON 2008-09

Talent was given the chance to flourish at Goldington Road during the 2008/09 season with a number of gifted individuals plying their trade, but it was team work that led to the Blues third place finish.

After the departure of 17 squad members at the end of 2007/08 many could have been forgiven for thinking that a mid table finish would be on the cards for a club adjusting to so many changes. Nothing could have been further from the truth.

A comprehensive 62-0 win over new boys Manchester on the opening day of the season saw four of the Blues new signings crossing the whitewash. Mike Howard and Gregor Gillanders got one apiece while pacey winger Ian Davey scored a brace but it was Billy Twelvetrees who stole the headlines and became an instant classic with four tries on his debut.

Things continued to get better for Bedford as they brushed aside Rotherham and Newbury before getting the upper hand on London Welsh at Old Deer Park. The first taste of defeat came for Mike Rayer's men against Exeter when the visitors slotted a penalty in the ninth minute of stoppage time to seal victory.

The Blues brushed themselves down and went on a three game winning streak before suffering three defeats on the bounce including a terrible home performance against Cornish Pirates. Although victory against Plymouth looked to have the Blues back on track, Doncaster dampened spirits as they ran in 50 points at Castle Park.

Christmas has tended to be a tough time for Bedford but they strung five wins together and things looked good for the new year. The team had flourished under the guidance of Rayer, Martin Hynes, Rob Crowle, Matt Volland and Nick Walshe while players such as Paul Tupai, Sacha Harding, Ian Vass, Brendan Burke, Ollie Dodge and Ryan Owen were coming more and more into their element.

Despite slip ups against London Welsh and Exeter, Bedford finished the season with a ten game winning streak which saw them revenge the defeats of the Pirates and Knights as well as putting one over on champions Leeds.

James Pritchard once again finished as top points scorer with 216 and Twelvetrees was the leagues joint top try scorer with 18. Bedford ran in 123 tries in all with Karl Dickson, Will Harries, Davey, Dodge, and Owen all reaching double figures.

The Blues will say a fond farewell to Twelvetrees and Dickson who are heading to the Premiership with Leicester Tigers and Harlequins respectively but Rayer has moved quickly to secure new signings Myles Dorrian from Coventry as well as Luke Fielden and Mike Guess from Cambridge as well as securing the services of the majority of the squad for the coming season.

BLUES' SEASON - 2008-09

Date	H/A	Opponents	Result & Score	Att.	15	14	13	12	11
\multicolumn{10}{l}{**NATIONAL ONE**}
30-08	H	Manchester	W 62-0	1933	Pritchard/7c	Owen/t	Twelvetrees/4t	Vass	Davey/2t
07-09	A	Rotherham	W 33-10	642	Pritchard/t2c3p	Owen	Burke	Twelvetrees/t	Davey/t
13-09	H	Newbury	W 53-12	2133	Pritchard/t4cp	Harries/t	Twelvetrees/c	Vass/t	Davey/t
20-09	A	London Welsh	W 32-23	1931	Pritchard/c5p	Owen/t	Burke/t	Vass(b/t)	Davey
27-09	H	Exeter	L 23-26	2986	Pritchard/2c3p	Dodge	Burke	Twelvetrees	Davey/2t
03-10	A	Coventry	W 26-3	1700	Pritchard/c3p	Harries	Burke	Twelvetrees/t	Davey/2t
11-10	H	Otley	W 37-12	2464	Burke	Harries/t	Roberts	Twelvetrees/4c3p	Owen(c/t)
18-10	H	Sedgley Park	W 53-7	2717	Pritchard/5cp	Harries/t	Roberts/t(e/t)	Twelvetrees	Davey/t
26-10	A	Nottingham	L 7-15	2019	Burke	Harries	Roberts	Twelvetrees/tc	Davey
01-11	H	Cornish Pirates	L 6-26	2514	Burke	Harries	Roberts	Twelvetrees/2p	Owen
09-11	A	Leeds Carnegie	L 8-19	3051	Harries/t	Owen	Burke	Roberts	Dodge
15-11	H	Plymouth Albion	W 37-9	2010	Harries/t	Owen(c/t)	Burke	Roberts/t	Dodge
22-11	A	Doncaster	L 21-50	1735	Harries	Dodge/2t	Burke	Roberts	Davey
28-11	H	Moseley	W 17-15	2406	Harries	Dodge(h/c)	Burke	Roberts	Davey/t
06-12	A	Esher	W 18-13	1081	Pritchard/c2p	Harries	Roberts	Twelvetrees/t	Davey/t
13-12	H	Manchester	W 25-5	324	Pritchard/cp	Owen	Burke	Vass	Davey/t
20-12	A	Rotherham	W 32-18	2338	Pritchard/2cp	Owen	Burke(j/t)	Vass	Davey
27-12	A	Newbury	W 34-0	878	Harries	Owen	Roberts	Vass	Dodge/t
03-01	H	London Welsh	L 32-33	3171	Pritchard/t3c2p	Harries/t	Burke	Vass	Dodge
10-01	A	Exeter	L 21-40	4092	Harries	Owen	Burke	Roberts	Davey
24-01	H	Coventry	W 23-9	2506	Pritchard/p	Dodge/t(l/t)	Burke	Vass	Owen
31-01	A	Otley	W 23-17	522	Pritchard/c2p	Harries/t	Twelvetrees	Vass	Owen/t
21-02	H	Nottingham	W 23-16	2918	Pritchard/p	Harries/t	Burke	Vass	Dodge
08-03	A	Cornish Pirates	W 6-5	4764	Harries	Dodge	Burke/p	Vass	Davey
14-03	H	Leeds Carnegie	W 27-24	2955	Harries/t	Owen/t	Burke	Vass	Dodge/t
21-03	A	Sedgley Park	W 64-0	436	Pritchard/t7c	Owen/3t	Roberts	Twelvetrees	Dodge/2t
28-03	A	Plymouth Albion	W 31-14	3363	Pritchard/2c	Owen/t	Burke/t	Vass	Dodge/t
04-04	H	Doncaster	W 42-20	3048	Pritchard/4c3p	Owen/t	Burke	Vass	Dodge/t
11-04	A	Moseley	W 26-23	1118	Pritchard/3c	Owen/t	Burke/t	Vass	Dodge/t
25-04	H	Esher	W 50-8	3307	Pritchard/6cp	Owen	Burke	Vass	Dodge(l/t)
\multicolumn{10}{l}{**EDF ENERGY NATIONAL TROPHY**}
4 17-01	A	Tynedale	W 30-23		Pritchard/3c3p	Dodge/t	Burke	Vass	Davey/t
5 14-02	A	Exeter	L 11-12		Pritchard/p	Harries/t	Burke	Vass	Dodge

SCORING BREAKDOWN

WHEN	Total	First Half	Second Half	1/4	2/4	3/4	4/4
the POINTS were scored	892	419	473	172	247	172	296
the POINTS were conceded	472	233	239	106	127	107	132
the TRIES were scored	123	53	70	20	33	24	45
the TRIES were conceded	51	23	28	8	15	11	17

HOW	Total	Pen. Try	Backs	Forwards	F Back	Wing	Centre	H Back	F Row	Lock	B Row
the TRIES were scored	123	-	88	35	7	42	17	22	6	10	19
the TRIES were conceded	51	1	37	13	5	16	9	7	4	2	7

KEY: * after opponents name indicates a penalty try.
Brackets after a player's name indicates he was replaced. eg (a) means he was replaced by replacement code "a" and so on.
/ after a player or replacement name is followed by any scores he made - eg /t, /c, /p, /dg or any combination of these

10	9	1	2	3	4	5	6	7	8
Davies/dg	Dickson	Cecere	Sammons	Boulton	Botha(a/t)	Hoy	Gillanders/t	Daynes	McKay
Davies	Dickson/t	Walsh	Richmond	Boulton	Howard	Botha	Gillanders	Daynes	McKay
Walshe	Dickson/2t	Walsh	Locke	Boulton	Howard/t	Botha	Gillanders/t	Daynes	McKay
Davies	Dickson	Cecere	Richmond	Boulton	Howard	Botha	Gillanders	Daynes	McKay
Walshe	Dickson	Cecere	Richmond	Boulton	Howard	Botha	Tupai	Harding	Gillanders
Walshe	Dickson	Walsh	Sammons	Boulton	Howard	Botha	Tupai	Harding	Gillanders
Vass	Walshe	Walsh	Sammons	Graham	Howard(d/t)	McKay	Tupai	Daynes	Gillanders/t
Vass	Dickson/t	Graham	Richmond	Boulton	Howard	Botha/2t	Tupai	Harding	McKay/t
Vass	Dickson	Cecere	Richmond	Boulton	Howard	Botha	Tupai	Harding	Gillanders
Vass	Walshe	Walsh	Sammons	Boulton	Cannon	Botha	Tupai	Daynes	Gillanders
Twelvetrees/p	Walshe	Cecere	Richmond	Boulton	Cannon	Botha	Gillanders	Harding	McKay
Twelvetrees/2cp	Walshe	Cecere	Richmond/t	Graham	Howard	Cannon	Botha	Harding/t	McKay(f/t)
Twelvetrees/2p	Walshe(g/t)	Walsh	Richmond	Boulton	Howard	Cannon	Botha	Harding	Tupai
Davies/cp	Walshe	Walsh	Richmond	Boulton	Cannon	Botha	Tupai	Harding	McKay/t
Davies	Dickson	Walsh	Richmond	Graham	Howard	Cannon	Gillanders	Harding	McKay
Twelvetrees	Dickson/t	Cecere	Locke/t(i/t)	Boulton	Howard	Cannon	Gillanders	Daynes	McKay
Twelvetrees	Dickson/t	Walsh	Richmond	Boulton/t	Howard(d/t)	Cannon	Gillanders	Daynes	Tupai/t
Twelvetrees/tc(e/c)	Walshe(g/t)	Cecere	Locke	Boulton	Cannon	Botha	Gillanders	Daynes/t	Tupai(k/t)
Twelvetrees	Dickson	Walsh	Richmond	Boulton	Howard	Cannon	Gillanders/t	Harding/t	Tupai
Twelvetrees/2t3c	Walshe	Cecere	Richmond	Walsh	Howard	Botha/t	Gillanders	Harding	McKay
Twelvetrees	Dickson	Cecere	Richmond	Boulton	Howard	Botha/t	Gillanders	Harding	Tupai/t
Davies	Walshe	Cecere	Sammons	Walsh	Botha	Cannon	Gillanders/t	Harding	Pienaar
Twelvetrees/2tcp	Dickson	Cecere	Richmond	Boulton	Botha	Cannon	Gillanders	Harding	Tupai
Twelvetrees	Dickson	Walsh	Richmond	Boulton	Howard	Botha	Gillanders	Harding	Tupai
Twelvetrees/t2cp	Dickson	Walsh	Richmond	Boulton	Howard	Botha	Gillanders	Harding	Tupai
Walshe	Dickson/t	Cecere	Sammons	Walsh	Howard/t	McKay	Gillanders/t	Daynes	Tupai/t
Twelvetrees/c	Dickson/t	Cecere	Richmond	Boulton	Howard	Botha/t	Gillanders	Harding	Tupai
Twelvetrees/t	Dickson/t	Walsh	Richmond	Boulton	Howard	Botha	Gillanders/t	Harding	Tupai
Twelvetrees	Dickson/t	Cecere	Richmond	Boulton	Howard	Botha	Gillanders	Harding	Tupai
Twelvetrees/2t	Dickson/t	Cecere	Richmond(m/t)	Boulton	Howard	Botha	Gillanders	Harding/t	Tupai(k/t)
Twelvetrees	Dickson/t	Cecere	Richmond	Boulton	Howard	Botha	Gillanders	Harding	Tupai
Twelvetrees/p	Walshe	Cecere	Richmond	Boulton	Botha	Cannon	Gillanders	Harding	Tupai

REPLACEMENTS

a- M Howard   b- W Twelvetrees   c- I Davey   d- M Botha
e- B Burke   f- G Gillanders   g- C Dickson h- J Pritchard
i- D Richmond j- O Dodge   k- R McKay   l- W Harries
m- C Locke

LEAGUE APPEARANCES

- 28 William Twelvetrees (1)
- 26 Gregor Gillanders (4)
- 24 Mouritz Botha (5), Philip Boulton (4)
- 23 Michael Howard (5), Brendan Burke (3)

NUMBER OF PLAYERS USED

29 plus 3 as a replacement only

LEAGUE POINTS SCORERS

Pts	Player	T	C	P	DG
216	James Pritchard	4	53	30	-
158	Will Twelvetrees	18	16	12	-
70	Ian Davey	14	-	-	-
65	Karl Dickson	13	-	-	-
55	Will Harries	11	-	-	-
55	Ollie Dodge	11	-	-	-

CHAMPIONSHIP

BEDFORD STATISTICS

LEAGUE

TEAM RECORDS

MOST POINTS
Scored at Home: 79 v Newbury 29.4.06
Scored Away: 68 v Pertemps Bees 11.3.06
Conceded at Home: 106 v Richmond 16.5.99
Conceded Away: 76 v Bath 13.1.90

MOST TRIES
Scored in a match: 11 v Blackheath 22.2.97
Conceded in a match: 16 v Richmond 16.5.99 (H)

BIGGEST MARGINS
Home Win: 57pts - 79-22 v Newbury 29.4.06
Away Win: 64pts - 64-0 v Sedgley Park 21.3.09
Home Defeat: 94pts - 106-12 v Richmond 16.5.99
Away Defeat: 76pts - 0-76 v Bath 13.1.90

MOST CONSECUTIVE
Victories: 18
Defeats: 15

INDIVIDUAL RECORDS

MOST APPEARANCES
by a forward: 116 (30) Matt Volland
by a back: 153 (1) Ben Whetstone

MOST CONSECUTIVE
Appearances: 46 Paul Alston 19.9.92-12.4.95
Matches scoring Tries: 6
Ben Whetstone & Martin Offiah
Matches scoring points: 36 Andy Finnie

MATCH RECORDS

Most Points
34 Ali Hepher   v Newbury 29.4.06 (H)

Most Tries
4 Jason Forster   v Fylde 17.1.98 (H)

Most Conversions
9 Ali Hepher   v Pertemps Bees 29.3.06 (A)

Most Penalties
8 James Pritchard   v Otley 2.11.02 (H)

Most Drop Goals
2 Andy Finnie   v Coventry 27.3.94 (H)
                  v Clifton 14.1.95 (A)
Ed Barnes   v Plymouth 23.3.03 (H)

SEASON RECORDS

Most Points	374	James Pritchard	02-03
Most Tries	18	Will Twelvetrees	08-09
Most Conversions	67	Mike Rayer	96-97
Most Penalties	72	James Pritchard	02-03
Most Drop Goals	5	Tony Yapp	98-99
		Ed Barnes	02-03

CAREER RECORDS

Most Points	1306	James Pritchard	01-09
Most Tries	74	Ben Whetstone	92-05
Most Conversions	233	James Pritchard	01-09
Most Penalties	205	James Pritchard	01-09
Most Drop Goals	22	Andy Finnie	87-96

LAST TEN SEASONS

	Division	P	W	D	L	F	A	P.D.	Pts	Pos	Most Points	Most Tries
99-00	P1	22	1	0	21	396	802	-406	3	12	70 Andy Gomersall	9 Paul Sackey
00-01	N1	26	9	1	16	463	616	-153	47	11	99 Ben Whetstone	9 James Hinkins
01-02	N1	26	12	3	11	654	600	54	68	6	239 James Pritchard	12 James Shanahan
02-03	N1	26	13	1	12	675	760	-85	64	7	374 James Pritchard	12 James Pritchard
03-04	N1	26	12	1	13	623	627	-4	61	7	144 Ed Barnes	9 Ben Whetstone
04-05	N1	26	16	1	9	679	536	143	77	7	347 Leigh Hinton	10 Leigh Hinton
05-06	N1	26	19	1	6	906	542	364	100	2	204 Mark Harris	9 Chris Johnson
06-07	N1	30	18	1	11	827	566	261	95	7	276 James Pritchard	12 James Pritchard
07-08	N1	30	18	0	12	705	542	163	85	6	196 James Pritchard	11 Alex Page
08-09	N1	30	23	0	7	892	472	420	111	3	216 James Pritchard	18 Will Twelvetrees

RFU SENIOR CUP

OVERALL PLAYING RECORD

	P	W	O	L	F	A	Pts Diff
Home	34	20	0	14	708	505	203
Away	27	9	0	18	501	525	-24
Neutral	1	1	0	0	28	12	16
TOTAL	62	30	0	32	1237	1042	195

TEAM RECORDS
Highest Score: 76 v Staines 97/98
Biggest Winning Margin: 60 (66-6) v Bournemouth 74/75 (76-16) v Staines 97/98
Highest Score Against: 54 v Saracens 00/01
Biggest Losing Margin: 37 (37-0) v Bristol 96/97

SEASON BY SEASON

71-72	2R	78-79	QF	85-86	2R	92-93	3R	99-00	4R
72-73	1R	79-80	2R	86-87	3R	93-94	2R	00-01	4R
73-74	DNQ	80-81	3R	87-88	3R	94-95	4R	01-02	3R
74-75	Winners	81-82	3R	88-89	3R	95-96	5R	02-03	3R
75-76	1R	82-83	4R	89-90	3R	96-97	5R	03-04	5R
76-77	QF	83-84	3R	90-91	2R	97-98	4R	04-05	6R
77-78	1R	84-85	3R	91-92	3R	98-99	4R		

European Shield - 99-00 Gp Stage
NATIONAL TROPHY

05-06	R-up	06-07	5 R	07-08	Q.F.	08-09	5 R

PLAYERS

	Position	D.o.B.	Apps.	Pts.	T	C	P	DG
Brendan Burke	Full Back	01/10/1981	49 (7)	55	10	1	1	-
Karl Dickson	Scrum half	02/08/1982	71 (28)	150	30	-	-	-
Ollie Dodge	Wing/Centre	27/08/1987	41 (7)	100	20	-	-	-
Ian Davey	Winger		15 (4)	70	14	-	-	-
Will Twelvetrees	Centre/Fly Half	15/11/1988	28 (1)	158	18	16	12	-
James Pritchard	Winger	21/07/1979	114 (4)	1306	45	233	205	-
Ryan Owen	Winger	04/10/1986	19 (2)	50	10	-	-	-
Will Harries	Winger	30/03/1987	18 (4)	55	11	-	-	-
Liam Roberts	Centre	12/12/1981	62 (15)	85	17	-	-	-
Nick Walshe	Scrum half	01/11/1973	13 (11)	-	-	-	-	-
Ian Vass	Scrum half/ Wing	17/8/1981	20 (5)	5	1	-	-	-
Marco Cecere	Prop	12/05/1982	28 (20)	5	1	-	-	-
Sam Walsh	Prop		16 (7)	-	-	-	-	-
Dan Richmond	Hooker	12/02/1979	44(14)	40	8	-	-	-
Chris Locke	Hooker		3 (6)	10	2	-	-	-
Greg Sammons	Hooker	31/12/1987	13 (20)	5	1	-	-	-
Mouritz Botha	Lock	29/01/1982	53 (16)	50	10	-	-	-
Greg Gillanders	Back row	12/04/1988	26 (4)	40	8	-	-	-
Michael Howard	Lock		23 (5)	15	3	-	-	-
Sacha Harding	Back row	03/02/1983	75(25)	80	16	-	-	-
Marc Comb	Lock	26/11/1982	24 (37)	15	3	-	-	-
Paul Tupai	Back row	14/02/1985	20 (5)	15	3	-	-	-
Rory McKay	Back row	09/02/1979	31 (14)	25	5	-	-	-
Ben Pienaar	Back row	10/09/1986	22 (21)	30	6	-	-	-

BIRMINGHAM & SOLIHULL

KEY PERSONNEL

Chairman	Brian Marshall	
Hon. Club Secretary	Tony Moir	
Commercial Manager	Robin Eaves	Tel: 07944 106236
Mini & Junior Chairman	Dai Philips	Tel: 07968 289209 (M)
Mini & Junior Match Sec.	John Dunn	Tel: 01773 713715
Head Coach	Russell Earnshaw	
Public Relations Manager	Jo Kilby	Tel: 07958 655728

Founded: 1989 (Birmingham RFC & Solihull RUFC merged)

Nickname: The Bees

Colours: Black, red and amber

Change colours: White, black and amber

Website: www.beesrugby.com

CONTACT DETAILS
Sharmans Cross Road, Solihull, West Midlands B91 1RQ
Tel. 0121 705 0409   Fax. 0121 705 8253
email: tsmith@beesrugby.com

GROUND DETAILS
Address:
Sharmans Cross Road, Solihull.B91 1RQ
Tel: 0121 705 0409
Fax: 0121 705 8253
email: tsmith@beesrugby.com

Capacity: 3,500
Covered Seating : 1000

Directions:
Junction 5 of M42, exit towards Birmingham (on to Solihull By-pass/ Seven Star Road). Turn right at fourth set of lights (on to Warwick Road), take second left (on to Broad Oaks Road). At end of road turn right into Streetsbrook Road. Take second left into Sharmans Cross Road, and ground is on left after approx. 0.2 mile.

Nearest BR Station: Solihull

Car Parking: 70 spaces available at the ground.

Admission
Matchday tbc
Season tbc

Clubhouse:
Open Sat. 12-11pm, Sun 10-3pm, Thur 7-11.30pm.
Functions: Capacity 150 contact Trish Smith 0121 705 0409

Club Shop:
Open on match days. contact Club office 0121 705 0409

PROGRAMME
Size: A5   Pages: 36
Price: £2
Editorial: Geoff Lightfoot Media.
Advertising Rates
Contact Robin Eaves 07944 106236

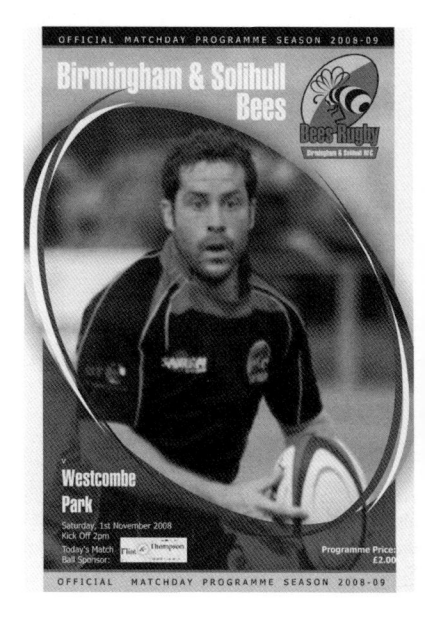

L-R - **Standing**: Emma Mark (Physio), Steve Hughes (Team Manager), Jimmy Aston, Ricky Davies, Andi Lawrence, Andy Daish, Cameron Mitchell, Russell Earnshaw, Simon Hunt, Craig Voisey, Matt Long, Jack Preece, Mark Woodrow, Chris Kemp (Strength & Conditioner) and Eugene Martin (Assistant/Backs Coach).
Seated: Adam Clayton, Luke Ward, Ryan Tomlinson, Chris Brightwell, Mitch Culpin, Alex Davidson, Ben Phillips (Captain), Rob Connolly, Sam Brown, Reece Spee, Scott Young and Dale Garner.
Absent: Rod Petty, Kyle Palm, Shaun Pammenter, Ed Orgee, Jim Jenner, Tom Collett and Leo Halavatau.

REVIEW OF THE SEASON 2008-09

Having been relegated from National One by the end of the 2008/09 season Birmingham & Solihull's Bees set about radically changing the face of the team from the inside out. Lynch-pin Russell Earnshaw was retained as Head Coach and given license to form the clubs first ever fully professional playing side. Former Waikato Chiefs fly-half Eugene Martin joined the Bees from Rotherham Titans as Earnshaw's right hand man and Backs Coach, his impact colossal as Bees finished the season just shy of 1,100 points in attack, securing an incredible four try bonus point in 21 out of their 26 league fixtures, but not everything went 100% to plan.

Being touted as one of the pre-season favourites the West Midlanders then proceeded to lose two of their first six including their season opener to Redruth and a rather humbling loss to eleventh placed Wharfedale.

With lessons learnt Bees moved onwards and upwards, crushing the likes of Mounts Bay, Westcombe Park, Southend and Cinderford whilst hard fought wins against tricky opponents Blackheath and last year's also relegated party, the Cornish All Blacks proved valuable confidence boosters. That the likes of Simon Hunt, Reece Spee, Mark Woodrow, Cameron Mitchell and Rob Connolly were firing on all cylinders just served to reinforce Bees deadly intent but with another twist still to be administered it was the quietly efficient Tynedale that collapsed Bees proud home record. The 24-28 loss at Sharmans Cross Road, whilst Earnshaw was away on England Sevens duty however proved a turning point and a new, refocused Bees was unveiled.

New signing Chris Brightwell having been little-used following the Wharfedale debacle, where he made his debut, was recalled and what an impact he made – nine tries in sixteen appearances. With the forwards finding their feet Ben Phillips, Craig Voisey and second row enforcers Alex Davidson and Shaun Pammenter in particular the appropriate inspiration was administered to eventually put Bees atop National Division 2 with just a handful of games remaining. That Bees had to face four of the top six before they could claim the Champions title was no mean feat, Tynedale away personifying this with an unbelievable 38 game unbeaten streak on the line, but Bees were in no mood for negotiating and by the half time whistle they were already 8-24 up and by the final one Hunt had not only grabbed his hat-trick but smashed Nick Baxter's eleven year National 2 All-time Try scorers record (final tally 31) to ensure Bees just had to win at home against Redruth to claim the season and promotion with a game to spare.

Redruth were hardly swept aside but a brace from fullback Spee sealed things and with it the title and entryway back to the now newly titled, Championship, despite the firm attentions of a strong finishing Cambridge.

A quarter-final finish in the EDF Energy National Trophy to National One's champions elect, Leeds Carnegie was almost a fairy tale come true – Bees leading 24-12 with 5 minutes remaining – but whilst the rub of the green favoured the men from the north from the performance comes great confidence that Bees will be a side to be reckoned with come September 2009.

145

BEES' CHAMPIONSHIP SEASON - 2008-09

CHAMPIONSHIP

Date	H/A	Opponents	Result & Score	Att.	15	14	13	12	11
NATIONAL TWO									
06-09	A	Redruth	L 28-35	851	Spee/t	Hunt/t	Young	Mitchell	Aston
13-09	H	Stourbridge	W 31-14	500	Spee	Hunt/2t	Young	Mitchell/t	Culpin
20-09	A	Cambridge	W 33-29	840	Spee	Hunt/3t	Young	Mitchell/t	Culpin
27-09	A	Mounts Bay*	W 61-8	550	Spee	Hunt/2t	Young	Mitchell/3t	Culpin
04-10	H	Blaydon	W 32-12	610	Spee/t	Hunt/t	Young	Mitchell	Culpin
11-10	A	Wharfedale	L 12-41	520	Spee	Hunt	Connolly	Mitchell	Aston
18-10	H	Launceston	W 23-19	548	Spee/t	Hunt	Young	Mitchell	Culpin/t
25-10	A	Blackheath	W 35-28	827	Spee/2t	Hunt/t	Young	Mitchell	Culpin
01-11	H	Westcombe Park	W 47-7	380	Spee/t	Hunt	Young/t	Mitchell	Culpin/t
08-11	A	Southend	W 39-14	250	Spee	Hunt/t	Young	Mitchell/t	Culpin/t
15-11	H	Cinderford	W 53-3	429	Spee	Hunt/3t	Young	Mitchell/t	Culpin(b/t)
29-11	A	Waterloo	W 52-16	246	Spee/2t	Hunt	Young	Mitchell/2t	Culpin
06-12	H	Tynedale	L 24-28	475	Spee	Hunt	Young	Mitchell/t	Culpin
20-12	A	Stourbridge	W 35-25	650	Spee	Hunt	Young	Mitchell	Culpin
24-01	A	Blaydon	W 31-15	417	Spee	Hunt	Young	Mitchell	Culpin/t
31-01	H	Wharfedale	W 55-13	497	Spee	Hunt/2t	Young/3t	Mitchell	Culpin
21-02	H	Blackheath	W 58-12	748	Spee/t	Hunt/3t	Young	Mitchell	Culpin
07-03	A	Westcombe Park	W 29-11	213	Spee	Hunt	Young	Mitchell/t	Culpin/t
14-03	H	Mounts Bay	W 80-5	314	Spee/t	Hunt/t	Young/t	Petty	Aston/t
21-03	A	Southend	W 49-27	407	Culpin/t	Hunt/2t	Tomlinson	Mitchell	Aston
28-03	A	Cinderford	W 36-10	410	Spee	Hunt	Young	Petty/t	Aston
04-04	H	Waterloo	W 115-0	447	Spee/2t	Hunt/3t	Tomlinson	Petty/3t	Culpin/t(f/t)
10-04	A	Launceston	W 35-16	882	Spee/t	Hunt/2t	Tomlinson	Petty	Culpin
18-04	A	Tynedale	W 45-22	710	Spee	Hunt/3t	Tomlinson	Petty/t	Culpin
25-04	H	Redruth	W 31-7	1177	Spee/t	Hunt/t	Tomlinson	Petty/t	Culpin
02-05	H	Cambridge	L 29-45	720	Spee(f/2t)	Hunt	Tomlinson	Petty/t	Culpin
EDF ENERGY NATIONAL TROPHY									
3 13-12	H	Redruth	W 31-8	300	Spee	Hunt	Young/t	Mitchell(a/c)	Culpin/t
4 17-01	A	Launceston	W 15-10		Culpin	Hunt	Tomlinson	Mitchell	Aston
5 15-02	H	Cinderford	W 38-26		Spee/t	Hunt/t	Culpin	Mitchell	Aston
Q.F. 28-02	H	Leeds Carnegie	L 24-26		Spee/t	Hunt/t	Young	Mitchell/t	Palm

SCORING BREAKDOWN

WHEN	Total	First Half	Second Half	1/4	2/4	3/4	4/4
the POINTS were scored	1098	502	596	202	300	228	368
the POINTS were conceded	462	266	196	99	167	118	78
the TRIES were scored	150	65	85	25	40	31	54
the TRIES were conceded	57	29	28	10	19	18	10

HOW	Total	Pen. Try	Backs	Forwards	F Back	Wing	Centre	H Back	F Row	Lock	B Row
the TRIES were scored	150	1	96	53	18	40	23	15	11	8	34
the TRIES were conceded	57	-	44	13	4	21	13	6	5	2	6

KEY: ** after opponents name indicates a penalty try.*
Brackets after a player's name indicates he was replaced. eg (a) means he was replaced by replacement code "a" and so on.
/ after a player or replacement name is followed by any scores he made - eg /t, /c, /p, /dg or any combination of these

10	9	1	2	3	4	5	6	7	8
Woodrow/2c3p	Brown	Long	Phillips	Voisey	Davidson	Orgee/t	Connolly	Preece	Earnshaw
Woodrow/4cp	Petty	Long	Phillips	Voisey	Davidson	Orgee	Connolly/t	Earnshaw	Jenner
Woodrow/2c3p	Petty	Voisey	Phillips	Long	Davidson	Orgee	Earnshaw	Connolly	Jenner
Woodrow/8c	Petty	Long	Collett	Davies	Davidson	Pammenter	Connolly/3t	Clayton	Earnshaw
Woodrow/3c2p	Petty/t	Long	Phillips	Voisey	Davidson	Orgee	Connolly/t	Earnshaw	Jenner
Woodrow/4p	Petty	Long	Phillips	Voisey	Davidson	Pammenter	Brightwell	Preece	Earnshaw
Woodrow/c2p	Petty	Long	Phillips	Voisey	Davidson	Pammenter	Connolly	Earnshaw	Jenner/t
Woodrow/3c3p	Petty	Long	Phillips	Voisey	Orgee	Pammenter	Connolly/t	Earnshaw	Jenner
Woodrow/t5c(a/tc)	Brown	Long	Phillips/2t	Voisey	Earnshaw	Pammenter	Connolly	Clayton	Jenner
Woodrow/4c2p	Neil	Long	Phillips	Voisey	Pammenter	Orgee/t	Connolly	Clayton/t	Earnshaw
Woodrow/t5cp	Brown	Long	Phillips/t	Voisey	Pammenter	Orgee	Connolly/t	Earnshaw	Jenner
Woodrow/5c	Brown	Long	Phillips/2t	Voisey	Pammenter	Orgee	Clayton/t(c/c)	Connolly/t	Halavatua
Woodrow/c4p	Petty/t	Long	Phillips	Voisey	Earnshaw	Pammenter	Connolly	Clayton	Jenner
Woodrow/3c2pdg	Brown	Davies	Phillips/2t	Voisey	Orgee	Pammenter	Brightwell/2t	Earnshaw	Jenner
Woodrow/2c4p	Brown	Long	Phillips	Voisey	Davidson	Pammenter/t	Connolly/t	Earnshaw	Halavatua
Woodrow/4c(a/c)	Brown	Long	Phillips/2t	Voisey	Davidson	Pammenter	Connolly(c/2t)	Earnshaw	Halavatua
Woodrow/2t6c2p	Brown	Long	Phillips	Voisey	Davidson	Pammenter/t	Brightwell/t	Earnshaw	Halavatua
Petty/3cp	Brown	Davies	Phillips	Voisey	Davidson/t	Pammenter	Brightwell/t	Connolly	Halavatua
Woodrow/t10c	Brown	Long/t	Preece/t	Voisey	Davidson/t	Pammenter	Connolly/2t	Clayton/t(c/t)	Earnshaw
Woodrow/5c3p	Petty/3t	Davies	Phillips	Voisey	Earnshaw	Pammenter	Brightwell	Clayton	Connolly
Woodrow/t4cp	Brown	Davies	Phillips	Voisey	Davidson	Pammenter	Brightwell	Connolly/t	Halavatua/t(d/t)
Woodrow/t15c	Brown/t	Lawrence	Preece/t	Voisey	Davidson	Pammenter	Brightwell/t	Clayton(e/t)	Halavatua/t(g/t)
Woodrow/5c	Brown	Long	Preece/t	Voisey	Davidson	Pammenter	Brightwell	Earnshaw	Halavatua(e/t)
Woodrow/t5c	Brown	Long	Phillips	Voisey	Davidson/t	Pammenter	Brightwell	Connolly/t	Earnshaw
Woodrow/3c	Brown	Long	Phillips	Voisey	Davidson	Pammenter	Brightwell/t	Connolly	Earnshaw
Woodrow/3cp	Brown	Davies	Phillips	Voisey	Davidson(d/t)	Daish	Earnshaw	Connolly	Halavatua
Woodrow/3c	Brown	Davies	Phillips	Voisey/t	Pammenter	Orgee	Brightwell	Connolly/t	Earnshaw
Woodrow(a/t)	Brown(h/t)	Davies	Phillips	Lawrence	Davidson	Pammenter	Connolly/t	Clayton	Halavatua
Woodrow/5cp	Brown	Davies	Phillips/t	Voisey	Davidson	Orgee/t	Daish	Brightwell	Halavatua/t
Woodrow/2c	Petty/t	Long	Phillips	Davies	Davidson	Pammenter	Clayton	Connolly	Halavatua

REPLACEMENTS

a- R Petty b- R Tomlinson c- R Brightwell d- A Clayton
e- R Connolly f- J Aston g- A Daish h- J Preece

LEAGUE APPEARANCES

26 Simon Hunt
25 Craig Voisey (1), R Spee (1), Mark Woodrow
23 Mitchell Culpin (2)
22 Ben Phillips (3), Rob Connolly (4),
    Russell Earnshaw

NUMBER OF PLAYERS USED

25 plus 3 as a replacement only

LEAGUE POINTS SCORERS

Pts	Player	T	C	P	DG
373	Mark Woodrow	8	108	38	1
155	Simon Hunt	31	-	-	-
78	Rod Petty	13	5	1	-
75	Reece Spee	15	-	-	-
75	Rob Connolly	15	-	-	-
55	Cameron Mitchell	11	-	-	-

CHAMPIONSHIP

BEES' STATISTICS

LEAGUE
BIRMINGHAM & SOLIHULL

CHAMPIONSHIP

TEAM RECORDS

MOST POINTS
Scored at Home: 115 v Waterloo 4.4.09
Scored Away: 72 v Aspatria 30.8.97
Conceded at Home: 68 v Bedford Blues 29.3.06
Conceded Away: 79 v Roundhay 26.11.88

MOST TRIES
Scored in a match: 17 v Waterloo 4.4.09
Conceded in a match: 14 v Roundhay 26.11.88

BIGGEST MARGINS
Home Win: 115pts - 115-0 v Waterloo 4.4.09
Away Win: 62pts - 72-10 v Aspatria 30.8.97
Home Defeat: 47pts - 3-50 v Wakefield 31.10.87
Away Defeat: 79pts - 0-79 v Roundhay 26.11.88

MOST CONSECUTIVE
Victories: 12 (20.12.08 - 25.4.09)
Defeats: 13

INDIVIDUAL RECORDS

MOST APPEARANCES
by a forward: 123 (3) Julian Hyde
by a back: 145 (12) Dave Knight

MATCH RECORDS

Most Points	35	Mark Woodrow	v Waterloo 4.4.09
Most Tries	4	Steve Chapman	v Hinckley 31.1.98
Most Conversions	15	Mark Woodrow	v Waterloo 4.4.09
Most Penalties	6	Matt Birch	v Hinckley 8.11.97
		Steve Gough	v Leeds 9.9.00
Most Drop Goals	1	by 8 players - Luis Criscuolo (4 times) Jonathan Smart (3), Steve Gough (2), Mark Woodrow (3), Tim Walsh (3), Peter Glackin, Luke Smith, Alex Grove.	

SEASON RECORDS

Most Points	373	Mark Woodrow	08-09
Most Tries	31	Simon Hunt	08-09
Most Conversions	108	Mark Woodrow	08-09
Most Penalties	55	Matt Birch	97-98
Most Drop Goals	4	Luis Criscuolo	01-02

CAREER RECORDS

Most Points	531	Mark Woodrow	03/05 & 08-09
Most Tries	62	Nick Baxter	01-06
Most Conversions	154	Mark Woodrow	03-05 & 08/09
Most Penalties	90	Matt Birch	97-99
Most Drop Goals	4	Luis Criscuolo	01-02

LAST TEN SEASONS

	Division	P	W	D	L	F	A	P.D.	Pts	Pos	Most Points	Most Tries
99-00	JN1	26	21	1	4	659	346	313	43	2p	166 Jon anthan Smart	14 Paul Lydster
00-01	N1	26	7	5	14	427	481	-54	48	9	176 Steve Gough	6 Chris Budgen
01-02	N1	26	10	1	15	432	626	-194	52	8	102 Dave Knight	15 Nick Baxter
02-03	N1	26	12	2	12	630	569	61	63	8	146 Luke Smith	16 Nick Baxter
03-04	N1	26	16	1	9	691	526	165	83	4	138 Mark Woodrow	15 Dave Knight
04-05	N1	26	10	0	16	541	667	-126	49	9	192 Tim Walsh	15 Nick Baxter
05-06	N1	25	6	2	17	501	735	-234	35	14	140 Ben Harvey	8 Nick Baxter
06-07	N1	30	13	2	15	736	911	-175	76	8	140 Jon Higgins	16 Akapusi Qera
07-08	N1	30	7	0	23	474	696	-222	41	15r	82 Jonathan Higgins	8 Andrew Daish
08-09	N2	26	22	0	4	1098	462	636	111	1p	373 Mark Woodrow	31 Simon Hunt

RFU SENIOR CUP

OVERALL PLAYING RECORD

	P	W	O	L	F	A	Pts Diff
Home	16	14	0	2	362	189	173
Away	20	10	0	10	419	546	-127
Neutral	0	0	0	0	0	0	0
TOTAL	36	24	0	12	781	735	46

TEAM RECORDS

Highest Score: 59 v Preston 01/02
Biggest Winning Margin: 44 (59-15) v Preston 01/02
Highest Score Against: 81 v Leeds 04-05 (A)
Biggest Losing Margin: 64 (81-17) v Leeds 04-05 (A)

SEASON BY SEASON

71-72	1R / DNQ	78-79	DNQ / DNQ	85-86	DNQ / DNQ	92-93	DNQ	99-00	5R
72-73	DNQ / DNQ	79-80	DNQ / DNQ	86-87	1R / 2R	93-94	4R	00-01	5R
73-74	DNQ / DNQ	80-81	1R / DNQ	87-88	DNQ / DNQ	94-95	1R	01-02	6R
74-75	DNQ / 1R	81-82	DNQ / DNQ	88-89	DNQ / DNQ	95-96	2R	02-03	5R
75-76	DNQ / DNQ	82-83	2R / DNQ	89-90	DNQ	96-97	2R	03-04	SF
76-77	1R / 1R	83-84	DNQ / 1R	90-91	DNQ	97-98	2R	04-05	6R
77-78	DNQ / DNQ	84-85	DNQ / DNQ	91-92	DNQ	98-99	2R		

From 71-72 until 88-89 the figure on the left shows **Birmingham RFC** and that on the right **Solihull RUFC**

NATIONAL TROPHY

05-06	6 R	06-07	S.F.	07-08	5 R	08-09	Q.F.

PLAYERS

	Position	D.o.B.	Apps.	Pts.	T	C	P	DG
Reece Spee	Full back	22/04/1978	79 (5)	150	30	-	-	-
Simon Hunt	Winger		26	155	31	-	-	-
Scott Young	Centre	25/07/1981	26 (2)	25	5	-	-	-
Cameron Mitchell	Centre	25/07/1983	32 (4)	65	13	-	-	-
Mitchell Culpin	Centre	14/03/1989	24 (3)	40	8	-	-	-
Ryan Tomlinson	Centre		6 (5)	5	1	--	--	-
James Aston	Winger	19/01/1981	19 (10)	40	8	-	-	-
Mark Woodrow	Fly half	06/09/1980	46 (5)	531	8	154	58	3-
Rod Petty	Scrum half		28 (19)	105	15	12	2	-
Sam Brown	Scrum half	24/07/1987	16 (7)	5	1	-	-	-
Craig Voisey	Prop		25 (1)	168	15	15	21	-
Matt Long	Prop	25/05/1973	104 (41)	35	7	-	-	-
Ricky Davies	Prop		6 (11)	-	-	-	-	-
Andrew Lawrence	Prop		1 (4)	-	-	-	-	-
Ben Phillips	Hooker		22 (3)	45	9	-	-	-
Tom Collett	Hooker		1 (6)	-	-	-	-	-
Shaun Pammenter	Lock		21	10	2	-	-	-
Alex Davidson	Lock	12/03/1981	109 (31)	60	12	-	-	-
Rob Connolly	Back row		22 (4)	75	15	-	-	-
Andrew Daish	Back row	06/09/1984	21 (7)	45	9	-	-	-
Jack Preece	Back row	01/08/1989	22 (13)	20	4	-	-	-
Chris Brightwell	Back row		10 (3)	47	9	1	-	-
Russell Earnshaw	Back row	08/04/1975	47 (1)	-	-	-	-	-
Adam Clayton	Back row		8 (14)	25	5	-	-	-
Jim Jenner	Back row	27/11/1971	71 (12)	35	7	-	-	-
Leo Halavatua	Back row	21/11/1983	34 (17)	35	7	-	-	-

BRISTOL RUGBY

KEY PERSONNEL

Chief Executive	Steve Gorvett	Tel: 0117 958 1630
Financial Controller	Alec Bellamy	Tel: 0117 958 1630
Club Administrator	Nikki Locke	Tel: 0117 958 1639
Media	Nicol McClelland	Tel: 0117 958 1634
Commercial Manager	Suzanne Roper	Tel: 0117 958 1635
Ticketing Manager	Steve Gray	Tel: 0117 958 1640
Head Coach	Paul Hull	Tel: 0117 958 1630

BRISTOL RUGBY

Founded: 1888
Nickname: Bris
Colours: Blue and white
Change colours: Burgundy
Website: www.bristolrugby.co.uk

CONTACT DETAILS

Bristol Rugby Club Limited, c/o Clifton RFC, Station Road, Henbury, Bristol BS10 7TT

TEL: 0117 958 1630   FAX: 0117 958 1631   SHOP: 0871 208 2234

GROUND DETAILS

Address:
The Memorial Stadium, Filton Avenue, Horfield, Bristol. BS7 0AQ
Capacity: 11,848
Seated capacity: 2,370   Covered capacity: 9,878
Directions: M4 to Junction 19, M32 to junction 2 (3 miles), join B4469, Muller Road, towards Horfield (1.5 miles) to junction with Filton Avenue, which is the second set of traffic lights past Brunel Ford and the Bus Station (on your right). Turn left into Filton Avenue and the Memorial Stadium is on your left
Nearest BR Station: Bristol Parkway or Bristol Temple Meads.
Car Parking: 375 spaces
Admission:
Season tickets:
Centenary and West Stands   Adult £275, Concession £220, U16 £165
South Stand   Adult £195, Concession £165, U16 £40
West Enclosure, Centenary Terrace
 & Family Enclosure   Adult £165, Concession £135, U16 £40
Bass Terrace   Adult £155, Concession £110, U16 £40
Match day:
Centenary and West Stand   Adult £28, Concession £23, U16 £15
South Stand   Adult £20, Concession £18, U16 £8
West Enclosure, Centenary Terrace
 & Family Enclosure   Adult £18 Concession £15, U16 £8
Bass Terrace   Adult £15 Concession £13, U16 £8
24 hour on-line ticketing at: www.bristolrugby.co.uk
Club Shop: Unit 3, The Arcade, Broadmead, Bristol
Open Monday to Saturday 9am – 5pm   Tel: 0871 208 2234
Shop Manager: Helen Russell
Matchday Club Shop: Open 12noon - 5pm.
Clubhouse: Snacks and bar meals available.

PROGRAMME

Size: B5

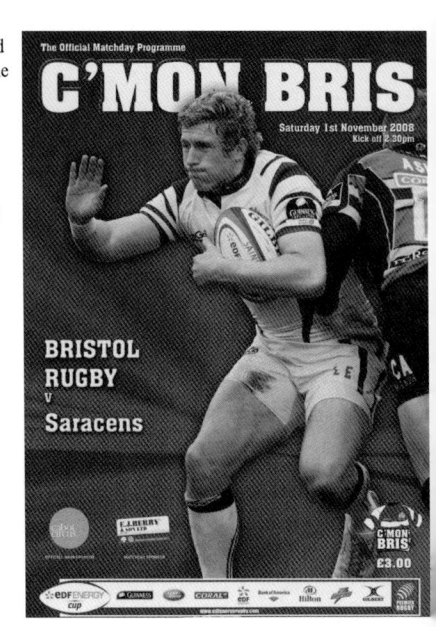

REVIEW OF THE SEASON 2008-09

2008-09 was a disappointing season for Bristol Rugby Club.

We have enjoyed 4 years in the Guinness Premiership, the highlights of which were a third place finish in the 06-07 season, followed by a Heineken cup place the following year, where the French giants Stade Francais were unable to score a single point against us at the Memorial Stadium, a feat not often achieved.

Relegation has not seen the Bristol Rugby support dwindle and on writing this our Season ticket sales for the up-coming campaign have remained at the same level as last season, which is very positive news.

When Bristol Rugby Club was last relegated from the Guinness Premiership at the end of the 2002 -2003 season, the club saw a large number of players leave. This time round and things are a lot different, the Club have a good financial footing and strong team spirit which has seen 22 senior players remain to fight their way back up to the Premiership.

In addition to this we see eight new players arrive, who will undoubtedly fit straight in to the Bristol family ethos. We also see a new leader in Head Coach Paul Hull who, after being assistant coach to Richard Hill for the last few seasons, is now looking forward to taking charge for a full season campaign.

It will be an interesting season in the newly formed Championship and Bristol can't wait for the challenge.

BRISTOL RUGBY

BRISTOL'S SEASON - 2008-09

Date	H/A	Opponents	Result & Score	Att.	15	14	13	12	11
GUINNESS PREMIERSHIP									
07-09	H	Bath	L 20-33	11021	L Arscott	T Arscott	Fatialofa	Maggs	Lemi/t
13-09	A	Harlequins	L 13-31	9497	L Arscott	T Arscott	Ne Brew	Maggs	Lemi/t
19-09	H	Sale Sharks	L 6-9	8111	L Arscott	T Arscott	Ne Brew	Barnes/p	Lemi
26-09	A	Newcastle Falcons	L 3-17	6056	Lilo	T Arscott	Ne Brew	Arscott	Lemi
01-10	H	Saracens	L 16-23	7215	L Arscott	T Arscott	Ne Brew	Barnes/2p	Lemi/t
16-11	H	Northampton Saints	W 14-13	6310	Lilo	T Arscott	Ne Brew	Barnes/c	Lemi
21-11	A	Gloucester	L 10-39	15297	L Arscott	T Arscott	Ne Brew	Barnes/c	Lemi/t
30-11	H	London Irish	L 13-18	6225	L Arscott	Robinson	Ne Brew	Eves/t	Lemi
20-12	A	Worcester	D 20-20	10015	L Arscott	Robinson/t	Ne Brew	Eves	Lemi
27-12	H	Gloucester	L 10-29	11845	L Arscott	Robinson	Ne Brew	Eves	Lemi/t
03-01	A	Northampton Saints	L 8-30	13090	L Arscott	Robinson	Ne Brew	Eves	Lemi/t
11-01	A	Saracens	L 13-37	5881	Lilo	Turner	Ne Brew	Barnes/c2p	Na Brew
13-02	N	Newcastle Falcons	L 3-35	8108	T Arscott	Robinson	Ne Brew	NaBrew	Lemi
20-02	A	Sale Sharks	L 13-32	8605	T Arscott	Robinson	Ne Brew	Eves	Lemi
01-03	H	Harlequins*	L 14-17	5005	T Arscott	Robinson	Ne Brew/t	Eves	Lemi
07-03	A	Bath	L 8-45	10600	T Arscott	Robinson/t	Ne Brew	Eves	Na Brew
13-03	H	Leicester Tigers	L 17-23	6037	L Arscott/t	T Arscott	Ne Brew	Na Brew	Lemi/t
22-03	N	London Wasps	L 19-21	8498	T Arscott	Robinson/2t	L Arscott	Fatialofa	Lemi/t
29-03	H	Worcester	W 37-18	5403	T Arscott/tdg	Robinson/2t	Ne Brew	Fatialofa/t	Lemi
04-04	A	London Irish	L 21-38	11262	L Arscott	Robinson	Eves/t	Fatialofa	T Arscott/3c
19-04	N	London Wasps	L 18-36	6508	L Arscott	Robinson/t	Eves	Fatialofa	Lemi
25-04	A	Leicester Tigers	L 3-73	18816	L Arscott/p	Robinson	Eves	Fatialofa	Lemi
EUROPEAN CHALLENGE CUP									
10-10	N	Montpellier	L 15-33	9040	Lilo	Robinson/t	Barden	Maggs	T Arscott
17-10	N	Toulon	W 39-11	5445	Lilo/t	Robinson	Ne Brew	Barnes	T Arscott
06-12	A	Northampton Saints	L 3-66	12607	Lilo	T Arscott	Eves	Maggs	Elliott
14-12	N	Northampton Saints	L 21-25	5220	L Arscott/t	T Arscott(j/t)	Ne Brew	Eves	Lemi
16-01	N	Toulon	W 37-19	5300	L Arscott	Robinson/2t	Ne Brew	Na Brew	T Arscott
25-01	H	Montpellier	W 25-14	4503	L Arscott	Robinson	Ne Brew	Na Brew	Lemi/t
EDF ENERGY CUP									
04-10	A	Northampton Saints	L 17-30	11301	Lilo/t	Robinson	Eves	Maggs	Turner/2t
24-10	A	Llanelli	L 0-27	10800	Elliott	Robinson	Eves	Fatialofa	Turner
01-11	H	Saracens	L 22-24	5025	Lilo	T Arscott	Ne Brew(h/2p)	Eves	Lemi/2t

SCORING BREAKDOWN

WHEN	Total	First Half	Second Half	1/4	2/4	3/4	4/4
the POINTS were scored	299	152	147	78	74	44	103
the POINTS were conceded	637	279	358	118	161	176	182
the TRIES were scored	33	16	17	8	8	4	13
the TRIES were conceded	77	30	47	13	17	21	26

HOW	Total	Pen. Try	Backs	Forwards	F Back	Wing	Centre	H Back	F Row	Lock	B Row
the TRIES were scored	33	1	24	8	2	15	4	3	2	1	5
the TRIES were conceded	77	2	48	27	11	13	15	9	7	7	13

KEY: * after opponents name indicates a penalty try.
Brackets after a player's name indicates he was replaced. eg (a) means he was replaced by replacement code "a" and so on.
/ after a player or replacement name is followed by any scores he made - eg /t, /c, /p, /dg or any combination of these

10	9	1	2	3	4	5	6	7	8
Jarvis/2c2p	Thomas	Irish	Linklater	Hobson	Budgett	Sidoli	Blowers/t	El Abd	Ward-Smith
Jarvis/c2p	Thomas	Irish	Linklater	Hobson	Sambucetti	Sidoli	Budgett	El Abd	Blowers
Jarvis/p	Beveridge	Clarke	Linklater	Hobson	Sambucetti	Budgett	Tooala	El Abd	Ward-Smith
Barnes/p	Beveridge	Clarke	Linklater	Hobson	Winters	Budgett	Salter	El Abd	Ward-Smith
Jarvis/cp	Beveridge	Clarke	Linklater	Hobson	Sambucetti	Budgett	Tooala	El Abd	Ward-Smith
Jarvis/c(a/t)	Beveridge	Clarke	Regan	Hobson	Winters	Sidoli	Tooala	El Abd	Ward-Smith/t
Jarvis/p	Beveridge	Clarke	Regan	Crompton	Winters	Sidoli	Tooala	El Abd	Ward-Smith
Barnes/c2p	Perry	Clarke	Regan	Crompton	Winters	Sidoli	Tooala	El Abd	Ward-Smith
Barnes/2c2p	Perry	Clarke	Regan	Hobson	Sambucetti	Sidoli	Budgett	Tooala	Ward-Smith/t
Barnes/p(b/c)	Perry	Crompton	Linklater	Hobson	Sambucetti	Sidoli	Budgett	Tooala	Ward-Smith
Barnes/p	Perry	Irish	Regan	Crompton	Winters	Sidoli	Budgett	Tooala	Ward-Smith
Jarvis	Perry	Irish	Linklater/t	Crompton	Budgett	Sidoli	Salter	Tooala	Ward-Smith
Barnes/p	Perry	Irish	Regan	Crompton	Winters	Budgett	Salter	Tooala	Ward-Smith
Jarvis/c2p	Perry	Irish	Linklater	Crompton	Attwood	Budgett	Tooala	El Abd	Ward-Smith/t
Jarvis(c/2c)	Perry	Irish	Blaney	Crompton	Attwood	Budgett	Pennycook	El Abd	Ward-Smith
Barnes/p	Perry	Irish	Blaney	Crompton	Winters	Budgett	Pennycook	El Abd	Ward-Smith
Barnes/2cp	Perry	Clarke	Regan	Crompton	Winters	Sidoli	Tooala	El Abd	Ward-Smith
Barnes/2c	Perry	Irish	Linklater	Crompton	Winters	Sidoli	Pennycook	El Abd	Tooala
Barnes/2c	Perry(d/t)	Irish	Linklater	Crompton	Sambucetti/t	Sidoli	Pennycook	El Abd	Ward-Smith
Barnes(f/t)	Thomas	Irish	Linklater/t	Crompton	Sambucetti	Sidoli	Pennycook	El Abd	Ward-Smith
Barnes/c2p	Perry	Irish	Linklater	Thompson	Sambucetti	Sidoli	Tooala(e/t)	Pennycook	Ward-Smith
Barnes	Perry	Irish	Linklater	Crompton	Sambucetti	Sidoli	Phillips	Pennycook	Ward-Smith
Jarvis/cp	Thomas	Irish	Blaney	Bracken	Sambucetti	Sidoli	Salter	Pennycook	Grieve/t
Jarvis/2c6p(h/c)	Beveridge	Clarke	Regan	Hobson	Winters	Budgett	Tooala	El Abd/t	Grieve(k/t)
Jarvis/p	Beveridge	Irish	Linklater	Bracken	Sambucetti	Attwood	Salter	Pennycook	Phillips
Barnes/c3p	Perry	Irish	Blaney	Crompton	Attwood	Sidoli	Salter	El Abd	Ward-Smith
Barnes/4c3p	Perry/t	Irish	Blaney	Crompton	Winters	Sidoli	Budgett/t	Salter	Ward-Smith
Barnes/2c2p	Perry	Irish/t	Blaney	Crompton	Winters	Sidoli	Salter	Tooala(i/t)	Ward-Smith
Ashwin	Thomas(g/c)	Irish	Regan	Bracken	Winters	Sidoli	Salter	Pennycook	Grieve
Ashwin	Thomas	Irish	Linklater	Crompton	Sambucetti	Sidoli	Salter	Pennycook	Blowers
Jarvis/2p	Beveridge	Clarke	Regan	Hobson	Winters	Budgett	Salter	El Abd	Ward-Smith

REPLACEMENTS

a- L Eves   b- A Jarvis   c- E Barnes   d- H Thomas
e- J Phillips   f- D Lemi   g- S Alford   h- C Ashwin
i- R Pennycook   j- L Robinson   k- D Ward Smith

Ne - Neil Brew, Na = Nathan Brew

LEAGUE APPEARANCES

20 Dan Ward-Smith (2)
19 David Lemi (1)
18 Ed Barnes (3)
17 Neil Brew

NUMBER OF PLAYERS USED

34 plus 7 as a replacement only

LEAGUE POINTS SCORERS

Pts	Player	T	C	P	DG
81	Ed Barnes	-	15	17	-
45	David lemi	9	-	-	-
41	Adrian Jarvis	-	7	9	-
35	Lee Robinson	7	-	-	-
15	Luke Eves	3	-	-	-
15	Dan Ward-Smith	3	-	-	-

BRISTOL STATISTICS

LEAGUE

TEAM RECORDS

MOST POINTS
Scored at Home: 68 v Exeter 27.03.05
Scored Away: 68 v Nottingham 2.10.04
Conceded at Home: 50 v Newcastle 27.12.97
Conceded Away: 76
v Bath 30.10.96
v Sale 9.11.97

MOST TRIES
Scored in a match: 10 v Rugby 28.3.92
Conceded in a match: 12 v Sale 9.11.97 (A)

BIGGEST MARGINS
Home Win: 53pts - 68-15 v Exeter 27.03.05
Away Win: 48pts -53-5 v Orrell 9.04.05
Home Defeat: 42pts: 8-50 v Newcastle 27.12.97
Away Defeat: 76pts: 0-76 v Sale 9.11.97

MOST CONSECUTIVE
Victories: 8
Defeats: 12

INDIVIDUAL RECORDS

MOST APPEARANCES
by a forward: 107(1) Dave Hinkins
by a back: 146 (4) Paul Hull

MOST CONSECUTIVE
Appearances: 81 Derek Eves 11.3.88 - 4.3.95
Matches scoring Tries: 4 Luke Nabaro
Matches scoring points: 31 Mark Tainton

MATCH RECORDS

Most Points
31   Felipe Contepomi   v Northampton 16.4.01 (H)

Most Tries
5   Luke Nabarro   v Blackheath 13.3.99 (H)

Most Conversions
5   Jason Strange   v Nottingham 2.10.04 (A)

Most Penalties
7   Mark Tainton   v Leicester 5.11.94 (H)
    Felipe Contepomi   v Wasps 8.9.02 (A)
    Jason Strange   v Penzance 5.9.04 (A)

Most Drop Goals
2   Simon Hogg   v Leicester 9.3.91 (H)

SEASON RECORDS

Most Points	287	Jason Strange	04-05
Most Tries	21	Sean Marsden	04-05
Most Conversions	64	Jason Strange	04-05
Most Penalties	56	Mark Tainton	94-95
Most Drop Goals	3	Simon Hogg	88-89
		Arwel Thomas	95-96

CAREER RECORDS

Most Points	706	Jason Strange	04-08
Most Tries	34	Sean Marsden	98-02, 03-05
Most Conversions	115	Jason Strange	04-08
Most Penalties	165	Mark Tainton	87-97
Most Drop Goals	6	Mark Tainton	87-97

LAST TEN SEASONS

	Division	P	W	D	L	F	A	P.D.	Pts	Pos	Most Points	Most Tries
99-00	P1	22	12	1	9	632	602	30	34	6	178 Henry Honiball	9 Spencer Brown
00-01	P1	22	9	1	12	443	492	-49	44	11	168 Felipe Contepomi	5 Jamie Mayer
01-02	P	22	9	1	12	591	632	-41	50	8	221 Felipe Contepomi	9 Felipe Contepomi
02-03	P	22	7	1	14	504	633	-129	36	12r	184 Felipe Contepomi	8 Brendon Daniel
03-04	N1	26	10	0	16	547	650	-103	51	9	157 Danny Gray	9 James Bailey
04-05	N1	26	22	0	4	940	355	585	105	1p	287 Jason Strange	21 Sean Marsden
05-06	P	22	8	1	13	393	445	-52	41	11	244 Jason Strange	8 David Lemi
06-07	P	22	14	1	7	398	394	4	64	3	80 Jason Strange	11 David Lemi
07-08	P	22	7	1	14	393	473	-80	38	9	95 Jason Strange	7 Tom Arscott
08-09	P	22	2	1	19	299	637	-338	17	12r	81 Ed Barnes	9 David Lemi

RFU SENIOR CUP

OVERALL PLAYING RECORD

	P	W	O	L	F	A	Pts Diff
Home	45	30	1	14	1032	566	466
Away	36	22	0	14	688	434	254
Neutral	5	1	0	4	105	131	-26
TOTAL	86	53	1	32	1825	1131	694

Other detail - Wasps Disq. 6R 04-05

TEAM RECORDS

Highest Score: 61 v Nottingham 04-05
Biggest Winning Margin: 55 (55-0) v Sandal 98/99
Highest Score Against: 46 v London Welsh 03/04
Biggest Losing Margin: 39 (43-4) v Leicester 84/85

SEASON BY SEASON

71-72	2R	78-79	DNQ	85-86	3R	92-93	3R	99-00	SF
72-73	Runners up	79-80	2R	86-87	QF	93-94	5R	00-01	5R
73-74	2R	80-81	4R	87-88	Runners up	94-95	5R	01-02	6R
74-75	2R	81-82	4R	88-89	QF	95-96	QF	02-03	6R
75-76	QF	82-83	Winners	89-90	QF	96-97	6R	03-04	6R
76-77	2R	83-84	Runners up	90-91	4R	97-98	4R	04-05	QF
77-78	QF	84-85	3R	91-92	QF	98-99	4R		

Anglo-Welsh Cup

05-06	Gp Stage
06-07	Gp Stage
07-08	Gp Stage
08-09	Gp Stage

Premiership Championship

02-03	-	07-08	-
03-04	-	08-09	-
04-05	-		
05-06	-		
06-07	SF		

EUROPEAN COMPETITIONS

TEAM RECORDS

Highest Score
89 v Viadana 18.12.05

Biggest Winning Margin
84 (89-5) v Viadana 18.12.05

Highest Score Against
66 v Northampton 06.12.08

Biggest Losing Margin
63 (3-66) v Northampton 06.12.08

INDIVIDUAL RECORDS

Most Points in a match
31 Steven Vile v Mont de Marsan 00/01
31 Felipe Contepomi v Parma 00/01

Most Tries in a match
4 David Lemi v Viadana 18.12.05

Most Conversions in a match
10 Jason Strange v Viadana 18.12.05

Most Penalties in a match
9 Steven Vile v Mont de Marsan 00/01

Most Drop Goals in a match
1 Paul Burke v Narbonne 96/97

CAREER RECORDS

Most Appearances
27 (12): Craig Short
27: Darren Crompton (10)
25: Matt Salter (4)
21: Paul Johnstone,

Most Points
195: Felipe Contepomi
109: Paul Burke
99: Steven Vile

Most Tries
10: David Lemi., Lee Robinson
6: Adam Vander, David Rees, Sean Marsden.

SEASON BY SEASON

1996-97	S	2nd Rd
1997-98	S	1st Rd
1998-99	-	-
1999-00	S	3rd Rd
2000-01	S	2nd Rd
2001-02	S	QF
2002-03	C	Gp Stage
2003-04	N.A.	-
2004-05	N.A.	-
2005-06	CC	Gp Stage
2006-07	CC	QF
2007-08	C	Gp Stage
2008-09	CC	Gp Stage

OVERALL PLAYING RECORD

	P	W	D	L	F	A	Pts Diff
Home	30	22	1	7	916	512	404
Away	33	12	0	21	704	892	-188
Neutral	-	-	-	-	-	-	-
Total	63	34	1	28	1620	1404	216

COVENTRY

Founded: 1874
Nickname: Cov
Colours:
Navy blue and white
Change colours: White
Website:
www.coventryrugby.co.uk

KEY PERSONNEL

President	Peter Rossborough
Chairman	Andrew Green
Operations Director	Michael Doyle
Sales & Marketing Director	Perry Deakin
Rugby Director	Phil Maynard - 0783 354 1029
Team Manager	Tony Gulliver - 0790 038 2297
Office Administrator	Joanne Davies
Email: office@coventryrfc.co.uk
Conference & Events Sales Manager	Jo Bayliss
Email: jbayliss@coventryrfc.co.uk
Press Liaison	John Butler
01543 432 654 (H)   0796 191 7200 (M)
Email: john@johnbutler4.wanadoo.co.uk

CONTACT DETAILS

Coventry RFC, Butts Park Arena, The Butts, Coventry. CV1 3GE.
Tel: 0871 750 9100   Fax: 0871 750 5580
email: office@coventryrfc.co.uk

GROUND DETAILS

Address:
Butts Park Arena, The Butts, Coventry. CV1 3GE.
Tel: 0871 750 9100
Fax: 0871 750 5580
email: office@coventryrfc.co.uk

Capacity: 7,000
Covered Seating: 3,000

Directions:
From Junction 7 of inner ring road, straight on up to and over traffic lights. Past Coventry Technical College on left, ground just past on left hand side.

Nearest BR Station: Coventry (15 mins walk)

Car Parking: Ample available at the ground (£3.00)

Admission:
Match day - Adult £15
Senior Citizen & Student £10;
Under 16 £5
Family (2 adults 2 children u16) £35
Season - Adult £195
Senior Citizen & Student £130;
Under 16 £65
Family (2 adults 2 children u16) £455

PROGRAMME

Size: A5   Pages: 32
Price: £2   Editor: John Butler
Advertising- Contact Dan Hardie
Tel: 0791 713 0218
Email: dhardie@coventryrfc.co.uk

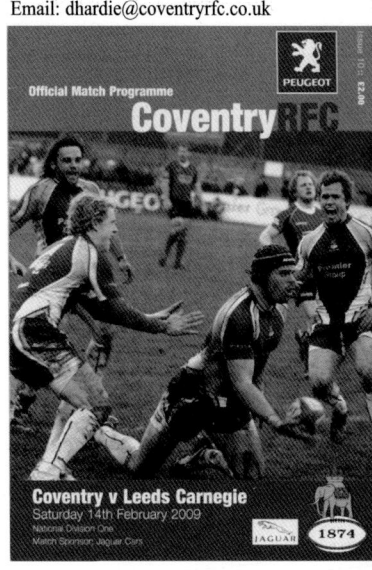

CoventryRFC
National League Division 1
2008 - 2009
Players and Coaches

Coventry squad pictured at the Butts Park Arena, September 2008
(Photograph courtesy of Sportrait.net)

REVIEW OF THE SEASON 2008-09

Coventry ended the 2008/9 season in 9th position, which equalled the efforts of a year earlier. The end result however having finished in the top eleven secured the essential spot in the new Championship, which in common with most clubs in the Division had been the major target for the season.

After a difficult summer of 2008, new Rugby Director Phil Maynard largely inherited a squad that in terms of numbers was not particularly large and despite magnificent work behind the scenes, with some injuries still kicking in, there were times when the squad and subsequent selection was severely hampered.

Consequently, although at one stage a higher position looked a possibility, a tough end to the campaign finished those hopes with finally 14 wins being achieved against 16 defeats. Highlights were clearly the home wins achieved over Exeter Chiefs and Doncaster, the Boxing Day win over arch rivals Moseley and the double over London Welsh. Indeed five wins were achieved overall against sides from the top half of the table.

Top try scorer for the second season running was New Zealand number eight Laurie McGlone with 11, followed by Myles Dorrian and Donovan Sanders both with 9. Long serving wing Kurt Johnson, who's appearances were cut short by injury finished the season on 99 league tries for the club, although his overall total had previously passed century mark. Dorrian finished as top points scorer with 150, whilst the number of appearances were led by Chris Whitehead and prop forward Rob Dugard both with 32.

The squad for the inaugural Championship season will be much changed from 2008/9, two of the earliest recruits being lock forward Arthur Brenton from Plymouth Albion and previously Bedford Blues, whilst another lock, Louis Mc Gowan has returned to the club from Rotherham Titans having previously had one season with "Cov" in 2001/2. There can be no doubt, 2009/10 will be tough with a top eight finish clearly being the target.

1874
COVENTRY

COVENTRY'S SEASON - 2008-09

CHAMPIONSHIP

Date	H/A	Opponents	Result & Score	Att.	15	14	13	12	11
NATIONAL ONE									
30-08	A	Plymouth Albion	L 5-37	2892	Parry	Montague	Russell	Winter	Slater/t
06-09	H	Cornish Pirates	W 16-0	1269	Russell	Parry	McLean/c3p	Winter	Slater
13-09	A	Moseley	L 12-34	1090	Russell	Parry	McLean/c	Winter	Slater
20-09	H	Esher	W 33-8	892	Russell/t	McLean/tc2p	Dixon	Winter	Parry/2t
27-09	A	Sedgley Park	W 30-27	638	Russell	McLean/3c3p	Dixon/t	Winter	Parry
03-10	H	Bedford	L 3-26	1700	Russell	McLean/p	Dixon	Sanders	Parry
11-10	A	Doncaster	L 22-34	1443	Dorrian/t	McLean/2cp	Dixon	Sanders	Winter
19-10	A	Leeds Carnegie	L 5-57	2972	Russell	McLean	Dixon	Sanders/t	Winter
25-10	H	Manchester	W 29-18	978	Russell	Montague	Dixon	Sanders/t	Winter
01-11	H	Newbury	W 31-7	1204	Russell	Johnson	Dixon	Sanders/t	Winter
08-11	A	Rotherham	L 27-28	892	Russell	Johnson	Dixon	Sanders/2t	Winter
15-11	H	Otley	W 48-3	838	Russell	McLean/5cp	Dixon	Sanders	Winter/2t
22-11	A	Exeter	L 8-45	4256	Russell	McLean/p	Dixon	Sanders	Winter
29-11	A	London Welsh	W 23-21	710	Russell	Hurrell	Dixon	Sanders	Winter
13-12	H	Plymouth Albion	L 6-7	961	Russell	Hurrell	Dixon	Sanders	Winter
21-12	A	Cornish Pirates	L 14-32	2877	Russell	Hurrell/t	Dixon	Sanders	Winter
26-12	H	Moseley	W 27-10	3638	Russell	Hurrell	Grove/t	Sanders	Winter
24-01	A	Bedford	L 9-23	2506	Toft	Hurrell	Dixon	Sanders	Winter
31-01	H	Doncaster	W 26-20	1252	Toft	Slater/t	Dixon	Sanders/t	Winter
14-02	H	Leeds Carnegie	L 11-15	1600	Russell	Johnson	Dixon	Sanders	Winter
21-02	A	Manchester	W 41-24	347	Russell	Toft	Lewis/t	McLean/t3c	Winter(d/t)
28-02	H	Sedgley Park	W 29-24	1297	Russell	Toft(d/2t)	Dixon/t	Sanders	Winter
07-03	A	Newbury	L 10-14	590	Toft/t	Parry	Dixon	Sanders	Winter
14-03	H	Rotherham	L 31-32	1228	Toft	Parry/2t	Dixon	Sanders	McLean/3c
21-03	A	Esher	L 18-27	1104	Russell	Johnson/t	Dixon	Sanders	Parry
28-03	A	Otley	W 32-13	463	Winter	Parry	Dixon	Sanders/2t	Hurrell
04-04	H	Exeter	W 35-28	1229	Winter	Johnson	Dixon/t	Sanders	Toft/t
11-04	H	London Welsh	W 36-30	1319	Russell/2c4p	Winter/t	Dixon	Sanders	Toft
19-04	A	Nottingham	L 0-55	1088	Russell	Winter	McLean	Sanders	Toft
25-04	H	Nottingham	L 22-37	1554	Winter	Johnson/t	Russell	Sanders	Hurrell

EDF ENERGY NATIONAL TROPHY

4 17-01	A	Rotherham	W 26-16		Russell	Hurrell/t	Dixon	Sanders/t	Winter
5 08-02	A	Leeds Carnegie	L 0-52		Toft	Johnson	Winter	McLean	Parry

SCORING BREAKDOWN

WHEN	Total	First Half	Second Half	1/4	2/4	3/4	4/4
the POINTS were scored	639	316	323	148	168	140	183
the POINTS were conceded	712	379	333	141	238	162	171
the TRIES were scored	83	39	44	16	23	19	25
the TRIES were conceded	94	46	48	17	29	23	25

HOW	Total	Pen. Try	Backs	Forwards	F Back	Wing	Centre	H Back	F Row	Lock	B Row
the TRIES were scored	83	-	51	32	3	17	14	17	9	4	19
the TRIES were conceded	94	3	70	21	10	34	17	9	5	7	9

KEY: * after opponents name indicates a penalty try.
Brackets after a player's name indicates he was replaced. eg (a) means he was replaced by replacement code "a" and so on.
/ after a player or replacement name is followed by any scores he made - eg /t, /c, /p, /dg or any combination of these

10	9	1	2	3	4	5	6	7	8
Dorrian	Jones	Dugard	Whitehead	Brits	Burgess	Walton	Ventner	Clayton	McGlone
Dorrian/t	Jones	Maddocks	Whitehead	Brits	Herrington	Walton	Ventner	Miller	McGlone
Dorrian	Walls/t	Maddocks/t	Whitehead	Dugard	Herrington	Walton	Miller	Clayton	McGlone
Dorrian/t	Slater	Whitehall	Whitehead	Dugard	Herrington	Walton	Ventner	Miller	McGlone
Dorrian	Slater/t	Whitehall	Whitehead	Dugard/t	Herrington	Burgess	Ventner	Clayton	McGlone
Dorrian	Slater	Whitehall	Whitehead	Dugard	Herrington	Burgess	Ventner	Clayton	McGlone
Hayes	Jones/t	Whitehall	Whitehead	Dugard	Walton	Burgess	Miller/t	Clayton	McGlone
Dorrian	Jones	Ovens	Whitehead	Dugard	Thomas	Burgess	Miller	Pons	McGlone
Dorrian/3cp	Jones	Ovens	Whitehead	Dugard	Herrington	Burgess	Miller	Bell	McGlone/3t
Dorrian/2t3c	Jones	Ovens	Whitehead	Dugard	Herrington	Burgess	Ventner	Miller/t(a/t)	McGlone
Dorrian/3c2p	Jones	Ovens	Whitehead	Dugard	Herrington	Burgess	Ventner	Miller	McGlone/t
Dorrian	Jones	Ovens	Pearl(b/t)	Dugard	Herrington/t	Lyons	Ventner	Miller/t	Thomas/t
Dorrian	Jones	Ovens	Whitehead	Dugard	Herrington	Lyons	Ventner	Miller	Thomas(c/t)
Dorrian/2c2pdg	Jones	Ovens	Whitehead/t	Brits	Burgess	Lyons	Ventner	Miller	McGlone/t
Dorrian/2p	Jones	Ovens	Whitehead	Brits	Burgess	Lyons	Ventner	Miller	McGlone
Dorrian/3p	Jones	Ovens	Whitehead	Brits	Burgess	Lyons	Ventner	Pons	McGlone
Dorrian/3c2p	Jones/t	Dugard	Whitehead	Brits	Herrington	Burgess	Ventner	Miller	McGlone/t
Dorrian/3p	Jones	Dugard	Whitehead	Brits	Herrington	Burgess	Ventner	Miller	McGlone
Dorrian/3c	Jones	Dugard	Whitehead	Brits	Herrington	Burgess	Ventner	Miller/2t	McGlone
Dorrian/2p	Walls/t	Dugard	Whitehead	Brits	Herrington	Burgess	Ventner	Miller	McGlone
Dorrian	Walls	Dugard/t	Whitehead/t	Brits	Herrington/2t	Burgess	Ventner	Miller	McGlone
Dorrian/t2c	Walls	Dugard	Whitehead/t	Brits	Herrington	Burgess	Ventner	Miller	McGlone
Walls	Slater	Dugard	Pearl	Brits	Herrington	Atkinson	Ventner	Clayton	McGlone/t
Hayes/t	Walls/t	Whitehall	Whitehead	Brits	Herrington	Burgess	Ventner	Clayton	McGlone/t
Hayes/tc2p	Walls	Whitehall	Whitehead	Dugard	Herrington	Atkinson	Ventner	Clayton	McGlone
Russell/t3cp(e/p)	Walls	Dugard	Whitehead	Brits	Herrington	Atkinson	Miller	Clayton	McGlone/t
Russell/2c2p(e/tc)	Walls/tdg	Dugard	Whitehead	Brits	Herrington	Ventner	Miller	Clayton	McGlone
Dorrian/t	Walls	Dugard	Whitehead/t	Brits/t	Herrington	Ventner	Miller	Clayton	McGlone
Dorrian	Walls	Davis	Whitehead	Dugard	Herrington	Atkinson	Ventner	Miller	McGlone
Dorrian/2cp	Walls	Davis	Whitehead	Dugard	Herrington/t	Atkinson	Ventner	Miller/t	McGlone
Dorrian/2t3c	Jones	Dugard	Whitehead	Brits	Herrington	Burgess	Ventner	Miller	McGlone
Hayes	Walls	Whitehall	Pearl	Brits	Atkinson	Lyons	Clayton	Pons	Thomas

REPLACEMENTS a- B Pons   b- C Whitehead   c- L McGlone
d- L Parry   e- T Hayes

LEAGUE APPEARANCES

28 Chris Whitehead (2), Laurie McGlone (2)
27 Oliver Winter (2)
25 Ben Russell (1), Rob Dugard (5), Neeno Ventner (2), Myles Dorrian

LEAGUE POINTS SCORERS

Pts	Player	T	C	P	DG
134	Myles Dorrian	7	21	18	1
84	Ronnie McLean	2	19	12	-
55	Laurie McGlone	11	-	-	-
45	Ben Russell	2	7	7	-
40	Donovan Sanders	8	-	-	-
35	Lee Parry	7	-	-	-

NUMBER OF PLAYERS USED

36 plus 3 as a replacement only

COVENTRY STATISTICS

LEAGUE

TEAM RECORDS

MOST POINTS
Scored at Home: 102 v Nottingham 5.10.96
Scored Away: 61 v Rugby 14.9.96
Conceded at Home: 57 v Worcester 10.04.04
Conceded Away: 68 v Leeds Tykes 03.04.01

MOST TRIES
Scored in a match: 14 v Nottingham 5.10.96
Conceded in a match: 12 v Leeds Tykes 03.04.01

BIGGEST MARGINS
Home Win: 80pts - 102-22 v Nottingham 5.10.96
Away Win: 58pts - 61-3 v Rugby 14.9.96
Home Defeat: 39pts - 6-45 v Rotherham 15.04.00
18-57 v Worcester 10.04.04
Away Defeat: 62pts - 3-65 v Northampton 24.11.08

MOST CONSECUTIVE
Victories: 9
Defeats: 13

INDIVIDUAL RECORDS

MOST APPEARANCES
by a forward: 216 (36) Dave Addleton
by a back: 197 (13) Kurt Johnson

MOST CONSECUTIVE
Appearances: 35
Richard Angell & Warwick Bullock
Matches scoring Tries: 5 Ally McLean, Kurt Johnson
Matches scoring points: 19 Gareth Cull 03-04

MATCH RECORDS

Most Points
42 Jez Harris v Nottingham 5.10.96 (H)
Most Tries
4 Andy Smallwood v Wakefield 8.5.99 (H)
Most Conversions
13 Jez Harris v Nottingham 5.10.96 (H)
Most Penalties
9 Matt Leek v Otley 13.11.04 (H)
Most Drop Goals
2 Mark Lakey v Moseley 3.4.93 (H)
v Lon Irish 8.10.94 (H)
Jez Harris v Wakefield 21.9.96 (H)

SEASON RECORDS

Most Points	305	Steve Gough	98-99
Most Tries	17	Andy Smallwood	96-97
Most Conversions	48	Jez Harris	96-97
		SteveGough	98-99
Most Penalties	53	Steve Gough	98-99
Most Drop Goals	5	Jez Harris	96-97

CAREER RECORDS

Most Points	571	Steve Gough	98-00
Most Tries	101	Kurt Johnson	99-09
Most Conversions	95	Steve Gough	98-00
Most Penalties	102	Steve Gough	98-00
Most Drop Goals	10	Mark Lakey	87-95

LAST TEN SEASONS

	Division	P	W	D	L	F	A	P.D.	Pts	Pos	Most Points	Most Tries
99-00	P2	26	15	0	11	714	589	125	30	6	266 Steve Gough	12 A Smallwood & Kurt Johnson
00-01	N1	26	14	0	12	565	604	-39	66	5	239 Martyn Davies	14 Kurt Johnson
01-02	N1	26	16	3	7	730	559	171	82	4	223 Martyn Davies	14 Kurt Johnson
02-03	N1	26	14	0	12	761	684	77	68	6	128 Lee Rust	14 Kurt Johnson
03-04	N1	26	6	2	18	488	733	-245	37	12	184 Gareth Cull	8 Kurt Johnson
04-05	N1	26	16	1	9	666	565	101	78	6	92 Richard Davies	10 Kurt Johnson
05-06	N1	26	9	0	17	593	732	-139	53	10	251 James Moore	9 Kurt Johnson
06-07	N1	30	12	2	16	569	745	-176	65	10	217 Ben Russell	9 George Dixon
07-08	N1	30	11	1	18	637	731	-94	63	9	145 Ben Russell	9 Laurie McGlone
08-09	N1	30	14	0	16	639	712	-73	72	9	134 Myles Dorrian	11 Laurie McGlone

RFU SENIOR CUP

OVERALL PLAYING RECORD

	P	W	O	L	F	A	Pts Diff
Home	42	25	0	17	910	678	232
Away	41	26	0	15	830	608	222
Neutral	2	2	0	0	53	21	32
TOTAL	85	53	0	32	1793	1307	486

TEAM RECORDS

Highest Score: 83 v Sheffield 97/98
Biggest Winning Margin: 64 (83-19) v Sheffield 97/98
Highest Score Against: 61 v Rotherham 02/03
Biggest Losing Margin: 49 (12-61) v Rotherham 02/03

SEASON BY SEASON

Season	Result	Season	Result	Season	Result	Season	Result	Season	Result
71-72	SF	78-79	2R	85-86	3R	92-93	3R	99-00	5R
72-73	Winners	79-80	2R	86-87	QF	93-94	4R	00-01	4R
73-74	Winners	80-81	4R	87-88	4R	94-95	4R	01-02	4R
74-75	SF	81-82	SF	88-89	2R	95-96	5R	02-03	3R
75-76	2R	82-83	SF	89-90	2R	96-97	6R	03-04	3R
76-77	1R	83-84	QF	90-91	3R	97-98	4R	04-05	5R
77-78	SF	84-85	SF	91-92	3R	98-99	3R		

NATIONAL TROPHY

05-06	6 R	06-07	Q.F.	07-08	5 R	08-09	5 R

PLAYERS

	Position	D.o.B.	Apps.	Pts.	T	C	P	DG
Ben Russell	Full back	09/07/1984	77 (2)	407	7	72	74	2
Kurt Johnson	Winger	23/06/1977	197 (13)	505	101	-	-	-
Ben Toft	Winger	18/03/1986	39 (11)	35	7	-	-	-
George Dixon	Winger	02/09/1983	50 (6)	75	15	-	-	-
Will Hurrell	Winger		7	5	1	-	-	-
Donovan Sanders	Centre	15/02/1981	91 (6)	120	24	-	-	-
Lee Parry	Winger	12/02/1987	15 (12)	35	7	-	-	-
Oliver Winter	Winger	12/2/1987	27 (2)	15	3	-	-	-
Ronnie McLean	Centre	05/06/1985	20 (10)	170	5	35	25	
Myles Dorrian	Fly half	26/11/1982	78 (3)	213	18	27	21	2
Tom Slater	Scrum half	11/10/1986	17 (23)	25	5	-	-	-
Nathan Jones	Scrum half	24/02/1984	27 (5)	5	1	-	-	-
Michael Walls	Scrum half	14/03/1980	60 (25)	48	9	-	-	1
Rod Dugard	Prop		25 (5)	10	2	-	-	-
Dave Maddocks	Prop	20/01/1983	17 (8)	25	5	-	-	-
Ricky Whitehall	Prop	31/05/1986	8 (14)	-	-	-	-	-
Rudi Brits	Prop	08/10/1980	63 (22)	10	2	-	-	-
Stuart Pearl	Hooker	08/06/1980	2 (23)	-	-	-	-	-
Chris Whitehead	Hooker	09/05/1986	53 (7)	40	8	-	-	-
Sam Herrington	Lock		24 (2)	10	2	-	-	-
Carl Burgess	Lock		18 (6)	-	-	-	-	-
Heeno Ventner	Back row	22/06/1981	91 (21)	20	4	-	-	-
Jamie Miller	Back row	08/02/1987	32 (17)	40	8	-	-	-
Laurie McGlone	Back row	26/03/1979	57 (3)	100	20	-	-	-
Darren Clayton	Back row	12/12/1985	41 (16)	20	4	-	-	-

DONCASTER RFC

KEY PERSONNEL

President: Tony DeMulder   **Chairman:** Steve Lloyd

Chief Executive
Rhonda Job
c/o Donaster RFC   Tel/Fax as club
(M) 07901 517602   email: rhondajob@castle-park.co.uk

Championship Contact
John Lowe
c/o Donaster RFC   Tel/Fax as club
(M) 07977 112706   email: johnlowe@drfc.co.uk

Director of Rugby
Lynn Howells
c/o Donaster RFC   Tel/Fax as club
(M) 07908 815744   email dor@castle-park.co.uk

1st XV Manager / Match Officials' Contact
Paul Turton
c/o Donaster RFC   Tel/Fax as club
(M) 07767 877083

Community Programme Manager
(DIRECT Reg.1117762)
Suzie Hill
c/o Donaster RFC   Tel/Fax as club
(M) 07946 868018
email: funding@castle-park.co.uk

Media Manager
Martin Haythorn
c/o Donaster RFC   Tel/Fax as club
(M) 07908 342105   email: press@castle-park.co.uk

Founded: 1875

Nickname
The Knights

Colours: Navy blue, with red & white trim

Change colours: Red, with navy blue and white trim

Website
www.drfc.co.uk

GROUND DETAILS

Address:
Castle Park, Armthorpe Road, Doncaster DN2 5QB
Tel: 01302 831388   Fax: 01302 836300
e-mail: reception@castle-park.co.uk

Capacity: 5,000
Seated: 1,600
Covered: 1,600

Directions: Leave M18 at J4 and follow A630 to Doncaster for 1 Mile. At 2nd r'about turn left to Armthorpe. At the next r'about in Armthorpe go right and the club is then 1.3 miles on the left beyond the built up area.

Nearest BR station: Doncaster (East Coast main line) 3 miles.

Local Airport: Doncaster Airport (DSA) is 7 miles from club.

Car Parking: Spaces for 1000 cars at the ground

Admission:
Matchday: Standing £12, Seated £15, concessions available.
Season: Standing £144, Seated £175

Clubhouse
Open every day & evening.
Food available before & after all matches only.
Functions: Five rooms available with full in-house facilities, contact Chris Elliott on 01302 831496

Club Shop
Open Mon-Fri 8-5.30pm, 1st XV matchdays and Sunday mornings in season. Contact club office on 01302 831388

CONTACT DETAILS

c/o Doncaster RFC,
Castle Park,
Armthorpe Road,
Doncaster DN2 5QB
Tel: 01302 831388
Fax: 01302 836300
email: reception@castle-park.co.uk

PROGRAMME

Size: A5   Pages: 48   Price: £2
Editor: James Criddle
Advertising: Contact Jon Kaye 01302 831388

REVIEW OF THE SEASON 2008-09

Doncaster Knights started the season with a much changed squad with 21 changes as Director of Rugby Lynn Howells endeavoured to reduce the average age. Early on they took some time for the team to settle and they lost 4 and drew 1 of their first 11 games. Once they had settled however their performance improved significantly and they only lost 3 and drew 1 of their last 19.

Highlights of the season were probably the three home victories against Bedford, Nottingham and Leeds, with the latter one being the eventual league winner's first defeat of the season. Away highlights were a first ever win at Cornish Pirates and a draw at Exeter in the last two games of the season. The six Yorkshire local derbies involving Leeds, Rotherham and Otley also presented a mini-contest within the league with the Knights winning 5 out of these 6 matches. They were also involved in two exciting home games against Exeter which, unfortunately, the Knights lost on both occasions by a single score. Looking to the coming season, the Knights will be encouraged with their improved performances against the other top 5 sides in the league as compared with the three previous seasons.

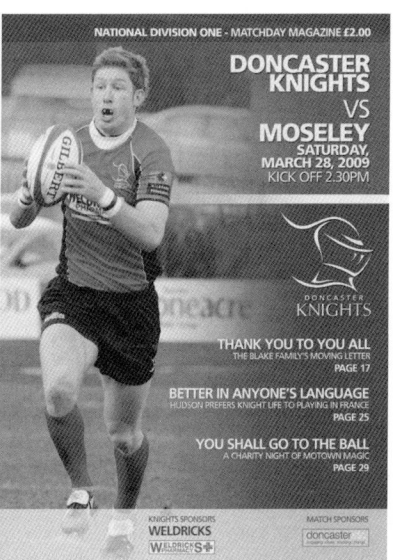

With the fight for promotion, the decision to reduce the size of the league and the possibility of the top four being possibly involved in an Anglo-Welsh Tournament kept the excitement going through right to the very end. With Leeds and Exeter assured of the top two places, the Knights, Nottingham and Bedford were involved in a mini-battle for league positions which went down to the very last day.

Doncaster Knights were one of several full-time clubs who lead the fight for a the new Championship and British and Irish Cup Competitions and, in spite of some teething problems, they see both as exciting concepts that will auger well for the future of a 2nd tier of professional rugby provided they get full financial and logistic support from the RFU

DONCASTER'S SEASON - 2008-09

CHAMPIONSHIP

NATIONAL ONE

Date	H/A	Opponents	Result & Score	Att.	15	14	13	12	11
30-08	H	Otley	W 36-15	868	Carter/t	Wright	Hughes	Tonga'uiha	Hughes/t
07-09	A	London Welsh*	L 16-31	960	Goss	Davies	Hughes	Tonga'uiha	Bishop
14-09	H	Rotherham	W 28-22	1613	Carter/t	Bishop	Tonga'uiha	Armitage	Hughes
20-09	A	Manchester	W 39-23	423	Lennard/3c2p	Hughes/t	Tonga'uiha	Armitage/t	van Vuuren/t
27-09	H	Newbury*	W 37-9	846	Carter/t	Hughes	Tonga'uiha	McColl	van Vuuren
05-10	A	Nottingham	L 9-18	1345	Carter	Hughes	Tonga'uiha	McColl	Bishop(c/2p)
11-10	H	Coventry*	W 34-22	1443	Carter	Davies	Tonga'uiha	Armitage/t	van Vuuren/t
18-10	H	Cornish Pirates	D 24-24	1102	Carter	Davies	Tonga'uiha	Armitage	van Vuuren
25-10	A	Sedgley Park	W 41-3	595	Carter	Davies	Tonga'uiha/t	Armitage	van Vuuren/t
01-11	A	Leeds Carnegie	L 13-28	3415	Carter	Davies	Tonga'uiha	Armitage/t	Hughes
08-11	A	Plymouth Albion	L 18-21	1983	Carter	Davies	Armitage	Tonga'uiha/t	Goss
15-11	A	Moseley	W 19-12	682	Carter	Davies	Armitage	Tonga'uiha	van Vuuren/t
22-11	H	Bedford	W 50-21	1735	Lennard/4c3p	Davies/2t	Tonga'uiha	Armitage	van Vuuren/t
29-11	A	Esher*	W 23-10	694	Lennard/2c2p	Davies/t	Tonga'uiha	Armitage	van Vuuren
06-12	H	Exeter	L 29-34	1388	Lennard/2c	Davies/3t	Tonga'uiha	Armitage	van Vuuren
13-12	A	Otley	W 27-16	457	Lennard/2cp	Davies	Armitage	McColl/t	van Vuuren/t
20-12	H	London Welsh	W 26-13	1300	Lennard/2p	Davies/t	Armitage/t	Tonga'uiha	van Vuuren
27-12	A	Rotherham	W 29-26	2548	Carter/t	Davies/t	Tonga'uiha	Armitage	van Vuuren
03-01	H	Manchester	W 52-10	1169	Carter/2t	Davies	Armitage	Tonga'uiha	Wright
24-01	H	Nottingham	W 25-14	1872	Carter	Davies/t	Tonga'uiha/t	Armitage	van Vuuren
31-01	A	Coventry*	L 20-26	1252	Carter	Davies/t	Armitage	McColl	van Vuuren
21-02	H	Sedgley Park	W 42-5	1194	Carter	Davies/2t	McColl/t	Armitage	Wright
07-03	H	Leeds Carnegie	W 27-12	2203	Carter	Davies	Tonga'uiha/dg	Armitage/t	Wright
14-03	H	Plymouth Albion	W 28-23	1027	Carter	Wright/t	McColl	Armitage	van Vuuren
21-03	A	Newbury*	W 50-17	310	Carter	Davies	Armitage/t	Tonga'uiha/t	Wright
28-03	H	Moseley	W 41-17	1438	Carter	Davies/t	Tonga'uiha/t	Armitage/t	Wright
04-04	A	Bedford	L 20-42	3048	Carter(e/t)	Davies	Armitage	Tonga'uiha	van Vuuren/t
11-04	H	Esher	W 50-25	1322	Carter	Davies	Tonga'uiha	Armitage/t	van Vuuren
19-04	N	Cornish Pirates*	W 33-23	2437	Carter	Davies	McColl	Armitage	Wright
25-04	A	Exeter	D 9-9	4972	Carter	Davies	Armitage	Tonga'uiha	Wright

EDF ENERGY NATIONAL TROPHY

4	17-01	H	Plymouth Albion	W 21-3		Carter	Davies	Armitage	McColl/t	Wright
5	14-02	A	Sedgley Park	W 28-6		Lennard/2c3p	Davies/t	Armitage	Tonga'uiha/t	Wright
Q.F.	28-02	H	Exeter	L 17-20		Carter	Davies	Tonga'uiha	Armitage	Wright/t

SCORING BREAKDOWN

WHEN	Total	First Half	Second Half	1/4	2/4	3/4	4/4
the POINTS were scored	895	416	479	186	230	234	240
the POINTS were conceded	571	325	246	135	190	123	123
the TRIES were scored	109	49	60	22	27	28	31
the TRIES were conceded	66	35	31	13	22	14	17

HOW	Total	Pen. Try	Backs	Forwards	F Back	Wing	Centre	H Back	F Row	Lock	B Row
the TRIES were scored	109	7	58	44	7	24	15	12	10	6	28
the TRIES were conceded	66	1	48	17	7	20	6	15	5	1	11

KEY: * after opponents name indicates a penalty try.
Brackets after a player's name indicates he was replaced. eg (a) means he was replaced by replacement code "a" and so on.
/ after a player or replacement name is followed by any scores he made - eg /t, /c, /p, /dg or any combination of these

10	9	1	2	3	4	5	6	7	8
Warnock/t3c	Hallam	List(a/t)	Boden	Tau	Smith	Kenworthy	Griffiths/t	Grainger	Kettle/t
Warnock/c3p	Albinson	Davies	Boden	Tau	Griffiths	Kenworthy	Cochrane	Grainger	Kettle
Warnock/c3p	Albinson(b/t)	List	Boden	Tau	Smith	Kenworthy	Griffiths	Grainger/t	Kettle
Warnock/c	Albinson/t	Davies	Boden	Cusack	Smith	Kenworthy	Griffiths	Cochrane	Kettle/t
Warnock/c2p(c/2c)	Albinson	List	Boden	Cusack(a/t)	Griffiths/t	Kenworthy	Kettle/t	Grainger	Planchant
Warnock/dg	Hallam	List	Boden	Tau	Griffiths	Kenworthy	Kettle	Grainger	Planchant
Lennard/4c2p	Hallam	List	Boden	Cusack	Smith	Kenworthy	Griffiths/t	Cochrane	Afu
Lennard/tc4p	Albinson	List	Boden	Tau	Smith	Kenworthy	Griffiths	Grainger/t	Afu
Lennard/3c4pdg	Albinson	Toke	Jenkins/t	Cusack	Griffiths/t	Kenworthy	Afu	Grainger	Planchant
Lennard/cpdg	Hallam	List	Jenkins	Tau	Griffiths	Kenworthy	Afu	Grainger	Planchant
Warnock/c2p	Hallam	List	Jenkins	Tau	Griffiths	Kenworthy	Afu	Cochrane	Planchant/t
Lennard/2c	Albinson/t	List	Jenkins	Cusack	Griffiths/t	Kenworthy	Afu	Grainger	Planchant
Warnock/dg	Hallam	List	Jenkins/t	Tau	Griffiths	Kenworthy	Afu/t	Cochrane/t	Planchant
Warnock/dg	Albinson	Davies	Jenkins	Cusack	Griffiths	Kenworthy	Afu	Cochrane	Planchant
Warner	Albinson	List	Jenkins	Tau	Griffiths	Kenworthy	Afu	Cochrane	Planchant/t
Warnock	Albinson	Davies/t	Jenkins	Tau	Smith	Kenworthy	Afu	Cochrane/t	Planchant
Warnock/cp	Hallam	Davies	Boden	Tau	Griffiths/t	Kenworthy	Afu	Cochrane	Planchant
Warnock(c/c4p)	Hallam	Davies	Boden	Tau	Griffiths	Kenworthy	Afu/t	Grainger	Planchant
Lennard/6c	Hallam(d/t)	List	Boden/t	Cusack	Griffiths	Kenworthy	Kettle/t	Cochrane/t	Planchant/2t
Lennard/t2cpdg	Hallam	List	Boden	Tau	Griffiths	Kenworthy	Afu	Cochrane	Planchant
Lennard/2c2p	Hallam	List	Boden	Tau	Griffiths	Kenworthy	Kettle	Cochrane	Planchant
Warnock/3c2p	Hallam	Davies	Boden	Tau	Griffiths	Smith	Afu	Grainger/t	Kettle/2t
Lennard/c3pdg	D'Arcy	Davies	Boden	Cusack	Smith/t	Kenworthy	Afu	Grainger	Planchant
Lennard/t2c3p	D'Arcy	List	Boden	Cusack	Smith	Kenworthy	Afu/t	Grainger	Kettle
Lennard/t5c	D'Arcy/t	Davies	Boden	Cusack/t	Smith	Kenworthy	Afu	Cochrane/t	Planchant
Lennard/tc3pdg(e/c)	D'Arcy	Davies	Boden	Tau	Smith	Kenworthy/t	Afu	Cochrane	Kettle
Lennard/2c2p	D'Arcy	List	Boden	Tau	Griffiths	Kenworthy	Afu	Grainger	Kettle
Lennard/6cp	D'Arcy	Davies/t	Boden	Cusack	Griffiths	Kenworthy	Kettle/t	Cochrane/2t	Afu/2t
Lennard/2c2pdg	D'Arcy/t	Davies/2t	Boden	Cusack	Griffiths	Kenworthy	Kettle	Cochrane	Afu
Lennard/2pdg	D'Arcy	Davies	Boden	Cusack	Griffiths	Kenworthy	Cochrane	Grainger	Afu
Lennard/c3p	Albinson	Davies	Jenkins	Tau	Smith	Griffiths	Afu	Kettle	Grainger/t
Warnock/t	Hallam	Davies	Boden	Cusack	Smith	Kenworthy	Afu	Grainger	Kettle
Lennard/4p	Hallam	List	Boden	Tau	Griffiths	Smith	Afu	Grainger	Kettle

REPLACEMENTS

a- T Toke   b- C Hallam   c- J Lennard
d- J Albinson   e- A Warnock

LEAGUE APPEARANCES

- 29 Glen Kenworthy (1)
- 26 Bevon Armitage (2)
- 25 Hudson Tonga'uiha (4). David Griffiths (1)
- 24 Wes Davies
- 23 Anthony Carter (3)

NUMBER OF PLAYERS USED

32 plus 1 as a replacement only

LEAGUE POINTS SCORERS

Pts	Player	T	C	P	DG
298	Jamie Lennard	5	57	46	7
84	Ali Warnock	2	13	13	3
65	Wes Davies	13	-	-	-
40	Bevon Armitage	8	-	-	-
40	D van Vuuren	8	-	-	-
40	Adam Kettle	8	-	-	-

DONCASTER STATISTICS

LEAGUE
Records relate to National league rugby only.

TEAM RECORDS

MOST POINTS
Scored at Home: 95 v West Hartlepool 24.11.01
Scored Away: 72 v Scunthorpe 30.3.02
Conceded at Home: 49 v Wharfedale 14.9.02
Conceded Away: 63 v Cornish Pirates 23.3.08

MOST TRIES
Scored in a match: 15 v W Hartlepool 24.11.01
Conceded in a match: 9 v Cornish Pirates 23.3.08

BIGGEST MARGINS
Home Win: 83 pts: 86-3 v Darlington MP 13.4.02
Away Win: 45pts: 48-3 v Rosslyn Park 22.1.05
Home Defeat: 31pts: 18-49 v Wharfedale 14.9.02
Away Defeat: 45pts
5-50 v Nuneaton 22.1.00 & 0-45 v Harlequins 12.2.06

MOST CONSECUTIVE
Victories: 19
Defeats: 6

INDIVIDUAL RECORDS

MOST APPEARANCES
by a forward: 127: Ngazu Tau (18)
by a back: 95 (4) : Donovan van Vuuren

MOST CONSECUTIVE
Appearances: 42 Gavin Baldwin 25.11.00 - 14.9.02
Matches scoring Tries: 8 Chris Conway 19.1.02 - 30.3.02
Matches scoring points: 20 John Liley 10.11.01 - 31.8.02

MATCH RECORDS

Most Points
32   John Liley   v Scunthorpe 30.3.02 (A)

Most Tries
7   Matt Donkin   v Whitchurch 10.11.01 (H)

Most Conversions
10   John Liley   v W Hartlepool 24.11.01 (H)

Most Penalties
9   John Liley   v Sheffield 4.12.99 (H)

Most Drop Goals
1   19 times by 8 players including
Richard Poskitt (2) Mark Woodrow (3),
Ali Warnock (3), Jamie Lennard (7) .

SEASON RECORDS

Most Points	359	John Liley	01-02
Most Tries	25	Jason Forster	06-07
Most Conversions	89	John Liley	01-02
Most Penalties	57	Rob Liley	02-03
		Rob Liley	04-05
Most Drop Goals	7	Jamie Lennard	08-09

CAREER RECORDS

Most Points	1013	Rob Liley	02-06
Most Tries	59	Chris Conway	99-03
Most Conversions	181	Rob Liley	02-06
Most Penalties	184	Rob Liley	02-06
Most Drop Goals	7	Jamie Lennard	08-09

LAST TEN SEASONS

	Division	P	W	D	L	F	A	P.D.	Pts	Pos	Most Points	Most Tries
99-00	N2N	26	12	2	12	656	539	117	26	6	279 John Liley	19 Chris Conway
00-01	N3N	*23	16	0	7	579	352	227	32	4	244 John Liley	13 Derek Eves
01-02	N3N	26	25	0	1	1074	357	717	50	1p	359 John Liley	24 Derek Eves & Chris Conway
02-03	N2	26	14	0	12	630	551	135	28	7	196 Rob Liley	11 Derek Eves
03-04	N2	26	17	0	9	692	487	205	34	4	268 Rob Liley	12 Nick Wakley
04-05	N2	26	23	1	2	818	379	439	106	1p	321 Rob Liley	20 Donovan van Vuuren
05-06	N1	26	10	1	15	555	697	-142	52	10	128 Rob Liley	10 Michael Wood
06-07	N1	30	22	1	7	855	474	381	110	3	197 Mark Woodrow	25 Jason Forster
07-08	N1	30	21	0	9	785	551	234	98	4	263 Mark Woodrow	13 Donovan van Vuuren
08-09	N1	30	21	2	7	895	569	326	105	5	303 Jamie Lennard	13 Wes Davies

RFU SENIOR CUP

OVERALL PLAYING RECORD

	P	W	O	L	F	A	Pts Diff
Home	5	3	0	2	171	90	81
Away	9	3	0	6	129	184	-55
Neutral	0	0	0	0	0	0	0
TOTAL	14	6	0	8	300	274	26

TEAM RECORDS

Highest Score: 79 v Sandal 01/02
Biggest Winning Margin: 71 (79-8) v Sandal 01/02
Highest Score Against: 58 v Richmond 97/98
Biggest Losing Margin: 50 (58-8) v Richmond 97/98

SEASON BY SEASON

Season	Result	Season	Result	Season	Result	Season	Result	Season	Result
71-72	DNQ	78-79	DNQ	85-86	DNQ	92-93	DNQ	99-00	1R
72-73	DNQ	79-80	DNQ	86-87	DNQ	93-94	DNQ	00-01	2R
73-74	DNQ	80-81	DNQ	87-88	DNQ	94-95	DNQ	01-02	2R
74-75	DNQ	81-82	DNQ	88-89	DNQ	95-96	DNQ	02-03	2R
75-76	DNQ	82-83	DNQ	89-90	DNQ	96-97	DNQ	03-04	2R
76-77	DNQ	83-84	DNQ	90-91	DNQ	97-98	4R	04-05	3R
77-78	DNQ	84-85	DNQ	91-92	DNQ	98-99	2R		

NATIONAL TROPHY

05-06	5 R	06-07	Q.F.	07-08	5 R	08-09	Q.F.

PLAYERS

	Position	D.o.B.	Apps.	Pts.	T	C	P	DG
Anthony Carter	Full back	02/02/1981	60 (9)	80	16	-	-	-
Andy Wright	Winger	12/04/1986	9	5	1	-	-	-
Wes Davies	Winger	20/01/1978	66 (9)	150	30	-	-	-
Donovan van Vuuren	Winger	06/01/1977	95 (4)	280	56	-	-	-
Hudson Tonga'uiha	Centre	16/11/1983	25 (4)	28	5	-	-	1
Bevon Armitage	Centre	05/08/1982	26 (2)	40	8	-	-	-
Stephen McColl	Centre		7 (6)	10	2	-	-	-
Jamie Lennard	Fly Half	23/02/1987	22 (7)	298	5	57	46	7
Ali Warnock	Fly Half	11/08/1982	14 (7)	84	2	13	13	3
Chris Hallam	Scrum Half	28/02/1984	12 (10)	5	1	-	-	-
Jamie Albinson	Scrum Half	25/06/1984	10 (7)	15	3	-	-	-
Ngazu Tau	Prop	15/01/1969	127 (18)	50	10	-	-	-
Richard List	Prop	01/05/1981	42 (48)	25	5	-	-	-
Michael Cusack	Prop	11/07/1984	13 (17)	5	1	-	-	-
Tom Davies	Prop	24/03/1986	23 (49)	25	5	-	-	-
Simon Jenkins	Hooker	27/06/1981	8 (6)	10	2	-	-	-
Steven Boden	Hooker	04/09/1982	88 (22)	75	15	-	-	-
Glen Kenworthy	Lock	15/03/1974	100 (9)	10	2	-	-	-
Dan Smith	Lock	23/10/1984	11 (8)	5	1	-	-	-
David Grffiths	Lock	08/03/1982	53 (7)	95	19	-	-	-
Simon Grainger	Back row	12/11/1980	94 (18)	90	18	-	-	-
Joshua Afu	Back row		22 (1)	25	5	-	-	-
Chris Planchant	Back row	24/07/1981	37 (5)	40	8	-	-	-
Adam Kettle	Back row	25/05/1982	14 (5)	40	8	-	-	-
Neil Cochrane	Back row	04/01/1984	17 (10)	30	6	-	-	-

EXETER

Founded: 1872
Nickname: The Chiefs
Colours: Black and white
Change colours: White and black
Web site: www.exeterchiefs.co.uk

GROUND DETAILS
Address:
Sandy Park, Sandy Park Way, Exeter EX2 7NN

Email: info@exeterchiefs.co.uk
Tel: +44 (0)1392 890890   Fax: +44 (0)1392 890888

Capacity: 7500
Covered Seating: 2500   Standing: 3300

Directions: By road - From junction 30 on the M5 take the A379 for Exeter and Dawlish. Sandy Park is the first exit left off the dual carriageway - 1 minute drive.
By rail - Nearest rail station is Exeter Digby & Sowton - 10 minutes walk. Mainline station is Exeter St David's - 4 miles.
By bus - Match day specials.
By air - Exeter International Airport - 10 minutes drive.
Car Parking: Disabled only at ground.
                  Signposted public car parking nearby
Club Shop: Open Matchdays only
Stadium: Public Bar open from mid day match days
For conferencing and non-rugby events contact June Hutchings on 01392 427427 or e-mail june@sandy-park.co.uk

Admission:

Matchday	Adult	Child	Student
West Grandstand	£24	£10	£14
SW Communications Stand	£20	£8	£12
East Terrace (Covered Standing)	£17	£5	£10
Ground	£15	£3	£7

Season	Adult	Child	Student	Family (1adult + 1 child)	Addit Adult	Addit. Child
West Grandstand	£280	£120	£180	£370	£260	£110
SW Communications Stand	£230	£105	£145	£290	£210	£90
East Terrace (Covered Standing)	£205	£60	£120	£240	£185	£55
Ground	£180	£35	£85	£200	£150	£35

KEY PERSONNEL

Honorary President	Dick Manley
Chief Executive	Tony Rowe
	tonyrowe@exeterchiefs.co.uk
Deputy Chief Executive	Keiron Northcott
	keironnorthcott@exeterchiefs.co.uk
Matchday Sponsorship Account Executive	Michael Churcher
	01392 890904, 07973 909371
	michaelchurcher@exeterchiefs.co.uk
Head Coach	Rob Baxter 01392 890890
	robbaxter@exeterchiefs.co.uk
Operation & Events Manager	Natasha Pavis 01392 890990
	natashagreen@exeterchiefs.co.uk
Communications Manager	Caroline Moore 07703 322268
	carolinemoore@exeterchiefs.co.uk
Administration	Zoe Coulman 01392 890890
	zoecoulman@exeterchiefs.co.uk

CONTACT DETAILS
Exeter Rugby Club
Sandy Park Stadium, Sandy Park Way, Exeter EX2 7JW
Tel: 01382 890890 Fax: 01392 427582

PROGRAMME
Size A5   Pages 48   Price: £2
Advertising: Michael Churcher
01392 890904 / 07973 909371

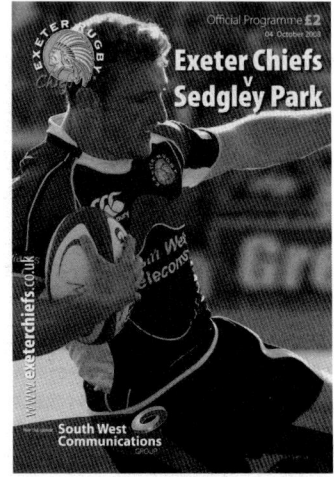

EXETER CHIEFS 2008-2009 SEASON

Back Row L. to R; Ed Lewsey, Nic Sestaret, Gareth Steenson, Ben Breeze, Simon Alcott, Sean Marsden, Andy Miller, Matt Jess, Wade Kelly, Tom Johnson, Chris Cracknell, Bryan Rennie.
Third Row L. to R; Neil Clark, Shane Kingsland, Tom Bedford, Matt Cornwell, Emyr Lewis, Jamie Fleming, Josh Drauniniu, Billy Moss, Joe Horn-Smith, Chris Budgen, Richard Pugh, Saul Nelson, John Andress.
Second Row L. to R; Keith Fleming (Commuity Development Manager), Paddy Asonn (Strength & Conditioning Coach), Clive Stuart-Smith, Richard Bolt, Toby Freeman, Tommy Hayes, Dan Touhy, Lewis Stephenson, Chris Bentley, Tom Skelding, Cormack Marshall, Ben Moon, Danny Gray, Mark Twiggs (Conditioning Coach), Tony Walker (Community Development Manager).
Front Row L. to R; John Moore (Physio), Jason Luff, Kevin Barrett, Sam Blythe, Tony Yapp, Gary KIngdom, Peter Drewett (Director of Rugby), Richard Baxter (Captain), Rob Baxter (Coach) Mark Fatialofa, James Hanks, Stephen Ward, Dan Parkes, Alan Miller, Jo Davey, (Physio).

REVIEW OF THE SEASON 2008-09

By communications manager Caroline Moore

The Chiefs began the 2008/09 season with another raft of changes to their squad's personnel with centre Matt Cornwell and Bryan Rennie joining the Sandy Park ranks from Premiership clubs Leicester Tigers and London Irish respectively, along with lock Dan Tuohy from Gloucester and prop Chris Budgen from Northampton Saints. Players also moved to Exeter from neighbouring south west teams with flanker Chris Cracknell and fly-half Gareth Steenson moving from Cornish Pirates, wing Matt Jess and hooker Neil Clark from Launceston, and full-back Emyr Lewis, flanker/lock Tom Hayes, wing Nic Sestaret and scrum-half Ed Lewsey from Plymouth Albion. A late addition in Ulster's Paul McKenzie has also paid dividends with the Irishman gradually competing for top try-scorer honours.

The coaching team began the season with the former England U21s manager Pete Drewett, Rob Baxter and Paul Larkin on board and long-serving Chief Richie Baxter also retaining the captain's armband.

Pre-season saw wins over Bristol and Launceston as well as the club's first ever Open Day and the installation of the new South West Communications Stand, which brought the capacity up to 7,312.

Exeter began their season with a trip to Esher where they won comfortably before playing their first home game in front of the new stand... against Leeds Carnegie. The Yorkshiremen scored two swift tries that would be enough to seal victory. The Chiefs fought back to get back to 13 points, but they were painfully one point short.

Such an early disappointment proved to put some fire in the bellies of the Exeter players and the size of the Chiefs squad allowed the coaches to rotate their players on a regular basis and this has paid dividend in keeping players fresh and hungry for a first team start.

Notable wins included away victories against Cornish Pirates, Bedford Blues and Nottingham while try bonus points proved invaluable to Exeter with five 70-plus victories in 2008/09 to keep them in touch with Leeds. The fight came for the top spot came to an abrupt halt however with a double-header loss to Moseley that saw Chiefs miss out on a final place in the trophy and a chance to draw level with Leeds.

Two days after this result and the club and Drewett parted company with the club and Baxter took the reigns for the rest of the season aided by temporary manager Robin Cowling. Baxter had since been officially appointed as head coach and Northampton Saints Academy coach Ali Hepher selected as backs coach.

Throughout the season, Exeter players were called up for international duty with Josh Drauniniu wearing England colours for the first time for the sevens team along with team Cracknell and Kevin Barrett. The Six Nations saw call-ups for England U20s prop Ben Moon and Ireland A prop John Andress.

Wins on the park saw Chiefs' gates rise by 25 per cent and the club's main sponsor, South West Communications Group, investing a further £1 million-plus for the next three years to take them to their 18th consecutive year of sponsorship.

169

EXETER'S SEASON - 2008-09

CHAMPIONSHIP

Date	H/A	Opponents	Result & Score	Att.	15	14	13	12	11
NATIONAL ONE									
30-08	A	Esher*	W 46-8	650	Kingdom	Sestaret	Rennie	Cornwell	Drauniniu/t
06-09	H	Leeds Carnegie	L 13-14	5693	Kingdom	Sestaret	Rennie	Cornwell	Drauniniu/t
14-09	H	Cornish Pirates	W 32-23	4913	Marsden/t	Sestaret	Rennie	Cornwell	Drauniniu/t
20-09	H	Moseley*	W 70-10	3724	Marsden/2t	Jess/2t	Rennie	Fatialofa/t	Drauniniu/t
27-09	A	Bedford	W 26-23	2986	Marsden/t	Sestaret	Rennie	Cornwell	Drauniniu/t
04-10	H	Sedgley Park	W 71-5	4016	Marsden/2t	Jess/3t	Ward	Fatialofa	Drauniniu/t
11-10	A	Plymouth Albion	W 41-14	6871	Marsden	Sestaret/t	Rennie	Cornwell/t	Drauniniu/t
18-10	A	Otley	W 69-0	460	Marsden/t	Jess/2t	Cornwell	Ward	Drauniniu/t
25-10	H	London Welsh	W 10-3	4813	Marsden	Jess	Cornwell	Ward	Drauniniu
01-11	A	Manchester	W 26-19	374	Lewis/t	Sestaret	Cornwell	Ward	Jess/t
08-11	H	Nottingham	W 29-18	4634	Marsden	Sestaret/t	Cornwell	Ward/t	Drauniniu/t
15-11	A	Newbury	W 37-20	703	Marsden/t	Jess/t	McKenzie/t(h/t)	Bedford/t	Sestaret
22-11	H	Coventry	W 45-8	4256	Breeze/2t	Sestaret/t	McKenzie/2t	Fatialofa/t	Jess/t
29-11	H	Rotherham	W 76-21	3965	Marsden/2t	Sestaret/t	McKenzie/2t	Fatialofa(i/t)	Jess/t
06-12	A	Doncaster	W 34-29	1388	Marsden	Sestaret/t	McKenzie/t	Bedford	Jess/t
13-12	H	Esher	D 12-12	3848	Breeze	Sestaret	Bedford	Rennie	Jess
20-12	A	Leeds Carnegie	L 16-18	5463	Marsden	Sestaret	McKenzie	Bedford	Drauniniu/t
27-12	A	Cornish Pirates	W 38-7	7345	Marsden/2t	Jess/t	McKenzie/t	Bedford/t	Drauniniu/t
10-01	H	Bedford	W 40-21	4092	Marsden/t	Jess/t	Rennie/t	Bedford	Drauniniu/t
24-01	A	Sedgley Park	W 35-12	431	McKenzie	Jess/t(j/t)	Bedford	Cornwell	Drauniniu/t
31-01	H	Plymouth Albion	W 29-0	6658	Marsden/t	McKenzie/2t	Rennie	Cornwell	Drauniniu
21-02	A	London Welsh	W 21-16	1420	Marsden/t	McKenzie	Bedford	Cornwell	Drauniniu
07-03	H	Manchester	W 40-5	3949	Marsden	Bedford/2t	Rennie/t	Fatialofa	McKenzie/t
15-03	A	Nottingham	W 15-14	1305	Marsden	McKenzie	Rennie	Bedford	Drauniniu
21-03	H	Moseley	L 24-32		Breeze	McKenzie	Bedford	Fatialofa	Lewsey/2t
28-03	H	Newbury	W 44-5	4120	Breeze	Bedford	Rennie	Fatialofa/t	McKenzie/2t
04-04	A	Coventry	L 28-35	1229	Breeze	Bedford	Rennie	Fatialofa	McKenzie/2t
11-04	A	Rotherham	L 21-35	1749	Lewis	Jess	McKenzie	Fatialofa	Rennie
18-04	H	Otley	W 80-17	2899	Lewis/t	Jess/t	Rennie/3t	Bedford/t	Ward
25-04	H	Doncaster	D 9-9	4972	Lewis	Jess	Rennie	Bedford	McKenzie
EDF ENERGY NATIONAL TROPHY									
4 17-01	H	Preston Grasshoppers	W 115-0		Breeze/2t	McKenzie/4t	Rennie/2t(i/t)	Cornwell	Drauniniu/3t(c
5 14-02	H	Bedford	W 12-11		Marsden	McKenzie	Bedford	Cornwell	Drauniniu
Q.F. 28-02	A	Doncaster	W 20-17		Marsden	Bedford/t	Rennie	Fatialofa	McKenzie
S.F. 21-03	A	Moseley	L 24-32		Breeze	McKenzie	Bedford	Fatialofa	Lewsey/2t

SCORING BREAKDOWN

WHEN	Total	First Half	Second Half	1/4	2/4	3/4	4/4
the POINTS were scored	1077	568	509	245	323	307	310
the POINTS were conceded	830	377	453	183	194	203	250
the TRIES were scored	152	76	76	31	45	38	38
the TRIES were conceded	53	19	34	8	11	10	24

HOW	Total	Pen. Try	Backs	Forwards	F Back	Wing	Centre	H Back	F Row	Lock	B Row
the TRIES were scored	151	2	101	49	21	46	22	12	19	9	21
the TRIES were conceded	52	1	37	14	4	19	8	6	4	4	6

KEY: * after opponents name indicates a penalty try.
Brackets after a player's name indicates he was replaced. eg (a) means he was replaced by replacement code "a" and so on.
/ after a player or replacement name is followed by any scores he made - eg /t, /c, /p, /dg or any combination of these

10	9	1	2	3	4	5	6	7	8
Steenson/4cp	Stuart-Smith(b/t)	Budgen	Clark/t(a/t)	Andress/t	Stevenson	Tuohy/t	Johnson	Miller	Baxter
Steenson/c2p	Barrett	Budgen	Clark	Andress	Stevenson	Tuohy	Cracknell	Miller	Baxter
Steenson/2c6p	Barrett	Budgen	Clark	Andress	Stevenson	Tuohy	Cracknell	Miller	Baxter
Steenson/t7c2p	Barrett/t	Parkes	Clark	Andress	Stevenson/t	Skelding	Johnson	Pugh	Baxter
Steenson/2c4p	Stuart-Smith	Budgen	Clark	Andress	Stevenson	Tuohy	Johnson	Pugh	Baxter
Gray/t8c	Barrett/t	Parkes	Blythe/t	Moon/t	Stevenson	Skelding	Johnson	Miller/t	Hayes
Steenson/5c2p	Stuart-Smith	Parkes	Clark	Andress	Stevenson/t	Tuohy	Johnson/t	Pugh	Baxter
Gray/6c(c/c)	Stuart-Smith	Budgen/3t	Blythe/t	Andress	Stevenson(d/t)	Hayes	Johnson	Miller/t	Baxter/t
Gray	Barrett	Budgen/t	Clark	Andress	Stevenson/t	Hayes	Johnson	Pugh	Baxter
Steenson/2c(f/c)	Barrett	Moon	Blythe	Andress	Tuohy	Skelding	Cracknell/t(e/t)	Miller	Hayes
Steenson/3cp	Stuart-Smith	Budgen	Blythe(g/t)	Andress	Stevenson	Hayes	Johnson	Pugh	Baxter
Gray/2cp	Barrett	Kingsland	Blythe	Budgen/t	Stevenson	Tuohy	Johnson	Miller	Hayes
Steenson/3c(f/2c)	Stuart-Smith	Sturgess	Blythe	Andress	Stevenson	Tuohy	Johnson	Pugh	Baxter
Gray/7cp(c/2c_	Stuart-Smith	Budgen/t	Blythe	Andress	Stevenson	Hayes	Johnson/2t	Pugh/t	Baxter
Steenson/3cp	Stuart-Smith	Budgen/t	Blythe	Andress	Stevenson	Hayes	Johnson/t	Pugh	Baxter
Gray/c	Stuart-Smith	Sturgess	Clark	Budgen/t	Bentley/t	Tuohy	Slade	Pugh	Baxter
Steenson/c3p	Stuart-Smith	Sturgess	Blythe	Budgen	Stevenson	Hayes	Johnson	Pugh	Baxter
Steenson/2c(f/2c)	Stuart-Smith	Sturgess	Blythe	Budgen	Stevenson	Hayes	Johnson	Pugh	Baxter
Steenson/t3c3p	Stuart-Smith	Sturgess	Blythe	Andress	Stevenson	Hayes	Johnson	Pugh	Baxter
Gray/p(c/c)	Barrett	Sturgess	Blythe	Andress	Tuohy	Hayes/t	Johnson/c	Miller	Baxter
Steenson/3cp	Stuart-Smith	Sturgess	Blythe	Andress	Stevenson	Hayes	Johnson	Miller	Baxter/t
Steenson/2p	Stuart-Smith	Sturgess	Blythe	Budgen	Stevenson	Hayes	Johnson	Miller	Baxter/2t
Gray/3c(c/2c)	Lewsey/t(k/t)	Budgen	Nelson	Andress	Bentley	Hayes	Johnson	Miller	Baxter
Steenson/cp	Stuart-Smith	Sturgess/t	Blythe	Andress	Stevenson	Hayes	Johnson	Pugh	Baxter/t
Steenson/c(f/tc)	Stuart-Smith	Sturgess	Blythe	Andress	Stevenson	Hayes	Johnson/t	Pugh	Baxter
Gray/c2p(c/3c)	Bolt/t	Sturgess	Blythe	Kingsland/t	Stevenson	Hayes	Slade(l/t)	Miller	Baxter
Steenson/tc2p	Bolt	Moon	Blythe	Andress	Tuohy	Hayes	Slade	Miller	Baxter
Gray/3c	Stuart-Smith	Sturgess	Blythe	Kingsland	Slade/t	Hayes	Johnson	Miller/t	Baxter/t
Steenson/7c(m/t3c)	Stuart-Smith	Moon/t	Nelson	Budgen	Bentley/t	Hayes(n/t)	Johnson/t	Miller	Baxter/t
Yapp/3p	Stuart-Smith	Moon	Nelson	Budgen	Bentley	Hayes	Johnson	Miller	Baxter
Gray/10c	Barrett/t	Budgen	Nelson	Andress	Stevenson	Tuohy/t	Cracknell/2t	Miller	Baxter/t(p/t)
Steenson/4p	Stuart-Smith	Sturgess	Blythe	Budgen	Stevenson	Hayes	Johnson	Miller	Baxter
Gray/2c(c/pdg)	Stuart-Smith	Sturgess	Blythe	Andress	Tuohy	Hayes	Johnson/t	Miller	Baxter
Steenson/c(f/tc)	Stuart-Smith	Sturgess	Blythe	Andress	Stevenson	Hayes	Johnson/t	Pugh	Baxter

REPLACEMENTS

a- S Alcott
b- K Barrett
c- G Steenson
d- D Tuohy
e- C Slade
f- D Gray
g- N Clark
h- B Breeze
i- T Bedford
j- S Marsden
k- R Bolt
l- T Johnson
m- T Yapp
n- T Hanks
o- E Lewsey
p- Alan Miller

LEAGUE APPEARANCES

27 Richard Baxter
24 Tom Johnson (3)
22 Tom Bayes (4), Lewis Stevenson (3)
20 John Andress (8)

NUMBER OF PLAYERS USED

40 plus 2 as a replacement only

LEAGUE POINTS SCORERS

Pts	Player	T	C	P	DG
228	Gareth Steenson	3	60	31	-
99	Danny Gray	2	37	5	-
80	Sean Marsden	16	-	-	-
80	Matthew Jess	16	-	-	-
75	Paul McKenzie	15	-	-	-
65	Josh Drauniniu	13	-	-	-

EXETER STATISTICS

LEAGUE

TEAM RECORDS

MOST POINTS
Scored at Home: 89 v Rugby Lions 14.9.02
Scored Away: 69 v Otley 18.10.08
Conceded at Home: 43 v Cornish Pirates 24.09.05
Conceded Away: 70 v Harlequins 22.10.05

MOST TRIES
Scored in a match: 14 v Rugby Lions 14.9.02 (H)
Conceded in a match: 10 v Leeds Tykes 16.12.00 (A)

BIGGEST MARGINS
Home Win: 81pts - 81-0 v W Hartlepool 6.5.00
Away Win: 69pts - 69-0 v Otley 18.10.08
Home Defeat: 34pts - 0-34 v Rotherham 22.1.00
Away Defeat: 65pts - 5-70 v Harlequins 22.10.05

MOST CONSECUTIVE
Victories: 14
Defeats: 8

INDIVIDUAL RECORDS

MOST APPEARANCES
by a forward: 275 Rob Baxter
by a back: 142 (4) Andy Maunder

MOST CONSECUTIVE
Appearances: 88 Andy Maunder 12.9.87- 17.9.94
Matches scoring Tries: 6 Richard Baxter (13.11.04 - 15.1.05)
Matches scoring points: 35 Tony Yapp

MATCH RECORDS

Most Points
31   Sam Howard   v W. Hartlepool 6.5.00 (H)

Most Tries   4   Simon Dovell   v Havant 21.12.96 (H)
John Fabian   v Waterloo 17.10.98 (H)
Gary Kingdom   vSedgley P 19.11.05(H)
Ali Murdoch   v Sedgley Park 28.4.07(H)
Jason Luff v London Welsh 13.10.07 (H)

Most Conversions
10   Sam Howard   v W. Hartlepool 6.5.00 (H)
Tony Yapp   v Manchester 28.2.04 (H)

Most Penalties
7   Andy Green   v Fylde 5.4.97 (H)
Tony Yapp   v Otley 20.09.03 (A)

Most Drop Goals
2   Andy Green   v Sheffield 23.4.88 (H)
Tony Yapp   v Plymouth 19.4.03 (H)

SEASON RECORDS

Most Points	349	Tony Yapp	02-03
Most Tries	22	Josh Drauniniu	07-08
Most Conversions	75	Tony Yapp	02-03
Most Penalties	54	Sam Howard	99-00
Most Drop Goals	7	Chris Malone	01-02

CAREER RECORDS

Most Points	1526	Tony Yapp	02-09
Most Tries	81	Richard Baxter	95-06
Most Conversions	338	Tony Yapp	02-09
Most Penalties	213	Andy Green	87-97
Most Drop Goals	22	Andy Green	87-97

LAST TEN SEASONS

	Division	P	W	D	L	F	A	P.D.	Pts	Pos	Most Points	Most Tries
99-00	P2	26	19	0	7	742	466	276	38	4	312 Sam Howard	10 Andrew Beattie
00-01	N1	26	14	0	12	677	563	114	71	3	131 Jon Hill	8 Martin Ridley & To'o Vaega
01-02	N1	26	19	1	6	707	448	259	92	3	247 Chris Malone	16 Richard Baxter
02-03	N1	26	20	2	4	940	459	481	104	3	349 Tony Yapp	11 Ed Lewsey & Tony Yapp
03-04	N1	26	15	1	10	706	499	207	74	6	320 Tony Yapp	11 Hayden Thomas
04-05	N1	26	20	0	6	805	511	294	101	2	285 Tony Yapp	13 Richard Baxter
05-06	N1	26	14	0	12	594	602	-8	71	6	158 Tony Yapp	8 Gary Kingdom, Stephen Ward
06-07	N1	30	21	1	8	774	507	267	101	4	280 Tony Yapp	16 Jason Luff
07-08	N1	30	24	0	6	899	424	475	116	2	172 Danny Gray	22 Josh Drauniniu
08-09	N1	30	23	2	5	1077	463	614	119	2	228 Gareth Steenson	16 Matthew Jess, Sean Marsden

RFU SENIOR CUP

OVERALL PLAYING RECORD

	P	W	O	L	F	A	Pts Diff
Home	32	21	0	11	674	417	257
Away	37	21	0	16	682	662	20
Neutral	0	0	0	0	0	0	0
TOTAL	69	42	0	27	1356	1079	277

TEAM RECORDS

Highest Score: 81 v Whitchurch 98/99
Biggest Winning Margin: 78 (78-0) v Manchester 04-05 (H)
Highest Score Against: 76 v Leicester 92/93
Biggest Losing Margin: 76 (0-76) v Leicester 92/93

SEASON BY SEASON

71-72	2R	78-79	2R	85-86	DNQ	92-93	QF	99-00	4R
72-73	2R	79-80	1R	86-87	2R	93-94	1R	00-01	4R
73-74	DNQ	80-81	4R	87-88	DNQ	94-95	QF	01-02	5R
74-75	DNQ	81-82	4R	88-89	3R	95-96	4R	02-03	6R
75-76	DNQ	82-83	1R	89-90	4R	96-97	3R	03-04	4R
76-77	1R	83-84	DNQ	90-91	3R	97-98	4R	04-05	5R
77-78	2R	84-85	DNQ	91-92	2R	98-99	5R		

NATIONAL TROPHY

05-06	S.F.	06-07	R-up	07-08	R-up	08-09	S.F.

PLAYERS

	Position	D.o.B.	Apps.	Pts.	T	C	P	DG
Ben Breeze	Full back	08/04/1974	33 (1)	60	12	-	-	-
Wade Kelly	Centre	08/02/1980	15 (17)	20	4	-	-	-
Sean Marsden	Winger	17/01/1980	44 (8)	125	25	-	-	-
Gary Kingdom	Winger	02/11/1982	92 (10)	250	31	25	15	-
Mark Fatialofa	Centre	12/11/1973	98 (10)	110	22	-	-	-
Paul McKenzie	Centre		16	75	15	-	-	-
Matthew Jess	Winger	04/04/1984	16 (2)	80	16	-	-	-
Tom Bedford	Wing/Centre		15 (4)	30	6	-	-	-
Nicholas Sestaret	Winger	26/07/1987	13	25	5	-	-	-
Tony Yapp	Fly half	26/07/1977	129 (10)	1526	41	338	204	11
Kevin Barrett	Scrum half	06/07/1980	64 (17)	65	13	-	-	-
Danny Gray	Fly half	21/05/1983	29 (10)	271	4	79	28	3
Gareth Steenson	Fly Half	05/04/1984	19 (8)	228	3	60	31	-
Josh Drauniniu	Winger	17/08/1985	44 (1)	175	35	-	-	-
Clive Stuart Smith	Scrum half	17/05/1983	42 (8)	20	4	-	-	-
Chris Budgen	Prop	21/03/1973	17 (7)	40	8	-	-	-
John Andress	Prop	20/01/1984	36 (4)	15	3	-	-	-
Dan Parkes	Prop	14/08/1975	32 (21)	5	1	-	-	-
Brett Sturgess	Prop	16/11/1981	22 (10)	10	2	-	-	-
Saul Nelson	Hooker	11/04/1980	13 (18)	10	2	-	-	-
Sam Blythe	Hooker	17/11/1976	135 (28)	125	25	-	-	-
Chris Bentley	Lock	24/05/1979	61 (16)	50	10	-	-	-
Tom Skelding	Lock	01/02/1982	4 (6)	-	-	-	-	-
Lewis Stevenson	Lock	01/06/1984	22 (4)	15	3	-	-	-
Tom Hayes	Lock	31/05/1980	22 (4)	5	1	-	-	-
Richard Baxter	Back row	23/06/1978	259 (20)	475	95	-	-	-
Tom Johnson	Back row	16/07/1982	41 (12)	60	12	-	-	-
Alan Miller	Back row	09/10/1981	58 (1)	45	9	-	-	-

LONDON WELSH

KEY PERSONNEL

President	S J Dawes OBE
Chairman	Kelvin Bryon
Chief Executive	Peter Thomas
Finance Manager	Andy Knights
Rugby Manager/League Contact	Gerald Davies
Head Coach	Danny Wilson
Commercial Department	Mike Davies
Press Officer	Damian Dolan

Founded: 1885
Nickname: The Dragons
Colours: Scarlet
Change colours: tba

Web site: www.london-welsh.co.uk

CONTACT DETAILS

c/o London Welsh RFC,
Old Deer Park, Kew Road, Richmond, Surrey TW9 2AZ
Tel: 020 8940 2368   Fax: 020 8940 1106

GROUND DETAILS

Address:
Old Deer Park, Kew Road, Richmond, Surrey TW9 2AZ
Tel: 0208 940 2368
Fax: 0208 940 1106
e-mail: commercial@london-welsh.co.uk

Capacity: 4,500
Covered Seating: 854

Directions: Half mile north of Richmond BR station into Kew Road. Ground on left before Kew Gardens
Nearest BR Station: Richmond (& Underground)
Car Parking: 200, public car park close by.

Admission:
Matchday - Ground: Adult £12, Concessions £6
            Grandstand £17
Children under 16 accompanied by an adult - Free
Season Tickets - On application

Club Shop:
Open matchdays. Other times by arrangement call 020 8940 2368

Clubhouse:
Open during normal licensing hours.
Snacks & bar meals available match days
Functions: From 50-200 contact David Thomas, facilities manager, 020 8332 6696

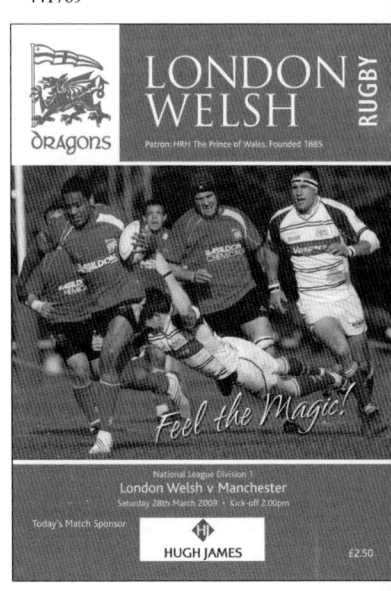

PROGRAMME

Size: A5
Pages: 44
Price: £2.50
Editor: Damian Dolan – 07810 828562
Advertising Contact Mike Davies – 07917 441789

Back Row: Dorian Williams, Simon Etheredge, Gavin O'Meara, Robert Bell, Aaron Hopkins, James Storey, Greg Evans, Alec Jenkins, Robin Boot, Adam Kwasnicki, Pete Lowe (Kit Manager), Richard Martin Redman (Club Captain).
Middle Row: Danny Wilson (Head Coach), Gerald Davies (Rugby Manager), Chris Walton (Fitness Adviser), Alun Rise (Academy Manager), Andy Brown, Aaron Liffchak, Nathan Bonner-Evans, Wame Ratu Lewaravu, Matt Corker, Jonathan Mills, Tom Audley, Dan George, Tom Brown, Ed Lewis-Pratt, Laura Saker, Phil Greening (Assistant Coach), Chris Jenkins (Head Physiotherapist), Joe Jones (Club Designer).
Front Row: Michael Tagicakibau, Peter Murchie, Allen Chilten, Paul Sampson, Paul Mackey, Mike Powell (1st XV Captain), Aled Thomas, Paul Doran Jones, Tom Rock, Mark Harris, Nick Runciman, Sunia Koto Vuli.

REVIEW OF THE SEASON 2008-09

The 2008/09 season was destined to go down in the annuals as an historic one for London Welsh RFC, long before a ball was kicked or a tackle made.

For the first time in the clubs history, Old Deer Park would play host to a professional London Welsh side. New arrivals over the summer included the likes of Tom Brown (Newbury), Mike Powell (Ospreys), Aled Thomas (Dragons), Tom Rock (Leeds Carnegie), Dan George (Dragons), Ed Lewis-Pratt (London Irish) and Gavin O'Meara (Leinster), to be subsequently joined by former Bedford full back Mark Harris.

They would join familiar faces such as Paul Sampson, Allen Chilten, Paul Mackey, Jon Mills, Sunia Koto Vuli, Michael Tagicakibau, Paul Doran Jones, and Matt Corker, while the coaching set up would be augmented by the addition of former WRU and Cardiff Blues skills coach Danny Wilson – although he would find himself thrust into the role of head coach before the year was out.

A pre-season win over Connacht in Galway would raise expectations and the Dragons would take that form in to their league campaign, winning their opening three matches. Bedford halted Welsh's run and Leeds outlined their intent for an immediate return to the Guinness Premiership with a 38-0 win at Old Deer Park.

Welsh bounced back with wins over Newbury and London rivals Esher, as they racked up five wins in six matches together with a Herculean bonus point at Exeter, but a run of three consecutive home defeats saw the Dragons lose ground on the early pace setters.

A 60-0 win over Sedgley Park got the Dragons back on track and Mark Harris' touchline conversion gave Welsh a thrilling 33-32 win at Bedford as they brought in the New Year in style.

Hopes were raised of a first Twickenham Cup final since 1985, following wins over Newbury and Cambridge, but they were dashed in the quarter-finals as Welsh threw away an 18-0 lead to lose to eventual winners Moseley with the last play of the game.

But while the Dragons were putting their cup disappointment behind them with a hard fought win at Rotherham the following week, fly half Aled Thomas was busy helping Wales to World Cup Sevens glory in Dubai, scoring the winning try in the final.

A bonus point win at Esher would effectively end their London rivals hopes of escaping the drop. While wins over Cornish Pirates and Moseley ensured the Dragons eclipsed last season's tally of 15 wins and 70 points, by notching up 19 wins and 91 points.

175

WELSH'S SEASON - 2008-09

Date	H/A	Opponents	Result & Score	Att.	15	14	13	12	11
NATIONAL ONE									
30-08	A	Moseley	W 15-9	815	Lewis Pratt/p	Sampson/t	Rock	Mackey	Jenkins
07-09	H	Doncaster	W 31-16	960	Lewis Pratt/t	Sampson	Rock	Mackey	Tombleson
13-09	A	Sedgley Park	W 43-11	698	Lewis Pratt(b/t)	Sampson	Rock	Hopkins/t	Tombleson
20-09	H	Bedford	L 23-32	1931	Lewis Pratt	Sampson	Rock	Hopkins	Jenkins/t
27-09	A	Plymouth Albion*	W 25-24	2602	Lewis Pratt	Sampson	Murchie	Mackey	Odejobi
04-10	H	Leeds Carnegie	L 0-38	1449	Lewis Pratt	Sampson	Murchie	Mackey	Jenkins
11-10	A	Newbury*	W 20-9	875	Thomas/2c2p	Sampson	Murchie	Mackey	Tombleson/t
18-10	H	Esher*	W 43-19	1480	Harris/tp	Sampson	Rock	Mackey	Tombleson
25-10	A	Exeter	L 3-10	4813	Harris	Sampson	Rock	Mackey	Tombleson
01-11	H	Rotherham	W 27-17	1070	Harris/t	Sampson	Rock	Mackey	Tagacakibau/t(
08-11	A	Otley	W 9-6	1053	Harris/p	Sampson	Hopkins	Mackey	Tombleson
15-11	A	Manchester	W 19-14	293	Thomas	Sampson/t	Murchie	Mackey	Tagacakibau
22-11	H	Nottingham	L 30-36	820	Lewis Pratt	Sampson	Murchie	Mackey/t	Tagacakibau/t
29-11	H	Coventry	L 21-23	710	Lewis Pratt	Sampson/t	Rock	Mackey	Tagacakibau
06-12	H	Cornish Pirates*	L 23-38	1265	Harris	Sampson	Rock	Mackey	Tagacakibau
20-12	A	Doncaster	L 13-26	1300	Harris	Sampson/t	Murchie	Mackey	Rock/t
27-12	H	Sedgley Park*	W 60-0	1110	Harris/t6cp	Sampson/t	Murchie/t	Mackey(e/t)	Tagacakibau/t
03-01	A	Bedford*	W 33-32	3171	Harris/t4c	Sampson	Murchie	Mackey/t(f/t)	Tagacakibau
25-01	A	Leeds Carnegie	L 10-35	2471	Harris/cp	Sampson(g/t)	Murchie	Lawson	Tagacakibau
31-01	H	Newbury	W 40-12	980	Harris/3c3p	Sampson/2t	Murchie/t	King	Tagacakibau
21-02	H	Exeter	L 16-21	1420	Harris/c3p	Lewis Pratt	Murchie	Mackey	Tagacakibau/t
07-03	A	Rotherham*	W 20-7	1142	Sampson/t	Murchie	Mackey	Shabbo	Tagacakibau
14-03	H	Otley	W 39-25	780	Sampson/t	Murchie	Shabbo/t	Mackey/t	Tagacakibau
22-03	H	Plymouth Albion	W 22-9	390	Sampson/2t	Shabbo	Murchie	Mackey	Tagacakibau
28-03	H	Manchester	W 57-10	920	Sampson	Lewis Pratt	Rock	Mackey	Tagacakibau/t
05-04	A	Nottingham	L 24-30	1321	Harris/t3cp	Sampson/t	Rock	Mackey	Lewis Pratt
11-04	A	Coventry	L 30-36	1319	Harris/t2c2p	Sampson	Rock	Mackey	Tagacakibau/2
18-04	A	Esher	W 32-21	1984	Harris/t2c2p(g/t)	Sampson/t	Murchie	Mackey/t	Tagacakibau
25-04	A	Cornish Pirates*	W 10-8	2616	Sampson	Evans	Murchie	Mackey	Lewis Pratt
02-05	N	Moseley	W 50-37	750	Sampson/t	Murchie	Evans/2t	Storey	Jenkins/2t
EDF ENERGY NATIONAL TROPHY									
4 17-01	H	Newbury	W 42-17		Harris/3c2p	Sampson/t	Murchie	Lawson	Tagacakibau/2
5 14-02	H	Cambridge	W 23-22		Harris/t2c3p	Sampson/t	Hopkins	Mackey	Tagacakibau
Q.F. 28-02	H	Moseley	L 21-27		Harris/c3p	Sampson	Murchie	Lawson	Tagacakibau

SCORING BREAKDOWN

WHEN		Total	First Half	Second Half	1/4	2/4	3/4	4/4
the POINTS were scored		788	444	344	201	243	176	168
the POINTS were conceded		611	289	322	141	148	125	197
the TRIES were scored		97	55	42	25	30	22	20
the TRIES were conceded		71	31	40	14	17	13	27

HOW	Total	Pen. Try	Backs	Forwards	F Back	Wing	Centre	H Back	F Row	Lock	B Row
the TRIES were scored	97	8	59	30	15	23	12	9	10	5	15
the TRIES were conceded	71	2	45	24	9	21	9	6	6	4	14

KEY: *after opponents name indicates a penalty try.
Brackets after a player's name indicates he was replaced. eg (a) means he was replaced by replacement code "a" and so on.
/ after a player or replacement name is followed by any scores he made - eg /t, /c, /p, /dg or any combination of these

10	9	1	2	3	4	5	6	7	8
Thomas/c	Walker	Doran-Jones	George(a/t)	Liffchak	Lewaravu	Powell	Mills	Ball	Brown
Thomas/t2c4p	Runciman	Doran-Jones/t	Koto Vuli	Liffchak	Lewaravu	Powell	Mills	Ball	Brown
Thomas/5cp	Chilten/t	Williams	George/t	Doran-Jones	Corker	Powell	Mills	Ball/t	Brown/t
Thomas/t2c3p	Walker	Doran-Jones	Koto Vuli	Liffchak	Corker	Powell	Mills	Audley	Brown
Thomas/2cpdg	Runciman	Williams	Koto Vuli/t	Liffchak	Thomas	Powell	Mills	Audley	Brown/t
Thomas	Chilten	Doran-Jones	Koto Vuli	Liffchak	Thomas	Powell	Ellis	Audley	Brown
Marks	Runciman	Williams	Koto Vuli	Doran-Jones	Corker	Powell	Thomas	Audley	Brown
Thomas/3c3p	Chilten/t	Williams	George	Doran-Jones	Corker	Powell	Ellis/t	Etheredge/t	Brown
Thomas/p	Runciman	Williams	Koto Vuli	Doran-Jones	Corker	Spencer	Mills	Etheredge	Brown
Thomas/2cp	Chilten/t	Williams	Koto Vuli	Doran-Jones	Corker	Powell	Ball	Etheredge	Brown
Thomas/2p	Runciman	Holford	George	Doran-Jones	Corker	Powell	Ball	Audley	Brown
Harris/3p	Walker	Doran-Jones	O'Meara	Liffchak	Thomas	Powell	Ball	Audley	Brown/t
Harris/3c3p	Chilten	Doran-Jones	O'Meara	Liffchak/t	Corker	Powell	Mills	Ball	Brown
Harris/cpdg(d/p)	Chilten	Doran-Jones/t	O'Meara	Liffchak	Thomas	Corker	Mills	Audley	Brown
Thomas/2c2pdg	Chilten	Doran-Jones	Koto Vuli	Liffchak	Corker	Powell	Mills	Ball	Brown/t
Thomas/p	Walker	Beech	Koto Vuli	Doran-Jones	Corker	Powell	Mills	Ellis	Brown
Thomas/t	Chilten	Doran-Jones	Koto Vuli	Liffchak/t	Lewaravu	Powell	Corker	Mills	Brown/t
Thomas/t	Chilten	Doran-Jones	Koto Vuli	Liffchak	Lewaravu	Powell	Corker	Mills	Brown
Thomas	Chilten	Holford	Koto Vuli	Doran-Jones	Corker	Powell	Mills	Audley	Brown
Thomas	Chilten	Ruwers	O'Meara	Doran-Jones	Corker/t	Powell/t	Mills	Audley	Brown
Thomas	Runciman	Doran-Jones	Koto Vuli	Liffchak	Lewaravu	Corker	Mills	Strauss	Brown
Harris/2cpdg	Runciman	Ruwers	Koto Vuli	Liffchak	Lewaravu	Corker	Mills	Bell	Bonner-Evans
Harris/4cpdg	Alford	Doran-Jones	Koto Vuli	Liffchak/t	Lewaravu/t	Corker	Mills	Bell	Bonner-Evans
Lewis Pratt/2cp	Runciman	Doran-Jones	Koto Vuli/t	Liffchak	Corker	Powell	Mills	Audley	Brown
Thomas/6c	Runciman	Williams	Koto Vuli	Doran-Jones/t	Corker	Powell	Mills(h/2t)	Audley	Brown/5t
Thomas/t	Runciman	Williams	Koto Vuli	Doran-Jones	Corker	Powell	Mills	Audley	Bonner-Evans
Thomas	Runciman/t	Williams	O'Meara	Doran-Jones	Corker	Lewaravu	Mills	Audley	Brown
Thomas/c	Chilten	Williams	Koto Vuli	Doran-Jones	Corker	Powell	Mills	Audley	Brown
Thomas/cp	Chilten	Williams	Koto Vuli	Liffchak	Corker	Powell	Mills	Audley	Brown
Lewis Pratt/6cp	Chilten	Boot	Koto Vuli	Hopkins	Lewaravu/2t	Powell	Bell	Audley	Corker
Thomas/t	Runciman	Liffchak	Koto Vuli/t	Doran-Jones/t	Lewaravu	Corker	Mills	Audley	Brown
Thomas	Chilten	Beech	O'Meara	Doran-Jones	Corker	Powell	Strauss	Audley	Brown
Thomas	Runciman	Doran-Jones/t	Koto Vuli	Liffchak	Corker	Powell	Mills/t	Strauss	Brown

REPLACEMENTS

a- S Koto Vuli   b- P Murchie   c- T Tombleson   d- A Thomas
e- T Rock   f- W Lawson   g- E Lewis Pratt h- N Bonner-Evans

LEAGUE APPEARANCES

29 Paul Sampson
26 Tom Brown (2), Paul Doran Jones (1)
25 Paul Mackay (1), Matt Corker (4),
24 Aled Thomas (2), Mike Powell (5)

LEAGUE POINTS SCORERS

Pts	Player	T	C	P	DG
180	Mark Harris	7	32	24	3
158	Aled Thomas	5	29	23	2
70	Paul Sampson	14	-	-	-
50	Tom Brown	10	-	-	-
40	Ed lewis Pratt	8	-	-	-
35	M Tagackibau	7	-	-	-

NUMBER OF PLAYERS USED

43 plus 6 as a replacement only

LONDON WELSH STATISTICS

LEAGUE

TEAM RECORDS

MOST POINTS
Scored at Home: 88 v Sudbury 25.3.95
Scored Away: 49 v Sidcup 16.11.91
Conceded at Home: 53 v Worcester 12.10.02
Conceded Away: 63 v Coventry 10.10.98

MOST TRIES
Scored in a match: 12 v Sudbury 25.3.95 (H)
Conceded in a match: 9
v Wharfedale 15.2.97 (A)
v Harrogate 1.3.97 (A)
v Coventry 10.10.98 (A)

BIGGEST MARGINS
Home Win: 81pts - 88-7 v Sudbury 25.3.95
Away Win: 43pts - 49-6 v Sidcup 16.11.91
Home Defeat: 46pts - 7-53 v Worcester 12.10.02
Away Defeat: 49pts - 0-49 v Orrell 24.04.04

MOST CONSECUTIVE
Victories: 10
Defeats: 9 (14.10.06 - 9.12.06)

INDIVIDUAL RECORDS

MOST APPEARANCES
by a forward: 113 (5) Graeme Peacock
by a back: 101 (10) Peter Shaw

MOST CONSECUTIVE
Appearances: 33 Graeme Peacock
Matches scoring Tries: 5
Mickey Bell (x2), Adam Jones & Andy Currier
Matches scoring points: 23 Craig Raymond

MATCH RECORDS

Most Points
30 Andy Lee   v Rugby 18.12.99 (H)

Most Tries
5   Tom Brown   v Manchester 28.03.09 (H)

Most Conversions
8   Craig Raymond   v Wharfedale 21.3.98 (H)
                    v Blackheath 17.4.99 (H)
    Andy Lee   v Rugby 18.2.99 (H)
    Daffyd Lewis   v Rugby 8.2.03 (H)

Most Penalties
6   Craig Raymond (3 times),
    Seb Fitzgerald (Twice)

Most Drop Goals
2   Craig Raymond   v Exeter 27.4.96 (A)
                    v Liverpool St H 31.8.96 (A)

SEASON RECORDS

Most Points	300	Craig Raymond	96-97
Most Tries	17	Scott Roskell	97-98
		Matt Vines	00-01
Most Conversions	64	Craig Raymond	97-98
Most Penalties	57	Craig Raymond	96-97
Most Drop Goals	7	Craig Raymond	96-97

CAREER RECORDS

Most Points	916	Craig Raymond	94-99
Most Tries	36	Andy Currier	97-00
Most Conversions	160	Craig Raymond	94-99
Most Penalties	148	Craig Raymond	94-99
Most Drop Goals	14	Craig Raymond	94-99

LAST TEN SEASONS

	Division	P	W	D	L	F	A	P.D.	Pts	Pos	Most Points	Most Tries
99-00	P2	26	16	0	10	712	476	236	32	5	198 Andy Lee	14 Simon Frost
00-01	N1	26	13	0	13	525	616	-91	64	6	179 Andy Lee	17 Matt Vines
01-02	N1	26	15	0	11	580	557	23	69	5	133 Jon Ufton	8 Matt Vines
02-03	N1	26	15	0	11	627	565	62	76	5	120 Daffyd Lewis	9 John Swords & Chris Ritchie
03-04	N1	26	12	0	14	531	605	-74	58	8	150 Seb Fitzgerald	7 Adam Bidwell & John Swords
04-05	N1	26	7	0	19	494	754	-260	37	12	139 Dylan Pugh	6 Dylan Pugh, Mark Meenan
05-06	N1	26	8	1	17	536	700	-164	45	12	76 Lee Cholewa	9 Tim Holgate
06-07	N1	30	11	1	18	572	794	-222	56	12	225 Sam Ulph	6 Chris Ritchie, Sam Ulph
07-08	N1	30	15	0	15	542	661	-119	70	7	106 Matthew Jones	11 Paul Sampson
08-09	N1	30	19	0	11	788	611	177	*91	6	180 Mark Harris	14 Paul Sampson

RFU SENIOR CUP

OVERALL PLAYING RECORD

	P	W	O	L	F	A	Pts Diff
Home	45	29	0	16	921	665	256
Away	34	18	0	16	541	482	59
Neutral	1	0	0	1	15	24	-9
TOTAL	80	47	0	33	1477	1171	306

TEAM RECORDS

Highest Score: 65 v Clifton 97/98
Biggest Winning Margin: 48 Pts - 65-17 v Clifton
Highest Score Against: 67 v Exeter 04-05 (H)
Biggest Losing Margin: 48 Pts (19-67) v Exeter 04-05 (H)

71-72	QF	78-79	QF	85-86	QF	92-93	3R	99-00	QF
72-73	SF	79-80	2R	86-87	4R	93-94	3R	00-01	5R
73-74	1R	80-81	DNQ	87-88	3R	94-95	2R	01-02	4R
74-75	1R	81-82	4R	88-89	2R	95-96	4R	02-03	5R
75-76	QF	82-83	QF	89-90	3R	96-97	3R	03-04	3R
76-77	SF	83-84	4R	90-91	3R	97-98	3R	04-05	3R
77-78	2R	84-85	Runners-up	91-92	DNQ	98-99	4R		

NATIONAL TROPHY

05-06	Q.F.	06-07	5 R	07-08	5 R	08-09	Q.F.

PLAYERS

	Position	D.o.B.	Apps.	Pts.	T	C	P	DG
Ed Lewis Pratt	Full back		14 (9)	40	3	8	3	-
Mark Harris	Full back		19 (1)	180	7	32	24	2
Paul Sampson	Full Back/Winger		65	130	26	-	-	-
James Storey	Centre		56 (3)	60	12	-	-	-
Tom Rock	Centre		13 (3)	10	2	-	-	-
Peter |Murchie	Centre		17 (4)	15	3	-	-	-
Aaron Hopkins	Centre		7 (15)	30	6	-	-	-
Michael Tagacakibau	Winger		22 (1)	40	8	-	-	-
Tom Tombleson	Winger		6 (2)	10	2	-	-	-
Paul Mackay	Centre		48 (3)	35	7	-	-	-
Aled Thomas	Fly half		24 (2)	158	5	29	23	2
Allen Chiltern	Scrum half		75 (13)	55	11	-	-	-
Nick Runciman	Scrum half		11 (5)	5	1	-	-	-
Aaron Liffchak	Prop		31 (9)	25	5	-	-	-
Paul Doran Jones	Prop		34 (5)	15	3	-	-	-
Dorrian Williams	Prop		45 (15)	-	-	-	-	-
Sunia Koto Vuli	Hooker		37 (4)	15	3	-	-	-
Gavin O'Meara	Hooker		5 (11)	-	-	-	-	-
Wame Lewaravu	Lock		25 (8)	30	6	-	-	-
Mike Powell	Lock		24 (5)	5	1	-	-	-
Matt Corker	Lock		41 (5)	5	1	-	-	-
Tom Brown	Back row		26 (2)	50	10	-	-	-
Jonathan Mills	Back row		48 (3)	10	2	-	-	-
Tom Audley	Back row		16 (6)	-	-	-	-	-

CHAMPIONSHIP

MOSELEY FC

Founded: 1873
Nickname: Mose
Colours:
Red and black hoops
Change colours:
White with red and black flashes
Training Nights:
Mon, Tues, Wed, Thurs.
Website:
www.moseleyrugby.co.uk

KEY PERSONNEL

President	John Beale
Chief Executive	David Warren
Treasurer	Tony Newby
Secretary	Dave Warren, c/o Moseley Rugby Ltd., Yardley Wood Road, Billesley, Birmingham B13 0PT. Tel: 0121 443 3631 email: info@moseleyrugby.co.uk
Fixture Secretary	Dave Ireland, 52, Bibury Road, Hall Green, Birmingham B28 0HQ Tel: 0121 694 9942 (H) 07813 666729 (M) email: irelands@blueyonder.co.uk
Chairman of Playing	Derek Nutt, c/o Moseley Rugby Ltd. (as above)
First XV Coach	Ian Smith with Don Caskie
Team Manager	John Caves Tel: 01216083383 (H) 07967056319 (M)
General Manager	Alan Potter Tel: 0121 443 3631 (O) 07796 171214 (M)

GROUND DETAILS

Address: Billesley Common, Yardley Wood Road, Billesley, Birmingham B13 0PT.
Tel: 0121 443 3631 email: info@moseleyrugby.co.uk
Capacity: 3,000   Covered Seating: 650

Directions: All road travellers are advised to approach from the South of Birmingham via the M42
From M42, J 3 head North on the A435 towards Birmingham.
After 1.5 miles, go across roundabout at Becketts Farm, continuing on the A435.
After 2.5 miles at roundabout (Large Sainsbury's opposite) take 3rd exit (signed to Warstock, Shirley & Solihull) into Maypole Lane.
After 1 mile turn left opposite Peterbrook Primary School into Yardley Wood Road.
Continue straight across a large roundabout (3rd exit).
Continue past the bus garage on left.
Continue across a double-mini-roundabout complex.
After 0.5 miles, cross two pedestrian crossings, and immed. turn left (before the bright green health centre) onto Billesley Common.

Nearest BR Station: Hall Green
Car Parking: 700 spaces
Admission: Matchday: Adult £15   Season: Adult £155
Club Shop: Open Saturday or Sunday, or through web-site. Contact Alan Potter
Clubhouse: Open Mon - Sat 9am-11pm, Sun 9am-3pm. Food is available. Functions contact Alan Potter

PROGRAMME

Size: A5   Pages: 44
Price: £2   Editor: Darren Andrews
Advertising:
Contact Alan Potter or see website.

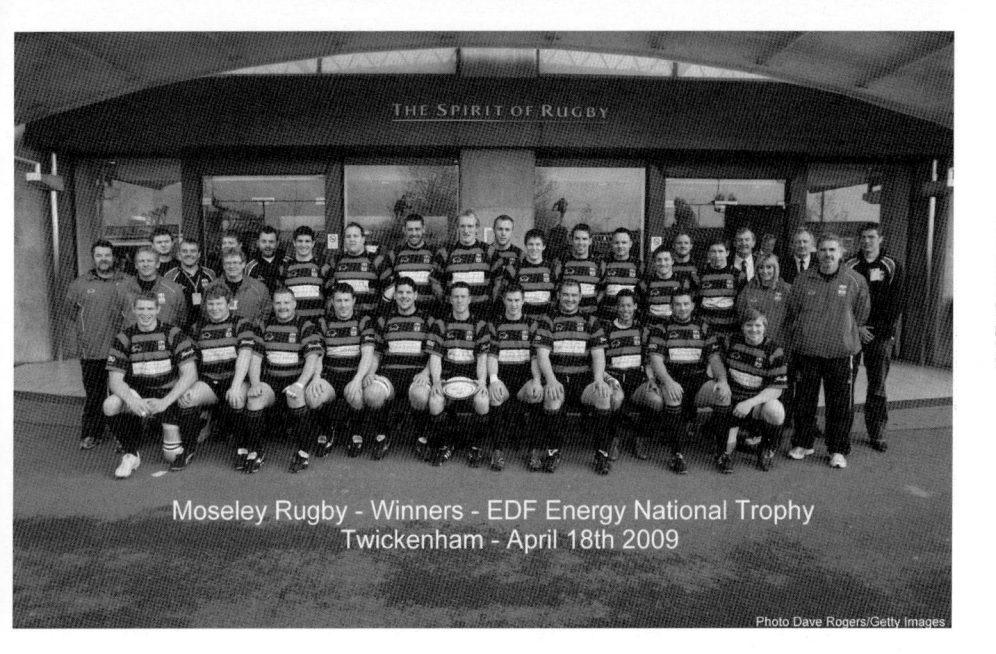

Moseley Rugby - Winners - EDF Energy National Trophy
Twickenham - April 18th 2009

Photo Dave Rogers/Getty Images

REVIEW OF THE SEASON 2008-09

The revival of this famous old club continued in 2008/09 with history being made on a number of fronts and success throughout its sixteen teams

Moseley won the EDF Trophy at Twickenham defeating Premiership bound Leeds Carnegie 23-17. Although this was Moseley's fourth visit to Twickenham for a National Cup final it was the club's first outright victory having shared the Cup with Gloucester in 1982. Andy Binns scored a vital try in his last season after fifteen years with the club.

In the League, the reduction of the 16 team ND1 to a 12 team "Championship" from 2009 meant that achieving 11th place or better became the focus. An excellent Cup run and weather problems played havoc with the fixture list, necessitating an appeal to win an extended season. Despite the disruption, Moseley finished a creditable 8th.

Representative honours included James Rodwell and Dan Norton in England 7's, and the dual registration arrangement with Gloucester saw many England U20's appearances for Dan Williams, Charlie Sharples, Henry Trinder and Jordi Pasqualin.

Moseley Women then followed up their unbeaten season in 2007/08 with a second successive promotion.

The Senior Colts won the North Midlands Cup, and only lost in the quarter-finals of National Cup to the eventual winners. Meanwhile the Junior Colts went all the way to the National Plate Final.

The ever growing Mini & Junior section held a successful 30th anniversary Mini tournament with over 1,250 children participating. The club's exceptional community department once again coached over 15,000 children in Birmingham.

A successful first year for sister club Moseley Oak provided a full range of rugby opportunities for every level of player as the dynamic development of the Billesley Common rugby centre of excellence continued.

MOSELEY'S SEASON - 2008-09

CHAMPIONSHIP

Date	H/A	Opponents	Result & Score	Att.	15	14	13	12	11
NATIONAL ONE									
30-08	H	London Welsh	L 9-15	815	Binns	Sharples	Adams	Reay	Bressington
06-09	A	Newbury	W 30-12	488	Binns	Sharples/t	Adams	Reay	Bressington(a/2t)
13-09	H	Coventry	W 34-12	1090	Binns	Sharples/2t	Adams	Reay	Bressington
20-09	A	Exeter	L 10-70	3724	Lavery	Norton	Adams(b/c)	Reay	Bressington
27-09	N	Otley	W 36-26	836	Binns	Sharples/t(c/t)	Adams/t	Reay	Bressington/t
04-10	A	Rotherham	L 23-47	1021	Binns	Sharples/t	Cox/t	Reay	Bressington
11-10	H	Nottingham	L 24-26	998	Binns	Sharples/t	Adams	Reay	Trinder/t
18-10	A	Plymouth Albion	L 17-26	2406	Binns	Bressington	Adams	Reay	Trinder
26-10	A	Cornish Pirates	L 15-19	2530	Binns	Sharples/t	Trinder	Reay	Bressington
01-11	H	Esher	W 22-13	750	Binns/t	Norton	Trinder	Reay	Bressington/2t
08-11	A	Sedgley Park	W 44-17	556	Thomas/2cp	Sharples	Adams/2t	Reay	Trinder/t
15-11	H	Doncaster	L 12-19	682	Thomas/4p	Sharples	Trinder	Reay	Bressington
23-11	A	Leeds Carnegie	L 20-53	2203	Thomas/2c2p	Sharples	Adams	Reay	Bressington/t
28-11	A	Bedford	L 15-17	2406	Thomas/cp	Roberts	Binns	Reay	Bressington/t
06-12	H	Manchester	W 48-7	822	Thomas/cp	Roberts/t	Trinder/3t	Reay	Bressington
20-12	A	Newbury*	W 36-9	700	Binns	Sharples	Trinder/t	Roberts	Bressington
26-12	A	Coventry	L 10-27	3638	Binns	Sharples	Trinder	Reay	Bressington
24-01	H	Rotherham*	W 43-21	974	Binns	Bressington	Adams/t	Reay	Norton/t
01-02	A	Nottingham	L 17-44	1107	Binns	Bressington	Adams	Reay/t	Thomas
21-02	H	Cornish Pirates*	L 26-37	965	Binns	Bressington	Adams/t	Reay	Norton
07-03	A	Esher	L 17-23	1612	Thomas/p	Bressington	Binns	Reay	Norton
14-03	H	Sedgley Park*	W 51-17	796	Binns(e/c)	Bressington/t	Adams	Reay	Norton/2t
21-03	H	Exeter	W 32-24		Binns	Bressington/t	Adams	Reay	Norton/2t
28-03	A	Doncaster	L 17-41	1438	Thomas/3p	Bressington	Adams	Reay	Norton
04-04	H	Leeds Carnegie	L 26-31	832	Binns	Bressington	Adams(a/2t)	Reay	Norton/t
11-04	H	Bedford	L 23-26	1118	Binns	Bressington/t(e/p)	Adams	Reay	Norton
25-04	H	Manchester	W 50-21	387	Thomas/2c	Bressington	Binns/t	Reay/2t	Norton
29-04	H	Plymouth Albion	W 50-32	1124	Binns	Bressington	Adams/2t	Reay/t	Norton
02-05	A	London Welsh	L 37-50	750	Vasey	Thomas/t	Binns	Reay	Norton/4t
		Otley	W 20-0		The match was cancelled with the agreement of the RFU at Otley's request.				
EDF ENERGY NATIONAL TROPHY									
4	17-01	H	Henley Hawks	W 34-6		Thomas/tc	Norton/t	Binns	Reay/t	Bressington/t
5	14-02	A	Bridgwater	W 43-10		Binns/t	Bressington	Adams/t	Reay	Thomas/t
Q.F.	28-02	A	London Welsh	W 27-21		Binns	Bressington	Adams	Reay	Norton/t
S.F.	21-03	H	Exeter	W 32-24		Binns	Bressington/t	Adams	Reay	Norton/2t
Final	18-04	N	Leeds Carnegie	W 23-18	10000	Binns/t(e/dg)	Trinder	Adams	Reay	Norton/t

SCORING BREAKDOWN

WHEN	Total	First Half	Second Half	1/4	2/4	3/4	4/4
the POINTS were scored	814	410	404	224	186	191	213
the POINTS were conceded	782	388	394	174	214	193	201
the TRIES were scored	105	48	57	27	21	25	32
the TRIES were conceded	104	50	54	22	28	25	29

HOW	Total	Pen. Try	Backs	Forwards	F Back	Wing	Centre	H Back	F Row	Lock	B Row
the TRIES were scored	105	8	59	38	1	33	19	6	7	9	22
the TRIES were conceded	104	2	78	24	11	30	15	22	5	9	10

182

KEY: * after opponents name indicates a penalty try.
Brackets after a player's name indicates he was replaced. eg (a) means he was replaced by replacement code "a" and so on.
/ after a player or replacement name is followed by any scores he made - eg /t, /c, /p, /dg or any combination of these

10	9	1	2	3	4	5	6	7	8
Vasey/3p	Taylor	Williams	Caves	Sigley	Arnold	Stott	Atkinson	Bignell	Rodwell
Vasey/3c3p	Taylor	Williams	Caves	Sigley	Arnold	Stott	Mason	Bignell	Rodwell
Vasey/4c2p	Taylor	Williams	Caves	Sigley	Arnold/t	Stott	Mason	Bignell	Rodwell/t
Roberts/p	Taylor	Williams	Oselton	Sigley	Arnold/t	Stott	Mason	Wirachowski	Rodwell
Vasey/3c	Taylor	Williams	Caves	Sigley	Arnold	Stott	Mason/t	Bignell	Rodwell/t
Vasey/c2p	Taylor	Williams	Caves	Sigley	Arnold	Evans	Atkinson	Bignell	Rodwell
Vasey/2pdg	Taylor	Williams	Caves	Sigley	Muldowney	Stott	Mason	Bignell	Rodwell/t
Vasey/3pdg	Taylor	Thomas	Caves	Williams	Muldowney	Stott	Mason	Bignell	Rodwell/t
Vasey/cdg	Taylor	Williams	Caves	Sigley	Muldowney	Stott	Whitney	Mason	Rodwell/t
Vasey/2cp	Pasqualin	Williams	Caves	Sigley	Muldowney	Stott	Mason	Bignell	Rodwell
Vasey/c	Taylor	Williams	Caves/t	Sigley	Arnold	Muldowney/3t	Evans	Bignell	Rodwell
Vasey	Taylor	Williams	Caves	Sigley	Arnold	Muldowney	Evans	Bignell	Rodwell
Vasey	Pasqualin	Sigley	Caves	Davis	Muldowney(d/t)	Stott	Mason	Bignell	Evans
Vasey	Taylor	Williams/t	Caves	Sigley	Muldowney	Williams	Mason	Whitney	Evans
Vasey/t4c	Pasqualin	Williams	Caves	Davis(d/t)	Muldowney	Stott	Mason/t	Bignell	Evans
Vasey/4cp	Taylor	Williams	Caves	Davis	Arnold	Muldowney	Mason	Evans	Rodwell/3t
Vasey/cp	Taylor	Williams	Caves	Davis	Arnold	Muldowney/t	Mason	Evans	Rodwell
Roberts/5cp	Taylor	Williams	Caves	Sigley	Muldowney	Stott	Mason/t	Bignell	Rodwell/2t
Roberts/cp(b/c)	Taylor	Sigley	Caves/t	Davis	Muldowney	Stott	Mason	Bignell	Evans
Roberts/c4p(b/c)	Pasqualin	Williams	Caves	Sigley	Muldowney	Stott	Mason	Bignell	Rodwell
Roberts/t2c	Taylor	Williams	Caves	Sigley	Muldowney/t	Stott	Mason	Bignell	Evans
Roberts/2cp	Taylor	Williams	Caves(f/t)	Sigley/t	Arnold/t	Stott	Mason	Bignell	Rodwell/t
Roberts/3c2p	Taylor	Williams	Caves	Sigley/t	Muldowney	Stott	Mason	Bignell	Rodwell
Vasey/dg	Taylor	Williams	Oselton	Sigley	Muldowney	Stott	Williams	Whitney/t	Mason
Roberts/t3c	Taylor	Williams	Caves	Sigley	Muldowney	Stott	Mason	Bignell	Williams
Roberts/2c2p	Taylor	Williams	Caves	Sigley	Muldowney	Stott	Mason	Bignell	Rodwell/t
Roberts/t4cp	Taylor/t	Williams	Caves	Sigley	Muldowney	Stott	Mason	Bignell	Rodwell/2t
Roberts/5cp(b/c)	Taylor	Williams	Caves	Sigley	Muldowney	Stott	Mason/t	Bignell	Rodwell/2t
Roberts/t2cp	Pasqualin	Thomas	Oselton	Williams	Arnold	Stott	Mason	Whitney	Evans

The result was recorded as a 20 - nil win for Moseley (5 league points).

Vasey/c	Taylor	Williams	Caves	Sigley	Stott	Muldowney(d/t)	Mason	Bignell	Rodwell/t
Roberts/4c	Taylor	Williams	Caves	Sigley	Muldowney/t	Stott	Mason/t	Bignell	Arnold/t
Vasey/p(g/2c)	Taylor	Williams	Caves/t	Sigley/t	Arnold/t	Stott	Mason	Bignell	Evans
Roberts/3c2p	Taylor	Williams	Caves	Sigley/t	Muldowney	Stott	Mason	Bignell	Rodwell
Roberts/2c2p	Taylor	Williams	Caves	Sigley	Muldowney	Stott	Mason	Sigley	Rodwell

REPLACEMENTS
a- H Trinder b- R Vasey c- T Roberts d- P Arnold
e- O Thomas f- D Oselton g- T Roberts

LEAGUE APPEARANCES
28 Andy Reay
27 Nathan Williams (2)
26 Adam Caves, Nathan Bressington
25 Neil Mason (2)
24 Gareth Taylor(4)

LEAGUE POINTS SCORERS

Pts	Player	T	C	P	DG
135	Tristan Roberts	6	30	15	-
127	Richard Vasey	1	28	18	4
85	James Rodwell	17			
67	Olly Thomas	1	10	14	-
50	Daniel Norton	10	-	-	-
50	Henry Trinder	10	-	-	-

NUMBER OF PLAYERS USED
32 plus 4 as a replacement only

MOSELEY STATISTICS

LEAGUE

TEAM RECORDS
MOST POINTS
Scored at Home: 51 v Sedgley Park 14.3.09
Scored Away: 50 v Manchester 25.4.09
Conceded at Home: 87 v Richmond 5.10.96
Conceded Away: 88 v Newcastle 22.3.97

MOST TRIES
Scored in a match: 9 v Sale 4.4.92
Conceded in a match: 14
v Richmond 5.10.96 (H) & v Newcastle 22.3.97 (A)

BIGGEST MARGINS
Home Win: 44pts - 47-3 v Barking 10.12.05
Away Win: 29pts - 42-13 v Wakefield 29.03.97
Home Defeat: 72pts - 15-87 v Richmond 5.10.96 v Manchester 50-21 25.4.09
Away Defeat: 69pts - 19-88 v Newcastle 22.3.97

MOST CONSECUTIVE
Victories: 13 (17.1.06 - 22.4.06)
Defeats: 8

INDIVIDUAL RECORDS
MOST APPEARANCES
by a forward: 157 (25) RIchard Stott
by a back: 247 (12) Andy Binns

MOST CONSECUTIVE
Appearances: 90 Gareth Taylor 25.1.03 - 29.4.06
Matches scoring Tries: 5 Darragh O'Mahoney
Matches scoring points: 11 Carl Arntzen

MATCH RECORDS
Most Points
28   Ollie Thomas   v Nottingham 7.4.07 (H)

Most Tries
4   Nathan Bressington   v Harrogate 18.2.06 (H)

Most Conversions
6   Richard LeBas   v Rotherham 26.4.97(H)

Most Penalties
8   Alastair Kerr   v Waterloo 17.2.96 (H)

Most Drop Goals
2   Alastair Kerr   v Plymouth 21.12.92 (H)
     A Houston   v Blackheath 14.1.95 (H)
     Matt Jones   v Orrell 25.10.97 (H)

SEASON RECORDS
Most Points	328	Ollie Thomas	04-05
Most Tries	20	Nathan Bressington	05-06
Most Conversions	49	Ollie Thomas	05-06
Most Penalties	64	Ollie Thomas	04-05
Most Drop Goals	5	Matt Jones	97-98
		Ollie Thomas	04-05

CAREER RECORDS
Most Points	1074	Ollie Thomas	03-09
Most Tries	60	Nathan Bressington	04-09
Most Conversions	165	Ollie Thomas	03-09
Most Penalties	218	Ollie Thomas	03-09
Most Drop Goals	10	Ollie Thomas	03-09

LAST TEN SEASONS

	Division	P	W	D	L	F	A	P.D.	Pts	Pos	Most Points	Most Tries
99-00	P2	26	14	0	12	595	526	69	28	7	116 Owen Doyle	11 Peter Buckton
00-01	N1	26	9	2	15	497	646	-149	47	10	181 Ben Harvey	6 Andy Gray & Rod Martin
01-02	N1	26	9	1	16	448	695	-247	46	11	126 Lee Hinton	7 R Protherough
02-03	N1	26	4	0	22	399	1178	-779	23	13r	123 Stephen Nutt	7 Geoff Gregory & J Hinkins
03-04	N2	26	11	2	13	535	524	11	24	10	151 Ollie Thomas	18 James Aston
04-05	N2	26	17	0	9	665	505	160	81	3	328 Ollie Thomas	16 Nathan Bressington
05-06	N2	26	23	0	3	785	415	370	112	1p	253 Ollie Thomas	20 Nathan Bressington
06-07	N1	30	7	0	23	527	943	-416	37	14	285 Ollie Thomas	8 Nathan Bressington
07-08	N1	30	12	1	17	519	744	-225	58	10	75 Matt Jones	9 Daniel Norton
08-09	N1	30	13	0	17	814	782	32	73	8	140 Tristan Roberts	17 James Rodwell

RFU SENIOR CUP

OVERALL PLAYING RECORD

	P	W	D	L	F	A	Pts Diff
Home	48	35	0	13	922	616	306
Away	32	15	0	17	359	520	-161
Neutral	3	0	1	2	30	44	-14
TOTAL	83	50	1	32	1311	1180	131

TEAM RECORDS

Highest Score: 79 v Liverpool St H 97/98
Biggest Winning Margin: 69 Pts 79-10 v Liverpool St H 97-98
Highest Score Against: 76 v Plymouth Alb. 04-05 (A)
Biggest Losing Margin: 70 Pts - 76-6 v Plymouth 04-05 (A)

71-72	Runners-up	78-79	Runners-up	85-86	4R	92-93	QF	99-00	4R
72-73	2R	79-80	2R	86-87	QF	93-94	QF	00-01	3R
73-74	2R	80-81	SF	87-88	SF	94-95	4R	01-02	4R
74-75	QF	81-82	Shared Cup	88-89	3R	95-96	4R	02-03	3R
75-76	2R	82-83	3R	89-90	SF	96-97	5R	03-04	2R
76-77	QF	83-84	4R	90-91	QF	97-98	6R	04-05	4R
77-78	2R	84-85	4R	91-92	2R	98-99	4R		

NATIONAL TROPHY

05-06	6 R	06-07	4 R	07-08	4 R	08-09	Winners

MOSELEY PLAYERS

	Position	D.o.B.	Apps.	Pts.	T	C	P	DG
Charlie Sharples	Winger		31	65	13	-	-	-
Daniel Norton	Winger		26 (6)	95	19	-	-	-
Henry Trinder	Winger		10 (2)	50	10	-	-	-
Nathan Bressington	Winger		119 (4)	300	60	-	-	-
Andy Binns	Full Back		247 (12)	315	33	27	31	1
Jack Adams	Centre		38	65	13	-	-	-
Andy Reay	Full back		46	30	6	-	-	-
Ollie Thomas	Fly half		107 (22)	1084	14	165	218	10
Richard Vasey	Fly Half		18 (6)	127	1	28	18	4
Tristan Roberts	Fly Half		15 (3)	135	6	30	15	-
Gareth Taylor	Scrum half		127 (10)	40	8	-	-	-
Jordi Pasqualin	Scrum half		5 (13)	-	-	-	-	-
Ben Buxton	Prop	09.11.79	121 (32)	20	4	-	-	-
George Davis	Prop		5 (15)	-	-	-	-	-
Nathan Williams	Prop		48 (7)	5	1	-	-	-
Terry Sigley	Prop		85 (12)	46	8	-	2	-
Adam Caves	Hooker		118 (40)	115	23	-	-	-
Dan Oselton	Hooker		3 (16)	5	1	-	-	-
Paul Arnold	Lock		50 (26)	35	7	-	-	-
Richard Bignell	Lock		54 (11)	5	1	-	-	-
Richard Stott	Back row		157 (29)	25	5	-	-	-
Neil Mason	Back row		92 (5)	75	15	-	-	-
James Rodwell	Back row		82 (3)	155	31	-	-	-
Mark Evans	Back row		123 (38)	45	9	-	-	-
Ali Muldowney	Lock		21 (3)	25	5	-	-	-

NOTTINGHAM RFC

NOTTINGHAM RUGBY

Founded: 1877

Nickname:
The Green and whites

Colours:
Green and white shirts, blue shorts.

Change Colours:
White shirts, blue shorts

Website:
www.nottinghamrugby.co.uk

KEY PERSONNEL

President	Nigel Bettinson-Eatch
Chairman	Geoff Huckstep
Treasurer	Mark Doleman
Club Secretary	Andi Starr
	email:andi.starr@nottinghamrugby.co.uk
Fixture Sec.	Glenn Delaney see below
Commercial Manager	Rob Harding
	email: Rob.harding@nottinghamrugby.co.uk
Director Of Rugby	Glenn Delaney
	email: glenn.delaney@nottinghamrugby.co.uk
Communication & Media Manager	Annie Bowden
	Tel: 0115 9850742 Mob: 07841 848376

CONTACT DETAILS

Nottingham Rugby,
The Bay, 1 Holme Road, West Bridgford, Nottingham, NG5 5AA
Tel: (0115) 907 0070   Fax: (0115) 907 0079
email: enquiries@nottinghamrugby.co.uk

GROUND DETAILS

Address
The Bay, 1 Holme Road, West Bridgford,
Nottingham, NG5 5AA
Tel: (0115) 907 0070
Fax: (0115) 907 0079
email: enquiries@nottinghamrugby.co.uk

Simple Directions
The ground is situated alongside the A6011 by the junction with Radcliffe Road.

Please note all First XV games in the 2008/09 season will be played at Meadow Lane, home of Notts County Football Club

Total Capacity: 18,000 - all covered seating

Car Parking: 200 spaces @ £5.

Nearest BR Station: Nottingham Midland

Admission Prices
Matchday: £18 adult, £12 concession, £7 Students, £4 U16

Season: £210 adults, £140 concession,£55 Students, £30 U16

Clubhouse
Open matchdays and training nights
Contact: Richard Garland

PROGRAMME

Size: A5   Pages: 56   Price: £2.50
Editorial & Advertising:
Rob Harding / Annie Bowden - see above.

REVIEW OF THE SEASON 2008-09

Having finished third, level on points with Exeter, the previous season Nottingham started well in their bid to go at least one better. Although they lost at Leeds on the opening day, a run of nine straight wins put them in genuine contention.

That run came to an end at Exeter in November, by which time the club had to make the painful announcement that financial difficulties threatened their continued existence at this level. The response to that announcement though was truly heartwarming, with players taking pay cuts and supporters showing passion and commitment, and plenty of imagination, in their fundraising efforts.

It was enough to see the club through one of the most difficult phases in its history.

On the field the Green and Whites just got on with the job and by the turn of the year had won fourteen of their eighteen games.

Attention then turned to the National Trophy, and again there was the incentive of improving on the previous year's placing.

Big wins over Blaydon, Cornish Pirates and Mounts Bay again took them to the semi finals as the season reached a thrilling climax in March, with consecutive home games against the top two sides in Division One.

A single point defeat against Exeter in the league was hardly the best preparation for their cup showdown with Leeds, but they dominated long periods against the Champions elect. In what was one of the best, and most dramatic games seen at Meadow Lane they again lost out by the narrowest of margins as a try deep into injury time put Leeds through to the final.

Those two games clearly took a lot out of Nottingham, but despite a poor performance at Rotherham the following week, they completed their league campaign in style, winning their last six games to finish fourth.

NOTTINGHAM RUGBY

NOTTINGHAM'S SEASON - 2008-09

CHAMPIONSHIP

Date	H/A	Opponents	Result & Score	Att.	15	14	13	12	11
\multicolumn{10}{l}{**NATIONAL ONE**}
31-08	A	Leeds Carnegie	L 19-34	3703	Jackson/c4p	Savage	Nirmalendran	Molenaar	Dodge
07-09	H	Plymouth Albion	W 43-19	1100	Jackson/t3c4p	Savage	Nirmalendran	Molenaar	Dodge
13-09	A	Esher	W 25-3	380	Jackson/tcp	Cobden/t	Nirmalendran	Molenaar	Dodge(a/t)
21-09	H	Sedgley Park	W 32-24	1207	Jackson/t3c2p	Cobden/t	Nirmalendran	Molenaar	Thompson
28-09	A	Cornish Pirates	W 31-20	2750	Jackson/t3c	Cobden/t(c/t)	Nirmalendran	Molenaar	Dodge
05-10	H	Doncaster	W 18-9	1345	Jackson/tp	Savage	Nirmalendran	Molenaar	Dodge
11-10	A	Moseley	W 26-24	998	Jackson	Savage	Nirmalendran/t	Molenaar	Dodge/t
19-10	H	Newbury	W 48-3	1277	Jackson/t5cp	Savage	Nirmalendran/t	Dodge/t	Thompson/t
26-10	A	Bedford	W 15-7	2019	Jackson/tcp	Savage	Nirmalendran	Molenaar	Dodge
01-11	A	Otley	W 43-3	952	Jackson/t	Savage/t	Nirmalendran	Molenaar/t	Cobden/t
08-11	A	Exeter	L 18-29	4634	Jackson	Savage	Nirmalendran	Molenaar	Dodge/t
16-11	H	Rotherham	W 33-13	2226	Nirmalendran	Savage/t	Tonks	Dodge	Cobden/t
22-11	A	London Welsh	W 36-30	820	Jackson/t	Savage/t	Tonks	Dodge	Cobden
30-11	H	Manchester	W 57-8	1247	Jackson/3t4c	Savage	Erinle	Tonks	Cobden/3t(f/t)
14-12	A	Leeds Carnegie	L 12-19	2663	Jackson	Savage	Tonks/t	Erinle	Cobden
20-12	A	Plymouth Albion	L 25-26	3102	Jackson/t	Nirmalendran	Tonks/c	Dodge	Cobden
28-12	H	Esher	W 36-14	1463	Savage/t	Dodge	Tonks/3cp	Erinle/t	Cobden/t
11-01	H	Cornish Pirates*	W 23-19	1705	Savage	Jackson	Cobden	Tonks/2c3p	Dodge
24-01	A	Doncaster	L 14-25	1872	Savage	Cobden	Erinle	Tonks/2c	Dodge/t
01-02	H	Moseley	W 44-17	1107	Savage/t	Cobden/t	Nirmalendran	Dodge	Jackson/t
21-02	A	Bedford	L 16-23	2918	Savage	Cobden	Nirmalendran	Starling	Jackson/t
08-03	H	Otley	W 95-5	1318	Savage/t(g/t)	Thompson	Nirmalendran/2t	Molenaar	Jackson/t3c
15-03	H	Exeter	L 14-15	1305	Jackson/2c	Cobden	Nirmalendran	Molenaar	Dodge
28-03	A	Rotherham	L 6-20	1237	Jackson/2p	Cobden	Tonks	Molenaar	Dodge
01-04	A	Sedgley Park	W 50-5	296	Savage	Jackson/5c	Tonks(h/t)	Dodge	Hayter/2t
05-04	H	London Welsh	W 30-24	1321	Tonks/tp	Jackson/3c2p	Nirmalendran	Molenaar/t	Dodge/t
11-04	A	Manchester	W 49-23	324	Jackson/t7c	Thompson	Hayter/t	Molenaar/t	Dodge
15-04	A	Newbury*	W 23-16	514	Jackson/2c3p	Thompson	Tonks/t	Molenaar	Dodge
19-04	H	Coventry	W 55-0	1088	Tonks	Cobden/t	Dodge/t	Molenaar	Jackson/t6cp
25-04	A	Coventry*	W 37-22	1554	Tonks/2t	Cobden/2t	Dodge	Molenaar	Jackson/2cp

EDF ENERGY NATIONAL TROPHY

4	17-01	H	Blaydon	W 33-22		Savage/2t	Nirmalendran	Cobden	Tonks/4c	Jackson/t
5	15-02	H	Cornish Pirates	W 39-8	908	Savage	Cobden	Nirmalendran	Dodge	Jackson
Q.F.	28-02	A	Mounts Bay	W 66-7	367	Jackson/3t	Cobden/t	Nirmalendran	Molenaar	Thompson/t
S.F.	22-03	H	Leeds Carnegie	L 13-14		Jackson/c2p	Cobden	Nirmalendran	Molenaar	Dodge

SCORING BREAKDOWN

WHEN	Total	First Half	Second Half	1/4	2/4	3/4	4/4
the POINTS were scored	973	421	552	197	224	227	325
the POINTS were conceded	499	280	219	125	155	89	130
the TRIES were scored	130	55	75	26	29	28	47
the TRIES were conceded	54	27	27	15	12	10	17

HOW	Total	Pen. Try	Backs	Forwards	F Back	Wing	Centre	H Back	F Row	Lock	B Row
the TRIES were scored	130	3	82	45	21	30	15	16	14	11	20
the TRIES were conceded	55	-	40	15	9	14	11	6	4	3	8

188

KEY: * after opponents name indicates a penalty try.
Brackets after a player's name indicates he was replaced. eg (a) means he was replaced by replacement code "a" and so on.
/ after a player or replacement name is followed by any scores he made - eg /t, /c, /p, /dg or any combination of these

10	9	1	2	3	4	5	6	7	8
Taylor	Usasz	Parr	Duffy	Hall	Morley	Rouse	Hammond	Sherriff/t	Montague
Taylor/t	Usasz	Parr	Duffy	Hall	Morley/t	Rouse/t	Hammond	Sherriff/t	Montague
Taylor	Usasz	Parr	Duffy	Hall	Morley	McDonald	Hammond	Sherriff	Montague/t
Taylor/t	Usasz	Fowkes	Duffy	Hall	Montague	McDonald	Hammond	Sherriff/t	McComb
Taylor/t	Usasz	Parr(b/t)	Duffy	Hall	Morley	Rouse	Hammond	Sherriff	Montague
Taylor/2t	Usasz	Parr	Duffy	Hall	Morley	Rouse	Hammond	Sherriff	Montague
Taylor/tc3p	Usasz	Parr	Duffy	Harris	Morley	Rouse	Hammond	Sherriff	McComb
Taylor	Pilgrim	Parr	Duffy/2t	Harris	Morley	McDonald	Hammond	Sherriff/t	Hemingway
Taylor	Usasz	Parr	Duffy/t	Hall	Morley	Rouse	Hammond	Sherriff	Montague
Taylor/5cp	Pilgrim	Harris	Duffy	Hall/t(d/t)	Rouse	McDonald	Hammond	Sherriff	McComb
Taylor/c2p	Usasz	Parr	Duffy	Hall	Morley	Rouse	Hemingway	Sherriff	Montague(e/t)
Taylor/t2c3p	Usasz	Parr	Duffy/t	Harris	Morley	Rouse	Hemingway	Sherriff	Montague
Taylor/t4cp	Usasz	Parr	Duffy	Harris	Morley	Rouse	McComb	Sherriff/t	Montague/t
Taylor/3cp	Pilgrim	Fowkes	Duffy/t	Harris	Morley	Rouse	McComb	Sherriff	Montague
Taylor/c	Usasz	Parr	Duffy	Harris	Morley	Rouse	Hammond	Sherriff/t	Montague
Taylor/c2p	Usasz	Parr	Duffy/t	Harris	Montague	Rouse/t	Hammond	Sherriff	Elphinston
Taylor/tc	Usasz	Parr	Duffy/t	Harris	Montague	Rouse	Hammond	Sherriff	Elphinston
Taylor	Usasz	Parr	Duffy	Cole	Morley	Rouse	Hammond	Sherriff	Montague/t
Taylor/t	Pilgrim	Parr	Duffy	Harris	Morley	Rouse	Hammond	Sherriff	Montague
Taylor/4c2p	Pilgrim/t	Parr	Duffy/t	Harris	Morley	Rouse/t	Hammond	Sherriff	Montague
Taylor/2p	Pilgrim	Parr	Duffy	Cole	Morley	Rouse	Hammond	Sherriff	Montague/t
Taylor/t9c2p	Pilgrim	Fowkes	Loney	Harris	Nimmo/t	Montague/2t	Corcoran/t	Hammond/2t	Elphinston/t
Taylor	Usasz	Parr	Duffy	Harris	Nimmo	Rouse/t	Hammond	Sherriff/t	Montague
Thompson	Usasz	Fowkes	Duffy	Parr	Nimmo	Rouse	Hammond	Sherriff	Montague
Taylor	Usasz/t	Fowkes	Loney	Duffy/t	McDonald	Rouse/t	Hammond	Elphinston	Montague
Taylor	Usasz	Parr	Duffy	Holford	Nimmo	Rouse	Hammond	Sherriff	Montague
Taylor	Davies/t	Parr	Loney/t	Holford	McDonald/t	Rouse	Montague	Eggleshaw	Elphinston/t
Taylor	Pilgrim	Parr	Loney	Holford	McDonald	Nimmo	Hammond	Eggleshaw	Elphinston
Taylor	Usasz(i/2t)	Parr	Duffy/t	Holford	Nimmo	Rouse/t	Hammond	Sherriff	Montague/t
Taylor	Usasz	Parr	Duffy	Holford	Nimmo	Rouse	Hammond	Sherriff	Montague/t
Thompson	Pilgrim	Fowkes	Duffy	Harris	McDonald	Rouse/t	Montague	Hammond	Elphinston/t
Taylor/t3c5pdg	Pilgrim(h/t)	Fowkes	Duffy	Harris	Morley	Rouse/t	Hammond	Sherriff	Montague
Taylor/t8c	Pilgrim/t	Fowkes	Duffy	Parr	McDonald/t	Rouse/t	Hammond/t	Eggleshaw	Montague
Taylor/t	Usasz	Parr	Duffy	Harris	Nimmo	Rouse	Hammond	Sherriff	Montague

REPLACEMENTS

a- B Thompson   b- R Harris   c- A Savage   d- N Fowkes
e- G McComb   f- R Nirmalendran   g- J Cobden   h- C Davies

LEAGUE APPEARANCES

- 29 Tim Taylor
- 27 David Jackson (3), Joe Duffy (3)
- 26 Luke Sherriff (1), Dan Montague (1)
- 25 Matt Parr (4), Nic Rouse (1), Craig Hammond (1)

NUMBER OF PLAYERS USED

31 plus 10 as a replacement only

LEAGUE POINTS SCORERS

Pts	Player	T	C	P	DG
261	David Jackson				
176	Tim Taylor	11	32	19	-
70	Jack Cobden	14	-	-	-
56	Greg Tonks	5	8	5	-
50	Joe Duffy	10	-	-	-
40	Dan Montague	8	-	-	-

NOTTINGHAM STATISTICS
LEAGUE

CHAMPIONSHIP

TEAM RECORDS
MOST POINTS
Scored at Home: 95 v Otley 8.3.09
Scored Away: 58 v Lydney 24.1.04
Conceded at Home: 74 v Newcastle 14.9.96
Conceded Away: 102 v Coventry 5.10.96

MOST TRIES
Scored in a match: 12 v Morley 24.10.92 (H)
Conceded in a match: 14 v Coventry 5.10.96 (A)

BIGGEST MARGINS
Home Win: 90pts - 95-5 v Otley 8.3.09
Away Win: 55pts - 55-0 v Liverpool St H 28.11.98
Home Defeat: 65pts - 5-70 v Richmond 16.11.96
Away Defeat: 80pts - 22-102 v Coventry 5.10.96

MOST CONSECUTIVE
Victories: 9 (7.8.08 - 30.11.08)
Defeats: 12

INDIVIDUAL RECORDS
MOST APPEARANCES
by a forward: 211(4) Mark Bradley
by a back: 191 (14) David Jackson

MOST CONSECUTIVE
Appearances: 51 Mark Bradley 20.1.01 - 14.12.02
Matches scoring Tries: 4 Andy Smallwood & Richard Lloyd
Matches scoring points: 38 Chris Atkinson

MATCH RECORDS
Most Points
29   Tim Taylor   Otley v 8.3.09 (H)

Most Tries
4   Gary Hartley   v Morley 24.10.92 (H)
     Alan Royer   v Liverpool St H 28.11.98 (A)

Most Conversions
9   Guy Gregory   v Morley 24.10.92 (H)
     Tim Taylor   v Otley 8.3.09 (H)

Most Penalties
6   Guy Gregory   v Saracens 12.3.94 (H)
     Chris Atkinson   v Camberley 19.9.98 (A)

Most Drop Goals
2   By three players Guy Gregory (4 times),
     Andy Sutton, Simon Hodgkinson

SEASON RECORDS
Most Points	272	Chris Atkinson	98-99
Most Tries	19	Richard Lloyd	02-03
Most Conversions	61	Tom Barlow	06-07
Most Penalties	64	Chris Atkinson	97-98/99
Most Drop Goals	9	Guy Gregory	92-93

CAREER RECORDS
Most Points	651	Russell Southam	00-03
Most Tries	59	David Jackson	00-09
Most Conversions	106	Neil Stenhouse	03-06
Most Penalties	142	Simon Hodgkinson	87-93, 95-97
Most Drop Goals	19	Guy Gregory	91-94

LAST TEN SEASONS

	Division	P	W	D	L	F	A	P.D.	Pts	Pos	Most Points		Most Tries	
99-00	JN1	26	8	1	17	460	574	-114	17	11	155	Tom Rolt	7	Tom Rolt
00-01	N2	26	10	0	16	544	584	-40	20	11	219	Russell Southam	16	Jamie Morley
01-02	N2	26	12	0	14	539	658	-119	24	8	203	Russell Southam	6	Russell Southam
02-03	N2	26	10	0	16	530	629	-99	20	11	229	Russell Southam	19	Richard Lloyd
03-04	N2	26	19	2	5	761	535	226	40	2p	238	Neil Stenhouse	11	David Jackson
04-05	N1	26	7	0	19	525	752	-227	40	11	147	Neil Stenhouse	12	Richard Lloyd
05-06	N1	26	13	0	13	642	604	38	66	7	166	Neil Stenhouse	11	Chris Wyles
06-07	N1	30	13	0	17	805	718	87	73	9	230	Tom Barlow	9	Rohan Nirmalandren
07-08	N1	30	23	0	7	818	520	298	116	3	77	David Jackson	13	Luke Sherriff
08-09	N1	30	22	0	8	973	499	474	*106	4	261	David Jackson	18	David Jackson

RFU SENIOR CUP

OVERALL PLAYING RECORD

	P	W	D	L	F	A	Pts Diff
Home	37	20	0	17	637	537	100
Away	29	14	0	15	460	623	-163
Neutral	0	0	0	0	0	0	0
TOTAL	66	34	0	32	1097	1160	-63

TEAM RECORDS

Highest Score: 50 v Preston 98/99
Biggest Winning Margin: 47 (50-3) v Preston 98/99
Highest Score Against: 61 v Bristol 04-05 (A)
Biggest Losing Margin: 52 (52-0) v Bath 91/92

SEASON BY SEASON

71-72	2R	78-79	DNQ	85-86	QF	92-93	4R	99-00	4R
72-73	1R	79-80	2R	86-87	4R	93-94	4R	00-01	2R
73-74	1R	80-81	QF	87-88	3R	94-95	4R	01-02	2R
74-75	1R	81-82	3R	88-89	QF	95-96	5R	02-03	4R
75-76	1R	82-83	QF	89-90	QF	96-97	5R	03-04	2R
76-77	DNQ	83-84	SF	90-91	SF	97-98	2R	04-05	4R
77-78	1R	84-85	4R	91-92	3R	98-99	4R		

NATIONAL TROPHY

| 05-06 | S.F. | 06-07 | 5 R | 07-08 | S.F. | 08-09 | S.F. |

PLAYERS

	Position	D.o.B.	Apps.	Pts.	T	C	P	DG
David Jackson	Full back	28/05/1982	191 (14)	537	52	74	41	2
Rohan Nirmalendran	Winger	19/05/1983	59 (14)	90	18	-	-	-
Alex Dodge	Winger		24 (4)	30	6	-	-	-
Jack Cobden	Winger		18 (6)	70	14	-	-	-
Greg Tonks	Centre		23 (1)	113	6	28	9	-
Tim Molenaar	Centre	19/02/1981	103 (1)	120	24	-	-	-
Alex Dodge	Centre	17/10/1984	79 (4)	90	18	-	-	-
Andrew Savage	Centre	27/01/1987	45 (11)	60	12	-	-	-
Ben Thompson	Fly half	03/12/1980	79 (40)	175	23	18	6	2
Tim Yaylor	Fly Half		29	176	11	32	19	-
Chris Pilgrim	Scrum half	13/01/1986	16 (40)	25	5	-	-	-
Tim Usasz	Scrum half	21/06/1983	43 (5)	20	4	-	-	-
Matt Parr	Prop	29/09/1982	69 (13)	15	3	-	-	-
Nigel Hall	Prop	23/11/1978	92 (14)	85	17	-	-	-
Neil Fowkes	Prop	05/11/1980	82 (71)	20	4	-	-	-
Robert Lee Harris	Prop		13 (8)	5	1	-	-	-
Joe Duffy	Hooker	22/06/1982	105 (33)	175	35	-	-	-
Alex Loney	Hooker	29/09/1983	64 (39)	60	12	-	-	-
Lee Morley	Lock	19/08/1982	94 (13)	35	7	-	-	-
Craig Hammond	Lock	11/02/1979	178 (5)	90	18	-	-	-
Vic Rouse	Lock	10/02/1981	78 (2)	50	10	-	-	-
Sam McDonald	Lock		7 (10)	5	1	-	-	-
Ian Nimmo	Lock		7 (2)	5	1	-	-	-
Ian Montague	Back row	10/09/1983	64 (7)	60	12	-	-	-
Luke Sherriff	Back row	15/02/1979	51 (2)	125	25	-	-	-

PENZANCE & NEWLYN

KEY PERSONNEL

Chairman of the Board	Dicky Evans
Chief Executive	Rod Coward, c/o the club as below
	Tel: 01736 335313 Fax: 01736 335319
	email: rod.coward@cornish-pirates.com
President	Robin Turner
Chairman	Sid Thomas
High Performance Manager	Chris Stirling, c/o the club as below
	Tel: 01736 335311 Fax: 01736 335319
	email: chris.stirling@cornish-pirates.com
Media Contact	Phil Westren, c/o the club as below
	Tel: 01736 335317 mobile 07817 998879
	email: phil.westren@cornish-pirates.com
Team Manager	Jan Rendall, c/o the club as below
	Tel: 07773 330012
	email: chris@rendall817.fsnet.co.uk
Club Administrator	Terry Drew, c/o the club as below
	Tel: 01736 351568 Fax: 01736 335319
	email: terry.drew@cornish-pirates.com

Founded: 1945

Nickname: Cornish Pirates

Colours: Black, red & white

Change colours: Black & gold

Web site: www.cornish-pirates.com

CONTACT DETAILS

c/o Penzance & Newlyn RFC,
Westholme, Alexandra Road, Penzance, Cornwall. TR18 4LY

PROGRAMME

Size: A5   Price: £2.50   Pages: 48
Advertising: c/o Phil Westren   Tel: 07817 998879

GROUND DETAILS

Address:
The Recreation Ground, Cranbury Road, Camborne, TR14 7PY.   Tel: 01209 712684

Capacity: 6,000   Covered Seating: 1,400

Directions: Leave A30 westbound at Camborne West junction, take the first left and left again at the roundabout into Camborne. Carry straight on for approx 1/4 a mile, turn right into Coronation Avenue (bungalows) opposite the fire station on the left and then right when you reach Cranberry Road.

Nearest BR Station: Camborne - approx 10 minutes walking distance from the ground

Car Parking: 250 adjacent to ground, and ample extra parking in the vicinity.

Admission: Matchday £20/£15/£12 (adults)
Season: £289/ £199/ £159 (all tbc) - Ticket Office contact Rudi Grenfell 01736 331961

L-R - Back: Sam Heard, Bruce Cumming, Heino Senekal, Bertrand Bedes, Mike Burak, Matt Evans, Joe Beardshaw, Ben Gulliver, Ollie Thomas, Chris Morgan, Aisea Havili. **Middle:** Lauren Devlin (Physio), Phil Angove (Scrummaging Coach), Simon Raynes (Strength & Conditioning Coach), Alan Paver, Brian Tuohy, Richard Bright, Steve Winn, Iva Motusaga, Paul Andrew, Sam Betty, Dan Seal, Tom Luke, Doug Sanft, Marika Vakacegu, Jan Rendall (Kit Man), Brett Davey (Assistant Coach), Jeff Till (Physio Assistant).
Front: Rhys Jones, Nick Griffiths, Rob Elloway, Darren Dawidiuk, Rhodri McAtee, Adryan Winnan (capt), Mark Hewitt (Coach), Ed Fairhurst, Peter Cook, Paul Devlin, Mark Ireland, Simon Whatling, Jimmy Moore

REVIEW OF THE SEASON 2008-09

Finishing fifth in National One the previous season, the aim at the start of the 2008-09 campaign was to hopefully finish in the top four. Disappointingly, however, the Pirates never played with any prolonged consistency, with their home form in particular being somewhat below par. In total, eight games were lost at Camborne, and the team ultimately finished seventh. It was not a disaster, but it was less than hoped for, and was frustrating for all involved.

Losing 16-0 at Coventry in the second game of the season was a disappointment, as was losing three homes games on the trot against Exeter Chiefs (23-32), Nottingham (20-31), and Rotherham (28-32). However, the mood was lifted after drawing 24-all draw at Doncaster, winning at home against Moseley (albeit by just 19-15 points), and then recording a superb 26-6 points win away to Bedford Blues.

2008, however, was to end with a 38-7 points drubbing away to Exeter Chiefs and going into 2009 the form continued to frustrate. The first game in February was away to Nottingham in Round 5 of the EDF Energy National Trophy, which everyone knew would be tough. In the league game played at Meadow Lane a month earlier the Cornish side had proved a match for the 'Green & Whites' losing 23-19 in injury-time, but on this occasion was well and truly beaten (39-8).

A few days later coach Mark Hewitt departed the club and Brett Davey took over the reins. Although the Pirates initially picked themselves up they were still unable to achieve any prolonged consistency right to the end of the season.

Despite a feeling of overall under achievement, a number of new faces certainly impressed in the Cornish Pirates colours during the season, including Fijian full-back/wing Marika Vakacegu, the club's top try-scorer on 13, who is now moving up to the Premiership with Sale Sharks.

Rhodri McAtee, Rhys Jones and Heino Senekal all played for the Barbarians, whilst three members of the Cornish Pirates squad, scrum-half Ed Fairhurst, lock Mike Burak, and prop Scott Franklin featured for Canada on their autumn tour.

Having mentioned Rhodri McAtee, he is also a proud holder of a Rugby World Cup Sevens gold medal, won as a member of the Wales team in Dubai. It was a successful and enjoyable tournament, with congratulations also to Brian Tuohy who played for Ireland.

Looking ahead to the new 'Championship' season, the Cornish Pirates have already been busy in recruitment. Kiwi Chris Stirling, as High Performance Manager, heads a new-look coaching team, whilst new players on board offer an exciting blend of experience (including former captain Gavin Cattle) and potential.

With reference to a number of players departing, Cornish Pirates CEO Rod Coward stated: "The Club wishes to record its grateful thanks for many years of commitment, unswerving loyalty and effort to stalwarts – Dan Seal, Heino Senekal and Iva Motusaga and also to the more recent Pirates who are moving on."

PIRATES' SEASON - 2008-09

Date	H/A	Opponents	Result & Score	Att.	15	14	13	12	11
NATIONAL ONE									
31-08	H	Newbury	W 48-5	2846	Winnan/t	McAtee/t	Ireland(a/t)	Winn	Vakacegu/t
06-09	A	Coventry	L 0-16	1269	Winnan	McAtee	Devlin	Winn	Vakacegu
14-09	H	Exeter	L 23-32	4913	Winnan	Vakacegu	Devlin	Luke	Havili
20-09	A	Otley	W 31-25	675	Winnan	Vakacegu/t	Devlin	Luke	Havili/2t
28-09	H	Nottingham	L 20-31	2750	Vakacegu/3t	Havili	Devlin	Luke	McAtee
04-10	A	Manchester	W 12-6	341	Vakacegu/t	Tuohy	Ireland	Winn	McAtee
12-10	H	Rotherham	L 27-32	2488	Vakacegu	Havili	Devlin	Luke/3c2p	Tuohy/t
18-10	A	Doncaster	D 24-24	1102	Winnan	Tuohy	Devlin	Luke	McAtee/2t
26-10	H	Moseley	W 19-15	2530	Winnan	Tuohy/t	Devlin	Luke	McAtee
01-11	A	Bedford	W 26-6	2514	Winnan	Tuohy	Devlin	Winn/t	McAtee
08-11	A	Esher	W 19-3	589	Winnan	Tuohy/2t	Devlin	Winn	Vakacegu
16-11	H	Leeds Carnegie	L 23-25	3853	Winnan	Tuohy	Devlin	Luke	Vakacegu
23-11	H	Sedgley Park*	W 56-14	2324	Vakacegu	Havili/2t	Ireland	Luke	Tuohy/c
29-11	A	Plymouth Albion*	L 12-20	5421	Vakacegu	Moore/c	Ireland	Winn	Tuohy/t
06-12	A	London Welsh	W 38-23	1265	Vakacegu	Devlin	Ireland/t	Luke/cp	Tuohy/3t
21-12	H	Coventry	W 32-14	2877	Vakacegu/2t	Tuohy/t	Ireland/t	Luke(d/t)	Devlin
27-12	A	Exeter	L 7-38	7345	Vakacegu	Devlin	Ireland	Luke	Tuohy(f/t)
03-01	H	Otley	W 55-13	2073	Vakacegu	Havili/t(g/t)	Devlin	Winn	McAtee/t
11-01	A	Nottingham	L 19-23	1705	Vakacegu	Tuohy	Devlin	Luke	McAtee
25-01	H	Manchester	W 25-10	2068	Vakacegu/t	Tuohy/t	Ireland	Luke	McAtee/t
31-01	A	Rotherham	W 34-28	1523	Vakacegu/2t	Tuohy(a/t)	Ireland	Luke	Devlin
21-02	A	Moseley	W 37-26	965	Winnan	Vakacegu	Devlin/t	Winn	Moore/4c3p
28-02	A	Newbury	W 39-10	433	Vakacegu	Havili	Devlin	Winn	Moore/2t
08-03	H	Bedford	L 5-6	4764	Winnan	Devlin	Ireland	Winn	Moore
15-03	H	Esher	L 7-16	1894	Winnan	McAtee	Ireland	Winn	Tuohy
29-03	A	Leeds Carnegie	L 9-33	3806	Winnan	Tuohy	Devlin	Winn	McAtee
04-04	A	Sedgley Park	W 35-27	524	Winnan	Havili/t	Ireland	Devlin/t	McAtee/t
12-04	H	Plymouth Albion	W 30-14	4306	Winnan(j/t)	Tuohy	Ireland	Luke	McAtee
19-04	H	Doncaster	L 23-33	2437	Vakacegu/t	Tuohy	Devlin	Luke	McAtee
25-04	H	London Welsh	L 8-10	2616	Vakacegu/t	Havili	Devlin	Ireland	McAtee
EDF ENERGY NATIONAL TROPHY									
4 18-01	H	Southend	W 24-0		Winnan	Moore/2c	Ireland	Winn	McAtee/t
5 15-02	A	Nottingham	L 8-39	908	Vakacegu	Winnan	Ireland	Winn/t	Devlin

SCORING BREAKDOWN

WHEN	Total	First Half	Second Half	1/4	2/4	3/4	4/4
the POINTS were scored	743	319	424	126	193	178	246
the POINTS were conceded	578	264	314	124	140	143	171
the TRIES were scored	95	36	59	11	25	22	37
the TRIES were conceded	64	24	40	12	12	16	24

HOW	Total	Pen. Try	Backs	Forwards	F Back	Wing	Centre	H Back	F Row	Lock	B Row
the TRIES were scored	95	2	65	28	14	29	7	15	7	4	17
the TRIES were conceded	64	7	39	18	9	17	6	7	5	3	10

KEY: * after opponents name indicates a penalty try.
Brackets after a player's name indicates he was replaced. eg (a) means he was replaced by replacement code "a" and so on.
/ after a player or replacement name is followed by any scores he made - eg /t, /c, /p, /dg or any combination of these

10	9	1	2	3	4	5	6	7	8
Sanft/4cp	Fairhurst	Paver	Elloway(b/t)	Heard	Senekal	Gulliver	Cumming	Morgan/t	Bedes/t
Sanft	Griffiths	Paver	Elloway	Heard	Senekal	Gulliver	Cumming	Morgan	Bedes
Sanft/2c3p	Fairhurst	Paver	Elloway	Heard	Senekal	Gulliver	Evans	Morgan(c/2t)	Bedes
Jones/3c	Fairhurst	Paver	Elloway/t	Heard	Burak/t	Gulliver	Cumming	Motusaga	Bedes
Sanft/cp	Fairhurst	Paver	Elloway	Seal	Burak	Gulliver	Cumming	Motusaga	Evans
Jones/c	Griffiths/t	Paver	Dawiduik	Franklin	Senekal	Gulliver	Betty	Motusaga	Bedes
Sanft	Fairhurst	Paver	Elloway	Seal/t	Senekal	Gulliver	Morgan	Motusaga	Bedes/t
Jones/3cp	Fairhurst	Paver	Elloway	Heard	Senekal	Gulliver	Morgan	Motusaga/t	Bedes
Jones/2pdg	Griffiths	Paver	Elloway	Heard	Senekal	Gulliver	Morgan	Motusaga	Bedes/t
Jones/2c4p	Griffiths/t	Paver	Dawiduik	Franklin	Senekal	Gulliver	Morgan	Motusaga	Bedes
Jones/3p	Griffiths	Paver	Dawiduik	Franklin	Senekal	Gulliver	Morgan	Betty	Bedes
Jones/6p	Griffiths	Paver	Dawiduik/t	Heard	Senekal	Gulliver	Morgan	Motusaga	Bedes
Whatling/dg	Moore/t4cp	Cook/t	Dawiduik	Heard	Senekal	Gulliver	Betty	Motusaga/2t	Evans/t
Whatling	Fairhurst	Paver	Dawiduik	Heard	Senekal	Gulliver	Morgan	Betty	Evans
Whatling/2dg	Fairhurst/t	Paver	Dawiduik	Heard	Senekal	Gulliver	Bedes	Morgan	Evans
Whatling/tc	Fairhurst	Paver	Dawiduik	Heard	Senekal	Gulliver	Betty	Motusaga	Morgan
Whatling(e/c)	Griffiths	Cook	Dawiduik	Heard	Senekal	Gulliver	Betty	Motusaga	Morgan
Jones/t7c2p	Griffiths	Cook	Dawiduik(h/t)	Seal	Senekal	Gulliver	Betty	Motusaga	Morgan/t
Jones/c4p	Griffiths/t	Cook	Elloway	Heard	Raven	Gulliver	Morgan	Betty	Evans
Jones	Griffiths	Cook	Elloway	Heard	Raven	Gulliver	Morgan	Motusaga/t(i/t)	Evans
Jones/3cp	Fairhurst	Cook	Elloway	Heard	Senekal	Gulliver	Cowan	Motusaga/t	Evans
Whatling	Griffiths/3t	Paver	Dawiduik	Heard	Senekal	Gulliver	Betty	Motusaga	Bedes
Jones/4c2p	Griffiths/t	Paver	Dawiduik/t	Seal	Burak	Gulliver	Morgan	Betty	Bedes/t
Jones/t	Griffiths	Paver	Dawiduik	Heard	Senekal	Gulliver	Morgan	Motusaga	Bedes
Whatling/tc	Fairhurst	Paver	Dawiduik	Franklin	Senekal	Gulliver	Cowan	Betty	Evans
Jones/2pdg	Fairhurst	Cook	Elloway	Heard	Burak	Gulliver	Cowan	Morgan	Evans
Whatling/2c2p	Griffiths	Paver	Elloway	Franklin	Burak/t	Senekal/t	Cowan	Betty	Bedes
Jones/t2p3dg	Griffiths	Paver	Elloway	Heard	Senekal	Gulliver	Cowan/t	Morgan	Evans
Jones/c2p	Griffiths/t	Paver	Elloway	Heard	Senekal/t	Burak	Cowan	Morgan	Evans
Whatling(e/p)	Fairhurst	Paver	Elloway	Heard	Senekal	Gulliver	Morgan	Motusaga	Bedes
Whatling	Fairhurst(k/t)	Andrew/t	Elloway	Heard	Evans	Gulliver	Morgan	Motusaga/t	Cowan
Jones/p	Fairhurst	Cook	Dawiduik	Heard	Senekal	Gulliver	Cowan	Morgan	Evans

REPLACEMENTS

a- J Moore   b- D Dawiduik   c- I Motusaga   d- S Winn
e- R Jones   f- R McAtee   g- B Tuohy   h- R Elloway
i- B Cowan   j- P Devlin   k- N Griffiths

LEAGUE APPEARANCES

28 Ben Gulliver (2)
24 Heino Senekal (2)
23 Alan Paver (2), Paul Devlin (5)
22 Chris Morgan (7)

LEAGUE POINTS SCORERS

Pts	Player	T	C	P	DG
178	Rhys Jones	3	26	32	5
65	Marika Vakacegu	13	-	-	-
64	James Moore	6	11	4	-
57	Brian Tuohy	11	1	-	-
40	Nick Griffiths	8	-	-	-

NUMBER OF PLAYERS USED

33 plus 3 as a replacement only

PENZANCE & NEWLYN STATISTICS

LEAGUE

All records relate to National league rugby only.

TEAM RECORDS

MOST POINTS
Scored at Home: 136 v Met Police 15.4.00
Scored Away: 76 v Tabard 23.2.02
Conceded at Home: 53 v Esher 24.1.04
Conceded Away: 71 v Worcester 6.12.03

MOST TRIES
Scored in a match: 22 v Met Police 15.4.00
Conceded in a match: 11 v Worcester 6.12.03

BIGGEST MARGINS
Home Win: 136pts: 136-0 v Met Police 15.4.00
Away Win: 65pts: 76-11 v Tabard 23.2.02
Home Defeat: 36pts: 12-48 v Pertemps Bees 14.12.03
Away Defeat: 61pts: 10-71 v Worcester 6.12.03

MOST CONSECUTIVE
Victories: 16 - 30.11.02-26.4.03 (Nat.2)
Defeats: 4 (twice 03/04)

INDIVIDUAL RECORDS

MOST APPEARANCES
by a forward: 149 (21) Alan Paver
by a back: 127 (1) Steve Evans

MOST CONSECUTIVE
Appearances: 79 Steve Evans 22.4.00 - 29.3.03
Matches scoring Tries: 10 Richard Newton

MATCH RECORDS

Most Points
    41 Nat Saumi v Met Police 15.4.00 (A)
Most Tries
    7 Richard Newton v Met Police 15.4.00 (A)
Most Conversions
    13 Nat Saumi v Met Police 15.4.00 (A)
Most Penalties
    6 Rhys Jones v Leeds Carnegie 16.11.08 (H)
Most Drop Goals
    3 Rhys Jones v Plymouth Albion 12.04.09 (H)

SEASON RECORDS

Most Points	374	Nat Saumi	01-02
Most Tries	38	Richard Newton	99-00
Most Conversions	91	Nat Saumi	01-02
Most Penalties	56	Alberto di Bernardo	06-07
Most Drop Goals	5	Rhys Jones	08-09

CAREER RECORDS

Most Points	1148	Nat Saumi	99-03
Most Tries	88	Victor Olonga	99-03
Most Conversions	257	Nat Saumi	99-03
Most Penalties	123	Nat Saumi	99-03
Most Drop Goals	5	Rhys Jones	08-09

LAST TEN SEASONS

	Division	P	W	D	L	F	A	P.D.	Pts	Pos	Most Points	Most Tries
99-00	N2S	26	20	1	5	1055	479	576	41	2	204 Nat Saumi	38 Richard Newton
00-01	N3S	26	18	2	6	823	492	331	38	3	336 Nat Saumi	20 Victor Olonga
01-02	N3S	26	24	1	1	1158	423	735	49	1p	374 Nat Saumi	28 Richard Newton
02-03	N2	26	22	1	3	849	442	407	45	1p	234 Nat Saumi	19 Victor Olongo
03-04	N1	26	8	1	17	474	892	-418	43	10	85 Rob Thirlby	11 Matthew Jess
04-05	N1	26	17	0	9	698	526	172	85	4	235 Lee Jarvis	12 Wes Davies
05-06	N1	26	19	0	7	682	460	122	90	3	140 Tom Barlow	15 Richard Welding
06-07	N1	30	20	2	8	812	493	319	101	5	293 Alberto di Bernardo	16 Rhodri McAtee
07-08	N1	30	20	1	9	800	583	217	*91	5	287 Gareth Steenson	11 Paul Devlin
08-09	N1	30	16	1	13	744	578	166	82	7	178 Rhys Jones	13 Marika Vakacegu

RFU SENIOR CUP

OVERALL PLAYING RECORD

	P	W	O	L	F	A	Pts Diff
Home	10	6	0	4	341	168	173
Away	7	4	0	3	173	119	54
Neutral	0	0	0	0	0	0	0
TOTAL	17	10	0	7	514	287	227

TEAM RECORDS

Highest Score: 80 v Cinderford 01/02
Biggest Winning Margin: 68 (80-12) v Cinderford 01/02
Highest Score Against: 30 v Saracens 03/04
Biggest Losing Margin: 16 (5-21) v Reading 98/99

SEASON BY SEASON

Season	Result	Season	Result	Season	Result	Season	Result	Season	Result
71-72	DNQ	78-79	DNQ	85-86	DNQ	92-93	DNQ	99-00	3R
72-73	DNQ	79-80	DNQ	86-87	DNQ	93-94	DNQ	00-01	3R
73-74	DNQ	80-81	DNQ	87-88	DNQ	94-95	DNQ	01-02	2R
74-75	DNQ	81-82	DNQ	88-89	DNQ	95-96	DNQ	02-03	3R
75-76	DNQ	82-83	DNQ	89-90	DNQ	96-97	DNQ	03-04	6R
76-77	DNQ	83-84	DNQ	90-91	DNQ	97-98	DNQ	04-05	4R
77-78	DNQ	84-85	DNQ	91-92	DNQ	98-99	2R		

NATIONAL TROPHY

05-06	6R	06-07	Winners	07-08	4R	08-09	5R

PLAYERS

	Position	D.o.B.	Apps.	Pts.	T	C	P	DG
Adryan Winnan	Full back	28/03/1983	72 (4)	65	13	-	-	-
James Moore	Winger	27/10/1982	41 (37)	239	23	32	20	-
Marika Vakacegu	Winger	23/06//1981	22	65	13	-	-	-
Brian Tuohy	Winger	19/09/1982	50 (11)	144	28	2	-	-
Rhodri McAtee	Wing/Scrum half	02/08/1984	90 (27)	245	49	-	-	-
Steve Winn	Centre	06/11/1977	56 (40)	40	86	-	-	-
Thomas Luke	Centre	13/04/1983	16 (7)	17	-	4	3	-
Paul Devlin	Centre	19/02/1981	65 (15)	85	17	-	-	-
Mark Ireland	Centre		35 (14)	20	4	-	--	-
Rhys Jones	Fly half	23/08/1987	16 (5)	178	3	26	32	5
Simon Whatling	Fly half	16/09/1984	9 (5)	33	2	4	2	3
Ed Fairhurst	Scrum half	07/05/1979	31 (10)	25	5	-	-	-
Nick Griffiths	Scrum half	07/04/1985	16 (8)	40	8	-	-	-
Sam Heard	Prop	10/03/1983	49 (18)	10	2	-	-	-
Alan Paver	Prop	28/11/1977	149 (20)	15	3	-	-	-
Dan Seal	Prop	23/10/1979	102 (80)	25	5	-	-	-
Peter Cook	Prop	25/12/1982	23 (18)	10	2	-	-	-
Darren Dawidiuk	Hooker	21/09/1987	15 (26)	20	4	-	-	-
Rob Elloway	Hooker	09/11/1983	35 (9)	15	3	-	-	-
Ben Gulliver	Lock	13/03/1981	28 (2)	-	-	-	-	-
Michael Burak	Lock	09/10/1980	6 (9)	10	2	-	-	-
Heino Senekal	Back row	20/10/1975	94 (11)	50	10	-	-	-
Iva Motusaga	Back row	16/11/1978	97 (15)	155	31	-	-	-
Chris Morgan	Back row	06/11/1981	22 (7)	10	2	-	-	-
Bertrand Bedes	Back row	06/05/1981	17 (3)	20	4	-	-	-
Matt Evans	Back row	30/05/1982	62 (31)	40	8	-	-	-

PLYMOUTH ALBION

Founded: 1876
Nickname: Albion
Colours: White, red and green.
Change colours: Black and white
Training Nights: Tuesday & Thursday
Website: www.plymouthalbion.com

KEY PERSONNEL

Chairman of Company & Club	Dr Graham Stirling
President	Mr Paul Woods
Company Secretary	Mr Don Seymour
Director of Rugby	Mr Graham Dawe
Commercial Director	Mr Wayne Harris
	Tel: 01752 566420 Fax: 01752 569802
	email: wayne@plymouthalbion.com
Marketing Director	Louise Uncles
	Tel: 01752 566421 Fax: 01752 569802
	email: louise@plymouthalbion.com
Finance Director	Mr Charles Evans
Fixture Secretary & Referee Contact	Mr Terry Brown
Travel Club	Mr Keith Colpitts

CONTACT DETAILS

Brickfields Recreation Ground, 25 Damerel Close, Plymouth, PL1 4NE
Tel: 01752 565064   Fax 01752 569802   email: info@plymouthalbion.com

GROUND DETAILS

Address: Brickfields, 25 Damerel Close, Plymouth, PL1 4NE
Tel: 01752 565064   Fax 01752 569802
email: info@plymouthalbion.com

Capacity: 8,400   Seated: 3500   Covered: 2200

Directions: Approach Plymouth along the A38 until you reach the Manadon intersection which is signposted for the A386, City Centre. Follow the A386 towards the City Center. Follow signs for Torpoint (ferry) A374 along Milehouse Road then Devonport Road through a small shopping area. Shortly after this shopping area there is a mini r'about turn right into Albert Rd. At the next set of traffic lights turn left. Proceed to mini r'about carry straight on following signs for the City Centre and signed as the A374. Within 400 meters there is a yellow AA sign indicating the left turn (into Madden Road) for Brickfields Recreation Ground.

Nearest BR Station: Plymouth 15 mins walk
Car Parking: 500 spaces at ground

Admission: Matchday - Grandstand £18, Covered Stand £16 & Ground £13

Season - Grandstand £234, Covered Stand £208 & Ground £169

Clubhouse: Open 9am - 11pm Mon - Fri. Open weekends
Food - Lunch 12 – 2pm
Functions: 6 function suites, catering for up to 400.
Contact Events 01752 566427

Club Shop: Open matchdays & Mon, Tue & Thur evening

PROGRAMME

Size: A5
Pages: 48
Price: £2
Advertising: Contact Louise Uncles

Picture Courtesy of The Plymouth Herald

REVIEW OF THE SEASON 2008-09

PLYMOUTH Albion finished the 2008-09 season as the second best supported team outside the Premiership.

The club managed to pull in an average of more than 3,400 supporters for their home games and broke their record league crowd for a fourth successive season when 6,871 turned up to see their derby match with Exeter.

They managed yet another annual improvement in their gates despite a tough injury-hit season on the field that resulted in the team being dragged into the relegation mix.

At the start of January, when plans for the new 12-team Championship were being finalised, nobody would have predicted Albion would be battling to secure their place in the new league a few months later.

Albion sat sixth in the table at the start of 2009 and were on a good run, having recorded impressive home wins over Doncaster, Cornish Pirates and Nottingham.

But the club, already missing long-term injury victims Martin Rice, James Tideswell and David Palu, suddenly lost a host of other key players due to injury, including fly-half Kieran Hallett, number eight Kyle Marriott, full-back Geoff Griffiths and centre Keni Fisilau, and their form and confidence deserted them. They also were not helped by having only three home games in the final three months of the season.

But they managed to secure their place in the new league and they will be looking to build on the potential their young side showed in the first half of 2008-09 this term.

Summer signing Hallett proved a real find. He managed to score 143 in just 13 starts before suffering a season ankle injury. But that was enough for him to finish as the club's top points scorer and claim their player-of-the-year award. Fellow fly-half Alex Davies was voted the club's young player-of-the-year.

Albion do like to bring through young talent from their successful development team and last term was no exception.

Devon-born centre Matt Hopper certainly grabbed his first team chance with both hands when handed it in November. He scored two tries on his debut against Esher and finished the season as joint top try-scorer alongside Canadian winger Justin Mensah-Coker.

As well as setting a new attendance record, there was also another record broken last season with player-coach Danny Thomas setting a new league appearance record for the club, breaking Richard Thompson's previous mark of 176.

Meanwhile, Graham Dawe, who celebrated his 10th anniversary as chairman of rugby in June, broke the 150 mark for league appearance for Albion, while Keni Fisilau clocked up the same figure of league and cup games for the club.

Off the field, Albion, who once again provided the majority of players for Devon's County Championship campaign, continued to improve their Brickfields ground. The stadium held its first international match in March when England under-18s played Japan, while the Combined Services again used it to stage their annual fixture with the Barbarians.

ALBION'S SEASON - 2008-09

Date	H/A	Opponents	Result & Score	Att.	15	14	13	12	11
NATIONAL ONE									
30-08	H	Coventry	W 13-5	2892	Jarvis	Gibson	Cruickshank	Fisilau	Mensah Coker
07-09	A	Nottingham	L 19-43	1100	Jarvis	Gibson	Cruickshank/t	Fisilau/t	Mensah Coker
13-09	H	Manchester	W 47-6	2163	Griffiths/t	Gibson/t	Cruickshank	Fisilau/t	Mensah Coker/t
20-09	A	Newbury	L 11-19	395	Griffiths	Gibson	Cruickshank	Fisilau	Mensah Coker
27-09	H	London Welsh	L 24-25	2602	Griffiths/t	Gibson(a/2c)	Cruickshank	Fisilau	Mensah Coker
04-10	A	Otley	W 31-16	550	Griffiths	Jarvis	Cruickshank/t	Fisilau/t	Mensah Coker/t
11-10	H	Exeter	L 14-41	6871	Saumi	Griffiths	Cruickshank	Fisilau	Mensah Coker
18-10	H	Moseley	W 26-17	2406	Saumi	Jarvis/t	Cruickshank	Fisilau	Mensah Coker
25-10	A	Rotherham	D 10-10	1011	Saumi	Jarvis	Fisilau	Allen(d/t)	Mensah Coker
01-11	H	Sedgley Park	W 31-7	2143	Saumi(e/t)	Cruickshank	Allen	Fisilau	Mensah Coker/2t
08-11	H	Doncaster	W 21-18	1983	Saumi	Cruickshank	Allen	Fisilau	Jarvis/t
15-11	A	Bedford	L 9-37	2010	Saumi	Cruickshank	Fisilau	Allen	Jarvis
22-11	H	Esher	W 36-14	1742	Griffiths	Gibson	Hopper/2t	Fisilau	Jarvis
29-11	H	Cornish Pirates	W 20-12	5421	Griffiths	Gibson	Hopper/t	Fisilau	Jarvis
07-12	A	Leeds Carnegie	L 18-49	2528	Griffiths	Gibson	Hopper/t	Allen	Jarvis
13-12	A	Coventry	W 7-6	961	Griffiths	Gibson	Hopper	Allen	Jarvis
20-12	H	Nottingham	W 26-25	3102	Griffiths/t	Gibson	Hopper	Allen	Jarvis
27-12	A	Manchester	W 31-5	410	Griffiths/t	Gibson	Hopper/t	Allen/t	Jarvis
03-01	H	Newbury	D 17-17	4087	Griffiths/t	Gibson	Hopper	Allen	Jarvis
24-01	H	Otley	W 23-15	3799	Jarvis	Gibson	Hopper	Allen	Mensah Coker
31-01	A	Exeter	L 0-29	6658	Griffiths	Gibson	Hopper	Allen	Jarvis
21-02	H	Rotherham	L 20-33	3478	Laidlaw	Gibson/t	Hopper	Allen	Jarvis
07-03	A	Sedgley Park*	W 27-11	362	Ireland	Gibson	Hopper/t	Cruickshank	Jarvis
14-03	A	Doncaster	L 23-28	1027	Ireland	Gibson	Hopper	Cruickshank	Mensah Coker/t
22-03	A	London Welsh	L 9-22	390	Ireland	Gibson	Hopper	Cruickshank	Mensah Coker
28-03	H	Bedford	L 14-31	3363	Ireland	Jarvis	Hopper	Cruickshank/t	Mensah Coker/t
04-04	A	Esher	L 28-31	1664	Ireland/t	Gibson/t	Hopper	Cruickshank/t	Mensah Coker
12-04	A	Cornish Pirates*	L 14-30	4306	Ireland	Gibson	Hopper	Cruickshank	Mensah Coker
25-04	H	Leeds Carnegie	L 6-17	4998	Ireland	Gibson	Cruickshank	Allen	Mensah Coker
29-04	A	Moseley*	L 32-50	1124	Ireland/t	Gibson/2t	Cruickshank	Allen	Mensah Coker
EDF ENERGY NATIONAL TROPHY									
17-01	A	Doncaster	L 3-21		Jarvis	Gibson	Hopper	Allen	Mensah Coker

SCORING BREAKDOWN

WHEN		Total	First Half	Second Half	1/4	2/4	3/4	4/4
the POINTS were scored		607	346	261	139	207	106	155
the POINTS were conceded		669	331	338	156	175	177	161
the TRIES were scored		67	34	33	15	19	12	21
the TRIES were conceded		85	38	47	17	21	25	22

HOW	Total	Pen. Try	Backs	Forwards	F Back	Wing	Centre	H Back	F Row	Lock	B Row
the TRIES were scored	67	3	42	22	8	14	14	6	10	1	11
the TRIES were conceded	85	2	43	40	8	16	12	7	9	8	23

KEY: ** after opponents name indicates a penalty try.*
Brackets after a player's name indicates he was replaced. eg (a) means he was replaced by replacement code "a" and so on.
/ after a player or replacement name is followed by any scores he made - eg /t, /c, /p, /dg or any combination of these

10	9	1	2	3	4	5	6	7	8
Laidlaw/c2p	Nicholls	Rice	Owen	Hopkins/t	Stewart	Brenton	Thomas	Denbee	Marriott
Hallett/p2dg	Nicholls	Rice	Owen	Hopkins	Stewart	Brenton	Lewis	Thomas	Denbee
Laidlaw/2c3p(a/2c)	Nicholls/t	Rice	Evans	Tideswell	Stewart	Brenton	Thomas	Denbee(b/t)	Lewis
Laidlaw/2p(a/t)	Nicholls	du Toit	Dawe	Tideswell	Stewart	Brenton	Stephen	Thomas	Marriott
Laidlaw/cp	Nicholls	Rice/t	Evans	du Toit	Lewis	Brenton	Stephen	Thomas(b/t)	Marriott
Hallett/4cp	Palu	Rice	Owen(c/t)	du Toit	Stewart	Brenton	Stephen	Thomas	Marriott
Hallett/3p	Palu	Rice/t	Owen	du Toit	Lewis	Brenton	Stephen	Thomas	Evans
Hallett/2c4p	Nicholls	Rice	Owen	du Toit	Lewis	Brenton	Stephen	Denbee	Evans/t
Hallett/cp	Nicholls	Rice	Owen	du Toit	Stewart	Brenton	Stephen	Denbee	Evans
Hallett/c3p	Nicholls	Rice	Owen	du Toit	Lewis	Brenton	Stephen	Denbee/t	Evans
Hallett/c3p	Nicholls	Rice	Owen	du Toit/t	Lewis	Brenton	Sprangle	Denbee	Evans
Hallett/2p(f/p)	Nicholls	Rice	Owen	Hopkins	Lewis	Brenton	Sprangle	Denbee	Evans
Laidlaw/4cp	Nicholls	Hopkins/t	Owen/t	du Toit	Lewis	Brenton	Sprangle	Denbee	Marriott/t
Hallett/2c2p	Nicholls	du Toit	Owen	Hopkins	Lewis	Brenton	Sprangle/t	Denbee	Marriott
Hallett/c2p	Nicholls	du Toit	Evans/t	Hopkins	Lewis	Brenton	Sprangle	Denbee	Marriott
Hallett/c	Nicholls	du Toit	Evans	Hopkins/t	Lewis	Brenton	Stephen	Denbee	Marriott
Hallett/t2c4p	Nicholls	du Toit	Salter	Hopkins	Stewart	Brenton	Stephen	Denbee	Marriott
Hallett/4cp	Nicholls	du Toit	Salter	Hopkins	Lewis	Brenton	Stephen	Denbee/t	Marriott
Laidlaw/tcp(g/c)	Nicholls	du Toit	Salter	Hopkins	Lewis	Brenton	Stephen	Denbee	Marriott
Davies/2c3p	Nicholls/t	Black	Owen	Hopkins	Lewis	Brenton	Sprangle	Thomas	Stephen/t
Davies	Nicholls	du Toit	Owen	Hopkins	Lewis	Brenton	Sprangle	Denbee	Stephen
Davies/t2c2p	Nicholls	du Toit	Owen	Hopkins	Lewis	Brenton	Sprangle	Denbee	Stephen
Davies/2c2p(f/c)	Nicholls	du Toit	Owen	Hopkins	Lewis	Brenton	Stephen/t	Denbee	Marriott
Davies/c2p	Nicholls	Porte	Owen/t	Hopkins	Stewart	Brenton	Stephen	Denbee/t	Marriott
Davies/3p	Nicholls	du Toit	Owen	Hopkins	Stewart	Brenton	Stephen	Denbee	Evans
Davies(f/2c)	Nicholls	Rice	Owen	Hopkins	Stewart	Brenton	Stephen	Denbee	Evans
Laidlaw/c2p	Nicholls	Rice	Owen	Porte	Stewart	Brenton	Stephen	Sprangle/t	Denbee
Laidlaw/c(g/c)	Nicholls	Rice	Owen	Porte	Stewart	Brenton/t	Stephen	Sprangle	Denbee
Laidlaw/2p	Newman	Rice	Owen	Porte	Stewart	Brenton	Stephen	Sprangle	Marriott
Laidlaw/3c2p	Newman	Rice	Owen	Hopkins	Stewart	Brenton	Stephen	Sprangle	Marriott
Laidlaw/p	Nicholls	Black	Owen	Hopkins	Lewis	Brenton	Sprangle	Stephen	Denbee

REPLACEMENTS
a- K Hallett b- W Sprangle c - G Evans d- A Cruickshhank
e- T Jarvis f- R Laidlaw g- A Davies

LEAGUE APPEARANCES

30	Arthur Brenton
26	Greg Nicholls (2)
23	Mike Denbee (3)
22	Liam Gibson, James Owen, Sean Michael Stephen (2)

LEAGUE POINTS SCORERS

Pts	Player	T	C	P	DG
143	Kieran Hallett	2	23	27	2
90	Ross Laidlaw	1	17	17	-
59	Alex Davies	1	9	12	-
30	Justin Mensah Coker	6	-	-	-
30	Matthew Hopper	6	-	-	-

NUMBER OF PLAYERS USED
33 plus 7 as a replacement only

CHAMPIONSHIP

PLYMOUTH STATISTICS

LEAGUE

TEAM RECORDS

MOST POINTS
Scored at Home: 73 v Charlton Park 29.03.97
Scored Away: 55 v Manchester 14.02.04, London Welsh 2.12.06
Conceded at Home: 64 v Bracknell 03.04.99
Conceded Away: 70 v Esher 07.02.98

MOST TRIES
Scored in a match: 11
v Charlton Park 29.03.97 & v Basingstoke 23.12.00
Conceded in a match 10: v Esher 07.02.98

BIGGEST MARGINS
Home Win: 66pts: 72-6 v Basingstoke 23.12.00
Away Win: 48pts: 55-7 v Manchester 14.02.04
Home Defeat: 52pts: 12-64 v Bracknell 03.04.99
Away Defeat: 70pts: 0-70 v Esher 07.02.98

MOST CONSECUTIVE
Victories: 41
Defeats: 8

INDIVIDUAL RECORDS

MOST APPEARANCES
by a forward: 182 (3) Danny Thomas
by a back: 164 (4) Richard Thompson

MOST CONSECUTIVE
Appearances: 174 Dan Ward Smith 2.9.00 - 12.3.05
Matches scoring Tries: 9 Dan Ward Smith
Matches scoring points: 19 Chris Atkinson

MATCH RECORDS

Most Points	25	
	Domonic Cundy	v Met Police 26.11.88 (H)
	Nick Burt	v Charlton Park 29.3.97 (H)
	Nicholas Sestaret	v Moseley 31.3.07 (H)
Most Tries	5	
	Nicholas Sestaret v Moseley 31.3.07 (H)	
Most Conversions	8	
	Dominic Cundy	v Met Police 26.11.88 (H)
Most Penalties	6	
	Mark Slade	v Bedford 14.12.91 (H)
Most Drop Goals	3	
	Mark Slade	v Liverpool St H 9.2.96 (H)

SEASON RECORDS

Most Points	260	Chris Atkinson	99-00
Most Tries	28	Nicholas Sestaret	06-07
Most Conversions	42	Tom Barlow	00-01
Most Penalties	59	Chris Atkinson	99-00
Most Drop Goals	6	Tom Barlow	02-03

CAREER RECORDS

Most Points	784	Tom Barlow	00-04
Most Tries	93	Dan Ward-Smith	99-05
Most Conversions	149	Tom Barlow	00-04
Most Penalties	93	Martin Thompson	89-99
Most Drop Goals	16	Martin Thompson	89-99
		Tom Barlow	00-04

LAST TEN SEASONS

	Division	P	W	D	L	F	A	P.D.	Pts	Pos	Most Points	Most Tries
99-00	N2S	26	17	2	7	664	382	282	36	4	260 Chris Atkinson	15 Steve Walklin
00-01	N3S	26	26	0	0	910	240	670	52	1p	255 Tom Barlow	20 Dan Ward-Smith
01-02	N2	26	23	0	3	895	314	581	46	2p	211 Tom Barlow	23 Dan Ward-Smith
02-03	N1	26	10	1	15	679	697	-18	60	9	166 Brett McCormack	21 Dan Ward-Smith
03-04	N1	26	19	1	6	752	417	335	92	3	185 Tom Barlow	23 Lee Robinson
04-05	N1	26	19	2	5	653	494	159	94	3	256 James Pritchard	13 James Pritchard
05-06	N1	26	14	0	12	639	537	102	75	5	106 Nat Saumi	12 Nicholas Sestaret
06-07	N1	30	19	1	10	789	450	339	97	6	162 Wihan Neethling	28 Nicholas Sestaret
07-08	N1	30	12	1	17	530	528	2	64	8	209 Ross Laidlaw	6 Ed Lewsey
08-09	N1	30	13	2	15	604	669	-62	66	11	143 Kieran Hallett	6 Matthew Hopper & Justin Mensah Coker

RFU SENIOR CUP

OVERALL PLAYING RECORD

	P	W	D	L	F	A	Pts Diff
Home	20	10	0	10	465	320	145
Away	24	7	0	17	317	491	-174
Neutral	0	0	0	0	0	0	0
TOTAL	44	17	0	27	782	811	-29

TEAM RECORDS

Highest Score: 76 v Moseley 04-05 (H)
Biggest Winning Margin: 70 (76-6) v Moseley 04-05 (H)
Highest Score Against: 49 v Rosslyn Park 92-93
Biggest Losing Margin: 46 (49-3) v Rosslyn Park 92-93

SEASON BY SEASON

Season	Result	Season	Result	Season	Result	Season	Result	Season	Result
71-72	1R	78-79	1R	85-86	3R	92-93	2R	99-00	1R
72-73	DNQ	79-80	DNQ	86-87	DNQ	93-94	3R	00-01	4R
73-74	DNQ	80-81	DNQ	87-88	QF	94-95	2R	01-02	2R
74-75	1R	81-82	DNQ	88-89	3R	95-96	2R	02-03	5R
75-76	1R	82-83	3R	89-90	3R	96-97	2R	03-04	4R
76-77	DNQ	83-84	4R	90-91	2R	97-98	1R	04-05	6R
77-78	DNQ	84-85	3R	91-92	2R	98-99	2R		

NATIONAL TROPHY

05-06	Q.F.	06-07	S.F.	07-08	S.F.	08-09	4 R

PLAYERS

	Position	D.o.B.	Apps.	Pts.	T	C	P	DG
Wihan Neethling	Full back	25/03/1981	18 (12)	179	7	36	24	-
Geoff Griffiths	Full back/winger		13 (3)	25	5	-	-	-
Tom Jarvis	Winger	21/03/1985	19 (6)	15	3	-	-	-
Justin Mensah Coker	Winger	18/11/1983	18 (5)	30	6	-	-	-
Aaron Cruickshank	Centre	10/12/1986	50 (19)	50	10	-	-	-
Matthew Hopper	Centre		16	30	6	-	-	-
Keni Fisilau	Centre	04/05/1976	143 (3)	160	32	-	-	-
Nat Saumi	Centre	03/09/1970	80 (19)	164	10	18	26	-
Ross Allen	Centre	14/03/1985	18 (6)	5	1	-	-	-
Alex Davies	Fly half		7 (3)	59	1	9	12	-
Ross Laidlaw	Fly half	08/10/1983	34 (14)	299	2	47	65	-
Kieran Hallett	Fly half	02/06/1985	13 (3)	143	2	23	27	2
Greg Nicholls	Scrum half	10/12/1983	26(2)	10	2	-	-	-
Matthew Newman	Scrum half	30/04/1980	2 (14)					
Martin Rice	Prop	26/06/1982	69 (3)	60	12	-	-	-
Gareth Evans	Prop	18/03/1982	15 (15)	15	3	-	-	-
Ryan Hopkins	Prop	20/09/1980	39 (16)	17 (11)	15	3	-	-
Jannie du Toit	Prop		20 (3)	5	1	-	-	-
James Owen	Hooker	28/06/1976	54 (27)	50	10	-	-	-
Jamie Salter	Hooker		3 (2)	-	-	-	-	-
Arthur Brenton	Lock	11/02/1981	30	5	1	-	-	-
Colin Stewart	Lock	06/01/1980	48 (4)	10	2	-	-	-
Mike Denbee	Back row		31 (6)	25	5	-	-	-
Wayne Sprangle	Back row	28/10/1982	12 (14)	20	4	-	-	-
Kyle Marriott	Back row	12/04/1987	20 (9)	10	2	-	-	-
Sean Michael Stephen	Back row	27/10/1982	22	10	2	-	-	-
Michael Lewis	Back row	05/01/1986	33 (6)	-	-	-	-	-

ROTHERHAM

ROTHERHAM TITANS

Founded: 1923

Nickname: Titans

Colours
Maroon and blue

Change colours:
Blue and maroon

Website:
www.rotherhamrugby.co.uk

KEY PERSONNEL

Management Team
Martin Jenkinson, Nick Cragg, Neil License, Ian Anderson, Allan McHale

Head Coach
Craig West
Tel: 01709 388548 email: craigwest@rotherhamrugby.co.uk

Fitness & Conditioning Coach
Dave Hembrough
Tel: 01709 388548 email: d.hembrough@shu.ac.uk

Rugby Administration
Keith Haynes
Tel: 01709 388548 email: keithhaynes49@hotmail.com

Finance
Bruce Allen
Tel: 01709 388540 email: bruceallen@rotherhamrugby.co.uk

Commercial
Jonathan Abbott
Tel: 07796 182510 email: jonathanabbott@rotherhamrugby.co.uk

Communications
Ian Anderson
Tel: 01709 388540 email: iananderson@rotherhamrugby.co.uk

Titans Community Foundation
Richard Finney, Chief Executive.
Tel: 01709 388540 richardfinney@rotherhamrugby.co.uk

GROUND DETAILS

Address:
Rotherham Titans, Clifton Lane, Rotherham, S60 2SN   Tel: 01709 388 540   Email: info@rotherhamrugby.co.uk

Capacity: 5,000   Seated: 200   Covered: 800

Directions:
From the M1 - M1 J33 onto Rotherway, at the roundabout turn right onto A631 marked Bawtry. Go straight ahead at Whiston traffic lights onto the dual carriageway. At the next roundabout, turn left onto B6410 (Broom Lane) then left onto A6021 (Broom Road). In 1/2 mile there is a roundabout, turn right into Badsley Moor Lane. The clubhouse is the second entrance on right.
From the A1(M) - join the M18.
From the M18 - M18 J1 onto A631 towards Rotherham. After 1 mile or so, go straight ahead at Wickersley Island. After 1 more mile turn right at the Brecks roundabout onto A6021. Go straight on at the Stag roundabout and after 2 miles or so there is a roundabout, turn right into Badsley Moor Lane. The clubhouse is the second entrance on right.

Matchday Parking
From the clubhouse entrance, take the next turning on the right (Badsley Street South). After 100 yards or so, bear left into the grounds of the Herringthorpe Pavilion. The car park is beyond the pavilion.

Nearest BR Station: Rotherham

Admission: Matchday - Adults £12, Concessions £6, Under 16's £3

Clubhouse: Open Weekday evenings and all day weekends. Traditional food served on match days.

Club room available for private hire, contact Mike

Club Shop: Open Tues eve. 7pm-8pm and match days or Shop on-line at www.rotherhamrugby.co.uk/shop

REVIEW OF THE SEASON 2008-09

Our opening day defeat ay Sedgley Park followed by three defeats against the eventual top sides put us under pressure from the start of the season. However, the character and quality of the squad, which was evident throughout the season, brought us through despite some close defeats and off-field mishaps.

The extreme measures taken to restructure the division meant that the bottom five sides would be relegated so each game was of enormous significance.

Like many clubs we had highs and lows. Our derby games against Doncaster, both unfortunately decided by single scores, were excellent high quality games. Losing away to Moseley after establishing a 21 point lead was difficult to take. However we had many highlights including away wins in the notoriously difficult South West against Cornish Pirates, and Plymouth, our late fight-back away at Coventry and critical home wins later in the season against two of the top four sides, Nottingham and Exeter.

Our belief that we should finish above the dreaded 12th place was never shaken but our end of season run in was exciting to say the least.

Captain and leading points scorer, Mike Whitehead had another influential season assisting coaches Craig West and Colin Noon develop an effective attacking style of play. This, in part, enabled our wingers to become our leading try scorers, Jon Feeley with 16 and Errie Claassens with 15.

All our new signings gelled and had a positive impact on the squad and hope that the majority will be with us next season.

As with every season players move on for different reasons and we will particularly miss those who have been with us for a number of years. We thank Errie Claassens, Stuart Corsar, Louis McGowan and Barry Jacobsz for all they have done for us and wish them well for the future.

PROGRAMME

Size: A5   Pages: 32   Price: £2.50
Editorial & Advertising: Michael Temple
Tel: 01709 388540
email: michaeltemple@rotherhamrugby.co.uk
Advertising Costs:
£600 full page full season (15 editions)
£400 half page full season (15 editions)

205

TITANS' SEASON - 2008-09

CHAMPIONSHIP

NATIONAL ONE

Date	H/A	Opponents	Result & Score	Att.	15	14	13	12	11
30-08	A	Sedgley Park	L 12-20	596	Claasans/t	Feeley	Hunt	Allen	Briers
07-09	H	Bedford	L 10-33	642	Whitehead	Briers	Buckley	Hunt/t	Claasans
14-09	A	Doncaster	L 22-28	1613	Whitehead	Allen	Hunt	Briers/2t	Claasans
21-09	H	Leeds Carnegie	L 24-41	2021	Whitehead	Feeley	Hunt	Briers/t	Claasans
27-09	A	Esher	W 59-32	710	Whitehead/t	Feeley/t	Hunt/2t	Briers/t	Claasans/t
04-10	H	Moseley	W 47-23	1021	Whitehead/t	Feeley	Hunt	Briers	Claasans/t
12-10	A	Cornish Pirates	W 32-27	2488	Whitehead/tp	Feeley/t	Hunt	Briers	Claasans
18-10	A	Manchester	W 54-35	471	Whitehead	Feeley/t	Hunt	Briers/2t	Claasans/3t
25-10	H	Plymouth Albion	D 10-10	1011	Whitehead	Feeley	Allen	Briers	Claasans
01-11	A	London Welsh	L 17-27	1070	Whitehead/c	Briers	Hunt	Buckley	Feeley
08-11	H	Coventry	W 28-27	892	Whitehead/tp	Feeley/t	Hunt	Buckley	Briers
16-11	A	Nottingham	L 13-33	2226	Hunt	Feeley/t	Buckley	Briers	Allen
23-11	H	Newbury	W 62-5	1127	Hunt/t	Feeley/4t	Buckley	Briers	Claasans
29-11	A	Exeter	L 21-76	3965	Hunt	MacDonald/t	Buckley	Allen	Claasans
06-12	H	Otley	W 42-13	1067	Hunt/t	Feeley	Buckley	Briers/t	Claasans/t
13-12	H	Sedgley Park*	W 22-0	848	Hunt	Feeley	Allen	Briers	Claasans/t
20-12	A	Bedford	L 18-32	2338	Hunt	Feeley	Buckley	Briers/t	Claasans
27-12	H	Doncaster	L 26-29	2548	Hunt	Feeley	Buckley	Briers	Claasans
04-01	A	Leeds Carnegie	L 3-28	3271	Whitehead/dg	Feeley	Buckley	Hunt	Claasans
24-01	A	Moseley	L 21-43	974	Hunt	Feeley/2t	Buckley	Briers	Claasans
31-01	H	Cornish Pirates*	L 28-34	1523	Hunt	Feeley	Buckley	Briers	Claasans
14-02	H	Manchester*	W 15-13	792	Hunt	Feeley	Buckley	Briers	Claasans
21-02	A	Plymouth Albion	W 33-20	3478	Whitehead/p	Feeley	Hunt/t	Buckley	Claasans
28-02	H	Esher	L 19-40	1107	Whitehead/2c	Feeley/t	Hunt	Briers	Claasans/2t
07-03	H	London Welsh	L 7-20	1142	Hunt	Feeley	Maggs	Briers	Claasans
14-03	A	Coventry	W 32-31	1228	Hunt/t	Feeley/2t	Maggs	Briers/t	Claasans
28-03	H	Nottingham	W 20-6	1237	Hunt	Feeley	Buckley	Maggs	Claasans/t
04-04	A	Newbury	W 23-21	446	Hunt	Feeley/t	Maggs/t	Briers	Claasans/t
11-04	H	Exeter	W 35-21	1749	Hunt	Feeley	Buckley	Maggs/t	Claasans/t
25-04	A	Otley*	W 39-7	1249	Hunt/t	Feeley/t	Maggs	Buckley	Claasans/2t

EDF ENERGY NATIONAL TROPHY

4 17-01	H	Coventry	L 16-26		Whitehead/t	Feeley	Allen/t	Briers	MacDonald

SCORING BREAKDOWN

WHEN	Total	First Half	Second Half	1/4	2/4	3/4	4/4
the POINTS were scored	794	368	426	208	160	241	185
the POINTS were conceded	775	393	382	182	211	201	176
the TRIES were scored	100	41	59	23	18	33	26
the TRIES were conceded	97	45	52	17	28	26	25

HOW	Total	Pen. Try	Backs	Forwards	F Back	Wing	Centre	H Back	F Row	Lock	B Row
the TRIES were scored	100	4	65	31	9	31	15	10	4	5	22
the TRIES were conceded	97	2	57	37	10	25	11	11	10	1	26

KEY: *after opponents name indicates a penalty try.*
Brackets after a player's name indicates he was replaced. eg (a) means he was replaced by replacement code "a" and so on.
/ after a player or replacement name is followed by any scores he made - eg /t, /c, /p, /dg or any combination of these

10	9	1	2	3	4	5	6	7	8
Whitehead/c	Chivers	Corsar	Conroy	Prescott	Hayter	McGowan	Jacobsz/t	Du Plessis	Skurr
Barlow/cp	Chivers	Corsar	Conroy	Prescott	Challinor	Raven	Jacobsz	Du Plessis	Skurr
Barlow/2cp	Chivers	Corsar	Horn	O'Donnol	Challinor	Raven	Jacobsz	Du Plessis/t	Skurr
Barlow/c4p	Erskine(a/t)	Corsar	Horn	Prescott	Challinor	Raven	Burrows	Du Plessis	Skurr
Barlow/5c3p	Chivers(b/t)	Corsar	Conroy	Prescott	Hayter	McGowan/t	Burrows	Du Plessis	Skurr
Barlow/5c(d/c)	Chivers/t	Corsar	Conroy(c/t)	Prescott	Hayter/t	Challinor	Burrows/t	Du Plessis/t	Skurr
Barlow/t3cp	Chivers	Corsar	Conroy	Prescott	Hayter	Challinor	Burrows	Du Plessis	Skurr/t
Barlow/5c3p	Chivers	Corsar	Conroy	Prescott	Challinor	Hayter/t	Burrows	Du Plessis	Skurr
Barlow/cp	Chivers/t	Corsar	Horn	Prescott	Hayter	McGowan	Burrows	Du Plessis	Skurr
Barlow/cp	West	Tea	Conroy	Prescott	Hayter	McGowan	Raven(e/2t)	Du Plessis	Burrows
Barlow/2c2p	Chivers	O'Donnol	Conroy	Prescott	McGowan	Hayter/t	Jacobsz	Burrows	Skurr
Barlow/c2p	Chivers	O'Donnol	Horn	Prescott	Challinor	Raven	Burrows	Du Plessis	Skurr
Whitehead	West/6cp	Corsar/t	Horn	Prescott	Challinor	Hayter	Burrows/2tc	Du Plessis	Skurr/t
Whitehead	West/3c	O'Donnol/t	Horn	Tea	Challinor	McGowan	Burrows	Du Plessis	Skurr(f/t)
Whitehead/tc	West/2c2p	Corsar	Conroy	Prescott	Challinor	Hayter	Burrows	Du Plessis	Skurr/2t
Whitehead/2c	West/p	Corsar	Conroy	Prescott	Challinor	Hayter/t	Barnes	Du Plessis	Skurr
Whitehead/2p	West/c	Corsar/t	Conroy	Prescott	Challinor	Hayter	Barnes	Du Plessis	Skurr
Whitehead/2c4p	Chivers/t	Corsar	Conroy	Prescott	Challinor	Hayter	Barnes	Du Plessis	Skurr/t
Barlow	Erskine	Corsar	Horn	Prescott	Ault	Barnes	Burrows	Du Plessis	Skurr
Whitehead/t3c	Erskine	Corsar	Conroy	Prescott	Challinor	Hayter	Barnes	Du Plessis	Skurr
Whitehead/t2c3p	Erskine	Corsar	Conroy	Prescott	Challinor	Hayter	Barnes	Du Plessis	Burrows/t
Whitehead/cp	Erskine	O'Donnol	Conroy	Prescott	Barnes	Hayter	Burrows	Du Plessis	Skurr/t
Barlow/cp	Chivers	O'Donnol	Conroy	Prescott	Barnes	Hayter	Burrows/2t	Du Plessis	Skurr/2t
Barlow	Chivers	Tea	Conroy	O'Donnol	Ault	Hayter	Barnes	Du Plessis	Burrows
Whitehead/c	Chivers	Corsar	Conroy	O'Donnol	Challinor	McGowan	Hayter	Barnes	Burrows/t
Whitehead/2cp	Chivers/t	Corsar	Conroy	O'Donnol	Challinor	Hayter	Burrows	Du Plessis	Skurr
Whitehead/2c2p	Chivers	Corsar	Conroy	O'Donnol	McGowan	Hayter	Burrows	Du Plessis	Skurr/t
Whitehead/c2p	Chivers	Corsar	Conroy	O'Donnol	Hayter	McGowan	Barnes	Du Plessis	Skurr
Whitehead/2c7p	Chivers	Corsar	Conroy	O'Donnol	Hayter	McGowan	Challinor	Du Plessis	Skurr
Whitehead/4c2p	Chivers	Corsar	Conroy	O'Donnol	Challinor	McGowan	Ault	Burrows	Skurr
Barlow/2p	Chivers	Tea	Horn	O'Donnol	Ault	McGowan	Barnes	Du Plessis	Skurr

REPLACEMENTS
a- N Chivers b- C Erskine c- H Horn d- J West
e- J Skurr f- S Raven

LEAGUE APPEARANCES
29 Brad Hunt (1), Michael Whitehead
27 Tinus Du Plessis (1), Jon Feeley (1), Errie Claassans
26 Jon Skurr (2)
24 Chris Briers (4)

NUMBER OF PLAYERS USED
29 plus 3 as a replacement only

LEAGUE POINTS SCORERS

Pts	Player	T	C	P	DG
173	Michael Whitehead	7	27	27	1
121	Tom Barlow	1	28	20	-
80	Jon Feeley	16	-	-	-
75	Errie Claasans	15	-	-	-
55	Jon SKurr	11	-	-	-
45	Chris Briers	9	-	-	-

ROTHERHAM STATISTICS

LEAGUE

TEAM RECORDS

MOST POINTS
Scored at Home: 102 v Moseley 6.10.02
Scored Away: 76 v Moseley 8.2.03
Conceded at Home: 68 v Bath 14.4.01
Conceded Away: 76 v Exeter 29.11.08

MOST TRIES
Scored in a match: 14 v Moseley 6.10.02
Conceded in a match: 11 v Newcastle 4.5.97 (A), Northampton 1.3.08 (A) & Exeter 29.11.08

BIGGEST MARGINS
Home Win: 99pts - 102-3 v Moseley 2.10.02
Away Win: 69pts - 76-7 v Moseley 8.2.032
Home Defeat: 56pts - 12-68 v Bath 14.04.01
Away Defeat: 73pts - 0-73 v Northampton 1.3.08

MOST CONSECUTIVE
Victories: 38 (17.11.01 - 15.3.03)
Defeats: 22 (13.9.03-28.4.04)

INDIVIDUAL RECORDS

MOST APPEARANCES
by a forward: 165 (26) John Dudley
by a back: 123 (3) Mike Umaga

MOST CONSECUTIVE
Appearances: 89 Richard Selkirk 12.9.87-1.4.94
Matches scoring Tries: 10 Michael Wood 1.9.02 - 16.11.02
Matches scoring points: 14 Kevin Plant (twice)

MATCH RECORDS

Most Points
41 Simon Binns v W Hartlepool 2.10.99 (H)

Most Tries
6 Paul Scott v Westoe 8.4.89 (H)

Most Conversions
10 Simon Binns v W Hartlepool 2.10.99 (H)
   Ramiro Pez v Moseley 6.10.02 (H)
   Jon Benson v Moseley 8.2.03 (A)

Most Penalties
6 David Francis v Keighley 8.4.89 (H)
  Dean Lax v Lon Scottish 2.11.96 (H)

Most Drop Goals
2 Kevin Plant v Coventry 28.10.95 (H)

SEASON RECORDS

Most Points	264	Ramiro Pez	02-03
	264	Gareth Steenson	06-07
Most Tries	22	Michael Wood	02-03
Most Conversions	79	Gareth Steenson	06-07
Most Penalties	41	Kevin Plant	90-91
		Simon Binns	97-98
Most Drop Goals	5	Kevin Plant	95-96

CAREER RECORDS

Most Points	922	Kevin Plant	87-96
Most Tries	42	Paul Scott	87-96
		Michael Wood	
Most Conversions	142	Ramiro Pez	01-05
Most Penalties	182	Kevin Plant	87-96
Most Drop Goals	17	Kevin Plant	87-96

LAST TEN SEASONS

	Division	P	W	D	L	F	A	P.D.	Pts	Pos	Most Points	Most Tries
99-00	P2	26	24	0	2	1045	267	778	48	1	251 Mike Umaga	18 Dean Lax
00-01	P1	22	2	0	20	335	813	-478	12	12r	139 Mike Umaga	3 James Naylor & Mike Umaga
01-02	N1	26	24	0	2	1099	325	774	120	1	197 Ramiro Pez	14 Oriol Ripol
02-03	N1	26	24	0	2	1077	336	741	116	1p	264 Ramiro Pez	22 Michael Wood
03-04	P	22	0	0	22	309	770	-461	3	12r	74 Phil Jones	4 Geraint Lewis
04-05	N1	26	12	0	14	598	543	55	62	8	120 Ramiro Pez	18 David Strettle
05-06	N1	26	15	1	10	715	613	102	79	4	200 Micheal Whitehead	20 Scott Donald
06-07	N1	30	23	1	6	937	501	436	118	2	264 Gareth Steenson	16 Brian Tuohy
07-08	N1	30	11	0	19	593	856	-263	58	11	93 Micheal Whitehead	8 by three players
08-09	N1	30	15	1	14	794	777	17	*70	10	173 Mike Whitehead	16 Jon Feely

208

RFU SENIOR CUP

OVERALL PLAYING RECORD

	P	W	D	L	F	A	Pts Diff
Home	15	8	0	7	485	332	153
Away	13	7	0	6	310	277	33
Neutral	0	0	0	0	0	0	0
TOTAL	28	15	0	13	795	609	186

TEAM RECORDS

Highest Score: 83 v Rosslyn Park 02/03
Biggest Winning Margin: 76 (83-7) v Rosslyn Park 02/03
Highest Score Against: 43
v Sale 89/90 & Saracens 01/02
Biggest Losing Margin: 33 (43-10) v Sale

SEASON BY SEASON

Season	Result	Season	Result	Season	Result	Season	Result	Season	Result
71-72	DNQ	78-79	DNQ	85-86	DNQ	92-93	DNQ	99-00	3R
72-73	DNQ	79-80	DNQ	86-87	DNQ	93-94	1R	00-01	5R
73-74	DNQ	80-81	DNQ	87-88	DNQ	94-95	4R	01-02	5R
74-75	DNQ	81-82	DNQ	88-89	DNQ	95-96	2R	02-03	QF
75-76	DNQ	82-83	DNQ	89-90	2R	96-97	6R	03-04	6R
76-77	DNQ	83-84	DNQ	90-91	DNQ	97-98	5R	04-05	3R
77-78	DNQ	84-85	DNQ	91-92	DNQ	98-99	4R		

NATIONAL TROPHY

05-06	Q.F.	06-07	4 R	07-08	Q.F.	08-09	4 R

PLAYERS

	Position	D.o.B.	Apps.	Pts.	T	C	P	DG
Mike Whitehead	Full back/Fly half		62 (6)	414	11	85	59	4
Jon Feeley	Winger		50 (6)	125	25	-	-	-
Tom Allen	Centre		48 (24)	35	7	-	-	-
Nick Buckley	Centre	03/02/1980	17 (1)	-	-	-	-	-
Kevin Maggs	Centre	03/06/1974	6	10	2	-	-	-
Chris Briers	Centre		24 (4)	45	9	-	-	-
Eric Claasens	Full back/Winger		84 (3)	190	38	-	-	-
Brad Hunt	Centre	07/12/1982	29 (1)	40	8	-	-	-
Tom Barlow	Fly half		14 (2)	121	1	28	20	-
Jono West	Scrum half		6 (11)	38	-	13	4	-
Chad Erskine	Scrum half		5 (4)	5	1	-	-	-
Neil Chivers	Scrum half		32 (17)	35	7	-	-	-
Stuart Corsar	Prop		44 (4)	10	2	-	-	-
Anton O'Donnel	Prop		18 (33)	5	1	-	-	-
Nigel Conroy	Hooker		71 (38)	5	1	-	-	-
Hugo Horn	Hooker		7 (16)	5	1	-	-	-
Ben Prescott	Prop	31/07/1978	23 (2)	-	-	-	-	-
Philip Boulton	Prop		23(4)	5	1	-	-	-
Gregor Hayter	Lock	13/08/1976	23 (3)	20	4	-	-	-
Matt Challinor	Lock		19 (7)	-	-	-	-	-
Louis McGowan	Lock		83 (22)	50	10	-	-	-
Andrew Barnes	Back row		11 (4)	-	-	-	-	-
Tinus du Plessis	Back row	20/05/1984	27 (1)	10	2	-	-	-
Ryan Burrows	Back row		21 (6)	37	7	1	-	-
Jon Skurr	Back row	08/07/1979	26 (2)	55	11	-	-	-

RECORDS SECTION
DIVISION TWO
(CURRENTLY NATIONAL LEAGUE ONE)

DIVISION TWO
ROLL OF HONOUR

	CHAMPIONS	Runners-up	Nos of Clubs/Games	Leading Points Scorer	
1987-88	Rosslyn Park	Liverpool St Helens	12/11	75	Andy Finnie (Bedford)
1988-89	Saracens	Bedford	12/11	138	Andy Kennedy (Saracens)
1989-90	Northampton	Liverpool St Helens	12/11	107	Ian Aitchison (London Irish)
1990-91	Rugby	London Irish	13/12	117	Brian Mullen (London Irish)
1991-92	London Scottish	West Hartlepool	13/12	147	David Johnson (Newcastle)
1992-93	Newcastle	Waterloo	13/12	136	David Johnson (Newcastle)
1993-94	Sale	West Hartelpool	10/18	172	Guy Gregory (Nottingham)
1994-95	Saracens	Wakefield	10/18	213	Mike Jackson (Wakefield)
1995-96	Northampton	London Irish	10/18	301	Michael Corcoran (London Irish)
1996-97	Richmond	Newcastle	12/22	334	Simon Mason (Richmond)
1997-98	Bedford	West Hartlepool	12/22	289	Mike Rayer (Bedford)
1998-99	Bristol	Rotherham	14/26	305	Steve Gough (Coventry)
99-2000	Rotherham	Leeds Tykes	14/26	312	Sam Howard (Exeter)
2000-01	Leeds Tykes	Worcester	14/26	349	Sateki Tuipulotu (Worcester)
2001-02	Rotherham	Worcester	14/26	283	Simon Binns (Otley)
2002-03	Rotherham	Worcester	14/26	374	James Pritchard (Bedford)
2003-04	Worcester	Orrell	14/26	320	Tony Yapp (Exeter)
2004-05	Bristol	Exeter	14/26	347	Leigh Hinton (Bedford)
2005-06	NEC Harlequins	Bedford	14/26	251	James Moore (Coventry)
2006-07	Leeds Tykes	Rotherham Titans	16/30	302	Leigh Hinton (Leeds)
2007-08	Northampton Saints	Exeter	16/30	287	Gareth Steenson (Penzance)
2008-09	Leeds	Exeter	16/30	303	Jamie Lennard (Doncaster)

RELEGATED CLUBS
87-88 - No relegation
88-89 - London Welsh, London Scottish
89-90 - No relegation
90-91 - Richmond, Headingley
91-92 - Plymouth, Liverpool St Helens
92-93 - Bedford, Rosslyn Park, Richmond, Blackheath, Coventry, Fylde & Morley
93-94 - Rugby, Otley
94-95 - Fylde, Coventry
95-96 - No relegation
96-97 - Rugby, Nottingham

97-98 - No relegation
98-99 - Blackheath, Fylde
99-00 - Rugby Lions, West Hartlepool
00-01 - Orrell, Waterloo
01-02 - Henley Hawks, Bracknell
02-03 - Moseley, Rugby Lions
03-04 - Wakefield, Manchester
04-05 - Henley Hawks, Orrell
05-06 - No relegation
06-07 - Otley, Waterloo
07-08 - Birmingham Solihull, Launceston
08-09 - Esher, Sedgley Park, Newbury, Otley, Manchester

LEEDS - NATIONAL LEAGUE ONE CHAMPIONS 2008-09

		MOST TRIES		MOST PENALTIES		MOST CONVERSIONS
87-88	10	Dave McLagan (Saracens)	19	Andy Finnie (Bedford)	12	Nick Holmes (Saracens)
88-89	7	Dave McLagan (Saracens)	30	Andy Kennedy (Saracens)	18	Simon Irving (Headinglet)
89-90	7	Jim Fallon (Richmond)	22	Ian Aitchison (London Irish) & John Steele (Northampton)	24	Martin Livesey (Richmond)
90-91	9	Lindsay Renwick (London Scottish)	22	Brian Mullen (London Irish)	16	Nick Grecian (London Scottish)
91-92	11	Nick Grecian (London Scottish)	26	David Johnson (Newcastle) & John Stabler	31	David Johnson (Newcastle)
92-93	7	Jon Sleighthome (Wakefield)	30	David Johnson (Newcastle)	16	David Johnson (Newcastle)
93-94	16	Simon Verbickas (Sale)	43	Guy Gregory (Nottingham)	29	Paul Turner (Sale)
94-95	8	Tony Penn (Newcastle)	57	Michael Jackson (Wakefield)	21	Simon Mason (Richmond) & Andy Tunningley (Saracens)
95-96	20	Matt Allen (Northampton)	63	Michael Corcoran (London Irish)	76	Paul Grayson (Northampton Saints)
96-97	23	John Bentley (Newcastle)	47	John Steele (London Scottish)	95	Rob Andrew (Newcastle)
97-98	17	Darragh O'Mahony (Moseley) & Ben Whetstone (Bedford)	66	Lyndon Griffiths (Waterloo)	65	Mike Rayer (Bedford)
98-99	18	Dean Lax (Rotherham)	53	Steve Gough (Coventry) & Sateki Tui	48	Steve Gough (Coventry)
99-00	18	Dean Lax (Rotherham)	55	Matt Jones (Henley) & Steve Swindell (Manchester)	60	Mike Umaga (Rotherham)
00-01	19	Graham Mackay (Leeds Tykes)	51	Martyn Davies (Coventry)	72	Richard Le Bas (Leeds Tykes)
01-02	25	Chris Garrard (Worcester)	63	Simon Binns (Otley)	60	Ramiro Pez (Rotherham)
02-03	26	Duncan Roke (Worcester)	72	James Pritchard (Bedford)	75	Tony Yapp (Exeter)
03-04	23	Leigh Hinton (Orrell) & Lee Robinson (Plymouth Alb.)	65	Simon Binns (Otley)	98	Tommy Hayes (Worcester)
04-05	21	Sean Marsden (Bristol)	69	Leigh Hinton (Bedford)	72	Tony Yapp (Exeter)
05-06	20	Scott Donald (Rotherham)	43	James Moore (Coventry)	51	Andrew Mehrtens (Harlequins)
06-07	28	Nicholas Sestaret (Plymouth A.)	56	Alberto di Bernardo (Penzance) Oliver Thomas (Moseley)	79	Gareth Steenson (Rotherham)
07-08	39	Chris Ashton (Northampton Saints)	49	Gareth Steenson (Penzance)	61	Mark Woodrow (Doncaster)
08-09	18	Will Twelvetrees (Bedford) & David Jackson (Notingham)	46	Jamie Lennard (Doncaster)	64	Alberto di Bernardo (Leeds)

DIVISION TWO

CHAMPIONSHIP

Constitution	12 87-88	12 88-89	12 89-90	12 90-91	13 91-92	13 92-93	13 93-94	10 94-95	10 95-96	12 96-97
Bedford	5	2p		8	10	7r			10	4
Birmingham Solihull										
Blackheah	11	8	10	10	11	10r			7	10
Bracknell										
Briol										
Covenry		5	4	4	6	11r		10r		3
Doncaer										
Eher										
Exeer										
Fylde						12r		9r		
Goforh/Newcale	10	10	12	6	4	1		3	8	2p
Harlequin										
Headingley	4	7	8	13r						
Henley										
Launceon										
Leed										
Liverpool S. Helen	2p		2p		13r					
London Irih	8	6	5	2p				5	2p	
London Scoih	7	11r		5	1		8	4	3	5
London Welh	9	12r								
Mancheer										
Morley					9	13r				
Moeley					7	6	5	6	6	8
Newbury										
Norhampon	12	3	1						1	
Noingham						4	6	7	9	12r
Orrell										
Oley							10r			
Penzance & Newlyn										
Plymouh Albion			7	11	12r					
Richmond	6	9	3	12r		9r				1
Rolyn Park	1					8r				
Roherham										7
Rugby			6	1			9r			11r
Sale		4	9	7	8	5	1			
Saracen	3	1					3	1		
Sedgley Park										
Wakefield				3	5	3	4	2	4	6
Waerloo			11	9	3	2	7	8	5	9
We Harlepool					2p		2p			
Worceer										

212

YEAR BY YEAR RECORDS

12 97-98	14 98-99	14 99-00	14 00-01	14 01-02	14 02-03	14 03-04	14 04-05	14 05-06	16 06-07	16 07-08	16 08-09
1			11	6	7	7	7	2	7	6	3
			9	8	8	4	9	14	8	15r	
9	13r										
				14r							
	1					9	1p				
7	7	6	5	4	6	12	6	10	10	9	9
								9	3	4	5
										12	12r
11	5	4	3	3	3	6	2	6	4	2	2
12	14r										
								1p			
		9	7	13r		11	13r				
										16r	
	6	2	1p						1p		1p
3p											
	4	5	6	5	5	8	12	11	12	7	6
			8	8	12	12	14r				16r
6	10	7	10	11	13r			14	10	8	
								12	11	13	14r
										1p	
						11	7	9	3	4	
5	8	11	13r		4	2	14r				
			12	7	11	5	5	8	15r		15r
						10	4	3	5	5	7
				9	3	3	3	5	6	8	11
4	2	1		1	1p		8	4	2	11	10
	11	13r		10	14r						
							10	13	13	14	13r
10	12	10	4	9	10	13r					
8	9	12	14r						16r		
2p		14r									
	3	3	2	2	2	1p					

CHAMPIONSHIP

213

DIVISION TWO

ALL TIME RECORDS

SEASON RECORDS

MOST POINTS
EVOLUTION OF RECORD
75	Andy Finnie	Bedford	1987-88
138	Andy Kennedy	Saracens	1988-89
147	David Johnson	Newcastle Gos	1991-92
172	Guy Gregory	Nottingham	1993-94
213	Mike Jackson	Wakefield	1994-95
310	Michael Corcoran	London Irish	1995-96
324	Simon Mason	Richmond	1996-97
349	Sateki Tuipulotu	Worcester	2000-01
374	James Pritchard	Bedford	2002-03

The ALL-TIME RECORDS can be found overleaf.

MOST TRIES
EVOLUTION OF RECORD
10	Dave McLagan	Saracens	1987-88
11	Nick Grecian	Lon. Scottish	1991-92
16	Simon Verbickas	Sale	1993-94
20	Matt Allen	Northampton	1996-97
23	John Bentley	Newcastle	1996-97
25	Chris Garrard	Worcester	2001-02
26	Duncan Roke	Worcester	2002-03
28	Nicholas Sestaret	Plymouth Albion	2006-07
39	Chris Ashton	Northampton	2007-08

ALL-TIME RECORDS
39	Nick Ashton	Northampton	2007-08
28	Nicholas Sestaret	Plymouth Albion	2006-07
28	Bruce Reihana	Northampton	2007-08
26	Duncan Roke	Worcester	2002-03
25	Chris Garrard	Worcester	2001-02
25	Jason Forster	Doncaster	2006/07
23	John Bentley	Newcastle	1996-97
23	Lee Robinson	Plymouth Albion	2003-04
23	Leigh Hinton	Orrell	2003-04
22	Michael Wood	Rotherham	2002-03
22	Josh Drauniniu	Exeter	2007-08
21	Gary Armstrong	Newcastle	1996-97
21	Scott Quinnell	Richmond	1996-97
21	Ben Hinshelwood	Worcester	2001-02
21	Dan Ward Smith	Plymouth	2002-03
21	Sean Marsden	Bristol	2004-05
20	Matt Allen	Northampton	1995-96
20	Jim Fallon	Richmond	1996-97
20	Scott Donald	Earth Titans	2005-06
19	Graham Mackay	Leeds Tykes	2000-01
19	Nmandi Ezulike	Worcester	2002-03
19	Daren O'Leary	Worcester	2002-03
19	Jason Luff	Exeter	2007-08
18	Dean Lax	Rotherham	1998-99
18	Dean Lax	Rotherham	1999-00
18	Shaun Woof	Leeds Tykes	2000-01
18	Gavin Pfister	Worcester	2003-04
18	Dave Strettle	Rotherham	2004-05
18	Simon Keogh	Harlequins	2005-06
18	David Jackson	Nottingham	2008-09
18	Will Twelvetrees	Bedford	2008-09

MOST CONVERSIONS
EVOLUTION OF RECORD
14	Andy Kennedy	Saracens	1988-89
24	Martin Livesey	Richmond	1989-90
31	David Johnson	Newcastle Gosforth	1991-92
76	Paul Grayson	Northampton	1995-96
95	Rob Andrew	Newcastle	1996-97
98	Tommy Hayes	Worcester	2003-04

ALL-TIME RECORDS
98	Tommy Hayes	Worcester	2003-04
95	Rob Andrew	Newcastle	1996-97
83	Simon Mason	Richmond	1996-97
79	Gareth Steenson	Earth Titans	2006-07
76	Paul Grayson	Northampton	1995-96
75	Tony Yapp	Exeter	2002-03
72	Richard Le Bas	Leeds Tykes	2000-01
72	Tony Yapp	Exeter Chiefs	2004-05
69	Leigh Hinton	Orrell	2003-04
68	Leigh Hinton	Leeds Tykes	2006-07
68	Phil Jones	Orrell	2002-03
67	Mike Rayer	Bedford	1996-97
67	Tony Yapp	Exeter	2003-04
65	Mike Rayer	Bedford	1997-98
64	Jason Strange	Bristol	2004-05
64	Alberto di Bernardo	Leeds	2008-09

MOST PENALTIES
EVOLUTION OF RECORD
30	Andy Kennedy	Saracens	1988-89
30	David Johnson	Newcastle	1992-93
43	Guy Gregory	Nottingham	1993-94
57	Mike Jackson	Wakefield	1994-95
63	Michael Corcoran	London Irish	1995-96
65	Lyndon Griffiths	Waterloo	1997-98
72	James Pritchard	Bedford	2002-03

ALL-TIME RECORDS
72	James Pritchard	Bedford	2002-03
69	Leigh Hinton	Bedford	2004-05
65	Lyndon Griffiths	Waterloo	1997-98
65	Simon Binns	Otley	2003-04
63	Michael Corcoran	London Irish	1995-96
63	Simon Binns	Otley	2001-02
57	Mike Jackson	Wakefield	1994-95
56	Alberto Di Bernardo	Cornish Pirates	2006-07
56	Ollie Thomas	Moseley	2006-07
55	Steve Swindells	Manchester	1999-00
55	Matt Jones	Henley	1999-00
54	Blair Feeney	Sedgley Park	2004-05
53	Steve Gough	Coventry	1998-99
53	Sateki Tuipulotu	Leeds Tykes	1998-99
53	Barry Reeves	Henley Hawks	2003-04
52	Simon Binns	Otley	2002-03
51	Bryan Easson	Exeter	1998-99
51	Martyn Davies	Coventry	2000-01
51	Simon Binns	Otley	2004-05
50	Sateki Tuipulotu	Worcester	2000-01
50	Rob Liley	Wakefield	2001-02

ALL TIME RECORDS

MOST DROP GOALS

EVOLUTION OF RECORD
4	Simon Smith	Bedford	1987-88
4	David Johnson	Gosforth	1987-88
8	Jon King	Blackheath	1988-89
9	Guy Gregory	Nottingham	1992-93
9	David Sleman	Orrell	2000-01

ALL-TIME RECORDS
9	Guy Gregory	Nottingham	1992-93
9	David Sleman	Orrell	2000-01
8	Jon King	Blackheath	1988-89
7	Chris Malone	Exeter	2001-02
7	Jamie Lennard	Doncaster	2008-09
6	Andy Lee	Saracens	1994-95
6	Rob Liley	Wakefield	2001-02
6	Tom Barlow	Plymouth	2002-03

MATCH RECORDS

MOST POINTS

EVOLUTION OF RECORD
26	Andy Mitchell	London Scot v North	03.10.87
28	David Johnson	New Gos v Morley	11.01.92
30	Michael Corcoran	L. Irish v Waterloo	23.09.95
42	Jez Harris	Coventry v Nott	05.10.96

The ALL-TIME RECORDS can be found overleaf.

MOST TRIES

EVOLUTION OF RECORD
3	Jerry Macklin	Lon Scot v Northampton	03.10.87
3	Peter Shillingford	Moseley v Wasps	05.02.88
5	Simon Verbickas	Sale v Otley	12.02.94
5	Pat Lam	Newcastle v Rotherham	04.05.97
5	Luke Nabaro	Bristol v Blackheath	13.03.99
5	Chris Garrard	Worcester v Otley	09.03.02
5	Michael Wood	Rotherham v Birm Sol	13.04.02
5	Richard Welding	Cornish P v Earth Titans	18.09.05
5	Ugo Monye	Harlequins v Exeter	22.10.05
5	Nicholas Sestaret	Plymouth A v Moseley	31.03.07
6	Chris Ashton	Northampton v Launceston	26.04.08

The ALL-TIME RECORDS can be found overleaf.

DIVISION TWO

MOST CONVERSIONS

EVOLUTION OF RECORD
6	Chris Howard	Rugby v Gosforth	11.11.89
9	David Johnson	New Gos v Morley	11.01.92
9	Guy Gregory	Nott v Morley	24.10.92
9	Paul Turner	Sale v Otley	12.02.94
18	Rob Andrew	Newcastle v Rugby	05.10.96

ALL-TIME RECORDS
18	Rob Andrew	Newcastle v Rugby	05.10.96
13	Jez Harris	Coventry v Nottingham	05.10.96
13	Bruce Reihana	Northampton v Sedgley P.	26.01.08
12	Jason Strange	Leeds v Manchester (A)	08.04.09
10	Simon Binns	Rotherham v W Hartlepool	02.10.99
10	Mike Umaga	Rotherham v Waterloo	11.03.00
10	Sam Howard	Exeter v W Hartlepool	06.05.00
10	Ramiro Pez	Rotherham v Moseley	06.10.02
10	Jon Benson	Rotherham v Moseley	08.02.03
10	Alberto di Bernardo	Leeds v Newbury (A)	29.11.08

MOST PENALTIES

EVOLUTION OF RECORD
7	Michael Corcoran	Lon Irish v Lon Scottish	13.01.96
8	Alastair Kerr	Moseley v Waterloo	17.02.96
9	Marcus Barrow	Manchester v Wakefield	20.12.01

ALL-TIME RECORDS
9	Marcus Barrow	Manchester v Wakefield	20.12.01
9	Matthew Leek	Coventry v Otley	13.11.04
8	Alastair Kerr	Moseley v Water	17.02.96
8	James Pritchard	Bedford v Otley	02.11.02
8	Luke Smith	Coventry v Exeter	09.04.03
7	Michael Corcoran	Lon Irish v Lon Scottish	13.01.96
7	Matt Inman	Rotherham v Richmond	14.09.96
7	Sateki Tuipulotu	Leeds v Coventry	03.01.99
7	Steve Gough	Coventry v Worcester	11.03.00
7	Jon Benson	Leeds v Manchester	08.04.00
7	Richard Le Bas	Leeds Tykes v Manchester	07.10.00
7	Tony Yapp	Exeter v Otley	20.09.03
7	Jason Strange	Bristol v Penzance	05.09.04
7	James Moore	Coventry v Newbury	11.03.06

MOST DROP GOALS

ALL-TIME RECORDS
3	Martin Livesey	Richmond v Northampton	19.11.88
3	Murray Walker	London Scot v W Hartlepool	23.04.94
3	Chris Malone	Exeter v Rotherham	10.11.01
3	Danny Gray	Plymouth v Exeter	08.09.07
3	Michael Whitehead	Rotherham v Exeter	11.04.09
3	Rhys Jones	Penzance v Plymouth	12.04.09

ALL TIME RECORDS
DIVISION TWO
MOST TRIES IN A MATCH

6	Chris Ashton	Northampton v Launceston	26.04.08
5	Simon Verbickas	Sale v Otley	12.02.94
	Pat Lam	Newcastle v Rotherham	04.05.97
	Luke Nabaro	Bristol v Blackheath	13.03.99
	Chris Garrard	Worcester v Otley	09.03.02
	Michael Wood	Rotherham v Birmingham & S.	13.04.02
	Richard Welding	Penzance v Rotherham	18.09.05
	Ugo Monye	Harlequins v Exeter	22.10.05
	Nicholas Sestaret	Plymouth A. v Moseley	31.03.07
	Paul Diggin	Northampton v Sedgley Park	26.01.08
	Tom Brown	London Welsh v Manchester	28.03.09
4	Craig Moir	Northampton v Waterloo	13.04.96
	Gary Armstrong	Newcastle v Nottingham	14.09.96
	Scott Quinnell	Richmond v Waterloo	02.11.96
	John Bentley	Newcastle v Wakefield	08.03.97
	John Clarke	Blackheath v Fylde	20.09.97
	Jason Forster	Bedford v Fylde	17.01.98
	Ben Wade	Rotherham v Exeter	25.04.98
	John Fabian	Exeter v Waterloo	17.10.98
	Lennie Woodward	Lon. Welsh v Fylde	12.12.98
	Jonathon Scales	Leeds Tykes v Exeter	07.02.99
	Dean Lax	Rotherham v Orrell	13.02.99
	Ian Breheny	Wakefield v Moseley	24.04.99
	Andy Smallwood	Coventry v Wakefield	08.05.99
	Andy Currier	London Welsh v Waterloo	06.10.99
	Chris Garrard	Worcester v Manchester	01.09.01
	Jamie Greenlees	Manchester v Bracknell	15.09.01
	Drew Hickey	Orrell v Rugby Lions	01.09.02
	Dan Ward-Smith	Plymouth Albion v Rugby Lions	26.10.02
	Dan Ward-Smith	Plymouth Albion v Manchester	04.01.03
	Duncan Roke	Worcester v Rugby Lions	26.04.03
	Dan Ward-Smith	Plymouth Albion v Henley Hawks	20.03.04
	Richard Welding	Orrell v Manchester	10.04.04
	Dan Ward-Smith	Plymouth Albion v Coventry	09.10.04
	Sean Marsden	Orrell v Bristol	09.04.05
	Gary Kingdom	Exeter v Sedgley Park	19.11.05
	Claasans, Eric	Newbury v Rotherham	28.04.07
	Murdoch, Alastair	Exeter v Sedgley Park	28.04.07
	Jason Luff	Exeter v London Welsh	13.10.07
	Chris Ashton	Rotherham v Northampton	27.10.07
	Chris Ashton	Northampton v Sedgley Park	26.01.08
	Chris Ashton	Doncaster v Northampton	10.02.08
	Bruce Reihana	Northampton v Launceston	26.04.08
	William Twelvetrees	Bedford v Manchester	30.08.08
	Jon Feeley	Rotherham v Newbury	23.11.08
	John Goodridge	Leeds Carnegie v Moseley	23.11.08
	Lee Blackett	Newbury v Leeds Carnegie	29.11.08
	George Lowe	Manchester v Esher	31.01.09
	Tom Biggs	Manchester v Leeds Carnegie	08.04.09
	Daniel Norton	London Welsh v Moseley	02.05.09

DIVISION TWO   ALL TIME RECORDS
MOST POINTS IN A MATCH

42	Jez Harris	Coventry v Nottingham	05.10.96
41	Simon Binns	Rotherham v West Hartlepool	02.10.99
37	Ramiro Pez	Rotherham v Moseley	06.10.02
36	Rob Andrew	Newcastle v Rugby	05.10.96
	Bruce Reihana	Northampton v Sedgley Park	26.01.08
34	Steve Gough	Coventry v London Welsh	10.10.98
	Alastair Hepher	Bedford v Newbury	29.04.06
33	Mike Umaga	Rotherham v Waterloo	11.03.00
32	Sateki Tuipulotu	Worcester v Hanley Hawks	19.01.02
	Leigh Hinton	Orrell v Bedford	06.12.03
	Aberto di Bernardo	Penzance v Moseley	17.09.06
	Chris Ashton	Northampton v Launceston	26.04.08
	Bruce Reihana	Northampton v Launceston	26.04.08
31	Sam Howard	Exeter v West Hartlepool	06.05.00
	Sateki Tuipulotu	Worcester v Henley Hawks	20.01.01
	James Pritchard	Bedford v Moseley	16.02.03
	Leigh Hinton	Orrell v Henley Hawks	29.11.03
30	Michael Corcoran	London Irish v Waterloo	23.09.95
	John Steele	London Scottish v Rugby	29.03.97
	Andy Lee	London Welsh v Rugby	08.12.99
	Ramiro Pez	Rotherham v Coventry	15.09.01
	Tony Yapp	Exeter v Manchester	28.02.04
29	Simon Mason	Richmond v Rotherham	14.09.96
	Simon Verbickas	Orrell v Wakefield	25.04.98
	Tony Yapp	Worcester v Wakefield	16.10.99
	Andy Lee	London Welsh v Bracknell	20.10.01
	James Pritchard	Bedford v Waterloo	27.01.07
	Tim Taylor	Nottingham v Otley	08.03.09
28	David Johnson	Newcastle Gosforth v Morley	11.01.92
	David Johnson	Newcastle Gosforth v Liverpool StH	29.02.93
	Oliver Thomas	Moseley v Nottingham	07.04.07
27	Simon Hodgkinson	Moseley v London Irish	08.04.95
	Simon Verbickas	Orrell v Waterloo	08.05.99
	Marcus Barrow	Manchester v Wakefield	15.12.01
	Dafyyd Lewis	London Welsh v Rugby Lions	08.02.03
	Matthew Leek	Coventry v Otley	13.11.04
	Ramiro Pez	Rotherham v Orrell	18.09.04

ALL TIME RECORDS — DIVISION TWO

MOST POINTS IN A SEASON

Points	Player	Club	Season	Tries	Cons.	Pens.	D.G.
374	James Pritchard	Bedford	2002-03	12	49	72	-
349	Sateki Tuopulotu	Worcester	2000-01	17	57	50	-
349	Tony Yapp	Worcester	2002-03	11	75	44	4
347	Leigh Hinton	Bedford	2004-05	10	45	69	-
346	Phil Jones	Orrell	2002-03	15	68	45	-
333	Richard Le Bas	Leeds Tykes	2000-01	9	72	48	-
324	Simon Mason	Richmond	1996-97	10	83	36	-
320	Tony Yapp	Exeter	2003-04	9	67	45	2
313	Leigh Hinton	Orrell	2003-04	23	69	20	-
312	Sam Howard	Exeter	99-2000	5	55	54	5
310	Michael Corcoran	London Irish	1995-96	8	36	63	-
310	Simon Binns	Otley	2003-04	5	45	65	-
305	Steve Gough	Coventry	1998-99	10	48	53	0
303	Tommy Hayes	Worcester	2003-04	7	98	24	-
302	Leigh Hinton	Leeds Tykes	2006-07	8	68	42	-
298	Jamie Lennard	Doncaster	2008-09	5	57	46	7
297	Rob Andrew	Newcastle	1996-97	7	95	23	1
293	Alberto Di Bernardo	Penzance	2006-07	2	56	56	1
289	Mike Rayer	Bedford	1997-98	6	65	43	-
287	Jason Strange	Bristol	2004-05	3	64	47	1
287	Gareth Steenson	Cornish Pirates	2007-08	5	56	49	1
285	Tony Yapp	Exeter	2004-05	6	72	34	3
285	Oliver Thomas	Moseley	2006-07	5	43	56	2
283	Simon Binns	Otley	2001-02	5	30	63	3
280	Tony Yapp	Exeter	2006-07	7	55	45	-
276	James Pritchard	Bedford	2006-07	12	60	32	-
274	Phil Jones	Sedgley Park	2006-07	12	44	42	-
266	Steve Gough	Coventry	99-2000	5	47	49	-
265	Simon Binns	Otley	2002-03	4	43	52	1
264	Ramiro Pez	Rotherham	2002-03	5	58	40	1
264	Gareth Steenson	Rotherham	2006-07	2	79	31	1
263	Mark Woodrow	Doncaster	2007-08	3	61	41	1
262	Bruce Reihana	Northampton Saints	2007-08	28	49	8	-
261	Lyndon Griffiths	Waterloo	1997-98	1	29	66	-
261	David Jackson	Nottingham	2008-09	18	51	23	-
256	John Steele	Northampton	1996-97	5	39	47	4
256	Luke Smith	Birmingham/Coventry	2002-03	4	46	47	1
256	James Pritchard	Plymouth Albion	2004-05	13	40	37	-
253	Blair Feeney	Sedgley Park	2004-05	4	34	54	1
251	Mike Umaga	Rotherham	99-2000	5	60	33	-
251	James Moore	Coventry	2005-06	8	41	43	-
250	Sateki Tuipulotu	Leeds Tykes	1998-99	3	38	53	-
249	Barry Reeves	Henley Hawks	2003-04	4	32	53	2
247	Chris Malone	Exeter	2001-02	5	45	37	7
244	Simon Binns	Rotherham	1997-98	8	39	41	-
241	Steven Vile	West Hartlepool	1997-98	8	33	43	2
241	Bryan Easson	Exeter	1998-99	2	39	51	-
241	Simon Binns	Otley	2004-05	3	35	51	1
239	Martyn Davies	Coventry	2000-01	4	33	51	-
239	James Pritchard	Bedford	2001-02	7	42	40	-
238	Mike Rayer	Bedford	1996-97	7	67	23	-

DIVISION TWO — ALL TIME RECORDS

TEAM RECORDS

Highest score:	156	Newcastle 156 Rugby 5. 5.10.96
Highest aggregate:	161	As above
Highest score by a losing side:	45	Sedgley Park 47 Newbury 45 21.04.07
Highest scoring draw:	33	Sedgley Park v Pertemps Bees 24.09.05
Most consecutive wins:	30	Northampton Saints 2007-08
Most consecutive defeats:	26	Rugby Lions 2002-03
Most points for in a season:	1321	Northampton Saints 2007-08 (30 games)
	1255	Newcastle 1996-97 (22 games)
Least points for in a season:	81	Northampton 1987-88 (11 games)
Most points against in a season:	1178	Moseley 2002-03 (26 games)
	1206	Sedgley Park 2008-09 (30 games)
Least points against in a season:	80	Saracens 1989-90 (11 games)
Most tries for in a season:	189	Newcastle 1996-97 (22 games)
Most tries against in a season:	168	Moseley 2002-03 (26 games)
Least tries for in a season:	7	Morley 1992-93 (12 games)
Least tries against in a season:	5	Sale 1992-93 (12 games)
Most conversions for in a season:	119	Newcastle 1996-97 (22 games)
Most conversions against in a season:	101	Orrell 1996-97 (22 games)
Most penalties for in a season:	72	Bedford 2002-03 (26 games)
Most penalties against in a season:	72	Birmingham & Sol 2001-02 (26 games)
Least penalties for in a season:	6	Gosforth 1987-88 (11 games)
Least penalties against in a season:	8	Saracens 1987-88, Sale 1990-91 (12 games)
Most drop goals for in a season:	11	London Scottish 1994-95 (18 games)
Most drop goals against in a season:	12	London Irish 1994-95 (18 games)

INDIVIDUAL RECORDS

Most points in a season:	374	James Pritchard (Bedford) 2002-03
Most tries in a season:	39	Chris Ashton, (Northampton Saints) 2007-08
Most conversions in a season:	95	Rob Andrew (Newcastle) 1996-97
Most penalties in a season:	72	James Pritchard (Bedford) 2002-03
Most drop goals in a season:	8	Guy Gregory (Nottingham) 1992-93
Most points in a match:	42	Jez Harris, *Coventry* v Nottingham 5.10.96
Most tries in a match:	6	Chris Ashton. *Northampton* v Launceston 26.04.08
Most conversions in a match:	18	Rob Andrew, *Newcastle* v Rugby 5.10.96
Most penalties in a match:	9	Marcus Barrow, *Manchester* v Wakefield 15.12.01
		Matthew Leek Coventry v Otley 13.11.04
Most drop goals in a match:	3	Martin Livesey, Richmond v Northampton 9.11.88
		Murray Walker, Lon. Scottish v W. Hartlepool 23.4.94
		Chris Malone, Exeter v Rotherham 10.11.01
		Danny Gray, Plymouth v Exeter 08.09.07

Support the RFU Injured Players Foundation

The Foundation helps and supports players from all levels of the game who suffer injuries whilst playing rugby which may cause permanent and severe disability.

Injury Management

Everyone involved in rugby has a role to play in making the game enjoyable and above all as safe as possible. Those who hold a coaching position or have a volunteer role providing pitch side care also have a specific responsibility to provide a safe and competent level of care to any injured player.

Rugby is a contact sport and in common with all contact sports, playing the game carries a risk of injury and while serious injuries are rare*, those involved will need to be prepared to deal with the full range of incidents that could occur on the training ground or pitch.

In addition to supporting the injured players after the event, the RFU IPF is working with experts in the field and the other Unions to ensure that wherever possible these injuries are prevented; that where injuries occur they have appropriate immediate injury management; and that the necessary specialist trauma care can be readily accessed

The RFU Injured Players Foundation works with the RFU to develop training courses and advice on this subject which can be accessed across the game.

Visit www.rfuipf.org.uk to discover more and see how you can help

*The risk of suffering a catastrophic injury while playing rugby in England is 0.8 per 100,000 people per annum and lower than other sports globally in the following order: American football (1.0 person per 100,000 people per annum), swimming (1.8), rugby league (2.0), skiing (2.5), ice hockey (4.0), gymnastics (8.2), and horse riding (29.7) - Dr Colin Fuller, Centre for Sports Medicine, University of Nottingham: ' Catastrophic Injuries in Rugby Union: An assessment of risk' (July 2007)

NATIONAL LEAGUE ONE

2008-2009 SEASON Review & Statistics 222-231

2009-10 CLUBS

Club	Page
Blackheath	232
Blaydon	236
Cambridge	240
Cinderford	244
Esher	248
Launceston	254
London Scottish	258
Manchester	264
Newbury	270
Nuneaton	276
Otley	282
Redruth	288
Sedgley Park	292
Stourbridge	298
Tynedale	302
Wharfedale	306

RECORDS SECTION
(previously National 2 & Division 3)

Roll of Honour	310
Year by Year Records	312

ALL-TIME RECORDS

All Time Team & Individual Records		314
All Time Records		316
Most Tries	in a Match	318
Most Points	in a Match	319
	in a Season	320

FIXTURES 2009-10

	Blackheath	Blaydon	Cambridge	Cinderford	Esher	Launceston	London Scottish	Manchester	Newbury	Nuneaton	Otley	Redruth	Sedgley Park	Stourbridge	Tynedale	Wharfedale
Blackheath		06.03	30.01	05.12	20.02	17.10	19.12	27.03	12.09	31.10	126.01	10.01	03.10	24.04	09.01	14.11
Blaydon	07.11		28.11	26.09	12.12	03.04	10.10	09.01	24.10	17.04	05.09	23.01	20.03	13.02	27.02	12.09
Cambridge	10.10	27.03		19.12	06.03	31.10	12.09	10.04	26.09	14.11	20.02	24.04	13.02	09.01	23.01	05.12
Cinderford	03.04	16.01	17.04		02.01	05.09	27.02	30.01	20.03	19.09	17.10	24.10	12.12	07.11	28.11	03.10
Esher	24.10	10.04	07.11	12.09		20.03	26.09	24.04	10.10	05.12	27.03	09.01	27.02	23.01	13.02	19.12
Launceston	13.02	05.12	27.02	24.04	14.11		09.01	19.12	23.01	27.03	06.03	12.09	24.10	26.09	10.10	10.04
London Scottish	17.04	30.01	02.01	31.10	16.01	19.09		20.02	03.04	03.10	14.11	06.03	05.09	28.11	12.12	17.10
Manchester	28.11	19.09	12.12	10.10	05.09	17.04	24.10		07.11	02.01	03.10	13.02	03.04	27.02	20.03	16.01
Newbury	02.01	20.02	16.01	14.11	30.01	03.10	05.12	06.03		17.10	19.12	27.03	19.09	10.04	05.09	31.10
Nuineaton	27.02	19.12	20.03	09.01	03.04	28.11	23.01	12.09	13.02		10.04	26.09	07.11	10.10	24.10	24.04
Otley	26.09	24.04	24.10	13.02	28.11	07.11	20.03	23.01	17.04	12.12		27.02	10.10	03.04	12.09	09.10
Redruth	12.12	03.10	05.09	20.02	19.09	02.01	07.11	17.10	28.11	16.01	31.10		17.04	20.03	03.04	30.01
Sedgley Park	23.01	14.11	17.10	10.04	31.10	20.02	24.04	05.12	09.01	06.03	30.01	19.12		12.09	26.09	27.03
Stourbridge	05.09	17.10	19.09	06.03	03.10	16.01	27.03	31.10	12.12	30.01	05.12	14.11	02.01		17.04	20.02
Tynedale	19.09	31.10	03.10	27.03	17.10	30.01	10.04.010	14.11	24.04	20.02	02.01	05.12	16.01	19.12		06.03
Wharfedale	20.03	02.01	03.04	23.01	17.04	12.12	13.02	26.09	27.02	05.09	19.09	10.10	28.11	24.10	07.11	

2008-09 LEAGUE TABLE

		P	W	D	L	F	A	PD	4T	<7	Pts
1	Birmingham Solihull	26	22	0	4	1098	462	636	21	2	111
2	Cambridge	26	22	0	4	908	434	474	17	3	108
3	Redruth	26	19	1	6	752	411	341	13	3	94
4	Tynedale	26	18	1	7	667	513	154	13	2	89
5	Cinderford	26	16	0	10	733	598	135	10	3	77
6	Blackheath	26	14	1	11	691	612	79	8	5	71
7	Launceston	26	13	1	12	695	578	117	10	6	70
8	Stourbridge	26	11	0	15	644	586	58	11	7	62
9	Wharfedale	26	11	0	15	546	643	-97	8	7	59
10	Blaydon	26	9	1	16	599	609	-10	11	6	55
11	Westcombe Park	26	9	1	16	468	746	-278	6	4	48
12	Southend	26	5	0	21	574	797	-223	5	7	32
13	Mounts Bay	26	6	0	20	402	849	-447	3	4	29
14	Waterloo	26	4	0	22	432	1371	-939	6	1	23

NATIONAL ONE

2008-09 RESULTS GRID

	Birmingham	Blackheath	Blaydon	Cambridge	Cinderford	Launceston	Mounts Bay	Redruth	Southend	Stourbridge	Tynedale	Waterloo	Westcombe P	Wharfedale
Birmingham Sol.		58-12	32-12	29-45	53-3	23-19	80-5	31-7	49-27	31-14	24-28	115-0	47-7	55-13
Blackheath	28-35		25-14	41-43	14-41	33-17	55-21	15-30	15-39	23-17	28-3	48-12	30-19	19-15
Blaydon	15-31	27-13		24-54	7-14	18-16	40-7	13-13	28-43	37-16	24-5	83-33	35-22	27-35
Cambridge	29-33	26-20	39-28		27-3	21-23	76-3	21-18	31-22	8-6	32-18	91-0	22-17	52-7
Cinderford	10-36	15-26	35-30	17-21		46-15	41-12	20-25	48-6	20-12	29-22	67-17	72-0	26-19
Launceston	16-35	18-18	23-19	0-24	22-20		6-8	19-8	33-23	37-29	29-27	103-5	45-19	38-10
Mounts Bay	8-61	28-22	12-0	3-28	26-45	15-19		16-35	40-15	9-14	14-32	41-16	14-40	14-18
Redruth	35-28	29-17	38-12	18-19	51-12	19-13	41-10		48-14	18-14	15-5	96-5	44-10	14-15
Southend	14-39	23-30	14-24	13-58	20-21	23-30	20-0	7-32		23-24	12-28	64-26	25-35	33-24
Stourbridge	25-35	19-24	46-7	5-38	31-37	37-36	44-16	15-26	18-15		27-31	51-20	36-14	43-6
Tynedale	22-45	16-15	8-5	49-15	31-10	29-17	14-7	35-24	29-20	24-15		50-20	46-14	45-30
Waterloo	16-52	24-85	8-46	18-13	5-46	9-58	51-31	17-35	27-26	10-5	14-38		33-40	27-42
Westcombe Park	11-29	10-13	12-10	5-40	18-21	34-19	8-26	13-15	28-21	21-55	18-18	22-7		13-10
Wharfedale	41-12	13-22	15-14	14-35	52-14	26-24	28-16	15-18	32-12	20-26	10-14	23-12	13-18	

2008-09 LEADING SCORERS

MOST POINTS

			T	C	P	DG
373	Mark Woodrow	Birmingham Solihull	8	108	38	1
250	Alastair Bressington	Stourbridge	12	44	34	-
246	Mark Bedworth	Wharfedale	11	40	36	1
197	Daniel Hawkes	Mounts Bay	4	30	36	3
183	Ben Patston	Cambridge	4	53	19	-
169	Adam Staniforth	Launceston	2	39	27	-
161	Andy Frost	Southend	8	29	21	-
161	Mark Scrivener	Redruth	-	37	28	1
155	Simon Hunt	Birmingham Solihull	31	-	-	-
152	Matthew Leek	Blackheath	3	34	23	-
150	Craig Evans	Cambridge	7	41	10	1
138	Daniol Trigg	Cinderford	2	31	22	-
120	Luke Fielden	Cambridge	24	-	-	-
101	Robert Miller	Tynedale	4	24	11	-
97	Andrew Fenby	Blaydon	18	2	1	-
90	Rob Thirlby	Redruth	18	-	-	-
85	Paul Thirby	Redruth	7	13	8	-
85	James O'Brien	Waterloo	10	7	7	-
85	Simon Hoult	Southend	7	7	12	-
85	Christoff Lombaard	Cambridge	17	-	-	-

MOST TRIES

			First Half	Second Half	Home	Away
31	Simon Hunt	Birmingham Solihull	12	19	18	13
24	Luke Fielden	Cambridge	14	10	9	15
18	Rob Thirlby	Redruth	7	11	11	7
18	Andrew Fenby	Blaydon	10	8	14	4
17	Christoff Lombaard	Cambridge	10	7	9	8
15	Rob Connolly	Birmingham Solihull	5	10	6	9
15	Reece Spee	Birmingham Solihull	9	6	9	6
14	Jack Harrison	Tynedale	6	8	5	9
13	Rod Petty	Birmingham Solihull	6	7	11	2
12	Paul Knight	Cinderford	7	5	8	4
12	Chris Malherbe	Wharfedale	6	6	5	7
12	Marc Dibble	Launceston	10	2	7	5
12	Alastair Bressington	Stourbridge	5	7	4	8
11	Brendon Daniel	Blaydon	4	7	7	4
11	Dave Knight	Cinderford	7	4	4	7
11	Mark Bedworth	Wharfedale	6	5	9	2
11	Cameron Mitchell	Birmingham Solihull	8	3	3	8
11	Mark Bright	Redruth	7	4	6	5
11	Jake Carter	Cinderford	7	4	8	3
11	Matt Williams	Waterloo	1	10	7	4

MOST PENALTIES
38 Mark Woodrow Birmingham Solihull

MOST CONVERSIONS
108 Mark Woodrow Birmingham Solihull

MOST DROP GOALS
3 Daniel Hawkes Mounts Bay

TRIES FOR
By Position

	TOTAL	BACKS	FORWARDS	Full Backs	Wing	Center	Half Backs	Front Row	Second Row	Back Row	Penalty Tries
Birmingham Solihull	149	96	53	18	40	23	15	11	8	34	1
Blackheath	82	60	22	9	22	15	14	6	3	13	9
Blaydon	85	51	34	5	35	8	3	12	4	18	1
Cambridge	123	79	44	17	24	23	15	10	3	31	3
Cinderford	97	73	24	6	26	19	22	5	3	16	1
Launceston	89	55	34	8	18	19	10	6	8	20	1
Mounts Bay	40	18	22	3	6	3	6	8	4	10	3
Redruth	99	64	35	21	27	11	5	6	8	21	2
Southend	66	49	17	10	20	14	5	10	3	4	4
Stourbridge	86	59	27	16	16	19	8	8	8	11	0
Tynedale	92	64	28	6	27	22	9	8	7	13	0
Waterloo	55	47	8	12	21	9	5	4	0	4	1
Westcombe Park	66	42	24	2	17	12	11	6	2	16	0
Wharfedale	67	51	16	7	13	20	11	7	1	8	1
Totals :	1196	808	388	140	312	217	139	107	62	219	27

TRIES AGAINST
By Position

	TOTAL	BACKS	FORWARDS	Full Backs	Wing	Center	Half Backs	Front Row	Second Row	Back Row	Penalty Tries
Birmingham Solihull	57	44	13	4	21	13	6	5	2	6	0
Blackheath	81	58	23	13	20	17	8	6	4	13	0
Blaydon	81	54	27	13	17	17	7	7	5	15	2
Cambridge	54	43	11	7	17	13	6	4	2	5	1
Cinderford	82	57	25	10	18	15	14	6	2	17	1
Launceston	75	49	26	8	24	10	7	9	3	14	1
Mounts Bay	111	74	37	8	30	26	10	11	4	22	1
Redruth	47	34	13	8	17	5	4	1	5	7	0
Southend	103	71	32	12	30	14	15	7	2	23	3
Stourbridge	69	39	30	5	16	13	5	9	2	19	3
Tynedale	61	43	18	5	11	14	13	5	5	8	2
Waterloo	197	130	67	29	51	30	20	18	15	34	3
Westcombe Park	96	59	37	13	21	14	11	9	7	21	1
Wharfedale	82	53	29	5	19	16	13	10	4	15	1
Totals :	1196	808	388	140	312	217	139	107	62	219	27

KICKING STRIKE RATE

S/R%	(Minimum 20 attempts)	Conversions Att	Suc	Penalties Att	Suc	TOTAL Att	Suc
92.00	Frank Lynch (Waterloo)	12	10	13	13	25	23
85.71	Jake Sharp (Southend)	12	10	9	8	21	18
83.33	Robert Miller (Tynedale)	28	24	14	11	42	35
82.76	Ben Patston (Cambridge)	64	53	23	19	87	72
79.31	Andrew Murray (Tynedale)	18	14	11	9	29	23
79.17	Freddie Burns (Cinderford)	21	16	3	3	24	19
78.92	Mark Woodrow (Birmingham Solihull)	141	108	44	38	185	146
75.86	Daniel Hawkes (Mounts Bay)	40	30	47	36	87	66
75.76	Andy Frost (Southend)	37	29	29	21	66	50
71.88	Gareth Hunter (Westcombe Park)	20	15	12	8	32	23
71.43	Mark Scrivener (Redruth)	57	37	34	28	91	65
70.37	Simon Hoult (Southend)	12	7	15	12	27	19
70.37	Rory Clegg (Blaydon)	21	14	6	5	27	19
67.86	Matthew Leek (Blackheath)	52	34	32	23	84	57
65.52	Mark Bedworth (Wharfedale)	65	40	51	36	116	76
65.35	Adam Staniforth (Launceston)	62	39	39	27	101	66
64.71	Tom White (Blackheath)	24	17	10	5	34	22
64.63	Daniol Trigg (Cinderford)	52	31	30	22	82	53
63.93	Alastair Bressington (Stourbridge)	78	44	44	34	122	78
63.64	Mal Roberts (Launceston)	11	6	11	8	22	14
63.64	James O'Brien (Waterloo)	13	7	9	7	22	14
61.70	Andrew Baggett (Blaydon)	35	21	12	8	47	29
61.45	Craig Evans (Cambridge)	61	41	22	10	83	51
60.61	Tim Stevenson (Cinderford)	15	8	18	12	33	20
60.00	Paul Thirby (Redruth)	22	13	13	8	35	21
56.36	Gavin Beasley (Tynedale)	44	24	11	7	55	31
56.10	Liam Reeve (Waterloo)	27	16	14	7	41	23
55.00	Matt Vaughan (Blackheath)	14	10	6	1	20	11
50.94	James Whittingham (Westcombe Park)	36	19	17	8	53	27
50.00	Brett Rule (Redruth)	17	9	11	5	28	14
42.86	Charlie Rayner (Blaydon)	16	8	12	4	28	12

DISCIPLINE RECORD

Sin Bin Breakdown

	SIN BIN			Violent Conduct			Professional Foul			RED		
	Total	H	A	Total	H	A	Total	H	A	Total	H	A
Birmingham Solihull	1	1	0	14	4	10	15	5	10	-		
Blackheath	1	1	0	11	6	5	12	7	5	1	1	0
Blaydon	-			17	7	10	17	7	10	-		
Cambridge	1	0	1	18	7	11	19	7	12	-		
Cinderford	-			13	6	7	13	6	7	1	1	0
Launceston	1	1	0	10	5	5	11	6	5	-		
Mounts Bay	-			17	5	12	17	5	12	2	1	1
Redruth	-			2	1	1	2	1	1	-		
Southend	2	2	0	15	7	8	17	9	8	-		
Stourbridge	1	1	0	10	3	7	11	4	7	-		
Tynedale	2	0	2	25	11	14	27	11	16	-		
Waterloo	-			12	9	3	12	9	3	1	1	0
Westcombe Park	1	1	0	9	4	5	10	5	5	-		
Wharfedale	2	1	1	10	4	6	12	5	7	-		
TOTAL	12	8	4	183	79	104	195	87	108	5	4	1

NATIONAL ONE

2008-09 REVIEW

- Birmingham Solihull take the National Two title at the first attempt to bounce right back into National One by three points from Cambridge
- National Two had just seven players start all 26 league matches down from 19 last season, five were forwards and two backs
- Birmingham Solihull's Mark Woodrow led the scoring with 373, the third highest ever in the division after Steve Gough 404 (Fylde 96/97) and 398 Neil Hallett Esher (06/07)
- Woodrow smashes the record for most conversions in a season with 108 which is 28 more than Barry Reeves (Henley Hawks 02/03) and Neil Hallett (Esher 06/07)
- Birmingham Solihull winger Simon Hunt sets a new National two record for tries in a season with 31, two more than Nick Baxter scored for Worcester back in the 1997/98 season. He also set a new record for conversions in a match with 15 against Waterloo in the 115-0 win, two more than Redruth's Mark Scrivener who broke the record in March also against the hapless Waterloo
- 15 was the most tries scored by a forward during the season, flanker Rob Connolly for champions Birmingham Solihull but it was some way off the record for a forward which stands at 23 by Dan Ward Smith for Plymouth Albion back in 2001/02
- Cambridge Full back/centre Luke Fielden finished with a club record 24 tries which was enough for joint third on the all time list for the division, with 15 of them coming away from home the highest number in the division, he also bucked the trend by scoring most of his tries in the first half 14 to 10, again the most in the division
- Only five players were sent off during the season and three of them were backs and two were forwards with Mounts Bay the only side to have two players dismissed
- Two players were sin binned five times during the season, Tynedale scrum half Ross Samson and Launceston second row Tim Collier
- Matthew Fieldhouse sat on the bench 20 times for Tynedale during the season, two more than Mounts Bay utility back Adrian Bick
- Blackheath hooker Liam Wordley was the most subbed player in the division coming off 18 times
- Birmingham Solihull set a new record high score beating Waterloo 115-0 in April which beat Cambridge's record form last season when they beat Harrogate 107-5
- Waterloo conceded 1371 points which is the most ever in a season in the division beating the previous record of 1347 set by Clifton in a 30 match season
- Birmingham Solihull scored 150 tries which is eight fewer than the all time record set by Leeds in the 1996/97 season when they played four games more
- Waterloo concede a record 201 tries in a season in the division, 17 more than the previous record from four games fewer set by Clifton in the 1996/97 campaign
- Two players topped scored in a match with 35 points which was enough to put them joint third on the all time list for the division, the two players were Mark Woodrow and Ali Bressington, with only Paul Brett 39 points and Mike Scott 42 points ahead of them
- Both Simon Hunt (Birmingham Solihull) and Luke Fielden (Cambridge) score four hat tricks during the season
- Mark Woodrow was the only player to score 20 or more points three times during the season
- Of all the players to have taken 40 kicks at goal Tynedale's Rob Miller has the best strike rate 83.33 with 35 of his 42 kicks on target

Birmingham Solihull
- They bounce back after relegation to take the National Two title and are now in the new Championship next season
- They picked up 21 try bonus points in 26 matches - four more than any other side in the division
- Topped 1000 points the only side in the division to do so scoring 190 points more than any other side
- Fly half Mark Woodrow smashed the club record of 296 points in a season with 373, the previous record was held by Matt Birch and set in the 1997/98 season
- Winger Simon Hunt ran in an incredible 31 tries, 15 more than the Bees previous record
- Woodrow kicked 108 conversions to beat the Bees' previous record by 50
- Winger Hunt was the only player to start all 26 league matches for the club, Craig Voisey and Reece Spee started 25 and come on as a replacement in the games they did not start

- In six matches against the other top four sides they ended the season with a 50% record
- They set a club record when they beat Waterloo 115-0 in early April running in 17 tries another club record, their previous highest score was 72 v Aspatria back in 1997 when they also set the club record for most tries with 11
- Mark Woodrow set a new club record with 28 points against Mounts Bay in mid March beating the previous record of 25 set by Steve Gough back in September 2000 including a new record of 10 conversions, two more than the previous record. He was not done though as in early April he scored 35 points against Waterloo including a new record of 15 conversions. It was the third highest points total in a match in the division ever and the most conversions ever in a match, three more than the previous record set by Paul Brett of Liverpool St Helens

Cambridge

- Continued their improvement, in their third season of National Two rugby, 9th the first season, 6th last season and now second just three points behind the Champions with both sides winning 22 matches but try bonus points proving crucial and only one promotion spot due to reorganisation
- Cambridge have now finished 1st or 2nd in three of their last five seasons of league rugby
- Picked up losing bonus points in three of their four defeats, the exception was at Tynedale
- With 17 try bonus ponts only the Champions got more with 21
- Former Bedford Blues star Ben Patston topped scored with 183, the best return by a Cambridge player since Dafydd Lewis scored 213 in their National three South Championship season in 05/06
- Patston broke the club record for points in a National League match with 26 against Mounts Bay with 10 conversions and two penalty goals, later in the season Craig Evans equalled the record in the match against Waterloo with 13 conversions which was a club record on its own. The previous record for a match was 25 by winger Christoff Lombaard with five tries against Harrogate the previous season
- Full back Luke Fielden was the leading try scorer with a new club record of 24 tries and ended wing Christoff Lombaard's run over the last three seasons, Lombaard was second with 17
- Lombaard took his all time record to an impressive 81 in four seasons as he failed to reach the 20 try mark for the first time in his Cambridge career
- No Cambridge player started all 26 league matches, three players started 25 matches flanker Darren Fox, Winger Christoff Lombaard and centre/fly half Craig Evans, both started on the bench in the other match and came on as replacements
- In matches against the top four they won four out of six, this after losing their first two early in the season

Redruth

- Long time leaders Redruth fell away and finished third in the end some 14 points behind second placed Cambridge
- This was their best finish since returning to the division four seasons ago beating their 4th place in 2006/07
- They finished the season with the best defensive record conceding just 411 points 23 fewer than Cambridge
- Fly half Mark Scrivener top scored with 161 points
- Rob Thirlby was the leading try scorer with an impressive 18, which was joint third in the division and more than doubled his total for the club from 16 to 34
- Winger Lewis Vinnicombe added nine tries to his all time total for the club and now has 66 tries in 122 starts
- No Redruth player started all 26 league matches the best was 24 by three players, Rob Thirlby and forwards, James Mann and Luke Collins
- Only managed two wins in six matches against the other top four sides including losing their last four
- Nathan Pedley and Darren Jacques passed 100 league starts for the club and Paul Thirlby and Damian Cook are just short but if you include appearances as replacements they have passed the 100 mark
- Centre Craig Bonds took his all time Redruth appearance record to 189 (5) with 22 starts and one from the bench
- In the forwards flanker Nathan Pascoe closed to within two of John Navin with 112 starts and both players have come on 24 times as a replacement
- Fly half Mark Scrivener scores a record 26 points in the clubs win over Redruth with 13 conversions, he broke Stephen Larkins record of 23 points in a match and Michael Hook's record on nine conversions. The 13 conversions was also a league record beating the 12 scored by Paul Brett for Liverpool St Helens back in 1997 v Clifton
- In the same match full back Emyr Lewis ran in a new club record five tries beating the old record of four set by No 8 Mark Bright back in March 2007
- Redruth's 96-5 win over Waterloo was also their highest ever score beating the 78 they scored against Bradford & Bingley back in April 2007 and the 14 tries they scored in that match was also a new club record three more than they scored against Weston super mare back in 1998

2008-09 REVIEW

Tynedale
- In their first ever season of National Two rugby Tynedale finished a highly creditable fourth after coming up as National Three North Champions the season before
- Tynedale have finished in the top 10 for at least the last 11 seasons of league rugby
- Rob Miller, in between playing for Newcastle Falcons and England under 20's top scored with 101 points, the lowest points for a season by a Tynedale player since they got into the National Leagues back in the 2000/01 season
- Centre jack Harrison was leading try scorer with 14 tries which was the best ever by a Tynedale player in the National Leagues, beating the record of 13 set by Will Massey three seasons ago, Harrison scored six tries more than the next player on the list, scrumhalf Ross Samson
- Prop Rupert Harden was the only Tynedale player to start all 26 league matches last season whilst Jack Harrison and scrumhalf Ross Samson started 25 and Harrison came on in the match he did not start
- Tynedale saw their 37 match winning run at home come to an end in their last home match of the season against Champions Birmingham Solihull, you have to go back to September 2006 for their last home defeat when beaten 37-18 by local rivals Blaydon
- In matches against the other top four sides they had three wins and three defeats, beating them all once

Cinderford
- Cinderford in their first ever season of National Two rugby finished an impressive fifth with a late surge some 12 points behind the other National two debut boys Tynedale
- Finished the season with five wins and a draw, only Cambridge had a better record over the last six matches of the season
- In matches against the top four they managed just one win to go with seven defeats, the win was at home to Tynedale back in October
- Full back Daniel Trigg was leading scorer for the fourth time in six seasons and the first time in three with 138 points, his lowest total when finishing top points scorer for the club
- Trigg has now scored 914 points for the club in league rugby as he closes in on the 1000 point mark
- Trigg also extended his all time totals for conversions and penalty goals to 186 149 respectively
- In a late season flourish England under 20 star Freddie Burns chipped in with 67 points including 30 points against Westcombe Park
- Paul Knight was the top try scorer with 12, one more than winger Jake Carter
- The most appearances by a Cinderford player was 22 by six players but prop Phil Kennedy also came on in three other matches and make a total of 25 appearances the most by any player
- Last season flanker Chris McNeil scored an impressive 19 tries but this season managed just one in 23 appearances
- Winger James Copsey scored seven tries to equal the all time record for tries the club of 26 set by winger Richard Bazeley

Blackheath
- Blackheath's fifth consecutive season in National Two saw them drop two places on last season's sixth place and their lowest in three seasons
- Managed just eight try bonus points which was the lowest of any side in the top eight
- Matthew Leek top scored for the second season running with 152 points, 42 more than last season
- Centre Steve Hamilton finished as the clubs leading try scorer with nine tries two more than winger Sam Smith
- In eight matches against the top four sides they managed just one win to go with seven defeats, the win was at home to new boys Tynedale
- Blackheath had two players start all 26 leagues matches - both forwards - prop Des Brett and second row Ali Vanner
- Vanner's 26 appearances took his club record for appearances by a forward to 158 but he is still some way behind all time leader Dave Fitzgerald who is on 191
- Before joining London Scottish full back Frankie Neale scored 13 points in four matches to take his club record to 439, six behind all time leader Jon Griffin
- His two conversions saw him extend his club all time record to 89
- Blackheath set a new club record for most points in a match, home or away, when they scored 85 points at Waterloo. They also scored a club record 13 tries in a match, both records which were previously set in the match against Bradford & Bingley in February 2007

228

Launceston

- After finishing bottom of National One last season the Cornish All Blacks finished seventh back in National Two
- In six of their 12 defeats they managed a losing bonus point, a 50% rate, the third best in the league after the top two
- Finished the season poorly with just a win and a draw in their last six matches slumping to four defeats
- In eight matches against the top four sides they actually managed three wins including a win at Cambridge
- The All Blacks had no ever presents and two players on 23 started the most matches during the league campaign, backs Adam Staniforth and Jon Fabian, both also came on in two more matches so taking part in all but one of the clubs matches
- Former Exeter Chiefs fly half Adam Staniforth top scored with 169 points in his debut season at the club
- Marc Dibble was the leading try scorer with 12 tries which is the worst total for four seasons since Nigel Simpson topped the list with nine
- Against the trend Dibble scored 10 of his 12 tries in the first half of matches
- Centre Steven Perry passed 100 league starts for the club and ended the season on 109 plus eight as a replacement
- Launceston set a new club record when they beat Waterloo 103-5 at Polson Bridge in January running in a record 16 tries

Stourbridge

- Stourbridge completed their eighth successive season in National Two achieving eighth place - a drop of five places from last season's third.
- They picked up seven losing bonus points in their 15 defeats, the joint most in the division
- They managed 11 try bonus points which was the joint fifth highest total in the division
- Full back Ali Bressington was the leading scorer for a fourth consecutive season with 250 points, his second best return for the club in a league season behind the 290 he scored in 2006/07
- Ali Bressington was also the clubs leading try scorer with 12 tries but that was some down on his club record of 19 set in the 2006/07 season
- Bressington has now scored 863 points for the club in league rugby in four seasons
- Jon Hall increases his all time try scoring record by five tries to 50 whilst Bressington closes in on him with his 12 tries taking him to 41
- Hooker Ben Gerry was the clubs only ever present during the season and was taken off just the once
- Jon Hall started 12 matches for Stour and in the process passed 200 league starts - just - he finished the season with 201 plus 23 appearances as a replacement
- Bressington's 44 conversions this season took his club career total to 170, passing Ben Harvey's previous record of 166
- Veteran prop Rob Merritt came back during the season and sat on the bench three times late in the campaign but did not get on to add to his 175 appearances for a forward for the club
- Bressington scored 35 points against Westcombe Park back in October to break his own club record of 31 points in a match, he scored three tries, kicked seven conversions and slotted a couple of drop goals
- Those seven conversions equalled the club record held by Duncan Hughes against Whitchurch back in 2000 when they were in National Three North

Wharfedale

- 14th consecutive season in National Two but they slipped out of the top half for the first time in five seasons
- Centre Mark Bedworth top scored with 246 points for the third time in four seasons since joining the club and with his highest ponts return, beating the 241 he scored in 2005/06
- Centre Chris Malherbe was the leading try scorer with 12, one more than Bedworth, to take his career total at the club to 69 in 156 starts
- Centre Andrew Hodgson, the clubs all time leading try scorer reached the magical 100 league try mark during the season
- Adam Whaites was the clubs only ever present and was replaced just once in his 26 league starts
- Two other backs Luke Gray and James Doherty started all but one of the clubs 26 league matches
- In matches against the top four Wharfedale managed two wins, including a win at then table toppers Redruth
- In the last match of the season against Cinderford at Threshfields Bedworth scored a club record 32 points beating the previous record of 29 which was shared by two of the clubs all time leading scorers Adam Mounsey and Jonathan Davies. Bedworth scored three tries kicked four conversions and slotted three penalty goals
- Second row David Lister became the second player at the club to pass 300 league appearances and finished the season with 315 starts and eight matches as a replacement which broke Hedley Verity's club and National League record of 312

2008-09 REVIEW

Blaydon
- Blaydon's second season in National two saw then again finish in 10th place but with two points more 55 but from a win fewer nine compared to 10
- They collected 11 try bonus points which was joint fifth best in the league
- Again failed to find a top line kicker with try scoring sensation Andrew Fenby leading the way with 97 points, including 18 tries and seven points from the boot
- Fenby finished top try scorer for the third consecutive season and forced his way into the Newcastle Falcons side in the Premiership, his 18 tries came from 18 starts. Fenby has now scored 72 tries in 75 starts over four seasons a pretty amazing strike rate
- Former Wharfedale player Andrew Baggett led the way in the kicking stakes with 69 and was one of six players who kicked during the season
- Blaydon did not have an ever present but No 8 Jason Smithson started all but one of their league games and was only replaced twice all season.
- Props James Isaacson and Robert Kalbraier both started 24 out of 26 league matches during the season
- Second row David Guthrie in his final season at the club before retiring breaks the record for most appearances in the league with his 18 starts taking him to 155 and passing the record held by prop Paul Winter of 142
- Nick Gandy extends his club record for National League appearances by a back to 76 which is only one ahead of Andrew Fenby now
- In matches against the top four Blaydon managed a win and a draw to go with six defeats, the draw was at home to Redruth and the win over local rivals Tynedale

Westcombe Park
- Westcombe Park's second season in National Two saw them relegated after a great first season when they finished fifth as they finished some seven points behind Blaydon and safety
- This was Combe's first ever relegation since coming into the National Leagues some 10 years ago
- Although relegated they were 16 points ahead of third bottom Southend
- They finished the season well with five wins in their last eight matches including a season best of fourth consecutive wins
- Gareth Hunter finished as top points scorer with just 72 points whilst last season's leading points scorer James Whittingham finished on 67 points way down on his 187, with 552 points in the three previous seasons he had been a crucial part of their success
- Centre Tyrone Child was the leading try scorer with 10 tries
- No 8 Tom Hayman scored just six tries during the season but it was enough to increase his all time record for tries in the league for the club to 58 tries in just 73 starts, an impressive record for a No 8
- Second row John Chance was the clubs only ever present during the league campaign starting all 26 matches and never being replaced
- In the backs, centre Tyrone Child started most matches, 24 out of 26 and was taken off just twice
- In matches against the other bottom four sides they did well with five wins and just one defeat
- Prop Ben McKinnell passed the 100 league appearances mark with his 16 starts taking him to 105 plus 28 as a replacement

Southend
- After two seasons in National two Southend are relegated back into National Three South
- They managed seven losing bonus points which was the joint most but did lose 21 matches
- Full back/wing Andrew Frost was again the leading points scorer for the club with 161, it is the fourth consecutive season he has finished as leading scorer but his lowest return and the first time he has failed to reach the 200 point mark
- Frost only started 11 matches during the season having only missed one match in the previous three seasons at the club
- In the process Frost passed the 1000 point mark for the club and ended the season at 1036 in four season averaging over 250 a season and came in just 88 starts
- Despite only starting 11 matches Frost also finished as the leading try scorer for the club with eight one more than winger Simon Hoult
- Chris Green switched from centre to back row and chipped in with four tries in 20 starts and took his all time try scoring record to 61

Southend cont.
- Prop Mark Williams took over Phil Bailey's record for most appearances by a forward as he moved onto 85 (plus 10 as a replacement), 10 more than second row Bailey
- Southend did not have an ever present last season with second row Andrew McClintock making the most starts, 23 out of a possible 25 with the Mounts Bay match not played
- Andy Frost broke the club record for most points in a match with 29, which broke his own previous record by two, in the home win over Waterloo in October, with two tries eight conversions and a penalty goal, later in the season he broke the old record again with 28 points against Wharfedale

Mounts Bay
- After six successive promotions Mounts Bay hit the brick wall and were relegated in their first season of rugby in National Two as they endured their first ever losing season since being formed in 1999
- Former Plymouth Albion player Dan Hawkes finished as leading points scorer with 197
- Forwards Steve Dyer, back row, and Ben Hilton, second row, played in all 25 league matches with the match against Southend not being played and Hilton was only taken off once in those 25 starts whilst Dyer went off nine times
- In the try scoring stakes flanker Brett Stroud led the way with just six tries which was still two more than anyone else
- Bay made a dreadful start to the season with eight straight defeats, which was as many defeats as they had suffered in the three previous seasons put together, the win was in the Cornish derby against Launceston who were flying high in the table at the time, one of the shock results of the season
- They then finished the season with nine straight defeats if you include the match against Southend which they forfeited
- In matches against the bottom four they had three wins and three defeats
- They had the worst return in the division for try bonus points managing just three all season

Waterloo
- Waterloo are back in National Three North after a break of five seasons which saw them climb back into National One but they have suffered two relegations in three seasons
- They finished bottom of the table with just four wins and six points adrift, although they did manage six try bonus points which was more than the two sides above them in the table
- In 22 defeats they only managed one losing bonus point
- They scored more points than second bottom Mounts Bay but conceded over 400 points more than the Cornish side
- James O'Brien ended the season as top points and leading try scorer for the club with 85 points and 10 tries, his 10 tries was enough for second place in the Waterloo try scoring list
- Winger Matt Williams finished the season on 11 tries the first Waterloo player for four seasons since Neil Kerfoot scored 18, to get into double figures, when they won promotion to National One. Williams scored just once in the first half of matches and 10 times in the second 40 minutes
- Returning Centre Freeman Payne took his club all time record for tries to 91 with eight during the season after a season away at Sedgley Park
- Winger Neil Kerfoot after one try in his two previous seasons was second top try scorer with nine and now has a career total of 85 league tries playing for both Orrell and Waterloo dating back to the 199/00 season in 160 starts in the league, including 61 for Waterloo and 24 for Orrell
- Payne started 25 of Waterloo's 26 league matches during the season and came on as a replacement in the other one along with fellow centre Jason Duffy

BLACKHEATH FC

**BLACKHEATH
1858 RUGBY**

Founded: 1858
Nickname: Club

Colours:
Black & red hooped shirts, black shorts, black & red socks
Change colours: Black

Website:
www.blackheathrugby.co.uk

KEY PERSONNEL

President	Mike Newson	
Chairman	Barry Nealon	
Treasurer	Chris Davies	
Club Secretary	Barry Shaw	c/o Blackheath FC
	barry.shaw@dsl.pipex.com	
Fixtures Secretary	Jim Collett	
	020 8858 7571 (H) email:jimcollettjm@aol.com	
Director of Operations	Fran Cotton	c/o Blackheath FC
	020 8850 0210 (O) 020 8293 0854 (Fax) 07831 667755(M)	
	francotton@blackheathrugby.co.uk	
Director of Rugby	Yusuf Ibrahim	c/o Blackheath FC
	020 8293 0853 (O)	
	joe.ibrahim@axiseurope.com	
Rugby General Manager	Albert Patrick	c/o Blackheath FC.
	matpatrick@yahoo.com	
Press Liaison	Jack Kay	
	07971 580889 (M)	

GROUND DETAILS

Only the 1st XV play at The Rectory Field.
All other teams, including Juniors and Minis, play at Club @ Well Hall.
1st Ground Address:
The Rectory Field, Charlton Road, Blackheath. SE3 8SR.
Tel: 020 8293 0853   Fax: 020 8293 0854
e-mail: info@blackheathrugby.co.uk
Capacity: 6,000   Seated: 572   Covered: 572
Directions: The entrance to the Rectory Field is in Charlton Road B210, 800m.from the junction of Stratheden Road and Westcombe Hill towards Charlton Village.
Nearest BR Station: Blackheath or Westcombe Park
Nearest Tube Station: North Greenwich - Jubilee Line
Car Parking: 250 spaces available on ground
Admission: Season: £120   Matchday: £12 incl. programme

Office & 2nd Ground Address: Club @ Well Hall, Kidbrooke Lane, Eltham, London SE9 6TE Tel: 020 8850 0210
Directions: The ground is at the junction of the A2 and the South Circular A205. From this junction head North towards Woolwich. Kidbrooke Lane is 100m on the right.
Car Parking: 200
Nearest BR Station: Eltham (5 minutes walk)

Club Shop:
Open matchdays and Sunday morning. Contact Mandy Allen

Both Clubhouses: Normal Licensing hours, Light refreshments available. Hot food available on matchdays.
Functions: Contact club office 020 8850 0210

PROGRAMME

Size: A5   Pages: 36
Price: £2   Editor Peter Brown
Advertising: Contact club office 020 8850 0210

v Barbarian F.C.
Wednesday March 18th 2009
Kick off 8pm
Sesquicentennial Celebration Match
Season 2008-2009

THE OLDEST OPEN RUGBY CLUB FOUNDED **1858**

NATIONAL ONE

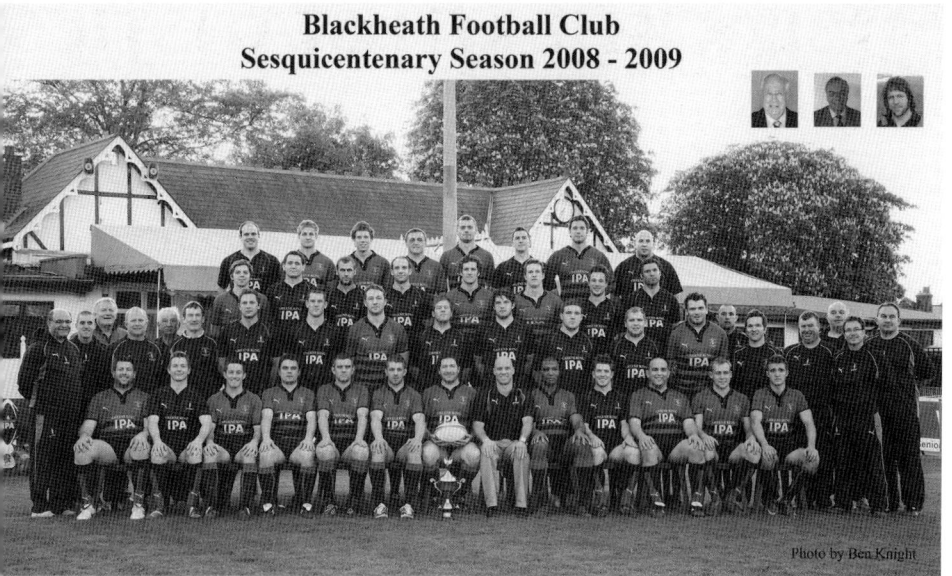

Blackheath Football Club
Sesquicentenary Season 2008 - 2009

Photo by Ben Knight

Back row left: Richard Pike Will Matthews Sam Smith Jack Knight Steve Hamilton Dave Brown Chris York Alastair Lyon
2nd Back: Tom White David Packer Jonny Smith Romain Perret Richard Windsor Sean Moan Lee Amzeleg Tom Lawy
3rd row: Yusuf Ibrahim (1st Squad Manager) Craig Walker (Physio) Albert Patrick (Rugby General Manager) Bobby Howe (Coach)
Paul Curry (Kit Technician) Andy Wolstenholme (Coach) Seb Pilecki Gavin Wallis Neil Dewale Danny Buckland Mark Davey Jimmy Stanford
Billy Sanderson Gareth Jones Alex Natera (Coach) Ben Ashworth (Physio) Iain Dinning (4th Official)
Ron Squires (Coach) Mike Friday (Coach) Steve Pope (Director Youth Development)
Sitting: Nick Winwood Alex Page Matt Vaughan Matt Leek Alastair Vanner Dave Allen Liam Wordley (Captain)
Harvey Biljon (Director of Coaching) Ken Aseme Jonnie Williams Simon Legg James Catt Ben Ibrahim
Inset: Mike Newsom (President) Barry Nealon (Immediate Past President) Desmond Brett

REVIEW OF THE SEASON 2008-09

It was a momentous season for Blackheath who celebrated their 150th anniversary with a series of events both on and off the pitch. The highlight was a superb game against the Barbarians in front of a full house. The Baa Baa's winning 57-45. As for the league itself, the Club finished a very creditable sixth place having started the season with a home win against local rivals Westcombe Park. It was generally accepted that our best opponents were Birmingham/Solihull and although they whipped the Club 58-12 at their place, it was a different story at the Rectory Field were they were relieved to scrape a 35-28 result in a cracking game.

Blackheath's involvement in the EDF Energy trophy lasted just eighty minutes going out at home to Division Three (North) side Kendal, 22-8. Then Blackheath struggled with the weather like the rest of the country, the first game affected was at home to Launceston, the game being abandoned in the second half with the Club leading. Then they lost out to the elements with postponements against Cinderford, Launceston (again) and Waterloo.

The Club picked up a trophy at the end of the season when they lifted the Kent Cup with a 29-8 victory over Gravesend. Blackheath said farewells to coach Harvey Biljon (going to Cornish Pirates). He will be replaced by Mike Friday and Bobby Howe sharing the coaching duties with Yusuf Ibrahim as 1st Squad manager. Also leaving the Club are skipper Liam Wordley, along with back rows, Will Matthews and Ken Aseme. The Rectory Field faithful can look forward to next season with anticipation as the young bloods are now establishing themselves as genuine first team material. Players like Steve Hamilton (leading try scorer) Sam Smith, James Catt, Peter Squires, Ben Ibrahim, Paul Humphries, Tom White and Jack Knight will all make their presence felt.

Jack Kay

BLACKHEATH 1858 RUGBY

233

BLACKHEATH STATISTICS
LEAGUE NATIONAL ONE

TEAM RECORDS

MOST POINTS
Scored at Home: 75 v Bradford & B 17.2.07
Scored Away: 85 v Waterloo 28.2.09
Conceded at Home: 72 v Newcastle 16.4.97
Conceded Away: 103 v Otley 4.12.99

MOST TRIES
Scored in a match: 13 v Waterloo 28.2.09 (A)
Conceded in a match: 16 v Otley 4.12.99 (A)

BIGGEST MARGINS
Home Win: 68pts -75-7 v Bradford & B 17.2.07
Away Win: 61pts - 85-24 v Waterloo 28.2.09
Home Defeat: 62pts - 10-72 v Newcastle 16.4.97
Away Defeat: 100pts - 3-103 v Otley 4.12.99

MOST CONSECUTIVE
Victories: 8 - 30.11.02 to 18.1.03
Defeats: 18 - 30.10.99 to 22.04.00

INDIVIDUAL RECORDS

MOST APPEARANCES
by a forward: Ali Vanner 157
by a back: Dave Fitzgerald 191

MOST CONSECUTIVE
Appearances: 46 Mike Friday 1993-96
Matches scoring Tries: 5
John Clarke & Charles Abban 8.2.03-29.3.03
Matches scoring points: 12
Derek Coates 13.9.03-13.12.03

MATCH RECORDS

Most Points
30 Frankie Neale v Bradford & B (H) 17.02.07

Most Tries
4 John Clarke v Fylde (H) 20.9.97

Most Conversions
10 Frankie Neale v Bradford & B (H) 17.02.07
Matthew Leek v Waterloo (A) 28.2.09

Most Penalties
7 Jon Griffin v Redruth (H) 14.12.02

Most Drop Goals
2 John King on 3 occasions
Chris Braithwaite v Nottingham (H) 22.3.97

SEASON RECORDS

Most Points	368	Derek Coates	03-04
Most Tries	15	Charles Abban	02-03
Most Conversions	62	Derek Coates	03-04
Most Penalties	78	Derek Coates	03-04
Most Drop Goals	8	John King	88-89

CAREER RECORDS

Most Points	445	Jon Griffin	00-03
Most Tries	43	Dave Fitzgerald	94-06
Most Conversions	87	Frankie Neale	05-08
Most Penalties	87	Derek Coates	03-04
Most Drop Goals	16	John King	87-91

LAST TEN SEASONS

	Division	P	W	D	L	F	A	P.D.	Pts	Pos	Most Points	Most Tries
99-00	N1	26	2	1	23	316	1037	-721	5	14r	48 Mitch Hoare	5 Nick Daniel
00-01	N3S	26	10	0	16	562	641	-79	20	9	130 Jon Griffin	13 Charles Abban
01-02	N3S	26	11	3	12	538	476	62	25	7	121 Chris Trace	12 Charles Abban
02-03	N3S	26	17	1	8	606	479	137	35	3	204 Jon Griffin	15 Charles Abban
03-04	N3S	26	22	0	4	839	350	489	44	1p	368 Derek Coates	12 Nick Maurer
04-05	N2	26	11	1	14	496	560	-64	57	9	228 Steve McCashin	6 Chris Trace
05-06	N2	26	10	0	16	503	622	-119	52	9	92 Frankie Neale	7 Paul Sampson / Ken Aseme
06-07	N2	26	16	0	10	687	527	160	77	5	237 Frankie Neale	10 Frankie Neale
07-08	N2	26	15	0	11	596	602	-6	75	4	110 Matthew Leek	9 David Allen / Joe Simpson
08-09	N2	26	14	1	11	691	612	79	71	6	152 Matthew Leek	9 Steve Hamilton

RFU SENIOR CUP

OVERALL PLAYING RECORD

	P	W	D	L	F	A	Pts Diff
Home	25	12	0	13	448	390	58
Away	30	13	0	17	436	686	-250
Neutral	0	0	0	0	0	0	0
TOTAL	55	25	0	30	884	1076	-192

TEAM RECORDS

Highest Score: 40
v Sutton & Epsom 84/85 & Sevenoaks 99/00
Biggest Winning Margin: 34 (40-6) v Sutton & E. 99/00
Highest Score Against: 72 v Harlequins 92/93
Biggest Losing Margin: 69 (3-72) v Harlequins 92/93

SEASON BY SEASON

71-72	2R	78-79	1R	85-86	4R	92-93	3R	99-00	2R
72-73	1R	79-80	DNQ	86-87	2R	93-94	4R	00-01	2R
73-74	DNQ	80-81	2R	87-88	3R	94-95	4R	01-02	2R
74-75	2R	81-82	3R	88-89	3R	95-96	4R	02-03	3R
75-76	DNQ	82-83	4R	89-90	3R	96-97	5R	03-04	2R
76-77	DNQ	83-84	4R	90-91	3R	97-98	4R	04-05	2R
77-78	1R	84-85	4R	91-92	2R	98-99	3R		

NATIONAL TROPHY

05-06	5R	06-07	3R	07-08	5R	08-09	3R

BLACKHEATH PLAYERS

	Position	D.o.B.	Apps.	Pts.	T	C	P	DG
Sam Smith	Winger		16	35	7	-	-	-
Mark Odejobi	Winger		10	15	3	-	-	-
Johnny Williams	Winger		10 (3)	10	2	-	-	-
Martin Olima	Winger		29 (6)	35	7	-	-	-
Matt Leek	Fly half		46 (2)	262	4	58	42	-
Sean Moan	Centre		29 (8)	30	6	-	-	-
Richard Windsor	Centre		9 (1)	10	2	-	-	-
Steve Hamnilton	Centre		15 (5)	45	9	-	-	-
Tom White	Centre		9 (3)	74	5	17	5	-
Frankie Neale	Outside half		51 (3)	439	12	89	66	1
Matt Vaughan	Fly Half		42 (27)	169	13	19	20	2
James Honeyben	Scrum Half		14 (1)	30	6	-	-	-
Ben Ibrahim	Scrum Half		16 (4)	25	5	-	-	-
Alex Page	Scrum half/wing		14 (1)	20	4	-	-	-
Simon Legg	Prop		87 (31)	5	1	-	-	-
Des Brett	Prop		125 (15)	45	9	-	-	-
Alistair Lyons	Prop		1 (10)	12	2	1	-	-
Tom Lindsay	Hooker		3 (5)	-	-	-	-	-
Liam Wordley	Hooker		24 (1)	30	6	-	-	-
Thomas Bason	Lock		91 (2)	85	17	-	-	-
Dave Allen	Back row		95 (7)	90	18	-	-	-
Ali Vanner	Lock		158 (4)	20	4	-	-	-
Kem Aseme	Back row		107 (19)	95	19	-	-	-
Neil Dewale	Back row		68 (20)	25	5	-	-	-
Gareth Jones	Back row		17 (5)	15	3	-	-	-

NATIONAL ONE

235

BLAYDON RFC

KEY PERSONNEL

President: R Hedley Redpath Te: 0191 267 3805
Chairman of Executive: Bruce Costello Tel: 07891 15498
Treasurer: Peter W Stokoe ACA Tel: 0191 413 1979
Club Secretary & 1st XV Manager, Press & Media & League Contact: James M Huxley
Tel/Fax: 0191 488 7280, 07884 358060 (M) email: jimhux@btopenworld.com
Director of Rugby: Nick Gandy Tel: 07737 378240
Chairman of Rugby: Jim Knight Tel: 0191 4887670
email : jim.knight@kdi-systems.com
House Manageress: Sharon Reed Tel: 0191 420 0505 (club) 07748 605549 (M)
Sportique (Gymnasium) Manager: David Silver Tel: 0191 4200508
Programme/Sponsorship: Jim Huxley, Sharon Reed, Mark Nordmann & Tom Rock

Founded: 1888
Nickname: Crows
Colours: Red with white trim & blue piping, blue shorts, red, white & blue socks.
Change shirts: White with blue piping
Training Nights: Tuesday & Thursday (seniors)
Website: www.blaydonrfc.co.uk

NATIONAL ONE

CONTACT DETAILS

c/o Blaydon RFC, Crow Trees Ground,
Hexham Road, Swalwell, Newcastle upon Tyne NE16 3BM
Tel: 0191 420 0505 (club), 0191 420 0506 (office)   Fax: 0191 420 0506
email brfcdevelopment@hotmail.com

PROGRAMME

Size: A5   Pages: 36
Price: with admission
Editors: Jim Huxley/Tom Rock
Advertising: Contact Editors

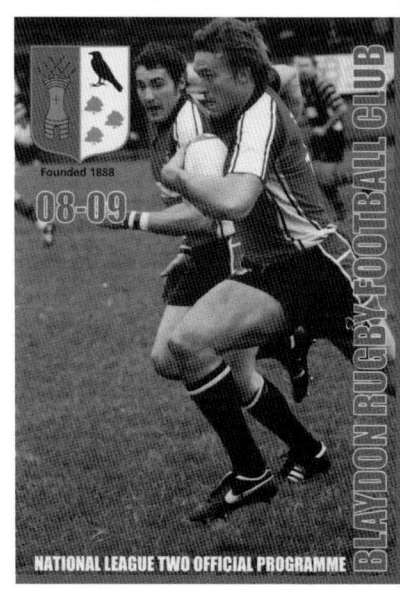

GROUND DETAILS

Address:
Crow Trees Ground, Hexham Road, Swalwell,
Newcastle upon Tyne NE16 3BN
Tel: 0191 420 0505 (club), 0191 420 0506 (office),
0191 420 0508 (gymnasium)
email: brfcdevelopment@hotmail.com

Capacity: 5,000
Covered seating: 400

Directions
Take A1 north past Gateshead Metro Centre, then take the next exit for Swalwell (B6316). Over mini roundabout, through the village to the lights and the ground is straight ahead.

Car Parking: 1,000 spaces
Nearest BR station: Newcastle upon Tyne
Admission:
Matchday: £8 incl. programme   Season Tickets £75

Clubhouse
Open 7pm - 11pm Monday - Friday, All day Saturday & Sunday.
Food available on request.
3 function suites available for private hire. Contact Sharon Reed

Club Shop: Open as clubhouse, contact David Silver.

236

REVIEW OF THE SEASON 2008-09

Having had a successful pre-season programme, the season began under the guidance of the same personnel as in the previous campaign and following an emphatic victory on day one at Waterloo, our sights were set for at least a top six finish.

A good result against neighbours Tynedale, followed by away defeats at Redruth and Birmingham Solihull, was interspersed with easy victories at home over Stourbridge and Mounts Bay, setting the pattern for the season with Blaydon always struggling on their travels.

However, a good result over one of the early season promotion candidates Launceston 18 – 16 with two excellent tries by Brendon Daniel gave us a lift, and despite losing at Blackheath when their pack decimated us, gaining one of their many penalty tries, we comfortably beat Westcombe Park at home, Southend away, and had a heroic match against Nottingham in the National Cup when we led 23 – 19 until the closing stages courtesy of, in the words of Glen Delaney 'the best ever try seen at Meadow Lane' when Andrew Fenby produced an amazing score from well within his own 22 finally handing off the home full-back to streak over, Charlie Rayner adding the way out conversion. A yellow card changed the game and two tries in the final five minutes saw Nottingham through.

Andrew Fenby was the top try scorer for a third successive season and made his Premiership debut for Newcastle Falcons

The cup tie was our peak and when the bad weather arrived and the injury list lengthened, our squad was too small and after losing the return game at Tynedale – this with 85% possession – we lost six games out of seven with only a home draw against Redruth to show, slipping rapidly down the table. Only a succession of bonus points kept us out of the bottom four.

On the plus side, we were still playing attractive rugby with wingers Andrew Fenby (averaging a try per game) Brendon Daniel – eleven tries and prop Robbie Kalbraier with eight – our leading scorers. Goal kicking was always a problem.

In the end, other results went our way and with one game to go, we were free of relegation worries after the demolition of Waterloo.

This coming season is all change with the departure of Director of Rugby Nick Gandy to pastures new, the retirement of long serving Captain Dave Guthrie, and several other members of the squad.

Tom Rock formerly of Leeds Carnegie/London Welsh, commences as Director of Rugby at Crow Trees and several new names have been added to the squad. Blaydon look forward with enthusiasm to what promises to be a highly competitive season with the newly promoted London Scottish and Nuneaton together with relegated sides Esher, Newbury, Otley and Manchester undoubtedly adding to the strength of the league.

JIM HUXLEY

BLAYDON STATISTICS

LEAGUE

TEAM RECORDS

MOST POINTS
Scored at Home: 124 v Orrell 24.3.07
Scored Away: 57 v Cleckheaton 31.3.07
Conceded at Home: 48 v Tynedale 22.3.03
Conceded Away: 64 v Manchester 8.3.08

MOST TRIES
Scored in a match: 18 v Orrell 24.3.07 (H)
Conceded in a match: 10 v Manchester 8.3.08

BIGGEST MARGINS
Home Win: 124 (124-0) v Orrell 24.3.07
Away Win: 52 pts (57-5) v Cleckheaton 31.3.07
Home Defeat: 33 pts (48-15) v Tynedale 22.3.07
Away Defeat: 54 pts (64-10) v Manchester 8.3.08

MOST CONSECUTIVE
Victories: 9 on two ocassions
Defeats: 6 (9.10.04 - 27.11.04)

INDIVIDUAL RECORDS

MOST APPEARANCES
by a forward: Paul Winter 142 (19)
by a back: 71 Nick Gandy (11)

MATCH RECORDS

Most Points
    34   Anthony Mellalieu v Orrell 24.3.07 (H)
Most Tries
    5   Peter Altona v Orrell 24.3.07 (H)
         Andrew Fenby v Orrell 24.3.07 (H)
Most Conversions
    17   Anthony Mellalieu v Orrell 24.3.07 (H)
Most Penalties
    6   James Lofthouse v New Brighton 6.10.01 (H)
Most Drop Goals
    1   Lee Hogarth v Halifax 15.3.03 (A)
         David Dalrymple v Halifax 1.11.03 (H)
         Richard Windle v Tynedale 9.9.06 (A)
         Jason Smithson v Southend 19.04.08 (H)

SEASON RECORDS

Most Points	190	James Lofthouse	01-02
Most Tries	25	Andrew Fenby	06-07
Most Conversions	40	Dan Clappison	05-06
Most Penalties	36	James Lofthouse	01-02
Most Drop Goals	1	Lee Hogarth	02-03
		David Dalrymple	03-04
		Richard Windle	06-07
		Jason Smithson	07-08

CAREER RECORDS

Most Points	381	Dan Clappison	03-07
Most Tries	72	Andrew Fenby	05-09
Most Conversions	77	Dan Clappison	03-07
Most Penalties	54	Dan Clappison	03-07
Most Drop Goals	1	Lee Hogarth	01-05
		David Dalrymple	01-04
		Richard Windle	03-07
		Jason Smithson	07-08

LAST TEN SEASONS

	Division	P	W	D	L	F	A	P.D.	Pts	Pos	Most Points		Most Tries	
99-00	North 1	22	10	1	11	402	457	-55	21	6				
00-01	North 1	21	19	0	2	588	306	282	40	2p	189	Ryan Roberts	23	Gareth King
01-02	N3N	26	13	0	13	625	494	131	26	7	190	James Lofthouse	15	Andrew Foreman
02-03	N3N	26	12	0	14	568	645	-77	24	8	70	Tom McLaren	14	Tom McLaren
03-04	N3N	26	14	1	11	587	434	153	29	4	166	David Dalrymple	10	Peti Keni
04-05	N3N	25	11	0	14	439	508	-69	53	10	148	Dan Clappison	9	Simon Barber
05-06	N3N	26	20	0	6	789	386	403	95	3	158	Dan Clappison	12	Iosua Segi
06-07	N3N	26	21	0	5	849	448	401	101	1p	118	Richard Windle	25	Andrew Fenby
07-08	N2	26	10	0	16	528	676	-148	53	10	93	Andrew Fenby	18	Andrew Fenby
08-09	N2	26	9	1	16	599	609	-10	55	10	97	Andrew Fenby	18	Andrew Fenby

RFU SENIOR CUP

OVERALL PLAYING RECORD

	P	W	D	L	F	A	Pts Diff
Home	5	3	0	2	106	94	12
Away	7	3	0	4	90	127	-37
Neutral	-	-	-	-	-	-	-
TOTAL	12	6	0	6	196	221	-25

TEAM RECORDS

Highest Score: 39 v Blackburn 04/05
Biggest Winning Margin: 39 pts - 39-0 v Blackburn 04/05
Highest Score Against: 36
v Bedford Athletic 02/03, v Orrell 04/05
Biggest Losing Margin: 36 Pts - 0-36 v Orrell 04/05

SEASON BY SEASON

71-72	DNQ	78-79	DNQ	85-86	DNQ	92-93	DNQ	99-00	2R
72-73	DNQ	79-80	DNQ	86-87	DNQ	93-94	DNQ	00-01	DNQ
73-74	DNQ	80-81	DNQ	87-88	DNQ	94-95	DNQ	01-02	2R
74-75	DNQ	81-82	DNQ	88-89	DNQ	95-96	DNQ	02-03	1R
75-76	DNQ	82-83	DNQ	89-90	DNQ	96-97	2R	03-04	2R
76-77	DNQ	83-84	DNQ	90-91	DNQ	97-98	DNQ	04-05	3R
77-78	DNQ	84-85	DNQ	91-92	DNQ	98-99	DNQ		

NATIONAL TROPHY

05-06	6R	06-07	3R	07-08	5R	08-09	4R

BLAYDON PLAYERS

	Position	D.o.B.	Apps.	Pts.	T	C	P	DG
Charlie Rayner	Full Back		14 (2)	38	2	8	4	-
Andrew Fenby	Winger		75	367	72	2	1	-
Brendon Daniel	Winger		21 (1)	55	11	-	-	-
Adam Dehatty	Centre		26 (1)	40	8	-	-	-
Nick Gandy	Centre		76 (12)	113	21	4	-	-
Martin Shaw	Centre		89 (2)	120	24	-	-	-
Simon Barber	Centre		68 (7)	115	23	-	-	-
Chris Clark	Winger		10 (8)	10	2	-	-	-
Richard Windle	Fly half		48 (14)	357	12	75	47	2
Rory Clegg	Fly half		4	43	-	14	5	-
Ben Mercer	Centre		27 (1)	40	8	-	-	-
James Clark	Scrum Half		3 (6)	5	1	-	-	-
James Isaacson	Prop		44	30	6	-	-	-
Selwyn St Bernard	Prop/Flanker		34 (19)	20	4	-	-	-
Robert Kalbraier	Prop		24	45	9	-	-	-
Andrew Harrison	Prop		16 (16)	-	-	-	-	-
Matthew Hall	Hooker		122 (11)	94	18	2	-	-
Ross Batty	Hooker		5 (6)	15	3	-	-	-
David Guthrie	Lock		155 (1)	65	13	-	-	-
Dave Whihehead	Lock		27 (6)	-	-	-	-	-
Chris Wearmouth	Lock		59 (3)	55	11	-	-	-
Jason Smithson	Back row		46 (1)	78	15	-	-	1
Will Welch	Back row		13 (2)	5	1	-	-	-
Duncan Brown	Back row		17 (6)	10	2	-	-	-
Scott Riddell	Back row		16	15	3	-	-	-

NATIONAL ONE

CAMBRIDGE RUFC

NATIONAL ONE

Founded: 1923
Colours:
Blood and sand
Change colours:
Black
Training Nights:
see website
Website:
www.crufc.co.uk

KEY PERSONNEL

CRUFC Executive
President:	Jerry Otter	01480 466880
		email: jerry@gunite.co.uk
Chairman:	Ian Wilson	07885 672492
		email: wilsonatlinton@aol.com
Treasurer:	Steve Bowller	07956 491286
		email: sbowller@yahoo.co.uk
Secretary:	Joe Lyons	07966 048611
		email: joelyons50@aol.com

Playing Group:
Director of Rugby:	James Shanahan	07738 586489
		email: shanners10@hotmail.com
Forwards Coach:	Bob Crooks	07771 627713
Fixture Secretary:	Keith Davis	07792 982804
		email: krdavis@btinternet.com
NCA/RFU contact & National Squad Administration:	Mal Schofield	07505359554
		email: pamal.schofield@live.co.uk
Match Day Organisation and 4th Official:	Kenny Isbister	07770 682546

Commercial Group:
Commercial Director:	Jeremy Grundy	07889 965065
		email: jeremy@jeremygrundy.com
Commercial Manager:	Phil Harvey	01638 667615
		email: philipharvey@tiscali.co.uk
Conference Centre:	Steve Wilson	08450 200350
		email: steve@hotelres.co.uk

GROUND DETAILS

Address:
Wests Renault Park, Grantchester Road, Cambridge CB3 9ED
Tel/Fax: 01223 312437   email: info@crufc.co.uk
Capacity: 2500   Covered: 500   Seated: 250
Directions:
Leave the M11 at junction 12, turn to go east towards Cambridge on the A603.
Turn first right into Grantchester Road after 1 mile.
Ground entrance 300 yards after the turn and on the right
Nearest BR Station: Cambridge, 1 mile.
Car Parking: 500
Admission: Matchday £12 (£10 members)
Club Shop: Open on match days 1.30-6pm, and Sundays 10.30-12.30pm for mini and youth rugby
Clubhouse: We have fully equipped new conference facilities and presentation rooms.
Catering facilities, formal meal, for up to 250.
Contact Steve Wilson 0845 0200 350
steve@hotelres.co.uk or events@crufc.co.uk

PROGRAMME

Size: A5   Pages: 24, incl. 8 pages editorial.
Price: with admission

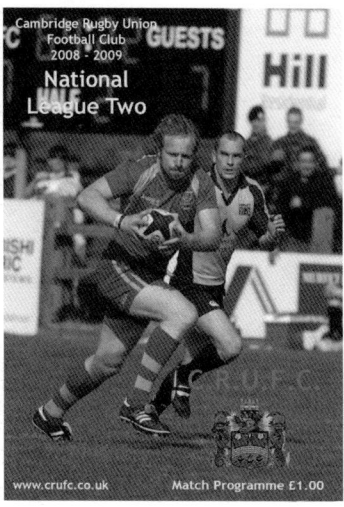

REVIEW OF THE SEASON 2008-09

Firstly ambitions were for some at CRUFC, to aim for promotion. For others it was to continue a further 3 rungs up the league ladder. Ninth to sixth to third. Task certainly more than accomplished closing down on Bees and taking the runners up spot, not through luck or good fortune, but by thorough preparation over the season. Not only did we raise the calibre of the squad, adding both experience and numbers, but more than doubled the coaching capacity, balancing on-field management with off-field direction. Bob Crooks as our second full time coach, added attention to detail at a microscopic level that made even me feel superficial. Whatever your standards, both James Shanahan and Bob set good examples for us all. There will always be tensions in competitive league sport over a testing season. It is how you deal with them that marks out the best from the rest.

Matt Miles and Karl Rudski were not yet available and injuries to other key players made us light on experience in the early games.

The Bees hit us hard after Stourbridge had run us close. Easier games followed but we were winning away from home against sides that deserved respect. The wheels most certainly came off at Waterloo. The warnings were there as we scraped home two weeks earlier, with luck well on our side, at Cinderford. Tynedale, and their the spongy pitch most certainly favoured the Miller/Smales/Harrison combo and gave us a second lesson, after the Bees 20 minute blitz, in joined up flowing rugby. November became the low point with just 1 win in 4 matches, CAB doing the ultimate damage to our promotion hopes with a try in extra time. Then came Redruth away. Dogged defence kept Redruth out of that infamous corner in the first half. That we then penetrated their defence with two kicks from our own half was nothing short of tales of the unexpected. Ben Paxton's penalty and Craig Evans' dropkick stunned the Redruth supporters. A win by a single point and so began our unbroken run of 15 league games.

Then the Waterloo win by 91-0 and invincibility grabbing hold.

The rest is now history but to win our last 4 matches away from home was in itself worthy of celebration, irrespective of our league position.

One final word of credit for Stefan Liebenberg consistently superb at 9. He missed the last two games and a chance for his able alternate "Deputy Dan Hunter" to demonstrate equal talent. To end with a flourish we gave Bees a master class in so many ways. They leave for the uncharted waters of the Championship and CRUFC look forward to the more exciting and predictable prospect of the 16 team National League 1.

CAMBRIDGE STATISTICS

LEAGUE

Records relate to National league rugby only.

TEAM RECORDS

MOST POINTS
Scored at Home: 107 v Harrogate 28.04.07
Scored Away: 57
v Old Patesians 10.12.05 & v Bradford & B 3.3.07
Conceded at Home: 47 v Otley 12.04.08
Conceded Away: 46 v Havant 8.10.05

MOST TRIES
Scored in a match: 17 v Harrogate 28.4.07
Conceded in a match: 8 v Havant 8.10.05

BIGGEST MARGINS
Home Win: 102pts - 107-5 v Harrogate 28.04.07
Away Win: 45pts - 57-12 v Old Patesians 10.12.05
Home Defeat: 25pts - 22-47 v Otley 12.4.08
Away Defeat: 32pts - 6-38 v Launceston 21.4..07

MOST CONSECUTIVE
Victories: 15 (29.11.08 - 2.05.09)
Defeats: 5 (4.11.06 - 16.12.06)

INDIVIDUAL RECORDS

MOST APPEARANCES
by a forward: 64 Glen Remnant
by a back: 100(2) Christoff Lombaard

MOST CONSECUTIVE
Appearances: 51 Christoff Lombaard
Matches scoring Tries: 6 James Shanahan 7.1.06 - 18.2.06
Matches scoring points: 16 Dafydd Lewis 3.9.05 - 28.1.06

MATCH RECORDS

Most Points
26 Craig Evans   v Waterloo (H) 21.2.09
    Ben Patston   v Mounts Bay (H) 4.10.08

Most Tries
5   Christoff Lombaard v Harrogate (H) 28.04.07

Most Conversions
11 Dafydd Lewis   v Harrogate (H) 28.04.07

Most Penalties
4   Dafydd Lewis   v Reading(H) 3.9.05

Most Drop Goals
1   Dafyyd Lewis   v Dings (A) 10.9.06
    Phil Read   v Nuneaton 16.9.06 (A)

SEASON RECORDS

Most Points	213	Dafydd Lewis	05-06
Most Tries	24	Luke Fielden	08-09
Most Conversions	57	Dafydd Lewis	05-06
Most Penalties	22	Dafydd Lewis	05-06
		Gareth Cull	07-08
Most Drop Goals	1	Dafydd Lewis	05-06
	1	Phil Read	06-07

CAREER RECORDS

Most Points	405	Christoff Lombard	05-09
Most Tries	81	Christoff Lombard	05-09
Most Conversions	101	Dafyyd Lewis	05-07
Most Penalties	43	Dafydd Lewis	05-07
Most Drop Goals	1	Dafydd Lewis	05-06
		Phil Reed	06-07

LAST TEN SEASONS

	Division	P	W	D	L	F	A	P.D.	Pts	Pos	Most Points		Most Tries	
99-00	L1	15	10	1	4	376	245	131	21	4				
00-01	L1	20	6	2	12	329	437	-108	14	8				
01-02	L1	22	5	1	16	229	490	-261	7(-4)	12r				
02-03	L2N	22	13	0	9	392	292	100	26	4				
03-04	L2N	22	17	0	5	710	259	451	34	2p*	*Most Points*		*Most Tries*	
04-05	L1	22	19	0	3	874	397	477	38	1p	154	*Thomas Dann*	21	*Mike Campbell*
05-06	N3S	26	23	0	3	865	381	484	106	1p	213	Dafydd Lewis	22	Christoff Lombaard
06-07	N2	26	12	0	14	639	607	32	61	9	161	Dafydd Lewis	21	Christoff Lombaard
07-08	N2	26	14	0	12	619	569	50	69	6	142	Gareth Cull	21	Christoff Lombaard
08-09	N2	26	22	0	4	908	434	474	108	2	183	Ben Patston	24	Luke Fielden

RFU SENIOR CUP

OVERALL PLAYING RECORD

	P	W	D	L	F	A	Pts Diff
Home	2	1	-	1	29	42	-13
Away	7	2	-	5	89	235	-146
Neutral	-	-	-	-	-	-	-
Total	9	3	-	6	118	277	-159

TEAM RECORDS

Highest Score: 23 v Reading 03/04
Biggest Winning Margin: 15 (21-6) v Westcombe Park 93/94
Highest Score Against: 85 v Esher 03/04
Biggest Losing Margin: 85 (85-0) v Esher 03/04

SEASON BY SEASON

71-72	DNQ	78-79	DNQ	85-86	DNQ	92-93	DNQ	99-00	DNQ
72-73	DNQ	79-80	DNQ	86-87	DNQ	93-94	3R	00-01	DNQ
73-74	DNQ	80-81	DNQ	87-88	DNQ	94-95	DNQ	01-02	DNQ
74-75	DNQ	81-82	DNQ	88-89	DNQ	95-96	DNQ	02-03	DNQ
75-76	DNQ	82-83	DNQ	89-90	DNQ	96-97	DNQ	03-04	2R
76-77	DNQ	83-84	DNQ	90-91	DNQ	97-98	1R	04-05	1R
77-78	DNQ	84-85	DNQ	91-92	DNQ	98-99	1R		

NATIONAL TROPHY

05-06	3R	06-07	5R	07-08	4R	08-09	5R

NATIONAL ONE

PLAYERS

	Position	Apps.	Pts.	T	C	P	DG
	Full back	25(3)	55	11	-	-	-
Luke Fielden	Full back	52(1)	224	37	12	5	-
Paul Kendal	Winger	27 (4)	65	13	-	-	-
James Hinkins	Winger	16 (2)	20	4	-	-	-
Craig Evans	Centre/Fly half	25 (1)	150	7	41	10	1
Christoff Lombaard	Wing/centre	100(2)	405	81	-	-	-
James Shanahan	Centre	95	192	37	2	1	-
Ben Patston	Fly half	14 (9)	183	4	53	19	-
Adam Barnard	Centre	30	30	6	-	-	-
Simon Lincoln	Winger	8 (2)	-	-	-	-	-
Johannes Schmidt	Winger	5 (2)	10	2	-	-	-
Steffan Liebenberg	Scrum half	41 (3)	75	15	-	-	-
Tom Laws	Prop	36 (10)	10	2	-	-	-
Matt Miles	Hooker	11 (2)	15	3	-	-	-
Mike Guess	Prop	19	20	4	-	-	-
James Ross	Prop	61 (28)	35	76	-	-	-
Callum Powell	Hooker	8 (2)	-	-	-	-	-
Peter Kolakowski	Lock	25 (7)	-	-	-	-	-
Robbie Hurrell	Lock	14 (3)	10	2	-	-	-
Karl Rudzki	Lock	12	-	-	-	-	-
Daniel Legge	Back row	23	30	6	-	-	-
David Archer	Back row	20 (4)	40	8	-	-	-
Lawrence White	Back row	8 (4)	-	-	-	-	-
Darren Fox	Back row	25	35	7	-	-	-
Tom Powell	Back row	29 (4)	65	13	-	-	-
Matthew Otter	Back row	26 (43)	-	-	-	-	-

243

CINDERFORD RFC

Founded: 1886

Training Nights:
Tuesday & Thursday

Colours:
Red, black & amber hoops

Change colours:
Mainly blue

Website: www.cinderfordrfc.com

NATIONAL ONE

KEY PERSONNEL

President	Peter Bell
Chairman	Rob Worgan Tel: 07929 468103 (M)
Treasurer	Barry Holmes Tel: 07831 303244 (M)
Club Secretary	John Wood Splinters II Buckshaft Road, Cinderford, Glos. Tel: 01594 823566 email: cinderfordrfc@hotmail.com
Fixture Secretary & Team Sec.	Rob Worgan. Parkland, Stockwell Green, Cinderford Glos.GL14 2EH Tel: 01594 826129 (H) 07929 468103 (M) email: cinderfordrfc@hotmail.com
Director of Rugby	Pete Glanville Tel: 07774 997399
Commercial Manager	Matt J Bayliss Tel: 07971 737578 (M)
Press Officer	Nigel Wilce 52 Mount Pleasant Rd., Cinderford, Glos. GL14 3BX Tel: 07905 689675
Coaches	Mark Cornwell and Phil Greenaway

GROUND DETAILS

Address:
The Recreation Ground, Dockham Rd., Cinderford, Glos. GL14 2AQ

Clubhouse: 01594 822673
Office & Fax: 01594 822400
email: cinderfordrfc@hotmail.com

Capacity: 2500   **Covered Seating**: 400

Directions:
From Gloucester take the A48 or A40 westbound and follow the signs for Cinderford. In town centre, at mini roundabout outside Swan Hotel, turn into Dockham Road. Ground is 100 yards on left just past Co-Op County Store.

Nearest BR Station: Gloucester (14 miles)

Car Parking: 200 spaces at the ground

Admission: Matchday: Full £10, Concessions £6, Junior £1
Season tickets not available.

Clubhouse: Opening hours are Weekdays 7pm-11pm, Weekends 12 noon-11pm. Food available on matchdays. Three bars, Functions cater for 200 standing, 130 seated. Functions such as wedding receptions, christening and birthday parties etc. are regularly catered for in our main function room or in 'Beavis Lounge'. Contact Sue Roberts on 01594 822673 (evenings) for further information.

Club Shop: Open matchdays, contact Sue Roberts as above.

PROGRAMME

Size: A5   Pages: 30
Price: £1
Editorial & Advertising: Matt Bayliss
Tel: 01452 501157 or 07971737578
e-mail mattbayliss1@btinternet.com

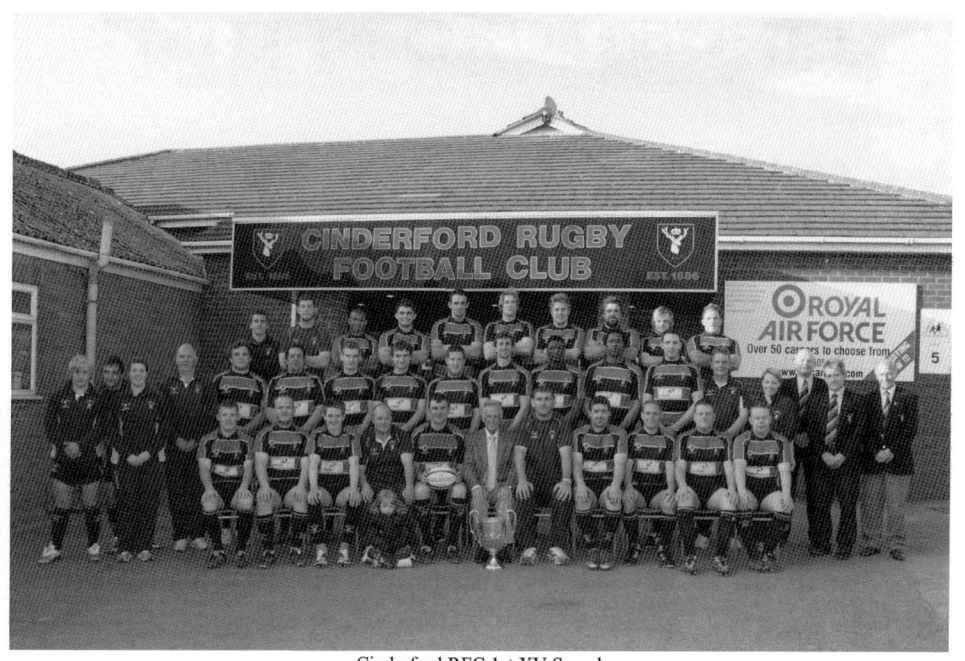

Cinderford RFC 1st XV Squad
Photo: Paul Smith, Dean Forest studios

REVIEW OF THE SEASON 2008-09

Cinderford exceeded all expectations to finish fifth in National Two at their first attempt. The Foresters won nineteen of thirty matches despite suffering a mid season hiatus of seven weeks inaction because of bad weather and the rescheduled EDF National Trophy matches of league opponents.

The season began with a narrow win against visitors Wharfedale and a narrower loss at Launceston. Heavier losses at Redruth and Birmingham were countered by good wins against Tynedale and Stourbridge. Cinderford won seven of their first twelve matches before the elements and the vagaries of cup rugby saw them left without a game from 29th November until the 17th of January.

A rusty team struggled to win a cup game against Hull Ionians and the following Saturday won by the odd point at Southend. Nevertheless the team grew in confidence as the days lengthened and finished strongly by winning eight of their last eleven league matches and also picked up the Gloucestershire County Cup along the way.

It is difficult to pick out stars amongst a squad where so many players, including those who stepped up from the very successful United/Development XV, grew in stature as the season progressed and no less than seven squad members represented Gloucestershire on the road to Twickenham. Youngsters Freddie Burns and Jaike Carter hit hot streaks as the season wound down but it was Cornishman and blind-side flanker Adam Nicholls who scooped both the 'Bob Beavis Cup' for players 'player of the year' and the Cinderford RFC Supporters Club Shield. Prop Phil Kennedy lifted the 'Carpenter Cup' for the front-row forward of the year

Danny Trigg was once again top scorer with 169 points in league and cup. Paul Knight was top try scorer with 14 closely followed by Carter with 13 and Dave Knight with 12.

CINDERFORD STATISTICS

LEAGUE

NATIONAL ONE

TEAM RECORDS

MOST POINTS
Scored at Home: 115 v Truro 6.3.04
Scored Away: 83 v Gloucester OB 9.4.05
Conceded at Home: 47 v Southend 29.10.05
Conceded Away: 85 v North Walsham 6.10.01

MOST TRIES
Scored in a match: 18 v Truro 6.3.04
Conceded in a match: 14 v North Walsham 6.10.01

BIGGEST MARGINS
Home Win: 115pts (115-0) v Truro 6.3.04
Away Win: 73pts (83-10) v Gloucester OB 9.4.05
Home Defeat: 42pts (0-42) v Westcombe Park 25.2.06
Away Defeat: 80pts (5-95) v North Walsham 6.10.01

MOST CONSECUTIVE
Victories: 15 - 03/04 through 04/05
Defeats: 5 twice

INDIVIDUAL RECORDS

MOST APPEARANCES
by a forward: 105 (9) Rob James
by a back: 112 (1) Michael Hart

MATCH RECORDS

Most Points
36 Jon Paul Goatley v Keynsham 15.3.03

Most Tries
5 Ronnie Patea v Gloucester O.B. 9.4.05

Most Conversions
11 Daniel Trigg v Truro 6.3.04

Most Penalties
5 by numerous players

Most Drop Goals
1 by seven players
   most Tristan Roberts (6)

SEASON RECORDS

Most Points	295	Daniel Trigg	04-05
Most Tries	19	Chris McNeil	07-08
Most Conversions	63	Daniel Trigg	04-05
Most Penalties	43	Daniel Trigg	04-05
Most Drop Goals	4	Tristan Roberts	06-07

CAREER RECORDS

Most Points	914	Daniel Trigg	03-09
Most Tries	26	Richard Bazeley	01-06
Most Conversions	186	Daniel Trigg	03-09
Most Penalties	149	Daniel Trigg	03-09
Most Drop Goals	6	Tristan Roberts	06-08

LAST TEN SEASONS

	Division	P	W	D	L	F	A	P.D.	Pts	Pos	Most Points		Most Tries	
99-00	SW1	22	15	0	7	685	348	337	30	3				
00-01	SW1	22	21	0	1	576	225	351	42	2p				
01-02	N3 S	26	6	0	20	390	649	-259	12	14r	125	Mark Roberts	7	Oliver Lamb
02-03	SW1	22	16	0	6	549	313	236	32	3				
03-04	SW1	22	17	0	5	616	367	249	34	2	181	Daniel Trigg		
04-05	SW1	22	20	0	2	811	264	547	40	1p	295	Daniel Trigg	21	Ronnie Patea
05-06	N3 S	26	11	0	15	508	743	-235	53	10	210	Daniel Trigg	7	Nigel Matthews
06-07	N3 S	26	12	0	14	520	513	7	58	8	105	Tristan Roberts	7	L Stapleton
07-08	N3 S	26	20	2	4	719	305	414	95	2p/po	187	Tristan Roberts	19	Chris McNeil
08-09	N2	26	16	0	10	728	598	130	77	5	138	Daniel Trigg	12	Paul Knight

RFU SENIOR CUP

OVERALL PLAYING RECORD

	P	W	D	L	F	A	Pts Diff
Home	2	1	-	1	48	41	7
Away	1	-	-	1	12	80	-68
Neutral	-	-	-	-	-	-	-
Total	3	1	-	2	60	121	-61

TEAM RECORDS

Highest Score: 27 v Norwich 99/00
Biggest Winning Margin: 9 (27-18) v Norwich 99/00
Highest Score Against: 80 v Penzance & Newlyn 01/02
Biggest Losing Margin: 68 (80-12) v Penzance & N 01/02

SEASON BY SEASON

71-72	DNQ	78-79	DNQ	85-86	DNQ	92-93	DNQ	99-00	2R
72-73	DNQ	79-80	DNQ	86-87	DNQ	93-94	DNQ	00-01	DNQ
73-74	DNQ	80-81	DNQ	87-88	DNQ	94-95	DNQ	01-02	IR
74-75	DNQ	81-82	DNQ	88-89	DNQ	95-96	DNQ	02-03	DNQ
75-76	DNQ	82-83	DNQ	89-90	DNQ	96-97	DNQ	03-04	DNQ
76-77	DNQ	83-84	DNQ	90-91	DNQ	97-98	DNQ	04-05	DNQ
77-78	DNQ	84-85	DNQ	91-92	DNQ	98-99	DNQ		

NATIONAL TROPHY

05-06	4R	06-07	1R	07-08	1R	08-09	5R

PLAYERS

	Position	D.o.B.	Apps.	Pts.	T	C	P	DG
Michael Hart	Winger		112	179	25	6	14	-
James Copsey	Winger		60 (3)	130	26	-	-	-
Jake Carter	Winger		14(1)	55	11	-	-	-
Andy Macrea	Winger		17	10	2	-	-	-
Dave Knight	Centre		22	50	10	-	-	-
Daniel Trigg	Full Back/Winger		109 (11)	814	19	186	149	-
Toby Wilson	Centre		52 (13)	50	10	-	-	-
Dewi Scourfield	Centre		93 (3)	72	14	1	-	-
Tim Stevenson	Fly half		22	77	5	8	12	-
Freddie Burns	Fly half		5 (10)	67	4	16	3	2
Paul Knight	Scrum half		22	77	13	3	2	-
Will Merivale	Scrum half		61 (14)	75	15	-	-	-
Andrew Deacon	Prop		67 (12)	25	5	-	-	-
Jake Meadows	Prop		12 (28)	5	1	-	-	-
Neil Baylis	Prop		7 (8)	5	1	-	-	-
Phil Kennedy	Prop		84 (12)	50	10	-	-	-
Nigel Matthews	Hooker		96 (16)	125	25	-	-	-
Chris Hall	Hooker		12 (5)	-	-	-	-	-
Mark Cornwell	Lock		37	5	1	-	-	-
Rob Fidler	Lock		22	10	2	-	-	-
Adisinia Obileye	Lock		16(18)	25	5	-	-	-
Dan Wright	Lock		12 (3)	5	1	-	-	-
Chris Jones	Lock		15	5	1	-	-	-
Rob James	Back row		105 (9)	80	16	-	-	-
Jed Hooper	Back row		16 (6)	55	11	-	-	-
George Evans	Back row		40 (17)	65	13	-	-	-
Chris McNeil	Back row		50 (4)	105	21	-	-	-

ESHER RFC

NATIONAL ONE

Founded: 1923-24
Nickname: The EEE's
Colours: Black with amber trim
Change Colours: Amber with black trim
Training Nights: Tuesday & Thursday 7pm
Website: www.esherrugby.com

KEY PERSONNEL

President	Ross Howard
Chairman	Bob Stratton
Treasurer	Julian Brigstocke
Club Secretary	Tim Bale c/o Esher RFC Tel: 01932 220 295 email timbale@esherrugby.com
Fixtures Secretary	Simon Gardner email: fixtures@esherrugby.com
1st XV Team Manager	Dave Page Tel: 07973 488142 (M) email: davidpage@esherrugby.com
Director of Rugby	Mike Schmid email: mikeschmid@esherrugby.com
Chairman of Rugby	John Inverdale
Media Liaison	David Page
Marketing Manager	Nicki Dent Tel: 01932 220 295 Fax 01932 254 627 email nickident@esherrugby.com

CONTACT DETAILS

c/o Esher RFC, 369 Molesey Road, Hersham, Surrey KT12 3PF
Tel: 01932 220295   Fax: 01932 254627   email: seniorrugby@esherrugby.com

GROUND DETAILS

Address:
The Rugby Ground, 369 Molesey Road, Hersham, Surrey KT12 3PF
Tel: 01932 220295 (Office)   Fax: 01932 254627
Capacity: 3,000   Seated: 1,300   Covered 1,200

Directions:
M25 Junc 10, A3 to London. After 1 mile left to Walton-on-Thames (A245), after 1/4 mile right at lights into Seven Hills Road (B365).

By Car: Turn right at r/about into Burwood Road & follow into Hersham Village. 2nd exit at r'about into Molesey Road. After the railway bridge (Hersham BR) the ground is 300yds on the left. NB Low bridge at Hersham BR station.

By Coach: At r/about straight on, at next r/about 2nd exit (Queens Rd A317) to Walton on Thames. At r/about left into Ashley Rd (B365). 1st right into Station Ave. Straight on at traffic lights into Rydens Rd. At T Junction turn right into Molesey Road. Ground is 300 yds on the right.

Nearest BR Station: Hersham (Waterloo-Woking line)
Car Parking: 300 on ground
Admission: TBA, both matchday & season tickets
Clubhouse: Open Mon - Fri 9-5pm, matchdays & training nights. Full onsite catering. Matchday hospitality; corporate & private functions available. Contact Trish Hassall 01932 220295
Club Shop: Open matchdays & and ordering available on line through link to Stash Rugby.

PROGRAMME

Size: A5   Pages: 40+
Price: £2
Advertising: Contact Nicki Dent as above

REVIEW OF THE SEASON 2008-09

Esher will resume life in the 3rd tier of the English game bloodied but unbowed after a tortuous year fighting both relegation and the RFU rule-changers.

After a second season in National Division One that was more successful than the first, not only in terms of points achieved but also in terms of the rugby played, it was immensely frustrating for the club to find itself demoted following the decision to move the relegation goalposts mid-season.

Having said that, a hugely disappointing first half of the season left Esher in the position of playing a dozen must-win games on consecutive weekends after Christmas - a task that in the end proved beyond them.

In a second half of the season that provided some of the most outstanding rugby ever played by the club, it would be invidious to single out individuals, but George Lowe deservedly won the player of the year award for some dazzling exhibitions of centre-play that will surely see him performing at the highest levels in seasons to come.

The most encouraging aspects for Esher for the year ahead is that the over-riding majority of players involved in the relegation fight have stayed to confront the battles ahead. Dave Slemen will captain the side again, and key figures such as seasoned campaigners Lee Starling and Neil Hallett will maintain long-standing continuity within the squad. Mike Schmid has signed a two-year contract to remain at the helm, and in what is bound to be a hugely competitive league, the club are cautiously optimistic that they'll be in contention come the end of the season.

249

ESHER'S SEASON - 2008-09

Date	H/A	Opponents	Result & Score	Att.	15	14	13	12	11
NATIONAL ONE									
30-08	H	Exeter	L 8-46	650	Flockhart	Stegmann	Taylor	Jewell/t	Loizides
06-09	A	Otley	W 18-12	516	Slemen	Stegmann	Taylor	Jewell	Flockhart
13-09	H	Nottingham	L 3-25	380	Slemen	Flockhart	Taylor	Jewell	Stegmann
20-09	A	Coventry	L 8-33	892	Hallett	Flockhart/t	Taylor	Barbini	Stegmann
27-09	H	Rotherham	L 32-59	710	Hallett	Stegmann	Lowe	Barbini	Flockhart/t
04-10	A	Newbury	W 14-8	680	Hallett	Flockhart	Lowe	Barbini	Briggs
11-10	H	Manchester	W 36-19	827	Flockhart/t	Stegmann/t	Lowe/t	Barbini	Briggs
18-10	A	London Welsh	L 19-43	1480	Flockhart/t	Briggs	Barbini	Lowe	Stegmann/t
25-10	H	Leeds Carnegie	L 8-52	1124	Flockhart	Loizides	Taylor	Barbini/t	Briggs
01-11	A	Moseley	L 13-22	750	Hallett/c2p	Flockhart	Lowe/t	Barbini	Loizides
08-11	H	Cornish Pirates	L 3-19	589	Hallett/p	Flockhart	Barbini	Baumberg	Loizides
15-11	A	Sedgley Park	L 26-27	525	Hallett/t3c	Flockhart/t	Barbini	Clouston/t	Loizides
22-11	A	Plymouth Albion	L 14-36	1742	Hallett/2c	Flockhart	Barbini	Clouston	Loizides
29-11	H	Doncaster	L 10-23	694	Hallett/cp	Flockhart/t	Barbini	Clouston	Loizides
06-12	H	Bedford	L 13-18	1081	Hallett/c2p	Flockhart	Barbini	Jewell	Stegmann
13-12	A	Exeter	D 12-12	3848	Hallett/c	Flockhart/2t	Lowe	Jewell	Loizides
20-12	H	Otley	W 48-16	956	Hallett/2c3p	Flockhart/t	Lowe/2t	Jewell	Loizides/2t
28-12	A	Nottingham	L 14-36	1463	Flockhart/t	Stegmann	Lowe	Jewell/t	Loizides
24-01	H	Newbury*	W 49-18	1049	Hallett/5c2p	Flockhart/t	Lowe	Jewell/dg	Stegmann/t
31-01	A	Manchester	W 40-28	283	Hallett/5c	Flockhart/t	Lowe/4t	Jewell	Loizides/t
22-02	A	Leeds Carnegie	L 21-47	2945	Hallett/3c	Flockhart	Lowe/2t	Jewell	Loizides
28-02	A	Rotherham	W 40-19	1107	Hallett/4c4p	Flockhart/t	Barbini	Jewell	Loizides/t
07-03	H	Moseley	W 23-17	1612	Hallett/2c3p	Flockhart	Lowe/t	Jewell	Loizides
15-03	A	Cornish Pirates	W 16-7	1894	Ulph/t2p	Flockhart/t	Amesbury	Jewell	Loizides
21-03	H	Coventry	W 27-18	1104	Hallett/3c2p	Flockhart	Amesbury/t	Jewell	Loizides/t
28-03	H	Sedgley Park	W 76-10	1258	Hallett/8c	Flockhart/t	Amesbury/2t	Jewell	Loizides/t
04-04	H	Plymouth Albion	W 31-28	1664	Hallett/t4cp	Flockhart	Lowe	Jewell/t	Amesbury/t
11-04	A	Doncaster	L 25-50	1322	Ulph	Flockhart	Lowe	Jewell/t	Stegmann/2t
18-04	H	London Welsh	L 21-32	1984	Ulph	Flockhart/t	Lowe	Jewell	Amesbury/t
25-04	A	Bedford	L 8-50	3307	Ulph	Flockhart	Lowe	Jewell	Amesbury
EDF ENERGY NATIONAL TROPHY									
17-01	A	Mounts Bay	W 43-5	200	Hallett/t4c	Flockhart/2t	Lowe/2t	Jewell	Stegmann

SCORING BREAKDOWN

WHEN	Total	First Half	Second Half	1/4	2/4	3/4	4/4
the POINTS were scored	676	347	329	195	152	174	155
the POINTS were conceded	830	377	453	183	194	203	250
the TRIES were scored	86	41	45	24	17	22	23
the TRIES were conceded	111	47	64	22	25	14	17

HOW	Total	Pen. Try	Backs	Forwards	F Back	Wing	Centre	H Back	F Row	Lock	B Row
the TRIES were scored	86	1	62	23	6	26	21	9	8	4	11
the TRIES were conceded	111	4	72	35	12	29	9	6	4	4	6

KEY: * after opponents name indicates a penalty try.
Brackets after a player's name indicates he was replaced. eg (a) means he was replaced by replacement code "a" and so on.
/ after a player or replacement name is followed by any scores he made - eg /t, /c, /p, /dg or any combination of these

10	9	1	2	3	4	5	6	7	8
Hallett/p	Barnes	Millard	Goldsmith	Lambert	Walker	Barker	Starling	Stitcher	Renwick
Hallett/c2p	Barnes	Millard	Goldsmith	Hannan	Barker	Walker	Starling/t	Stitcher	Renwick
Hallett/p	Barnes	Millard	Goldsmith	Lambert	Barker	Walker	Starling	Stitcher	Renwick
Jewell/p	Barnes	Millard	Goldsmith	Rogers	Barker	Walker	Starling	Stitcher	Renwick
Jewell/2c2p(b/c)	Barnes	Millard	Goldsmith(c/t)	Rogers	Walker	Barker	Starling	Stitcher/2t	Renwick
Jewell/3p	Shaw	Millard	Hayter	Hannan	Ayling	Waterhouse	Starling	Stitcher	Blakeburn/t
Hallett/4cp	Shaw	Millard	Hayter/t	Hannan	Ayling	Waterhouse	Starling/t	Stitcher	Blakeburn
Hallett/t2c	Shaw	Rogers	Goldsmith	Hannan	Inglis	Waterhouse	Starling	Stitcher	Blakeburn
Hallett/p	Barnes	Millard	Corrigan	Hannan	Ayling	Inglis	Blakeburn	Starling	Renwick
Jewell	Shaw	Millard	Corrigan	Hannan	Waterhouse	Inglis	Starling	Stitcher	Blakeburn
Jewell	Barnes	Millard	Corrigan	Hannan	Waterhouse	Ayling	Starling	Stitcher	Blakeburn
Slemen	Barnes	Millard	Corrigan	Croall	Walker	Ayling	Waterhouse/t	Stitcher	Renwick
Slemen	Barnes	Millard	Corrigan	Croall/t	Ayling	Walker	Starling	Stitcher(d/t)	Renwick
Slemen	Barnes	Millard	Corrigan	Croall	Ayling	Walker	Waterhouse	Starling	Renwick
Slemen	Shaw	Millard	Corrigan	Elosu	Barker(e/t)	Walker	Waterhouse	Tubasei	Starling
Slemen	Shaw	Millard	Goldsmith	Elosu	Inglis	Walker	Waterhouse	Tubasei	Renwick
Slemen	Shaw	Millard	Corrigan	Elosu	Inglis	Walker/t	Waterhouse	Tubasei	Starling/t
Slemen/2c	Shaw	Hannon	Corrigan	Elosu	Inglis	Walker	Waterhouse	Stitcher	Starling
Slemen	Shaw/t	Millard	Corrigan	Hannan/2t	Inglis	Barker	Waterhouse	Stitcher	Blakeburn
Slemen	Shaw	Millard	Lindsay	Hannan	Barker	Inglis	Starling	Stitcher	Renwick
Slemen/t	Shaw	Reid	Lindsay	Hannan	Inglis	Barker	Waterhouse	Stitcher	Renwick
Slemen	Shaw	Hannan	Corrigan	Elosu	Barker	Inglis	Waterhouse	Stitcher	Renwick/2t
Slemen/t	Shaw	Hannan	Corrigan	Elosu	Barker	Inglis	Waterhouse	Stitcher	Renwick
Slemen	Shaw	Rogers	Corrigan	Elosu	Barker	Ayling	Waterhouse	Stitcher	Renwick
Slemen	Shaw	Rogers	Corrigan	Elosu	Barker	Inglis	Waterhouse	Stitcher/t	Renwick
Slemen/t	Shaw/3t	Rogers/t	Corrigan(f/t)	Elosu/t	Barker	Inglis/t	Waterhouse	Yellowlees	Blakeburn
Slemen	Shaw	Rogers	Corrigan	Elosu	Barker	Inglis/t	Waterhouse	Stitcher	Renwick
Hallett/2c2p	Shaw	Tunnicliffe	Corrigan	Hannan	Barker	Inglis	Waterhouse	Stitcher	Starling
Hallett/c3p	Shaw	Rogers	Corrigan	Hannan	Barker	Ayling	Waterhouse	Stitcher	Renwick
Hallett/p	Shaw/t	Tunnicliffe	Corrigan	Hannan	Barker	Inglis	Waterhouse	Stitcher	Renwick
Slemen/t(a/t)	Shaw	Reid	Corrigan	Hannon	Inglis	Barker	Waterhouse	Stitcher	Blakeburn

REPLACEMENTS a- D Shabbo   b- D Slemen   c- J Hayter   d- J Tubasei
e- J Englis   f- S Goldsmith

LEAGUE APPEARANCES

30	Douglas Flockhart
28	Neil Hallett
24	Seb Jewell (2), Sam Stitcher (2)
22	James Waterhouse (2)
20	Robbie Shaw (2)

NUMBER OF PLAYERS USED

39 plus 13 as a replacement only

LEAGUE POINTS SCORERS

Pts	Player	T	C	P	DG
224	Neil Hallett	3	55	33	-
80	Doug Flockhart	16	-	-	-
60	George Lowe	12	-	-	-
45	Seb Jewell	4	2	6	1
30	Tom Lozides	6	-	-	-

NATIONAL ONE

ESHER STATISTICS

LEAGUE

TEAM RECORDS

MOST POINTS
Scored at Home: 104 v Met Police
Scored Away: 57 v Met Police 14.2.98 & Bradford B 7.4.07
Conceded at Home: 59 v Rotherham 27.9.08
Conceded Away: 74 v Northampton 20.10.07

MOST TRIES
Scored in a match: 17 v Met Police
Conceded in a match: 12 v Northampton 20.10.07 (A)

BIGGEST MARGINS
Home Win: 97pts - 104-7 v Met Police
Away Win: 43pts - 56-13 v Norwich
Home Defeat: 44pts - 8-52 v Leeds Carnegie 25.10.08
Away Defeat: 64pts -10-74 v Northampton 20.10.07

MOST CONSECUTIVE
Victories: 15 (Twice)
Defeats: 8 (18.10.08 - 6.12.08)

INDIVIDUAL RECORDS

MOST APPEARANCES
by a forward: 205 (24) Mark Butterworth
by a back: 131(1) Jonathan Gregory

MOST CONSECUTIVE
Appearances: Chris Wilkins
Matches scoring points: Jon Gregory

MATCH RECORDS

Most Points
34   Michael Corcoran v Cheltenham 13.2.99 (H)

Most Tries
4   Nana Dontah   v Plymouth 10.10.98 (H)
     M Corcoran   v Cheltenham 13.2.99 (H)
     Nyasha Shumba v Stourbridge 8.2.03 (A)

Most Conversions
8   Jon Gregory   v Clifton 2.10.99 (H)
                        v W Hartlepool 8.4.01 (H)
     Neil Hallett v Sedgley Park 28.3.09 (H)

Most Penalties
8   Jon Gregory   v Preston 1.12.01 (H)

Most Drop Goals
2   Chris Finch   v Kendal 28.9.02 (H)

SEASON RECORDS

Most Points	398	Neil Hallett	06-07
Most Tries	24	Matt Moore	05-06
Most Conversions	80	Neil Hallett	06-07
Most Penalties	76	Jon Gregory	01-02
Most Drop Goals	4	Chris Finch	02-03

CAREER RECORDS

Most Points	1609	Jon Gregory	98-04
Most Tries	60	Matt Moore	04-08
Most Conversions	272	Jon Gregory	98-04
Most Penalties	290	Jon Gregory	98-04
Most Drop Goals	7	Chris Finch	01-03

LAST TEN SEASONS

	Division	P	W	D	L	F	A	P.D.	Pts	Pos	Most Points	Most Tries
99-00	N2S	26	23	0	3	1018	356	662	46	1p	351 Jon Gregory	15 Michael Corcoran
00-01	N2	26	11	1	14	577	484	93	23	8	260 Jon Gregory	7 John Gregory
01-02	N2	26	12	0	14	547	587	40	24	7	311 Jon Gregory	9 Spencer Bromley
02-03	N2	26	16	1	9	697	550	147	33	3	214 Jon Gregory	18 Nysha Shumba
03-04	N2	26	12	1	13	641	612	29	25	6	164 Jon Gregory	11 Piers Gregory
04-05	N2	26	10	0	16	665	744	-79	53	11	223 Neil Hallett	10 J P O'Reilly
05-06	N2	26	18	1	7	741	407	334	91	3	302 Neil Hallett	24 Matt Moore
06-07	N2	26	23	1	2	967	441	526	115	1p	398 Neil Hallett	23 Matt Moore
07-08	N1	30	10	0	20	481	850	-369	49	12	95 Neil Hallett	11 Douglas Flockhart
08-09	N1	30	12	1	17	676	830	-154	61	12r	224 Neil Hallett	16 Douglas Flockhart

RFU SENIOR CUP

OVERALL PLAYING RECORD

	P	W	O	L	F	A	Pts Diff
Home	15	10	0	5	394	237	157
Away	13	4	0	9	231	331	-100
Neutral	0	0	0	0	0	0	0
TOTAL	28	14	0	14	625	568	57

TEAM RECORDS

Highest Score: 85 v Cambridge 03/04
Biggest Winning Margin: 85 (85-0) v Cambridge 03/04
Highest Score Against: 64 v Penzance & Newlyn 04-05 (A)
Biggest Losing Margin: 64 (64-0) v Penzance 04-05 (A)

SEASON BY SEASON

71-72	DNQ	78-79	1R	85-86	DNQ	92-93	DNQ	99-00	3R
72-73	DNQ	79-80	1R	86-87	DNQ	93-94	DNQ	00-01	4R
73-74	DNQ	80-81	DNQ	87-88	DNQ	94-95	2R	01-02	2R
74-75	DNQ	81-82	DNQ	88-89	DNQ	95-96	DNQ	02-03	2R
75-76	DNQ	82-83	DNQ	89-90	DNQ	96-97	4R	03-04	4R
76-77	1R	83-84	DNQ	90-91	DNQ	97-98	1R	04-05	3R
77-78	1R	84-85	DNQ	91-92	DNQ	98-99	4R		

NATIONAL TROPHY

05-06	6 R	06-07	3 R	07-08	Q.F.	08-09	4 R

ESHER PLAYERS

	Position	D.o.B.	Apps.	Pts.	T	C	P	DG
Neil Hallett	Full back/Fly half	18/02/1980	112 (2)	1242	23	247	211	-
Douglas Flockhart	Winger	25/11/1984	59	135	27	-	-	-
Toby Clouston	Centre	21/11/1978	105 (21)	90	18	-	-	-
Matteo Barbini	Centre	08/06/1982	16 (5)	20	4	-	-	-
Seb Jewell	Centre	20/12/1987	24 (2)	45	4	2	6	1
George Lowe	Centre		16 (50	60	12	-	-	-
David Slemen	Fly half	12/09/1978	29 (4)	68	6	13	4	-
Seb Stegmann	Winger	12/04/1989	11	25	5	-	-	-
Tom Lozides	Winger		17 (2)	30	6	-	-	-
Charlie Amesbury	Winger	08/04/1986	24 (1)	50	10	-	-	-
Robbie Shaw	Scrum half		22 (2)	25	5	-	-	-
Ian Barnes	Scrum half	08/06/1983	11 (20)	-	-	-	-	-
Dave Millard	Prop	11/01/1987	25 (12)	-	-	-	-	-
Alex Rogers	Prop	16/12/1986	8 (3)	5	1	-	-	-
Colm Hannon	Prop		16 (6)	10	2	-	-	-
James Campbell	Hooker	21/02/1973	21 (2)	15	3	-	-	-
Kevin Corrigan	Hooker		19 (2)	-	-	-	-	-
Simon Goldsmith	Hooker	15/01/1977	23 (39)	40	8	-	-	-
Paul Barker	Lock	17/01/1979	78 (6)	5	1	-	-	-
Mike Blakeburn	Lock	15/08/1980	71 (19)	55	11	-	-	-
James Waterhouse	Back row		22 (20	5	1	-	-	-
Sam Stitcher	Back row	24/11/1986	24 (2)	15	3	-	-	-
Shaun Renwick	Back row		19 (9)	10	2	-	-	-
Lee Starling	Back row	02/04/1980	80 (16)	80	16	-	-	-
James Inglis	Back row	26/08/1986	34 (2)	20	4	-	-	-

LAUNCESTON

Founded: 1948
Nickname: Cornish All Blacks
Colours: All Black strip with offset white cross on shirt
Change colours: White shirt with offset black cross
Training Nights: Tuesday & Thursday Mini/Juniors - Wednesday
Website: www.cornishallblacks.co.uk

KEY PERSONNEL

President	Tony Randel
Chairman	Tim Fox
Treasurer	Clive Miles
Club Secretary	Sarah Goodwin, Ogbeare Hall, North Tamerton, Holsworthy EX22 6SE Tel: 01409 271208 & 01566 773406 (Club) email sarah.ogbeare@virgin.net
Fixture Secretary	Suzanne Cleave, 35 Rockhead St., Delabole, Cornwall. PL33 9BY Tel: 01840 213615 email:fixturescornishallblacks.co.uk@
1st Team Manager	Jim O'Hara Marantha, Highcliffe, Polzeath, PL27 6TN Tel: 01208 862725, & 07979 392411 email: jimolrfc@aol.com
Sales & Marketing Manager	Neil Plummer Tel: 07968 687994 (M) & 01566 773406 (Afternoon)
Club Admin Manager	Ian Morgan Tel: 07830 393085 & 01566 773406 (Morning)
Joint Head Coaches	Chris Brown 07971 668496 Jon Hill 07816 846955
Academy Manager	Ian Goldsmith 01579 343313
Merchandising Manager	Paul Harrison 01566 779653

GROUND DETAILS

Address:
Polson Bridge, Launceston, Cornwall PL15 9QT
Tel: 01566 773406
e-mail: administrator@cornishallblacks.co.uk

Capacity: 4,000
Seating: 220
Covered: 220

Directions
M5 to Exeter, then A30 to Launceston. After 45 minutes look for sign on left "Tavistock, Liftondown, Lifton" - turn left, down to T junction, left again, down hill to river Tamar, ground on the left.

Nearest BR Station: Bodmin Parkway, 40 mins via A30

Car Parking: Ample available at the ground

Admission:
Membership details - Membership@cornishallblacks.co.uk
Matchday: Ground: Adults: £10 OAP: £7.   Stand transfer £3
Season tickets: £120 (League matches only) OAPs £84

Clubhouse: Open matchdays from Noon, training nights 7-11pm & most Sundays (Mini/Juniors). Food available on matchdays and Sundays. Clubhouse available for hire for small functions "Lanson Suite" - Corporate Hospitality & Conferencing Facility - Available for private hire. Contact - Admin Manager
Club Shop: Open matchdays from noon and by request.
Contact Paul Harrison 01566 779653.   See website also.

PROGRAMME

Size: A5   **Price:** £1   **Pages:** 12
Matchday insert with/without yearbook
Editor: Contact Admin Manager.
Advertising Rates: Contact editor.

Cornish All Blacks squad 2008-09

REVIEW OF THE SEASON 2008-09

After a busy summer full of recruitment in an effort to bounce straight back to Division One at the first attempt, the Cornish All Blacks were rather disappointed to finish in 7th place. Form displayed away from Polson Bridge would be the key reason for the mid-table finish in a season that promised so much at the beginning, but fell away towards the end.

That said, on their day the Cornish All Blacks were a match for everyone, and Birmingham were the only side in the division to do the double over them. Victories away at Cambridge, at home to Redruth and a 100 point victory against Waterloo are the highlights, whilst a disappointing loss at home to Mounts Bay and a first ever loss against Redruth away would be the huge disappointments.

The loss of Tight Head Prop Hamish Mitchell due to family reasons, and the unavailability of injured key players such as Steve Perry, Ron Ireland, Steve Pape, and Glen Remnant were costly, but also provided opportunities for a number of promising youngsters to take centre stage and build for the future. Lock Bryn Jenkins, Back Rower Sam Hocking, Half Back Lewis Webb and Centre Jake Murphy all made significant contributions, and benefited from long term exposure in the first xv. Sam Hocking gained the player of the year award for some fantastic performances, whilst winger Marc Dibble was the highest try scorer.

Joint Head Coach Chris Brown left the club towards the end of the season due to family reasons, and former Club Captain Keith Brooking has since been appointed as his replacement in a new look coaching team alongside Tony Yapp, Tony Roques and Jon Fabian with Jon Hill as Director of Rugby. Mal Roberts and Tom Rawlings have been appointed 1st xv Captain and Club Captain respectively.

LAUNCESTON STATISTICS

LEAGUE

TEAM RECORDS

MOST POINTS
Scored at Home: 103 v Waterloo 3.1.09
Scored Away: 62 v Redruth 13.4.02,
 & v Tabard 6.3.04 & Harrogate 11.11.06
Conceded at Home: 40 v Harrogate 4.3.06
Conceded Away: 67 v Sedgley Park 8.2.03

MOST TRIES
Scored in a match: 16 v Waterloo 3.1.09 (H)
Conceded in a match: 13 v Northampton 26.4.08

BIGGEST MARGINS
Home Win: 67pts 74-7 v Barking 23.2.02
Away Win: 62pts 62-0 v Harrogate 11.11.06
Home Defeat: 25pts 10-35 v Esher 29.10.06
Away Defeat: 51pts 12-63 v Doncaster 19.2.05

MOST CONSECUTIVE
Victories: 14 (22.11.03 - 13.3.04)
Defeats: 5 (21.12.02 - 25.1.03)

INDIVIDUAL RECORDS

MOST APPEARANCES
by a forward: 141 Dave Risdon (21)
by a back: 129 Andy Birkett (26)

MOST CONSECUTIVE
Appearances: 56 Jimmy Tucker
Matches scoring Tries: 5 Mark Fatialofa 1.12.01-12.10.02
Matches scoring points: 18 Simon Porter 1.11.03 - 13.3.04

MATCH RECORDS

Most Points
  32   Simon Porter   v Tabard 6.3.04 (A)

Most Tries
  4   Matt Bradshaw   v Cheltenham 30.0.00 (H)
       Mark Fatialofa   v Old Patesians 23.3.02 (H)
       Ashley Rescorla   v Old Colfeians 7.2.04 (H)

Most Conversions
  10   Simon Porter   v Old Colfeians 7.2.04 (H)

Most Penalties
  8   Stuart Alred   v Blackheath 21.1.06 (H)

Most Drop Goals
  1   Andrew Birkett (3 times),
       Anthony Alatini, Stuart Alred & Mike Provis

SEASON RECORDS

Most Points	288	Danny Sloman	00-01
Most Tries	20	Mark Fatialofa	01-02
Most Conversions	63	Simon Porter	03-04
Most Penalties	48	Stuart Alred	05-06
Most Drop Goals	1	Andrew Birkett	00-01/02/03
		Anthony Alatini	02-03
Mike Provis 08-09		Stuart Alred	05-06

CAREER RECORDS

Most Points	464	Danny Sloman	00-02
Most Tries	36	Eddie Nancekivell	00-05
Most Conversions	82	Danny Sloman	00-02
Most Penalties	80	Danny Sloman	00-02
Most Drop Goals	2	Andrew Birkett	00-07

LAST TEN SEASONS

	Division	P	W	D	L	F	A	P.D.	Pts	Pos	Most Points	Most Tries
99-00	SW1	21	19	0	2	693	266	427	38	1	Danny Sloman	
00-01	N3S	26	20	1	5	777	396	381	41	2	288 Danny Sloman	13 Mark Fatialofa
01-02	N3S	26	24	0	2	876	397	479	48	2p	191 Barend Vorster	20 Mark Fatialofa
02-03	N2	26	10	0	16	532	643	-111	20	12r	186 Scott Martin	11 Jimmy Tucker
03-04	N3S	26	22	0	4	832	371	461	44	2p*	274 Simon Porter	16 Mike Heyes
04-05	N2	26	13	2	11	570	609	-39	70	5	149 Steven Perry	12 Martin Lacey
05-06	N2	26	16	2	8	584	538	46	76	4	232 Stuart Alred	9 Nigel Simpson
06-07	N2	26	19	1	6	795	448	347	96	2p	254 Sam Young	13 Wayne Sprangle
07-08	N1	30	8	0	22	441	906	-465	40	16r	124 Jon Fabian	17 Matthew Jess
08-09	N2	26	13	1	12	695	578	117	70	7	169 Adam Staniforth	12 Marc Dibble

RFU SENIOR CUP

OVERALL PLAYING RECORD

	P	W	D	L	F	A	Pts Diff
Home	15	9	0	6	443	276	167
Away	10	4	0	6	177	265	-88
Neutral	0	0	0	0	0	0	0
TOTAL	25	13	0	12	620	541	79

TEAM RECORDS

Highest Score: 59 v Fylde 03/04
Biggest Winning Margin: 52 (58-6) v Bicester 97/98
Highest Score Against: 67 v Rotherham 97/98
Biggest Losing Margin: 52 (67-15) v Rotherham 97/98

SEASON BY SEASON

Season	Result	Season	Result	Season	Result	Season	Result	Season	Result
71-72	DNQ	78-79	DNQ	85-86	DNQ	92-93	DNQ	99-00	1R
72-73	DNQ	79-80	DNQ	86-87	DNQ	93-94	DNQ	00-01	3R
73-74	DNQ	80-81	DNQ	87-88	DNQ	94-95	3R	01-02	3R
74-75	DNQ	81-82	DNQ	88-89	DNQ	95-96	1R	02-03	2R
75-76	DNQ	82-83	DNQ	89-90	DNQ	96-97	1R	03-04	4R
76-77	DNQ	83-84	1R	90-91	DNQ	97-98	3R	04-05	3R
77-78	DNQ	84-85	DNQ	91-92	DNQ	98-99	2R		

NATIONAL ONE

NATIONAL TROPHY

| 05-06 | 4 R | 06-07 | 4 R | 07-08 | Q.F. | 08-09 | 4R |

LAUNCESTON PLAYERS

	Position		Apps.	Pts.	T	C	P	DG
Hamish Smales	Winger		17 (2)	15	3	-	-	-
Ryan Westran	Full back	26/10/1984	60 (12)	59	11	2	-	-
Jon Fabian	Winger	18/09/1976	52 (2)	174	11	19	26	1
Gary Kingdom	Winger		16	42	6	6	-	-
Steven Perry	Centre	01/04/1981	109 (8)	188	6	43	24	-
Adam Staniforth	Centre/Fly half		23 (2)	169	2	39	27	-
Mal Roberts	Centre		14 (1)	51	3	6	8	-
Lewis Webb	Centre		16 (5)	20	4	-	-	-
Jason Luff	Winger		2 (2)	30	6	-	-	-
Jake Murphy	Full Back		4 (2)	-	-	-	-	-
Marc Dibble	Scrum half	12/06/1985	75 (26)	190	38	-	-	-
Ben Turner	Scrum half	28/04/1986	13 (10)	10	2	-	-	-
Hamish Mitchell	Prop		8	5	1	-	-	-
Danny Porte	Prop		6	-	-	-	-	-
Jason Bolt	Prop	13/03/1980	70 (60)	15	3	-	-	-
Billy Moss	Hooker		5 (2)	-	-	-	-	-
Glenn Cooper	Hooker		14 (8)	10	2	-	-	-
Keith Brooking	Hooker	07/05/1973	62 (12)	-	-	-	-	-
Tim Collier	Lock		11 (1)	15	3	-	-	-
Steven Pape	Lock	27/01/1983	50 (11)	25	5	-	-	-
Mike Myerscough	Lock	28/05/1986	30 (7)	25	5	-	-	-
Tom Skelding	Lock	01/02/1982	16	-	-	-	-	-
Josh Lord	Back row	11/06/1982	86 (13)	65	13	-	-	-
Sam Hocking	Back row		30 (18)	40	8	-	-	-
Glen Remnant	Back row		13 (3)	15	3	-	-	-
Anthony Roques	Back row	07/09/1978	35 (7)	10	2	-	-	-

LONDON SCOTTISH FC

KEY PERSONNEL

President	Rod Lynch, c/o London Scottish FC
Treasurer	Ross Luke, c/o London Scottish FC
Club Secretary	Hugh Mackay, c/o London Scottish FC
	0208 946 9173 (H) 0208 940 7156 (O) 0208 940 0342 (F)
	email: secretary@londonscottish.com
Fixture Secretary	Ally Hart Tel: 07748 024845 email: allyhart@ezspk.com
Director of Rugby	Brett Taylor Tel: 07739 430812
Team Manager / 1st XV Matchday Correspondence	Buffy Mair Tel: 0208 940 7156 email: buffy@londonscottish.com
Club Administrator	Buffy Mair, c/o London Scottish FC Tel: 0208 940 7156 email:admin@londonscottish.com
PR & Commercial	Helena Searcaigh Tel: 0208 940 7156 email:Helena.searcraigh@londonscottish.com
Club Physio	Russell Kelsey Tel: 07515 282346 email: russell.kelsey@londonscottish.com

Founded: 1878

Colours: Navy blue shirts, white shorts, red stockings.

Change strip: Red and navy hooped shirts

Training nights: Monday and Wednesday

Website: www.londonscottish.com

CONTACT DETAILS

London Scottish FC, The Athletic Ground, Kew Foot Road, Richmond, Surrey TW9 2SS
Tel: 0208 940 - 7156 or 8289 **Fax** 0208 940 0342 **email:** admin@londonscottish.com

GROUND DETAILS

Address
London Scottish FC, The Athletic Ground, Kew Foot Road, Richmond, Surrey TW9 2SS
Tel: 0208 940 - 7156 or 8289
Fax 0208 940 0342
email:admin@londonscottish.com

Directions:
From Richmond Station (BR and District Line) turn right to a major roundabout. Cross A316 at crossing and turn left. Ground is 100m on right.

Capacity: 3,000
Covered seating: 950

Admission: No prices available at this time.

Nearest BR Station: Richmond (BR & District Line)

Parking 100 cars.

Clubhouse: Open matchdays & training eves. Cafeteria. Functions: Contact Richmond Athletic Association. Natalie Hostcombe 0208 940 0397

Club shop: Open Saturdays and Sundays during season.

PROGRAMME

Size: A5   Editor: Contact Helena Searcaigh

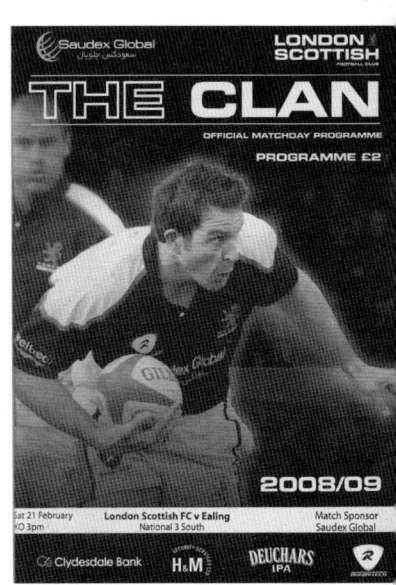

Photo: James Hann

REVIEW OF THE SEASON 2008-09

Only very rarely does a national league side go unbeaten, and London Scottish emulated the feat of the side captained by Gavin Hastings two decades ago when there were only eleven league fixtures to survive, not 26. The club has now secured six promotions since 2000 following the demise of the Premiership club.

The mixture of experience and youth proved too much for the other promotion hopefuls. Indeed the awards of the Players' Player trophy to the 40-year-old Andrew Smith, back from serving in Afghanistan, and the Supporters' trophy to a 22-year-old former minis, juniors and colts star Rory Damant, highlighted the blend achieved by the coaching team of Jim Kelly, Simon Amor and, from October, head coach Brett Taylor.

The key signings were former England Sevens captain Amor from Wasps, and the Worcester pair James Brown and Gary Trueman. Brown's orchestration ensured that the backs exploited the strong platform provided by former full-time pros Volley, Fullarton, Gotting, Ward and Soden, augmented by club stalwarts such as Johnston, Millard, Leek, Silvester, Livingston, Smith, Wasps academy player Lipp, Jope, and others.

Skipper Trueman and fellow centre Naca had, as it happened, nightmare seasons with injuries but with Scotland Sevens expert McInroy alongside him in the centre for much of the season, Damant was the side's leading a scorer, and the outside backs Broughton - another junior product - Piotrowski, Neale and the rest drove the points tally well over the thousand mark.

At the same time opportunities were given to several Academy players, taking into double figures the tally of Scots who played.

The stand-out performances were the second half at arch rival Ealing, where Scottish came from a man down and a point behind to grab not only victory but a try-scoring bonus point as well, and at Rosslyn Park where a defensive display of exceptional heart and quality shut out the most dangerous side faced all season.

259

SCOTTISH'S SEASON - 2008-09

Date	H/A	Opponents	Result & Score	Att.	15	14	13	12	11
NATIONAL THREE SOUTH									
06-09	H	Chinnor	W 45-3	700	Swailes	Yiend	Nacamavuto	Truman/2t	Piotrowski/t
13-09	A	Bridgwater	W 36-15	907	Petzer	Greenslade-Jones/t	Nacamavuto/t	Truman	Piotrowski/3t
20-09	H	Worthing	W 45-11	700	Petzer/3c	Greenslade-Jones	McInroy/2t	Truman(a/t)	Piotrowski/t
27-09	A	Richmond	W 21-12	1685	Swailes/t	Greenslade-Jones/t	Damant	McInroy	Piotrowski
04-10	H	Rosslyn Park	W 25-17	1200	Swailes	Greenslade-Jones	Damant	McInroy/t	Piotrowski/t
11-10	A	Canterbury	W 43-28	336	Swailes	Greenslade-Jones	Damant	McInroy/2t	Yiend/2t
25-10	H	Dings Crusaders	W 43-0	1200	Swailes/t	Broughton	Damant/t	McInroy	Yiend/3t
02-11	A	Ealing	W 38-17	210	Swailes	Broughton(b/t)	Damant/t	McInroy	Piotrowski
08-11	H	Havant	W 45-8	112	Swailes/3t	Broughton/t	Damant/t	McInroy	Piotrowski
15-11	A	Lydney	W 45-10	410	Swailes/2t	Broughton	Damant	McInroy	Piotrowski
29-11	A	Rugby Lions	D 18-18	239	Neale	McInroy/t	Damant	Truman	Piotrowski
06-12	H	Barking	W 80-14	600	Neale/4t	Broughton/2t	Damant/t	Truman	Piotrowski/t
20-12	A	Henley Hawks	W 19-9	580	Neale	Broughton	Damant	Truman	Piotrowski
24-01	H	Richmond	W 33-8	2100	Rust/t	Broughton	McInroy	Truman/t(g/t)	Piotrowski
31-01	A	Rosslyn Park	W 18-7	1210	Rust/2t	Yiend	McInroy	Truman	Piotrowski
14-02	A	Dings Crusaders	W 18-16	269	Rust	Yiend	Damant	McInroy	Piotrowski
21-02	H	Ealing	W 19-16	1200	Neale/t	Yiend	Damant/t	McInroy	Piotrowski
28-02	A	Havant	W 61-10	170	Neale/t	Broughton/t	Damant/2t	McInroy	Piotrowski/2t
07-03	H	Lydney	W 76-11	400	Neale	Broughton/t (a/t)	Damant/4t	McInroy	Piotrowski
14-03	A	Bridgwater	W 52-7	300	Neale/2t	Broughton/4t	Damant	McInroy	Piotrowski
21-03	H	Rugby Lions	W 85-3	1000	Neale/t3c	Broughton/t	Damant/2t	McInroy	Piotrowski/t
28-03	A	Barking	W 21-19	300	Neale	Broughton	Damant	McInroy	Piotrowski
04-04	H	Henley Hawks*	W 38-5	700	Neale	Broughton/2t	Damant	McInroy	Piotrowski
11-04	A	Worthing	W 71-13	350	Neale/t8c	Broughton/2t	Damant	Truman/t	Piotrowski/(a
18-04	A	Chinnor	W 59-29	250	Neale	Broughton/t	Damant/2t	Truman	Swailes/t
25-04	H	Canterbury	W 38-22	1109	Neale/t	Swailes/t	Damant/t	Truman/t	Piotrowski/t
EDF ENERGY NATIONAL TROPHY									
1 18-10	H	St Marys Old Boys	W 36-22		Broughton	Brabant	Petzer	Dunlop	Yiend/t
2 23-11	H	Richmond*	W 30-13		Neale	Greenslade-Jones	Hayward	Truman	Piotrowski
3 20-12	H	Basingstoke	W 40-27		Swailes/t	Finch/t	Hayward	Dunlop	Rust/t
4 17-01	A	Manchester	W 33-25		Neale	Broughton/t	McInroy	Truman	Piotrowski/t
5 07-02	A	Mounts Bay	L 5-6	171	Neale	Broughton	Damant	Peel	Yiend

NATIONAL ONE

SCORING BREAKDOWN

WHEN		Total	First Half	Second Half		1/4	2/4	3/4	4/4
the POINTS were scored		1092	528	564		232	296	279	278
the POINTS were conceded		328	151	177		57	94	68	109
the TRIES were scored		157	77	80		33	44	39	40
the TRIES were conceded		41	15	26		3	12	9	17

HOW	Total	Pen. Try	Backs	Forwards	F Back	Wing	Centre	H Back	F Row	Lock	B Row
the TRIES were scored	157	1	109	47	21	40	30	18	17	7	23
the TRIES were conceded	41	-	30	11	2	19	6	3	5	-	6

KEY: * after opponents name indicates a penalty try.
Brackets after a player's name indicates he was replaced. eg (a) means he was replaced by replacement code "a" and so on.
/ after a player or replacement name is followed by any scores he made - eg /t, /c, /p, /dg or any combination of these

10	9	1	2	3	4	5	6	7	8
Brown/4c	Amor/tc	Millard	Leek	Fahey/t	Smith	Fullerton	Volley	Grinter/2t	Stewart
Brown/4cp	Amor	Fahey	Leek	Ward	Smith	Fullerton	Lipp	Volley	Soden
Brown/t2c	Amor	Millard	Leek	Ward	Smith	Smith	Lipp/2t	Grinter	Soden
Brown/c3p	Walbyoff	Fahey	Leek	Ward	Smith	Smith	Volley	Lipp	Soden
Brown/2cpdg	Amor/t	Fahey	Silvester	Ward	Livingstone	Fullerton	Lipp	Volley	Soden
Brown/4c	Amor	Millard	Leek	Ward	Smith	Livingstone	Lipp	Volley	Jope/3t
Brown/4c	Amor	Johnston	Gotting	Ward	Livingstone/t	Fullerton	Karonias	Volley	Jope/t
Brown/3c4p	Amor	Johnston	Silvester	Ward	Fullerton	Livingstone/t	Soden	Volley	Jope/t
Amor/3c(c/t/2c)	Walbyoff/t	Millard	Silvester	Fahey	Livingstone	Smith	Lipp	Volley	Soden
Amor/5c(d/t)	Walbyoff/t	Bruce/t	Silvester	Fahey	Smith	Fullerton/2t	Lipp	Volley	Soden
Brown/c2p	Walbyoff	Johnston	Silvester	Ward	Livingstone(e/t)	Fullerton	Soden	Lipp	Jope
Brown/10c	Amor	Fahey/t	Silvester(f/t)	Ward	Karonias/t	Livingstone	Soden/t	Volley	Lipp
Brown/c4p	Walbyoff	Johnston	Silvester	Ward/t	Smith	Livingstone	Lipp	Volley	Soden
Brown/3c	Amor/c	Fahey	Silvester	Johnson	Fullerton	Livingstone/t	Lipp	Volley	Soden/t
Brown	Amor/tp	Fahey	Silvester	Johnson	Fullerton	Livingstone	Soden	Volley	Jope
Hadden/c2p	Heeks/t	Fahey	Leek	Johnston	Livingstone	Fullerton	Soden	Volley	Jope/t
Brown/p	Amor/2p	Millard	Gotting	Ward	Fullerton	Livingstone	Lipp	Volley	Soden
Brown/8c	Amor	Johnson/t	Gotting	Ward(h/t)	Smith	Livingstone	Karonias	Volley	Soden/t
Brown/8c	Walbyoff/2t	Millard	Gotting/t	Fahey/t	Smith	Livingstone	Karonias/2t	Lipp	Soden
Brown/t6c	Walbyoff/t	Millard	Gotting	Ward	Smith	Livingstone	Karonias	Volley	Lipp
Brown/8cp	Amor/2t	Millard	Gotting/t	Ward/t	Smith	Livingstone	Karonias	Volley	Soden
Brown/c3p	Amor	Millard	Gotting/t	Ward	Smith	Livingstone	Karonias	Volley	Soden/t
Brown/5cp	Amor	Millard	Gotting	Ward(j/t)	Smith	Livingstone	Karonias	Volley	Soden
Brown	Amor/t	Johnston	Gotting/t	Ward(h/t)	Smith	Fullerton	Karonias/t	Volley/t	Soden/t
Brown/7c	Walbyoff	Johnston(j/t)	Gotting/t	Fahey	Smith	Fullerton	Karonias(k/2t)	Volley	Lipp/t
Brown/t4c	Walbyoff	Johnston	Gotting	Johnson	Smith	Livingstone	Grinter	Volley	Lipp
Hadden/3t3c	Grant/t	Johnston	Baker	Johnson	Karonias	Smith	Grinter/t	Kaplan	Taft
Hadden/2c2p	Heeks	Johnston	Box	Ward	Smith	Karonias/t	Volley	Lipp/t	Fitzgerald
Hadden/t2c3p	Grant	Bruce	Leek	Johnson	Smith	Karonias/t	Grinter	Breerton	Fitzgerald
Brown/2c3p	Amor/t(l/t)	Johnston	Silvester	Fahey	Smith	Fullerton	Lipp	Volley	Soden
Hadden	Walbyoff	Millard	Leek	Ward	Smith	Smith/t	Karonias	Lipp	Fitzgerald

REPLACEMENTS

a- G Swales   b- R Greenslade Jones   c- S Hadden   d- D Hayward
e- A Karonias f- D Box   g- R Damant   h- A Fahey
i- C Johnson   j- L Ward   k- G Livingstone   l- O Walbyoff

LEAGUE APPEARANCES

23	Paul Volley, Roman Piotrowski, James Brown
21	Rory Damant (1)
20	Mark Soden
19	Grant Livingstone (3), Ian McInroy (3)

NUMBER OF PLAYERS USED

37 plus 7 as a replacement only

LEAGUE POINTS SCORERS

Pts	Player	T	C	P	DG
253	James Brown	3	86	21	1
90	Rory Damant	18	-	-	-
77	Frankie Neale	11	11	-	-
75	Charles Broughton	15	-	-	-
60	Roman Piotrowski	12	-	-	-
60	Gareth Swales	12	-	-	-

LONDON SCOTTISH STATISTICS

LEAGUE (National Leagues only)

NATIONAL ONE

TEAM RECORDS

MOST POINTS
Scored at Home: 85 v Rugby Lions 21.03.09
Scored Away: 71 v Worthing 11.04.09
Conceded at Home: 59 v Northampton 27.4.96
Conceded Away: 76 v Bath 15.5.99

MOST TRIES
Scored in a match: 12 v Rugby Lions 21.03.09 & v Worthing 11.04.09 & v Lydney v 07.03.09
Conceded in a match: 12 v Bath 15.5.99

BIGGEST MARGINS
Home Win: 82pts - 85-3 v Rugby Lions 21.03.09
Away Win: 58pts -71-13 v Worthing 11.04.09
Home Defeat: 40pts - 19-59 v Northampton 27.4.96
Away Defeat: 63pts - 13-76 v Bath 15.5.99

MOST CONSECUTIVE
Victories: 15 (06.12.08 - 25.04.09)
Defeats: 6 (twice)

INDIVIDUAL RECORDS

MOST APPEARANCES
by a forward: 148 Paul Burnell
by a back: 97 (14) Dave Millard

MOST CONSECUTIVE
Appearances: 53 Nick Grecian 10.9.88-21.11.92
Matches scoring Tries: 6 Nick Grecian

Matches scoring points: 12 Nick Grecian/Jannie de Beer

MATCH RECORDS

Most Points
30   John Steele   v Rugby 29.3.97 (A)

Most Tries
4   Charles Broughton   v Bridgwater 14.03.09 (H)
     Rory Damant   v Lydney 07.03.09 (H)
     Frankie Neale   v Barking 06.12.08 (H)

Most Conversions
10   James Brown   v Barking 06.12.08 (H)

Most Penalties
6   Ian McAusland   v Sale 5.9.98 (H)

Most Drop Goals
3   Murray Walker   v W Hartlepool 23.4.94 (H)

SEASON RECORDS

Most Points	256	John Steele	96-97
Most Tries	18	Rory Damant	08-09
Most Conversions	86	James Brown	08-09
Most Penalties	47	John Steele	96-97
Most Drop Goals	6	Jannie de Beer	98-99

CAREER RECORDS

Most Points	474	John Steele	94-97
Most Tries	28	DaveMillard	89-99
Most Conversions	86	James Brown	08-09
Most Penalties	91	John Steele	94-97
Most Drop Goals	10	John Steele	94-97

LAST TEN SEASONS

	Division	P	W	D	L	F	A	P.D.	Pts	Pos	Most Points		Most Tries	
99-00	Did not compete in the leagues													
00-01	HM1	18	17	0	1	554	118	436	34	2p				
01-02	L4NW	18	14	0	4	533	214	319	28	1p				
02-03	L3NW	18	16	0	2	560	199	361	32	1p				
03-04	Lon 2N	22	20	1	1	752	277	475	41	1p				
04-05	Lon 1	22	15	0	7	676	343	333	30	4				
05-06	Lon 1	22	16	1	5	840	324	516	33	3				
06-07	Lon 1	22	20	0	2	997	235	762	40	1p				
07-08	N3 S	26	17	0	9	633	410	223	83	5	71	Lee Cholewa	12	Matt Fitzgerald
08-09	N3 S	26	25	1	0	1092	328	764	120	1p	253	James Brown	18	Rory Damant

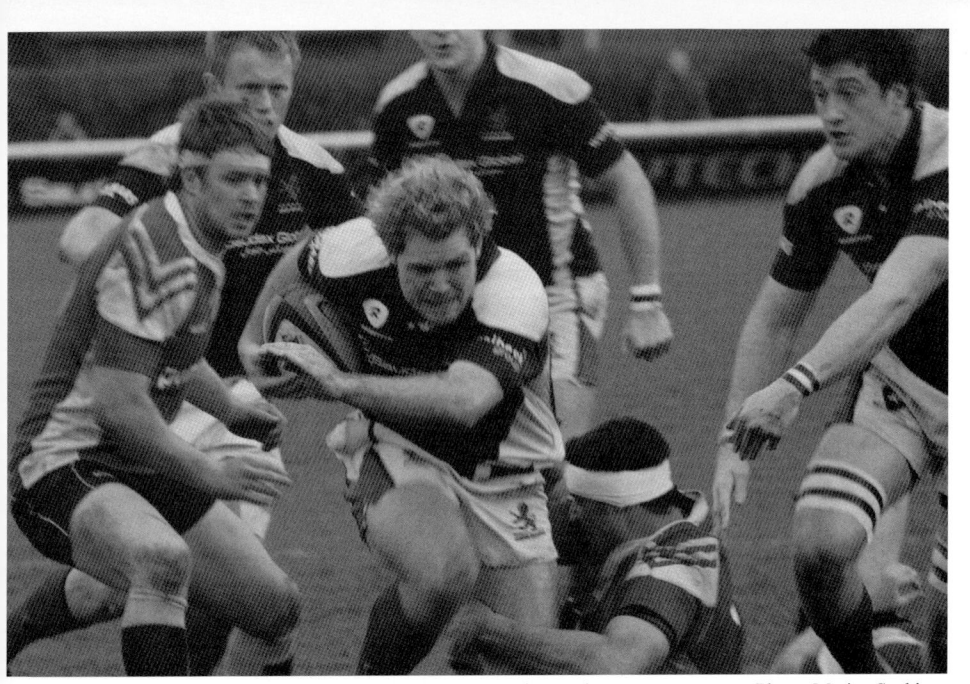

Rory Damant breaks clear on the way to one of his four tries against Lydney. Photo: Marina Scukina

PLAYERS

	Position	D.o.B.	Apps.	Pts.	T	C	P	DG
Frankie Neale	Full back		13 (1)	77	11	11	-	-
Roman Piotrowski	Winger		23	60	12	-	-	-
Charles Broughton	Winger		33 (2)	112	22	1	-	-
Gareth Swales	Winger		27 (6)	105	21	-	-	-
Rory Damant	Centre		21 (1)	90	18	-	-	-
Ian McInroy	Centre		19 (3)	30	6	-	-	-
Gary Truman	Centre		11 (2)	25	5	-	-	-
James Brown	Fly half		23	253	3	86	21	1
Simon Amor	Scrum half		18 (3)	59	6	10	3	-
Owain Walbyoff	Scrum half		28 (12)	25	5	-	-	-
Lorne Ward	Prop		17 (7)	15	3	-	-	-
Steve Millard	Prop		21 (15)	20	4	-	-	-
Matt Johnson	Prop		52 (5)	35	7	-	-	-
Andy Fahey	Hooker		12 (13)	25	5	-	-	-
Stuart Silvester	Hooker		23 (12)	15	3	-	-	-
Ben Gotting	Hooker		11 (1)	25	5	-	-	-
Andrew Smith	Lock		36 (8)	5	1	-	-	-
Iain Fullerton	Lock		13 (4)	10	2	-	-	-
Grant Livingstone	Lock		27 (4)	35	7	-	-	-
Paul Volley	Back row		23	5	1	-	-	-
Mark Soden	Back row		20	25	5	-	-	-
William Lipp	Back row		16 (4)	15	3	-	-	-
Alexander Karonias	Back row		10 (3)	25	5	-	-	-

MANCHESTER

Founded: 1860

Colours:
Red & white hooped shirt, blue shorts

Change colours:
Navy shirt with red & white trim

Website:
www.manchesterrugby.co.uk

KEY PERSONNEL

President	Ian Brown
Club Secretary	Jenni Deakin 44 Deva Close, Poynton, Cheshire SK12 1HH Tel: 07990 534986 Fax: 0161 485 1115 Jennideakin@yahoo.co.uk
Fixture Secretary	Jenni Deakin as above Tel: 0161 485 1115 Fax: 0161 485 1115
Team Secretary	Gareth Jones c/o the club Tel: 0161 485 1115 Fax: 0161 485 1115 garethgsjones@lineone.net

CONTACT DETAILS

Manchester Rugby Club,
Grove Park, Grove Lane, Cheadle Hulme, Cheshire SK8 7NB
Tel: 0161 485 1115 Fax: 0161 485 1115
e-mail: enquiries@manchesterrugby.co.uk

GROUND DETAILS

Address:
Grove Park, Grove Lane, Cheadle Hulme, Cheshire. SK8 7NB.
Tel: 0161 485 1115
Fax: 0161 485 1115
e-mail: enquiries@manchesterrugby.co.uk

Capacity: 4,500
Covered Seating: 275
Covered Standing 700

Directions:
From North: Exit M60 at junc 3, Cheadle Royal, head south on A34 (Wilmslow) for 2.5 miles to second roundabout. Exit left (B5095) club is 400 meters on the right.
From South: M56 Manchester Airport to A34 (Heald Green) then towards Wilmslow, left onto B5095 to Bramhall. Club is approx a mile on right
Nearest BR Station: Bramhall.

Car Parking:
120 spaces available within the ground.

Admission:
Match day: Members £10, non members £14,   u-16: Free
Season Ticket: £115 members, £190 non members

Club Shop:
Open Sat. & Sun. 10-5pm. Contact Iain Stewart 0771 121 7825

Clubhouse:
Open every day 11am-11pm. Three bars with food available throughout the day. **Functions**: up to 160 for a seated meal.
Contact Steward, Simon Ramsden-Smith 0161 483 3733

PROGRAMME

Size: A5   Pages: 16
Price: FOC
Editor: Jenni Deakin
Advertising Rates- contact Jenni Deakin

FOUNDED IN 1860
AS MANCHESTER
FOOTBALL CLUB

REVIEW OF THE SEASON 2008-09

Manchester's return to National One after a four year absence lasted just one season as they finished bottom of the table with just two wins in 30 matches, some four points behind Otley, who were also promoted the previous season along with Manchester into the division.

Their two wins were a narrow 16-12 away win at local rivals Sedgley Park just before Christmas which ended a 16 matches losing streak from the start of the season, which was a club record, and then in March they finally secured a home win after 11 straight defeats with a 35-17 win at Grove Park against Newbury.

Winger Gareth Wynne was again the leading points scorer for the club with 121 and that made it three successive years at top points scorer, but this was his lowest return. In the try scoring stakes centre Andre Wilson led the way with seven tries, one more than Richard Wainwright, which took him to 40 in his career at Manchester as he passed 100 league appearances.

Bizarrely they suffered their worst ever home defeat away from home, late in the season they switched their match with Leeds Carnegie to Headingley from Grove Park for a mid week match under lights and were beaten 104-0.

Prop Nick Flynn started the most matches 29 as he extended his club record for appearances to 168 (+13 as sub) after being an ever present last season in National Two.

Despite being relegated Manchester were well represented in the English Counties squad on their tour of Asia with Matt Owen, Pat Leach, Tom Eaton, Seb Moss all selected.

MANCHESTER'S SEASON - 2008-09

NATIONAL ONE

Date	H/A	Opponents	Result & Score	Att.	15	14	13	12	11
30-08	A	Bedford	L 0-62	1933	Coulbeck	Wynne	Wilson	Rawlings	O'Regan
06-09	H	Sedgley Park	L 35-51	631	Coulbeck	Wynne/3c3p	Wilson/t	Rawlings	O'Regan
13-09	A	Plymouth Albion	L 6-47	2163	Coulbeck	Wynne/2p	Wilson	Rawlings	O'Regan
20-09	H	Doncaster*	L 23-39	423	Coulbeck	Wellock	Parrott	Rawlings	Wynne/c3p
28-09	A	Leeds Carnegie	L 0-57	3092	Coulbeck	Wellock	Parrott	Rawlings	Knowles
04-10	H	Cornish Pirates	L 6-12	341	Coulbeck	Wellock	Parrott	Rawlings	Wynne/2p
11-10	A	Esher	L 19-36	827	Coulbeck	Wynne/t3p	Wilson/t	Rawlings	Wellock
18-10	H	Rotherham	L 35-54	471	Coulbeck	Wynne/3c3p	Parrott	Rawlings/t	O'Regan
25-10	A	Coventry	L 18-29	978	Coulbeck	Knowles/tc2p	Wilson/t	Parrott	O'Regan
01-11	A	Exeter	L 19-26	374	Coulbeck/t	Knowles/t	Wilson	Parrott	Wynne/3p
08-11	A	Newbury	L 6-26	434	Coulbeck	Wynne/2p	Wilson	Parrott	Wainwright
15-11	H	London Welsh	L 14-19	293	Coulbeck	Wynne/2t2c	Wilson	Rawlings	Wainwright
22-11	H	Otley	L 14-15	393	Coulbeck/t	Wainwright	Wilson	Rawlings	Wynne/3p
30-11	A	Nottingham	L 8-57	1247	Knowles	Wynne/p	Parrott	Rawlings	Irlam
06-12	A	Moseley	L 7-48	822	Knowles/tc	Wynne	Wilson	Rawlings	Irlam
13-12	H	Bedford	L 5-25	324	Knowles	Wynne	Wilson	Parrott	Irlam
20-12	A	Sedgley Park	W 16-12	526	Wainwright	Knowles/c3p	Wilson	Rawlings	Irlam
27-12	H	Plymouth Albion	L 5-31	410	Wainwright	Knowles	Wilson	Rawlings	Irlam
03-01	A	Doncaster	L 10-52	1169	Wainwright	Wynne	Wilson	Rawlings	Irlam
25-01	A	Cornish Pirates	L 10-25	2068	Knowles	Irlam	Wilson/t	Parrott	O'Regan
31-01	H	Esher*	L 28-40	283	Knowles/2c3p	Styles/t	Wilson	Rawlings	Blackwell
14-02	A	Rotherham	L 13-15	792	Knowles	Styles	Wilson	Rawlings	Blackwell
21-02	H	Coventry	L 24-41	347	Wainwright	Styles	Wilson/2t	Rawlings	O'Regan
07-03	A	Exeter	L 5-40	3949	Coulbeck	Wainwright	Parrott(d/t)	Leach	O'Regan
14-03	H	Newbury	W 35-17	314	Coulbeck/2t	Wainwright/2t	Parrott	Leach	O'Regan
28-03	A	London Welsh	L 10-57	920	Coulbeck	Wainwright	Parrott	Leach/t	O'Regan
04-04	A	Otley	L 18-29	450	Coulbeck	Styles	Parrott	Leach/t	O'Regan
08-04	A	Leeds Carnegie	L 0-104	1781	Coulbeck	O'Regan	Parrott	Knight	Taylor
11-04	H	Nottingham	L 23-49	324	Taylor(e/t)	O'Regan/t	Parrott	Eaton	Wynne/2c3p
25-04	H	Moseley	L 21-50	387	Wainwright	O'Regan	Parrott/t	Leach	Wynne

EDF ENERGY NATIONAL TROPHY

4 17-01	H	London Scottish	L 25-33		Wainwright	Wynne/t2c2p	Parrott	Leach/t	O'Regan

SCORING BREAKDOWN

WHEN	Total	First Half	Second Half	1/4	2/4	3/4	4/4
the POINTS were scored	433	190	243	83	107	112	131
the POINTS were conceded	1165	581	584	320	261	141	338
the TRIES were scored	50	16	34	8	8	15	19
the TRIES were conceded	171	84	87	46	38	35	51

HOW	Total	Pen. Try	Backs	Forwards	F Back	Wing	Centre	H Back	F Row	Lock	B Row
the TRIES were scored	50	2	30	18	3	12	6	9	6	3	9
the TRIES were conceded	171	1	109	61	13	47	33	16	15	6	40

KEY: * after opponents name indicates a penalty try.
Brackets after a player's name indicates he was replaced. eg (a) means he was replaced by replacement code "a" and so on.
/ after a player or replacement name is followed by any scores he made - eg /t, /c, /p, /dg or any combination of these

10	9	1	2	3	4	5	6	7	8
Wainwright	Runciman	Gadd	Oxley	Flynn	Owen	Norris	Lloyd	Dew	Moss
Wainwright/2t	Runciman	Gadd	Oxley	Flynn/t	Owen	Norris	Lloyd	Dew	Moss
Wainwright	Stringer	Mantell	Oxley	Flynn	Collier	Norris	Lloyd	Dew	Moss
Wainwright/tc	Stringer	Gadd	Oxley	Flynn	Ralph	Norris	Owen	Dew	Moss
Wainwright	Stringer	Gadd	Platt	Flynn	Collier	Norris	Owen	Lewis	Moss
Wainwright	Runciman	Gadd	Platt	Flynn	Ralph	Norris	Owen	Dew	Moss
Wainwright	Runciman	Gadd	Platt	Flynn	Ralph	Norris	Owen	Dew	Moss
Wainwright	Runciman/t	Gadd	Platt	Flynn/t	Ralph	Norris	Lloyd/t	Dew	Moss
Eaton	Stringer	Gadd	Platt	Flynn	Ralph	Norris	Lloyd	Dew	Moss
Eaton	Stringer	Gadd	Oxley	Flynn	Ralph	Norris	Owen	Lewis	Lloyd
Eaton	Stringer	Gadd	Oxley	Flynn	Ralph	Norris	Owen	Dew	Lloyd
Eaton	Stringer	Gadd	Oxley	Flynn	Ralph	Norris	Owen	Dew	Moss
Eaton	Runciman	Birchall	Oxley	Flynn	Ralph	Norris	Owen	Dew	Moss
Wainwright	Runciman	Birchall	Wilson	Flynn	Ralph	Norris	Williams/t	Lewis	Lloyd
Wainwright	Runciman	Birchall	Oxley	Flynn	Ralph	Norris	Lloyd	Dew	Moss
Eaton	Runciman	Birchall	Oxley	Irvine	Ralph/t	Norris	Lloyd	Dew	Moss
Eaton	Stringer	Birchall	Oxley	Flynn	Ralph	Norris	Lloyd	Dew	Moss/t
Eaton	Stringer	Birchall	Oxley	Flynn	Ralph	Norris	Lloyd	Dew	Moss(a/t)
Eaton	Runciman/t	Birchall	Oxley	Flynn	Ralph	Norris	Owen	Dew/t	Moss
Eaton	Runciman	Birchall/t	Oxley(b/t)	Flynn	Collier	Norris	Williams	Dew	Owen
Wainwright/t	Runciman	Birchall	Oxley	Flynn	Ralph	Norris	Collier	Dew	Owen
Eaton/c2p	Runciman	Birchall/t	Oxley	Flynn	Ralph	Norris	Collier	Dew	Owen
Eaton/2c	Runciman	Birchall	Oxley	Flynn	Ralph(c/2t)	Norris	Collier	Holmes	Owen
Eaton	Runciman	Birchall	Oxley	Flynn	Holmes	Norris	Owen	Dew	Moss
Eaton/2c2p	Runciman	Birchall	Oxley	Flynn/t	Ralph	Collier	Holmes	Porter	Moss
Eaton/p(f/c)	Runciman	Birchall	Oxley	Flynn	Ralph	Collier	Holmes	Dew	Moss
Eaton/cp(f/p)	Runciman	Birchall	Oxley	Flynn	Ralph/t	Norris	Owen	Dew	Moss
Wainwright	Runciman	Mantell	Oxley	Flynn	Collier	Norris	Williams	Moss	Owen
Wainwright	Runciman	Birchall	Wilson	Flynn	Ralph	Norris	Moss	Dew	Owen
Eaton/2p	Runciman/t	Birchall/t	Wilson	Flynn	Ralph	Norris	Moss	Dew	Owen
Eaton	Runciman	Mantell	Oxley	Flynn/t	Ralph	Norris	Owen	Dew	Lloyd

REPLACEMENTS a- T Mantell   b- C Wilson   c- D Ward   d- A Wilson
                 e- S Williams   f- A Taylor

LEAGUE APPEARANCES

- 29 Nick Flynn
- 28 Ed Norris (1)
- 24 Gareth Dew (2), Richard Wainwright (4)
- 23 Seb Moss (1), Paul Ralph (2)

NUMBER OF PLAYERS USED

35 plus 6 as a replacement only

LEAGUE POINTS SCORERS

Pts	Player	T	C	P	DG
121	Gareth Wynne	3	11	28	-
49	Joe Knowles	3	5	8	-
36	Tom Eaton	-	6	8	-
35	Andre Wilson	7	-	-	-
32	Richard Wainwright	6	1	-	-
20	Ben Coulbeck	4			

MANCHESTER STATISTICS

LEAGUE

NATIONAL ONE

TEAM RECORDS

MOST POINTS
Scored at Home: 101 v Nuneaton 25.04.98
Scored Away: 70 v Barking 14.4.07
Conceded at Home: 72* v Rotherham 6.04.02
Conceded Away: 85 v Exeter 28.2.04
* conceded 104 (104-0) at Headingley when they were the designated home side after changing the venue 8.4.09

MOST TRIES
Scored in a match: 15 v Nuneaton 25.4.98
Conceded in a match: 13 v Exeter 28.2.04

BIGGEST MARGINS
Home Win: 89pts - 101-12 v Nuneaton 25.4.98
Away Win: 55pts - 70-15 v Barking 14.4.07
Home Defeat: 65pts - 7-72 v Rotherham 6.04.02
Away Defeat: 79pts - 6-85 v Exeter 28.2.04

MOST CONSECUTIVE
Victories: 9
Defeats: 16 (30/8/2008 - 13.12.2008))

INDIVIDUAL RECORDS

MOST APPEARANCES
by a forward: 168 (13) Nick Flynn
by a back: 126 Isaac Richmond

MOST CONSECUTIVE
Matches scoring Tries: 6 Tim Burgon
Matches scoring points: Steve Swindell

MATCH RECORDS

Most Points
28 Steve Swindells v Hereford 22.3.97 (H)

Most Tries
5 Matt Hoskins v Camberley

Most Conversions
10 Steve Swindells v Nuneaton 25.4.98

Most Penalties
9 Marcus Barrow v Wakefield 15.12.01 (H)

Most Drop Goals
2 Rod Ellis v Orrell 2.10.99 (H)

SEASON RECORDS

Most Points	398	Steve Swindells	97-98
Most Tries	24	Lucas Onyango	04-05
Most Conversions	91	Steve Swindells	97-98
Most Penalties	70	Steve Swindells	98-99
Most Drop Goals	3	Rod Ellis	98-99 & 99-00

CAREER RECORDS

Most Points	1413	Steve Swindells	96-01
Most Tries	46	Tim Burgon	96-01
Most Conversions	242	Steve Swindells	96-01
Most Penalties	267	Steve Swindells	96-01
Most Drop Goals	6	Rod Ellis	96-00

LAST TEN SEASONS

	Division	P	W	D	L	F	A	P.D.	Pts	Pos	Most Points	Most Tries
99-00	P2	26	11	0	15	513	617	-104	22	8	237 Steve Swindells	6 Matt Kirke
00-01	N1	26	12	0	14	471	549	-78	53	8	162 Steve Swindells	7 Stuart Williams
01-02	N1	26	8	0	18	381	758	-377	36	12	141 Marcus Barrow	6 Dave Muckalt
02-03	N1	26	7	0	19	484	791	-307	39	12	152 Simon Verbickas	7 Martin Worthington
03-04	N1	26	1	2	23	363	1007	-644	13	14r	107 Stuart Brown	6 Isaac Richmond
04-05	N2	26	12	2	12	694	541	153	68	6	120 Lucas Onyango	20 Lucas Onyango
05-06	N2	26	13	2	11	475	545	-70	63	6	146 Andre Wilson	10 Jonathan Lowden
06-07	N2	26	12	1	13	605	490	115	64	8	147 Gareth Wynne	8 Gareth Wynne
07-08	N2	26	21	0	5	803	461	342	104	2p	286 Gareth Wynne	15 Richard Wainwright
08-09	N1	30	2	0	28	444	1165	-721	17	16r	121 Gareth Wynne	7 Andre Wilson

RFU SENIOR CUP

OVERALL PLAYING RECORD

	P	W	D	L	F	A	Pts Diff
Home	14	9	0	5	373	235	138
Away	14	8	0	6	316	442	-126
Neutral	0	0	0	0	0	0	0
TOTAL	28	17	0	11	689	677	12

TEAM RECORDS

Highest Score: 57 v Blackheath 02/03 (H)
Biggest Winning Margin: 57 (57-0) v Blackheath 02/03 (H)
Highest Score Against: 78 v Exeter 04-05 (A)
Biggest Losing Margin: 78 (78-0) v Exeter 04-05 (A)

SEASON BY SEASON

Season	Result	Season	Result	Season	Result	Season	Result	Season	Result
71-72	DNQ	78-79	DNQ	85-86	DNQ	92-93	DNQ	99-00	QF
72-73	DNQ	79-80	DNQ	86-87	DNQ	93-94	DNQ	00-01	5R
73-74	DNQ	80-81	DNQ	87-88	DNQ	94-95	DNQ	01-02	5R
74-75	DNQ	81-82	DNQ	88-89	DNQ	95-96	1R	02-03	4R
75-76	DNQ	82-83	DNQ	89-90	DNQ	96-97	2R	03-04	3R
76-77	DNQ	83-84	DNQ	90-91	DNQ	97-98	4R	04-05	4R
77-78	DNQ	84-85	DNQ	91-92	4R	98-99	2R		

NATIONAL TROPHY

05-06	4R	06-07	5R	07-08	5R	08-09	4R

MANCHESTER PLAYERS

	Position	Apps.	Pts.	T	C	P	DG
Ben Coulbeck	Full back	51	87	17	1	-	-
Selorm Kaudey	Winger	12	50	10	-	-	-
Andrew Vilk	Winger	10	25	5	-	-	-
Matt O'Regan	Winger	8(5)	15	3	-	-	-
Will Cliff	Scrum half	2(8)	5	1	-	-	-
Gareth Wynne	Winger	42(6)	433	16	79	64	1
Scott Rawlings	Centre	51	139	14	15	13	-
Andre Wilson	Fly half	91	359	33	37	38	2
Richard Wainwright	Fly half	47(1)	120	21	3	1	2
Jim Bramhall	Scrum half	115(7)	126	17	13	3	2
Nick Flynn	Prop	139(13)	105	21	-	-	-
Marshall Gadd	Prop	16(9)	5	1	-	-	-
Thomas Mantell	Prop	14(32)	-	-	-	-	-
Henry Platt	Hooker	55(6)	15	3	-	-	-
Craig Wilson	Hooker	8(4)	5	1	-	-	-
Matt Owen	Lock	125(7)	25	5	-	-	-
Paul Ralph	Lock	23	40	8	-	-	-
Stuart Eboral	Back row	14(2)	10	2	-	-	-
Seb Moss	Back row	21(3)	5	1	-	-	-
Gareth Dew	Back row	15(4)	15	3	-	-	-
Jonathan Keep	Back row	36(6)	30	6	-	-	-

NEWBURY RFC

KEY PERSONNEL

All unfinished email addresses are @newburyrfc.co.uk

President	David Smith	07801 666116 (M)	email: president@
Chairman	Bill Brogden	07775 678231 (M)	email: chairman@
Treasurer	tbc		email: treasurer@
Club Secretary	Dave Smith	07824 994717 (M)	email: secretary@
Chairman Commercial	Chris Dunn		email: commercial@
Chairman of Youth Rugby	Bill Brogden	07775 678231 (M)	
Fixture Secretary	Brian Lee	01635 552678	email: fixtures@
1st Team Manager	Andy Widdop	07747 535799 (M)	
			email: andyphysio@aol.com
1st Team Coach	Ben Sturnham		email: coach@

Founded: 1928
Nickname: The Blues
Colours: Navy, sky & white irregular hooped shirts, blue shorts & socks
Change colours: White with red hoop
Training Nights: Tuesday & Thursday 7-9pm
Web site: www.newburyrfc.co.uk

CONTACT DETAILS

Except where shown separately above all correspondence to:
c/o Newbury RFC, Monks Lane, Newbury. RG14 7RW
Tel: 01635 40103   Fax: 01635 40533   email: info@newburyrfc.co.uk

GROUND DETAILS

Address:
Monks Lane, Newbury, Berkshire RG14 7RW
Tel : 01635 40103   Fax: 01635 40533
e-mail: info@newburyrfc.co.uk

Capacity: 8,000
Covered Seating: 200

Directions: From M4, take A34 south towards Winchester, ignore immediate signs to Newbury and at the 3rd exit take the signs to Highclere and Wash Common. At the resulting roundabout turn left. After about a mile you'll come to a double roundabout (The Gun & The Bell PH's), turn right onto Monks Lane. The Club is 400 yards on your RHS.
Nearest BR Station: Newbury (10 mins walk from ground)
Car Parking: 300 on ground, 1000 nearby @ £2.
Admission:
Matchday: Adults £10, Students/OAP's £8, u16 Free
Season: £130.00
Club Shop:
Open Sat 12-5pm, Sun 10-1pm.
email: info@newburyrfc.co.uk
Clubhouse:
Open 7am – 9pm daily. Normal licensing hours.
Business Conferencing, Banqueting, Private Celebrations, Corporate Hospitality, Fitness Studio, Aerobics Suite, 4 Conference Rooms and hosts of International Rugby. Contact Andy McKelvie 01635 40103

PROGRAMME

Size: A5   Pages: 40
Price: £2

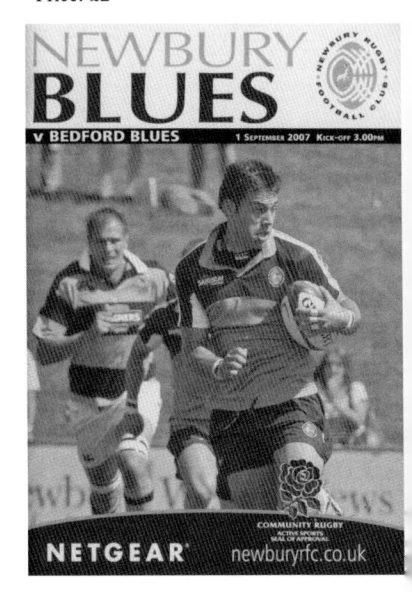

REVIEW OF THE SEASON 2008-09

Despite losing 75% of their squad due to budget cuts Newbury RFC exceeded expectations last season finishing 14th in National Division one which would normally have been enough to survive relegation. The RFU reorganisation of level two however has seen the Blues unexpectedly placed in the new National One at Level Three.

They remained competitive throughout the season helped by loan players from Bath and Bristol. They also uncovered new talent with new comer Ross Noonan becoming the club's player of the season. During the season Noonan played in every back 5 forward position, including his favoured position of 6. Noonan's versatility and industry sums up the season for the Blues where they had to be creative to remain competitive.

New coach Ben Sturnham pulled together a remarkable squad from a virtual standing start. Blues now find themselves in a much better position for this season having retained the services of Sturnham and several key players.

Ben Stevenson finished the season as leading points scorer with 95 points just one more than Gareth Griffiths.

During the season they suffered their worst ever home defeat in league rugby going down 89-12 to eventual Champions Leeds Carnegie and in the process conceded a club record 13 tries.

Scoring tries was a problem and they only picked up two try bonus points all season which was the lowest number in the division as their four year stay in the second tier of English rugby came to an end.

NEWBURY'S SEASON - 2008-09

Date	H/A	Opponents	Result & Score	Att.	15	14	13	12	11
NATIONAL ONE									
31-08	A	Cornish Pirates	L 5-48	2846	Williams	Humphries/t	Sweeney	Henderson	Defty
06-09	H	Moseley	L 12-30	488	Williams	Nutt	Henderson	Humphries	Ridgers/t
13-09	A	Bedford	L 12-53	2133	Williams	Perry	Henderson	Humphries	Nutt
20-09	H	Plymouth Albion	W 19-11	395	Williams	Henderson	Wakeling	Humphries	Nutt
27-09	A	Doncaster	L 9-37	846	Williams	Hylton	Henderson	Humphries	Nutt
04-10	H	Esher	L 8-14	680	Williams	Hylton	Henderson	Burns	Nutt/t
11-10	H	London Welsh	L 9-20	875	Williams	Hylton	Sweeney	Burns	Nutt
19-10	A	Nottingham	L 3-48	1277	Williams	Henderson	Sweeney	Burns	Hylton
25-10	H	Otley	W 26-20	499	Williams/t	Henderson	Hylton	Burns	Nutt
01-11	A	Coventry	L 7-31	1204	Williams	Ridgers	Hylton/t	Burns	Nutt
08-11	H	Manchester	W 26-6	434	Williams	Hylton	Henderson/2t	Burns	Ridgers
15-11	H	Exeter	L 20-37	703	Hylton/t	Nutt	Henderson	Burns	Ridgers
23-11	A	Rotherham	L 5-62	1127	Hylton	Williams	Henderson	Burns	Nutt
29-11	H	Leeds Carnegie	L 12-89	316	Williams/t	Henderson	Sweeney	Humphries	Hylton/t
06-12	A	Sedgley Park	L 37-42	564	Hylton	Henderson	Sweeney	Humphries	Scott(c/t)
20-12	A	Moseley	L 9-36	700	Hylton	Henderson	Sweeney	Burns	Scott
27-12	H	Bedford	L 0-34	878	Hylton	Nutt	Scott	Burns	Crane
03-01	A	Plymouth Albion	D 17-17	4087	Hylton	Nutt	Sweeney	Humphries	Scott/t
24-01	A	Esher	L 18-49	1049	Hylton	Scott	Sweeney/t	Humphries	Crane
31-01	A	London Welsh	L 12-40	980	Hylton	Nutt	Scott	Sweeney	Perry
21-02	A	Otley	D 12-12	450	Hylton	Nutt	Sweeney	Humphries	Crane
28-02	H	Cornish Pirates	L 10-39	433	Perry	Crane	Scott	Humphries	Nutt
07-03	H	Coventry	W 14-10	590	Hylton	Perry	Sweeney	Scott	Ridgers
14-03	A	Manchester	L 17-35	314	Hylton	Perry	Sweeney	Scott	Ridgers(e/2t)
21-03	H	Doncaster	L 17-50	310	Hylton	Perry	Sweeney	Scott	Crane/t
28-03	A	Exeter	L 5-44	4120	Hylton	Nutt	Henderson	Sweeney/t	Crane
04-04	H	Rotherham	L 21-23	446	Hylton	Crane/t	Henderson	Scott	Nutt/t
12-04	A	Leeds Carnegie	L 14-57	3564	Perry	Scott	Henderson(g/t)	Sweeney	Ridgers/t
15-04	H	Nottingham	L 16-23	514	Hylton	Nutt	Henderson	Scott	Crane
25-04	H	Sedgley Park	L 27-30	603	Hylton	Nutt	Henderson	Scott	Williams
EDF ENERGY NATIONAL TROPHY									
17-01	A	London Welsh	L 17-42		Hylton	Nutt	Sweeney/t	Henderson	Crane

SCORING BREAKDOWN

WHEN	Total	First Half	Second Half	1/4	2/4	3/4	4/4
the POINTS were scored	419	178	241	92	86	137	104
the POINTS were conceded	1047	481	566	239	242	267	299
the TRIES were scored	48	17	31	7	10	17	14
the TRIES were conceded	146	64	82	32	32	35	47

HOW	Total	Pen. Try	Backs	Forwards	F Back	Wing	Centre	H Back	F Row	Lock	B Row
the TRIES were scored	48	-	30	18	3	12	6	9	6	3	9
the TRIES were conceded	146	8	91	47	12	42	20	17	14	6	27

KEY: ** after opponents name indicates a penalty try.*
Brackets after a player's name indicates he was replaced. eg (a) means he was replaced by replacement code "a" and so on.
/ after a player or replacement name is followed by any scores he made - eg /t, /c, /p, /dg or any combination of these

10	9	1	2	3	4	5	6	7	8
Griffiths	Gasson	Green	Fincken	Fidler	Ashcroft Leigh	Brown	Lee	Fox	Noonan
Griffiths/c	Gasson	Green	Fincken	Fidler	Ashcroft Leigh	Griffiths	Lee/t	Bentall	Noonan
Griffiths/c	Kessell(a/t)	Burgess	Fincken	Fidler	Ashcroft Leigh	Noonan	Edwards	Lee/t	Witcombe
Griffiths/3p	Gasson/t	Green	Fincken/t	Fidler	Ashcroft Leigh	Noonan	Clark	Fox	Witcombe
Griffiths/3p	Gasson	Green	Fincken	Fidler	Ashcroft Leigh	Noonan	Clark	Fox	Witcombe
Stevenson/p	Gasson	Green	Clark	Fidler	Ashcroft Leigh	Noonan	Perkins	Fox	Witcombe
Griffiths/3p	Gasson	Catt	Clark	Fidler	Griffiths	Noonan	Lee	Fox	Witcombe
Griffiths/p	Gasson	Catt	Clark	Burgess	Griffiths	Attwood	Lee	Fox	Pennycook
Griffiths/2c3pdg	Gasson	Catt/t	Clark	Fidler	Griffiths	Brown	Lee	Pennycook	Noonan
Griffiths(b/c)	Kessell	Catt	Clark	Fidler	Griffiths	Brown	Lee	Pennycook	Phillips
Stevenson/3c	Gasson/t	Catt	Fincken	Fidler	Griffiths	Mockford	Lee	Fox/t	Witcombe
Stevenson/2c2p	Gasson/t	Catt	Fincken	Fidler	Griffiths	Mockford	Fox	Pennycook	Witcombe
Stevenson	Gasson/t	Green	Fincken	Fidler	Griffiths	Mockford	Lee	Fox	Witcombe
Griffiths/c	Avery	Catt	Clark	Fidler	Attwood	Griffiths	Noonan	Pennycook	Phillips
Griffiths/dg	Stevenson/3cp	Green	Clark	Catt/t	Griffiths	Mockford/t	Bentall/2t	Pennycook	Lee
Griffiths	Stevenson/3p	Catt	Clark	Ion	Griffiths	Mockford	Lee	Bentall	Pennycook
Griffiths	Stevenson	Catt	Fincken	Ion	Ashcroft Leigh	Mockford	Pennycook	Fox	Griffiths
Griffiths/4p	Gasson	Fidler	Fincken	Ion	Ashcroft Leigh	Mockford	Noonan	Fox	Witcombe
Griffiths/2p(b/c)	Gasson	Green	Fincken	Fidler(d/t)	Ashcroft Leigh	Noonan	Witcombe	Fox	Phillips
Stevenson/c	Gasson	Green	Clark	Fidler	Ashcroft Leigh	Mockford/t	Witcombe/t	Fox	Phillips
Griffiths/c	Gasson	Catt	Clark/t	Fidler	Ashcroft Leigh	Mockford	Bentall/t	Fox	Griffiths
Griffiths/p(b/tc)	Gasson	Green	Clark	Fidler	Ashcroft Leigh	Mockford	Bentall	Fox	Phillips
Stevenson/3p	Kessell/t	Green	Fincken	Pendleton	Ashcroft Leigh	Mockford	Noonan	Fox	Phillips
Stevenson/c	Kessell	Green	Fincken	Pendleton	Witcombe	Mockford	Noonan	Fox(f/t)	Phillips
Griffiths/t	Stevenson/2cp	Clark	Fincken	Pendleton	Ashcroft Leigh	Mockford	Noonan	Fox	Witcombe
Griffiths	Stevenson	Clark	Fincken	Fidler	Ashcroft Leigh	Mockford	Bentall	Fox	Noonan
Griffiths	Stevenson/c3p	Clark	Fincken	Fidler	Ashcroft Leigh	Mockford	Pennycook	Bentall	Noonan
Griffiths/2c	Kessell	Green	Clark	Pendleton	Noonan	Griffiths	Pennycook	Fox	Witcombe
Griffiths/dg	Stevenson/c2p	Green	Clark	Fidler	Griffiths/t	Mockford	Bentall	Pennycook	Noonan
Griffiths/2c	Stevenson/c2p(a/t)	Green	Clark	Fidler/t	Kench	Mockford	Ashcroft Leigh	Noonan	Griffiths/t
Griffiths/tc	Gasson	Catt	Fincken	Fidler/t	Ashcroft Leigh	Mockford	Noonan	Fox	Witcombe

NATIONAL ONE

REPLACEMENTS

a- W Gasson b- B Stevenson c- C Ridgers d- N Catt
e- R Crane   f- M Lee   g- M Nutt

LEAGUE APPEARANCES

24	John Hylton (1)
23	Gareth Griffiths (6)
22	Tom Fidler (4)
20	Sean Fox (1)

LEAGUE POINTS SCORERS

Pts	Player	T	C	P	DG
95	Ben Stevenson	1	18	18	-
94	Gareth Griffiths	1	10	20	3
30	Waylon Gasson	6	-	-	-
20	Rhys Crane	4	-	-	-

NUMBER OF PLAYERS USED

40 plus 8 as a replacement only

NEWBURY STATISTICS

LEAGUE

TEAM RECORDS

MOST POINTS
Scored at Home: 91 v Tabard 28.3.97
Scored Away: 74 v Askeans 19.4.97
Conceded at Home: 89 v Leeds Carnegie 29.11.08
Conceded Away: 79 v Bedford Blues 29.4.06

MOST TRIES
Scored in a match: 15 v Tabard 28.3.97
Conceded in a match: 13 v Leeds Carnegie 29.11.08

BIGGEST MARGINS
Home Win: 87pts - 87-0 v Met. Police 22.2.97
Away Win: 69pts - 74-5 v Askeans 19.4.87
Home Defeat: 50pts - 3-53 v Bracknell 7.4.01
Away Defeat: 58pts - 13-71 v Rotherham 12.4..08

MOST CONSECUTIVE
Victories: 26
Defeats: 8 (4.3.06 to 9.9.06)

INDIVIDUAL RECORDS

MOST APPEARANCES
by a forward: 152 Chris Hart
by a back: 140 (27) Mal Roberts

MOST CONSECUTIVE
Appearances: 30 Colin Hall
Matches scoring Tries: 5 Brian Johnson
Matches scoring points: 24 Nick Grecian

MATCH RECORDS

Most Points
    32   Nick Grecian   v Charlton Park 25.1.97 (H)
                                     v Met Police 22.2.97 (H)
Most Tries
    4   Brian Johnson   v Askeans 19.4.97 (A)
                                     v Plymouth 26.4.97 (H)
Most Conversions
    11   Nick Grecian   v Charlton Park 25.1.97 (H)
Most Penalties
    6   Fraser Jones   v Esher 6.9.03 (A)
Most Drop Goals
    1   By eight different players

SEASON RECORDS

Most Points	391	Nick Grecian	96-97
Most Tries	27	Brian Johnson	96-97
Most Conversions	100	Nick Grecian	96-97
Most Penalties	44	Dave Harvey	04-05
Most Drop Goals	5	Dave Harvey	04-05

CAREER RECORDS

Most Points	563	Nick Grecian	96-98
Most Tries	63	Craig Davies	96-02
Most Conversions	135	Nick Grecian	96-98
Most Penalties	84	Mal Roberts	98-06
Most Drop Goals	5	Dave Harvey	04-05

LAST TEN SEASONS

	Division	P	W	D	L	F	A	P.D.	Pts	Pos	Most Points	Most Tries
99-00	JN1	26	15	1	10	550	483	67	31	5	123 Dave Griffiths	10 Jeremy Griffiths
00-01	N2	*25	10	1	14	437	502	-65	21	9	85 Mal Roberts	8 Jeremy Griffiths
01-02	N2	26	12	0	14	548	723	-175	24	9	165 Ian Morgan	8 Craig Davies
02-03	N2	26	11	0	15	491	618	-127	22	9	152 Mal Roberts	6 Jo Czerpak
03-04	N2	26	12	0	14	589	546	43	24	9	128 Mal Roberts	9 Marcus McCluggage
04-05	N2	26	20	0	6	635	390	245	93	2p	285 Dave Harvey	11 Martin Nutt
05-06	N1	26	8	2	16	614	905	-291	46	11	225 Blair Feeney	10 Chris Cracknell
06-07	N1	30	11	0	19	661	774	-113	57	11	217 Tim Walsh	13 Mal Roberts, Martin Nutt
07-08	N1	30	8	1	21	497	792	-295	45	13	98 Tim Walsh	8 Martin Nutt
08-09	N1	30	4	2	24	419	1047	-628	27	14r	95 Ben Stevenson	6 Waylon Gasson

NATIONAL ONE

RFU SENIOR CUP

OVERALL PLAYING RECORD

	P	W	D	L	F	A	Pts Diff
Home	10	8	0	2	414	154	260
Away	17	9	0	8	400	410	-10
Neutral	0	0	0	0	0	0	0
TOTAL	27	17	0	10	814	564	250

TEAM RECORDS

Highest Score: 114 v Spalding 02/03
Biggest Winning Margin: 114 (114-0)v Spalding 02/03
Highest Score Against: 46 v Richmond 98/99
Biggest Losing Margin: 34 (46-12) v Richmond 98/99

SEASON BY SEASON

Season	Result	Season	Result	Season	Result	Season	Result	Season	Result
71-72	DNQ	78-79	DNQ	85-86	DNQ	92-93	1R	99-00	3R
72-73	DNQ	79-80	DNQ	86-87	DNQ	93-94	DNQ	00-01	3R
73-74	DNQ	80-81	DNQ	87-88	DNQ	94-95	DNQ	01-02	5R
74-75	DNQ	81-82	DNQ	88-89	DNQ	95-96	DNQ	02-03	3R
75-76	DNQ	82-83	DNQ	89-90	DNQ	96-97	5R	03-04	3R
76-77	DNQ	83-84	DNQ	90-91	DNQ	97-98	5R	04-05	3R
77-78	DNQ	84-85	DNQ	91-92	DNQ	98-99	4R		

NATIONAL TROPHY

| 05-06 | 5 R | 06-07 | Q.F. | 07-08 | 4 R | 08-09 | 4 R |

NATIONAL ONE

PLAYERS

Name	Position	D.o.B.	Apps.	Pts.	T	C	P	DG
John Hyltton	Winger	06/04/1981	48 (4)	45	9	-	-	-
Matt Williams	Full Back		14 (2)	10	2	-	-	-
Martin Nutt	Winger	18/10/1981	98 (16)	182	36	1	-	-
Matt Humphries	Winger		11 (2)	5	1	-	-	-
Matt Humphreies	Winger		11 (2)	5	1	-	-	-
Rhys Crane	Winger		8 (2)	20	4	-	-	-
Marc Sweeney	Centre		15 (2)	10	2	-	-	-
Nick Scott	Centre		14 (4)	5	1	-	-	-
Andrew Henderson	Centre	11/11/1987	42 (9)	29	5	2	-	-
Gareth Griffiths	Fly half		23 (6)	94	1	10	20	3
Ben Stevenson	Fly half		15 (6)	95	1	18	18	-
Waylon Gasson	Scrum half		16 (4)	30	6	-	-	-
Luke Burns	Scrum half		10	-	-	-	-	-
Robert Green	Prop		15 (9)	-	-	-	-	-
Nathan Catt	Prop		11 (2)	15	3	-	-	-
Tom Fidler	Prop		24 (8)	5	1	-	-	-
Joe Clark	Hooker		19 95)	5	1	-	-	-
Paul Fincken	Hooker		40 (6)	30	6	-	-	-
Ian Ashcroft Leigh	Lock	08/09/1987	42 (13)	5	1	-	-	-
Bradley Mockford	Lock		17 (1)	10	2	-	-	-
Ross Noonan	Back row		19 (7)	-	-	-	-	-
Mark Lee	Back row		11 (5)	15	3	-	-	-
Cheevy Pennycook	Back row		16 (5)	-	-	-	-	-
Scott Witcombe	Back row		14 (7)	5	1	-	-	-

275

NUNEATON RFC

KEY PERSONNEL

President	Keith J Howells	Tel: 07714 293436
Chairman	Robert Ryan	Tel: 07887 688518
Treasurer	Susan Ryan	Tel: 07709 303363
Secretary	Maggie Mander	

Homeland, Weddington Rd., Caldecote, Nuneaton CV10 0TS
Tel: 02476 381893 or 07808-734054 (M)
Telephone first for fax or send to club fax
email: margaret.mander@btopenworld.com

Fixture Secretary	Steve Bird

c/o Nuneaton RFC as below
Tel: 02476 348279 Fax: 02467 383925 Mob: 07740 747960
email: hangingjudgebird@yahoo.co.uk

Team Manager	To be advised
Director of Rugby	Mike Umaga
Match Liaison:	David Cadden Tel: 07870-408625
Bar Manager:	Diane Packer Tel: 07989-691803

Founded: 1879
Nickname: The Nuns
Colours: Red, white & black hoops
Change colours: White, red, black
Training Nights: Tuesday and Thursday
Website: www.nuneatonrugby.com

CONTACT DETAILS
Nuneaton RFC Ltd.,
Liberty Way, Attleborough Fields, Nuneaton, Warks. CV10 0TS.
Tel: 02476 383206   Fax: 02476 383925

GROUND DETAILS
Address:
Liberty Way, Attleborough Fields, Nuneaton, Warks. CV10 0TS.
   Tel: 02476 383206   Fax: 02476 383925
   email: margaret.mander@btopenworld.com
Capacity: Unlimited standing
Directions:
M1 (from south) to M6, A444 town centre and M5 to M42, M6, A444 town centre, Follow M69 (Leicester) and crematorium.
M1 (from north) to M69, A5, A47 to town centre, left at first roundabout (Eastborough Way), follow sign for crematorium.
Club is situated on Eastborough Way opposite crematorium.
Nearest BR Station: Nuneaton, 5 mins by taxi
Car Parking: Unlimited
Admission: Matchday: £8 Adult (including programme) Season £85
Clubhouse: Normal licensing hours.
Food available Tues, Thur, matchdays & Sun morning.
Functions: Room and marquee available for hire.
Contact Diane Packer Tel:07989-631803
Club Shop: Open Training Nights, Match Days and Sundays.
Contact Teresa Bird 02476-348279

PROGRAMME
Size: A5   Pages: Approx 30   Price: £1
Editor: John Green
Advertising: Geraldine Blake 02476-383925

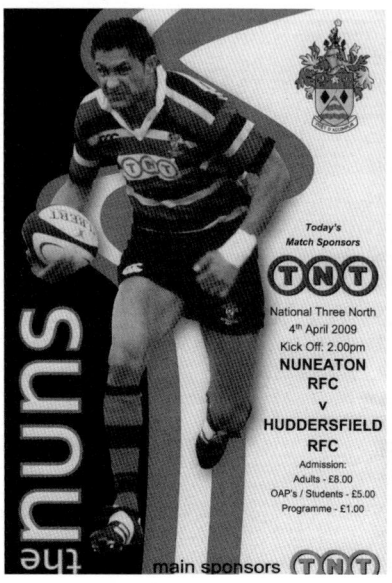

Insets L-R - Top: Llyr Griffiths, Nathan Roy-Smith, Lucas Roy-Smith, Jamie Taylor
Bottom: Brook Davies, Ian Critchley, Rickie Aley, Adam Woodfield.
L-R - Back Row: John Green (Team Manager), Lee Young (Physio), Richard Johnson, Scott Wright, Mark White, Adam Jones, Stuart Friswell (Coach), Mike Umaga (Director of Rugby).   **Middle Row:** Mickey Moore, Alex Taylor, Will Cave, Dan Hurst, Matt Aston, Arron Turner, Tim Pickard, Ben Gilbert, Paul Ryan, Nick Smith.
Front Row: Rob Cook, Adam Bray, Huw Thomas, Nick Murray (TNT), David Warden (Chairman), Gary Holmes (Captain), Keith Howells (President), Maggie Mander Howells (Secretary), Aaron Takarangi, Simon Brocklehurst, Tim Douglas

REVIEW OF THE SEASON 2008-09

None of us thought after losing our first game of last season to Leicester Lions that we would be celebrating as league winners some eight months later. Credit for this remarkable achievement has to be bestowed upon our Director of Rugby, Mike Umaga, and his team.

Throughout the season the squad jelled together and worked as a unit. This camaraderie was also present off the pitch and in training sessions. Mike's "clear and simple" game plan paid off and areas of weakness from the previous season were worked upon and improved. Thirty-seven players were used during the season to cover a total of thirty-one games (including friendlies and Cup). Eleven had twenty or more starts and of these eleven five played twenty-eight games. In the EDF cup we beat Longton (away) but then lost at home to Hull.

Highlights of our year included the selection to England Counties of Ricky Aley, Rob Cook and Huw Thomas. As well as his selection for England Counties, Huw also played for Warwickshire and was our top points scorer of the season (184 points). Our top try scorer was Will Cave with 18 tries to his credit.

Our 2nd XV once again played in the North Midlands Reserve League and finished in 3rd position just six points behind the league winners.

Unlike the previous year, our Colts side did not progress past the second round of the National Cup. They did, however, reach the final of the Warwickshire Cup but failed to secure the Cup for a second year in succession. Our Ladies Team did not have such a good season but we are hopeful they will continue and build on successes of previous years.

We are looking forward to the season in the newly formed National 1 and it will be good to meet some old friends and make new acquaintances.

NUN'S CHAMPIONSHIP SEASON - 2008-09

Date	H/A	Opponents	Result & Score	Att.	15	14	13	12	11
NATIONAL THREE NORTH									
06-09	H	Leicester Lions	L 16-19	237	Cook(a/t)	Cave	Johnson	Taylor	Takarangi
13-09	H	Loughborough Students	W 41-30	175	Cook	Cave	Johnson	Douglas	Takarangi/t
20-09	A	Fylde	D 27-27	410	Moore/t	Cave/t	Johnson	Douglas	Takarangi
27-09	H	Halifax	W 39-10	230	Cook/2tc	Cave	Johnson	Douglas	Takarangi
04-10	A	Harrogate	W 23-17	150	Cook	Cave	Johnson	Douglas	Takarangi/t
11-10	H	Macclesfield	W 41-35	213	Cook	Cave/2t	Johnson	Douglas	Takarangi/t
01-11	H	Caldy	L 23-31	148	Cook	Cave/t	Johnson	Douglas	Takarangi/2t
08-11	A	Darlington MP	W 44-17	143	Brocklehurst	Cave/t	Blackmore	Douglas	Takarangi/t
15-11	H	Hull Ionians	W 29-6	127	Cook/t	Cave	Brocklehurst	Douglas/t	Takarangi/t
29-11	A	Bradford Bingley	W 19-16	225	Cook/t	Moore	Cave	Douglas	Takarangi
06-12	H	Preston Grasshoppers	W 46-22	175	Moore/t	Cave/3t	Taylor	Douglas	Takarangi/2t
20-12	A	Huddersfield	W 20-6	283	Moore	Cave	Taylor/t	Douglas	Takarangi
03-01	A	Loughborough Students	W 23-7	150	Moore	Cave	Taylor	Douglas	Takarangi(b/p)
24-01	A	Halifax	W 37-14	167	Jones	Cave/2t	Taylor(c/t)	Douglas	Takarangi/t
31-01	H	Harrogate	W 32-9	153	Moore	Cave/2t	Taylor	Douglas	Takarangi
14-02	H	Kendal	W 21-13	330	Moore	Cave/t	Taylor	Douglas	Takarangi
21-02	A	Caldy	W 15-7	413	Moore	Cave/t	Taylor	Douglas	Takarangi
07-03	A	Hull Ionians	W 30-8	300	Cave	Johnson	Taylor	Douglas	Takarangi/t
21-03	H	Bradford Bingley	W 51-10	210	Jones	Johnson	Taylor(d/t)	Douglas	Takarangi
28-03	A	Preston Grasshoppers	W 50-24	301	Cook	Johnson/2t	Taylor	Douglas/t	Takarangi/t
04-04	H	Huddersfield	W 42-22	283	Moore/2t	Johnson	Taylor	Douglas/t	Takarangi
11-04	A	Kendal	L 29-44	650	Moore	Johnson	Taylor	Douglas/t	Takarangi/t
18-04	A	Leicester Lions	W 25-20	200	Cook	Cave/t	Brocklehurst	Douglas/t	Takarangi
25-04	H	Darlington MP	W 31-25	225	Cook/3t	Moore/t	Cave/t	Douglas	Takarangi
02-05	A	Macclesfield	L 16-21	250	Moore	Johnson	Cave	Douglas	Takarangi
09-05	H	Fylde	W 50-5	203	Cook	Gilbert/3t	Takarangi/tc	Douglas	Moore/2t

NATIONAL ONE

EDF ENERGY NATIONAL TROPHY

1	18-10	A	Longton	W 20-13		Cook	Cave/t	Johnson	Douglas	Takarangi
2	22-11	H	Hull	L 16-22		Cook/t	Cave/t	Johnson	Douglas	Takarangi

SCORING BREAKDOWN

WHEN	Total	First Half	Second Half	1/4	2/4	3/4	4/4
the POINTS were scored	820	432	388	199	233	161	227
the POINTS were conceded	465	234	231	120	114	110	116
the TRIES were scored	101	50	51	23	27	20	31
the TRIES were conceded	56	24	32	11	13	14	17

HOW	Total	Pen. Try	Backs	Forwards	F Back	Wing	Centre	H Back	F Row	Lock	B Row
the TRIES were scored	101	-	72	29	12	36	10	14	11	1	17
the TRIES were conceded	55	1	34	21	4	17	6	7	4	5	12

KEY: * *after opponents name indicates a penalty try.*
Brackets after a player's name indicates he was replaced. eg (a) means he was replaced by replacement code "a" and so on.
/ after a player or replacement name is followed by any scores he made - eg /t, /c, /p, /dg or any combination of these

10	9	1	2	3	4	5	6	7	8
Aley/c3p	Thomas	Davies	Wright	Pickard	Hurst	Mitchell	Holmes	Critchley	Aston
Aley/t3c4pdg	Thomas	Davies/t	Bray	Pickard/t	Hurst	Aston	Smith	Critchley	Holmes
Cook	Thomas/c5p	Davies	Bray	Pickard	Hurst	Holmes	Smith	Critchley	Naivalu
Aley/3c2p	Thomas	Davies/t	Bray	Pickard/t	Hurst	Aston	Smith	Critchley/t	Holmes
Aley/6p	Thomas	Davies	Bray	Pickard	Hurst	Aston	White	Critchley	Holmes
Aley/3c2p3dg	Thomas/t	Ryan	Bray	Pickard	Hurst	Aston	Turner	Critchley	Holmes
Aley/cpdg	Thomas	Ryan	Bray	Pickard	Hurst	Griffiths	Holmes	White	Taylor
Aley/4c2p	Thomas/t	Davies	Bray	Pickard	Hurst	Griffiths	Holmes/2t	Critchley/t	Taylor
Aley/3cp	Thomas	Davies	Bray	Pickard	Hurst	Griffiths	Holmes/t	Critchley	Taylor
Aley/p3dg	Thomas/c	Davies	Bray	Ryan	Hurst	Griffiths	Holmes	Critchley	Aston
Cook	Thomas/t4cp	Davies	Bray	Pickard	Hurst	Griffiths	Smith	Holmes	Aston
Cook	Thomas/t2c2p	Davies	Bray	Ryan	Hurst	Griffiths	Smith	Holmes	Aston
Cook/tdg	Thomas/2cp	Davies	Bray	Ryan	Hurst	Griffiths	Smith	Holmes/t	Aston
Cook/t	Thomas/3c2p	Davies	Bray	Ryan	Hurst	Griffiths	Smith	Holmes	Aston
Cook	Thomas/3c2p	Davies	Bray	Ryan	Hurst	Griffiths	Smith	Holmes/t	Aston/t
Cook	Thomas/c3p	Davies	Bray/t	Ryan	Hurst	Griffiths	Smith	Holmes	Aston
Cook/t	Thomas/cp	Davies	Bray	Ryan	Hurst	Griffiths	Smith	Holmes	Aston
Cook/tc	Thomas/tc2p	Davies	Bray	Ryan	Hurst	Griffiths	Smith	Holmes/t	Aston
Cook/2t	Thomas/5c2p	Davies/2t	Bray	Ryan	Hurst	Griffiths	Critchley	Holmes/2t	Aston
Thomas/t6cp	Roy Smith	Davies	Bray	Ryan	Hurst/t	Griffiths	Smith	Holmes/t	Aston
Cook/t	Thomas/3c2p	Davies/t	Bray/t	Ryan	Hurst	Griffiths	Holmes	Critchley	Aston
Cook	Thomas/2c	Davies	Bray/t	Ryan	Hurst	Griffiths	Holmes/2t	Critchley	Aston
Aley/2cpdg	Thomas	Davies	Bray/t	Ryan	Hurst	Griffiths	Smith	Critchley	Holmes
Aley/3c	Thomas	Davies	Bray	Ryan	Hurst	Griffiths	Smith	Roy Smith	Holmes
Cook	Thomas/c3p	Davies	Bray	Ryan	Hurst	Turner	Critchley	Roy Smith	Holmes/t
Thomas/3c	Roy Smith	Davies	Bray	Ryan	Hurst	Griffiths	Smith	Holmes/2tc	Aston
Aley/2c2p	Thomas/t	Ryan	Wright	Pickard	Hurst	Holmes	Turner	Marston	Taylor
Aley/2p	Thomas	Davies	Bray	Pickard	Hurst	Griffiths	Holmes	White	Aston

REPLACEMENTS

a- M Moore b- R Aley c- R Johnson d- S Brocklehurst

LEAGUE APPEARANCES

26 Daniel Hurst, Gary Holmes, Huw Thomas, Aaron Takarangi,
25 Tim Douglas (1), Rob Cook, Adam Bray (1)
24 Brook Davies (1)

NUMBER OF PLAYERS USED

32 plus 6 as a replacement only

LEAGUE POINTS SCORERS

Pts	Player	T	C	P	DG
189	Huw Thomas	6	39	27	-
150	Rickie Aley	1	23	24	9
80	Will Cave	16	-	-	-
77	Rob Cook	14	2	-	1
72	Garry Holmes	14	1	-	-
72	Aaron Takarangi	14	1	-	-

NATIONAL ONE

NUNEATON STATISTICS

LEAGUE

TEAM RECORDS

MOST POINTS
Scored at Home: 91 v Lydney 24.1.04
Scored Away: 50 v Preston G 28.3.09
Conceded at Home: 51 v Doncaster 16.3.02
Conceded Away: 101 v Manchester 25.4.98

MOST TRIES
Scored in a match: 15 v Lydney 24.1.03 (H)
Conceded in a match: 15 v Manchester 25.4.98 (A)

BIGGEST MARGINS
Home Win: 91pts - 91-0 v Lydney 24.1.04
Away Win: 37pts - 37-0 v Winnington Park 1.3.97
Home Defeat: 25pts - 14-39 v Sheffield 26.9.98
Away Defeat: 89pts -12-101 v Manchester 25.4.98

MOST CONSECUTIVE
Victories: 14 (08.11.08 - 4.04.09)
Defeats: 9 (22.11.97 - 31.1.98)

INDIVIDUAL RECORDS

MOST APPEARANCES
by a forward: 150 Alan Roberts
by a back: 159 (3) Jody Peacock

MOST CONSECUTIVE
Appearances: 45 Richard Moore 12.9.98 - 26.2.00
Matches scoring Tries:
9 Gary Marshall 02/03, Nick Hill 03/04
Matches scoring points: 18 Jody Peacock 02/03

MATCH RECORDS

Most Points
25 Gareth Cull v Harrogate 14.4.07 (H)

Most Tries
4 Alistair Baron v Sandal 20.10.01 (H)
   Jordan Hands v Lydney 24.1.04 (H)
   Tristan Prosser Shaw v Kendal 22.4.06 (A)

Most Conversions
10 Gareth Cull v Harrogate 14.4.07 (H)

Most Penalties
5 M Drane v Exeter 8.10.88 (A)
   Vasile Ion v Roundhay 23.11.91 (H)
   Gareth Cull Four times

Most Drop Goals
3 Rickie Aley v Bradford 29.11.08 (A)
              v Macclesfield 11.10.08 (H)

SEASON RECORDS

Most Points	259	Gareth Cull	05-06
Most Tries	21	Jody Peacock	02-03
		Gary Marshall	02-03
		Phil Read	05-06
Most Conversions	49	Gareth Cull	05-06
Most Penalties	51	Gareth Cull	06-07
Most Drop Goals	9	Rickie Aley	08-09

CAREER RECORDS

Most Points	688	Jody Peacock	99-06
Most Tries	79	Jody Peacock	99-04
Most Conversions	119	Gareth Cull	04-07
Most Penalties	120	Gareth Cull	04-07
Most Drop Goals	13	Rickie Aley	07-09

LAST TEN SEASONS

	Division	P	W	D	L	F	A	P.D.	Pts	Pos	Most Points	Most Tries
99-00	N2 N	26	11	1	14	610	665	-55	23	8	145 Marc Thomas	11 Steve Carter
00-01	N3 N	26	15	1	10	597	605	-8	31	5	139 Warwick Masser	20 Gary Marshall
01-02	N3 N	26	12	0	14	599	585	14	24	8	119 Jody Peacock	14 Alistair Baron
02-03	N3 N	26	23	0	3	802	406	396	46	1p	176 Jody Peacock	21 G Marshall & Jody Peacock
03-04	N2	26	17	1	8	655	405	250	35	3	201 Jody Peacock	17 Jody Peacock
04-05	N2	26	10	2	14	447	660	-213	52	12r	128 Gareth Cull	7 Jody Peacock
05-06	N3 N	26	21	1	4	705	382	323	97	2p/sp	259 Gareth Cull	21 Phil Read
06-07	N2	26	12	0	14	600	573	27	58	10	254 Gareth Cull	11 Lee Parry
07-08	N2	26	6	0	20	456	747	-291	32	12r	110 Hugh Thomas	9 Aaron Takarangi
08-09	N3 N	26	21	1	4	819	465	354	103	1p	189 Huw Thomas	16 Will Cave

NATIONAL ONE

RFU SENIOR CUP

OVERALL PLAYING RECORD

	P	W	D	L	F	A	Pts Diff
Home	26	14	0	12	488	429	59
Away	17	6	0	11	220	442	-222
Neutral	-	-	-	-	-	-	-
Total	43	20	0	23	708	871	-163

TEAM RECORDS

Highest Score: 39 v Macclesfield 02/03
Biggest Winning Margin: 27 (27-0) v Stockwood Park 89/00
Highest Score Against: 118 v Northampton 99/00
Biggest Losing Margin: 115 (118-3) v Northampton 99/00

SEASON BY SEASON

Season	Result	Season	Result	Season	Result	Season	Result	Season	Result
71-72	DNQ	78-79	DNQ	85-86	1R	92-93	DNQ	99-00	4R
72-73	DNQ	79-80	DNQ	86-87	DNQ	93-94	1R	00-01	2R
73-74	DNQ	80-81	DNQ	87-88	1R	94-95	1R	01-02	4R
74-75	DNQ	81-82	3R	88-89	2R	95-96	1R	02-03	3R
75-76	DNQ	82-83	DNQ	89-90	3R	96-97	1R	03-04	4R
76-77	DNQ	83-84	3R	90-91	1R	97-98	2R	04-05	2R
77-78	DNQ	84-85	2R	91-92	1R	98-99	2R		

NATIONAL TROPHY

05-06	3R	06-07	5R	07-08	4R	08-09	2R

PLAYERS

	Position	Apps.	Pts.	T	C	P	DG
Rickie Aley	Full back/Fly half	17 (1)	193	1	31	29	13
Aaron Takarangi	Winger	49	117	23	1	-	-
William Cave	Winger	33	110	22	-	-	-
Michael Moore	Winger	18 (5)	45	9	-	-	-
Tim Douglas	Centre	36 (1)	35	7	-	-	-
Simon Brocklehurst	Centre	67 (7)	68	13	-	1	-
Richard Johnson	Centre	13 (9)	15	3	-	-	-
Alex Taylor	Centre	13 (3)	5	1	-	-	-
Rob Cook	Fly half/Centre	47(1)	125	25	-	-	-
Hugh Thomas	Scrum half	68 (18)	304	11	51	49	-
Lucas Roy Smith	Scrum half	1 (9)	-	-	-	-	-
Brook Davies	Prop	24 (1)	25	5	-	-	-
Paul Ryan	Prop	18 (7)	-	-	-	-	-
Adam Woodfield	Prop	(7)	-	-	-	-	-
Adam Bray	Hooker	55 (8)	25	5	-	-	-
Scott Wright	Hooker	1 (18)	-	-	-	-	-
Daniel Hurst	Lock	28 (2)	10	2	-	-	-
Llyr Griffiths	Lock	19	-	-	-	-	-
Aaron Turner	Lock	2 (1)	-	-	-	-	-
Nick Smith	Back row	14 (5)	-	-	-	-	-
Garry Holmes	Back row	52	87	17	1	-	-
Matthew Aston	Back row	20 (1)	5	1	-	-	-
Ian Critchley	Back row	50 (9)	45	9	-	-	-
Nathan Roy Smith	Back row	3 (14)	-	-	-	-	-

NATIONAL ONE

OTLEY R.U.F.C.

Founded: 1865
Colours:
All Black
Change colours:
White shirts, black shorts
Training Nights:
Tuesday & Thursday
Websites:
otleyrugbyclub.co.uk
otleyrugby.co.uk

KEY PERSONNEL

President	Mike K Henry
Chairman	Paul Carter
Treasurer	Neil Blenkin
Club Secretary & Fixture Sec.	Ronnie Franks
	38 Ings Lane, Guiseley, Leeds LS20 8DA
	Tel: 01943 877086 (H) 07759 819345 (M)
	email: ronniefranks@aol.com
Director of Rugby	Mike Wright
Commercial Secretary	Paul H Whatmuff and Mike Gillson
Head Coach	Mark Luffman
Press Officer	John Finch Tel: 01943 872491

CONTACT DETAILS

c/o Otley RFC, Cross Green, Otley. LS21 1HE
Tel: 01943 461180   Fax: 01943 850142
email: otleyrugby@btconnect.com

PROGRAMME

Size: A5   Pages: 40
Price: £2
Editor: Peter Thompson

Advertising Rates:
Contact Mike Gillson 07930 926648

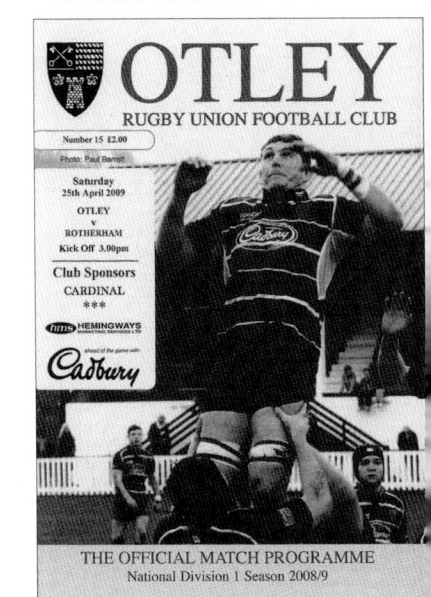

GROUND DETAILS

Address:
Cross Green, Otley. LS21 1HE
Tel: 01943 461180   Fax: 01943 850142
email: otleyrugby@btconnect.com

Capacity: 7,000
Seated: 499
Covered capacity: 1000

Directions:
400 yards from town centre on A659 Pool Road.

Nearest BR Station: Leeds
Car Parking:
100 on ground and opposite the club down Bremner Street.

Admission:
Matchday - £12, Concessions £8;
Season - £150, Concessions £100

Club Shop:
Franchised to J R Sports, Jonathan Ross. 01943 466775

Clubhouse:
Normal licensing hours
with snacks available matchdays only
Functions: Capacity up to 140

REVIEW OF THE SEASON 2008-09

The aim of the season was to establish a foothold in National 1 and it soon became obvious this was going to be harder than was first thought. Head Coach Peter Clegg strengthened the side by recruiting well but last years 'Player of the Year' Richard Snowball never played a game all season due to injury & Guy Easterby retired from the game.

Otley lost the first 12 games of the season and never recovered from this point. The announcement in December that 5 teams will be demoted put the 'tin hat' on the rest of the season.

The team was held together by the loyal support from all its members, the loan of some young talented players from Leeds Carnegie to whom we are very grateful and hard work from the head coach and Mark Luffman (1st team coach).

We broke an unenvious record this season with our record league loss of 95-5 at Nottingham in March but at least Ian Shuttleworth put us on the board with our solitary try.

Suffered a club record 12 straight defeats from the opening day of the season till they narrowly beat Manchester in November. Fly half Tom Rhodes was the top points scorer in his debut season with 104 points whilst winger Peter Wackett was the leading try scorer with five. Scrum half Dave McCormack played most matches, 27, including 25 starts.

Although we are a small market town with only 14,000 inhabitants, we have been punching well above our weight for the last ten seasons but we will have to wait and see if we can sustain this.

At the time of writing, preparations are well under way for the new season

Photos: Paul Barrett
Above: Prop Kris Pullman demonstrating good technique.
Below: Ben Steele touches down against Manchester.

283

OTLEY'S SEASON - 2008-09

Date	H/A	Opponents	Result & Score	Att.	15	14	13	12	11
NATIONAL ONE									
30-08	A	Doncaster	L 15-36	868	Shuttleworth	Kitching/tcp	Buchanan	Dench	Smith
06-09	H	Esher	L 12-18	516	Shuttleworth	Parsons	Buchanan	Dench	Kitching/4p
14-09	A	Leeds Carnegie	L 14-58	4112	Shuttleworth	Parsons	Dench	Buchanan	Smith/t
20-09	H	Cornish Pirates	L 25-31	675	Shuttleworth	Kitching	Buchanan	Dench	Smith(a/2t)
27-09	A	Moseley	L 26-36	836	Shuttleworth	Kitching	Dench	Mooney/2t	Parsons
04-10	H	Plymouth Albion	L 16-31	550	Shuttleworth	Wackett	Burrell	Mooney	Kitching/t
11-10	A	Bedford	L 12-37	2464	Wackett	Dench	Burrell	Mooney	Kitching
18-10	H	Exeter	L 0-69	460	Monks	Kitching	Dench	Mooney	Smith
25-10	A	Newbury	L 20-26	499	Shuttleworth	Dench	Burrell/t	Mooney	Kitching/2t
01-11	H	Nottingham	L 3-43	952	Shuttleworth	Kitching	Buchanan	Burrell	Wackett
08-11	H	London Welsh	L 6-9	1053	Wackett	Dench	Burrell	Mooney	Kitching
15-11	A	Coventry	L 3-48	838	Wackett	Dench	Burrell	Mooney	Smith
22-11	A	Manchester	W 15-14	393	Wackett	Dench/t	Burrell/t	Mooney	Smith
29-11	H	Sedgley Park	W 14-7		Wackett	Dench	Buchanan	Mooney	Andre
06-12	A	Rotherham	L 13-42	1067	Wackett	Andre	Burrell	Mooney	Smith
13-12	H	Doncaster	L 16-27	457	Wackett	Andre	Burrell/t	Buchanan	Smith
20-12	A	Esher	L 16-48	956	Greendale	Wackett/t	Burrell	Buchanan	Smith
26-12	H	Leeds Carnegie	L 10-66	2610	Shuttleworth	Buchanan	Whatmuff	Dench	Smith
03-01	A	Cornish Pirates	L 13-55	2073	McCormack	Roberts	Dench	McCormish	Smith
24-01	A	Plymouth Albion	L 15-23	3799	Shuttleworth/cp	Parsons	Burrell	Dench	Andre
31-01	H	Bedford	L 17-23	522	Wackett	Parsons	Burrell	Dench	Andre/t
21-02	H	Newbury	D 12-12	450	Shuttleworth	Wackett/t	Burrell	Dench	Andre
08-03	A	Nottingham	L 5-95	1318	Shuttleworth/t	Parsons	Buchanan	Dench	Kitching
14-03	A	London Welsh	L 25-39	780	Wackett	Parsons	Burrell	Buchanan/t	Whittaker
28-03	H	Coventry	L 13-32	463	Shuttleworth	Wackett	Parsons	Dench	Andre
04-04	H	Manchester	W 29-18	450	Monks/t	Parsons/t	Buchanan	Dench	Wackett
11-04	A	Sedgley Park*	L 29-36	497	Wackett/t	Parsons	Burrell/t	Buchanan	Andre
18-04	A	Exeter	L 17-80	2899	Wackett/2t	Silau	Dench	Buchanan	Parsons/c
25-04	H	Rotherham	L 7-39	1249	Monks	Parsons/t	Dench	Buchanan	Wackett
		Moseley	L 0-20		The match was cancelled with the agreement of the RFU at Otley's request.				

EDF ENERGY NATIONAL TROPHY

| 4 | 17-01 | H | Cambridge | L 6-34 | | Dench | Andre | Burrell | Buchanan | Smith |

SCORING BREAKDOWN

WHEN		Total	First Half	Second Half		1/4	2/4	3/4	4/4
the POINTS were scored		418	232	186		145	87	99	87
the POINTS were conceded		1118	517	601		266	251	299	302
the TRIES were scored		47	22	25		17	5	12	13
the TRIES were conceded		154	67	87		34	33	45	42

HOW	Total	Pen. Try	Backs	Forwards	F Back	Wing	Centre	H Back	F Row	Lock	B Row
the TRIES were scored	47	1	30	16	5	13	8	4	4	5	7
the TRIES were conceded	154	5	89	60	13	37	28	11	16	13	31

KEY: * after opponents name indicates a penalty try.
Brackets after a player's name indicates he was replaced. eg (a) means he was replaced by replacement code "a" and so on.
/ after a player or replacement name is followed by any scores he made - eg /t, /c, /p, /dg or any combination of these

10	9	1	2	3	4	5	6	7	8
Monks	McCormack/t	Trethewey	Parkes	Fullman	Williams	Parr	McCormish	Stockdale	Lewis
Rhodes	McCormack	Trethewey	Parkes	Fullman	Parr	Williams	Lewis	Bland	McCormish
Rhodes/2c	McCormack	Wederell	Kay	Fullman	Parr	Williams	Lewis	McCormish	Baldwin/t
Rhodes/2c2p	McCormack	Wederell	Parkes	Fullman	Lewis	Williams	Baldwin/t	Bland	McCormish
Rhodes/3c	McCormack/t	Wederell	Parkes	Fullman	Parr	Williams/t	Lewis	Baldwin	McCormish
Rhodes/2p	McCormack	Trethewey	Parkes	Fullman	Denton	Williams	Baldwin/t	Rowan	McCormish
Rhodes/4p	McCormack	Trethewey	Steele	Wederell	Denton	Williams	Baldwin	Rowan	McCormish
Rhodes	McCormack	Trethewey	Steele	Fullman	Parr	Williams	McNeil Matthews	Rowan	Baldwin
Rhodes/cp	McCormack	Trethewey	Steele	Wederell	Denton	Williams	Baldwin	Hyde	McCormish
Rhodes/p	McCormack	Trethewey	Steele	Steele	Parr	Denton	Baldwin	Hyde	McCormish
Rhodes/2p	McCormack	Trethewey	Kay	Black	Denton	Williams	Baldwin	Hyde	McCormish
Whittaker/p	McCormack	Trethewey	Kay	Black	Parr	Williams	Baldwin	Rowan	Hyde
Rhodes/cp	McCormack	Wederell	Kay	Fullman	Denton	Williams	Baldwin	Hyde	McCormish
Rhodes/3p	McCormack	Wederell(b/t)	Kay	Hopcroft	Parr	Denton	Baldwin	Rowan/t	McCormish
Rhodes/c2p	McCormack	Trethewey	Kay	Hopcroft	Parkes	Williams	Baldwin	Rowan	Hyde
Rhodes/2p(c/cp)	McCormack	Trethewey	Kay	Hopcroft	Denton	Williams	Parr	Hyde	Baldwin
Rhodes/c3p	Brown	Wederell	Kay	Hopcroft	Williams	Parr	McCormish	Hyde	Baldwin
Rhodes/cp	Brown	Trethewey	Kay	Fullman	Parr/t	Williams	McCormish	Hyde	Baldwin
Rhodes/c2p	Brown	Trethewey	Kay	Fullman	Parr	Williams	Lewis	Hyde/t	Baldwin
Greendale	Brown	Wederell/t	Kay	Fullman	Craig	Denton/t	Lewis	Rowan	Hyde
Shuttleworth/2cp	Brown	Wederell	Steele	Fullman	Craig	Denton	Parr	Hyde/t	Lewis
Greendale/tc	McCormack	Wederell	Kay	Fullman	Craig	Williams	Lewis	Hyde	McCormish
Monks	McCormack	Wederell	Kay	Fullman	Parr	Lewis	Steele	Andre	Hyde
Greendale/t2c2p	McCormack	Wederell	Kay	Fullman	Denton/t	Craig	Lewis	Andre	Hyde
Greendale/c2p	McCormack	Wederell/t	Steele	Fullman	Denton	Williams	Lewis	Hyde	McCormish
Greendale/3cp	McCormack	Wederell	Steele/t	Fullman	Lewis	Williams	Andre	Hyde/t	McCormish
Monks/3cp	McCormack	Wederell	Steele	Swainston	Craig	Williams/t	Lewis	Hyde	McCormish
McCormack	White	Wederell	Steele(d/t)	Swainston	Craig	Williams	Lewis	Rowan	McCormish
Greendale/c	McCormack	Wederell	Steele	Fullman	Craig	Williams	Parr	Rowan	McCormish

The result was recorded as a 20 - nil win for Moseley.

| Rhodes/2p | Brown | Wederell | Kay | Fullman | Denton | Williams | Lewis | Hyde | McCormish |

REPLACEMENTS
a- S Parsons   b- S Trethewey   c- A Greendale   d- S Nute

LEAGUE APPEARANCES

25	Dave McCormack (2)
23	Paul Williams (3)
22	Kyle Dench (2)
21	Michael McCormish

NUMBER OF PLAYERS USED
38 plus 6 as a replacement only

LEAGUE POINTS SCORERS

Pts	Player	T	C	P	DG
104	Tom Rhodes	-	13	26	-
46	Adam Greendale	2	9	6	-
37	Robin Kitching	4	1	5	-
25	Peter Wackett	5	-	-	-
22	Stephen Parsons	4	1	-	-
20	Luther Burrell	4	-	-	-

OTLEY STATISTICS

LEAGUE

TEAM RECORDS

MOST POINTS
Scored at Home: 103 v Blackheath 04.12.99
Scored Away: 55 v Blackheath 15.04.00
Conceded at Home: 69 v Exeter 18.10.08
Conceded Away: 95 v Nottingham 8.3.09

MOST TRIES
Scored in a match: 16 v Blackheath 04.12.99 (H)
Conceded in a match: 14 v Sale 12.2.94 (A)

BIGGEST MARGINS
Home Win: 100pts - 103-3 v Blackheath 04.12.99
Away Win: 47pts - 55-8 v Blackheath 15.04.00
Home Defeat: 69pts - 0-69 v Exeter 18.10.08
Away Defeat: 90pts - 5-95 v Nottingham .8.3.09

MOST CONSECUTIVE
Victories: 12 (17.11.07 - 1.3.08)
Defeats: 12 (30.8.08 - 15.11.08))

INDIVIDUAL RECORDS

MOST APPEARANCES
by a forward: 205(19) Ian Carroll
by a back: 196 (20) Robert Whatmuff

MOST CONSECUTIVE
Appearances: 44 Neil Hargreaves 10.2.96 - 11.10.97
Duncan Sayers 24.10.98 - 25.3.2000
Matches scoring Tries: 5 Glyn Melville
Matches scoring points: 18 Peter Rutledge

MATCH RECORDS

Most Points
27 Robin Kitching v Blackheath 19.4.08 (H)

Most Tries
5 Mark Kirkby v Redruth 8.2.97 (A)

Most Conversions
10 Dan Clappison v Blackheath 4.12.99 (H)

Most Penalties
6 Peter Rutledge v Harrogate 29.10.94 (A)
Simon Binns v Henley 22.9.01 (H)

Most Drop Goals
2 Richard Petyt v Nottingham 11.9.93 (A)
Dan Clappison v Birmingham 11.12.99 (A)

SEASON RECORDS

Most Points	310	Simon Binns	04-05
Most Tries	22	Mark Kirkby	96-97 & 99-00
Most Conversions	61	Dan Clappison	99-00
Most Penalties	65	Simon Binns	03-04
Most Drop Goals	7	Richard Petyt	93-94

CAREER RECORDS

Most Points	1350	Simon Binns	01-07
Most Tries	68	Mark Kirkby	96-03
Most Conversions	185	Simon Binns	01-06
Most Penalties	289	Simon Binns	01-06
Most Drop Goals	10	Richard Petyt	91-94

LAST TEN SEASONS

	Division	P	W	D	L	F	A	P.D.	Pts	Pos	Most Points	Most Tries
99-00	JN1	26	22	1	3	817	399	418	45	1p	262 Dan Clappison	22 Mark Kirkby
00-01	N1	26	9	1	16	455	630	-175	46	12	131 Dan Clappison	8 Andy Brown
01-02	N1	26	11	1	14	601	675	-74	56	7	283 Simon Binns	7 Mark Kirkby
02-03	N1	26	9	0	17	597	839	-242	45	11	265 Simon Binns	13 Neil Law
03-04	N1	26	17	0	9	609	484	125	75	5	310 Simon Binns	9 Neil Law
04-05	N1	26	17	1	8	573	436	137	80	5	241 Simon Binns	9 Waisale Sovatabua
05-06	N1	26	10	1	15	540	627	-87	52	9	143 Simon Binns	9 Mark Luffman
06-07	N1	30	6	0	24	457	907	-447	31	15r	108 Simon Binns	11 Danny Smith
07-08	N2	26	23	0	3	782	379	403	105	1p	230 Robin Kitching	15 Robin Kitching
08-09	N1	30	3	1	26	421	1126	-705	*21	15r	104 Tom Rhodes	5 Peter Wackett

RFU SENIOR CUP

OVERALL PLAYING RECORD

	P	W	D	L	F	A	Pts Diff
Home	14	6	0	8	298	335	-37
Away	14	7	0	7	334	288	46
Neutral	0	0	0	0	0	0	0
TOTAL	28	13	0	15	632	623	9

TEAM RECORDS

Highest Score: 76 v Whitchurch 99/00
Biggest Winning Margin: 76 (76-0) v Whitchurch 99/00
Highest Score Against: 83 v Leicester 00/01
Biggest Losing Margin: 72 (83-11) v Leicester 00/01

SEASON BY SEASON

71-72	DNQ	78-79	DNQ	85-86	DNQ	92-93	2R	99-00	3R
72-73	DNQ	79-80	DNQ	86-87	DNQ	93-94	5R	00-01	4R
73-74	DNQ	80-81	DNQ	87-88	DNQ	94-95	2R	01-02	4R
74-75	DNQ	81-82	DNQ	88-89	DNQ	95-96	3R	02-03	4R
75-76	DNQ	82-83	DNQ	89-90	2R	96-97	4R	03-04	4R
76-77	DNQ	83-84	DNQ	90-91	DNQ	97-98	3R	04-05	5R
77-78	DNQ	84-85	DNQ	91-92	1R	98-99	2R		

NATIONAL TROPHY

05-06	Q.F.	06-07	4 R	07-08	4 R	08-09	4 R

PLAYERS

	Position	D.o.B.	Apps.	Pts.	T	C	P	DG
Ian Shuttleworth	Full back		187 (5)	330	39	29	28	1
Xavier Andre	Winger/Back row		36 (31)	70	14	-	-	-
Peter Wackett	Winger		18 (2)	25	5	-	-	-
Robin Kitching	Winger		44 (16)	341	23	53	39	1
Danny Smith	Winger		56 (9)	105	21	-	-	-
Stephen Parsons	Winger		40 (2)	82	16	1	-	-
Robert Whatmuff	Centre		196 (14)	170	34	-	-	-
Luther Burrell	Centre		16 (4)	20	4	-	-	-
Jon Buchanan	Centre		28 (6)	25	5	-	-	-
Paul Mooney	Centre		83 (15)	35	7	-	-	-
Kyle Dench	Centre		85 (19)	50	10	-	-	-
Adam Greendale	Fly half		14 (3)	140	5	29	23	-
Tom Rhodes	Fly half		17 (2)	104	-	13	26	-
Dave McCormack	Scrum half		25 (2)	10	2	-	-	-
Andy Brown	Scrum half		177 (51)	199	34	4	7	-
Kristyn Fulman	Prop		110 (1)	25	5	-		
Ryan Wederall	Prop		32 (22)	20	4	-	-	-
Stephen Trethewey	Prop		53 (25)	10	2	-	-	-
Adam Hopcroft	Prop		4	-	-	-	-	-
Ben Steele	Hooker		48 (37)	25	5	-	-	-
Will Kay	Hooker		14 (8)	-	-	-	-	-
Howard Parr	Lock		46 (19)	45	9	-	-	-
Jacob Rowan	Back row		9 (5)	5	1	-	-	-
Robert Baldwin	Back row		17 (2)	15	3	-	-	-
Michael McCormish	Back row		21	-	-	-	-	-
Dan Hyde	Back row		50 (1)	45	9	-	-	-
Max Lewis	Back row		20 (2)	15	3	-	-	-
Paul Williams	Lock		187 (24)	120	24	-	-	-

REDRUTH RFC

KEY PERSONNEL

President	Derek Collins
Chairman of Executive Committee	Ron Spencer
Joint Treasurers	Ron Spencer and Robert Hamer email: rhhjb@aol.com
Secretary	Roger Watson Trelawny House, 30 Fore St., Tregony, Truro, Cornwall TR2 5RN Tel & Fax: 01872 530687 (H); 07790 365250 (M) e-mail: watson_roger@hotmail.com
Fixtures Secretary	Peter Flack 110 Trefusis Road, Redruth, TR15 2JN Tel: 01209 218405 (H), 07789 670438 (M)
Director of Rugby	David Penberthy 2 Wheal Uny, Trewergie Hill, Redruth TR15 2TD Tel: 07966 532404 email: david-penberthy@tiscali.co.uk
Head Coach	Nigel Hambly Tel: 07974 311074 (M)

Founded: 1875
Nickname: The Reds
Colours: Red with black trim
Change colours: Black with red trim
Training Nights: Tuesday & Thursday
Website: www.redruthrfc.com

NATIONAL ONE

GROUND DETAILS

Address:
The Recreation Ground, Redruth, Cornwall TR15 1SY
Tel: 01209 215520
Fax: 01209 314438

Capacity: 10,000
Covered Seating: 670

Directions:
A30 West through Cornwall, leave at Redruth exit over roundabout, down through council estate, 1/4 mile to crossroads, then left.

Nearest BR Station: Redruth, walk thro Town Centre, down Green Lane grd at end, 10 mins

Car Parking:
£2 on ground, 500 on Industrial Estate - free.

Admission:
Standing £10 incl. programme Grandstand £3
Season Ticket (includes membership) £150

Clubhouse:
Open Training Nights, Matchdays (inc Sundays) and Special events
Hot food on Matchdays. All functions catered for, contact Clubhouse Manager 01209 215520

Club Shop:
Open matchdays. Contact Jeff Knuckey 01736 850039

PROGRAMME

Size: A5   Pages: 56
Price: with admission
Editor: Nick Serpell 01579 348853
Advertising Rates contact Dave Thomas
email: davidredruthrfc@aol.com

REVIEW OF THE SEASON 2008-09

No one could have predicted the huge strides the team and the club would make during the past 12 months. The club topped the table for 21 matches, went 11 games unbeaten at the start of the season, had the best defensive record in the league, produced four players who represented England Counties and one who represented the Barbarians in the annual Mobbs Memorial match.

Our season started with a home match against relegated Birmingham & Solihull Bees who kept a full time squad together and wanted to get their campaign off to a good start, however they did not build into their planning process a vibrant Reds side who had their own ideas and in a pulsating match the Reds came out on top by 35 points to 28.

Good wins followed with the pick against Wharfedale, our first ever victory on their patch, and a first ever league victory over the Cornish All Blacks. The win at Blackheath was notable for a wonderful bonus point clinching try from Rob Thirlby. Cambridge were to be the team that put a stop to our wonderful start with a single point victory at the Rec. Defeats at home to Wharfedale, their first ever at the Rec, and away to the Cornish All Blacks coupled with a draw at Blaydon saw the pressure mount.

The game against Blackheath at the end of January saw the boys hit top form again and wins against Westcombe Park, Southend, Waterloo and Cinderford took the team into the toughest end of season imaginable. Back to back defeats against Tynedale and Cambridge ended any hopes of promotion and with a difficult challenge on the last day of the season against Birmigham our slip to 3rd place was disappointing.

Our EDF Trophy experience was short lived with a defeat at Birmingham, however the match was used for our Development Team to gain experience and they did the club proud. Jason Pengilly must take a lot of credit for his tireless efforts throughout the season.

All in all a season to be remembered and with 23 ex Colts representing the 1st XV , the infrastructure still remains the strongest around.

289

REDRUTH STATISTICS

LEAGUE

TEAM RECORDS

MOST POINTS
Scored at Home: 96 v Waterloo 21.3.09
Scored Away: 62 v Tabard 5.2.05
Conceded at Home: 62 v Launceston 13.4.02
Conceded Away: 84 v Leeds 9.11.96

MOST TRIES
Scored in a match: 14 v Waterloo 21.3.09
Conceded in a match: 14 v Leeds 9.11.96

BIGGEST MARGINS
Home Win: 91pts (96-5) v Waterloo 21.3.09
Away Win: 55pts (62-7) v Tabard 5.2.05
Home Defeat: 47pts (15-62) Launceston 13.4.02
Away Defeat: 68pts (3-71) v Reading 15.2.97

MOST CONSECUTIVE
Victories: 16 (6.11.04 - 12.3.05)
Defeats: 13 (11.1.96 - 5.4.97)

INDIVIDUAL RECORDS

MOST APPEARANCES
by a forward: 114 John Navin (24)
by a back: 189 Craig Bonds (5)

MOST CONSECUTIVE
Appearances: 61 Tony Cook
Matches scoring Tries: 4 Richard Newton 97-98

MATCH RECORDS

Most Points
   26   Mark Scrivener   v Waterloo 21.3.09 (H)

Most Tries
   5   Emtr Lewis   v Waterloo 21.3.09 (H)

Most Conversions
   13   Mark Scrivener   v Waterloo 21.3.09 (H)

Most Penalties
   6   Michael Hook   v Cambridge 7.10.06 (H)

Most Drop Goals
   2   Bede Brown   v Plymouth 18.11.00

SEASON RECORDS

Most Points	271	Michael Hook	06-07
Most Tries	21	Mark Bright	06-07
Most Conversions	56	Michael Hook	06-07
Most Penalties	47	Michael Hook	06-07
Most Drop Goals	7	Bede Brown	00-01

CAREER RECORDS

Most Points	769	Steve Larkins	98-03
Most Tries	66	Lewis Vinnicombe	03-06/07-09
Most Conversions	131	Steve Larkins	98-03
Most Penalties	104	Steve Larkins	98-03
Most Drop Goals	8	Bede Brown	00-05

LAST TEN SEASONS

	Division	P	W	D	L	F	A	P.D.	Pts	Pos	Most Points	Most Tries
99-00	N2S	26	16	0	10	597	523	74	32	5	195 Steve Larkins	10 Jamie Knight
00-01	D3S	26	14	1	11	691	600	91	29	5	207 Steve Larkins	12 Luke Waqunivere
01-02	N3S	26	12	0	14	629	736	-107	24	8	217 Steve Larkins	11 Steve Larkins
02-03	N3S	26	12	1	13	583	588	-5	25	7	122 Bede Brown	9 James Lancaster
03-04	N3S	26	16	0	10	581	473	108	32	4	197 Scott Martin	11 Lewis Vinnicombe
04-05	N3S	26	22	1	3	726	303	423	104	2	169 Bede Brown	19 Nathan Pedley
05-06	N2	26	10	1	15	430	486	-56	51	10	70 Gavin Donald	13 Lewis Vinnicombe
06-07	N2	26	19	1	6	726	406	320	92	4	271 Michael Hook	21 Mark Bright
07-08	N2	26	14	0	12	545	514	31	*58	9	151 Gareth Griffiths	13 Lewis Vinnicombe
08-09	N2	26	19	1	6	752	411	341	94	3	161 Mark Scrivener	18 Rob Thirlby

RFU SENIOR CUP

OVERALL PLAYING RECORD

	P	W	D	L	F	A	Pts Diff
Home	18	10	0	8	280	271	9
Away	19	8	0	11	294	497	-203
Neutral	0	0	0	0	0	0	0
TOTAL	37	18	0	19	574	768	-194

TEAM RECORDS

Highest Score: 32 v Walsall 03-04 (A)
Biggest Winning Margin: 17 (26-9) v Old Culverhayians 97/88
Highest Score Against: 96 v Leeds 96/97
Biggest Losing Margin: 90 (96-6) v Leeds 96/97

SEASON BY SEASON

71-72	DNQ	78-79	DNQ	85-86	DNQ	92-93	4R	99-00	3R
72-73	DNQ	79-80	DNQ	86-87	DNQ	93-94	2R	00-01	2R
73-74	DNQ	80-81	3R	87-88	2R	94-95	3R	01-02	1R
74-75	DNQ	81-82	DNQ	88-89	2R	95-96	3R	02-03	2R
75-76	DNQ	82-83	DNQ	89-90	2R	96-97	3R	03-04	3R
76-77	DNQ	83-84	DNQ	90-91	DNQ	97-98	1R	04-05	3R
77-78	DNQ	84-85	3R	91-92	1R	98-99	1R		

NATIONAL TROPHY

05-06	6R	06-07	4R	07-08	4R	08-09	3R

PLAYERS

	Position	D.o.B.	Apps.	Pts.	T	C	P	DG
Lewis Vinnicombe	Winger		122 (1)	330	66	-	-	-
Emyr Lewis	Full Back		8	45	9	-	-	-
Rob Thirlby	Winger		45 (4)	170	34	-	-	-
Nathan Pedley	Winger		104 (2)	205	41	-	-	-
Paul Thirlby	Centre		95 (14)	329	43	24	20	2
Brett Rule	Centre		7 (3)	33	-	9	5	-
Craig Bonds	Centre		189 (4)	248	49	-	1	-
PJ Gidlow	Centre		84 (1)	95	19	-	-	-
Mark Scrivener	Fly half		35 (8)	308	3	61	56	1
Mark Richards	Scrum half		161 (2)	98	16	6	2	-
Ashley Morcom	Prop		21 (36)	-	-	-	-	-
Darren Jacques	Prop		112 (18)	30	6	-	-	-
Peter Joyce	Prop		60 (33)	10	2	-	-	-
Owen Hambley	Hooker		31 (3)	25	5	-	-	-
Luke Collins	Lock		49 (1)	25	5	-	-	-
Chris Fula	Back row		41 (25)	10	2	-	-	-
Damian Cook	Lock		97 (4)	20	4	-	-	-
Richard Carroll	Lock		64 (8)	50	10	-	-	-
Mark Bright	Back Row		62 (1)	170	34	-	-	-
Nathan Pascoe	Back row		112 (26)	75	15	-	-	-
Dave Roberts	Back row		12 (7)	-	-	-	-	-
James Mann	Back row		70 (7)	125	25	-	-	-

SEDGLEY PARK RUFC

KEY PERSONNEL

Chief Executive — Geoff Roberts
Salesis Farm, Salesis Lane, Walmersley, Bury BL9 6TH
Daytime Tel & Fax as club. 0161 764 6914 (H), 07793 184818 (M)

President — John W Smith   Tel: 0161 798 4147 (H)
20 Ringstone Close, Prestwich, Manchester M25 9PJ

Chairman of Rugby — David H Smith   Tel: 0161 280 2921 (H), 0161 280 3509 (B)
95 Bury Old Road, Whitefield, Manchester M45 7AY.

Club Secretary — Mark G Mold   Tel: 0161 486 0496 (H), 0161 254 1721 (B)
32 Vicarage Avenue, Cheadle Hulme, Cheadle, Ches. SK8 7JW
email: mark.mold@eu.bovislendlease.com

Treasurer — Peter Ratcliffe   Tel: 01625 535542 (H)
22 Hilltop Avenue, Wilmslow, Cheshire SK9 2JE

Fixture Secretary — Stuart Tattersall   Tel: 0161 723 6539 (B)
10 Butler Street, Ramsbottom, Greater Manchester. BL0 9PG

FDR Director — Ernie Neely   Tel: 0161 773 3750

League Contact — 16 Carlisle Close, Whitefield, Manchester. M45 6TH

Joint Chairs - Mini & Junior Section
Carol Allen   Tel: 0161 794 5419 (H)
21 Allenby Road, Swinton, Manchester. M27 0ES
and
Fiona Smith   Tel: 0161 280 2921 (H)
95 Bury Old Road, Whitefield, Manchester M45 7AY

Press Officer — Peter Collins   Tel: 077175 71542 (M)

---

www.sedgleytigers.com
Founded: 1932
Nickname: Tigers
Colours: Claret & gold broad hooped shirts and socks with claret shorts
Change: None
Training Nights:
Seniors - Tues & Thur.,
Juniors - Wed.
Website:
www.sedgleytigers.com

GROUND DETAILS

Address:
Park Lane, Whitefield, Manchester M45 7DZ
Tel: 0161 766 5050   Fax: 0161 796 2646
e-mail: admin@sedgleyrugby.wanadoo.co.uk

Capacity: 2,500   Seated: 350

Directions
From M60/M62 junction 17 onto A56 for Bury. Take the left filter at the 2nd set of traffic lights, left at the next lights (Park Lane), past School on left and ground is 1/2 mile on left

Nearest BR Station: Whitefield (Manchester Metro Line) served frequently from Manchester Piccadilly Mainline Station (via Victoria Station) – 20 mins journey time.
Ground is a good mile walk (Taxi £5 ish)

Car Parking: 150 on ground, 200 nearby free.

Admission:
Matchday: Adults £10
Concessions £5   Under 16's £1
Season: Adults POA (League matches only)

Clubhouse:
Flexible licensing hours, snacks & bar meals available
Sit-down 2 Course Lunch also available if pre-booked.
Functions: 2 Function rooms and Lounge Bar.
Capacity 150 in larger Function Room.
Contact John Grundy 07774 637064 (M), 0161 280 5752 (H)

Club Shop: Yes, in clubhouse

PROGRAMME
Size: B5   Pages: 72   Price: £2
Editorial & Advertising: Contact Geoff Roberts.
Advertising Rates: Page £360; 1/2 £200
Perimeter Board £450 + £130 set up costs

REVIEW OF THE SEASON 2008-09

Wow - Shortest season on record – we didn't know until 23rd June 2008 whether we would be relegated or not instead of PerTemps Bees (following a protracted appeal to the RFU) and by first week of November 2009 the RFU confirmed their Restructuring plans meant 5 teams would be relegated. To finish 6th from bottom would have meant winning half our games and that had proved beyond us in our previous 4 seasons in National 1, so there was little optimism of a Great Escape at Park Lane. Nevertheless we headed the table for a dizzy 24 hours after Week 2 until the Sunday games were played !

Tim Fourie, Player-Coach and 2nd Row for 7 years, including 5 seasons at National 1, did not deserve for his magical journey to end with enforced relegation. Rich Senior, former 1st XV Back Row has taken over as Coach after coaching our Seconds to back to back BMW League Championships, with Andy Craig and Phil Jones as Assistant Coaches.

We had been no strangers to relegation tussles in National 1 with our best finish being 13th position with 10 wins and 52 points, but there was no tussle last season. Results-wise it resembled a sandwich with 2 wins at the start and 2 at the end with a couple of wins at the halfway point. This meant 2 long runs without a League win which was demoralising for all and led to us shipping a record 1206 points. The season became an opportunity to introduce home-grown players into the First Team Squad as they would need to be our backbone for the future seasons at the lower level.

Statistics : Leading starting appearances : Glen Townson, Second Row, 29 starts and played every minute of each game. Adam "Dog" Newton, Flanker 29 starts (rested for 1 midweek re-arranged game meaning he clocked 89 out of 90 possible League appearances in 3 seasons. Pete Swatkins was leading try scorer with 14 from 28 starts.

Low Points – Record losing Run of 12 matches starting 13 December to 4 April 2009. Conceding a record 1206 points and 172 tries (average 40.2 and 5.73 per game respectively), including record home defeat to Bedford Blues 64-0.

Painful - Home loss to Manchester and away loss to Otley. Losses home and away to Coventry. 4 games that were very much winnable. Big defeats to Exeter , Leeds Carnegie and Bedford Blues.

High Points – Winning first 2 games. Gutsy performances against Exeter at home and Nottingham away. Positive approach to playing open and attacking rugby and fielding our home grown talent. Our only Double against fellow strugglers Newbury.

Again we were unable to make inroads against the established final top 6 teams (all full-time sides of course). Further our inability to move up a gear in the second half continues to hurt us. Defensive patterns and first-up tackles will be the priorities in pre-season training for the Coaching Team..

Players leaving the Club include Tim Fourie, Player Coach and 2nd Row to Rossendale, Adam "Dog" Newton, Flanker to VRAC Valladolid, Spain, Glen Towson, Second Row to Doncaster Knights, Oliver Cook, No 8 to Huddersfield, Petrus "Parra" Du Plessis, Prop to Nottingham and Pete Swatkins Winger to Titans.

Players rejoining the club include Ed Norris, 2nd Row and Richard Oxley, Hooker both ex Manchester, Steve Nutt, Fullback and Fly Half ex Fylde.

New signings include Nick Flynn, Prop (ever present at Manchester last season), Richard Wainwright, Fly Half , Paul Williams, 2nd Row ex Otley, Barry Jacobsz Back Row ex Huddersfield.

With all Clubs struggling for financial resources to boost their squads, it looks like a real scrap for the one promotion place to the Championship will develop. Having lost several key inspirational players from last season's squad, it remains to be seen if we can hit the ground running with new captain, Chris Wilkinson for what looks like a very tough season ahead.

293

PARK'S SEASON - 2008-09

Date	H/A	Opponents	Result & Score	Att.	15	14	13	12	11
NATIONAL ONE									
30-08	H	Rotherham	W 20-12	596	Riley	Swatkins	Craig	Tafa	Wilcock/t
06-09	A	Manchester	W 51-35	631	Riley	Swatkins/t	Hall	Tafa/t	Wilcock/3t
13-09	H	London Welsh	L 11-43	698	Riley	Swatkins/t	Hall	Tafa	Wilcock
21-09	A	Nottingham	L 24-32	1207	Riley/t2cp	Swatkins	Hall	Tafa	Wilcock/t
27-09	H	Coventry	L 27-30	638	Riley/c5p	Swatkins/t	Hall	Tafa	Wilcock
04-10	A	Exeter	L 5-71	4016	Riley	Swatkins	Hall	Tafa/t	Wilcock
11-10	H	Leeds Carnegie	L 7-52	886	Riley	Swatkins/t	Hall	Tafa	Wilcock
18-10	A	Bedford	L 7-53	2717	Riley	Swatkins/t	Hall	Tafa	Wilcock
25-10	H	Doncaster	L 3-41	595	Riley	Swatkins	Hall	Weedon	Wilcock
01-11	A	Plymouth Albion	L 7-31	2143	Riley	Swatkins	Weedon	Tafa	Wilkinson/t
08-11	H	Moseley	L 17-44	556	Riley	Swatkins/2t	Weedon	Tafa	Wilkinson/t
15-11	H	Esher	W 27-26	525	Riley/tc	Swatkins	Weedon/t(c/t)	Tafa	Wilkinson
23-11	A	Cornish Pirates	L 14-56	2324	Hall	Swatkins/t	Riley	Tafa	Wilcock
29-11	A	Otley	L 7-14		Hall	Swatkins	Riley	Tafa	Wilcock
06-12	H	Newbury	W 42-37	564	Riley	Swatkins/2t	Hall	Tafa	Wilcock/t(d/t)
13-12	A	Rotherham	L 0-22	848	Swatkins	Largen	Hall	Tafa	Wilcock
20-12	H	Manchester	L 12-16	526	Riley	Swatkins/t	Hall	Tafa	Wilcock
27-12	A	London Welsh	L 0-60	1110	Swatkins	Hall	Riley	Tafa	Wilcock
24-01	H	Exeter	L 12-35	431	Riley	Largen	Tafa	Jones/c	Monsell
01-02	A	Leeds Carnegie	L 0-66	2029	Riley	Largen	Tafa	Jones	Monsell
21-02	A	Doncaster	L 5-42	1194	Riley	Swatkins	Hall	Tafa	Largen
28-02	A	Coventry	L 24-29	1297	Riley/3cp	Swatkins/t	Hall	Tafa/t	Largen
07-03	H	Plymouth Albion	L 11-27	362	Riley/2p	Swatkins	Hall	Tafa	Largen
14-03	A	Moseley	L 17-51	796	Riley	Swatkins/t	Hall/t	Tafa	Largen
21-03	H	Bedford	L 0-64	436	Swatkins	Monsell	Hall	Riley	Largen
28-03	A	Esher	L 10-76	1258	Riley	Monsell	Swatkins	Hall/t	Largen
01-04	H	Nottingham	L 5-50	296	Riley	Swatkins	Wilkinson/t	Jones	Largen
04-04	H	Cornish Pirates	L 27-35	524	Riley/2t	Swatkins	O'Hare	Jones/2cp	Largen/t
11-04	H	Otley	W 36-29	497	Riley	Swatkins	Hall/t	Jones/2t4cp	Largen
25-04	A	Newbury	W 30-27	603	Riley/c	Swatkins/t	Hall	Jones/c2p	Largen
EDF ENERGY NATIONAL TROPHY									
4 17-01	H	Kendal	W 50-27	487	Swatkins/2t	Hall(d/t)	Riley	Tafa	Wilcock/t
5 14-02	H	Doncaster	L 6-28		Riley	Largen	Tafa	Jones/2p	Monsell

SCORING BREAKDOWN

WHEN		Total	First Half	Second Half		1/4	2/4	3/4	4/4
the POINTS were scored		458	201	257		80	121	95	162
the POINTS were conceded		1206	599	607		294	305	304	303
the TRIES were scored		64	27	37		9	18	12	25
the TRIES were conceded		172	81	91		39	42	45	46

HOW	Total	Pen. Try	Backs	Forwards	F Back	Wing	Centre	H Back	F Row	Lock	B Row
the TRIES were scored	64	-	50	14	4	24	11	11	2	4	8
the TRIES were conceded	172	7	98	67	14	43	2	20	21	18	28

KEY: *after opponents name indicates a penalty try.
Brackets after a player's name indicates he was replaced. eg (a) means he was replaced by replacement code "a" and so on.
/ after a player or replacement name is followed by any scores he made - eg /t, /c, /p, /dg or any combination of these

10	9	1	2	3	4	5	6	7	8
Jones/2c2p	Leck	Gazzola	Roddam	Du Plessis	Fourie	Townson	Crous	Newton/t	Cook
Jones/t5c2p	Leck	Gazzola	Roddam	Du Plessis	Fourie	Townson	Crous	Newton	Cook/t
Jones/2p	Leck	Gazzola	Roddam	Evans	Fourie	Townson	Crous	Newton	Cook
Jones/c	Leck	Livesey	Roddam	Evans	Fourie	Townson/t	Townson/t	Newton	Cook
Wilkinson	Leck/t	Gazzola	Roddam	Du Plessis	Fourie	Townson	Jones	Newton	Cook
Atkinson	Wilkinson	Gazzola	Roberts	Du Plessis	Fourie	Townson	Jones	Newton	Cook
Jones/c	Leck	Gazzola	Roddam	Du Plessis	Fourie	Townson	Jones	Newton	Cook
Jones/c	Leck	Evans	Roddam	Du Plessis	Fourie	Townson	Jones	Newton	Cook
Jones/p	Wilkinson	Gazzola	Roddam	Du Plessis	Fourie	Townson	Jones	Newton	Cook
Jones/c	Leck	Gazzola	Roddam	Du Plessis	Crous	Townson	Jones	Newton	Cook
Jones/c	Cliff	Evans	Roddam	Du Plessis	Crous	Townson	Jones	Newton	Cook
Jones	Cliff(a/t)	Evans	Roddam(b/t)	Du Plessis	Fourie	Townson	Crous	Jones	Cook
Jones/2c	Wilkinson	Evans	Roberts	Du Plessis/t	Fourie	Townson	Crous	Jones	Newton
Jones/c	Wilkinson	Evans	Roddam	Du Plessis	Fourie	Townson	Crous/t	Newton	Jones
Jones/2t3c2p	Wilkinson	Evans	Roddam	Du Plessis	Fourie	Townson	Crous	Newton	Cook
Jones	Wilkinson	Evans	Roddam	Du Plessis	Fourie	Townson	Crous	Newton	Cook
Jones/tc	Wilkinson	Livesey	Roddam	Du Plessis	Fourie	Townson	Crous	Newton	Cook
Jones	Wilkinson	Greenhalgh	Roddam	Livesey	Woods	Townson	Crous	Newton	Cook
Kohler(e/t)	Wilkinson	Evans	Roddam	Du Plessis	Fourie/t	Townson	Crous	Newton	Cook
Kohler	Wilkinson	Evans	Roddam	Du Plessis	Fourie	Townson	Williams	Newton	Cook
Jones/t	Wilkinson	Evans	Roddam	Du Plessis	Williams	Townson	Crous	Newton	Cook
Kohler	Wilkinson/t	Greenhalgh	Roddam	Du Plessis	Lloyd	Townson	Crous	Newton	Cook
Wilkinson	Stringer	Greenhalgh	Roddam	Livesey	Lloyd	Townson/t	Crous	Newton	Cook
Jones/c	Wilkinson/t	Greenhalgh	Roddam	Du Plessis	Lloyd	Townson	Crous	Newton	Cook
Jones	Wilkinson	Simpson	Greenhalgh	Livesey	Fourie	Townson	Crous	Newton	Lloyd
Jones	Wilkinson	Greenhalgh	Roberts	Du Plessis	Fourie	Townson	Crous	Newton	Lloyd/t
Kohler	Stringer	Simpson	Roberts	Livesey	Lloyd	Williams	Cook	Livesey	Lamprey
Atkinson	Wilkinson	Greenhalgh	Roddam	Du Plessis	Lloyd	Townson/t	Crous	Newton	Cook
Atkinson/t	Wilkinson	Simpson	Roddam	Du Plessis	Lloyd	Townson	Crous/t	Newton	Cook
Atkinson	Wilkinson	Simpson	Roddam	Du Plessis	Lloyd	Townson	Crous/t(f/t)	Newton/t	Cook
Jones/3t5c	Wilkinson	Evans	Roddam	Greenhalgh	Woods	Townson	Crous	Newton	Cook/t
Kohler	Wilkinson	Evans	Roddam	Du Plessis	Williams	Townson	Crous	Newton	Cook

REPLACEMENTS
a- C Hall   b- A Newton   c- P Wilcock   d- P Largen
e- D O'Hare   f- M Lamprey

LEAGUE APPEARANCES
- 29 Glen Townson, Matt Riley
- 28 Peter Swatkins, Adam Newton (1),
- 26 Oliver Cook (1), Phil Jones
- 25 Johnny Roddam (1)
- 24 Chris Wilkinson (6), Petrus du Plessis

NUMBER OF PLAYERS USED
34 plus 7 as a replacement only

LEAGUE POINTS SCORERS

Pts	Player	T	C	P	DG
130	Phil Jones	7	28	13	-
70	Peter Swatkins	14	-	-	-
63	Matt Riley	4	8	9	-
35	Paul Wilcock	7	-	-	-
25	Chris Wilkinson	5	-	-	-
20	Chris Hall	4	-	-	-

NATIONAL ONE

SEDGLEY PARK STATISTICS
LEAGUE

TEAM RECORDS
MOST POINTS
Scored at Home: 70 v Winnington Park 05.12.98
Scored Away: 66 v Sandal 17.03.01
Conceded at Home: 64 v Bedford Blues 21.3.09
Conceded Away: 96 v Northampton 26.01.08

MOST TRIES
Scored in a match: 11 v Sandal 17.03.01
Conceded in a match: 14 v Northampton 26.01.08

BIGGEST MARGINS
Home Win: 69pts 69-0 v Bedford Ath 10.02.01
Away Win: 51pts 51-0 v Whitchurch 10.10.98
Home Defeat: 64pts 0-64 v Bedford Blues 21.3.09
Away Defeat: 93pts 3-96 v Northampton 26.01.08

MOST CONSECUTIVE
Victories: 13 - 2000-01
Defeats: 13 (13.12.08 - 1.4.09))

INDIVIDUAL RECORDS
MOST APPEARANCES
by a forward: 200 (26) Tim Fourie
by a back: 123 Mike Wilcock

MOST CONSECUTIVE
Appearances: 52 Kern Yates 02/03 - 03/04
Matches scoring Tries: 6 Christian Raducanu 1999-00
Matches scoring points: 19 Colin Stephens 2000-01

MATCH RECORDS
Most Points
  34   Rob Moon   v Bedford Ath 10.2.01 (H)
Most Tries
  4   Ben Cohen   v Winnington Park 27.12.98 (H)
       Mike Wilcock v Whitchurch 2.12.00 (H)
Most Conversions
  8   Rob Moon   v Bedford Ath 10.2.01 (H)
Most Penalties
  8   Neil Lomax   v Stourbridge 27.3.99 (H)
Most Drop Goals
  2   Colin Stephens v Fylde 8.12.01 (A)

SEASON RECORDS
Most Points	274	Phil Jones	06-07
Most Tries	18	Mike Wilcock	00-01
Most Conversions	50	Colin Stephens	00-01
Most Penalties	54	Blair Feeney	04-05
Most Drop Goals	4	Colin Stephens	00-01, 01-02

CAREER RECORDS
Most Points	848	Phil Jones	05-09
Most Tries	54	Rob Moon	98-03
Most Conversions	140	Phil Jones	05-09
Most Penalties	139	Phil Jones	05-09
Most Drop Goals	8	Colin Stephens	00-02

LAST TEN SEASONS

	Division	P	W	D	L	F	A	P.D.	Pts	Pos	Most Tries		Most Points	
99-00	N2N	26	14	2	10	686	484	202	30	5	141	Rob Moon	12	Elijah Sobanjo
00-01	N3N	*25	21	0	4	887	327	560	42	2	235	Colin Stephens	18	Mike Wilcock
01-02	N2	26	20	1	5	684	468	216	41	3	244	Colin Stephens	12	Rob Moon
02-03	N2	26	15	0	11	702	567	135	30	6	223	Arno De Jager	13	James Naylor
03-04	N2	26	20	1	5	658	487	171	41	1p	177	Ryno Ueckermann	12	Ross Bullough
04-05	N1	26	8	0	18	515	772	-257	40	10	253	Blair Feeney	13	Jon Feeley
05-06	N1	26	6	3	17	529	856	-327	41	13	219	Phil Jones	15	Jon Feeley
06-07	N1	30	10	0	20	614	936	-322	52	13	274	Phil Jones	12	Phil Jones
07-08	N1	30	7	1	22	506	821	-315	44	14	225	Phil Jones	14	Chris Briers
08-09	N1	30	6	0	24	466	1209	-743	34	13r	130	Phil Jones	14	Peter Swatkins

RFU SENIOR CUP

OVERALL PLAYING RECORD

	P	W	D	L	F	A	Pts Diff
Home	7	3	0	4	124	177	-53
Away	8	3	0	5	148	214	-66
Neutral	0	0	0	0	0	0	0
TOTAL	15	6	0	9	272	391	-119

TEAM RECORDS

Highest Score: 34 v Bromsgrove 98/99
Biggest Winning Margin: 24 (34-10) v Bromsgrove 98/99
Highest Score Against: 53 v Wasps 98/99
Biggest Losing Margin: 50 (53-3) v Wasps 98/99

SEASON BY SEASON

71-72	DNQ	78-79	DNQ	85-86	DNQ	92-93	1R	99-00	2R
72-73	DNQ	79-80	DNQ	86-87	DNQ	93-94	DNQ	00-01	3R
73-74	DNQ	80-81	DNQ	87-88	DNQ	94-95	DNQ	01-02	3R
74-75	DNQ	81-82	DNQ	88-89	DNQ	95-96	DNQ	02-03	2R
75-76	DNQ	82-83	DNQ	89-90	DNQ	96-97	DNQ	03-04	2R
76-77	DNQ	83-84	DNQ	90-91	DNQ	97-98	1R	04-05	3R
77-78	DNQ	84-85	DNQ	91-92	DNQ	98-99	4R		

NATIONAL TROPHY

05-06	5 R	06-07	4 R	07-08	5 R	08-09	5 R

PLAYERS

	Position	D.o.B.	Apps.	Pts.	T	C	P	DG
Matt Riley	Full back		58 (6)	98	7	18	9	-
Peter Swatkins	Winger		28	70	14	-	-	-
Henry Monsell	Winger		5 (4)	-	-	-	-	-
Paul Wilcock	Winger		15 (3)	35	7	-	--	-
Philip Largen	Winger		14 (6)	10	2	-	-	-
Chris Hall	Centre		52 (3)	78	15	-	-	1
Chris Briers	Centre		79 (4)	115	23	-	-	-
Lisiate Tafa	Centrte		23 (1)	15	3	-	-	-
Phil Jones	Fly half		106 (2)	848	29	150	139	2
Chris Leck	Scrum half		25 (19)	5	1	-	-	-
Chris Wilkinson	Scrum half		71 (25)	40	8	-	-	-
Gareth Roberts	Prop		59 (82)	35	7	-	-	-
Petrus du Plessis	Prop		84 (42)	30	6	-	-	-
Phil Gazzola	Prop		48 (26)	-	-	-	-	-
Danny Greenhalgh	Prop		7 (18)	-	-	-	-	-
Gerault Evans	Hooker		61 (7)	5	1	-	-	-
Johnny Roddam	Hooker		80 (5)	20	4	-	-	-
Tim Fourie	Lock		200 (26)	130	30	-	-	-
Glen Townson	Lock		44 (10)	20	4	-	-	-
Dave Livesey	Lock		2 (24)	-	-	-	-	-
Juan Crous	Back row		36 (18)	15	3	-	-	-
Adam Newton	Back row		88 (2)	65	13	-	-	-
Oliver Cook	Back row		26 (1)	5	1	-	-	-
James Jones	Back row		11 (4)	-	-	-	-	-

STOURBRIDGE RFC

Founded: 1876

Colours: Navy blue and narrow white hooped jerseys, navy blue shorts

Change colours: Primarily white with navy & red detail jerseys, navy blue shorts

Training Nights: Tuesday and Thursday

Website: www.stourbridge-rugby.com

KEY PERSONNEL

President
Malcolm Jones
(h) 01384 370927 (m) 07885 221943 (e) malcolm.jones@macmail.com

Chairman of Management Committee
Dick Jeavons-Fellows
(h) 01299 896155 (m) 07967584051 (e) playrugby@stourton-park.com

Treasurer
Neil Smith
(h) 01384 372396 (m) 07801 762364 (e) ns@fwca.co.uk

Club Secretary
Huw Jenkins, 23 Agenoria Drive, Stourbridge. DY8 3TJ
(h) 01384 824193 (m) 07977 911957 (e) hjenkins@blueyonder.co.uk

Chairman of Professional Rugby
Andrew Ferguson
(h) 01384 377625 (m) 07799 348119 (e) janda.ferguson@btinternet.com

Membership Secretary
Richard Simmonds
(h) 01384 833002 (m) 07527 053233 (e) richard.rugby@blueyonder.co.uk

Director of Rugby
Neil Mitchell
(m) 07812 210022 (e) mitchsrfc@hotmail.com

1st Team Manager
Andrew Verlander
(m) 07801 454862 (e) A.Verlander@fbcmb.co.uk

Hon. Press Officer
David Garratt, 9 Bridle Road, Wollaston, Stourbridge. DY8 4QE.
(h) 01384 374704 (m) 07757 331809 (e) dave_garratt@hotmail.com

NCA Representative
Peter Thompson, 6 Ryecroft, Pedmore, Stourbridge. DY9 9EH
(h) 01384 373800 (m) 07836 562221 (e) ceo@thompsonandbryan.com

NCA Representative
Norman Robertson, 3 Crabtree Close, West Hagley, Stourbridge. DY9 0PU
(h) 01562 886011 (m) 07802 226767 (e) njr90@hotmail.com

Club Manager
Sara Milkins
(w) 01384 395000 (m) 07792 216729 (e) rugby@stourtonpark.com

Club Administrator
Hannah Walker
(w) 01384 395000 (e) rugby@stourtonpark.com

GROUND DETAILS

Address: Stourton Park, Bridgnorth Road, Stourton, Stourbridge, W. Mids. DY7 6QZ
Tel & Fax: 01384 395000 email: rugby@stourtonpark.com
Capacity: 2500   Seated: 700
Covered: 450. Free access to the covered stand.
Directions: On A458 Bridgnorth Road, midway between Stourbridge town centre & Stewponey junction with A449.
Nearest Station: Stourbridge Town or Stourbridge Junction
Car Parking: Ample on site, free access.
Admission (2009/10): Matchday: Members £8, non-members £12, all u16s free.
Season Ticket: Individual £150.00, Family £240
Clubhouse: Open Saturdays & Sundays from 11am, training nights from 8pm.
Food is available indoor & outdoor, large parties should pre-book with club administrator.
Club Shop: Open matchdays & Sunday morning. At other times contact Club administrator.

PROGRAMME

Size: A5   Price: £2
Pages: 56
Editor & Club archive:
Vernon Davies, 36, Beckman Road, Pedmore, Stourbridge, DY9 0TZ
(h) 01562 883640 (f) 01562 720534 (e) vernondavies36@hotmail.com
Ian Cole (m) 07979 703784) (e) iircole@googlemail.com

Standing L-R: Marcus Cook (Coach), Malcolm Jones (Medical Officer), Neil Mitchell (Director of Rugby), Harry Collins, John Holtby, Alistair Bressington, Duncan White. Peter Knight, Duncan Hughes, Rupert Cooper, Simon Homer, Keith Fowles, Ben Barkley, Ramsay Dean, Will Foden, Martin Freeman, Ben Griffiths, Jon Higgins, Jim Williams (Physio), John White (Coach), Francis Trinham.

Seated L-R: Miles Edge, Adam Billig, Danny Pointon, Alex Bristow, Alan McCreadie (Rugby Executive), Adam Sturdy, Frank Kendrick (President), Ben Gerry, Peter Trinham (Chairman), Jon Hall, Tom Richardson, Ollie Bache, Andrew Verlander (1st XV Manager)

REVIEW OF THE SEASON 2008-09

As feared, the outstanding performances of 2007/8 attracted the interest of clubs further up the league structure, and before the season had started we had lost last season's captain, player of the season and top try scorer. This left Director of Rugby Neil Mitchell an unenviable squad rebuilding exercise. Mitch built a team blending the enthusiasm of youth with the experience and leadership of a few older heads - a great example being the centre pairing, where Ben Barkley's raw talent fed off the vintage performances of Adam Billig.

With the extra relegation slot adding to the pressure, it duly proved to be a tough season. The team had a difficult start, and with just two victories from the opening seven games we found ourselves near the bottom of the table. The latter end of 2008 saw us play three in-form opponents, and yielded little for our efforts despite some excellent performances. But a corner had been turned, and the young side had found a steely determination and never-say-die attitude. They ground out do-or-die victories at fellow strugglers Mounts Bay and Wharfedale, and then came from behind for a tremendous home victory against Launceston. This sequence propelled us up the table and appeared to offer security.

But at the end of March, with the injury toll mounting, a much-depleted side subsided to a shock 10-5 defeat at Waterloo and we were dragged into the relegation mix. The run in was uncomfortable, as we lost 5 of our final 6 games and were constantly looking over our shoulders. The resolve and commitment of the team came through however, and crucial bonus points secured in several hard-fought games kept us just ahead of the pack. With safety finally guaranteed we produced a grand finale at home against Blaydon, running in 8 tries to secure eighth place.

Simon Homer – a mid-season convert from lock to tighthead - secured both the Director's Player of the Year and Stourbridge News' 'Sports Personality of the Year' awards, the latter following John Hall's 2007/8 win. Tremendous progress in his first season saw Ben Barkley win the Faye Newton Player's Player of the Year award.

In the last game of 2007/8 Jon Hall had made his 200th 1st XV league appearance. The last game of 2008/9 – again in front of a home crowd – saw him run in for his 51st league try, making him the club's record league try scorer.

299

STOURBRIDGE STATISTICS

LEAGUE

TEAM RECORDS

MOST POINTS
Scored at Home: 72 v Morley 02.09.90
Scored Away: 74 v Lichfield 17.04.99
Conceded at Home: 52 v Henley 7.9.02
Conceded Away: 74 v Henley 12.4.03

MOST TRIES
Scored in a match: 12
v Morley 02.09.00 & v Lichfield 17.04.99
Conceded in a match 10 v Sedgley Park 12.4.03

BIGGEST MARGINS
Home Win: 58pts - 65-7 v Whitchurch 14.10.00
Away Win: 74pts - 74-0 v Lichfield 17.04.99
Home Defeat: 40pts -3-43 v Waterloo 29.10.05
Away Defeat: 50pts - 24-74 v Henley Hawks 12.4.03

MOST CONSECUTIVE
Victories: 12 - 1998-99
Defeats: 8 (31.8.02 - 2.11.02)

INDIVIDUAL RECORDS

MOST APPEARANCES
by a forward: 175 Bob Merritt
by a back: 201 (23) Jon Hall

MOST CONSECUTIVE
Appearances: 48 Bob Merritt
Matches scoring Tries: 6 Rob Myler 2000-01
Matches scoring points: 40 Ben Harvey 10.11.01- 1.3.03

MATCH RECORDS

Most Points
35   Ali Bressington   v Westcombe P 25.10.08 (A)
Most Tries
4   Nathan Bressington   v Wharfedale 10.01.04 (H)
     Tom Richardson   v Barking 16.12.06 (H)
Most Conversions
7   Duncan Hughes   v Whitchurch 14.10.00 (H)
7   Ali Bressington   v Westcombe P 25.10.08 (A)
Most Penalties
8   Steve Baker   v Hereford 26.1.91 (H)
     Ben Harvey   v Rosslyn Park 25.10.03
Most Drop Goals
2   Chris Mann   v Birmingham 30.9.95 (H)

SEASON RECORDS

Most Points	315	Ben Harvey	02-03
Most Tries	19	Alistair Bressington	06-07
Most Conversions	60	Alistair Bressington	06-07
Most Penalties	59	Ben Harvey	01-02
Most Drop Goals	2	Andy Dickens	87-88
		Chris Mann	95-96

CAREER RECORDS

Most Points	987	Ben Harvey	01-05
Most Tries	50	Jon Hall	00-09
Most Conversions	170	Ben Harvey	06-09
Most Penalties	179	Ben Harvey	01-05
Most Drop Goals	4	Chris Mann	93-99

LAST TEN SEASONS

	Division	P	W	D	L	F	A	P.D.	Pts	Pos	Most Points	Most Tries
99-00	N2N	26	21	1	4	730	411	319	43	2	116 Hamish Pearson	10 Jacob John, Spencer Bradley
00-01	N3N	*25	21	1	3	861	368	493	43	1p	224 Duncan Hughes	15 Duncan Hughes
01-02	N2	26	9	1	16	600	702	-102	19	11	298 Ben Harvey	9 Ben Harvey, Duncan Hughes
02-03	N2	26	11	1	14	628	783	-155	23	8	315 Ben Harvey	9 Marcus Cook
03-04	N2	26	12	0	14	614	655	-41	24	11	210 Ben Harvey	17 Nathan Bressington
04-05	N2	26	10	2	14	576	695	-119	59	7	164 Ben Harvey	6 By three players
05-06	N2	26	11	1	14	462	605	-143	54	8	88 Alistair Bressington	7 Cameron Mitchell
06-07	N2	26	13	0	13	661	537	124	72	7	290 Alistair Bressington	19 Alistair Bressington
07-08	N2	26	21	0	5	677	432	245	99	3	235 Alistair Bressington	9 Tom Jarvis
08-09	N2	26	11	0	13	642	583	59	62	8	250 Ali Bressington	12 Ali Bressington

RFU SENIOR CUP

OVERALL PLAYING RECORD

	P	W	D	L	F	A	Pts Diff
Home	15	7	1	7	290	289	1
Away	18	7	0	11	311	462	-151
Neutral	0	0	0	0	0	0	0
TOTAL	33	14	1	18	601	751	-150

Other detail - Walk-over v North Walsham 2R 04-05

TEAM RECORDS

Highest Score: 69 v Taunton 97/98
Biggest Winning Margin: 64 (69-5) v Taunton 97/98
Highest Score Against: 78 v Coventry 95/96
Biggest Losing Margin: 58 (20-78) v Coventry

SEASON BY SEASON

Season	Result	Season	Result	Season	Result	Season	Result	Season	Result
71-72	DNQ	78-79	DNQ	85-86	1R	92-93	DNQ	99-00	2R
72-73	DNQ	79-80	DNQ	86-87	1R	93-94	4R	00-01	3R
73-74	DNQ	80-81	DNQ	87-88	DNQ	94-95	2R	01-02	2R
74-75	DNQ	81-82	2R	88-89	DNQ	95-96	3R	02-03	3R
75-76	DNQ	82-83	DNQ	89-90	DNQ	96-97	1R	03-04	2R
76-77	DNQ	83-84	3R	90-91	DNQ	97-98	3R	04-05	3R
77-78	DNQ	84-85	2R	91-92	1R	98-99	3R		

NATIONAL TROPHY

05-06	5R	06-07	3R	07-08	3R	08-09	3R

STOURBRIDGE PLAYERS

	Position	D.o.B.	Apps.	Pts.	T	C	P	DG
Alistair Bressington	Full back		78 (21)	863	41	170	106	-
Martin Freeman	Winger		44 (5)	100	20	-	-	-
Jon Hall	Winger	20.04.78	201 (23)	263	50	2	3	-
John Holtby	Centre		5	15	3	-	-	-
Adam Billig	Centre		38	30	6	-	-	-
Scott Morris	Centre		12 (7)	20	4	-	-	-
Mark Eastwood	Centre		60(4)	45	9	-	-	-
Ben Bartley	Centre		21	40	8	-	-	-
Marcus Cook	Centre		102 (10)	148	29	-	-	1
Jon Higgins	Fly half		24	12	1	2	1	-
Tom Richardson	Scrum half		61 (5)	112	22	1	-	-
Harry Collins	Hooker		3 (4)	5	1	-	-	-
Chris Rowland	Hooker		10 (14)	10	2	-	-	-
Adam Sturdy	Prop		95 (37)	45	9	-	-	-
Joe Baker	Prop		1 (7)	5	1	-	-	-
Ben Gerry	Hooker		66 (2)	40	86	-	-	-
Simon Homer	Lock		55 (23)	15	3	-	-	-
Ben Griffiths	Lock		17 (3)	15	3	-	-	-
Ben Hughes	Lock		41 (2)	45	9	-	-	-
Duncan White	Back row		36 (5)	50	10	-	-	-
Thomas Jordan	Back row		68 (15)	60	12	-	-	-
Peter Knight	Back row		40 (7)	-	-	-	-	-
Rupert Cooper	Back row		21 (4)	15	3	-	-	-

301

TYNEDALE RFC

KEY PERSONNEL

President	Andrew Deacon	
Chief Executive	Douglas Hamilton	
Club Secretary	Bill Stewart	2 Beech Hill, Hexham NE46 3AG
		01434 603970 (T/F) 07719 698235 (M)
		email: billandbren@btopenworld.com
Fixture Secretary	Craig Johnston	44 Kingsgate Terrace, Hexham NE46 3EP
		01434 607696 (T/F) 07759 020052 (M)
		email: jcjohnston@supanet.com
Chairman of Senior Rugby & League Contact & Press Officer	John Shotton	2 Millfield Gardens, Hexham NE46 3EG
		01434 607546 (T) 01434 321650 (Fax)
		07968 839043 (M) email: jbs@agma.co.uk
1st XV Coach	Tom Borthwick	016973 21379 (H) 07909 740740 (M)
1st XV Asst. Coach	Ian Peel	07764 933302
1st XV Manager	Peter Simpson	07810 180880
Club Physio	Catherine Cotterill	07968 283793
	Graeme Stevenson	07825 372628
Club Doctor	Dr Rachel Scurfield	07939 138821
Video Analyst	Tom Bramald	07904 729999
Conditioner	Kirk Barclay	07713 122155

Founded: 1876
Nickname: 'Tyne'
Colours: Royal blue & white
Change colours: Yellow, with royal blue trim
Training Nights: Tuesday & Thursday, 7pm.
Web site: www.tynedalerfc.co.uk

GROUND DETAILS

Address:
Tynedale Park, Station Rd., Corbridge, Northumberland NE45 5AY
Tel / Fax: 01434 632966
e-mail: tynedalerfc@hotmail.com

Capacity: Unlimited
Covered Seating: 400

Directions:
From A69 westbound: 2nd exit at Styford roundabout (signed Corbridge) follow signs for Hexham. Cross single lane bridge to roundabout. First exit signed Gateshead. 250 yds to left fork into Station Road - 150 yards to entrance.

Nearest BR Station: Corbridge, next to ground entrance

Car Parking: plentiful, within ground

Admission
Matchday: £8 adult, incl. programme
Season: Adults - £80; £70 Members
Concessions - £50; £40 Members

Clubhouse:
Open training nights(Tues & Thur) 6.30-11 and matchdays.
Food is available.
Functions: contact Douglas Hamilton 01661 852017 (T&F) or Peggy Verkooien 07534 244683

Club Shop:
Open matchdays, contact Edward Robson 077878 11058 (M)

PROGRAMME

Size: A5   **Pages:** 20
Price: With admission
Editor: Douglas Hamilton

Advertising Rates: Contact
Douglas Hamilton 01661 852017 (T&F)

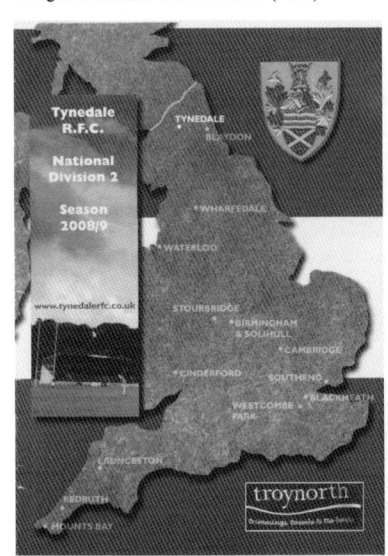

REVIEW OF THE SEASON 2008-09

After all the excitement and euphoria at the end of season 2007/08 there was a great sense of anticipation for the season ahead in our first ever venture into National League 2

It was very much a case of going into the unknown, literally in some cases travelling to all corners of the country. After all the hard work on and off the field the first fixture at home was a 'bit of a damp squib', with torrential rain spoiling the occasion. However, our first points in league 2 were achieved, but because of the conditions it gave us no idea of the quality of sides that lay ahead.

It was after our second half performance away at Launceston that the players themselves realised that they were more than capable of competing at this level. This gave us the spring board for the rest of the season and the squad must be congratulated on some outstanding performances, especially at home and be proud of extending our consecutive home league wins to 38. Again it was our disappointing away form that initially was the main concern and crucial points were thrown away due to lack of consistency and in some cases discipline and our yellow card culture!

Our initial away performances certainly cannot be blamed on distances travelled, because the organisation for every away game was excellent and one that a fully professional club would be proud of.

The one away game where the squad eventually put everything together both in attack an defence and gave us a very satisfactory away win was at eventual league champions Birmingham Solihull, this set the yardstick for the professionalism on an off the field that needed to be applied for such a result.

At the end of the season a very satisfying league position of 4th was achieved. An outstanding effort by everyone concerned, particularly with the quality of opposition teams, players, travel and even the new ELV's to be taken into consideration.

The impact the club as a whole has made in the league has been tremendous and some recognition of this has been shown by two of our players, Ross Samson and Rupert Harden being chosen by other coaches in the league for National League 2 Dream Team. Further recognition was also shown by the selection of Rupert Harden, Gavin Beasley and Jack Harrison for the England Counties games versus Ireland and France. Then Jack Harrison, Eniola Gesinde and Joseph Graham being selected for the England Counties tour to Japan and Korea and that squad of 26 will be under the guidance of Tynedales Head Coach, Tom Borthwick.

Finally, as a club we must make sure we do not rest on our laurels, the 'honeymoon' period is over! Perhaps it was fitting that our tremendous home league record fell to the eventual league champions. It was the impact of this game more than any other that showed us that the areas of conditioning and physicality should be our main focus in pre season if we are to aspire to greater success next season.

303

TYNEDALE STATISTICS

LEAGUE

TEAM RECORDS

MOST POINTS
Scored at Home: 102 v Orrell 17.2.07
Scored Away: 48 v Blaydon 22.3.03
Conceded at Home: 58 v Waterloo 15.3.03
Conceded Away: 42 v Nuneaton 29.3.03

MOST TRIES
Scored in a match: 16 v Orrell 17.2.07 (H)
Conceded in a match: v Waterloo 15.3.03 (H)

BIGGEST MARGINS
Home Win: 102pts (102-0) v Orrell 17.2.07
Away Win: 36pts (46-10) v Fylde 24.9.05
Home Defeat: 42pts (16-58) v Waterloo 15.3.03
Away Defeat: 36pts (6-42) v Nuneaton 29.3.03

MOST CONSECUTIVE
Victories: 12 (twice)
Defeats: 5 18.1.03 - 22.2.03

INDIVIDUAL RECORDS

MOST APPEARANCES
by a forward: 189 Andrew Murray (87)
by a back: 129 Ben Duncan (3)

MATCH RECORDS

Most Points
29 Alastair Murray   v Longton 16.10.03 (H)

Most Tries
3 On eight occasions by six players
   Will Massey (x3)

Most Conversions
11 Phil Belgian   v Orrell 17.2.07 (H)

Most Penalties
7 Alan Moses v Liverpool St Helens 2.9.00 (A)

Most Drop Goals
1 17 times by three players - Phil Belgian (8),
   Gavin Beasley (5), Alan Moses (4)

SEASON RECORDS

Most Points	224	Phil Belgian	02-03
Most Tries	14	Jack Harrison	08-09
Most Conversions	49	Phil Belgian	07-08
Most Penalties	45	Phil Belgian	02-03
Most Drop Goals	4	Phil Belgian	01-02

CAREER RECORDS

Most Points	1070	Phil Belgian	01-08
Most Tries	37	Will Massey	04-08
Most Conversions	219	Phil Belgian	01-08
Most Penalties	181	Phil Belgian	01-08
Most Drop Goals	8	Phil Belgian	01-08

LAST TEN SEASONS

	Division	P	W	D	L	F	A	P.D.	Pts	Pos	Most Points		Most Tries
99-00	North1	22	22	0	0	710	221	489	44	1	246	Alan Moses	13 Simon Clayton-Hibbott & Epi Taione
00-01	N3 N	*18	6	1	11	282	311	-29	13	8	159	Alan Mose	7 Simon Clayton-Hibbott
01-02	N3 N	26	14	0	12	530	528	2	28	5	120	Phil Belgian	8 Edward Holmes & A Murray
02-03	N3 N	26	12	1	13	561	582	-21	25	7	224	Phil Belgian	10 B Hills
03-04	N3 N	26	12	1	13	462	407	55	25	7	159	Phil Belgian	7 Ben Duncan
04-05	N3 N	26	13	1	12	512	598	-86	63	5	187	Will Massey	11 Will Massey
05-06	N3 N	26	16	1	9	650	430	220	80	4	165	Phillip Belgian	12 Will Masey & Hamish Smailes
06-07	N3 N	26	21	1	4	805	367	438	100	2	183	Phillip Belgian	13 Will Massey
07-08	N3 N	26	24	1	1	715	280	435	112	1p	157	Phillip Belgian	11 Robert Miller
08-09	N2	26	18	1	7	667	513	154	89	4	101	Rob Miller	14 Jack Harrison

RFU SENIOR CUP

OVERALL PLAYING RECORD

	P	W	D	L	F	A	Pts Diff
Home	19	15	0	4	464	369	95
Away	18	6	0	12	240	301	-61
Neutral	-	-	-	-	-	-	-
Total	37	21	0	16	704	670	34

TEAM RECORDS

Highest Score: 47 v Winnington Park 98/99 (H)
Biggest Winning Margin: 37 Pts (47-10) v Winnington Park 98/99
Highest Score Against: 76 v Worcester 00/01 (H)
Biggest Losing Margin: 64 Pts (76-12) v Worcester 00/01

SEASON BY SEASON

Season	Result	Season	Result	Season	Result	Season	Result	Season	Result
71-72	DNQ	78-79	DNQ	85-86	2R	92-93	3R	99-00	DNQ
72-73	DNQ	79-80	DNQ	86-87	1R	93-94	1R	00-01	4R
73-74	DNQ	80-81	DNQ	87-88	3R	94-95	3R	01-02	1R
74-75	DNQ	81-82	DNQ	88-89	3R	95-96	DNQ	02-03	2R
75-76	DNQ	82-83	DNQ	89-90	3R	96-97	2R	03-04	3R
76-77	DNQ	83-84	DNQ	90-91	DNQ	97-98	3R	04-05	1R
77-78	DNQ	84-85	DNQ	91-92	3R	98-99	2R		

NATIONAL TROPHY

05-06	4R	06-07	4R	07-08	4R	08-09	4R

PLAYERS

Name	Position	D.o.B.	Apps.	Pts.	T	C	P	DG
Rob Miller	Full Back		24 (1)	214	15	32	25	-
Will Massey	Full Back		78 (3)	406	37	55	37	-
Ben Duncan	Winger		129 (2)	210	42	-	-	-
Jack Harrison	Centre		74 (4)	135	27	-	-	-
James Hoyle	Winger		14 (3)	30	6	-	-	-
Peter Cole	Winger		17 (1)	20	4	-	-	-
Fraser Shaw	Winger		11 (10)	30	6	-	-	-
Charlie Ingall	Winger		10	35	7	-	-	-
Tim Visser	Centre		4	25	5	-	-	-
Gavin Beasley	Fly half		101 (3)	196	16	34	11	5
Ross Samson	Scrum half		57	90	18	-	-	-
Peter Southern	Prop		166 (27)	45	9	-	-	-
Johnny Williams	Prop		32 (15)	25	5	-	-	-
Rupert Harding	Prop		53 (4)	25	5	-	-	-
Aaron Charlton	Hooker		93 (69)	15	3	-	-	-
Matthew Fieldhouse	Hooker		22 (40)	62	12	1	-	-
Ben Marshall	Lock		72 (6)	5	1	-	-	-
Kevin Showler	Lock		10 (13)	5	1	-	-	-
Eniola Gesinde	Lock		15 (2)	20	4	-	-	-
Graeme McGilchrist	Back Row		14 (25)	15	3	-	-	-
Grant Rastall	Back Row		89 (16)	55	11	-	-	-
Andrew Murray	Back Row		189 (7)	378	37	41	37	-
Greg Irvin	Back row		18 (2)	20	4	-	-	-
Grant Beasley	Back row		10 (7)	10	2	-	-	-

NATIONAL ONE

WHARFEDALE RUFC

KEY PERSONNEL

President John Spencer
Garsleigh, The Avenue, Threshfield, Skipton BD23 5BT
Tel: 01756-753908; 07885-932129 (M)
Fax: 01756 753020   email: jss@spencerdavies.co.uk

Chairman Chris Baker
email: info@wharfedalerufc.co.uk

Club Secretary Antony Davies   email: amd@spencerdavies.co.uk
21 Raikeswood Drive, Skipton, N. Yorks. BD23 1NA
01756 798435 (H), 01756 753015 (B), 01756 753020 (F)

Chairman of Rugby Michael Harrison
& Fixture Secretary Old Hall Stable, Threshfield, Skipton, N. Yorks. BD23 5PL
Tel: 01756 752777 (H & B & Fax)

Press Officer Chris Ellwood
Green Lea, Kettlewell, N Yorks BD23 5RN
Tel: 01756 760251
email:chrisellwood06@btinternet.com

Founded: 1923
Nickname: Green Machine
Colours:
Emerald green
Change colours:
Scarlet & white hoops
Training Nights:
Monday & Wednesday
Website:
www.wharfedalerufc.co.uk

NATIONAL ONE

GROUND DETAILS

Address:
Wharfeside Avenue, Threshfield, Skipton, N Yorks BD23 5BS
Tel : 01756 752547
email: email: info@wharfedalerufc.co.uk

Capacity: 3,000
Seated: 120
Standing: Covered 180, Uncovered 2,700

Directions:
Take B6265 from Skipton bypass (signed Grassington). At Threshfield (8 miles), turn right after passing the Old Hall Inn on your left. 400 metres, then left down Wharfeside Avenue.

Nearest BR Station: Skipton, limited bus service. Group transport may be arranged with club secretary

Car Parking: 120 adjacent, no charge

Admission
Matchday - Adults (incl. prog.) £8,   u16 No Charge

Club Shop:
Open 1 hour before & after 1st XV matches.
Contact Toni Birch   01535 652764
email: wharfedaleshop@hotmail.com

Clubhouse:
Open matchdays. Hot snacks etc available.
Functions: Capacity 120
Bookings Terry Bell 01756 752657

PROGRAMME
Size: A5   Price: Free
Editor: Gordon Brown 01756 752410
Advertising: Terry Bell   01756-752657
tb@bell-company.co.uk

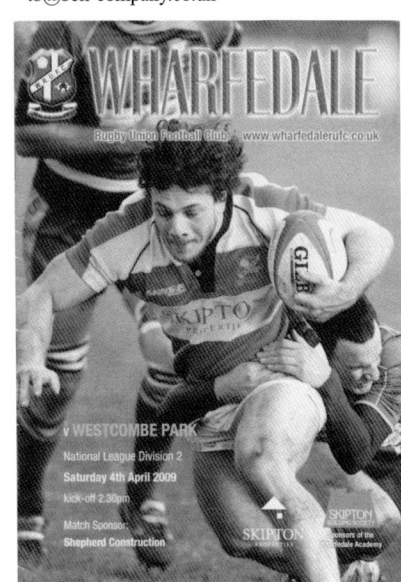

REVIEW OF THE SEASON 2008-09

A season of high emotion at Wharfedale. A shadow was cast over the club with the deaths of Chairman Graham Currier and Team Manager Peter Hartley – huge personalities (in every sense!) who earned affection and respect in the wider world of rugby.

On the pitch, fans endured another season of now almost traditional 'ups and downs', culminating in an anxious finale in which only victory in the last match, at home to Cinderford, would guarantee safety from relegation. As results panned out elsewhere, the 52-14 win was 'excess to requirements', but it ended a run of defeats that, combined with Westcombe Park's stirring finish to the campaign as they fought to overtake the Greens, had racked up tension to 'sleepless nights' level.

High points there certainly were, but consistency was a rare commodity indeed. Ultimate champions Birmingham/Solihull suffered their heaviest defeat – 41-12 (and 5 tries to nil) – at The Avenue in October. This followed hot on the 43-6 drubbing the Dalemsn had received at the hands of Stourbridge just 7 days earlier. Then, narrow wins at Mounts Bay, and at home to Blaydon, preceded a depressing run of 5 defeats – shipping over 150 points in the process. Next stop: table-topping Redruth and a splendid, fighting victory 15-14. A search for logic seemed futile.

Things settled down somewhat after that, and 5 wins in 8 matches – including 2 home games switched to Giggleswick School when snow hit the Dales – looked to have done the necessary. One more win, from 5 remaining fixtures, was all that was needed. True to 2008/09 form, the erratic Greens tortured their faithful followers to the end, finally proving that they had had it in them all along with an exhilarating last-gasp flourish.

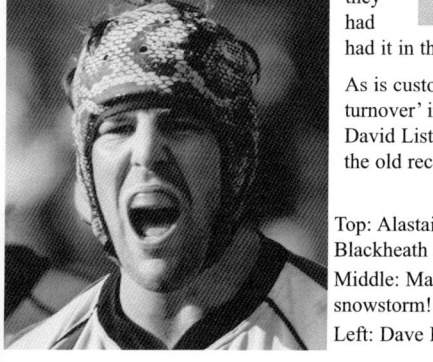

As is customary with a club that surely has the lowest 'labour turnover' in senior rugby, there is a national record to report. Lock David Lister set a new mark at 317 for league match starts – beating the old record of one Hedley Verity (of Wharfedale, of course).

PHOTOS - All courtesy of the Craven Herald

Top: Alastair Allen succumbs - with good grace - to the attentions of Blackheath defenders.

Middle: Mark Bedworth fights through the Stourbridge defence - plus a snowstorm!

Left: Dave Lister

NATIONAL ONE

307

WHARFEDALE STATISTICS
LEAGUE

TEAM RECORDS

MOST POINTS
Scored at Home: 72 v Fylde 23.9.00
Scored Away: 68 v Lichfield 30.3.96
Conceded at Home: 53 v Worcester
Conceded Away: 71 v London Welsh 21.3.98

MOST TRIES
Scored in a match: 12 v Sandbach 29.2.92
Conceded in a match: 11 v London Welsh 21.3.98 (A)

BIGGEST MARGINS
Home Win: 67pts - 67-0 v Harrogate 23.12.06
Away Win: 34pts - 68-34 v Lichfield 30.3.96, 52-18 Barking 3.3.07, 44-10 v Bradford & B 31.3.07
Home Defeat: 42pts - 8-50 v Walsall 25.3.95
Away Defeat: 47pts - 24-71 v London Welsh 21.3.98

MOST CONSECUTIVE
Victories: 14 x 2
Defeats: 8 (18.4.98 - 10.10.98 & 16.11.02 - 18.1.03)

INDIVIDUAL RECORDS

MOST APPEARANCES
by a forward: 315 David Lister (8)
by a back: 208 (8) Jonathan Davies

MOST CONSECUTIVE
Appearances: 153 David Lister 14.3.98 - 14.2.04
Matches scoring Tries: 6 Andrew Hodgson
Matches scoring points: 50 Adam Mounsey

MATCH RECORDS

Most Points
32 Mark Bedworth v Cinderford 25.4.09 (H)

Most Tries
6 Les Ingham v Sandbach 29.2.92

Most Conversions
8 David Pears v Fylde 23.9.00

Most Penalties
6 Mark Toesland v Lymm 14.1.98
   David Pears v Liverpool St H 7.11.98

Most Drop Goals
1 On 28 occasions
   including 9 by Russ Buckroyd

SEASON RECORDS

Most Points	278	Jonathan Davies	01-02
Most Tries	21	Andrew Hodgson	96-97
Most Conversions	44	Jonathan Davies	01-02
Most Penalties	55	Adam Mounsey	97-98/99/00
Most Drop Goals	4	David Pears	98-99

CAREER RECORDS

Most Points	987	Jonathan Davies	94-07
Most Tries	95	Andrew Hodgson	96-04/05-09
Most Conversions	147	Jonathan Davies	94-06
Most Penalties	175	Adam Mounsey	96-01
Most Drop Goals	10	Russ Buckroyd	87-97

LAST TEN SEASONS

	Division	P	W	D	L	F	A	P.D.	Pts	Pos	Most Points	Most Tries
99-00	JN1	26	19	1	6	646	317	329	39	3	274 Adam Mounsey	19 Andrew Hodgson
00-01	N2	*25	14	0	11	594	475	119	28	6	171 Adam Mounsey	7 Adam Mounsey, Chris Armitage
01-02	N2	26	11	2	13	603	638	-35	24	6	278 Jonathan Davies	15 Andrew Hodgson
02-03	N2	26	10	1	15	517	579	-62	21	10	191 Jonathan Davies	11 Andrew Hodgson
03-04	N2	26	13	0	13	484	505	-21	26	5	137 David Pears	7 A Hodgson B Wade C Malherbe
04-05	N2	26	11	1	14	481	528	-47	58	8	214 Jonathan Davies	10 Chris Malherbe
05-06	N2	26	12	4	10	531	550	-19	69	5	241 Mark Bedworth	11 Simon Horsfall
06-07	N2	26	13	2	11	677	517	160	74	6	209 Mark Bedworth	14 Simon Horsfall, Chris Malherbe
07-08	N2	26	12	1	13	600	559	41	67	7	168 Andrew Baggett	10 Simon Horsfall
08-09	N2	26	11	0	15	546	641	-95	59	9	246 Mark Bedworth	12 Chris Malherbe

RFU SENIOR CUP

OVERALL PLAYING RECORD

	P	W	D	L	F	A	Pts Diff
Home	8	5	0	3	185	136	49
Away	14	5	0	9	311	283	28
Neutral	0	0	0	0	0	0	0
TOTAL	22	10	0	12	496	419	77

TEAM RECORDS

Highest Score: 59 v Scunthorpe 93/94
Biggest Winning Margin: 53 (59-6) Scunthorpe 93/94
Highest Score Against: 34 v Otley 96/97
Biggest Losing Margin: 21 (8-29) v Worcester

SEASON BY SEASON

71-72	DNQ	78-79	DNQ	85-86	DNQ	92-93	DNQ	99-00	2R
72-73	DNQ	79-80	DNQ	86-87	DNQ	93-94	4R	00-01	3R
73-74	DNQ	80-81	DNQ	87-88	DNQ	94-95	3R	01-02	2R
74-75	DNQ	81-82	DNQ	88-89	DNQ	95-96	1R	02-03	2R
75-76	DNQ	82-83	DNQ	89-90	DNQ	96-97	3R	03-04	4R
76-77	DNQ	83-84	DNQ	90-91	DNQ	97-98	3R	04-05	2R
77-78	DNQ	84-85	DNQ	91-92	DNQ	98-99	3R		

NATIONAL TROPHY

05-06	5R	06-07	4R	07-08	4R	08-09	3R

WHARFEDALE PLAYERS

	Position	D.o.B.	Apps.	Pts.	T	C	P	DG
Adam Whaites	Full back		76 (2)	116	22	-	2	-
Dave Hall	Winger		15 (2)	35	7	-	-	-
Joel Gill	Centre		8 (6)	5	1	-	-	-
Thomas Cokell	Centre/Wing		8 (3)	-	-	-	-	-
Mark Bedworth	Centre		81 (5)	773	39	118	112	2
Chris Malherbe	Centre		156 (1)	347	69	1	-	-
Daniel Hart	Centre		23 (3)	20	4	-	-	-
Luke Gray	Centre		40 (7)	35	5	2	2	-
Tom Ball	Centre		11 (6)	-	-	-	-	-
James Doherty	Scrum half		75 (2)	65	13	-	-	-
Tom Horner	Prop		23 (9)	-	-	-	-	-
Ben Fear	Prop		15 (11)	-	-	-	-	-
Peter Hall	Prop		11 (5)	10	2	-	-	-
Chris Steel	Prop		53 (5)	20	4	-	-	-
Scott Freer	Hooker		5 (7)	5	1	-	-	-
Gavin Hindle	Hooker		114 (14)	60	12	-	-	-
Dave Charnley	Hooker		8 (11)	5	1	-	-	-
Oliver Renton	Lock		40 (30)	35	7	-	-	-
David Lister	Lock	19.10.73	315(8)	150	30	-	-	-
Anthony Capstick	Lock	26.12.74	216 (8)	15	3	-	-	-
Gavin Jones	Back row		2 (12)	5	1	-	-	-
Alistair Allen	Back row		95 (13)	25	5	-	-	-
Robert Baldwin	Back row		83 (43)	75	15	-	-	-
Daniel Solomi	Back row		16	10	2	-	-	-
Dave Muckalt	Back row		10 (7)	10	2	-	-	-

RECORDS SECTION
DIVISION THREE
(NOW NATIONAL LEAGUE ONE)

ROLL OF HONOUR

	CHAMPIONS	Runners-up	Nos of Clubs/Game	Leading Points Scorer
1987-88	Wakefield	West Hartlepool	12/11	121 Steve Burnage (Fylde)
1988-89	Plymouth Albion	Rugby	12/11	123 Chris Howard (Rugby)
1989-90	London Scottish	Wakefield	12/11	102 Andy Higgin (Vale of Lune)
1990-91	West Hartlepool	Morley	13/12	108 Mark Rodgers (Sheffield)
1991-92	Richmond	Fylde	13/12	106 Mike Jackson (Fylde)
1992-93	Otley	Havant	12/11	122 Andy Green (Exeter)
1993-94	Coventry	Fylde	10/18	172 Andy Finnie (Bedford)
1994-95	Bedford	Blackheath	10/18	228 Andy Finnie (Bedford)
1995-96	Coventry	Richmond	10/18	215 Ralph Zoing (Harrogate)
1996-97	Exeter	Fylde	16/30	404 Steve Gough (Fylde)
1997-98	Worcester	Leeds	14/26	322 Sateki Tuipulotu (Leeds)
1998-99	Henley	Manchester	14/26	365 Steve Swindells (Manchester)
99-2000	Otley	Birmingham Solihull	14/26	274 Adam Mounsey (Wharfedale)
2000-01	Bracknell	Rugby Lions	14/26	260 Jonathan Gregory (Esher)
2001-02	Orrell	Plymouth Albion	14/26	343 Phil Jones (Otley)
2002-03	Penzance & Newlyn	Henley Hawks	14/26	327 Barry Reeves (Henley Hawks)
2003-04	Sedgley Park	Nottingham	14/26	268 Rob Liley (Doncaster)
2004-05	Doncaster	Newbury	14/26	328 Oliver Thomas (Moseley)
2005-06	Moseley	Waterloo	14/26	302 Neil Hallett (Esher)
2006-07	Esher	Launceston	14/26	398 Neil Hallett (Esher)
2007-08	Otley	Manchester	14/26	286 Gareth Wynne (Manchester)
2008-09	Birmingham & Solihull	Cambridge	14/26	373 Mark Woodrow (Birmingham)

RELEGATED CLUBS

87-88 - Morley, Birmingham
88-89 - Maidstone, Met Police
89-90 - None
90-91 - Met Police, Vale of Lune
91-92 - Lydney, Nuneaton
92-93 - Sheffield, Leeds, Clifton, Askeans, Liverpool St Helens, Aspatria, Plymouth Albion, Broughton Park.
93-94 - Havant, Redruth.
94-95 - Clifton, Exeter.
95-96 - None
96-97 - Walsall, Havant, Redruth, Clifton.

97-98 - None
98-99 - Morley, Liverpool St Helens,
99-00 - Reading, Blackheath.
00-01 - Camberley, Lydney, West Hartlepool
01-02 - Rosslyn Park, Waterloo, Preston
02-03 - Launceston, Kendal, Fylde.
03-04 - Rugby Lions, Lydney
04-05 - Nuneaton, Bracknell, Rosslyn Park
05-06 - Orrell
06-07 - Bradford & Bingley, Barking, Harrogate
07-08 - Nuneaton, Henley, Halifax
08-09 - Westcombe Park, Mounts Bay, Southend, Waterloo

BIRMINGHAM & SOLIHULL - NATIONAL LEAGUE TWO CHAMPIONS 2008-09

		MOST TRIES		MOST PENALTIES		MOST CONVERSIONS
87-88	10	Brendan Hanavan (Fylde)	22	John Stabler (W Hartlepool)	30	Steve Burnage (Fylde)
88-89	8	Steve Walklin (Plymouth) & Dave Scully (Rotherham)	24	Steve Burnage (Fylde)	19	Chris Howard (Rugby)
89-90	7	Mike Harrison (Wakefield) & Brendan Hanavan (Fylde)	25	Andy Green (Exeter)	13	Gavin Hastings (Lon Scot)
90-91	9	Jonathan Wrigley (W Hartlepool)	22	Andy Green (Exeter) & Mark Rodgers (Sheffield)	19	John Stabler (W Hartlepool)
91-92	8	Matt Brain (Clifton)	26	Mike Jackson (Fylde)	16	Simon Hogg (Clifton)
92-93	8	Martin Kelly (Broughton P) & Mark Sephton (Liverpool St H)	31	Andy Green (Exeter)	14	Peter Rutledge (Otley)
93-94	12	Brendan Hanavan (Fylde)	45	Andy Finnie (Bedford)	23	Richard Angell (Coventry)
94-95	8	David Bishop (Rugby)	56	Andy Finnie (Bedford)	24	Andy Finnie (Bedford)
95-96a	12	Colin Phillips (Reading)	53	Ralph Zoing (Harrogate)	28	Jonathan Gregory (Esher)
96-97	22	Mark Kirkby (Otley)	82	Steve Gough (Fylde)	63	Ralph Zoing (Harrogate)
97-98	29	Nick Baxter (Worcester)	64	Chris Atkinson (Nottingham)	64	Craig Raymond (London Welsh)
98-99	15	Lafaele Filipo (Otley) & Adam Standeven (Morley	70	Steve Swindells (Manchester)	60	Steve Swindells (Manchester)
99-00	22	Mark Kirkby (Otley)	61	Lee Osborne (Lydney)	61	Dan Clappison (Otley)
00-01	17	Ed Smithies (Harrogate)	47	Jonathan Gregory Esher)	44	Mike Scott (Kendal)
01-02	23	Dan Ward Smith (Plymouth)	76	Jonathan Gregory (Esher)	68	Lee Cholewa (Harrogate)
02-03	20	Nmandi Obi (Henley Hawks)	59	Ben Harvey (Stourbridge)	80	Barry Reeves (Henley)
03-04	18	James Aston (Moseley)	50	Rob Liley (Doncaster)	56	Lee Cholewa (Harrogate)
04-05	24	Lucas Onyango (Manchester)	64	Ollie Thomas (Moseley)	70	Rob Liley (Doncaster)
05-06	24	Matt Moore (Esher)	51	Neil Hallett (Esher)	57	Neil Hallett (Esher)
06-07	23	Matt Moore (Esher)	61	Neil Hallett (Esher)	80	Neil Hallett (Esher)
07-08	21	Christoff Lombardi (Cambridge)	40	Gareth Wynne (Manchester)	63	Gareth Wynne (Manchester)
08-09	31	Simon Hunt (Birmingham Sol.)	38	Mark Woodrow (Birmingham Sol.)	108	Mark Woodrow (Birmingham Sol.)

DIVISION THREE

NATIONAL ONE

Constitution	12 87-88	12 88-89	12 89-90	13 90-91	13 91-92	12 92-93	10 93-94	10 94-95	10 95-96	16 96-97
Askeans		8	5	6	7	10r				
Aspatria						9r				
Barking										
Birmingham	12r									
Birmingham & Solihul										
Bedford							3	1		
Blackheath							4	2p		
Blaydon										
Bracknell										
Bradford & Bingley										
Broughton Park					8	6	11r			
Camberley										
Cambridge										
Cinderford										
Clifton				5	3	8r		9r		16r
Coventry							1		1	
Doncaster										
Esher										
Exeter	9	9	6	4	4	3	6	10r		1
Fylde	6	10	8	3	2p		2p		10	2p
Halifax										
Harrogate								7	6	5
Havant						2	9r			14r
Headingley					11					
Henley										
Kendal										
Launceston										
Leeds						6r				3
Liverpool St Helens						7r				12
London Scottish				1						
London Welsh				12r						11
Lydney				11	11	13r				10
Maidstone	8	12r								
Manchester										
Metropolitan Police	7	11r			12r					
Morley	11r				2p		8	5	5	4
Moseley										
Mounts Bay										
Newbury										
Nottingham										
Nuneaton	10	5	10	7	12r					
Orrell										
Otley					9	1		6	7	9
Penzance & Newlyn										
Plymouth Albion	3	1p				12r				
Preston Grasshoppers										
Reading									8	6
Redruth					5	4	10r			15r

312

YEAR BY YEAR RECORDS

97-98	98-99	99-00	00-01	01-02	02-03	03-04	04-05	05-06	06-07	07-08	08-09
14	14	14	14	14	14	14	14	14	14	14	14
							7	13r			
	11	2p									1p
		14r					9	9	5	4	6
										10	10
		7	1p		5		7	13r			
									12r		
	9	12	12r								
									9	6	2
											5
					7	4	1p				
			8	7	3	6	11	3	1p		
		9	9	5	14r						
								11	11	14r	
14	12	6	5	4	4	8	10	13	14r		
	1p				2p			12	3	13r	
			4	10	13r						
					12r		5	4	2p		7
2p											
11	14r										
3p											
12	8	10	13r			14r					
	2p						6	6	8	2p	
13	13r										
						10	3	1p			
											13r
6	6	5	10	9	9	2p					
7	4	11	11	8	11						
						3	12r		10	12r	
			1p						14r		
9	5	1								1p	
					1p						
					2p						
	8	7	14r								
8	10	13r									
								10	4	9	3

NATIONAL ONE

313

DIVISION THREE

Constitution	12 87-88	12 88-89	12 89-90	13 90-91	13 91-92	12 92-93	10 93-94	10 94-95	10 95-96	16 96-97
Richmond					1		7	8	2p	
Rosslyn Park							5	4	9	8
Rotherham									4p	
Roundhay			7	9	10					
Rugby		2p						3	3p	
Sedgley Park										
Sheffield	4	6	4	10	8	5r				
Southend										
Stourbridge										
Tynedale										
Vale of Lune	5	7	9	13r						
Wakefield	1	3	2p							
Walsall										13r
Waterloo										
Wharfedale										7
Westcombe Park										
West Hartlepool	2	4	3	1p						
Worcester										

NATIONAL ONE

ALL TIME TEAM RECORDS

Highest score:	115	Birmingham 115 Waterloo 0, 4.04.09
Highest aggregate:	115	As above
Highest score by a losing side:	43	Stourbridge 55 Esher 43. 8.2.03
Highest scoring draw:	36	Wharfedale v Esher 28.04.07
Most consecutive wins:	16	Penzance & Newlyn 2002-03
Most consecutive defeats:	26	West Hartlepool 2000-01
Most points for in a season:	1209	Leeds 1996-97
Least points for in a season:	46	Birmingham Solihull 1987-88
Most points against in a season:	1371	Waterloo 2008-09
Least points against in a season:	89	Plymouth 1988-89
Most tries for in a season:	158	Leeds 1996-97
Most tries against in a season:	201	Waterloo 2008-09
Least tries for in a season:	3	Birmingham Solihull 1987-88
Least tries against in a season:	5	Plymouth 1988-89
Most conversions for in a season:	113	Birminham Solihull 2008-09
Most conversions against in a season:	125	Clifton 1996-97
Most penalties for in a season:	85	Fylde 1996-97
Most penalties against in a season:	74	Otley 1996-97
Least penalties for in a season:	8	Morley 1987-88
Least penalties against in a season:	10	West Hartlepool 1990-91
Most drop goals for in a season:	8	Morley 1994-95, London Welsh 1996-97
Most drop goals against in a season:	8	Rotherham 1995-96, Havant 1996-97

314

YEAR BY YEAR RECORDS cont.

14 97-98	14 98-99	14 99-00	14 00-01	14 01-02	14 02-03	14 03-04	14 04-05	14 05-06	14 06-07	14 07-08	14 08-09
5	3	4	3	12r		12	14r				
4p			2p			13r					
				3	6	1p					
										8	12r
				11	8	11	7	8	7	3	8
											4
				13r			4	2p		11	14r
10	7	3	6	6	10	5	8	5	6	7	9
										5	11r
			14r								
1p											

ALL TIME INDIVIDUAL RECORDS

Most points in a season:	**404**	Steve Gough (Fylde) 1996-97
Most tries in a season:	**31**	31 Simon Hunt (Birmingham Solihull) 2008-09
Most conversions in a season:	**108**	Mark Woodrow (Birmingham Solihull) 2008-097
Most penalties in a season:	**82**	Steve Gough (Fylde) 1996-97
Most drop goals in a season:	**8**	Jamie Grayson (Morley) 1995-96
Most points in a match:	**42**	Mike Scott *Kendal* v W Hartlepool 27.1.01
Most tries in a match:	**6**	Nick Baxter, *Worcester* v Otley 21.2.98
Most conversions in a match:	**15**	Mark Woodrow, *Birmingham* v Waterloo 4.04.09
Most penalties in a match:	**9**	Paul Morris, *Lydney* v Otley 14.9.96
		Rob Ashworth, *Havant* v Clifton 21.9.96
Most drop goals in a match:	**4**	Andy Rimmer, *Broughton Park* v Sheffield 17.11.90

DIVISION THREE

ALL TIME RECORDS

SEASON RECORDS

MOST POINTS

EVOLUTION OF RECORD

121	Steve Burnage	Fylde	1987-88
123	Chris Howard	Rugby	1988-89
172	Andy Finnie	Bedford	1993-94
228	Andy Finnie	Bedford	1994-95
404	Steve Gough	Fylde	1996-97

The ALL-TIME RECORDS can be found overleaf.

MOST TRIES

EVOLUTION OF RECORD

10	Brendan Hanavan	Fylde	1987-88
12	Brendan Hanavan	Fylde	1993-94
12	Colin Phillips	Reading	1994-95
22	Mark Kirkby	Otley	1996-97
29	Nick Baxter	Worcester	1997-98
31	Simon Hunt	Birmingham Sol.	2008-09

ALL-TIME RECORDS

31	Simon Hunt	Birmingham Sol.	2008-09
29	Nick Baxter	Worcester	1997-98
24	Lucas Onyango	Manchester	2004-05
24	Matt Moore	Esher	2005.06
23	Dan Ward-Smith	Plymouth	2001-02
23	Matt Moore	Esher	2006-07
22	Mark Kirkby	Otley	1996-97
22	Mark Kirkby	Otley	1999-00
21	Andrew Hodgson	Wharfedale	1996-97
21	Mark Bright	Redruth	2006-07
21	Christoff Lombaard	Cambridge	2006-07
21	Christoff Lombaard	Cambridge	2007-08
20	Donovan van Vuuren	Doncaster	2004-05
20	Mark Preston	Fylde	1996-97
20	Nnamdi Obi	Henley Hawks	2002-03
20	Nathan Bressington	Moseley	2005-06
19	Andrew Hodgson	Wharfedale	1999-00
19	Andy Craig	Orrell	2001-02
19	Neil Kerfoot	Orrell	2001-02
19	Richard Lloyd	Nottingham	2002-03
19	Victor Olonga	Penzance	2002-03
19	Ali Bressington	Stourbridge	2006-07
18	Nyasha Shumba	Esher	2002-03
18	James Aston	Moseley	2003-04
18	Neil Kerfoot	Waterloo	2005-06
18	Andrew Fenby	Blaydon	2007-08

MOST CONVERSIONS

EVOLUTION OF RECORD

63	Ralph Zoing	Harrogate	1996-97
64	Craig Raymond	London Welsh	1997-98
68	Lee Cholewa	Harrogate	2001-02
80	Barry Reeves	Henley	2002-03
109	Mark Woodrow	Birmingham Sol.	2008-09

ALL-TIME RECORDS

109	Mark Woodrow	Birmingham Sol.	2008-09
80	Barry Reeves	Henley	2002-03
80	Neil Hallett	Esher	2006-07
70	Rob Liley	Doncaster	2004-05
68	Lee Cholewa	Harrogate	2001-02
64	Craig Raymond	London Welsh	1997-98
63	Ralph Zoing	Harrogate	1996-97
63	Gareth Wynne	Manchester	2007-08
61	Jason Dance	Reading	1996-97
61	Dan Clappison	Otley	1999-00
60	Sateki Tuipulotu	Leeds Tykes	1997-98
60	Richard LeBas	Worcester	1997-98
60	Steve Swindells	Manchester	1998-99
60	Ali Bressington	Stourbridge	2006-07
59	Phil Jones	Orrell	2001-02

MOST PENALTIES

EVOLUTION OF RECORD

21	Ray Adamson	Wakefield	1987-88
22	Andy Higgin	Vale of Lune	1989-90
26	Mike Jackson	Fylde	1991-92
31	Andy Green	Exeter	1992-93
45	Andy Finnie	Bedford	1993-94
56	Andy Finnie	Bedford	1994-95
82	Steve Gough	Fylde	1996-97

ALL-TIME RECORDS

82	Steve Gough	Fylde	1996-97
81	Richard Mills	Walsall	1996-97
76	Jonathan Gregory	Esher	2001-02
70	Steve Swindells	Manchester	1998-99
66	Paul Morris	Lydney	1996-97
64	Chris Atkinson	Nottingham	1997-98
64	Chris Atkinson	Nottingham	1998-99
64	Ollie Thomas	Moseley	2004-05
61	Neil Hallett	Esher	2006-07
59	Ben Harvey	Stourbridge	2002-03
57	Craig Raymond	London Welsh	1996-97
57	Mike Scott	Kendal	2001-02
57	Rob Liley	Doncaster	2002-03
57	Rob Liley	Doncaster	2004-05
56	Andy Finnie	Bedford	1994-95
55	Adam Mounsey	Wharfedale	1999-00
55	Ben Harvey	Stourbridge	2001-02

ALL TIME RECORDS

MOST DROP GOALS

EVOLUTION OF RECORD

ALL-TIME RECORDS

MATCH RECORDS

MOST POINTS

EVOLUTION OF RECORD

28	Steve Burnage	Fylde v Birmingham	07.11.87
29	Paul Morris	Lydney v Otley	14.09.96
29	Rob Ashworth	Havant v Clifton	21.09.96
30	Paul Brett	Liverpool v Redruth	01.02.97
39	Paul Brett	Liverepool v Clifton	15.02.97
42	Mike Scott	Kendal v W Hartlepool	27.01.01

The ALL-TIME RECORDS can be found overleaf.

MOST TRIES

EVOLUTION OF RECORD
(Only the first to reach the figure is shown)

3	Kevin Norris	Plymouth v Sheffield	12.09.87
4	Brendan Hanavan	Fylde v Exeter	03.10.87
5	Mark Kirkby	Otley v Redruth	08.02.97
6	Nick Baxter	Worcester v Otley	21.02.98

The ALL-TIME RECORDS can be found overleaf.

MOST DROP GOALS

ALL-TIME RECORD

4	Andy Rimmer	Broughton P v Sheffield	17.11.90

DIVISION THREE

MOST CONVERSIONS

EVOLUTION OF RECORD

9	Steve Burnage	Fylde v Birmingham	07.11.87
9	Gerry Ainscough	Leeds v Clifton	07.12.96
12	Paul Brett	Liverpool v Clifton	15.02.96
13	Craig Evans	Cambridge v Waterloo	21.02.09
15	Mark Woodrow	Birmingham v Waterloo	4.04.09

ALL-TIME RECORDS

15	Mark Woodrow	Birmingham S v Waterloo	4/04/09
13	Mark Scrivener	Redruth v Waterloo	21/03/09
13	Craig Evans	Cambridge v Waterloo	21/02/09
12	Paul Brett	Liverpool v Clifton	15.02.96
11	Mike Scott	Kendal v W Hartlepool	27.01.01
11	Dafyyd Lewis	Cambridge v Harrogate	28.04.07
10	Dan Clappison	Otley v Blackheath	04.12.99
10	Chris Glynn	Preston v Camberley	25.03.00
10	Gareth Cull	Nuneaton v Harrogate	14.04.07
10	Frankie Neale	Blackheath v Bradford & B	17.02.07
10	Mark Woodrow	Birmingham v Mounts Bay	14/03/09
10	Matthew Leek	Waterloo v Blackheath	28/02/09
10	Ben Patston	Cambridge v Mounts Bay	04/10/08

MOST PENALTIES

EVOLUTION OF RECORD

6	John Stabler	W Hart v Met Police	06.01.88
7	Andy Finnie	Bedford v Coventry	23.04.94
9	Paul Morris	Lydney v Otley	14.09.96

ALL-TIME RECORDS

9	Paul Morris	Lydney v Otley	14.09.96
9	Rob Ashworth	Havant v Clifton	21.09.96
8	Richard Mills	Walsall v Leeds	12.10.96
8	Jonathan Gregory	Esher v Preston	01.12.01
8	Ben Harvey	Stourbridge v Rosslyn Park	25.10.03
8	Corrado Pilat	Barking v Manchester	17.09.05
8	Stuart Alred	Launceston v Blackheath	21.01.06
7	Andy Finnie	Bedford v Coventry	23.04.94
7	Denzil Evans	Rugby v Richmond	15.10.94
7	Phil Belshaw	Reading v Morley	14.10.95
7	Jamie Grayshon	Morley v Rugby	21.10.95
7	Andy Green	Exeter v Fylde	05.04.97
7	Richard Mills	Walsall v Redruth	19.04.97
7	Nat Saumi	Redruth v Clifton	03.05.97
7	Guy Gregory	Camberley v Birm & Solihull	19.12.98
7	Ben Stafford	Camberley v Nottingham	10.10.99
7	Chris Glynn	Sedgley Park v Wharfedale	31.08.02
7	Ben Harvey	Stourbridge v Kendal	16.11.02
7	Neil Hallett	Esher v Stourbridge	03.02.07
7	Dan Hawkes	Mounts Bay v Southend	15.11.08

NATIONAL ONE

ALL TIME RECORDS

DIVISION THREE

MOST TRIES IN A MATCH

6	Nick Baxter	Worcester v Otley	21.02.98
5	Mark Kirkby	Otley v Redruth	08.02.97
	Simon Middleton	Leeds v Morley	14.02.98
	Matt Hoskin	Manchester v Camberley	12.09.98
	John Carter	Doncaster v Lydney	07.02.04
	Christoff Lombard	Cambridge v Harrogate	28.04.07
	Emyr Lewis	Redruth v Waterloo	21.03.09
4	Brendan Hanavan	Fylde v Exeter	03.10.87
	Steve Walklin	Plymouth v Birmingham	17.10.87
	Ian Russell	Plymouth v Fylde	31.10.87
	Brendan Hanavan	Fylde v Birmingham	07.11.87
	Dan Cottrell	Clifton v Askeans	04.01.92
	Mark Sephton	Liverpool St H v Aspatria	13.03.93
	Dean Crompton	Liverpool St H v Aspatria	13.03.93
	Mark Farrar	Otley v Askeans	27.03.93
	Brendan Hanavan	Fylde v Redruth	09.04.94
	Richard Matthias	Leeds v Clifton	07.12.96
	Simon Dovell	Exeter v Havant	21.12.96
	Ben Wade	Morley v Clifton	18.01.97
	Mark Sephton	Liverpool StH v Clifton	15.02.97
	Colin Stephens	Leeds v Lydney	15.03.97
	Toby Rakison	Rosslyn Park v Otley	29.03.97
	Steve Bartliffe	Leeds v Havant	26.04.97
	Nick Baxter	Worcester v L St Helens	21.03.98
	Alan Royer	Nottingham v L St. Helens	28.11.98
	Jeremy Griffiths	Newbury v Harrogate	02.01.99
	Lafaele Filipo	Otley v Reading	03.04.99
	Mark Kirby	Otley v Blackheath	04.12.99
	Iain Bruce	Preston G. v Camberley	25.03.00
	Mike Scott	Kendal v West Hartlepool	27.01.01
	Mark Farrar	Preston G.v Harrogate	06.04.02
	Victor Olonga	Penzance v Kendal	07.12.02
	Nyasha Shumba	Esher v Stourbridge	08.02.03
	Nathan Bressington	Stourbridge v Wharfedale	10.01.04
	Jordan Hands	Nuneaton v Lydney	24.01.04
	Felise Ah - Ling	Barking v Launceston	03.09.05
	Nathan Bressington	Harrogate v Moseley	18.02.06
	Tom Richardson	Stourbridge v Barking	16.12.06
	Mark Bright	Redruth v Barking	17.03.07
	Adam Slade	Westcombe Park v Nuneaton	20.10.07
	Nathan Pedley	Redruth v Birmingham Solihull	06.09.08
	Luke Fielden	Cambridge v Waterloo	21.02.09

DIVISION THREE ALL TIME RECORDS

MOST POINTS IN A MATCH

42	Mike Scott	Kendal v W Hartlepool	27.01.01
39	Paul Brett	Liverpool St Helens v Clifton	15.02.97
35	Ali Bressingham	Westcombe Park v Stourbridge	25.10.08
	Mark Woodrow	Birmingham v Waterloo	04.04.09
32	Sam Howard	Rosslyn Park v Bracknell	03.01.04
	Mark Bedworth	Wharfedale v Cinderford	25.04.09
31	Alastair Bressington	Bradford Bingley v Stourbridge	23.09.06
	Neil Hallett	Blackheath v Esher	11.11.06
30	Paul Brett	Liverpool St Helens v Redruth	01.02.97
	Nick Baxter	Worcester v Otley	21.02.98
	Ben Harvey	Stourbridge v Esher	06.04.02
	Colin Stephens	Sedgley Park v Wharfedale	15.12.01
	Jonathon Gregory	Esher v Lydney	13.12.03
	Frankie Neale	Blackheath v Bradford Bingley	17.02.07
	Freddie Burns	Cinderford v Westcombe Park	02.05.09
29	Paul Morris	Lydney v Otley	14.09.96
	Rob Ashworth	Havant v Clifton	21.09.96
	Adam Mounsey	Wharfedale v Reading	15.01.00
	Jonathan Davies	Wharfedale v Preston G.	19.01.02
	Jonathan Davies	Wharfedale v Nuneaton	09.10.04
	Frankie Neale	Harrogate v Blackheath	21.04.07
	Andy Frost	Southend v Waterloo	11.10.08
28	Steve Burnage	Fylde v Birmingham	07.11.87
	Craig Raymond	London Welsh v Clifton	28.12.96
	Jaques Steyn	Rugby v Camberley	02.12.00
	Rob Moon	Nottingham v Sedgley Park	22.09.01
	Jonathan Gregory	Esher v Preston G.	01.12.01
	Lee Cholewa	Harrogate v Preston G.	15.12.01
	Jonathan Davies	Wharfedale v Kendal	12.04.03
	Chris Glynn	Sedgley Park v Wharfedale	31.08.02
	Rob Liley	Doncaster v Launceston	19.02.05
	Neil Hallett	Stourbridge v Esher	03.02.07
	Mark Woodrow	Birmingham v Blackheath	21.02.09
	Andy Frost	Southend v Wharfedale	18.04.09
27	Ralph Zoing	Harrogate v Fylde	14.10.95
	Gerry Ainscough	Leeds v Rosslyn Park	14.09.96
	Craig Raymond	London Welsh v Lydney	09.11.96
	Gerry Ainscough	Leeds v Walsall	01.03.97
	Nat Saumi	Redruth v Clifton	03.05.97
	Adam Standeven	Morley v Newbury	25.04.98
	David Pears	Wharfedale v Fylde	23.09.00
	Rob Liley	Doncaster v Kendal	15.03.03
	Neil Hallett	Bracknell v Esher	13.09.03
	Mark Bedworth	Wharfedale v Harrogate	23.12.06
	Scott Rawlings	Manchester v Bradford Bingley	28.04.07
	Robin Kitching	Otley v Blackheath	19.04.08

DIVISION THREE — ALL TIME RECORDS

MOST POINTS IN A SEASON

Points	Player	Club	Season	Tries	Cons.	Pens.	D.G.
404	Steve Gough	Fylde	1996-97	7	57	82	3
398	Neil Hallett	Esher	2006-07	11	80	61	-
373	Mark Woodrow	Birmingham Solihull	2008-09	8	108	38	1
365	Steve Swindells	Manchester	1998-99	7	60	70	0
343	Phil Jones	Orrell	2001-02	15	59	50	-
338	Richard Mills	Walsall	1996-97	1	42	81	2
328	Oliver Thomas	Moseley	2004-05	5	48	64	5
327	Barry Reeves	Henley Hawks	2002-03	4	80	46	3
322	Sateki Tuipulotu	Leeds	1997-98	11	60	49	
321	Rob Liley	Doncaster	2004-05	2	70	57	-
315	Ben Harvey	Stourbridge	2002-03	8	49	59	-
311	Jonathan Gregory	Esher	2001-02	5	29	76	-
307	Gerry Ainscough	Leeds	1996-97	14	45	49	
305	Ralph Zoing	Harrogate	1996-97	4	63	48	5
302	Neil Hallett	Esher	2005-06	7	57	51	-
300	Andy Green	Exeter	1996-97	5	58	50	3
300	Craig Raymond	London Welsh	1996-97	6	39	57	7
298	Ben Harvey	Stourbridge	2001-02	9	44	55	-
296	Rob Liley	Doncaster	2002-03	10	36	57	1
290	Alastair Bressington	Stourbridge	2006-07	19	60	25	-
289	Lee Cholewa	Harrogate	2001-02	9	68	35	1
287	Peter Rutledge	Otley	1996-97	8	56	45	
286	Gareth Wynne	Manchester	2007-08	8	63	40	-
285	Dave Harvey	Newbury	2004-05	8	49	44	5
282	Andy Frost	Southend	2007-08	11	58	36	1
281	Jason Dance	Reading	1996-97	6	61	43	
278	Jonathan Davies	Wharfedale	2001-02	5	44	54	1
275	Paul Morris	Lydney	1996-97	3	31	66	
274	Adam Mounsey	Wharfedale	99-2000	7	37	55	
272	Chris Atkinson	Nottingham	1998-99	2	35	64	
271	Mike Scott	Kendal	2001-02	2	36	57	6
271	Michael Hook	Redruth	2006-07	3	56	47	1
268	Rob Liley	Doncaster	2003-04	6	44	50	-
267	Sam Howard	Rosslyn Park	2003-04	11	49	35	-
264	Craig Raymond	London Welsh	1997-98	8	64	29	3
262	Chris Atkinson	Nottingham	1997-98	6	30	64	
262	Dan Clappison	Otley	99-2000	1	61	42	3
260	Jonathan Gregory	Esher	2000-01	7	42	47	-
254	Gareth Cull	Nuneaton	2006-07	3	43	51	-
254	Sam Young	Launceston	2006-07	6	55	38	-
253	Oliver Thomas	Moseley	2005-06	1	49	49	1
250	Ali Bressington	Stourbridge	2008-09	12	44	34	=
248	Lee Osborne	Lydney	99-2000	3	25	61	
248	Neil Hallett	Bracknell, Esher	2004-05	1	39	55	
247	Adam Mounsey	Wharfedale	1997-98	4	31	55	
246	Jason Dance	Reading	1997-98	4	35	52	
246	Mark Bedworth	Wharfedale	2008-09	11	40	36	1
244	Colin Stephens	Sedgley Park	2001-02	4	37	46	4
241	Mark Bedworth	Wharfedale	2005-06	8	30	47	-
239	Neil Hallett	Bracknell	2003-04	8	35	41	2
238	Neil Stenhouse	Nottingham	2003-04	2	48	40	4
237	Frankie Neale	Blackheath	2006-07	10	47	30	1

NATIONAL LEAGUE TWO NORTH

2008-2009 SEASON   Review & Statistics   322-329

2009-2010 CLUBS

Club	Page
Bradford & Bingley	330
Broadstreet	332
Caldy	334
Fylde	336
Harrogate	338
Huddersfield	340
Hull	342
Hull Ionians	344
Kendal	346
Leicester Lions	348
Loughborough Students	350
Macclesfield	352
Preston Grasshoppers	354
Rugby lions	356
Waterloo	358
Westoe	360

RECORDS SECTION
(previously National 3 North, Division 4 North, Division 5 North & Area League North)

Roll of Honour	362
Year by Year Records	364
All Time Records	366
All-Time Team & Individual Records	368

FIXTURES 2009-10

	Bradford & B	Broadstreet	Caldy	Fylde	Harrogate	Huddersfield	Hull	Hull Ionians	Kendal	Leicester Lions	Loughborough	Macclesfield	Preston G.	Rugby lions	Waterloo	Westoe
Bradford & B.		24.04	16.01	30.01	14.11	09.01	10.04	17.10	19.12	03.10	27.03	20.02	05.12	31.10	12.09	06.03
Broadstreet	05.09		05.12	19.09	20.02	17.04	14.11	16.01	27.03	02.01	31.10	03.10	07.11	29.01	12.12	17.10
Caldy	26.09	03.04		24.10	09.01	12.09	27.02	07.11	20.03	10.10	23.01	28.11	13.02	12.12	17.04	05.09
Fylde	10.10	09.01	20.02		05.12	23.01	24.04	31.10	12.09	13.02	10.04	06.03	19.12	14.11	26.09	27.03
Harrogate	20.03	24.10	19.09	03.04		07.11	10.10	12.12	13.02	28.11	26.09	17.04	23.01	05.09	27.02	02.01
Huddersfield	19.09	19.12	02.01	03.10	06.03		05.12	30.01	10.04	16.01	14.11	17.10	27.03	20.02	24.04	31.10
Hull	12.12	20.03	31.10	05.09	30.01	03.04		02.01	07.11	17.04	17.10	19.09	20.02	16.01	28.11	03.10
Hull Ionians	13.02	26.09	06.03	27.02	10.04	10.10	12.09		09.01	24.10	19.12	14.11	24.04	27.03	23.01	05.12
Kendal	17.04	28.11	14.11	02.01	17.10	12.12	06.03	19.09		05.09	20.02	16.01	31.10	03.10	03.04	30.01
Leicester Lions	23.01	12.09	30.01	17.10	27.03	26.09	19.12	20.02	24.04		05.12	31.10	10.04	06.03	09.01	14.11
Loughborough	28.11	27.02	03.10	12.12	16.01	20.03	13.02	17.04	24.10	03.04		05.09	10.10	02.01	07.11	19.09
Macclesfield	24.10	23.01	27.03	07.11	19.12	13.02	09.01	20.03	26.09	27.02	24.04		12.09	05.12	10.10	10.04
Preston G.	03.04	06.03	17.10	17.04	03.10	28.11	24.10	05.09	27.02	12.12	30.01	02.01		19.09	20.03	16.01
Rugby Lions	27.02	9.10	10.04	20.03	24.04	24.10	26.09	28.11	23.01	07.11	12.09	03.04	09.01		13.02	19.12
Waterloo	02.01	10.04	19.12	16.01	31.10	05.09	27.03	03.10	05.12	19.09	06.03	30.01	14.11	17.10		20.02
Westoe	07.11	13.02	24.04	28.11	12.09	27.02	23.01	03.04	10.04	10.04	20.03	09.01	12.12	26.09	17.04	24.10

2008-09 LEAGUE TABLE

		P	W	D	L	F	A	PD	Bonus Pts 4T	<7	Pts
1	Nuneaton	26	21	1	4	820	465	355	15	2	103
2	Caldy	26	17	1	8	678	485	193	10	4	84
3	Macclesfield	26	16	2	8	643	518	125	7	6	81
4	Fylde	26	15	2	9	762	541	221	12	5	81
5	Harrogate	26	16	0	10	632	606	26	11	4	79
6	Loughborough Students	26	15	2	9	605	509	96	10	1	75
7	Leicester Lions	26	15	0	11	623	497	126	6	4	70
8	Kendal	26	13	1	12	646	522	124	9	4	63
9	Preston Grasshoppers	26	11	0	15	610	638	-28	7	4	55
10	Huddersfield	26	10	2	14	549	618	-69	2	5	51
11	Hull Ionians	26	9	2	15	519	555	-36	6	5	51
12	Bradford Bingley	26	9	1	16	560	869	-309	6	2	46
13	Darlington MP	26	6	1	19	467	692	-225	3	9	38
14	Halifax	26	1	1	24	339	938	-599	2	2	10

2008-09 RESULTS MATRIX

	Bradford & Bingley	Caldy	Darlington M. P.	Fylde	Halifax	Harrogate	Huddersfield	Hull Ionians	Kendal	Leicester Lions	Loughborough Students	Macclesfield	Nuneaton	Preston Grasshoppers
Bradford Bingley		6-50	32-17	15-54	32-12	43-24	25-25	28-19	0-68	14-64	20-38	13-26	16-19	23-51
Caldy	41-10		16-16	33-23	52-7	28-14	22-13	20-19	31-20	29-12	15-25	25-39	7-15	16-12
Darlington MP	14-20	18-13		18-39	38-31	15-21	26-28	19-22	22-19	20-21	8-20	19-31	17-44	29-15
Fylde	27-8	23-22	61-15		36-5	62-13	35-18	38-14	24-24	18-7	52-30	17-24	27-27	41-25
Halifax	22-67	15-39	17-19	17-35		11-10	35-43	20-35	11-21	13-57	13-36	13-13	14-37	13-24
Harrogate	28-11	41-44	33-10	36-19	29-12		27-20	37-27	31-30	15-14	31-19	11-14	17-23	45-17
Huddersfield	18-22	9-37	19-13	44-32	24-3	43-25		31-29	17-26	13-27	15-15	19-18	6-20	24-9
Hull Ionians	30-10	27-29	33-10	10-21	43-8	12-16	31-18		28-13	16-19	19-11	22-22	8-30	17-12
Kendal	35-29	35-12	34-13	17-18	23-12	5-24	23-8	13-18		20-29	28-23	44-29	33-12
Leicester Lions	23-28	7-9	13-12	25-21	83-3	35-14	16-9	27-10	12-40		19-36	16-10	20-25	49-33
Loughborough S.	44-23	14-22	19-17	15-10	20-0	25-26	16-27	3-3	33-5	20-6		27-18	7-23	29-24
Macclesfield	20-39	19-16	24-29	15-12	35-15	27-28	27-23	33-16	29-14	26-6	33-17		21-16	35-14
Nuneaton	51-10	23-31	31-25	50-5	39-10	32-9	42-22	29-6	21-13	16-19	41-30	41-35		46-22
Preston G.	49-16	23-19	36-8	14-12	48-7	8-27	17-13	23-10	23-15	34-8	19-27	22-26	24-50	

2008-09 LEADING SCORERS

MOST POINTS

			T	C	P	DG
290	Gavin Roberts	Caldy	10	54	44	-
286	Ross Winney	Macclesfield	3	41	59	4
248	Chris Johnson	Huddersfield	5	29	48	7
224	Jon Boden	Leicester Lions	7	54	27	-
216	Stephen Nutt	Fylde	9	45	27	-
189	Hugh Thomas	Nuneaton	6	39	27	-
186	Marcus Jackson	Preston Grasshoppers	2	22	44	-
150	Rickie Aley	Nuneaton	1	23	24	9
146	Steve Brimacombe	Bradford Bingley	4	33	20	-
145	Gareth Collins	Leicester Lions	29	-	-	-
144	Iain Gordon	Halifax	1	26	29	-
140	Lewis Boyd	Kendal	28	-	-	-
138	Jon Benson	Darlington MP	1	17	33	-
120	Nicholas Royle	Fylde	24	-	-	-
120	Ollie Brennand	Fylde	24	-	-	-
120	Grant Pointer	Loughborough Students	5	25	15	-
111	Mike Aspinall	Harrogate	6	27	9	-
101	Dan Stephens	Kendal	1	21	18	-
100	James Ferguson	Hull Ionians	-	20	20	-

MOST TRIES

			First Half	Second Half	Home	Away
29	Gareth Collins	Leicester Lions	15	14	18	11
28	Lewis Boyd	Kendal	12	16	15	13
24	Nicholas Royle	Fylde	11	13	14	10
24	Ollie Brennand	Fylde	15	9	12	12
16	William Cave	Nuneaton	9	7	10	6
15	Mark Turner	Caldy	9	6	6	9
15	Fergus Mulchrone	Macclesfield	7	8	6	9
14	Aaron Takarangi	Nuneaton	6	8	8	6
14	Andrew Soutar	Caldy	8	6	8	6
14	Gary Holmes	Nuneaton	7	7	6	8
14	Rob Cook	Nuneaton	6	8	9	5
13	Sam Bottomley	Harrogate	6	7	8	5
12	Ed Smithies	Harrogate	5	7	9	3
12	Phil Burgess	Loughborough Students	6	6	5	7
11	Russell Flynn	Preston Grasshoppers	6	5	6	5
11	Darren Wilson	Preston Grasshoppers	4	7	5	6
10	Mark Kirkby	Bradford Bingley	5	5	3	7
10	Craig Aikman	Fylde	7	3	9	1
10	Gavin Roberts	Caldy	5	5	6	4

MOST PENALTIES
59 Ross Winney (Macclesfield)

MOST CONVERSIONS
54 Gavin Roberts (Caldy) & Jon Boden (Leicester Lions)

MOST DROP GOALS
8 Rickie Aley (Nuneaton)

TRIES FOR
By Position

	TOTAL	BACKS	FORWARDS	Full Backs	Wing	Center	Half Backs	Front Row	Second Row	Back Row	Penalty Tries
Bradford Bingley	70	51	19	6	19	18	8	6	8	5	1
Caldy	82	57	25	15	18	18	6	11	1	13	0
Darlington MP	57	36	21	4	14	10	8	11	1	9	0
Fylde	107	86	21	1	55	10	20	4	2	15	1
Halifax	38	24	14	1	13	8	2	2	2	10	2
Harrogate	89	57	32	14	23	10	10	12	4	16	0
Huddersfield	54	33	21	2	13	9	9	3	0	18	1
Hull Ionians	58	44	14	5	14	18	7	2	5	7	1
Kendal	88	57	31	2	39	13	3	7	5	19	0
Leicester Lions	82	59	23	17	31	7	4	6	5	12	1
Loughborough Students	80	46	34	11	18	11	6	1	8	25	4
Macclesfield	71	39	32	11	16	5	7	10	6	16	0
Nuneaton	101	72	29	12	36	10	14	11	1	17	0
Preston Grasshoppers	71	47	24	9	15	8	15	5	6	13	0
Totals :	1048	708	340	110	324	155	119	91	54	195	11

TRIES AGAINST
By Position

	TOTAL	BACKS	FORWARDS	Full Backs	Wing	Center	Half Backs	Front Row	Second Row	Back Row	Penalty Tries
Bradford Bingley	118	83	35	12	40	17	14	10	5	20	1
Caldy	56	46	10	7	27	5	7	4	1	5	0
Darlington MP	94	57	37	9	22	12	14	5	6	26	1
Fylde	64	43	21	6	25	8	4	5	4	12	0
Halifax	127	91	36	19	34	24	14	14	5	17	4
Harrogate	76	50	26	8	25	10	7	8	6	12	0
Huddersfield	73	55	18	10	18	16	11	6	2	10	0
Hull Ionians	67	47	20	7	22	12	6	6	4	10	0
Kendal	67	41	26	8	17	11	5	9	3	14	1
Leicester Lions	53	29	24	4	14	7	4	7	2	15	0
Loughborough Students	57	30	27	4	13	6	7	6	3	18	2
Macclesfield	57	40	17	4	19	9	8	4	2	11	1
Nuneaton	55	34	21	4	17	6	7	4	5	12	0
Preston Grasshoppers	84	62	22	8	31	12	11	3	6	13	0
Totals :	1048	708	340	110	324	155	119	91	54	195	11

NATIONAL 2 NORTH

KICKING STRIKE RATE

		Conversions		Penalties		TOTAL	
S/R%		Att	Suc	Att	Suc	Att	Suc
78.40	Gavin Roberts (Caldy)	72	54	53	44	125	98
75.00	Matt Booth (Bradford Bingley)	11	7	9	8	20	15
74.16	Marcus Jackson (Preston Grasshoppers)	36	22	53	44	89	66
71.43	Ross Winney (Macclesfield)	67	41	73	59	140	100
69.37	Chris Johnson (Huddersfield)	42	29	69	48	111	77
68.97	Karl Birch (Hull Ionians)	13	9	16	11	29	20
68.75	Hugh Thomas (Nuneaton)	61	39	35	27	96	66
68.07	Jon Boden (Leicester Lions)	77	54	42	27	119	81
67.92	Mike Aspinall (Harrogate)	43	27	10	9	53	36
66.67	James Ferguson (Hull Ionians)	30	20	30	20	60	40
66.67	Grant Pointer (Loughborough Students)	37	25	23	15	60	40
66.67	Matthew Johnson (Huddersfield)	10	7	17	11	27	18
66.25	Steve Brimacombe (Bradford Bingley)	55	33	25	20	80	53
65.28	Rickie Aley (Nuneaton)	34	23	38	24	72	47
65.22	Nick Cooper (Hull Ionians)	8	5	15	10	23	15
64.91	Robert Aloe (Kendal)	38	22	19	15	57	37
64.71	Iain Gordon (Halifax)	38	26	47	29	85	55
63.64	Cerith Rees (Harrogate)	9	6	13	8	22	14
63.16	Stephen Nutt (Fylde)	77	45	37	27	114	72
60.98	Jon Benson (Darlington MP)	39	17	43	33	82	50
57.69	Nicholas Smith (Preston Grasshoppers)	16	8	10	7	26	15
57.35	Dan Stephens (Kendal)	43	21	25	18	68	39
57.14	Neil Hunter (Fylde)	17	11	4	1	21	12
54.05	James Murray (Harrogate)	27	14	10	6	37	20
50.00	Benjamin Snook (Darlington MP)	17	8	21	11	38	19
45.83	Paul Trendell (Loughborough Students)	16	8	8	3	24	11

DISCIPLINE RECORD

Sin Bin Breakdown

	SIN BIN			Violent Conduct			Professional Foul			RED		
	Total	H	A	Total	H	A	Total	H	A	Total	H	A
Bradford Bingley	2	1	1	19	11	8	21	12	9	2	2	0
Caldy	4	3	1	12	5	7	16	8	8	-		
Darlington MP	2	1	1	8	5	3	10	6	4	-		
Fylde	2	0	2	11	5	6	13	5	8	1	1	0
Halifax	6	0	6	20	9	11	26	9	17	1	1	0
Harrogate	2	0	2	13	7	6	15	7	8	-		
Huddersfield	-			16	9	7	16	9	7	-		
Hull Ionians	1	1	0	23	10	13	24	11	13	-		
Kendal	-			12	3	9	12	3	9	-		
Leicester Lions	2	1	1	13	8	5	15	9	6	1	1	0
Loughborough Students	-			18	8	10	18	8	10	-		
Macclesfield	2	1	1	10	6	4	12	7	5	-		
Nuneaton	1	0	1	14	8	6	15	8	7	1	1	0
Preston Grasshoppers	2	1	1	11	7	4	13	8	5	1	1	0
TOTAL	26	9	17	200	101	99	222	108	114	7	7	0

NATIONAL 2 NORTH

2008-09 STATS REVIEW

> Nuneaton win National Three North by some 19 points from Caldy. They previously won the title back in 2002/03

> Halifax after a seven season stay in the National Leagues are relegated back to North One, finally managing a win in their last match of the season

> Darlington Mowden Park after an eight season stay in National Three South are relegated back to North One finishing some eight points form safety despite a late rally which saw them gain three wins and a draw in their last six matches

> Caldy centre Gavin Roberts tops the point's scorers list with 290 points, the best since New Brighton's Anthony Birley scored 316 points in the 2003/04 season. It was the ninth highest ever total points in a Three North season

> Leicester Lions full back/wing Gareth Collins ran in 29 tries which is the second highest total ever in the division after the 31 scored by Fylde's Nick Royle in the 2006/07 season

> Second in the try scoring was Kendal wing Lewis Boyd with 38, enough for third place on the all time list

> Ross Winney kicked 58 penalty goals for Macclesfield which takes him into fifth on the all time list in the division but some way behind the all time record of 73 set by Fylde's Mike Scott in 2003/04

> Nuneaton's Rickie Alley nine drop goals in the season equalled the record set by Preston Grasshoppers fly half Steve Kerry in the 1996/97 season.

> Twice Aley drops three goals in a match to fall one short of the record of four set by Hoppers Steve Kerry in the 1996/97 season

> Rob Cook also dropped a goal for Nuneaton as they equalled Preston Grasshopper's record of 10 drop goals in that season.

Nuneaton

- Nuneaton bounce back at the first attempt after relegation from National two last season to take the National Three North title for the second time having already won it in the 2002/03 season
- They took the most try bonus points, 15, three more than anyone else
- They were the top scorers in the division and had the best defensive record
- Huw Thomas tops the scoring charts for the second successive season with 189 points
- Winger William Cave is the top try scorer with 16 tries, seven more than Aaron Takarangi scored last season
- Fly half Rickie Aley set a new record for drop goals in a season with nine which is also a division record and twice he dropped three goals in a match which is also a club record
- In matches against the other top four side they have three wins, two defeats and one draw
- They had the best home record in the division with 11 wins and two defeats and took try bonus points in ten of those 11 wins
- Nuneaton had four ever presents during the season, second row Daniel Hurst, flanker Gary Holmes, fly half Huw Thomas and winger Aaron Takarangi, plus they also had three further players who started all but one of their league games

- **Caldy**
- In their second season of National League rugby Caldy improved three places to finish as runners up after leading the table for much of the season
- Started the season with 12 wins in their opening 14 matches but finished with just one win in their last five
- Despite finishing second they were only the seventh highest try scorers in the division with 82
- Centre Gavin Roberts was the top points scorer in the division with 290 including 10 tries
- Full back Mark Turner, a summer transfer from West Park, topped the try scorers list with 15 - one more than winger Andrew Soutar who also moved from West Park in the summer. Soutar was the only Caldy player to start all 26 league matches with centre Shaun Woof and second row Paul White missing just one
- In matches against the other top four sides they started the season with two wins but then went on to lose the last four, although in three of them they did take losing bonus points
- Caldy had a great defensive record in the first half of matches only conceding 14 tries, 10 fewer than anyone else during this period

Macclesfield

- After three seasons at the wrong end of the table Macclesfield recovered to finish third, their second best finish in six seasons after their second place back in 2004/05
- In six of their eight defeats they took losing bonus points, but they only managed seven try bonus points - only joint seventh in the division. With 71 tries they were only 10th in the try scoring list.
- Fly half Ross Winney again top scored for the club with an impressive 277 his best return by some 62 points and the third time he has topped 200 points in a season
- In four seasons at Macclesfield Winney has now scored 859 points in 95 starts
- During the season Winney passed the 1000 point mark in league rugby and ended the season on 1075 from 187 starts plus 28 as a replacement whilst playing for Wakefield, Plymouth and Orrell as well as Macc
- Full back Fergus Mulchrone was the leading scorer with 15 tries - the most by a Macclesfield player in league rugby
- In matches against the other top four sides Macclesfield had a great record with five wins and just one defeat the best record of any side - the only match they lost was their first against Nuneaton back in October, four of the wins were close affairs with the losers picking up a losing bonus point

Fylde

- Fylde were the top try scorers in the division with 109 - eight more than Champions Nuneaton
- They took 12 try bonus points - the second best total in the division and were also the second highest scorers
- Fly half Stephen Nutt finished the season as leading points scorer with 216.
- In try scoring it was a tie between Ollie Brennand and Nick Royle on 24 tries - joint third in the division.
- Royle has been top try scorer for three of his four seasons at Fylde scoring 85 tries in just 80 starts. Overall in his league career he has now scored 99 tries having scored 10 for Liverpool St Helens and four for Manchester in his debut season 2002/03 in National One
- Brennand is not far behind with his strike rate scoring 62 tries in 66 starts
- No Fylde player started all 26 matches. Craig Aikman with 25 started the most - one more than winger Brennand
- In matches against the other top four sides they only managed one win to go with a draw and four defeats although in two of the defeats they did manage a losing bonus point

Harrogate

- Harrogate finished fifth a one place better than last season when they returned to the division after a 14 year absence
- Michael Aspinall was the leading scorer with 111 having previously been leading scorer four seasons.
- Leading try scorer was wing Sam Bottomley with 13 tries - one more than full back Ed Smithies who had been leading scorer four times previously
- 34 year old Smithies has now scored 98 leagues tries for the club in 232 starts plus seven more appearances as a replacement. His return of 12 was his best for seven seasons when he scored also scored 12.
- They collected 11 try bonus points - the third highest total in the division
- In matches against the top four sides they managed just two wins to go with six defeats
- No ever presents, but backs Ed Smithies and Sam Bottomley and prop Simon Davies all started 24 matches. Davies also came on as a replacement in a further match bringing his appearances to 25
- Hooker Aaron Yorke also appeared in 25 matches starting 23 and twice coming on as a replacement

Loughborough Students

- Loughborough Students in their first ever season of League Rugby finished a highly creditable sixth - four points behind fifth placed Harrogate and five points in front of Leicester Lions
- They picked up 10 try bonus points - the fourth highest total in the division but only managed one losing bonus point in nine defeats - the lowest total of any side
- Only conceded 509 points which was the fourth lowest total in the division although they only played 25 matches
- Full back Grant Pointer top scored with 120 points
- In the try scoring stakes No 8 Phil Burgess led the way with 12 tries which was also the second most by a forward in the division, two behind Nuneaton flanker Gary Holmes
- In their eight matches against the top four sides they lost the first five but finished with three straight wins
- No player played all 26 matches the best was 20 by wing Simon Lilley, three more than three players on 17 including leading try scorer Burgess
- They did though have the meanest defence at home conceding just 22 tries five fewer than any other side

Leicester Lions

- Lions finished in seventh place - three places down on last season in their fourth season of National League rugby
- They had the meanest defence in terms of fewest tries conceded just 53 in 26 matches, three fewer than first and second placed Nuneaton and Caldy
- They only conceded 497 points which was the third lowest total in the division
- They only managed six try bonus points all season which was the lowest of any top nine sides
- Gareth Collins was the leading try scorer for the third time in four seasons but with his best return yet, 29 which topped the division. He finished the season strongly with a run of 18 tries in six matches, twice scoring six tries in a match - one off the division record
- In his four seasons at the club he has now scored 69 tries in 94 appearances and had previously scored 14 league tries for Rugby Lions
- Fly half Jon Boden was the leading points scorer for a 3rd consecutive season with 224 and in his Lions career is averaging over 10 points a game with 598 in 58 starts. In all he has scored 953 National League points.

Kendal

- After a two year absence Kendal return to National League rugby and finish in eighth place some eight points clear of the next side in the division
- Winger Lewis Boyd was the leading try scorer with a club record 28 tries. This put him in second place in the division just one behind leader Gareth Collins (Leicester Lions)
- Boyd was also the leading point's scorer with 140 but from the boot Dan Stephens led the way with 96
- In matches against the top four sides they did well with three wins and a draw to go with four defeats
- Centre Ian Voortman was the only ever present and played in every minute of every match apart from the two occasions when he was sin binned
- Winger Boyd also played in every match starting 25 and coming on as a replacement once as well which was the same story for No 8 Craig Wilson
- Kendal were one of just three sides to concede more tries at home than on the road
- They had 10 players start 22 matches or more which was the most in the division

Preston Grasshoppers

- Hoppers finished in ninth place which is down two places on last season and their lowest in their four year stint in the division having finished third the season before
- Fly half Marcus Jackson was top points scorer with 186 which was the seventh highest total in the division in his first full season for the club having played four matches the previous season
- In the try scoring stakes there was a tie for top spot between scrum half Darren Wilson and winger Russell Flynn with 11 which was four more than Oliver Viney managed the previous season to top the try charts
- In matches against the top four they managed two wins - at home against Caldy and against Fylde
- Back row forward Andrew Dochray played the most matches starting 25 of the 26 matches whilst prop Richard Carlton started 23 matches but came on in two others to make it 25 appearances
- Only had 13 sin binnings which was the four lowest total in the division
- Hoppers half backs scored 15 tries which was the second most by a half back pairing in the division after Fylde who scored 20 from there

Huddersfield

- In their first ever season of National League rugby Huddersfield finished in 10th place some 13 points off the relegation zone
- They only managed two try bonus points all season and they were both picked up late in the season
- Winger Alex Shaw and back rower Nick Sharpe were joint leading try scorers with seven as Huddersfield struggled to score tries
- Shaw was the only player to start all 26 matches and play in every minute of every match, just behind him with 25 starts were prop Anthony Stringwell and back row man Mike Whitehead
- In the points scoring Chris Johnson again led the way with 248 points from his 22 starts after playing a huge roll last season in their promotion to the National Leagues
- 18 of their 55 tries came from the back row, 33% their highest % in the division

Hull Ionians
- In their fourth season back in Three North Hull Ionians had their worst finish - three places lower than last season
- They struggled to score with only the two relegated sides scoring fewer points but did better defensively with having a better record than three of the sides above them in the table
- Fly half James Ferguson was the leading scorer with just 100 points which was 72 less than he managed last season when the topped Ionians scoring for the first time
- James Greene was the top try scorer with nine, two more than centre Travis Plumridge, and was an improvement on the two previous seasons when six and eight were enough to finish top try scorer
- Second row Richard Hill made the most starts with 23, one more than flanker Richard Wigham, and these were the only two players to start over 20 matches for the club
- With 24 they had the second most players sin binned during the season
-

Bradford & Bingley
- Finished two places lower than last season when they returned to the division after a one season run in National Two and made it five seasons of National League rugby since winning North One back in 2003/04
- Fly half Steve Brimacombe topped scored with 146 points for the first time in his first full season at the club
- In the try scoring stakes wing Mark Kirkby led the way with 10 tries and has now scored 46 tries in his four seasons at the Bees from 86 matches
- Back row forward Neil Spence started all 26 league matches and apart from being replaced one as a temporarily played every minute of every match. Wing Kirkby played 25 matches missing just one game all season.
- Were the only side to have two players sent off during the season
- Although finishing third bottom the Bees were the eighth highest try scorers in the division
- Only five of their 71 tries came from their back row - the worst return in the division.

Darlington Mowden Park
- DMP's eight year stay in the National Leagues came to an end as they finished second bottom and some eight points from safety, but it could have been so different
- Picked up nine losing bonus points from their 19 defeats - the most in the division & three more than anyone else
- Prop Dan Miller started 25 of the clubs 26 league matches and came on as a replacement in the other, one more appearance than fellow front rowers Danny Brown and Howard Murray
- Jon Benson topped scored for DMP for a second successive season and during the season passed 1000 league points which he has accumulated playing for West Hartlepool, Leeds, Rotherham, Doncaster & Otley
- Topping the try scoring list were two players who scored eight tries - scrum half Martin Lithgow and centre/wing Adam McKenzie. McKenzie, a Scottish U20 International this season, scored his 8 tries in just seven starts.
- Despite their league position only had 10 players sin binned during the season - the lowest number in the division
- Their front row scored 11 tries which was the second best by a front row in the division, one behind Harrogate

Halifax
- Halifax are relegated back to North One after a seven year run in the National Leagues which included three seasons in National Two as they suffer back to back relegations
- It took until the last match of the season to achieve their only win - a home success over Harrogate
- They were the lowest scorers and conceded the most points and just managed two try bonus points all season and two losing bonus points in their 24 defeats
- Iain Gordon was the leading points scorer with 144 which was the 11th best return in the division
- In the try scoring stakes flanker Dominic Moon led the way with seven one more than centre Tim Mennell
- Gordon and Moon were ever presents for the club starting all 25 matches the club played and Gordon was not replaced in any of them.

BRADFORD & BINGLEY RFC

KEY PERSONNEL

President:	Mick Waterhouse	mickwaterhouse@btinternet.com 0788 978 4236
Secretary:	Nick Patterson	nickpatt@me.com 0781 203 9277
Press Secretary:	as above	
Membership Secretary:	Andy Dean	beesmembership@googlemail.com 0771 358 4152
Chairman of Rugby:	Glen Shaw	glen@shaw2505.freeserve.co.uk 0795 805 9162
Treasurer:	Chris Hemsley	hemsleycrh@aol.com 0788 789 1969
Head Coach:	Stuart Dixon	centyorkscrc@hotmail.co.uk 0779 236 7658
Coach :	Robin Kay	0798 929 1488
First Team Manager:	Benji Pickin	benjipickin@hotmail.com 0797 157 3211
Director of Rugby:	Chris Hemsley	hemsleycrh@aol.com 0788 789 1969
Fixture Secretary:	Jimmy Lawrence	lawrence.james@blueyonder.co.uk 0759 520 4345
League Contact:	as above	
Referee Coordinator	John Gray	johngray53@hotmail.co.uk 0776 628 0652
Marketing	Peter Harrison	peter.harrison26@btopenworld.com 0751 713 8056

Formed: 1982
(Bradford RFC & Bingley RUFC amalgamated)

Nickname: The Bees

Website: www.bradfordandbingleyrfc.co.uk

Colours: Black shirt with an amber and white honeycombed front, black shorts & socks

Change colours: White shirt with black, red and amber stripes on the sides; black shorts & socks

Training nights: Tuesday & Thursday

GROUND DETAILS

Address:
Aireview, Wagon Lane, Bingley, BD16 1 LT
Tel: 01274 775441 Fax: 01274 775442
email: Thebeessportsclub@yahoo.co.uk

Directions: On the main road south of Bingley, (not the new by-pass) turn into Wagon Lane by Beckfoot School.

Capacity: 2000   Covered Seating: 300

Car Parking: Ample at ground

Nearest Railway Station: Bingley (1 mile away in town centre)

Admission: Matchday £8 or £6 advance purchase. Concessions available.

Kick Off Times: 3pm in September, October, March & April; 2.15pm November through to February.

Clubhouse:
Open weekday evenings 5-11pm and 11am-11pm Sat. & Sun.
Food is available.

Functions available - contact the Club Office as above.

Club Shop:
Open matchday afternoons and selected other times. See website for specific details or contact the Secretary Nick Patterson.

CONTACT DETAILS

Correspondence should be addressed to the Secretary, Five Rise Locks House, 1 Five Rise, Bingley, BD16 4DT

PROGRAMME

Size: A5
Price: with admission
Advertising: Contact Phil Greaves
email: PhilG@cumminspapyrus.co.uk

NATIONAL 2 NORTH

REVIEW OF THE SEASON 2008-09

At the start of the 2008-09 season the aim was to finish safely positioned in the top half of National League 3 North. By this standard the final place of 12th was disappointing. However, staying in the National leagues for a sixth consecutive season is a satisfactory outcome.

It certainly was a mixed season with terrific away wins at Macclesfield, Darlington Mowden Park, Huddersfield, Leicester Lions & the thumping of Halifax 22 – 67. Home wins came against Hull Ionians, Halifax, Darlington Mowden Park and Harrogate.

On the other foot we were too easily beaten by some hefty scores which left both the coaches and committee bemused.

Again we suffered with injuries throughout the season with a major loss of Captain Baz Clark who missed most of the season with a broken arm, and Benny Greaves having more time out than in any other season on memory.

New players had been drafted in from local clubs as we looked to cut our cloth accordingly in these times of financial restraint.

A good nucleus of up and coming "home grown" talent have been given the opportunity to sample 1st XV rugby for the first time, and add to a very youthful Bees squad, which should only improve over the coming seasons.

As a club we are striving to be as competitive as possible in the National leagues and aim not to get into the financial turmoil that has bestowed some of the local clubs around us.

Our 2nd XV had a fantastic season Winning the Aire Wharfe Cup and finishing in second place in the league. The 2nd XV will be joining the newly formed 2nd Team Yorkshire Premier league, with some very strong opposition to look forward to in the coming months.

The Junior section, a very important part of our club have been working very hard, and I can now announce that through their efforts we have now obtained The RFU Seal of Approval and sport England Clubmark.

LAST TEN SEASONS

	Division	P	W	D	L	F	A	P.D.	Pts	Pos	Most Pts		Most Tries	
99-00	North 1	22	13	1	8	559	415	144	27	4				
00-01	North 1	22	12	0	10	503	392	111	24	3				
01-02	North 1	22	8	1	13	474	438	36	17	10r				
02-03	North 2E	22	21	0	1	1013	245	768	42	1p				
03-04	North 1	22	20	1	1	975	366	609	41	1p	Most Pts		Most Tries	
04-05	N3N	26	17	1	8	680	451	229	84	3	275	Tom Rhodes	12	Latu Makaafi, Renier Volshenk, Richard Tafa
05-06	N3N	26	23	1	2	934	465	469	110	1p	270	Tom Rhodes	17	Mark Kirkby
06-07	N2	26	5	0	21	410	942	-532	26	12r	145	Tom Rhodes	8	Mark Kirkby
07-08	N3N	26	10	1	15	551	593	-42	58	10	176	Tom Rhodes	12	Richard Tafa
08-09	N3 N	26	9	1	16	558	869	-311	46	12	146	Steve Brimacombe	10	Mark Kirby

331

BROADSTREET RFC

KEY PERSONNEL

President: Mr. Don Branston

Chairman: Mr. Richard Skene

Treasurer: Mr. Peter Garlick

Club Secretary: Mr. Charlie McGinty
14 Glendower Ave., Whoberley, Coventry CV5 8BE
Tel: 07801 869730 (M) email: cmcginty@eircom.net

Fixture Secretary: Mr. Dave Wilkinson
4 Court Leet, Binley Woods, Coventry CV3 2JP
Tel: 02476 543548 (H) email: dave.ros.wilkinson10@btinternet.com

Chairman of Playing Committee: Mr. Richard Skene
14, Hallams Close, Brandon, Coventry. CV8 3NZ
Tel: 01926 813561 (H) 01926 407717 (W) 07720 441355 (M)
email: skenefhpm@aol.com

Founded: 1929

Nickname: 'The Street'

Website:
www.broadstreet-rugby.co.uk

Colours: Green with red & white hoops, navy shorts

Change colours: Red with green & white hoops, or white with red & green hoops

Training Nights:
Tues & Thur 7pm

GROUND DETAILS

Ground Address: Ivor Preece Field, Rugby Road, Binley Woods, Coventry CV3 2AY

Tel: 02476 541070 (Clubhouse)
02476 541068 (Club Steward)
Fax: 02476 541069
email: broadstreetrfc@btconnect.com

Directions: Leave M6 at J2. Follow signs for Warwick/Stratford/Banbury along the A46. Look for signs for Binley Woods. At the island junction with the A428 (Coventry/Rugby road) turn left towards Rugby. The ground is 100m on the left in the village of Binley Woods.

Capacity: Unlimited.   **Seating**: 250

Admission: tbc

Nearest BR Station: Coventry, approx. 4 miles.

Car Parking: 150 spaces plus overspill. Coach Parking: First left off access road.

Clubhouse: Bar open every evening plus Sat & Sun lunchtimes. Full catering facilities. Functions: Private Parties, Weddings, Corporate and Conference Facilities. Contact Keith Williams or Kay Finch. 02476 541070.

Club Shop: Open match days, Sunday lunchtimes and training evenings. Contact Richard Skene

PROGRAMME

Size: A5 **Pages**: 40 **Price**: with admission
Editorial & Advertising:
Contact Charlie. McGinty (as above)

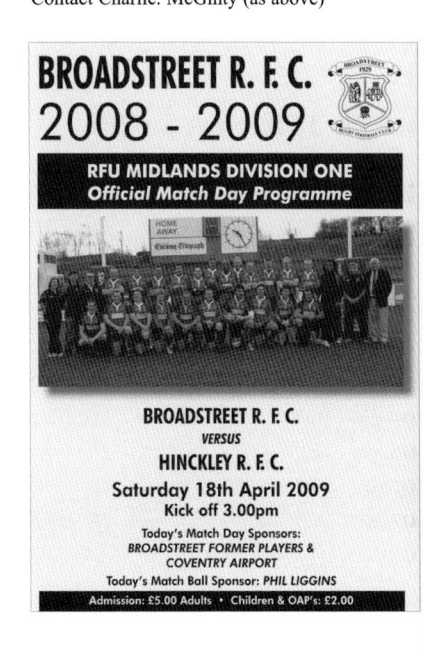

BROADSTREET R. F. C.
2008 - 2009

RFU MIDLANDS DIVISION ONE
Official Match Day Programme

BROADSTREET R. F. C.
VERSUS
HINCKLEY R. F. C.
Saturday 18th April 2009
Kick off 3.00pm

Today's Match Day Sponsors:
BROADSTREET FORMER PLAYERS &
COVENTRY AIRPORT
Today's Match Ball Sponsor: PHIL LIGGINS

Admission: £5.00 Adults • Children & OAP's: £2.00

REVIEW OF THE SEASON 2008-09

After our final league match of season 2007-08 which saw us finish in third place we obviously thought we had good chance of winning promotion this season but anyone who saw our first league match of the season against Bedford Athletic would have thought we had more chance of being relegated. However I have come to the conclusion that was a clever tactical ploy to lull the rest of the league into complacency as what happened afterwards was one for the history books.

We won promotion to the National Leagues, reached the fourth round of the RFU Cup and then went on to win the Warwickshire Cup (for the fourteenth time and the sixth time in succession) by beating a very determined Dunlop team in the final at Coventry. Our second team won the Warwickshire 2nd Tier League Division One and the Coventry & Mid Warwickshire 2nd Team Cup. Our third team won the 3rd division in the Warwickshire 2nd Tier League competition and we also won the plate in the County Floodlit Forties midweek competition. In the Sevens Competitions we won the Coventry & Mid Warwickshire Competition and lost in the final of the plate at the Earlsdon Sevens.

Congratulations are due to Lee Crofts and the rest of the coaching and management team for the efforts put in this season. I would also like to congratulate and thank all of the players for the effort they have put in during the season.

Our facilities, hospitality and organisation at the Ivor Preece Field continue to be highly praised from all quarters and we host games and competitions from all levels of the game including the semi final stages of the Daily Mail Schools competition and the Gulliver's Travel Schools Festival.

Charlie McGinty

LAST TEN SEASONS

	Division	P	W	D	L	F	A	P.D.	Pts	Pos
99-00	Mid 1	16	10	0	6	338	273	65	20	5
00-01	Mid 1	22	14	0	8	474	394	80	28	4
01-02	Mid 1	22	18	0	4	573	340	233	36	1p
02-03	N3N	26	8	1	17	477	795	-318	17	12r
03-04	Mid 1	22	9	1	12	473	488	-15	19	9
04-05	Mid 1	22	4	0	18	291	610	-319	8	11r
05-06	Mid 2W	22	21	0	1	748	177	571	42	1p
06-07	Mid 1	22	11	1	10	421	415	6	23	4
07-08	Mid 1	22	14	0	8	394	415	-21	28	3
08-09	Mid 1	22	18	1	3	674	252	422	37	1p

CALDY RFC

Formed: 1924

Colours: Sable, with claret, silver & gold.

Change Colours: White & maroon

Training Nights: Tuesday & Thursday 7pm

Website: www.caldyrugby.co.uk

NATIONAL 2 NORTH

KEY PERSONNEL

President:	James Churchill	
Chairman:	Graham Armitage	
Treasurer:		
Club Secretary:	Roger Flashman, 26 Milton Crescent, Heswall, Wirral CH60 5ST	
Fixture Secretary:	Tel: (H) 0151 342 5300	
	(W) 0151 653 1824	
	(M) 07772 027409	
	email: roger.flashman@btinternet.com	
Director of Rugy:	Matt Holt	Tel: 07727 158844
		email: Theholtmeisters@live.com
Rugby Manager:	Gareth Davies	Tel: 07920 180533
		email: gd@cheryllewis.co.uk
Chairman of Youth:	Iain Corlett	Tel: 07747 842143
		email: iaincorlett@tiscali.co.uk
Chairman of Mini:	Jonathan Aitkinson	Tel: 07714 206567
		email: jonathan@atkinsonloller.co.uk
Welfare:	Lynn Ridgway	Tel: 07714 992685
		email: lynn.ridgway@medix-uk.com
Commercial:	James Brown	email: Jimbo.brown@hotmail.com

GROUND DETAILS

Address:
Paton Field, Thurstaston Road, West Kirby, Wirral CH41 7ED
Tel: 0151 625 8203   email: admin@caldyrugby.co.uk

Directions:
M56-M53, exit J2 signed A551. Straight on to 2nd r'about, turn right, opposite cricket ground, to West Kirby. Go passed 'Twelfth Man' and 'Red Cat', over r'about and left after church (St. John the Divine). Right opposite 'Farmers Arms', left at r'about and ground is 300 metres on the left.

Nearest BR Station: West Kirby

Car Parking: 500

Capacity: 1000, all uncovered standing.

Admission:
Matchday: £7 incl programme
Season ticket: Adult £60 members, £75 non-members
   Concessions (Over 65) £50 members, £65 non members

Clubhouse:
Open Tues & Thurs 7.30-11, Sat 12.30-midnight.
Available for functions.

Club Shop:
Open Thurs 7-10pm, Sat 1-4pm & Sun 11-1pm.
Contact M Walker - admin@caldyrugby.co.uk.
Orders: via website www.caldyrugby.co.uk

PROGRAMME

Size: A5   **Pages**: 18
Price: £7 incl. admission
Editor:
Advertising: Contact Jane Corlett at admin@caldyrugby.co.uk

Caldy RFC : 1st team squad 2008-9

REVIEW OF THE SEASON 2008-09

Caldy in their second year of National League Rugby finished a highly successful season in 2nd place a three place improvement on their 5th place the previous season.

After competing with Nuneaton for most of the season for top spot in the division they fell away late in the season and in the end finished some 19 points adrift of Champions Nuneaton. They made a super start to the season with 12 wins in their opening 14 matches with the two defeats coming away at Darlington Mowden Park and Macclesfield and in both matches they took a losing bonus point. At the end of January they suffered a third defeat but successive defeats a few weeks later threw them off course losing to title rivals Nuneaton at home and away at Fylde.

They stopped the run with a win at home to Halifax and then won an amazing match at Harrogate overcoming a 21 point deficit going into the last quarter to come through 44-41. After that they lost three and drew one in a four match winless streak which ended their hopes completely.

Centre Gavin Roberts top scored with 290 points, which also the top in the division, and he scored 10 tries in that total as well. But that was only good enough for third place in the try scoring stakes as the former West Park St Helens pair of Mark Turner and Andrew Soutar led the way with 15 and 14 respectively, Turner played at full back and Soutar on the wing.

Ahead of the new season Caldy announce that Tony Walker is to return to the club to take up the role of Commercial Director overseeing all aspects of sponsorship, sales, marketing and the overall development of the club's commercial profile.

'I am delighted to return to Caldy in this new role and look forward to working with the club as it continues to consolidate its remarkable success on the field'

These are challenging times for business and especially for sports clubs. However with the continued valued support of members and sponsors, I am confident that we can build on the strong commercial foundation created over the past few years.'

LAST TEN SEASONS

	Division	P	W	D	L	F	A	P.D.	Pts	Pos
99-00	NW1	18	13	0	5	382	206	176	26	3
00-01	N2W	21	10	1	10	373	363	10	21	6
01-02	N2W	22	4	0	18	266	573	-307	8	12r
02-03	SLC 1	22	20	1	1	863	205	658	41	1p
03-04	N2W	22	16	0	6	551	288	263	32	2
04-05	N2W	22	18	0	4	671	247	424	36	1p
05-06	North 1	22	8	1	13	368	493	-125	17	9
06-07	North 1	22	19	0	3	717	255	462	38	1p
07-08	N3 N	26	13	2	11	555	493	62	67	5
08-09	N3 N	26	17	1	8	678	488	190	84	2

Most Points		Most Tries	
164	Simon Mason	11	Craig Ross
290	Gavin Roberts	15	Mark Turner

NATIONAL 2 NORTH

FYLDE

Founded: 1919

Colours: Claret, gold & white /white/ claret

Change colours: Maroon

Training Nights: Tuesday and Thursday.

Website: www.fylderugby.co.uk

KEY PERSONNEL

President	Alan Townsend	01253 735605 (H), 07960 139826 (M)
Chairman	Mike Brennand, Cranbrook, Islay Road, Lytham FY8 4AD Tel: 07966 341801 (M)	
Treasurer	Nigel Pollard	01253 734733 (C)
Club Secretary	Mike Hornby	01253 734733 (C) 07802 591280 (M)
Director of Coaching	tba	01253 734733 (C)
1st Team Manager	tba	01253 734733 (C)
Coaches	Stuart Connell	07977 261302 (M)
	Martin Scott	01254 853589 (H) 07971 114050 (M)
1st XV Admin/Press	Stewart Brown	01253 883100 (H)
	179 Hardhorn Road, Poulton-le-Fylde, Lancs. FY6 8ES	
Commercial Manager	Fred Harrison	01253 734733 (C)

CONTACT DETAILS

Unless shown separately above all correspondence is: c/o Fylde RFC, Woodlands Memorial Ground, Blackpool Rd., Ansdell, Lytham St. Annes. FY8 4EL
Tel: 01253 734733   **Fax**: 01253 739137   **email**: info@fylderugby.co.uk

PROGRAMME

Size: A5   Pages: 44   Editor: Allan Foster
Price: Free with admission
Advertising
Colour - Page £650, 1/2 £350, 1/4 £200
Two Tone - Page £450, 1/2 £250, 1/4 £150

GROUND DETAILS

Address
Woodlands Memorial Ground,
Blackpool Road, Ansdell, Lytham St. Annes. FY8 4EL
Tel: 01253 734733   Fax: 01253 739137
email: info@fylderugby.co.uk
Capacity: 5,440   Covered Seating: 440

Directions:
From the end of the M55 follow signs for Lytham St. Annes -B5230 then B5261 onto Queensway - ground is three miles on the left opposite Blossoms P.H. and R.C. Church.

Nearest BR Station: Ansdell & Fairhaven.
Left outside station, down the hill away from the sea, along Woodlands Rd to T junction (R.C. Church & Blossoms PH) - ground is opposite to the right.

Car Parking: 120 spaces (incl. disabled) available at the ground.

Admission: (Standing only)
Matchdays: Non members £8, Senior Citizens £6. Membership & season tickets: various categories, such as £110 for adult member including season ticket.

Club Shop:
Open matchdays 1-6pm & Sundays 10-Noon.
Contact Fred Harrison, General Manager, 01253 734733.

Clubhouse:
Open Matchdays: 11.30-midnight; Sundays: 11.30-16.30; Mon-Thurs 18.30-23.00; Friday 15.30-23.00. 4 bars; 3 course lunches in Woodlands Suite; Snacks and bar meals in Bill Beaumont Bar. Functions: Approx 500. Contact Sue Wild on 01253 734733.

NATIONAL 2 NORTH

REVIEW OF THE SEASON 2008-09

Fylde RFC finished 4th in National Three (North) after a roller coaster 2008/9 season. There was a palpable feeling of disappointment around the Woodlands that, with a strong and well assembled squad, they ultimately fell short of their promotion chasing ambitions. But there were a number of positive factors too – the winning of the Lancashire Senior Cup over old rivals Preston Grasshoppers at Lightfoot Lane, the 1st team's only silverware for a long time, being the outstanding moment. This also contributed to the Club being named as Lancashire's Senior Club of 2008/9.

The team thrilled crowds with some exhilarating performances during the eight months campaign and won some tough, hard fought games scoring more tries than any other club in the division. As usual, England Counties wingers Nick Royle & Oliver Brennand led the way with 24 each and Steve Nutt was top scorer with 216 points. But Director of Rugby Mark Nelson is brutally honest in his assessment: "It's the nature of ambition that if you aim high the fall you take if you fail is harder. The vast majority of clubs in our league would have been pleased with a top four finish and a cup win. But my aim was to win the league and I have come up short."

"Perhaps the most important long term reassurance I can offer to the Club and its many followers is that the promotion of young talent, from the immediate local area and the wider Lancashire community, is extremely healthy. We've been able to introduce a number of teenagers to the hard national league rugby environment and some have made the transition as if they were born to it." The re-branding of its academy to the externally funded Centre of Rugby Excellence (CORE) is already paying off with a cohort of excellent young players making their mark at county and national levels. The U'16s team are Lancashire champions and a major breakthrough is the establishment of the Fylde Vixens Women's team.

There were many other off the pitch highlights of the season - the completion of the superb 3G all-weather pitch, the installation of floodlights on three pitches & the new gym. The Club has a healthy financial position and remains as the best supported team in its division.

LAST TEN SEASONS

	Division	P	W	D	L	F	A	P.D.	Pts	Pos	Most Points	Most Tries
99-00	JN1	26	10	1	15	387	485	-98	21	9	194 Nick Booth	6 Richard Kenyon, Greg Anderton
00-01	N2	26	11	1	14	377	594	-217	21$^{(-2)}$	10	84 Ben Godfrey	7 Greg Anderton
01-02	N2	26	14	0	12	462	549	-87	28	5	112 Ben Godfrey	8 Brent Wilson
02-03	N2	26	3	0	23	457	774	-317	6	14r	173 Morne Loxton	7 Dylan O'Grady
03-04	N3 N	26	14	0	12	529	531	-2	28	6	289 Mike Scott	10 Mark Evans
04-05	N3 N	26	13	2	11	599	506	93	65	4	136 Paul Green	14 Quentin King
05-06	N3 N	26	13	2	11	569	539	30	64	7	264 Mike Scott	16 Nicholas Royle
06-07	N3 N	26	16	1	9	659	390	269	79	5	247 John Armstrong	31 Nicholas Royle
07-08	N3 N	26	15	2	9	579	485	94	76	3	141 John Armstrong	22 Ollie Brennand
08-09	N3 N	26	15	2	9	762	541	221	81	4	216 Stephen Nutt	24 Nick Royle, Ollie Brennand

HARROGATE RUFC

KEY PERSONNEL

President: Allen Tattersfield

Chairman: Paul Barnard Contact via Harrogate RUFC email: chairman@harrogaterugby.co.uk

Treasurer: David Wheat. Contact via Harrogate RUFC email: accounts@harrogaterugby.co.uk

Club Secretary: Bill Barrack
15 Eastgate Close, Bramhope, Leeds LS16 9AR
0113 284 2540 (T)   01423 509073 (Fax)

Fixtures Secretary: Bill Barrack
15 Eastgate Close, Bramhope, Leeds LS16 9AR
0113 284 2540 (T)   01423 509073 (Fax)

Chairman of Rugby: Graham Siswick
22A Hillway, Tranmere Park, Guiseley, Leeds LS20 8HB
01943 875620 (T & Fax) 07957 297684 (M) email: sizzythekid@yahoo.co.uk

Commercial Secretary: David Belward Contact via Harrogate RUFC

Membership Secretary: Stuart Young
email: membership@harrogaterugby.co.uk

Founded: 1871

Nickname: Gate

Colours:
Red, amber & black hoops

Change colours:
tba

Training Nights:
Tuesday & Thursday

Web site:
www.harrogaterufc.co.uk

GROUND DETAILS

Address:
The County Ground, Claro Road, Harrogate. HG1 4AG
Tel : 01423 566966
Fax: 01423 509073
email: info@harrogaterufc.co.uk

Capacity: 1500
Seated: 450   **Covered:** 450

Directions:
Claro Road is on the north side of the A59 (York- Skipton road), just off the Stray (open grassed area) adjacent to the town centre).

Nearest BR Station: Harrogate. Exit to East Parade turn left, right onto Parkview continues into Kingsway & Walkers passage, cross Stray to Claro Rd (10mins).

Car Parking: 120 at the ground, unlimited nearby

Admission: Matchday: £8   Season: NA

Club Shop:
Open 12-4pm Sat. & Sun. Contact Kevin Ellis 01423 566566
email kellis@ellisadvertising.co.uk

Clubhouse:
Mon - Fri 7-11pm, Sat Matchdays 12-11.
Food available.
Functions: Contact Colette Dunn 01423 566966

PROGRAMME

Size: A5
Pages: Variable
Price: £1
Editor: TBA
Advertising:
Contact Ian Dunn 07968 480920

REVIEW OF THE SEASON 2008-09

The measure of Harrogate 's progression over the last 2 seasons can be assessed by the disappointment that we could only manage to finish the league programme in 5th place.

A promising start with a hattrick of wins then led to a downturn with 4 successive losses and so the rollercoaster went on.Whilst a plethora of postponements and an abandonment disrupted the middle section of the league programme another good run gave hopes of a 2nd place finish but three losses in the final four games resulted in 5th place at the end.

On many occassions Harrogate played some exhilarating rugby and often edged some tight and exciting encounters making some thrilling afternoons for the faithful following.

In a club total of 632 points scored Mike Aspinall contributed the highest number with 116 and Sam Bottomley led the try scorers with 13. Ed Smithies the captain broke the all time league appearances for the club overtaking Peter Taylor's 222 to finish with 236 games in which he has scored 98 league tries.47 players were used in total.

LAST TEN SEASONS

	Division	P	W	D	L	F	A	P.D.	Pts	Pos		Most Points		Most Tries
99-00	JN1	26	14	1	11	508	449	59	29	6	190	Matt Duncombe	11	Ed Smithies
00-01	N1	26	14	2	10	617	422	195	30	5	161	Lee Cholewa	17	Ed Smithies
01-02	N2	26	16	1	9	744	556	188	33	4	284	Lee Cholewa	16	John Dudley
02-03	N2	26	16	0	10	606	493	113	32	4	187	Lee Cholewa	11	Ed Smithies, James Tapster
03-04	N2	26	11	2	13	668	578	90	24	8	222	Lee Cholewa	16	Jamie Barker
04-05	N2	26	10	1	15	607	764	-157	54	10	196	Lee Cholewa	13	James Tapster
05-06	N2	26	5	1	20	476	682	-206	39	13	90	Mike Aspinall	15	Stephen Parsons
06-07	N2	26	1	0	25	261	1196	-935	6	14r	99	Nick Wainwright	5	Ed Smithies
07-08	N 3 N	26	13	0	13	464	428	36	66	6	144	Nick Wainwright	10	Ryan Peacey
08-09	N3 N	26	16	0	10	632	606	26	79	5	111	Mike Aspinall	13	Sam Bottomley

HUDDERSFIELD RFC

KEY PERSONNEL

President: Mark Birch

Chairman: Mike Brown

Treasurer: Dereck Tasker

Club/Match Secretary: Ian Cleave
2 Clough Way, Fenay Bridge, Huddersfield HD8 0JL
Tel: 01484 306 045
email: ian.cleave@ntlworld.com

Fixtures Secretary: James Nixon
9 Meadow View, Skelmanthorpe, Huddersfield HD8 9ET
Tel: 07713 607906 Fax: 01484 469880
email: james@theosmosisagency.com

Director of Rugby: Mark Sowerby

Commercial Secretary: Mrs Jenny Shaw

Formed: 1870, reformed 1909

Training Nights: Tuesday & Thursday 7pm

Colours: White, claret & gold

Change colours: Black and claret

Website: www.huddersfieldrugby.com

PROGRAMME
Size: A5   **Pages:** 40
Price: With admission
Advertising: On request via the club.

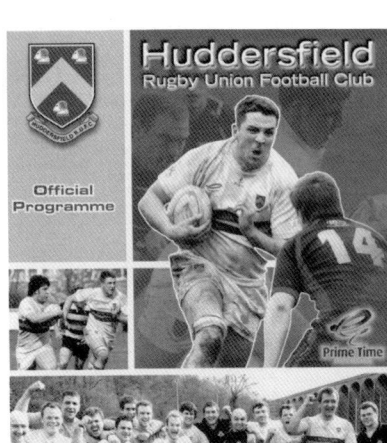

GROUND DETAILS

Ground Address:
Lockwood Park, Brewery Drive, Huddersfield HD4 6EN
Tel: 01484 469 801   Fax: 01484 469 880
email: info@huddersfieldrugby.com

Directions: From M62 take J23 (eastbound) or J24 (westbound) following the Huddersfield signs to the ring road and then take the A616 marked Holmfirth/Sheffield. At the third set of traffic lights at Lockwood Bar with the Red Lion pub on the right go straight ahead through the traffic lights for half a mile and you will see our main entrance on the left just before a huge viaduct.

Capacity: 1500   **Seating:** 499

Car Parking: 300 at ground

Nearest BR Station: Huddersfield

Admission: Matchday £6   Season: contact the club

Clubhouse: Open every evening and all day Sat & Sun. Full catering available.
Functions: Up to 120, 4 conference rooms.
Contact Lisa Hendry   email lisa@huddersfieldrugby.com

Club Shop: Contact main club

REVIEW OF THE SEASON 2008-09

Huddersfield in their first ever season of National League Rugby finished a creditable 10th level on points with Hull Ionians who they headed on the more wins rule and four points behind Preston Grasshoppers.

They only managed two try bonus points all season which was the joint lowest in the division along with bottom of the table Halifax, and they were picked up late in the season in successive home wins over Fylde and Harrogate in April.

Winger Alex Shaw was the leading try scorer along with back row man Nick Sharpe with seven each. Shaw was the only player to start all 26 matches and play in every minute of every match, just behind him with 25 starts were prop Anthony Stringwell and back row forward Mike Whitehead.

They adapted to National League Rugby quickly and started the season well with six wins and a draw in their opening 10 matches including away wins at Loughborough and Darlington Mowden Park by the end of November.

After that they suffered a bad patch with just one win in 12 matches and that was against bottom of the table Halifax. They did though finish the season with a flourish picking up three successive wins before losing away at Kendal in their final match of the season in the middle of May.

Fly half Chris Johnson was the leading points scorer with 248 and continued to be a huge influence on the club and its results just as he was the season before as Huddersfield won promotion to the National Leagues.

LAST TEN SEASONS

	Division	P	W	D	L	F	A	P.D.	Pts	Pos		
99-00	North 2	22	16	1	5	675	282	393	33	3		
00-01	North 2E	20	12	1	7	470	270	200	25	4		
01-02	North 2E	22	18	2	2	565	301	264	38	2p		
02-03	North 1	22	6	0	16	329	482	-153	12	10		
03-04	North 1	22	2	0	20	290	744	-454	4	12r		
04-05	N2E	22	18	1	3	576	203	373	37	2p		
05-06	North 1	22	13	0	9	420	330	90	26	4		
06-07	North 1	22	14	0	8	437	334	103	28	4		
07-08	North 1	22	19	0	3	506	255	251	38	2p/po	Most Points	Most Tries
08-09	N3 N	26	10	2	14	549	618	-69	51	10	248 Chris Jonson	7 Nick Sharpe, Alex Shaw

HULL RUFC

KEY PERSONNEL

President:	Ron Gibbin.
Chairman:	Leroy McKenzie
Fixture Secretary:	Dominic Ward
	78 St. Margarets Ave., Cottingham HU16 5NB
	Tel: 01482 325242
Team Secretary:	Ron Gibbin
	307 Chanterlands Avenue, Hull HU4 4DY
	Tel: 01482 342589
Director of Rugby:	Tevita Vaikona
Head Coach:	Lee Radford
Commercial Chairman:	John Beal.
Rugby Chairman:	Richard Beal.
Press Officer:	Alistair Horsley
	email: alistairhorsley@gmail.com

Founded: 1992

Colours: Black & gold and red

Change colours: Gold, black & red.

Training Nights: Tuesday & Thursday 6.30pm

Website: www.hullrugbyunion.co.uk

PROGRAMME
Size: A5 Pages: 10
Price: with admission
Editor: Richard Beal

GROUND DETAILS

Address: Hull Sports Centre, Ferens Ground, Chanterlands Ave., Hull HU5 4EF
Tel: 01482 448907

Brief Directions: see website for interactive map.

Capacity: Unlimited uncovered standing.

Car Parking: Available on site

Nearest BR Station: Hull

Admission:
Matchday £5 incl programme.
No season tickets available.

Clubhouse:
Open weekday evenings, Sat & Sun afternoon and evenings.
Bar food is available.
Functions: Contact Kris Renwick

Club Shop: Open Training nights and home matchdays

REVIEW OF THE SEASON 2008-09

The move from Haworth Park to the new Ferens Ground on Chanterlands Avenue was completed during the summer months and Hull began their fifth season in North One in the hope that promotion to the National Leagues would be the icing on the cake.

A very good season saw Hull head the table from day one up to December 20th and from then on they occupied second spot before winning the play-off game against Chester to gain the promotion they desired.

The move has resulted in attendances almost doubling with crowds of 250 about standard - the opening game attracted 350 spectators and the local derby against Beverley brought 300, while we had about 450 for the play-off game.

The season began with a 64-7 victory at West Park St. Helens to be followed by the first game at the new ground which saw Hull defeat eventual champions Westoe by 63-8, giving probably the finest display of rugby ever given by a Hull side. Hull lost just one game in the run-up to Christmas and after losing the return game at Westoe continued their good form with just two defeats in the second half of the season.

The side made progress in the EDF Energy Cup with a first round win at New Brighton followed by a stunning 22-16 win at National Three North leaders Nuneaton in the second round. They could not maintain that form on a rain-soaked pitch at Preston Grasshoppers, going down 27-10 in the third round.

Unlike the previous season Hull suffered very few injury problems and among the forwards especially the appearance figures were very high. The signings of county players Scott Plevey and Rob Devonshire along with Tongan forwards Latu Makaafi, Sione Onesi and later on Makoni Finau added strength to a pack which already included the outstanding second-row pairing of Chris Murphy and Dan Cook along with the versatile Kiwi Darren Wigg.

The appointment of former Rugby League and Rugby Union legend Tevita Vaikona as Director of Rugby at the end of the previous season carriedf on the good groundwork started by the previous incumbent Geoff Wappett and the efforts of the club's three development officers Dan Cook, Maea David and Alex Piercy have seen the mini and junior sections blossom to about 200 members as these three have taken the rugby union word into the local schools in what is a rugby league heartland. This work was acknowledged with Hull RUFC being awarded the RFU President's XV Recognition Award for the best club-to-school link in England.

The undoubted find of the season was young fly-half James Cameron who scored a record breaking 24 points on his debut against West Park SH while also setting up new club records for both goal-kicking and points scoring. Tongan winger Mateo Malupo scored 16 tries in ten games before returning home in December.

Tevita Vaikona had the final say after the play-off victory when he said, "It is what we aspired to be and now the hard work really begins".

Hull RUFC are ready for National League rugby.

LAST TEN SEASONS

	Division	P	W	D	L	F	A	P.D.	Pts	Pos
99-00	NE2	18	8	0	10	327	372	-45	16	7
00-01	York1	22	6	2	14	315	531	-216	14	9
01-02	York1	22	19	1	2	526	237	289	31	1p
02-03	N2E	22	15	0	7	525	336	189	30	3
03-04	N2E	22	21	0	1	773	245	528	42	1p
04-05	North 1	22	16	0	6	625	334	291	32	3
05-06	North 1	22	11	0	11	485	430	55	22	6
06-07	North 1	22	10	0	12	459	419	40	20	7
07-08	North 1	22	10	1	11	522	457	65	21	5
08-09	North 1	22	18	0	4	702	241	461	36	2

HULL IONIANS RUFC

Founded: 1989
Nickname: 'I's'
Colours: White, with red, blue and green trim
Change colours: Red, with white, blue and green trim
Training Nights: Tuesday & Thursday
Website: www.hull-ionians.com

KEY PERSONNEL

President	Roger Gosling
Chairman	Trevor Stephenson
Treasurer	Matthew Moore
Club Secretary	Andy Jenkinson Tel: 01482669749 (H) 07966 595288 (M) email: andyjenkinson@yahoo.co.uk
Fixture Secretary	John Clayton 45 Chestnut Ave., Willerby HU10 6PD Tel: 01482 651667 (H) 07775 755758 (M) email: jclayton@lewisgroup.co.uk
1st XV Secretary & Press Sec.	Brian Norman c/o the club Tel 01482 666014 (H); 07770 377368 email brian@bcnorman.karoo.co.uk
Director of Rugby	Stephen Townend
Rugby Manager	Graeme Simm Tel: 07702 307201 (M)
Mini-Junior Chairman	John Doris c/o the club

NATIONAL 2 NORTH

GROUND DETAILS

Address:
Brantingham Park, Brantingham, E. Yorks. HU15 1HX
Tel: 01482 667342   Fax: 01482 666695
email: office@hullionians.karoo.co.uk

Capacity: 2,500   Covered Seating: 225

Directions:
Take M62 East. Becomes A63. Take first exit and follow signs to Brough. After 1 mile take left turn to Brantingham (2nd of two left turns). At T junction turn right. Club 1/2 mile on RHS.

Nearest BR Station: Brough

Car Parking:
Spaces for 120 cars plus large overspill area.

Admission:
Matchday £6 incl programme, season tickets unavailable.

Clubhouse:
Open 9-5 plus 9-Late on matchdays & training nights.
Food available on matchdays & Sunday.

Club Shop:
Open as clubhouse, contact Peter Sharp 07887 842252.

PROGRAMME

Size: A5   Pages: 30
Price: with admission
Editorial & Advertising: Brian Norman
email: brian@bcnorman.karoo.co.uk

REVIEW OF THE SEASON 2008-09

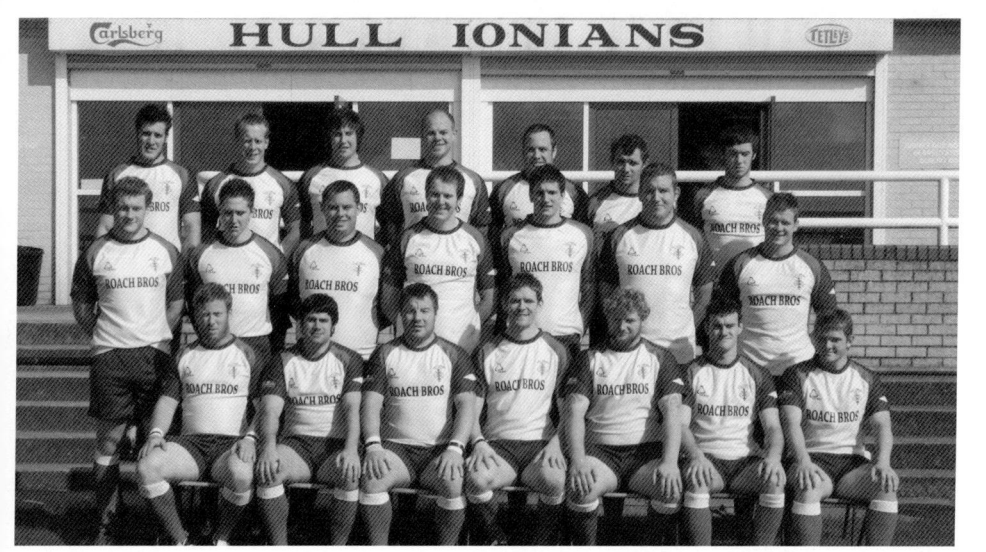

Hull Ionians approached the start of the season with confidence having gathered, what appeared on paper, probably the best squad the club has had for a long time. The first matches saw 4 good home wins and an away draw but the season was already showing signs of the Curates Egg, as we struggled to play well and win away from Brantingham Park.

Hull Ionians had one of their best cup runs but were hoping for a more local draw than Cinderford away. After a long break due to the bad weather conditions the first game of 2009 was the long trip to Cinderford, when after a Stirling performance the lads went down 10-3 and did great credit to National 3 rugby and the club. The team then won the next three games and started to play rugby that they had been striving for from the start of the season. There followed a roller coaster of win one, lose one that never really allowed the team to play consistent winning rugby.

Further success included Captain Jimmy Rule included in the England Counties Squad with the future looking bright with many more young players coming through the Junior and Academy system to progress into the young team. Two players were in the Scotland U18 squad and one Player was in the England U16 squad. In addition the club teams were Yorkshire Cup winners at Under 19, Under 16 and Under 15 level.

Hull Ionians are proud to be a young Yorkshire based team and aim to keep the squad together and continue to blend youth and experience to build for the future, the aim is to climb higher up the leagues. Plans are starting to fall into place for next season and hopefully we can achieve our potential.

LAST TEN SEASONS

	Division	P	W	D	L	F	A	P.D.	Pts	Pos		Most Points		Most Tries
99-00	North 1	22	17	0	5	663	327	336	34	2				
00-01	North 1	22	8	0	14	399	516	-117	16	8				
01-02	North 1	22	16	1	5	599	411	188	33	2p		Most Points		Most Tries
02-03	N3 N	26	6	1	19	515	747	-232	13	13r	195	Nick Cooper	11	Nick Cooper
03-04	North 1	22	8	1	13	524	624	-100	17	9				
04-05	North 1	22	17	0	5	616	265	351	34	2				
05-06	N3 N	26	12	1	13	565	581	-16	62	8	140	Glenn Boyd	14	Derek Eves
06-07	N3 N	26	11	0	15	474	588	-114	56	10	141	Karl Birch	8	Garry Stephenson
07-08	N3 N	26	13	0	13	441	540	-99	62	8	172	James Ferguson	6	Robert Kench
08-09	N3 N	26	9	2	15	519	555	-36	51	11	100	James Ferguson	9	James Greene

KENDAL RUFC

KEY PERSONNEL

President of Club: Ian Hutton

Board Members of Club:
Chairman: Dr Stephen Green
Burt Boardley, Chris Hayton,
Craig Hine, Mike Miller,
Andrew Peill, Roger Wilson

Company Secretary: Fraser Rae

All Board correspondence: c/o Kendal RUFC Tel: 01539 734039

Founded: 1905

Nickname: The Black & Ambers

Colours: Black and amber

Change colours: Amber jerseys with black trim

Training Nights: Tuesday & Thursday

Website: www.kendal-rugby.com

Fixture Secretary: Craig Hine
Tel: 07815 745075 (M) email: hiney3@btopenworld.com

Rugby Secretary & RFU Contact:
Roger Wilson, 31 Hillswood Drive, Kendal, Cumbria LA9 5BT
Tel: 01539 740449 (H) email: rog.w@dsl.pipex.com

Cumbria RFU & NCA Rep.: John Hutton
Tel: 01539 733152(H) email: scoophutton@aol.com

PROGRAMME

Size: A5   Pages: 32
Editor: tbc
Advertising : Richard Berrie Tel:01539 734039
email: rdbkendal@hotmail.com

GROUND DETAILS

Address: Kendal RUFC, Mint Bridge, Shap Road, Kendal, Cumbria LA9 6DL.
Tel: 01539 734039

Directions: From the M6 junction 36 take A591. Then A6 (Kendal to Penrith). Keep left at the `Duke of Cumberland' and the ground is 400 metres on the left.

Capacity: 1900   Seated: 400   Covered: 400

Car Parking: Space for 200 cars on ground.

Nearest BR Station: Kendal (via Oxenholme)

Admission: £7 non members, £5 members, £4 concessions (programme included in admission price)

Clubhouse: Open matchdays and training evenings only. Snacks and bar meals are available.
Functions: Capacity up to 200.
Contact Geoff Wilson, c/o the club.

Club Shop: Open matchdays only.
Contact Richard Berrie Tel:01539 734039
email: rdbkendal@hotmail.com

REVIEW OF THE SEASON 2008-09

Kendal's first season back in the National Leagues system got off to a good start with a win in their opening league game at home to Darlington Mowden Park. However a week later Kendal lost away to Hull Ionians. Kendal held on at home against a fierce Bradford & Bingley fight back after building a commanding lead and then produced a flowing performance of running rugby to defeat Leicester Lions on the road after narrowly losing at Lightfoot Lane, as local league rivalries were once again resumed against Preston Grasshoppers.
At the start of November a large crowd witnessed an enthralling game against Fylde at Woodlands which ended in a 28-28 draw.
Kendal's season was badly disrupted by the weather as three games had to be postponed before Christmas and three more early in the New Year which meant Kendal's season ran on until the 16th May 2009.
Kendal's excellent run in the EDF National Trophy came to an end in early January, as National League One side Sedgley Park ensured the difference in League status told, but not before Kendal had recorded a famous victory away at Blackheath just before Christmas, one which has now gone down with legendary status in the annals of 'Black & Amber' history.
The second half of the League season started well for Kendal as they won against Hoppers' at Mint Bridge and the following week overcame Huddersfield in the second half. However indifferent performances, not helped by several injuries, saw Kendal lose 6 out of 7 League games in February and March.
But Kendal showing true character & determination came back strongly recording back to back victories over Caldy and then Nuneaton at Mint Bridge, producing some electrifying rugby in the process, in April.
Kendal's inconsistent season continued with losses away at Darlington Mowden Park and Loughborough Students completing the double over Kendal in the last week of April at Mint Bridge.
Kendal completed the season on a high with victories over Hull Ionians and Bradford & Bingley (where they played some scintillating rugby) before they finished off with a win against Huddersfield at Mint Bridge to maintain their unbeaten record against the Yorkshire side.

LAST TEN SEASONS

	Division	P	W	D	L	F	A	P.D.	Pts	Pos	Most Points	Most Tries
99-00	N2N	26	24	0	2	817	305	512	48	1p	273 Casey Mee	15 Jason Balmer
00-01	N2	26	16	1	9	622	467	155	33	4	235 Mike Scott	7 by Three players
01-02	N2	26	10	0	16	576	607	-31	20	10	271 Mike Scott	10 Jason Balmer & Ian Voortman
02-03	N2	26	6	0	20	446	837	-391	13	13r	201 Mike Scott	10 Jason Balmer
03-04	N3N	26	11	1	14	417	681	-264	23	8	71 Adam Pate	8 Luke Ladell
04-05	N3N	26	10	1	15	506	584	-78	54	9	154 Dan Stephens	19 John Ladell
05-06	N3N	26	1	1	24	297	923	-626	8	14r	67 Chris Park	6 Martin Armstrong & Simon Mulholland
06-07	North 1	22	12	0	10	468	482	-14	24	5	-	-
07-08	North 1	22	22	0	0	584	204	380	44	1p	-	-
08-09	N3 N	26	13	1	12	646	522	124	63	8	140 Lewis Boyd	28 Lewis Boyd

NATIONAL 2 NORTH

LEICESTER LIONS RFC

KEY PERSONNEL

President	Melv Wright
Chairman	Roger Hill
Treasurer	Paul Pugh
Club Secretary	Martin Evans
	21 Long Meadow Wigston Leicester LE18 3TY
	Tel: 0116 2812629
	email: martingmevans@ntlworld.com
	email: secretary@leicesterlionsrfc.com
Fixtures Secretary	Malc Wright
	12 Poplar Avenue Countesthorpe Leicester LE8 5SP
	Tel: 07984 300966
	email: fixtures@leicesterlionsrfc.com
Director of Rugby	Glyn Evans
	email: g.evans@13-amp.co.uk

Founded 1999
Westleigh (Founded 1904)
& Wigston (Founded 1946)
merged 1999

Nickname: Lions

Colours:
Purple, black & white

Change Colours:
Light grey, purple & black

Website:
www.leicesterlionsrfc.com

Training Nights:
Tuesday & Thursday

NATIONAL 2 NORTH

CONTACT DETAILS
Unless shown otherwise - c/o the club

PROGRAMME
Size: A5   Pages: 28
Price: £5 incl. admission
Editorial & Advertising: Glyn Evans Tel: 0797 1796020   email: g.evans@13-amp.co.uk

GROUND DETAILS

Address:
Lutterworth Road, Blaby, Leicester LE8 4DY
Tel: 0116 277 1010   email: rugby@leicesterlionsrfc.com
Contact: Glyn Evans Tel: 0797 1796020
email: g.evans@13-amp.co.uk

Directions: From M1/M69 Depart M69, Leicester on Local road(s) (East) At r'about, take the 3rd exit Exit r'about onto A5460 Continue (East) on Ramp Bear LEFT (South) onto A563 [Lubbesthorpe Way] Bear LEFT (South) onto B4114 [Narborough Road] Continue (South) on B4114 [St Johns] At r'about, take the 1st exit Exit r'about onto B582 [Blaby Road] Continue (East) on B582 [Enderby Road] At r'about, take the 4th exit Exit r'about onto A426 [Blaby By Pass] At r'about, take the 2nd exit Exit r'about onto A426 [Blaby By Pass] At r'about, take the 1st exit Exit r'about onto Lutterworth Road Bear LEFT (North-West) onto Local road(s)

Nearest BR Station: Narborough & Leicester

Car Parking: 150

Capacity: 2,000 all uncovered standing

Admission: £5 incl programme

Clubhouse:
Open Tue, Wed & Thur 7-11pm, Sat 11-11pm, Sun 12-3pm.

Club Shop: Open matchdays & Sunday morning.
For Clubhouse & Club Shop contact Chris Stanley -
Tel: 0116 277 1010 or 07811 276698 (M)

REVIEW OF THE SEASON 2008-09

Leicester Lions made an excellent start to the season with a close away win, 16-19, in the local derby against Nuneaton. Hopes for the season where further raised with home wins against very strong Fylde and Harrogate teams.

October brought a reality check for the squad when they travelled to Macclesfield and were comprehensively beaten by a more hungry and streetwise outfit. A disappointing loss to Kendal at home followed, with Lions unable to deal with Kendal's uncompromising forward play. A further loss to Caldy away left Lions with a mountain to climb if they were to realistically compete for a top end of the table finish. Playing for the full 80 minutes saw well deserved victories against Darlington and Hull but the wheels were to fall off again with a heavy defeat in thick fog at Preston Grasshoppers in November.

The squad's determination to succeed was shown in the New Year fixture at Fylde. A great game, played in atrocious weather conditions saw Fylde lead 8-7 at halftime. Due to the weather Lions were forced to run the ball from their own line in the 2nd half and, with veteran Jody Peacock to the fore, they built numerous long phases of play that put the home side under enormous pressure. Unfortunately Lions had to chase the game and conceded a try in the last minutes to lose the game 7-18, however the style of play and effort of the players was to set the tone for the rest of the season. Some sound displays followed with a particularly pleasing 16-10 home win against a strong Macclesfield side and a narrow loss 7-9 to promotion favourites Caldy. March saw new arrival Gerhard Boshoff control the game at Bradford and Bingley where Gareth Collins bagged a double hatrick of tries resulting in a 64 point haul for the Lions and one of the best team performances of the season. The ever exuberant Collins went on to score another 4 tries in the thrilling 49-33 home victory over Preston, when Lions played much of the game with 14 men, and repeated the double hatrick feat in the 83-3 mauling of relegated Halifax. Lions were still prone to 'a bad day at the office' losing at home to Loughborough with the normally sound defence unable to cope with the students pace and precision.

The last game of the season was the home fixture against local rivals Nuneaton. A glorious start saw Lions race to a 17 point lead but a number Lions mistakes allowed Nuns to muscle their way back and level the scores at halftime. A tense second half ended 20-25 to Nuns and fittingly guaranteed their place as league winners. It was definitely a game that was there for the taking and the Lions need to learn from the experience if they wish to be serious contenders for the league in the coming season.

Player of the season Gareth Collins finished as top try scorer in National 3 North with 29 tries and was deservedly rewarded with selection for the England counties tour to South Korea and Japan.

LAST TEN SEASONS

	Division	P	W	D	L	F	A	P.D.	Pts	Pos
99-00	Mid 1	16	4	1	11	222	470	-248	9	13
00-01	Mid 1	22	19	0	3	574	183	391	38	2
01-02	Mid 1	22	12	0	10	543	347	196	24	5
02-03	Mid 1	22	12	0	10	506	443	63	24	5
03-04	Mid 1	22	11	2	9	479	432	47	24	6
04-05	Mid 1	22	19	1	2	535	250	285	39	1p
05-06	N3 N	26	9	2	15	484	732	-248	52	12
06-07	N3 N	26	13	1	12	520	548	-28	63	7
07-08	N3 N	26	13	3	10	658	466	192	73	4
08-09	N3 N	26	15	0	11	626	495	131	70	7

	Most Points		Most Tries
05-06	174 Dan Yuill	14	Gareth Collins
06-07	92 Jon Boden	12	Feofaaku Lea
07-08	282 Jon Boden	16	Gareth Collins
08-09	229 Jon Boden	29	Gareth Collins

LOUGHBOROUGH STUDENTS RFC

KEY PERSONNEL

Director of Rugby
Alan Buzza
Tel: 01509 226110   email a.j.buzza@lboro.ac.uk

Head Coach / Head of Coach Development [BOOST project]
Dave Morris
Tel: 01509 226129   email: d.f.morris@lboro.ac.uk

Both at:
Sport Development Centre, Loughborough University, Loughborough LE11 3TU

Fixture Secretary
Ken Palfreyman
79 Eastway Road, Wigston, Leciester
Tel: 0116 2881311 (H)   07740 604495 (M)
email: kpalfreyman@btinternet.com

Formed: 1919

Colours:
Maroon and white shirts, black shorts, maroon and white socks

Change colours:
White shirts

Website: www.loughboroughrugby.com

CONTACT

All club correspondence, other than Fixture/Match secretary work, should be addressed to
Rugby Club Coordinator, Sport Development Centre, Loughborough University, Loughborough LE11 3TU
Email: lsrfcadmin@lboro.ac.uk   Tel: 01509 226110

GROUND DETAILS

Ground Location:
LE11 3TT
Office hours: 01509 226116 Other times: Tel: 01509 226110

Directions: Junction 23 of M1. Follow signs to University. Pitch within site of main gates.

Nearest BR Station:
Loughborough Station 2 miles from ground.

Car Parking: Unlimited

Capacity: 3,000 uncovered standing.

Admission: By Programme

Programme: £3

REVIEW OF THE SEASON 2008-09

Off the pitch, the tragic losses of Jeff Trendell, Dan James and Paula Wild meant it was a highly emotional year. Each made a substantial contribution to the club and will be greatly missed.

On the pitch a young Loughborough side got off to a poor start in their first year of National League rugby and at Christmas looked slightly precarious in 10th position without a win away from home.

The New Year saw a very different Loughborough side go from strength to strength and finish 6th in the table. With recruitment looking extremely strong there is a lot of excitement in the club about how we might perform in 2009-10.

Apart from the National League Loughborough had mixed experiences in their two biggest fixtures. We underperformed in the BUCS semi-final losing to a strong Hartpury side, but came good at the end of the year with a stunning 23-20 win over England U20 in their warm up for the U20 World Cup.

LAST TEN SEASONS

	Division	P	W	D	L	F	A	P.D.	Pts	Pos
99-00	EM/L 1	22	20	0	2	860	254	606	40	2
00-01	Mid 4ES	18	11	0	7	422	192	230	22	3
01-02	Mid 4EN	18	16	0	2	651	192	459	32	1p
02-03	Mid 3EN	18	13	1	4	510	231	279	27	2p/po
03-04	Mid 2E	22	10	0	12	583	461	122	20	7
04-05	Mid 2E	22	12	2	8	563	385	178	26	4
05-06	Mid 2E	22	16	0	6	759	294	465	32	4
06-07	Mid 2E	22	19	1	2	802	196	606	39	1p
07-08	Mid 1	22	17	0	5	712	348	364	34	1p
08-09	N3 N	26	15	2	9	605	506	99	75	6

	Most Points	Most Tries
	120 Grant Pointer	12 Phil Burgess

MACCLESFIELD RUFC

KEY PERSONNEL

President	Peter Jones
Chairman	Alan Johnson
Treasurer	Clive Hammond
Hon. Secretary	All enquiries direct to the club office.

Founded: 1877

Nickname: The Blues

Colours: Royal blue and navy blue

Change colours: Red and navy

Training Nights: Tues., Wed. & Thur.

Website: www.macclesfieldrufc.com

Club Secretary (Admin)	Bev Roberts	c/o the club Tel: 01625 827899 Fax: 01625 829056 email: bev@maccrugby.co.uk
1st XV Fixture Secretary:	Brendan Thomas Tel: 07976 719439.	
Rugby Operations Manager	Brendan Thomas	
Gen & Commercial Mgr.	D J Roberts	email: bill@maccrugby.co.uk
Head Coach	Geoff Wappett	
Press Officer	Geoff Allen	Tel: 01625 432345(H) 01244 613499
Referee Liaison Officer	Albert Simpson	Tel: 01625 429100
Youth Welfare Officer	Mark Sharples	

NATIONAL 2 NORTH

GROUND DETAILS

Address
Macclesfield RUFC, Priory Park,
Priory Lane, Prestbury, Macclesfield, Cheshire SK10 4AF
Tel: 01625 827899
Fax: 01625 829056
email: info@maccrugby.co.uk

Capacity: 6,000   **Covered Seating:** 200
Facilities: Match floodlights & Astroturf training pitch.

Directions:
Leave or enter Macclesfield on B5087 Alderley Edge Road. Turn into Priory Lane on the outskirts of town. Club is approx 100 metres on right hand side.

Nearest BR Station: Macclesfield (in town centre)

Car Parking: 400 spaces.

Admission: Matchday - £8 incl. programme & parking; Concessions £6; u16 free. **Season** - £85, Concessions £65

Clubhouse: Daytime - permanently open. Tue/Wed/Thur/Fri evenings from 6.30pm, Sat all day & Sun from 9.30 am.
Food available on matchdays only.
Contact Club Steward

Club Shop: Open Sat matchdays 1-3pm & Sundays 10-1pm

PROGRAMME
Size: A5   Pages: 48
Price: With admission
Editorial: Geoff Allen
Advertising: D J Roberts

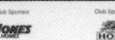

352

REVIEW OF THE SEASON 2008-09

After having had to work very hard over the past few seasons to ensure that Macclesfield retained it's National League status, we started afresh, to immediately achieve quite a few Ws in the early stages to give promise for the rest of the season. And so it continued, under the control of the new Coaching Team of Geoff Wappett and Andy Northey, who brought in their vast past experience to the benefit of a mix of established experienced players plus newcomers attracted to the club.

These early successes continued as the Season progressed, to the delight of Coaches and the club, by a continuation of winning ways throughout the season. In the top 4 of this League throughout, despite one or two close disappointments, the team eventually continued their winning ways to show a record, in finishing third, of having beaten every other team in the league, at least once and included in that, the eventual, champions and promoted club – Nuneaton.

In doing all that, the team were consistently successful in playing a style of attractive rugby throughout, that brought 15 tries for full back Fergus Mulchrone (6th in the League rankings) and especially thankful for the efforts again of captain/No.10, Ross Winney, who, with 241 points, finished at the top of the League rankings as kicker. In the pack Dan Baines, despite a lay off due to injury was always at the forefront of their efforts in every game.

The club, also benefitted from the infusion of some home developed talent such as Sam Moss at hooker and young Pete Hardwick on the wing, plus the returning Jonathon Keep back from Manchester. They, together with newcomers such as Rob McDermott, Martin Kemp and Alan Marsh maintained a consistent quality of play throughout the season, despite suffering considerably, as did most clubs, from injuries throughout the Season. With an extra 4 league matches to be played in the season to come, it will be essential for this club – and all others – to have strong back up squad of players if they are to remain competitive through to the end of the season. In that respect, Macclesfield are lucky to have in a strongly developing Seconds (the Lions) a successful mix of experienced and promising young players.

To crown the season the club again won the Cheshire Cup as well as providing 8 players to the County Championship winning teams at Twickenham, of Cheshire and Lancashire.

LAST TEN SEASONS

	Division	P	W	D	L	F	A	P.D.	Pts	Pos	Most Points		Most Tries	
99-00	North 1	22	11	0	11	301	409	-108	22	5				
00-01	North 1	*21	12	0	9	403	293	110	24	4				
01-02	North 1	*20	11	1	8	400	391	9	23	6				
02-03	North 1	22	17	0	5	645	354	291	34	2p*	326	Gary Bell	10	Jonathon Keep
03-04	N3 N	26	10	2	14	507	642	-135	22	9	229	Gary Bell	9	Stephen Campbell
04-05	N3 N	26	19	1	6	607	402	205	88	2	219	Michael Newell	12	Mark Frost
05-06	N3 N	26	10	2	14	560	520	40	57	9	167	Ross Winney	9	Ben Coulbeck
06-07	N3 N	26	11	0	15	573	541	32	59	9	200	Ross Winney	9	Richard Jones
07-08	N3 N	26	9	2	15	443	488	-45	50	11	215	Ross Winney	5	Chris Jones
08-09	N3 N	26	16	2	8	645	518	127	81	3	277	Ross Winney	15	Fergus Mulchrone

353

PRESTON GRASSHOPPERS RFC

KEY PERSONNEL

President	Peter Ashcroft
Chairman	George Erdozain
Treasurer	Robert Bailey
Club Secretary	Mike Forshaw
	c/o Preston Grasshoppers
	Tel: 01772 863546 Fax: 01772 861605
	email: info@pgrfc.co.uk
	forshaws@ashtonbank.freeserve.co.uk
General Manager	Lisa Knowles
	c/o Preston Grasshoppers
Fixtures Secretary	John Powell
	121 Bare Lane, Morecambe, Lancs. LA4 4RD
	Tel: 01524 424514 Fax: 01254 849586
	email: jm.p@btopenworld.com
Team Secretary	Richard Morton
	c/o Preston Grasshoppers
	Tel: 01772 863546 Fax: 01772 861605
	email: info@pgrfc.co.uk
Chairman of Rugby	Mike Bailey
Head Coach	Alex Keay
Press Officer	Ken Moore

Founded: 1869
Nickname: Hoppers
Colours: White shirts with narrow navy hoops; navy shorts & socks.
Change colours: Emerald green
Training Nights: Tuesday & Thursday
Website: www.pgrfc.co.uk

NATIONAL 2 NORTH

GROUND DETAILS

Address:
Lightfoot Green, Fulwood, Preston, Lancs. PR4 0AP
Tel: 01772 863546
Fax: 01772 861605
email: info@pgrfc.co.uk

Capacity: 3250
Covered Seating: 250

Directions: Leave the M6 at Junct. 32 and take slip road for Garstang / Preston. Turn left at the end of the slip road towards Preston. Take first left and follow signs for Ingol. The ground is 1/2 mile on the right.

Nearest BR Station: Preston (3 miles)

Car Parking: 300 spaces available adjacent to the ground.

Admission: Matchday: Adult Members £5, Others £7, OAPs/Students/Juniors £3 (incl. programme) Under 14s Free

Clubhouse: Open Mon-Thurs 4-11pm, Fri 12-12, Sat 12-11, Sun 12-10.30. Food available at weekends. Full conference & banqueting facilities. Contact Club Office on 01772 863546

Functions: Full catering service to 300.
Contact Gill Parkinson, Lisa Knowles or Head Chef, Allan Nutter.

Club Shop: Open Sat. 11.30 am–3.00 pm Sun. 9.30 am – 1.30 pm
Contact Gill Parkinson on 01772 863546

PROGRAMME

Size: A5   Pages: 40
Price: £2 (incl. with admission)
Editor: Ken Moore
Advertising: Contact Ken Moore

354

Preston Grasshoppers First XV Squad, Coaches and Support Staff 2008/09

REVIEW OF THE SEASON 2008-09

Captain, full back and leading try-scorer for the last 3 seasons, Olly Viney, went 'rugby walkabout' down under but hopes to be back this season and, when successor Glyn Dewhurst became unavailable due to work commitments, Darren Wilson stepped in and was a (figurative) tower of strength with 11 league tries, culminating in his selection for the Barbarians in the Annual Mobbs Memorial match at Bedford in April.

A promising start saw Hoppers win comfortably at Halifax but it proved a bit of a false dawn, since the Yorkshire club struggled throughout the season and the next 7 away league games all ended in defeat until Bradford & Bingley were put to the sword in February. Fortunately, home form was better, producing 7 victories in a row which maintained a mid-table spot, although a late spell of injuries had its effect. Hoppers finished the season in 9th spot, again turning to youth with another influx of young players coming through and, during the campaign, turned out arguably their youngest side for some seasons if not ever.

A welcome run in the EDF National Trophy ended in Round 4 at the hands of Premiership pretenders, Exeter Chiefs and the season finished with a Lancashire Cup Final appearance after impressive victories against Sedgley Park and Waterloo but Fylde had the edge on the day to take the trophy. Meanwhile, strength in depth was demonstrated by the 2nd XV finishing 3rd in the Bateman Premier and being runners-up in the Halbro Cup.

Darren Wilson was Player of the Season, Mark Rigbye Players' Player and Dan Waller Best Newcomer. Most of last year's squad are retained with the principle losses being prop Richard Carleton, who has returned to his native Ireland, while a new job takes back row Andrew Dockray to the Midlands.

LAST TEN SEASONS

	Division	P	W	D	L	F	A	P.D.	Pts	Pos	Most Points	Most Tries
99-00	JN1	26	12	0	14	608	580	28	24	8	110 Chris Glynn	15 Iain Bruce
00-01	N2	26	12	2	12	569	517	52	26	7	219 Chris Glynn	10 Josh Williams
01-02	N2	26	4	0	22	401	959	-558	8	14r	210 Chris Glynn	6 Chris Glynn
02-03	N3 N	26	11	1	14	617	625	-8	23	9	135 S Tuihalamaka	19 Oliver Viney
03-04	N3 N	26	7	0	19	443	754	-311	14	12r	100 Paul Bailey	18 Oliver Viney
04-05	North 1	22	19	0	3	700	326	374	38	1p	*231 Paul Bailey*	*12 Richard Morton*
05-06	N3 N	26	13	3	10	763	605	158	74	6	269 Paul Bailey	20 Oliver Viney
06-07	N3 N	26	17	1	8	706	482	224	85	3	202 Paul Bailey	16 Oliver Viney
07-08	N3 N	26	14	0	12	463	586	-123	63	7	137 Gerhard Boshoff	7 Oliver Viney
08-09	N3 N	26	11	0	15	610	639	-29	55	9	186 Marcus Jackson	11 Russell Flynn, Darren Wilson

NATIONAL 2 NORTH

355

RUGBY LIONS

RUGBY LIONS

Founded: 1873

Nickname: The Lions

Club Colours: White with red lion

Change colours: Black with red lion

Training Nights:
Mon., Tues. & Thur. evenings 6pm

Website:
www.therugbylions.com

KEY PERSONNEL

Chairman:	David Owen
Directors:	Mal Malik, Eddie Saunders
Hon. Secretary:	Mal Malik
	e-mail: mal@therugbylions.com
Mini & Junior Chairman:	Andy Machon Tel: 07976 181939
Fixtures Secretary:	Fred Empy Tel: 07850 491845
Director of Rugby:	Mal Malik
1st Team Coaches:	Peter Glackin & Steve Halsey
1st Team Captain:	Alex Nash
Vice Captain:	Matt Goode
Managers:	Steve King & Ron Everton
Player Development Director:	Tony Smith

CONTACT DETAILS

Rugby FC, Webb Ellis Road, Rugby, Warwickshire CV22 7AU
Tel: 01788 334466   Fax: 01788 334888
e-mail: mal@therugbyfootballclub.com

PROGRAMME

Size: B4   Pages: 30
Price: £1.50
Editor: Dennis Keen
Advertising:
Contact Linda Dainty 01788 34882

GROUND DETAILS

Address:
Webb Ellis Road, Rugby. CV22 7AU
Tel: 01788 334466
Fax: 01788 334888
email: mal@therugbylions.com

Capacity: 3,396   Seated: 240   Standing: Covered 600

Directions:
2nd turn right, half mile south west of town centre on A4071, Bilton Rd.
From NW: M6 Jnc 1 A426 Rugby A4071
From NE: M1 Jnc 20 A426 Rugby A4071
From SE: M1 Jnc 17/M45/A4071 towards Rugby.

Nearest BR Station: Rugby - recommend taxi 2 miles to ground

Car Parking: Available at ground

Admission:
Season: V.P. membership: £60, OAP/Student: £35;
Matchday (incl programme): Adults £8, OAPs £5

Club Shop
Matchday 1-5pm, Mon-Fri 9-5 by appointment.

Clubhouse
Matchdays 12-late & training nights
Functions: Capacity 120-200. Manager: Tracy Garrett

NATIONAL 2 NORTH

REVIEW OF THE SEASON 2008-09

Rugby Lions set out on their first season in National League 3 South after level transfer from 3 North looking forward to meeting friends old and new.

Lions were expecting to face a more open style of rugby but didn't realise they would be coming up against such big packs in virtually every game.

A mainly stable squad was boosted by the arrival of former Scotland international Craig Moir, who unfortunately suffered a bad injury early on and then moved to Wales with his job.

Lions began with 2 wins out of 3 but a big defeat at Rosslyn Park started a slide only ended by a National Trophy win against Leicester Lions, the first of a superb run of nine games unbeaten which included draws against top sides Ealing, Henley and, best of all, London Scottish to become the only side to hold the runaway champions in a brilliant all-round display.

Come the New Year, Rugby suffered the same slump as in the previous season, this time not helped by six away games in the last eight fixtures.

The young Lions squad, led by inspirational back row Alex Nash, showed they could give anyone a game on their day but they lacked the essential consistency and some performances were more than disappointing.

Rugby will be looking to develop the talents of rising stars such as Tom Harris, Justin Parker, Alex Waller, Brett Ford and Lloyd Saunders while a good group of experienced players will continue to form the backbone of the League side.

Guiding the Lions will be Peter Glackin and Steve Halsey, previously backs and forwards coaches under Mark Ellis, when they meet five new League opponents with the meetings with near-neighbours Broadstreet the obvious highlight.

LAST TEN SEASONS

	Division	P	W	D	L	F	A	P.D.	Pts	Pos	Most Points		Most Tries	
99-00	P2	26	6	1	19	408	905	-497	13	13r	179	Martyn Davies	6	Oscar Wingham
00-01	N2	*25	19	2	4	888	320	568	40	2p	120	Jaques Steyn	16	Eddie Saunders
01-02	N1	26	9	1	16	518	668	-150	47	10	127	Richard Davies	12	Phil Read
02-03	N1	26	0	0	26	422	1067	-745	7	14r	137	Jon Boden	9	James Baker
03-04	N2	26	9	0	17	511	697	-186	18	13r	137	Jon Boden	9	Lloyd Warner
04-05	N3 N	26	9	2	15	532	523	9	49*	12r	142	Alan Mitchell	8	Gareth Collins
05-06	Mid1	22	20	0	2	738	320	418	40	1p	177	*Glenn Bond*	12	*James Hawken*
06-07	N3 N	26	17	1	8	652	476	176	81	4	266	James Hawken	18	Ade Hales
07-08	N3 N	26	13	0	13	533	600	-67	61	9	189	James Hawken	15	Ade Hales
08-09	N3 S	26	10	4	12	573	653	-80	58	8	169	James Hawken	10	Ade Hales

WATERLOO RFC

Founded: 1882

Colours:
Solid green, red shoulders, white chest band

Change colours:
Green, red & white hoops

Training Nights:
Monday and Thursday

Website:
www.waterloorugby.com

GROUND DETAILS

Address:
The Pavillion, St Anthony's Rd.,
Blundellsands, Liverpool. L23 8TW
Tel: 0151 924 4552
Fax: 0151 924 0900
email: admin@waterloorugby.com

Capacity: 3,000
Covered Seating: 486

Directions:
From the end of the M57/58 follow signs for Crosby. Waterloo FC is then sign-posted to the ground.

Nearest BR Station:
Blundellsands & Crosby/Hall Road.

Car Parking: On street parking around the ground.

Admission: Matchday (incl programme):
Adults £10.00, Concessions (Students, OAP's) £5.00.
Stand Transfer £2.00
Season: Full single membership £125;
Full joint membership £150

Club Shop:
Open on matchdays and Sunday 12-1pm.
Contact Andrea Davidson

Clubhouse: Open from 12 noon.
Three bars, with snacks and meals available.
Functions: Capacity 150, contact the club.

KEY PERSONNEL

President: Phil Mahon

Chairman: Simon Robb

Club Secretary: Andrea Davidson
c/o Waterloo Rugby Club
Tel: 0151 924 4552
email: admin@waterloorugby.com

Fixtures Secretary: John Rimmer
2 Chapel Meadow, Longton, Preston PR4 5NR
Tel: 01772 614277 (H) 01772 885000 (B)
email: jandjrimmer@compurserve.com

Club Captain: Martin O'Keefe

Director of Rugby: Colin D Fisher

Company Director of Finance: Ian Robins

Chairman of Mini & Junior Rugby: John Wainwright
Tel: 0151 924 4552

Head Coach: Chris O'Callaghan

Performance Consultant: Joe Lydon

CONTACT DETAILS

Unless shown otherwise, all correspondence to:
c/o Waterloo Rugby Club,
The Pavillion, St Anthony's Rd.,
Blundellsands, Liverpool. L23 8TW
Tel: 0151 924 4552
Fax: 0151 924 0900
email: admin@waterloorugby.com

PROGRAMME

Size: A5
Pages: 48 (Full colour)
Price: £2
Editor: Geoff Lightfoot
Advertising Rates: Contact Eddie Bentley
Colour: Page £400, Half £225, 1/4 £120

WATERLOO STATISTICS

LEAGUE

TEAM RECORDS

MOST POINTS
Scored at Home: 91 v Preston G. 28.2.04
Scored Away: 57 v Scunthorpe 15.2.03
Conceded at Home: 85 v Blackheath 28.2.09
Conceded Away: 115 v Birmingham Sol 4.4.09

MOST TRIES
Scored in a match: 14 v Preston G. 28.2.04
Conceded in a match: 17 v Birmingham Sol 4.4.09

BIGGEST MARGINS
Home Win: 86pts - 91-5 v Preston G. 28.2.04
Away Win: 57pts - 57-0 v Scunthorpe 15.2.03
Home Defeat: 66pts - 3-69 v Northampton 28.10.96
Away Defeat: 115pts (0-115) v Birmingham Sol 4.4.09

MOST CONSECUTIVE
Victories: 22 (03-04)
Defeats: 11 on two occasions

INDIVIDUAL RECORDS

MOST APPEARANCES
by a forward: 232 (12) David Blyth
by a back: 239 (8) Tony Handley

MOST CONSECUTIVE
Appearances: 133 Freeman Payne 01-02 to 17.9.06
Matches scoring Tries: 4 Steve Bracegirdle
Neil Kerfoot 14.2.04-6.3.04
Matches scoring points: 44 Lyndon Griffiths

MATCH RECORDS

Most Points
26 John Broxson v Preston G. 28.2.04 (H)

Most Tries
4 Fergus Griffies v Broadstreet 8.2.03 (H)
v Scunthorpe 15.2.03 (A)

Most Conversions
9 John Broxson v Preston G. 28.2.04 (H)

Most Penalties
6 Ian Aitchison v Blackheath 25.4.92 (A)
Steve Swindells v Otley 12.3.94 (A)
v Newcastle G. 10.9.94 (H)
v Rugby Lions 25.9.99 (H)

Most Drop Goals
2 on 6 occasions by 4 players

SEASON RECORDS

Most Points	293	Tony Handley	02-03
Most Tries	23	Neil Kerfoot	03-04
Most Conversions	73	Tony Handley	02-03
Most Penalties	66	Lyndon Griffiths	97-98
Most Drop Goals	6	Paul Grayson	92-93

CAREER RECORDS

Most Points	918	Tony Handley	01-07
Most Tries	91	Freeman Payne	00-09
Most Conversions	195	Tony Handley	01-05
Most Penalties	175	Lyndon Griffiths	96-00
Most Drop Goals	11	Tony Handley	01-06

LAST TEN SEASONS

	Division	P	W	D	L	F	A	P.D.	Pts	Pos	Most Points	Most Tries
99-00	P2	26	6	2	18	441	830	-389	14	12	201 Lyndon Griffiths	5 Gareth Davies & Karelle Dixon
00-01	N1	26	6	1	19	450	676	-226	35	14r	190 Phil Belgian	6 Matt Holt
01-02	N2	26	4	2	20	476	792	-316	10	13r	160 Tony Handley	16 Freeman Payne
02-03	N3N	26	21	0	5	888	458	430	42	3	293 Tony Handley	18 Freeman Payne
03-04	N3N	26	25	0	1	979	343	636	50	1p	269 Tony Handley	23 Neil Kerfoot
04-05	N2	26	14	1	11	650	510	140	72	4	138 Stephen Nutt	12 Jay van Deventer
05-06	N2	26	22	2	2	803	370	433	110	2p	208 Neil Hunter	18 Neil Kerfoot
06-07	N1	30	3	0	27	470	1175	-705	18	16r	60 Dan Loader	9 Freeman Payne
07-08	N2	26	11	1	14	488	517	-29	*52	11	154 Alex Davies	7 Nicola Mazzucato
08-09	N2	26	4	0	22	432	1371	-939	23	14r	85 James O'Brian	11 Matt Williams

WESTOE RFC

Founded: 1875

Website:
www.westoerfc.com

Colours: Red,
sky blue and dark blue

Change colours: Red

Training Nights:
Tuesday & Thursday

NATIONAL 2 NORTH

KEY PERSONNEL

Chairman:	Duncan Murray
	3 Ascot Court, E West Boldon, NE36 0DA
	Tel. 0191 536 7838
Treasurer:	J Duncan
	11 Park Road, Jarrow NE32 5JH
Club Secretary:	J. Wells
	240 Mowbray Rd, South Shields, Tyne & Wear NE33 4EA
	Tel. 0191 455 2260
	e-mail: a.wells3@btopenworld.com
Fixture Secretary:	D. McNulty
	8 Westoe Village South Shields
	Tel 0191 456 1192
Director Of Rugby:	A Howells
	c/o Westoe RFC
Match Secretary:	K Bannon
	51 Basil Way, South Shields, NE34 8UA
	Tel: 0191 426 1558 (H) 07887 510753 (M)

GROUND DETAILS

Address: Wood Terrace, Dean Road, South Shields, Tyne & Wear NE33 4EA
Tel: 0191 456 1506

Directions: Map on website under directions

From the North: Travel through the Tyne Tunnel and head South on the A19. After approx 400 yards (nope not metric) take slip road on the left signposted "South Shields". Turn left at roundabout onto the A194. After 100 yards turn right at roundabout for the A1300. See below A1300

From the West: Travel along A69 to junction with A1 West of Newcastle. Follow A1 South past the Metro Centre and Angel of the North. Take slip road to the left marked "Washington". This is just before the motorway starts. Follow road straighton for approx half a mile until a roundabout is reached. Turn left onto the motorway A194(M) and then the A194 following signs for "South Shields". About two miles from end of motorway turn right at roundabout for the A1300. See below A1300

From the South (we recommend the A19 as the better route): A19 travel North past Nissan factory and straight ahead at next roundabout. Take slip road to the left signposted "South Shields".Turn right at roundabout and after 100 yards turn right at roundabout for the A1300. See below A1300

A1 travel North until Washington Services and then take A194(M)and then the A194 following signs for "South Shields". About two miles from end of motorway turn right at roundabout for the A1300. See below A1300

A1300: Follow A1300 for two miles (passing Hospital on the left) until reaching the A1018. Turn left towards town centre and straight ahead for 3/4 of a mile. After passing the "County" pub on your left within 100yds you will reach a roundabout. Turn left and the ground is directly on your left (opposite the Mecca Bingo).

Nearest BR station: Newcastle, then the Metro to Chichester

Capacity: 2,000   Covered 400   **Admission:** £5   **Car Parking:** Ample

Clubhouse: Open Monday to Friday, 7 to 11pm, Saturday 12 to 11pm, Sunday am and 7 to 11pm

Club Shop: Online or contact Susan Tighe email: susan@tighe.uk.com Tel. 07984 723325

Programme: Size: A5   Pages: 24

REVIEW OF THE SEASON 2008-09

For the first time in many years Westoe entered the new season as Durham County Cup holders after a tight and high scoring final against Darlington. In addition they retained the 3rd XV cup and the 4th XV shield, this for the 7th time.

The senior cup success brought automatic entry to the EDF National Trophy, where convincing wins at Bedford and at home against Loughborough Students brought an away game in the 3rd round against Broadstreet and a loss by a single point.

After a third position for a third time in the league Westoe looked to strengthen their coaching team to ensure a presence on match day which had not been the case in the previous season. A steady if somewhat lacklustre victory against Beverley opened the season followed by a devastating loss against Hull marking them out as a team to watch in the promotion stakes.

It says much for Westoe that this defeat was followed by 13 successive league victories including the return match against Hull. By mid-February Westoe led the league by 6 points but 2 away defeats reduced this lead to 2 points with 5 matches to play. This situation remained unchanged to the last match of the season when a blistering first half display at Beverley ensured promotion to the National Leagues at the 4th attempt.

In gaining this success Westoe had played the best rugby seen at Wood Terrace in its long history.

A tribute must be paid to the work of the junior section over many years through its Mini and Junior teams and no praise can be high enough for the army of volunteers who continue to produce such a large number of talented players on which the senior success has been built.

LAST TEN SEASONS

	Division	P	W	D	L	F	A	P.D.	Pts	Pos
99-00	NE3	18	15	0	3	442	192	250	30	1
00-01	D/N 1	22	21	0	1	666	232	434	40*	1p
01-02	N2E	22	12	2	8	452	371	81	26	4
02-03	N2E	22	13	1	8	447	417	30	27	4
03-04	N2E	22	12	0	10	443	403	40	24	4
04-05	N2E	22	19	0	3	821	260	561	38	1p
05-06	North 1	22	14	1	7	553	342	211	29	3
06-07	North 1	22	15	0	7	457	362	95	30	3
07-08	North 1	22	16	1	5	455	286	169	33	3
08-09	North 1	22	19	0	3	737	264	473	38	1p

NATIONAL 2 NORTH

RECORDS SECTION
DIVISION FOUR NORTH
(CURRENTLY NATIONAL LEAGUE TWO NORTH)
Previously also Area League North, Division Five North & National 3 North

ROLL OF HONOUR

	CHAMPIONS	Runners-up	Nos of Clubs/Games		Leading Points Scorer
1987-88	Rugby	Durham	11/10	118	Steve Kerry (Preston)
1988-89	Roundhay	Broghton Park	11/10	94	Jamie Grayshon (Morley)
1989-90	Broughton Park	Morley	11/10	78	Jamie Grayshon (Morley)
1990-91	Otley	Lichfield	13/12	105	Paul Grayson (Preston)
1991-92	Aspatria	Hereford	13/12	127	Paul Grayson (Preston)
1992-93	Harrogate	Rotherham	13/12	131	Ralph Zoing (Harrogate)
1993-94	Rotherham	Preston	13/12	118	Kevin Plant (Rotherham)
1994-95	Walsall	Kendal	13/12	164	Richard Mills (Walsall)
1995-96	Wharfedale	Worcester	13/12	143	Alex Howarth (Wharfedale)
1996-97	Worcester	Birmingham Solihull	14/26	317	Steve Kerry (Preston)
1997-98	Birmingham Solihull	Manchester	14/26	398	Steve Swindells (Manchester)
1998-99	Preston Grasshoppers	Stourbridge	14/26	246	Ian Shuttleworth (Sandal)
99-2000	Kendal	Stourbridge	14/26	302	Paul Brett (New Brighton)
2000-01	Stourbridge	Sedgley Park	14/26	258	Paul Brett (New Brighton)
2001-02	Doncaster	Dudley Kingswinford	14/26	359	John Liley (Doncaster)
2002-03	Nuneaton	New Brighton	14/26	293	Tony Handley (Waterloo)
2003-04	Waterloo	Halifax	14/26	316	Anthony Birley (New Brighton)
2004-05	Halifax	Macclesfield	14/26	275	Tom Rhodes (Bradford & Bingley)
2005-06	Bradford & Bingley	Nuneaton	14/26	270	Tom Rhodes (Bradford & Bingley)
2006-07	Blaydon	Tynedale	14/26	266	James Hawken (Rugby Lions)
2007-08	Tynedale	Darlington M.P.	14/26	282	Jon Boden (Leicester Lions)
2008-09	Nuneaton	Caldy	14/26	290	Gavin Roberts (Caldy)

RELEGATED CLUBS
87-88 - Derby, Solihull, Birkenhead Park
88-89 - Birmingham
89-90 - None
90-91 - Stoke on Trent, Birmingham & Sol
91-92 - Vale of Lune, Northern
92-93 - Towcestrians
93-94 - Bradford & Bingley, Durham City
94-95 - Hereford, Barkers Butts
95-96 - Broughton Park
96-97 - Hereford, Stoke on Trent
97-98 - None

98-99 - Hinckley, Lichfield, Winnington Park
99-00 - Sheffield
00-01 - Walsall, Aspatria
01-02 - Whitchurch, Morley, Sandal, West Hartlepool
02-03 - Bedford Athletic, Broadstreet, Hull Ionians, Scunthorpe
03-04 - Preston Grasshoppers, Liverpool St Helens, Longton
04-05 - Rugby Lions, Dudley Kingswinford, Bedford Athletic
05-06 - New Brighton, Kendal
06-07 - Darlington, Cleckheaton, Orrell
07-08 - Morley, West Park St Helens, Beverley
08-09 - Darlington M.P., Halifax

NUNEATON - NATIONAL LEAGUE THREE NORTH CHAMPIONS 2008-09

		MOST TRIES		MOST PENALTIES		MOST CONVERSIONS
87-88	7	Eddie Saunders (Rugby)	21	Steve Kerry (Preston)	12	Steve Kerry (Preston) & Chris Howard (Rugby)
88-89	10	Jim Mallinder (Roundhay)	23	Jamie Grayshon (Morley)	13	Gary Walker (Roundhay)
89-90	5	Paul White (Morley)	15	Jamie Grayshon (Morley)	8	Jamie Grayshon (Morley)
90-91	16	Jon Walker (Otley)	28	Paul Grayson (Preston)	17	Jon Howarth (Otley)
91-92	7	Jimmy Miller (Aspatria)	25	Paul Grayson (Preston)	13	Andrew Harrison (Aspatria)
92-93	9	Guy Easterby & Steve Baker (both Harrogate)	31	Simon Pennington (Stourbridge)	28	Ralph Zoing (Harrogate)
93-94	8	John Dudley (Rotherham)	23	Richard Mills (Walsall)	22	Kevin Plant (Rotherham)
94-95	11	Jon Rowe (Walsall)	31	Richard Mills (Walsall)	29	Richard Mills (Walsall)
95-96	10	Neil Heseltine (Wharfedale) & Spencer Bradley (Worcester)	29	Alex Howarth (Wharfedale)	23	Alex Howarth (Harrogate)
96-97	18	Nick Baxter (Worcester)	64	Steve Kerry (Preston)	61	Tim Smith (Worcester)
97-98	21	Matt Hoskins (Manchester)	62	Steve Swindells (Manchester)	91	Steve Swindells (Manchester)
98-99	27	Michael Lough (Preston)	35	Martin Emmett (Preston)	53	Martin Emmett (Preston)
99-00	22	Chris Hall (Morley)	55	Paul Brett (New Brighton)	53	Casey Mee (Kendal)
00-01	20	Gary Marshall (Nuneaton)	48	Simon Worsley (Liverpool St H.)	50	Colin Stephens (Sedgley Park)
01-02	25	Shaun Perry (Dudley K)	47	Paul Brett (New Brighton)	89	John Liley (Doncaster)
02-03	21	Jody Peacock & Gary Mashall (both Nuneaton)	45	Phil Belgian (Tynedale)	73	Tony Handley (Waterloo)
03-04	23	Neil Kerfoot (Waterloo)	73	Mike Scott (Fylde)	69	Tony Handley (Waterloo)
04-05	21	Anzac Luteru (Halifax)	48	Tom Rhodes (Bradford &Bingley)	58	Douglas Sanft (Halifax)
05-06	25	Alan Brown (Darlington)	54	Mike Scott (Fylde)	86	Tom Rhodes (Bradford &Bingley)
06-07	31	Nicholas Royle (Fylde)	44	James Hawken (Rugby Lions)	61	Anthony Mellalieu (Darlington MP/ Blaydon)
07-08	22	Ollie Brennand (Fylde)	47	John Boden (Leicester Lions)	55	John Boden (Leicester Lions)
08-09	29	Gareth Collins (Leicester Lions)	59	Ross Winney (Macclesfield)	54	Gavin Roberts (Caldy) & John Boden (Leicester Lions)

NATIONAL 2 NORTH

363

The league positions used for the 2000-01 season are those as amended by the RFU to take into account uncompleted fixtures.

DIVISION FOUR NORTH

Constitution	11 87-88	11 88-89	11 89-90	13 90-91	13 91-92	13 92-93	13 93-94	13 94-95	13 95-96	14 96-97
Aspatria					1					10
Barkers Butts								12r		
Bedford Athletic										
Beverley										
Birkenhead Park	9r									
Birmingham		11r								
Birmingham Solihull				13r			9	10	3	2
Blaydon										
Bradford & Bingley							13r			
Broadstreet										
Broughton Park	6	2	1						13r	
Caldy										
Cleckheaton										
Darlington										
Darlington Mowden Park										
Derby	10r									
Doncaster										
Dudley Kingswinford										
Durham City	2	7	4	10	10	8	12r			
Fylde										
Halifax										
Harrogate				6	7	1				
Hereford				11	2	11	8	13r		13r
Hinckley										
Huddersfield										
Hull Ionians										
Kendal			5	5	3	6	10	2	9	9
Leicester Lions										
Lichfield	8	9	7	2	5	5	7	5	12	11
Liverpool St. Helens										
Longton										
Loughborough Students										
Macclesfield										
Manchester										4
Morley		8	2p							
New Brighton										
Northern	5	4	8	7	13r					
Nuneaton						12	11	11	10	12
Orrell										
Otley				1p						
Preston Grasshoppers	4	6	6	3	4	3	2	3	8	3
Rotherham						2	1p			
Roundhay	3	1p								
Rugby	1p									
Sandal									6	5
Sedgley Park										
Scunthorpe										
Sheffield								9	5	8
Solihull	11r									
Stoke on Trent			10	11	12r		4	6	7	11	14r
Stourbridge	7	3	3	8	6	9	5	6	7	6
Towcestrians					9	13r				
Tynedale										
Vale of Lune					12r					
Walsall			10	9	11	7	3	1		
Waterloo										
West Hartlepool										
West Park St Helens										
Winnington Park		5	9	4	8	10	4	8	4	7
Wharfedale								4	1p	
Whitchurch										
Worcester									2	1p

NATIONAL 2 NORTH

364

YEAR BY YEAR RECORDS

14 97-98	14 98-99	14 99-00	14 00-01	14 01-02	14 02-03	14 03-04	14 04-05	14 05-06	14 06-07	14 07-08	14 08-09
9	10	12	14r								
		9	10	10	11r		14r				
										14r	
1p											
				7	8	4	10	3	1p		
							3	1p		10	12
					12r						
										5	2
							11	10	13r		
						10	8	5	12r		
				5	5	3	7	11	8	2	13r
		6	4	1p							
			6	2	10	11	13r				
						6	4	7	5	3	4
					4	2	1p				14r
										6	5
12	12r										
											10
					13r			8	10	8	11
3	4	1p				8	9	14r			8
								12	7	4	7
13	13r										
		13	9	3	6	13r					
						14r					
											6
					9	2	9	9	11	3	
2p											
		7	11	12r					6	12r	
	3	3	3	4	2	5	6	13r			
7	5	8	5	8	1p		2				1p
									14r		
4	1p				9	12r		6	3	7	9
							12r		4	9	
8	7	10	12	13r							
5	8	5	2p								
				9	14r						
10	6	14r									
6	2	2	1p								
			8	6	7	7	5	4	2	1p	
11	9	4	13r								
					3	1p					
				14r							
										11	13r
14	14r										
	11	11	7	11r							

NATIONAL 2 NORTH

365

DIVISION FOUR (NORTH) ALL TIME RECORDS

SEASON RECORDS

MOST PENALTIES

EVOLUTION OF RECORD

21	Steve Kerry	Preston G'hoppers	1987-88
23	Jamie Grayshon	Morley	1988-89
28	Paul Grayson	Preston G'Hoppers	1990-91
31	Simon Pennington	Stourbridge	1992-93
31	Richard Mills	Walsall	1994-95
64	Steve Kerry	Preston G'hoppers	1996-97
73	Mike Scott	Fylde	2003-04

ALL-TIME RECORDS

73	Mike Scott	Fylde	2003-04
64	Steve Kerry	Preston G.	1996-97
63	Anthony Birley	New Brighton	2003-04
62	Steve Swindells	Manchester	1997-98
59	Ross Winney	Macclesfield	2008-09
55	Matt Birch	Birmingham & Sol.	1997-98
55	Ian Shuttleworth	Sandal	1997-98
55	Gary Bell	Macclesfield	2003-04
54	Mike Scott	Fylde	2005-06
53	Mark Hardcastle	Sandal	1996-97
50	Douglas Sanft	Halifax	2003-04
48	Mike Scott	Aspatria	1996-97
48	Simon Worsley	Liverpool St H	2000-01
48	Tom Rhodes	Bradford & Bingley	2004-05
48	Chris Johnson	Huddersfield	2008-09
47	Paul Brett	New Brighton	2001-02
47	Gareth Cull	Nuneaton	2005-06
47	Jon Boden	Leicester Lions	2007-08
46	Ross Winney	Macclesfield	2007-08
45	Phil Belgian	Tynedale	2002-03
44	Mark Bedworth	Darlington MP	2002-03
44	James Hawken	Rugby Lions	2006-07
44	Gavin Roberts	Caldy	2008-09
44	Marcus Jackson	Preston G.	2008-09

MOST DROP GOALS

EVOLUTION OF RECORD

5	Steve Kerry	Preston G'hoppers	1987-88
6	Paul Grayson	Preston G'hoppers	1991-92
9	Steve Kerry	Preston G'hoppers	1996-97

ALL-TIME RECORDS

9	Steve Kerry	Preston G'hoppers	1996-97
8	Michael Newell	Macclesfield	2004-05
8	Rickie Aley	Nuneaton	2008-09
7	Tom Rhodes	Bradford & Bingley	2004-05
7	Chris Johnson	Huddersfield	2008-09
6	Paul Grayson	Preston G'hoppers	1991-92
6	Simon Worsley	Liverpool St Helens	2002-03
6	John Armstrong	Fylde	2007-08

MOST DROP GOALS - ALL-TIME RECORDS cont.

5	Steve Kerry	Preston G'hoppers	1987-88
5	Simon Worsley	Liverpool St Helens	2000-01
4	Richard Mills	Walsall	1990-91
4	Ian Shuttleworth	Sandal	1997-98
4	Rob Pound	Sheffield	1997-98
4	Colin Stephens	Sedgley Park	2000-01
4	Tim Robinson	Scunthorpe	2001-02
4	Philip Belgian	Tynedale	2001-02
4	Mike Scott	Bradford & Bingley	2005-06

MOST CONVERSIONS

EVOLUTION OF RECORD

12	Steve Kerry	Preston G'hoppers	1987-88
	Chris Howard	Rugby	1987-88
13	Gary Walker	Roundhay	1988-89
17	Jon Howarth	Otley	1990-91
28	Ralph Zoing	Harrogate	1992-93
29	Richard Mills	Walsall	1994-95
61	Tim Smith	Worcester	1996-97
91	Steve Swindells	Manchester	1997-98

ALL-TIME RECORDS

91	Steve Swindells	Manchester	1997-98
89	John Liley	Doncaster	2001-02
86	Tom Rhodes	Bradford & Bingley	2005-06
73	Tony Handley	Waterloo	2002-03
67	Tony Handley	Waterloo	2003-04
65	Paul Bailey	Preston Grasshoppers	2005-06
61	Tim Smith	Worcester	1996-97
61	Anthony Mellalieu	Blaydon	2006-07
59	Steve Smart	Dudley K	2001-02
58	Douglas Sanft	Halifax	2004-05
58	Matt Birch	Birmingham & Solihull	1997-98
55	Jon Boden	Leicester Lions	2007-08
54	Gavin Roberts	Caldy	2008-09
54	Jon Boden	Leicester Lions	2008-09
53	Martin Emmett	Preston	1998-99
53	Casey Mee	Kendal	1999-00
53	Douglas Sanft	Halifax	2003-04
52	James Hawkens	Rugby Lions	2006-07
51	Paul Brett	New Brighton	1999-00
51	John Amrstrong	Fylde	2006-07
50	Colin Stephens	Sedgley Park	2000-01
50	Chris Mann	Stourbridge	1996-97
50	Colin Stephens	Sedgley Park	2000-01
50	Tom Rhodes	Bradford & Bingley	2004-05
49	Steve Swindells	Manchester	1996-97
49	Phil Belgian	Tynedale	2007-08
47	Jonathan Smart	Birmingham & Solihull	1996-97
47	Simon Worsley	Liverpool St. Helens	2001-02
47	Mark Bedworth	Darlington M.P.	2002-03
47	Paul Brett	New Brighton	2002-03

ALL TIME RECORDS

DIVISION FOUR (NORTH)

MOST POINTS

EVOLUTION OF RECORD

118	Steve Kerry	Preston G'hoppers	1987-88
127	Paul Grayson	Preston G'hoppers	1991-92
131	Ralph Zoing	Harrogate	1992-93
164	Richard Mills	Walsall	1994-95
317	Steve Kerry	Preston G'hoppers	1996-97
398	Steve Swindells	Manchester	1997-98

ALL-TIME RECORDS

398	Steve Swindells	Manchester	1997-98
359	John Liley	Doncaster	2001-02
320	Steve Smart	Dudley K	2001-02
317	Steve Kerry	Preston G.	1996-97
316	Anthony Birley	New Brighton	2003-04
302	Paul Brett	New Brighton	1999-00
296	Matt Birch	Birmingham & Sol.	1997-98
293	Tony Handley	Waterloo	2002-03
290	Gavin Roberts	Caldy	2008-09
289	Mike Scott	Fylde	2003-04
288	Paul Brett	New Brighton	2001-02
286	Ross Winney	Macclesfield	2008-09
282	Jon Boden	Leicester Lions	2007-08
275	Tom Rhodes	Bradford & Bingley	2004-05
273	John Liley	Doncaster	1999-00
273	Casey Mee	Kendal	1999-00
271	Jonathon Smart	Birmingham & Sol.	1996-97
270	Douglas Sanft	Halifax	2004-05
270	Tom Rhodes	Bradford & Bingley	2005-06
269	Tony Handley	Waterloo	2003-04
269	Paul Bailey	Preston Grasshoppers	2005-06
268	Ian Shuttleworth	Sandal	1997-98
266	Douglas Sanft	Halifax	2003-04
266	James Hawken	Rugby Lions	2006-07
254	Mike Scott	Fylde	2005-06
259	Gareth Cull	Nuneaton	2005-06
258	Paul Brett	New Brighton	2000-01
254	Mark Bedworth	Darlington MP	2002-03
251	Mike Scott	Aspatria	1996-97
251	Steve Swindells	Manchester	1996-97
248	Mark Hardcastle	Sandal	1996-97
248	Chris Johnson	Huddersfield	2008-09
247	John Armstrong	Fylde	2006-07
244	John Liley	Doncaster	2000-01
243	Rob Pound	Sheffield	1997-98
242	Tim Smith	Worcester	1996-97

MOST TRIES

EVOLUTION OF RECORD

7	Eddie Saunders	Rugby	1987-88
10	Jim Mallinder	Roundhay	1988-89
16	Jon Walker	Otley	1990-91
18	Nick Baxter	Worcester	1996-97
21	Matt Hoskin	Manchester	1997-98
27	Michael Lough	Preston	1998-99
31	Nick Royle	Fylde	2006-07

ALL-TIME RECORDS

31	Nick Royle	Fylde	2006-07
29	Gareth Collins	Leicester Lions	2008-09
28	Lewis Boyd	Kendal	2008-09
27	Michael Lough	Preston	1998-99
25	Iain Bruce	Preston	1998-99
25	Shaun Perry	Dudley K	2001-02
25	Alan Brown	Darlington	2005-06
25	Andrew Fenby	Blaydon	2006-07
24	Chris Conway	Doncaster	2001-02
24	Derek Eves	Doncaster	2001-02
24	Nick Royle	Fylde	2008-09
24	Ollie Brennand	Fylde	2008-09
23	Neil Kerfoot	Waterloo	2003-04
22	Chris Hall	Morley	1999-00
22	Sean Casey	Liverpool St H	2001-02
22	Ollie Brennand	Fylde	2007-08
21	Matt Hoskin	Manchester	1997-98
21	Jody Peacock	Nuneaton	2002-03
21	Gary Marshall	Nuneaton	2002-03
21	Jay Van Deventer	Waterloo	2003-04
21	Anzac Luteru	Halifax	2004-05
21	Phil Reed	Nuneaton	2005-06
20	Gary Marshall	Nuneaton	2000-01
20	Oliver Viney	Preston Grasshoppers	2005-06
20	Peter Altona	Blaydon	2006-07
19	Chris Conway	Doncaster	1999-00
19	Stephen Hanley	Aspatria	1997-98
19	Oliver Viney	Preston Grasshoppers	2002-03
18	Nick Baxter	Worcester	1996-97
18	Mike Wilcock	Sedgley Park	2000-01
18	Olly Ryan	Bedford Athletic	2001-02
18	Freeman Payne	Waterloo	2002-03
18	Ian Gowland	Dudley Kingswinford	2003-04
18	Ade Hayles	Rugby Lions	2006-07
18	John Hampsey	Morley	2007-08

DIVISION FOUR NORTH — ALL TIME RECORDS

TEAM RECORDS

Highest score:	124	Blaydon 124 Orrell 0, 24.03.07
Highest aggregate:	124	as above
Highest score by a losing side:	41	Harrogate 41 v Caldy 44
Highest scoring draw:	35	Fylde v Hull Ionians 8.04.06
Most consecutive wins:	31	Halifax 2003-04 throu 2004-05
Most consecutive defeats:	22	Kendal 23.04.05 - 11.03.06
Most points for in a season:	1029	Manchester 1997-98
Least points for in a season:	29	Birmingham Solihull 1988-89
Most points against in a season:	1219	Orrell 2006-07
Least points against in a season:	67	Roundhay 1987-88
Most tries for in a season:	135	Stourbridge 1998-99
Most tries against in a season:	152	New Brighton 2005-06
Most conversions for in a season:	98	Manchester 1997-98
Most conversions against in a season:	82	Hereford 1996-97
Most penalties for in a season:	73	Sheffield 1996-97, Fylde 2003-04
Most penalties against in a season:	63	Longton 2003-04
Most drop goals for in a season:	10	Preston Grasshoppers 1996-97 Nuneaton 2008-09
Most drop goals against in a season:	8	Aspatria 1996-97

INDIVIDUAL RECORDS

Most points in a season:	398	Steve Swindells (Manchester) 1997-98
Most tries in a season:	31	Nick Royle (Fylde) 2006-07
Most conversions in a season:	91	Steve Swindells (Manchester) 1997-98
Most penalties in a season:	73	Mike Scott (Fylde) 2003-04
Most drop goals in a season:	9	Steve Kerry (Preston Grasshoppers) 1996-97 Rickie Aley (Nuneaton) 2008-09
Most points in a match:	44	Jamie Morley, *Sheffield* v Lichfield 7.9.97
Most tries in a match:	7	Nick Royle, Orrell v *Fylde*, 31.03.07
Most conversions in a match:	17	Anthony Mellalieu, *Blaydon* v Orrell, 24.03.07
Most penalties in a match:	8	Steve Baker, *Stourbridge* v Hereford 26.1.91
Most drop goals in a match:	4	Steve Kerry, *Preston G.* v Aspatria 7.9.96

NATIONAL LEAGUE TWO SOUTH

2008-2009 SEASON Review & Statistics 370-377

2009-2010 CLUBS

Club	Page
Barking	378
Barnes	380
Bridgwater	382
Canterbury	384
Clifton	386
Dings Crusaders	388
Ealing	390
Henley	392
Lydney	394
Mounts Bay	396
Richmond	398
Rosslyn Park	400
Shelford	402
Southend	404
Westcombe Park	406
Worthing	408

RECORDS SECTION
(previously National 3 South, Division 4 South, Division 5 South & Area League South)

Roll of Honour	410
Year by Year Records	412
All Time Records	414
All-Time Team & Individual Records	416

FIXTURES 2009-10

	Barking	Barnes	Bridgwater	Canterbury	Clifton	Dings Crusaders	Ealing	Henley	Lydney	Richmond	Rosslyn Park	Shelford	Southend	Westcombe Park	Worthing
Barking		28/11	23/01	12/09	20/03	09/01	26/09	13/02	17/04	12/12	10/10	05/09	27/02	07/11	24/10
Barnes	27/03		24/04	05/12	13/02	10/04	19/12	09/01	14/11	06/03	12/09	20/02	23/01	10/10	26/09
Bridgwater & Alb.	03/10	05/09		30/01	17/04	17/10	20/02	20/03	16/01	19/09	07/11	31/10	03/04	12/12	28/11
Canterbury	02/01	03/04	10/10		28/11	26/09	23/01	24/10	05/09	17/04	13/02	19/09	07/11	20/03	27/02
Clifton	14/11	17/10	19/12	27/03		05/12	10/04	12/09	06/03	31/10	24/04	30/01	26/09	23/01	09/01
Dings Crusaders	19/09	12/12	13/02	16/01	03/04		10/10	27/02	02/01	05/09	24/10	03/10	20/03	28/11	07/11
Ealing	16/01	17/04	24/10	03/10	12/12	30/01		07/11	19/09	02/01	27/02	17/10	28/11	03/04	20/03
Henley	17/10	19/09	14/11	20/02	02/01	31/10	06/03		30/01	03/10	27/03	05/12	17/04	05/09	12/12
Lydney	19/12	20/03	26/09	24/04	07/11	12/09	09/01	10/10		03/04	23/01	10/04	24/10	27/02	13/02
Richmond	10/04	07/11	09/01	19/12	27/02	24/04	12/09	23/01	05/12		26/09	27/03	13/02	24/10	10/10
Rosslyn Park	30/01	02/01	06/03	17/10	05/09	20/02	31/10	28/11	03/10	16/01		14/11	12/12	17/04	03/04
Shelford	24/04	24/10	27/02	09/01	10/10	23/01	13/02	03/04	12/12	28/11	20/03		12/09	26/09	17/04
Southend	31/10	03/10	05/12	06/03	16/01	14/11	27/03	19/12	20/02	17/10	10/04	02/01		19/09	24/04
Westcombe Park	06/03	30/01	10/04	14/11	03/10	27/03	05/12	24/04	31/10	20/02	19/12	16/01	09/01		12/09
Worthing	20/02	16/01	27/03	31/10	19/09	06/03	14/11	10/04	17/10	30/01	05/12	19/12	05/09	02/01	

2008-09 LEAGUE TABLE

		P	W	D	L	F	A	PD	Bonus Pts 4T	<7	Pts
1	London Scottish	26	25	1	0	1092	328	764	18		120
2	Rosslyn Park	26	22	0	4	639	338	301	10		98
3	Ealing	26	17	1	8	833	434	399	17	5	92
4	Richmond	26	15	2	9	566	510	56	8	2	74
5	Canterbury	26	13	1	12	658	599	59	11	4	69
6	Dings Crusaders	26	12	2	12	514	580	-66	5	4	61
7	Barking	26	11	2	13	572	522	50	6	8	59
8	Rugby Lions	26	10	4	12	573	653	-80	6	4	58
9	Henley Hawks	26	10	3	13	497	553	-56	6	3	55
10	Bridgwater	26	11	0	15	486	665	-179	4	2	49
11	Lydney	26	8	1	17	463	699	-236	4	7	45
12	Worthing	26	8	1	17	471	698	-227	5	5	44
13	Chinnor	26	7	2	17	455	703	-248	3	5	40
14	Havant	26	3	0	23	345	882	-537	4	5	19

2008-09 RESULTS MATRIX

	Barking	Bridgwater	Canterbury	Chinnor	Dings	Ealing	Havant	Henley	Lon. Scottish	Lydney	Richmond	Rosslyn Park	Rugby Lions	Worthing
Barking		50-0	16-29	19-23	28-0	27-8	52-14	12-12	19-21	48-18	8-11	5-11	31-10	48-9
Bridgwater	22-15		38-12	25-20	9-15	17-39	13-10	29-12	15-36	20-0	39-15	15-25	22-20	47-15
Canterbury	23-30	27-11		10-10	24-8	19-48	75-0	25-14	28-43	19-16	13-17	12-27	39-27	35-17
Chinnor	30-22	29-3	19-53		14-20	20-13	13-24	14-22	29-59	25-27	21-35	11-18	3-37	20-32
Dings Crusaders	30-13	33-24	25-20	15-19		33-29	55-14	21-6	16-18	33-29	13-13	14-16	35-27	25-26
Ealing	55-0	30-8	38-22	46-26	46-9		50-5	37-15	17-38	53-16	51-10	19-8	25-26	53-6
Havant	11-18	39-25	18-25	17-25	32-10	10-46		5-34	10-61	7-25	0-17	13-18	9-23	27-55
Henley Hawks	16-17	41-20	21-14	19-7	24-32	10-15	42-17		9-19	24-18	28-19	22-28	26-26	3-17
London Scottish	80-14	52-7	38-22	45-3	43-0	19-16	45-8	38-5		76-11	33-8	25-17	85-3	45-11
Lydney	10-11	41-12	24-29	20-20	16-7	17-5	29-22	20-26	10-45		8-27	0-42	24-23	28-10
Richmond	18-18	45-15	37-25	23-21	13-16	22-27	47-12	32-22	12-21	18-12		30-16	37-24	19-5
Rosslyn Park	21-18	6-3	26-6	42-0	32-19	26-21	23-5	45-14	7-18	28-17	23-6		53-6	14-9
Rugby Lions	17-14	23-28	20-32	10-20	32-17	18-18	31-10	20-20	18-18	24-7	26-18	23-26		15-12
Worthing	23-19	15-19	11-20	47-13	13-13	7-26	25-6	6-10	13-71	43-20	13-17	7-41	24-44	

2008-09 LEADING SCORERS

MOST POINTS

			T	C	P	DG
253	James Brown	London Scottish	3	86	21	1
232	Ben Ward	Ealing	9	56	25	-
223	Gert De Kock	Canterbury	9	56	22	-
223	Mark Davies	Lydney	1	25	53	3
204	Adam Westall	Dings Crusaders	4	35	37	1
202	Matt Hart	Richmond	3	41	35	-
181	Ben Coulson	Worthing	8	24	31	-
173	Dylan Pugh	Rosslyn Park	3	34	30	-
169	James Hawken	Rugby Lions	4	28	31	-
165	Luke Cozens	Bridgwater	4	38	23	-
165	David Howells	Ealing	33	-	-	-
110	Michael Melford	Canterbury	22	-	-	-
103	Craig Ratford	Barking	2	18	19	-
101	Peter Hodgkinson	Ealing	10	15	7	-
99	James Cathcart	Chinnor	-	18	21	-
94	Danny Wells	Henley Hawks	6	17	10	-
90	Rory Damant	London Scottish	18	-	-	-
85	Thomas Turner	Henley Hawks	-	14	19	-
84	Ben Hewitt	Chinnor	3	12	15	-
77	Frankie Neale	London Scottish	11	11	-	-
75	Charles Broughton	London Scottish	15	-	-	-

MOST TRIES

			First Half	Second Half	Home	Away
33	David Howells	Ealing	15	18	19	14
22	Michael Melford	Canterbury	15	7	13	9
18	Rory Damant	London Scottish	6	12	13	5
15	Charles Broughton	London Scottish	7	8	11	4
12	Gareth Swailes	London Scottish	4	8	7	5
12	Roman Piotrowski	London Scottish	9	3	7	5
11	Pat Sykes	Canterbury	9	2	9	2
11	Owen Bruynseels	Ealing	4	7	6	5
11	Frankie Neale	London Scottish	7	4	9	2
10	Chris Simmons	Rosslyn Park	7	3	4	6
10	Ade Hales	Rugby Lions	4	6	7	3
10	Kiba Richards	Ealing	4	6	9	1
10	Nick Canty	Rosslyn Park	7	3	5	5
10	Scott Shaw	Barking	4	6	5	5
10	Peter Hodgkinson	Ealing	4	6	8	2
9	Phil Read	Rugby Lions	4	5	4	5
9	James Strong	Rosslyn Park	5	4	5	4
9	Gert De Kock	Canterbury	3	6	4	5
9	Ben Ward	Ealing	6	3	5	4
9	Jonathan Wehbe	Richmond	4	5	8	1
9	Chris Jones	Barking	4	5	5	4

MOST PENALTIES
53 Mark Davies Lydney

MOST CONVERSIONS
86 James Brown London Scottish

MOST DROP GOALS
3 Mark Davies (Lydney) & Joe Govett (Worthing)

TRIES FOR
By Position

	TOTAL	BACKS	FORWARDS	Full Backs	Wing	Center	Half Backs	Front Row	Second Row	Back Row	Penalty Tries
				BACKS				**FORWARDS**			
Barking	69	45	24	6	21	8	10	11	3	10	2
Bridgwater	61	27	34	4	13	4	6	4	13	17	0
Canterbury	91	71	20	8	30	24	9	4	1	15	0
Chinnor	56	44	12	6	21	9	8	7	1	4	0
Dings Crusaders	55	32	23	3	9	11	9	9	7	7	2
Ealing	117	99	18	11	54	19	15	4	2	12	0
Havant	48	21	27	1	6	12	2	7	8	12	0
Henley Hawks	63	40	23	6	13	15	6	5	2	16	0
London Scottish	156	109	47	21	40	30	18	17	7	23	1
Lydney	46	35	11	6	18	10	1	4	2	5	1
Richmond	71	50	21	6	24	11	9	9	6	6	1
Rosslyn Park	82	62	20	12	29	11	10	7	4	9	0
Rugby Lions	65	49	16	7	22	16	4	3	3	10	0
Worthing	54	36	18	4	16	10	6	3	9	6	0
Totals :	1034	720	314	101	316	190	113	94	68	152	7

TRIES AGAINST
By Position

	TOTAL	BACKS	FORWARDS	Full Backs	Wing	Center	Half Backs	Front Row	Second Row	Back Row	Penalty Tries
				BACKS				**FORWARDS**			
Barking	64	44	20	7	20	8	9	8	2	10	0
Bridgwater	87	65	22	8	33	16	8	8	6	8	1
Canterbury	81	53	28	7	26	16	4	6	3	19	1
Chinnor	89	55	34	9	21	19	6	7	11	16	1
Dings Crusaders	69	45	24	4	23	11	7	7	5	12	1
Ealing	48	28	20	7	11	7	3	5	5	10	0
Havant	118	87	31	14	38	27	8	9	7	15	1
Henley Hawks	61	40	21	6	20	7	7	9	5	7	1
London Scottish	41	30	11	2	19	6	3	5	0	6	0
Lydney	92	65	27	8	16	20	21	9	6	12	1
Richmond	66	44	22	3	20	13	8	6	6	10	0
Rosslyn Park	42	30	12	7	10	5	8	2	3	7	0
Rugby Lions	80	59	21	10	27	12	10	7	6	8	0
Worthing	96	75	21	9	32	23	11	6	3	12	0
Totals :	1034	720	314	101	316	190	113	94	68	152	7

NATIONAL 2 SOUTH

KICKING STRIKE RATE

		Conversions		Penalties		TOTAL	
S/R%	Minimum 20 attempts	Att	Suc	Att	Suc	Att	Suc
81.48	Peter Hodgkinson (Ealing)	18	15	9	7	27	22
75.51	Craig Ratford (Barking)	27	18	22	19	49	37
75.00	Thomas Turner (Henley Hawks)	18	14	26	19	44	33
73.29	James Brown (London Scottish)	117	86	29	21	146	107
71.95	James Hawken (Rugby Lions)	36	28	46	31	82	59
69.90	Adam Westall (Dings Crusaders)	46	35	57	37	103	72
69.09	Matt Hart (Richmond)	65	41	45	35	110	76
68.09	Dylan Pugh (Rosslyn Park)	51	34	43	30	94	64
67.83	Mark Davies (Lydney)	46	25	69	53	115	78
67.07	Ben Coulson (Worthing)	38	24	44	31	82	55
67.03	Luke Cozens (Bridgwater)	49	38	42	23	91	61
66.67	Gert De Kock (Canterbury)	86	56	31	22	117	78
66.67	Matthew McLean (Worthing)	14	10	10	6	24	16
64.29	Ben Ward (Ealing)	96	56	30	25	126	81
63.93	James Cathcart (Chinnor)	27	18	34	21	61	39
60.71	Thomas Luktaniec (Dings Crusaders)	10	6	18	11	28	17
58.70	Danny Wells (Henley Hawks)	26	17	20	10	46	27
58.33	Harry Owens (Barking)	14	7	22	14	36	21
58.33	Harry Owens (Rugby Lions)	14	7	22	14	36	21
58.06	Rhys Gosling (Rosslyn Park)	18	10	13	8	31	18
56.67	Matt Goode (Rugby Lions)	14	7	16	10	30	17
56.41	Ollie Crosby (Barking)	23	10	16	12	39	22
55.10	Ben Hewitt (Chinnor)	24	12	25	15	49	27
45.00	Keith Molyneux (Havant)	14	6	6	3	20	9

DISCIPLINE RECORD

	SIN BIN			Sin Bin Breakdown Violent Conduct			Professional Foul			RED		
	Total	H	A	Total	H	A	Total	H	A	Total	H	A
Barking	2	1	1	10	4	6	12	5	7	-		
Bridgwater	2	1	1	11	3	8	13	4	9	1	0	1
Canterbury	4	1	3	15	9	6	21	12	9	1	0	1
Chinnor	-			15	6	9	15	6	9	-		
Dings Crusaders	3	0	3	19	6	13	22	6	16	-		
Ealing	4	2	2	12	6	6	16	8	8	1	1	0
Havant	3	0	3	11	6	5	14	6	8	-		
Henley Hawks	3	2	1	23	15	8	26	17	9	1	0	1
London Scottish	4	3	1	8	3	5	12	6	6	2	0	2
Lydney	2	2	0	22	13	9	24	15	9	-		
Richmond	-			11	5	6	11	5	6	-		
Rosslyn Park	1	0	1	16	9	7	17	9	8	-		
Rugby Lions	-			15	7	8	15	7	8	1	0	1
Worthing	-			11	6	5	11	6	5	-		
	28	12	16	199	98	101	223	110	113	7	1	6

NATIONAL 2 SOUTH

2008-09 REVIEW

- Ealing winger David Howells scores 33 tries during the season which is the second best ever return in the division after Penzance & Newlyn winger Richard 'Rocky' Newton ran in 38 tries in the 2001/02 season, with only three players topping 30 tries in a season in the division
- He is the second Ealing player to top the try scoring in the division as last season wing Owen Bruynseels scored 20 as Ealing returned to the National leagues
- London Scottish fly half James Brown kicks 86 conversions which gets him into fourth place on the all time list behind Nick Grecian (Newbury 100), Andy Frost (Southend 97) and Nat Saumi (Penzance 91)
- Scottish scored 157 tries during the season 10 fewer than Newbury managed in the 1996/97 season
- Scottish set a new record for 113 conversions during the season, James Brown (86), Frankie Neale (11), Simon Amor (10), Scott Haddon (3) and Anton Petzer (3), 10 more than Newbury managed in the 96/97 season in their 26 match winning season
- Ealing winger David Howells ran in six hat tricks during the season which is a division record
- Chinnor are relegated for the second time in three seasons from the division
- Relegated Chinnor had the 10th best try scoring record in the division with the backs dominating the scoring 44 to 12
- Lydney fly half Mark Davies slotted 53 penalty goals during the season

London Scottish
- London Scottish made it two promotions in three seasons having won the London One title in 2006/07 and in nine seasons since they returned to the League structure they have won six promotions and in five of them they have been the Champions
- Went unbeaten all season winning 25 and drawing one of their 26 league matches
- At home they won all 13 matches and took a try bonus point in 11 of them to make it 63 points out of a possible 65
- Former Worcester fly half James Brown led the way with 253 points, 21 more than anyone else in the league
- Brown had a strike rate of 73.29% which was the highest of any player to take 50 or more kicks at goal finding the target with 107 of his 146 attempts
- Scored 1000 points for the first time ever in League rugby and a club record 157 tries and had the meanest defence in the division conceding 10 points fewer than runners up Rosslyn Park
- Centre Rory Damant was the leading try scorer with 18 tries, three more than winger Charles Broughton, he managed just one hat trick along with six other Scottish players during the league campaign
- Scottish did not have any ever presents but three players started 23 of their 26 matches, Paul Volley, Roman Piotrowski and James Brown
- Their front row contributed 17 tries six more than any other front row in the division

Rosslyn Park
- Park were runners up in National Three South, their best position since returning to the division four seasons ago and a seven place improvement on last season
- Had their first winning season in three and suffered just one defeat at home when losing to Champions London Scottish but only took six try bonus points in their 12 wins
- Had the second meanest defence only conceding 10 points more than the Champions, 338 to 328 and one try more, 42 to 41, including just 24 on the road which was the lowest total in the division
- Former London Welsh star Dylan Pugh top scored for the club in his debut season with 173
- Captain and centre Rob Jewell was Park's only ever present, two more than the second row pair of Howard Quigley and Russell Forster
- It was tight at the top of the try scorers list with Chris Simmons and Nick Canty joint leaders with 10 one more than James Strong
- Finished the season well with nine wins in their last 10 matches including a run of six straight wins at the end
- Rosslyn Park picked up 48 tries in the first half of matches and just 34 in the second the highest % in the division

Ealing
- In the end after challenging early in the season they fell away to finish third just as they did the season before
- Took 17 try bonus points - just one behind Champions London Scottish
- In five of their eight defeats they managed a losing bonus point
- Lost seven of their last 12 matches including three in a row at the end of the season
- They had the second best home record in the division with 11 wins and just two defeats, London Scottish and Rugby Lions and took try bonus points in all their 11 wins
- Winger David Howells was the leading try scorer in all the National Leagues with 33 tries in 21 starts
- Ealing had three players start all 26 league matches, Ben Ward (fly Half), James Winterbottom (Second row) and Harry Rowland (Flanker), and Ward played in every minute of every match, the only player to do so
- Ben Ward was the top scorer with 232 points and was second leading scorer in the division

Richmond
- On their return to the National Leagues Richmond finished the season well to take fourth place with eight wins and a draw in their last 11 matches losing just twice to London Scottish and Ealing
- Fourth place equals their lowest finish since returning to league rugby nine seasons ago
- Their 566 points scored was only the eighth highest total in the division but defensively they had the fourth best record in the division the same as their league position
- In matches against the other top four sides they managed just one win in five when winning 30-16 at home to Rosslyn Park
- Matt Hart finished the season as leading point's scorer with 202 whilst wing Jonathan Wehbe was leading try scorer with nine including four in the final league match of the season at home to Bridgwater & Albion, and finished two clear of anyone else
- Richmond picked up just 11 sin bins during the season which was the joint lowest in the division

Canterbury
- They collected 11 try bonus points which was the third highest in the division and ran in 91 tries
- Full back Gert De Kock topped scored for the second successive season with 223 points which was an increase of 102 on last season
- Winger Michael Melford was again the leading try scorer with 22 tries, seven more than he managed last season and two more than De Kock's National League record for the club set in 2006/07
- In four seasons of league rugby De Kock has scored an impressive 59 tries in 98 starts
- Overall he has now topped the 500 point mark for the club in his four seasons with 524, in his 98 starts he has only been replaced twice
- Back row forward Christoff Blom was the only ever present starting all 26 matches whilst five other players started 25 matches and one of them, prop, Matt Pinnock came on in the match he did not start and so took part in all 26
- Gert De Kock was the only player in the division to score 20 points or more four times during the season

Ding Crusaders
- Dings Crusaders equal their best ever finish in National Three South with sixth place which they achieved last season as they completed a sixth successive season in the division, the longest current run of any side
- Adam Westall top scored for Dings in his first season at the club with 201 points from 21 starts, the first Dings player to top 200 points in a season in the National Leagues. Westall is now 17 points short of 1500 league points since making his debut for Newbury back in the 2000/01 season
- Westall topped 200 points for the third time in his career but for the first time in five seasons
- The most tries was five by three players, second row Dave Bufton, centre Sam Caven and hooker Dave Wheeler whilst the normally prolific Sylvan Edwards managed just three in 18 starts, his worst return in six seasons of National League rugby as he took his Dings all time career record to 60 tries in 128 starts
- Second row Dave Bufton started the most matches for Dings during the season, 25 out of 26, one more than the trio of centre Sam Caven, winger Chris Wright Hyder and No 8 Michael Panoho
- Dings only managed 57 tries all season and only the bottom four sides scored fewer and their 18 on the road was the lowest of any side in the division
- In their eight away defeats they failed to claim a single losing bonus point
- They were the only side to finish in the top half of the table who had a negative point's difference

Barking
- Barking finished in seventh place in their second season back in National Three South a four place leap on last season as they finished a point in front of Rugby Lions
- They picked up the moist losing bonus points, eight in 13 defeats and took six try bonus points which was the joint fifth best in the division
- In all they got 14 bonus points the third most in the division after London Scottish and Ealing
- Fly half Craig Ratford top scored with just 103 points but only played nine matches to average over 10 points a match, it was the third lowest points return to top the point's scorers list in the last 10 years of league rugby at Barking
- Winger Scott Shaw was the top try scorer with 10 in 23 starts and was the first Barking player to get into double figures since Felise Ah Ling Back in 2005/06
- Winger Shaw also started the most matches for the club with 23, one more than flanker James Kellard although Kellard did part in 23 matches coming on as a replacement in another match
- Barking had the fifth meanest defence letting in just 522 points and 65 tries including just 18 at home which was the joint second lowest figure in the division

Rugby Lions
- Finished in eighth place in their first season in National Three South having transferred from National Three North, and it was a one place improvement on last season
- Rugby were the draw specialists with four of their 26 matches ending all square
- James Hawken finished as leading scorer despite missing the start of the season and started just 16 matches and racked up 169 points as he topped the scoring charts for a third consecutive season the Webb Ellis Road
- Hawken passed 100 league appearances during the season and has scored 752 points for the Lions in 101 starts over four seasons
- Winger Ade Hales was top try scorer for the club for the third consecutive season as he again hit double figures but his total of 10 was his lowest in those three seasons but did come from just 16 starts, altogether he has scored 56 tries for the Lions in just 69 starts plus seven as a replacement

Henley Hawks
- Henley Hawks finished ninth in their first season in this division in over a decade after relegation last season form National Two, they last played in this division in the 1997/98 season when they went up as runners up to Camberley
- They managed to draw three matches - the most they have ever drawn in a season
- Centre Danny Wells top scored for the second successive season with 94 points, better than last season's 70 points
- In the try scoring centre Neil Baggett and No 8 Matt Payne led the way with eight tries each
- In eight matches against the top four sides they managed just one win, they beat Richmond at home back in October and after that lost seven in a row although all three home defeats were by less than 10 points
- The Hawks picked up the most sin bins in the division, 26, three more than Lydney and had a player sent off, the most Sin Bins went to flanker Stern Williams with five
- Although down in ninth place they had the fourth best defensive record in terms of tries conceded just 62, only the top three in the league table conceded fewer

Bridgwater & Albion
- In their fourth season in National Three South they have their worst ever finish 10th, two places worse than last season having finished in the top half of the table in their first two season in the division
- They managed just four try bonus points only Chinnor with three got fewer
- They also only managed two losing bonus points which was the lowest of any of the bottom 10 sides in the division
- Fly half Luke Cozens top scored with 165 points which was the best return by an Albion player since Jarvis Manupenu scored the same amount of point back in 2005/06 and he scored his points in just 18 starts
- The top try scorer with eight was back row forward Dave Kimberley, who started just 11 matches although he came on in 12 more, which was the lowest ever return by an Albion player in National League rugby
- Kimberley scored four tries as a starter and four as a replacement
- Albion had two ever presents, Flanker Dan Kemmish and centre Tito Elisara and Elisara played every minute of every game whilst Kemmish was replaced just once
- In matches against the bottom four they won five and lost three, they won all their home matches and were winners away at Worthing

Lydney

- Lydney are the second longest serving side in the division after Dings Crusaders as they complete a fifth season with easily their lowest ever finish, 11th, prior to this it was seventh last season
- They were second when it came to losing bonus points taking seven in their 17 defeats, only Barking with eight took more and it was two more than any other side in the division
- In matches against the other bottom four sides they did really well with four wins and a draw and their only defeat came at Worthing late in the season
- In matches against the top four they lost seven out of eight with their only win coming in their last match when they were 17-7 winners over Ealing having lost all before that
- Lydney had three ever present who started all 26 matches for the club, fly half Mark Davies, hooker Ben Lewis and second row Paul Kiely, and had another eight players who started 20 or more matches
- Fly half Davies was the top point's scorer with 223 points, the first Lydney layer to top 200 league points in a season since Adam Westall back in 2004/05. He scored almost half of the clubs 458 points
- Centre Chris Holder was the leading try scorer with eight tries one more than utility back Craig Jones
- Only once recorded back to back wins all season in late March early April as they finished the season with three wins in their last five matches

Worthing

- Worthing in their first ever season of National League rugby survived for another season after finishing 12th four points clear of relegated Chinnor
- In matches against the other three bottom four sides they did really well with five wins and just one defeat but in matches against the top four they lost all eight taking just two losing bonus points
- Winger Ben Coulson was again the clubs leading scorer, and has been now for the last four seasons, with 181 points his best return since he scored 252 back in the 2004/05 season
- In his 21 appearances he was also the clubs leading try scorer with eight two more than anyone else
- Coulson also started the most matches, 21, one more than flanker Jody Levett
- Worthing only picked up 11 sin binning during the season which was the joint lowest in the division along with Richmond

Chinnor

- Chinnor again fail to make a second season in National Three South as they are again relegated after winning South West One for the second time in three seasons
- Chinnor missed out by four points although they did finish 21 points ahead of bottom of the table Havant
- They only managed three try bonus points which was the lowest of any side in the division
- In matches against the other bottom four sides they were beaten four times and managed one win and one draw and in just one of the four defeats did they take a losing bonus point
- Top scorer with 99 points was fly half James Cathcart who missed the early part of the season and only started 14 matches
- In his two previous seasons for Chinnor he has topped the 200 point mark and in total scored 680 points in 69 starts, an impressive average in any league and overall playing or four clubs has passed 1000 league points

Havant

- Havant after a five season stay in the division are relegated back to London One finishing some 21 points behind Chinnor and 25 points from safety, just three seasons ago they were third in the league table
- They were the lowest scorers and had the worst defensive record in the division
- In matches against the other bottom four sides they managed just the one win to go with five defeats when winning 24-13 away at Chinnor, although in the five defeats they managed just one losing bonus points
- Centre Greg Sullivan was the leading try scorer with eight in 18 starts
- In the points scoring winger Keith Molyneux led the way just with 41 points, one more than Sullivan, as they struggled to find a top line goal kicker

BARKING RUFC

Founded: 1930
Colours:
Cardinal and grey
Change colours: Blue
Training Nights:
Tues. & Thurs. (Seniors)
Youth: Mon & Wed
Minis: Sat. morning
Website:
www.barkingrfc.com

KEY PERSONNEL

President	Jason Leonard
Chairman	Paul Page 07875 561539 (M)
Club Secretary	Jim Marner
	Meadow View, Kirkham Rd, Horndon-on-the-Hill,
	Essex SS17 8QE
	07957 328363 (M), Club: 0208 595 7324 Fax: 0208 517 3706
	email: jmarner@barkingrugby.info
Treasurer	Alan Bultitude
	18 Grantham Ave., Great Notley, Braintree, Essex CM77 7FP
	07730 648715 (M) email: alanbultitude@hotmail.com
Director of Rugby	Peter Mahoney 07977 219928 (M)
	e-mail: peter.mahoney@barkingrfc.com
Director of Coaching	Alex Codling 07833 727352 (M)
Forwards Coach	Alex Codling
Backs Coaches	Kevin Sorrell / Chris Jones
Fixture Secretary	Andy Pudney 07917 344751 (M)
	email: andypudney@yahoo.co.uk
Youth Chairman	Andy Pudney 07917 344751, email: andypudney@yahoo.co.uk
Youth Fixture Secretary	Brian Wren 07951 025590, email: brianwren@geodan.co.uk

NATIONAL 2 SOUTH

GROUND DETAILS

Address
Goresbrook, Gale St., Dagenham, Essex RM9 4TX
Tel: 0208 595 7324
Fax: 0208 517 3706

Capacity: 2,000
Seated: 300   Covered Standing: 200

Directions:
By Road:
From Dartford Tunnel, follow A13 London bound, go past Ford Works for another 2 miles and take the next roundabout located beneath a flyover. Take 4th exit and return back onto the A13 in the opposite direction. The ground is 1/2mile on the left
From M11, take the A406 east bound towards the A13; turn left onto the A13 signposted Dartford Tunnel. The ground is 4 miles on the left.
By Rail: Take District Line tube to Becontree Station, exit the station and turn left, the ground is 3/4 mile on the left hand side.
Car Parking: 200 spaces available at ground
Admission: Matchday: £8   Season: £85 incl. programme
Clubhouse:
Open 11am -11pm, snacks available.
Functions: Capacity 120, contact Dawn Abrahams
Club Shop: Open 11-3pm. Manager Alan Bultitude

PROGRAMME
Size: A5
Pages: 32
Price: £2
Editor: Peter Mahoney

Advertising Rates
Full Page £350, Half Page £200

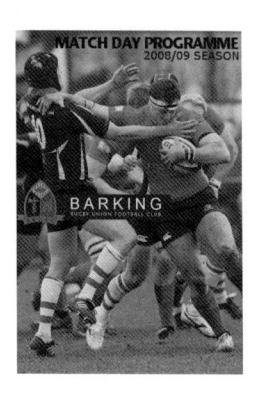

REVIEW OF THE SEASON 2008-09

After narrowly avoiding relegation on the final day of the previous season, all at Barking were hoping for a better campaign in 2008/09.

First up were relegated Henley at Goresbrook, a match the East Enders would have won but for a last minute penalty which salvaged a draw for the visitors.

A run of three consecutive defeats, including a 55-0 drubbing at the hands of Ealing, followed before Mark Robinson's men secured their first win of the campaign, 50-0 at home against Bridgwater & Albion.

That result sparked a mini-winning streak, the Essex side earning victory in each of their next three matches against Havant, Worthing and Lydney respectively.

But then the wheels came off and a run of five consecutive league defeats in the run up to Christmas – including an 80-14 thumping by eventual champions London Scottish - saw Robinson end his tenure at the club.

He was replaced at the helm by former England international Alex Codling, who won his first match against Dings Crusaders handsomely (28-0).

A disappointing away defeat at Chinnor followed, before Barking pulled off the result of the season by defeating Ealing 27-8 at Goresbrook.

But their away form continued to vex Codling, who saw his side slump at Bridgwater and then Worthing over consecutive weekends.

A relegation battle loomed but commanding home wins over Lydney, Rugby Lions and Havant saw Barking ease away from the danger zone.

Unbeaten at home in 2009, Codling's men then faced unbeaten London Scottish in one of the matches of the season at Goresbrook.

Despite leading for long periods of the match, Barking eventually fell foul of a fightback from the Exiles who emerged 21-19 winners.

Two fine away victories over Canterbury (30-23) and then Henley (17-16), brought the curtain down on Barking's season, finishing National Three South in a creditable seventh position.

LAST TEN SEASONS

	Division	P	W	D	L	F	A	P.D.	Pts	Pos	Most Points	Most Tries
99-00	N2 S	26	15	0	11	628	523	105	23	6	88 Justin Azzopardi	13 Scott Gregory
00-01	N3 S	26	15	1	10	611	481	130	31	4	192 Billy Murphy	15 Fred Lewis
01-02	N3 S	26	8	1	17	407	623	-216	17	10	105 Justin Azzopardi	11 Droston McDonald
02-03	N3 S	26	11	2	13	473	578	-105	24	8	172 Justin Azzopardi	5 Paul Pickworth
03-04	N3 S	26	15	0	11	648	522	126	30	5	146 Casey Mee	10 Casey Mee
04-05	N3 S	26	24	1	1	904	346	558	116	1p	236 Ben Montgomery	20 Lloyd Williams
05-06	N2	26	11	1	14	471	518	-47	58	7	197 Corrado Pilat	13 Felise Ah Ling
06-07	N2	26	3	0	23	413	924	-511	16	13r	52 Harry Bryan	9 Jonathan Marlin
07-08	N3 S	26	8	1	17	488	708	-220	41	11	170 Harry Bryan	8 Adam Bishop
08-09	N3 S	26	11	2	13	572	522	50	59	7	103 Craig Ratford	10 Scott Shaw

BARNES RFC

KEY PERSONNEL

President: Monique Bruce-Copp
Chairman: Michael Whitfield
Treasurer: Michael Whitfield
Vice Chairman: Anthony Joyce
Past Presidents: Neil Bruce-Copp OBE, Colin Wright and Paul Kirby
Hon. Secretary: David Doonan
Tel: 07799 471085 email:daviddoonan@btinternet.com
Fixture Secretary: None appointed at time of going to press but email fixtures@barnesrfc.org Tel 07799 471085
Media Liaison: Peter Boyd
Tel: 0208 398 2634 email: peter_m_boyd@yahoo.co.uk
Director of Rugby: Carson Russell
Sponsorship Manager: Robert Orr

Formed: 1839
Nickname: Green & golds
Colours: Green and gold
Change colours: Black
Training Nights: Tues & Thur 7-9pm.
Website: www.barnesrfc.org

NATIONAL 2 SOUTH

GROUND DETAILS

Clubhouse Address:
Barnes RFC, 10 Queen Elizabeth Walk, London SW13 9SA
Tel.: Ground 020-8876 7685   Clubhouse 020-8487 1100
email: information@barnesrfc.org
Ground Address: Barn Elms Sports Centre, Queen Elizabeth Walk, Barnes, London SW13 0DG   Tel: 020-8876 9873
Directions: From Central London cross Hammersmith Bridge, (coaches excepting) and proceed down Castlenau 3/4 mile, turn sharp left into Queen Elizabeth Walk at the Red Lion P.H. Barnes RFC Clubhouse is 50 yards on the left. For changing rooms and ground, continue down Q.E. Walk, through gates into Barn Elms Sports Centre.
Nearest BR Station:
Barnes, 1/2 mile, Hammersmith Underground 1 mile
Capacity: 2,500   Seated: 150   Covered: 100
Car Parking: 90 cars & 12 coaches.
Admission:
Matchday, incl programme £5 - £10.
Clubhouse:
Open normal licensing hours, Food available 12-9pm.
Functions contact Tony Joyce.

PROGRAMME

Size: A5   Pages: 40
Price: with admission   Editor: Ron Holley
Advertising: Page - colour £750, b/w £500.
Contact Commercial Managers.

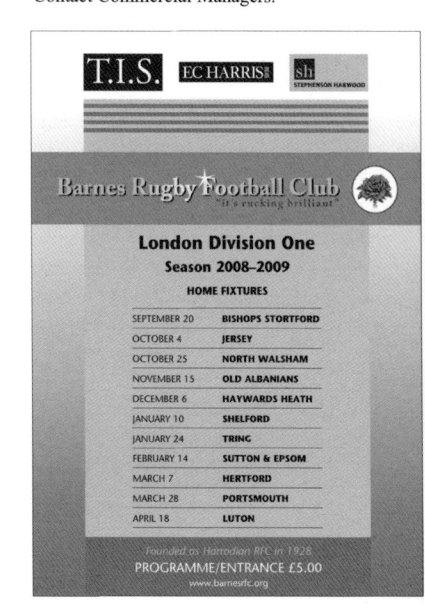

Barnes Rugby Football Club
"it's rucking brilliant"

London Division One
Season 2008-2009
HOME FIXTURES

SEPTEMBER 20	BISHOPS STORTFORD
OCTOBER 4	JERSEY
OCTOBER 25	NORTH WALSHAM
NOVEMBER 15	OLD ALBANIANS
DECEMBER 6	HAYWARDS HEATH
JANUARY 10	SHELFORD
JANUARY 24	TRING
FEBRUARY 14	SUTTON & EPSOM
MARCH 7	HERTFORD
MARCH 28	PORTSMOUTH
APRIL 18	LUTON

Founded as Hattodian RFC in 1928
PROGRAMME/ENTRANCE £5.00
www.barnesrfc.org

BACK ROW:- Jamie Turner (Coach) - Carson Russell (Director of Rugby) - Michael Whitfield (Chairman) - Andrew Pickering (Club Captain) - Tom Archer - Marcel Du Toit - Daniel Hopkirk - Jonnie Fennell - Chris Brown - James Lumby - Ali Smith - James Keany - Jim Brownrigg - Josh Clements - Phill Cooper - Pat Crossley - Rob Argles (Fitness Coach) - Sally Brown (Physio) - Ian Moss - Becky (Physio) - Matt Hill
FRONT ROW:- Brock Baillie - Rob Westworth - Chow Mezger - Warren Gower - Adrian Penzhorn - Simon Givens (Captain) - Al Buchanan - Dainel Sutherland - Matt Clarke - Ross Blake - Gareth Williams Davies

REVIEW OF THE SEASON 2008-09

Barnes Rugby Club is looking forward to a fantastic season in National 2 in 2009/2010. Although we are a small village club we have lofty ambitions and last season, as runners up in London League One, we beat Bracknell 39-19 in the play offs to win promotion. Barnes has risen up 8 leagues over the last 15 years and has done this at a sensible pace maintaining our integrity as a local community rugby club with flair and fun being at our core.

We have an enviable coaching staff, which attracts players from all over the UK and the innovation shown by Director of Rugby, Carson Russell, and his team of coaches is fast gathering an excellent reputation for all budding rugby players.

Our strategies that have been so successful to date will not change and we will not move away from the "core rugby values" that have been integral to the club. We remain as ambitious as before but continue to believe in playing for each other and playing for enjoyment, training will always be skill based and we will always play to our own abilities and not focus too much on our opposition, the quality of our performances is down to us and no one else.

We operate 5 senior men's teams, including a Vets team, a Ladies XV and last season we launched a highly successful minis section which trains on a Saturday and plays tournaments on a Sunday which has proved very popular for the Mums and Dads in South West London. At the moment this is for ages 6-12 but will expand as we get more players.

Barnes RFC is a really friendly, unpretentious rugby club, doing what rugby clubs do best - play hard on the field and play hard off the field and next season will not be any different although we know we are in for a challenge.

LAST TEN SEASONS

	Division	P	W	D	L	F	A	P.D.	Pts	Pos
99-00	Lon 3SW	16	7	2	7	273	324	-51	16	8
00-01	Lon 4SW	20	14	0	6	550	259	291	28	3
01-02	Lon 4SW	22	19	0	3	962	289	673	38	2p
02-03	Lon 3SW	18	15	1	2	706	220	486	31	2p
03-04	Lon 2S	22	16	0	6	536	261	275	32	2
04-05	Lon 2S	22	18	0	4	646	254	392	36	1p
05-06	Lon 1	22	9	2	11	422	365	57	20	5
06-07	Lon 1	22	10	0	12	456	576	-120	20	6
07-08	Lon 1	22	14	0	8	614	399	215	*26	4
08-09	Lon 1	22	19	1	2	616	349	267	39	2

BRIDGWATER & ALBION RFC

Founded: 1875
Nickname: Bridgy; Albion
Colours: Black with red & amber trim
Change colours: Grey with black, red & amber trim.
Training Nights: Tuesday & Thursday 7pm
Website: www.barfc.co.uk

KEY PERSONNEL

President	Mike Berry email: mrb@maxwellsaccountants.co.uk
Chairman	Steve Smith sms21@btinternet.com
Treasurer	Debbie Villis email: debbiev@maxwellsaccountants.co.uk
Club Secretary	Jamie Driver Stonewall, Fiddington, Bridgwater TA5 1JP Tel: 01278 732293 email: Jamie90@hotmail.com
Chairman of Rugby, Referee Contact, NCA Rep. &, 4th Official	Tony Pomeroy Hafod-Y-Gan, Newton Road, North Petherton, Bridgwater TA6 6SN Tel: 01278 662181 email: pomeroyhome@aol.com
Fixtures Secretary	Steve Bryant 18 Withiel Drive, Cannington, Nr Bridgwater, Somerset Tel: 01278 652796
Director of Rugby	Mike Tewkesbury Tel: 07740 445952
Press Officer	Richard Walsh Tel: 07971 100 418 email: richardwalsh@sportsouthwest.co.uk

GROUND DETAILS

Address: College Way, Bath Road, Bridgwater, Somerset. TA6 4TZ
    Tel: 01278 423900   Fax: 01278 446608   email: barfc@btinternet.com
Capacity: 4,000   Covered Seating: 630   Covered Standing: 1,600
Directions:
From south - leave M5 at Junction 24 (Huntworth), follow signs A38/A39 Bridgwater. At major traffic lights turn right A38 Bristol A39 Glastonbury. Keep right after 1st lights on dual carriageway. Follow signs for A39 Glastonbury. Ground is on right after railway bridge.
From north - leave M5 at Junction 23 (Dunball). Bear left and take A39 Glastonbury/Wells. Go up and down Puriton Hill. Turn right for Bridgwater A39. Follow road for 2 miles. Ground on left after factory on right hand side and adjacent to Bridgwater College.
Nearest BR Station: Bridgwater (BR) (Bristol to Exeter line). 10 minute walk to the ground
Car Parking: 300 spaces at ground
Admission: Matchday £7   Season £70
Clubhouse: Open daily 9am-10pm, Sun 9-3pm.
Food available matchdays only.
Functions: Capacity 10-300
Club Shop: Open Matchdays 12.30-3pm.
Programme: Size: A5   Pages: 32   Price: £1   Editor: Tony Pomeroy

REVIEW OF THE SEASON 2008-09

The 2008/9 season was very mixed for Bridgwater & Albion. A good run in the EDF Energy National Trophy where they lost to the eventual winners, Moseley, in the fifth round, only served to emphasise the disappointment at some of the league performances.

At the end of a season that saw Bridgwater & Albion finish in tenth place in the league, the club Director of Rugby, Mike Tewkesbury reflected " If we are honest we have to say that the team lacked consistency throughout the season but we did put in some good performances together, especially at the end of the season."

The situation – in the bottom two of the league - the club found themselves in towards the end of the season was a result of postponed matches following the cup run. The players responded magnificently to the pressure with some excellent rugby ensuring that National League rugby will continue at Bridgwater.

Skipper, Ben Purcell, was again very influential at No 8. When he was absent through injury, he was considerably missed. His deputy, scrum half Matt Britton, also missed the early part of the season but brought stability to the side once he regained match fitness.

Bridgwater also missed young prop, David Morton, for a large part of the season as he was playing for Scotland Under 20's in the Six Nations Championships. The club wish him well as he has joined Plymouth Albion for next season. Fly Half, Luke Cozens, was invited to join the England Counties XV in March but had to withdraw with injury.

Bridgwater & Albion will be concentrating their resources on younger players in the future. Some of those given their chance last season showed their potential and the club has high hopes for Rob Allen, Ali Blundell, Dan Johnson and James Stark amongst others.

LAST TEN SEASONS

	Division	P	W	D	L	F	A	P.D.	Pts	Pos	Most Points	Most Tries
98-99	N2 S	26	8	0	18	523	729	-206	16	12r	149 Nick Edmonds	9 John Batchelor
99-00	SW1	22	11	1	10	478	434	44	23	5		
00-01	SW1	22	11	1	10	489	426	63	23	6		
01-02	SW1	22	7	2	13	453	496	-43	16	10		
02-03	SW1	22	9	0	13	450	456	-6	18	9		
03-04	SW1	22	18	0	4	1,008	308	700	36	2p*	256 Andrew George	23 Neil Meyer
04-05	N3 S	26	13	0	13	725	571	154	71	7	165 Jervis Manapenu	19 Faapoloo Soolefai
05-06	N3 S	26	15	1	10	645	499	146	78	6	136 Christian Wulff	14 John Edwards & C Wulff
06-07	N3 S	26	13	0	13	495	558	-63	62	8	119 Christian Wulff	10 John Edwards & Sam Osborne
07-08	N3 S	26	11	0	15	486	665	-179	49	10	165 Luke Cozens	8 David Kimberley

CANTERBURY RFC

KEY PERSONNEL

President	Dickie Ovenden	
Chairman	Giles Hilton	Tel: 01227 752272 07711 773 306 email: ghilton@shepherd-neame.co.uk
Club Secretary	Alison Williams	15 Weatherall Close, Boughton-under-Blean, Faversham, Kent ME13 9UL. Tel: 01227 752143 email: alisonhelen.williams@googlemail.com
Fixture Secretary	Jerome Weigh	40 Westmeads Road, Whitstable, Kent CT5 1LP 077977 016516 (M) email: fixtures@cantrugby.co.uk
Press Officer	David Haigh	Brambletye, Grove Road, Wickhambreaux, Canterbury, Kent CT3 1SJ 01227 721411 (T & Fax) 07986 972076 (M) email: davidhaigh@airwise.com
First Team Manager	Chris Fullbrook	01227 711972 (H) 07919 408385 (M) 01227 596851 (B) email: christopher.fullbrook@jobcentreplus.gsi.gov.uk or vinnie.67@hotmail.co.uk

NATIONAL 2 SOUTH

Founded: 1929

Colours: Black with amber, black shorts

Change Colours: Light blue with black, black shorts.

Training Nights: Tuesday & Thursday

Website: www.cantrugby.co.uk

PROGRAMME

Size: A5   Pages: 64
Price: with admission
Editor: David Haigh
Advertising: Page £150, 1/2 £100, 1/4 £75.
Contact John Pratt
Tel: 07824 702 436;
e-mail: jbpratt_1@hotmail.com

GROUND DETAILS

Ground Address:
Merton Lane North, Nackington Road, Canterbury, Kent
Tel: 01227 761301
email: info@cantrugby.co.uk

Directions: Exit A2 into Canterbury. At the 4th r'about take 3rd Exit (Old Dover Road). After approx. 1 mile turn right at lights at corner of Kent Cricket Ground into Nackington Road (signed Hythe). After 9/10ths of a mile turn right at sign to club. Do not cross bypass.

Car Parking: Ample at ground

Nearest BR Station: Canterbury East

Capacity: 1000 uncovered standing   Covered 200

Admission: Matchday £8, Members £5 incl. programme
Season N/A

Clubhouse: Open training nights and weekends. Food available.
Functions: Contact Alison Williams   01227 752143
e-mail alisonhelen.williams@googlemail.com

Club Shop: Open match days & Sunday am.
Contact Giles Hilton or John Pratt

REVIEW OF THE SEASON 2008-09

Canterbury's attacking strengths saw them emerge from a pack of mid-table clubs to end their third season in National League rugby in fifth position. The team's ability to score tries and collect important bonus points made the difference in a group of clubs tightly bunched behind the dominant top three.

Canterbury's total of 91 tries was bettered only by London Scottish and Ealing and 15 bonus points gathered was, again, third highest figure in the league. Wing Mike Melford showed the way by finishing second in the list of the league's top try scorers and another strong contribution, with both goals and tries, came from full back Gert de Kock.

National 3 South was, by common consent, at its strongest for a number of seasons so this was an encouraging outcome for Head Coach Danny Vaughan and skipper Chris Hinkins who was leading the side for a fourth season.

With a relatively small squad a realistic appraisal of the club's prospects pointed to a mid-table finish. Mixed performances in the first half of the season, which brought six defeats, a draw and only four victories, seemed to confirm that judgement. However, a good win at Barking in the final game before the Christmas break galvanised the side and their form, apart from a couple of off-colour days, improved steadily in the New Year. This was despite the loss of two fly halves to long term injuries. The side was reinforced in January with the arrival of Michael Coman, a member of the Canterbury Crusaders Academy and a former New Zealand Under-19 player, who brought added power to an already formidable back row made up of Hinkins and Cristoff Blom.

One disappointment for the club was the failure to retain the Kent Cup for a fifth consecutive season. New rules forced the county's National League clubs to enter their second teams in the competition.

Another unsatisfactory area concerned the second team's membership of the Canterbury Shield competition where far too many games were called off. As a consequence the important second string played very little rugby and will compete elsewhere next season.

In contrast, a positive note was struck by the Development side who tested themselves successfully in a tougher league and where several young players of high potential are emerging. That promise for the future was reinforced by the Junior section where Canterbury sides swept almost everything before them in the age group competitions.

Centre Pat Sykes on his way to scoring a try against Lydney.

LAST TEN SEASONS

	Division	P	W	D	L	F	A	P.D.	Pts	Pos	Most Points	Most Tries
99-00	Lon 2S	16	15	0	1	424	194	230	30	1		
00-01	Lon 2S	22	18	0	4	778	162	616	36	2		
01-02	Lon 2S	22	19	0	3	778	228	552	38	1p		
02-03	Lon 1	22	9	0	13	437	463	-26	18	8		
03-04	Lon 1	22	14	1	7	604	277	327	29	4		
04-05	Lon 1	22	12	1	9	489	536	-47	25	6		
05-06	Lon 1	22	21	0	1	809	260	549	42	1p	Most Points	Most Tries
06-07	N3 S	26	17	0	9	778	516	262	85	4	103 David Dorton	20 Gert de Kock
07-08	N3 S	26	18	0	8	608	473	135	*83	4	121 Gert de Kock	15 Michael Melford
08-09	N3 S	26	13	1	2	658	599	59	69	5	233 Gert de Kock	22 Michael Melford

385

CLIFTON RFC

KEY PERSONNEL

President: Norman Golding Tel: 0117 927 3707 (H)
Treasurer: Keith Bonham Tel: 0117 968 4972
Chairman: Richard Clifton
Tel: 0117 9506214   e mail: Richard_Clifton@nfumutual.co.uk
Club Secretary: Roger Bealing
13 Frobisher Road, Ashton, Bristol BS3 3AU
Tel/Fax: 0117 968 1532 (H) 07790 727670 (M)
email: roger.bealing@talktalk.net
Fixtures Secretary / League Contact & Media Liaison: Brian 'Ben' Jordan,
17 Royal Close, Henbury, Bristol BS10 7XF
Tel: 0117 950 4723 (H) 07732 406910 (M) Fax: 0117 950 2855
e-mail: brainjordan@blueyonder.co.uk
Marketing Manager: Mike Anderton
Tel: 07817 639061 (M) or 0117 968 8092
Director of Rugby: Darren Lloyd
Tel: 0780 3022 875 (M), 0117 9650742 (H),
e mail: Darren.lloyd@origin-uk.co.uk or d.lloyd@united-uk.com
1st XV Coach: John Barnes
Tel: 07921 924386 (M) e mail jbarnes@bristolrugby.co.uk

Founded: 1872

Nickname: 'The Club'

Colours: Lavender, black and white

Change colours:
White, black & lavender

Training Nights:
Tuesday & Thursday

Website:
www.cliftonrugby.co.uk

GROUND DETAILS

Address: Station Road, Henbury, Bristol BS10 7TT.
Club: 0117 950 0445 Fax: 0117 950 0445
e-mail: clubhouse@cliftonrugby.co.uk

Steward: Sue Adams Tel 07710 82546

Directions: M5 J 17, take A4018 (dual carriageway) towards Bristol West/Clifton. At first r'about go straight on passing through 2 sets of traffic lights to next r'about.
a. Coaches approaching this r'about move to outside lane and leave on second exit (Bus lane only) and entrance to ground 100 metres on right
b. Cars leave r'about on first exit and pass through 2 sets of pedestrian lights to next r'about. Take 3rd exit returning down other side of dual carriageway through 2 sets of pedestrian lights before passing on left hand side a new second hand car lot. Approx 100 metres after car lot turn left into a short lane. At end of lane turn right and entrance to ground is on the left.

Car Parking: 200 spaces

Nearest BR Station: Bristol Parkway, taxi 15 minutes

Capacity: 2,500   Covered Seating: 250

Admission: Matchday: Adults £7, OAPs £5, Students & u16s Free

Clubhouse: Normal licensing hours though closed some weekday eves.
Bar food available matchdays.
Functions available contact Sue Adams 07710 829546

Club Shop: Open match days & Sun morning

REVIEW OF THE SEASON 2008-09

After the disappointments of the previous season when they lost their place in the National Leagues Clifton's new Director of Rugby, Darren Lloyd and Head Coach, John Barnes set themselves two objectives. The first was to re-establish the club's National League status and the second was to win the Bristol Combination Cup, a trophy the club had never won. The summer saw very few departures from the previous seasons side and Lloyd's astute recruitment including the return of former scrum half Dan Frost, who lead the side, enabled him to establish a small competitive squad. He also added Mark Regan to his coaching team the former England hooker developed a highly competitive pack.
The opening game with Chippenham produced a narrow victory but demonstrated the potential of the side with pacey backs and a mobile pack. This was the start of an 11 match winning run which clearly established their promotion potential. Bracknell provided them with their hardest test when Clifton demonstrated the character of the side coming from behind to score twice in the stages to snatch a win which appeared unlikely five minutes from time.
The weather and a run in the EDF Cup played havoc with the fixtures and on a heavy pitch in January the side's colours were lowered for the first time at Old Patesians. They also took a dislike to traveling down the M5 as they lost their next 2 away games to Devon sides. The crucial game was the away trip to Bournemouth on Easter Saturday. In a cup final atmosphere both sides gave of their all with Clifton establishing a 17 point lead early in the second half and then producing a fine defensive display as the home side came back to narrow the lead to 3 points but we closed out the game and with it achieved the first objective of returning to the National Leagues. The second objective was achieved on a Wednesday evening in early May when they overcame St Mary's in the final in an excellent game.
The league is a marathon not a sprint with games being played all conditions. To top the league a side has to be capable of adapting their style of play to suit the prevailing conditions and this our boys did with fluent running in the dry and excellent forward play in the wet and all times brilliant defense
The unexpected bonus was to reach the final of the EDF Intermediate Cup. They combined with the winners, Hartpury College, to produce a final which was a credit to both sides. It was a fabulous experience for all involved and I am sure the memory of the Clifton day at Twickenham will live with those involved for many years.

LAST TEN SEASONS

	Division	P	W	D	L	F	A	P.D.	Pts	Pos	Most Points		Most Tries	
99-00	N2S	26	12	1	13	575	549	26	25	7	149	Rhys Oakley	9	Chris Randall
00-01	N3S	26	10	1	15	509	628	-119	21	8	228	Jonathan Martin	14	Barnaby Kent
01-02	N3S	26	6	0	20	469	698	-229	12	13	126	John Barnes	13	Chris Randall
02-03	SW1	22	10	0	12	405	383	22	20	6	*185*	*John Barnes*	*10*	*Barnaby Kent*
03-04	SW1	22	11	0	11	574	472	102	22	5	146	John Barnes	19	Rob Viol
04-05	SW1	22	18	0	4	879	291	588	36	3	*318*	*John Barnes*	*22*	*Rob Viol*
05-06	SW1	22	16	2	4	737	226	511	34	2p/po	*250*	*John Barnes*	*12*	*Rob Viol*	*incl PO*
06-07	N3S	26	8	1	17	531	675	-144	46	11	210	John Barnes	15	Rob Viol
07-08	N3S	26	8	1	17	476	852	-376	40	12r	166	John Barnes	15	Rob Viol
08-09	SW1	21	17	0	4	592	369	223	34	1p	*137*	*John Barnes*	*13*	*Ollie Sills*

NATIONAL 2 SOUTH

387

DINGS CRUSADERS RFC

Founded: 1897

Nickname: The Dings

Training Nights:
Tuesday & Thursday 7-9pm

Colours:
Royal blue & black hoops, black shorts

Change colours:
Gold and black hoops

Website: www.dingsrfc.org.uk
Contact:
richard.fackrell@sky.com

NATIONAL 2 SOUTH

KEY PERSONNEL

President	Floyd Waters, 86 Coldharbour Road, Redland, Bristol Tel: H 0117 924 7404 B 01934 862006
Chairman	Steve Lloyd, 53 Wades Rd, Filton, Bristol. Tel. H 0117 9094795 B 0117 967 0014 M 07717 860839 email: steve@hillselectricalsw.co.uk
Treasurer	Richard Fackrell, 48 Station Road, Filton, Bristol BS14 7JQ Tel H 0117 931 1630 Email: richard.fackrell@sky.com
Club Secretary	Pete Jones Tel: 01275 846789 email: petejones@talktalk.net
Fixture Secretary	Pete Boyes, 692 Whitchurch Lane, Whitchurch, Bristol BS14 OEJ email: peteboyes@aol.com Tel: 01275 543932 (H) 07971 929498 (M)
Team Secretary	Richard Grant, 24 Selworthy, Kingswood, Bristol, BS15 9RJ Tel: 0117 9476835 Mob: 07866097743 email: grant.richard@btinternet.com
Commercial Manager	Chris Lloyd, Mendip House, Northdown Lane, Shipham, Somerset BS25 1SL email: chris.lloyd1@btinternet.com
Director of Rugby	Alan Martinovich
Gloucestershire County Representative	John Davis ,

GROUND DETAILS

Address: Landseer Avenue, Lockleaze, Bristol. BS7 9YS
Tel: 0117 969 1367
email: info@dingsrfc.org.uk

Capacity: 1,000
Seated: Nil   Covered : 30

Directions:
M4, J19 to M32 J2 (B4469) towards Horfield. Turn right at second set of traffic lights before railway bridge towards Lockleaze. After about a mile turn left into Hogarth Walk and right at the end into Landseer Avenue. Or see website.

Car Parking:
Spaces for 100 cars

Nearest BR Station: Bristol Parkway

Admission:
Matchday Non members £8, members £3.
Season Tickets not available
Club membership available – contact Chris Lloyd

Clubhouse: Open Tues, Wed & Thur 6-10.30pm, Sat & Sun 12-10.30pm. Available for private function hire. Contact Pam Cole.

Club Shop: Open Tues & Thur 6.30-9pm & Sat & Sun 12.30-6.30pm. contact Chris Lloyd.

PROGRAMME

Size: A5   Pages: 12   Price: 50p
Editor: Richard Grant
Advertising:
Contact Commercial Manager, Chris Lloyd

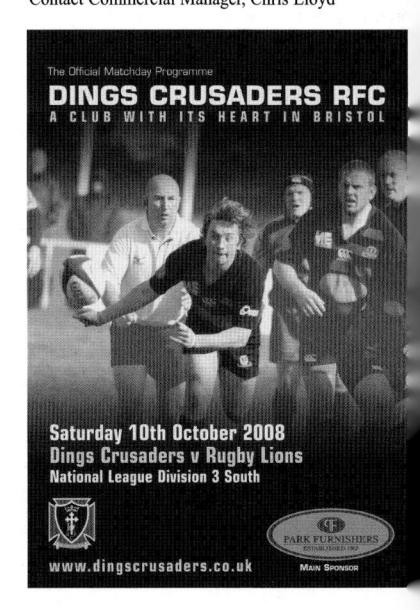

The Official Matchday Programme
DINGS CRUSADERS RFC
A CLUB WITH ITS HEART IN BRISTOL

Saturday 10th October 2008
Dings Crusaders v Rugby Lions
National League Division 3 South

www.dingscrusaders.co.uk   MAIN SPONSOR
PARK FURNISHERS ESTABLISHED 1907

REVIEW OF THE SEASON 2008-09

Dings Crusaders finished in sixth place which was their equal highest ever finish in league rugby following on from last season as they finished a sixth successive season in the division the longest current run of any side in the league.

They had an excellent home record with eight wins and a draw to go with just four defeats and they took a losing bonus point in all four of the defeats at Lockleaze and pushed Champions London Scottish all the way before going down 18-16 to a late penalty goal.

They were the only side in the top half of the table to finish the season with a negative points difference.

They finished the season disappointingly with four defeats in their last six matches but the two wins were good ones at Richmond at home to Ealing both sides who finished above them in the league table. They also suffered a mid-season blip with a five match winless run which incuded back to back 13 all draws which is very rare.

They struggled to score tries managing on 58 with only the bottom four scoring fewer and the 18 they scored on the road was the lowest of any side in the division. With just five try bonus points it was the lowest return from any side in the top half of the table.

Adam Westall in his first season at the club was top scorer with 201 points from 21 starts, the first Dings player to top 200 points in the National Leagues.

The most tries was five by three players, second row Dave Bufton, centre Sam Caven and hooker Dave Wheeler whilst the normally prolific Sylvan Edwards managed just three in 18 starts, his worst return in six seasons of National League rugbyas he took his all time Dings try scoring record to 60 in 128 starts.

LAST TEN SEASONS

	Division	P	W	D	L	F	A	P.D.	Pts	Pos		Most Points		Most Tries
99-00	SW2W	22	14	1	7	430	281	117	*27	4				
00-01	SW2W	22	19	0	3	604	237	367	38	1p				
01-02	SW1	22	15	0	7	409	315	94	30	2				
02-03	SW1	22	19	0	3	463	291	172	38	1p		Most Points		Most Tries
03-04	N3S	26	8	1	17	386	624	-238	17	12	160	Waylon Gasson	10	Sylvan Edwards
04-05	N3S	26	13	0	13	516	538	-22	62	8	136	Waylon Gasson	17	Sylvan Edwards
05-06	N3S	26	11	1	14	551	648	-97	59	8	129	Iestyn Williams	10	Sylvan Edwards & Paul Flincken
06-07	N3S	26	9	3	14	445	628	-183	51	9	93	Gareth Griffiths	9	Sylvan Edwards
07-08	N3 S	26	13	1	12	492	441	51	67	6	122	Waylon Gasson	13	Michael Panoho
08-09	N3 S	26	12	2	12	514	580	-66	61	6	201	Adam Westall	5	by three players

EALING FC (RU)

Formed: 1871

Colours:
Green & white

Change colours:
White & green

Training Nights:
Tuesday & Thursday

Website:
www.ealingrugby.co.uk

KEY PERSONNEL

President:	Brendan Kelly
Chairman:	Damian Bugeja
Treasurer:	Les O'Gorman
Director of Rugby:	Mike Cudmore
Chairman, Senior Rugby:	David Steene
Chairman, Youth Rugby:	Andy Killeen
Chairman, Mini Rugby:	Bill Grist
Club Secretary	Les O'Gorman
	Trailfinders Sports Club, Vallis Way, Ealing, London W13 0DD
	Tel: 020 8998 7928, (M) 07887 485477
	email: secretary@ealingrugby.co.uk
Fixture Secretary & Team Secretary	Ben Ward
	Trailfinders Sports Club, as above
	Tel: 07852 142495
	email: benward_10@yahoo.co.uk
Fixture Secretary: Minis & Youth	Charles Miller
	email: charlesm.miller@lineone.net

PROGRAMME

Size: A5   Pages: 44   Price: £2.5
Editorial & Advertising:
David Steene Tel: 07952 749891,
email: dsteene@Tullib.com

GROUND DETAILS

Address:
Trailfinders Sports Club, Vallis Way, Ealing, London W13 0DD
Tel: 020 8998 7928
email: les.ogorman@btinternet.com

Directions:
By Road - From A40 take the B452 turn to Ealing (Perivale). over two sets of traffic lights.
At the 1st r'about (about .5km) turn right into vallis way. entrance is at the end of the road.

By Bus: many buses stop in the vicinity including the 297, E1, E2, E7, E9 & E10.

By Rail Either take a train to Ealing Broadway and then a bus. Or take a train to Castlebar Park, cross over the bridge and walk

Capacity: 5,000   Seated: 460   Covered: 160

Car Parking: Available adjacent to clubhouse.

Nearest BR station: Castle Bar Park

Admission: Matchday - £5

Clubhouse: For all enquires contact Dave Robinson or Stephanie Cudmore of Trailfinders Sports Club on 020 8998 7928 or check the website: www.tfsc.co.uk

Club Shop: Open League Match Days – check website for times, & Sundays 10-1pm. Contact Shelley Blake

NATIONAL 2 SOUTH

REVIEW OF THE SEASON 2008-09

Entering the 2008/09 season in National 3 south for our second season following an absence of 15 years, after finishing a creditable 3rd place, was always going to be hard to eclipse

Early season form was good. Wins over local rivals Rosslyn Park, was followed by 6 consecutive wins before the trend was broken by a defiant Rugby Lions team who kept Ealing to an 18-18 draw at Webb Ellis Road. The home defeat against title favourites London Scottish drew a crowd of 3500 to Vallis Way, for what was a great game of rugby. Scottish took advantage of a sin bin early in the first half, and ran out 17-38 winners.

Winning form returned as did the free flowing style play that we have been renowned for. Wingers David Howells, Owen Bruynseels & Kiba Richards were to be the season chief beneficiaries of the free flowing style of play, with 32,11 & 10 tries respectively. Indeed David Howells was to end the season as the top try scorer in league rugby. Ben Ward with 187 points was the leagues 3rd top highest points' scorer.

Going into the New Year saw us sitting in second place behind unbeaten London Scottish. It was at this time the RFU introduced their plans for the top end of professional rugby in England and the reorganisation of league rugby at our level. This meant that the usual route for promotion via winning the league or via a play off was changed. One automatic slot was all that was open to us.

The weather began to play havoc with fixtures, we were lucky in losing only a couple of games, but a back log would occur. Pre-Christmas recruitment by teams also changed the landscape. February put a real dent in our title ambitions with consecutive losses to Rugby (25-26) and our last chance saloon away at London Scottish, in a game that could have easily been won, 19-16.

March & April saw win over Bridgewater, Worthing, a comprehensive demolition of rivals Richmond 51-10, and Henley. However defeats against Chinnor, who were fighting for survival, Dings, Park and Lydney, meant that we were not to better last season's final third place finish.

Some great rugby was seen at Vallis Way. The team was captained by number 8 Mark Lock & hooker Andy Dalgleish. Full back Pete Hodgkinson was voted the supporters player of the season, whilst second row Matt Garvey and the leagues top try scorer, David Howells were the joint player's player of the season. Flanker Jay King took the coaches player of the season for the second year running.

The clubs success is not only about the 1st & 2nd XV. The Cougars won the league & cup double for the second season running, whilst the Exiles narrowly missed out on promotion. The Evergreens produced some strong performances, whilst the Women's XV, the Jades again enjoyed a good season. The Mini's & Youth section continued to grow, and are an integral part of the club, and something that will continue to feed the senior section for many years to come.

LAST TEN SEASONS

	Division	P	W	D	L	F	A	P.D.	Pts	Pos
99-00	L 3NW	16	15	0	1	556	134	422	30	2
00-01	L 3NW	18	7	0	11	291	278	13	14	7
01-02	L 3NW	18	14	1	3	447	231	216	29	3
02-03	L 3NW	18	15	0	3	521	149	372	30	2
03-04	Lon 2N	22	16	0	6	754	285	469	32	3
04-05	Lon 2N	22	21	0	1	795	262	533	42	1p
05-06	Lon 1	22	14	0	8	526	446	80	28	4
06-07	Lon 1	22	19	0	3	1077	304	773	38	2p/po
07-08	N3 S	26	18	1	7	689	402	287	91	3
08-09	N3 S	26	17	1	8	833	434	399	92	3

Most Points		Most Tries	
212 Ben Ward		20 Owen Bruynseels	
232 Ben Ward		33 David Howells	

HENLEY HAWKS

KEY PERSONNEL

President	Noel Armstead
Chairman	Philip Woodall
Finance Director	Allan Hannah
Administration Secretary	Mary Wordsell, Henley RFC see below Tel. 01491 574499 Fax: 01491 412335 email: mary_worsdell@henleyrugbyclub.org.uk
Fixture Secretary	Contact office for details
Press Secretary	Noel Armstead Tel: 01628 474398 (Office) 8, Chiswick Lodge, Liston Road, Marlow SL& 1AG email: henleyscoop@yahoo.co.uk
Head Coach	Jason Forster, c/o Henley RFC see below Tel. 01491 574499, 07917 774272

Founded: 1930
Nickname: The Hawks
Colours:
Bottle green, gold panels, navy shorts & socks
Change colours:
Gold with navy side panels
Training Nights:
Mon., Tues. and Thurs.
Website:
www.henleyhawks.co.uk

CONTACT DETAILS

Henley RFC, 'Dry Leas', Marlow Road, Henley-on-Thames, Oxfordshire RG9 2JA
01491 574499 (Office) 01491 412335   email: admin@henleyrugbyclub.org.uk

GROUND DETAILS

Address:
Dry Leas, Marlow Rd, Henley-on-Thames, Oxon RG9 2JA
Tel. 01491 574499   Fax: 01491 412335
email: admin@henleyrugbyclub.org.uk
Capacity: 4,000   Covered Seating: 150
Directions:
From M4 – Exit J 8/9. Take A404(M) north, after passing under the A4 Thicket r'about, take next exit left signposted Henley, then A4130 West to Henley, over Henley Bridge and turn right at T Juction with Town Hall in front of you. Proceed until you reach two mini r'abouts, straight across at first mini r'about and then right at second mini r'about into Marlow Road. Ground 150 yards on left hand side.
From M40 – Exit Junction 4, Turn onto A404 south for 5 miles to r'about. Carry straight over onto A404, after 1 mile, exit left to large r'about, take third exit signposted Henley on A4130 West to Henley, then as above from Henley Bridge.
Car Parking: 1000 at ground
Nearest BR station: Henley-on-Thames
Admission:
Matchday: Seating: £13 Seating Concession £10;
Ground: £10 Ground Concessions: £7
Season: Ground £110, Concession (Over 65) £75
Members Grandstand Upgrade £35
Clubhouse: Open matchdays.
Pre-match hospitality (booking via club office).
Hot & cold food selection, outside bars & refreshments.
Available for private hire, contact Sarah Astbury 07971 092488
Club Shop: Open matchdays.
No Sweat - Brian Rosier email: brianrosier52@hotmail.com
Tel: 07973 391665

PROGRAMME

Size: A5   Pages: 64   Price: £2
Editor: Noel Armstead
Advertising
Page from £500   1/2 page from £250
Contact 01491 574499

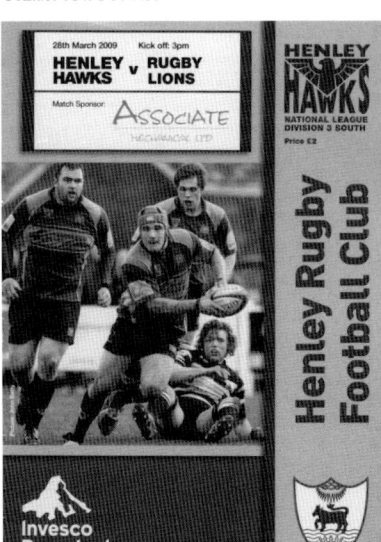

392

REVIEW OF THE SEASON 2008-09

Henley Hawks started the season suffering from the fallout consequent upon relegation from National League 2, all the more painful as they had started the season as one of the favourites for promotion to National 1.

Director of Rugby Jason Forster, appointed in late February, had to pick up the pieces of a squad which had been decimated by the departure to other clubs of all but nine who had had played some games in the previous season.

He filled the enormous gap with 25 young players, four from the sister junior club Henley Wanderers. Thorough pre-season preparation led to a promising start with four victories and a draw before a comprehensive defeat, 45-14, at Rosslyn Park. The remaining pre-Christmas games brought mixed results with the defeat of second division Stourbridge, 11-9, in the third round of the EDF Trophy, the highlight

A tough game in the next round after the Christmas saw them go down to the eventual winners Moseley. This and the postponement of three fixtures in the cold spell knocked the Hawks out of their rhythm and this was compounded by a devastating run of injuries amongst the backs with six out of action on three occasions so that outstanding flanker Stean Williams started two games in the centre. This was responsible, in no small way, for a run of six consecutive league defeats.

Thoughts of another relegation were dispelled by three wins and a draw in March. Leading them through a roller coaster of a season was Matt Payne. At No. 8 he led by example, scored eight tries and had the double distinction of being voted the player's player of the year and the supporters player of the year.

Payne is a product on Henley youth and with four other home juniors also featuring in the Hawks' side the future of the club will be assured if the burgeoning talent in the lower echelons of the club is harnessed effectively.

LAST TEN SEASONS

	Division	P	W	D	L	F	A	P.D.	Pts	Pos	Most Points	Most Tries
99-00	P2	26	10	1	15	599	696	-97	21	9	236 Matt Jones	17 Duncan Roke
00-01	N1	26	12	2	12	517	589	-72	62	7	171 Matt Jones	6 Bruce Rowland
01-02	N1	26	6	1	19	449	767	-318	33	13r	199 John Fabian	6 Peter Davies
02-03	N2	26	19	1	6	782	473	309	39	2p	327 Barry Reeves	20 Nmandi Obi
03-04	N1	26	6	2	18	488	780	-202	39	11	249 Barry Reeves	12 Nmandi Obi
04-05	N1	26	6	0	20	483	811	-328	32	13r	82 Matt Honeybun	9 Nmandi Obi
05-06	N2	26	9	0	17	475	544	-69	48	12	150 Mitch Burton	10 Chris Simmons
06-07	N2	26	20	0	6	614	318	296	95	3	194 Mitch Burton	11 Liam Wordley
07-08	N2	26	6	1	19	333	617	-284	31	13r	70 Daniel Wells	3 by four players
08-09	N3 S	26	10	3	13	497	553	-56	55	9	94 Danny Wells	8 Neil Bagggett, Matt Payne

NATIONAL 2 SOUTH

LYDNEY RFC

KEY PERSONNEL

President	Derek Pomeroy
Chairman	J Nelmes
Vice Chairman	Chris Whitehead
Hon. Treasurer	Chris Wathen
	Tel: 07912 890467 email: wath@fsmail.net
Club Secretary	Richard Powell, Skalnimesto, Park Hill, Whitecroft, Lydney, Glos. GL15 4PL
	Tel: 01594 562820 (H) email: rbpowell@tiscali.co.uk
Fixture Sec.	Richard Powell, as above
League Contact	D J Nelmes
	12 Naas Lane, Lydney, Glos, GL15 6LX
	Tel: 01594 842217 (H), 07713 872338 (M)
1st XV Manager Media Liaison	C Henderson
	12 Maypole Road, Bream, Lydney, Glos. GL15 6XN
	Tel: 01594 562430 (H) 01452 300100 (B) 07760 161006 (M) email: colinandgeraldine456@btinternet.com

Formed: 1887
Nickname: The Severnsiders
Colours: Black & white hoops
Change Colours: Red
Training Nights: Tuesday & Thursday
Website: www.lydneyrfc.co.uk

NATIONAL 2 SOUTH

PROGRAMME

Size: A5   Pages: 40
Price: £1
Editor: Club Secretary Dave Kent
Advertising: Contact Commercial Manager - Maria Davies, Tel: 01594 845605 07824 346607
email: ria.davies@btinternet.com

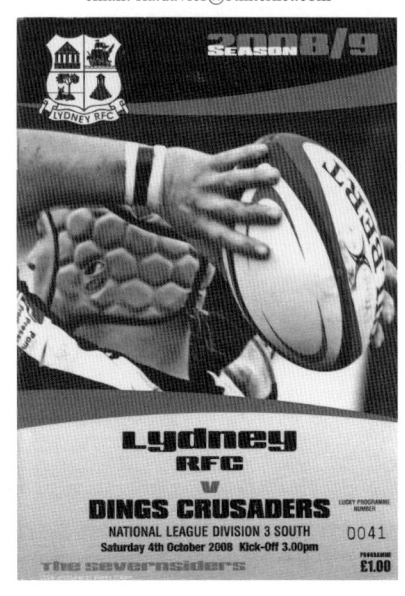

GROUND DETAILS

Address
Regentsholme, Regent Street, Lydney, Glos, GL15 5RN
Tel: 01594 842479 (Clubhouse)
Tel & Fax: 843064 (Office)
email: kentparkend@screaming.net

Simple Directions: See Website

Total Capacity 3,900
Seated Capacity: 500
Covered Capacity: 500

Car Parking: Restricted at ground, other spaces nearby
Nearest BR Station: Lydney (1 mile)

Admission Prices
Matchday: £6 incl. programme
Season: £160

Clubhouse
Open 7-11pm Mon to Fri, 12-12 Sat, 12-11 Sun
Food available on Match days
Available for functions, enquire at clubhouse

REVIEW OF THE SEASON 2008-09

Last year's report predicted a hard struggle for survival, and so it was.

There were times when relegation seemed inevitable, but at the end the old Lydney 'dog', the spirit that has kept the club competitive with bigger, wealthier and more fashionable clubs reasserted itself.

It's impossible to overestimate the influence that outside half Mark Davies had on Lydney's season. His record as the league's second highest points scorer from the boot kept the club in this league. Lydney were jointly at the bottom of the league's try scoring table, and that poor record would have been much worse if the dozen or so tries by grateful Lydney wingers picking up deadly accurate Davies' crosskicks had not been scored.

After a reasonable start to the season the club threw away two victories deep into injury time in the second half. Chinnor escaped with a draw with a late try, and against Barking it was even worse, with an 85th minute try giving the visitors a victory by a single point.

A barren mid season put Lydney in deep trouble, and with fellow strugglers winning unexpected matches, prospects looked bleak with 2 matches to go. But then, in a stunning victory that Lydney fans will remember for a long time, they overcame second in the table Ealing with an epic display of controlled possession rugby that ensured survival. A losing bonus point with a rare four try bonus point against Canterbury in the last match brought the season to a satisfactory conclusion.

Lydney were delighted to welcome back Ben Slatter and Paul Price at the end of the season to provide the necessary late impetus. With some younger players making a mark, there is great hope for the future. Jimmy Williams, outstanding scrum half and full back progressed well this season, and featured in the County Under 20 triumph, with George Porter, prop and county captain. Tony Wicks was another younger player to shine, becoming increasingly more confident at full back.

Of the established players, captain and club legend Paul Kiely again led from the front and did not miss a match for the fourth consecutive season. We were pleased to welcome Matt Taylor to make up an effective back row with the experienced Dean Jenkins and Will Jones. The club was also encouraged by the great work of the coaching team, veteran Paul Williams and Nick Bartlett, the latter growing in authority every match.

LAST TEN SEASONS

	Division	P	W	D	L	F	A	P.D.	Pts	Pos	Most Points	Most Tries
99-00	JN1	26	9	2	15	496	632	-136	20	10	248 Lee Osborne	6 Paul Price, Charles Vine & Ross Armstrong
00-01	N2	*22	6	0	16	308	565	-257	12	13	70 Stephen Ward	4 by four players
01-02	N3 S	26	13	0	13	513	520	-7	26	6	117 Julian Hill	10 Charles Vine
02-03	N3 S	26	23	0	3	695	422	273	46	2	373 Adam Westall	14 Adam Westall
03-04	N2	26	2	1	23	352	1044	-692	5	14r	180 Adam Westall	5 Regan Torua & Charles Vines
04-05	N3 S	26	17	1	8	767	463	304	87	4	332 Adam Westall	19 Andy Macrae
05-06	N3 S	26	17	1	8	618	477	141	83	4	133 Adam Westall	9 Tom Beechy
06-07	N3 S	26	17	0	9	710	562	148	83	5	134 Adam Westall	14 Andy Macrae
07-08	N3 S	26	13	0	13	501	485	16	63	7	127 Adam Westall	Andy Macrae & Dean Jenkins
08-09	N3 S	26	8	1	17	463	699	-236	45	11	223 Mark Davies	8 Chris Holder

MOUNTS BAY RFC

Founded 1999

At Mounts Bay RFCs AGM at the Bath Inn, Penzance on 23rd July 2009, it was unanimously decided that the club should fold. There was 'no other avenues that could have been explored' according to Chairman Arthur Edwards, and there were simply not the finances there to prove to the RFC the club could be sustained without the support from Redruth RFC.
The club's thanks go out to everyone concerned with the club.

Statement from Arthur Edwards, Chairman Mounts Bay RFC on 24th July 2009

'I addressed the AGM last evening and ensured those present that all that could have been done was done, however, the time had finally come when Mounts Bay Rugby had become a name in the history of the game. Fortunately, in the short history of the club we have many achievements and lasting memories to savour, and as the meeting closed there were many wet eyes in the room, which proved that Mounts Bay RFC meant so much to many people in the club, and I would suggest in the West Penwith area. Penzance has lost another rugby club and it is sad to reflect that there will be no senior rugby played on the Mennaye Field for the first time in its history. I am saddened by what has happened but will re-live many of the happy memories of the club for many years ahead.'

Arthur Edwards

The most successful club in the history of the game rising from level 11 to National League 2 is an outstanding record that all involved with the running of the club was justly proud of.
From its humble beginnings the club climbed to the upper echelons of the RFU League Structure, and many former famous clubs such as Blackheath, Rosslyn Park, London Scottish, Birmingham Solihull, Waterloo to name but a few, all played at the Mennaye Field. Trips to Newcastle to play against Tynedale and Blaydon were also memorable occasions last year. Last season also saw local derbies against Launceston and Redruth which brought in good crowds, and exceptional competitive games which reminded Penzance people of past glories. The club lost 13-10 in a National Cup Junior Vase semi-final match in extra time at North Ribblesdale, a small club in the Yorkshire Dales, which meant the club's dream of a Twickenham appearance was lost. However, the Twickenham dream came about when in 2006-07 season the club achieved its ultimate ambition by playing at Twickenham in the EDF Energy Cup final when we beat a competitive Dunstablians side from Luton 46-36 in the final having fought back from a double score against us in the opening minutes of the game. Phil Western wrote in our programme 2007-08 'Can it get any better? Who knows, but for all involved it has been an amazingly successful short journey'. This success was followed by yet another promotion to National League 2.
At all levels attained by the club, this was usually followed by a new influx of talented players who played outstandingly for the club, and gave the club a good name because of its commitment to playing fast running open rugby. Jarvis, Child Cheun-Fook, Mosey, Evans, Griffiths, Burnett, Marlin, Dyer, Flide, Reid, Nonu etc. etc. as well as, local lads such as Hilton, Pellow, Larkins, the Semmens brothers, Nicholls, Clackworthy, Salter, Outram etc. etc. etc. In the early days Bernard Durrant was instrumental encouraging players to play for the 'Bay', and in the past five or six years the club's financier Mr Michael Leah and Chief Executive Roger Moyle continued with player development producing players who have and would have graced the game at a much higher level. The rugby played was outstanding and a pleasure to watch. This encouraged spectators to turn up in their hundreds.

MOUNTS BAY STATISTICS
LEAGUE

TEAM RECORDS
MOST POINTS
Scored at Home: 64 v Luton 15.03.08
Scored Away: 55 v Clifton 06.10.07
Conceded at Home: 61 v Birmingham Sol 27.9.08
Conceded Away: 80 v Birmingham Sol 14.3.09

MOST TRIES
Scored in a match: 10 v Luton
Conceded in a match: 12 v Birmingham Sol 14.3.09

BIGGEST MARGINS
Home Win: 53 - 63-10 v Barking 1.09.07
Away Win: 36 - 55-19 v Clifton 6.10.07
Home Defeat: 53 - (61-8) v Birmingham Sol 27.09.08
Away Defeat: 75 - (5-80) v Birmingham Sol 14.03.09

MOST CONSECUTIVE
Victories: 12 (1.09.07 - 1.12.07)
Defeats: 8 (14.02.09 - 25.04.09)

INDIVIDUAL RECORDS
MOST APPEARANCES
by a forward: 49 Ben Hilton (1)
by a back: 24 Lee Jarvis

MOST CONSECUTIVE
Appearances: Ben Hilton 45 - 20.10.07 - 25.04.09
Matches scoring Tries: 3 Jonathan Marlin 07-08
Matches scoring points: 8 Lee Jarvis 07-08

MATCH RECORDS
Most Points
27 Lee Jarvis v Bridgwater & A 8.09.07 (A)

Most Tries
3 Tim Mosey v Barking 1.09.07 (H)
   William Harris v Rosslyn Park 29.09.07(H)

Most Conversions
9 Lee Jarvis v Barking 1.09.07 (H)

Most Penalties
7 Dan Hawkes v Southend 15.11.08 (H)

Most Drop Goals
1 Lee Jarvis (4), Dan Hawkes (3), Josh Matavasi

SEASON RECORDS
Most Points	266	Lee Jarvis	07-08
Most Tries	12	Jonathan Marlin	07-08
Most Conversions	65	Lee Jarvis	07-08
Most Penalties	28	Lee Jarvis	07-08
Most Drop Goals	4	Lee Jarvis	07-08

CAREER RECORDS
Most Points	266	Lee Jarvis	07-08
Most Tries	12	Jonathan Marlin	07-08
Most Conversions	65	Lee Jarvis	07-08
Most Penalties	28	Lee Jarvis	07-08
Most Drop Goals	4	Lee Jarvis	07-08

LAST TEN SEASONS

	Division	P	W	D	L	F	A	P.D.	Pts	Pos	Most Points	Most Tries
99-00												
00-01	Corn 2	14	13	0	1	432	97	335	26	1p		
01-02	Corn 1	16	13	0	3	339	191	148	26	2		
02-03	Corn 1	16	13	0	3	596	189	407	26	2p/po		
03-04	C&Dev	22	20	0	2	861	173	688	40	1p		
04-05	WCo.W	22	19	2	1	1027	252	775	40	1p		
05-06	SW 2W	22	21	0	1	1023	343	680	42	1p	Most Points	Most Tries
06-07	SW 1	22	17	1	4	734	368	366	35	1p	265 *Lee Jarvis*	11 *Lee Jarvis*
07-08	N3 N	26	23	0	3	772	337	435	107	1p	266 Lee Jarvis	12 Jonathan Marlin
08-09	N2	26	6	0	20	399	844	-445	*29	13r	197 Daniel Hawkes	6 Brett Stroud

NATIONAL 2 SOUTH

RICHMOND FC

Founded: 1861

Training Nights:
Tuesdays and Thursdays

Colours:
Old Gold, red & black hoops

Change Colours:
Black with gold collar

Website:
www.richmondfc.co.uk

KEY PERSONNEL

President	Robert Vallings
Chairman	David Corben
Finance Director	Peter Moore
General Manager, Club Secretary & Press Secretary,	Andrew Gordon c/o the club Tel: 020 8332 7112, Fax: 020 8332 7113 email: andrewg@richmondfc.co.uk
League Contact & Fixture Secretary:	Andy Quigley 46 Coval Road, East Sheen, London SW14 7RL Tel: 020 8878 2838 (H) 07980 309006 (M) email: quigas@aol.com
Director of Rugby	Geoff Richards Tel: 07948 530662 (M) email: geoffr@richmondfc.co.uk

GROUND DETAILS

Address: The Athletic Ground,
Kew Foot Road, Richmond, Surrey TW9 2SS
Tel: 020 8332 7112   Fax: 020 8332 7113
email: andrewg@richmondfc.co.uk

Directions:
The Athletic Ground lies on the North side of the A316 just West of Richmond Circus r'about and adjacent to Royal Mid Surrey Golf Club and the swimming pool, Pools on the Park. The main entrance is from the A316 not Kew Foot Road.

Capacity: 3000   **Covered Seating:** 900

Car Parking: 400+

Nearest BR Station: Richmond

Admission: Matchday - Adult: members £5, non members £10; Over 65, Student, under 21: members £3, non members £6; Members of HM Armed Forces & under 16: Free.
Season tickets (Members only) Adult £55, Concessions £30

Clubhouse: Open Mon – Thurs & Sat 9am – 10pm,
Fri 9 – 6pm, Sun 9 – 5pm.
Food available at weekends and by request.
Cluhouse Manager Natalie Hostcombe 020 8940 0397.
Functions: 2 rooms available for hire, contact Patrick Tolland on 020 8940 0397   email: admin@the-raa.co.uk

Club Shop: Open Sat 12-3 & Sun 9-1.
Contact Jen Gadsby Peet on 07885 700517

PROGRAMME

Size: A5   **Pages:** 52   **Price:** £3
Editor: Harry Hooper 07850 951156
Advertising: Colour page £800, 1/2 page £500
Contact Andrew Saunders 020 8939 1190

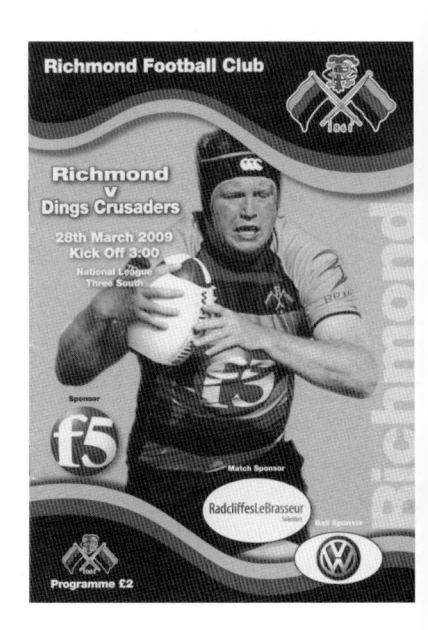

NATIONAL 2 SOUTH

Back Row: (L/R) Simon Hallett, Pete Clarke, Luke Cousins, Jo Ajuwa, Danny Parkinson, Gavin Hart, Johnny Wehbe, Ricky Lutton, David West, Dave Burr, Adam Wheatley Second Row: (L/R) Tony Gadsby Peet (Director), Peter Moore (Finance Director), David Corben (Chairman), Gregg Marsh (Fitness Coach), Tom George, Iain Buzza, Jono Farmer, Tristan Wesley, Colin O'Keefe, Henry Head, Chris Butt, Andy Saunders, Francois van Schalkwyk, Tim Cook, Richard Scott, Buster White (Assistant Head Coach), Andy Quigley (Manager), Geoff Richards (Director of Rugby), Jen Gadsby Peet (Assistant Secretary)
Sitting/kneeling: (L/R) James Platt, Tom Gregory, Ed Rosa, Tom Nuttall, Martin Bolton, Michael Hodgson-Hess (President), Matt Hart (Captain), Rupert Allhusen, Paul Wilson, Nick Gaskell, Nick Wheatley, Kris Greene Absent: Alastair Simmie and Guillaume Schueller

REVIEW OF THE SEASON 2008-09

Pre-season saw the 1st XV full of confidence for their return to the national leagues until such time as Director of Rugby, Brett Taylor, announced he was jumping ship to go to London Scottish of all clubs, being co-tenants at the Athletic Ground. Unsurprisingly this caused some mayhem but a new Head Coach in the guise of Geoff Richards, who had recently coached the England Women's team for 7 years, was appointed. He was appointed Director of Rugby later on.

Despite the indignation the team felt at the mode of Taylor's departure, it took some time for them to settle and by the end of October they were fourth from bottom of the league table and the pessimists were wondering if London 1 beckoned again. However from this nadir the team gelled and some of the disappointing defeats of the early season were reversed on the re-match, none more pleasingly than Rosslyn Park, league runners up, where a 23 – 6 away defeat in November was turned into a 30 – 16 home win in March. They finished the season in a highly satisfactory fourth place behind the big spending London Scottish, Rosslyn Park and Ealing.

The last cup season was rather disappointing losing to London Scottish in the second round, which added to a double defeat to them in the league made for a bitter pill to swallow! It is a shame that there will no longer be the opportunity of meeting teams from other leagues in future.

Once again strength in depth was a key factor to the successful outcome of the season. The 2nd XV, Vikings, also newly promoted to Canterbury Shield Div 1 established themselves competitively finishing seventh in stark contrast to their last appearance there in 2006/7. The 3rd XV, Saxons, were promoted to Canterbury Shield Div 2 where they consolidated well ending in fifth place, mid table. The Barbarians played an extensive list of friendly fixtures, winning the majority, but will play in the Surrey Premier league in 2009/10.

Elsewhere the Heavies won the Surrey Veterans league again, the Women's 1st XV were the National Cup winners finishing second in the league, as did the 2nd XV and the 3rd XV gained promotion by winning their league. The Student U 21s made some amends by beating London Scottish but narrowly lost to Rosslyn Park. The Youth and Minis sections continued successfully with increased numbers.

Altogether a highly creditable season!

LAST TEN SEASONS

	Division	P	W	D	L	F	A	P.D.	Pts	Pos
99-00	Did not compete in the leagues									
00-01	HM1	18	17	0	1	816	72	744	34	1p
01-02	L4SW	22	22	0	0	1142	115	1027	44	1p
02-03	L3SW	18	18	0	0	885	113	772	36	1p
03-04	Lon 2S	22	22	0	0	991	155	836	44	1p
04-05	Lon 1	22	16	0	6	616	291	325	32	3
05-06	Lon 1	22	19	0	3	850	337	513	38	2
06-07	Lon 1	22	14	0	8	756	418	338	28	4
07-08	Lon 1	22	21	0	1	870	180	690	42	1p
08-09	N3 S	26	15	2	9	566	510	56	74	4

	Most Points		Most Tries
199	Matt Hart	9	Jon Wehbe

ROSSLYN PARK RFC

KEY PERSONNEL

President	Dr John Thurston
Chairman	Mr John Adair
Treasurer	Mr Peter Curry
Club Secretary	Mr Robert Evans
	29 Drayton Avenue, Orpington, Kent BR6 8JN
	Tel: 01689-853002 (H)
	email: robert.evans666@ntlworld.com
Fixtures Secretary	David Booth
	Tel: 020 8876 6044
	email: botthyda@hotmail.com
Team Secretary	Kojo Jecty
	Tel: 07976 747660 (M)
Director of Rugby	Shaun Justice Tel: 07912 650287 (M)
Commercial Secretary	Steve Kearns
	Tel: 0208 876 6044 (B) 07870 686445 (M)
Chief Coach	Florient Rossigneux

Founded: 1879
Nickname: 'Park'
Colours:
Red and white hoops.
Change colours:
Dark blue
Training Nights:
Tuesday & Thursday
Website:
www.rosslynpark.co.uk

NATIONAL 2 SOUTH

GROUND DETAILS

Address:
Priory Lane, Roehampton, London SW15 5JH
Tel: 0208 876 1879   Fax: 0208 878 7527
email: admin@rosslynpark.co.uk

Capacity: 4,000
Covered Seating: 700

Directions: The Ground situated at the junction of Upper Richmond Rd (Sth Circular) and Roehampton Lane.

Nearest BR Station: Barnes - BR Southern Region

Car Parking: 150 in the ground

Admission
Matchday: Adults £10
Membership & Season £145

Clubhouse:
Open daily 6-10pm.
Snacks, bar meals available on Tues, Thur. & Sat..
Functions: Contact Steve Kearns 0208 876 6044

Club Shop:
Open matchdays 1-4pm.

PROGRAMME

Size: A5   Pages: up to 16
Price: £2
Editor: Ben Gilbey
email: aussierockboy@aol.com
Advertising: Steve Kearns 0208 876 6044

Rosslyn Park FC
Now in our 130th Season

Saturday 28th March 2009
National League Three South
Rosslyn Park v Canterbury

Today's Match Sponsored by: THE BUTCHER & GRILL

400

REVIEW OF THE SEASON 2008-09

The season opened for Park with great expectations. Director of rugby Shaun Justice had recruited well and the coaches had worked hard in pre season to settle all the new players into a cohesive unit. The first game though away to powerful Ealing ended in a narrow defeat. Undaunted the whole squad worked even harder to produce a teal showing a formidable combination of talent and team work which then produced twenty two wins during the season- the only defeats being two close affairs against eventual league winners London Scottish and a stumble against a spirited Richmond side fired up for a local derby. Revenge was satisfied at the end of the season when Ealing were beaten in the return fixture and in so doing Park secured second spot in the league.

Throughout the season the team showed an exciting blend of solid forward play and sparkling pace and verve in the backs. In the pack there were many outstanding performers- not least veteran hooker Chris Ritchie- showing his usual motivational drive- who was ably supported by many others in a well drilled and powerful unit. Young prop Dan Frazier, who in his two year loan spell from Harlequins has contributed immensely, is now going on to higher things in the world of rugby and everyone at the club wishes him well for the future.

Leading try scorers were Nick Canty, James Strong and Chris Simmons who all finished with ten- in the case of James from only nine matches in, for him, an injury ravaged season whilst Dylan Pugh was a reasonably consistent kicker with over 150 points.

Cementing everything together both on and off the field was 'Player of the Season' and skipper Rob Jewell who in his first season at Park showed great leadership as well as consummate playing skills in the centre.

Further recruitment has produced an even stronger squad for 09/10 and everyone at Park is eager now for the season to start.

LAST TEN SEASONS

	Division	P	W	D	L	F	A	P.D.	Pts	Pos	Most Points		Most Tries	
99-00	JN1	26	17	2	7	694	371	323	36	4	145	Stuart Hibbert	12	Crawford Henderson
00-01	N2	*25	19	2	4	752	439	313	40	3	157	Paul Roblin	18	James Justice
01-02	N2	26	8	1	17	490	605	-115	17	12r	74	James Hendy	8	John Allen
02-03	N3 S	26	24	0	2	1055	395	660	48	1p	359	Sam Howard	15	James Justice
03-04	N2	26	9	1	16	672	646	26	19	12	267	Sam Howard	15	James Justice
04-05	N2	26	6	0	20	415	671	-256	35	14r	61	Sam Howard	4	By three players
05-06	N3 S	26	15	0	11	549	444	105	72	6	180	Richard Mahony	12	Marcus McCluggage
06-07	N3 S	26	10	0	16	485	664	-179	48	10	201	Richard Mahony	5	By three players
07-08	N3 S	26	12	0	14	502	463	39	59	9	215	Richard Mahony	7	Nick Harlock
08-09	N3 S	26	22	0	4	639	338	301	98	2	173	Dylan Pugh	10	Nick Canty, Chris Simmonds

SHELFORD RFC

Founded: 1933

Nickame:
Shelford Peacocks

Website:
www.shelfordrugby.co.uk

Colours:
Maroon & white hoops

Change colours: Blue

Training Nights:
Seniors Tuesday & Thursday

NATIONAL 2 SOUTH

KEY PERSONNEL

President:	Colin Astin
Chairman:	Anthony Roberts
Treasurer:	Annaleaza Finlayson
Director of Rugby:	Sam Tovo
Club Secretary:	Tony Roberts Tel: 01480 463725 email: anthonyroberts@hotmail.com
Fixture Secretary:	Sanjay Mistry 16 Campion Close, Soham, Ely, Cambs. CB7 5FX Tel H 01223 835276, M 07980 389882 email sanjmistry31@hotmail.com
Youth Chairman	Rory Finlayson Tel: 01223 834207
PR & Web Admin.:	Ross Seymour Tel: 07947 355469 email: ross@shelfordrugby.co.uk Andrew Baron Tel: 01223 834363 email: beefnlola@googlemail.com

GROUND DETAILS

Ground Address: The Davy Field, Cambridge Road, Great Shelford, Cambridge, CB2 5JJ
     Tel: 01223 843 357   email: info@shelfordrugby.co.uk

Directions: Shelford RFC is situated 1 mile S East of Cambridge city centre.

Approaching either Southbound or Northbound on M11, exit at junction 11 taking A1309 towards Cambridge. Turn Right at first traffic lights onto Cambridge Road (the Waitrose Shopping Centre will be on your left). The ground entrance is 1 mile on the right hand side (Opposite Scotsdales Garden Centre)

Note. From winter 09/10 a new slip road may be open leading to Addenbrookes Hospital from the A1309 just after exiting the M11. Unless this has been marked 'hospital only' this is a short cut that takes you directly to the Cambridge Road, Shelford.

Nearest BR station: Cambridge

Car Parking: Space for approx 400 cars

Capacity: 3,000   Seated: 100   Covered: 150

Admission: Matchday £10

Clubhouse: Substantially extended in 2000 the clubhouse now offers a large hall, opening out onto open ground, a long bar and kitchen facilities, a first floor executive lounge & committee room. Available for private hire, contact Jackie Burgoyne, Club Administrator on 01223 504744   email: jackie.burgoyne@shelfordrugby.co.uk.

Club Shop: Open Saturday matchdays 12-5pm, Sundays 10-1pm.

Programme: None

Shelford celebrate winning London 1

REVIEW OF THE SEASON 2007-08

Shelford's meteoric rise up the RFU league pyramid system continues with yet another promotion as they move into the National Leagues for the first time. Shelford have now had four promotions in the last eight years coming up from London Three North East in 2001/02.

It has only taken them three season's of level five rugby, to move up into National Two South with a gradual improved over the three years. In their first season of London One rugby they were fifth, then they were third and this season they made the big step which was the perfect way to celebrate the clubs 75th Year.

The side were again coached by Sam Tovo and the scrum half Alex Birkby led by example on the field as captain as they took the London One title with a last day of the season win over Old Albanians

They got off to a great start and were undefeated in their opening 12 matches with the only blemish a 6-6 draw away at Jersey. Just after Christmas they suffered their first defeat going down at Barnes and they followed that up with a disappointing defeat at Davy Field against Jersey. That proved to be their last defeat of the season as they got back on track to take the London One title after a number of close encounters. They were pushed all the way by Old Albanians before coming through 18-14 despite being out played for much of the match in the final match of the season.

The returning Ed Gough made a huge contribution with his excellent goal kicking after three years away in Cardiff, with superb kicking displays second to none in the division and provided valuable and unexpected points in many close encounters.

Also making a big impression were three newcomers in the back five, New Zealander Matt Shane-Berryman in the back row along with Tony Begovich and Will McLintock, both Begovich and McLintock have had National League experience in the past with Blaydon and Southend respectively which can only bode well for the future.

LAST TEN SEASONS

	Division	P	W	D	L	F	A	P.D.	Pts	Pos
99-00	Lon 3NE	16	11	0	5	413	233	180	22	5
00-01	Lon 3NE	18	6	1	11	260	364	-104	*11	7
01-02	Lon 3NE	18	17	0	1	453	211	242	34	1p
02-03	Lon 2N	22	8	0	14	340	414	-74	16	10r
03-04	Lon 3NE	18	14	1	3	474	221	253	29	1p
04-05	Lon 2N	22	14	1	7	494	367	127	29	3
05-06	Lon 2N	22	20	0	2	856	244	61	40	1p
06-07	Lon 1	22	11	0	11	580	611	-31	20	5
07-08	Lon 1	22	16	0	6	711	483	228	32	3
08-09	Lon 1	22	19	1	2	576	281	295	39	1p

NATIONAL 2 SOUTH

403

SOUTHEND RFC

KEY PERSONNEL

President — Dick Collie   email: Richard.collie@gmail.com
24 Basingbourne Road, Fleet, Hampshire GU52 6TE
Tel: Tel: 01252 617715 (H)   07974 102255 (M)

Chairman — Neil Harding   email: agh477799@aol.com
77 Hillside Crescent, Leigh-on-Sea, Essex SS5 1HH
Tel: 01702 477799h   07778 126098(M)

C.E.O. — Nick Fleming
The Gables, 146 Stambridge Road, Rochford SS4 1DT
Tel 01702 542937 (H)   07711 945375 (M)

Hon. Secretary — Michael Jones   email: mdjessex@btinternet.com
29 Glencrofts, Hockley, Essex SS5 4GN
Tel: 01702 0202042 (H)   07932 755187 (M)

Marketing Director — Nathan Strange   Tel: 07908 222005
email: nathanstrange007@hotmail.com

Fixtures Secretary — Frank Dyton   email: cathite@btconnect.com
1 The Crossways, Westcliffe-on-Sea, Essex SS0 8PU
Tel: 01702 475075 (H)

Director of Rugby — Ben Green   Tel: 07974 237247

1st XV Manager & Operations Manager — Kevin Scully   Tel: 07766 414576

Youth & Mini Section
Chairman: Lee McDowell
Club Coaching Co-ordinator: Wayne Hallett
Welfare Officer: Jackie Flynn   email: hlwy6@aol.com

Founded: 1870
Club Colours: Chocolate brown & white
Change colours: Blue and gold
Training Nights: Tuesday & Thursday
Website: wwww.southendrugby.com

NATIONAL 2 SOUTH

GROUND DETAILS

Address
Warners Bridge Park, Sumpters Way, Southend-on-Sea. SS2 5RR
Tel: 01702 546682   email: agh477799@aol.com

Capacity: 5,000
Covered Seating: 220

Directions
A127 to Southend, turn left Sutton Road, turn right at r'about into Chandlers Way, left into Sumpters Way and club is 50 yds over the bridge.

Car Parking: 100 spaces at ground.
Nearest BR station: (Southend) Prittlewell : Liverpool St.

Admission: Members £5, non-members £8

Clubhouse: Open daily 11-11pm, bar snacks available.
Functions: Contact Jane Vaufrouard 07766 880857

Club Shop: Open Saturday & Sunday.
Contact Jane Vaufrouard 07766 880857

PROGRAMME
Size: A5   Pages: 48   Price: Free
Editor: Nathan Strange   07908 222005

REVIEW OF THE SEASON 2008-09

We started the season with a good young group of local players and a couple of overseas imports to strengthen the squad. It became apparent after a few weeks that injuries to our more experienced players would cost us dearly. After an early season win at Blackheath we managed to lose a number of matches by less than one score and this coupled with our inexperience to close a game down ultimately cost us our place in the league.

The standard of National League 2 clearly improved with the amount of former Premier Squad players contracted to various clubs the resulting rugby was mostly of the highest quality. Our coaching staff under DOR Ben Green worked very hard to gel our squad into a team and they performed extremely well under pressure for most of the season; they still managed to walk of the pitch head held high on all occasions with late season performances away to both Cambridge and Birmingham Solihull being memorable.

It is good to report that our 2nd XV the Priors won their league; Canterbury 2 and our Abbotts, Deacons & Bishops all had very good results competing in the excellent BL Merit Table.

The club's Youth & Mini Section continues to grow now having in excess of 300 members and a wide spectrum of young talent can be seen on a Sunday morning at Warners Bridge Park.

I would like to thank 1st team Stand Off Joel Johnston for his total commitment to the club both as a player and also as our Administrator of our Schools Programme which he has helped to develop over the last four years. We wish him well as he returns to his native Australia.

We also welcome on board Dick Collie our new President who replaces the ever-popular Peter Thomas who stands down after four years.

With 9 weeks to go we are looking forward to competing at National 2 South and renewing old rivalries with our fellow Essex club Barking (who did let the dogs out?) and many other London based clubs.

As I write this piece London Welsh are in administration, Mounts Bay are hoping to regroup and Halifax have dropped out of the National Leagues. It is tough for the semi-professional game but with sound management and players support the game will continue to grow with or without some of our central administrators support.

Photo shows Andrew Frost leading the breakaway against Launceston.

LAST TEN SEASONS

	Division	P	W	D	L	F	A	P.D.	Pts	Pos	Most Points		Most Tries	
99-00	Lon 2N	16	1	2	13	150	399	-249	4	14r				
00-01	Lon 3NE	18	16	0	2	484	190	294	32	1p				
01-02	Lon 2N	22	19	0	3	568	245	323	38	2p	Most Points		Most Tries	
02-03	Lon 1	22	19	0	3	713	296	417	38	1p	298	Ali Chambers	11	A Barker
03-04	N3S	26	13	0	13	702	703	-1	26	6	198	Ali Chambers	16	Chris Green
04-05	N3S	26	10	0	16	494	611	-117	49	10	177	Simon Hoult	9	Craig Green
05-06	N3S	26	15	2	9	697	561	136	78	5	258	Andy Frost	14	Jaco du Toit
06-07	N3S	26	22	0	4	944	542	402	107	1p	335	Andy Frost	32	Faapolou Soolefai
07-08	N2	26	12	0	14	666	620	46	66	8	282	Andy Frost	15	Faapolou Soolefai
08-09	N2	26	5	0	21	574	797	-223	32	12r	161	Andy Frost	8	Andy Frost

WESTCOMBE PARK RFC

KEY PERSONNEL

President: John Ward Turner
Westerham Lodge, Westerham Road, Keston Kent BR2 6DA
01689 854868 (H), 07802 986682 (M), e-mail: president@westcombeparkrugby.co.uk

Chairman: John Bellinger
32A Courtyard, Eltham, London SE9 5QE
020 8850 7280 (H), 07939 130049 (M)   chairman@westcombeparkrugby.co.uk

Secretary: David Barnes
59 Warren Road, Orpington, Kent BR6 6JF   Tel: 07707 058158
email: hon.sec@westcombeparkrugby.co.uk

Treasurer: Stephen Jones
Heathview, 17 Knoll Road, Bexley Kent DA5 1AY
Tel: 01322 558960 (H), 020 8318 1417 (W), 07970 561206 (M)
email: hon.treas@westcombeparkrugby.co.uk

Fixture Secretary: John Day
23, Glyndebourne Park, Locks Bottom, Orpington, Kent
Tel: 01689 854221 (H),   07768 827958 (M)
email: fixtures.sec@westcombeparkrugby.co.uk

Chairman of Rugby Playing: Ian Taylor
14 Broughton Road, Orpington, Kent BR6 8EQ
Tel: 01689 856308 (H),   07855 483958 (M)
email: chair.rugby@westcombeparkrugby.co.uk

Chairman of Marketing & Programme Editor: Denes Nemestothy
Ashbury Villa, 36 Worlds End Lane, Orpington, Kent BR6 6AQ
01689 600858 (H)   020 8254 5150 (O)   07801 292938 (M)
e-mail: marketing@westcombeparkrugby.co.uk

1st XV Team Manager: John Ward Turner
Westerham Lodge, Westerham Road, Keston Kent BR2 6DA
01689 854868 (H)   07802 986682 (M)   01689 860246 (F) e-mail: pr@wardturner.com

Head Coach: Darren Molloy   07770 221331

1st XV Backs Coach: Jaco du Toit

Director 1st XV Rugby: Steve Reynolds
01580 892478 (H)   07812 136063 (M)
email: director.1stXV@westcombeparkrugby.co.uk

Founded: 1904

Nickname: "Combe"

Colours: Blue & white hoops

Change colours: White & blue hoops

Training Nights: Monday and Wednesday

Web site: www.westcombeparkrugby.co.uk

GROUND DETAILS

Address:	Goddington Dene, Goddington Lane, Orpington, Kent BR6 9SX Tel: 01689 834902 (T & F)
Capacity:	2000 uncovered Covered seating: 200
Directions:	From M25 - exit at J4. At next round-about exit A244 (Orpington), at 40 MPH sign (2.8 miles from M25) turn right into Goddington Lane, opposite the Highway. From A20 - Leave A20 at Crittall's Corner (Orpington A224). Take A224 to Orpington, Sevenoaks Way, Continue into Court Road, following sign, M25-Sevenoaks. After six sets of lights turn LEFT into Goddington Lane (opposite Volvo show room) From Croydon - follow A232 into Orpington, over War Memorial roundabout, up Spur Road to A224. Turn Right into Court Road at lights, 1/4 mile turn Left into Goddington Lane.
Nearest BR Station	Chelsfield **Car Parking:** 200
Admission:	Matchday - £8 including programme
Club Shop:	Open Saturday & Sundays mornings. Contact Lew Barnett - see below
Clubhouse:	Open during normal licensing hours, snacks and bar meals available. Function Rooms available. Contact Lew Barnett email:house.manager@westcombeparkrugby.co.uk
Programme	**Size:** A5 **Pages:** 36 **Price:** with admission **Editorial & Advertising:** Denes Nemestothy

REVIEW OF THE SEASON 2008-09

The 2008/2009 season was 'Combe's ninth in the National Leagues and our second in Division 2. The second season at this level is difficult for any club and to have the ELVs introduced made life even more interesting.

The team needed to be reconstituted, which was very well done, and after some results narrowly going against us in the middle of the season the team came good towards the end and would easily have maintained the National Division 2 status (going forward as National 1) if it were not for the RFU's League reorganisation which meant that we will be playing in National League Division 2 South for 2009/2010 which we look forward to.

Despite a long season we were delighted with the commitment of the first team squad and, particularly, the superb dedication of Fraser Thomson and Darren Molloy our two coaches.

The other group that never wavered was the faithful band of traveling supporters who enjoyed our first victory in Cornwall with the customary 'Combe celebrations.

We are greatly looking forward to 2009/2010 in the excellent National League Division 2 South, which is broadly around the London area, renewing old acquaintances and making new friends.

For those who are not familiar with Westcombe Park's history we were founded in 1904 in Westcombe Park, South East London, eventually settling in Orpington in 1937. We moved to our current location in Goddington Dene in 1990. We manage a major sports facility known as Westcombe Park & Orpington Sports Club. Comprising 23 acres of superb playing facilities it caters for Rugby at all levels being 1st XV plus five senior sides, a youth Academy and junior and mini rugby. We also run soccer, cricket and tennis.

As a club we are looking forward to welcoming new clubs and their supporters to our facilities and at the same time renewing friendships with old rivals.

WORTHING RFC

KEY PERSONNEL

President: Richard Mowbray

Chairman: Allan Imrie

Chairman of Administration: Brian Vincent
email: admin@worthingrfc.co.uk

Commercial Manager: Mike Perring
Tel: 01903 784706
email: mike@worthingrfc.co.uk

League Contact: David Hinchliffe
Tel: 01903 775506, 07802 488939 (M)
email: davidh@ipdconsultants.com

Head Coach: Will Green
Tel. 07802 460002 (M)
email: will.green@ccas.uk.com

Fixture Secretary: Nigel Lyons
Tel: 07808 094883 (M)
email: fixtures@worthingrfc.com

Match Secretary: Paul Baker
Tel: 07730 596422 (M)

Founded: 10.9.1920

Training Nights: Tuesday & Thursday

Colours: Blue & gold.

Change colours: Brown & gold

Website: www.worthingrfc.co.uk

GROUND DETAILS

Ground Address:
Worthing RFC, Rugby Park,
Roundstone Lane, Angmering, W. Sussex BN16 4AX

Tel/Fax: 01903 784706
email: rugby@worthingrfc.co.uk

Directions:
West or east on A259, Worthing to Littlehampton road, turn right or left at Roundstone Pub (depending on approach) into Roundstone Lane. Ground 800 metres on left.
Full details & location map on the website

Nearest BR Station: Angmering

Car Parking: 175 cars

Capacity: 3,000 Covered seating: 150

Admission: £8 non members, £5 members

Clubhouse: 8.30am-11pm. Food available weekends. Functions: contact Mike Perring at the club.

Club Shop: Open 6-8pm Mon/Fri, 10am-3pm Sat/Sun. Contact Lisa Simms e-mail lisa@worthingrfc.co.uk

PROGRAMME

Size: A5   **Pages:** 50   **Price:** £3

Editorial: Heather Simmons e-mail heather@worthingrfc.co.uk

Advertising: Contact Mike Perring

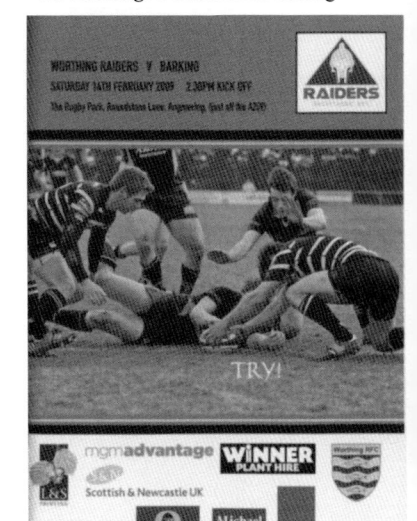

NATIONAL 2 SOUTH

REVIEW OF THE SEASON 2008-09

Worthing RFC is proud to be more than just a 1st XV and 2008-9 proved to be a vintage season across senior, junior and mini rugby.

In highly competitive National 3 South, the 1st XV climbed a steep learning curve, initially made even steeper by injuries to a number of key players. By Christmas the foundations were in place for a strong push for survival and, though safety was not guaranteed until the last home game and a stirring victory over Lydney, the team did the business. Indeed, had the first half of the season mirrored the second, a mid table place would have been secured. We look forward to the new challenges offered in National 2 South 2009-10.

The 2nd XV secured the Canterbury Shield Division 3 title and manager Dave Roberts and his young squad are to be congratulated on their commitment given the amount of travelling this league requires.

The Development XV won the Sussex Intermediate league and topped the table by a 13 point margin. Their promotion takes them into the heady realms of the RFU leagues, the first time the club has had two teams in the RFU structure. The season was capped by a 33-5 victory over Eastbourne 2nd XV in the Sussex Bowl final.

The 4th XV finished mid table in Sussex Two West league and made the final league of the Sussex Vase competition, losing 25-13 to East Grinstead 2nd XV.

The 5th XV secured the Sussex Three West league title by a 5 point margin. The past three seasons under captain Dean Widdows have seen the Mighty Vs take their place as another serious competitive side in the club's senior rugby set up.

Not to be outdone the Colts XV secured a league and cup double.

With strong performances by both mini and junior sides throughout the sections, Worthing can look back on a long, hard but successful season with much satisfaction, the award of the Sussex Champion Club Trophy setting the seal on our successes.

LAST TEN SEASONS

	Division	P	W	D	L	F	A	P.D.	Pts	Pos	Most Points	Most Tries
99-00	Lon 3SE	16	13	0	3	450	179	271	26	2		
00-01	Lon 3SE	18	14	1	3	429	145	284	29	3		
01-02	Lon 3SE	18	15	1	2	414	133	281	31	1p		
02-03	Lon 2S	22	18	0	4	532	222	310	36	1p		
03-04	Lon 1	22	12	0	10	523	404	119	24	6		
04-05	Lon 1	22	19	0	3	732	275	457	38	2		
05-06	Lon 1	22	9	2	11	517	464	53	20	6		
06-07	Lon 1	22	19	0	3	945	248	697	38	3		
07-08	Lon 1	22	19	0	3	770	237	533	38	2	Most Points	Most Tries
08-09	N3 S	26	8	1	17	471	698	-227	44	12	191 Ben Coulson	8 Ben Coulson

RECORDS SECTION
DIVISION FOUR SOUTH
(CURRENTLY NATIONAL LEAGUE THREE SOUTH)
Previously also Area League South & Division Five South

ROLL OF HONOUR

	CHAMPIONS	Runners-up	Nos of Clubs/Game		Leading Points Scorer
1987-88	Askeans	Sidcup	11/10	69	John Field (Askeans)
1988-89	Lydney	Havant	11/10	--	N/A
1989-90	Met Police	Clifton	11/10	83	Simon Harvey (Clifton)
1990-91	Redruth	Basingstoke	13/12	122	Melvin Badger (Weston)
1991-92	Havant	Basingstoke	13/12	129	Pete Russell (Havant)
1992-93	Sudbury	London Welsh	13/12	123	Steve Dyble (Sudbury)
1993-94	Reading	Lydney	13/12	133	Phil Belshaw (Reading)
1994-95	London Welsh	Lydney	13/12	119	Paul Thatcher (Weston-s-Mare)
1995-96	Lydney	Weston-s-Mare	13/12	176	Richard Perkins (Henley)
1996-97	Newbury	Henley	14/26	391	Nick Grecian (Newbury)
1997-98	Camberley	Henley	14/26	256	Rob Thirlby (Redruth)
1998-99	Bracknell	Esher	14/26	313	Jonathon Gregory (Esher)
99-2000	Esher	Penzance & Newlyn	14/26	351	John Gregory (Esher)
2000-01	Plymouth Albion	Launceston	14/26	336	Nat Saumi (Penzance & Newlyn)
2001-02	Penzance & Newlyn	Launceston	14/26	374	Nat Saumi (Penzance & Newlyn)
2002-03	Rosslyn Park	Lydney	14/26	374	Adam Westall (Lydney)
2003-04	Blackheath	Launceston	14/26	368	Derek Coates (Blackheath)
2004-05	Barking	Redruth	14/26	332	Adam Westall (Lydney)
2005-06	Cambridge	North Walsham	14/26	258	Andy Frost (Southend)
2006-07	Southend	Westcombe Park	14/26	335	Andy Frost (Southend)
2007-08	Mounts Bay	Cinderford	14/26	266	Lee Jarvis (Mounts Bay)
2008-09	London Scottish	Rosslyn Park	14/26	253	James Brown (Lon. Scottish)

RELEGATED CLUBS
87-88 - Streatham/Croyden
88-89 - Sidcup, Stroud, Ealing
89-90 - Salisbury
90-91 - Maidenhead, Cheltenham
91-92 - Sidcup, Ealing
92-93 - Thurrock
93-94 - Southend, Maidstone
94-95 - Sudbury, Basingstoke
95-96 - Camborne
96-97 - Berry Hill, Askeans, High Wycombe, Charlton Park
97-98 - None
98-99 - Havant
99-00 - Bridgwater, Norwich & Met. Police
00-01 - Basingstoke, Cheltenham, Reading & Weston-s-Mare
01-02 - Clifton, Cinderford
02-03 - Havant, Camberley
03-04 - Dings Crusaders, Basingstoke, Old Colfeians
04-05 - Weston-s-Mare, Tabard, Haywards Heath
05-06 - Reading, Bracknell
06-07 - Hertford, Old Patesians, Chinnor
07-08 - Clifton, North Walsham, Luton
08-09 - Chinnor, Havant

LONDON SCOTTISH - NATIONAL THREE SOUTH CHAMPIONS 2008-09
Photo James Hann

		MOST TRIES		MOST PENALTIES		MOST CONVERSIONS
87-88			13	John Field (Askeans)	9	John Field (Askeans)
88-89	7	Jon Willis (Redruth)				
89-90			15	Simon Harvey (Clifton)	10	Simon Harvey (Clifton)
90-91	8	Melvin Badger (Weston)	27	Rob Ashwoth (Havant)	16	Simon Blake (Redruth)
91-92	9	Will Knight (Havant)	24	Pete Russell (Havant)	23	Pete Russell (Havant)
92-93	12	Steve Titcombe (Sudbury)	25	Andy Holford (Lydney)	28	Mike Hamlin (London Welsh)
93-94			34	Phil Belshaw (Reading)		
94-95			31	Paul Thatcher (Weston)		
95-96	10	Richard Perkins (Henley) & Tommy Adams (Camborne)	28	Paul Thatcher (Weston) & Richard Larkins (Askeans)	27	Richard Perkins (Henley)
96-97	27	Brian Johnson (Newbury)	53	Nick Churchman (Tabard)	100	Nick Grecian (Newbury)
97-98	17	Rob Thirlby (Redruth)	51	James Shanahan (N Walsham)	48	Rob Thirlby (Redruth)
98-99	16	Nana Dontah (Esher) & Andy Carter (Met Police)	58	Jonathan Gregory (Esher)	52	Jonathan Gregory (Esher)
99-00	38	Richard Newton (Penzance & N)	59	Chris Atkinson (Plymouth)	78	Jonathan Gregory (Esher)
00-01	20	Dan Ward-Smith (Plymouth A.) & Victor Olonga (Penzance & N.)	46	Derek Coates (Westcombe P.)	67	Nat Saumi (Penzance & N.)
01-02	28	Richard Newton (Penzance & N)	64	Derek Coates (Westcombe P.)	91	Nat Saumi (Penzance & N.)
02-03	21	Andy Thorpe (N Walsham)	69	Adam Westall (Lydney)	77	Sam Howard (Rosslyn Park)
03-04	19	Gert De Kock (Westcombe Park)	78	Derek Coates (Blackheath)	63	Simon Porter (Launceston)
04-05	23	Cam Avery (Havant)	42	Neil Barella (Hertford)	62	Adam Westall (Lydney)
05-06	24	Tom Hayman (Westcombe Park)	46	James Cathcart (Reading)	63	Andrew Dickson (North Walsham)
06-07	32	Faapoloo Soolefai (Southend)	42	John Barnes (Clifton)	92	Andy Frost (Southend)
07-08	20	Owen Bruynseels (Ealing)	49	Richard Mahony (Rosslyn Park)	65	Lee Jarvis (Mounts Bay)
08-09	33	David Howells (Ealing)	53	Mark Davies (Lydney)	86	James Brown (Lon. Scottish)

411

DIVISION FOUR SOUTH

Constitution	11 87-88	11 88-89	11 89-90	13 90-91	13 91-92	13 92-93	13 93-94	13 94-95	13 95-96	14 96-97
Askeans	1p							t	8	14r
Barking								5	4	3
Basingstoke			8	2	2	5	11	13r		
Berry Hill						7	7	11	5	11r
Blackheath										
Bracknell										
Bridgwater & Albion										
Camberley									7	4
Camborne	4	3	4	4	6	4	4	8	13r	
Cambridge										
Canterbury										
Charlton Park										13r
Cheltenham	10	6	9	13r					6	5
Chinnor										
Cinderford										
Clifton				2p						
Dings Crusaders										
Ealing		9r		10	13r					
Esher										
Havant	5	2	5	8	1p					
Haywards Heath										
Henley								9	3	2
Hertford										
High Wycombe					5	8	9	10	10	12r
Launceston										
London Welsh				3	3	2	6	1p		
London Scottish										
Luton										
Lydney	3	1p				3	2	2	1p	
Maidenhead				12r						
Maidstone			10	11	8	12	13r			
Metropolitan Police			1p		10	9	10	7	12	7
Mounts Bay										
Newbury										1p
North Walsham				6	7	11	8	4	11	10
Norwich										
Old Colfeians										
Old Patesians										
Penzance & Newlyn										
Plymouth Albion										6
Reading							1p			
Redruth			4	3	1p					
Richmond										
Rosslyn Park										
Rugby Lions										
Salisbury	9	7	11r							
Sidcup	2	11r			12r					
Southend	7	8	7	9	11	6	12r			
Stroud	6	10r								
Streatham/Croydon	11r									
Sudbury	8	5	6	7	4	1p		12r		
Tabard							3	6	9	8
Thurrock							13r			
Westcombe Park										
Weston super Mare				5	9	10	5	3	2	9
Worthing										

412

YEAR BY YEAR RECORDS

14 97-98	14 98-99	14 99-00	14 00-01	14 01-02	14 02-03	14 03-04	14 04-05	14 05-06	14 06-07	14 07-08	14 08-09
3	4	6	4	10	8	5	1p		t	11	7
			13r		12	13r					
			9	7	3	1p					
	1p						t	14r			
8	10	12r						7	6	8	10
1p			t	12	14						
								1p			
									4	4	5
5	13	11	14r						14r		13r
				14r				10	8	2	
11	7	7	8	13r					11	12	
						12	8	8	9	6	6
										3	3
4	2	1p									
12	14r				13r		7	9	3	10	14r
						10	14r				
2p										t	9
							5	11	12r		
			2	2p		2p					
										5	1p
										14r	
			t	6	2p	t	4	4	5	7	11
14	5	14r									
											1p
7	3	3	6	3	4	3	3	2	7	13r	
	6	13r									
				11	9	14r					
				5	5	7	11	12	13r		
		2	3	1p							
13	12	4	1p								
			11r				6	13r			
9	11	5	5	8	7	4	2p				
											4
				t	1p		t	6	10	9	2
								Transferred from N3N			8
						6	10	5	1p		
6	8	8	10	9	10	11	13r				
		10	7	4	11	9	9	3	2po		
10	9	9	12r		6	8	12r				
											12

NATIONAL 2 SOUTH

DIVISION FOUR (SOUTH)   ALL TIME RECORDS

SEASON RECORDS

MOST PENALTIES

EVOLUTION OF RECORD

13	John Field	Askeans	1987-88
15	Simon Harvey	Clifton	1989-90
27	Rob Ashworth	Havant	1990-91
34	Phil Belshaw	Reading	1993-94
53	Nick Churchman	Tabard	1996-97
58	Jon Gregory	Esher	1998-99
59	Chris Atkinson	Plymouth	1999-00
64	Derek Coates	Westcombe Park	2001-02
69	Adam Westall	Lydney	2002-03
78	Derek Coates	Blackheath	2003-04

ALL-TIME RECORDS

78	Derek Coates	Blackheath	2003-04
69	Adam Westall	Lydney	2002-03
64	Derek Coates	Westcombe Park	2001-02
60	Matthew Townsend	Old Colfeians	2001-02
59	Chris Atkinson	Plymouth	1999-00
58	Jon Gregory	Esher	1998-99
53	Nick Churchman	Tabard	1996-97
53	Neil Coleman	Weston	1999-00
53	Mark Davies	Lydney	2008-09
51	James Shanahan	N Walsham	1997-98
50	Nick Edmonds	Bridgwater & A	1997-98
50	Jon Gregory	Esher	1999-00
50	Derek Coates	Westcombe Park	2002-03
49	Derek Coates	Westcombe Park	1999-00
49	Richard Mahony	Rosslyn Park	2007-08
46	Derek Coates	Westcombe Park	2000-01
46	James Cathcart	Reading	2005-06
45	Carson Russell	Bracknell	1998-99
45	Danny Sloman	Launceston	2000-01
45	Scott Martin	Redruth	2003-04

MOST DROP GOALS

EVOLUTION OF RECORD

2	Andy Perry	Havant	1987-88
6	Simon Harvey	Clifton	1989-90
10	Simon Cattermole	Weston-s-Mare	1996-97
11	Nick Edmonds	Bridgwater & Alb.	1997-98

ALL-TIME RECORDS

11	Nick Edmonds	Bridgwater & Alb.	1997-98
10	Simon Cattermole	Weston-s-Mare	1996-97
7	Bede Brown	Redruth	2000-01
6	Simon Harvey	Clifton	1989-90
6	James Shanahan	N Walsham	1997-98
6	Stewart Whitworth	Redruth	1999-00

MOST CONVERSIONS

EVOLUTION OF RECORD

9	John Field	Askeans	1987-88
10	Simon Harvey	Clifton	1989-90
16	Simon Blake	Redruth	1990-91
23	Pete Russell	Havant	1991-92
28	Mike Hamlin	London Welsh	1992-93
100	Nick Grecian	Newbury	1996-97

ALL-TIME RECORDS

100	Nick Grecian	Newbury	1996-97
97	Andy Frost	Southend	2006-07
91	Nat Saumi	Penzance & Newlyn	2001-02
86	James Brown	London Scottish	2008-09
78	Jon Gregory	Esher	1999-00
77	Sam Howard	Rosslyn Park	2002-03
67	Nat Saumi	Penzance & Newlyn	2000-01
67	James Whittingham	Westcombe Park	2006-07
65	Lee Jarvis	Mounts Bay	2007-08
63	Simon Porter	Launceston	2003-04
63	Andrew Dickson	North Walsham	2005-06
62	Derek Coates	Blackheath	2003-04
62	Adam Westall	Lydney	2004-05
59	Danny Sloman	Launceston	2000-01
57	Dafydd Lewis	Cambridge	2005-06
56	Jervis Manupenu	Bridgwater & Albion	2005-06
56	Ben Ward	Ealing	2008-09
56	Gert de Kock	Canterbury	2008-09
55	Nat Saumi	Penzance & Newlyn	1999-00
52	Jon Gregory	Esher	1998-99
52	Derek Coates	Westcombe Park	2001-02
51	Ngapaku Ngapaku	Havant	2006-07
51	Ben Ward	Ealing	2007-08
48	Robert Thirlby	Redruth	1997-98
48	Adam Westall	Lydney	2002-03
48	Andy Frost	Southend	2005-06
46	Steve Larkins	Redruth	2000-01
46	Ian Calder	Basingstoke	2002-03
45	Berend Vorster	Launceston	2001-02
42	Tom Barlow	Plymouth Albion	2000-01
41	Derek Coates	Westcombe Park	2002-03
41	Neil Barella	Hertford	2004-05
41	Matt Hart	Richmond	2008-09
40	Rob Colbourne	Tabard	2003-04
40	Daniol Trigg	Cinderford	2005-06
40	Tristan Roberts	Cinderford	2007-08

414

ALL TIME RECORDS DIVISION FOUR (SOUTH)

MOST POINTS

EVOLUTION OF RECORD
69	John Field	Askeans	1987-88
83	Simon Harvey	Clifton	1989-90
122	Melvin Badger	Weston-s-Mare	1990-91
129	Pete Russell	Havant	1991-92
133	Phil Belshaw	Reading	1993-94
176	Richard Perkins	Henley	1995-96
391	Nick Grecian	Newbury	1996-97

ALL-TIME RECORDS
391	Nick Grecian	Newbury	1996-97
374	Nat Saumi	Penzance & Newlyn	2001-02
373	Adam Westall	Lydney	2002-03
368	Derek Coates	Blackheath	2003-04
359	Sam Howard	Rosslyn Park	2002/03
351	Jon Gregory	Esher	1999-00
336	Nat Saumi	Penzance & Newlyn	2000-01
335	Andy Frost	Southend	2006-07
332	Adam Westall	Lydney	2004-05
326	Derek Coates	Westcombe Park	2001-02
313	Jonathan Gregory	Esher	1998-99
298	Neil Barella	Hertford	2004-05
288	Danny Sloman	Launceston	2000-01
274	Simon Porter	Launceston	2003-04
267	Derek Coates	Westcombe Park	2002/03
266	Lee Jarvis	Mounts Bay	2007-08
264	Nick Churchman	Tabard	1996-97
260	Chris Atkinson	Plymouth	1999-00
258	Andy Frost	Southen	2005-06
256	Rob Thirlby	Redruth	1997-98
255	Tom Barlow	Plymouth	2000-01
253	James Shanahan	North Walsham	1997-98
253	James Brown	London Scottish	2008-09
248	Nick Thomson	Barking	1996-97
248	Matthew Townsend	Old Colfeians	2001-02
245	Ian Calder	Basingstoke	2002-03
243	Derek Coates	Westcombe Park	1999-00
242	Nick Edmonds	Bridgwater & Albion	1997-98
239	Nick Churchman	Tabard	1997-98
238	James Whittingham	Westcombe Park	2006-07
236	Ben Montgomery	Barking	2004-05
232	Ben Ward	Ealing	2008-09
230	Neil Coleman	Weston	1999-00
229	Ian Calder	Basingstoke	2003-04
228	Jon Martin	Clifton	2000-01
227	James Cathcart	Reading	2005-06
224	Andrew Dickson	North Walsham	2005-06
223	Mark Slevin	Met. Police	1996-97
223	Gert de Kock	Canterbury	2008-09
223	Mark Davies	Lydney	2008-09
217	Justin Azzopardi	Barking	1998-99
217	Steve Larkins	Redruth	2001-02
216	Carson Russell	Bracknell	1998-99
215	Derek Coates	Westcombe Park	2000-01
215	Richard Mahony	Rosslyn Park	2007-08
213	Dafydd Lewis	Cambridge	2005-06
212	Ben Ward	Ealing	2007-08

MOST TRIES

EVOLUTION OF RECORD
7	John Willis	Redruth	1988-89
8	Melvin Badger	Weston-s-Mare	1990-91
9	Will Knight	Havant	1991-92
12	Steve Titcombe	Sudbury	1992-93
27	Brian Johnson	Newbury	1996-97
38	Richard Newton	Penzance & Newlyn	1999-00

ALL-TIME RECORDS
38	Richard Newton	Penzance & Newlyn	1999-00
33	David Howells	Ealing	2008-09
32	Faalapou Soolefai	Southend	2006-07
28	Richard Newton	Penzance & Newlyn	2001-02
27	Brian Johnson	Newbury	1996-97
25	Craig Davies	Newbury	1996-97
24	Victor Olonga	Penzance & Newlyn	1999-00
24	Tom Hayman	Westcombe Park	2005-06
23	Victor Olonga	Penzance & Newlyn	2001-02
23	Laka Waqanivere	Penzance & Newlyn	2001-02
23	Cam Avery	Havant	2004-05
22	Christoff Lombaard	Cambridge	2005-06
22	Sam Greenaway	Westcombe Park	2006-07
22	Michael Melford	Canterbury	2008-09
21	James Shanahan	North Walsham	1999-00
21	Andy Thorpe	North Walsham	2002-03
20	Victor Olonga	Penzance & Newlyn	2000-01
20	Dan Ward-Smith	Plymouth	2000-01
20	Mark Fatialofa	Launceston	2001-02
20	Lloyd Williams	Barking	2004-05
20	Andy Thorpe	North Walsham	2006-07
20	Gert De Koch	Canterbury	2006-07
20	Owen Bruynseels	Ealing	2007-08
19	Tom Holloway	Newbury	1996-97
19	Gert de Kock	Westcombe Park	2003-04
19	Nathan Pedley	Redruth	2004-05
19	Andy Macrea	Lydney	2004-05
19	Faapoloo Soolefai	Bridgwater	2005-06
19	Tom Hayman	Westcombe Park	2006-07
19	Chris McNeil	Cinderford	2007-08
18	Neil Barella	Hertford	2004-05
18	Andy Thorpe	North Walsham	2005-06
18	Rory Damant	London Scottish	2008-09
17	Robert Thirlby	Redruth	1997-98
17	Nat Saumi	Penzance & Newlyn	2000-01
17	Peter Redgrave	Penzance & Newlyn	2000-01
17	Marc Richards	Penzance & Newlyn	2001-02
17	Andy Thorpe	North Walsham	2003-04
17	Tom Johnson	Reading	2004-05
17	Sylvan Edwards	Dings Crusaders	2004-05
17	Adam Westall	Lydney	2004-05
17	Chris Green	Southend	2006-07

NATIONAL 2 SOUTH

DIVISION FOUR SOUTH ALL TIME RECORDS

TEAM RECORDS

Highest score:	136	Penzance & Newlyn 136 Met Police 6, 15.04.00
Highest aggregate:	142	as above
Highest score by a losing side:	41	Southend 42 Reading 41, 14.01.06
Highest scoring draw:	30	Chinnor v Dings Crusaders, 23.09.06
Most consecutive wins:	26	Plymouth Albion 2000-01
Most consecutive defeats:	28	Metropolitan Police 1998-99/1999-2000
Most points for in a season:	1170	Newbury 1996-97
Least points for in a season:	64	Maidstone 1989-90
Most points against in a season:	1308	Met Police 1999-2000
Least points against in a season:	61	Reading 1993-94
Most tries for in a season:	167	Newbury 1996-97
Most tries against in a season:	188	Met Police 1999-2000
Most conversions for in a season:	103	Newbury 1996-97
Most conversions against in a season:	95	Charlton Park 1996-97
Most penalties for in a season:	81	Blackheath 2003-04
Most penalties against in a season:	65	Plymouth Albion 1997-98
Most drop goals for in a season:	14	Bridgwater 1997-98
Most drop goals against in a season:	8	Metropolitan Police 1997-98

INDIVIDUAL RECORDS

Most points in a season:	385	Nick Grecian (Newbury) 1996-97
Most tries in a season:	38	Richard Newton (Penzance & Newlyn) 1999-00
Most conversions in a season:	96	Nick Grecian (Newbury) 1996-97
Most penalties in a season:	78	Derek Coates (Blackheath) 2003-2004
Most drop goals in a season:	11	Nick Edmonds (Bridgwater) 1997-98
Most points in a match:	42	Adam Westall, Haywards Heath v *Lydney* 12.3.05
Most tries in a match:	7	Richard Newton, *Penzance* v Met Police 15.4.00
		James O'Brien Old Patesians v Old Colfeians 27.3.04
Most conversions in a match:	13	Nat Saumi, *Penzance* v Met Police 15.4.00
Most penalties in a match:	7	Carson Russell, *Bracknell* v N Walsham 27.3.99
		Jon Gregory, *Esher* v Tabard 18.03.00
		Jon Griffin Blackheath v Redruth 14.12.02
		John Barnes Clifton v Lydney 21.10.06
		Kieron Davies Hertford v Rosslyn Park 30.09.06
Most drop goals in a match:	4	Simon Cattermole, *Weston-s-M.* v Berry Hill 16.11.96

NORTHERN DIVISION

WESTOE RFC - NORTH ONE CHAMPIONS 2008-09

NORTHERN

STRUCTURE

Level			
5			NATIONAL LEAGUE 3 NORTH
6		NORTH 1 EAST	
7	Durham & Northumberland 1		Yorkshire 1
8	Durham & Northumberland 2		Yorkshire 2
9	Durham & Northumberland 3		Yorkshire 3
10			Yorkshire 4
11			Yorkshire 5
12			Yorkshire 6

418

NORTHERN DIVISION
CONTENTS

Northern Division	Officials & League Secretaries	420
National League 3 North	08-09 League Table & 09-10 Fixture List	422
	Year by Year record - the last 10 years	423
	2009-10 Clubs	424
North 1 East	08-09 League table & 09-10 Fixture Grid	440
	2009-10 Clubs	441
North 1 West	08-09 League table & 09-10 Fixture Grid	446
	2009-10 Clubs	447
Other Northern	2008-09 League Tables	452
	2009-10 Fixture Grids	456
	Level 7-12 Clubs	462

A complete club index appears at the back of the book, showing which league each club is in for the 2009-10 season

DIVISION

2009-2010

	Level
NATIONAL LEAGUE 3 NORTH	5
NORTH 1 WEST	6
North Lancs & Cumbria — South Lancs & Cheshire 1	7
North Lancs 1 — Cumbria — South Lancs & Cheshire 2	8
North Lancs 2 — South Lancs & Cheshire 3	9

NORTHERN

419

NORTH OFFICIALS 2009-10

COMMITTEE Position

Mike Smith — Chairman / Hon Secretary
The Lowe, Wainstalls, Halifax, West Yorkshire HX2 7TR
Tel: 01422 882879 Mob: 07850 233019 Fax: 01422 882879 email: TheLowe@aol.com

Stephen McCafferty — RFU Competitions / Cheshire Rep
The Stanley Arms, Old Road, Anderton, Northwich, Cheshire. CW9 6AG
Tel: 01606 782371 (H) Mob: 07810 861185 email: stephenmccafferty@hotmail.com

Dave Thompson — Hon Treasurer / Durham Rep
12 Aldsworth Close, Springwell, Gateshead. NE9 7PG
Tel: 0191 416 9839 Mob: 07778 809125 email: dat_rugby@hotmail.com

Bill Scott — Fines Treasurer / Durham Rep
131 Kepier Chare, Crawcrook, Tyne & Wear NE40 4UY
Tel: 0191 413 6293 Mob: 0792 911 7261 email: billscott80@btinternet.com

Dudley Gibbs — Northumberland Rep
'Sandyford', Healey, Northumberland. NE44 6BA
Tel: 01434 682496 Fax: 01434 682019 Mob: 07766 117410 email: rugby@dudleygibbs.com

Terry Owen Smith — Northumberland Rep
3 Lindisfarne Rd, Alnwick, Northumberland NE66 1AU
Tel: 01665 602160 Mob: 07803 454377 email: terry@owensmith.f2s.com

Mike Brown — Yorkshire Rep
Holmroyd Nook Farm, 66, Deanhouse, Netherthong, Holmfirth. HD9 3UR
Tel: 05602436073 email: michaelbrown909@btinternet.com

David Clarke — Lancashire Rep
224 Billinge Road, Pemberton, Wigan, WN5 8HX
Tel: 01942 207771 (H) email: david.clarke51@yahoo.co.uk

Ken Potter — Lancashire Rep
109A Ormskirk Rd, Upholland, Lancs. WN8 0AL
Tel/Fax: 01695 624441 Mob: 07773 664065 email: Ken.potter@hotmail.co.uk

Mike Lord — Cheshire Rep
68 Hoole Road, Chester, Cheshire, CH2 3NL
Tel: 01244 312702 Mob: 07801 283506 Email: S33mjl@talktalk.net

Frank Sheppard — Cumbria Rep
74 Meadow Field, Gosforth, Cumbria, CA20 1HX
Tel: 01946 725327 email: Fjsheppard@aol.com

Ian Shovelton — Cumbria Rep
10 Buttermere Drive, Millom, Cumbria, LA18 4PL
Tel: 01229 773743 Mob: 07871 486617 email: Danshovelton1@aol.com

LEAGUE SECRETARIES

Terry Owen Smith — National 3 North
3 Lindisfarne Rd, Alnwick, Northumberland NE66 1AU
Tel: 01665 602160 Mob: 07803 454377 email: terry@owensmith.f2s.com

John Ker — North 1 East
4 Anlaby Close, Billingham, Cleveland, TS23 3RA
Tel: 01642 560536 Mob: 07842 119 664 email: john.ker@ntlworld.com

Ken Potter — North 1 West
109A Ormskirk Rd, Upholland, Lancs. WN8 0AL
Tel/Fax: 01695 624441 Mob: 07773 664065 email: Ken.potter@hotmail.co.uk

W. G. (Bill) Scott	**Durham Northumberland 1**

131 Kepier Chare, Crawcrook, Tyne & Wear NE40 4UY
Tel: 0191 413 6293   Mob: 0792 911 7261   email: billscott80@btinternet.com

Tony Brown	**Durham Northumberland 2**

22 Mill Crescent, Hebburn, Tyne & Wear NE31 1UQ
Tel: 0191 4693716   Mob: 07850 082791   email: robson-brown@supanet.com

Peter Spencer	**Durham Northumberland 3**

3 St. Lucia Close, Whitley Bay, NE26 3HT
Tel: 0191 252 4811   Mob: 07960 230606 (Sats)   email: ps002h5078@blueyonder.co.uk

Aiden Philips	**Yorkshire 1**

7 Thornhill Road, Steeton, Keighley, BD20 6SU
Tel: 01535 654125   Mob: 07931 737417   email: naresfield@talktalk.net

Bill Cooper	**Yorkshire 2**

Moorcroft, Lucy Hall Drive, Baildon, West Yorkshire BD17 5BG
Tel/Fax: 01274 584355   email: wfcooper1934@uk2.net

Ron Lewis	**Yorkshire 3**

17 Harewood Drive, Wrenthorpe, Wakefield, Yorkshire WF2 0DS
Tel: 01924 299874   email: ron.lws1@googlemail.com

Kathleen McNally	**Yorkshire 4**

28 Cherry Tree Road, Armthorpe, Doncaster, Yorks, DN3 2HP
Tel: 01302 834252   Mob: 07730 090135   email: kathmcnally@aol.com

Graham Mapplebeck	**Yorkshire 5**

46 Cranmore Crescent, Belle Isle, Leeds LS10 4AN
Tel/Fax: 0113 270 4935   email: gmapp1954@yahoo.co.uk

Anthony McNally	**Yorkshire 6**

28 Cherry Tree Road, Armthorpe, Doncaster, Yorks DN3 2HP
Tel: 01302 834252   Mob: 07734 022629   email: tonymacepes@aol.com

Mike Massey	**South Lancs Cheshire 1**

10 Laburnum Lane, Hale, Altrincham, Cheshire. WA15 0JR
Tel: 0161 928 2997   Mob: 07967 530019   email: masseysquip@tiscali.co.uk

Dave Clarke	**South Lancs Cheshire 2**

224 Billinge Road, Pemberton, Wigan WN5 9HX
Tel: 01942 207771   Mob: (Sat only) 07712 582423   email: david.clarke51@yahoo.co.uk

Mike Harrison	**South Lancs Cheshire 3**

439 Parrswood Rd, Didsbury, Manchester M20 5NE
Tel: 0161 445 9254   Mob: 0777 206 5305   Email: pe.Harrison@ntlworld.com

Ian Scott Brown	**North Lancs Cumbria**

3 New Street, Carleton in Craven, Skipton, North Yorkshire, BD23 3DS
Tel: 01756 701107   email: brownianscott@aol.com

Vic Thomas	**North Lancs 1**

5 Portree Close, Winton, Eccles, Manchester M30 8LX
Tel: 0161 788 7540   email: vicshe@supanet.com

Brian H. Stott	**North Lancs 2**

8 Barlea Avenue, New Moston, Manchester M40 3WL
Tel: 0161 682 3835 (H)   0161 947 3980 (B)   Mob 07974 141122   Email: leaguesec.bhstott@virgin.net

Ian Shovelton	**Cumbria**

10 Buttermere Drive, Millom, Cumbria, LA18 4PL
Tel: 01229 773773   Mob: 07871 486617   email: Danshovelton1@aol.com

NATIONAL LEAGUE THREE
NORTH

2008-09 LEAGUE TABLE (North 1)

		P	W	D	L	F	A	PD	Pts
1	Westoe	22	19	0	3	737	264	473	38
2	Hull	22	18	0	4	702	241	461	36
3	Morley	22	16	0	6	497	224	273	32
4	Sheffield Tigers	22	15	0	7	495	307	188	30
5	Birkenhead Park	22	14	1	7	370	328	42	29
6	Middlesbrough	22	11	0	11	477	421	56	22
7	West Hartlepool	22	9	0	13	356	420	-64	18
8	Stockport	22	8	0	14	416	520	-104	16
9	Beverley	22	8	0	14	311	425	-114	16
10	Cleckheaton	22	5	1	16	290	651	-361	11
11	West Park (St Helens)	22	5	0	17	273	599	-326	10
12	Darlington	22	3	0	19	245	769	-524	6

2009-10 FIXTURES GRID

	Beverley	Birkenhead Park	Chester	Cleckheaton	Darlington M.P.	Middlesbrough	Morley	Penrith	Rochdale	Rossendale	Sheffield Tigers	Stockport	West Hartlepool	West Park St. H.
Beverley		12/09	19/12	26/09	16/01	30/01	24/10	20/02	07/11	13/03	10/10	28/11	27/03	05/09
Birkenhead Park	12/12		26/09	16/01	10/10	24/10	20/02	07/11	13/03	28/11	30/01	27/03	05/09	19/09
Chester	19/09	09/01		10/10	30/01	20/02	07/11	13/03	28/11	27/03	24/10	05/09	12/12	03/10
Cleckheaton	09/01	03/10	23/01		24/10	07/11	13/03	28/11	27/03	05/09	20/02	12/12	19/09	17/10
Darlington M. P.	03/10	23/01	17/10	13/02		13/03	28/11	27/03	05/09	12/12	07/11	19/09	09/01	31/10
Middlesbrough	17/10	13/02	31/10	06/03	14/11		05/09	12/12	19/09	09/01	20/03	03/10	23/01	05/12
Morley	13/02	31/10	06/03	14/11	20/03	10/04		19/09	09/01	03/10	05/12	23/01	17/10	12/12
Penrith	31/10	06/03	14/11	20/03	05/12	12/09	19/12		03/10	23/01	10/04	17/10	13/02	09/01
Rochdale	06/03	14/11	20/03	05/12	10/04	19/12	26/09	16/01		17/10	12/09	13/02	31/10	23/01
Rossendale	14/11	20/03	05/12	10/04	12/09	26/09	16/01	10/10	30/01		19/12	31/10	06/03	13/02
Sheffield Tigers	23/01	17/10	13/02	31/10	06/03	28/11	27/03	05/09	12/12	19/09		09/01	03/10	14/11
Stockport	20/03	05/12	10/04	12/09	19/12	16/01	10/10	30/01	24/10	20/02	26/09		14/11	06/03
West Hartlepool	05/12	10/04	12/09	19/12	26/09	10/10	30/01	24/10	20/02	07/11	16/01	13/03		20/03
West Park (St H.)	10/04	19/12	16/01	30/01	20/02	27/03	12/09	26/09	10/10	24/10	13/03	07/11	28/11	

YEAR BY YEAR RECORD
THE LAST 10 YEARS

Nos. of Clubs/Games	99-00 12/22	00-01 12/22	01-02 12/22	02-03 12/22	03-04 12/22	04-05 12/22	05-06 12/22	06-07 12/22	07-08 12/22	08-09 12/22
Altrincham Kersal						8	4	6	12r	
Aspatria			8	9	11r					
Beverley								2po		9
Birkenhead Park				6	6	7	7	9	4	5
Blaydon	7	2								
Bradford & Bingley		4	3	10r		1p				
Broughton Park										
Caldy							9	1p		
Chester		7	5	4	7	5	8	11r		
Cleckheaton				3	2				8	10
Darlington			4	1p					9	12r
Darlington Mowden Park		1p								
Driffield	3	5	7	8	10r					
Halifax			1p							
Huddersfield				10	12r		5	4	2po	
Hull						3	6	7	5	2p/po
Hull Ionians	2	8	2		9	2				
Kendal								5	1p	
Liverpool St. H.						11r			10r	
Longton							10			
Macclesfield	6	4	6	2						
Middlesbrough	5	9	11r			9	11r		6	6
Morley				5	3	6	1p			3
New Brighton								12r		
Northern	10	12r								
Penrith								8	11r	
Preston G.						1p				
Sandal				12r						
Sheffield			6	9r		8	12r			
Sheffield Tigers									7	4
Stockport								10r		8
Stockton	9	11r								
Tynedale	1p									
Vale of Lune					5	10r				
Vestoe							3	3	3	1p
West Hartlepool				11r						7
West Park St. H.			3	7	4	4	2			11
Whitchurch							12r			
Widnes	12r									
Wigton	8	10	12r							
Winnington Park	11r									

BEVERLEY R.U.F.C.

President: David Holmes Tel: 01482 863899
Chairman: Malcolm Cunningham   Tel: 07802 348484
Treasurer: Tim Hebb Tel: 01482 882538
Club Secretary: Andrew Wilson, 3 Denton Street, Beverley, East Yorkshire HU17 0PX
Tel: 01482 874941   email: Andy.Wilson@birse.co.uk
Fixture Secretary: Rob Jenner, 42 Normandy Avenue, Beverley, E. Yorkshire HU17 8PE
Tel: (H) 01482 868 944. Mob. 07940 296114   email: Robert_Jenner@hotmail.com
Team Secretary: Chris Dexter Tel: 07852 141610
Junior Section Chairman: Andy Ellis   Tel: 07960 703743
Address: Beaver Park, Norwood, Beverley HU17 9HT   Tel: 01482 870 306
Directions: 1 mile from Town Centre on Hornsea Road, behind Lady le Gross pub.
Nearest BR station: Beverley   **Car Parking:** 150
Capacity: All uncovered standing   **Admission:** Matchday: £4.   **Membership:** £75
Clubhouse: Open Saturday & Sunday. Available for private hire. Contact Dave Kneeshaw Tel: 07836 264160 (M)
Club Shop: Open as Clubhouse. Contact Dave Holmes Tel: 07958 118620
Founded: 1959 as Longcroft Old Boys renamed Beverley RUFC 1965   **Nickname:** The Beavers
Training Nights: Tuesday & Thursday   **Colours:** Green, white & brown.   **Change colours:** White, green & brown
Programme: Size: A5   Pages: 12   Price: Free with admission.   **Website:** www.beverleyrufc.co.uk
Editor: John Nursey   Advertising: Dave Holmes   07958 118620

REVIEW OF THE SEASON 2008-09

Beverley after a year in the National Leagues returned to North One and for the first time in six years they were not promoted or relegated. They were promoted in four successive seasons from Yorkshire 2, Yorkshire 1, North Two Eat and North One before relegation last season.

So there second season in North One say them finish ninth, the season has by no means been a failure. It was nearly half over before they were able to field anything like a settled side and in the later months they have come back strongly to put together a string of good results. Had it not been for a couple of inexplicable lapses in recent weeks they would have finished several places higher.

At the AGM Chairman Malcolm Cunningham, in reviewing the season, paid tribute to Coaches James McKay and Junior Tupai who, together with skipper Dave Worrall stepped into the breach created when former coach Anthony Posa left the club immediately before the start of the season. His departure was compounded by Director of Rugby Graham Hodgson also leaving his post due to work and family commitments.

Despite these setbacks the 1st XV achieved all that was expected of it in the league programme, consolidating it's position in North 1 when many expected another relegation. They then capped of the season in magnificent style by reaching the final of the Yorkshire Cup.

At the end of the season they failed to become the first East Yorkshire side, still in existence, in 50 years to win the Yorkshire Cup when they were beaten 23-13 by the youngsters at Leeds Carnegie at Brantingham Park .

LAST TEN SEASONS

	Division	P	W	D	L	F	A	P.D.	Pts	Pos	Most Points	Most Tries
99-00	N E1	18	10	0	8	313	389	-76	20	5		
00-01	N 2E	*21	7	1	13	355	435	-80	15	9r		
01-02	Yorks 1	22	9	0	13	316	426	-110	18	9r		
02-03	Yorks 2	22	10	0	12	325	420	-95	20	6		
03-04	Yorks 2	22	20	0	2	706	225	481	40	1p		
04-05	Yorks 1	22	21	0	1	722	214	508	42	1p		
05-06	N 2E	22	19	0	3	671	211	460	38	2p/po		
06-07	North 1	22	16	0	6	493	371	122	32	2p/po		
07-08	N3 N	26	5	0	21	410	750	-340	30	14r	79 Philip De Boulay	10 Jade Gardiner
08-09	North 1	22	8	0	14	311	425	-114	16	9		

BIRKENHEAD PARK F.C.

President: Mark McNally   **Chairman:** Greg Casey   **Treasurer:** Elizabeth Briscoe
Administration Officer: Barry Fitzgerald, c/o the club.
Tel: 07873 766 397 (M) email: fitzjb@btinternet.com
Fixture Secretary: Barry Tilston, 40 Cornelius Drive, Pensby, Wirral, CH61 9PS
Tel 0151 648 2141   email: barry.tilston@tesco.net
Coaching Co-ordinator: John McNally, c/o club Tel: 07815 136487
Chairman of Youth Rugby: Joe McGowan, c/o the club
Tel: 07960 732576   email: jpmcg@postmaster.co.uk
Ground Address: The Upper Park, Park Road North, Birkenhead CH41 8AA
Tel: 0151 652 4646 (Clubhouse) 0151 653 6070 (Office) email: as Admin. Officer.
Capacity: 3000 uncovered standing. **Car Parking:** 40 in ground, good on road parking. **Admission:** Matchday £5, Season n/a
Nearest BR station: Birkenhead Park - 5 stops on Merseyrail u/ground from Liverpool Lime St.
Directions: M53 J1, follow signs for Birkenhead centre. Straight on at junction with church in centre, signed Birkenhead Park. Take 1st right after passing Aldi Supermarket (on right) into Park Road North. Club is on left.
Clubhouse: Weekdays 7-11pm, Sat. Noon-11pm, Sun. from Noon. Bar snacks available, pre-match lunches available if pre-booked with club office. Functions contact Secretary.   **Club Shop:** Online shop, see website
Programme: Size: A5   **Pages:** approx. 28   **Price:** with admission   **Editor:** Peter Greville   **Advertising:** contact editor.
Founded: 1871   **Nickname:** 'Park'   **Website:** www.birkenheadparkrugby.com
Colours: Red, white and blue hoops   **Change colours:** Black with red trim.   **Training Nights:** Tues. & Thur. 7pm

REVIEW OF THE SEASON 2008-09

Birkenhead Park enjoyed another good season in North 1 and they achieved their highest ever points total at this level (29) to finish in fifth place. Park proved to be strong contenders and they beat all the other sides in the division at least once apart from champions Westoe to prove their pedigree.

Park achieved the double over Darlington, West Park, West Hartlepool and Middlesbrough but a lack of consistency saw them miss out on the promotion places as they were left to rue a last minute defeat at Stockport, a draw at Cleckheaton and a narrow defeat at Beverley. Highlights were the away wins at Morley and Middlesbrough and the defeat of Hull at the Upper Park.

Hooker Chris Jones captained the side and was leading try scorer with just six tries compared to the remarkable 32 he notched the previous year. Full back Dave Hall had an excellent season and was named as the Player of the Year, he finished second in the North 1 kicking table and scored 212 points in all league and cup games. The return of centre Steven Dodd from Waterloo added class to the back division and winger Anthony Molloy showed considerable promise in his first season. Colin Campbell played with distinction in all three rows of the scrum and he along with prop Gareth Jones appeared in all 26 matches. Colt Joe Spencer also impressed after joining the side during the latter stages of the season.

Park just failed in their bid to retain the Cheshire Cup after an excellent contest in a repeat of last year's final against Macclesfield. Park fought back from an 18-0 deficit at half time but Macclesfield just held on to win 18-14 but only after a storming second half performance from Park. Park disappointed in the National Trophy losing at Newark at the first attempt.

Park will now take their place in the new National 3 North and look forward to renewing local rivalry with neighbours Chester as well as competing against other North West newcomers Rochdale and Rossendale and traditional rivals Halifax.

LAST TEN SEASONS

	Division	P	W	D	L	F	A	P.D.	Pts	Pos
99-00	NW 1	18	8	0	10	367	322	35	16	6
00-01	SL&C 1	22	20	0	2	762	222	540	40	1p
01-02	North 2W	22	19	0	3	690	290	400	38	1p
02-03	North 1	22	11	2	9	521	369	152	24	6
03-04	North 1	22	10	1	11	515	547	-32	21	6
04-05	North 1	22	10	0	12	484	524	-40	20	7
05-06	North 1	22	10	0	12	369	536	-167	20	7
06-07	North 1	22	9	0	13	388	463	-75	18	9
07-08	North 1	22	11	0	11	442	327	115	22	4
08-09	North 1	22	14	1	7	370	328	42	29	5

CHESTER R.F.C.

President: B Hayes   **Chairman:** P G Youdan   **Treasurer:** P Crompton   **Director of Rugby:** T Doig
Club Secretary: M J Dangerfield, Arran Cottage, Chapel Lane, Rossett LL12 0EE
Tel: 01244 570457   email: mike.dangerfield@oakbase.co.uk
Fixture Secretary: M Christmas, 9 Ash Bank, Hare Lane, Pipers Ash, Chester CH3 7EH
Tel: 01244 332212   email: crufcfixtures@aol.com
Sponsorship Manager: Lorenzo Mansutti   Tel. 07788 618845, mansutti@hotmail.co.uk
Youth Manager: J Armstrong   Tel: 01829 740527   email: jj.armstrong@btinternet.com
Squash Chairman: J Goodall   Tel: 01244 621626   email: johnnygoodall@tiscali.co.uk
Ground Address: Hare Lane, Littleton, Chester CH3 7DB   Tel: 01244 336017   Fax: 01244 332619   email: info@chester-rufc.com
Capacity: 2,000   Seating: 400   Covered: 499
Directions: From the A55 (Chester outer ring road) take the A51(Nantwich) turning and Hare Lane is the first left. From the M6, J18 or 19, you approach along the A51. Hare Lane is the last right before the A55 junction.
Car Parking: 500 spaces   **Nearest BR Station:** Chester   **Admission:** Matchday £4, Season £25
Clubhouse: Opening hours during the season - Mon-Thur 7-11pm, Sat 11-11, Sun 11-4.
Food is available. Available for private functions, contact Danielle Winter.
Club Shop: Open Tues & Thur 6.30-10pm, Sat 1-5pm, Sun 9-2pm. Contact Tim Doig/Lorenzo Mansutti
Founded: 1925   **Training Nights:** Tuesday & Thursday   **Website:** www.chester-rufc.com
Colours: Red shirts with black trim, black shorts   **Change colours:** Black shirts with red trim, black shorts
Programme: Size: A5   Pages: 16   Price: With admission   Editorial/Advertising: Lorenzo Mansutti as above

REVIEW OF THE SEASON 2008-09

The highs of the previous season, gaining promotion and winning the EDF Intermediate Cup, were going to be a very difficult act to follow for Chester. Having gained promotion out of North West 1 they found themselves in unfamiliar territory in Midlands 1 and with three away games out of the first four, life in the higher division was never going to be easy.

Chester's away form from the very start was indifferent to say the least and it was not until they visited Kettering in late October that they final recorded an away win and by a convincing margin. At home, however, it was a very different story and it wasn't until late March that they were final beaten by champions to be Broadstreet.

Their disastrous away form also included defeat in the Intermediate Cup, away to league rivals Malvern, although they did gain revenge two weeks later in the league.

Apart from Broadstreet all the rivals for the championship managed to either beat each other or lose to sides lower down in the league. This ensured that the play-off position was up for grabs until the final day, with four sides all in touching distance. With all the results going the right way Chester found themselves finishing in second and facing the long trip across the Pennines for the play-off game against Hull, a game that Chester found themselves losing to the better side.

With the first team achieving their highest ever league position, the second team followed suit achieving their highest finish in Miller League Premiership. Not to be outdone, the third team won promotion from their Miller League, having been relegated the season before. Chester's strong Junior section all competed for honours at many age levels.

LAST TEN SEASONS

	Division	P	W	D	L	F	A	P.D.	Pts	Pos
99-00	North 2	22	20	1	1	767	278	489	*39	2p
00-01	North 1	22	11	1	10	517	393	124	23	7
01-02	North 1	22	12	0	10	494	484	10	24	5
02-03	North 1	22	16	0	6	512	417	95	32	4
03-04	North 1	22	10	0	12	555	450	105	20	7
04-05	North 1	22	16	0	6	506	378	128	32	5
05-06	North 1	22	9	0	13	457	410	47	18	8
06-07	North 1	22	6	0	16	358	619	-261	12	11r
07-08	N 2W	22	19	2	1	747	225	522	40	1p
08-09	Mid 1	22	15	0	7	529	297	232	30	2

CLECKHEATON R.F.C.

Chairman: Steve Hutton Tel: 07860 250607 (M)
Treasurer: Keith Gatenby Tel: 01422 311628
Hon. Secretary: Mr Ian Johnson, 20, St Andrews Cres, Oakenshaw, Bradford BD12 7EL.
Tel: 01274-601043(H), secretary@cleckheatonrugbyclub.com
Fixture Secretary: Alan Bentley, 15 Sycamore Drive, Cleckheaton, W. Yorks BD19 6AP
Tel: 01274 869264, 07753 438042 (M) email: fixturesecretary@cleckheatonrugbyclub.com
Press Officer / Match Day Organisation: Alan Bentley
Programme Editor: Andrew Foster Tel: 01274 861345 email: programmeeditor@cleckheatonrugbyclub.com
Referee Coordinator – Alan Bentley as above
Head Coach: Dave Harrison   **Assistant Coach:** Pete Murphy
Ground Address: Cleckheaton Sports Club, Moorend, Cleckheaton BD19 3UD Tel. 01274 873410
Directions: From J 26 of the M62, take the A638 to Dewsbury and in 200 yds turn left into Cleckheaton Sports Club.
Capacity: 1500 inc 250 covered seating   **Admission prices:** Matchday: £5, members £4   **Season:** N/a
Nearest BR station - Dewsbury   **Car Parking:** 150 at ground
Clubhouse: Open Mon. - Fri. 7 - 11pm, Sat.& Sun. 12 noon - 11pm. Food available at weekends
Functions up to 150 formal, contact Irene Hall 01274-873041.
Founded: 1924   **Nickname:** 'Cleck'   **Training nights:** Tue. & Thur. eves.   **Website:** www.cleckheatonrugbyclub.com
Colours: Red & white hoops, black shorts, red socks with 2 white hoops.   **Change colours:** Black.
Programme: Size A5   **Pages**: 36   **Price**: with admission   **Editorial & Advertising:** Andrew Foster

REVIEW OF THE SEASON 2008-09

The squad assembled for Season 2008-09 had, for the first time at Cleck, a cosmopolitan feel about it. Three South Africans, a New Zealander, an Australian, and a Samoan, plus a local lad with an Italian name. Would this exotic mix blend with young and inexperienced players left at the end of the previous season work?

In the event the season started encouragingly with two narrow defeats, before the first win against Beverley. Then came the multi – talented, and even more exotic, Hull. This was a reality check with a comprehensive defeat after only being down by four points at the break. However, the team bounced back with good spell up to Christmas, including a last minute two point loss to the eventual League winners Westoe, after leading for the entire second half, and a home victory against arch rivals Morley, meaning a mid-table place looked secure.

This season the weather meant that the Christmas break was longer than usual. When play resumed at the end of January the squad had a totally different feel about it. The overseas contingent had gradually drifted away and with them, went the confidence that had been increasingly evident.

Cleck would start games encouragingly but as soon as the opposition scored, however fortuitously, the heads went down and frustration went up, hence an inordinate number of yellow cards, and games they should have won were lost. Defeats to teams that had been propping up the table all season were especially disappointing, when the experience and potential ability of the sides fielded by Cleck were viewed in context. Relegation was avoided, but only just, and the fact that 38 players were used on 1st XV duty illustrates the revolving door of selection and availability.

The non-availability syndrome seriously affected the rest of the senior sides fielded by Cleck post Christmas, the second string, the Kestrels, folded, although the 3rd and 4th XVs continued to function and thrive in their inimitable and effective manner.

LAST TEN SEASONS

	Division	P	W	D	L	F	A	P.D.	Pts	Pos
99-00	North E2	18	12	0	6	416	198	218	24	2
00-01	Yorks 1	22	21	0	1	613	197	416	42	1p
01-02	North 2E	22	18	2	2	698	293	405	38	1p
02-03	North 1	22	16	0	6	592	413	179	32	3
03-04	North 1	22	19	0	3	725	393	332	38	2p*
04-05	N3N	26	10	0	16	458	646	-188	51	11
05-06	N3N	26	11	0	15	476	550	-74	*53	10
06-07	N3N	26	5	2	19	381	674	-293	32	13r
07-08	North 1	22	7	2	13	367	525	-158	16	8
08-09	North 1	22	5	1	16	290	651	-361	11	10

As did the Junior – Mini section, fielding teams all the way through from U7's to U16's. The fact that the Section took five coaches full of players and supporters to the sea–side at Bridlington in their end of season away day fixture, is evidence that rugby will continue to flourish at Cleckheaton RUFC in seasons to come.

DARLINGTON MOWDEN PARK R.F.C.

President: Robert Wilson   **Chairman:** John Widdall   **Chairman of Rugby:** Mike Keeligan
Hon. Secretary & Senior Coach: Kevin Robinson Tel: 01642 783985 Mob: 07977 409324 email: info@dmprfc.com
Hon. Treasurer: John Ritchie Tel: 01325 483063 Mob: 07913 387147 email: ciacia@hotmail.co.uk
Fixture Secretary: Trevor Alley
1ST XV Manager: Gus Miller Tel: 07976 586974 (M) email: gus.miller64@ntlworld.com
1ST XV Coach: Peter Taylor Tel: 07811 954907
Ground Address: 22 Yiewslew Drive, Darlington, Co. Durham DL3 9XS Tel: 01325 465932 email: info@dmprfc.com
Capacity: 1500   Seated: 300   Covered: 300   **Website:** www.dmprfc.com
Directions From the A1 (M) follow A66 (M). At the 2nd r'about, take the first exit (signposted Barnard Castle) and turn left at next r'about on to A67 Barnard Castle Road. Just before the 40 mph sign (half mile) turn right into Edinburgh Drive past the school on the left. Continue some way until you come to the 'Model T' pub and the shopping precinct. Yiewsley Drive is on the left just before the bend.   **Car Parking:** 68 (tarmac) plus grass overspill
Nearest BR Station: Darlington - Victoria Rd, Darlington DL1 4AA. Tel: 0845 7484750. Approx 3 miles away.
Admission: Matchday (incl. prog.) Adults: £5, Concessions £4, under 16 £2   Season Ticket £60
Clubhouse: Open 6.30 - 11.00pm Snacks available on match days only. Contact Stuart at the club
Functions / Private Hire: Contact Geoff Chandler 07778 215437   **Club Shop**: Enquire at club or via website.
Founded: 1946 RFU Membership 1950   **Colours:** Navy blue/white shirts, navy blue shirts, navy blue/white socks
Change colours: Maroon shirt, navy blue shorts, maroon socks   **Training Nights:** Tuesday & Thursday 19.00-20.30
Programme: Size: A5   Price: £1   Pages: 32 + 4 page inset   Advertising: Contact Graham Sykes 07717 311174

REVIEW OF THE SEASON 2008-09

After the heroics of the previous season, when promotion was so narrowly missed at Cinderford, the 2008-09 campaign was always going to be tough going and so it proved. The off-season began with an almost total rebuild of the team, as some fifteen senior players had decided to move on in various directions. This gave the new management team, under the direction of Chairman of Rugby, Mike Keeligan, assisted by Kevin Robinson, Gus Miller and 1st xv Coach Peter Taylor obvious initial problems, but once new recruits were welcomed and added to a nucleus of senior stalwarts, the makings of a side capable of competing in the league, came together.

Unfortunately, a good team takes time to evolve and that time was in short supply against the well-established sides of National League Three (North), as we quickly fell behind in our attempts to find a settled side. Losses soon mounted and our league position rarely changed during the course of the season. We had the unenviable title of being 'losing bonus point kings', as many of our losses were by the smallest of margins, which was no consolation, but proved that the squad assembled were not far away.

At one stage, towards the latter part of the season, we did establish a settled side and began to string together some decent results, giving a glimmer of hope. But it was all too late, as we joined Halifax RFC in the drop. Many congratulations to Nuneaton RFC, who were by far the best side in the league.

Due to the reshuffling of the leagues, we find ourselves relegated to…….. National League Three (North)……… funny old game isn't it!

On a sad note, all at the club were deeply saddened by the death of our fixture secretary Ted Irons, who will be greatly missed.

LAST TEN SEASONS

	Division	P	W	D	L	F	A	P.D.	Pts	Pos	Most Points	Most Tries
99-00	North 2	22	21	0	1	893	277	616	42	1p	224 Kevin Oliphant	21 Mick Kent
00-01	North1	20	20	0	0	719	163	556	40	1p	171 Kevin Oliphant	17 Mark Bedworth
01-02	N3 N	26	14	1	11	583	587	-4	27*	6	116 Kevin Oliphant	8 Kevin McCallum
02-03	N3 N	26	14	0	12	688	491	197	28	5	254 Mark Bedworth	13 P Kelekolio
03-04	N3 N	26	16	0	10	602	439	163	32	3	135 Mark Bedworth	13 Andrew Foreman & Iain Dixon
04-05	N3 N	26	12	1	13	505	531	-26	61	7	168 Mark Bedworth	8 Mark Bedworth
05-06	N3 N	26	10	1	15	472	578	-106	52	11	66 Iain Dixon	9 Pieter Booysen
06-07	N3 N	26	12	2	12	570	629	-59	62	8	124 Anthony Mellalieu	9 Lewis Farrar
07-08	N3 N	26	17	0	9	721	494	227	83	2	188 Jon Benson	11 James Clark
08-09	N3 N	26	6	1	19	470	692	-222	38	13r	138 Jon Benson	8 Martin Lithgow, Adam McKenzie

MIDDLESBROUGH R.U.F.C.

President: Keith Bircham   **Chairman**: Mike Wright   **Treasurer:** Richard Ward
Secretary: Don Brydon, 20 Westwood Avenue, Linthorpe, Middlesbrough, TS5 5PY
Tel & Fax: 01642 819954   Mob: 07817 211942   email: brydon@ts55py.fsnet.co.uk
Fixture Secretary: E R Scott, 7 Lambfield Way, Ingleby Barwick, Stockton-on-Tees, TS17 5BF
Tel (H) 01642 761386; (M) 07894 422 644 & 0777 202 5773
email eddie.scott@hotmail.co.uk & eddie.scott@sata.com
Match Secretary: Andy Murray, 19 Cattistock Close, Guisborough, TS14 7NL
Tel: 01287 637803   email: a.murray14@ntlworld.com
Director of Rugby: Colin McNeill   **Commercial Secretary:** Walter Hibbert
Coaching Co-ordinator: Bernie Coyne   **Press Officer:** Mike Read 01609 883525
Volunteer Co-ordinator: Paul Johnson

Ground address: Acklam Park, Green Lane, Acklam, Middlesborough TS5 7SL   Tel: 01642 818 567
Directions: From A19 north/south, take A1130 exit to Middlesbrough/Acklam and first exit (left fork) from mini roundabout. At the bollards turn right onto Croft Avenue, then at lights go straight across onto Green Lane. Acklam Park is 600m on right.
Capacity: 800   Covered Seating: 200   **Parking**: 150   **Nearest BR Station:** Middlesbrough
Admission: Matchday £5 incl prog.   **Clubhouse**: open from 5pm every evening, Thur and Fri lunchtime, all day Saturday and Sunday. Food available Sat & Sun lunch. Private parties catered for contact Keith Bircham (Treasurer)
Club Shop: Open training nights, Sat & Sun mornings. Contact Keith Bircham (Treasurer)
Programme: Size: A5   Pages: 24   Price: with admission   Editor: Don Brydon (Sec.) Advertsing: Walter Hibbert
Founded: 1872   **Website**: www.middlesbroughrufc.co.uk   **Training Nights:** Tuesday and Thursday
Nickname: Boro   **Colours**: Maroon shirts with gold hoops, maroon shorts   **Change Colours**: White

REVIEW OF THE SEASON 2008-09

Prior to the start of the season we lost several players for a variety of reasons, and then during the season suffered long term injuries to others. This meant that resources were stretched to the limit. Fortunately we had a Colts squad of quite exceptional ability, and although the intention was always to introduce some of them to first team rugby, we hadn't envisaged the tremendous impact they would make. Impressively 15 Colts made first team appearances and at some time during the season every position was filled by a Colt. The fast and adventurous style of rugby played by these young men resulted in the team scoring more points and conceding fewer than last season. Far from being a season of consolidation it was one of regeneration, with the promise of more to come.

This success has been repeated throughout the club, with the second team topping their division in the CANDY league, the third team achieving a momentous treble for the second consecutive year, winning two leagues and the North Yorkshire KO Trophy, and a fourth team again playing regularly fixtures. The Colts had a very successful year, winning the Yorkshire League, the U19 'Cock o' the North' Cup and losing the semi final of the National Cup to the eventual winners. Middlesbrough Colts played for the North of England, Yorkshire, Durham, Scottish Exiles, the Independent Schools Barbarians and five were selected for the Yorkshire Terriers summer tour to New Zealand.

Our Junior Section also grows from strength to strength, with the highlight being the return of our U13s with the Yorkshire Cup before the first team kicked off in their game against the Wooden Spoon Anti Assassins to commemorate the official opening of our fabulous new clubhouse. A fitting end to a successful season.

LAST TEN SEASONS

	Division	P	W	D	L	F	A	P.D.	Pts	Pos
99-00	North 1	22	12	0	10	443	483	-40	24	5
00-01	North 1	21	8	1	12	472	402	70	15(-2)	9
01-02	North 1	22	4	1	17	393	619	-226	9	9r
02-03	North 2E	22	10	1	11	461	349	112	21	7
03-04	North 2E	22	16	2	4	564	310	254	34	2p*
04-05	North 1	22	7	0	15	429	517	-88	14	9
05-06	North 1	22	7	0	15	360	510	-150	14	11r
06-07	North 2E	22	21	0	1	803	256	547	42	1p
07-08	North 1	22	9	0	13	421	448	-27	18	6
08-09	North 1	22	11	0	11	477	421	56	22	6

MORLEY R.F.C.

President: David Bradshaw
Chairman: David Bradshaw Tel: 0113 2520412   **Treasurer:** Mark Earnshaw
Secretary: Dennis Elam   26 The Roundway, Morley Leeds LS27 0JS   Tel /Fax 0113 252 4248 (H)
Tel: 0113 201 2266 (B)   Fax 0113 201 2268 (B) email: dennis.elam@btinternet.com
Chairman of Rugby: Mr. John Firth Tel: 07730 116937   **Head Coach:** Peter Seabourne Tel: 07866 263847
Fixture Secretary: Mr. John Firth 07730 116937 / Mr. Mick Coates 0113 2525825   **Programme Editor:** tbc
Ground Address: Morley RFC, Scatcherd Lane, Morley, West Yorkshire LS27 0JJ
Tel.: 0113 253 3487 e-mail: dennis.elam@btinternet.com
Capacity: 2,899   Seated: 499   Covered: 800
Directions: From West: M62 J27 take M621/A650 towards Wakefield for 1.2 miles turn left St. Andrews Ave. Ground 0.3 miles on left. From other directions: Leave M62 J28 follow A650 towards Bradford for 1.7 miles, turn right into St Andrews Ave.   **Nearest BR Station:** Morley Low Station   **Car Parking:** 110 in & around ground
Admission: Season: Adult £50   Matchday: Adults £6, Children/OAPs £3
Clubhouse: Mon-Fri 7-11, Sat 12-11, Sun 12-4.30 & 8-11. Three bars with snacks & bar meals available.
Functions: Up to 200 Contact Bar Manager 0113 253 3487
Club Shop: Open matchdays & training nights. Contact Shop Manager 0113 253 3487
Founded: 1878   **Colours**: Maroon & white quarters   **Change colours:** Cambridge blue.
Training Nights: Tuesday & Thursday   **Website**: www.morleyrfc.co.uk
Programme: Size: A5   Pages: 16   Price: with admission

REVIEW OF THE SEASON 2008-09

With the departure of 17 players from the first team squad, Morley RFC knew they were in for a tough time following their relegation to North 1. Although brave words were spoken about a "Top 4 spot", the overriding worry was a second relegation. The departure of so many experienced players and the disappearance of the bulk of the second team through over reliance on the local university led to a very small squad at the start of 2008-9. The positive side to the departures was that those who stayed played with a passion and spirit not seen the previous year.

The season started well with a narrow win away to Stockport, thereby equalising the number of away victories of the previous season. Despite losing at home to Birkenhead Park through lack of experience, it was clear by the end of October that Morley were not relegation candidates. November included defeats by Westoe and Hull showing that promotion was unlikely and probably unwelcome. The former battered and bullied Morley into defeat; the latter won due to South Sea Islanders' class. December confirmed the feeling with defeats at Sheffield Tigers and at Cleckheaton. This latter match was the worst display and low point of the season, showing the importance of spirit and attitude.

The final 4 months showed Morley lose only one more match – away to promoted Hull. Again this turned on a moment of class from Vaikona. The highlights being a victory away to Birkenhead Park, revenge at home with a 40-5 victory over Cleckheaton and a hard won battle with Champions Westoe in one of the most thrilling matches seen at Scatcherd Lane for many a season. In a tense, thrilling match in which Westoe played their full part, Sean Burke's try was arguably the best try seen at Scatcherd Lane for over 20 years.

With 6 out of the 7 Officers of the club standing down next season, 2009-10 will be a season of change as Morley seek to build on the "One Club" philosophy. Two age groups at Colts level and a return of the Cavaliers will hopefully increase the strength in depth. The thirds will add their considerable contribution to rugby, the bar and life in general. The club recognise the importance of the Juniors in the building of a community club and were very pleased to have received the RFU Seal of Approval.

The new season brings opportunities to make new friends at Penrith, Rochdale and Rossington, whilst renewing acquaintances with Chester and Darlington MP but sadly not with Halifax. As financial realities hit hard at national and local clubs, players will chose clubs for benefits other than cash and Morley are in a good position to consolidate and move forward. The majority of players are staying, more are available from the Colts and we hope to introduce a few new players who share our philosophy of rugby. Although we may struggle against clubs with "Sugar Daddies", Morley hope to compete at the top end of the table, to have fun doing it and to live within our means.

LAST TEN SEASONS

	Division	P	W	D	L	F	A	P.D.	Pts	Pos
99-00	JN2N	26	12	1	13	611	547	64	25	7
00-01	N3N	*25	8	0	17	468	720	-252	16	11
01-02	N3N	26	8	1	17	541	600	-59	17	12r
02-03	North 1	22	13	0	9	397	378	19	26	5
03-04	North 1	22	15	1	6	455	395	60	31	3
04-05	North 1	22	12	0	10	415	397	18	24	6
05-06	North 1	22	18	2	2	708	268	440	38	1p
06-07	N3 N	26	13	1	12	558	558	0	68	6
07-08	N3 N	26	8	3	15	446	568	-122	46	12r
08-09	North 1	22	16	0	6	497	224	273	32	3

PENRITH R.F.C.

President: Keith Davis Tel: 01768 866089
Treasurer: Chris Lilley
Chairman of Rugby: Stuart Mills Tel: 01768 898616   email: white-ox@btconnect.com
Club Secretary: Ian Davidson, 3 Coldsprings Court, Penrith, Cumbria CA11 8EX
Tel: (H) 01768 863151 email: secretary@penrithrufc.org.uk
Fixture Secretary: Willie Mounsey, The Luham, Edenhall, Penrith, Cumbria CA11 8TA Tel: (H) 01768 881202
Coaches: Mark Bowman, Keith Robinson
Team Managers: Colin Titterington (League Contact),4 Orchard Grove, Newton Reigny, Penrith CA11 0AS
Tel 01768 890354 (H), 01768 863594 (W)
Ian Thompson, 5 Pear Tree Way, High Carleton, Penrith CA11 8WA Tel: 01768 864965 (H)
Director of Rugby: Nigel Beaty,9 Beckside,Penrith CA11 8RW.Tel 01768 899655(H), 07793 121104
Press Officer: Mike Sanderson Tel: 01768 352988 (H) 01768 351324 (W)
Ground Address: Winters Park, Penrith, Cumbria CA11 8RG
Tel: 01768 863151 or 863462 email:rugby@penrithrufc.org.uk   **Website**: www.penrithrufc.org.uk
Directions: M6 J40, A66 east for 0.5 mile, then A686 east for 0.5 mile down hill past Police HQ on right and the club is on the left going back up hill.
Capacity: 2000 Covered Seating: 200 **Car Parking:** 350 spaces + 3 dedicated bus areas.   **Nearest BR station:** Penrith
Clubhouse: open every day with various commercial, social & sporting activities. In-house caterers provide for evry occasion. Full disabled access. Contact Stewardess Caren Bainbrdge 01768 863462.
Club Shop: Club merchandise is available from Richard Ellwood (Sat.) or Karen Mounsey (Sun.)
Programme: Size: A5   Price: With admission.   Advertising: Richard Ellwood 01768 863637 (W)
Founded: 1882.   **Colours**: Myrtle green & white hoops, white shorts   **Change Colours:** Dark & light blue panels.

LAST TEN SEASONS

	Division	P	W	D	L	F	A	P.D.	Pts	Pos
99-00	N W1	18	9	0	9	313	287	26	18	5
00-01	N2 W	*16	6	0	10	196	282	-86	12	11r
01-02	NL&C	22	15	1	6	616	212	404	31	3
02-03	NL&C	22	18	1	3	573	168	405	37	2p
03-04	N2 W	22	10	1	11	306	404	-98	21	8
04-05	N2 W	22	16	0	6	622	296	326	32	3
05-06	N2 E	22	20	0	2	657	209	448	40	1p
06-07	North 1	22	10	0	12	379	470	-91	20	8
07-08	North 1	22	7	0	15	390	539	-149	14	11r
08-09	N2 E	22	17	0	5	706	373	333	34	1p

ROCHDALE R.U.F.C.

President: Mrs. Wendy Sunderland **Chairman:** Mr. Michael Holden
Treasurer: Mr. Chris Collins, 38 Greenview Drive, Rochdale, OL11 5YQ
Tel: 07714 430422   email: cj.collins@virgin.net
Secretary: Mr Tim Taylor, 10 Pargate Chase, Rochdale, OL11 5DZ
Tel: 01706 345971 (H) 07770 854982 (M) 0161 214 5001 (W)   email: tmst@btopenworld.com
Fixture Secretary: Mr Mike Deasey, 405 Shawclough Road, Rochdale, OL12 7HR
Tel: 07887 580043 (M) 01706 693500 (W)   email: mike.deasey@eu.sunchem.com
Team Secretary: as Fixture Secretary   **Director of Rugby:** Mick Gould
Ground Address: Moorgate Avenue, Bamford, Rochdale, OL11 5LU
Tel.: 01706 646863   email: club@rrufc.org
Directions: M62 J20 - Follow A627M to Rochdale. At the end of the motorway keep left for town centre. At next set of traffic lights (Tesco on left) go straight through onto the B6452 to Blackburn. Down and up the hill to traffic lights. Turn left, the Club is third right Moorgate Avenue. Club is at the top of the avenue.
Capacity: All uncovered standing   **Admission:** Matchday £3
Nearest BR station: Rochdale   **Car Parking:** 120+ spaces at club.
Formed: 1921   **Website:** www. rrufc.org
Colours: Maroon & white hoops   **Training Nights:** Tuesday & Thursday

REVIEW OF THE SEASON 2008-09

The season turned out to be very competitive with almost any side being able to win against any other.

Rochdale had a bright start with notable early wins against a strong Rossendale team (30 – 5) and Wilmslow (50 – 13). Most other games were hard fought up front with the well organised Rochdale backs (aided by a mobile back row) often having the edge to win these games.

Our three quarter line frequently contained three teenagers and eighteen years old Phil Cowburn was top try scorer with 20 tries. Our 'little General' at out half, Steven Collins ended as top scorer with 202 league points and had the distinction of being selected by County Champions Lancashire, coming on as second half substitute against Warwickshire and scoring a try.

An indication of the tight nature of the league was shown in consecutive games. In the first, against bottom club Blackburn, we had to fight hard to come from behind in the second half to secure a narrow victory. In the next game we travelled to the then top side Altrincham Kersal and played some excellent rugby to win 35 – 18.

The crucial game was the three times postponed game at Rossendale where we fronted their powerful pack on a narrow pitch to end up narrowly in front by 22 – 20 which gave us the North 2 West championship. This takes us to the highest level ever in our history even though we maintain our strictly amateur, family ethos.

In the Lancashire Trophy we struggled to find anyone who would play us. Luckily Vale of Lune turned up for the Final where after opening an early 14 point lead we were pressurised by Vale but finished in style to win 21 – 5 and clinch a League and Cup double.

LAST TEN SEASONS

	Division	P	W	D	L	F	A	P.D.	Pts	Pos
99-00	NW3	18	17	0	1	609	118	491	34	1
00-01	NL/C	*18	12	1	5	365	219	146	25	3
01-02	NL/C	*19	17	1	1	493	201	292	35	1p
02-03	N2 W	22	15	1	6	449	358	91	31	2
03-04	N2 W	22	6	1	15	333	462	-129	13	11r
04-05	SL/C	22	18	1	3	639	185	454	37	1p
05-06	N2 W	22	14	1	7	532	307	225	29	3
06-07	N2 E	22	10	2	10	368	384	-16	22	6
07-08	N2 W	22	11	1	10	430	363	67	23	6
08-09	N2 W	22	17	0	5	502	335	167	34	1p

432

ROSSENDALE R.U.F.C.

President: Francis Jelly **Chairman:** Nick Ingham Tel: 07774 284700 (M)
Hon Sec: Alec Graham 636 Newchurch Road Rossendale Lancs. BB4 9HG
Tel: 01282 855400   email: a.graham@sjlaw.co.uk
Fixtures Sec: Terence Kelly 111 Broadway Haslingden Rossendale Lancs. BB4 4EH
Tel: (H) 01706 217361 (M) 07967 020195 email: terencekelly@ktdinternet.com
Director of Rugby: Simon Bond Tel: 07719 363911
Senior section: David Wood Tel: 07968 944585
Ladies section: Bryn Clement Tel: 07779 323963
Junior section: Jim Rylance Tel: 07828 937851

Ground Address: Marl Pits Sports Centre, Newchurch Road, Rossendale, Lancs. BB4 7SN
Clubhouse: 01706 229152   email: info@rossendalerugby.co.uk
Directions: A56 onto Newchurch Road at the market. Ground 1 mile up on the left.
Nearest BR station: Burnley   **Car Parking:** 100 spaces
Capacity: Unlimited uncovered standing   **Admission:** £4 by programme
Clubhouse: Open Tuesday & Thursday 18:00 - 23:00, Friday 17:30 - Close, Saturday 11:30 - Close, Sunday 10:00 - 20:00
Founded: 1969   **Website:** www.rossendalerugby.co.uk
Colours: Maroon & white   **Change colours:** Yellow and green   **Training Nights**: (Seniors) 6.45 for 7pm

LAST TEN SEASONS

	Division	P	W	D	L	F	A	P.D.	Pts	Pos
99-00	North W3	18	11	1	6	312	182	130	23	5
00-01	N Lancs/C*19	11	1	7	341	215	126	23	5
01-02	N Lancs/C*21	12	0	9	419	301	118	24	5
02-03	N Lancs/C*21	12	0	9	420	375	45	24	6
03-04	N Lancs/C	22	18	0	4	576	246	330	36	2
04-05	N Lancs/C*21	16	0	5	466	211	255	32	1p
05-06	North 2W*21	3	1	17	235	637	-402	7	11
06-07	N Lancs/C	22	9	0	13	313	476	-163	18	8
07-08	N Lancs/C	20	17	0	3	618	169	449	34	2p/po
08-09	North 2W	22	14	1	7	407	308	99	29	2p/po

ROCHDALE 2008-09

SHEFFIELD TIGERS R.U.F.C.

Chairman: John Joel   Tel: 0114 2663552
Treasurer: Mike Hewitt   e-mail:g4ayo@aol.co.uk
Club Secretary: Alick Bush, 210 Bradway Road, Sheffield, South Yorkshire, S17 4PE
Tel: (H) 0114 236 1129, (M) 07967 475 588, (W) 0114 271 6962, email: alick.bush@shsc.nhs.uk
Fixtures Secretary: Brett Speddings, 134 Green Oak Road, Sheffield, S17 4FS
(H) 0114 236 1021, (M) 07794 323721, (W) 0114 294 3048, email: spedz@sky.com
Director Of Rugby: Richard Senior   Tel: (M) 07841 460217
Ground Address: Dore Moor, Hathersage Road, Sheffield, S17 3AB
Tel: 0114 236 0075   email: tigers@sheffieldtigers.co.uk

Directions: Leave M1 at Junction 33 and head for Sheffield City Centre. Turn left onto the Ring road (A6102). Follow the Ring road for 4-5 miles until you come to the Meadowhead roundabout. Straight across and turn right after about 100m (signed for Castleton). At the bottom of the hill, at the roundabout, turn left. Go through the next set of lights (at Beauchief Hotel), follow the road uphill for a mile, bending left, until you come to a T Junction. Turn left (onto the A625 to Hathersage). After a mile go past the Dore Moor Inn on the right and the ground is on the right after 200 yards.

Nearest BR Station: Sheffield   **Car Parking:** 80 spaces at ground
Capacity: 500 uncovered standing; 80 uncovered seats   **Admission:** £5 incl. programme.
Clubhouse: Open training eves, match days & Sun am. Food is available. Clubhouse available for private hire.
Club Shop: Opening hours Saturday 2-00 to 4-00, Sunday 11-00 to 1-00. Contact Sue Bradshaw.
Programme: Size A5   Pages 20   Price: with admission   Editor: Stuart Headford (club e-mail)
Programme Advertising: Contact Sarah Brown (club e-mail).
Formed: 1932   **Nickname:** Tigers   **Website:** www.sheffieldtigers.co.uk   **Training Nights:** Tuesday and Thursday
Colours: Maroon shirts & socks, black shorts.   **Change colours:** White shirts.

REVIEW OF THE SEASON 2008-09

Sheffield Tigers enjoyed their most successful season in the Club's history, finishing fourth in North 1 and the semi-finalists in the EDF Intermediary Cup. The achievements could have been even greater if they had not gone off the boil in the final weeks of the season. This success owes a lot to the team work of the whole club over several seasons, both on and off the field.

The playing side has been steered from Yorkshire 2 in 2004/5 by the coaching team of Richard Selkirk and David Holmes under Director of Rugby, Richard Senior. This consistency has provided a highly effective blend of local players, combining both experience and youth. This season saw the addition of the experienced Dave Scully as player/coach. The success of the 1st XV has been built upon a strong and experienced pack under the captaincy of Richard Joel, and props Simon Bunting and Harry Toews. This has provided a strong platform for the backs going forward, and contributed to an excellent defensive record. The half-backs, Alex Drage and Dave Scully have consistently unleashed the young three-quarters to produce some exciting attacking rugby. Nick (Biffa) Pearson thoroughly deserved his 'player of the year' award and received his County cap. Tom Bray was awarded the young player of the year trophy for his strong performances. The top try scorers were Gareth Morley and Alex Drage, while Charles Spon-Smith and Tom Outram shared the kicking successes.

Sheffield Tigers regularly put out 4 sides, ensuring that everyone can enjoy competitive game, whatever their level of experience or skill. This 'whole club' ethos provides the backbone of the club, on which the league success is built. The award of the S Yorkshire Whistlers Trophy was a fitting reflection of the way in which the club looks after visiting officials as well as club members.

LAST TEN SEASONS

	Division	P	W	D	L	F	A	P.D.	Pts	Pos
99-00	Yorks 2	*17	13	0	4	335	200	135	26	2
00-01	Yorks 2	22	17	1	4	527	298	229	35	2p/po
01-02	Yorks 1	22	9	2	11	356	435	-79	20	8
02-03	Yorks 1	22	2	2	18	230	604	-354	*2	12r
03-04	Yorks 2	22	15	1	6	487	300	187	31	4
04-05	Yorks 2	22	21	1	0	712	194	518	43	1p
05-06	Yorks 1	22	20	1	1	547	199	348	41	1p
06-07	North 2E	22	16	0	6	575	309	266	32	2p/po
07-08	North 1	22	9	0	13	329	438	-109	18	7
08-09	North 1	22	15	0	7	495	307	188	30	4

The 2nd XV won more games than they lost, and lifted the S Yorkshire trophy. The 3rd XV were the team of the year, clocking up over 1000 points with only 2 losses all season on their way to winning the S Yorkshire merit table. The 4th XV/Vets have provided some excellent social rugby, entertaining touring sides as well as travelling abroad themselves.

The Club is now looking firmly to the future and has built a south Yorkshire under 20 development side. This is helping young players make the transition from the Club's Juniors into the senior teams. We have already seen several of the under 20's play in the 1st and 2nd XV's last season, and more players should progress through the club's sides over the coming months.

STOCKPORT R.U.F.C.

President: Julie Fuller, Julie Fuller Recruitment, Bank House, 147 Buxton Road, Stockport, Cheshire SK2 6EQ
Tel: 0161 482 2512, 07880 737017 (M) email: julie@juliefullerrecruitment.com
Treasurer: Hugh Oldham 0161 439 9590 (H)
Chairman: Stewart Bertenshaw Tel: 0161 427 1108 07836 605178 (M) email: thebertenshaws@hotmail.com
Club Secretary: Gillian Stone, 17 Highfield Close, Davenport, Stockport SK3 8UB
Tel: 0161 419 9854 07904 535968 email: gillianlstone@aol.com
Director of Rugby: Mike Drew Tel: 01625 539037 (B) 07976 623361 (M) email: mike@cardwell-drew.co.uk
Head Coach: Tim Burgon
Match Secretary: David Illingworth Tel: 01625 875635 Mobile 07747 131372
Press Officer: Richard Hope Tel 07793 134464 email Rambler@stockportrugby.co.uk
Ground Address: Bridge Lane Memorial Ground, Headlands Road, Bramhall, Stockport SK7 3AN
Tel: 0161 439 2150 email: info@stockportrugby.co.uk **Website:** www.stockportrugby.co.uk
Directions: Leave M56 following signs for Manchester Airport. Cont. until you reach a r'about. Take 2nd exit (Ringway Rd). 1.5 miles until you reach traffic lights, turn left (Styal Rd). Next lights turn right. (Finney Lane) Travel to the next lights. Into centre lane-turn left & then immed. right (Etchells Rd). Next lights straight on. (Albert Rd). Next lights turn right (Station Rd) Cont. to a small r'about - straight on (Manor Rd), continue until you meet a 't' junction. Turn left to the big r'about where you take 2nd exit (Bridge Lane). Headlands Rd is on right (approx 450 yds). Full directions are available on website.
Nearest BR Station: Bramhall or Davenport **Matchday Admission:** £5 inc programme
Founded: 1923 **Nickname:** Port **Training Nights:** Tues & Thur.
Colours: Red, white & green hooped shirts, black shorts & socks **Change colours:** Black and white

REVIEW OF THE SEASON 2008-09

After a reasonable first half of the season when hopes were high following our return to North 1, a top 6 place looked likely. Unfortunately and following a series of injuries, our relatively young side slipped to 8th position, somewhat below our expectations. The reorganisation of the leagues was not a factor; it was our inability to win games that we had controlled for substantial periods.

Despite this, there were plenty of positives, with the continuing development of the younger players and a relatively successful season for the 2nd XV in the Miller Homes Premiership.

Captain Dave Marwick again was rewarded with the Player of the Season award at the annual Player's Dinner. His selection for the county side a just reward for his splendid leadership throughout the season.

The 3rd XV won promotion again and will now play in Miller Homes League 2.

Such is the enthusiasm around the Club that we shall be fielding a 5th XV in addition to an occasional Vets team.

Embarking on the new season, the 1st XV have now achieved National League status following the reorganisation of leagues. With three long term injured returning to action, modest recruitment in key positions and with an overall stronger squad we hope to challenge for a top three position.

Last season Stockport maintained their record of having produced strong Junior and Senior Colts teams with both finishing as losing finalists in well-contested encounters. Whilst it may be too early to contemplate the introduction of some of the Senior Colts in to the 1st XV, a number will be knocking on the door in the next couple of seasons underlining the strength of our Mini and Junior Section.

Mike Drew, Director of Rugby

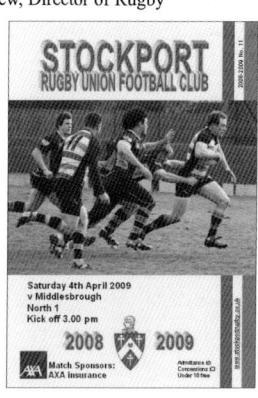

LAST TEN SEASONS

	Division	P	W	D	L	F	A	P.D.	Pts	Pos
99-00	N W1	18	15	0	3	467	191	276	30	2
00-01	N 2W	22	11	1	10	462	418	44	*21	5
01-02	N 2W	22	14	0	8	485	375	110	28	3
02-03	N 2W	22	14	2	6	504	321	183	30	3
03-04	N 2W	22	13	0	9	350	339	11	26	4
04-05	N 2W	22	18	0	4	643	227	416	36	2
05-06	N 2W	22	20	1	1	787	202	585	41	1p
06-07	North 1	22	8	0	14	395	544	-149	16	10r
07-08	N 2W	22	17	0	5	626	210	416	34	2p/po
08-09	North 1	22	8	0	14	416	520	-104	16	8

WEST HARTLEPOOL R.F.C.

President: Reg Turner **Chairman:** Peter Olsen
Treasurer: Peter Olsen, Oakland, 40 Victoria Road, Hartlepool, TS26 8DD
Tel: 01429 272797   email: Peter.Olsen@horwath.co.uk
Club Secretary: Geoff Hainsworth, 23 Fens Crescent, Hartlepool TS26 2QN
Tel: 01429 420724 email: captainbeff@hotmail.com
Chairman of Rugby / Fixture Secretary: Les Smith   01429 422765
Correspondence to: West Hartlepool RFC, Oakland House, 40 Victoria Road, Hartlepool TS26 8DD
Ground Address: Brinkburn, Catcote Road, Hartlepool   Contact Les Smith 07892 681122
Directions: From the North From A19 take the A179 signposted Hartlepool. At the first r'about take third exit. Enter Hartlepool and at mini-r'about [with ALDI on the right] go straight on. In 300 yards turn right at lights. Continue straight on at r'about [White House pub on the right] and continue for half a mile when you come to Brinkburn Pavilion on your left. From the South From A19 or A1 approach Hartlepool on the A689 dual carriageway. Go straight ahead at lights on outskirts of town [signposted Greatham] and again straight on at next set which provide access to an industrial estate and Cleveland Fire Brigade HQ. At next set of lights turn left into Truro Drive. At T-junction turn right into Catcote Road. Continue along Catcote Road for 3 miles until you reach the Brinkburn playing fields on your right.
Space is reserved beside the pavilion for coaches.
Nearest BR Station: Hartlepool
Car Parking: 150 spaces at the ground
Capacity: 2,500 uncovered standing   76 covered seating   **Admission:** £5   **Club Shop:** Open matchdays 1-2pm
Programme: Size: A5   Pages: 24.   Price: Free.   Editor: Dave Picken.   Advertising: Malcom Wallis
Founded: 1881   **Website:** www.west-rugby.org.uk   **Training Nights:** Tuesday and Thursday
Colours: Green, red & white hooped shirts, navy shorts, green socks.   **Change colours:** All dark green

REVIEW OF THE SEASON 2008-09

West Hartlepool continued their revival after the downward spiral from the heady days of life at the very top level. The first team finished in mid-table in their first season back in North One and reached the quarter final of the Intermediate Cup - succumbing to the eventual winners from Hartpury College in Gloucestershire.

West were left to rue the luck of the draws which saw them playing away in every round – at Durham City, Penrith and Burton before that defeat in the West Country.

It was a creditable first season for the new coaching team of Tim Sawyer, a front row player with the England Deaf XV, and former fly half Kevan Oliphant who returned to his home club after a coaching stint with Darlington Mowden Park in National Three.

The newly formed second team - the Stags – won the CaNDY league against the second strings of National League clubs Tynedale, Blaydon and Mowden Park.

West also fielded a third team for the first time in many years, The Bucks, mainly last season's Colts, fared well in the Tees Valley league against bigger and more experienced opponents while the next generation of West players , the Under 18s, won their own league and the Durham County Cup.

Off the field the club is continuing to make progress in developing a new at home at Brinkburn. The club has negotiated a long term lease with partners Hartlepool Sixth Form college which provides four excellent playing pitches together with space to develop extra changing rooms and clubhouse facilities.

LAST TEN SEASONS

	Division	P	W	D	L	F	A	P.D.	Pts	Pos
99-00	P2	26	1	0	25	216	1114	-898	2	14r
00-01	N2	26	0	0	26	240	1266	-1026	0	14r
01-02	N3 N	26	3	0	23	412	1018	-606	6	14r
02-03	North 1	22	4	1	17	250	655	-405	9	11r
03-04	North 2E	22	10	5	7	375	354	21	*23	5
04-05	North 2E	22	10	0	12	267	417	-150	20	6
05-06	North 2E	22	11	1	10	488	337	151	23	6
06-07	North 2E	22	14	0	8	483	383	100	28	3
07-08	North 2E	22	19	0	3	591	256	335	38	1p
08-09	North 1	22	9	0	13	356	420	-64	18	7

WEST PARK R.F.C.

President: Denis Glynn
Chairman: Malcolm Worsley, Old Lodge Farm, Clay Lane, Burtonwood, WA5 4DQ
Tel: 01925 225845   email: chair@westparksthelens.co.uk
Club Secretary: Liam Fortune, 30 Alexandra Road, Stockton Heath, Warrington, WA4 2UT
Tel: 01925 604360   email: honsec@westparksthelens.co.uk
Treasurer: Mike Simmons, 417 Prescot Road, St. Helens, WA10 3AJ
Tel: 07779 657194   email: hontreasurer@westparksthelens.co.uk
Chairman of Rugby: Ian Worsley, Tel: 07714226374   Email Ian.Worsley@pilkington.com
Fixture Secretary: Mr Alan Clarke, 9 St. Nicholas Road, Whiston, Prescot, Merseyside L35 3SN
Tel: 0151 4260362   email: discipline@westparksthelens.co.uk
Match Secretary: David Griffiths, 26 Derwent Close, Rainhill. Tel: 0151 426 1821
Press Secretary: Geoff Lightfoot, c/o West Park RFC
Coach: Chris Chudleigh Tel: 07968071030   email: chrisc@rugbyperformance.co.uk
Membership Sec.: Richard Chesworth, 1 Moss Brow, Rainford, St.Helens, WA11 8AE
Tel: 07921 709666   email: membership.secretary@hotmail.com

Address: West Park RFC, Prescot Road, St. Helens WA10 3AG   **Website:** www.westparksthelens.co.uk
Tel: 01744 26138 (club) 01744 617285 (office/fax)
Nearest BR Station: Eccleston Park   **Car Parking:** 80 spaces at ground
Capacity: 3000   Covered Standing: 250   **Admission:** Matchday £5 incl prog & parking
Directions: M62 off at J6 & take M57 towards Liverpool Docks, take exit at Prescott turnoff (Knowlsey safari park).
Follow signs for Safari park & St. Helens A58. Through lights at 'Wellington' PH (on right), passed 'Grapes' PH (on right) follow road for 1/2 mile and clubhouse is on the left just before right hand bend.
Clubhouse: Open every evening except Sunday.   Bar Manager Lorraine Clark
Founded: 1947   **Training Nights:** Tuesday & Thursday (Seniors)
Colours: Green & gold hooped shirts, green shorts   **Change colours:** Black, green & gold hoops
Programme: Size: A5   Pages: 32   Price: with admission   Editor: Geoff Lightfoot Media 01744 603199

REVIEW OF THE SEASON 2008-09

Another difficult season, which saw us finish just above the relegation zone.

We had a good preseason with good numbers attending, but we unfortunately lost 14 of the previous season's first team squad which left us with some large holes to fill! We managed to recruit some talent from Liverpool University through Chris Chudleigh and also managed to set up a South African exchange programme which saw us bring over 6 lads from SA who played all or part of the season.

For the early part of the season we struggled to gel as a side, putting in some good performances but ultimately falling short of winning. Despite some agonisingly close results we had to wait till 8th Nov to register our first league victory.

However after the new year we seemed to have turned a corner and have registered a further 4 league wins and looked comfortably like a North 1 team.

Kevin Greaves is now back on board as 1st team coach with Chris Chudleigh continuing in a broader coaching role at the club. Some strong recruitment in preseason and a talented colts section maturing fast, will hopefully bode well for a successful season.

LAST TEN SEASONS

	Division	P	W	D	L	F	A	P.D.	Pts	Pos			
99-00	North W1	18	17	1	0	623	188	435	35	1			
00-01	North 2W	22	19	0	3	616	263	353	38	1p			
01-02	North 1	*21	14	0	7	574	300	274	28	3			
02-03	North 1	22	11	0	11	600	482	118	22	7			
03-04	North 1	22	13	1	8	575	519	56	27	4			
04-05	North 1	22	16	0	6	565	353	212	32	4			
05-06	North 1	22	16	1	5	519	322	197	33	2	**Most Points**		**Most Tries**
06-07	N3 N	26	9	2	15	572	599	-27	53	11	206 Andrew Souter		11 Mark Turner
07-08	N3 N	26	7	2	17	460	668	-208	43	13r	172 Andrew Souter		10 Andrew Souter
08-09	North 1	22	5	0	17	273	599	-326	10	11			

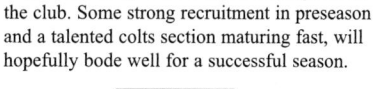

437

SHEFFIELD TIGERS 2008-09

WEST PARK R.F.C. 2008-09

WEST HARTLEPOOL 1st XV 2008-2009. Inset are - Left: Andy Dixon who captained Durham County in season, Centre: club skipper Anth Carr and Right leading try scorer Iain Dixon.

NORTH PHOTO CALL

CLECKHEATON 2008-09

Photo courtesy of the Spenborough Guardian

Shirt Sponsor PZ Engineering

L-R - Back Row: Tom Lauriston, Gordon Piper, Lance Hamilton, Richard Piper, Edu Hanekom, Dave Malton, Tom Denton, Ian Gresser, Johnn Dudley, Ross Hayden, Ben Wade, Doug Trivella, Mark Waite.
Front Row: Waisail Sovatubua, Marlon Miller, Craig Blackburn, Craig Rika (Captain), Andy Piper, Matt Piper, Bossie Muller, Marthinus Venter.

STOCKPORT 2008-09

439

NORTH ONE EAST

2008-09 LEAGUE TABLE North Two East

		P	W	D	L	F	A	PD	Pts	Adj
1	Penrith	22	17	0	5	706	373	333	34	
2	Old Crossleyans	22	16	0	6	441	343	98	32	
3	Sandal	22	15	0	7	488	306	182	30	
4	Billingham	22	15	0	7	498	323	175	30	
5	Pontefract	22	14	0	8	444	401	43	28	
6	Morpeth	22	12	1	9	495	392	103	25	
7	Carlisle	22	9	2	11	375	470	-95	20	
8	Gateshead	22	9	1	12	451	424	27	19	
9	Driffield	22	7	2	13	428	499	-71	16	
10	Aspatria	22	7	1	14	385	501	-116	15	
11	Durham City	22	6	0	16	333	522	-189	12	
12	Ilkley	22	1	1	20	261	751	-490	3	

2009-10 FIXTURES GRID

	Billingham	Carlisle	Darlington	Driffield	Durham City	Gateshead	Hartlepool Rovers	Ilkley	Morpeth	Old Brodleians	Old Crossleyans	Percy Park	Pontefract	Sandal
Billingham		12/09	19/12	26/09	16/01	10/10	30/01	24/10	20/02	05/09	07/11	13/03	28/11	27/03
Carlisle	12/12		26/09	16/01	10/10	30/01	24/10	20/02	07/11	19/09	13/03	28/11	27/03	05/09
Darlington	19/09	09/01		10/10	30/01	24/10	20/02	07/11	13/03	03/10	28/11	27/03	05/09	12/12
Driffield	09/01	03/10	23/01		24/10	20/02	07/11	13/03	28/11	17/10	27/03	05/09	12/12	19/09
Durham City	03/10	23/01	17/10	13/02		07/11	13/03	28/11	27/03	31/10	05/09	12/12	19/09	09/01
Gateshead	23/01	17/10	13/02	31/10	06/03		28/11	27/03	05/09	14/11	12/12	19/09	09/01	03/10
Hartlepool Rovers	17/10	13/02	31/10	06/03	14/11	20/03		05/09	12/12	05/12	19/09	09/01	03/10	23/01
Ilkley	13/02	31/10	06/03	14/11	20/03	05/12	10/04		19/09	12/12	09/01	03/10	23/01	17/10
Morpeth	31/10	06/03	14/11	20/03	05/12	10/04	12/09	19/12		09/01	03/10	23/01	17/10	13/02
Old Brodleians	10/04	19/12	16/01	30/01	20/02	13/03	27/03	12/09	26/09		10/10	24/10	07/11	28/11
Old Crossleyans	06/03	14/11	20/03	05/12	10/04	12/09	19/12	26/09	16/01	23/01		17/10	13/02	31/10
Percy Park	14/11	20/03	05/12	10/04	12/09	19/12	26/09	16/01	10/10	13/02	30/01		31/10	06/03
Pontefract	20/03	05/12	10/04	12/09	19/12	26/09	16/01	10/10	30/01	06/03	24/10	20/02		14/11
Sandal	05/12	10/04	12/09	19/12	26/09	16/01	10/10	30/01	24/10	20/03	20/02	07/11	13/03	

BILLINGHAM R.F.C.

President: Ian Brown   **Chairman**: Mark Armstrong   **Financial Director**: Kate Baucherel
Hon Secretary: Keith Blenkinsopp 10 Severn Grove Billingham ClevedonTS22 5BJ
Tel: 07736 224671   email: k.blenkinsopp@ntlworld.com
Fixture Secretary: Stewart Evans; 38 York Crescent, Billingham, Cleveland TS23 1AS
Tel: 01642 651968
Director of Rugby: Stewart Evans   **Director of Rugby Development**: Colin Snowdon
Commercial Director: John Ker   **Commercial Manager**: Ken Potts
Ground Address: Greenwood Road, Billingham, Cleveland TS23 4BA
Contact Number: 07736 224671   email: k.blenkinsopp@ntlworld.com
Directions: From the A19, northbound or southbound, take the exit signposted for Billingham A1027. Heading eastbound into Billingham, go straight over at the first two roundabouts onto Central Avenue. At the next roundabout turn left onto Cowpen Lane. Just after the traffic lights at Marsh House Avenue, turn right into Greenwood Road. Billingham Rugby Club is situated on the left hand side, approximately halfway along Greenwood Road.
Clubhouse: An excellent modern facility. Available for private hire, catering up to 100. Contact Ken Potts.
Formed: 1924   **Website**: www.billinghamrugby.co.uk
Colours: Green & Thin White Hoops, White Shorts

CARLISLE R.F.C.

President: John Tiffen Tel: 01228 519983 email: johnrugby@fsmail.net
Chairman: Bill Swarbrick Tel: 01228 529287 email: billswarbrick@tinyworld.co.uk
Club Secretary: David Morton, 14 Naworth Drive, Lowry Hill, Carlisle, CA3 0DD
Tel: 01228 515486 H) 0771 992 7758 (M) email: mortwas82@aol.com
Fixture Sec.: Martin Burnett, Hilldene, School Road, Cumwhinton, Carlisle, CA4 8OU
Tel: 01228 560119 (H) 01228 888999 (B) 0791236 3665 (M) email: mburnett@bpkcumbria.co.uk
1st XV Manager: Paul Grealish, 156 Dalston Road, Carlisle, CA2 5 PJ Tel: 01228 546226 (H) 07912 110783 (M)
Director of Rugby: Martin Plummer Tel: 01228 590091 (H) 07919 621 118 email: plumpots1@hotmail.com
Ground Address:: The Rugby Ground, Warwick Road, Carlisle CA1 1LW   Tel: 01228 521300 email: mortwas82@aol.com
Directions: M6, J 43 (A69). Follow A69 into Carlisle through three sets of traffic lights (approx 1 mile). 250/300 yards beyond the third set (where you will see Carlisle United AFC) the club is on the right.
Capacity: Standing: 2,500   Covered Seating: 250   **Admission**: By programme @ £3
Nearest BR Station: Citadel Station, Carlisle, 15 mins walk   **Car Parking**: 150 cars & ample matchday coach parking
Clubhouse: Open daily 11am-11.30pm. Snacks normally available. All types of functions catered for. Contact the club secretary in the first instance on 01228 515486   **Club Shop**: Open matchdays & training evenings
Programme: Size: A5   Pages: 16   Price: £3   Editorial & Advertising: David Morton, details above
Formed: 1873   **Training Nights**: Tues & Thur. @ 6.45pm   **Website**: www.carlislerugby.co.uk
Colours: Navy shirts with red & white trim **Change Colours**: (1) White shirts with red & navy trim; (2) Red shirts.

441

DARLINGTON R.F.C.

President: Ian Taylor 01325 265346 email: ian_marilyn@yahoo.co.uk **Treasurer:** Gary Hinton 01325 266102
Chairman: Paul Barkes 07909 910255 email: info@thorpefarm.co.uk **Director of Rugby:** Brian Baldwin 07533 718635
Rugby Secretary: Chris de Jong, 5 Wheatear Lane, Ingleby Barwick, Stockton-on-Tees, TS17 0TB
Tel: 01642 769629 (H) 07905 285116 (M) email:darlingtonrfc@gmail.com
Fixtures Secretary: Tony Stowe - 20 The Meadows, Middleton St. George, Darlington
Tel: 01325 335120 (H) 07971 575862 (M) email: tonystowe@hotmail.com
Commercial Contact: Steve Thompson 07891 450940 email: genuinearmysurplus@hotmail.com
Senior Coach: Lee Richardson **Ladies Captain:** Jessica Cheesman 07801 069263
GroundAddress: Blackwell Meadows, Grange Road, Darlington. DL1 5NR Tel: 01325 363777 Fax: 01325 363888
Directions: Northbound on A1(M), exit at A66 sign then head for town centre. Club can be seen on the right.
Southbound on A1(M), exit on A68. At shopping precinct pick up Teeside (A66) sign. After approx. 1.5 miles turn left at roundabout (signed for Town Centre). Club can be seen on the right.
Nearest BR Station: Darlington, 2 miles. **Car Parking:** Spaces for 200 cars
Capacity: 1000 all uncovered standing **Admission:** Matchday:£5 incl. programme **Season Ticket:** Not available.
Clubhouse: Open Monday to Sunday 11am - 11pm. Food available evenings only, Monday to Friday, all day Saturday. For private hire contact Sandra Appleyard. **Club Shop:** Open match days, training nights and Sunday morning.
Founded: 1863 **Training Nights:** Tuesday & Thursday **Web site:** www.darlingtonrfc.co.uk
Colours: Red shirt with black chest band **Change colours:** Red
Programme: Size: A5 Pages: 16 Price: With admission Editor: Bill Jones Advertising: Contact Bill Jones

DRIFFIELD R.U.F.C.

President: Charles Booth Tel: 01377 254433 **Chairman:** Andrew Kitching Tel: 01377 229373
Hon. Treasurer: Mark Goodson Tel: 01377 253186 **Director of Rugby:** Patrick Burdass Tel: 07814 119081
Director of Commercial Sponsorship: Dave Stephenson Tel: 01262 420294, 07774 416630 (M)
Club Secretary: Mrs Karen Clark; 26 Heather Garth, Driffield YO25 UT
Tel: 07791 420404 email: kjclark22@aol.com
Fixture Secretary: John Leason, 15 Albion Street, Driffield, YO25 6PZ Tel: 01377 254036 (H&B)
Director of Mini Junior Rugby: Andrew Chapman Tel: 01377 236696, 07970 074297 (M)
Ground Address: The Clubhouse, Kelleythorpe, Driffield, YO25 9DW
Tel: 01377 256598 Fax: 01377 250302 email: durfc@aol.com
Directions: One mile south of Driffield town centre between the A163 and the A164.
Nearest BR station: Driffield, 1 mile. **Car Parking:** Unlimited
Capacity: 1000+ Covered Standing: 50 **Admission:** Matchday £4
Clubhouse: Open every day. Hot food available on matchdays.
Available for private hire, contact Club Manager: Richard Mitchell-Williams 01377 256598. **Club Shop:** Open Sun luchtime
Programme: Size: A5 Pages: 16 Price: with admission **Website:** www.www.driffieldrufc.co.uk
Founded: 1926 **Colours:** Black, royal blue & white hoops, navy shorts **Change colours:** Red & black

DURHAM CITY R.F.C.

President: Harry Johnson **Chairman:** Michael Littlechild **Treasurer:** Chris Roberts
Club Secretary: Bob Elston c/o the club (see below)
Fixture Secretary: Mark Berriman c/o the club (see below)
Executive Manager: Derek Best c/o the club (see below) **Director Of Rugby:** Mark Davison
Ground Address: Durham City RFC, Hollow Drift, Green Lane, Old Elvet, Durham City. DH1 3JU
Tel: 0191 386 1172 Fax: 0191 384 7571 email: dcrfc@talk21.com
Directions: Leave A1M at J 62 Carrville. Signed A690 Durham / Sunderland. Follow Dual Carriageway to Durham City Centre, at first r'about take second junction signposted City Centre, descend hill, keeping left on r'about and Cross Bridge, signposted Bowburn & Coxhoe keeping to the inside lane, Traffic Lights at Royal County Hotel, Turn left into Old Elvet. Proceed to the top of Old Elvet, est. 400m turn left into Green Lane, 300m turn right into Wycliffe House car park. Follow road around to the left DCRFC Club House on left.
Nearest BR station: Durham **Car Parking:** 150 vehicles
Capacity: 7,000 Covered Seating: 450 **Admission:** Matchday £3, concessions £2
Clubhouse: Open mid-week 12–2.30pm & 6–11pm, Sat 12–11pm, Sun 10.30–6pm. Food available lunch times and game days. 2 rooms available for private hire. Contact Derek & Julie Best. **Club Shop:** open as Clubhouse.
Founded: 1873 **Website:** www.durhamcityrfc.co.uk **Programme:** Size A5, Pages 6, Price with admission
Colours: Navy & gold, navy shorts **Change colours:** Red **Training Nights:** Tues. & Thurs.

442

GATESHEAD R.F.C.

President: D.A.Thompson **Chairman:** P.A.Douglas **Treasurer:** D.A.Thompson
Hon Secretary: Mrs Ann Nunn, 30 Limetrees Gardens, Low Fell, Gateshead, Tyne and Wear NE9 5BE
Tel: 0191 420 3089 email: anunn@blueyonder.co.uk
Fixtures Secretary: John Davison, 9 Torver Place, Gateshead, Tyne and Wear NE9 6YL
Tel: (H) 0191 4823778 email: JohnD.Rugby@blueyonder.co.uk
Team Secretary: P Walton, 4 Eastwood Gardens, Low Fell, Gateshead, Tyne & Wear NE9 5UB
Tel: 0191 4826696 email: waltonpip@blueyonder.co
Chairman of Rugby: T.Tate Tel: 0191 4913083 **Bookings Secretary:** M. A. Nunn Tel: 0191 4203089
Youth Development Officer: Mrs.C-A Scott Tel. 0191 4411273 **Membership Secretary:** J. M. Wilson Tel. 0191 2847036
Ground Address: Hedley Lawson Park, Eastwood Gardens, Low Fell, Gateshead, Tyne & Wear NE9 5UB
Tel: 0191 420 0207 email: anunn@blueyonder.co.uk **Website:** www.gatesheadrfc.co.uk
Directions: Travelling North on the A167 into Gateshead pass two sets of main lights turn right into Joicey Road second left into Eastwood Gardens; travelling South on the A167 turn left at the Snooker Hall and Gym into Dryden Road continue 300 yards up Dryden Road turn left into Evistones Road
Capacity: 2,000 Covered Seating: 500 **Car Parking:** Use roadside. **Nearest BR station:** Newcastle upon Tyne Central
Clubhouse: M,T,W & Th 8-11pm, Fri 5-11pm, Sat 12-11pm, Sun 12-3pm & 8-11pm. Sandwiches and snacks are available, available for private hire contact M A Nunn (see above) **Club Shop:** Open as Clubhouse **Admission:** Matchday £2
Founded: 1998 **Colours:** Red, pale blue band surrounded by navy blue. **Change colours:** Royal blue
Programme: Size: A5 Pages: 8 Price: with admission Editor: P Walton Advertising: Contact J.M.Wilson 0191 2847036

HARTLEPOOL ROVERS R.F.C.

President: W.M. Bowden FRCS.Ed **Chairman:** Phillip Mitchell **Treasurer:** tbc
Club Secretary: John Ainsley, 'Inglethorpe', Elwick Road, Hartlepool, TS26 0DE Tel: 01429 861793
Fixtures Secretary: Chris Collins, 'Sea Change', The Oval, Hartlepool, TS26 9QH
Tel: 01429 298061 email: chris.collins250@ntlworld.com
Director of Rugby: Brian Hall **Commercial Secretary:** Darren Atter
Club Steward: Don Foreman **Rugby Development Director:** Alby Pattison
Head Coach: Jonathan Wrigley **Club Captain:** Mark Power
Ground Address: The Friarage, Low Warren, West View Road, Hartlepool, TS24 0BP Tel: 01429 267741
Directions: From North or South on A19 approach Hartlepool via A179, continue straight ahead over 4 roundabouts, continue under railway bridge, club is 100 yard on left
Car Parking: Ample on site **Nearest Station:** Hartlepool
Capacity: All uncovered standing **Admission:** Matchday £3 Season tickets available on request.
Clubhouse: Open Mon – Fri 7pm to 11pm, Sat - Sun 12pm – 11pm. Late license available for functions. Food is available match days & Sunday morning. Club rooms available for functions – contact club house for details
Club Shop: Contact club house for details **Programme:** Size A5, approx 20 pages, Price: with admission.
Founded: 1879 **Nickname:** Rovers, Friargatemen **Website:** http://official.sportnetwork.net/main/s219.htm
Colours: White shirts, black shorts, red socks **Change colours:** Black or red shirts **Training Nights:** Tues & Thur.

ILKLEY R.F.C.

President: Ronald Obank **Chairman:** Richard Scargill
Hon Secretary: Ken Bernard, 36 Dale View, Ilkley, West Yorks. LS29 9BP
Tel: 01943602945 email: j.k.bernard@btinternet.com
Fixtures Secretary: Brian Crane; 96 Valley Drive Ben Rhydding, Ilkley West Yorks. LS29 9PG
Tel: 07968 195702
Chairman of Junior and Youth section: Tom Gillon Tel: 07947 604165 (M) email: tgillon@blueyonder.co.uk
Chairman of Rugby, Development Officer: Dave Duxbury Tel: 07811 331427
Head Coach: Hamish Pratt Tel: 07764 336702
Ground Address: Stacks Field Ilkley West Yorks. LS29 0BZ
Contact Number: 01943 607 237 email: webmaster@ilkleyrugby.co.uk
Website: www.ilkleyrugby.co.uk
Directions: At traffic lights in centre of town (with Church, a gents outfitters, Dalesway Hotel/Pub, Crescent Hotel on the 4 corners) turn left if coming from Skipton/Silsden, or right if coming from Leeds/Bradford/Otley. Go about 1/4 mile over bridge and club is visible on your right. Turn right down Denton Rd. the gates are about 30yds along right.
Covered Seating; 200
Clubhouse: Available for private hire. **Training Nights:** (Seniors) Tuesday & Thursday 7pm prompt.
Colours: Red, Black, White

NORTHERN

443

MORPETH R.F.C.

President: Martin Calder.   **Chairman**: Mike Brunskill   **Treasurer**: Mike Brunskill
Club Secretary: Ken. Fraser, Solway House, De Merley Road, Morpeth, Northumberland NE61 1HZ
   Tel: (H) 01670 511 208   (W) 01642 736541   email: k.fraser@macmillan-academy.org.uk
   Fixture Secretary: Bill Hewitt   Tel: (H) 01670 787757   email: w.g.hewitt@btinternet.com
   Team Manager: Peter Forsythe   **Chairman of Rugby**: Gary Stephenson
Ground Address: Grange House Field, Mitford Road, Morpeth NE61 1RJ
   Tel: 01670 512 508   email: mail@morpethrfc.co.uk
Directions: Come off the A1 north signposted Morpeth A197. Follow the signs into the town centre, go over the bridge and take a left at the mini roundabout. Follow the road through the town and up the hill through a set of traffic lights until you see a signpost directing you left to Mitford. This is Dogger Bank, follow the road down the hill for 500 metres and the club is on your right hand side
Nearest BR station: Morpeth   **Car Parking**: Ample at the ground
Capacity: Unlimited uncovered standing   **Admission**: £3
Club Shop: On-line from September 2009
Founded: 1947   **Website**: www.morpethrfc.co.uk   **Training Nights**: Tues & Thur 7pm
Colours: Red & white hoops, navy blue shorts   **Change colours**: Purple

OLD BRODLEIANS R.U.F.C.

President: Harold Smith   **Chairman**: Richard Turner   **Treasurer**: Stephen Rooks
Club Secretary: Colin Green, 13 Yew Trees Avenue, Northowram, Halifax, West Yorkshire HX3 7JD
   Tel: 01422 201502   email: colin.greenyta@btinternet.com
   Fixtures Secretary: Michael Hey, 2 Sunnybank Crescent, Sowerby Bridge, West Yorkshire HX6 2PL
   Tel: 01422 839614
   Head Coach: Nick O'Connor   **First Team Coach**: Ian Armitage
   Youth Coordinator: Marc Turnbull Tel: 07738 020502
   Mini Coordinator: Chris Ramsden Tel: 07920 572002
Ground Address: Woodhead Denholme Gate Road, Hipperholme, Halifax, West Yorkshire HX3 8JU
Tel: 01422 201502   email: as Secretary   **Website**: www.oldbrodleians.co.uk
Directions: M62 - Exit 26 - Take A58 to Halifax - After 3.8 miles turn right at traffic lights (Whitehall Pub on the corner) - Club 0.5 miles up on the left after the Jet garage
Capacity: Mainly uncovered standing   **Car Parking**: Ample at ground   **Nearest BR Station**: Halifax
Clubhouse: Available for private hire (up to 120 for a Dinner Dance) contact Susan Turner Tel: 01484 714010
Club Shop: Open 2-4pm Sat and 10-1pm Sun during the season..
Founded: 1930
Colours: Black - red hoops on white ban   **Training Nights**: Tues & Thur.

OLD CROSSLEYANS R.U.F.C.

President: Graham Thomas   **Chairman**: Barry Thompson
Treasurer: David Knight
Club Secretary: Richard A. Davies, 4, Warley Dene, Warley, Halifax HX2 7RS
   Tel: 01422 832218 email: c/o   maxuttley@blueyonder.co.uk
Fixture Secretary: Hanson Haigh, 24, Bankhouse Lane, Salterhebble, Halifax. HX3 0QJ
   Tel: 01422 354989   email: hansonh@pulmans.co.uk
Ground: Standeven House, Broomfield Avenue, Savile Park, Halifax. HX3 0JE
Tel: 01422 363000   email: maxuttley@blueyonder.co.uk   **Website**: www.oldcrossleyans.co.uk
Directions: M62 Exit 24. A629 towards Halifax. At 4th set of lights, left on A646 signposted Savile Park and King Cross. Left at 2nd set of lights along Birdcage Lane. Club is 200 metres on left
Capacity: circa 200   **Covered Seating**: 100   **Car Parking**: 75   **Nearest BR Station**: Halifax
Admission: Matchday £4   Season tickets not available.
Clubhouse: Open training evenings and matchdays only. Food is available. Functions Contact Hugh Robinson 01422 363000
Programme: Size: A5   Pages: 20   Price: With admission
         Editorial & Advertising: Max Uttley.   email: maxuttley@blueyonder.co.uk
Formed: 1923   **Nickname**: Crocs   **Training Nights**: Tuesday and Thursday
Colours: Blue, amber and white.   **Change Colours**: Amber, blue and white

PERCY PARK R.F.C.

President: Albi Duhrin
Chairman: Michael Dunn michaeld@hadaway.co.uk   **Treasurer:** Eileen Shepherd Eileen@percyparkrfc.co.uk
Club Secretary: Chris Baker, c/o The Clubhouse, Preston Avenue, North Shields, Tyne & Wear, NE30 2BE
Tel: 0191 4144689   email: chris@bakergray.co.uk
Fixtures Secretary: Mick Ishida, 2a Kennersdene, Tynemouth, Tyne & Wear NE30 2LT
Tel: 0191 2516236 (W)   07769 705558 (M)   email: Mri.newgatefinancialservices@btconnect.com
Director of Rugby & Team Sec.: Thomas Turnball   Tel: 07511 642447   email: thomas@percyparkrfc.co.uk
Mini Chairman: Lee Weatherley lee.weatherley@talktalk.co.uk   **Youth Chairman:** Kevin Dale Kevin.dale@blueyonder.co.uk
Ground Address: Percy Park RFC, Preston Avenue, North Shields, Tyne & Wear, NE30 2BE
Tel: 0191 2575710   email: brian@percyparkrfc.co.uk
Directions: From the A19 northbound, go through the Tyne Tunnel and on exiting, continue up the A19. At the roundabout turn right onto the A1058 (eastbound, fourth exit). Continue to the Billy Mill Roundabout and take the second exit (past the front of the Tesco Garage). Continue to the next roundabout (Swimming pool on right, Morrisons on left) and turn right (third exit). Continue straight across mini roundabout and take the second left into Preston Avenue. Continue down Preston Avenue and Percy Park RFC is on the left hand side.   **Car Parking:** Yes   **Nearest Station:** Tynemouth or North Shields
Capacity: Ample with 250 seat grandstand   **Admission** £3   **Clubhouse Manager:** Brian Scorer brian@percyparkrfc.co.uk
Club Shop: None.   **Programme:** Size: A5   Price with admission   Editor: Mick Ishida
Founded: 1872   **Website:** www.percyparkrfc.co.uk   **Training Nights:** Mon & Wed.
Colours: Black & white hooped shirts, black shorts, black socks with white tops   **Change colours:** Red shirts

PONTEFRACT R.F.C.

President: Neil Bowmer   **Chairman:** Alan Boyd   **Treasurer:** Mike Spears
Hon Secretary: Tony Brown, 70 Carleton Road, Pontefract, West Yorkshire WF8 3NF
Tel: (H) 01977 704176   (M) 07966 928056   email: tonyjoany.brown@tiscali.co.uk
Fixtures Secretary: D. L. Howdle, 7 Mill Lane Close, Darrington, Pontefract   Tel: (H) 01977 704 615
Director of Rugby: Derek Eves   **Chairman of Junior Rugby:** Owen Peacock
Club Captain: Matty Williams   **1st XV Captain:** Simon Spears
Youth Development Officer: Derek Eves
Ground Address: Moor Lane, Carleton, Pontefract, West Yorkshire WF8 3RX
Tel: 01977 702650   email: club@pontefractrufc.co.uk   Website: www.pontefractrufc.co.uk
Directions: Exit A1 at Darrington, follow signs for Pontefract, 2 miles to Moor Lane which is 1st left after 30 mph sign on outskirts of Pontefract.   **Nearest Stations:** Pontefract Monkhill, Pontefract Baghill & Pontefract Tanshelf (all within 1.5 miles)
Ground Capacity: 1000   **Stand Capacity:** 150 covered seats   **Parking** for 200 cars
Clubhouse: Open Tuesday evening, Thursday evening, Saturday all day (food available) & Sunday morning for junior rugby. Clubhouse available for hire; seating for 100 or seating/dancing 150.
Colours: Royal blue shirts & shorts   **Change colours:** White or Red   **Training Nights:** Tuesday & Thursday 7.15pm
Founded: Rugby Union has been played in Pontefract since the late 19th century. The Old Pomfretians, as they were then known, re-formed after the Second World War. In 1967 the club's name was changed to Pontefract.

SANDAL R.F.C.

President: Malcolm Smith
19 Heather Croft, Sharlaston Common, Wakefield WF4 1TJ
Please send all Club correspondence to above.
Chairman: Chris Dix   **Director of Finance:** Andrew Wright
Director of Rugby / Fixtures Secretary: Angus Moran, 8 St James Rise, Wakefield, WF2 8YL
Tel (H) 01924 299019   (M)07917 618684   email: angusmoran2@yahoo.co.uk
Chair of Mini/Junior Rugby: Pete Stephenson
Ground Address: Milnthorpe Green Standbridge Lane, Sandal, Wakefield, West Yorks. WF2 7DY
Clubhouse: 01924 250661   email: info@sandalrufc.co.uk
Directions: M1 Junction 39 Follow signs for Wakefield. Continue on dual-carriageway to second roundabout, turn right towards Sandal. Continue past Pugney's lake and ASDA, Straight on at both mini roundabouts. Entrance to Sandal RUFC Car Park 150m on left.
Kick Off Times: Sept., Oct, March & April 3.00pm; November - February 2.15pm
Founded: 26th August 1927   **Website:** www.sandalrugby.co.uk
Colours: Amber, maroon & white

NORTH ONE WEST

2008-09 LEAGUE TABLE North Two West

		P	W	D	L	F	A	PD	Pts	Adj
1	Rochdale	22	17	0	5	502	335	167	34	
2	Rossendale	22	14	1	7	407	308	99	29	
3	Lymm	22	14	0	8	381	346	35	28	
4	Altrincham Kersal	22	13	1	8	439	260	179	27	
5	Leigh	22	12	0	10	355	373	-18	24	
6	New Brighton	22	10	2	10	407	376	31	22	
7	Broughton Park	22	10	1	11	370	371	-1	21	
8	Wilmslow	22	10	0	12	356	364	-8	20	
9	Sandbach	22	8	1	13	346	430	-84	17	
10	Northwich	22	8	1	13	373	491	-118	17	
11	Liverpool St Helens	22	8	0	14	302	361	-59	16	
12	Blackburn	22	4	1	17	254	477	-223	9	

2009-10 FIXTURES GRID

	Altrincham Kersal	Aspatria	Blackburn	Broughton Park	Burnage	Leigh	Liverpool St H.	Lymm	New Brighton	Northwich	Sandbach	Tyldesley	Vale of Lune	Wilmslow
Altrincham Kersal		12/09	19/12	26/09	16/01	10/10	30/01	24/10	20/02	07/11	13/03	28/11	27/03	05/09
Aspatria	12/12		26/09	16/01	10/10	30/01	24/10	20/02	07/11	13/03	28/11	27/03	05/09	19/09
Blackburn	19/09	09/01		10/10	30/01	24/10	20/02	07/11	13/03	28/11	27/03	05/09	12/12	03/10
Broughton Park	09/01	03/10	23/01		24/10	20/02	07/11	13/03	28/11	27/03	05/09	12/12	19/09	17/10
Burnage	03/10	23/01	17/10	13/02		07/11	13/03	28/11	27/03	05/09	12/12	19/09	09/01	31/10
Leigh	23/01	17/10	13/02	31/10	06/03		28/11	27/03	05/09	12/12	19/09	09/01	03/10	14/11
Liverpool St Helens	17/10	13/02	31/10	06/03	14/11	20/03		05/09	12/12	19/09	09/01	03/10	23/01	05/12
Lymm	13/02	31/10	06/03	14/11	20/03	05/12	10/04		19/09	09/01	03/10	23/01	17/10	12/12
New Brighton	31/10	06/03	14/11	20/03	05/12	10/04	12/09	19/12		03/10	23/01	17/10	13/02	09/01
Northwich	06/03	14/11	20/03	05/12	10/04	12/09	19/12	26/09	16/01		17/10	13/02	31/10	23/01
Sandbach	14/11	20/03	05/12	10/04	12/09	19/12	26/09	16/01	10/10	30/01		31/10	06/03	13/02
Tyldesley	20/03	05/12	10/04	12/09	19/12	26/09	16/01	10/10	30/01	24/10	20/02		14/11	06/03
Vale of Lune	05/12	10/04	12/09	19/12	26/09	16/01	10/10	30/01	24/10	20/02	07/11	13/03		20/03
Wilmslow	10/04	19/12	16/01	30/01	20/02	13/03	27/03	12/09	26/09	10/10	24/10	07/11	28/11	

ALTRINCHAM KERSAL RFC

President: David Elliott **Chairman**: John Wilks **Treasurer**: Michael Meaney
Club Secretary: Rob Neyton, Bridge Cottage, 20 BradburnsLane, Hartford, Cheshire CW8 1LT
Tel: 01606 75078 (H) 07870 399774 (M) email: robneyton.akrfc@btinternet.com
Fixture Secretary: Mike Fletcher, 47 Heyes Lane, Timperley, Altrincham, Cheshire WA15 6DZ
07810 757185 (M) 0161 903 5678 (W) 0161 976 1043 (H) email: mike.fletcher@cis.co.uk
Team Secretary & Director of Rugby: Chris Smith, 10 Bonville Chase, Altrincham WA14 4QA
0161 929 4200 (W) 07976 868444 (M) email: chris@dunhaminvestment.co.uk
Commercial Secretary: Mark Weeden Tel: 07971 870591 email: mweeden@graingerplc.co.uk
Head Coach: Dylan O'Grady **Press Officer**: Alec Forbes **Mini & Junior Chairman**: Dominic Leach
Address: Stelfox Avenue, Timperley, Altrincham, Cheshire WA15 6UL Tel: 0161 973 9157 email: info@akrfc.co.uk
Directions: Jtn 3A M56 – A560 Altrincham. Pass Tesco then 400 yds r'bout 3rd exit to Timperley. Stelfox Ave first right.
Capacity 1500 - all uncovered standing **Car Parking**: 100 in car park. **Nearest Station**: Altrincham
Admission: Matchday: £5.00 adults. Children free. Season: N/A
Clubhouse: Open Mon – Thurs 7-11, Sat 10am – 11pm Sun 9.30-5pm. Food available on match days & training nights
Functions Contact Chris Barlow Tel: 0161 976 3221 email: chrisbarlow69@btinternet.com. **Club Shop**: Contact tbc
Programme: Size: A5 Pages: 16 Price: With admission Editorial & Advertising: John Emerson 0161 941 1362
Founded: 1897 **Nickname**: Kersal **Website**: www.akrfc.co.uk **Training Nights**: Tuesday & Thursday 7pm
Colours: Red, white, black hooped shirts **Change Colours**: All Black

ASPATRIA R.U.F.C.

President: Melvin Hanley **Chairman**: John Heyworth **Treasurer**: Barney Clegg
Club Secretary: David Wilson Esq. 9 Lawn Terrace, Silloth-on-Solway, Cumbria CA7 4AW
Tel: 016973-23919 email: davidwilsonathousenrigg@ukonline.co.uk
Fixture Secretary: Peter Gray, 5 Morningside, Plumbland, Aspatria, Cumbria. CA7 2EY
Tel: 016973-21760 email: petpengray@aol.com
Team Secretary: Mike Ray, 67 North View, Aspatria, Cumbria. CA7 3EL Tel/Fax: 016973-21313
Director of Rugby: Mark Richardson **Commercial Secretary**: Barney Clegg
Ground Address: Bower Park, Station Road, Aspatria, Cumbria CA7 2AJ Tel: 01697 320420
Directions: M6 Junc 41, B5305 to Wigton. then the A596 to Aspatria **Car Parking**: 300
Nearest Railway Station: Aspatria, 300yds from ground.
Capacity: 2,500 Covered Seating: 300 **Admission**: Matchday £4 Season: £10 + £3 admission
Clubhouse: Open 10am-1am except Monday. Snacks & bar meals available match days only
Functions contact Barney Clegg 01697 320285
Club Shop: Open 12-6 matchdays only. Contact Andrew Marshall 01697 320420
Programme Size: A5 Price: £1 Pages: 66 Editorial & Advertising: Barney Clegg 01697 320285
Founded: 1875 **Nickname**: Black reds **Training Nights**: Tuesday & Thursday
Colours: Black & red hoops **Change colours**: Black **Website**: www.aspatriarufc.co.uk

BLACKBURN R.U.F.C.

President: Dave Morris Tel: 01706 216545 (M) 07785 972360 email: morris_d@btconnect.com
Chairman: Ray Pemberton Tel: 01254 775894 (H), 07768 276927 (M) email: ray.pemberton@btopenworld.com
Treasurer: Nick Westhead Tel: 01254 248574 (H), 07768 833846 (M) email:nick.westhead@mdalimited.co.uk
Hon Secretary: Bill Neild, 16 Dandy Row, Hoddlesden, Blackburn, Lancs BB3 3BL
Tel: (H) 01254 705704 (M) 07860 820922 email: billneild@usa.net
Fixtures Secretary: John Toms Tel: 01254 682209 (M) 07718 209210 email: jptoms51@talktalk.net
Head Coach: Dave Muckalt Tel: 07958 574047 (m) email: dnmuckalt@giggleswick.n-yorks.sch.uk
Mini & Youth Chairman: Ian Gibbs Tel: 01200 423894 (H), 07976 757684 (M) email: gibbs.ian@btinternet.com
Ground Address: Blackburn RUFC, Ramsgreave Drive, Blackburn, Lancs. BB1 8NB
Tel: 01254 247669 Fax: 01254 246834 email: info@brufc.com
Directions: M6 J31, follow A677 for 5 miles to traffic lights. Turn left A6119 (M66, M65) Ground is 1.5 miles on left.
Nearest BR Station: Blackburn **Car Parking:** Space for approx. 130 cars
Admission: £4 **Training Nights:** Tuesdays and Thursday 7pm
Founded: 1877 **Nickname:** 'Burn' **Website:** www.brufc.com
Colours: Royal blue with crimson trim, blue shorts **Change colours:** Crimson with royal blue trim

BROUGHTON PARK R.F.C.

President: Christine Barber Tel: 0161 286 3596 (H) 0790 007 3954 (M)
Chairman: David Poppitt Tel: 0161 434 4808 (H) 0778 572 8700 (M) Fax: 0161 434 1847
Treasurer: Jim Rochford email: treasurer@broughton-park.org.uk
Club Secretary: Rob Loveday, 2 Devonshire Road, Heaton Moor, Stockport SK4 6LB Tel: 0161 947 9157 (H)
0161 832 0060 (B) 07740 180182 (M) Fax: 0161 832 0061 (B), email: secretary@broughton-park.org.uk
Fixtures Secretary & Director of Rugby: Kevin O'Brien, 106 Windsor Road, Denton, Manchester M34 2HE
Tel: 0161 320 5077 (H), 0161 235 5921 (B), 07739 191932 (M) email: fixtures@broughton-park.org.uk
Press Officer: Alan Bramall Tel: 0161 485 1683, 07768 283366 (M) email: press@broughton-park.ork.uk
Ground Address: 2 Houghend Crescent, Off Mauldeth Road West, Manchester M21 7TA Tel: 0161 861 0854
Directions: From the M56 J3 or the M60 J5 get onto the A5103 going north. After 3 or 2 miles respectively, turn left, at the large Hough End Playing Field sign, into Mauldeth Road West. The ground is 3/4 mile on the left down Houghend Crescent.
Capacity: 2000 **Admission:** £4 **Nearest BR Station:** Manchester Picadilly **Car Parking:** 200 spaces at ground
Clubhouse: New clubhouse available for hire, contact Operations Manager Michelle on 0161 861 0854
Club Shop: Open 1st XV matchdays 2-5pm
Founded: 1882 **Nickname:** Park **Website:** http://www.broughton-park.org.uk/contactus.htm
Colours: Black & White Hoops. **Change colours:** Red **Training Nights:** Tuesday & Thursday.

BURNAGE R.F.C.

President: Stephen Willcock **Treasurer:** Paul Wilson
Chairman: Simon Coop; Delft House, 59 Waggs Road, Congleton Cheshire CW12 4BT
Tel: 01260 275440 email: sicoop@btinternet.com
Club Secretary: Johnathan Scholes Tel: 07792 851970
Fixtures Secretary: Mr Paul Quare, 17 Erica Drive, Burnage, Manchester M19 1NP
Tel: 0161 4429849 email: pq@cs.man.ac.uk
Club Manager: Andy Green Tel: 0161 432 2150
Ground Address: Varley Park, Battersea Road, Stockport, Cheshire SK4 3EA
Tel: 0161 432 2150 email: burnage@btconnect.com
Directions: From A34 - Turn left or right at the junction with the A5145 / Parrs Wood Lane (towards Stockport). Continue for about .5 mile, then turn right into Station Road. Follow this for approx. .3 mile then take right fork into Vale Road. After approx. 100 metres turn right into Battersea Road. Club at the end.
Capacity: All uncovered standing **Car Parking:** Ample at the clubhouse **Nearest Station:** East Didsbury
Clubhouse: The clubhouse is available for private hire.
Founded: 1936 **Website:** www.burnagerugby.co.uk
Colours: Black **Change colours:** Amber **Training Nights:** Tues & Thur.

NORTHERN

LEIGH R.U.F.C.

President: Joe Downs   Chairman: Dave Phillips   Treasurer: Margaret Hampson
Hon Secretary: Mike Hampson, 12 Briar Close, Hindley Green, Wigan, Lancashire WN2 4RH
Tel: (H) 01942 523 496   email: m.hampson54@btinternet.com
Fixtures Secretary: Tommy Hughes, 2 Launceston Road, Hindley Green, Wigan, Lancashire WN2 4TQ
Tel: (H) 01942 257427
First Team Captain: David Wood
Press Officer: Mark Downs   email: Mark.downs@jacobi.net
Ground Address: Round Ash Park, Hand Lane, Leigh, Lancashire WN7 3NA
Tel: 01942-673526   email: leigh.rufc@btinternet.com   Website: www.leighrufc.co.uk
Directions: 1. From Liverpool & M6 - Follow A580 towards Manchester, go past Lane Head lights (Kings Arms pub on right) until next set of lights. Turn left onto A579 and turn right at first set of lights. Continue along St Helens Road and take 3rd turning right, Beech Walk, the club is at bottom on the left.
2. From Manchester & M60 , M62 - Follow A 580 towards Liverpool and past the Greyhound Motel. First set of lights turn right onto A 579 and turn right at first set of lights. Then as above.
Formed: 1949   **Colours**: Black & Amber
Club Shop: Leigh RUFC shirts and equipment can be bought at Scrumdownunder.com

LIVERPOOL ST. HELENS R.F.C.

President: Ray French   Club Secretary: John Robertson
Chairman & Treasurer: John Bithell   Tel: 0151 426 2464   email: j.bithel@tiscali.co.uk
Fixture Secretary: Ron Hall, 21 Childwall Abbey Road, Liverpool. L16 0JL
Tel: 0151 722 3588 (H)   email: rahall@which.net
Team Secretary: Ged Garvey   Tel: 01744 25296   Director of Rugby: Martin Jones Tel: 0151 220 4964
Press Officer: John Williams   Tel: 07767 441978   email: johnawilliams@blueyonder.co.uk
Secretary of Rugby Management Committee: Ian Harrison   Tel: 01744 884077, 07830 360716 (M)
Ground Address: Moss Lane, (off Rainford Road), Windle, St Helens, WA11 7PL
Tel/Fax: 01744 25708   email: liverpool.rugby@which.net   Website: liverpoolsthelensrugby.co.uk
Directions: Ground is located on Moss Lane off Rainford Road at Junction of A570 & A580 (Windle Island) St Helens
See website for map & detailed directions.   **Nearest BR Station**: St. Helens Central   **Car Parking**: Yes
Capacity: 2000   Covered Seating: 260   **Admission**: Matchday £4 incl. programme
Clubhouse: Open Every day as required for match and function commitments.. Pre match buffet and delicious food bar available.   Available for private function hire, contact Paul Poulton 01744 757838   **Club Shop**: Open matchdays.
Programme: Size: A5 Pages: 32 Price: with admission   Editorial & Advertising: contact John Williams 07767 441978
Founded: 1857   **Nickname**: LSH   **Training Nights**: Tuesday and Thursday generally.
Colours: Red, white, black and blue hoops   **Change Colours**: Blue and red.

LYMM R.F.C.

President: Tony Wright   Chairman: Danny McNichol   Treasurer: J Cartwright
Club Secretary: Cameron Haworth, 35, Mill Lane, Lymm, Cheshire. WA13 9SD
Tel: 01925 755 411   email: CameronsAddress@aol.com
Fixture Secretary: Jim Fergusson, 25 Rushes Meadow, Lymm, Cheshire WA13 7WS
Tel: 07973 496 078   email: james.fergy@tesco.net
Team Secretary: Paul Maguire, 2 Shuldham Close, High Legh, Cheshire WA16 6UE
Tel: 07932 005 378   email: pvmaguire@hotmail.com
Director of Rugby: Paul Maguire (as above)   Commercial Secretary: Rick Condo - Club Manager
Ground Address: Beechwood, Crouchley Lane, Lymm, Cheshire WA13 0AT
Tel: 01925 753212   email: admin@lymmrfc.co.uk   Website: www.lymmrfc.co.uk
Directions: From the M6 J 20/ M56 J 9 follow signs for Lymm along B5158. Follow the road for approx. 1.5 miles to the end, then turn right at T-junction onto A56 towards Altrincham, follow the road for approx. 1/2 mile then turn right, just after the Church Green Pub on your right, onto Crouchley Lane, the club entrance is 300 yards on your right.
Capacity: All uncovered standing   **Admission**: £3   **Car Parking**: Free   **Nearest BR station**: Warrington Bank Quay
Clubhouse: open Tues & Thur 7-11pm, Sat 12-11pm. Available for private hire, contact Rick Condo.
Founded: 1960   **Training nights**: Tuesday and Thursday 7pm start
Colours: Green, black & white   **Change colours**: Red, black & white
Programme: Size: A5   Pages: 24   Price: with admission   Editor: Gordon Kennedy   Advertising: Contact Rick Condo

NEW BRIGHTON FC

President: Chris Roberts **Chairman:** Bill Kerr **Treasurer:** Paul Horner
Club Secretary: Mrs Beryl Bowes, 4 Murrayfield Drive, Moreton, Wirral, Cheshire CH46 3RS
Tel: 0151 678 2654 email: berylbowes@btinternet.com.com
Fixtures & Team Secretary: Guy Hughes: c/o New Brighton FC (RU)
0151 677 2442 Fax: 0151 606 9745 email: nbrugby@hotmail.com
Chairman of Rugby: Dr Neville Waters, 196 Meols Parade, Meols, Wirral, CH47 6AW
Tel : 0151 632 3008: email : nevillewaters@hotmail.com
Address: New Brighton FC (RU), Hartsfield, Reeds Lane, Leasowe, Wirral CH46 3RH Tel: 0151 677 2442 / 0151 677 1873
Capacity: 5,400 Covered Seating: 400 **Car Parking:** 400 at ground
Directions: M53 Jnct 1, direction for New Brighton, then 1st left (signposted Moreton, NBFC) onto Leasowe Rd. Approx. 1 mile turn left at first traffic lights onto Reeds Lane. At about 200 yards turn left into Hartsfield.
Nearest BR Station: Liverpool Lime St.; Leasowe (Wirral line - West Kirby) **Car Parking:** Yes
Admission: Matchday: Adults £5 including programme.
Clubhouse: Open 7 days a week. Snacks always available, hot food on matchdays Functions: Capacity 300. Contact Guy Hughes at club office. **Club Shop:** Open matchdays & training eves., contact club office.
Founded: 20th March 1875 **Nickname:** The Blues **Website:** www.newbrightonrugby.org.uk
Colours: Light blue, navy blue & white quarters. **Change colours:** All white **Training Nights:** Tuesday & Thursday
Programme: Size: A5 Price: with admission Pages: 40
Advertising rates: Colour - Page £500, 1/2 Page 275; 2 colours - Page £220, 1/2 £145. Contact Terry Webster

NORTHWICH R.U.F.C.

President: John Cosgrove **Treasurer:** Tomoas Lewis
Chairman: Colin (Sam) Naylor Tel: 01606 871547 email: snaylor@northwichrufc.co.uk
Hon Secretary: Trevor Rawling, Hartford House, 49 School Lane, Hartford, Northwich, Cheshire CW8 1NT
Tel: (H) 01606 871636 email: trawling@northwichrufc.co.uk
Fixtures Secretary: Ken Houghton, 7 Hareswood Close, Winsford, Cheshire CW7 2TP
Tel: 01606 558317 (H) 07740 896845 (M) email: khoughton@northwwichrufc.co.uk
Junior Section Chairman: Bob Phillips Tel: 01606 810601 email: bphillips@northwichrufc.co.uk
Vice Chairmen - Rugby: Steve Wood Administration: Trevor Rawling Community Development: Phil Clarke
Ground Address: Moss Farm Recreation Centre, Moss Farm, Winnington, Northwich, Cheshire CW8 4BH
Moss Farm Centre Office (staffed/managed by Cheshire West and City of Chester Council) Tel: 01606 783823
Club Contact - Tel: 01606 871636 email: club-secretary@northwichrufc.co.uk
Official Club Address: Northwich Rugby Union Football Club, Moss Farm Recreation Centre, rest as above
Directions: Moss Farm is also the site of Northwich swimming pool. Follow the signs for Moss Farm when you get to Northwich. Please note that Moss Farm is public amenity run by the local authority and has a 'No dogs' policy. So please do not bring your dog along to the match. For detailed directions see the club website - www.northwich rufc.co.uk
Club Shop: Open Sat & Sun. Contact Eleri Phillips ephillips @northwichrufc.co.uk or see website.
Formed: 1965 **Training Nights:** Tuesday & Thursday (Seniors) 6.30pm
Colours: Black shirts with gold collar & trim, black shorts **Website:** www.northwichrufc.co.uk

SANDBACH R.U.F.C.

President: Keith Jones **Treasurer:** John Pemberton **Director of Rugby:** Nigel Burrows
Chairman: Robin Astles, Smethwick House, Smethwick Lane, Sandbach, Cheshire CW11 2ST
Tel: 01477 500221 email: chairman@sandbachrufc.co.uk
Team Secretary: Alex Burton, 11 Brownlow Heath, Brownlow, Congleton, Cheshire, CW12 4TH
Tel: 07714 0133655 email: coach@sandbachrufc.co.uk
Hon Secretary: Chris Tapper, c/o Gorse Fields Barn, Booth Lane, Kinderton, Middlewich, Cheshire, CW10 0LE
Tel: (M) 07795 467502 Email: secretary@sandbachrufc.co.uk
Fixtures Secretary: Simon Price, 117 Abbey Road, Sandbach, Cheshire CW11 3HB
Tel: 01270 764739 email: fixtures@sandbachrufc.co.uk
Commercial Secretary: Chris Butler **House Secretary:** Jon Stubbs **Mini/Junior Chairman:** Tony Barry
Ground Address: Bradwall Road, Sandbach, Cheshire, CW11 1RA Tel: 01270 762475 email: webmaster@sandbachrufc.co.uk
Directions: Junction 17 on the M6, follow signs to Sandbach, turn right on to Congleton Road, opposite petrol station, turn right onto Offley Road, turn right at mini r'about, on to Bradwall Road, Club 200 meters on right.
Capacity: 1,500 all uncovered standing **Car Parking:** Space for 400 cars **Nearest BR station:** Sandbach
Clubhouse: Variable opening hours. Available for private hire. Contact jon Stubbs 07771 570121
Programme: Size: A5 Pages: 12 Price: Free Editor: Jon Stubbs Advertising: £100 page; £50 1/2 page; £25 1/4 page
Founded: 1934 **Colours:** Green and red **Change colours:** Black and red **Website:** www.sandbachrufc.co.uk
Club Shop: Variable opening hours. contact Karen Stubbs 01270 766944 **Training Nights:** Tuesday & Thursday

450

TYLDESLEY R.U.F.C.

President: Terry Alexander **Chairman:** Keith Sharratt **Treasurer:** Susan Broad
Club Secretary: Howard Hughes, 81 Astley Street, Tyldesley, Lancashire, M29 7BA
Tel: 01133 828251 (W) 01942 877055 (H) 07736 854060 (M) email: howard.3.hughes@bt.com
Fixtures Secretary: Adrian Jones, 363 Manchester Road, Blackmoor, Astley, M29 7DX
Tel: 01942 883348 (W) 01942 876938 (H) email: adyjonesblackmoor@hotmail.co.uk
Team Secretary: Ian Lysons Tel: 07770 691398 **Director of Rugby:** Lee Cunliffe **Commercial Secretary:** Paul Woodward
Ground Address: St. Georges Park, Astley Street, Tyldesley, Lancs. M29 8HN
Tel: 01942 882967 (Club) 01942 877055 (Admin) email: bongsrugby@hotmail.co.uk
Directions: Follow Astley/Tyldesley signs from the A580 as you head up the hill into Tyldesley the Club is on the left hand side facing Standish Street and the Public Park. **Car Parking:** 250cars **Nearest Station:** Atherton 2.5 miles
Capacity: 4000 - all uncovered standing. **Admission** - Matchday £3, Season Ticket £25
Clubhouse: Open from 6pm weekdays, 11am weekends until 12 midnight. Food available only on matchdays until 6pm.
Available for private hire, contact Jim Redmond 01942 882967.
Club Shop: Open Saturday 12 noon – 1.30pm, contact Mike Prendergast
Programme: Size: A5 Pages: 20 Price: with admission Editor: Paul Woodward
Advertising Rates: Full Page £150, Half Page £90, Third of a Page £55
Founded: 1881 **Nickname:** Bongs **Website:** www.tyldesleyrufc.co.uk
Colours: Royal blue shirts, white shorts **Change colours:** Red shirts, white shorts **Training Nights:** Tues & Thur.

VALE OF LUNE R.U.F.C.

President: Phil Sutcliffe **Chairman:** Brian McCann **Treasurer:** Tony Whiteway
Club & Commercial Secretary: Peter Lovett-Horn c/o the club Tel: 01524 64029 email: valerugby@btconnect.com
Fixtures Secretary: Fred Swarbrick, Oxendale, Wyresdale Road, Lancaster, LA13JJ
Tel: 01524 37601 email: f.swarbrick@homecall.co.uk
Team Secretary: Stuart Hesketh, 1 Mallard Court, Lancaster LA1 1TL Tel: 07943 175122
Directors Of Rugby: Andy Higgin, Steven Swarbrick
Press Secretary: Stuart Vernon, 01524 822092
Coach: Graham Murphy **Colts Academy chair:** Neil McSporran, 07970153264
Ground chair: Geoff Marsden, 01524 824280 **Junior Rugby Chair:** Michelle Fish, 07764 960224
Ground Address: Powderhouse Lane, Lancaster LA1 2TT Tel: 01524 64029 email: valerugby@btconnect.com
Directions: Ground located off Torrisholme Road between Lancaster and Morecambe.
Capacity: 4000 Covered Seating: 300 **Admission:** Matchday £4 Season: £40
Car Parking: 300 cars **Nearest Station:** Lancaster
Clubhouse: Open 6.30pm – 11.30. Food available. Available for private hire, contact Derrick Freedman 01525 64029
Club Shop: Open saturday & Sunday afternoons. Contact the Secretary.
Programme: Size: A5 Pages: 16 Price: with admission Editor: Stuart Vernon Advertising contact the Secretary
Founded: 1900 **Nickname:** The Vale **Website:** www.valeoflune.co.uk
Colours: Cherry and white hoops **Change colours:** Navy and blue hoops **Training Nights:** Tues & Thur. at 7pm

WILMSLOW R.U.F.C.

President: David Barker 01625 829008 pottiebarker@hotmail.com
Chairman: John Harries 01625 521159 (H) 07946 894253(M) jananjon@ic24.net
Hon. Treasurer: Tony Kersh 01625 421394 (H) 07979 505637(M) tkersh-acf@btconnect.com
Hon Secretary: Grant Mckechnie, 18 Nursery Lane, Wilmslow, Cheshire SK9 5JQ
Tel: 01625 517663 email: Grant.Mckechnie@AstraZeneca.com
Hon. Fixtures Secretary & Referees Convenor: Simon Muckle
Tel: 07980 565563 (M) simon.muckle@wilmslowrugby.com
Director of Rugby: Darren 'Daz' Lucas 01625 527725 (H) 07720 459500 (M) email: Darren.lucas@ntlworld.com
Ground Address: Memorial Ground, Kings Road, Wilmslow SK9 5PZ
Tel: 01625 522 274 email: info@wilmslowrugby.com
Directions: Kings Road is off the A538 Wilmslow to Altrincham, approx. 4 miles from the M56 junction 6. It is on the left as you enter the town., just after the Texaco garage.
Clubhouse: Club Steward - Keith Booth 01625 522274 (Club) 07787 351681 (M) postmaster@keithbooth.plus.com
Club Shop: Manager - Elaine Hill 01625 536387 (H) 07813 871976 (M) elaine.k.hill@btinternet.com
Colours: Sky Blue with Maroon & White Hoops
Founded: 1884, reformed 1923 **Website:** www.wilmslowrugby.com

451

NORTH 1 EAST

Yorkshire 1 ▲   ▲ Durham/Northumberland 1

Yorkshire 1	P	W	D	L	PF	PA	PD	Pts	Adj
1 Old Brodleians	22	19	0	3	581	235	346	38	
2 Bridlington	22	18	0	4	524	219	305	36	
3 Bradford Salem	22	16	0	6	554	326	228	32	
4 Heath	22	14	1	7	473	408	65	29	
5 York	22	10	1	11	410	431	-21	21	
6 Keighley	22	10	0	12	335	401	-66	20	
7 Selby	22	8	3	11	417	486	-69	19	
8 Sheffield	21	8	1	12	335	370	-35	17	
9 Malton and Norton	22	8	0	14	345	467	-122	16	
10 Skipton	22	7	1	14	396	440	-44	15	
11 Scarborough	21	5	1	15	312	499	-187	11	
12 Glossop	22	4	0	18	238	638	-400	8	

Yorkshire 2	P	W	D	L	PF	PA	PD	Pts	Adj
1 Wheatley Hills Doncaster	20	18	1	1	552	203	349	37	
2 Castleford	20	14	1	5	508	296	212	29	
3 Dinnington	20	14	1	5	447	249	198	29	
4 Yarnbury	20	9	1	10	323	490	-167	19	
5 Pocklington	20	8	2	10	423	386	37	18	
6 Moortown	20	9	0	11	332	354	-22	18	
7 North Ribblesdale	20	9	0	11	286	365	-79	16	-2
8 Leodiensian	20	7	1	12	258	399	-141	15	
9 Knottingley	20	7	0	13	309	363	-54	14	
10 Ripon	20	7	0	13	317	451	-134	14	
11 Huddersfield Y.M.C.A.	20	4	1	15	335	534	-199	7	-2

Yorkshire 3	P	W	D	L	PF	PA	PD	Pts	Adj
1 West Park Leeds	22	19	1	2	552	248	304	39	
2 Hullensians	22	18	0	4	730	282	448	36	
3 Barnsley	22	16	0	6	565	397	168	32	
4 Hessle	22	16	0	6	496	338	158	32	
5 Goole	22	10	3	9	474	416	58	23	
6 West Leeds	22	11	1	10	442	448	-6	23	
7 Doncaster Phoenix	22	9	1	12	445	459	-14	19	
8 Aireborough	22	7	0	15	434	595	-161	14	
9 Old Otliensians	22	7	0	15	343	592	-249	14	
10 Baildon	22	5	1	16	254	469	-215	11	
11 Roundhegians	22	5	1	16	316	567	-251	11	
12 Wath Upon Dearne	22	5	0	17	292	532	-240	10	

Yorkshire 4	P	W	D	L	PF	PA	PD	Pts	Adj
1 Old Rishworthian	22	19	0	3	685	190	495	38	
2 Bramley Phoenix	22	16	1	5	548	255	293	33	
3 Thornensians	22	14	0	8	455	296	159	28	
4 Old Modernians	22	14	0	8	479	348	131	28	
5 Halifax Vandals	22	13	1	8	339	314	25	27	
6 Garforth	22	10	3	9	432	368	64	23	
7 Northallerton	22	10	1	11	373	390	-17	21	
8 Rotherham Phoenix	22	9	1	12	336	412	-76	19	
9 Leeds Corinthians	22	7	2	13	344	437	-93	14	-2
10 York Railway Institute	22	5	2	15	257	550	-293	12	
11 Hornsea	22	5	0	17	267	678	-411	10	
12 Burley	22	4	1	17	222	499	-277	9	0

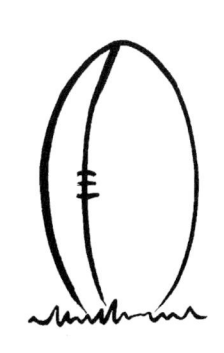

NORTHERN DIVISION LEAGUE TABLES 2008-09

Yorkshire 5A	P	W	D	L	PF	PA	PD	Pts	Adj
1 Sheffield Medicals	16	14	0	2	508	129	379	28	
2 Hemsworth	16	13	0	3	435	144	291	26	
3 Ossett	16	13	0	3	346	152	194	26	
4 Harrogate Pythons	16	11	0	5	416	226	190	22	
5 Knaresborough	16	8	0	8	414	325	89	16	
6 Mosborough	16	4	0	12	234	329	-95	8	
7 Pontefract Pythons	16	5	0	11	244	392	-148	8	-2
8 Stocksbridge	16	4	0	12	133	399	-266	6	-2
9 Sheffield Oaks	16	0	0	16	48	682	-634	0	

Yorkshire 5B	P	W	D	L	PF	PA	PD	Pts	Adj
1 Leeds Met. University	15	15	0	0	741	83	658	26	-2
2 Leeds Medics	16	12	0	4	505	155	350	24	
3 Old Grovians	16	10	0	6	388	342	46	20	
4 Adwick Le Street	16	9	1	6	324	325	-1	17	-2
5 Stanley Rodillians	16	7	0	9	251	337	-86	12	-2
6 Marist	16	5	0	11	208	370	-162	10	
7 Wibsey	16	5	0	11	147	576	-429	10	
8 Rossington Hornets	15	4	1	10	193	281	-88	7	-2
9 Wetherby	16	3	0	13	114	402	-288	4	-2

Durham/N'thm'land 1	P	W	D	L	PF	PA	PD	Pts	Adj
1 Hartlepool Rovers	22	21	0	1	899	269	630	42	
2 Percy Park	22	20	0	2	704	230	474	40	
3 Alnwick	22	16	0	6	452	324	128	32	
4 Northern	22	15	0	7	587	400	187	30	
5 Horden	22	14	0	8	618	375	243	28	
6 Gosforth	22	9	0	13	324	511	-187	18	
7 Ashington	22	7	2	13	338	455	-117	16	
8 Stockton	22	7	1	14	342	556	-214	15	
9 Wallsend	22	7	1	14	309	523	-214	13	-2
10 Ryton	22	5	0	17	267	614	-347	10	
11 Sunderland	22	3	1	18	315	604	-289	7	
12 Consett	22	5	1	16	322	616	-294	5	-6

Durham/N'thm'land 2	P	W	D	L	PF	PA	PD	Pts	Adj
1 Team Northumbria	22	18	0	4	725	308	417	36	
2 Hartlepool	22	18	0	4	540	231	309	36	
3 Redcar	22	16	0	6	631	351	280	32	
4 Barnard Castle	22	13	0	9	419	340	79	26	
5 Novocastrians	22	13	0	9	459	386	73	26	
6 Ponteland	22	12	0	10	383	323	60	24	
7 Medicals	22	10	1	11	490	422	68	21	
8 Winlaton Vulcans	22	8	0	14	424	463	-39	16	
9 Whitley Bay Rockcliff	22	7	2	13	269	419	-150	16	
10 North Shields	22	6	1	15	320	667	-347	13	
11 Acklam	22	5	1	16	271	484	-213	11	
12 Houghton	22	3	1	18	232	769	-537	7	0

NORTHERN DIVISION LEAGUE TABLES 2008-09

Durham/N'thm'land 3

		P	W	D	L	PF	PA	PD	Pts	Adj
1	Seaton Carew	20	20	0	0	837	168	669	40	
2	Bishop Auckland	20	16	0	4	579	150	429	32	
3	Blyth	20	15	0	5	592	228	364	30	
4	Yarm	20	14	0	6	336	291	45	28	
5	Guisborough	20	12	0	8	505	228	277	24	
6	Whitby	20	10	0	10	350	258	92	20	
7	South Tyneside College	20	9	0	11	341	478	-137	18	
8	Hartlepool Athletic	20	6	0	14	200	621	-421	10	-2
9	Hartlepool B.B.O.B.	20	3	1	16	230	551	-321	5	-2
10	Chester-Le-Street	20	2	1	17	156	685	-529	5	
11	Seaham	20	2	0	18	174	642	-468	4	

NORTH 1 WEST

North Lancs/Cumbria ↑   ↑ South Lancs/Cheshire 1

North Lancs/Cumbria

		P	W	D	L	PF	PA	PD	Pts	Adj
1	Tyldesley	22	19	0	3	547	254	293	38	
2	Vale of Lune	22	17	1	4	585	240	345	35	
3	Kirkby Lonsdale	22	16	0	6	458	245	213	32	
4	Heaton Moor	22	13	2	7	550	412	138	28	
5	Wigton	22	13	1	8	477	242	235	27	
6	Workington	22	13	0	9	425	331	94	26	
7	Keswick	22	9	1	12	315	498	-183	19	
8	Oldham	22	8	0	14	355	495	-140	16	
9	Fleetwood	22	7	0	15	291	518	-227	14	
10	Aldwinians	22	6	1	15	278	395	-117	13	
11	Upper Eden	22	5	0	17	318	602	-284	10	
12	Burnley	22	3	0	19	238	605	-367	6	

North Lancs 1

		P	W	D	L	PF	PA	PD	Pts	Adj
1	Furness	22	17	2	3	512	241	271	36	
2	Eccles	22	17	1	4	527	190	337	35	
3	Didsbury Toc H	22	17	0	5	553	232	321	34	
4	Littleborough	22	14	0	8	384	259	125	28	
5	De La Salle (Salford)	22	16	1	5	427	200	227	21	-12
6	Trafford MV	22	10	1	11	395	348	47	21	
7	Birchfield (Lancs)	22	9	2	11	346	384	-38	20	
8	Ashton-Under-Lyne	22	10	0	12	286	399	-113	20	
9	Bury	22	6	0	16	242	444	-202	12	
10	Bolton	22	4	1	17	202	518	-316	9	
11	Garstang	22	4	0	18	197	502	-305	8	
12	Old Bedians	22	4	0	18	250	604	-354	8	

North Lancs 2

		P	W	D	L	PF	PA	PD	Pts	Adj
1	Hutton	17	16	0	1	846	82	764	32	
2	Windermere	18	15	0	3	548	260	288	30	
3	Hawcoat Park	18	12	0	6	367	279	88	24	
4	Tarleton	18	11	0	7	431	202	229	22	
5	Chorley	18	10	0	8	289	344	-55	20	
6	North Manchester	17	9	0	8	321	351	-30	18	
7	Colne & Nelson	17	5	1	11	178	368	-190	11	
8	Clitheroe	18	5	1	12	256	475	-219	11	
9	Blackpool	17	2	0	15	189	586	-397	4	
10	Carnforth	18	2	0	16	151	629	-478	4	

Cumbria

		P	W	D	L	PF	PA	PD	Pts	Adj
1	Netherhall	21	18	0	3	643	137	506	36	
2	St Benedicts	18	16	1	1	562	98	464	33	
3	Whitehaven	20	14	2	4	623	127	496	30	
4	Egremont	19	14	0	5	712	166	546	28	

NORTHERN DIVISION LEAGUE TABLES 2008-09

		P	W	D	L	PF	PA	PD	Pts	
5	Millom	20	14	0	6	511	189	322	28	
6	Cockermouth	20	9	0	11	215	362	-147	18	
7	Gosforth Greengarth	11	5	0	6	126	317	-191	10	
8	Wigton Wanderers	19	5	0	14	256	485	-229	10	
9	Aspatria Eagles	20	4	1	15	208	635	-427	9	
10	Creighton	19	4	0	15	281	636	-355	8	
11	Workington Steelers	20	3	0	17	183	908	-725	6	
12	Moresby	13	2	0	11	127	387	-260	4	

South Lancs/Cheshire 1

		P	W	D	L	PF	PA	PD	Pts	Adj
1	Burnage	20	17	1	2	620	274	346	35	
2	Widnes	20	16	0	4	715	338	377	32	
3	Sale	20	15	0	5	509	325	184	30	
4	Wirral	20	13	1	6	545	274	271	27	
5	Bowdon	20	11	0	9	440	359	81	22	
6	Ormskirk	20	10	0	10	516	474	42	20	
7	Hoylake	20	8	0	12	302	465	-163	16	
8	Vagabonds (I.O.M.)	20	6	0	14	286	645	-359	12	
9	Winnington Park	20	5	1	14	378	486	-108	11	
10	Wigan	20	5	0	15	267	531	-264	10	
11	Dukinfield	20	2	1	17	206	613	-407	5	

South Lancs/Cheshire 2

		P	W	D	L	PF	PA	PD	Pts	Adj
1	Anselmians	22	17	1	4	572	279	293	35	
2	Warrington	22	17	0	5	446	292	154	34	
3	Oswestry	22	16	1	5	410	313	97	29	-4
4	Sefton	22	14	0	8	420	346	74	28	
5	Ruskin Park	22	13	1	8	368	293	75	27	
6	Douglas (I.O.M.)	22	11	2	9	360	342	18	22	-2
7	Trentham	22	7	2	13	231	428	-197	16	
8	Ashton-on-Mersey	22	7	2	13	345	390	-45	14	-2
9	Wallasey	22	7	1	14	339	479	-140	13	-2
10	Southport	22	6	0	16	235	339	-104	12	
11	Orrell Anvils	22	9	0	13	313	313	0	8	-10
12	Crewe and Nantwich	22	3	0	19	288	513	-225	6	

South Lancs/Cheshire 3

		P	W	D	L	PF	PA	PD	Pts	Adj
1	Oldershaw	22	19	1	2	852	125	727	39	
2	Liverpool Collegiate	22	19	0	3	695	219	476	38	
3	Moore	22	16	0	6	521	300	221	32	
4	Marple	22	13	0	9	574	393	181	26	
5	Holmes Chapel	22	12	2	8	443	352	91	26	
6	Knutsford	22	10	0	12	420	535	-115	16	-4
7	St Edward's O.B.	22	9	0	13	309	485	-176	16	-2
8	Prenton	22	8	1	13	276	432	-156	15	-2
9	Ellesmere Port	22	7	0	15	209	603	-394	14	
10	Eagle	22	7	0	15	398	511	-113	12	-2
11	Newton-le-Willows	22	6	1	15	307	574	-267	9	-4
12	Mossley Hill	22	3	1	18	241	716	-475	7	

South Lancs/Cheshire 4

		P	W	D	L	PF	PA	PD	Pts	Adj
1	West Park Warriors	18	16	0	2	405	242	163	32	
2	Linley	18	13	1	4	473	149	324	27	
3	Parkonians	18	13	1	4	506	228	278	27	
4	Ramsey (IoM)	18	13	1	4	431	154	277	27	
5	Capenhurst	18	9	1	8	293	334	-41	19	
6	St Mary's O.B. (Lancs)	18	7	0	11	316	327	-11	14	
7	Port Sunlight	17	7	1	9	266	377	-111	13	-2
8	Congleton	18	4	1	13	201	506	-305	9	
9	Helsby	18	4	0	14	294	445	-151	8	
10	Merseyside Police	17	0	0	17	152	575	-423	-4	-4

455

NORTH DIVISION FIXTURE GRIDS 2009-2010

YORKSHIRE ONE

	Bradford Salem	Bridlington	Castleford	Dinnington	Heath	Keighley	Malton and Norton	Scarborough	Selby	Sheffield	Skipton	Wheatley Hills	Yarnbury	York
Bradford Salem		12/09	13/03	28/11	30/01	26/09	16/01	19/12	24/10	10/10	20/02	27/03	05/09	07/11
Bridlington	12/12		28/11	27/03	24/10	16/01	10/10	26/09	20/02	30/01	07/11	05/09	19/09	13/03
Castleford	14/11	20/03		31/10	26/09	10/04	12/09	05/12	16/01	19/12	10/10	06/03	13/02	30/01
Dinnington	20/03	05/12	20/02		16/01	12/09	19/12	10/04	10/10	26/09	30/01	14/11	06/03	24/10
Heath	17/10	13/02	09/01	03/10		06/03	14/11	31/10	05/09	20/03	12/12	23/01	05/12	19/09
Keighley	09/01	03/10	05/09	12/12	07/11		24/10	23/01	13/03	20/02	28/11	19/09	17/10	27/03
Malton and Norton	03/10	23/01	12/12	19/09	13/03	13/02		17/10	28/11	07/11	27/03	09/01	31/10	05/09
Scarborough	19/09	09/01	27/03	05/09	20/02	10/10	30/01		07/11	24/10	13/03	12/12	03/10	28/11
Selby	13/02	31/10	03/10	23/01	10/04	14/11	20/03	06/03		05/12	19/09	17/10	12/12	09/01
Sheffield	23/01	17/10	19/09	09/01	28/11	31/10	06/03	13/02	27/03		05/09	03/10	14/11	12/12
Skipton	31/10	06/03	23/01	17/10	12/09	20/03	05/12	14/11	19/12	10/04		13/02	09/01	03/10
Wheatley Hills Doncaster	05/12	10/04	07/11	13/03	10/10	19/12	26/09	12/09	30/01	16/01	24/10		20/03	20/02
Yarnbury	10/04	19/12	24/10	07/11	27/03	30/01	20/02	16/01	12/09	13/03	26/09	28/11		10/10
York	06/03	14/11	17/10	13/02	19/12	05/12	10/04	20/03	26/09	12/09	16/01	31/10	23/01	

DURHAM & NORTHUMBERLAND 1

	Alnwick	Ashington	Consett	Gosforth	Hartlepool	Horden	Northern	Novocastrians	Redcar	Ryton	Stockton	Sunderland	Team Northumbria	Wallsend
Alnwick		13/03	07/11	10/10	28/11	20/02	30/01	27/03	05/09	16/01	26/09	12/12	19/09	24/10
Ashington	14/11		16/01	10/04	17/10	26/09	12/09	13/02	31/10	05/12	20/03	06/03	23/01	19/12
Consett	06/03	03/10		05/12	23/01	19/12	10/04	17/10	13/02	20/03	14/11	31/10	09/01	12/09
Gosforth	23/01	05/09	27/03		12/12	28/11	07/11	19/09	09/01	13/02	17/10	03/10	31/10	13/03
Hartlepool	20/03	30/01	10/10	12/09		16/01	19/12	31/10	06/03	10/04	05/12	14/11	13/02	26/09
Horden	31/10	09/01	19/09	20/03	03/10		05/12	23/01	17/10	14/11	06/03	13/02	12/12	10/04
Northern	17/10	12/12	05/09	06/03	19/09	27/03		09/01	03/10	31/10	13/02	23/01	14/11	28/11
Novocastrians	05/12	24/10	30/01	19/12	20/02	10/10	26/09		14/11	12/09	10/04	20/03	06/03	16/01
Redcar	10/04	20/02	24/10	26/09	07/11	30/01	16/01	13/03		19/12	12/09	05/12	20/03	10/10
Ryton	03/10	27/03	28/11	24/10	05/09	13/03	20/02	12/12	19/09		23/01	09/01	17/10	07/11
Stockton	09/01	28/11	13/03	30/01	27/03	07/11	24/10	05/09	12/12	10/10		19/09	03/10	20/02
Sunderland	12/09	07/11	20/02	16/01	13/03	24/10	10/10	28/11	27/03	26/09	19/12		05/09	30/01
Team Northumbria	19/12	10/10	26/09	20/02	24/10	12/09	13/03	07/11	28/11	30/01	16/01	10/04		27/03
Wallsend	13/02	19/09	12/12	14/11	09/01	05/09	20/03	03/10	23/01	06/03	31/10	17/10	05/12	

LEVEL SEVEN

SOUTH LANCASHIRE & CHESHIRE

	Anselmians	Bowdon	Dukinfield	Glossop	Hoylake	Ormskirk	Oswestry	Sale	Vagabonds (IoM)	Warrington	Widnes	Wigan	Winnington Park	Wirral
Anselmians		05/12	12/09	03/10	20/03	19/12	13/02	14/11	23/01	09/01	06/03	17/10	10/04	31/10
Bowdon	27/03		13/03	05/09	13/02	28/11	09/01	17/10	12/12	31/10	23/01	19/09	07/11	03/10
Dukinfield	12/12	14/11		19/09	06/03	05/09	23/01	31/10	09/01	05/12	13/02	03/10	20/03	17/10
Glossop	16/01	10/04	19/12		05/12	26/09	31/10	20/03	17/10	23/01	14/11	13/02	12/09	06/03
Hoylake	28/11	24/10	07/11	27/03		13/03	19/09	23/01	05/09	17/10	03/10	12/12	20/02	09/01
Ormskirk	19/09	20/03	10/04	09/01	14/11		17/10	06/03	03/10	12/12	31/10	23/01	05/12	13/02
Oswestry	24/10	26/09	10/10	20/02	19/12	30/01		12/09	07/11	20/03	10/04	13/03	16/01	05/12
Sale	13/03	30/01	20/02	28/11	10/10	07/11	12/12		27/03	03/10	09/01	05/09	24/10	19/09
Vagabonds (I.O.M.)	10/10	12/09	26/09	30/01	10/04	16/01	06/03	05/12		13/02	20/03	31/10	19/12	14/11
Warrington	26/09	20/02	27/03	10/10	30/01	12/09	28/11	16/01	24/10		19/12	07/11	13/03	10/04
Widnes	07/11	10/10	24/10	13/03	16/01	20/02	05/09	26/09	28/11	19/09		27/03	30/01	12/12
Wigan	30/01	19/12	16/01	24/10	12/09	10/10	14/11	10/04	20/02	06/03	05/12		26/09	20/03
Winnington Park	05/09	06/03	28/11	12/12	31/10	27/03	03/10	13/02	19/09	14/11	17/10	09/01		23/01
Wirral	20/02	16/01	30/01	07/11	26/09	24/10	27/03	19/12	13/03	05/09	12/09	28/11	10/10	

NORTH LANCASHIRE & CUMBRIA

	Aldwinians	Burnley	Eccles	Fleetwood	Furness	Heaton Moor	Kswick	Kirkby Lonsdale	Netherall	Oldham	St Benedicts	Upper Eden	Wigton	Workington
Aldwinians		13/02	12/12	27/03	19/09	17/10	07/11	03/10	09/01	05/09	31/10	28/11	13/03	23/01
Burnley	24/10		05/09	28/11	12/12	23/01	20/02	09/01	19/09	27/03	17/10	13/03	07/11	03/10
Eccles	12/09	10/04		10/10	31/10	05/12	19/12	14/11	06/03	30/01	13/02	16/01	26/09	20/03
Fleetwood	05/12	20/03	23/01		17/10	14/11	10/04	31/10	13/02	03/10	09/01	19/12	12/09	06/03
Furness	19/12	12/09	20/02	30/01		10/04	26/09	20/03	14/11	24/10	06/03	10/10	16/01	05/12
Heaton Moor	30/01	10/10	27/03	13/03	05/09		24/10	19/09	12/12	28/11	03/10	07/11	20/02	09/01
Keswick	06/03	31/10	19/09	05/09	09/01	13/02		23/01	03/10	12/12	14/11	27/03	28/11	17/10
Kirkby Lonsdale	16/01	26/09	13/03	20/02	28/11	19/12	10/10		27/03	07/11	05/09	24/10	30/01	12/09
Netherall	26/09	19/12	07/11	24/10	13/03	12/09	16/01	05/12		20/02	20/03	30/01	10/10	10/04
Oldham	10/04	05/12	17/10	16/01	13/02	20/03	12/09	06/03	31/10		23/01	26/09	19/12	14/11
St Benedicts	20/02	30/01	24/10	26/09	07/11	16/01	13/05	10/04	28/11	10/10		12/09	27/03	19/12
Upper Eden	20/03	14/11	03/10	19/09	23/01	06/03	05/12	13/02	17/10	09/01	12/12		10/04	31/10
Wigton	14/11	06/03	09/01	12/12	03/10	31/10	20/03	17/10	23/01	19/09	05/12	05/09		13/02
Workington	10/10	16/01	28/11	07/11	27/03	26/09	30/01	12/12	05/09	13/03	19/09	20/02	24/10	

NORTH DIVISION FIXTURE GRIDS 2009-2010

YORKSHIRE TWO

		1	2	3	4	5	6	7	8	9	10	11	12	13	14
1	Barnsley		19/09	09/01	03/10	10/04	23/01	14/11	05/12	31/10	20/03	06/03	13/02	17/10	12/12
2	Doncaster Phoenix	19/12		03/10	23/01	12/09	17/10	20/03	10/04	06/03	05/12	14/11	31/10	13/02	09/01
3	Goole	26/09	16/01		17/10	19/12	13/02	05/12	12/09	14/11	10/04	20/03	06/03	31/10	23/01
4	Hessle	16/01	10/10	30/01		26/09	31/10	10/04	19/12	20/03	12/09	05/12	14/11	06/03	13/02
5	Huddersfield Y.M.C.A.	05/09	12/12	19/09	09/01		03/10	06/03	20/03	13/02	14/11	31/10	17/10	23/01	05/12
6	Hullensians	10/10	30/01	24/10	20/02	16/01		12/09	26/09	05/12	19/12	10/04	20/03	14/11	06/03
7	Knottingley	13/03	28/11	27/03	05/09	07/11	12/12		20/02	03/10	24/10	23/01	09/01	19/09	17/10
8	Leodiensian	27/03	05/09	12/12	19/09	28/11	09/01	31/10		17/10	06/03	13/02	23/01	03/10	14/11
9	Moortown	20/02	07/11	13/03	28/11	24/10	27/03	16/01	30/01		10/10	26/09	12/12	05/09	19/09
10	North Ribblesdale	28/11	27/03	05/09	12/12	13/03	19/09	13/02	07/11	23/01		17/10	03/10	09/01	31/10
11	Pocklington	07/11	13/03	28/11	27/03	20/02	05/09	10/10	24/10	09/01	30/01		19/09	12/12	03/10
12	Ripon	24/10	20/02	07/11	13/03	30/01	28/11	26/09	10/04	12/09	16/01	19/12		27/03	05/09
13	West Leeds	30/01	24/10	20/02	07/11	10/04	13/03	19/12	16/01	10/04	26/09	12/09	05/12		20/03
14	West Park Leeds	12/09	26/09	10/10	24/10	27/03	07/11	30/01	13/03	19/12	20/02	16/01	10/04	28/11	

YORKSHIRE THREE

		1	2	3	4	5	6	7	8	9	10	11	12
1	Aireborough		12/09	31/10	20/02	14/11	13/03	12/12	30/01	10/04	03/10	05/09	16/01
2	Baildon	09/01		20/02	14/11	13/03	12/12	10/04	31/10	05/09	30/01	26/09	03/10
3	Bramley Phoenix	13/02	07/11		05/09	09/01	26/09	23/01	20/03	17/10	28/11	19/12	06/03
4	Garforth	07/11	06/03	17/04		26/09	23/01	17/10	19/12	13/02	20/03	09/01	28/11
5	Halifax Vandals	06/03	28/11	12/09	16/01		17/10	13/02	17/04	07/11	19/12	23/01	20/03
6	Northallerton	28/11	20/03	16/01	03/10	30/01		07/11	12/09	06/03	17/04	13/02	19/12
7	Old Modernians	20/03	19/12	03/10	30/01	31/10	20/02		16/01	28/11	12/09	06/03	17/04
8	Old Otliensians	17/10	13/02	12/12	10/04	05/09	09/01	26/09		23/01	06/03	28/11	07/11
9	Old Rishworthian	19/12	17/04	30/01	31/10	20/02	14/11	13/03	03/10		16/01	20/03	12/09
10	Roundhegians	23/01	17/10	13/03	12/12	10/04	05/09	09/01	14/11	26/09		07/11	13/02
11	Thornensians	17/04	16/01	10/04	12/09	03/10	31/10	14/11	13/03	12/12	20/02		30/01
12	Wath Upon Dearne	26/09	23/01	14/11	13/03	12/12	10/04	05/09	20/02	09/01	31/10	17/10	

YORKSHIRE FOUR

		1	2	3	4	5	6	7	8	9	10	11	12
1	Adwick Le Street		19/12	16/01	03/10	28/11	20/03	30/01	07/11	06/03	12/09	13/02	17/04
2	Burley	10/04		14/11	13/03	26/09	23/01	12/12	05/09	09/01	20/02	17/10	31/10
3	Harrogate Pythons	26/09	06/03		05/09	13/02	07/11	09/01	23/01	17/10	20/03	19/12	28/11
4	Hemsworth	23/01	28/11	17/04		07/11	06/03	26/09	17/10	13/02	19/12	09/01	20/03
5	Hornsea	13/03	16/01	31/10	20/02		12/09	14/11	12/12	10/04	30/01	05/09	03/10
6	Leeds Corinthians	12/12	03/10	20/02	14/11	09/01		13/03	10/04	05/09	31/10	26/09	30/01
7	Leeds Medics	17/10	20/03	12/09	16/01	06/03	28/11		13/02	07/11	17/04	23/01	19/12
8	Old Grovians	20/02	17/04	03/10	30/01	20/03	19/12	31/10		28/11	16/01	06/03	12/09
9	Ossett	14/11	12/09	30/01	31/10	19/12	17/04	20/02	13/03		03/10	20/03	16/01
10	Rotherham Phoenix	09/01	07/11	12/12	10/04	17/10	13/02	05/09	26/09	23/01		28/11	06/03
11	Sheffield Medicals	31/10	30/01	10/04	12/09	17/04	16/01	03/10	14/11	12/12	13/03		20/02
12	York Railway Institute	05/09	13/02	13/03	12/12	23/01	17/10	10/04	09/01	26/09	14/11	07/11	

YORKSHIRE FIVE

		1	2	3	4	5	6	7
1	Knaresborough		26/09	12/12	17/10	09/01	07/11	23/01
2	Marist	28/11		17/10	09/01	07/11	23/01	12/09
3	Mosborough	03/10	19/12		07/11	23/01	12/09	28/11
4	Pontefract Pythons	19/12	31/10	16/01		12/09	28/11	03/10
5	Stanley Rodillians	31/10	16/01	14/11	30/01		03/10	19/12
6	Stocksbridge	16/01	14/11	30/01	26/09	12/12		31/10
7	Wibsey	14/11	30/01	26/09	12/12	17/10	09/01	

DURHAM & NORTHUMBERLAND TWO

		1	2	3	4	5	6	7	8	9	10	11	12
1	Acklam		31/10	13/03	12/12	03/10	20/02	30/01	14/11	10/04	16/01	12/09	05/09
2	Barnard Castle	13/02		26/09	23/01	28/11	05/09	20/03	09/01	17/10	06/03	07/11	19/12
3	Bishop Auckland	28/11	16/01		07/11	17/04	03/10	12/09	30/01	06/03	19/12	20/03	13/02
4	Blyth	20/03	03/10	20/02		12/09	30/01	16/01	31/10	28/11	17/04	19/12	06/03
5	Houghton	23/01	13/03	05/09	09/01		12/12	14/11	10/04	26/09	13/02	17/10	07/11
6	Medicals	07/11	17/04	23/01	17/10	20/03		19/12	26/09	13/02	28/11	06/03	09/01
7	North Shields	17/10	12/12	09/01	26/09	06/03	10/04		05/09	23/01	07/11	13/02	28/11
8	Ponteland	06/03	12/09	17/10	13/02	19/12	16/01	17/04		07/11	20/03	28/11	23/01
9	Seaton Carew	19/12	30/01	14/11	13/03	16/01	31/10	03/10	20/02		12/09	17/04	20/03
10	Whitley Bay Rockcliff	26/09	14/11	10/04	05/09	31/10	13/03	20/02	12/12	09/01		23/01	17/10
11	Winlaton Vulcans	09/01	20/02	12/12	10/04	30/01	14/11	31/10	13/03	05/09	03/10		26/09
12	Yarm	17/04	10/04	31/10	14/11	20/02	12/09	13/03	03/10	12/12	30/01	16/01	

DURHAM & NORTHUMBERLAND THREE

		1	2	3	4	5	6	7	8	9	10	11	12	13
1	Chester-Le-Street		30/01	12/09	19/12	24/10	20/02	10/10	07/11	13/03	28/11	16/01	27/03	26/09
2	Guisborough	17/10		13/02	31/10	05/09	12/12	20/03	19/09	09/01	03/10	14/11	23/01	06/03
3	Hartlepool Athletic	12/12	24/10		26/09	20/02	07/11	30/01	13/03	28/11	27/03	10/10	05/09	16/01
4	Hartlepool B.B.O.B.	19/09	20/02	09/01		07/11	13/03	24/10	28/11	27/03	05/09	30/01	12/12	10/10
5	Newton Aycliffe	13/02	10/04	31/10	06/03		19/09	05/12	09/01	03/10	23/01	20/03	17/10	14/11
6	Prudhoe & Stocksfield	31/10	12/09	06/03	14/11	19/12		10/04	03/10	23/01	17/10	05/12	13/02	20/03
7	Seaham	23/01	28/11	17/10	13/02	27/03	05/09		12/12	19/09	09/01	06/03	03/10	31/10
8	Sedgefield	06/03	19/12	14/11	20/03	26/09	16/01	12/09		17/10	13/02	10/04	31/10	05/12
9	Seghill	14/11	26/09	20/03	05/12	16/01	10/10	19/12	30/01		31/10	12/09	06/03	10/04
10	South Park Rangers	20/03	16/01	05/12	10/04	10/10	30/01	26/09	24/10	20/02		19/12	14/11	12/09
11	South Tyneside College	03/10	13/03	23/01	17/10	28/11	27/03	07/11	05/09	12/12	19/09		09/01	13/02
12	Washington	05/12	10/10	10/04	12/09	30/01	24/10	16/01	20/02	07/11	13/03	26/09		19/12
13	Whitby	09/01	07/11	03/10	23/01	13/03	28/11	20/02	27/03	05/09	12/12	24/10	19/09	

NORTH DIVISION FIXTURE GRIDS 2009-2010

SOUTH LANCASHIRE & CHESHIRE TWO

		1	2	3	4	5	6	7	8	9	10	11	12	13	14
1	Ashton-on-Mersey		07/11	12/09	26/09	13/03	28/11	27/03	05/09	16/01	30/01	24/10	10/10	20/02	19/12
2	Buxton	06/03		14/11	05/12	17/10	13/02	31/10	23/01	10/04	19/12	26/09	12/09	16/01	20/03
3	Crewe and Nantwich	12/12	13/03		16/01	28/11	27/03	05/09	19/09	10/10	24/10	20/02	30/01	07/11	26/09
4	Douglas (I.O.M.)	09/01	27/03	03/10		05/09	12/12	19/09	17/10	24/10	07/11	13/03	20/02	28/11	23/01
5	Liverpool Collegiate	14/11	30/01	20/03	10/04		31/10	06/03	13/02	12/09	26/09	16/01	19/12	10/10	05/12
6	Marple	20/03	24/10	05/12	12/09	20/02		14/11	06/03	19/12	16/01	10/10	26/09	30/01	10/04
7	Moore	05/12	20/02	10/04	19/12	07/11	13/03		20/03	26/09	10/10	30/01	16/01	24/10	12/09
8	Oldershaw	10/04	10/10	19/12	30/01	24/10	07/11	28/11		20/02	27/03	12/09	13/03	26/09	16/01
9	Orrell Anvils	03/10	05/09	23/01	13/02	12/12	19/09	09/01	31/10		13/03	28/11	07/11	27/03	17/10
10	Ruskin Park	17/10	19/09	13/02	06/03	09/01	03/10	23/01	05/12	14/11		05/09	20/03	12/12	31/10
11	Sefton	13/02	09/01	31/10	14/11	03/10	23/01	17/10	12/12	20/03	10/04		05/12	19/09	06/03
12	Southport	23/01	12/12	17/10	31/10	19/09	09/01	03/10	14/11	06/03	28/11	27/03		05/09	13/02
13	Trentham	31/10	03/10	06/03	20/03	23/01	17/10	13/02	09/01	05/12	12/09	19/12	10/04		14/11
14	Wallasey	19/09	28/11	09/01	10/04	27/03	05/09	12/12	03/10	30/01	20/02	07/11	24/10	13/03	

SOUTH LANCASHIRE & CHESHIRE THREE

		1	2	3	4	5	6	7	8	9	10	11
1	Capenhurst		12/12	13/02	10/04	07/11	06/03	05/09	09/01	26/09	17/10	23/01
2	Congleton	20/03		07/11	05/09	06/03	28/11	09/01	26/09	23/01	13/02	17/10
3	Ellesmere Port	31/10	20/02		14/11	03/10	30/01	13/03	12/12	10/04	09/01	05/09
4	Helsby	19/12	17/04	06/03		28/11	20/03	26/09	23/01	17/10	07/11	13/02
5	Holmes Chapel	20/02	14/11	23/01	13/03		31/10	12/12	10/04	05/09	26/09	09/01
6	Knutsford	14/11	13/03	17/10	12/12	13/02		10/04	05/09	09/01	23/01	26/09
7	Linley	17/04	12/09	28/11	16/01	20/03	19/12		17/10	13/02	06/03	07/11
8	Parkonians	12/09	16/01	20/03	03/10	19/12	17/04	30/01		07/11	28/11	06/03
9	Port Sunlight	16/01	03/10	19/12	30/01	17/04	12/09	31/10	20/02		20/03	28/11
10	Prenton	30/01	31/10	12/09	20/02	16/01	03/10	14/11	13/03	12/12		10/04
11	Ramsey (IoM)	03/10	30/01	17/04	31/10	12/09	16/01	20/02	14/11	13/03	19/12	

NORTH LANCASHIRE ONE

		1	2	3	4	5	6	7	8	9	10	11
1	Ashton-Under-Lyne		12/12	07/11	10/10	30/01	24/10	26/09	19/09	27/03	13/03	20/02
2	Birchfield (Lancs)	12/09		20/02	16/01	10/10	30/01	19/12	05/09	28/11	07/11	24/10
3	Bolton	06/03	31/10		05/12	10/04	12/09	14/11	09/01	17/10	03/10	19/12
4	Bury	23/01	03/10	27/03		07/11	13/03	17/10	31/10	19/09	05/09	28/11
5	De La Salle (Salford)	17/10	23/01	05/09	06/03		28/11	13/02	14/11	09/01	12/12	27/03
6	Didsbury Toc H	13/02	17/10	12/12	14/11	20/03		31/10	05/12	03/10	19/09	05/09
7	Garstang	09/01	19/09	13/03	30/01	24/10	20/02		03/10	05/09	28/11	07/11
8	Hawcoat Park	19/12	10/04	26/09	20/02	13/03	27/03	16/01		07/11	10/10	12/09
9	Hutton	05/12	20/03	30/01	19/12	26/09	16/01	10/04	06/03		24/10	10/10
10	Littleborough	14/11	06/03	16/01	10/04	12/09	19/12	20/03	23/01	13/02		26/09
11	Old Bedians	31/10	13/02	19/09	20/03	05/12	10/04	06/03	12/12	23/01	09/01	
12	Tarleton	10/04	05/12	24/10	26/09	16/01	10/10	12/09	20/03	13/03	20/02	30/01
13	Trafford MV	03/10	09/01	28/11	24/10	20/02	07/11	23/01	17/10	12/12	27/03	13/03
14	Windermere	20/03	14/11	10/10	12/09	19/12	26/09	05/12	13/02	31/10	30/01	16/01

NORTH LANCASHIRE TWO

		1	2	3	4	5	6	7	8	9	10	11
1	Blackpool		17/10	13/02	07/11	12/12	10/04	05/09	06/03	09/01	26/09	23/01
2	Carnforth	30/01		12/09	16/01	31/10	20/02	14/11	03/10	13/03	12/12	10/04
3	Chorley	31/10	09/01		03/10	20/02	14/11	13/03	30/01	12/12	10/04	05/09
4	Colne & Nelson	20/02	26/09	23/01		14/11	13/03	12/12	31/10	10/04	05/09	09/01
5	Eagle	20/03	13/02	07/11	06/03		05/09	09/01	28/11	26/09	23/01	17/10
6	Mossley Hill	19/12	07/11	06/03	28/11	17/04		26/09	20/03	23/01	17/10	13/02
7	Newton-le-Willows	17/04	06/03	28/11	20/03	12/09	16/01		19/12	17/10	13/02	07/11
8	North Manchester	14/11	23/01	17/10	13/02	13/03	12/12	10/04		05/09	09/01	26/09
9	St Edward's O.B.	12/09	28/11	20/03	19/12	16/01	03/10	30/01	17/04		07/11	06/03
10	St Mary's O.B. (Lancs)	16/01	20/03	19/12	17/04	03/10	30/01	31/10	12/09	20/02		28/11
11	West Park Warriors	03/10	19/12	17/04	12/09	30/01	31/10	20/02	16/01	14/11	13/03	

CUMBRIA

		1	2	3	4	5	6	7	8	9	10
1	Aspatria Eagles		12/09	14/11	26/09	05/12	10/10	19/12	24/10	16/01	05/09
2	Cockermouth	07/11		26/09	05/12	10/10	19/12	24/10	16/01	05/09	19/09
3	Creighton	19/09	28/11		10/10	19/12	24/10	16/01	05/09	07/11	03/10
4	Egremont	28/11	03/10	12/12		24/10	16/01	05/09	07/11	19/09	17/10
5	Gosforth Greengarth	03/10	12/12	17/10	09/01		05/09	07/11	19/09	28/11	31/10
6	Millom	12/12	17/10	09/01	31/10	23/01		19/09	28/11	03/10	07/11
7	Moresby	17/10	09/01	31/10	23/01	12/09	14/11		03/10	12/12	28/11
8	Whitehaven	09/01	31/10	23/01	12/09	14/11	26/09	05/12		17/10	12/12
9	Wigton Wanderers	31/10	23/01	12/09	14/11	26/09	05/12	10/10	19/12		09/01
10	Workington Steelers	23/01	14/11	05/12	19/12	16/01	12/09	26/09	10/10	24/10	

NORTHERN LEVEL 7-10 & NON LEAGUE CLUBS

Acklam RUFC
Ground Address: Acklam R.U.F.C. c/o 12 Salcombe Close Tollesby Hall Middlesbrough Cleveland
Contact: 01642 321397
Email: markzachory@hotmail.com
Website: www.acklamrufc.co.uk
Directions: A19 to A174 Redcar/Teesport/Whitby, take B1380 Acklam, right at T junction, continue for 1 mile past golf course etc. turn left into estate. Go straight on, down cycle path, club 500 yds
Honorary Secretary: Mrs Paula Atkin; 1 St. Ives Close Middlesbrough Cleveland TS8 9AA Tel: 01642 316262
Fixtures Secretary: Mr James Ward; 107 Guisborough Road Nunthorpe Middlesbrough TS7 0JD Tel: 01642 319302
email: j.w.ward@hotmail.co.uk
Club Colours: Black, Green & White
League: Durham-N'Thm'Land 2 (level 8)

Adwick Le Street RUFC
Ground Address: The Bullcroft Memorial Hall Chestnut Avenue Carcroft Doncaster South Yorkshire DN68AP
Contact: 01302 724253
Email: oldshep@compuserve.com
Directions: We are located just off the B1220 between the A1 and the A19. From the A19 take the B1220 signposted Skellow and Carcroft - Just past the Asda Superstore take half right turn at the Bet Davis Betting shop into Chestnut Avenue. Northbound on the A1 by-pass Doncaster and go on to the Pontefract turn at Barnsdale Bar, filter off left then turn right onto the flyover which takes traffic over the A1 and back down onto the southbound carriageway and then follow the southbound directions.Southbound on the A1 turn left onto the B1220 just before the Redhouse junction, signposted Skellow and Carcroft. After the second zebra crossing take first left into Chestnut Avenue.
Honorary Secretary: Mr John Sheppard; 23 Finghall Road Skellow Doncaster DN6 8PB Tel: 07801 537130
email: oldshep@talktalk.net
Fixtures Secretary: Mr Michael Leach-Flanagan; 31 Alexandra Road Bentley Doncaster South Yorkshire DN5 0PA Tel: 07810 631404
email: leach-flanaganM@freightliner.co.uk
Club Colours: Navy with White, Orange Hoops
League: Yorkshire 4 (level 10)

Aireborough RUFC
Ground Address: ANSA Aireborough Rugby Club Nunroyd Park Yeadon LEEDS LS19 7HR
Contact: 01943 878299
Email: jameskinghorn@btinternet.com
Website: www.aireboroughrufc.org
Directions: We are based at Nunroyd Park between Guiseley and Rawdon on the A65 from Leeds to Ilkley. Please visit our web page for details of how to get to the ground.
Honorary Secretary: Mr James Kinghorn; 11 Keelham Drive Rawdon Leeds LS19 6SG Tel: 07769 692185
email: jameskinghorn@btinternet.com
Fixtures Secretary: Mr John Holdsworth; 11 Kingsdale Drive Menston Ilkley West Yorkshire LS29 6QN Tel: 01943 871210
email: john.holdsworth@vocalink.com
Club Colours: Navy Blue / Maroon / White
League: Yorkshire 3 (level 9)

Aldwinians RUFC
Ground Address: Audenshaw Park, Droylsden Road, Audenshaw, Greater Manchester M34 5SN
Contact: 0161 3366814
Email: sylviadonley57@hotmail.com
Website: www.aldwiniansrufc.org.uk
Directions: Located 3/4 mile west of Junction 23 of the M60 at the Snipe Retail Park. Road signs direct you to the club at regular intervals. The club was awarded Year 3 Seal of Approval status in June 1997
Honorary Secretary: Mrs Sylvia Donley; 43 Hulme Road Denton Manchester M34 2WX Tel: 07947 018175
email: sylviadonley57@hotmail.com
Fixtures Secretary: Mr Alan Whalley; 190 Greenside Lane Droylsden Manchester M43 7UR
Tel: 0161 2231353
email: allen.whalley1@btinternet.com
Club Colours: Red & White hoops, Navy shorts
League: North Lancs-Cumbria (level 7)

Alnwick RUFC
Ground Address: Greensfield St. James Alnwick NorthumberlandNE66 1BG
Contact: 01665 602342
Email: clare@owensmith.f2s.com
Website: www.alnwickrugby.com
Directions: A1 slip (south) of Alnwick signed Alnwick from N/Castle, after slip 1st left, Club 300yds on left. From Edinburgh, after slip straight over roundabout, ground as above
Honorary Secretary: Miss Clare Owen-Smith Tel: 01665 603490
email: clare@owensmith.f2s.com
Fixtures Secretary: John Dixon Tel: 01665 711509
Club Colours: Royal Blue + Gold Lion Rampant
League: Durham-N'Thm'Land 1 (level 7)

462

Ambleside RFC
Ground Address: Galava Park Borrans Road Borrans Road Ambleside LA22 0EN
Contact: 01539 432536
Email: jeanette@irwin200.fsnet.co.uk
Directions: A591 Kendal to Ambleside. Take Coniston, Hawkshead road at traffic lights. Ground is half a mile on the left after lights.
Honorary Secretary: Mrs Jeanette Irwin; 20 School Knott Drive Windermere LA23 2DY Tel: 01539 442025
email: jeanette@irwin200.fsnet.co.uk
Fixtures Secretary: Mr John Dixon; 55 Sandgate Kendal LA9 6HZ Tel: 01539 722190
Club Colours: Black & Amber
Non League

Anselmians
Ground Address: Malone Field Eastham Village Road Eastham Wirral Merseyside CH62 0BJ
Contact: 0151 3271613
Website: www.arufc.com
Directions: Leave M53 motorway at junction 5 take A41 in direction of Birkenhead. Take first turning on the right Eastham Village Road and follow this road through the village until reaching the ground on the far side of the village. Or take A41 from Birkenhead until you reach Eastham then turn left into Eastam Village Road the ground is 100 yds along on the right.
Honorary Secretary: Mr Trevor Petterson; 27 Queens Drive Prenton Merseyside CH43 0RR
Tel: 07880 781522
email: petterst@msn.com
Fixtures Secretary: Mr Tony McArdle; 18 Greenbank Drive Pensby Wirral Merseyside CH61 5UF
Tel: 0151 3421470
email: tony.mcardle@btinternet.com
Club Colours: Blue & Yellow Jerseys Navy Blue Shorts
League: South Lancs-Cheshire 1 (level 7)

Ashington Joint Welfare RFC
Ground Address: Recreation Ground Ellington Road Ashington NorthumberlandNE63 8TP
Contact: 01670 814123
Website: www.ashingtonrugbyclub.co.uk
Directions: Take A1 to Seaton Burn (A19) turn off - 6 miles North of Newcastle. Straight over at r'about heading for Tyne Tunnel, ignoring second left A1068 turn to Ashington. At next roundabout (Cramlington) take second left onto A189. Continue on this road crossing the rivers Blyth and Wansbeck. Straight on at r'about junction with B1334. You will pass Wansbeck Hospital on your left before taking first left at next r'about , bear right at next r'about - signposted Morpeth, straight on at next two r'abouts passing Lidl and ASDA supermarkets and Ashington Football Clubs former ground on left. Straight over 2 r'abouts right and then left at double roundabout. (Maxwells and Aldi on your right.) After 200yds past JET filling station turn right onto A1068. In about 500yds. - past new housing development on bend of road - make a full right turn into Recreation Ground

Honorary Secretary: Mr Albert Armstrong; 25 Dunsdale Drive Cramlington NorthumberlandNE23 2GA
Tel: 07798 665555
email: aarmstrong@northumberland.gov.uk
Fixtures Secretary: Mr Albert Armstrong; 25 Dunsdale Drive Cramlington NorthumberlandNE23 2GA
Tel: 07798 665555
email: aarmstrong@northumberland.gov.uk
Club Colours: Royal Blue and Amber Shirts
League: Durham-N'Thm'Land 1 (level 7)

Ashton-on-Mersey RFC
Ground Address: Banky Lane (off Carrington Lane) Ashton on Mersey Sale M33 5SL
Contact: 0161 9736637
Email: john.bolton57@ntlworld.com
Website: www.aomrufc.co.uk
Directions: M63 J63 Carrington Spur, towards Carrington, right at traffic lights, left at T junction, Club 300 yards on right.
Honorary Secretary: Mr John Bolton; 43 Barwell Road Sale Cheshire M33 5EE Tel: 0161 973 2960
email: john.bolton57@ntlworld.com
Fixtures Secretary: Mr Pat Stokes; 15 Poolcroft Sale Cheshire M33 2LF Tel: 0161 2823245
email: psns64@hotmail.com
Club Colours: Maroon Shirts, Navy Shorts, Maroon & White Socks
League: South Lancs-Cheshire 2 (level 8)

Ashton-Under-Lyne RFC
Ground Address: Gambrel Bank, St. Albans Avenue, Ashton-Under-Lyne. OL6 8TU
Contact: 0161 3301361
Email: aulrfc@supanet.com
Website: www.aulrfc.supanet.com
Directions: Directions follow the M60 to Jn 23, follow the signs for Ashton then Oldham (A627) and at the traffic lights at the Peugeot dealers (Robins & Day) turn right into Wilshaw Lane. At the roundabout take the first exit, Alt Road, and find the club 400 yds on right
Honorary Secretary: Mr Anthony Spafford; 22 Cravenwood Ashton-u-Lyne OL6 8AX
Tel: 07929 671097
email: a.spafford@ntlworld.com
Fixtures Secretary: Mr John Broomhead; 149 Cheetham Hill Road Dukinfield Cheshire SK16 5JU
Tel: 0161 3382672
email: jdbv@talktalk.net
Club Colours: Red, Black & Amber Hoops
League: North Lancs 1 (level 8)

LEVELS 7-12 & NON LEAGUE CLUBS

BAe Warton RUFC
Ground Address: Lightning Club, Mill Lane, Mill Lane, Warton, PR4 1AX
Contact: 07973 551535
Email: phil.mortimer@baesystems.com
Website: www.wartonrugby.com
Directions: From Motorway - Leave M6 at J32 and join the M55 towards Blackpool. - Leave M55 at J3. - At the end of the slip road turn left onto A585 towards Kirkham and Lytham St Annes - At the first r'about take the 2nd exit (straight on) - At the 2nd r'about take the second exit (straight on) - At the third (major) r'about (A585 and A583) take the 2nd exit (straight on) towards Wrea Green - Continue straight over the mini- r'about to Wrea Green Village. - In Wrea Green Village take the first exit (left) at the r'about. The Village Green is now on your right. - At the traffic lights at Warton (Church Road and Lytham Road - A584) turn right. - Turn into Bank Lane which is on the left and signposted to Bank Lane Caravan Park, you will find the pitches 500 yards on the left From Preston - Travel towards Blackpool on the A583. - Turn left onto the A584 - At the r'about take the 2nd exit (Freckleton by-pass) - Take position in the outside lane. At the 2nd r'about take the second exit (straight on) - You are now on Lytham Road in Warton. Go past the BAE Systems gates - Turn into Bank Lane which is on the left and signposted to Bank Lane Caravan Park, you will find the pitches 500 yards on the left
Honorary Secretary: Mr Phil Mortimer; 5 Barclay Road Longridge Preston PR3 3LD Tel: 07973 551535 email: phil.mortimer@baesystems.com
Fixtures Secretary: Mr Robert Cockrill; 7 Mornington Road Lytham St. Annes Lancashire FY8 5BA
Tel: 07515 258455 email: rob.cockrill@baesystems.com
Club Colours: Blue with White Chest/Arm Band
Non League

Baildon RUFC
Ground Address: Heygate Lane off Jenny Lane Baildon West Yorkshire BD17 6RS
Contact: 07799 586296
Email: catharine.oconnell@ccmh.co.uk
Website: www.baildon-rugby.co.uk
Directions: Leave Shipley North on A6038, at lights bear left on Baildon Road (B6151) up the hill. Across the roundabout onto Northgate. Right at Websters Fish and Chip shop onto Jenny Lane. At the end of Jenny Lane (200 metres) turn left Heygate Lane
Honorary Secretary: Mrs Catharine O'Connell; 15 Menin Drive Baildon Shipley West Yorkshire BD17 5PN
Tel: 0845 3860001
email: catharine.oconnell@beaumonts-insurance.co.uk
Fixtures Secretary: Mr Philip Francis; Parkway Fernhill Bingley West Yorkshire BD16 4AQ Tel: 07778 014794
email: pifran1@aol.com
Club Colours: Red/Black
League: Yorkshire 3 (level 9)

Barnsley RUFC
Ground Address:
Shaw Lane Barnsley South Yorkshire S70 6HZ
Contact: 01226 203509
Email: info@barnsleyrufc.co.uk
Website: www.barnsleyrufc.co.uk
Directions: M1 J37, towards Barnsley, through 1st major lights, past Polar Garage, 2nd turning right into Shaw Lane. Ground on right after 1st school. **N.B.** We do not allow dogs on site, with the exception of guide dogs.
Honorary Secretary: Mr Brian Johnson; 38 Vernon Way Gawber Barnsley S75 2NN Tel: 01226 289889
email: brijohn@fsmail.net
Fixtures Secretary: Mr Steve Bates; 0 Sackup Lane Darton Barnsley South Yorkshire S75 5AW
Tel: 07712 225868
email: steve.bates@peachorator.co.uk
Club Colours: Navy Blue Body Red and White
League: Yorkshire 2 (level 8)

Berwick Upon Tweed RFC
Ground Address: The Clubhouse 11 Derwentwater Terrace Scremerston Berwick Upon Tweed NorthumberlandTD15 2QY
Contact: 01289 302141
Email: admin@berwickrugbyclub.co.uk
Website: www.berwickrugbyclub.co.uk
Honorary Secretary: Mr S & B Spiers; 2 Greenlawalls Duddo Berwick upon Tweed NorthumberlandTD15 2PR
Tel: 01890 820328   email: bryanspiers@aol.com
Fixtures Secretary: Mr Chris Budzynski; Springfield Park 17 East Ord Berwick upon Tweed TD15 1FD
Tel: 01289 330044
email: cb@berwick-upon-tweed.gov.uk
Non League

Birchfield RUFC (Lancashire)
Ground Address: Birchfield Park Sports Club Birchfield Road Widnes Cheshire WA8 9ES
Contact: 0151-424-3397 (H)
Email: cliff.christie@britton-group.com
Directions: From M62 J7 follow A57 (Warrington). Turn right at first set of lights, then at T junction, 1st at r'about onto Birchfield Rd. Ground is 250 yds on the right.
Honorary Secretary: Mr Eddie Wiles; 2 Hartland Gardens The Larches Rainhill St Helens Merseyside WA9 5TZ Tel: 0044 7790772312
email: eddie@ewiles.fsnet.co.uk
Fixtures Secretary: Mr Cliff Christie; 47 Cowan Way Widnes Cheshire WA8 5BW Tel: 07786 228404
email: cliff.christie@britton-group.com
Club Colours: Black/ Gold
League: North Lancs 1 (level 8)

Bishop Auckland R.U.F.C.
Ground Address: West Mills Playing Fields Bridge Road Bishop Auckland Co. Durham DL14 7PA
Contact: 01388 602922
Website: www.bishopaucklandrugby.co.uk
Directions: Follow signs for Crook. Avoid new road over

viaduct. Take old road down hill past Newton Cap pub. Turn off left before River Wear.
Honorary Secretary: Mrs Penny Macnair
email: penny_macnair@hotmail.co.uk
Fixtures Secretary: Mr R Williamson; 19 Waddington Street Bishop Auckland Co. Durham DL14 6HG
Tel: 01388 600059
email: udoron_ron@yahoo.co.uk
Club Colours: Navy & Sky Blue, Red
League: Durham-N'Thm'Land 2 (level 8)

Blackpool RUFC
Ground Address: Fleetwood Road Norbreck Blackpool Lancashire FY5 1RN
Contact: 01253 868862
Email: ian.potts@barsbank.com
Website: www.blackpoolrugby.co.uk
Directions: M55 J4, right onto A583, right onto Whitegate Drive (still A583), bear right onto Devonshire Road, B5214. Club on right 0.5 mile past Red Lion Pub.
Honorary Secretary: Mr Ed Parlour; 11 Goldstone Drive Thornton-Cleveleys Lancashire FY5 3QF
Tel: 01253 867213
email: ed.parlour@baesystems.com
Fixtures Secretary: Mr Sean O'Brien; 424 Ashfield Road Thornton Cleveleys Blackpool Lancashire FY5 3PJ
Tel: 07778 115449
email: sean141064@aol.com
Club Colours: Red & Blue Squares
League: North Lancs 2 (level 9)

Blyth RFC
Ground Address:
Blyth R.F.C. Plessey Road Blyth NE24 3LE
Contact: 01670 352063
Email: dave.grey@bt.com
Directions: Take A1 north of Newcastle & turn off onto A19. After 2 miles take A189 (North) & then turn off towards Blyth on A1061. Follow town centre signs & turn left onto A193, turn left into Plessey Road.
Honorary Secretary: Mr David Grey; 12 Winchester Avenue Blyth NorthumberlandNE24 2EY
Tel: 07860 841701
email: dave.grey@bt.com
Fixtures Secretary: Mr Carlos Correia; 34 Teal Avenue Blyth NorthumberlandNE24 3PT Tel: 07738 477749
email: carlos.correia@eds.com
Club Colours: Black & Green, Black Shorts.
League: Durham-N'Thm'Land 2 (level 8)

Bolton RUFC
Ground Address: Mortfield Pavilion Avenue Street off Chorley Old Road Bolton Lancashire BL1 3AW
Contact: 01204 363710
Email: play@boltonrugby.co.uk
Website: www.boltonrugby.co.uk
Directions: From A58,south on Chorley Old Rd for 1.5m, 400yds past Morrisons. Avenue St on L. From A666,turn L, 2/3m onto Chorley Old Rd, 600yds. Avenue St on R. : LONGER DIRECTIONS : ** M62/M60, M61,

A666. At T/L turn L, thru T/L, at T/L bear R, thru T/L, thru T/L onto Chorley Old Rd, thru new T/L. Avenue Street on R, 100m after Shell garage. : **OR** : ** A58, at about "10 o'clock" on ring road head toward town from roundabout on B6226, for 1 mile, thru T/L, past Morrisons for 400m. Avenue Street on L, 100m before Shell garage.
Honorary Secretary: Mr Simon Clarke; 33 Kilcoby Avenue Swinton Manchester Lancashire M27 8AD
Tel: 0161 925 0959
email: honsec@boltonrugby.co.uk
Fixtures Secretary: Mr Shaun Crimmins; 5 Exford Drive Breightmet Bolton BL2 6TB Tel: 07766 665812
email: fixtures@boltonrugby.co.uk
Club Colours: Scarlet / White Hoops
League: North Lancs 1 (level 8)

Border Park RFC
Ground Address: Dargues Hope Rochester NorthumberlandNE19 1LE
Contact: 0161 499 4994
Email: info@borderparkrugby.com
Website:
Directions: The club is located at Butteryhaugh, Kielder Village, Northumberland, close to Kielder Castle. The postcode is NE48 1YX. Full location details are on the club's website.
Honorary Secretary: Mr Chris Galley; Dargues Hope Elishaw Otterburn NorthumberlandNE19 1LE
Tel: 0797 0187878
email: london@compuserve.com
Fixtures Secretary: Mr Tom Richards; Craig Villas Falstone Hexham NorthumberlandNE48 1AD
Tel: 01434 240401
Club Colours: Black and red
Non League

Bowdon RUFC
Ground Address:
Clay Lane Timperley Altrincham WA15 7AF
Contact: 0161 980 8321
Email: brufc.steward@hotmail.com
Website: www.bowdonrufc.com
Directions: M56 J6, follow signs to Hale, after 1.5 miles turn right at lights onto Delahays Road, through next set of lights, after 0.5 miles up Thorley Lane turn right at Mini roundabout on to Clay Lane. Club on left.
Honorary Secretary: Mr Myles Kitchiner; 67 Crofton Avenue Timperley Altrincham Cheshire WA15 6BZ
Tel: 07966 447510
email: m.kitchiner@talktalk.net
Fixtures Secretary: Mr Frank Norton; 36 Green Walk Timperley Altrincham Cheshire WA15 6JN
Tel: 01925 834639
email: fsjn@supanet.com
Club Colours: Claret, White & Black
League: South Lancs-Cheshire 1 (level 7)

LEVELS 7-12 & NON LEAGUE CLUBS 465

BP Chemicals RUFC
Ground Address: B.P. Chemicals Sports & Social Club Saltend, Hedon HU12 8DS
Contact: 01482 896113
Directions: Follow signs for A1033 Hendon Road and docks when coming into Hull. The dround is opposite the B.P plant at Saltend
Honorary Secretary: Mr Stuart Ladd; 837 Holderness Road Hull HU8 9AZ Tel: 07769 673933
email: stu@stuladd.karoo.co.uk
Fixtures Secretary: Mr Paul Drury; 3 Westfield Road Cottingham HU16 5PE Tel: 01482 892552
email: paul.drury@uk.bp.com
Club Colours: Maroon & Gold
Non League

Bradford Salem RFC
Ground Address: Bradford Salem RFC Shay Lane Heaton Bradford West Yorkshire BD9 6SL
Contact: 01274 496230
Email: brucestrachan@btinternet.com
Website: www.bradfordsalem.co.uk
Directions: From Bradford centre take A650 (towards Keighley) along Manningham Lane. Left at 'The Park' pub & up the hill go past shops on your right as the road bends to the left turn right onto Shay Lane. Ground is 300yds on the left.
Honorary Secretary: Mr Bruce Strachan; 272 Leaventhorpe Lane Thornton Bradford W. Yorks. BD13 3BJ Tel: 07816 662708
email: brucestrachan@btinternet.com
Fixtures Secretary: Mr John Dobson; Hilltop Kings Grove Bingley West Yorkshire BD16 4EZ
Tel: 07768 448236   email: johncdobson@hotmail.com
Club Colours: Black, Gold & Royal Blue
League: Yorkshire 1 (level 6)

Bramley Phoenix RFC
Ground Address: The Warrels Grosmont Terrace Warrels Road, Bramley Warrels Road, Bramley Leeds West Yorkshire LS13 3NY
Contact: 0113 2577787
Email: daz457@hotmail.com
Website: http://www.bramleyphoenix.co.uk/
Honorary Secretary: Mr Michael Ryan; 280 Whitehall Road Wyke Bradford West Yorkshire BD12 9DX
Tel: 01274 727782
email: michaelryan2@btconnect.com
Fixtures Secretary: Mr Trevor Smith; The Rein 200 Priestthorpe Road Farsley Leeds West Yorkshire LS28 5RD Tel: 0113 2576253
Club Colours: green/gold/black
League: Yorkshire 3 (level 9)

Bridlington RUFC
Ground Address:
Dukes Park Queens Gate Bridlington YO16 7LN
Contact: 01262 676405
Website: http: //clubs.rfu.com/Clubs/portals/BridlingtonRUFC/

Directions: See website http: //clubs.rfu.com/Clubs/portals/BridlingtonRUFC/directions.aspx Once in Bridlington: From the South/West: Traffic lights straight over (sign-posted Flamborough) Roundabout - 2nd exit - immediately onto a smaller roundabout - take 2nd exit onto St Johns Street (sign-posted town centre) Pass Old Ship Inn on left Traffic Lights - turn left into Queensgate Ground 400m on right (shared with Bridlington AFC) From the North(A165): Roundabout - first exit immediately onto a smaller r'about - take 2nd exit onto St Johns Street - then as above.
Honorary Secretary: Mrs Emma Ridley; Chatswood North Marine Road Flamborough Bridlington YO15 1LG Tel: 07980 459026
email: theridleys@dsl.pipex.com
Fixtures Secretary: Mr Dennis Catt; 38 St. Jude Road Bridlington YORKSHIRE YO16 7LB
Tel: 01262 671768
email: theridleys@dsl.pipex.com
Club Colours: Navy and Amber
League: Yorkshire 1 (level 7)

Burley RFC
Ground Address: The Club House Abbey Road Abbey Road Leeds West Yorkshire LS5 3NG
Contact: 07939 612438
Email: duncan.elsey@networkrail.co.uk
Website: burleyrufc.co.uk
Directions: Travel out of Leeds on the A65 until just past Kirkstall Abbey. The clubhouse is on the left opposite the Vesper Gate public house.
Honorary Secretary: Mr Duncan Elsey; 57 Vesper Gate Mount Kirkstall Leeds LS5 3NL Tel: 0113 2781823
email: Duncan.Elsey@networkrail.co.uk
Fixtures Secretary: Mr Jim Lewin; 6 Linden Place Leeds LS11 6HE Tel: 07881 626456
email: lewin15@hotmail.com
Club Colours: Maroon and White
League: Yorkshire 4 (level 10)

Burnley RUFC
Ground Address: Holden Road, Reedley, Reedley, Burnley. Lancashire BB10 2LE
Contact: 01282 424337
Email: s.jackson.770@btinternet.com
Website: www.burnleyrugbyclub.co.uk
Directions: M65 J12, right to Brierfield, through one set of traffic lights, Holden Road on left approx. 1/4 mile by Oaks Hotel.
Honorary Secretary: Steve Jackson; 17 Reedley Road Burnley Lancashire BB10 2LS Tel: 01282 697874
email: s.jackson.770@btinternet.com
Fixtures Secretary: Mr Mike Wilton; 93 Talbot Drive Briercliffe Burnley Lancashire BB102RT
Tel: 01282 457963
email: mike.wilton@hotmail.co.uk
Club Colours: Royal Blue & Gold Hoops
League: North Lancs-Cumbria (level 7)

Bury RUFC
Ground Address: Radcliffe Road, Bury. BL9 9JX
Contact: 0161 7235695
Email: texgriffin@aol.com
Website: www.buryrufc.co.uk
Directions: Leave M602 at J 17 follow A56 towards Bury. After 4 miles turn left at traffic lights into Radcliffe Road. Club 20yds on right.
Honorary Secretary: Mr Mike Griffin; 114 Turks Road Radcliffe Manchester M26 4WN Tel: 0161 7235695
email: texgriffin@tiscali.co.uk
Fixtures Secretary: Mr Christopher Bluer; 5 Belgrave Close Radcliffe Manchester M26 4DE
Tel: 07711 474926
email: chris.bluer@ntlworld.com
Club Colours: Red, Gold & Blue Hooped Jerseys
League: North Lancs 1 (level 8)

Buxton RUFC
Ground Address: Sunnyfields Brierlow Bar Road Harpur Hill, Buxton Derbyshire SK17 9PX
Contact: 01298 70455
Email: info@buxtonrugbyclub.com
Website: www.buxtonrugbyclub.com
Directions: Follow A515 from Buxton towards Ashbourne. After leaving the town into 50mph area take first right towards Harpur Hill. At end of road turn left and ground approx 500yds on left.
Honorary Secretary: Mrs Julie Vorheiss; 55 Pictor Road Buxton Derbyshire SK17 7TB Tel: 01298 22546
email: julesv2007@aol.com
Fixtures Secretary: Mr Patrick Leahy c/o the club
Tel: 01298 70455
email: PatPaula@leahy86.freeserve.co.uk
Club Colours: Blue, Red & Gold Hoops, Blue Shorts
League: South Lancs-Cheshire 2 (level 8)

Capenhurst RUFC
Ground Address: Capenhurst Sports Ground Capenhurst Lane, Capenhurst Nr Chester Cheshire CH1 6ER
Contact: 01244 378789
Email: ted@edwardroberts.plus.com
Directions: From Liverpool M53, A41, turn rt at lights for Capenhurst, lft at r/bout, over railway bridge, past BNFL wks, ground on rt. From Warrington/Cheshire, M56 to end, rt at r/bout, lft to Capenhurst, lft at T-junc, past BNFL wks, ground on rt.
Honorary Secretary: Mr Ted Roberts; 8 Chichester Street Chester CH1 4AD Tel: 07985 125099
email: ted@edwardroberts.plus.com
Fixtures Secretary: Graeme Ainsworth; 44 Upton Drive Upton Chester CH2 1BU Tel: 01244 381509
email: moxyainsworth@btopenworld.com
Club Colours: Blue and White or Black and White
League: South Lancs-Cheshire 3 (level 9)

Carnforth RFC
Ground Address: Carnforth High School, Kellett Road, Carnforth, Lancashire LA5 9LS
Contact: 01524 720462
Email: spoon@weath1008.fsnet.co.uk
Website: www.carnforthrufc.co.uk
Directions: Turn of M6 at Junction 35. Follow sign posts for Nether Kellett and Kirkby Lonsdale until you come of the end of the motorway restrictions. Turn RIGHT at the "T" junction. We play at the Carnforth High School approx 1/2 mile from the junction.
Honorary Secretary: Mr Paul Weatherill; 106 Lancaster Road Carnforth Lancashire LA5 9EA
Tel: 07767 774410
email: paul.weatherill@sky.com
Fixtures Secretary: Mr Alan Hardy; 16 Edward Street Carnforth Lancashire LA5 9DA Tel: 07733 130234
email: alanh@thetravelleruk.com
Club Colours: Green & Black Hooped shirts, black shorts, green socks
League: North Lancs 2 (level 9)

Carrington RFC
Ground Address: The Windmill Manchester Road Carrington M31 4BF
Contact: 0161 775 2251
Email: dhickman@kodak.com
Website: http://members.lycos.co.uk/montellrufc/index.html
Directions: From the M60 junction 7 follow signs for Carrington and Partington along the A6144(M). At the end of the A6144(M) at the traffic lights go straight ahead and follow the road for approx. 1fi miles, through the next set of traffic lights, passed Ackers Lane
Honorary Secretary: Dr. Derek Hickman; 37 Overdale Crescent Flixton Urmston Manchester M41 5GR
Tel: 0151 5476107
email: dhickman@kodak.com
Fixtures Secretary: as Hon. Sec.
Club Colours: Red and yellow quarters, black shorts
Non League

Castleford RUFC
Ground Address: Willowbridge Lane Whitwood Whitwood Castleford West Yorkshire WF10 5PD
Contact: 01924 896584
Email: stephenball85@live.com
Website: www.castlefordrufc.org
Directions: M62, exit J31, 2nd turn left off roundabout,towards Castleford. Go past Rising Sun on left and Mexboro Arms on right. Ground on right hand side. We have a website www.castlefordrufc.org that contains these details.
Honorary Secretary: Mr Stephen Ball; 36 Knightsway LEEDS West Yorkshire LS15 7BW Tel: 0113 2601300
email: stephenball85@live.com
Fixtures Secretary: Mr Dave Price; 10 Langdale Avenue Outwood Wakefield West Yorkshire WF1 3TX
Tel: 01924 825434
email: Davidprice10@talktalk.net
Club Colours: White with blue and red hoops
League: Yorkshire 1 (level 7)

LEVELS 7-12 & NON LEAGUE CLUBS

Chester-Le-Street RFC
Ground Address: David Owen Clark Centre Riverside Park Chester-le-Street DH3 4NT
Contact: 0191 387 1995
Directions: Take A1(M) to Chester-le-Street and follow directions to County Cricket Ground. Rugby Club is situated adjacent to the ground in the Donald Owen Clark Centre.
Honorary Secretary: Mr David Kilkenny; 64 Highfield Rise Chester le Street Co. Durham DH3 3UX
Tel: 0191 3888357
email: david.kilkenny@komatsu-uk.com
Fixtures Secretary: Mr Colin Wlison; 7 Fairaisle Ouston Chester Le Street Co. Durham Tel: 0191 4109874
Club Colours: Blue Shirts & Shorts, Red Socks
League: Durham-N'Thm'Land 3 (level 9)

Chorley RFC
Ground Address: Chorley RFC Brookfields, Chancery Road Astley Village, Chorley Lancashire PR7 1XP
Contact: 01257 268806
Email: nicksergeant@hotmail.com
Website: www.chorleyrugby.com
Directions: Exit Exit M61 J8 towards Chorley across first roundabout. Right at second roundabout past hospital on left. Left at next roundabout into Chancery Road. Club on the right after 200yds.
Honorary Secretary: Mr David Martin; 71 Ayrshire Close Buckshaw Village Chorley Lancashire PR7 1UY
Tel: 07854 908164
email: martind14@cpwplc.com
Fixtures Secretary: Mr John Witts; 54 Carrington Road Chorley Lancashire PR7 2DG Tel: 07715 755203
email: jwitts@forrestcontracts.co.uk
Club Colours: Black and White Hoops
League: North Lancs 2 (level 9)

Cockermouth RFC
Ground Address: Grasmoor Sports Centre, Strawberry How Strawberry How Lorton Road Cockermouth Cumbria CA13 9XQ
Contact: 010900 824884
Email: william.ford@btinternet.com
Directions: Leave by-pass along Lampugh Road & Station Street. Turn left 50 yards past Shell F/Station on right into Lorton Road. 0.5 mile past cemetry on left, turn left into Strawberry How - 100yds Club drive way on the right (then open fields).
Honorary Secretary: Mr William Ford; 45 Oaktree Crescent Cockermouth Cumbria CA13 9HP
Tel: 01900 824461
email: william.ford@btinternet.com
Fixtures Secretary: Mr W Mcdowel; 10 The Green Cockermouth Cumbria CA13 9AS Tel: 01900 824274
Club Colours: Black & Amber Hoops
League: Cumbria (level 8)

Colne & Nelson RFC
Ground Address: The Club House Holt House Harrison Drive Colne Lancashire BB8 9SF
Contact: 01282 863339
Email: rugby@colneandnelson.co.uk
Website: www.colneandnelson.co.uk
Directions: At end of M65 follow Skipton signs. Through traffic lights & left at large roundabout & follow the road to the top of hill.
Honorary Secretary: Mr Keith Thornton; 25 Gertrude Street Nelson Lancashire BB9 8RS Tel: 01282 602661
email: kitjel@supanet.com
Fixtures Secretary: Mr H Lambert; 13 Townley Street Colne Lancashire BB8 9LF Tel: 01282 433112
email: HLambert@gw-intl.com
Club Colours: All Black
League: North Lancs 2 (level 9)

Congleton RUFC
Ground Address: The Woodman 78 Park Street Congleton Cheshire CW12 1EG
Contact: 07730 691394
Email: davemccaddon@yahoo.co.uk
Website: www.congletonrufc.co.uk
Directions: Directions to the Ground: If lost follow the signs to Congleton Leisure Centre alongside Congleton Park. The senior pitch is alongside the Leisure Centre with the clubhouse and changing rooms 100 metres up the hill in Park Street (limited parking in the
Honorary Secretary: Mr Dave Mccaddon; 6 Pirie Road Congleton Cheshire CW12 2EE Tel: 07964 712119
email: davemccaddon@yahoo.co.uk
Fixtures Secretary: Mr Russell Williams; 8 Wensleydale Avenue Congleton Cheshire CW12 2DE
Tel: 01260 272685 email: rus.williams@tinyworld.co.uk
Club Colours: Red, White & Black
League: South Lancs-Cheshire 3 (level 9)

Consett & District RFC
Ground Address: The Demi Albert Road Albert Road Consett Co. Durham DH8 5QU
Contact: 0120 7590662
Email: consettrugbyfc@aol.com
Website: www.consettrugby.com
Directions: Behind & to the side of Consett Civic Centre only 400m from centre of Consett. Full details on web site. All major nearby roundabouts travelling into Consett you will see signs for the Civic Centre (On Menonsley Road) follow these and you will see a sign adjacent to the Civic Centre for the Rugby Club.
Honorary Secretary: Mr Melvyn Spratt; 47 Benfield Close Shotley Bridge Consett Co. Durham DH8 0RH
Tel: 01207 507183 email: melspratt@sky.com
Fixtures Secretary: Mr Derek Clark; 34 George Street Consett Co. Durham DH8 5LN Tel: 01207 591847
email: clark_nobby@hotmail.com
Club Colours: Black & amber with red trim, black short
League: Durham-N'Thm'Land 1 (level 7)

468

Creighton RFC
Ground Address: Sycamore Lane Parkland Carlisle Cumbria CA1 3SR
Contact: 01228524379B 535111H
Email: djt@halton-soal.co.uk
Directions: From North/East/South.Junction 42 M6 follow signs to City Centre.First traffic lights turn right into Cumwhinton Road.Straight on for about 800 metres until mini roundabout.Turn left Sycamore Lane approx 600 metres on right.From City Centre turn left at t
Honorary Secretary: Mr David Thomlinson; 146 Moorhouse Road Belle Vue Carlisle CA2 7QR
Tel: 01228 511119   email: djt@halton-soal.co.uk
Fixtures Secretary: Mr Roger Harrison; Royal Oak Gaitsgill Dalston Carlisle Cumbria CA5 7AH
Tel: 01697 476422
Club Colours: Navy, Red Collar & Cuffs, White Shorts
League: Cumbria (level 8)

Crewe and Nantwich
Ground Address: Crewe Vagrants Sports Club Newcastle Road, Willaston Nantwich CW5 7EP
Contact: 01270 569506
Email: secretarycnrufc@yahoo.com
Website: www.creweandnantwichrufc.com
Directions: please see website
Honorary Secretary: Miss Helena Crook; 105 Birchin Lane Nantwich Cheshire CW5 6JZ Tel: 07886 980699
Fixtures Secretary: Mr Les Briers; 13 Arran Close Woolstanwood Crewe CW2 8UQ Tel: 01270 585049
email: allansproston@hotmail.com
Club Colours: Black, white shoulders, red & gold ringlet
League: South Lancs-Cheshire 2 (level 8)

De La Salle (Salford)
Ground Address: Lancaster Road, Salford. M6 8FX
Contact: 0161-789-2161
Email: jbarrett@orange.net
Directions: South: Off M602 Eccles J2, follow Salford past Hope Hospital on right, next lights left onto Lancaster Road. From North: A580 East Lancs Road towards Salford, right at Lancaster Road, Club halfway on right.
Honorary Secretary: Mr Stephen Parrott; 11 Errington Drive Salford M7 1QP Tel: 07707 330974
email: stephenparrott649@hotmail.com
Fixtures Secretary: as Hon. Sec.
League: North Lancs 1 (level 8)

Didsbury Toc H RFC
Ground Address: Didsbury Toc H R.F.C. Clubhouse Simon Field Ford Lane Didsbury Gtr Manchester M20 2TJ
Contact: 0161 4462146
Email: info@didburyrfc.co.uk
Website: www.didsburyrfc.co.uk
Directions: From A34 follow signs for Didsbury to traffic lights at Shell Petrol Station. Left on to Dene Road immediate left for Ford Lane - down to bottom.

Honorary Secretary: Mr Ian Howells; 21 Heathwood road Manchester M19 1WU Tel: 0161 431 4364
email: howellsey@yahoo.co.uk
Fixtures Secretary: Mr Keith Price; 29 Cherry Holt Avenue Stockport Cheshire SK4 3PS Tel: 0161 4317838
email: keith.price@waitrose.com
Club Colours: Black & Amber
League: North Lancs 1 (level 8)

Dinnington RFC
Ground Address: Lodge Lane Dinnington Sheffield South Yorkshire S25 2PB
Contact: 01909 562044
Email: alanpeasgood@tiscali.co.uk
Website: www.dinningtonrugby.net
Honorary Secretary: Mr Alan Peasgood; 0 Woodsetts Road Anston Sheffield South Yorkshire S25 4EQ
Tel: 07726 322707
email: alanpeasgood@tiscali.co.uk
Fixtures Secretary: Mr Terry Young; 3 Milton Road Dinnington Sheffield S25 2QR Tel: 01909 567889
Club Colours: Blue,Gold White, Hoops
League: Yorkshire 1 (level 7)

Doncaster Phoenix RUFC
Ground Address:
Castle Park Armthorpe Road Doncaster DN2 5QB
Contact: 01302 831388
Email: will@shape-services.com
Honorary Secretary: Mr W Hircock; The Grange Top Road Barnby Dun Doncaster South Yorkshire DN3 1DB
Tel: 01302 391188
email: will@shape-services.com
Fixtures Secretary: Mr Graham Kitchen; 18 Broadway Dunscroft Doncaster South Yorkshire DN7 4AA
Tel: 01302 844700   email: grahamkitchen06@aol.com
Club Colours: Black and Red
League: Yorkshire 2 (level 8)

Douglas (I.O.M.)
Ground Address: Douglas R.F.C. Port-E-Chee Meadow, Port-E Chee Peel Road, Douglas, Isle of Man.
Correspondence: to Hon. Sec.
Contact: 01624 673187
Email: kcwmason@live.co.uk
Website: www.douglasrufc.com
Directions: The club house and grounds are just over a mile out from the centre of Douglas on the main Douglas to Peel Road the A1.After passing through the round abouts at the quarterbride the entrance is two hundred yards of the right hand side. The ground and Club House are at the end of the drive way.
Honorary Secretary: Mr Karl Mason; 17 Hatfield Grove Douglas Isle of Man IM1 3HE Tel: 07624 450996
email: karl.m@ctcprinters.co.uk
Fixtures Secretary: Mr Andrew Corris; 48 Sunningdale Drive Onchan Isle of Man IM3 1EJ Tel: 07624 240179
email: drewcorris@hotmail.com
Club Colours: Maroon with Gold Band
League: South Lancs-Cheshire 2 (level 8)

LEVELS 7-12 & NON LEAGUE CLUBS 469

Dukinfield RUFC
Ground Address: Blacksages Playing Fields Birch Lane Dukinfield Cheshire SK16 5AP
Contact: 07973 919026
Website: www.dukinfieldrugby.com
Directions: On the B6170 mid way between Ashton and Hyde, next to Dukinfield Baths.
Honorary Secretary: Mr Martin Garside; 98 Lodge Lane Dukinfield Cheshire SK16 5HY
Tel: 0161 3383317
email: m_garside@tiscali.co.uk
Fixtures Secretary: Mr Alan Hilton; 260 Huddersfield Road Stalybridge Cheshire SK15 3DZ
Tel: 0161 3383410
email: allan.hilton@cloneshall.co.uk
Club Colours: Royal Blue and Gold Hoops
League: South Lancs-Cheshire 1 (level 7)

Eagle RUFC
Ground Address: Eagle Sports and Social Thornton Road, Great Sankey, Warrington. WA5 2SZ
Contact: 0788 2640245
Email: info@eaglerufc.com
Website: www.eaglerufc.com
Directions: A57 west from Warrington towards Liverpool onto the dual carriageway, where road solts at roundabout take left hand road (A562) & at lights turn left into Thornton Road.
Honorary Secretary: Mr Iwan Evans; 48 Mottram Close Grappenhall Warrington WA4 2XU Tel: 07999 875908
email: iwanandjane@btinternet.com
Fixtures Secretary: Craig Harpur Tel: 07800 523180
Club Colours: Black & White
League: North Lancs 2 (level 9)

Eccles RFC
Ground Address: Gorton Street, Peel Green, Peel Green, Eccles, Manchester. Greater Manchester M30 7LZ
Contact: 0161 7892613
Email: info@ecclesrfc.org.uk
Website: www.ecclesrfc.org.uk
Directions: J 11 M60, A57 to Eccles, 2nd left, Gorton St.
Honorary Secretary: Mr Paul Thorpe; 19 Catherine Road Swinton Manchester M27 0EX Tel: 07766 512552
email: paul.thorpe@isg-technology.com
Fixtures Secretary: Mr Don Edmondson; 43 Coll Drive Davyhulme Urmston Manchester M41 7FX
Tel: 0161 7476697
email: donald.edmondson1@btinternet.com
Club Colours: Navy & White Hoops, White Shorts
League: North Lancs-Cumbria (level 7)

Edge Hill University
Ground Address: Edge Hill College St. Helens Road Ormskirk Lancashire L39 4PZ
Contact: 01695 584057
Email: gilbodk@edgehill.ac.uk
Fixtures Secretary: Ms Karen Gilbody; Edge Hill College Students Union St Helens Road Ormskirk Lancashire L39 4QP Tel: 01695 584057

email: gilbodk@edgehill.ac.uk
Club Colours: Green Black White
Non League

Egremont RFC
Ground Address:
Bleach Green Egremont Cumbria CA22 2NL
Contact: 01946 820645
Website: www.egremontrugbyuion.co.uk
Directions: M6 J36 . Follow A595 north towards Workington, Egremont is approx. 4 miles south of Whitehaven.
Honorary Secretary: Mrs Susan Peet; Lyndale Baybarrow Road Egremont CA22 2NG
Tel: 01946 824098
Club Colours: Black & Amber
League: Cumbria (level 8)

Ellesmere Port RUFC
Ground Address: Whitby Sports & Social Club Chester Road, Whitby Ellesmere Port Cheshire CH65 6QF
Contact: 0151 2007050
Directions: M6, M56, M53, J10, A5117 to forth roundabout. Turn right, club on right in 3/4 mile. (Whitby Sports & Social Club)
Honorary Secretary: Mr Mark Davies; 17 Cedardale Drive Whitby Ellesmere Port Cheshire CH66 2UW
Tel: 07981 002796   email: mark-davies1@ntlworld.com
Fixtures Secretary: Mr G Fenion; 19 Belgrave Drive Ellesmere Port CH65 7EJ Tel: 01244 283710
Club Colours: Black with 2 Single Red/Yellow Hoops
League: South Lancs-Cheshire 3 (level 9)

Fleetwood RUFC
Ground Address: Fleetwood Rugby Club Melbourne Avenue, Fleetwood. FY7 8AY
Contact: 01253 874774
Email: info@frufc.com
Website: www.frufc.com
Directions: From M55 J3 follow signs for Fleetwood along A585. Stay on the A585 for 10 miles (past the Morrison r'about) go straight on at the next lights and take the next left onto the B5409 (Rossall Lane) just before the Fleetwood Nautical Building on RHS, Take first right and follow road to lights turn right after 400m turn right into Melbourne Ave club entrance is 25 m on. left
Honorary Secretary: Barry Newbery; 32 Buttermere Avenue Fleetwood Lancashire Tel: 01253 874271
email: katy@the-barlows.co.uk
Fixtures Secretary: Mr Andrew Thompson; 67 Levens Drive Poulton Le Fylde Lancashire FY6 8EZ
Tel: 01253 882121   email: frufc@btinternet.com
Club Colours: Green & Gold Hoops
League: North Lancs-Cumbria (level 7)

Furness RFC
Ground Address: Furness R.U.F.C. Strawberry Grounds Croslands Park Road Barrow-in-Furness Cumbria LA13 9LA
Contact: 01229 825226
Email: frufc@frufc.net
Website: www.frufc.net

Directions: At 3rd roundabout on Dalton by-pass take left exit for hospital. At mini roundabout turn right onto Abbey Road after approx 1 mile turn left into Croslands Park Road, entrance 100yards on right, adjacent to bungalow and down a narrow drive.
Honorary Secretary: Mr Ken Oliver; 14 East Drive Birkrigg Park Ulverston Cumbria LA12 0UD
Tel: 01229 584546
email: secretary@furnessrugby.co.uk
Fixtures Secretary: Mr Graham Brannon; 7 Monks Vale Grove Barrow-in-Furness Cumbria LA13 9JQ
Tel: 01229 822505
email: fixtures@furnessrugby.co.uk
Club Colours: Blue & White Hoops
League: North Lancs-Cumbria (level 7)

Garforth RUFC
Ground Address: Garforth Community College Lidgett Lane, Garforth Leeds LS25 1LJ
Contact: 07974833516
Email: JonathanFallas@aol.com
Website: www.garforthrufc.org.uk
Directions: For **Directions** Please visit our Web-site www.garforthrufc.org.uk
Honorary Secretary: Mr Simon Horwell; 9 Granville Street Castleford West Yorkshire WF10 5HF
Tel: 07977 603746
email: garforthrugby@yahoo.com
Fixtures Secretary: Mr Jonathan Fallas; The Step 0 Westfield Lane Kippax Leeds LS25 7LY
Tel: 07974 833516   email: JonathanFallas@aol.com
Club Colours: All Black with Gold Trim
League: Yorkshire 3 (level 9)

Garstang RFC
Ground Address: Hudson Park, Garstang Sports & Social Club, High Street, Garstang. PR3 1JA
Contact: 07930 563441
Email: joinus@garstangrugby.com
Website: www.gastangrugby.com
Directions: see website
Honorary Secretary: Mr Frank Purkis; 5 Cyprus Road Heyshom Lancashire Lancashire LA3 2qr
Tel: 07877 854400   email: purkisfc@hotmail.com
Fixtures Secretary: Mr Adrian Bosson; 23 Norton Road PR3 IJX Tel: 01995 600881
email: adrian.louise@tiscali.co.uk
Club Colours: Sky Blue and Navy
League: North Lancs 1 (level 7)

Glossop RFC
Ground Address: Hargate Hill Lane Charlesworth Glossop SK13 5HG
Contact: 01457 857302
Email: glossop.rufc@btinternet.com
Website: http://www.glossop-rugbyufc.co.uk/
Directions: Through Glossop on A57, take A626 signed Marple, ground is 1.5 miles on left.

Honorary Secretary: Mr Paul Whiston; 18 Spring Rise Simmondley Glossop Derbyshire SK13 6US
Tel: 07748 332891
email: paul.whiston@btconnect.com
Fixtures Secretary: Mr Phil Littlewood
Tel: 07976 714706
email: phillip@oakmount76.freeserve.co.uk
Club Colours: Royal Blue Shirts, Black Shorts
League: South Lancs-Cheshire 1 (level 7)

Goole RFC
Ground Address:
Westfield Lane Hook Goole DN14 5PW
Contact: 01405 762018
Email: julian.patrick@butlergroup.com
Website: www.goolerfc.co.uk
Directions: Exit M62 at Jnc 37 (Signed Howden). At end of slip road follow signs for Goole (A614). Straight across mini roundabout and over Boothferry Bridge. Turn left at next roundabout (signed Hook). Rugby club is approx 1 mile down the road on the right.
Honorary Secretary: Mr Andy Barrass; 1 Mond Avenue Goole Humberside DN14 6LF Tel: 07989 190948
email: baz@mondave.co.uk
Fixtures Secretary: Mr Phil Shand; 4 Kings Close Pontefract West Yorkshire WF8 3PD Tel: 01977 600435
email: phil.shand@btopenworld.com
Club Colours: Blue and Gold
League: Yorkshire 2 (level 8)

Gosforth Greengarth RUFC
Ground Address: 5 Wastwater Rise Seascale gosforth Cumbria CA20 1LB
Contact: 019467 27922
Email: ruddpaul3@aol.com
Directions: Club house is adjacent to the A595 at Gosford crossroads. The pitch is on the other side of the A595.
Honorary Secretary: Paul Rudd; 5 Wastwater Rise Seascale Cumbria CA20 1LB Tel: 019467 27922
email: ruddpaul3@aol.com
Fixtures Secretary: Mr Steven Eastwood; 7 Meadowfield Gosforth Seascale Cumbria CA20 1HX
Tel: 019467 25790
League: Cumbria (level 8)

Gosforth RFC
Ground Address: Druid Park Ponteland Road Woolsington Newcastle Upon Tyne NE13 8DF
Contact: 01661 523425
Email: rugby@gosforthfrc.fsnet.co.uk
Website: www.Gosforth-rfc.co.uk
Honorary Secretary: Mr David Hall; 2 Heswall Road Northburn Dale Cramlington NorthumberlandNE23 3UU
Tel: 01670 732661
email: DavidAlanHall@btinternet.com
Fixtures Secretary: Mr Malcolm Bell; 3 Lansdowne Gardens Stakeford Choppington NorthumberlandNE62 5LF Tel: 07742 724729
Club Colours: Green & White Hoops & White Shorts
League: Durham-N'Thm'Land 1 (level 7)

LEVELS 7-12 & NON LEAGUE CLUBS   471

Guisborough
Ground Address: Guisborough Rugb Club Belmangate Guisborough North Yorkshire TS146BB
Contact: 01287 632966
Email: paulwren@guisboroughrugby.co.uk
Website: www.guisboroughrugby.co.uk
Directions: From South From A19 take A172 signposted Stokesley and Guisborough. When entering Guisborough - go straight on at Shell garage to far end of Westgate (High Street). At traffic lights turn right passing Fox Inn. At next lights go straight on. Club is 300 metres on the right hand side immediately before bridge.
From North Take A174 signed Redcar. Then take A171 exit for Guisborough and Whitby. Follow signs for Guisborough. When entering Guisborough - then as above.
Honorary Secretary: Mr Paul Wren; 4 Reid Terrace Guisborough Cleveland TS14 6EB Tel: 07904 702706
email: paulwren@guisboroughrufc.co.uk
Fixtures Secretary: Mr Matthew Paylor; 1 Cliff Terrace Liverton Saltburn-by-the-Sea Cleveland TS13 4QE
Tel: 07896 141052
email: matthew.paylor@googlemail.com
League: Durham-N'Thm'Land 3 (level 9)

Halifax Vandals RUFC
Ground Address: The Clubhouse Warley Town Lane Warley Halifax HX2 7SL
Contact: 01422 831703
Email: neilcrossley@live.com
Website: www.vandalsrugger.com
Directions: From M62: 1. Leave the motorway at J24 and follow A629 towards Halifax. 2. When A629 becomes single lane, turn left at lights and go straight on at the mini r'about towards Sowerby Bridge. 3. Travel through Copley along Wakefield Road. You will pass the HBOS plc on the right. 4. At lights turn left down hill into Sowerby Bridge town centre. 5. Go through pelican crossing. Turn right at next lights up Tuel Lane. 6. At top of hill turn left onto Burnley Road then take immediate right up Blackwall Lane. 7. At end of this road turn right. 8. Follow winding road into the village of Warley. 9. Keep left through village centre (church on left) up Warley Town Lane. 10. After fi mile you will come to new Clubhouse and car park. From Halifax: 1. From Halifax - Leave Halifax by following A58 going west towards Hebden Bridge/Burnley. 2. Follow this road through the major traffic lights/junction at King Cross. 3. After a mile or so turn right up Windle Royd Lane (directly before Peacock Inn). 4. Turn left at end of this road onto Stocks Lane and enter Warley village. 5. At village centre (Maypole Inn on left) keep right up Warley Town Lane. 6. After fi mile you will come to new Clubhouse and car park.
Honorary Secretary: Mr Neil Crossley; 44 Clifton Common Brighouse West Yorkshire HD6 1QW
Tel: 07789 923579   email: neilcrossley@live.com
Fixtures Secretary: Mr Peter Jones; Wells Court Flat 7 Rawson Street North Boothtown Halifax HX3 6PX
Tel: 01422 367134
Club Colours: Blue & White Hooped Shirts
League: Yorkshire 3 (level 9)

Harrogate Pythons
Ground Address: County Ground, Claro Road, Harrogate, North Yorkshire , HG1 4AG
Contact: 01423 566966
Email: info@harrogaterugby.co.uk
Website: http: //www.harrogaterugby.co.uk/index.php
Directions: Take A1 to J 47, signposted Harrogate and York, follow the road signs to Harrogate, turning right at the 3rd r'about. Follow Wetherby Road into Harrogate (passing Sainsbury's on your left), and go straight through the traffic lights, past the Harrogate Town ground and the Hospital on your right, to the main r'about on the A59 (Empress Roundabout). Go straight across this r'about, following signs for Skipton and A59. Go through the first set of lights (pedestrian crossing) and Claro Road is signposted at the next set of traffic lights. The ground is about 200 yards along on the right. There is plenty of onsite parking.
Honorary Secretary: Neil Summersall
email: nsummersall@hotmail.com
Club Colours: Yellow, black & red stripes, black shorts
League: Yorkshire 4 (level 10)

Hartlepool Athletic RFC
Ground Address: Oakesway Estate Hartlepool TS24 0RE
Contact: 01429 274715
Email: jimainslie1998@yahoo.co.uk
Website: www.kissthebadge.co.uk
Directions: Leave A19 at A179 Hartlepool turn off, follow signs for Headland, Ground 3 miles from A19 .
Honorary Secretary: Mr Jim Ainslie; 10 Regent Street Hartlepool Cleveland TS24 0QN Tel: 01429 260003
email: jimainslie1998@yahoo.co.uk
Fixtures Secretary: Mr John Bentham; 22 Tempest Road Hartlepool Cleveland TS24 9QH Tel: 01429 281012
Club Colours: Sky Blue, White, Royal Blue.
League: Durham-N'Thm'Land 3 (level 9)

Hartlepool B.B.O.B.
Ground Address: Old Friarage Moor Terrace, Headland Hartlepool TS24 0PS
Contact: 07887 555154
Email: fawcett1630@btinternet.com
Directions: Leave A19 at A179, follow A179 past Hart Village to 1st roundabout, follow signs for 'Headland' and ' Heugh Battery', take left at St. Hildas Church, then next left. Parking and pitch on the right hand side of road. Changing facilities adjacent to pitch.
Honorary Secretary: Mr Steve Fawcett; 5 Brooklime Close Hartlepool Cleveland TS26 0WH
Tel: 01388 776242
email: fawcett1630@btinternet.com
Fixtures Secretary: Mr William Gray; 25 Wentworth Grove Clavering Park Hartlepool Cleveland TS27 3PP
Tel: 07877 480212
Club Colours: Black and White Shirts, Black Band
League: Durham-N'Thm'Land 3 (level 9)

Hartlepool RFC
Ground Address: Mayfield Park Easington Road
Hartlepool TS24 9BA
Contact: 01429 236 177
Email: davejones50@hotmail.com
Website: www.hartlepool.co.uk
Directions: Leave A19 north of town on A179 over two roundabouts, right at 3rd, Ground 500m on left.
Honorary Secretary: Mr Dave Jones; 14 Turnberry Grove Hartlepool Cleveland TS27 3PX
Tel: 01429 231125   email: davejones50@hotmail.com
Fixtures Secretary: Mr Lee Dodgson; 32 Thornbury Close Hartlepool Cleveland TS27 3RA
Tel: 07737568696   email: leedodgson@hotmail.co.uk
Club Colours: Black and White
League: Durham-N'Thm'Land 1 (level 7)

Hawcoat Park RUFC
Ground Address: Hawcoat Park Sports & Social Club Hawcoat Lane Barrow in Furness Cumbria LA14 4HF
Contact: 01229 874643
Email: cafbaeb@tesco.net
Website: www.vrufc.co.uk
Directions: M6 J36. Follow A590 to Barrow. Follow signs to Barrow. At r'about signposted Dalton left Barrow straight on follow Barrow, continue on at next roundabout, * turn left at next r'about, turn right at next r'about, follow road for approx 1.5miles at Strawberry Hotel traffic lights turn right, club is 200m on the left From West Coast A591 after passing through Askam-in-Furness turn right at first r'about, then from * above.
Honorary Secretary: Mr Alan Troughton; 188 Yarlside Road Barrow-in-Furness Cumbria LA13 0EY
Tel: 01229 838023   email: troughton.a@hrl.co.uk
Fixtures Secretary: Mr Tony Skelton; 85 Hill Road Barrow-in-Furness Cumbria LA14 4EX
Tel: 01229 827791
email: anthony.skelton@baesystems.com
Club Colours: Maroon & White Shorts
League: North Lancs 1 (level 8)

Heath RUFC
Ground Address: Heath R.U.F.C. North Dean Stainland Road Greetland Halifax West Yorkshire HX4 8LS
Contact: 01422 372920
Email: heathrufcsec@btinternet.com
Website: www.heathrufc.com
Directions: M62 J24, follow Halifax signs at bottom of hill (end of dual carriageway). turn left towards Stainland, clubhouse approx. 500m on left after garden centre.
Honorary Secretary: Mr Peter Burton; 10 Castle Estate Ripponden Sowerby Bridge West Yorkshire HX6 4JY
Tel: 07720 843168
email: heathrufcsec@btinternet.com
Fixtures Secretary: Mr Michael Downsborough; 15 Hill Grove Salendine Nook Huddersfield W. Yorks. HD3 3TL
Tel: 01484 656890
Club Colours: Emerald Gold and Claret
League: Yorkshire 1 (level 7)

Heaton Moor RUFC
Ground Address: Heaton Moor R.U.F.C. Green Lane, Heaton Moor, Stockport. Cheshire SK4 2NF
Contact: 0161 4321757
Email: info@heatonmoorrugby.co.uk
Website: www.heatonmoorrugby.co.uk
Directions: Directions: - M60 - Junction 1 (Stockport Centre & West). Take A5145 off roundabout - signposted Didsbury. After approx. 1/2 mile, turn right into Bankhall Road at traffic lights at top of hill. Turn right at next set of lights into Green Lane. Club 250 yds. on left
Honorary Secretary: Mr Peter Heath; 3 Hepley Road Poynton Stockport Cheshire SK12 1RX
Tel: 07876 521462   email: pete_heath@hotmail.com
Fixtures Secretary: Mr M Jeskins; 5 Hazel Drive Manchester M22 5LY Tel: 0161 4364807
email: john.jeskins@talktalk.net
Club Colours: Red, Black and Amber
League: North Lancs-Cumbria (level 7)

Helsby RFC
Ground Address: Helsby Community sports clubClub Chester Road, Helsby Frodsham Cheshire WA6 0DL
Contact: 01928 722267
Email: allan.garner@helsbyrugby.com
Website: www.helsbyrugby.com
Directions: From Junction 14 of the M56 take the A56 towards Helsby. Go straight through the traffic lights after one mile (Helsby Arms pub on the left hand side). The club are based at Helsby Community Sports Club which is a further 400 metres along the road, on the left opposite the Total garage.
Honorary Secretary: Mr Allan Garner; 60 Mountain View Helsby Frodsham Cheshire WA6 0BG
Tel: 01928 724947   email: allan.garner@shell.com
Fixtures Secretary: Mr Anthony Ryder; 64 Chester Road Helsby Frodsham WA6 0DW Tel: 01928 723733
email: allan.garner@shell.com
Club Colours: Black & Amber Hoops, Black shorts
League: South Lancs-Cheshire 3 (level 9)

Hemsworth RUFC
Ground Address: Moxon Fields Lowfield Road, Hemsworth Pontefract West Yorkshire WF9 4JT
Contact: 01977 610078
Email: info@hemsworthrufc.co.uk
Website: http://www.hemsworthrufc.co.uk
Directions: From Hemsworth town centre take Pontefract Road. Lowfield Road is on the right just after the left hand bend.
Honorary Secretary: Mr John Lightfoot; 12 Haven Court Pontefract West Yorkshire WF8 4RU
Tel: 07967 990512
email: john.lightfoot@linde-jewsburys.co.uk
Fixtures Secretary: Mr Jason Crawford; 54 Parkland View Barnsley South Yorkshire S71 5LL
Tel: 01226 718182
email: juniorrugby4Hemsworth@talktalk.net
Club Colours: Maroon & Blue Quarters
League: Yorkshire 4 (level 10)

NORTHERN

LEVELS 7-12 & NON LEAGUE CLUBS   473

Hessle RUFC
Ground Address: Livingstone Road Hessle HU13 0EG
Contact: 01482 643430
Email: hesslerufcc@aol.com
Directions: Take A63 towards Hull. Pass under Humber Bridge approach road. Take next turn off - signposted Hessle. At traffic lights at top of slip road turn right and cross over A63. Turn right at next, immediate, set of traffic lights (mandatory) and go onto A63 Westbound slip road. DO NOT go onto A63 but take immediate left turn signposted Hessle Foreshore and Livingstone Road Insustrial Estate. Follow road, passing offices, garages, old shipyard, Hessle Haven, Italian Restaurant. Hessle RUFC clubhouse and ground is then approximately 200 metres on left.
Honorary Secretary: Mr Patrick Love; 3 The Coachings Hessle Yorkshire   Tel: 07788 598662
email: patrick.love@linertech.com
Fixtures Secretary: Mrs Julie Allinson; 1 Trinity Grove Hull HU9 3RP Tel: 0778 7365915
email: gordymarg@hotmail.com
Club Colours: Green, Black and White
League: Yorkshire 2 (level 8)

Holmes Chapel RFC
Ground Address: A P Club Station Road Holmes Chapel Cheshire CW4 8BE
Contact: 07881 828739
Website: www.pitchero.com/clubs/holmeschapl
Directions: From M6 follow signs for Congleton. Turn right into Chester Road and follow to Traffic Lights. Go Straight through the lights and club is first right turn after the railway bridge.
Honorary Secretary: Mr Edward Meyrick; 8 Wellcroft Gardens Lymm Cheshire WA13 0LU Tel: 078818 28739
email: eddie_meyrick@hotmail.com
Fixtures Secretary: Mr Mike Corfield; 72 St. Annes Road Middlewich Cheshire CW10 9BY
Tel: 07771 812218
email: Mike.corfield@shell.com
Club Colours: Royal Blue Shirts with Single Gold Band
League: South Lancs-Cheshire 3 (level 9)

Horden RFC
Ground Address: Horden RFC Northumberland Street, Peterlee SR8 4PX
Contact: 0191 5863501
Email: mac.995@btinternet.com
Website: www.hordenrugbyclub.co.uk
Directions: Directions from north, leave a 19 at easington/Horden slip road. Turn right at roundabout and follow road past walkers crisps on right and Horden hall on left.Turn rightat next roundabout and follow road till you reach a mini roundabout, turn left down Northumberland street and club is on the right. From the south leave a19 at peterlee slip road. Follow the road through Peterlee and follow signs for Horden.You reach a "T" junction and turn left. Follow road through Horden till you reach mini roundabout. Turn right down Northumberland Street and club is on right at bottom.
Honorary Secretary: Mr Richard Thirkell Snr; 2 Aspen Avenue Horden Peterlee Co. Durham SR8 4HB Tel: 07969 457850
email: richy@thirkell51.fsnet.co.uk
Fixtures Secretary: Mr Jonathon Hudson; 47 Eastdene Way Peterlee SR8 5TL
email: jon_hudson_83@hotmail.com
Club Colours: Claret and Blue
League: Durham-N'Thm'Land 1 (level 7)

Hornsea RUFC
Ground Address: The Hollis Recreation Ground Westwood Avenue Hornsea HU18 1EE
Contact: 01964 541064
Email: nom@postmaster.co.uk
Website: www.hornsearufc.co.uk
Directions: Leave Hornsea on Atwick & Bridlington Road. Turn left after 300m onto Westwood Avenue, opposite School playing fields.
Honorary Secretary: Mr Nicholas O'Mahony; Brazzock House Main Street Catwick Beverley HU17 5PH
Tel: 07515 154125
email: nom@postmaster.co.uk
Fixtures Secretary: Mr Roger Mclatchie; 7 Headland View Hornsea HU18 1NF Tel: 07836 559950
Club Colours: Black with Green & White Hoops
League: Yorkshire 4 (level 10)

Houghton RUFC
Ground Address: Houghton RUFC. Dairy Lane Houghton-Le-Spring DH4 5BH
Contact: 0191 584 1460
Email: tommy@tabeston.wanadoo.co.uk
Directions: Situated on A1052, Houghton to Chester-Le-Street Road, opposite Houghton Police Station, 0.25 mile west of A690.
Honorary Secretary: Mr Ralph Johnson; 21 Church Street Houghton-Le-Street DU5 8AA Tel: 0191 2343000
Fixtures Secretary: Mr Derek English; C/0 Club Tel: 07956 512080
Club Colours: Black / white hoop, black shorts & socks
League: Durham-N'Thm'Land 2 (level 8)

Hoylake RFC
Ground Address: Carham Road Hoylake Wirral Merseyside CH47 4FF
Contact: 0151 6322538
Email: stirling.dutton@excite.com
Website: www.hoylake.net
Directions: Turn at r'about in Hoylake towards Railway Station. After 500 yards, turn left down Carham Road.
Honorary Secretary: Mrs Tracy Kellaway; 43 Dovedale Road Wirral CH47 3AN Tel: 0151 6325742
email: ANNIE.KELLAWAY@TESCO.NET
Fixtures Secretary: Mrs Sue Kurton; 7 Meadowcroft Road Meols Wirral Merseyside CH47 6BG
Tel: 0151 6325540
email: jacsue.kurton@btinternet.com
Club Colours: Green with red/white hoops
League: South Lancs-Cheshire 1 (level 7)

Huddersfield YMCA RUFC
Ground Address: Laund Hill Sports Complex Laund Hill New Hey Road Salendine Nook Huddersfield HD3 3XF
Contact: 01484 654052
Email: gnasey@blueyonder.co.uk
Website: www.huddersfieldymcarugby.org.uk
Directions: From West: M62,J23, follow Huddersfield sign, ground 0.5 mile on left. From East: M62, J24, follow Rochdale sign at r'bout, along A643 for 1 mile, left at r'bout, follow Huddersfield sign, ground o.5 mile on left.
Honorary Secretary: Mr Grahame Nasey; 12 Deep Lane Clifton Brighouse Yorkshire HD6 4HF
Tel: 01484 384161   email: gnasey@blueyonder.co.uk
Fixtures Secretary: Mr Steve Metcalfe; 38 Marcus Way Mount Huddersfield HD3 3YA Tel: 01484 325844
email: steve.metcalfe1@ntlworld.com
Club Colours: Red and Black Hooped Shirts
League: Yorkshire 2 (level 8)

Hullensians RUFC
Ground Address: Springhead Lane Springfield Way, Anlaby Common Hull HU4 7RU
Contact: (01482) 505656
Email: info@hullensians.org
Directions: M62/A63 towards Hull. Turn off at Ferriby follow signs for Anlaby. Travel along Boothferry Road, left along First First Lane, right at the end, sharp left at roundabout,1st right Springhead Lane. Pitch visible from there behind Mormon Church.
Honorary Secretary: Mr P Jones; 5 Sherwood Drive Hull HU4 7RG Tel: 07796 144158
email: Pete.Jones@hullensians.org
Fixtures Secretary: Mrs Kath Smith Tel: 01482 667262
email: ksmith1950@ksmith1950.karoo.co.uk
Club Colours: Red & Black & White
League: Yorkshire 2 (level 8)

Hutton RFC
Ground Address: 29 Westerdale Drive Banks Southport Merseyside PR9 8DG ENGLAND
Contact: 07710 836500
Email: info@huttonrufc.co.uk
Website: www.huttonrufc.co.uk
Honorary Secretary: Mr Daniel Horton; Flat 6, Beech Grove 85 Garstang Road Preston Lancashire PR1 1UT
Tel: 07880 556418   email: d.b.horton@hotmail.co.uk
Club Colours: Blue & white stripe shirts, black shorts
League: North Lancs 1 (level 8)

Keighley RUFC
Ground Address: Skipton Road Utley Utley Keighley West Yorkshire BD20 6DT
Contact: 01535 602174
Email: michealgreaves@btinternet.co.uk
Website: www.keighleyrufc.org.uk
Directions: Ground is situated on North-West side of Keighley in suburb known as Utley on B6265 road (old A629) from Keighley towards Skipton. Facilities on right hand side of B6265, in fields after last house on righthand side travelliing out of Keighley
Honorary Secretary: Mr Michael Greaves; Holmelea Summerhill Lane Steeton Keighley W. Yorks. BD20 6RX
Tel: 01535 653192
email: michealgreaves@btinternet.com
Fixtures Secretary: Mr Joe Midgley; 21 Woodville Road Keighley BD20 6JA Tel: 01535 212145
email: naresfield@tiscali.co.uk
Club Colours: Scarlet, Emerald Green & White
League: Yorkshire 1 (level 7)

Keswick RFC
Ground Address:
Davidson Park Keswick Cumbria CA12 5EG
Contact: 01768780186
Email: etherdend@aol.com
Website: www.keswickrugbyclub.co.uk
Directions: From M6 Lunction 40 (Penrith) A66 (west) for 17 miles. Ignore first turnoff signed for Keswick & Windermere. Continue on A66 down hill to roundabout. Take 1st left off roundabout (signed Keswick) Continue 1/2 miles to T Junction. Turn Left. Continue 1/2 mile to mini roundabout - Turn Right After 50 yards turn right (twoards Booths Supermarket) Continue past Booths Supermarket Car Park and after 20 yards bear right - Keswick RUFC is 50 yards on your right This Route is valis for Cars & Coaches At ground follows Match day Parking Siigns PLEASE NOTE THE TARMAC CAR PARK AT THE ENTRANCE IS PAY & DISPLAY This Car Park is NOT operated by the Club but by Allerdale Borough Council - BE WARNED THEY LIKE ISSUING PARKING TICKETS !!
Honorary Secretary: Mr Elizabeth Weightman; Greengarth Eleventrees Keswick CA12 4LW
Tel: 01768 772448   email: lizziemint@hotmail.com
Fixtures Secretary: Mr Alan Gray; 49 Blencathra Street Keswick Cumbria CA12 4HX Tel: 017687 73051
email: alan.krfc@btopenworld.com
Club Colours: Navy, green & yellow hoops, navy shorts.
League: North Lancs-Cumbria (level 7)

Kirkby Lonsdale RFC
Ground Address: The Clubhouse Underley Park Underley Park Kirkby Lonsdale Cumbria LA6 2DS
Contact: 015242 71780
Email: admin@klrufc.co.uk
Website: www.klrufc.co.uk
Directions: M6 to Junction 36, after approx 5 miles it is signposted to Kirkby Lonsdale. At road junction, bear left and at bottom of hill turn left again. About 0.5 mile up the hill, turn right at small sign post for KLRUFC. Full details on website at www.klrufc.c
Honorary Secretary: Mr Jack Hamer; 55 Rushgreen Road Lymm Cheshire WA13 9PS Tel: 01925 752527
email: honsec@klrufc.co.uk
Fixtures Secretary: Mr Billy Whewell; The Clubhouse Underley Park Kirkby Lonsdale Cumbria LA6 2DS
Tel: 01524 782019   email: childprotection@klrufc.co.uk
Club Colours: Red, black & amber hoops, black shorts.
League: North Lancs-Cumbria (level 7)

LEVELS 7-12 & NON LEAGUE CLUBS

Knaresborough RUFC
Ground Address: Hay-A-Park Park lane (off Chain Lane) Knaresborough North Yorkshire HG5 0DQ
Contact: 01423 556219
Email: info@krufc.co.uk
Website: www.krufc.co.uk
Directions: Follow A59 to centre of Knaresborough, at traffic lights by Board Inn turn North, away from Calcutt (signposted), take 2nd right, at school, follow on to end of road. Continue on down lane under bridge. Pitch is 200 yds on right.
Honorary Secretary: Mr Ben cutting; B 42 Bachelor Gardens Harrogate North Yorkshire HG1 3EE
Tel: 01423 525911   email: pete.drew@ntlworld.com
Fixtures Secretary: Mr Peter Roberts; Whitestacks House Havikil Lane Scotton Knaresborough North Yorkshire HG5 9HN Tel: 07881 626876
email: p.roberts@skinmed.co.uk
Club Colours: Blue and gold hooped shirts, navy shorts
League: Yorkshire 5 (level 11)

Knottingley RUFC
Ground Address: Knottingley RUFC Howards Field, Marsh Lane Knottingley WF11 9DE
Contact: 07795 121609
Email: Ian.Beach@Rockware.co.uk
Directions: On to A645 main road towards Knottingley, turn off at town hall/St Botolophs Church, follow road 500m past Cherry Tree Pub, turn left just before lights at bridge to Howards Field.
Honorary Secretary: Mr Ian Beach; 71 Green Lane Selby North Yorkshire YO8 9AN Tel: 07795 121609
email: ian.beach@rockware.co.uk
Fixtures Secretary: Mr Mark Carley; 17 Stumpcross Way Pontefract West Yorkshire WF8 2DF
Tel: 01977 706830
Club Colours: Blue & White Shirt, Blue Shorts & Socks
League: Yorkshire 2 (level 8)

Knutsford RFC
Ground Address: Knutsford Sports Club Mereheath Lane Knutsford Cheshire WA16 6SZ
Contact: 01565 872588
Email: a.j.spark@btinternet.com
Website: www.knutsfordrugby.com
Directions: From the roundabout in Knutsford town centre, take the A50 heading North (Manchester). Go past the Heath on the Left and take the 4th road on the right (Garden Road). Take the 2nd road on the Left (Mereheath Lane) and the Ground is a quarter mile on the Left. On arrival please make your way round to the left of the car park where you will find the changing rooms. Our Club address is - Knutsford Rugby Club Mereheath Lane, Knutsford, Cheshire, WA16 6SZ
Honorary Secretary: Mr Neil Loftus; Sycamore Lodge Toft Road Cheshire WA16 9EE Tel: 01565 631807
email: hon_secretary@knutsfordrugby.com
Fixtures Secretary: Mr Gregg Sawyer; Knutsford Sports Club Mereheath Lane Knutsford Cheshire WA16 6SZ
Tel: 07738 150898

email: gregg@wombling.org
Club Colours: Blue & Gold
League: South Lancs-Cheshire 3 (level 9)

Leeds Corinthians RUFC
Ground Address: 'Nutty Slack' Middleton District Centre Middleton Leeds LS10 4RA
Contact: 0113 2711574
Website: www.leedscorinthiansrufc.co.uk
Directions: M62 J28 to Leeds or M1 City centre to Dewsbury, follow signs for A653, turn onto Middleton ring road at Tommy Wass pub, right at 1st roundabout & go to rear of super market onto shale track to Club.
Honorary Secretary: Mr Jamie Portrey; 4 Queensway Rothwell Leeds LS26 0NB Tel: 07736 865980
Fixtures Secretary: Mr Phillip Blong; 76 Manor Farm Drive Churwell Leeds LS27 7RN Tel: 0133 2525361
Club Colours: Black, Gold & White
League: Yorkshire 4 (level 10)

Leodiensian RUFC
Ground Address: Crag Lane off King Lane, Alwoodley off King Lane, Alwoodley Leeds LS17 5PR
Contact: 0113 2673409
Email: chairman@leodiensian.co.uk
Website: http: //www.leodiensian.co.uk
Directions: visit our website for directions & maps.
Honorary Secretary: Mr Matt Smith; 46 Park Place Leeds LS1 2RY Tel: 07966 167721
email: secretary@leodiensian.co.uk
Fixtures Secretary: Mr Alun Gabriel; 28 Denton Avenue Roundhay Leeds LS8 1LE Tel: 01422 322396
email: fixtures@leodiensian.co.uk
Club Colours: Navy blue & gold Shirts, navy shorts
League: Yorkshire 2 (level 8)

Linley & Kidsgrove RFC
Ground Address: Kidsgrove Cricket Club Clough Hall Road Kidsgrove ST7 1AW
Contact: 01782 250616
Email: trina@fsmail.net
Website: www.linleyandkidsgroverufc.co.uk
Directions: M6 J16, A500 towards Stoke-on-Trent, 2nd junction A34 Kidsgrove, follow signs for the ski centre.
Honorary Secretary: Mrs Trina Harding; 23 Cedar Avenue Butt Lane Talke Stoke On Trent Staffs. ST7 1LA
Tel: 01782 776856
email: trina@fsmail.net
Fixtures Secretary: Mr Phillip Briggs; 27 Bourne Road Kidsgrove Stoke on Trent Staffs. ST7 1EU
Tel: 07533 775931
email: Phil_briggs_435@fsmail.net
Club Colours: Green and gold quarters
League: South Lancs-Cheshire 3 (level 9)

Littleborough RUFC
Ground Address: Rakewood Hollingworth Lake Littleborough Lancashire OL15 0AP
Contact: 01706 379825
Email: chris.j.collins@sky.com
Website: www.rfu.com/clubs/littleborough

Directions: Exit M62 at J 21 turn left towards Rochdale, at first set of T-lights, turn right. At next mini r'about turn left, continue up hill for 300y and then vere left towards Hollingworth Lake. Follow for 1 mile and at next mini r'about turn right. Follow road round with lake on right hand side. At end of lake as you approach the Wine Press, turn right and follow until the end to find LRUFC. From Littleborough From centre of Littleborough (mini r'about) follow A58 east towards Halifax. Through T-lights and just after passing under railway bridge take immediate right. Follow for 1 mile until road bends sharply to the right and turn left onto Rakewood. Follow road to end and you will find LRUFC.
Honorary Secretary: Mr Mark Murgatroyd; 6 The Greens Whitworth Rochdale Lancashire OL12 8AQ Tel: 01706 853601
email: mark.murgatroyd@biwater.com
Fixtures Secretary: Mr Brian Hurst; 1 Tudor Avenue Chadderton Oldham OL9 9PG Tel: 07947 500956
email: brian_hurst@btinternet.com
Club Colours: Green, Yellow & Black hoops
League: North Lancs 1 (level 8)

Liverpool Collegiate RUFC
Ground Address: Liverpool Collegiate R.U.F.C. Liverpool Cricket Club Aigburth Road Grassendale Liverpool L19 3QF
Contact: 0787 6048801
Email: frank.carroll@unilever.com
Website: www.liverpoolcollegiaterugby.com
Directions: View directions on www.liverpoolcollegiaterugby.com or phone 07876048801.
Honorary Secretary: Mr Frank Carroll; 75 Moses Street Liverpool Merseyside L8 4SY Tel: 07876 048801
email: frankcarroll@hotmail.com
Fixtures Secretary: Mr Michael Deane; 39 Avonmore Avenue Mossley Hill Liverpool Merseyside L18 8AL Tel: 07727 635919 email: purplebins@hotmail.co.uk
Club Colours: Dark Blue with Sky Blue Hoop
League: South Lancs-Cheshire 2 (level 8)

Liverpool John Moores University RFC
Ground Address:
LSU The Haigh Maryland Street L1 9DE
Contact: 0151 231 3696 / 95
Fixtures Secretary: Miss Samantha Inman; Students Union Liverpool John Moore Uni Haigh Building Maryland Street Liverpool Merseyside L1 9DE
Tel: 0151 2314969 email: lsusinma@livjm.ac.uk
Club Colours: Blue and Gold
Non League

Lostock RFC
Ground Address: Lostock Lane Lostock Bolton Lancashire BL6 4BR
Contact: 01204 695779
Email: hawkrigg@ntlworld.com
Website: www.lostockrugby.com
Honorary Secretary: Mr Peter Hawkrigg; 11 Webb Street Horwich Bolton BL6 5Ns Tel: 01204 457006
email: hawkrigg@ntlworld.com
Fixtures Secretary: Mr Barry Jubb; 5 Lower Makinson Fold Horwich Bolton BL6 6PD Tel: 01204 696998
email: barry.jubb@googlemail.com
Club Colours: Black & Red
Non League

Malton and Norton RUFC
Ground Address: The Gannock Old Malton Road Malton Yorkshire YO17 7EY
Contact: 01751 472228
Email: laidler@wlaidler.fsnet.co.uk
Website: www.malton-norton-rfu.co.uk
Directions: A64 York-Scarborough take first turning for Malton. At traffic lights in town centre carry straight on towards Pickering. Ground is approx 600 yards on right after cricket club.
Honorary Secretary: Mr W Laidler; 8 Second Avenue Beacon Park Pickering North Yorkshire YO18 8AH Tel: 01751 472228
email: laidler@wlaidler.fsnet.co.uk
Fixtures Secretary: as Hon. Sec.
Club Colours: Red, Black, White Irregular Hoops
League: Yorkshire 1 (level 7)

Manchester Metropolitan University RFC
Ground Address: RUFC, Manchester Met. University, Students Union Martin Luther King Building 99 Oxford Road Manchester Lancashire M1 7EL
Contact: 0161 2476447
Email: s.u.sportsdev@mmu.ac.uk
Website: www.mmurugbyunion.co.uk
Directions: We currently play our home matches at Broughton Park Rugby Club which is just behind Hough End playing fields. We use there facilities for training and matches: Broughton Park R.F.C. 2 Houghend Crescent Manchester Lancashire M21 7TL
Honorary Secretary: Mr Sandy Kerr; MMU Union 99 Oxford Road Manchester Greater Manchester M1 7EL
Tel: 0161 2476447
email: s.kerr@mmu.ac.uk
Fixtures Secretary: as Hon. Sec.
Club Colours: royal blue with yellow
Non League

Manchester Village Spartans RFC
Ground Address: Rookwood Clarendon Crescent Sale Cheshire M33 2DE
Contact: 0784 1531722
Email: bshort001@btinternet.com
Website: www.villagespartans.co.uk
Honorary Secretary: Mr Ben Short; Riverside Court 207 254, The Quays Salford Manchester M50 3SE
Tel: 07841 531722
email: bshort001@btinternet.com
Fixtures Secretary: Richard Leech; Tel: 07973 498024
email: drahcirjl@hotmail.com
Non League

Marist RUFC
Ground Address: Cranbrook Avenue Cottingham Road Cottingham Road Hull HU6 7TT
Email: maristrufc@hotmail.co.uk
Website: www.maristrufc.com
Directions: From M62 follow signs for Universities, then continue to Cranbrook Avenue along Cottingham Road.
Honorary Secretary: Mr Sean Harkin; 69 Woldcarr Road Hull HU3 6TR Tel: 07813 087244
email: Sean.Harkin@smith-nephew.com
Fixtures Secretary: Mr Ralph Ayre; 92 Auckland Avenue Hull HU6 7SH Tel: 01482 804166
Club Colours: Blue Shirt,Navy Shorts
League: Yorkshire 5 (level 11)

Marple RUFC
Ground Address: Ridge Sports Pavillion Wood Lane Marple Stockport Cheshire SK6 7RE
Contact: 0161 4277915
Website: www.marplerugby.com
Directions: Leave the M60 motorway at juntion 27 Stockport. Follow the A626 Marple. At the second set of lights at the top of the rise, turn left still following the A626 Marple. Follow this road for approx 3 miles. As you enter Marple the Railway pub is on your right, continue for quarter of a mile. Take right hand turn, Cross Lane (before Texaco garage). Continue to Marple Tavern pub, turn right onto Wood Lane, bear right onto unmade road to club.
Honorary Secretary: Mr Dave Shaw; 43 Brookfield Avenue Bredbury Stockport Cheshire SK6 1DF Tel: 07963 947632 email: davejpshaw@tesco.net
Fixtures Secretary: Mr Neil Hawkley; 4 Tatton Gardens Woodley Stockport Cheshire SK6 1HT
Tel: 0161 494 1582 email: neil.hawkley@sky.com
Club Colours: Red and Black
League: South Lancs-Cheshire 2 (level 8)

Medicals RFC
Ground Address: Cartington Terrace Heaton Newcastle upon Tyne NE6 5QQ
Contact: 07792 035655
Email: jon.clayson@btinternet.com
Website: www.medicalsrfc.co.uk
Directions: From Newcastle City Centre Take A1058 towards the coast. After the Corner House pub, take the slip road up to the roadabout Take the third exit (turn right) onto Chillingham Road. Cartington Terrace is 200 yards on the right. From the A19 Take the A1058 towards Newcastle city centre. At the first set of traffic lights (at the Corner House pub) turn left onto Heaton Road Cartington Terrace is 200 yards on the left
Honorary Secretary: Mrs Jonathan Clayson; 37 Lesbury Road Heaton Newcastle-upon-Tyne NE6 5LB
Tel: 07792 035655 email: jon.clayson@btinternet.com
Fixtures Secretary: Mr Alan Dawes; 34 Tosson Terrace Heaton Newcastle upon Tyne NE6 5LW
Tel: 07734 435867 email: al_dawes1@yahoo.co.uk
Club Colours: Maroon shirt & socks, white shorts
League: Durham-N'Thm'Land 2 (level 8)

Millom
Ground Address:
Wilson Park Haverigg Millom LA18 4HB
Contact: 01229 772300
Email: secretary@mrufc.co.uk
Directions: As you arrive in Haverigg, turn onto the beach road at the Harbour Hotel, continue past the inshore rescue building. Wilson Park is on your left at the end of the tarmac road.
Honorary Secretary: Mr Neal Hartley; 78 Lowther Road Millom Cumbria LA18 4PN Tel: 01229 772115
email: millomite@millom63.freeserve.co.uk
Fixtures Secretary: Mr Tony Park
email: tbobpark@aol.com
Club Colours: Blue and White
League: Cumbria (level 8)

MMU Cheshire
Ground Address: MMU Cheshire Athletic Union Hassall Road, Alsager ST7 2HL
Contact: 0161 247 5588 / 5136
Email: phil.kynaston@mmu.ac.uk
Directions: Sign posted 'Alsager Campus' from J16 M6
Honorary Secretary: Mr Rob Ledley
MMUnion Cheshire Alsager Campus Hassall Road Alsager Staffs. ST7 2HL   Tel: 0161 2475324
email: rob.ledley@mmu.ac.uk
Fixtures Secretary: Mr Keith Haverty
address & tel. as Hon. Sec.
email: keithhavo2@hotmail.com
Club Colours: Green and Black
Non League

Moortown RUFC
Ground Address: Moortown R.U.F.C. Moss Valley King Lane Alwoodley Leeds West Yorkshire LS17 7NT
Contact: 0113 2678243
Website: www.moortownrufc.org
Directions: From the ring road turn up past the entrance to Sainsburys,1.5 miles turn right onto The Avenue , 0.5 mile turn right into Far Moss.
Honorary Secretary: Mr John Hesketh; 5 Grange Holt Leeds LS17 7TY Tel: 07595 826114
email: john@jchesketh.freeserve.co.uk
Fixtures Secretary: Mr Nick Webb; 8 Adel Wood Drive Adel Leeds West Yorkshire LS16 8ES Tel: 07809 468943
email: helen.webb90@ntlworld.com
Club Colours: Maroon with Green & White Hoops
League: Yorkshire 2 (level 8)

Moresby RUFC
Ground Address: Walkmill Park Moresby Whitehaven Cumbria CA28 8XW
Contact: 01946 695 984
Email: KELL@MORESBY1.FSNET.CO.UK
Directions: M6 J40 (Penrith) A66 for 35 miles. Turn left onto A595 for approx 7 miles, then left up Swallow Brow. Ground is approx. 2 miles.
Honorary Secretary: Mr Ian Johnstone; 41 Hillcrest Avenue Whitehaven Cumbria CA28 6SS

Tel: 01946 66713   email: johnsty@aol.com
Fixtures Secretary: Mr Steven Kellett; 26 Miterdale Close Whitehaven Cumbria CA28 6XH
Tel: 07710 680786   email: kell@moresby1.co.uk
Club Colours: Red Shirts, White Shorts
League: Cumbria (level 8)

Mosborough RUFC
Ground Address: Mosborough WMC Station Road Station Road Sheffield S20 5AA
Contact: 0114 2477290
Email: mosboroughrufc@btinternet.com
Website: www.mosboroughrufc.co.uk
Directions: M1 J30, take A616 towards Sheffield, at 2nd set of lights turn right, Clubhouse on left 50m.
Honorary Secretary: Mr Steven Sadler; 219 High Street Mosborough Sheffield S20 5AG Tel: 01924 887732
Fixtures Secretary: Mr Alistair Boswell
Tel: 0114 2879499   email: alistair.boswell@sheffcol.ac.uk
Club Colours: Red / Black
League: Yorkshire 5 (level 11)

Mossley Hill RUFC
Ground Address: Mossley Hill Road, Liverpool. L188BX
Contact: 0151 4231821
Email: andrewpealing@btopenworld.com
Website: www.mossleyhillrufc.com
Directions: From M62 take ring road towards Liverpool Airport. Turn left onto Allerton Road, right onto Rose Lane (at Tescos) Ground is behind Mossley Hill Church at top of Rose Lane.
Honorary Secretary: Mr Eddie McCarthy; 35 The Beeches Liverpool L18 3LT   Tel: 07966 487568
email: edwardpmccarthy@googlemail.com
Fixtures Secretary: Mr Peter Barnett; 49 Ferndale Road Wavertree Liverpool Merseyside L15 3JY
Tel: 0151 2805794
email: peter@barnett2278.freeserve.co.uk
Club Colours: Maroon and Gold
League: North Lancs 2 (level 9)

Nestle Rowntree RUFC
Ground Address: Nestle Rowntree Sportsground Mille Crux Haxby rd york
Contact: 01904 766122
Email: Brian.Cottom@portasilo.co.uk
Directions: From North: Use Northern Outer Ring Road (A1237). Turn off at the New Earswick Roundabout towards York for 2 miles. Ground is on the left opposite the factory. From West, South & East: From the A64 join the Northern Outer Ring Road (A1237) at the Scarborough junction turn left signposted thirsk A19 then left at turning to New Earswick ground on left after 2 miles. Do NOT use the YO91 postcode,in satnav this is a company code and will take you to a postbox in the city centre OOPS
Honorary Secretary: Mr Brian Cottom; Portasilo Ltd New Lane Huntington York North Yorkshire YO32 9PR
Tel: 01904 766122 email: Brian.Cottom@Portasilo.co.uk

Fixtures Secretary: Mr Graeme Lavender; 1 Carlton Fields, Carlton, Goole DN14 9RT Tel: 0772 5629248
email: yogiinyork@yahoo.co.uk
Club Colours: Balck, Red and White
Non League

Netherhall RFC
Ground Address: Netherhall R.F.C. Netherhall Park Netherhall Road Maryport Cumbria CA15 6NT
Contact: 01900 815833
Email: jimedmondson@supanet.com
Website: www.nrufc.co.uk
Directions: A66 to Cockermouth, go across r'about on outskirts of Cockermouth signed Workington. At next r'about take 2nd exit for Maryport. Take 1st exit at next r'about for Maryport for 7 miles. Head into Maryport, right at lights A596 to Carlisle, Club 400 yards on right.
Honorary Secretary: Mr David Atkinson; 53 Curzon Street Maryport Cumbria CA15 6LW
Tel: 01900 8144239
email: David.Atkinson@thomasarmstrong.co.uk
Fixtures Secretary: Mr Keith Edmondson; 13 Newlands Park Dearham Maryport Cumbria CA15 7ED
Tel: 01900 814253   email: as Hon. Sec.
Club Colours: Claret & Gold
League: North Lancs-Cumbria (level 7)

Newton Aycliffe RUFC
Ground Address: Moore Lane Newton Aycliffe Co. Durham DL5 5AG
Contact: 01325 312768
Email: admin@aycliffeuruby.co.uk
Website: www.aycliffeuruby.co.uk
Directions: Approach Newton Aycliffe on the A167. At the traffic lights to the North of the town turn onto the B6443, Central Avenue. Turn left at the first roundabout onto Shafto Way. Take the fourth left, Creighton Road. Moore Lane is 1st on Right.
Hon. Secretary: Doctor Stuart McIvor; 6 Luttryngton Court Newton Aycliffe Co. Durham DL5 7HL
Tel: 07732 268714   email: stuartdm@btinternet.com
Fixtures Secretary: Luke Tinkler Tel: 01325 315129
Club Colours: Green, Maroon & Amber
League: Durham-N'Thm'Land 3 (level 9)

Newton-le-Willows RUFC
Ground Address: Newton Sports Club Crow Lane East Newton-le-Willows Merseyside WA12 9XE
Contact: 07876 740114
Email: info@newtonrufc.co.uk
Website: www.newtonrufc.co.uk
Directions: Exit the M6 at J23. Turn left onto A49 for Newton. Approx. 1.5 miles, turn right at Oak Tree Pub. Club is 300 yards on the right.
Honorary Secretary: Nigel McNamara; 20 Park Road Warrington Cheshire WA2 9AZ Tel: 07984 415588
email: nigela.mcnamara@ntlworld.com
Fixtures Secretary: as Hon. Sec.
Club Colours: Royal Blue and Amber
League: North Lancs 2 (level 9)

North Manchester RUFC
Ground Address: Tudor Lodge Victoria Avenue East, Moston Manchester. M40 5SH
Contact: 0161 6829234
Email: info@northmanrugby.co.uk
Website: www.northmanrugby.co.uk
Directions: Intersection of Victoria Avenue East (A6104) and Greengate (B6239), Moston, Manchester.
Nearest M60 Junction: Clockwise 20 Anti Clockwise 21
Honorary Secretary: Mr Brian Stott; 8 Barlea Avenue Manchester M40 3WL Tel: 0161 6820541
email: bh.stott@virgin.net
Fixtures Secretary: Mr Anthony Donley; 12 Grange Street Salford Manchester M6 5PR Tel: 07740 100143
email: tony.donley@resource-group.com
Club Colours: Black, green & white hoops. black shorts
League: North Lancs 2 (level 9)

North Ribblesdale RFC
Ground Address:
Grove Park Lower Greenfoot Settle BD24 9QH
Contact: 01729 822755
Email: cvsharpe@lineone.net
Website: www.northribblesdale.co.uk
Directions: leave a65 at roundabout on southskirts of town,into town turning right 1st past falcon manor (signposted "rugby ground") head .25 mile grounds on left proceed along 1st team field entrance on left past large club sign.
Honorary Secretary: Mr Christopher Sharpe; Ash Grove 28 Keighley Road Cross Hills Keighley West Yorkshire BD20 7RU Tel: 07999 999145
email: cvsharpe@lineone.net
Fixtures Secretary: Mr Duncan Brown; 4 East View Settle North Yorkshire BD24 9AP Tel: 07812 958940
Club Colours: Royal Blue and White
League: Yorkshire 2 (level 8)

North Shields RFC
Ground Address: North Shields R.F.C. Preston Playing Field Preston Village North Shields NE29 9ND
Contact: 0191 2577352
Email: rugby@northshieldsrfc.co.uk
Directions: From Newcastle A167M to The Coast (A1058) A1058 (E) Coast Road to Billy Mill roundabout straight over roundabout to A1058 (E) Beach Road to next roundabout turn right (3rd exit) onto A192 towards North Shields Town Centre turn 1st right onto B1304
Honorary Secretary: Mr A Shield; 9 Cresswell Avenue North Shields Tyne & Wear NE29 9BQ
Tel: 0191 2590402
email: alastair.shield@blueyonder.co.uk
Fixtures Secretary: Mr Jonathan Kenny; 84 Paignton Avenue Monkseaton Tyne & Wear NE25 8SZ
Tel: 07932 045 420
email: j.kenny07@btinternet.com
Club Colours: Royal Blue with white shoulder
League: Durham-N'Thm'Land 2 (level 8)

Northallerton RUFC
Ground Address: Northallerton R.U.F.C. Brompton Lodge Northallerton Rd, Brompton Northallerton DL6 2PZ
Contact: 07751 787843
Email: secretary@northallertonrufc.co.uk
Website: www.northallertonrufc.co.uk
Directions: Enter Northallerton from the north or leave to the north on the A684 Stokesley Road. Turn left going north or right going south at filling station onto Brompton Road.The Club is 400m on left.
Honorary Secretary: Mr James Morton; 37 Northallerton Road Brompton Northallerton North Yorkshire DL6 2QA   Tel: 01609 778326
email: blueboar@tiscali.co.uk
Fixtures Secretary: Mr Alan Bradley; 15 Borrowby Avenue Northallerton North Yorkshire DL6 1AL
Tel: 01609 772743
Club Colours: Green, Amber & White
League: Yorkshire 3 (level 9)

Northern FC
Ground Address: McCracken Park Great North Road Newcastle Upon Tyne NE3 2DT
Contact: 0191 2363369
Email: admin@northernfc.co.uk
Website: www.northernrfc.co.uk
Directions: From either North or South: Travel on A1 to the junction with A1056 with at the north of Newcastle, head south along Great North Road (dual carriageway) for @ 3/4 mile. McCracken Park is immediately on left after first roundabout.
Honorary Secretary: Doctor Mel Vecsey; Marlborough Ave 52 Gosforth Newcastle upon Tyne NE3 2HU
Tel: 0191 2858494   email: mel.vecsey@unn.ac.uk
Fixtures Secretary: Tracey Young; 71 Nelson Avenue Nelson Village Cramlington Northumberland NE23 1HQ
Tel: 07887 925779   email: tracyyoung28@aol.com
Club Colours: Red, White and Blue
League: Durham-N'Thm'Land 1 (level 7)

Northumbria University RFC
Ground Address: Sport Northumbria, 6 North Street,Northumberland Road Northumberland Road University of Northumbria at Newcastle NE1 8DE
Contact: 0191 227 4871
Email: ian.elvin@unn.ac.uk
Website: www.sportnorthumbria.com
Honorary Secretary: Miss Suzi Newton; City Campus sports Centre Northumbria University Northhumberland Road Newcastle Upon Tyne NE1 8DE
Tel: 0191 2437751   email: suzi2.newton@unn.ac.uk
Fixtures Secretary: Richard Arnold; C/0 Club Address Sport Northumbria 6 North Street, Northumberland Road University of Northumbria at Newcastle NE1 8DE
Tel: 07970 741640   email: richard.arnold@unn.ac.uk
Club Colours: Black/Red
Non League

Old Bedians RFC
Ground Address: c/o Didsbury Sports Centre, Millgate Lane, Millgate Lane, Didsbury, Manchester. M205QX
Contact: 0161 9750875
Email: s_m_atherton@hotmail.com
Website: www.oldbedians.co.uk
Honorary Secretary: Declan Sealy Tel: 07834 183564 email: declansealy@yahoo.co.uk
Fixtures Secretary: Peter Tonge Tel: 07931 541520
Club Colours: Navy Blue
League: North Lancs 1 (level 8)

Old Grovians
Ground Address: Woodhouse Grove School, Apperley Bridge, Bradford BD10 0NR
Contact: Nick Fawcett (Hon. Secretary)
Email: fawcettna@yahoo.co.uk
Website: www.oldgroviansrugby.com
Honorary Secretary: Nick Fawcett (Tel) (H) 01274 610314 (M) 07969 157414 Email: fawcettna@yahoo.co.uk
Fixtures Secretary: As Hon. Sec.
Club Colours: Black/Gold
League: Yorkshire 4 (level 10)

Old Modernians RUFC
Ground Address:
Cookridge Lane Cookridge Leeds LS16 7ND
Contact: 0113 267 1075
Directions: A660 north from Leeds until 1/4 mile past junction with A6120 ring road at Lawnswood. Fork left at Cookridge. Ground 2 miles on the right.
Honorary Secretary: Mr John Bracewell; Pasture View 21 Brackenwell Lane North Rigton North Yorkshire LS17 0DG Tel: 07709 439249
email: jcb1750@hotmail.co.uk
Fixtures Secretary: Mr David Carter; 81 Green Lane Cookridge Leeds LS16 7ET Tel: 0113 2679718
Club Colours: Red & Black Hooped Shirt
League: Yorkshire 3 (level 9)

Old Otliensians RUFC Ltd
Ground Address: Chaffer's Field Pool Road Otley West Yorkshire LS21 1DY
Contact: 01943 461476
Website: www.oorufc.co.uk
Directions: From Otley town centre take A659 to Harrogate, turn right at Smiths Garden Centre, follow sign to Club house.
Honorary Secretary: Thomas Broadbent; Flat 8 King House Kings Road Ilkley West Yorkshire LS29 9AN Tel: 07809741970 email: tkbean87@hotmail.co.uk
Fixtures Secretary: Mr John Churchman; 28 Glen Road Eldwick, Bingley Bradford West Yorkshire BD16 3ET Tel: 01274 564134 email: joval@talktalk.net
Club Colours: Navy Blue, Royal Blue and White
League: Yorkshire 3 (level 9)

Old Rishworthian RUFC
Ground Address: The Clubhouse Copley Halifax West Yorkshire HX3 0UG
Contact: 01422 353919
Email: info@orrufc.co.uk
Website: www.orrufc.co.uk
Directions: Leave the M62 at junction 24. Take second exit and follow A629 to Halifax. At the first set of traffic lights, go across mini roundabout. Follow A6025 to Copley After 1/2 mile turn left at the traffic lights before Volunteer Arms. Continue along Copley Lane, over canal, under railway bridge. Club house is on left.
Honorary Secretary: Mr Peter Morgan; Burnal Bank Farm Stainland Rd Holywell Green Halifax West Yorkshire HX4 9AE Tel: 07799 338560
email: pgm18@aol.com
Fixtures Secretary: Mr Don Blakey; 4 Mountfields Hipperholme Halifax West Yorkshire HX3 8SS Tel: 07710 394726
Club Colours: Maroon & white hoops
League: Yorkshire 3 (level 9)

Oldershaw RFC
Ground Address: Belvidere Field Belvidere Road, Wallasey Wallasey CH45 4RZ
Contact: 0151 6371856
Website: www.oldershawrugbyclub.co.uk
Directions: From the M53 Follow the signs for Wallasey Docks at the round about turn left up Mill Lane carry on up the hill to the second set of traffic lights. Turn left into Marlowe Road and go through the next lights. The club is 200 yards on your left hand side
Honorary Secretary: Mr Will Gardner; 44 Montpellier Crescent Wallasey Merseyside CH45 9LA
Tel: 07803 298969   email: will.gardner@closeam.com
Club Colours: Navy Blue with Gold Hoops
League: South Lancs-Cheshire 2 (level 8)

Oldham RUFC
Ground Address: Manor Park Byrth Road Oldham Lancashire OL8 2TJ
Contact: 0 1616246383
Email: sue-burgess@hotmail.co.uk
Website: www.orufc.co.uk
Directions: Off the main A627 Oldham to Ashton road, behind Bardsley Church.
Honorary Secretary: Ms Susan Burgess; 20 Garthwaite Avenue Oldham OL8 4HS Tel: 0161 6789304
email: sue-burgess@hotmail.co.uk
Fixtures Secretary: Mr T Park; C/0 Club Address Manor Park Byrth Road Oldham Lancashire OL8 2TJ
Tel: 0161 8326753   email: tompark22@hotmail.com
Club Colours: Red & White Hoops, Navy Shorts
League: North Lancs-Cumbria (level 7)

LEVELS 7-12 & NON LEAGUE CLUBS

Ormskirk RUFC
Ground Address: Green Lane Ormskirk Lancs. L39 1ND
Contact: 01704 894503
Email: andrewmontrose@hotmail.com
Website: www.ormskirkrufc.co.uk
Directions: Ajacent A59 at junction with A570 opposite the Fiveways Pub.
Honorary Secretary: Mr Andy Montrose; 38 Hesketh Road Burscough Ormskirk Lancashire L40 7SQ
Tel: 07813 300373
email: andrewmontrose@hotmail.com
Fixtures Secretary: Mr Russ Brennan; Green Lane Ormskirk Lancashire L39 1ND Tel: 07866 216940
email: russbrennan@aol.com
Club Colours: Bottle Green/Blue flashes
League: South Lancs-Cheshire 1 (level 7)

Orrell RUFC
Ground Address: 2 Lawns Avenue Orrell Wigan Lancashire WN5 8UQ
Contact: 07736 802124
Email: richard@synapseconsulting.co.uk
Directions: Ground is about 2 miles from M6 J26. Left at traffic lights at end of slip road, then left at lights at the Stag Inn. After about 400 yards left again at lights & after another 400 yards left again at lights which take you into Edgehall Road.
Honorary Secretary: Mr Richard Fisher; 2 Lawns Avenue Tontine Orrell Wigan WN8 8UQ
Tel: 01695 624153   email: richard.fisher@rpsgb.org
Fixtures Secretary: Mr Mel Parker; 2 Warrington Road Golborne Dale Newton-le-Willows Merseyside WA12 0HZ
Tel: 01925 226679
Club Colours: Black & Amber
League: South Lancs-Cheshire 2 (level 8)

Ossett RUFC
Ground Address: Ossett Cricket & Athletic Club The Pavillion Queens Terrace Ossett WF5 8AP
Contact: 01924 273618
Email: patays@talktalk.net
Website: www.ossettrugby.co.uk
Directions: Home games played at Springmill, off Queens Drive Ossett. M1 Junction 40, follow A638 to Wakefield. Turn right at 2nd lights into Queens Drive. Go under motorway bridge and after 200 yards turn right at sign for Golf and follow track to ground.
Honorary Secretary: Mr Paul Taylor; 10 Grange Drive Ossett WF5 0SH   Tel: 07960 972208
email: paytays@talktalk.net
Fixtures Secretary: Mr I Whitehead; 20 Westfield Street Ossett West Yorkshire WF5 8JE   Tel: 01924 274345
Club Colours: Red shirts, black sleeves, white inserts.
League: Yorkshire 4 (level 10)

Parkonians RFC
Ground Address: Martin Curphey Memorial Ground Holm Lane, Oxton Birkenhead, Wirral CH43 2HU
Contact: 0151 6523105
Email: oldparkonians@hotmail.co.uk
Website: www.oldparkonians.org.uk
Directions: Off M53 at J3 head to B'head on A552. Turn off into Holm Lane at the Swan Hotel. Club is 400m on left - near top of Holm Lane
Honorary Secretary: Mr P Mullen; 8 Deerwood Crescent Little Sutton Ellesmere Port CH66 1SE
Tel: 0151 3391270
email: mullen55@btinternet.com
Fixtures Secretary: Mr Peter Evans; 24 Pine Tree Grove Moreton Merseyside CH46 9QX Tel: 0151 6773825
email: peter.evans@whnt.nhs.uk
Club Colours: Maroon Blue White Jerseys & St
League: South Lancs-Cheshire 3 (level 9)

Pocklington RUFC
Ground Address: Pocklington R.F.C. Feathers Field Percy Road Pocklington YO42 2QB
Contact: 01759 371706
Email: Robjacksonr@aol.com
Website: www.pocklingtonrufc.co.uk
Directions: The grounds lie at the junction of Percy Road and Burnby Lane near the centre of the town. Head towards Burnby and the Francis Scaife swimming pool.
Honorary Secretary: Mr Rob Jackson; Rose Cottage Low Catton York YO41 1EA Tel: 07903 456744
email: Robjacksonr@aol.com
Fixtures Secretary: Mr Graham Thurlow; 12 Kilnwick Close Pocklington York YO42 2PR Tel: 01759 306289
email: robjacksonr@aol.com
Club Colours: Navy & White Hoops
League: Yorkshire 2 (level 8)

Ponteland RFC
Ground Address: Ponteland Leisure Centre Callerton Lane Ponteland Northumberland NE20 9EG
Contact: 01661 825169
Email: wack7@talktalk.net
Website: www.Pontelandrfc.co.uk
Directions: From north or south, enter village via A696, at lights by Diamond Inn turn left to follow river, entrance to Sports centre 150 yards on left just after zebra crossing.
Honorary Secretary: Mr Paul Walker; 97 Thornhill Road 97 Thornhill Road Ponteland Newcastle upon Tyne NE20 9QE Tel: 01661 825169
email: wack7@talktalk.net
Fixtures Secretary: Mr Daniel Whaley; 72 Cheviot View Ponteland Newcastle Upon Tyne Tyne & Wear NE20 9BW Tel: 07885 205714
email: dcwhaleypont@yahoo.co.uk
Club Colours: Maroon black & white shirts, black shorts
League: Durham-N'Thm'Land 2 (level 8)

Pontefract Pythons RFC
Ground Address:
Moor Lane, Pontefract, West Yorkshire, WF8 3RX
Contact: 01977 702650
Website: http://www.pontefractpythons.co.uk
Directions: Leave the M62 at J 33 onto Great North Road (A1) South for 1 mile. Take Darrington turn off and

482

head for Pontefract. Moor Lane is 2 miles on the left.
Honorary Secretary: Mr Mark Cook
email: mcook@finning.co.uk
Club Colours: Red shirts with black stripe, black shorts
League: Yorkshire 5 (level 11)

Port Sunlight RFC
Ground Address: Leverhulme Playing Fields Green Lane, Bromborough Wirral CH62 3PU
Contact: 0151 3343677
Email: secretary@psrfc.co.uk
Website: www.psrfc.co.uk
Directions: A41 Bromborough at Traffic lights turn into Old Hall Road, at roundabput 3rd exit into Riverwood Road, take 1st right into lane signed PSRFC.
Honorary Secretary: Mr Michael Mcmillan; 114 Mark Rake Bromborough Wirral CH62 2DR
Tel: 07791 064286   email: mikewmcmillan@hotmail.com
Fixtures Secretary: Mr Franklin Williams; 20 Rawdon Close Palacefields Runcorn Cheshire WA7 2QQ
Club Colours: Black & White Narrow Hoops
League: South Lancs-Cheshire 3 (level 9)

Prenton RUFC
Ground Address: Prenton Dell Road Prenton Birkenhead Merseyside CH43 3BS
Contact: 0151 6081501
Email: chrismchugh@tiscali.co.uk
Website: www.prentonrufc.co.uk
Directions: from M53 J3 take turn off on round about heading for Birkenhead that is Woodchurch Rd take the 4th turning on the right into Prenton Dell Rd take 2nd on right into Club
Honorary Secretary: Mr John Bolton; 3 Carr House Lane Wirral Merseyside CH46 6EN Tel: 0151 6782532
email: jbolton@btinternet.com
Fixtures Secretary: as Hon. SEc.
Club Colours: Maroon, Gold & Black
League: South Lancs-Cheshire 3 (level 9)

Prudhoe and Stocksfield RFC
Ground Address: Stocksfield Sportsfield &Cricket Club Main Road Stocksfield NorthumberlandNE43 7NN
Contact: 0191 4133783
Email: pandsrufc@hotmail.com
Directions: On the A695 in the village of Stocksfield. Clubhouse and car park are next to Broomley School.
Honorary Secretary: Mr Chris Russell; 18 Riding Terrace Mickley Stocksfield NorthumberlandNE43 7BU
Tel: 07967 592838   email: chrisrussell55@hotmail.com
Fixtures Secretary: Mr Phil Bewick; 35 Rowan Grove Prudhoe NorthumberlandNE42 6PP Tel: 01661 834215
Club Colours: Shirts - Red, White & Blue hoops
League: Durham-N'Thm'Land 3 (level 9)

RAF Leeming RFC
Ground Address: Bldg 19 (90SU OP IT) Leeming Hawks RFC RAF Leeming Northallerton DL7 9NJ
Contact: 01677 457036
Email: aqmdbmanager@tcw.raf.mod.uk
Directions: Off A1 at RAF Leeming & Gatenby turn,
then left at roundabout.
Honorary Secretary: Mr Gavin Hainey; 90SU OP IT RAF Leeming Gatenby Northallerton North Yorkshire DL7 9NJ Tel: 01677 457036
email: amdbmanager@tcw.raf.mod.uk
Fixtures Secretary: Gaz Dunn; Bldg 19 (90SU OP IT) Leeming Hawks RFC RAF Leeming Leeming Northallerton North Yorkshire DL7 9NJ
Club Colours: Red & Black hoops
Non League

RAF Menwith Hill RFC
Ground Address: Menwith Hill Station Harrogate North Yorkshire HG3 2RF
Contact: 01423 777788
Honorary Secretary: Mr A Burton; Raf Menwith Hill Box 244 Harrogate North Yorkshire HG3 2RF
Tel: 01423 777959   email: burtona@menwith.army.mil
Non League

RAF Valley RFC
Ground Address: Medical Centre RAF Valley Holyhead LL65 3NY
Contact: 07979527835
Email: andy.thomas135@btopenworld.com
Club Colours: Airforce Blue
Non League

Ramsey RUFC
Ground Address: Mooragh Promenade Ramsey Isle of Man IM8 3EU
Contact: 01624 816044
Email: ramseyrufc@manx.net
Website: www.ramseyrugby.com
Directions: On entering Ramsey, follow signs for the Mooragh Park. Turn right off Bowring Road onto North Shore Road (opposite Bridge Inn). On reaching the Mooragh Promenade, turn left. Take second left for pitch which is clearly visible from the road.
Honorary Secretary: Mr Michael Jelski; Marlborough Way 7 Clifton Park Ramsey Isle of Man
Tel: 07624 498269   email: me@mikejelski.com
Fixtures Secretary: Mr Jason Walker; 3 Gladstone Avenue Ramsey Isle of Man IM8 2LE
Tel: 07624 473532   email: jw@manx.net
Club Colours: Red & Black
League: South Lancs-Cheshire 3 (level 9)

Rawmarsh RUFC
Ground Address: Rawmarsh Leisure Centre Barbers Avenue, Rawmarsh Rotherham South Yorkshire S62 6AE
Contact: 01709 719 952
Directions: From Sheffield or Doncaster approach the Rotherham ring road. Take A630 & enquire at the Mushroom Garage.
Honorary Secretary: Mr Eric Perkins; 21 Harding Avenue Rawmarsh Rotherham South Yorkshire S62 7ED
Tel: 01709 526786
Fixtures Secretary: as Hon. Sec.
Club Colours: Black with Amber Trim
League: Yorkshire 6 (level 12)

Redcar RUFC
Ground Address: McKinlay Park Green Lane Redcar Cleveland TS10 3RW
Contact: 01642 482733
Email: giorgio@ntlworld.com
Directions: From the a174 head towards redcar across the top of ici go straight across first two roundabouts turn left at third roundabout and right at next roundabout head towards marske in marske high st turn left and head towards the sea go round sharp left bend with bydales school on left go down the coast road for about a mile until you come to the first left turn after you turn club is 200 yards up on right
Fixtures Secretary: Mr Dave Pearson; 36 Henry Street Redcar Cleveland TS10 1BJ Tel: 01642 473736
email: dave.r.pearson@ntlworld.com
Club Colours: Black & Red
League: Durham-N'Thm'Land 1 (level 7)

Ripon RUFC Ltd.
Ground Address: The Clubhouse Mallorie Park Ripon NORTH YORKSHIRE HG4 2QD UNITED KINGDOM
Contact: 01765 604675
Email: duffja@hotmail.com
Website: www.riponrugby.co.uk
Directions: Mallorie Park is on Pateley Bridge road out of Ripon. Access from the South is via Harrogate Road and Skellbank; from the North via North Road and Pateley Road
Honorary Secretary: Mrs Gail Squires; 9 Mallory Close, Ripon HG4 2QE (Tel) 01765 604 282
Email: gailsquires@riponcathedral.org.uk
Fixtures Secretary: Mr Andy Proud, 1 Ure Bank Terrace, Ripon, N. Yorks. HG4 1JG (Tel) 07786 250672
Club Colours: White, light & dark blue narrow bands
League: Yorkshire 2 (level 8)

Rossington Hornets
Ground Address: Rossington Miners Welfare West End Lane Rossington Doncaster DN11 0DU
Email: andrewjgregory@btinternet.com
Directions: Enter Rossington and go over the railway crossings. Drive on to West End Lane and contiune till you see the sign Rossington Miners' Welfare Club.
Honorary Secretary: Mr Andrew Gregory; 7 St. Vincents Avenue Branton Doncaster DN3 3QR
Tel: 07738 786638 email: andrewjgregory@btinternet.com
Club Colours: Black and Yellow
League: Yorkshire 6 (level 12)

Rotherham Phoenix
Ground Address: Clifton Lane Sports Ground, Badsley Moor Lane, Rotherham, S65 2AA
Email: umplebybrian@yahoo.co.uk
Directions: From the M1 - M1 exit 33 onto Rotherway, at the r'about turn right onto A631 marked Bawtry. Go straight ahead at Whiston traffic lights onto the dual carriageway. At the next r'about, turn left onto B6410 (Broom Lane) then left onto A6021 (Broom Road). In 1/2 mile there is a r'about, turn right into Badsley Moor Lane. The clubhouse is the second entrance on right. From the A1(M) - join the M18.
From the M18 - M18 exit 1 onto A631 towards Rotherham. After 1 mile or so, go straight ahead at Wickersley Island. After 1 more mile turn right at the Brecks r'about onto A6021. Go straight on at the Stag r'about and after 2 miles or so there is a r'about, turn right into Badsley Moor Lane. The clubhouse is the second entrance on the right.
Honorary Secretary: Mr Brian c/o the club
Tel: 01709 510045
email: umplebybrian@yahoo.co.uk
Fixtures Secretary: Mr Steven Houghton; 150 Pear Tree Avenue Bramley Rotherham South Yorkshire S66 2NF
Club Colours: Maroon and Blue Hoops
League: Yorkshire 4 (level 10)

Roundhegians RUFC
Ground Address: Memorial Ground Chelwood Drive, Roundhay Leeds LS8 2AT
Contact: 0113 2667377
Website: www.roundhegians.org
Directions: A61 to junction with Street Lane. Follow Street Lane towards Roundhay Park, Chelwood Drive is a road off Street Lane.
Honorary Secretary: Mr Richard Tripp; Eversheds Solicitors Bridgewater Place Water Lane LS11 5DR
email: richardtripp@eversheds.com
Fixtures Secretary: Mr Jim Malia; 525 Ring Road Moortown Leeds LS17 8NR Tel: 07775 998233
email: jim.malia@tchamson.co.uk
Club Colours: Green, Black & White Hoops
League: Yorkshire 3 (level 9)

Runcorn RFC
Ground Address: Halton Sports Murdishaw Avenue Runcorn Cheshire WA7 6HP
Contact: 01928 751496
Email: jeffgore@saltunion.com
Directions: M56 J11 take exit and proceed sign posted Preston Brook / Dutton. Go down hill through 2 sets lifgts and 2 mini roundabouts untill you get to large roundabout over M. Way. Straight across on to Murdishaw Ave. Then 1st right into Halton Arms Pub.
Honorary Secretary: Mr Jeff Gore; 1 Beechways Appleton Warrington Cheshire WA4 5EL
Tel: 01928 712684 email: jeffgore@saltunion.com
Fixtures Secretary: Mr Tony Elliot Tel: 01928 715091
Club Colours: Black Body/Blue Shoulders
Non League

Ruskin Park RUFC
Ground Address: Ruskin Drive Sportsground Ruskin Drive, St. Helens. WA10 6RP
Contact: 07949 594069
Email: Ruskin.park@yahoo.co.uk
Website: www.ruskinpark.co.uk
Directions: Turn off A580 onto A570 towards St Helens. Travel approx. 1 mile & turn right into Dentons Green Lane. Ruskin Drive is 400 yards on the left.

Honorary Secretary: Mr Stuart Fisher; 43 Hollin Hey Close Billinge Wigan Lancashire WN5 7SA
Tel: 01744 893989
email: Stuart.fisher@talk21.com
Fixtures Secretary: Mr Barry Loftus
email: loftusb@blueyonder.co.uk
Club Colours: Blue with Black & White Band
League: South Lancs-Cheshire 2 (level 8)

Ryton RFC Ltd
Ground Address: Main Road Barmoor Ryton NE40 3AG
Contact: 0191 4132882
Email: dwroberts@dsl.pipex.com
Website: www.rytonrfc.co.uk
Directions: From the A1 (south): After the Washington Services, the road divides (A1 to the left, motorway to the right). Bear left on the A1 past the Angel of the North. Shortly after the Metro Centre, take the exit signposted A695 Blaydon. Continue on this road, going straight on at the r'abouts and get into the right hand lane on the approach to the Scotswood Bridge. When you reach a large r'about next to McDonalds, take the third exit which is the B6317 to Ryton. Continue on through Ryton until you see the Comprehensive School on your right then look out for the Ryton RFC sign on your left hand side
From the A1 (north): After passing Newcastle, take the exit signposted Blaydon. Take the second exit at the r'about and turn right over the Scotswood Bridge, keeping in the right hand lane. Follow the long sweeping left hand curve back under the bridge. When you reach a large r'about next to McDonalds, take the third exit which is the B6317 to Ryton. Continue on through Ryton until you see the Comprehensive School on your right then look out for the Ryton RFC sign on your left hand side. Bus services: The following bus services stop outside the ground: Go Ahead: 10, 11 Classic: 10C Arriva: 602, 604
Honorary Secretary: David Roberts; 47 Grange Drive Ryton NE40 3LF Tel: 0191 4132882
email: secretary@rytonrfc.co.uk
Fixtures Secretary: Mr K Dunn; 36 Mollyfair Close Crawcrook Ryton Tyne & Wear NE40 4UZ
Tel: 0191 4133890
email: clubhouse@rytonrfc.co.uk
Club Colours: Royal Blue with White Stripe
League: Durham-N'Thm'Land 1 (level 7)

Sale F.C.
Ground Address: Heywood Road Brooklands Sale Cheshire M33 3WB
Contact: 0161 283 1861
Email: secretary_salefc@yahoo.co.uk or info@salefc.com
Directions: See Website
Honorary Secretary: Mr Graham Oglethorpe; Sale F C Training Ground Carrington Lane Trafford Greater Manchester M31 4AE Tel: 0795 2519371
email: graham.oglethorpe@sky.com

Fixtures Secretary: Mr Mike Ramscar c/o the club
Tel: 0161 9733811
email: mikeramscar@btconnect.com
Club Colours: Blue & White hoops, Navy Shorts
League: South Lancs-Cheshire 1 (level 7)

Scarborough RFC
Ground Address: The J M Guthrie Clubhouse Scalby Scarborough North Yorkshire YO13 0NL
Contact: 01723357740
Email: admin@scarboroughrugby.co.uk
Website: www.scarboroughrugby.co.uk
Directions: A171 Scalby Road. Approx 2 miles from Town Centre heading towards Whitby.
Honorary Secretary: Mr C Adamson; 5 The Close Scarborough North Yorkshire YO12 6EG
Fixtures Secretary: Mr Andy Downes; 20 Lawrence Grove Newby Scarborough Tel: 07731 593954
email: downesa@hotmail.com
Club Colours: Navy (Main), Maroon and White or White (Main)
League: Yorkshire 1 (level 7)

Seaham RUFC
Ground Address: Vane Tempest Sports & Social Centre New Drive Seaham Co. Durham SR7 7BX
Contact: 0191 5812744
Email: seahamrufc@gmail.com
Website: www.seaham.intheteam.com
Directions: (Southbound): Leave the A19 at the B1404 junction and follow the signs for the coast and Seaham Hall. Go straight ahead at the traffic lights and over the railway level crossing. Bear right at the junction, bypass Seaham Hall and follow the meandering road past the Crow's Nest pub r'about and through a traffic calming junction (give way). Travel for 250 yards before taking the first right turn into Dene House Road. Follow the signs for the Seaham Railway Station. The Vane Tempest Sports & Social Centre lies 50 yards to the right of the station with the pitch a further 200 yards along a cinder track. (Northbound): Leave the A19 at the junction for Dalton Park. Turn right at the r'about and follow the A182 for Dawdon and the coast. Take a right turn at the third r'about and head for Seaham town centre and the coast. Bypass Asda and a number of shops and pubs on your left and go straight ahead (with right of way) at two traffic calming junctions before turning left into Dene House Road. Follow the signs for Seaham Railway Station. Then as above. If you get lost call the clubhouse on 0191 5812744 or wind your window and ask one of our friendly locals. Everyone knows where we are!!!
Honorary Secretary: Mr Neil Roseberry, 19 Vincent St. Princess Road Dawdon Seaham Co. Durham SR7 7QL
Tel: 07970 215240   email: roseberryk@tiscali.co.uk
Fixtures Secretary: Mr Stephen Wilkinson, 34 Viceroy Street Seaham Co. Durham SR7 7HZ
Tel: 07716 986034   email: s.wilka19@talktalk.net
Club Colours: Scarlet Jersey (white trim), White Shorts
League: Durham-N'Thm'Land 3 (level 9)

LEVELS 7-12 & NON LEAGUE CLUBS   485

Seaton Carew RUFC
Ground Address: Hornby Park, Elizabeth Way Seaton Carew Hartlepool TS25 2AZ
Contact: 01429 260945
Email: PMcManus1@doosanbabcock.com
Directions: From A19 Road take A689 to Hartlepool. Turn right at Owton Lodge Public House on to B1276 road to Seaton Carew sea front area. Turn right and follow the sea front road past the golf club. Seaton Carew Rugby club is on the right with the entrance in Elizabeth way. Nearest Railway Station is at Seaton Carew which exits into Station Lane turn right out of Station and then take the first right into Elizabeth way. Follow Elizabeth way down towards the sea Front and the Rugby club is the last building on your right before you come to the Tees Road.
Honorary Secretary: Mr Paul Mcmanus; 9 Ruswarp Grove Seaton Carew Hartlepool Cleveland TS25 2BA Tel: 01429 268835
email: pmcmanus1@doosanbabcock.com
Fixtures Secretary: Mr Andrew Sedgwick; Hornby Park, Elizabeth Way Seaton Carew Hartlepool TS25 2AZ Tel: 07826862261
email: andy.sedgwick@doosanbabcock.com
Club Colours: Maroon & Amber Hooped Shirts & socks
League: Durham-N'Thm'Land 2 (level 8)

Sedgefield District RUFC
Ground Address: Sedgefield Community College Hawthorn Road Sedgefield TS213DD
Contact: 01740 620234
Email: info@sedgefieldrugby.co.uk
Website: www.sedgefieldrugby.co.uk
Honorary Secretary: Neil Hetherington
Tel: 07946 353808
email: Secretary@sedgefieldrugby.co.uk
Club Colours: Black and Red
League: Durham-N'Thm'Land 3 (level 9)

Sefton RUFC
Ground Address: Sefton RUFC Thornhead Lane, Leyfield Road, Leyfield Road, Liverpool L12 9EY
Contact: 0151 2289092
Email: rugby@seftonrufc.com
Website: www.seftonrufc.co.uk
Directions: End of M62 take A5058 towards Bootle, at A57 turn right, left at lights, right in front of hospital, left at Bulldog Pub (Leyfield Road), right into lane by electricity substation.
Honorary Secretary: Mr Roy Spencer; 8 Stoneycroft Close Liverpool L13 0AT Tel: 0151 2289833
email: roy@rspencer.fsnet.co.uk
Fixtures Secretary: Mr Bernard Houghton; 14 Gateacre Vale Road Liverpool L25 5NP Tel: 0151 4283740
email: titchoughton@gmail.com
Club Colours: Red White & Blue Hooped Shirts
League: South Lancs-Cheshire 2 (level 8)

Seghill RFC
Ground Address: Seghill R.F.C. Welfare Park Seghill Cramlington NE23 7EZ
Contact: 0191 2370414
Directions: A19 through Tyne Tunnel, take sliproad for Seghill, right at junction, left at next junction, right at mini roundabout then 2nd left, right at T junction, Car park 150 yards on the right.
Honorary Secretary: Mrs Sheila Burgess; 19 Chester Grove Seghill Cramlington NorthumberlandNE23 7TR Tel: 0191 2374056
email: burgess_2@tiscali.co.uk
Fixtures Secretary: Mr Gavin Burgess; 7 Barras Mews Seghill Cramlington NorthumberlandNE23 7NZ Tel: 0191 2372287
Club Colours: Scarlet & black hooped shirts, white shorts
League: Durham-N'Thm'Land 3 (level 9)

Selby RUFC
Ground Address:
Sandhill Lane Leeds Road Selby YO8 4JP
Contact: 01757 703 608
Directions: Situated off Sandhill Lane 1 mile west of town centre off A63 Leeds road.
Honorary Secretary: Mr G Adamson; 70 Parkways Selby North Yorkshire YO8 9BB Tel: 07715 043893
email: Sec-garry.adamson@btopenworld.com
Fixtures Secretary: Mr John Philips; Greystones Chapel Street Hillam Nr Selby North Yorkshire YO8 9J Tel: 01757 213344 email: John.Phillips@selbyfoods.co.uk
Club Colours: Green, Red & Gold Narrow Hoops
League: Yorkshire 1 (level 7)

Sheffield Hallam University RFC
Ground Address: c/o Sports Union 814 Pearson Building, Broomgrove, Road, Sheffield South Yorkshire S10 2BP
Contact: 07920 014449
Honorary Secretary: Rick O'Toole; Collegiate Crescent Campus 0 Collegiate Crescent Pearson Building Broomgrove Road Sheffield S10 2BP
Tel: 0114 2253994   email: r.j.o'toole@shu.ac.uk
Fixtures Secretary: Ms Janet Beddus; Collegiate Crescent Campus 36 Collegiate Crescent Pearson Building Broomgrove Road Sheffield S10 2BP
Tel: 07834 322850   email: j.beddus@shu.ac.uk
Non League

Sheffield Oaks RUFC
Ground Address: Malin Bridge Sports & Social Club 22a Stannington Road, Malin Bridge Sheffield S6 5FL
Contact: 01142 363757
Email: sheffield_oaks@yahoo.com
Website: http: //sitekreator.com/sheffieldoaks/index.html
Directions: M1 J36 into Sheffield (north), A61 to Hillsborough Ground, 1st available right after Hillsborough Ground, Bradfield Road, to Holme Lane, left at end of Holme Lane onto Stannington Road, 1st right after car sales.
Honorary Secretary: Mr Richard Harrison; 44 St. Quentin Drive Bradway Sheffield S17 4PP

Tel: 0114 2363757   email: r.harrison4@sky.com
Fixtures Secretary: Mr Jamie Grace
email: grace.jamie@googlemail.com
Club Colours: Royal Blue with Gold Hoops
League: Yorkshire 6 (level 12)

Sheffield RUFC
Ground Address:
Abbeydale Park Totley Rise Sheffield S17 3LJ
Contact: 0114 2353414
Email: admin@sheffieldrufc.co.uk
Directions: **Directions** to Sheffield RUFC Abbeydale Sports Club Abbeydale Park Totley Rise Sheffield S17 3LJ Tel: 0114 235 3414 From the North via M1 Motorway By Coach 1. Exit M1 at Junction 33. From the roundabout follow A630 (Sheffield Parkway) towards c
Honorary Secretary: Mr Chris Wilson; 183 Rustlings Road Sheffield S11 7AD
Tel: 0114 2767481   email: chrisw@hlwlaw.co.uk
Fixtures Secretary: Roger Keegan Tel: 0114 2361714
email: rogermkeegan@tiscali.co.uk
Club Colours: Blue & White Hoops
League: Yorkshire 1 (level 7)

Skipton RFC
Ground Address: The Coulhurst Memorial Ground Sandylands Engine Shed Lane Skipton N. Yorks. BD23 2AZ
Contact: 01756 793148
Email: robin.hargrave@btinternet.com
Website: www.skiptonrfc.com
Directions: From the High Street follow signs for Keighley. At first set of traffic lights, just after the Esso garage turn right. Pass under the railway bridge and turn first right along Carleton New Road. Turn first left again, brings you to Skipton RFC. For more d
Honorary Secretary: Mr Julian Pointon
email: jpointon@jvl.co.uk
Fixtures Secretary: Mrs Tracy Murray; 74 Burnside Crescent Skipton North Yorkshire BD23 2BU
Club Colours: Red shirts,black shorts,red socks
League: Yorkshire 1 (level 7)

Southport RUFC
Ground Address:
Waterloo Road, HIllside, Southport. PR8 4QW
Contact: 01704 569906
Email: p.i.king@talktalk.net
Website: www.southportrufc.com
Directions: The Waterloo Road ground is situated on the main A565 Liverpool to Southport Road close to Merseyrail's Hillside station
Honorary Secretary: Mr Peter King; 48 Victoria Court York Rd Southport Merseyside PR8 2DN
Tel: 01704 569714   email: p.i.king@talktalk.net
Fixtures Secretary: Mr Don Devey; 30 Church Terrace Higher Walton Preston Lancashire PR5 4DY
Tel: 01772 334890   email: michelletowers@btinternet.com
Club Colours: Red / Amber / Black
League: South Lancs-Cheshire 2 (level 8)

St Benedicts RFC
Ground Address: Newlands Avenue Mirehouse Mirehouse Whitehaven CA28 9SH
Email: showse19@aol.com
Directions: **Directions** Leave M6 at Junc 40, take A66 towards Keswick. A595 towards Whitehaven. On entering town take left fork past BP Garage. Straight on through 2 sets of lights, roundabout straight on. Next right, down the hill and bear left following the road, g
Honorary Secretary: Mr Stephen Howse; 12 Castlerigg Close Whitehaven Cumbria CA28 9RJ
Tel: 01946 599657   email: showse19@aol.com
Fixtures Secretary: Mr Ian Maguire; 9 Grisedale Close Whitehaven Cumbria CA28 8DF
email: mscrumhalf@aol.com
Club Colours: Green, Yellow and Black irregular hoops
League: North Lancs-Cumbria (level 7)

St Edward's O.B
Ground Address: CIEA, Bishops Court, North Drive, Sandfield Park, West Derby, Liverpool. L12 2AR
Contact: 0151-228-1414
Email: simon@mail.cybase.co.uk
Directions: To end of M62 , traffic lights, right onto Queens Drive (A5080), downhill through lights, right at next lights onto Aider Road, left onto Eaton Road, playing fields on left.
Honorary Secretary: Carl Driscoll; 41 Blackmoor Drive Liverpool L12 9ED Tel: 0151 2805606
email: carl.driscoll@masonowen.com
Club Colours: Royal blue shirts with a single gold hoop
League: North Lancs 2 (level 9)

St Mary's O.B. RUFC (Lancs)
Ground Address: The Playing Fields Gorsey Lane Hightown Liverpool. L38 3RB
Contact: 0151-929-2020
Email: p.mccann@blueyonder.co.uk
Website: http:
//clubs.rfu.com/Clubs/portals/StMarysOldBoysRUFCLancs
Directions: At the end of the M57/M58 turn left (M57) or continue (M58) onto Dunningsbridge Road (A5036) and then turn right at the Police Station onto Copy Lane (A5207), leading into the Northern Perimeter Road (A5207) and Lydiate Lane (A5207). At the junction by the Grapes pub turn right onto Park View (A565), leading onto Ince Lane and Moor Lane (A565) and passing through Ince Woods. At the traffic lights by the Red Squirrel and Weld Blundell pubs turn left onto Orrell Hill Lane. At the end of Orrell Hill Lane turn left onto Moss Lane (B5193), passing the Pheasant pub on the left. After a series of bends turn right onto Gorsey Lane. Ground is at the junction of Gorsey Lane & Sandy Lane.
Honorary Secretary: Mr Paul McCann; 0 York Road Formby Liverpool L37 8BA Tel: 01704 386168
email: p.mccann@blueyonder.co.uk
Fixtures Secretary: Mr Peter Moore; 5 Moss Gardens Halsall Southport Lancashire PR8 4JD
Tel: 0151 9244898   email: pmoore000@btconnect.com
League: North Lancs 2 (level 9)

Stanley Rodillians RUFC
Ground Address: The Clubhouse Manley Park Lee Moor Road, Stanley Lee Moor Road, Stanley Wakefield West Yorkshire WF3 4EF
Contact: 01924 823619
Email: rodillians@blueyonder.co.uk
Website: www.rodillians.co.uk
Directions: M62 J30, head towards Wakefield, turn right opposite Gordons Tyres, top of hill turn right, past double junction on left, turn left just after Lee Moor Pub.
Honorary Secretary: Mr Martyn Thompson; 23 Cyprus Mount Wakefield West Yorkshire WF1 2RJ
Tel: 07981 757130 email: rodillians@blueyonder.co.uk
Fixtures Secretary: Mr Stuart Knight; 23 Nelson Place Morley Leeds LS27 8LX
Club Colours: Green, white, black hoops, black shorts
League: Yorkshire 5 (level 11)

Stocksbridge RFC
Ground Address: 634 Manchester Road Stocksbridge Sheffield Yorkshire S36 1DY
Contact: 0114 2885078
Email: mickgribbins@hotmail.co.uk
Directions: Ground: Just outside village of Bolsterstone. Club house: Just outside centre of Stocksbridge, opposite fire station.
Honorary Secretary: Mr Mick Gribbins; 7 Hole House Lane Stocksbridge Sheffield S36 1BN
Tel: 0114 2884995 email: mgribbins@hotmail.co.uk
Fixtures Secretary: Bob Woods; 62 St Mary Crescent Deepcar Sheffield S36 2TL Tel: 0114 2887955 email: woods-r3@sky.com
Club Colours: Royal Blue with 2 White Hoops
League: Yorkshire 5 (level 11)

Stockton RFC
Ground Address: Norton (Teesside) Sports Complex Station Road Norton Stockton On Tees TS20 1PE
Contact: 01642 554031
Email: enquiries@stocktonrfc.com
Website: www.stocktonrfc.com
Directions: From A19 North or South If coming from south after crossing River Tees do NOT take first exit signpost for Norton (A139) Take A1027 - signpost to Billingham & Norton. Take Norton exit. Dual carriageway 400 metres. Through one set of traffic lights and at first roundabout with old church on left turn right into Junction Road signpost B 1274 Carlton. In 60m turn right into Station Road. Clubhouse 300 metres on left before Norton Tavern Pub Turn left immediately before rail crossing for road to dressing rooms which goes behind Norton Tavern. From A1 / A689/ A177 On A177 turn left just after Tesco supermarket onto B1274 Junction Road. Go past Blakeston school on left, over 2 railway bridges , and past education centre on right . After 200 metres when road begins to bear right, turn immediate left into Station Road . Do not go as far as the roundabout. Then above .
Honorary Secretary: Mr Harry Buxton; 2 Winterton Av Sedgefield Co. Durham T21 3NH Tel: 01740 629545

email: harry_buxton@btopenworld.com
Fixtures Secretary: Mr Terry Wilson; 1 Brambling Close Norton Stockton On Tees TS20 1TX
Tel: 01642 550084 email: tandcwilson@btinternet.com
Club Colours: Red Shirts & Navy shorts
League: Durham-N'Thm'Land 1 (level 7)

Sunderland RFC
Ground Address: West Lawn Ashbrooke Sports Club Ashbrooke Sunderland Tyne & Wear SR2 7HH
Contact: 0191 5284536
Email: sunderlandrfc@hotmail.co.uk
Website: www.sunderlandrfc.com
Directions: A19 towards Sunderland, exit Durham/Sunderland junction, east 2.5 miles on Durham Road to Barns Htl, right then left onto Queen Alexanda Road, over 1st roundabout, 1st left W'bank Road. left Ashbrook Road, Club 200yards left.
Honorary Secretary: Mrs Gillian Geehan; 30 Fourstones Road Ford Sunderland & Wear SR4 6UX
Tel: 0191 5675041 email: sunderlandrfc@hotmail.co.uk
Fixtures Secretary: Mr Graham Waddell
Club Colours: Red, Black & Gold, White Shorts
League: Durham-N'Thm'Land 1 (level 7)

Tarleton RFC
Ground Address: Carr Lane, Tarleton, Preston. PR4 6BT
Contact: 07785 998388
Email: info@tarletonrugby.com
Website: www.tarletonrugby.com
Directions: Situated on the A59 between Preston and Liverpool just outside Southport - follow signs into the centre of the village and at the main roundabout turn left and Carr Lane comes up on the right - turn down the lane - the Club is situated 300 yards on the le
Honorary Secretary: Mrs Judy Newlove; 27 Jubilee Way Croston Leyland Lancashire PR26 9HD
Tel: 07590 717710
email: judith.newlove@btinternet.com
Fixtures Secretary: Mr Chris Malkin
Tel: 01704 531663   email: malkincj@aol.com
Club Colours: Black with red, gold and white
League: North Lancs 1 (level 8)

Team Northumbria
Ground Address: Bullocksteads Sports Ground, Ponteland, Kenton Bank Foot, Newcastle Upon Tyne, NE13 8AH
Website: www.teamnorthumbria.com
Honorary Secretary: Gaz Lee; 6th North Street East Newcastle upon Tyne NE1 8ST (Tel) 07970 478723
Email: Gaz.lee@northumbria.ac.uk
Fixtures Secretary: As Hon. Sec.
Club Colours: Black shirt with red side panels, black shorts and socks
League: Durham-N'Thm'Land 1 (level 7)

The Gentlemen of Moore RUFC
Ground Address:
Moss Lane Moore Warrington WA4 6UU
Contact: 01925 740473

Email: info@moorerufc.co.uk
Website: www.moorerufc.co.uk
Directions: M56 J11 follow A56 towards Warrington, straight over roundabout, left at 1st set of lights along Runcorn Road for 2 miles, right on 'S' bend into Moss Lane in Moore Village.
Honorary Secretary: Mrs Jayne Jones; Moore RUFC 0 Moss Lane Moore Warrington Cheshire WA4 6UU Tel: 07967 606235
email: lucky7travel@btinternet.com
Fixtures Secretary: Mr Stephen Woollacott c/o Club Address Tel: 01925 481462
email: woollacottsj@bigfoot.com
Club Colours: Black with broad gold band
League: South Lancs-Cheshire 2 (level 8)

Thornensians RUFC
Ground Address: Thornensians RUFC The Rugby Club Church Balk Thorne Doncaster S. Yorks. DN8 5BU
Contact: 01405 812746
Email: trufc@tisltd.plus.com
Website: www.thornensiansrufc.co.uk
Directions: Approach Thorne on the M18, leave at J6 taking the A614 into Thorne, in 300mm pass under a railway bridge, in 900m tn left at traffic lights, in 250m tn right at crossroads, in 800m tn left at 'T' junction in front of Church, in 600mm pass the Trinity Academy on the left and in 100mm turn right onto Thornensians RUFC car park.
Fixtures Secretary: Mr Kevin Jones; Belmont 59 Church Road Barnby Dun Doncaster South Yorkshire DN3 1BD Tel: 07912 606149
email: ksecrjones@aol.com
Club Colours: Blue, Black & White Hoops
League: Yorkshire 3 (level 9)

Trafford MV RFCC
Ground Address: MacPherson Park, Finney Bank Road, Finney Bank Road, Sale. M33 6LR
Contact: 0161 9737061
Email: traffordmv@btconnect.com
Website: www.traffordmv.co.uk
Directions: Take M60 to J7 follow signs for Sale & Altrincham at first lights turn right into Glebelands Rd 2/3 mile turn right into Finney Bank Rd. Or take M6 to J19 follow A556/A56 to Altrincham, continue on 3 miles to Sale, go past Volunteer pub & turn left at ne
Honorary Secretary: Mr Christopher Higgins; 41 Lulworth Road Eccles Manchester Lancashire M30 8WP Tel: 0161 7894258   email: cj.higgins@ntlworld.com
Fixtures Secretary: Mr Christopher Higgins; 41 Lulworth Road Eccles Manchester Lancashire M30 8WP Tel: 0161 7894258   email: cj.higgins@ntlworld.com
Club Colours: Black and White Hoops
League: North Lancs 1 (level 8)

Trentham RFC
Ground Address: Trentham RUFC New Inn Lane Trentham Stoke On Trent Staffs. ST4 8BE
Contact: 01782 642120
Email: janeprocter1@btinternet.com
Website: www.trenthamrufc.co.uk
Directions: M6 J15, A500 towards Stoke on Trent, A34 south signs to Trentham, at Trentham Gardens roundabout turn left onto Longton road, then 4th left onto New Inn Lane. Approx. 1/3rd of a mile on the right.
Honorary Secretary: Mrs Jane Procter; Holly House Barn Court Clayton Newcastle Staffs. ST5 4NL Tel: 01782 848603   email: ajphilpott@email.com
Fixtures Secretary: Mr Nicholas Wide; 4 Torridon Close Trentham Stoke On Trent Staffs. ST4 8YA
Tel: 07590. 046073   email: nick.wide@talktalk.net
Club Colours: Green & White Hoops
League: South Lancs-Cheshire 2 (level 8)

University of Chester (Chester Campus)
Ground Address: Rugby Union Club Captain University College Chester Parkgate Road CH1 4AG
Honorary Secretary: Honorary Secretary; Chester Students Union Parkgate Road University College Chester Chester Cheshire CH1 4BJ
Club Colours: Dark Green
Non League

University of Durham RFC
Ground Address: 1 Hillcrest Mews Durham DH1 1RD
Contact: 0191 3342178
Email: sports.union@dur.ac.uk
Website: www.sportdurham.com/unisport
Directions: DURFC play home matches at three grounds: Maiden Castle, The Racecourse and Durham City RFC.
Honorary Secretary: Mr Steven Colwell; 1 Hillcrest Mews Durham DH1 1RD Tel: 07813 697094
email: stevencolwell@gmail.com
Fixtures Secretary: David Astle Tel: 07962 181438
email: d.e.p.astle@durham.ac.uk
Club Colours: Palatinate Purple
Non League

University of Huddersfield RFC
Ground Address:
Contact: 07917582410
Email: huddrugbyunion@hotmail.com
Website: www.huddersfieldstudent.com/main/activities/sport/
Non League

University of Hull RFC
Ground Address: AU Cottingham Road Hull HU6 7RX
Contact: 01482 466256
Email: a.yarnley@hull.ac.uk
Website: www.rfu.com/clubs/hurfc
Directions: use a route finder...HU6 7RX
Honorary Secretary: Hon. Secretary; Athletic Union University of Hull Cottingham Road University House Hull Yorkshire HU6 7LS
Fixtures Secretary: Mr Sam Broderick; Thwaite Hall Thwaite Street Cottingham HU16 4RE
Tel: 07859 805631   email: sbroders27@hotmail.com
Club Colours: Blue and Yellow
Non League

LEVELS 7-12 & NON LEAGUE CLUBS

University of Leeds
Ground Address: LUU Rugby Club Leeds University Union PO Box 157 LS1 1UH
Email: hkjohnston83@hotmail.com
Directions: Training at University Sports Ground, Weetwood
Fixtures Secretary: Miss Wendy Voo; LUU Sports Office 157 Po Box Leeds West Yorkshire LS1 1UH Tel: 07824 663893 email: nutty_wendy@hotmail.com
Club Colours: Green/Maroon
League: Yorkshire 6 (level 12)

University of Liverpool RFC
Ground Address: Liverpool University RFC Sport Liverpool c/o Guild of Students 160 Mount Pleassant Liverpool L3 5TR
Contact: 0151 7085033
Email: swade@liv.ac.uk
Website: www.liv.ac.uk/sports
Honorary Secretary: David Beale; 160 Mount Pleasant Liverpool Merseyside L3 5TR Tel: 07789 966359 email: d.j.beale@student.liverpool.ac.uk
Fixtures Secretary: Katy Young; Sport Liverpool The Guild of Students 160 Mount Pleasant Liverpool Merseyside L3 5TR Tel: 07807 106560 email: kyoung@liv.ac.uk
Club Colours: Blue
Non League

University of Newcastle Upon Tyne RFC
Ground Address: Cochrane Park Etherstone Avenue Newcastle Upon Tyne
Contact: 0191 266 1164
Honorary Secretary: Mr John Fenn; Keswick House Newcastle Road Houghton Le Spring Tyne & Wear DH4 5PX Tel: 07984 377244
email: j.e.fenn@newcastle.ac.uk
Fixtures Secretary: As Hon. Sec.
Non League

University of Salford RFC
Ground Address: SUSU, University House The Crescent Salford M5 4WT
Contact: 0161 736 7811 ext 226
Email: SalfordUniRUFC@hotmail.co.uk
Website: www.rfu.com/clubs/salforduni
Honorary Secretary: Honorary Secretary; Athletic Union University of Salford RFC University House The Crescent Salford Lancashire M5 4WT
Fixtures Secretary: Robin Johnstone; University House Salford University Salford Tel: 07704 042179
Club Colours: Blue & Gold
Non League

University of Sunderland RFC 1
Ground Address: Blaydon RFC Crowstree Ground Hexham Rd, Swalwell Newcastle-upon-Tyne NE16 3BN
Contact: 0191 420 0505
Non League

University of Teeside RFC
Ground Address: Borough Road Middlesborough Cleveland TS1 3BA
Contact: 01642 342 245
Directions: http: //teessideunimru.co.uk/aboutus.html
Honorary Secretary: Chris Ellis; 31 Polopit Titchmarsh Kettering Northants. NN14 3DL Tel: 07772 641722
email: jediknightellis@hotmail.com
Fixtures Secretary: Mr Aidan Chapman
email: chappo10@hotmail.com
Club Colours: Maroon Shirt, Black Shorts
Non League

Upper Eden RUFC
Ground Address: Pennine Park Westgarth Rd Kirkby Stephen Cumbria CA17 4TF
Contact: 017683 71585
Email: dcpearson8@hotmail.com
Website: www.upperedenrufc.co.uk
Directions: M6 J36, 12 miles to Kirby Stephen, turn left by Spar shop (Westgarth), straight onto top of estate. A66 turn off at Brough, 4 miles to Kirby Stephen, right just after shop.
Honorary Secretary: Mr David Pearson; Castle Hill Cottage Warcop Appleby-in-Westmorland Cumbria CA16 6PD Tel: 01768 341847
email: dcpearson8@hotmail.com
Fixtures Secretary: Mr Trevor Braithwaite; 23 High Street Kirkby Stephen CA17 4SG Tel: 017683 71074
email: trevorbks@talktalk.net
Club Colours: Black & White Hoops
League: North Lancs-Cumbria (level 7)

Vagabonds RUFC
Ground Address: Mike Hailwood Centre TT Grandstand, Glencrutchery Road, Douglas Isle of Man IM2 6DA
Email: vagabonds@manx.net
Website: www.vagabondsiom.net
Directions: Clubhouse & Ground at Glencrutchery Road,Douglas Clubhouse behind the TT Grandstand.
Honorary Secretary: Miss Sally Aston; 2 Pandora Apartments 6 Clarence Terrace Central Promenade Douglas Isle of Man IM2 4LS Tel: 01624 649441
email: saston@doehle-iom.com
Fixtures Secretary: Mrs Jan Bell; Laureston Terrace 4 Douglas Isle of Man IM2 5DH Tel: 01624 628710
email: belljan@manx.net
Club Colours: White Yellow & Black
League: South Lancs-Cheshire 1 (level 7)

Wallasey RFC
Ground Address: Cross Lane Leasowe road Wallasey CH45 8NS
Contact: 0151 6303710
Email: cdunnachie@btinternet.com
Directions: The directions are Exit 1 on M53 towards Wallasey take 2nd slip road on to the A551 turn right at the lights into cross lane and proceed for approx 200 yards and the club is on the left
Honorary Secretary: Mr Colin Dunnachie; 3 Marlwood Avenue Wallasey Merseyside CH45 8NU
Tel: 07748 431857
email: cdunnachie@btinternet.com
Fixtures Secretary: Mr Andrew Mclean; 11 Hilbre Avenue Wallasey Merseyside CH44 5RR
Tel: 0151 6911285
email: Andy.McLean@eon-uk.com
Club Colours: Red, Black & White Hoops
League: South Lancs-Cheshire 2 (level 8)

Wallsend RFC
Ground Address: Benfield Community Association Sam Smith's Pavilion Benfield School Campus, Benfield Road NE6 4NU
Contact: 0191 2659357
Email: dheppell@blueyonder.co.uk
Website: www.wallsendrfc.co.uk
Directions: Just off A1058 Newcastle-Tynemouth (Coast road), turn on to C127 to Benfield School, Club at rear of school.
Hon. Secretary: Mr Brian Thirlaway; 29 Belmont Close Battle Hill Estate Wallsend Tyne & Wear NE28 9DX
Tel: 0191 2344877
email: bthirlaway@msn.com
Fixtures Secretary: Mr Stuart Robinson; 5 Dinsdale Avenue Wallsend Tyne & Wear NE28 9JD
Tel: 0191 2627485
email: stuartrobison@talktalk.com
Club Colours: Myrtle Green Jerseys with Gold Trim
League: Durham-N'Thm'Land 1 (level 7)

Warrington RUFC
Ground Address: Warrington Sports Club Walton Lea Road ,Higher Walton Walton Lea Road , Higher Walton Warrington Cheshire WA4 6SJ
Contact: 07825 705573
Email: peter.riley@warringtonrufc.com
Website: www.warringtonrufc.com
Directions: From the M6 North Shell Haydock Island (Junction 23) M6 Leave the M6 at junction 22, then at r'about take the 3rd exit onto the A49 (signposted Newton) A49 At r'about take the 1st exit onto the A49 (signposted Warrington) A49 At r'about take the 2nd exit onto the A49 (signposted Warrington) A49 At r'about take the 2nd exit onto the A49 (signposted Town Centre) A49 At r'about take the 2nd exit onto the A49 (signposted Town Centre) A49 At Cockhedge Green r'about take the 3rd exit onto the A49 (signposted Whitchurch, Chester) A49 At r'about take the 2nd exit onto the A49 (signposted Whitchurch, Macclesfield) A49 At Bridge Foot r'about take the 3rd exit onto the A49 (signposted Whitchurch, Chester) A49 At r'about take the 3rd exit onto the A5060 (signposted North Wales, Chester, Walton) A5060 Turn left onto the A56 (signposted Lymm, Stockton Heath) A56 Turn right onto Hill Cliffe Road Hill Cliffe Road Turn right onto Walton Lea Road Walton Lea Road Arrive at WA4 6SJ,Higher Walton M6 South Leave the M6 at junction 20, then at r'about take the 1st exit onto the A50 (signposted Warrington) A50 At r'about take the 2nd exit onto the A50 (signposted Warrington) A50 At traffic signals turn left onto the A56 (signposted Runcorn) A56 At traffic signals continue forward onto the A56 (signposted Runcorn, Walton) A56 Turn left onto Hill Cliffe Road Hill Cliffe Road Turn right onto Walton Lea Road Walton Lea Road M56 Leave the M56 at junction 11, then at r'about take the 2nd exit onto the A56 (signposted Warrington, Runcorn East) A56 At r'about take the 2nd exit onto the A56 (signposted Warrington) A56 Turn right onto Hill Cliffe Road Hill Cliffe Road Turn right onto Walton Lea Road Walton Lea Road
Honorary Secretary: Mr Peter Riley; 27 Grappenhall Road Stockton Heath Warrington WA4 2AH
Tel: 01925 604896
email: peterr@mortgageforce.co.uk
Fixtures Secretary: Mr Peter Riley; 27 Grappenhall Road Stockton Heath Warrington WA4 2AH
Tel: 01925 604896
email: peterr@mortgageforce.co.uk
Club Colours: Red white & green
League: South Lancs-Cheshire 1 (level 7)

Washington RFC
Ground Address: Biddick Sports College Biddick Lane Washington Tyne & Wear NE38 8AL
Contact: 0191 3873963
Email: matthew@omegaflex.co.uk
Website: www.intheteam.com/washington
Directions: Biddick Community College Washington

Wath Upon Dearne RUFC
Ground Address: Moor Road Wath-Upon-Dearne Rotherham S63 7RT
Contact: 01709 872 399
Directions: Moor Road is adjacent to Wath Swimming Baths on the main Rotherham to Barnsley (A630) road.
Honorary Secretary: Mr Steve Poxton; 5 Cortworth Place Elsecar Barnsley South Yorkshire S74 8HX
Tel: 07753 395604   email: s.poxton@barnsley.org
Club Colours: Blue with Maroon & Gold Bands
League: Yorkshire 3 (level 9)

LEVELS 7-12 & NON LEAGUE CLUBS

West End RFC
Ground Address: All Saints College West Denton Way Newcastle upon Tyne Tyne & Wear NE5 2SZ
Directions: Travelling from the North Take the exit for Westerhope off the A1. Turn right at the r'about. Turn left at the next r'about (McDonalds drive thorugh). Straight over at the next r'about. All Saints college is 500 yards on the right. Follow the road round in the school until you reach the sports centre. Travelling from the South Take the exit for Westerhope off the A1. Turn left at the r'about. Turn left at the next r'about (McDonalds drive through). Straight over at the next r'about. All Saints College is 500 yards on the right. Follow the road round in the school until you reach the sports centre. Travelling from the West Take the Lemington Road Ends turn off the A69. Turn left at the r'about. Go through the next set of traffic lights and take the next right, you will see the pitch on your left hand side. All Saints College is around 700 yards on the left. Follow the road round in the school until you reach the sports centre.
Honorary Secretary: Mr John Blair; 113 Burnstones West Denton Newcastle upon Tyne NE5 2DG
Tel: 0191 2431845   email: jpblair@blueyonder.co.uk
Fixtures Secretary: Mr Alan Smart; 2 Smailes Lane Highfield Rowlands Gill Tyne & Wear NE39 2LR
Tel: 07876 761436   email: bigalsmart@hotmail.com
Club Colours: Black
Non League

West Hartlepool Amateur RFC
Ground Address: Hartlepool 6th Form College Catcote Road Hartlepool TS25 4HG
Contact: 01429 273737
Email: tonywilson2@myway.com
Directions: Home Ground is Hartlepool Sixth Form College, Catcote lane entrance. Approaching Hartlepool on the A689 turn left at the first roundabout into Owton Manor Lane. At T junction, top of Owton Manor Lane, turn right into Catcote Road. Ground is approximat
Honorary Secretary: Mr Tony Wilson; 6 Harvey Walk Hartlepool Cleveland TS25 4PZ Tel: 07788 972827
email: tonywilson2@myway.com
Fixtures Secretary: Mr Graham Frankland; 16 Hardwick Court Hartlepool Cleveland TS26 0AZ
Tel: 01429 261716
email: Graham.Frankland1@ntlworld.com
Club Colours: Red & Blue with White Trim
Non League

West Leeds RUFC
Ground Address:
The Clubhouse Bluehill Lane Leeds LS12 4NZ
Contact: 0113 2639769
Email: barrybreakwell@btinernet.com
Website: www.westleedsrugby.org
Directions: From M621 to Leeds outer ring road take A6110 & turn right at second roundabout. After Ringways , turn right at lights follow road left at Fawcett Lane & Club is half a mile on the left.
Honorary Secretary: Mrs Jill Broadbent; 21 Butterbowl Road Farnley Leeds LS12 5JE Tel: 07720 297873

email: jillybroadbent@hotmail.com
Fixtures Secretary: Mr Colin Edwards; 59 Moorfield Gildersome Morley Leeds LS27 7BW
Tel: 07850 226393
Club Colours: Old gold, navy & white irregular hoops
League: Yorkshire 2 (level 8)

West Park Leeds RUFC
Ground Address: The Sycamores Bramhope Leeds West Yorkshire LS16 9JR
Contact: 0113 2671437
Email: mailbox@westparkleeds.co.uk
Website: www.westparkleeds.co.uk
Directions: From Leeds City Centre take A660 sign posted Skipton and Otley. Continue for approx 8 miles in Bramhope village take first exit at roundabout into The Sycamores, follow direct to Club.
Honorary Secretary: Mr Rob Storey; 7 Moseley Wood Way Leeds LS16 7HN Tel: 0113 2675266
email: bobskybob@sky.com
Fixtures Secretary: Mr Phil March; 202 Moseley Wood Gardens Cookridge Leeds LS16 7JE Tel: 0113 2268246
email: phil_m_2003@yahoo.co.uk
Club Colours: Black,Gold,Blue and White
League: Yorkshire 2 (level 8)

West Park Warriors RUFC
Ground Address:
Red Rocks, Prescot Road, St. Helens. WA10 3AG
Contact: 01744 26138
Email: aliduncan76@yahoo.co.uk
Honorary Secretary: Alison Duncan; 81 Chapel Street St. Helens Merseyside WA10 2BJ Tel: 07866 622344
email: aliduncan76@yahoo.co.uk
Fixtures Secretary: David Griffiths; 26 Derwent Close Rainhill Merseyside L35 0NP Tel: 0151 4261821
email: griffiths288@btinternet.com
Club Colours: Green & Gold
League: North Lancs 2 (level 9)

Wetherby RFC
Ground Address: Wetherby R.F.C. Grange Park Sports Club Grange Park Wetherby West Yorkshire LS22 5NB
Email: member@wetherbyrufc.com
Website: www.wetherbyrufc.co.uk
Directions: From Wetherby town centre head for A1 south, pass Police station on left, to roundabout, 2nd exit for A1 south, cross A1 & take left turn, follow the road along into Grange Park.
Honorary Secretary: Mr Phil Hill; 109 Birchwood Hill Shadwell Leeds LS17 8NT Tel: 07769 033205
email: phill@northcroft.co.uk
Fixtures Secretary: Mr Richard Watts; 8 Maple Drive Wetherby W. Yorks. LS22 6RS   Tel: 01937 584446
email: richard.watts@fss.pnn.police.uk
Club Colours: Red & White Hoops, White Shorts
League: Yorkshire 6 (level 12)

Wheatley Hills RUFC
Ground Address: Wheatley Hills Doncaster RUFC Brunel Road York Road Ind. Estate DN5 8PT

Contact: 07974 830878
Email: stevehanson56@hotmail.com
Directions: A638 1 mile north out of Doncaster on York Road, turn into Ind. Est next to the Range superstore and follow road around past Furniture Factors into cul-de-sac
Honorary Secretary: Mr Steve Hanson c/o the club
Tel: 07974 830878   email: stevehanson56@hotmail.com
Fixtures Sec.: Christopher Whitehouse; 4 Meadow Court South Elmsall Pontefract W. Yorks. WF9 2SP
Tel: 01302 321333
Club Colours: Gold, Maroon and White Stripes
League: Yorkshire 1 (level 7)

Whitby RUFC

Ground Address: 'Showfield' White Leys Road Whitby North Yorkshire YO21 3PB
Contact: 01947 602008
Email: Emma_Garbutt@redcar-cleveland.gov.uk
Website: www.whitbyrugbyclub.co.uk
Directions: come in on A171. at 1st roundabout turn left by the garage. follow road to junction and head right. then follow road passed two shops and we are 2nd left. Or see www.streetmap.co.uk
Honorary Secretary: Mrs Emma Garbutt; 1 St. Hildas Court Green Lane Whitby YO22 4BZ
Tel: 01947 820761
email: Emma_Garbutt@redcar-cleveland.gov.uk
Fixtures Secretary: Mr Peter Stentiford; Manor House Farm Newholm Whitby North Yorkshire YO21 3QY
Tel: 01947 820840   email: pete_stentiford@yahoo.co.uk
Club Colours: Maroon & Black
League: Durham-N'Thm'Land 3 (level 9)

Whitehaven RFC

Ground Address: The Playground Richmond Terrace Whitehaven Cumbria CA28 7QR
Contact: 01946 852644
Email: wrufc@hotmail.com
Directions: Behind the Whitehaven Sports Centre & next to Jacksons Timber Yard.
Honorary Secretary: Mrs Pamela McConnell; 33 Loop Road South Whitehaven Cumbria CA28 7SD
Tel: 01946 693379
Fixtures Secretary: Mr D Telford; 11 Thronton Road Fairfield Whitehaven Cumbria CA28 6UJ
Tel: 01946 61355
Club Colours: Maroon & White Hoops
League: Cumbria (level 8)

Whitley Bay Rockcliff RFC

Ground Address: Hillheads Lovaine Avenue Whitley Bay Tyne & Wear NE25 8RW
Contact: 01912 510748
Email: martinpage54@hotmail.com
Website: www.whitleybay-rockcliffrfc.co.uk
Directions: Travelling down hill on Hillheads Road past the Ice rink, turn 2nd right (Club signed) along Lovaine Avenue, 2nd right into Club.
Honorary Secretary: Mr John Mcgee; 49 Willoughby Drive Whitley Bay Tyne & Wear NE26 3DZ

Tel: 0191 2528997   email: johnmcgee@btinternet.com
Fixtures Secretary: Mr D Bennett; 4 Millfield Gardens North Shields Tyne & Wear NE30 2PX
Tel: 0191 2572174
Club Colours: Cardinal & Gold Shirts
League: Durham-N'Thm'Land 2 (level 8)

Wibsey RUFC

Ground Address: 143 High Street Wibsey Bradford West Yorkshire BD6 1RA
Contact: 07926159510
Directions: From top of M606 take 2nd exit towards Odsal roundabout, take 4th exit at side of Police Station, 0.75 mile on left joined onto White Swan Pub.
Honorary Secretary: Mr Paul Garside; 19 Thornaby Drive Clayton Bradford West Yorkshire BD14 6ER
Tel: 01274 813327
email: fastasarock@blueyonder.co.uk
Fixtures Secretary: Mr Daniel Horsfall; Highgate Rd Clayton Heights Bradford West Yorkshire
Club Colours: Red & Green Hoops
League: Yorkshire 5 (level 11)

Widnes RUFC

Ground Address: Heath Road, Widnes. WA8 7NU
Contact: 0151 4242575
Email: ianthompson@widnesrufc.co.uk
Website: www.widnesrufc.co.uk
Directions: Directions: M62 J6. Take A5080 to Cronton. Right at Traffic Lights. After 1 mile, take second exit from roundabout. Go over railway bridge, take first left into Heath Road. Clubhouse is on left.
Honorary Secretary: Ian Thompson; 3 Rushton Close Upton Rocks Widnes Cheshire WA8 9ZF
Tel: 0151 4234712   email: ianet@btinternet.com
Fixtures Secretary: Mr Derek Dyer; 19 Clincton Close Widnes Cheshire WA8 8JP Tel: 07713 260466
email: DEREKD_1213@FSMAIL.NET
Club Colours: Red and Black Jerseys, Black Shorts
League: South Lancs-Cheshire 1 (level 7)

Wigan RUFC

Ground Address: Douglas Valley, Wingates Lane, Leyland Mill Lane, Wigan. Lancashire WN1 2SJ
Contact: 01257 425056
Email: davorlia@aol.com
Website: www.wiganru.com
Directions: M6, J27, follow signs to Standish, take A49 towards Wigan, 2 miles, 1st left after Cherry Gardens Hotel into Leyland Mill Lane, then sign posted
Honorary Secretary: Mr David Wilkinson; 1 The Fields Standish Wigan WN6 0GF   Tel: 01257 425056
email: davorlia@aol.com
Fixtures Secretary: Mr David Clarke; 224 Billinge Road Pemberton Wigan Lancashire WN5 9HX
Tel: 07712 582423
email: david.clarke51@yahoo.co.uk
Club Colours: Black & White Irregular Hoops
League: South Lancs-Cheshire 1 (level 7)

NORTHERN

LEVELS 7-12 & NON LEAGUE CLUBS

Wigton RFC
Ground Address: Lowmoor Road Wigton CA7 9QT
Contact: 0 1697342206
Email: wigtonrufc@btconnect.com
Directions: Junction 41, M6, B3505 to Wigton to j/w A595, follow signs to Wigton. Club on right 3/4 mile approx. For vehicles not using motorway follow A595 to j/w as above and follow directions as above.
Honorary Secretary: Mr Alan Thompson; 9 Highmoor Park Wigton Cumbria CA7 9LZ Tel: 01697 345123
email: at.thompson@tiscali.co.uk
Fixtures Secretary: Mr David Allison; 23 Highmoor Bungalows Wigton Cumbria CA7 9LW
Tel: 01228 818920
email: bongo56@btinternet.com
Club Colours: Green jersey, white shorts
League: North Lancs-Cumbria (level 7)

Windermere RUFC
Ground Address: Dawes Meadow Longlands Bowness on Windermere LA23 3AS
Contact: 015394 43066
Email: colin.hetherington@etherway.net
Website: www.windermererufc.co.uk
Directions: Drive towards Bowness & the lake from Windermere, coming into Bowness, right just before cinema, right again past the bowling club, Club house is on the right.
Honorary Secretary: Mr Colin Hetherington; Sundown Keldwyth Drive Troutbeck Bridge Windermere Cumbria LA23 1HQ Tel: 015394 46500
email: colin.hetherington@etherway.net
Club Colours: Amber & Black
League: North Lancs 1 (level 8)

Winlaton Vulcans RFC
Ground Address: Axwell View Playing Fields Winlaton Blaydon-On-Tyne NE21 6NF
Contact: 0191 4142502
Email: winlatonvulcansrfc@hotmail.co.uk
Website: www.winlatonvulcansrfc.co.uk
Directions: Winlaton is situated 5 miles South West of Newcastle upon Tyne. Travelling from the South on the A1M After passing the service station at Birtley, follow the A1, and immediately after the Metro Centre, take the slip road to Swalwell and proceed past Blaydon Rugby Club until you reach the next roundabout. Travelling from the West on the A69 from Carlisle join the A1M and take the LEFT exist until 1.4 miles onto the A694 / B6317 / Consett / Whickham / Swalwell exit. At roundabout, take the 2nd exit onto A694 and at the next roundabout (0.6 miles), take the 3rd exit onto B6317. Swalwell Roundabout Follow the B6317 for Blaydon for half a mile, and on reaching the Swimming pool on the right hand side, turn left and proceed up Shibdon Bank where you will eventually see the rugby club on your left after 0.9 miles.

Honorary Secretary: Mr Richard Jones; 20 Meldon Way Winlaton Blaydon-on-Tyne Tyne & Wear NE21 6HJ
Tel: 07749 825580
email: richard_jones_8@hotmail.com
Fixtures Secretary: Mr I Bilclough; 6 Reay Gardens Westerhope Newcastle upon Tyne NE5 2NB
Tel: 0191 4147723
email: ian.bilclough@baesystems.com
Club Colours: Black & White
League: Durham-N'Thm'Land 2 (level 8)

Winnington Park RFC
Ground Address: Burrows Hill Hartford Northwich CW8 3AA
Contact: 01606 74242
Email: chairman@wprfc.com
Website: www.wprfc.com
Directions: Approach Northwich on the A556, turn off following the sign for Harford, turn right at the church, left at the first set of lights, right at the next T junction, next left into Burrows Hill. The Rugby Club is second on the right.
Honorary Secretary: April Wilkinson; 2 Lowwe Haigh Street Winsford Cheshire CW7 1HH Tel: 01606 556169
email: john@wilkinson6138.freeserve.co.uk
Fixtures Secretary: Mr Neil Marrs; 35 Longmeadow Weaverham Northwich Cheshire CW8 3JH
Tel: 07973 951465   email: neilmarr@warrington.gov.uk
Club Colours: Sky Blue, Royal Blue and White
League: South Lancs-Cheshire 1 (level 7)

Wirral RUFC
Ground Address: Memorial Ground Thornton Common Road Clatterbridge Bebington CH63 0LT
Contact: 0151 3341309
Email: wirralrfc@millsmediagroup.com
Website: http: //www.wirralrugbyclub.com/
Directions: Exit junction 4 off the M53, and take the B5151 to Neston/Clatterbridge, passing a hospital & a Texaco Petrol station on your right. Half a mile further down the road turn left at the roundabout, signposted Wirral RFC & CC Wirral Rugby Club is on your left. Main Car Park is by the club house Alternative Car Park is further down along side the 2nd Team pitch Nearest Train Station Spital, Bromborough or Bromborough Rake are all close. Served by Merseyrail services from Liverpool or Chester on the Wirral Line.
Honorary Secretary: Mr Andrew Mills; Edendale 32 Hooton Road Willaston Neston Cheshire CH64 1SJ
Tel: 0151 6493600
email: andrew@millsmediagroup.com
Fixtures Secretary: Mr Steve Fergusson; Memorial Ground Thornton Common Road Clatterbridge Bebington CH63 0LT Tel: 07939 950406
email: stevefergiwirral@hotmail.com
Club Colours: Maroon & White Hoops
League: South Lancs-Cheshire 1 (level 7)

Workington RFC
Ground Address: Ellis Sports Ground Mossbay Road Workington CA14 3XZ
Contact: 01900 602625
Email: workingtonzebras@talk21.com
Website: www.workingtonrfc.co.uk
Directions: Follow trunk roads to town centre, then follow B5296 (Harrington) for 1/2 mile. Entrance to ground on right 100m after traffic lights at TA Centre.
Honorary Secretary: Mr Michael Heaslip; 32 Elizabeth Street Workington CA14 4DB Tel: 07786 625859
email: Michael@heaslip.fslife.co.uk
Fixtures Secretary: Mr William Anderson; 18 Hensingham Road Hensingham Whitehaven Cumbria CA28 8PS Tel: 01946 692844
Club Colours: Black & White Hoops, Black shorts
League: North Lancs-Cumbria (level 7)

Yarm RUFC
Ground Address: c/o 5 Pinewood Road Eaglescliffe Stockton on Tees TS16 0AH
Contact: 07813 328258
Email: yarmrugbyclub@ntlworld.com
Website: www.yarmrugbyclub.co.uk
Directions: Wass Way, Eaglescliffe TS16 0PS. From Durham Lane into Cleasby Way then right into Sowerby Way and left into Wass Way. Entrance to ground is at the end of Wass Way on the left.
Honorary Secretary: Mr Andrew Perriman; 12 Severn Drive Guisborough Cleveland TS14 8AU
Tel: 01287 637161
email: andyperriman@hotmail.com
Fixtures Secretary: Mr Rob Ivey; 7 Mayfield Crescent Eaglescliffe Stockton on Tees Cleveland TS16 0NQ
Tel: 07838 381233
email: Robivey@hotmail.co.uk
Club Colours: Navy blue & light blue
League: Durham-N'Thm'Land 2 (level 8)

Yarnbury RFC
Ground Address: The Clubhouse Brownberrie Lane Horsforth Horsforth Leeds LS18 5HB
Contact: 0113 2581346
Email: proptrigg@hotmail.com
Website: www.yarnbury.co.uk
Directions: Follow signs on Leeds Outer Ring Road (A6120)to Horforth. Turn north onto Low Lane. At T-Junction turn left then after approx 300 yards come to 'Old Ball' roundabout. Take 3rd exit onto Brownberrie Lane. The Club is about half a mile up hill on the right
Honorary Secretary: Mrs Lynda Gomersall; 85 Cookridge Lane Leeds LS16 7NE Tel: 0113 2289324
email: lynda.gomersall@ntlworld.com
Fixtures Secretary: Mr John Riley; 65 Broadgate Lane Horsforth Leeds LS18 5AB Tel: 0113 2589131
email: johnriley801@btinternet.com
Club Colours: Blue, black and white
League: Yorkshire 1 (level 7)

York RI RFC
Ground Address: Railway Institute Sports Ground New Lane, Acomb York YORKSHIRE YO24 4NU
Contact: 01904 798930
Email: brynbates@freenetname.co.uk
Website: yorkrugby.co.uk
Directions: From the A1237 York ring road, take the B1224 signposted Acomb for 1.5 miles. After the Church of the Latter Day Saints on the right, take the 1st road (New Lane) on the right to the end. The gates for the Sports Ground are directly opposite.
Honorary Secretary: Mr Bryn Bates; 16 Beech Place Strensall York YO32 5AS Tel: 01904 692970
email: brynbates@freenetname.co.uk
Fixtures Secretary: Mr Bill Cooper; Moorcroft Lucy Hall Drive Baildon Shipley West Yorkshire BD17 5BG
Tel: 01274 584135
Club Colours: Royal Blue & White Hoops
League: Yorkshire 4 (level 10)

York RUFC
Ground Address: Clifton Park Shipton Road York YO30 6RE
Contact: 01904 623602
Email: brianmcclure@btinternet.com
Website: www.yorkrufc.co.uk
Directions: Turn south off the northern part of York outer ring road (A1237) towards city centre on A19 from Thirsk, Club situated on right after about 1.75 miles.
Honorary Secretary: Mr Brian Mcclure; 15 Stubden Grove Clifton Moor York YO30 4UY
Tel: 07739 714285
email: brianmcclure@btinternet.com
Fixtures Secretary: Mr Allan Robertshaw; 25 Manor Park Close York YO30 5UZ
Tel: 01904 626659
email: atrob@cwctv.net
Club Colours: Green, black & white shirts, black shorts
League: Yorkshire 1 (level 7)

York St John's College
Ground Address: c/o Students Union, St. John's College Lord Mayor's Walk York YO31 7EX
Honorary Secretary: Hon. Secretary; Athletic union St John's College York Cordukes Building Lord Mayors Walk York Y031 7EX
Fixtures Secretary: Emma Reeve; 34 Huntington Mews York North Yorkshire YO31 8JG
Tel: 07792 250976
email: emma.reeve@yorksj.ac.uk
Non League

Support the RFU Injured Players Foundation

The Foundation helps and supports players from all levels of the game who suffer injuries whilst playing rugby which may cause permanent and severe disability.

Welfare Support

Historically, the majority of rugby related injuries that initially appear catastrophic, make a full or near full recovery. For those that have a significant residual disability after completing their rehabilitation, RFU IPF welfare support will continue for as long as the individual wishes, and can be accessed through the Injured Player Welfare Officer (IPWO):

The IPWO is able to provide advice or facilitate advice and assistance on the following:

- Fundraising
- Trust funds
- Financial support (charity funding and grant applications)
- Government benefits
- Local authority support
- Local "rugby" support (through Constituent Bodies)
- NHS support
- Tickets for England Internationals

As a result of the RFU's "New Vision" the way insurance is managed has recently been improved. Rather than relying solely on an insurance-based system, on advice from spinal injury specialists, other spinal injury charities and injured players, the RFU IPF now delivers a system that could provide help and support in the early months of an injury as well as longer term support.

The aim of this is to provide effective benefits to supplement and/or facilitate those provided by the state, which can be accessed at the appropriate time during the rehabilitation and re-integration window, in order to optimise the care provided and the opportunities for achieving as high a level of independent living as possible.

Alongside this, the Foundation will also work much more closely with the spinal injuries units, contribute to their case management if required, and help players in obtaining the support they are entitled to from the NHS and Local Authorities.

Visit www.rfuipf.org.uk to discover more and see how you can help

MIDLANDS DIVISION

BROADSTREET RFC - MIDLANDS ONE CHAMPIONS 2008-09

MIDLANDS

STRUCTURE

MIDLANDS

Level			
5		NATIONAL LEAGUE 3 MIDLANDS	
6	MIDLANDS 1 WEST		
7	Midlands 2 West *North*	Midlands 2 West *South*	
8	Midlands 3 West *North*	Midlands 3 West *South*	
9	Midlands 4 West *North*	Midlands 4 West *South*	
10	Midlands 5 West *North*	Midlands 5 West *South West*	Midlands 5 West *South East*

MIDLANDS DIVISION
CONTENTS

Midlands Division	Officials & League Secretaries	500
National League 3 Midlands	08-09 League Table & 09-10 Fixture List	502
	Year by Year record - the last 10 years	503
	2009-10 Clubs	504
Midlands 1 East	08-09 League table & 09-10 Fixture Grid	522
	2009-10 Clubs	523
Midlands 1 West	08-09 League table & 09-10 Fixture Grid	528
	2009-10 Clubs	529
Other Midlands	2008-09 League Tables	534
	2009-10 Fixture Grids	538
	Level 7-10 Clubs	544

A complete club index appears at the back of the book,
showing which league each club is in for the 2009-10 season

DIVISION

2009-2010

	Level
NATIONAL LEAGUE 3 MIDLANDS	5
MIDLANDS 1 EAST	6
Midlands 2 East North — Midlands 2 East South	7
Midlands 3 East North — Midlands 3 East South	8
Midlands 4 East North — Midlands 4 & 5 East South	9
Midlands 5 East North	10

MIDLANDS

499

MIDLANDS OFFICIALS AND LEAGUE SECRETARIES

Midlands Leagues Organising Committee

Paul Kaminski — **Chairman**
Green Paddocks, 21 Kingsway, Whitchurch. SY13 1EH
Tel: 01948 662536 (H)   01948 662889 (B)   email: kami.rugby@paulkaminski.demon.co.uk

Roger Rees — **Secretary**
2 Wain Close, Alcester, Warwickshire. B49 6LA — North Midlands Rep
Tel 01789 400082   Email rogerwrees@sky.com

Ray Roberts — **Assistant Secretary**
261 Alwyn Road, Rugby, Warwickshire. CV22 7RP — Warwickshire Rep
Tel: 01788 810276 (H)   Fax: 01788 816520   email: rayrobwark@aol.com

Henri Ginvert — **Treasurer**
5 The Paddock, Markfield, Leicestershire. LE67 9RR — Leicestershire Rep
Tel: 01530 242761 (H)   07785 724989 (M)   email: henri.ginvert@btinternet.com

Keith Shurville — **RFU Council**
41 Churchill Avenue, Northampton. NN3 6NY — East Midlands Rep
Tel: 01604 494374 (H)   07721 368477 (M)   email: keith.shurville@emru.co.uk

David Miller — **Notts.Lincs.& Derbys. Rep**
37 Rosemary Drive, Alvaston, Derby. DE24 0TA   Tel:01332 755935 (H)   01332 246689 (B)
Mob: 07976 193344 (Weekday) 07733 116513 (Weekend)   e-mail: milleradmiller@aol.com

David Davies — **Staffordshire Rep**
14,Morris Drive, Kingston Hill, Stafford. ST16 3YE
Tel: 01785 215183 (H)   07974 237482 (M)   email: david.davies207@ntlworld.com

Ex-Officio Members

Bob Taylor — **Ex President RFU**
82 Bridgewater Drive, Northampton. NN3 3AG — East Midlands
Tel: 01604 638626 (H)   07775 800391 (M)   email: robert.taylor@emru.co.uk

Geoff Payne — **Ex RFU Council**
13 Knightly Close, Cubbington, Leamington Spa. CV32 7LB — Warwickshire
Tel: 01926 332840 (H)   01926 812195 (B)
Mob: 07771 731188   Fax: 01926 817401   email: paynegeoff@sky.com

Nicola Russell — **RFU Rugby Registrar**
The RFU Rugby Registrar, PO Box 183, Leicester. LE3 8BZ
Tel: 0116 233 2200 or 2205 (B)   Fax: 0116 233 2204   email: nicola-russell@rfumidlands.demon.co.uk

Midlands Leagues Secretaries

Keith Shurville — **National 3 Midlands**
Details as above

Stuart Hetherington — **Midlands 1 West**
87 Church Lane, Backwell, Bristol. BS48 3JW
Tel: 01275 463902 (H)   07779 126142 (M)   email: shethers@blueyonder.co.uk

Henri Ginvert — **Midlands 1 East**
Details as above

Nigel Banwell — **Midlands 2 West (N)**
16 Riverside Close, Upton-on-Severn. WR8 0JN
Tel: 01684 592046 (H)   07790 730688 (M)   email: nigel.banwell@tesco.net

Keith Dale   Midlands 2 West (S)
14 St. Anthony's Drive, Newcastle, Staffordshire. ST5 2JE
Tel: 01782 615770 (H)

Graham Ashley   Midlands 2 East (N)
2C, Dodington, Whitchurch, Shropshire. SY13 1DZ
Tel:01948 663925   email: gashley@supanet.com

Phil Osborne   Midlands 2 East (S)
Ashthorne, Teeton Road, Ravensthorpe, Northampton. NN6 8EJ
Tel: 01604 770772 (H) Tel: 01327 705785 (B)   email: annaliz.100@virgin.net

Dave Darlington   Midlands 3 West (N)
5 Moreton View, Gyfelia, Wrexham. LL13 0YN
Tel: 01978 842418 (H&B)   07714 659710 (M) email: david@darlington201.fsnet.co.uk

Martin Dolphin   Midlands 3 West (S)
10 Canobie Lea, Madeley, Telford, Shropshire. TF7 5RL
Tel: 01952 684904 (H) 07752 576304 (M)   email: mids4.ws@homecall.co.uk

Steve Allford   Midlands 3 East (N)
12 Hanbury Close, Chesterfield, Derbyshire. S40 4SQ
Tel 01246 297053 (H)   07759 489384 (M)   email: home@steveallford.go-plus.net

Kevan Curtis   Midlands 3 East (S)
21 Potton Road, St. Neots, Huntingdon, Cambs. PE19 2NP
Tel: 01480 390066 (H)   07835 623892 (M)   email: kevin.curtis@ntlworld.com

Mike Townsend   Midlands 4 West (N)
New Road Farm, Hanmer, Whitchurch, Shropshire SY13 3EJ
Tel: 01948 830650 (H&B)   0773 9582185 (M) email: scrum@half.fsbusiness.co.uk

Phil Green   Midlands 4 West (S)
28 Longdon Croft, Copt Heath, Knowle, West Midlands. B93 9LJ
Tel: 01564 777994 (H) 07971 573820 (M)   email: p.g.green@blueyonder.co.uk

Tim Bembridge   Midlands 4 East (N)
16 Davey Close, Boston, Lincolnshire. PE21 9JD
Tel: 07834 902940 (M)   email: timbembridge616@btinternet.com

Chris Rowan   Midlands 4 & 5 East (S)
17 Blethan Drive, Huntingdon, Cambridgeshire. PE29 6GN
Tel: 01480 434959 (H) Tel: 01480 892838 (B)
Fax: 01480 383121 Mob: 07808 184274 email: chris.rowan1@ntlworld.com

Peter Greenow   Midlands 5 West (N)
Hackford House, Dinedor, Hereford. HR2 6PD
Tel: 01432 870874 (H) 07808 336396 (M)   email: petegreenow@btinternet.com

Tim Day   Midlands 5 West (SW)
20 Daffodil Place, Orchard Hills, Walsall. WS5 3DX
Tel: 01922 611729 (H)   07738 220786 (M)   email: timday@tfday.freeserve.co.uk

Ray Roberts   Midlands 5 West (SE)
Details as above

Phil Gordon   Midlands 5 East (N)
Beggars Behind, Main Street, Morton, Nottinghamshire. NG25 0UT
Tel: 01636 831446 (H)   07783 740419 (M)   email: pgrog1@aol.com

Reserve League Secretaries

David Murphy   Ex Midlands 6 East (NE)
The Old Carpenters Arms, 32 High Street,   League Secretary (NLD)
Little Bytham, Grantham, Lincolnshire. NG33 4QX
Tel: 01780 410692 (H)   07879 425058 (M)   email: davhumurphy@tiscali.co.uk

NATIONAL LEAGUE THREE
MIDLANDS

2008-09 LEAGUE TABLE (Midlands 1)

		P	W	D	L	F	A	PD	Pts
1	Broadstreet	22	18	1	3	674	252	422	37
2	Chester	22	15	0	7	529	297	232	30
3	Luctonians	22	15	0	7	418	247	171	30
4	Kenilworth	22	14	1	7	525	325	200	29
5	Peterborough	22	14	0	8	495	346	149	28
6	Newport (Salop)	22	11	3	8	497	379	118	25
7	South Leicester	22	9	2	11	358	388	-30	20
8	Kettering	22	8	1	13	319	498	-179	17
9	Hinckley	22	7	2	13	298	538	-240	16
10	Malvern	22	7	0	15	367	477	-110	14
11	Longton	22	4	2	16	210	609	-399	10
12	Bedford Athletic	22	4	0	18	298	632	-334	8

2009-10 FIXTURES GRID

	Ampthill	Bedford Ath.	Bromsgrove	Hereford	Hinckley	Kenilworth	Kettering	Longton	Luctonians	Luton	Malvern	Newport	Peterborough	S. Leicester
Ampthill		12/09	19/12	26/09	16/01	10/10	30/01	24/10	20/02	27/03	07/11	13/03	28/11	05/09
Bedford Athletic	12/12		26/09	16/01	10/10	30/01	24/10	20/02	07/11	05/09	13/03	28/11	27/03	19/09
Bromsgrove	19/09	09/01		10/10	30/01	24/10	20/02	07/11	13/03	12/12	28/11	27/03	05/09	03/10
Hereford	09/01	03/10	23/01		24/10	20/02	07/11	13/03	28/11	19/09	27/03	05/09	12/12	17/10
Hinckley	03/10	23/01	17/10	13/02		07/11	13/03	28/11	27/03	09/01	05/09	12/12	19/09	31/10
Kenilworth	23/01	17/10	13/02	31/10	06/03		28/11	27/03	05/09	03/10	12/12	19/09	09/01	14/11
Kettering	17/10	13/02	31/10	06/03	14/11	20/03		05/09	12/12	23/01	19/09	09/01	03/10	05/12
Longton	13/02	31/10	06/03	14/11	20/03	05/12	10/04		19/09	17/10	09/01	03/10	23/01	12/12
Luctonians	31/10	06/03	14/11	20/03	05/12	10/04	12/09	19/12		13/02	03/10	23/01	17/10	09/01
Luton	05/12	10/04	12/09	19/12	26/09	16/01	10/10	30/01	24/10		20/02	07/11	13/03	20/03
Malvern	06/03	14/11	20/03	05/12	10/04	12/09	19/12	26/09	16/01	31/10		17/10	13/02	23/01
Newport (Salop)	14/11	20/03	05/12	10/04	12/09	19/12	26/09	16/01	10/10	06/03	30/01		31/10	13/02
Peterborough	20/03	05/12	10/04	12/09	19/12	26/09	16/01	10/10	30/01	14/11	24/10	20/02		06/03
South Leicester	10/04	19/12	16/01	30/01	20/02	13/03	27/03	12/09	26/09	28/11	10/10	24/10	07/11	

YEAR BY YEAR RECORD
THE LAST 10 YEARS

Nos. of Clubs/Games	99-00 17/16	00-01 12/22	01-02 12/22	02-03 12/22	03-04 12/22	04-05 12/22	05-06 12/22	06-07 12/22	07-08 12/22	08-09 12/22
Banbury	6	8	12r							
Barkers Butts	7	9	9	12r						
Bedford Athletic					1p		2	8	6	12
Belgrave	17r									
Broadstreet	5	4	1p		9	11r		4	3	1p
Bromsgrove				8r		7	12r			
Burton	11	11r					11r			
Camp Hill	13	7	11r							
Chester										2
Derby							10r			
Dudley Kingswinford	1p						5	2	12r	
Dunstablians			7	4	4	4	8	3	10r	
Hereford	8	6	10r							
Hinckley	15r			10r						9
Kenilworth	12	5	6	11r					7	4
Kettering					2	2	10r			8
Leicester Lions	4	2	5	5	6	1p				
Lichfield	16r									
Longton	3	3	3	1p		3	(to N1)	6	5	11
Loughborough Students									1p	
Luctonians			4	2	8		6	9	2	3
Luton					12r		4	1p		
Malvern			8	9r						10
Mansfield						12r				
Market Bosworth							7	12r		
Newbold	10	10r								
Newport (Salop)									9	6
Old Laurentians					11r					
Peterborough								10	8	5
Rugby Lions							1p			
Scunthorpe	2	1p			3	6	3	7	11r	
South Leicester								5	4	7
Spalding				6	10r					
Stoke on Trent	9	12r								
Syston	14r									
Walsall			2	7	5	8	9	11r		
Whitchurch				3	7	9	(to N1)			

AMPTHILL & DISTRICT R.U.F.C.

President: David Williams   **Chairman:** Colin Burke   **Treasurer:** Bill Warfield

Hon Secretary: Warren Kay, 20 Park Way, Woburn Sands, Milton Keynes, Bucks MK17 8UH
Tel: (H) 01908 585767   (M) 07768 583 131   Email: secretary@ampthillrufc.com

Fixtures Secretary: Keith Belcher, 64 Hitchin Road, Biggleswade, Beds SG18 9BU
Tel: (H) 01767 316409   Email: keith.belcher1@ntlworld.com

Director of Rugby: Mark Lavery   email: DirectorOfRugby@ampthillrufc.com

Ground Address: Dillingham Park, Woburn Street, Ampthill, Beds MK45 2HX   Tel: 01525 403303
Email: cliff.page@tinyworld.co.uk
Directions: Leave M1 at J13. Left at J13 exit lights, onto A421. Right at next lights (for Ridgemont). In Ridgemont turn left at top of hill onto A507 for Millbrook, Ampthill, Flitwick. Stay on A507 past Millbrook, then turn 1st left for Ampthill (B530, Woburn St). Rugby Club on the Right. Full directions & map available on website.   **Nearest BR station:** Flitwick
Capacity: approx. 500, uncovered standing   **Admission:** None   **Car Parking:** 50-60 cars
Clubhouse: Open 11am-6pm (Sat), 9:30am-3pm (Sun), 6:30pm-10pm (Tue, Wed, Thu). Food is available at weekends. Available for private hire, contact Vic Kaye. Club Steward, on 01525 403303
Club Shop: Open Sun. 09:450am-10:30 & Noon-1pm; Tue, Wed & Thur evenings. Contact Julie Woodward
Programme: Size: A5   Pages: approx 20   Price: £1   **Website:** www.ampthillrufc.com
Founded: 1881   **Nickname:** Amps or A's   **Training Nights:** Tues & Thur 7.30pm.   **Colours:** Maroon & amber

REVIEW OF THE SEASON 2008-09

On and off the field of play Ampthill had a season to remember in 2008-9.

The 1st XV won a Midlands 2 East (W20, L 2) & East Midlands Cup (Peterborough) double, reaching level 5 for the first time in their history while playing in a style which brought plaudits from opposition as well as home supporters.

The 2nd XV (second in East Midlands Merit Table 1), the 3rd XV (third in EMMT 2) and the Vets all had best ever seasons.

Under DoR Mark Lavery, coaches Alan Brown & Stuart Evans and physio Mick Dwyer, Ampthill's senior squad improved beyond recognition, a process likely to continue with the recruitment of Clive Griffiths and Simon Emms to the coaching team for the 2009-10 season.

The girls (U15 & U18) sides went from strength to strength, mini & youth reached record levels of registered players while producing performances which saw the U17s winning the National U17 Bowl at Worcester (the 3rd time in four years that an Amps U17 side had featured on finals day), many youth age groups were winners or runners up in their leagues and/or county cups with record numbers represented Bedfordshire & East Midlands, mini age groups achieved unprecedented success including appearing in all six age group Bedfordshire Festival finals, with the U11s not only winning there but also the regional Land Rover Premiership Cup at Northampton Saints, the East Midlands Mobbs competition at Bedford Blues, the 30 team Seapoint Irish festival and the Gulliver's National final at Twickenham in front of the Guinness Premiership Final crowd!

Off the field the club came to an agreement with a local land owner to purchase a field adjacent to Dillingham Park which will, with the help of the RFU, provide additional playing facilities and solve the most pressing issues preventing further expansion.

Ampthill are looking forward to the coming season's challenge with relish

LAST TEN SEASONS

	Division	P	W	D	L	F	A	P.D.	Pts	Pos
99-00	Mid 2	16	7	1	8	302	264	38	15	8
00-01	Mid 2E	22	5	4	13	310	487	-177	14	10
01-02	Mid2 E	22	11	0	11	457	423	34	22	6
02-03	Mid 2E	22	14	0	8	624	321	303	28	5
03-04	Mid 2E	22	11	1	10	568	528	40	23	5
04-05	Mid 2E	22	8	1	13	442	644	-202	17	9
05-06	Mid 2E	22	3	0	19	248	880	-632	6	12r
06-07	Mid 3ES	22	17	1	4	686	266	420	35	1p
07-08	Mid 2E	22	10	0	12	404	429	-25	20	7
08-09	Mid 2E	22	20	0	2	809	321	488	40	1p

BEDFORD ATHLETIC R.F.C.

Club Chairman	John Donnelly	Tel: 07732 311330 email donnellyja@ntlworld.com
Treasurer	Mr Colin Bennett	Tel: 01234 405196 email: colin.bennett307@ntlworld.co.uk
President / Legal Secretary	Mr Nic Davies	Tel: 01234 216051 email: ndavies@woodfines.co.uk
Club Secretary	Ms. Mandy Andrew	Tel: 07973 665176 email : mandy.andrew@btinternet.com
Fixture Secretary	Mr Jeremy Tyrrell	Tel: 07973 333974 email: jeremy.tyrrell@emru.co.uk
Team Secretary	Mr Michael Bowden	Tel: 07919 228911 email: michael.bowden@veolia.co.uk
Director of Rugby	Mr Val Jones	Tel: 07971 235416 email val78@btopenworld.com
Commercial Manager	Nigel Evans	Tel: 07971 480265 email:Nigel.Evans@espconsult.co.uk
Bar Secretary	Ms. Michelle Wilson	Tel: 07849 167149 email: shelby1985@yahoo.co.uk

Ground Address: Putnoe Wood Club House, Wentworth Drive, Bedford MK41 8QA Tel: 01234 350874
Directions: Leave M1 at J13 and follow A421 to Bedford. Exit at the A428 junction and follow A428 into Bedford. At 1st roundabout turn right into Norse Road, go straight over 3 roundabouts into Wentworth Drive and the clubhouse is on the right hand side just beyond school
Nearest BR station: Bedford Midland Road
Car Parking: Free
Capacity: 500 all uncovered standing
Admission: £5 incl. programme
Clubhouse: Open matchdays & training evenings.
Club Shop: Open matchdays.
Founded: 1908   **Nickname:** 'The Ath'   **Website:** www.bedfordathrugby.co.uk
Colours: Black & white hoops, black shorts & socks.   **Change colours:** Red shirts with black trim, black shorts & socks
Training Nights: Tues & Thur 7pm   **Programme:** Size: A5   Price: with admission

REVIEW OF THE SEASON 2008-09

This was very much a transitional season for Bedford Athletic with a new coach, new director of rugby, new captain and several summer departures on the playing front giving the side a young inexperienced look throughout the campaign. The highlight of a bleak season was the last day victory over Malvern which secured the club's status in the same league for the forthcoming season. In a match that had to be won the team trailed 31-8 with half an hour remaining but superbly marshalled by captain Garry Acton four converted tries saw the side home. However the joy at escaping relegation on the final day must be tempered by the fact that in any other season the club which was well adrift at the bottom of the league would have been relegated a lot earlier and it was thanks to the RFU league reorganisation that survival was even possible. Indeed a club record 12 consecutive competitive defeats was an unwanted record from the season.

Firm steps were taken before the end of the season to lay proper foundations for the forthcoming campaign. Hendry Rheeders the ex Coventry captain has been appointed as Head Coach and will bring with him both National 1 and Currie Cup experience to bolster the side. Several of the successful Colts side from 2007-08 will have benefitted from a year's rugby in the first team and with one or two players joining in key positions, the side should have greater strength in depth. However the increase in the league to 14 sides and the greater number of matches as a result will stretch the meagre resources of clubs like Bedford Athletic and with the number of changes the club has seen, a season of proper consolidation in the new National 3 Midlands would be most welcome.

LAST TEN SEASONS

	Division	P	W	D	L	F	A	P.D.	Pts	Pos
99-00	N2N	26	11	0	15	563	729	-162	22	9
00-01	N3N	*24	8	0	16	386	613	-227	16	10
01-02	N3N	26	10	1	15	599	624	-25	21	10
02-03	N3N	26	10	0	16	497	625	-128	20	11r
03-04	Mid 1	22	18	0	4	648	330	318	36	1p
04-05	N3N	26	6	0	20	468	687	-219	30	14r
05-06	Mid 1	22	19	0	3	617	354	263	*36	2
06-07	Mid 1	22	10	1	11	494	451	43	21	8
07-08	Mid 1	22	11	0	11	496	489	7	22	6
08-09	Mid 1	22	4	0	18	298	632	-334	8	12

BROMSGROVE R.U.F.C.

President: Phillip R Amphlett Tel: 01905 620514
Chairman: Mr M Leech 01527 578959 (H) 01527 879000 (B) 07946 383192 (M) email: mleech@ccsg.uk.com
Club Secretary: Miss Charlotte Wellington, 16 Alcester Road, Finstall, Bromsgrove Worcs. B60 1EJ
Tel 01527 836870 email: charlottewell@aol.com
Fixture Secretary: Andy Potter, Broomstick Cottage, 6 Churchfields Road, Bromsgrove B61 8EB
Tel: 01527 578204 (H), 07816 782500 (B). 07816 782500 (M) email: andypotter1@btinternet.com
Playing Officer: John Blackhall Tel: 0121 445 5881 (H) 07774 992489 (M) email: john@cdpbroms.co.uk
Commercial Officer: Jason Woodbine Tel: 07717 546039   email: jason.woodbine@barrattplc.co.uk
Press Officer: John Berlyn Tel: 0121 445 3011 (H) 07717 274396 (M) email: berlynjohn@googlemail.com
Colts Chairman: Paul Meads Tel: 07971 116604 email: paul.meads@sunlight.co.uk
Minis & Junior Chairman: Paul Wilkinson Tel: 07725 632846 email: paul.wilkinson@hotmail.com
Captain of the Club: Richard Arnold Tel: 07736 475146 email: richard.arnold@allen-ford.com
Ground Address: Finstall Park, Finstall Road, Bromsgrove, Worcs, B60 3DH Tel: 01527 874 690
Brief Directions: Situated between Aston Fields and Finstall on Finstall Road (B4184), Bromsgrove.
Web Address www.bromsgrovefc.co.uk
Colours: White with red/black/red hoops, white shorts.
Training Nights: Tuesday & Thursday 7.15pm.

REVIEW OF THE SEASON 2008-09

What a difference 12 months make. Ending season 2008/9 9th in Midlands Two West, Bromsgrove transformed themselves into League Champions with six weeks to spare! The success was based upon the strong management team of Clare Foster, Owen Sweeting and Mike Jesson, a 10 month professional fitness regime under Chris Hargreaves and physio Anna Curnow that made the team the fittest in the league, a back to basics game plan under coaches Ross Baxter, Duncan Roke and Mark Cornelius and an unbeaten home record for the season.

Add to this the total commitment of a young squad of players who sought to improve themselves at every turn and all the ingredients were there. The team set off at blistering pace stretching to eight straight wins and then maintained the pressure on their competitors with a further eleven wins to secure the league with a home win against Solihull. Central to the success was the league's top try scorer Duncan Roke with 18 tries, Richard Stockholm with 15, Nigel Burrows with 14 and the kicking boots of Ben Copson with 143 for the season. Player of the season Drew Harper at No8 and props Steve Blackburn and Kevin Salisbury plus second row Nick Wright (an ever present) all played huge roles.

The club also underlined its position as one of the biggest junior clubs in the Midlands running a further seven adult sides from U21 to Vets and a youth and mini section of over 400 players from U7-U17. Supported by a pro-active and enthusiastic Executive Committee, the club runs a strong schools' and colleges' community programme working closely with the RFU and the Local Authority.

Charlotte Wellington, Hon. Sec.

LAST TEN SEASONS

	Division	P	W	D	L	F	A	P.D.	Pts	Pos
99-00	Mid 2	16	12	0	4	407	229	178	24	2
00-01	Mid2 W	22	16	2	4	623	232	391	34	3
01-02	Mid 2W	22	21	0	1	894	245	649	42	1p
02-03	Mid 1	22	9	0	13	453	505	-52	18	8r
03-04	Mid 2W	22	20	1	1	712	236	476	41	1p
04-05	Mid 1	22	10	1	11	478	513	-35	21	7
05-06	Mid 1	22	0	0	22	331	891	-560	0	12r
06-07	Mid 2W	22	9	0	13	504	443	61	18	8
07-08	Mid 2W	22	9	1	12	365	477	-112	19	8
08-09	Mid 2W	22	19	0	3	630	314	316	38	1p

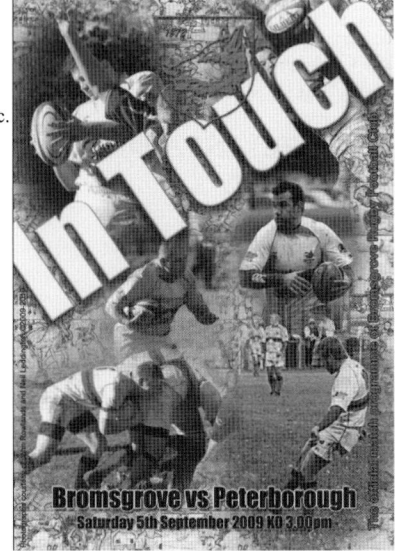

HEREFORD R.F.C.

President: Derek Miles   Tel: 01432 277129   email miles1ss@btinternet.com
Hon. Treasurer: Robin Davies
Chairman: Guy Griffiths, 4 Bullrush Close, Hereford HR1 2SU
Tel: 01432 268906   Fax: 01432 264179   email: guy.griffiths1@btinternet.com
Hon Secretary: Frank Dullehan, 10 Brockington Drive, Tupsley, Hereford
Tel: 01432 355323, 07786 453817 (M)   email: hftdulles@Talktalk.net
Youth & Junior Chair man: Malcolm Harris, Upper Court, Lugwardine, Herefordshire HR1 4AE
Tel: 01432 851170   email: MHatHERE@aol.com
Chairman of Rugby: John Watkins
Ground Address: Belvedere Lane, Wyeside, Hereford HR4 9UT
Contact Tel: 01432 273 410   Email: guy.griffiths1@btopenworld.com
Directions: Full directions and map are available on the website www.herefordrfc.co.uk
Club Shop: Open Saturdays & Sun am when juniors are at home
Formed: 1870   **Colours**: Red & Black   **Website**: www.herefordrfc.co.uk
Nearest BR Station:- Hereford (1.5. miles from ground)   **Car Parking**: free at ground
Capacity: 2000 plus. Covered stand.   **Admission**: £4 with programme. .
Club Shop: Open training nights, match days and Sunday morning.
Training nights:- Senior teams-Tuesday and Thursday evenings at 7.0 pm.
Clubhouse: Food available on match days.
Programme: Editorial & advertisements:- Treasurer Rob Davies or Secretary Frank Dullehan
Sponsorship:- Spencer Goodall   Tel: 01432 275238   email: Spencer.Goodall@btinternet.com

REVIEW OF THE SEASON 2008-09

A successful season, in which the 1st. XV reached the play-offs for the second successive season, thanks to an 11 game undefeated run after Christmas. Ten wins and one draw took the Club into second place in the league and earned a play-off at Scunthorpe which we won by sixteen points to nine.

It was a successful season for the whole Club. The 2nd. XV were runners-up n the North Midlands Reserve League and won the Luctonians Floodlit Cup for the third year in succession.

The 3rd. XV are champions of Worcestershire and Herefordshire League Division Two and won promotion to Division One.

The 4th. XV won the Worcestershire and Herefordshire League Division Three title and were promoted to Division Two

The Junior Section is a continuing success story. This year the Under 17 team were North Midlands (South) League Champions and were runners up in the Midlands final.

We are looking forward to meeting old friends next season.

LAST TEN SEASONS

	Division	P	W	D	L	F	A	P.D.	Pts	Pos
99-00	Mid 1	16	8	1	7	268	273	-5	17	8
00-01	Mid 1	22	10	0	12	330	439	-109	20	6
01-02	Mid 1	22	7	1	14	345	549	-204	15	10
02-03	Mid 2W	*21	11	0	10	443	366	77	22	6
03-04	Mid 2W	22	3	0	19	253	653	-400	6	11
04-05	Mid 3WS	22	16	1	5	493	303	190	33	3
05-06	Mid 3WS	22	17	0	5	776	252	524	34	2p/po
06-07	Mid 3WS	22	20	0	2	726	174	552	40	1p
07-08	Mid 2W	22	17	0	5	522	227	295	34	2
08-09	Mid 2W	22	16	1	5	620	256	364	33	2p/po

Hereford - v - Whitchurch
20th September 2008
Midlands 2 (West)

This year's captain in action against Burton last season.

Kick-Off: 3:00 pm
Entry & Programme: £3.00

HINCKLEY R.F.C.

President: Tom Swain **Treasurer:** Kim Swift
Chairman: John Tilley **Director of Rugby:** Paul Walsh
Contact the above through Secretary
Club Secretary: John Skelton, 146 Coventry Road, Hinckley, Leics. LE10 0JU
Tel: 01455 611322 (H) 07825 019325 (M) Email: hinckleyrugby@yahoo.co.uk
Fixtures Secretary: Wayne Spencer, 52 Welwyn road Hinckley LE10 2GZ
Tel: 01455 634185; 07809 710996 (M) email: wayne.spencer47@ntlworld.com

Ground Address: Hinckley RFC, Leicester Road, Hinckley, Leics LE10 3DR.
Tel: 01455 615010 **Website:** www.hinckleyrugby.co.uk
Directions: **From South via M69 Northbound**: leave at Junction 1 and take the B4109 (Rugby Road) into Hinckley and the A447/B4668 (Leicester Road) signposted to Leicester (A47).
From South/North via A5: take the A47 signposted to Leicester and follow over the north of Hinckley to end of the new road taking the A447/B4688 into Hinckley.
From North via A47: take the B4688 into Hinckley off of the A47 at a major roundabout at the foot of the hill shortly after passing through Earl Shilton.
From North via M69 Southbound: leave at Junction 2 and take the B4669 (Hinckley Road) into Hinckley and the A447/B4668 out of town signposted to Leicester (A47
Nearest BR station: Hinckley.   **Car Parking:** 200
Capacity: Unlimited - all uncovered standing.   **Admission**: Matchday £5 incl. programme
Clubhouse: Open Tues & Thur evenings and all day match days. Hot and cold food available. Available for private hire. Contact Mr John Skelton.
Programme: Size: A5 Pages: 6 Price: with admission.   Advertising: Contact Club Secretary.
Founded: 1893.   **Nickname**: Hincks   **Training Nights**: Tuesday & Thursday 7 pm.
Colours: Black & amber hoops, black shorts, black & amber socks **Change colours**: Maroon or green

REVIEW OF THE SEASON 2008-09

This was our first year back in the top flight of midlands rugby for many seasons. All the players from last season's campaign were retained and some notable new younger players added. Pre season training was well attended and went well.

Our season was really defined in two half's. When the grounds were hard and our young quick back division could run at opposition we played good attacking rugby. This brought about some notable victories and some very close fought narrow defeats.

As we entered the winter months the effect of wetter conditions and bigger packs neutralised this style of play. This led to a string of defeats a situation some of our younger players had not experienced before and a loss of confidence.

As the season came to an end we bounced back with a couple of notable results to steady the nerves.

Overall we were aware of the difficulties that lay ahead in this league and to the players credit the final league position was almost where it was predicted at the beginning of the campaign. Some notable results were achieved and two poor away defeats were conceded. Our ability to compete at this level was confirmed and with a couple of big forward recruits things are looking good.

LAST TEN SEASONS

	Division	P	W	D	L	F	A	P.D.	Pts	Pos
99-00	Mid 1	16	6	0	10	225	259	-34	12	15r
00-01	Mid 2W	22	17	0	5	621	262	359	34	4
01-02	Mid 2E	22	18	2	2	729	188	541	38	1p
02-03	Mid 1	22	8	1	13	475	410	65	17	10r
03-04	Mid 2E	22	19	0	3	609	294	315	38	2
04-05	Mid 2W	22	17	1	4	587	294	293	35	3
05-06	Mid 2W	22	13	1	8	455	417	38	27	3
06-07	Mid 2E	22	11	1	10	468	424	44	23	6
07-08	Mid 2E	22	16	2	4	444	236	208	34	2p/po
08-09	Mid 1	22	7	2	13	298	538	-240	16	9

KENILWORTH R.F.C.

President: Geof Jordan   **Chairman:** Peter Blakeman   **Treasurer:** John Davies
Club Secretary: Willie Whitesmith, 4 Glasshouse Lane, Kenilworth, Warwickshire CV8 2AJ
Tel: (W) 01926 851113   (H) 01926 859 465   email: willie.whitesmith@appliedgeology.co.uk
Fixture Secretary: Dean Stephenson, 13 Gretna Rd, Coventry CV3 6DY
Tel: 0797 4984195   email: deanstephenson@hotmail.com
Team Manager: Pete Lindsay, 07789 753345   email: peter.lindsay@ukngrid.com
Director of Rugby: Dom Carrick   **Coaches:** Mat Davies and Peter Roberts
Ground Address: The Jack Davies Memorial Ground, Glasshouse Lane, Kenilworth, Warwickshire CV8 2AJ
Tel: 01926 853 945   email: krfc@appliedgeology.co.uk
Directions: Take A452 off A46 to large roundabout, 3rd exit onto Birches lane which leads onto Glasshouse Lane. Ground is on southern side of Kenilworth.   **Nearest BR station:** Warwick Parkway, Coventry
Capacity: All uncovered standing   **Admission:** £5   **Car Parking:** Ample
Clubhouse: Closed on Tuesday. Food available on match days only. Function room available contact Ian Hadwin, 07931 908225.   **Club Shop:** Open matchdays and Sun morning. Contact Jenny Maisey
Programme: Size: A5   Price: with admission   Editor: W Whitesmith   Advertising: On aplication
Founded: 1924   **Nickname:** Ken   **Website:** www.kenilworthrugby.co.uk
Colours: Blue with yellow flashes, matching blue shorts   **Change colours:** Black or green shirts
Training Nights: Tuesday & Thursday plus Wednesdays (for third and fourth XV's)

REVIEW OF THE SEASON 2008-09

What a difference a year makes. At the end of season 07/08 Kenilworth played Luctonians in the last game needing a win to ensure survival in Midlands 1. This season second placed Kenilworth travelled to fourth placed Luctonians in the last game knowing a win would see them in the National League play off. The win was cruelly denied when, firstly, a superb penalty effort into the wind fell just short then the try line was denied in the dying minutes despite constant pressure. Ironically a 13-15 defeat meant that neither Luctonians nor Kenilworth made the play off.

It was the disappointing away form that counted in the end, particularly a miserable defeat at Malvern in January, and this needs to be improved if a serious challenge is to be sustained in 2009/10 season.

Whilst the club welcomed many new recruits it was very gratifying to see a large number of ex colts players (8) participating in the first XV squad.

No7 Francis Nock claimed the Player of the Season accolade and, with fellow back row player 'Griz' McGuire, shared the Players Player of the Year award.

The second XV had another successful season and finished second in their league and were cruelly denied another Warwickshire Second XV Cup when a last minute penalty went passed a post leaning at 45°. The third XV/Pirates collected the club's only trophy with a win in the Warwickshire Veterans Double Top competition. The colts played continually through the season and reached the semi final of the Warwickshire Colts cup, narrowly losing to Nuneaton. The Minis & Juniors section had another record breaking season and once again successfully hosted their annual Festival in April.

Season 2009/2010 will see a new coaching set up at Kenilworth following the departure of Ian Fergusson, our most successful coach ever.

LAST TEN SEASONS

	Division	P	W	D	L	F	A	P.D.	Pts	Pos
99-00	Mid 1	16	7	0	9	230	343	-*113	14	12
00-01	Mid 1	22	10	0	12	339	446	-107	20	5
01-02	Mid 1	22	12	0	10	620	434	186	24	6
02-03	Mid 1	22	5	0	17	312	676	-364	*8	11r
03-04	Mid 2W	22	13	0	9	404	391	13	26	5
04-05	Mid 2W	22	12	1	9	584	466	118	25	5
05-06	Mid 2W	22	18	0	4	696	323	373	36	2
06-07	Mid 2W	22	20	0	2	943	210	733	40	1p
07-08	Mid 1	22	10	2	10	503	521	-18	22	7
08-09	Mid 1	22	14	1	7	525	325	200	29	4

MIDLANDS 1
Bedford Athletic
Broadstreet
Chester
Hinckley
Kenilworth
Kettering
Longton
Luctonians
Malvern
Newport
Peterborough
South Leicester

509

KETTERING R.F.C.

President: John Horrell 01832 720645 (H)
Chairman: Len Brookes. 01536 267859 (H/B)   **Treasurer:** Stuart Bonham. 01536 392994 (H)
Club Secretary: Peter May 107, Pytchley Road, Kettering. NN15 6NA
Tel: 01536 415804 (H); 07704 336733 (M) email: secretary@ketteringrugbyclub.co.uk
Fixture Sec. & League Contact: Liz May, 107, Pytchley Road, Kettering. NN15 6NA
Tel: 01536 415804 (H); 01536 310770 (B), 07957 861221 (M) email: fixtures@ketteringrugbyclub.co.uk
Commercial Secretary: Peter May Tel: 01536 415804 (H)
Director of Rugby: Doug Bridgeman 01536 712684 (H)   **Mini/Junior Chairman:** Steve Wilson Tel: 01832 735869
Address: The Clubhouse, Waverley Road, (off Pipers Hill Road), Kettering. Northants. NN15 6NT
Tel.: 01536 485588 (Tel/Fax)   email: secretary@ketteringrugbyclub.co.uk   **Website:** www.ketteringrugbyclub.co.uk
Directions: From A14, take junction 10, follow A6 towards Kettering, at 2nd traffic lights (outside Wicksteed Park) Turn right (Windmill Ave.), then 1st left (Pipers Hill Road) and 1st left again into Waverley Rd, ground is at the end.
Nearest Station: Kettering   **Car Parking:** Free parking on the ground.   **Capacity:** Unlimited uncovered standing
Admission: Matchday: £5 including programme. Season ticket: £50 (a saving of £15)
Clubhouse: Open matchdays, Tues, Wed & Thur evenings and Sundays. Bar snacks are available.
Functions contact Jill Austin-Underwood 01536 485588
Club Shop: Open matchdays, training nights and Sundays. Contact Kerry Newman on 01536 485588
Programme: Size: A5   Pages: 32   Price: With admission   Editorial & Advertising: Peter May Tel: 01536 415804; 07704 336733
Founded: 1875   **Nickname:** 'The Blues'   **Training Nights:** Tues., Wed & Thur.
Colours: Blue & white hoops, blue shorts   **Change Colours:** Red and white shirts

REVIEW OF THE SEASON 2008-09

Lack of 'strength in depth' proved to be Kettering's main problem last season and when injuries to key players happened it took its toll and in a couple of games the effects were devastating. This problem hopefully will be rectified for the new season as twenty six league games will certainly stretch most clubs playing resources over the next eight months in a league where it is difficult to spot an easy game.

Although the side never really looked like being relegation candidates some good performances towards the end of the season made sure that the club would take its place in the new league structure come September.

It was a team effort last season with no outstanding 'stars' but mention must be made of skipper Ryan James whose power play and leadership were sorely missed when he was out injured.

The coaching team lead by Director of Rugby Doug Bridgeman, continued the clubs philosophy of being very fit in order to play an expansive game, but winning the good ball to do this sometimes proved difficult so former Scotland and British Lions hooker Colin Deans has been added to the coaching staff to work on this problem for the new season.

So what about the 2009/10 season? Although a couple of seasoned regulars have retired the squad will have a familiar if young look to it and there are already a number of strong contenders expected to join the squad from the successful Colts side, from other local sides and also from the Southern Hemisphere, so things once again look promising and the whole club is looking forward to its debut season in the new National League 3 Midlands on September 5th

Away from the first team the club continues to prosper on the playing side, still able to put out five sides and a Colts XV most Saturdays, with a Vets side playing once a month

LAST TEN SEASONS

	Division	P	W	D	L	F	A	P.D.	Pts	Pos
99-00	Mid 2	16	11	0	5	343	221	122	22	5
00-01	Mid 2E	22	14	1	7	572	306	266	29	4
01-02	Mid 2E	22	13	1	8	447	368	79	27	4
02-03	Mid 2E	22	18	2	2	622	223	399	40	1p
03-04	Mid 1	22	16	0	6	581	365	216	32	2
04-05	Mid 1	22	16	0	6	628	365	263	32	2
05-06	Mid 1	22	7	0	15	376	562	-186	14	10r
06-07	Mid 2E	22	16	1	5	651	365	286	33	3
07-08	Mid 2E	22	18	1	3	688	260	428	37	1p
08-09	Mid 1	22	8	1	13	319	498	-179	17	8

LONGTON R.F.C.

President: Terry Keeling **Chairman**: Mick Wheat email: mick.wheat@sky.com
Treasurer: Martin Hamer, 26, Beech Avenue, Worcester, WR3 8PZ
01905 759992 email phoenix15@talktalk.net
Secretary: John Till, Weston Barn, Bowers Court, Standon, Staffordshire, ST21 6JQ
01782 791120 email: secretary@longtonrugby.co.uk
Fixture Secretary: Tom Derrington, 12 Irvine Rd., Werrington, Stoke-on-Trent ST9 0DR
01782 258489 (H) 07788 900506 (M) email: fixtures@longtonrugby.co.uk
Team Secretary: Tony Wheat 07835876751 (m) email: anthony.wheat@staffsmoorlands.gov.uk
Commercial Manager: Martin Hamer, 26, Beech Avenue, Worcester, WR3 8PZ
01905 759992 email phoenix15@talktalk.net
Director of Rugby: Tony Wheat, contact details as above
Head of Junior Rugby: Doug Finney, email dcfinney@btinternet.com
Ground: Eastern Rise, off Sir Stanley Matthews Way, Trentham Lakes, Stoke-on-Trent ST4 8GR
Directions: Leave M6 at Jn 15 onto A500, then A50, take first exit onto Trentham Lakes . Follow Sir Stanley Matthews way to first set of lights and turn left. **Nearest BR station**: Stoke-on-Trent **Car Parking**: 180 spaces at the ground
Capacity: 500 - all uncovered standing **Admission**: Matchday: £4 Season Ticket: £40
Clubhouse: New clubhouse now open. 6 ensuite changing rooms, Members bar and function Room. Open Tues, Wed, Thurs and Saturday plus as required. Functions: 150 max; Contact Clubhouse Manager 01782 594016
Founded: 1952 **Previous Name**: Old Longtonians until 1994 **Training Nights**: Tuesday & Thursday
Colours: Black & amber, black shorts **Change colours**: Blue, black shorts **Website**: www.longtonrugby.co.uk
Programme: Size: A5 Pages: Varies Price: with admission Advertising: contact Commercial manager

REVIEW OF THE SEASON 2008-09

Last season was a time of major change and adjustment at Longton following relocation to their impressive new headquarters at Trentham Fields. Much time and effort was spent by managing the transition from Roughcote Lane, arguably to the detriment of the playing side.

On field it proved to be Longton's most challenging season yet in Midlands 1 with most of the previous season's back division leaving; four moved to National league sides with another three moving due to relocation. The situation was made worse by a lengthy injury list.

As such, over 50 players represented the 1st.XV during the season, including seven different scrum halves and seven fly halves. Inevitably, the team found it difficult to establish any consistency in their performance, especially as many of the players brought in were young and inexperienced at this level. There was further disruption when it was decided to change the coach, which also resulted in a new support team coming in for the latter part of the season. These changes have now been made with former first team stalwarts, Tony Wheat and Neil Smith, heading up the Management Team, with Craig Wilson as Head Coach. The new team have been busy drawing up plans for next season and it is anticipated that the playing strength will be improved.

Longton Ladies gained in numbers and strength towards the latter part of the season and with the return of the influential Gemma Hughes from long-term injury, prospects look good for the forthcoming season.

LAST TEN SEASONS

	Division	P	W	D	L	F	A	P.D.	Pts	Pos
99-00	Mid 1	16	11	0	5	336	262	74	22	3
00-01	Mid 1	22	15	3	4	545	255	290	33	3
01-02	Mid 1	22	14	0	8	519	434	85	28	3
02-03	Mid 1	22	19	1	2	648	212	436	39	1p
03-04	N3N	26	1	3	22	300	647	-347	5	14r
04-05	Mid 1	22	15	0	7	625	347	278	30	3
05-06	North 1	22	7	1	14	330	406	-78	15	10
06-07	Mid 1	22	12	0	10	372	405	-33	*22	6
07-08	Mid 1	22	12	0	10	373	407	-34	24	5
08-09	Mid 1	22	4	2	16	210	609	-399	10	11

Another bonus of the new facilities has been a rapid growth of the Junior Section under the guidance of Doug Finney and Mick Hibbert. It is anticipated that numbers will rise to around 200 from a figure of just over 40 only twelve months ago and with a good group of coaches in place exciting times lie ahead.

On reflection, it was far from a disastrous season with the 1st.XV maintaining their Midlands 1 status and winning the Staffordshire Cup for the fourth year running; the 2nd.XV finishing runners up in their Merit Table and the 3rd.XV winning theirs.

LUCTONIANS R.F.C.

Hon. President: David Burke   **Hon. Chairman:** Richard Powell   **Hon. Treasurer:** John Langley
Fulltime Administrator: Simon Green-Price c/o Club Office, Luctonians RFC as below
01568 709 080, 01568 708 169 inc Fax, 07967 806 678 email: cluboffice@luctonians.co.uk
Hon. Secretary: Mrs Julia Higgs c/o Luctonians Sports Club , Mortimer Park, Leominster HR6 9SB   Tel 01568 70 90 80
Fixtures Secretary: Simon Green-Price, as above
Director of Rugby: Simon Green-Price
Commercial Secretary: Tracy Fellows   07813 813 008
Chairman Youth Sport: Hugh Black Tel: 01568 611546 (H), 07966 237 818 (M) email: hugh.black@mdc.org.uk
Ground Address: Mortimer Park, Hereford Road, Kingsland, Leominster, Herefordshire. HR6 9SB
Tel: 01568 709080   Fax: 01568 708169   email: cluboffice@luctonians.co.uk
Directions: 4 miles north west of Leominster. On the side of the A4110 at the western end of Kingsland.
Car Parking: Plenty at ground   **Nearest BR Station**: Leominster   **Capacity**: Unlimited.   Covered seating: 22
Admission: Matchday - £5 including programme. No season tickets available.
Clubhouse: Open Sat, Sun, training nights. Food available. For private hire contact Tracy Fellows 07813 813008
Club Shop: Ring Clubsport 01544 231351. Contact Simon Hussey
Programme: Size: A5   Price: incl. with admission   Pages: 40   Editorial & Advertising: Dave Burke 07789 560252
Founded: 1948   **Training Nights:** Tuesday & Thursday 7.30pm   **Nickname**: 'Lucs'   **Website**: luctonians.co.uk
Colours: Black & white hoops, black shorts, b & w hooped socks   **Change colours**: Green

REVIEW OF THE SEASON 2008-09

A third place finish in the league and the retention of the North Mids Cup would spell success in most people's vocabulary but there was a tinge of disappointment at Luctonians as the goal of promotion again slipped by.

Lucs were flying high at Christmas, sitting on top of Midlands One with ten victories which included an away win over Broadstreet who would eventually win the league with something to spare. But the Christmas and New Year's break together with a January frost meant there had been a four week break when matches resumed and Lucs discovered that they had inexplicably lost their pre-Christmas form and momentum. Four losses in the next five matches meant that the team was playing catch up rugby from then on and was depending on the results of other matches to further their cause. They rallied strongly in March however and won five out of the remaining six but the loss of form in January and February was their undoing.

In the last match of the season the runners up spot was still available but a victory over second placed Kenilworth was of no avail as Chester also won on the day and pipped Lucs for the runners up spot with a better points for and against record. But Chester's fate in the play off match indicated that Lucs would have been unlikely to have survived had they gained promotion. Winning Midlands One with a few games in hand and a strengthening of the first team squad would be the minimum requirements for moving up a level and staying there.

The league statistics show that Lucs had the best defensive record but failed to match this in the points for department scoring only 57 tries (6th best) and lacking a first line goal kicker. The forwards however more than held their own with a tight front five and a competent back row where number 8 Paul Hulland was Lucs' top try scorer with 12. There is plenty of room for optimism however and the retention of Viv Wooley as Coach Co-ordinater for next season puts the first piece of the jigsaw in place.

Lucs had their day in the sun in May when they embarked upon their almost annual pilgrimage to Stourbridge where they won the North Mids Cup for the fourth time in five years with a victory over DK. There was good news on other fronts too. The second XV won the North Midlands Reserve League for the second season and both the Colts and the Under 16's won their North Mids Plate finals. The new floodlights were switched on in November and the Lucs' banner was flown overseas with the Colts visiting Spain and the usual eclectic mob of wrinklies enjoying their annual jaunt to the Hong Kong Sevens where they saw Luctonian Dan Woodside representing the West Indies.

A Lucs party of 25 is presently being kitted out with South Wales Borderers uniforms and will support the Lions in South Africa. It doesn't get much better than that.

Huw Davie.

LAST TEN SEASONS

	Division	P	W	D	L	F	A	P.D.	Pts	Pos
99-00	Mid 2	16	12	0	4	364	220	144	24	3
00-01	Mid 2W	22	18	1	3	522	251	271	37	2p
01-02	Mid 1	22	13	1	8	421	327	94	27	4
02-03	Mid 1	22	18	0	4	568	273	295	36	2
03-04	Mid 1	22	13	0	9	536	392	144	*22	8
04-05	Mid 1	22	13	2	7	451	392	59	28	5
05-06	Mid 1	22	12	0	10	393	388	5	24	6
06-07	Mid 1	22	10	1	11	412	393	19	21	9
07-08	Mid 1	22	13	2	7	557	254	303	28	2
08-09	Mid 1	22	15	0	7	418	247	171	30	3

LUTON R.F.C.

President: Phil Wilson   **Chairman**: Keith Butten   **Treasurer**: Pete Wardley
Club Secretary: Rob Thomas, 46, Redwood Glade, Leighton Buzzard, Beds LU7 3JT
Tel: 01525 374175   email: rob.thomas@lutonrugby.com
Fixture Secretary: Jimmy Hanahan, 7 St Johns Close, Luton, Beds. LU1 5PG.
Tel: 07806 716312   email: fixtures@lutonrugby.com
Director of Rugby: Denis Ormesher   **First Team Manager**: Mark Turner   **Physio**: Dean Payne
Address: Newlands Road, Luton, Beds LU1 4BQ   Tel: 01582 720355   email: info@lutonrugby.com
Directions: M1, J10 up to roundabout. Turn right at r'about along the A1081 to Harpenden. Tale first right into Newlands Road and the clubhouse is approx. 2 miles on the left..
Capacity: 2000   Covered Standing: 200   **Nearest Station**: Luton Parkway   **Car Parking**: 500
Admission: Matchday £5 including programme.   Season: N/A
Clubhouse: Open 11-11. Food is available on matchdays only.   Marquee and Newlands Rooms - Conferences, weddings, social, meetings (capacity up to 300). Contact Mark Bierton, Luton Rugby club
Club Shop: Open Sundays and 1st XV home match days. Contact Linda Butten
Formed: 1931   **Colours**: Green (predominantly), red & white   **Change colours**: White (predominantly), green & red.
Brand Name: Lutonians   **Training Nights**: Tuesday & Thursday   website: www.lutonrugby.com
Programme: Size: A5   Pages: 32   Editorial & Advertising: Keith Butten

REVIEW OF THE SEASON 2008-09

After relegation from national league in the previous season, Luton had a satisfying first season in a very strong London Division One. Luton club were level transferred to London from the Midlands due to an imbalance in number of teams in the leagues. Ironically, it resulted in Luton playing some teams that, in the era of friendlies before leagues were introduced, were regular fixtures e.g. Old Albanians, Bishops Stortford, Hertford.

The pre season progressed very well with 3 impressive wins, one of which was against National 3 side, Rosslyn Park. The season also started well with four straight wins. In the fifth match away at Bishops Stortford, having played the last 30 minutes with 14 players due to injuries, a last minute penalty denied them a win a deserved win. The defeat, immediately followed by a defeat at home to Hertford, took away the momentum from the promising start to the season. The rest of the season was a mix of highly competitive and indifferent performances. There were hard earned wins against North Walsham, Sutton and Bishops Stortford and, one of the best performances away at League winners, Shelford, when Luton almost scored a winning try with the last move of the match. However, the good performances were mixed with disappointing performances away to Portsmouth, Tring and Hertford.

There were many positive signs from the season on which the club can build for this season. The team were well led by ex Bedford and Northampton centre, Matt Allen. There were very encouraging performances from several new and young players which should provide a strong basis to build for next season. Player of the year, Mark Kohler, proved a dangerous runner against the best teams, Pepe Nanci capped a good all round season with selection for East Midlands, U20 players Tom Wilmore and Daryl Veedendaal made impressive contributions.

Director of Rugby, Denis Ormesher, in his first year at the club, brought a professional approach from his previous club, Bedford. He introduced many changes to team organisation, training and coaching, and player development at all levels in the club. It will provide many of the building blocks for progress of the club this season and in the future.

LAST TEN SEASONS

	Division	P	W	D	L	F	A	P.D.	Pts	Pos
99-00	Mid E1	16	15	0	1	585	161	424	30	2
00-01	Mid 2E	22	15	1	6	510	264	246	31	3
01-02	Mid 2E	22	7	3	12	398	432	-34	17	9
02-03	Mid 2E	22	18	1	3	712	301	411	37	2p
03-04	Mid 1	21	1	1	19	219	767	-548	*1	12r
04-05	Mid 2E	22	20	0	2	791	258	533	40	1
05-06	Mid 1	22	13	0	9	700	397	303	26	4
06-07	Mid 1	22	15	1	6	626	294	332	31	1p
07-08	N 3N	26	2	0	24	380	821	-441	16	14r
08-09	Lon 1	22	10	1	11	484	552	-68	*19	7

MALVERN R.U.F.C.

President: Ray Gillard **Chairman:** Martin S Pocock **Treasurer:** John E Tavener
Club Secretary: Bill Pomeroy, 50, Barnards Green Rd., Malvern Worcs. WR14 3LW
Tel: 01684 562279(H) 07980 302802 (Ml) email: secretary@malvernrfc.co.uk
Fixture Secretary: Brian Howells, 2, Bluebell Close, Ryall, Upton-on-Severn, Worcs WR8 0PP
Tel: 01684 594299(H); 07817 297731 (M) email: brian.howells4@btinternet.com`
Director of Rugby: David I Robins Tel: 07877 309441 (M)
Commercial Secretary: Tony Brook Tel: 07885 841553
Ground Address: Spring Lane, Malvern, Worcs WR14 1AJ Tel: 01684 573728
Directions: A449 South from Worcester (8 miles). At 1st set of traffic lights in Malvern Link turn left into Spring Lane. Club is 400m on right **Nearest BR station:** Malvern Link **Car Parking:** Limited on ground.
Capacity: Unlimited uncovered standing. **Admission:** Matchday by programme (£5)
Clubhouse: Open 7–11pm weekdays & 12–11pm on Saturdays. Food available matchdays only.
Available for function hire. Contact Jayne Payne at clubhouse number.
Club Shop: Open Saturday 12:00 - 2:00, Sundays 10:00 - 12:00. Contact Commercial Sec.
Programme: Size: A5 Pages: 12 Price: £5 Advertising: Contact Commercial Secretary, see above
Founded: 1934 **Website:** www.malvernrfc.co.uk **Training Nights:** Tuesday & Thursday
Colours: Maroon, light blue, gold edging **Change colours:** Light blue, maroon, gold edging

REVIEW OF THE SEASON 2008-09

Having gained promotion to Midlands One, Malvern had a terrible start to the season, a vast crop of injuries contributing to a sequence of nine league defeats and over thirty players featuring in those games.

The turning point came in the Intermediate Cup, where Malvern hosted holders Chester and comprehensively outplayed them for a first victory of the season. A more settled team and growing confidence saw the young Worcestershire side begin to win league games, first taking the scalps of other lowly placed sides, then upping the game considerably by beating high flyers Kenilworth and Peterborough.

As the season progressed, so did the standard of play and eventual champions Broadstreet were given a close call on their own turf by an impressive Malvern display. The game flourished throughout the club, the second team, although often depleted by first XV call-ups, finishing high up in the North Midlands Reserve League, whilst the 3rds won promotion in the Hereford and Worcester Merit Table with some impressive performances from a mixture of old heads and raw young talent.

Malvern's Youth Section continues to flourish and season 2009/10 will see the first steps towards establishment of a Malvern Rugby Academy, which will bridge the gap between youth and senior rugby. Like many clubs, Malvern have struggled to field colts teams in the last few years, but working with local schools and developing the existing Youth section should bring about the desired result – a constant feed of home grown talent through to the adult sides.

With excellent facilities being constantly improved at Spring Lane, Malvern RFC looks forward to a successful season in National Three Midlands and throughout the playing strength, senior and junior.

LAST TEN SEASONS

	Division	P	W	D	L	F	A	P.D.	Pts	Pos
99-00	Mid 2	16	15	0	1	552	208	344	28	1
00-01	Mid 2W	22	19	2	1	595	239	356	40	1p
01-02	Mid 1	22	11	0	11	482	467	15	22	8
02-03	Mid 1	22	9	0	13	465	539	-74	18	9r
03-04	Mid 2W	22	15	0	7	628	438	190	30	3
04-05	Mid 2W	22	18	1	3	691	248	443	37	2
05-06	Mid 2W	22	8	2	12	410	446	-36	18	9
06-07	Mid 2W	22	12	1	9	562	462	100	25	6
07-08	Mid 2W	22	17	1	4	591	303	288	35	1p
08-09	Mid 1	22	7	0	15	367	477	-110	14	10

NEWPORT (SALOP) R.U.F.C.

President: Andrew Watson-Jones **Treasurer:** Mark Atkinson
Chairman: Andrew Watson Jones, Howle Manor , Sambrook , Newport Shropshire TF10 8AY
01952 550308 (H&B)   07836 572064 (M); email: awj1@btconnect.com
Club Secretary: Chris Wilde, 12 Wordsworth Close Priorslee Telford Shropshire TF2 9 NR
0797 495 6848   email: chris.p.wilde@hotmail.co.uk
Fixture Secretary: Mike Redwood, Harebutts Cottage, Waters Upton, Telford Shropshire TF6 6PD
01952 541458 or 0798 9979424 (M)   email: mredwood@hotmail.com
Chair of Rugby: Ray Price, 25 Vineyard Road, Newport, Shropshire TF10 7HZ
Tel 01952 406878, 07834 037615 (M)
Club Coach: Ian Bletcher

Ground Address: The Old Showground, Forton Road, Newport, Shropshire TF10   Tel: 01952 810021
Directions: From M54 Junction 3 turn right and follow A41 to Newport. Take Newport by pass and then on third island on by pass turn left (A519) towards home. Club turning is 200 meters on right hand side
Nearest BR station: Stafford (Mainline, 14 miles) or Telford (8 miles).   **Car Parking:** Ample
Capacity: Unlimited uncovered standing.   **Admission:** TBA   **Club Shop:** Open on matchdays.
Clubhouse: Open on matchdays. Light refreshments available. Available for private hire. Contact: David Turner, Bar Secretary, Toads Castle, The Common, Edgmond Newport TF10 8ES Tel 01952 812229 (H)
Founded: 1946   **Nickname:** The Fishes   **Website:** www.thescrummage.co.uk
Colours: Maroon and white hooped shirts.   **Change colours:** None   **Training Nights:** Tuesday & Thursday

REVIEW OF THE SEASON 2008-09

Newport's second season in Midlands 1 was eagerly awaited by all at the club. A new club Captain in Craig Ingram eager to build on our success of the previous season. Although we were reduced in squad size by retirement and players leaving for various reasons, to the tune of nine 1st team squad members, we had recruited a new lock from Walsall, Steve Foulkes and joining his twin brother already a Newport player, Matthew Curgenven an exciting centre who looked very promising in training.

We had also secured the continued services of New Zealand prop Morgan Sikanen and South African back row, Lodewikus Van Staden. Both of whom played an enormous part in the continued success during the new season. Coming back to the club after university was Toby Mann, a superb scrum half who was to play at full back for most of the season.

Two weeks prior to our first league game, the club however were dealt a big setback with the resignation of our club Coach for personal reasons to do with club direction , strategy and authority. A training injury ruled our new lock, Steve Foulkes out for the whole season. This was a start we did not envisage and resulted in the whole squad digging deep, but come the start of the league season and our first game against Peterborough at home, Newport were up for it and ground out an excellent win. Watching the game was Ian Bletcher, RFU Coaching Development Manager, who expressed an interest in taking over the coaching role at Newport. Fortunately Ian was impressed with what he saw and decided to take on the position after two training sessions, on a permanent basis. This was to prove as the season unfolded, an excellent choice as Ian pushed us forward to play some, if not the best, Midlands 1 rugby seen during the whole of the season.

A league position of 2nd place at Christmas and another EDF cup run after wins at Sutton Coldfield and Mansfield, saw Newport on a playing high. The new coach and rejuvenated team spirit reaping excellent results.

Come the new year, a further EDF win at home against Maidenhead had Newport in the quarter finals at Sheffield Tigers. Our league form however, took a dip as injuries and unavailabilities resulted in some setbacks due to the very small squad Newport were operating with. We dropped to a comfortable 6th place in the league where we were to finish the season. An EDF cup exit at Sheffield with some noticeable player absentees was a disappointing result especially in front of our superb, much travelled Newport supporters who virtually out numbered their Sheffield counterparts.

In all a season to be remembered and one the club should be proud of. All the players are to be congratulated on their commitment and performances for the whole season. Our new 1st team Manager, Gareth Davies especially for his devotion to ensuring all comes together on a Saturday.

Well done and we look forward to the 2009/2010 season in our new look league set up.

LAST TEN SEASONS

	Division	P	W	D	L	F	A	P.D.	Pts	Pos
99-00	Mid 2	16	9	0	7	419	253	166	18	6
00-01	Mid 2W	22	7	1	14	376	601	-225	15	8
01-02	Mid 2W	22	1	0	21	188	856	-668	2	12r
02-03	Mid 3WN	18	2	2	14	211	455	-244	6	10r
03-04	Mid 4WN	18	15	0	3	523	202	321	30	2p/po
04-05	Mid 3WN	22	19	1	2	622	230	392	39	2p/po
05-06	Mid 2W	22	12	2	8	425	399	26	26	4
06-07	Mid 2W	22	17	1	4	692	266	426	35	2p/po
07-08	Mid 1	22	10	1	11	437	443	-6	21	9
08-09	Mid 1	22	11	3	8	497	379	118	25	6

515

PETERBOROUGH R.U.F.C.

President: Eddie Hein   Tel: 01780 783322 (h)   email: president@prufc.com
Chairman: Neil Pretsell   Tel: 07738 706606 (m)   email: chairman@prufc.com
Club Secretary: Paul Gardner, 10 Lawn Avenue, Peterborough, PE1 3RB
   Tel: 01733 766617 (h), 01733 569413 (f), 07595 020634 (m) email: secretary@prufc.com
Fixture Secretary & Director of Rugby: Paul Freeman   Tel: 07525 726931 (m)   email: pfreeman@prufc.com
Club Coach: Darian Uys   Tel: 07852 180418 (m) email: duys@prufc.com
General Manager: Nigel Cook   Tel: 07808 887833 (m), email: ncook@prufc.com
Mini & Junior Chairman: Darren King   Tel: 07960 870126, email: dking@prufc.com
Club Development Officer: Debbie Beecham   Tel: 07939 098569 (m), email: sponsorship@prufc.com
Ground Address: Second Drove, Fengate, Peterborough PE1 5XA   Tel/Fax: 01733 569413   email: enquiries@prufc.com
Directions: From the north or south follow A1 to junction with A1139. From the west (A47), join the A1 (south) at Wansford and follow to junction with A1139. From the east (A47) follow to junction with A1139. Follow A1139 to junction 5 (Showcase cinema & Halfords). Take the exit signposted Fengate (before Halfords). At next roundabout (Wickes on right) take 3rd exit. At the sharp left hand bend turn right. First Left into 2nd Drove, signposted rugby club. Our ground is at the bottom of the road.
Nearest BR station:Peterborough   **Car Parking**: 200
Capacity: 1,000 Covered Seating: 150   **Admission**: Matchday £5 including programme   Season: £45
Clubhouse: Open matchdays, training nights & Sundays. Bar snacks available. Functions contact Nigel Cook 07808 887833.
Club Shop: Open as clubhouse, contact Nigel Cook or Paul Gardner
Programme: Size: A5   Pages: 20   Price: With admission.   Editor: Paul Gardner   Advertising: Page £100 for season.
Founded: 1868, re-formed 1924   **Nickname**: Borough   **Website**: www.prufc.com
Colours: Red, gold & silver   **Change colours**: Navy with red, gold & silver hoops   **Training Nights**: Tues & Thurs.(seniors)

REVIEW OF THE SEASON 2008-09

What a season!! It coughed and spluttered into life as players and coaches adjusted to the requirements of the ELVs and each other. At one point we didn't look as if we would ever win away. As soon as we did we surrendered our home record! Time to have a sit down and chat about where we can improve! Eight wins from eight matches beating the top four sides along the way confirms the saying that "it's great to talk". All good things must come to an end and a couple of poor games halted this great run, but two wins from the last three games allowed us to complete our best ever league season.

The new coaching team of Richard Mardling and Jon Phillips was joined by Jon's brother Chris, who had a very successful year as coach of the 2nd XV. More games than ever have been played on the 'Mound' on training nights developing skills and decision making, and each Saturday is videoed and feedback provided to each player.

The success of any 1st XV is predicated upon the success of its supporting sides and this year the X-Men (4th XV) won their Merit Table, the 3rd XV (average age of 21) came second in their Merit Table and the 2s went one better than last year and won their Merit table. Furthermore, a total of 16 players were selected for the East Midlands squad that competed in the end of season county championship.

This coming season Paul Cook leads the 1st XV for the fifth successive season, taking us into new territory as the leagues have been re-organised, with our league gaining 2 extra teams.

Unfortunately we are losing a couple of influential players this summer due to work commitments, but old faces are returning after playing at higher levels and the club's development programme has brought through more youngsters into the 1st XV squad. Roll on September!

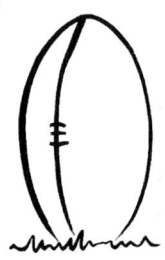

LAST TEN SEASONS

	Division	P	W	D	L	F	A	P.D.	Pts	Pos
97-98	Mid E1	16	8	0	8	336	268	68	16	7
98-99	Mid E1	16	6	0	10	319	363	-44	12	11
99-00	Mid 3ES	18	9	0	9	399	332	67	18	5
00-01	Mid 3ES	18	8	1	9	302	247	55	17	7
01-02	Mid 3ES	18	15	0	3	541	235	306	30	2
02-03	Mid 3ES	18	15	1	2	567	198	369	31	2
03-04	Mid 2E	22	18	0	4	737	334	403	36	3
04-05	Mid 2E	22	19	1	2	889	263	626	39	2
05-06	Mid 1	22	10	1	11	406	469	-63	21	10
06-07	Mid 1	22	11	0	11	451	512	-61	22	8
07-08	Mid 1	22	14	0	8	495	346	149	28	5

SOUTH LEICESTER R.U.F.C.

President: Peter Bale **Chairman**: tbc
Finance Chairman: Terry Bryan **Club Captain**: Len Fincham
Sponsorship Manager: Stewart/Wayne Marsden **Membership Secretary**: Robin Bosworth
Director of Rugby: Ian Smith **Mini & Junior Chairman**: Geoff. Brookes
Club Secretary: Brian Kirkpatrick 7, Penclose Road, Fleckney, Leicester. LE8 8TE
Tel 0116 2403 334 (H) 07967936339 (M) e-mail brian@bgkservices.co.uk
Fixture Secretary: Bob Colyer, 104, Overpark Avenue, Leicester LE3 1NL Tel: 0116 254 4863
Ground Address: Welford Road Ground, Wigston, Leicester LE18 1TE Tel: 0116 288 2066
Directions: M1/M69 Junction 21 head east on ring road towards Oadby and Wigston.
Turn right on the A50 towards Northampton. The Ground entrance is off the layby just beyond the final roundabout as you leave the built up area of Wigston. **Nearest BR Station**: South Wigston
Car Parking: Spaces for 75 cars plus a large lay by at the Clubhouse entrance.
Admission: Matchday - £5 including programme. Season ticket not available.
Clubhouse: For Bar opening and Clubhouse letting contact Jason Pinnock at the Clubhouse or mobile 07974 139579
Club Shop: Open training nights and weekends as well as being accesible through the web site.
Programme: No programme available. Considering producing one for the 06-07 season.
Founded: 1919 **Nickname**: 'South' **Website**: www.southleicesterrugby.com
Colours: Green & white hoops **Change colours**: Blue **Training Nights**: Monday & Wednesday

REVIEW OF THE SEASON 2008-09

South's season was one of consolidation although a little disappointing compared with the previous season's fourth place Midlands One finish. Although we retained the Leics County Cup against Hinckley (the only club to achieve back to back victories, following our 2008 success against Loughborough Students, in the long history of that competition).

South were inconsistent throughout. Losing three key members of last season's pack to the French Federal 2 league, Loughborough Students and Dorset respectively. Long term injuries to some key players, some coach rejigging, the unhelpful ELVs and the windy conditions that seemed to prevail throughout the season, both home and away, didn't help the cause.

Victories were achieved against all the clubs in the division with exception of the top two (Broadstreet and Chester) and inexplicably Kettering after dominating in both matches. Excellent victories at Luctonians and Peterborough were the away day highlights while Newport, Hinckley and Kenilworth victories brought cheer to the home faithful. Two away draws at Longton and Hinckley saw South break new ground in the league never before having drawn a game.

Fly half Mark Lord was top scorer with 254 points while winger Matt Thomas was top try scorer with 8 tries. Scrum half/Full back Kris McFredries was voted most valuable player of the season while hooker Dom Green gained the most improved player of the season award.

LAST TEN SEASONS

	Division	P	W	D	L	F	A	P.D.	Pts	Pos
98-99	Mid E2	16	15	0	1	513	131	382	30	2p
99-00	Mid E1	16	10	0	6	467	260	207	20	6
00-01	Mid 3ES	18	18	0	0	707	161	546	36	1p
01-02	Mid 2E	22	15	1	6	603	333	270	31	3
02-03	Mid 2E	22	15	2	5	734	305	429	32	4
03-04	Mid 2E	22	16	0	6	577	416	161	32	4
04-05	Mid 2E	22	10	2	10	479	392	87	22	5
05-06	Mid 2E	22	20	1	1	627	233	394	41	1p
06-07	Mid 1	22	11	0	11	587	463	124	22	5
07-08	Mid 1	22	12	0	10	416	360	56	24	4
08-09	Mid 1	22	9	2	11	358	388	-30	20	7

A total of twelve South players represented Leicestershire in their County Championship Shield campaign retaining Leics place in that competition for next season with victory over Cumbria and losses versus eventual winners Cheshire and North Midlands.

South now look forward to the extra games in National League 3 Midlands, bonus points and above all the return of the rolling maul.

MIDLANDS PHOTO CALL

Bromsgrove Rugby Football Club.
1st Team Squad 2008/2009
Midlands Two West Champions

Back Row: Chris Morgan, Dan Ingram, Nick Wright, Manny Samra, Sam Stiley, James Lloyd Jones, Steve Blackburn
Middle Row: Owen Sweeting (Asst Mngr), Anna Curnow (Physio), Sam Lofthouse, John Ward, Nigel Burrows, Tom Solomo, Kevin Foster, Drew Harper, Ben Copson, Warren Oliver, Chris Danks, Ross Baxter(Head Coach), Clare Foster (Mngr), Duncan Roke (Player/Coach)
Front Row: Richard Stockholm, Chris Hurcombe, Nick Copson, Richard Arnold (Captain),Mark Cornelius, Dan Quinn, Kevin Salisbury

Kenilworth RFC 2008-09

An aerial view of LUCTONIANS

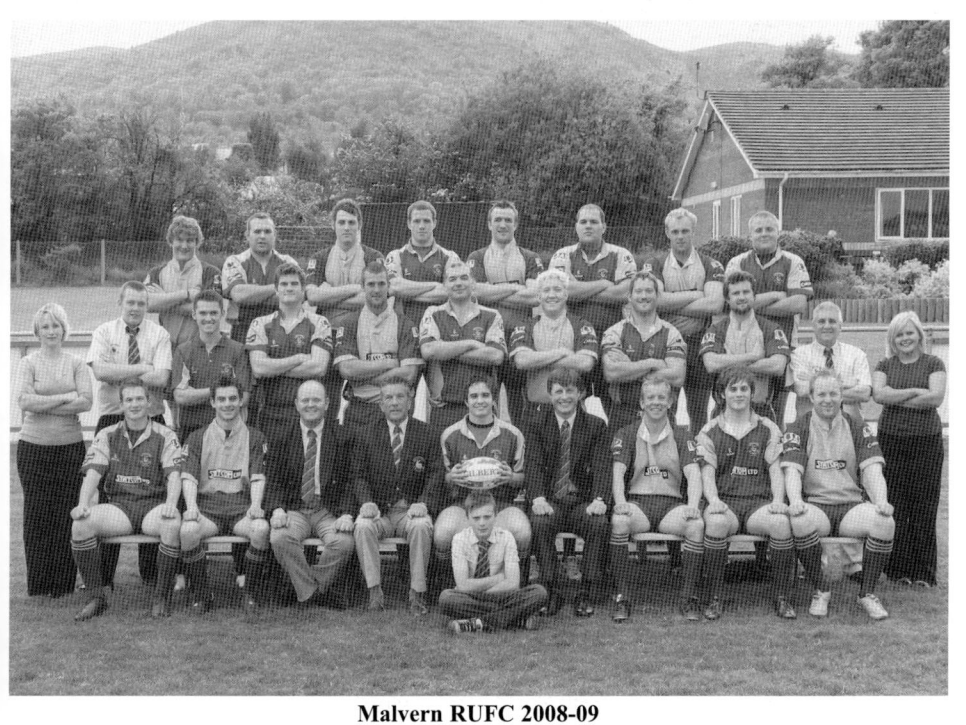

Malvern RUFC 2008-09

MIDLANDS PHOTO CALL

Newport (Salop) RFC 2008-09

PETERBOROUGH

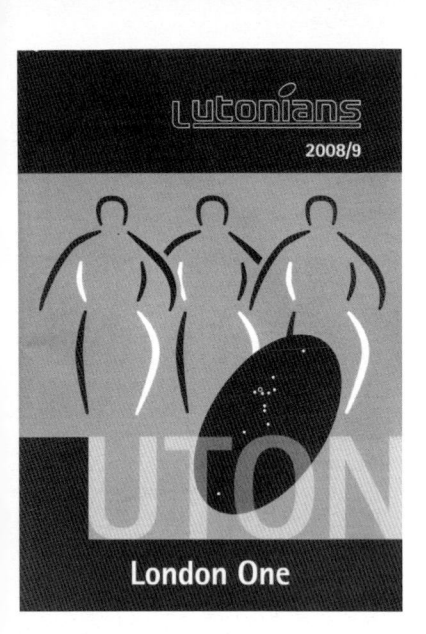

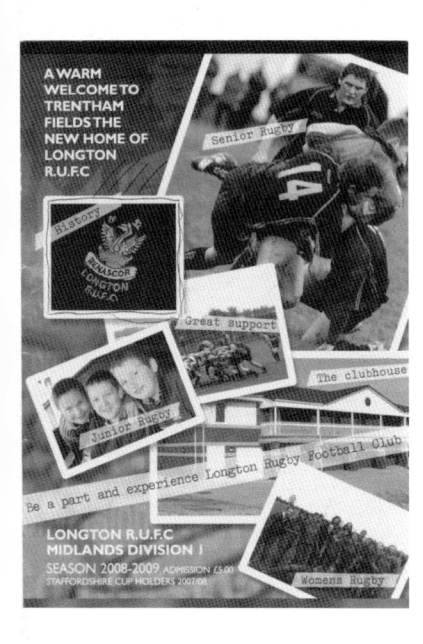

Right: BEDFORD ATHLETIC
- season 2008-09

MIDLANDS

MIDLANDS ONE EAST

2008-09 LEAGUE TABLE Midlands Two East

		P	W	D	L	F	A	PD	Pts	Adj
1	Ampthill	22	20	0	2	809	321	488	40	
2	Scunthorpe	22	17	0	5	636	329	307	34	
3	Paviors	22	16	0	6	532	368	164	23	
4	Syston	22	15	0	7	554	277	277	30	
5	Dunstablians	22	14	1	7	594	432	162	29	
6	Newark	22	13	1	8	534	349	185	27	
7	Mansfield	22	9	0	13	398	503	-105	18	
8	Leighton Buzzard	22	7	1	14	350	715	-365	15	
9	Matlock	22	6	0	16	370	422	-52	12	
10	Derby	22	5	1	16	267	563	-296	11	
11	Market Bosworth	22	5	0	17	323	542	-219	10	
12	Wellingborough	22	3	0	19	348	894	-546	6	

2009-10 FIXTURES GRID

	Derby	Dunstablians	Ilkeston	Leighton Buzzard	Mansfield	Market Bosworth	Matlock	Newark	Old Northamptonians	Paviors	Scunthorpe	Stewarts & Lloyd	Syston	Wellingborough
Derby		12/09	19/12	26/09	16/01	10/10	30/01	24/10	20/02	07/11	13/03	28/11	27/03	05/09
Dunstablians	12/12		26/09	16/01	10/10	30/01	24/10	20/02	07/11	13/03	28/11	27/03	05/09	19/09
Ilkeston	19/09	09/01		10/10	30/01	24/10	20/02	07/11	13/03	28/11	27/03	05/09	12/12	03/10
Leighton Buzzard	09/01	03/10	23/01		24/10	20/02	07/11	13/03	28/11	27/03	05/09	12/12	19/09	17/10
Mansfield	03/10	23/01	17/10	13/02		07/11	13/03	28/11	27/03	05/09	12/12	19/09	09/01	31/10
Market Bosworth	23/01	17/10	13/02	31/10	06/03		28/11	27/03	05/09	12/12	19/09	09/01	03/10	14/11
Matlock	17/10	13/02	31/10	06/03	14/11	20/03		05/09	12/12	19/09	09/01	03/10	23/01	05/12
Newark	13/02	31/10	06/03	14/11	20/03	05/12	10/04		19/09	09/01	03/10	23/01	17/10	12/12
Old Northamptonians	31/10	06/03	14/11	20/03	05/12	10/04	12/09	19/12		03/10	23/01	17/10	13/02	09/01
Paviors	06/03	14/11	20/03	05/12	10/04	12/09	19/12	26/09	16/01		17/10	13/02	31/10	23/01
Scunthorpe	14/11	20/03	05/12	10/04	12/09	19/12	26/09	16/01	10/10	30/01		31/10	06/03	13/02
Stewarts & Lloyds	20/03	05/12	10/04	12/09	19/12	26/09	16/01	10/10	30/01	24/10	20/02		14/11	06/03
Syston	05/12	10/04	12/09	19/12	26/09	16/01	10/10	30/01	24/10	20/02	07/11	13/03		20/03
Wellingborough	10/04	19/12	16/01	30/01	20/02	13/03	27/03	12/09	26/09	10/10	24/10	07/11	28/11	

DERBY R.F.C.

President: Gordon Stirling **Chairman:** Martyn Murney **Treasurer:** Gwent Paylor
Club Secretary: Dave Hall email: dave.hall@derbyrfc.com
Fixture Secretary: John Schofield email: john.schofield@derbyrfc.com
Match Secretary: Richard Lucas Tel: 01530 832296 email: richardlucas55@yahoo.com
Co-Rugby Chairman: Colin Cornfield & Richard Lucas
Mini & Jun. Chairman: Paul Fish email: paul.fish@derbyrfc.com **Patron:** Tony Bell
Ground Address: Haslams. Haslams Lane, Darley Abbey, Derby DE22 1EB Tel: 01332 344341
Directions: From the North From M1 take the A38 signed Derby. Take A61 towards Derby At the next r'about take 3rd exit (Alfreton Road). Go along Alfreton Road for 0.6 miles then turn right into Haslams Lane. Along Haslams Lane for 0.2 miles and the Club is on the left. **From Nottingham** Follow A52 towards Derby. At Pentagon Island take A61 exit signposted Chesterfield. Along A61 (aka Sir Frank Whittle Way) passing over 2 r'abouts. At 3rd r'about take 1st exit (Alfreton Rd). Then as above.
From the South Take A38 Northbound. Take the A61 towards Derby At the 1st r'about take the 3rd exit (Alfreton Rd). then as above.
Nearest BR station: Derby **Capacity:** Unlimited. Covered seating: 176 **Parking:** 140 at ground plus overspill
Admission: £3 incl. prog. **Programme:** Size: A5 Pages: 54 Advertising: Paul Richardson. email paulricho@aol.com
Clubhouse: Open Daily 12.00 noon – 11.00pm. Extensive menu available until 8.30pm. Open to the general public. For functions contact the Manager Tel: 01332 344341. **Club Shop:** Match days & Sunday am during season. Contact Karen Fearon.
Founded: 1892 **Nickname:** Tigers **Website:** www.Derbyrfc.com
Colours: Black & amber **Change Colours:** Green & burgundy **Training Nights:** Tuesday & Thursday.

DUNSTABLIANS RUFC.

President: Steve Carline **Chairman:** Graham White
Secretary & League Contact: Paul Freeman, 1 Station Road, Harlington, Dunstable, Beds, LU5 6LD
Tel: 07976 834932 (M) 01525 875277 email: paul.freeman@bigfoot.com
Fixtures Secretary : Jon Gilbert, 5 The Retreat, Dunstable, Beds, LU5 4PZ
Tel: 01582 759295 07775 803474 (M) email jon.gilbert340@ntlworld.com
Ground Address: Bidwell Park, Bedford Road, Houghton Regis, Dunstable, Beds. LU5 6JW.
Tel: 01582 866555 01582 864107 email: secretary@drufc.com Website: www.drufc.com
Directions: From Dunstable, head north on the A5. Cross the roundabout on the Leighton Buzzard by-pass and then turn right, sign posted to Thorn. At the end of this road, the ground is opposite. Turn right to the car park entrance, which is on the left.
From M1 J12, turn towards Toddington. Stay on the A5120 through the village and continue for about 3 miles. The ground is on an 'S' bend just before you enter Houghton Regis. From M1 J11, turn towards Dunstable. At the Halfway House pub roundabout, turn right towards Houghton Regis. In the centre of the town, turn right at the Kings Arms pub towards Toddington. The Club is half a mile further on, on the right before an 'S' bend. **Capacity:** 400 **Seating:** 80
Car Parking: 100+ cars at ground **Nearest BR Station:** Leagrave or Harlington **Admission:** £5 incl. programme
Clubhouse: Open Mon-Fri 7-11pm, Sat 11-1, Sun 10-6pm. Food available on matchdays.
Functions contact Sally Goddard 01582 866555 **Club Shop:** On request & Sun am. Contact Sally Goddard
Founded: 1948 **Nickname:** "Ds" **Colours:** Red, black, silver **Change colours:** All black **Training Nights:** Tues & Thur
Programme: Size: A5 Price: with admission Pages: 24 Editor: Peter Davis 01582 866555 Advertising: Contact Editor

ILKESTON R.U.F.C.

President: Pete Watson (07909567245) **Chairman:** Sean Ryan (07813 858007) **Treasurer:** Mark Cufflin (07968 738545)
Club Secretary: Mick Green, 62 Northern Drive, Trowell, Nottingham. NG9 3QL
Tel: 07792 486526 email: mick.green1@ntlworld.com
Fixtures Secretary: Paul Daykin, 61 Swingate, Kimberley, Nottingham. NG16 2PU
Tel: 07887 542181 email: paul.daykin@ntlworld.com
1st XV Manger: Bob Garland, 9 Crescent Road, Selston, Nottingham. NG16 6DT
Tel: 07900 882500 email: bob.garland@ntlworld.com
Director of Rugby: Scott Rudkin Tel: 07852 244934
Referee Liaison Officer: Paul Daykin **Referee Hospitality Officer:** Alan Jones **Junior Chairman:** Alan Pilbeam
Ground Address: The Stute, Hallam Fields Road, Ilkeston, Derbyshire. DE7 4AZ Tel: 01159 323244
Directions: From A609 Nottingham Road turn up alongside Rutland Windows up Thurman Street. At end turn left at T junction and ground is 250m on right hand side. **Admission:** Matchdays: £3 non members; £1 members Season: £80
Capacity: 1200 Covered standing: 100 **Car Parking:** 200 spaces **Nearest Station:** Nottingham
Clubhouse: Open Mon.-Thurs. 12:00-15:00; 19:00-23:00, Fri./Sat. 12:00-23:00 & Sun. 12:00-22:30. Hot food available lunchtimes 12:00-14:30. Function room with own bar/toilets available for hire, contact Lana Meakin **Club Shop:** matchdays or via website
Programme: Size: A5 Pages: 20 Price: incl. with admission. Editor: Bob Garland
Advertising: Full Page £250; Half Page £150; Quarter Page & Banner Adverts £75. All plus VAT
Founded: 1926 **Nickname:** The Elks **Website:** www.ilkestonrufc.co.uk
Colours: Green, blue and white **Change colours:** Maroon & yellow **Training Nights:** Tues & Thur.

LEIGHTON BUZZARD R.U.F.C.

President: Mark Hardy **Chairman**: Graham Blower **Treasurer**: Eric Cohen
Hon. Secretary: Lee Beaumont, c/o Leighton Buzzard RUFC
Tel: 01525 371322 e mail secretary@buzzardrugby.co.uk
Fixtures Secretary: Alan Perrey, 22 The Coppins, Ampthill, Bedford MK45 2SN
Tel: 01525 750877
Chairman of Rugby: David Yirrell
Mini & Junior Chairman: Mike Stacey mjchairman@buzzardrugby.co.uk
Ground Address: Wright's Meadow, Leighton Road, Stanbridge, Leighton Buzzard, Beds. LU7 9HR
Tel: 01525 371322 email: rugby@buzzardrugby.co.uk
Directions: Leave M1 at Junc 12. Take turning towards Toddington. In Toddington at main village green turn right at Bell Public House towards Tebworth. Follow this road through Tebworth for 2.5 miles to a T junction. Turn left onto A5 towards Dunstable. Follow A5 to Roundabout. Turn Right onto A505 Leighton By Pass. Take second right off Bypass (signposted Stanbridge Road Industrial Estate) LBRFC is half a mile up on right hand side.
Nearest BR Station: Leighton Buzzard
Club Shop: Open Saturdays and Sundays throughout the season.
Founded: 1934 **Training Nights**: Tuesday & Thursday **Website**: www.buzzardrugby.co.uk
Colours: White with blue hoops

MANSFIELD R.U.F.C.

Chairman: Andy Foster Tel: 01623 657509 (H), 07720 899996 (M)
Treasurer: Mike Copestake Tel: 01623 633071 (H)
Hon Secretary: Steven Troman 16 Daleside Cotgrave Nottingham NG12 3QA
Tel: 07966 220515 email: steventroman@btinternet.com
Membership Secretary: Kev Whale Tel: 01623 662198 (H)
Fixtures Secretary: Pete Steffen Tel: 07736 278862, 07971 281784 (M) email: peter.steffen@spsaerostructures.co.uk
Clubhouse Bookings: Martin Spencer Tel: 01623 623890 (H)
1st XV Senior Coach: Steve Shaw Tel: 07980 500230 (M)
Ground Address: Clubhouse Grounds & Sports Centre, Eakring Road, Mansfield NG18 3EW
Contact Number: 01623 649 834 **Email**: chairman@mansfieldrugby.co.uk
Directions: From Mansfield Town centre take A617 towards Newark. Travel 2 miles, turn left towards Ollerton. Travel 1 mile to T/lights turn right onto Eakring road.
Clubhouse: Offering excellent bar & catering facilities for up to 250 people - Club Steward Tony Wooley 07801 208292 (M) Available for private hire, contact Martin Spencer (above).
Founded: 1956 **Website**: www.mansfieldrugby.co.uk
Colours: Blue & white hooped shirts, blue shorts & socks

MARKET BOSWORTH R.F.C.

President: Harry Whitehead **Chairman**: Jonathon Chadburn 01455 273355 **Treasurer**: Rick Sykes
Club Secretary: Mike McKay, 20 Occupation Road, Orton-On-The-Hill, Atherstone Warks, CV9 3NE
Tel: 01827 880788, 07971 421104 (M) email: hoymckay@aol.com
Fixture Secretary: Tom Kilburn Tel: 07793 809363 (M) email tomkilburn@hotmail.com
Senior Coach: Robert Harding Tel: 07711 180344
1st XV Manager: Paul Jarvis Tel. 01455 291631, 0789 6057868 (M)
Commercial Secretary: Anna Clark Tel: 01455 293133, 07816 452498 (M)
Ground Address: Cadeby Lane, Market Bosworth, Nuneaton, Warks, CV13 0BA.
Tel: 01455 291340 email: mbrfc@mbrfc.co.uk
Directions: Off the A447, Hinckley to Ibstock Road. Turn at signs for Cadeby, through village in the direction of Market Bosworth, ground on left in one mile. Full details are available on the website. **Nearest BR Station**: Hinckley
Capacity: 1,000 uncovered standing **Admission**: £5 **Parking**: 100 - overflow in Bosworth Country Park.
Club House: Open Fri 6-9pm. Sat 2-9pm. Sun 12-2.30pm. Food available on matchdays. Manager: Leanne Saunders.
Club Shop: Open Sunday morning. Contact: Sharon Williams 01455 271564
Formed: September 1965 **Nickname**: Bos **Website**: www.mbrfc.co.uk **Training nights**: Tue, Wed, Thur & Fri.
Colours: Blue white and gold irregular hooped shirts, black shorts & socks.
Change Colours: Red shirt with narrow green & black band. black shorts & socks.

MATLOCK R.U.F.C.

President: Dave Ramsden **Chairman:** George Edwards **Treasurer:** Terry Lane
Club Secretary: Mike Overend, Rowley House, Sledgegate Lane. Lea, Matlock, Derbyshire DE4 5GL
Tel 01629 534364 email mikeoverend@hotmail.co.uk
Fixture Secretary: Dave Toone Tel. 01629 580243
Chairman of Rugby: Rob Siddall Tel. 01629 57519
Head Coach: Mike Brookes Tel. 01629 825074 email: mike@kohimo.com
Ground Address: Cromford Meadows, Mill Road, Cromford, Matlock DE4 3RQ
Tel: 01629 822821 email: rugby@matlockrugby.com

Directions: From **North**: Proceed south on A6 from Matlock towards Derby. At Cromford traffic lights turn left signposted Crich, Lea and Holloway. Pass the Cromford Mill on the left and 100m on the right is the entrance to Cromford Meadows. The clubhouse is at the far end of the meadow about 300m along the tarred road.   From **South**: Proceed north on A6 from Derby towards Matlock. At Cromford traffic lights turn right signposted Crich, Lea and Holloway. Pass the Cromford Mill on the left and 100m on the right is the entrance to Cromford Meadows.
NB If arriving by coach please notify the Club so that the overhead barrier at entrance to Cromford Meadows can be opened.
Nearest BR station: Cromford, 1/2 mile.   **Car Parking:** Unlimited grass parking and hard standing close to clubhouse
Capacity: Unlimited uncovered standing   **Admission:** Free
Clubhouse: Open matchdays from 1pm, Sunday (during season) 10-1pm. Snacks available on Sundays.
Clubhouse available for hire contact Adam Addis 01629 822821   **Club Shop:** Contact clubhouse
Programme: Size: A5   Price: £2   **Founded:** 1928   **Website:** www.matlocktugby.com
Colours: Shirts royal blue & gold, shorts navy blue, socks royal blue   **Training Nights:** Tues & Thur.

NEWARK R.U.F.C.

President: Andy Clay   **Chairman:** Chris Waddington   **Treasurer:** Peter Moore
Club Secretary: Tony Aspbury, 1 Millgate, Newark NG24 4TR
Tel: 01636 707765 (H); 0115 8528050 (W) and 07736 539832 (M) email: aspbury@btinternet.com
Fixture Secretary: Ernie Brummitt, 162 Winthorpe Rd, Newark, Notts, NG24 2AR
Tel: 01636 684257 (H) 07977-676403 (M) email: ernie_brummitt@hotmail.com
1st XV Manager: Billy Barker Tel: 01636-893616 or 07855-121967
Club Administrator: Wendy Boas, Club Office, Newark RUFC. Address, Tel. & email as club (below)
Director of Rugby: Alan Swain mobile 07776-208032
Ground Address: The Rugby Ground, Kelham Rd, Newark, Notts. NG24 1WN
Tel: 01636 702255 Fax: 01636 707601 email: post@newarkrugby.com
Directions: Club is on Newark to Mansfield road (A613) about one mile outside town.
Nearest BR station: Newark Northgate (London mainline) or Newark Castle (trains from Nottingham)
Capacity: Approx 1,000 Covered standing: 500   **Car Parking:** Ample
Admission: Matchday £2 with prog. Season: Membership £70, Patron £5
Clubhouse: Open training nights & matchdays. Snacks available on matchdays.   Clubhouse available for private hire, contact Andrea Wilkinson   **Club Shop:** Open matchdays & Thu eves. Contact Sheila Williams 01636-525419.
Programme: Size: A5 Pages: 32 Price: with admission Editor: Rob Wildman (07775-447730) Advertising: Wendy Boas
Founded: 1919   **Nickname:** Blue and whites   **Website:** www.newarkrugby.com
Colours: Navy blue shirt, white hoop, blue shorts. **Change:** Yellow jerseys   **Training Nights:** Tues & Thur 730pm.

Newark celebrate their 2nd successive victory in the Three Counties Cup.   Photo: Steve Yarnell

OLD NORTHAMPTONIANS R.F.C.

President: Barry Timms   **Chairman:** Peter Doughty   **Treasurer:** Chris Sugden
Club Secretary: Philip Watson, 78 Ashburnham Road, Northampton, NN1 4RA
Tel: 01604 712571,   07725 304774 (M)   email: pjwatto@aol.com
Fixtures Secretary: Philip Watson as above
Director of Rugby: Mark Kefford
Team Manager: Philip Watson as above
Mini & Junior Contact: Mark Russell Tel: 01604 518195
Ground Address: The Sports Field, Billing Road, Northampton, NN1 5RX
Tel: 01604 634045   email: Oldnorthamptonians@hotmail.co.uk   **Website:** www.oldnorthamptonians.co.uk
Directions: Leave M1 at Junct 15, follow dual carriageway A508 towards Northampton. Take exit signposted Northampton and Bedford. At r'about take 2nd exit into Rushmere Road. At traffic lights at top of road, turn left. Sports Field is 200 yrds on right.
Capacity: Unlimited uncovered standing   **Car Parking:** 200   **Nearest Station:** Northampton
Clubhouse: Open Tue., Wed., Thur., Fri 7-11pm; Sat 1-11pm & Sun 12-3pm. No food available.
Available for private hire; contact Bev Kevan 01604 634045.   **Club Shop:** Open Sun 11-1pm. Contact Bev Cheyne.
Programme: Size: A5   Pages: 24   Price: Free   Editor: Mike Hull   Advertising : Contact Mike Hull 07979661111
Founded: 1923   **Nickname:** ONs   **Training Nights:** Tues & Thur.
Colours: Cardinal red, navy and gold hoops   **Change colours:** Navy, cardinal red and gold

PAVIORS R.F.C.

President: Phil Molyneux   **Chairman:** Mark Britton   **Treasurer:** Graham Turner
Club Secretary: Chris Holdrick Tel:01636 812559,   07840 622158 (M) email: choldrick@btinternet.com
Fixture Secretary: Pete Laplanche, 37a Waterhouse Lane, Gedling, Nottingham NG44BP
Tel: 0115 9402073,   07966 245008 (M)   email: pete.laplanche@btinternet.com Note: e-mail or mobile preferred contact
Membership Secretary: Sue Arnold Tel: 0115 965 5683,   07778 483918 (M)   email: susan.arnold@ntlworld.com
Mini & Junior Sec.: Dave Monk   Tel: 0115 953 2513,   07825 326610 (M)   email: d.monk2@ntlworld.com
Ground Address: The Ron Rossin Ground, Burntstump Hill, Arnold, Nottingham, NG5 8PQ
Tel: 0115 963 0384   email: graham.turner11@btopenworld.com
Directions: A614 from Nottingham to Doncaster, 2 miles north of City turn left onto Burntstump Hill, after 100 metres take left turning passed the school on left, follow lane round to the right to rugby club.
Nearest BR station: Nottingham Midland station
Capacity: 500   Covered Seating: 25   **Admission:** By programme   **Car Parking:** 200+ cars
Clubhouse: Open match days & training nights. Hot & cold food on match days. Functions on request, contact Liz Stirland
Club Shop: Open Sat & Sun. Contact Phil Molyneux.
Programme: Size: A5   Pages: 20   Editorial & Advertising: Will Oates.
Founded: 1922   **Nickname:** Pavs   **Website:** www.paviorsrfc.co.uk
Colours: Green with red & black bands   **Change colours:** Blue   **Training Nights:** Tues. & Thur. from 7pm

SCUNTHORPE R.U.F.C.

President: D A Chapman   **Chairman:** Louie Clayton   **Treasurer:** Paddy Beggs
Club Secretary: Malcolm Yates, Farthing's Cottage Turner Street, Kirton in Lindsey. Gainsborough Lincs. DN21 4DB
Tel: 01652 648084,   07921 124619   email:malyates@aol.com
Fixture Secretary: Ray Wilson, 70 Wiltshire Avenue, Burton-on-Stather, Scunthorpe
Tel: 01724 720915 (H)   email: ezramorlock@aol.com
Director of Rugby: Liam Waldron   **Commercial Secretary:** Alan Bell 01724 843678 (H)
Colts Chairman: Terry Jackson
Ground: Heslam Park, Ashby Road, Scunthorpe DN16 2AG
Tel: 01724 843013 email: malyates@aol.com   **Website:** www.scunthorperufc.com
Directions: End of M181 take 3rd exit off roundabout. across miniroundabout 3rd exit at next roundabout (A18). 3rd exit of next roundabout (A159) through traffic lights ground on the left.   **Nearest BR Station:** Scunthorpe
Capacity: 1000   Covered seating: 200   **Admission:** Matchday £4   **Car Parking:** at the clubhouse
Clubhouse: Open daily during normal licensing hours. Sandwiches available on matchdays.
Available for private hire, contact club.   **Club Shop:** via Intersport Scunthorpe & at the club Sunday am
Founded: 1929   **Nickname:** The Greens   **Training Nights:** Tuesday & Thursday
Colours: Lincoln green with narrow black and white hoops   **Change colours:** Red with narrow black and white hoops
Programme: Size: A5   Pages: 6 + adverts   Price: with admission   Editors: M Yates & K. Robinson
Advertising K. Robinson Tel: 01724 721855

STEWARTS & LLOYDS R.F.C.
President: Mr Charles Veall **Chairman:** Mr Neil Campbell **Treasurer:** Mr Grant Cook
Club Secretary: Simon Mullin, 492 Gainsborough Road, Corby, NN18 0QD
Tel: 01536 267190 or 07930 842436 (M)   email: simon@simonmullin.wanadoo.co.uk
Fixtures Secretary: Peter Cleary, 8 Stanier Close, Corby, NN17 1XP
Tel: 01536 400652   email: peter@durlum.co.uk
Team Secretary: Simon Mullin, as above
Director of Rugby: Adey Mitchell
Ground Address: The Clubhouse, Occupation Road, Corby, NN17 1EH
Tel: 01536 400317   emaail: simon@simonmullin.wanadoo.co.uk   **Website:** www.slrfc.org.uk
Directions: From Kettering take A6003 to Oakham, at Corby RFC turn right into A6116, 1/4 mile turn right, just past game bird pub, into Occupation Road. 1st right into Cannock Road. Club on the right at end of road.
Capacity: All uncovered standing   **Admission:** Free   **Car Parking:** Yes   **Nearest BR Station:** Corby
Clubhouse: Open 6.30 -10pm Tues- Thurs, Sat 12-10pm. Contact Glen Brooks 01536 400317
Club Shop: See website contact Neil Carr/Paul Franklin 01536 400317
Programme: Price: £1   Editor & Advertising: Neil Campbell 01536 400317
Founded: 1936   **Training Nights:** Tues & Thur. 7-9 pm.
Colours: Black shirts & shorts, black & white hooped socks.   **Change colours:** White shirts

SYSTON R.F.C.
President: Ed Walker   **Chairman:** Neil Pickles   **Treasurer:** Mrs Joan Newton
Hon Secretary: Mark Puttnam, 41 Orchard Way, Syston, Leics LE7 2AL
Tel: (H) 0116 260 1574 (M) 07962 990374   Email: markputtnam@hotmail.com
Fixtures Secretary: Ivan Thorpe, 12 Perseverance Road, Birstall, Leics. LE4 4AU
Tel: (H) 0116 267 7950 (M) 07731 899472
Director of Rugby: Phil Smith   **Head Coach:** Chris Tarbuck   **Disciplinary Chairman:** Phil Smith
Club Physiotherapist: Nikki MacMannard   **Club Captain:** Brendan Coles   **Bar Steward:** Mrs Alison Toon
Ground Address: Barkby Road, Quenilborough, Leicester LE7 3FE.
Tel: 0116 2601223 (Clubhouse)   email: markputtnam@hotmail.co.uk
Simple Directions: On the Barkby Rd, between Queniborough and Syston.
Nearest BR Station: Syston   **Car Parking:** Parking for 200 cars
Capacity: All uncovered standing   **Admission:** No charge
Clubhouse: Open matchdays from 12 noon.
Programme: Size: A5   Pages: 32   Price: £1   Editor: Dr John Brindley
Founded: 1887   **Website:** www.systonrfc.org.uk
Colours: Navy and saxe (light blue)   **Change colours:** Green   **Training Nights:** Tuesday & Thursday

WELLINGBOROUGH R.F.C.
Chairman: Ken Morse, The Old Barn, 161 Ecton Lane, Sywell, Northants. NN6 0BB Tel: 01604 644062
Treasurer: Paul Hulse, 4b Palm Road, Rushden, Northants. NN10 6AS
Tel: 01933 411212   email: treasurerwrfc@tiscali.co.uk
Hon Secretary: Steve Hill, 11 Wilby Lane, Great Doddington, Northants. NN29 7TP Tel: 01933 273369
Fixtures Secretary: Paul Dodson, 53 Station Road, Earls Barton, Northants. NN6 0NT Tel: 01933 810412
Club Captain: Peter Vickers Tel: 07709 995429
Mini-Junior Chairman: Brian Hillson Tel: 07751 548679
Ground Address: Wellingborough R.F.C. Cut Throat Lane Great Doddington, Wellingborough, Northants NN29 7TZ
Tel: : 01933 222260   email: as Hon. Secretary   **Website:** www.wrfc.net
Directions: From M1 junction 15, take the A45 towards Northampton & Wellingborough. Take the Great Doddington / Earls Barton slip road, turn left at end of this slip road, then left again at a small crossroads in approximately 800 metres. The Clubhouse and ground is on the right, after going over the dual carriageway about 500 metres along the road.
Nearest BR Station: Wellingborough   **Car Parking:** Ample at the ground
Clubhouse: Available for private hire, contact David Wilson Tel: 01933 401261
Club Shop: Open Saturday 12-3pm & Sunday 10-1pm
Founded: 1879   **Colours:** White shirts with a red hoop   **Training Nights:** Tues & Thur. 6.45 for 7pm

MIDLANDS

MIDLANDS ONE WEST

2008-09 LEAGUE TABLE Midlands Two West

		P	W	D	L	F	A	PD	Pts	Adj
1	Bromsgrove	22	19	0	3	630	314	316	38	
2	Hereford	22	16	1	5	620	256	364	33	
3	Dudley Kingswinford	22	16	1	5	707	365	342	33	
4	Burton	22	13	1	8	537	475	62	27	
5	Sutton Coldfield	22	12	1	9	535	452	83	25	
6	Stoke on Trent	22	10	1	11	410	517	-107	21	
7	Stratford Upon Avon	22	10	1	11	507	481	26	19	-2
8	Walsall	22	8	0	14	491	573	-82	16	
9	Solihull	22	7	0	15	392	555	-163	14	
10	Whitchurch	22	7	0	15	323	678	-355	14	
11	Cheltenham North	22	5	1	16	341	557	-216	11	
12	Camp Hill	22	5	1	16	330	600	-270	11	

2009-10 FIXTURES GRID

	Bournville	Burton	Camp Hill	Cheltenham North	Dudley Kings.	Leamington	Nuneaton O.E.	Old Halesonians	Solihull	Stoke on Trent	Stratford u Avon	Sutton Coldfield	Walsall	Whitchurch
Bournville		12/09	19/12	26/09	16/01	10/10	30/01	24/10	20/02	07/11	13/03	28/11	27/03	05/09
Burton	12/12		26/09	16/01	10/10	30/01	24/10	20/02	07/11	13/03	28/11	27/03	05/09	19/09
Camp Hill	19/09	09/01		10/10	30/01	24/10	20/02	07/11	13/03	28/11	27/03	05/09	12/12	03/10
Cheltenham North	09/01	03/10	23/01		24/10	20/02	07/11	13/03	28/11	27/03	05/09	12/12	19/09	17/10
Dudley Kingswinford	03/10	23/01	17/10	13/02		07/11	13/03	28/11	27/03	05/09	12/12	19/09	09/01	31/10
Leamington	23/01	17/10	13/02	31/10	06/03		28/11	27/03	05/09	12/12	19/09	09/01	03/10	14/11
Nuneaton Old Edwardians	17/10	13/02	31/10	06/03	14/11	20/03		05/09	12/12	19/09	09/01	03/10	23/01	05/12
Old Halesonians	13/02	31/10	06/03	14/11	20/03	05/12	10/04		19/09	09/01	03/10	23/01	17/10	12/12
Solihull	31/10	06/03	14/11	20/03	05/12	10/04	12/09	19/12		03/10	23/01	17/10	13/02	09/01
Stoke on Trent	06/03	14/11	20/03	05/12	10/04	12/09	19/12	26/09	16/01		17/10	13/02	31/10	23/01
Stratford Upon Avon	14/11	20/03	05/12	10/04	12/09	19/12	26/09	16/01	10/10	30/01		31/10	06/03	13/02
Sutton Coldfield	20/03	05/12	10/04	12/09	19/12	26/09	16/01	10/10	30/01	24/10	20/02		14/11	06/03
Walsall	05/12	10/04	12/09	19/12	26/09	16/01	10/10	30/01	24/10	20/02	07/11	13/03		20/03
Whitchurch	10/04	19/12	16/01	30/01	20/02	13/03	27/03	12/09	26/09	10/10	24/10	07/11	28/11	

BOURNVILLE R.F.C.

President: Ivor Boehmer / George Foley   **Treasurer:** Mick O'Sullivan
Chairman: Ivor Boehmer, 116 Alcester Road South, King's Heath, Birmingham B14 7PR Tel: 0121 443 9639
Club Secretary: Jenny Allen, 219 Selly Oak Road, Bournville, Birmingham B30 1HR
Tel: 07970 661630   email: judo.jen@hotmail.co.uk
Fixtures Secretary: Ian Gay, 6 Brennand Close, Oldbury, West Midlands B68 0SD
Tel: 07748 708759   email: ian@wilsmore-mail.com
Director of Rugby: Rob Sigley   email: rob@tryhardsports.com
Commercial Secretary: Darren Clegg   email: Darren.clegg@shoosmiths.co.uk
Press Officer: Iestyn Pratt - iestynpratt@hotmail.com   **Hippo's (Vets):** Adam Hardy – adamnadine92@hotmail.com
Club Registrar: Ivor Boehmer – ivor.boehmer@hotmail.co.uk
Women's Captain: Charlotte Hulbert - captain_twink@hotmail.co.uk
Ground Address: Rowheath Pavilion, Heath Road, Bournville, Birmingham B30 1HH Tel: 0121 458 1711
Directions: Leave the M5 at J3 or the M42 at J2. From the motorway follow Cadbury World signs. The ground is second right after Cadburys heading south. Take Mary Vale Rd which crosses the A4123 (Linden Rd) this continues into Heath Road 1 mile south of Selly Oak and 0.5 mile north of Cotteridge. The Pavilion is on the left about 600 yds from the A4123.
Car Parking: Opposite pitches - f.o.c.   **Nearest Station:** Bournville Station   **Website:** www.bournvillerfc.co.uk
Founded: 1909 – Centenary Season 2009/10.   RFU Presidents XV Veterans Team of the Year 208/09 – Bournville Hippo's
Colours: Maroon with blue/gold stripes   **Change colours:** Pink with blue sleeves   **Training Nights:** Mon & Wed.

BURTON R.F.C.

President: Bill Leason   **Chairman:** John Lowe   **Treasurer:** Martyn Evans email: mwe7@hotmail.co.uk
Club Secretary: Mr Philip Stockbridge; Bretby Lane, Bretby, Burton On Trent DE15 0QP
Tel: 07900 892630   email: burtonrugby@btconnect.com
Fixture Secretary: Steve Harris, 56 Harehedge Lane, Burton upon Trent, Staffs DE130AS
Tel: 01283 516426   07840 967350 (M)   email: steve@burtonrugbyclub.co.uk
Ground Address: Peel Croft, Lichfield Street, Burton upon Trent DE14 3RH Tel: 01283 564510
Directions: The ground is in the centre of Burton on the town centre side of the river over St Peter's bridge (A444), between the new ASDA supermarket site and Halfords/Dunelm/Lidl
Nearest BR station: Burton upon Trent   **Car Parking:** Limited at ground, but surrounded by public Pay & Display
Capacity: 2,000   Covered: 1,000   Seated: 380   **Admission:** 1st XV Matchday: £4   Season: £45
Clubhouse: Open Tues & Thurs 7.30–11.00, Sat. 12.00–11.30, Sun 12.00–3.00. Filled cobs available.
Functions - Contact clubhouse steward Pete Cowling 07966 482841
Club Shop: The Club shop is normally open on Thursday evening from 7.15pm, Sunday 12-2pm and some Saturdays. At other times for enquires or to place an order, contact: fiona.reeve@sky.com or Rugbykitburton@aol.com (Steve Briggs)
Programme: Size: A5   Pages: 42   Price: With admission   Advertising: Contact Anthony Peverill Tel: 07736 522259
Founded: Oct 1870   **Website:** www.burtonrugbyclub.co.uk   **Training Nights:** Tues & Thur 7pm
Colours: White shirt, black diag. band over rt. shoulder, white shorts, black socks white tops.
Change colours: Black shirts.

MIDLANDS

CAMP HILL R.F.C.

Chairman: Dave Maiden Tel:0121 745 2030, (M) 07970 196089 email: dmaiden@blueyonder.co.uk
Hon Secretary: Karen Gibbons, 75 Bills Lane, Shirley, Solihull, West Midlands B90 2PE
Tel: 0121 745 9349, (M) 07956 170829 email: KpatCampHill@aol.com
Fixtures Secretary: Graham Scutt 130 Longmore Road, Shirley, Solihull, West Midlands B90 3EE
Tel: 0121 744 4495 email: gscutt2@tiscali.co.uk
Membership Secretary: Steve Terrace Tel:0121 624 4733 (M) 07753 539711
Press Officer: Paul "Oscar" Twilby Tel:0121 603 6501 (M) 07840 419909
1st XV Captain: Pete Koziot Tel: 07971 614382 (M)
Mini & Junior Section Chairman: Nick Freeman 0121 745-2573, 07966-465932 (M) email: nickf@tsgmedia.co.uk
Ground Address: Camp Hill RFC, Haslucks Green Road, Shirley, Solihull B90 2EF
Tel: 0121 744 4175 email: chrfc@sagesol.demon.co.uk
Directions: Leave M42 at Junction 4. Turn North onto A34
After 3 miles turn left at traffic lights onto Haslucks Green Road. Club entrance 400m on left.
Clubhouse: Open Thursday eve., Sat afternoon & eve. & Sun afternoon.
Website: www.chrfc.co.uk   **Colours**: Maroon & light blue
Training Nights: (Seniors) Tuesday & Thursday 7pm Minis & Juniors Sunday 10.30am.

CHELTENHAM NORTH R.F.C.

President: Bill Summers Tel: 01242 604638 email: williamsummers@btinternet.com
Chairman: Andy Page, 15 Cheriton Close, Up Hatherley, Cheltenham GL51 3NR
Tel: (H) 01242 510 932 (W) 01242 662700 email andrew_d.page@sky.com
Treasurer: Jo Parsons (M) 07712 887153 email jo@masstock.co.uk
Team & Match Secretary: Malcolm Kedward Tel: (m) 07802 166103 email bettykedward@popeselm.fsnet.co.uk
Fixtures Secretary: Niel Carpenter (m) 07946 752371 email n.carpenter@sky.com
Head Coach: Mike Stubbs (m) 07971 538139 email mstubbs@bhbs.hereford.sch.uk
Ground Address: Stoke Orchard Road, Bishops Cleeve, Gloucestershire GL52 7DG
Tel: 01242 675958 / 238341
Directions: Junction 10 or 11 Cheltenham, head out of Cheltenham past racecourse on A435 towards Bishops Cleeve, turn towards Stoke Orchard village, 500 yards on left.
See website for map & full directions.
Clubhouse: Contact Ann Pitman Tel: 01242 675968
Web: www.cnrfc.co.uk
Club Colours: Black with one red band
Programme Advertising/Sponsorship: Contact Jo Parsons

DUDLEY KINGSWINFORD R.F.C.

Chairman: Ken Crane Tel: 07970 855729 email: ken.crane@mbpmail.co.uk
Club Secretary: David Coyle, 67 Court Cresent, Kingswinford. West Midlands DY6 9RJ
Tel: 01384 830508 (h) 07899 792395 (m) email: dcoyle@junkers.co.uk
Treasurer: Martin Chard
Fixture Secretary: Bill Jones Tel: 01902 678427 (h) 07721 716500 (m) email: Bill.Jones@atotech.com or superted0408@fsmail.net
Match Confirmer/Team Secretary: Bill McLachlan, 32, Lynwood Avenue, Wall Heath, Kingswinford. DY6 9AJ
01384 831279 (h)   07802 749909 (m) email: fixtures@dkrfc.co.uk or willmacdk@blueyonder.co.uk
Rugby Administrator: Gordon Bannatyne Tel: 07850 395544 email: lastdrop@btinternet.com
Club Manager: Roger Port Tel: 01384 287006 or 07989 837215
Address: Heathbrook, Swindon Rd, Kingswinford, West. Midlands. DY6 0AW Tel/Fax: 01384 287006 email: rugby@dkrfc.co.uk
Capacity: 1500   Covered Seating: 250   **Admission**: Matchday: £5   Season tickets £60
Directions: Just off the A449 at Wall Heath, midway between Kidderminster and Wolverhampton.
Nearest BR Station: Stourbridge Junction   **Car Parking**: Spaces for 200+ at the ground
Clubhouse: Open Mon - Fri 7-11pm & 12-11pm Sat.. Food available matchdays. For Functions contact Martin Chard c/o club
Club Shop: Open training nights 7-8 & match days. contact Ian Bratt
Founded: 1928   **Nickname**: DK   **Colours**: Cambridge & navy blue hooped shirts, navy shorts
Training Nights: Tues. & Thur. 7pm   **Web site**: www.dkrfc.co.uk   **Change colours**: White with red chevrons
Programme: Size: A5   Price: Incl with admission   Editor: David Coyle   Advertising: Contact Roger Port or Martin Chard

LEAMINGTON R.U.F.C.

President: Peter Preece   **Chairman:** Hugh Smith   **Treasurer:** John Hodgetts
Club Secretary: John Lyons, 3 Denewood Way, Kenilworth, CV82NY
Tel: 01926 855787   email: johnlizlyons@btopenworld.com
Fixtures Secretary: Bryn Evans, 36 Southam Road, Radford Semele, leamington Spa
Tel: 01926 881879   email: Bryn.evans@pels.co.uk
Team Secretary: Kit Forrest, 96 Greville Road, Warwick, CV345PL
Tel: 01926 402395   email: sales@allianceandgeneral.co.uk
Director of Rugby: Peter Preece
Ground Address: Moorefields, Kenilworth Road, Leamington Spa CV32 6RG
Tel: 01926 425584   email: johnlizlyons@btopenworld.com   **Website:** www. leamingtonrugby.com
Directions: Join A46 Warwick by-pass (from north - M6 J2. From south - M40 J15). Leave A46 at Leamington/Kenilworth junction . Take A452 to Leamington. Ground on left after 1 mile, before town.
Capacity: All uncovered standing   **Car Parking:** 200   **Nearest Station:** Leamington, Warwick or Coventry
Admission: Matchday - By programme.   Season Ticket not available.   **Clubhouse:** None   **Club Shop:** None.
Programme: Size: A5 (8" x 5")   Pages: 16   Price: £3   Editor: John Warner   Advertising: £100 per page + VAT
Founded: 1926   **Nickname:** Leam   **Training Nights:** Tues & Thur.
Colours: Blue shirts with red & gold trim, blue shorts   **Change colours:** Red shirts with blue & gold trim

NUNEATON OLD EDWARDIANS R.F.C.

President: John Burdett   **Chairman:** Ken McBride   **Treasurer:** Juliet Perry
Club Secretary: John Jones, 137 Higham Lane, Nuneaton, Warks. CV1 6AL
Tel: 02476 387719,   07887 556869 (M),   email: johnmeredith@hotmail.com
Fixtures Secretary: John Burdett, 5 Henley Close, Nuneaton, Warks. CV11 6HF
Tel: 02476 341231 (W),   02476 347257 (H),   07909 884037 (M)
email: jandjburdett@talk21.com (H),   john.burdett@nwfinance.co.uk (W)
Director of Rugby: Paul Vowles
Ground Address: Weddington Road, Nuneaton CV10 0AL   Tel: 02476 386778   email: info@noerfc.co.uk
Directions: Off M6 at junction 3 follow A444 into and through Nuneaton club on left leaving town. Off A5 at A444 junction, follow A444 to Nuneaton for 2 miles club on right.
Capacity: All uncovered standing   **Car Parking:** Ample   **Nearest BR Station:** Nuneaton
Clubhouse: Normal opening hours are: Saturday open at 12pm; Sunday 12 - 3pm; Tuesday & Thursday open at 8pm
To hire the clubhouse, please call Gareth Edwards - Mobile: 07796 547922
Club Shop: None.   **Programme:** None
Founded: 18th Feb. 1910   **Nickname:** 'Old Eds'   **Website:** www.noerfc.co.uk
Colours: Red and white hoops, black shorts   **Change colours:** Black shirts   **Training Nights:** Normally Tues & Thur.

OLD HALESONIANS R.F.C.

President: Peter Sidaway   **Chairman:** Paul Gaynham   **Treasurer:** Tony Crocombe
Club Secretary: Mike Churchill, 10 Parkfield Close   Halesowen WestMidlands   B62 OHL
Tel: 0121 6023797,   07906 677824 (M)   email: mikechurchill@blueyonder.co.uk
Fixtures Secretary: Martin Head, 287 Hagley Road   Pedmore   Stourbridge   WestMidlands   DY9 ORJ
Tel: 01562 883525,   07973 696547 (M)   email: steadyheady@yahoo.co.uk
Director of Rugby: Gary Cox
Ground Address: Old Halesonians, Wassell Grove, Hagley, West Midlands
Tel: 01562 883250   **Website:** www.Oldhalesrfc.co.uk
Directions: Exit M5 at junction 3 and follow the A456 Kidderminster, pass pub on right, Badgers Set.
At next Island turn right into Wassell Grove Lane club 300yds on right
Capacity: 500 Covered Seating: 120   **Admission:** Free
Car Parking: 200+   **Nearest Station:** Stourbridge
Clubhouse: Open Mon to Sat eves & Sat & Sun   lunchtimes. Food is available.
Functions contact Dave Layton 07850 706394   **Club Shop:** None.
Programme: Size: A5   Pages 6   Price £2   Editor: Roy Western   Advertising: Paul Gaynham   07770442103
Founded: 1939   **Nickname:** Owen   **Training Nights:** Tues & Thur. 19.30
Colours: Royal blue, amber hoop and scarlet   **Change colours:** Black and white hoop

MIDLANDS

SOLIHULL R.U.F.C.
President: Mr Tony Smith   **Chairman:** Mr David Hull   **Treasurer:** Mr John Marsh
Club Secretary: Mark Tandy, 194 St Bernards Road, Solihull B92 7BJ
Tel: 07966 121528   email: thetandys@talktalk.net
Fixtures Secretary: Jason Goodwin, 110 Pitmaston Road, Hall Green, Birmingham, B28 9PN
Tel: 07941 619186, 0121 733 7596   email: jasegoodwin@hotmail.co.uk
Director of Rugby: Julian Hyde   **Commercial Secretary:** Andrew Smallwood
Ground Address: c/o Birmingham & Solihull RFC, Sharmans Cross Road, Solihull, West Midlands B91 1RQ
Club Number: 0121 705 7995   **Email:** as Secretary   **Website:** www.solihullrufc.com
Directions: From Solihull town centre take Streetsbrook road, through traffic lights past fire station,over bridge, then second turning on the right into Sharmans Cross road, the ground is 500 yards on the left hand side.
Alternative ground at Portway Please check location of game.
Car Parking: 100 spaces available at the ground   **Nearest BR Station:** Solihull, 2km.
Capacity: 3,500   Covered Seating: 1,000   **Admission:** matchday £3 - £5.
Programme: With admission. Advertising contact Secretary.
Colours: Gold shirts with black wings   **Change colours:** Black shirts with red sleeves
Formed: Reformed in 2000 following a merger with Birmingham Rugby Football Club in 1989 season - Solihull Rugby Club was originally formed in 1933.   **Training Nights:** Wednesday 7pm, Sharmans Cross Road

STOKE ON TRENT R.F.C.
President: John Evans   **Treasurer:** Keith Salt
Chairman: Brian Ellis, 6 Montfort Place , Newcastle under Lyme ST5 2HE
Tel: 01782 610244   email: cb-yregistrar-staffs@therfu.com
Honorary Secretary: David Potts; Greenhill, Station Road, Barlaston, Stoke-on-Trent ST12 9DE
Tel: 01782 715577   email: thepottskas@hotmail.com
Fixture Secretary: Eric Hardisty; 29 Kingston Drive, Stone Staffs. ST15 0JH
Tel: 01785 813641   email: erichardisty@tiscali.co.uk
Chairman of Playing: Jeremy Edwards
Ist XV Manager: Steve Maskrey
Ground Address: Hartwell Lane, Barlaston, nr Stone, Stoke on Trent ST15 8TL
Contact Tel.: 01782 372807   email: ian.godfrey@tesco.net   **Website:** www.stokerfc.co.uk
Directions: From M1 A38 to a50. Left at lights (A520) at town outskirts. Take road to Barlaston after 3m. Club 1m on left. From M6 leave J15 (A34 South) to Barlaston, Club on right.
Club Shop: See website for available items.
Founded: 1884   **Training Nights:** Tuesday & Thursday 7 for 7.30pm
Club Colours: Dark blue with light blue hoop, black shorts.   **Change colours:** Plain red or White with blue flashing

STRATFORD UPON AVON R.F.C.
President: Dr Ken Holley   **Treasurer:** Andy Urquhart
Chairman: Jim Leach , 01789 415718 (H) 07836 668490 (M) reachleach@ntlworld.com
Club Secretary: Charles Beighton, 15 Wetherby Way, Kings Acre, Stratford Upon Avon, Warwickshire CV37 9LU
Tel: (H) 01789 415462   email: Charles_beighton@nfumutual.co.uk
Fixtures & Match Secretary: Tony Wakelin, 99 Evesham Road, Stratford upon Avon, Warks CV37 9BE
Tel: 01789 552253 (H) 07778 465120 (M)   email: acanthus@dsl.pipex.com
Chairman of Playing Committee: John Butler, 7 Rushbrook Road , Stratford upon Avon CV 37 7JW
Tel: 01789 414144 (H) 07979 642717 (M)   email: Jr.butler@lineone.net
Joint Chair of Vice Presidents: David Young   email: dcmyoung@btopenworld.com
Club Steward and Grounds Manager: Adi Davey   Tel: 01926 624488 (H)   07790 436026 (M)
Ground Address: Pearcecroft, Loxley Road, Stratford Upon Avon, Warwickshire CV37 7DP
Tel: 01789 297796   email: info@stratforduponavonrugbyclub.co.uk   **Website:** www.stratforduponavonrugbyclub.co.uk
Directions: the club is situated in central Stratford, off Tiddington Road, alongside river on southern bank.Turn right into Loxley Road and the club is 400 yds down on left.   A location map is available on the website.
Clubhouse: Available for private hire, contact Adi Davey.
Colours: Black & white hoops, black shorts & socks.
Founded: 1877

SUTTON COLDFIELD R.F.C.

Chairman: Geoff Fletcher Tel: 07813 216707 Email: geoffreyfletcher@advantagewm.co.uk
Vice Chairman: Ken Lewis Tel: 0121 354 6009(H) 0778 698 2817 (M) Email: ken@kynochlewis.co.uk
Treasurer: Ben Bolt Tel: 0790 026 7590 (M) 0121 308 8275 (H) Email: ben.bolt@kaupthing.com
President: Paul 'Bodger' Rogers Tel: 0121 681 6547
Hon Secretary: Simon Yeo, Medway Court Flat 11, Garrard Gardens, Sutton Coldfield, West Midlands B73 6DT
Tel: (H) 0121 354 7529   (M) 07881957828   email: sj.y@btinternet.com
Fixtures Secretary: Richard Harries, 6, Warrington Close, Walmley, Sutton Coldfield, West Midlands
Tel: (H) 0121 351 7317   (M) 07941966788   email: richard.harries@talktalk.net
1st XV Head Coach: Matt Nevitt
Ground Address: Sutton Coldfield R.F.C., Walmley Road, Walmley, Sutton Coldfield B76 2QA
Tel: 0121 351 5123   email: sj.y@btinternet.com   **Website**: www.suttoncoldfieldrfc.com
Nearest BR Station: Sutton Coldfield   **Car Parking**: Spaces for 150 cars at ground
Capacity: 1500
Directions: M6 J5 take A452 (Brownhills) at Bagot Arms Pub, then right onto B4148 to Walmley.
Or A38 at A453 to Sutton Coldfield - T/Lights left to Walmley. See website for detailed map.
Founded: 1921   **Colours**: Emerald green, white shorts   **Change colours**: White and emerald green, white shorts

WALSALL R.F.C.

President: Chris Emes   **Treasurer**: Phil Pittaway
Club Secretary: David Rogers, 34 Canberra Rd, Walsall, West Mids, WS5 3NN Tel:. 07976 691568 (M) 0121 525 8766
email: david.rogers@constructionalsteework.fsnet.co.uk (B) davrog34@hotmail.com (H)
Fixtures Secretary: Matt Ellis, 97 Chester Road, Streetly, Sutton Coldfield
Tel: 0121 353 3510 (H) or 07967 180649 email: j.ellis67@btinternet.com
Club Administrator: Sara Taylor c/o Walsall RFC
Director of Rugby: Rob Harding Tel: 01905 23204 (B)   07973 561385 (M). email goodnewsworcs@point4.co.uk
Chairman of Mini/Juniors: Gary Taylor Tel: 01922 722780 (H) 07791 457124 (M) email: g-taylor@qmgs.walsall.sch.uk
GroundAddress: Delves Road, Walsall WS1 3JY Tel: 01922 626818 Fax 01922 613310 email: walsallrugbyclub@btopenworld.com
Capacity: 2,250   Covered Seating: 250   **Nearest BR Station**: Walsall BR 1.5 miles, hourly bus or taxi.
Directions: From South & SW, M6 J7, A34 to Walsall, after about 2 miles turn left at island by Quality Hotel onto ring road A4148. The
ground is about 1/2mile on the right, turn right into Delves Road. From Northwest. M6 J 9, turn left signed A461 Lichfield. Fork right at the
lights and follow signs to Lichfield A461 & Ring road A4148. Stay on this road, after passing The New Fullbrook PH the turning into Delves
Road is about 600m on the left.
Car Parking: 100 adjacent to Clubhouse, 200 within 5 mins walk.   **Club Shop**: Matchdays, Sun & Thur. eve.
Clubhouse: Matchdays 12-11. Eves (except Wed), 7-11 Sun. 12-6pm. Available for private hire contact Rob Taylor 07976 136493
Programme: Size: A5   Pages: 36 plus cover   Price: with admission   Editorial & Advertising: Chris Emes, Editor
Founded: 1922   **Training Nights**: Tuesday & Thursday   **Website**: www.walsallrugbyclub.com
Colours: Scarlet/black/scarlet   **Change colours**: Royal blue & amber/blue/blue & amber

WHITCHURCH R.F.C.

President: John Gregory   **Chairman**: Jim Mullock Tel: 01948 662203   **Treasurer**: Dave Speed
Secretary: Bob Thompson, 15 Richmond Terrace Station Road Whitchurch Shropshire SY 13 1RH
Tel: 01948 666391   email: toasthompson@ yahoo.co.uk
Fixture Sec.: Gary Evans, West View, Whixall Green, Whixall, Whitchurch SY13 2QR
Tel: 01244 686574   email: gary.evans@marks-and-spencer.com
Press & Media / League Contact: John Gregory Tel: 01948 663151   **1st XV Captain**: Chris Hares
Ground Address: Edgeley Park, Heath Road, Whitchurch, Shropshire SY13 1EU   Tel: 01948 663316
Directions: From South - From joint A41/49 follow signs for Town Centre. Pick up signs for Rugby Club and follow. Ground
is in Heath Road, opposite the cricket club. From north: join A41/49 and go round the Whitchurch by-pass. Take road marked
Newcastle & Nantwich. At next r'about turn left towards the town centre. The club is on the right opp. the cricket club.
Nearest BR Station: Whitchurch (7 mins walk - please phone for directions)   **Car Parking**: 500
Capacity: Unlimited   Covered standing: 50   **Admission**: Matchday £3   Season Tickets - £50
Clubhouse: Open Tue, Wed & Thur 7-11pm,. Sat 11am-11pm, Sun 12-7pm. Food available.
Functions: Contact Diane Tinsley 01948 663316   **Club Shop**: Contact Mike Townsend
Founded: 1936   **Training Nights**: Tues & Thur 7.30pm   **Website**: www.whitchurchrugbyclub.co.uk
Colours: Red shirts, white shorts, red socks   **Change colours**: Blue shirts
Programme   Size: A5   Price: with entry   Pages: 22   Advertising - contact Rob Slater 07803 856622

MIDLANDS DIVISION LEAGUE TABLES 2008-09

Midlands 3 West South

		P	W	D	L	F	A	PD	Pts	Adj
1	Leamington	22	17	0	5	527	270	257	34	
2	Nuneaton Old Edwardians	22	17	0	5	509	339	170	34	
3	Old Laurentians	22	16	0	6	541	296	245	32	
4	Earlsdon	22	11	1	10	338	379	-41	23	
5	Barkers Butts	22	11	0	11	335	387	-52	22	
6	Droitwich	22	9	1	12	318	337	-19	19	
7	Old Coventrians	22	9	1	12	327	424	-97	19	
8	Spartans (Midlands)	22	9	1	12	305	452	-147	19	
9	Newbold on Avon	22	9	0	13	395	415	-20	18	
10	Kidderminster	22	8	1	13	353	484	-131	17	
11	Silhillians	22	7	0	15	378	447	-69	14	
12	Berkswell & Balsall	22	6	1	15	287	383	-96	13	

Midlands 4 West South

		P	W	D	L	F	A	PD	Pts	Adj
1	Worcester Wanderers	22	20	0	2	690	248	442	40	
2	Bedworth	22	18	0	4	637	197	440	36	
3	Dunlop	22	16	0	6	618	275	343	30	-2
4	Ledbury	22	14	1	7	501	322	179	29	
5	Upton-on-Severn	22	14	0	8	347	317	30	28	
6	Pershore	22	13	2	7	560	257	303	26	-2
7	Old Leamingtonians	22	11	0	11	488	421	67	22	
8	Woodrush	22	9	0	13	339	405	-66	18	
9	Shipston on Stour	22	7	1	14	314	620	-306	15	
10	Southam	22	4	1	17	215	610	-395	7	-2
11	Edwardians	22	2	1	19	215	695	-480	5	
12	Kings Norton	22	1	0	21	202	759	-557	0	-2

Midlands 5 West South

		P	W	D	L	F	A	PD	Pts	Adj
1	Redditch	20	16	2	2	413	158	255	34	
2	Harbury	20	16	1	3	445	190	255	33	
3	Evesham	20	11	1	8	550	214	336	23	
4	Coventry Welsh	20	11	0	9	339	216	123	22	
5	Stoke Old Boys	20	9	3	8	312	344	-32	21	
6	Pinley	20	9	0	11	236	238	-2	18	
7	Keresley	20	8	2	10	272	304	-32	18	
8	Manor Park	20	8	2	10	280	328	-48	18	
9	Dudley Wasps	20	6	2	12	282	427	-145	14	
10	Coventrians	20	5	2	13	163	404	-241	12	
11	Copsewood	20	3	1	16	115	584	-469	5	-2

Midlands 6 West SW

		P	W	D	L	F	A	PD	Pts	Adj
1	Birmingham Exiles	18	13	1	4	324	198	126	27	
2	Warley	18	13	0	5	291	204	87	26	
3	Bromyard	18	11	1	6	355	184	171	23	
4	Claverdon	18	11	1	6	300	202	98	23	
5	Chaddesley Corbett	18	10	1	7	322	326	-4	19	-2
6	Tenbury	18	7	1	10	259	235	24	15	
7	Clee Hill	17	6	1	10	209	288	-79	13	
8	Bredon Star	18	7	1	10	240	310	-70	11	-4
9	Birmingham C.S.	17	7	0	10	254	238	16	10	-4
10	Highley	18	0	1	17	89	458	-369	-3	-4

Midlands 6 West SE

		P	W	D	L	F	A	PD	Pts	Adj
1	Rugby Welsh	16	14	1	1	464	146	318	29	
2	Alcester	16	14	0	2	397	130	267	28	
3	Trinity Guild	16	12	1	3	440	258	182	25	
4	Wellesbourne	16	6	0	10	231	311	-80	12	
5	Atherstone	15	7	1	7	253	204	49	11	-4
6	Old Wheatleyans	16	5	1	10	304	300	4	11	
7	Coventry Technical	16	6	0	10	311	304	7	8	-4
8	Warwickian	16	4	1	11	164	435	-271	5	-4
9	Coventry Saracens	15	0	1	14	62	538	-476	-3	-4

MIDLANDS 1 WEST

Midlands 3 West North ▲   ▲ Midlands 3 West South

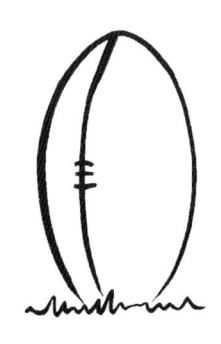

MIDLANDS DIVISION LEAGUE TABLES 2008-09

Midlands 3 West North	P	W	D	L	F	A	PD	Pts	Adj
1 Old Halesonians	22	20	0	2	549	176	373	40	
2 Bournville	22	20	0	2	523	202	321	40	
3 Lichfield	22	15	0	7	500	359	141	28	-2
4 Bridgnorth	22	14	0	8	425	291	134	28	
5 Aston Old Edwardians	22	13	0	9	511	313	198	26	
6 Ludlow	22	12	0	10	398	383	15	24	
7 Lordswood Dixonians	22	10	1	11	427	370	57	21	
8 Stafford	22	10	0	12	404	407	-3	20	
9 Old Saltleians	22	9	1	12	313	381	-68	19	
10 Wolverhampton	22	3	0	19	260	612	-352	6	
11 Stourbridge Lions	22	4	0	18	213	555	-342	4	-4
12 Wednesbury	22	1	0	21	253	727	-474	2	

Midlands 4 West North	P	W	D	L	F	A	PD	Pts	Adj
1 Willenhall	22	21	0	1	633	179	454	42	
2 Shrewsbury	22	19	0	3	612	229	383	38	
3 Burntwood	22	15	0	7	460	238	222	30	
4 Tamworth	22	14	1	7	511	217	294	29	
5 Veseyans	22	13	0	9	537	343	194	26	
6 Newcastle (Staffs)	22	11	1	10	379	364	15	23	
7 Old Yardleians	22	11	0	11	448	346	102	22	
8 Handsworth	22	9	1	12	373	486	-113	19	
9 Leek	22	7	0	15	379	441	-62	14	
10 Moseley Oak	22	6	0	16	252	728	-476	12	
11 Bishops Castle & Onny Valley	22	4	1	17	139	604	-465	9	
12 Cleobury Mortimer	22	0	0	22	193	741	-548	-2	-2

Midlands 5 West North	P	W	D	L	F	A	PD	Pts	Adj
1 Bloxwich	20	18	0	2	501	177	324	36	
2 Telford Hornets	20	16	0	4	550	173	377	32	
3 Yardley & District	20	15	0	5	502	178	324	30	
4 Harborne	20	14	0	6	373	254	119	28	
5 Eccleshall	20	12	0	8	293	258	35	24	
6 St Leonards	20	9	0	11	374	347	27	18	
7 Cannock	20	7	1	12	283	341	-58	13	-2
8 Old Griffinians	20	7	0	13	332	485	-153	12	-2
9 Barton-Under-Needwood	20	5	1	14	225	381	-156	11	
10 Stourport	20	3	0	17	228	516	-288	6	
11 Five Ways O.E.	20	3	0	17	162	713	-551	6	

Midlands 6 West North	P	W	D	L	F	A	PD	Pts	Adj
1 Essington	14	12	2	0	426	82	344	26	
2 Rugeley	14	10	1	3	297	133	164	21	
3 Market Drayton	14	10	0	4	364	164	200	20	
4 Whittington	14	9	0	5	375	161	214	18	
5 Aldridge	14	6	2	6	341	155	186	14	
6 Hanford	14	3	0	11	166	469	-303	4	-2
7 Wheaton Aston	14	2	0	12	83	529	-446	4	
8 Stone	14	1	1	12	71	430	-359	-1	-4

MIDLANDS

MIDLANDS DIVISION LEAGUE TABLES 2008-09

MIDLANDS 3 EAST NORTH	P	W	D	L	F	A	PD	Pts	Adj
1 Ilkeston	22	20	1	1	844	232	612	41	
2 Spalding	22	19	0	3	745	194	551	38	
3 Melton Mowbray	22	15	1	6	524	283	241	31	
4 Loughborough	22	14	1	7	659	344	315	29	
5 Bakewell Mannerians	22	11	0	11	526	490	36	22	
6 Ashbourne	22	10	1	11	356	440	-84	21	
7 Lincoln	22	8	1	13	393	591	-198	15	-2
8 Grimsby	22	6	0	16	304	849	-545	12	
9 Coalville	22	16	1	5	787	374	413	11	-22
10 Nottingham Moderns	22	4	0	18	357	635	-278	8	
11 Sleaford	22	4	0	18	272	795	-523	6	-2
12 West Bridgford	22	2	0	20	162	702	-540	4	

MIDLANDS 4 EAST NORTH	P	W	D	L	F	A	PD	Pts	Adj
1 Market Rasen & Louth	22	21	0	1	1,048	179	869	40	-2
2 Belgrave	22	18	0	4	607	206	401	36	
3 Mellish	22	18	0	4	551	232	319	36	
4 Ashby	22	14	1	7	544	362	182	29	
5 Nottingham Casuals	22	14	1	7	518	351	167	29	
6 Boston	22	13	0	9	457	421	36	26	
7 Oakham	22	10	2	10	488	499	-11	22	
8 Kesteven	22	6	2	14	263	462	-199	14	
9 Barton & District	22	7	0	15	324	596	-272	10	-4
10 Southwell	22	4	1	17	273	735	-462	7	-2
11 Amber Valley	22	2	0	20	195	641	-446	4	
12 Ashfield	22	1	1	20	169	753	-584	-1	-4

MIDLANDS 5 EAST NORTH	P	W	D	L	F	A	PD	Pts	Adj
1 Worksop	18	17	0	1	449	146	303	34	
2 Melbourne	18	15	0	3	388	144	244	30	
3 Rolls Royce	18	11	0	7	411	281	130	22	
4 Chesterfield Panthers	18	10	0	8	371	295	76	20	
5 Belper	18	9	1	8	350	226	124	19	
6 Leesbrook	18	7	0	11	211	274	-63	14	
7 East Leake	18	6	2	10	250	320	-70	14	
8 Nottinghamians	18	6	1	11	204	279	-75	13	
9 East Retford	18	6	0	12	234	352	-118	12	
10 Castle Donington	18	1	0	17	87	638	-551	2	

MIDLANDS 6 EAST NW	P	W	D	L	F	A	PD	Pts	Adj
1 Uttoxeter	14	12	0	2	558	75	483	24	
2 Dronfield	14	11	1	2	417	179	238	23	
3 Nottingham Boots Corsairs	14	11	0	3	436	127	309	22	
4 Tupton	14	7	2	5	370	258	112	14	-2
5 Long Eaton	14	6	0	8	223	283	-60	10	-2
6 All Spartans OB	14	2	2	10	134	403	-269	6	
7 University Of Derby	14	4	0	10	140	613	-473	6	-2
8 Meden Vale	14	0	1	13	121	461	-340	1	

MIDLANDS 6 EAST NE	P	W	D	L	F	A	PD	Pts	Adj
1 Cleethorpes	8	7	0	1	159	91	68	14	
2 Skegness	8	4	0	4	207	147	60	8	
3 Keyworth	8	4	0	4	129	94	35	8	
4 Ollerton	8	2	0	6	124	249	-125	4	
5 North Hykeham	8	3	0	5	112	150	-38	2	-4

MIDLANDS 1 EAST

Midlands 3 East North ↑   ↑ Midlands 3 East South

MIDLANDS 3 EAST SOUTH	P	W	D	L	F	A	PD	Pts	Adj
1 Old Northamptonians	22	22	0	0	1,036	140	896	44	
2 Stewarts & Lloyds	22	20	0	2	596	239	357	40	
3 Towcestrians	21	14	1	6	521	312	209	29	
4 Northampton Old Scouts	22	14	0	8	575	389	186	28	
5 Banbury	22	12	0	10	536	507	29	20	-4
6 Lutterworth	22	10	0	12	336	483	-147	20	
7 Leicester Forest	21	8	0	13	334	474	-140	16	
8 Old Newtonians	22	7	2	13	304	469	-165	16	
9 Vipers	22	9	0	13	377	585	-208	16	-2
10 Northampton BBOB	22	5	1	16	300	600	-300	11	
11 Aylestone St James	22	5	0	17	262	520	-258	10	
12 Huntingdon & District	22	3	0	19	224	683	-459	6	

MIDLANDS 4 EAST SOUTH	P	W	D	L	F	A	PD	Pts	Adj
1 Market Harborough	22	20	0	2	610	135	475	40	
2 Peterborough Lions	22	19	1	2	861	257	604	39	
3 Rugby St Andrews	22	14	1	7	471	343	128	29	
4 Daventry	22	13	1	8	419	228	191	27	
5 Bugbrooke	22	13	0	9	486	280	206	26	
6 Northampton Casuals	22	13	0	9	334	320	14	26	
7 Bedford Swifts	22	11	0	11	408	463	-55	22	
8 Deepings	22	11	0	11	407	422	-15	20	-2
9 Northampton Mens Own	22	10	0	12	405	425	-20	20	
10 Brackley	22	4	0	18	182	523	-341	6	-2
11 Vauxhall Motors	22	1	1	20	178	819	-641	3	
12 Long Buckby	22	1	0	21	112	658	-546	2	

MIDLANDS 5 EAST SOUTH	P	W	D	L	F	A	PD	Pts	Adj
1 Stockwood Park	18	17	0	1	418	135	283	34	
2 Queens	18	14	1	3	405	170	235	29	
3 Oundle	18	13	0	5	492	236	256	26	
4 Oadby Wyggestonians	18	11	0	7	325	223	102	22	
5 Rushden & Higham	18	11	0	7	386	287	99	22	
6 Aylestone Athletic	18	6	1	11	186	436	-250	13	
7 Biggleswade	18	4	1	13	206	379	-173	9	
8 Stoneygate	18	5	0	13	231	342	-111	8	-2
9 Wellingborough O.G.	18	2	0	16	200	563	-363	4	
10 Kempston	18	5	1	12	222	300	-78	-3	-14

MIDLANDS 6 EAST SOUTH	P	W	D	L	F	A	PD	Pts	Adj
1 St Neots	10	9	1	0	362	87	275	19	
2 Stamford	10	7	0	3	176	127	49	14	
3 St Ives (Midlands)	10	6	1	3	221	112	109	13	
4 Thorney	10	4	0	6	163	229	-66	8	
5 Westwood	10	3	0	7	155	169	-14	6	
6 Stamford College Old Boys	10	0	0	10	71	424	-353	0	

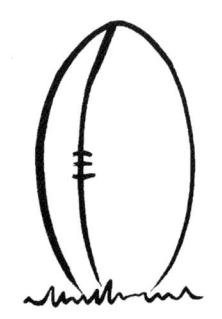

MIDLANDS DIVISION FIXTURE GRIDS 2009-2010

MIDLANDS TWO EAST NORTH	Bakewell Mann.	Belgrave	Coalville	Grimsby	Lincoln	Loughborough	Market Rasen & L.	Melton Mowbray	Nottingham Moderns	Sleaford	Spalding	West Bridgford
Bakewell Mannerians		26/09	09/01	10/10	23/01	31/10	13/02	14/11	06/03	05/12	10/04	12/09
Belgrave	19/12		10/10	23/01	31/10	13/02	14/11	06/03	05/12	10/04	12/09	03/10
Coalville	03/10	16/01		31/10	13/02	14/11	06/03	05/12	10/04	12/09	19/12	17/10
Grimsby	16/01	17/10	30/01		14/11	06/03	05/12	10/04	12/09	19/12	03/10	07/11
Lincoln	17/10	30/01	07/11	20/02		05/12	10/04	12/09	19/12	03/10	16/01	28/11
Loughborough	30/01	07/11	20/02	28/11	27/03		12/09	19/12	03/10	16/01	17/10	12/12
Market Rasen & Louth	07/11	20/02	28/11	27/03	12/12	17/04		03/10	16/01	17/10	30/01	19/12
Melton Mowbray	20/02	28/11	27/03	12/12	12/09	26/09	09/01		17/10	30/01	07/11	16/01
Nottingham Moderns	28/11	27/03	12/12	17/04	26/09	09/01	10/10	23/01		07/11	20/02	30/01
Sleaford	27/03	12/12	17/04	26/09	09/01	10/10	23/01	31/10	13/02		28/11	20/02
Spalding	12/12	17/04	26/09	09/01	10/10	23/01	31/10	13/02	14/11	06/03		27/03
West Bridgford	17/04	09/01	23/01	13/02	06/03	10/04	26/09	10/10	31/10	14/11	05/12	

MIDLANDS TWO EAST SOUTH	Aylestone St J.	Banbury	Huntingdon & D.	Leicester Forest	Lutterworth	Market Harborough	Northampton BBOB	N'mpton Old Scouts	Old Newtonians	Peterborough Lions	Towcestrians	Vipers
Aylestone St James		26/09	09/01	10/10	23/01	31/10	13/02	14/11	06/03	05/12	10/04	12/09
Banbury	19/12		10/10	23/01	31/10	13/02	14/11	06/03	05/12	10/04	12/09	03/10
Huntingdon & District	03/10	16/01		31/10	13/02	14/11	06/03	05/12	10/04	12/09	19/12	17/10
Leicester Forest	16/01	17/10	30/01		14/11	06/03	05/12	10/04	12/09	19/12	03/10	07/11
Lutterworth	17/10	30/01	07/11	20/02		05/12	10/04	12/09	19/12	03/10	16/01	28/11
Market Harborough	30/01	07/11	20/02	28/11	27/03		12/09	19/12	03/10	16/01	17/10	12/12
Northampton BBOB	07/11	20/02	28/11	27/03	12/12	17/04		03/10	16/01	17/10	30/01	19/12
Northampton Old Scouts	20/02	28/11	27/03	12/12	17/04	26/09	09/01		17/10	30/01	07/11	16/01
Old Newtonians	28/11	27/03	12/12	17/04	26/09	09/01	10/10	23/01		07/11	20/02	30/01
Peterborough Lions	27/03	12/12	17/04	26/09	09/01	10/10	23/01	31/10	13/02		28/11	20/02
Towcestrians	12/12	17/04	26/09	09/01	10/10	23/01	31/10	13/02	14/11	06/03		27/03
Vipers	17/04	09/01	23/01	13/02	06/03	10/04	26/09	10/10	31/10	14/11	05/12	

LEVEL SEVEN

MIDLANDS TWO WEST NORTH	Ashbourne	Aston Old Es	Bridgnorth	Lichfield	Lordswood Dix.	Ludlow	Old Saltleians	Shrewsbury	Stafford	Stourbridge Lions	Willenhall	Wolverhampton
Ashbourne		26/09	09/01	31/10	23/01	10/10	13/02	14/11	06/03	05/12	10/04	12/09
Aston Old Edwardians	19/12		10/10	13/02	31/10	23/01	14/11	06/03	05/12	10/04	12/09	03/10
Bridgnorth	03/10	16/01		14/11	13/02	31/10	06/03	05/12	10/04	12/09	19/12	17/10
Lichfield	30/01	07/11	20/02		27/03	28/11	12/09	19/12	03/10	16/01	17/10	12/12
Lordswood Dixonians	17/10	30/01	07/11	05/12		20/02	10/04	12/09	19/12	03/10	16/01	28/11
Ludlow	16/01	17/10	30/01	06/03	14/11		05/12	10/04	12/09	19/12	03/10	07/11
Old Saltleians	07/11	20/02	28/11	17/04	12/12	27/03		03/10	16/01	17/10	30/01	19/12
Shrewsbury	20/02	28/11	27/03	26/09	17/04	12/12	09/01		17/10	30/01	07/11	16/01
Stafford	28/11	27/03	12/12	09/01	26/09	17/04	10/10	23/01		07/11	20/02	30/01
Stourbridge Lions	27/03	12/12	17/04	10/10	09/01	26/09	23/01	31/10	13/02		28/11	20/02
Willenhall	12/12	17/04	26/09	23/01	10/10	09/01	31/10	13/02	14/11	06/03		27/03
Wolverhampton	17/04	09/01	23/01	10/04	06/03	13/02	26/09	10/10	31/10	14/11	05/12	

MIDLANDS TWO WEST SOUTH	Barkers Butts	Bedworth	Berkswell & B.	Droitwich	Earlsdon	Kidderminster	Newbold on Avon	Old Coventrians	Old Laurentians	Silhillians	Spartans (Midlands)	Worcester Wanderers
Barkers Butts		26/09	09/01	10/10	23/01	31/10	13/02	14/11	06/03	05/12	10/04	12/09
Bedworth	19/12		10/10	23/01	31/10	13/02	14/11	06/03	05/12	10/04	12/09	03/10
Berkswell & Balsall	03/10	16/01		31/10	13/02	14/11	06/03	05/12	10/04	12/09	19/12	17/10
Droitwich	16/01	17/10	30/01		14/11	06/03	05/12	10/04	12/09	19/12	03/10	07/11
Earlsdon	17/10	30/01	07/11	20/02		05/12	10/04	12/09	19/12	03/10	16/01	28/11
Kidderminster	30/01	07/11	20/02	28/11	27/03		12/09	19/12	03/10	16/01	17/10	12/12
Newbold on Avon	07/11	20/02	28/11	27/03	12/12	17/04		03/10	16/01	17/10	30/01	19/12
Old Coventrians	20/02	28/11	27/03	12/12	17/04	26/09	09/01		17/10	30/01	07/11	16/01
Old Laurentians	28/11	27/03	12/12	17/04	26/09	09/01	10/10	23/01		07/11	20/02	30/01
Silhillians	27/03	12/12	17/04	26/09	09/01	10/10	23/01	31/10	13/02		28/11	20/02
Spartans (Midlands)	12/12	17/04	26/09	09/01	10/10	23/01	31/10	13/02	14/11	06/03		27/03
Worcester Wanderers	17/04	09/01	23/01	13/02	06/03	10/04	26/09	10/10	31/10	14/11	05/12	

MIDLANDS DIVISION FIXTURE GRIDS 2009-2010

MIDLANDS 3 EAST NORTH

		1	2	3	4	5	6	7	8	9	10	11	12
1	Amber Valley		26/09	09/01	10/10	23/01	31/10	13/02	14/11	06/03	05/12	10/04	12/09
2	Ashby	19/12		10/10	23/01	31/10	13/02	14/11	06/03	05/12	10/04	12/09	03/10
3	Ashfield	03/10	16/01		31/10	13/02	14/11	06/03	05/12	10/04	12/09	19/12	17/10
4	Barton & District	16/01	17/10	30/01		14/11	06/03	05/12	10/04	12/09	19/12	03/10	07/11
5	Boston	17/10	30/01	07/11	20/02		05/12	10/04	12/09	19/12	03/10	16/01	28/11
6	Kesteven	30/01	07/11	20/02	28/11	27/03		12/09	19/12	03/10	16/01	17/10	12/12
7	Melbourne	07/11	20/02	28/11	27/03	12/12	17/04		03/10	16/01	17/10	30/01	19/12
8	Mellish	20/02	28/11	27/03	12/12	17/04	26/09	09/01		17/10	30/01	07/11	16/01
9	Nottingham Casuals	28/11	27/03	12/12	17/04	26/09	09/01	10/10	23/01		07/11	20/02	30/01
10	Oakham	27/03	12/12	17/04	26/09	09/01	10/10	23/01	31/10	13/02		28/11	20/02
11	Southwell	12/12	17/04	26/09	09/01	10/10	23/01	31/10	13/02	14/11	06/03		27/03
12	Worksop	17/04	09/01	23/01	13/02	06/03	10/04	26/09	10/10	31/10	14/11	05/12	

MIDLANDS 4 EAST NORTH

		1	2	3	4	5	6	7	8	9	10	11	12
1	Belper		26/09	09/01	10/10	23/01	31/10	13/02	14/11	06/03	05/12	10/04	12/09
2	Castle Donington	19/12		10/10	23/01	31/10	13/02	14/11	06/03	05/12	10/04	12/09	03/10
3	Chesterfield Panthers	03/10	16/01		31/10	13/02	14/11	06/03	05/12	10/04	12/09	19/12	17/10
4	Cleethorpes	16/01	17/10	30/01		14/11	06/03	05/12	10/04	12/09	19/12	03/10	07/11
5	Dronfield	17/10	30/01	07/11	20/02		05/12	10/04	12/09	19/12	03/10	16/01	28/11
6	East Leake	30/01	07/11	20/02	28/11	27/03		12/09	19/12	03/10	16/01	17/10	12/12
7	East Retford	07/11	20/02	28/11	27/03	12/12	17/04		03/10	16/01	17/10	30/01	19/12
8	Leesbrook	20/02	28/11	27/03	12/12	17/04	26/09	09/01		17/10	30/01	07/11	16/01
9	Nottinghamians	28/11	27/03	12/12	17/04	26/09	09/01	10/10	23/01		07/11	20/02	30/01
10	Rolls Royce	27/03	12/12	17/04	26/09	09/01	10/10	23/01	31/10	13/02		28/11	20/02
11	Skegness	12/12	17/04	26/09	09/01	10/10	23/01	31/10	13/02	14/11	06/03		27/03
12	Uttoxeter	17/04	09/01	23/01	13/02	06/03	10/04	26/09	10/10	31/10	14/11	05/12	

MIDLANDS 5 EAST NORTH

		1	2	3	4	5	6	7	8	9
1	All Spartans OB		16/01	31/10	30/01	14/11	20/02	12/12	27/03	26/09
2	Keyworth	17/10		14/11	20/02	12/12	27/03	26/09	09/01	07/11
3	Long Eaton	23/01	13/02		12/12	27/03	26/09	09/01	17/10	28/11
4	Meden Vale	07/11	28/11	06/03		26/09	09/01	17/10	23/01	19/12
5	North Hykeham	13/02	06/03	19/12	10/04		17/10	23/01	07/11	09/01
6	Nottingham Boots Corsairs	28/11	19/12	10/04	10/10	16/01		07/11	13/02	23/01
7	Ollerton	06/03	10/04	10/10	16/01	31/10	30/01		28/11	13/02
8	Tupton	19/12	10/10	16/01	31/10	30/01	14/11	20/02		06/03
9	University Of Derby	10/04	30/01	20/02	27/03	10/10	31/10	14/11	12/12	

MIDLANDS 3 EAST SOUTH

		1	2	3	4	5	6	7	8	9	10	11	12
1	Bedford Swifts		26/09	09/01	10/10	23/01	31/10	13/02	14/11	06/03	05/12	10/04	12/09
2	Brackley	19/12		10/10	23/01	31/10	13/02	14/11	06/03	05/12	10/04	12/09	03/10
3	Bugbrooke	03/10	16/01		31/10	13/02	14/11	06/03	05/12	10/04	12/09	19/12	17/10
4	Daventry	16/01	17/10	30/01		14/11	06/03	05/12	10/04	12/09	19/12	03/10	07/11
5	Deepings	17/10	30/01	07/11	20/02		05/12	10/04	12/09	19/12	03/10	16/01	28/11
6	Long Buckby	30/01	07/11	20/02	28/11	27/03		12/09	19/12	03/10	16/01	17/10	12/12
7	Northampton Casuals	07/11	20/02	28/11	27/03	12/12	17/04		03/10	16/01	17/10	30/01	19/12
8	Northampton Mens Own	20/02	28/11	27/03	12/12	17/04	26/09	09/01		17/10	30/01	07/11	16/01
9	Queens	28/11	27/03	12/12	17/04	26/09	09/01	10/10	23/01		07/11	20/02	30/01
10	Rugby St Andrews	27/03	12/12	17/04	26/09	09/01	10/10	23/01	31/10	13/02		28/11	20/02
11	Stockwood Park	12/12	17/04	26/09	09/01	10/10	23/01	31/10	13/02	14/11	06/03		27/03
12	Vauxhall Motors	17/04	09/01	23/01	13/02	06/03	10/04	26/09	10/10	31/10	14/11	05/12	

MIDLANDS EAST SOUTH A

		1	2	3	4	5	6	7
1	Biggleswade		26/09	28/11	12/12	31/10	10/10	09/01
2	Oundle	14/11		10/10	31/10	09/01	12/12	12/09
3	Rushden & Higham	03/10	05/12		09/01	12/09	31/10	14/11
4	St Ives (Midlands)	17/10	19/12	07/11		03/10	16/01	05/12
5	St Neots	19/12	07/11	16/01	28/11		26/09	17/10
6	Wellingborough O.G.	05/12	17/10	19/12	12/09	14/11		03/10
7	Westwood	07/11	16/01	26/09	10/10	12/12	28/11	

MIDLANDS EAST SOUTH B

		1	2	3	4	5	6	7
1	Aylestone Athletic		26/09	28/11	10/10	12/12	31/10	09/01
2	Kempston	14/11		10/10	12/12	31/10	09/01	12/09
3	Oadby Wyggestonians	03/10	05/12		31/10	09/01	12/09	14/11
4	Stamford	05/12	17/10	19/12		12/09	14/11	03/10
5	Stamford College Old Boys	17/10	19/12	07/11	16/01		03/10	05/12
6	Stoneygate	19/12	07/11	16/01	26/09	28/11		17/10
7	Thorney	07/11	16/01	26/09	28/11	10/10	12/12	

MIDLANDS DIVISION FIXTURE GRIDS 2009-2010

MIDLANDS 3 WEST NORTH

		1	2	3	4	5	6	7	8	9	10	11	12
1	Bishops Castle & Onny Valley		26/09	09/01	10/10	23/01	31/10	13/02	14/11	06/03	05/12	10/04	12/09
2	Bloxwich	19/12		10/10	23/01	31/10	13/02	14/11	06/03	05/12	10/04	12/09	03/10
3	Burntwood	03/10	16/01		31/10	13/02	14/11	06/03	05/12	10/04	12/09	19/12	17/10
4	Handsworth	16/01	17/10	30/01		14/11	06/03	05/12	10/04	12/09	19/12	03/10	07/11
5	Leek	17/10	30/01	07/11	20/02		05/12	10/04	12/09	19/12	03/10	16/01	28/11
6	Moseley Oak	30/01	07/11	20/02	28/11	27/03		12/09	19/12	03/10	16/01	17/10	12/12
7	Newcastle (Staffs)	07/11	20/02	28/11	27/03	12/12	17/04		03/10	16/01	17/10	30/01	19/12
8	Old Yardleians	20/02	28/11	27/03	12/12	17/04	26/09	09/01		17/10	30/01	07/11	16/01
9	Tamworth	28/11	27/03	12/12	17/04	26/09	09/01	10/10	23/01		07/11	20/02	30/01
10	Telford Hornets	27/03	12/12	17/04	26/09	09/01	10/10	23/01	31/10	13/02		28/11	20/02
11	Veseyans	12/12	17/04	26/09	09/01	10/10	23/01	31/10	13/02	14/11	06/03		27/03
12	Wednesbury	17/04	09/01	23/01	13/02	06/03	10/04	26/09	10/10	31/10	14/11	05/12	

MIDLANDS 4 WEST NORTH

		1	2	3	4	5	6	7	8	9	10
1	Barton-Under-Needwood		10/10	16/01	31/10	30/01	14/11	20/02	12/12	27/03	26/09
2	Cannock	09/01		31/10	30/01	14/11	20/02	12/12	27/03	26/09	17/10
3	Cleobury Mortimer	17/10	23/01		14/11	20/02	12/12	27/03	26/09	09/01	07/11
4	Eccleshall	23/01	07/11	13/02		12/12	27/03	26/09	09/01	17/10	28/11
5	Essington	07/11	13/02	28/11	06/03		26/09	09/01	17/10	23/01	19/12
6	Harborne	13/02	28/11	06/03	19/12	10/04		17/10	23/01	07/11	09/01
7	Old Griffinians	28/11	06/03	19/12	10/04	10/10	16/01		07/11	13/02	23/01
8	Rugeley	06/03	19/12	10/04	10/10	16/01	31/10	30/01		28/11	13/02
9	St Leonards	19/12	10/04	10/10	16/01	31/10	30/01	14/11	20/02		06/03
10	Yardley & District	10/04	16/01	30/01	20/02	27/03	10/10	31/10	14/11	12/12	

MIDLANDS 5 WEST NORTH

		1	2	3	4	5	6	7	8
1	Aldridge		10/10	16/01	31/10	20/02	28/11	27/03	26/09
2	Five Ways O.E.	19/12		31/10	20/02	28/11	27/03	26/09	17/10
3	Hanford	17/10	30/01		28/11	27/03	26/09	19/12	14/11
4	Market Drayton	30/01	14/11	06/03		26/09	19/12	17/10	12/12
5	Stone	14/11	06/03	12/12	10/04		17/10	30/01	19/12
6	Warley	06/03	12/12	10/04	10/10	16/01		14/11	30/01
7	Wheaton Aston	12/12	10/04	10/10	16/01	31/10	20/02		06/03
8	Whittington	10/04	16/01	20/02	27/03	10/10	31/10	28/11	

MIDLANDS 3 WEST SOUTH

		1	2	3	4	5	6	7	8	9	10	11	12
1	Dunlop		26/09	09/01	10/10	23/01	31/10	13/02	14/11	06/03	05/12	10/04	12/09
2	Edwardians	19/12		10/10	23/01	31/10	13/02	14/11	06/03	05/12	10/04	12/09	03/10
3	Harbury	03/10	16/01		31/10	13/02	14/11	06/03	05/12	10/04	12/09	19/12	17/10
4	Kings Norton	16/01	17/10	30/01		14/11	06/03	05/12	10/04	12/09	19/12	03/10	07/11
5	Ledbury	17/10	30/01	07/11	20/02		05/12	10/04	12/09	19/12	03/10	16/01	28/11
6	Old Leamingtonians	30/01	07/11	20/02	28/11	27/03		12/09	19/12	03/10	16/01	17/10	12/12
7	Pershore	07/11	20/02	28/11	27/03	12/12	17/04		03/10	16/01	17/10	30/01	19/12
8	Redditch	20/02	28/11	27/03	12/12	17/04	26/09	09/01		17/10	30/01	07/11	16/01
9	Shipston on Stour	28/11	27/03	12/12	17/04	26/09	09/01	10/10	23/01		07/11	20/02	30/01
10	Southam	27/03	12/12	17/04	26/09	09/01	10/10	23/01	31/10	13/02		28/11	20/02
11	Upton-on-Severn	12/12	17/04	26/09	09/01	10/10	23/01	31/10	13/02	14/11	06/03		27/03
12	Woodrush	17/04	09/01	23/01	13/02	06/03	10/04	26/09	10/10	31/10	14/11	05/12	

MIDLANDS 4 WEST SOUTH

		1	2	3	4	5	6	7	8	9	10
1	Alcester		10/10	16/01	31/10	30/01	14/11	20/02	12/12	27/03	26/09
2	Birmingham Exiles	09/01		31/10	30/01	14/11	20/02	12/12	27/03	26/09	17/10
3	Coventry Welsh	17/10	23/01		14/11	20/02	12/12	27/03	26/09	09/01	07/11
4	Dudley Wasps	23/01	07/11	13/02		12/12	27/03	26/09	09/01	17/10	28/11
5	Evesham	07/11	13/02	28/11	06/03		26/09	09/01	17/10	23/01	19/12
6	Keresley	13/02	28/11	06/03	19/12	10/04		17/10	23/01	07/11	09/01
7	Manor Park	28/11	06/03	19/12	10/04	10/10	16/01		07/11	13/02	23/01
8	Pinley	06/03	19/12	10/04	10/10	16/01	31/10	30/01		28/11	13/02
9	Rugby Welsh	19/12	10/04	10/10	16/01	31/10	30/01	14/11	20/02		06/03
10	Stoke Old Boys	10/04	16/01	30/01	20/02	27/03	10/10	31/10	14/11	12/12	

MIDLANDS 5 WEST SOUTH EAST

		1	2	3	4	5	6	7
1	Atherstone		10/10	16/01	31/10	30/01	20/02	12/12	27/03	26/09
2	Copsewood	09/01		31/10	30/01	14/11	12/12	27/03	26/09	17/10
3	Coventrians	17/10	23/01		14/11	20/02	27/03	26/09	09/01	07/11
4	Coventry Saracens	23/01	07/11	13/02		12/12	26/09	09/01	17/10	28/11
5	Coventry Technical	07/11	13/02	28/11	06/03		09/01	17/10	23/01	19/12
6	Old Wheatleyans	28/11	06/03	19/12	10/04	10/10		07/11	13/02	23/01
7	Trinity Guild	06/03	19/12	10/04	10/10	16/01	30/01		28/11	13/02
8	Warwickian	19/12	10/04	10/10	16/01	31/10	14/11	20/02		06/03
9	Wellesbourne	10/04	16/01	30/01	20/02	27/03	31/10	14/11	12/12	

MIDLANDS 5 WEST SOUTH WEST

		1	2	3	4	5	6	7
1	Birmingham C.S.		10/10	16/01	31/10	30/01	14/11	12/12	27/03	26/09
2	Bredon Star	09/01		31/10	30/01	14/11	20/02	27/03	26/09	17/10
3	Bromyard	17/10	23/01		14/11	20/02	12/12	26/09	09/01	07/11
4	Chaddesley Corbett	23/01	07/11	13/02		12/12	27/03	09/01	17/10	28/11
5	Claverdon	07/11	13/02	28/11	06/03		26/09	17/10	23/01	19/12
6	Clee Hill	13/02	28/11	06/03	19/12	10/04		23/01	07/11	09/01
7	Highley	06/03	19/12	10/04	10/10	16/01	31/10		28/11	13/02
8	Stourport	19/12	10/04	10/10	16/01	31/10	30/01	20/02		06/03
9	Tenbury	10/04	16/01	30/01	20/02	27/03	10/10	14/11	12/12	

MIDLANDS LEVEL 7-10 & NON LEAGUE CLUBS

Alcester RFC
Ground Address: Birmingham Road Kings Coughton Alcester Warwickshire B49 5QF
Contact: 01789 764061
Email: rugby@alcesterrfc.co.uk
Website: www.alcesterrfc.co.uk
Directions: The ground is situated on the West side of the A435 between Studley and Alcester approx. 1 mile north of Alcester at Kings Coughton.
Honorary Secretary: Mr Michael Edwards; 8 Icknield Row Alcester Warwickshire B49 5EW
Tel: 01789 764096
Email: mjedwards11@tiscali.co.uk
Fixtures Secretary: Mrs Kim Flynn; 3 Knottesford Close Studley Warwickshire B80 7RL
Tel: 01527 857482
Email: kandaflynn@btinternet.com
Club Colours: Red & Black Shirts, Black Shorts
League: Midlands 4 West (S) (level 9)

Aldridge RFC
Ground Address: Bourne Vale off Little Hardwick Road Aldridge WS9 0SH
Contact: 0121 3553770
Email: mikehalloran@blueyonder.co.uk
Website: www.aldridgerfc.co.uk
Directions: Sign posted off Little Hardwick Road. Situated at the end of Bourne Vale. Turn right before entrance to Woodlands Camp. Signposted.
Honorary Secretary: Mr Mike Halloran; 86 Eastern Road Sutton Coldfield Birmingham B73 5NX
Tel: 07980 672399
Email: mikehalloran@blueyonder.co.uk
Fixtures Secretary: Mr Anthony Harbutt
Tel: 07859848456
Email: anthonyharbutt@blueyonder.co.uk
Club Colours: Maroon, Black & Gold Hoops
League: Midlands 5 West (N) (level 10)

All Spartans OB RFC
Ground Address: 132 Chesterfield Road South Mansfield Nottinghamshire NG19 7AP ENGLAND
Contact: 01623 400515
Email: allspartansoldboys@hotmail.co.uk
Website: www.allspartansoldboys.org
Directions: M1 J28 - A38 to Mansfield follow this until you come to a large fourway juction with MacDonalds on your left. Carry on through following signs for Chesterfield for 1 and a half miles until you reach another fourway juction , turn right at this juction to town centre for 1 half mile then turn left at crossing into Queen Elizabeth School grounds.
Honorary Secretary: Mr Charles Chiverton; 28 Kempton Road Mansfield Nottinghamshire NG18 3FG
Tel: 01623 400515 Email: Chivertona@aol.com

Fixtures Secretary: Mr Dale Cattel; little john drive rainworth 10 mansfield Nottinghamshire ng21 ojj
Tel: 07971162250
Email: allspartansoldboys@hotmail.co.uk
Club Colours: RED BLACK WHITE
League: Midlands 5 East (N) (level 10)

Amber Valley RUFC
Ground Address: Pye Bridge Lower Somercotes Alfreton Derbyshire DE55 4NW
Contact: 01773 514308
Email: s_kirkup@hotmail.com
Website: www.ambervalleyrugbyclub.co.uk
Directions: M1 J28 follow A38 towards Derby, 2 miles B600 to Somercotes, follow B600 towards Selston club 2 miles on lcft.
Honorary Secretary: Mr Stewart Kirkup; 6 Mount Pleasant Ripley Derbyshire DE5 3DX
Tel: 01773 570157   Email: s_kirkup@hotmail.com
Fixtures Secretary: Terry Ellans; 32 Waggstaff lane Jacksdale Nottinghamshire NG16 5JJ
Tel: 01773 607913
Email: terence.ellans@ntlworld.com
Club Colours: Amber & Black
League: Midlands 3 East (N) (level 8)

Anstey RFC
Ground Address: no post - changing rooms only Anstey Martin High School Link Rd Anstey LE7 7EB
Email: ac@alanchapman.com
Website: www.ansteyrfc.co.uk
Directions: A5630 into Anstey off A46 (from J21A M1, or J22 A50 from North). From town centre roundabout take Bradgate Road. Link Road is 5th right. Park and change at Martin School, half-mile on left. Clubhouse is Old Hare and Hounds, Bradgate Rd.
Honorary Secretary: Mr Peter Carter; 22 Kingsbridge Cresent Anstey Heights Leicester LE4 1EG
Tel: 07594 876694   Email: degs1001@yahoo.co.uk
Fixtures Secretary: Mr Ian Pollock; 14 Pinewood Close Leicester LE4 1ER Tel: 07854 534115
Email: irp@arfc.fsnet.co.uk
Club Colours: Black shirts & shorts (change - red shirts)
League: Midlands 5 East (S) (level 10)

Ashbourne RUFC
Ground Address: The Recreation Ground Cockayne Avenue Ashbourne DE6 1EJ
Email: webmaster@ashbournerufc.co.uk
Website: http://www.ashbournerufc.co.uk
Directions: A52 Derby/Ashbourne. The ground is visible coming down the Derby Hill to your right. Visit our website for information about how to fund us.
Honorary Secretary: Mr Stephen Jones; 15 Lodge Farm Chase Ashbourne Derbyshire DE6 1GY
Tel: 07768 811150
Email: steve.jones@homeluxnenplas.com

544

Fixtures Secretary: Mr Andrew Bailey; Yeldersley Hall Yeldersley Ashbourne DE6 1LS Tel: 01335 343432
Email: awbailey@tiscali.co.uk
Club Colours: NAVY/AMBER HOOPS
League: Midlands 2 West (N) (level 7)

Ashby RFC
Ground Address: Ashby R.F.C. Clubhouse & Grounds Nottingham Road Ashby-de-la-Zouch LE65 1DQ UNITED KINGDOM
Contact: 01530 413992
Email: michaelensor@trecarn.co.uk
Website: www.ashbyrfc.com
Directions: M42 J13, signposted Ashby (A511), right at next roundabout, sign posted Lount Breedon (A453), 1000m on left hand side.
Honorary Secretary: Mr Michael Ensor; 47-49 Wood Street Ashby-de-la-Zouch Leicestershire LE65 1EL Tel: 01283 554780
Email: michaelensor@trecarn.co.uk
Fixtures Secretary: Mr Anton Stander; 15 Lower Packington Road Ashby de la Zouch, Leicestershire LE65 1GH Tel: 07810 297177
Email: ndlovumanuk@yahoo.co.uk
Club Colours: Maroon & sky blue hooped shirts
League: Midlands 3 East (N) (level 8)

Ashfield RFC
Ground Address: Moor Lane Community Centre Moor Lane Mansfield Nottinghamshire NG18 5SF
Contact: 01623 400411
Email: steve_trainer@hotmail.com
Directions: M1 junction 28, follow signs to Mansfield (A38) at McDonalds lights turn right towards Mansfield. Go through 3 sets of lights, Moor lane is on your right.
Honorary Secretary: Mrs Patricia Wilson; 2 The Shires Sutton In Ashfield Nottinghamshire NG17 1LW
Tel: 01623 517411
Email: patwilsonashfieldrufc@hotmail.co.uk
Fixtures Secretary: Mr Steve Trainer; 3 Ladybrook Lane Mansfield Nottinghamshire NG18 5JA
Tel: 01623 400411 Email: steve_trainer@hotmail.com
Club Colours: Red/Navy & Amber hoops Black Shorts
League: Midlands 3 East (N) (level 8)

Aston Old Edwardians RFC
Ground Address: Sunnybank Avenue Perry Common Birmingham West Midlands B44 0HP
Contact: 0121 3735746
Email: gordon.loffman@rlf.co.uk
Website: www.astonoldeds.com
Directions: Off College Road (A453) approx. half way between A452 and B4138. Seat garage located on corner of A453 and Sunnybank Avenue.
Honorary Secretary: Mr Glyn Brazell; 3 Bagshawe Croft Birmingham B23 5YR Tel: 0121 3778825
Email: glynbrazell@businesslilnkwm.co.uk

Fixtures Secretary: Mr Tony Stafford; 54 Station Rd Marston Green Solihull West Midlands B37 7BA
Tel: 0121 6842653
Email: tony.stafford@blueyonder.co.uk
Club Colours: Green, red & white hoops, white shorts
League: Midlands 2 West (N) (level 7)

Atherstone RFC
Ground Address: Ratcliffe Road Atherstone Warwickshire CV9 1PJ
Contact: 01827 714934
Email: steve.haddon@btinternet.com
Directions: See RFU Club Home page for directions.
Honorary Secretary: Mr Steve Haddon; 93 Coleshill Road Atherstone Warwickshire CV9 2AJ
Tel: 07799 785867 Email: steve.haddon@btinternet.com
Fixtures Secretary: Mr Keith Berry; 10 goodere drive polesworth tamworth Staffordshire b78 1bz
Tel: 01827 893138 Email: keith.berry@sky.com
Club Colours: Black and White
League: Midlands 5 West (SE) (level 10)

Aylestone Athletic RFC
Ground Address: The pavillon Victoria Park Leicester Leicestershire LE1 6UB
Contact: 07979 245267
Email: darren.watson@gistworld.com
Website: www.aylestoneathletic.co.uk
Directions: Victoria Park is apprx 1 mile to the South of the city centre on the A6 & the Pavilion is on the North side of the park.
Honorary Secretary: Mr Neil Weston; 49 Stretton Road Leicester Leicestershire LE3 6BL Tel: 07891 125289
Email: neil.weston@connells.co.uk
Fixtures Secretary: Mr Darren Watson; 12 Rivets Meadow Cloae Thorpe Astley Leicester LE3 3TB
Tel: 07979 245267 Email: darren.watson@gistworld.com
Club Colours: Blue Shirts, white and red sides
League: Midlands 4 East (S) (level 9)

Aylestone St James RFC
Ground Address: Aylestone St. James R.F.C. The Clubhouse Covert Lane, Scraptoft Covert Lane, Scraptoft Leicester Leicestershire LE7 9SP
Contact: 01530 242842
Email: jamie@jangro-leicester.com
Website: www.aylestonestjamesrfc.co.uk
Directions: Out of Leicester on A47 Uppingham Road, veer left onto Scraptoft Lane. Follow all the way up until you go past white house pub at mini island,go directly on onto Covert Lane. Half a mile along we are the 2nd clubhouse on left. Alternatively download a PD
Honorary Secretary: Mr Jamie Hargrave; 183 Markfield Rd Groby LE6 0FT Tel: 01530 242842
Email: jamie@jangro-leicester.com
Fixtures Secretary: Mr Pete Chapman; 8 Valentine Road Leicester LE5 2GH Tel: 07792 010068
Email: Glennc9@freenet.co.uk
Club Colours: Royal Blue & White Hoops, Navy Shorts
League: Midlands 2 East (S) (level 7)

Aylestonians RFC
Ground Address: Knighton Lane East Leicester leicester LE2 6FU
Contact: 01509557463
Email: CLIVE282@HOTMAIL.COM
Honorary Secretary: Mr Ian Manning; 105 oadby rd wigston leicester Leicestershire le2 8ax
Tel: 07915 054150   Email: ianmanning007@aol.com
Fixtures Secretary: Mr Kenneth Crane; 16 Ridley Close Blaby Leicestershire LE8 4AW Tel: 07944 749891
Club Colours: Red, white & navy hoops, navy shorts
League: Midlands 5 East (S) (level 10)

Bakewell Mannerians RUFC
Ground Address: The Showground Bakewell Derbyshire DE45 1AQ
Contact: 01629 735882
Email: bmrufc@bakewellrugby.org.uk
Website: www.bakewellrugby.org.uk
Directions: Follow the 'Agricultural Centre' signs from the A6. The pitch is on the right in front of the Agricultural Business Centre. Changing is at the pavilion across the river via the footbridge. See Club Website for maps, instructions & car parking.
Honorary Secretary: Mr Stephen Coates; The Homestead Wenslees Darley Bridge Matlock DE4 2JZ
Tel: 01629 735882
Email: stephencoates1@btinternet.com
Fixtures Secretary: Mr Roderick Bell; Ladywell Shippon Bar Road Baslow Bakewell Derbyshire DE45 1SF Tel: 01246 583564
Email: pdh@peak-district-holidays.co.uk
Club Colours: Navy, Light Blue & White Hoops
League: Midlands 2 East (N) (level 7)

Banbury RFC
Ground Address: Bodicote Park Oxford Road Banbury OX15 4AF
Contact: 01295 266010
Email: philmontanaro@aol.com
Website: http://www.banburyrufc.co.uk/index1.html
Directions: M40 Junction 11. Follow signs to Town Centre, Hospital, Adderbury A4260. The ground is situated on the left, 1.5 miles past the hospital on the A4260 towards Adderbury.
Honorary Secretary: Mr Tim Rogers; Castle House Bodicote Banbury Oxon OX15 4BS Tel: 01295 266010
Email: TVROG@AOL.COM
Club Colours: Navy & White Hoop Shirt, Navy Shorts
League: Midlands 2 East (S) (level 7)

Barkers Butts RFC
Ground Address: Bob Coward Memorial Ground Pickford Grange Lane Allesley Coventry CV5 9AR
Contact: 01676 522192
Email: barkersbuttsrfc@tiscali.co.uk
Website: www.barkersbuttsrfc.co.uk
Directions: From Birmingham A45 take Meriden turn , turn right at 3rd roundabout. From Coventry A45 take Meridan slip road, after 200yds turn left Ground 300yds on right Nearest Rail service Birmingham International or Coventry.
Honorary Secretary: Mr H Roberts; 84 Keresley Road Coventry CV6 2JD Tel: 02476 333244
Email: hboroberts@ntlworld.com
Fixtures Secretary: Mr Jon Barber; Barkers' Butts Rugby Club Pickford Grange Lane Allesley Coventry CV5 9AR Tel: 0779 6088865
Email: barkersbuttsrfc@tiscali.co.uk
Club Colours: Royal Blue & Amber
League: Midlands 2 West (S) (level 7)

Barton & District RUFC
Ground Address: Mill Lane Barrow Upon Humber Lincolnshire DN19 7BA
Contact: 01469 531119
Email: DGSHELTON@AOL.COM
Website: www.bartonrugby.co.uk
Directions: Take the A15 and turn off into Barton, right at mini-roundabout at bottom of hill, through Barton market place and head for Barrow, approx. 1 1/2 miles out of Barton. In Barrow, right at roundabout next sharp right into ground.
Honorary Secretary: Mr Darren Shelton; 11 St. Crispin Close North Killingholme Immingham Lincolnshire DN40 3JN Tel: 07971 454125
Email: dgshelton@aol.com
Fixtures Secretary: Mr LEIGH JOHNSON; 18 Hedgerow Close Barrow upon Humber Lincs. DN19 7TE
Tel: 01469 531240   Email: nobby72_@hotmail.com
Club Colours: Red & White Hoops
League: Midlands 3 East (N) (level 8)

Barton-Under-Needwood RFC
Ground Address: Barton under Needwood RFC Holland Sports & Social Club Efflinch Lane Barton-under-Needwood Staffordshire DE13 8ET
Contact: 01283 716440
Email: bartonrufc@yahoo.co.uk
Website: www.bartonrugby.com
Directions: Off A38 into village. Left at Three Horeshoes Pub onto Efflinch Lane. 400 yards on left.
Honorary Secretary: Miss Amy Spurrier; The Shoulder of Mutton, Main Street, Barton Under Needwood Burton On Trent Staffordshire DE13 8AA Tel: 01283 712568
Email: bartonrufc@yahoo.co.uk
Fixtures Secretary: Mr Nick Rigby; Forest Barn Cottage 2 Barton Gate Barton under Needwood Burton-on-Trent Staffordshire DE13 8BP Tel: 07947 672338
Email: nick.rigby@forestbarn.freeserve.co.uk
Club Colours: Red and White quarters
League: Midlands 4 West (N) (level 9)

Bedford Swifts RUFC
Ground Address: Bedford Athletics Stadium (01234 - 351115) Barkers Lane/Newham Avenue Bedford Bedfordshire MK41 9SB
Contact: 07710 972902
Email: seanwhite65@aol.com
Website: www.bedfordswifts.com

Directions: See Directions Given In Description Above
Honorary Secretary: Doctor Bernard Claxton; 77 Bower Street Bedford Bedfordshire MK40 3RB Tel: 01234 213228
Email: swifts@bernardclaxton.com
Fixtures Secretary: Mr Parvaz Khan; 72 Birkdale Road, Bedford Bedfordshire Tel: 07823 885740
Email: khan_parwaz@hotmail.com
Club Colours: Royal Blue and Gold Hooped Shirts
League: Midlands 3 East (S) (level 8)

Bedworth RUFC
Ground Address: Rectory Fields Smarts Road Bedworth CV12 0BP
Contact: 024 7631 2025
Directions: M6 J3. A444 [to Nuneaton] First left then left at bottom of slip road.Straight over lights and left again into Smarts Road at Cross Keys pub.Clubhouse is located at end of road.
Honorary Secretary: Mr Alan Sheppard; 15 Warwick Gardens Nuneaton Warwickshire CU10 8DB
Tel: 02476 742203
Email: alansheppard@hotmail.co.uk
Fixtures Secretary: Mr Keith Brown; 20 Rosemary Way Hinckley Leicestershire LE10 0LN Tel: 07775 8161606
Email: keithbrown@ntlworld.com
Club Colours: Emerald Green
League: Midlands 2 West (S) (level 7)

Belgrave RFC
Ground Address: Belgrave Pastures Thurcaston Road Abbey Lane LE4 2RG
Contact: 0116 266 3033
Email: mail@belgraverfc.com
Directions: Go To - www.belgraverfc.com - and select - "How To Find Us"
Honorary Secretary: Mr Bruce Ord; 10 Windmill Close Thurmaston Leicester LE4 8GX Tel: 07801 539664
Email: ordb99@aol.com
Fixtures Secretary: Mr Kevin Hick; 62 Goodes Lane Syston Leicester LE7 2JJ Tel: 0116 2739501
Club Colours: Red & black hoops, black shorts
League: Midlands 2 East (N) (level 7)

Belper RUFC
Ground Address: Herbert Strutt School Playing Fields Derby Road Belper Derbyshire DE56 1UU
Contact: 07850 024638
Email: belperrugbyclub@yahoo.co.uk
Website: www.belperrugbyclub.co.uk
Directions: Ground is off A6 in Belper between Morrisons supermarket and Babington Hospital - near town centre.
Honorary Secretary: Mr Anthony Laven
Tel: 07877 723075
Email: ajlaven@yahoo.co.uk
Fixtures Secretary: Mr Peter Rose Tel: 07919 691947
Email: peter.rose@uk.transport.bombardier.com
Club Colours: Black & White Hoops
League: Midlands 4 East (N) (level 9)

Berkswell & Balsall RFC
Ground Address: Honiley Road Meer End Kenilworth Warwickshire CV8 1NQ
Contact: 01676 534 862
Email: Lesley@dhscontractors.fsnet.co.uk
Directions: From Birmingham or Balsall Common follow main road to Warwick A4111 (not road to Kenilworth). Ground Approx 1 mile on right with entrance in Honiley Road
Honorary Secretary: Mrs Lesley Fahy; 7 Dalmeny Road Coventry CV4 8AX Tel: 02476 474093
Email: office@dhscontractorsltd.co.uk
Fixtures Secretary: Mr Keith Ballinger; 340 Kenilworth Road Balsall Common Coventry CV7 7ER
Tel: 01676 533020
Club Colours: Red & Black Shirts, Black Shorts
League: Midlands 2 West (S) (level 7)

Biggleswade RUFC
Ground Address: The Clubhouse Langford Road Biggleswade SG18 9RA
Contact: 01767 312463
Email: biggy.rugby@ntlworld.com
Directions: On the A6001 Biggleswade to Henlow Road, approx 1 mile from Biggleswade by the Broom turn off, on the right hand side coming from Biggleswade.
Honorary Secretary: Mr Simon Rutt; 11 The Dairy Henlow Bedfordshire SG16 6JD Tel: 07879 692067
Email: simon.rutt@virgin.net
Fixtures Secretary: Mr Peter Biernis; 12 Boothey Close Biggleswade Bedfordshire SG18 0DG
Tel: 01767 221347   Email: pete.biernis@ntlworld.com
Club Colours: Navy blue with broad red band
League: Midlands 4 East (S) (level 9)

Bingham RFC
Ground Address: The Town Pavilion Brendan Grove, Wynhill Bingham NG13 8TN
Contact: 0115 9892889
Directions: We play at the Town Pavillion, Brendon Grove, Bingham, NG13 8TN Bingham lies some eight miles to the east of Nottingham at the intersection of the A52 & A46 At the A46/A52 roundabout (where the Shell petrol station is), take Bingham exit then take the 1st left (small town pavilion sign), turn left at the T junction at the end of the road. Follow the road around taking the 5th left into Brendon Grove
Honorary Secretary: Mr Christopher Packer; 5 Wiverton Road Bingham Nottinghamshire NG13 8EY
Tel: 01949 876063
Email: chris.packer@ntlworld.com
Fixtures Secretary: Mr James Singer; The Town Pavilion Brendan Grove, Wynhill Bingham NG13 8TN
Tel: 07988 953574
Email: james.singer1@ntlworld.com
Club Colours: Red & Green Quarters with Black
League: Non League

MIDLANDS LEVELS 7-10 & NON LEAGUE CLUBS

Birmingham Barbarians RFC
Ground Address: The Pavilion UCE Sportsground Moor Lane Moor Lane Witton West Midlands B6 7AA
Contact: 0 1212470754
Email: play@bhambarbarians.co.uk
Website: www.bhambarbarians.co.uk
Directions: From City Centre Birmingham - A34 to Walsall. At Perry Barr onto A453 Aldridge Road. Continue half mile under motorway, stay on A453 into College Road. First right into Moor Lane, grounds and clubhouse on right, Witton Cemetery on left
Honorary Secretary: Mr Tom Townsend; 71 Knights Road Birmingham West Midlands B11 3QB
Tel: 07817291587
Email: tom@bhambarbarians.co.uk
Fixtures Secretary: Mr Paul Sturch; 132 Brantley Road Witton Birmingham West Midlands B6 7DP
Tel: 0121 6862648
Email: fixtures@bhambarbarians.co.uk
Club Colours: Green, Black & White
League: Non League

Birmingham Civil Service RFC
Ground Address: Old Silhillians Assoc Warwick Rd Copt Heath Knowle Solihull West Midlands B93 9LW
Contact: 07970 065536
Email: jimmoll500@hotmail.co.uk
Directions: Ground sharing with Silhillians RUFC J5 M42 then towards Knowle, ground 50yds on left
Honorary Secretary: Mr Tony Plant; 96 Ulverley Green Road Solihull West Midlands B92 8AJ
Tel: 0121 7081565
Email: tonyplant@madasafish.com
Fixtures Secretary: Mr James Mollison; 31 Stanbrook Road Solihul West Midlands B90 4UT
Tel: 07970 065536
Email: jimmoll500@hotmail.com
Club Colours: Red & White Shirts, Blue Shorts
League: Midlands 5 West (SW) (level 10)

Birmingham Exiles RFC
Ground Address: Catherine De Barnes Lane Bickenhill Solihull West Midlands B92 0DX
Contact: 01675 442995
Email: martin.whateley@focus.co.uk
Website: www.birminghamexilesrfc.co.uk
Directions: Leave M42 at J6 then leave A45 Coventry Road at Birmingham Airport junction and take Catherine de Barnes Lane exit.
Honorary Secretary: Mr Martin Whateley; 19 Wimbourne Road Sutton Coldfield West Midlands B76 2SU Tel: 07770 634782
Email: martin.whateley@midlandheart.org.uk
Fixtures Secretary: Mr Andy Evans
Tel: 0121 6665393
Club Colours: Navy Blue shirts with Red hoops
League: Midlands 4 West (S) (level 9)

Birmingham Wyvern RFC
Ground Address: Pickwick Athletic Club Windermere Road, Moseley Birmingham West Midlands B13 9JS
Contact: 07944850011
Email: mattportlock@hotmail.com
Website: birminghamwyvern.co.uk
Directions: off wake green road or yardley wood road, parking at pickwick cricket club
Honorary Secretary: Mr Dean Mills; 51 Middle Acre Road Bartley Green Birmingham West Midlands B32 3AR Tel: 07977 938882
Email: info@centralpr.co.uk
Fixtures Secretary: Mr Paul Urwin; 10 Orkney Close Nuneaton Warwickshire CV10 7LB Tel: 02476 386863
Email: purwin@jaguar.com
Club Colours: Green with gold and black hoops
League: Non League

Birstall RFC
Ground Address: Longslade Community College Wanlip Lane Birstall LE4 4GH
Contact: 0784 1584206
Email: david.bonser@hotmail.co.uk
Website: www.birstallrfc.co.uk
Honorary Secretary: Mr David Bonser; 33 Ryegate Crescent Birstall Leicester LE4 3HN Tel: 07841 584204
Email: david.bonser@hotmail.co.uk
Fixtures Secretary: Mr Steve Hill; Orchard Road Leicester Leicestershire LE4 4GD Tel: 07725 596823
Email: stevehill_brfcfixtures@live.co.uk
Club Colours: Green, Black, White Hoops
League: Non League

Bishops Castle & Onny Valley RFC
Ground Address: Love Lane Bishops Castle ShropshireSY9 5BW
Contact: 01743791692
Email: ajmeredith@supanet.com
Directions: On Eastern edge of town off the A484 Shrewsbury to Clun Road.
Honorary Secretary: Mr andrew Meredith; Sunnycroft Main Road Pontesbury Shrewsbury ShropshireSY5 0RR
Tel: 01743 791692
Email: ajmeredith@supanet.com
Fixtures Secretary: Mr D Lakelin; The Hazels Station Road Pontesbury Shrewsbury SY5 0QY
Tel: 07801 190960
Email: d-lewis-lakelin@hotmail.com
Club Colours: Greeen & Red
League: Midlands 3 West (N) (level 8)

Bloxwich RFC
Ground Address: Stafford Road Sports Club King George V Playing Fields Stafford Road Bloxwich Walsall West Midlands WS3 3NJ
Contact: 01922 405891
Email: bloxwichrfc@gmail.com
Website: www.bloxwichrfc.com
Directions: 1/4 mile outside Bloxwich Town on A34 going toward Cannock. Straight on at Bell Lane PH

traffic lights Driveway entrance is 50yds past traffic lights on left, signposted Bloxwich Stafford Road Sports Club The entrance is on the opposite side of road between Royal Exchange & Frances Drive marked by a tall black and white post. If you go past Frances Drive - you've gone too far ! Public Park Pitches are in King George Vth Playing Fields, 100 mtrs from clubhouse & changing rooms Please go to clubhouse NOT to the park
Honorary Secretary: Mrs Anita Chew; 29 Astoria Gardens Willenhall West Midlands WV12 5XR
Tel: 07522 834807
Email: anitachew@hotmail.com
Fixtures Secretary: Mr Lee Green; 28 Wych Elm Road Clayhanger Walsall West Midlands WS8 7QP
Tel: 07970 105821
Email: leegreen@live.com
Club Colours: RED with GREEN side panels
League: Midlands 3 West (N) (level 8)

Boston RFC
Ground Address: Boston R.F.C. Princess Royal Arena Great Fen Road Wyberton Boston Lincs. PE21 7PB
Contact: 01205 362683
Email: Keightley1@aol.com
Website: www.bostonrugbyclub.co.uk
Directions: Quarter of a mile west of Boston on A1121, which heads to A17 to Sleaford/Newark. Turn right into Great Fen Road, Club is situated 1/4 mile on left hand side, opposite the Ruddy Duck Public House, and Princess Royal Sports Arena
Honorary Secretary: Mr Martyn Keightley; 25 Manor Gardens Boston Lincolnshire PE21 6JG
Tel: 01205 364755
Email: keightley1@aol.com
Fixtures Secretary: Mr Tim Bembridge; 16 Davey Close Boston Lincolnshire PE21 9DJ Tel: 07834 902940
Email: timbembridge616@btinternet.com
Club Colours: Blue and White Hoops
League: Midlands 3 East (N) (level 8)

Brackley RUFC
Ground Address: P O Box 5964 Brackley NN13 6YF
Contact: 01280 700685
Email: hutch@hazelborough.com
Website: www.brackleyrufc.co.uk
Directions: Nightingale Close, Brackley NN13 6PN. From High Street turn into Halse Road (opp The Bell Inn and Greyhound) signposted Halse and Rugby Club. Follow towards Halse over two mini RB; at next RB turn left into Humphries Drive; next RB turn right into Nightingale Close and entrance to club.
Honorary Secretary: Mr John Hutchinson; 25 Burwell Hill Brackley NN13 7AS Tel: 01280 840918
Email: hutch@hazelborough.com
Fixtures Secretary: Mr Nigel Boot-Handford; 15 Pavillons Way Brackley Northamptonshire NN13 6LA
Tel: 01280 702491
Email: rugbyref@aol.com
Club Colours: Royal Blue and White
League: Midlands 3 East (S) (level 8)

Bredon Star RFC
Ground Address: Bredon Playing Fields Main Road, Bredon Nr. Tewkesbury GL20 7QN
Contact: 01684 773183
Email: kevin.falvey@btinternet.com
Directions: From Jct 9 of M5 take A46 to Evesham. Left after 2 miles at traffic lights onto B4079. Left at T junction in village and car park is 50 yards on right.
Honorary Secretary: Ms Linda Llewellyn; The Close Main Road Bredon Tewkesbury Gloucestershire GL20 7EG Tel: 07876 377966
Email: llewellyn@linda999880.fsnet.co.uk
Fixtures Secretary: Mr Neil Evans; Apple Orchard Chapel Lane Kinsham Tewkesbury Gloucestershire GL20 8HS Tel: 07973 171451
Club Colours: Red and Black
League: Midlands 5 West (SW) (level 10)

Bridgnorth RFC
Ground Address: 9 Bridge Street Bridgnorth Shropshire WV15 5AA
Contact: 01746 762796
Email: dougmcgil@aol.com
Website: www.bridgnorthrfc.co.uk
Directions: Severn Park off A442 Bridgnorth to Telford Road. Clubhouse adjacent to Old Bridge Low Town. Parking at Falcon Pub Car Park.
Honorary Secretary: Mr Doug McGill; 3 Northgate Mews Bridgnorth ShropshireWV16 4EF
Tel: 01746 767047
Email: dougmcgil@aol.com
Fixtures Secretary: Mr Alun Stoll; Ty'r Ysgol Vicarage Road Penn Wolverhampton West Midlands WV4 5HP
Tel: 01902 558355
Email: admin@pennhall.biblio.net
Club Colours: Black
League: Midlands 2 West (N) (level 7)

Bromyard RFC
Ground Address: Clive Richards Sports Ground Tenbury Road Bromyard Herefordshire HR7 4LW
Contact: 01885 483933
Email: warthog1@freeuk.com
Website: www.bromyardrfc.co.uk
Directions: From Bromyard, take the B4214 towards Tenbury Wells, the ground is on the right hand side, approx 0.5 mile from the town.
Honorary Secretary: Mr Paul Dawson; North Cottage Bringsty Worcester WR6 5UQ Tel: 07877 140751
Email: warthog1@freeuk.com
Fixtures Secretary: Mr Simon Irwin; Pine Tree Cottages 2 Tedstone Wafre Bromyard Herefordshire HR7 4QD
Tel: 01885 488322
Email: simon.irwin@westons-cider.co.uk
Club Colours: green and gold shirts and black shorts
League: Midlands 5 West (SW) (level 10)

MIDLANDS LEVELS 7-10 & NON LEAGUE CLUBS

Bugbrooke RUFC
Ground Address: Bugbrooke Rugby Union Football Club Camp Close Bugbrooke NN7 3RW
Contact: 07989 230033
Email: chairman@brufc.org
Website: www.brufc.org
Directions: From M1 J16, take the A45 towards Northampton. After approximately 1 mile take the 3rd exit (right) at the roundabout, signposted Kislingbury and Bugbrooke. Go through Kislingbury and enter Bugbrooke, keeping on the main road. Go through village following
Honorary Secretary: Mr Jonathan Goddard; 41 Badgers Close Bugbrooke Northamptonshire NN7 3BA
Tel: 01604 833525 Email: jon.goddard@amey.co.uk
Fixtures Secretary: Mr Robert (Soapy) Holding; 25 Greenaway Close Blisworth Northampton NN7 3EJ
Tel: 07812 997484
Club Colours: Green and Gold
League: Midlands 3 East (S) (level 8)

Burbage RFC
Ground Address: Britannia Road Burbage LE10 2HF
Contact: 01162 848237
Email: beckystartin@hotmail.com
Directions: From M69 East and West, exit at junction 1 and take 5th exit along Rugby Road. Continue over roundabout and take 1st right on to Coventry Road. Turn right onto Britannia Road just before The Sycamores Pub. Rugby ground is on your right.
Honorary Secretary: Mrs Kelly Withers; 18 Northfield Road Hinckley Leicestershire LE10 0LJ
Tel: 01455 458554
Email: kptrip02@yahoo.co.uk
Fixtures Secretary: Mr Richard Sansome; 39 Duport Road Burbage Leicestershire Tel: 01455 440412
Email: rjs.1@hotmail.co.uk
Club Colours: Green and White Hoops
League: Non League

Burntwood RUFC
Ground Address: Burntwood RFC The Sportsway Chasewater Chasetown Burntwood Staffs. WS7 3PH
Contact: 01543 676651
Email: raforsyth@hotmail.com
Website: www.burntwoodrugby.co.uk
Directions: Burntwood RUFC is midway between Cannock & Lichfield. The clubhouse is located and signposted on the Burntwood by-pass approximately half a mile from Jct T6 of the M6 Toll. The sportsway leads off the traffic island where the A5190 & A5195 meet.
Honorary Secretary: Mr Robert Forsyth; 25 Viscount Road Chase Terrace Burntwood Staffordshire WS7 1PU
Tel: 01543 305997
Email: raforsyth@hotmail.com
Fixtures Secretary: Mr Andrew Macey; 40 Holly Grove Lane Burntwood WS7 1QA Tel: 07970 554964
Email: yecam@live.co.uk
Club Colours: Scarlet, emerald & white hoops, black shorts
League: Midlands 3 West (N) (level 8)

Buxton RUFC
Ground Address: Sunnyfields Brierlow Bar Road Harpur Hill, Buxton Derbyshire SK17 9PX
Contact: 01298 70455
Email: info@buxtonrugbyclub.com
Website: www.buxtonrugbyclub.com
Directions: Follow A515 from Buxton towards Ashbourne.After leaving the town into 50mph area take first right towards Harpur Hill.At end of road turn left and ground approx 500yds on left.
Honorary Secretary: Mrs Julie Vorheiss; 55 Pictor Road Buxton Derbyshire SK17 7TB Tel: 01298 22546
Email: julesv2007@aol.com
Fixtures Secretary: Mr Patrick Leahy; Sunnyfields Brierlow Bar Road Brierlow Bar Road Harpur Hill, Buxton Derbyshire SK17 9PX Tel: 01298 70455
Email: PatPaula@leahy86.freeserve.co.uk
Club Colours: Blue, Red & Gold Hoops, Blue Shorts
League: Non League

Cannock RUFC
Ground Address: The Morgan Ground Stafford Road Huntington Cannock Staffordshire WS12 4NU
Contact: 01543 495211
Email: dianeevans57@hotmail.com
Website: www.rfu.com/Clubs/portals/CannockRUFC
Directions: Take the A34 between Cannock and Stafford. Turn off by the "Orissa" Indian restaurant. Continue up the lane past the restaurant, go round the youth centre at the end of the road and through the gates. The clubhouse is at the end of the track past the field
Honorary Secretary: Mrs Diane Evans; 13 Corsican Drive Hednesford Cannock Staffordshire WS12 4SZ
Tel: 01543 878293 Email: dianeevans57@hotmail.com
Fixtures Secretary: Mr John Evans; 13 Corsican Drive Hednesford Cannock Staffordshire WS12 4SZ
Tel: 01543 878293
Email: johnevansplaster@hotmail.com
Club Colours: Navy and Gold
League: Midlands 4 West (N) (level 9)

Castle Donington RUFC
Ground Address: The Spittal Pavillion The Spittal 07813 837963 Castle Donington Derbyshire DE74 2NL
Contact: 07813 837963
Email: steven.bradley5@googlemail.com
Website: www.castledoningtonrufc.co.uk
Directions: Travel into Castle Donington from A50 turning right into Trent Lane (at CO OP), continue to the end of Trent Lane, turn left at mini island into Darsway, then first left into The Spittal. Car park at the end of road.
Honorary Secretary: Mr Steven Bradley; 2 Moorfields Avenue Eastwood Nottingham NG16 3DF
Tel: 07813 837963
Email: steven.bradley5@googlemail.com
Fixtures Secretary: Daniel Robinson; 4 Trent Lane Castle Donington Derbys. DE74 2NX
Tel: 07974 712139
Club Colours: Red & Black Quarters, Black shorts
League: Midlands 4 East (N) (level 9)

Chaddesley Corbett RFC
Ground Address: Chaddesley Corbett R.F.C. Chaddesley Corbett Sports Club Fox Lane Chaddesley Corbett Worcestershire DY10 4RH
Directions: On A448 between Kidderminster & Bromsgrove. Do not enter village, turning to ground is on sharp corner between The Fox P.H. and Rowberrys farm shop. Signed CCRFC - turn right from Kidderminster, left from Bromsgrove.
Honorary Secretary: Mr Nigel Evans; Cherry Tree House 7 Mustow Green Nr.kidderminster DY10 4LQ
Tel: 01562 777070
Email: evans.nigel@btinternet.com
Fixtures Secretary: Mr Sean Tate; 26 Briar Hill Chaddesley Corbett Worcestershire DY10 4SQ
Tel: 01562 770112
Email: rugbysec@aol.com
Club Colours: Green with blue trim
League: Midlands 5 West (SW) (level 10)

Chesterfield Panthers RUFC
Ground Address: The Rugby Field Sheffield Road Stonegravels Chesterfield Derbyshire S41 7JH
Contact: 01246 232321
Email: thepells@btinternet.com
Website: www.chesterfieldpanthers.co.uk
Directions: From the Town Centre, the M1 the South, Sheffield and the North get onto the A61 dual carriageway. At the Tesco roundabout leave by the spur road following Town Centre. At next roundabout turn left onto Sheffield Road. Second right is Tapton View Road. Take that and 200 metres up on the left are gates into the ground and car park.
Honorary Secretary: Mr Fred Pell; 14 Williamthorpe Road North Wingfield Chesterfield Derbyshire S42 5PB
Tel: (01246) 857480
Email: thepells@btinternet.com
Fixtures Secretary: Mick Lord; 34 Pennine Way Chesterfield Derbyshire S40 4ND Tel: 01246 274105
Email: m.lord@sky.com
Club Colours: Red, Black and White Shirts; B
League: Midlands 4 East (N) (level 9)

Churchill College RFC
Ground Address: Churchill College Storey's Way Cambridge CB3 0DS
Email: mcy23@cam.ac.uk
Honorary Secretary: Christien mott Tel: 07971608768
Email: cjm94@cam.ac.uk
Fixtures Secretary: Christien mott Tel: 07971608768
Email: cjm94@cam.ac.uk
Club Colours: Brown/Pink
League: Non League

Claverdon RFC
Ground Address: Ossetts Hole Lane Yarningale Common Claverdon Warwickshire CV35 8HN
Contact: 0 1676529277
Email: andrew.hughes@phones4u.co.uk
Website: www.clavrfc.co.uk
Directions: Off A4189 Warwick to Henley in Arden
Honorary Secretary: Mr Andrew Hughes; 22 Whitehead Grove Balsall Common SOLIHULL West Midlands CV77US Tel: 01676 529277
Email: arh31@hotmail.com
Club Colours: Red/ white hooped jersey/socks ,white shorts
League: Midlands 5 West (SW) (level 10)

Clee Hill RFC
Ground Address: Tenbury Road Clee Hill Ludlow ShropshireSY8 3NJ
Contact: 01584 890868
Email: david.edwards@tarmac.co.uk
Directions: Between Ludlow and Cleobury Mortimer on A4117. Take B4214 at Clee Hill (signposted Tenbury Wells). Ground approx. 1 mile on right hand side.
Honorary Secretary: Mrs Penny Cooper; Studley Cottage Studley Clee Hill Ludlow ShropshireSY8 3NP
Tel: 01584 890990
Email: matt.pen@btinternet.com
Fixtures Secretary: Philip Edwards; Shop Farm Dhustone Lane Clee Hill Ludlow Shropshire SY8 3PQ
Tel: 07977111078
Club Colours: Maroon & Navy Quarters, Blue Shorts
League: Midlands 5 West (SW) (level 10)

Cleethorpes RUFC
Ground Address: Lucarleys Club Wilton Road Cleethorpes DN36 4AW
Contact: 01472 812936
Email: cphil1952@aol.com
Website: www.cleethorpesrufc.co.uk
Directions: At the last roundabout on A180 follow signs to Cleethorpes passing over flyover onto Cleethorpes Road. After approx 2 miles first roundabout turn right. Next roundabout turn left. Next roundabout straight on passing Pear Tree Pub. Next right is Wilton Road. Club is 100 yds on left.
Honorary Secretary: Mr Philip Cass; 29 Victoria Court Victoria Street Grimsby DN31 1PT Tel: 07834 986394
Email: cphil1952@aol.com
Fixtures Secretary: Mr Paul Capindale; 5 Worsley Close Holten-le-Clay Grimsby Humberside DN36 5EY
Tel: 01472 236601
Email: paulcapindale@yahoo.co.uk
Club Colours: Blue & Gold Hoops
League: Midlands 4 East (N) (level 9)

Cleobury Mortimer RFC
Ground Address: Cleobury Mortimer Sports & Social Club Love Lane, Cleobury Mortimer Kidderminster DY14 8PE
Contact: 01299 270364
Email: jeredfern@yahoo.com
Directions: Cleobury Mortimer is on the A4117 midway (11 miles) between Kidderminster and Ludlow. The ground is on the north side of the town on Lacon Childe School ground.
Honorary Secretary: Guy Turpin; 5 New Road Cleobury Mortimer Nr Kidderminster Worcestershire DY14 8AN Tel: 01299 271094
Email: guy@sunlab.co.uk
Fixtures Secretary: Mrs Kath Phillips; 5 Heath Close Cleobury Mortimer Kidderminster Worcs. DY14 8ED Tel: 01299 270381
Email: cm270381@yahoo.co.uk
Club Colours: Red & Green Quarters, Black Shorts
League: Midlands 4 West (N) (level 9)

Coalville RFC
Ground Address: Memorial Ground Hall Lane Whitwick Coalville Leicestershire LE67 5PF
Contact: 01530 812090
Email: info@coalvillerugby.com
Website: www.coalvillerugby.com
Directions: Leave M1 @ J22. Join road signposted Coalville A511. Go over 5 R/Abouts and then turn right at the traffic lights on to Broomleys Road, take the 1st turning on the left Hall Lane and Coalville RFC (sign-posted) is 500 yds on the left.
Honorary Secretary: Mr Peter Smith; 50 Parkdale Ibstock Leicestershire LE67 6JW Tel: 07903 943148
Email: leicesternum@ukinbox.co.uk
Fixtures Secretary: Mr Christopher Taylor; Memorial Ground Hall Lane Whitwick Coalville Leicestershire LE67 5PF Tel: 07879 205716
Email: seniorfixtures@coalvillerugby.com
Club Colours: Navy Blue with Amber Stripe
League: Midlands 2 East (N) (level 7)

Copsewood RFC
Ground Address: Pavilion Sports Bar Allard Way Allard Way Coventry CV3 1HS
Contact: 024 76506199
Email: rugby@copsewoodrfc.co.uk
Website: www.copsewoodrfc.co.uk
Directions: From M6, J2 join A46. After approx 2 miles right at r'about. Left at next r'about. Right at lights, right at next lights, then left at 2nd set of lights. Ground 300yds on the left.
Honorary Secretary: Mr Gavin Palk; 77 Whitemoor Road Kenilworth Warwickshire CV8 2BN
Tel: 07712661716 Email: gavin.palk@ericsson.com
Fixtures Secretary: Mr Phil Gaffney; 74 Cecily Road Cheylesmore Coventry CV3 5LA Tel: 07775 581487
Email: philgaffney@aol.com
Club Colours: Red, Green & Blue Hoops, Blue Shorts
League: Midlands 5 West (SE) (level 10)

Corby RFC
Ground Address:
Northern Park Rockingham Road Corby NN17 2AE
Contact: 01536 204466
Email: corbyrfc@hotmail.com
Website: www.pitchero.com/clubs/corbyrfc
Directions: Located at the junction of the A6003 (Corby to Oakham road) and the A6116 (Rockingham Road) Corby.
Honorary Secretary: Mr Michael Stark; 26 Primrose Close Corby Northamptonshire NN18 8LE
Tel: 07737 921699
Email: mike2212stark@msn.com
Fixtures Secretary: Mr Michael Stark; 26 Primrose Close Corby Northamptonshire NN18 8LE
Tel: 07737 921699
Email: mike2212stark@msn.com
Club Colours: Red & White Quarters, Blue Shorts
League: Non League

Cosby RFC
Ground Address: Victory Park Park Road Park Road Cosby Leicestershire LE9 1RN
Contact: 07740 205928
Email: cliveelliott56@aol.com
Website: www.cosbyrfc.co.uk
Directions: Victory Park, Cosby From M1/M69 towards Narborough, follow signs for railway station, over level crossing, follow sign for Cosby (turn right) follow road for about a mile, park on your right hand side. At mini-roundabout turn right, the immediate right i
Honorary Secretary: Mr Clive Elliott; 9 Wavertree Close Cosby Leicester LE9 1TN Tel: 07740 205928
Email: cliveelliott56@aol.com
Fixtures Secretary: Mr Clive Elliott; 9 Wavertree Close Cosby Leicester LE9 1TN Tel: 07740 205928
Email: cliveelliott56@aol.com
Club Colours: Black with Red Panels
League: Non League

Coventrians RFC
Ground Address: The Black Pad Yelverton Road, Radford Yelverton Road, Radford Coventry CV6 4AH
Contact: 02476 682885
Website: www.coventriansrfc.com
Directions: M6 J3 onto A444 to Coventry, second exit at 2nd roundabout to holbrooks,first exit at next roundabout on to Holbrooks lane Yelverton Road is 50yds on right just before the railway bridge.
Honorary Secretary: Mrs Jane Connolly; 147 Wheelwright Lane Ash Green Coventry West Midlands CV7 9HR Tel: 0770 2829313
Email: j_connolly@sky.com
Fixtures Secretary: Mr Steve Springate; 2 Goldthorn Close Coventry West Midlands CV5 7DY
Tel: 02476 470535
Email: SDSpringate@aol.com
Club Colours: Blue and White Quarters
League: Midlands 5 West (SE) (level 10)

Coventry Saracens RFC
Ground Address:
Bredon Avenue Binley Coventry CV6 2AR
Contact: 02476 453 557
Directions: From A46 (Eastern Bypass) take A428 to Coventry City Centre for approx. 1 mile, left into Brendon Ave, ground approx 200 mtrs on left.
Honorary Secretary: Mr Keiron Knights; 114 Roland Avenue Holbrooks Coventry CV6 4LX
Tel: 0247 6700399
Email: keironknights@hotmail.com
Fixtures Secretary: Mr I Riggs; C/0 114 Roland Avenue Holbrooks Coventry CV6 4LX
Club Colours: Black shirts, red/green "V", black shorts
League: Midlands 5 West (SE) (level 10)

Coventry Tech RFC
Ground Address: Mitchell Avenue Canley Canley Coventry West Midlands CV4 8DW
Contact: 024 76471733
Email: mtucker@lti.co.uk
Website: www.covtechrfc.co.uk
Directions: The club is only 5 mins from A45 Fletchhampstead Highway. Southbound take right turn at Canley Police Station & Fire Station and next right into Charter Ave. Northbound left at island by Canley Fire and Police Station, next right onto Charter Avenue. Clu
Honorary Secretary: Mr Richard Rees; 5 Anglesey Close Allesley Village Coventry West Midlands CV5 9GB Tel: 024 76404735
Email: richard.rees@hmrc.gsi.gov.uk
Fixtures Secretary: Mr Jim Kingsley-smith; 85 Sherbourne Cresent Coundon Coventry West Midlands CV5 8LG Tel: 0791 4889876
Email: kingsley_123@hotmail.com
Club Colours: Dark Green, Yellow & Brown
League: Midlands 5 West (SE) (level 10)

Coventry University/Lanchester RFC
Ground Address: Coventry University Students Union, Priory Street Coventry CV1 5FJ
Contact: 02476 887 688
Email: lanchtoursec@yahoo.co.uk
Honorary Secretary: Honorary Secretary; Athletic Union Coventry University RFC Priory Street Coventry West Midlands CV1 5FB
Fixtures Secretary: Mr Bryan Loftus; c/o Club Address
Email: lanchtoursec@yahoo.co.uk
Club Colours: Blue with yellow trim
League: Non League

Coventry Welsh RFC
Ground Address: 82 Burbages Lane Exhall Coventry Warwickshire CV6 6AY
Contact: 02476 673124
Email: johnrichards17@btinternet.com
Website: www.coventrywelsh.com
Directions: M6 J3, take bypass road A444 towards Coventry. At the next roundabout take the 3rd Exit and continue along this road for about 500 yards to Traffic Lights. At these traffic lights,turn right into Wheelright Lane. Continue along Wheelright Lanefor approx. half a mile and Burbages lane can be found on the right hand side. The Club is approximately 300 yards down Burbages lane on the left hand side. The only entrance is along an entryway.
Honorary Secretary: Mr John Richards; 17 Dulverton Avenue, Coundon, Coventry CV5 8HG
Tel: 07899 910900
Email: johnrichards17@btinternet.com
Fixtures Secretary: Mr Gary Greenway; 4 Kings Gardens, Bedworth Warwickshire CV12 8JG
Tel: 07787 686042
Email: k.greenway161@btinternet.com
Club Colours: Red Shirts, Black Shorts
League: Midlands 4 West (S) (level 9)

Cranfield University RFC
Ground Address: Cranfield University RFC Building 114 Wharley End MK43 0AL
Contact: 01234 754095
Email: csa@cranfield.ac.uk
Website: http://www.cranfield.ac.uk/socs/rugby
Directions: go out of Junction 13 on the M1 and follow signs for cranfield university
Fixtures Secretary: Mr Craig Wilde; Building 19, Sports Hall Cranfield University Cranfield Bedford MK43 0AL
Tel: 07884 470902
Email: c.wilde@cranfield.ac.uk
Club Colours: Dark Blue & Light Blue
League: Non League

Daventry RFC
Ground Address: Stefen Hill Western Avenue Daventry NN11 4ST
Contact: 01327 703802
Email: peterweckermann@btinternet.com
Directions: M1 J16, A45 west to Daventry, straight over roundabout heading for Daventry town centre, 3rd road on left and the ground is facing you.
Honorary Secretary: Mr P Weckermann; 3 Portland Close, Daventry Northamptonshire NN11 4SQ
Tel: 01327 311151
Email: peterweckermann@btinternet.com
Fixtures Secretary: Mr Peter Lyes; 13 The Glebe Daventry Northamptonshire NN11 4HR
Tel: 01327 872212
Email: p.lyes@sky.com
Club Colours: All Black
League: Midlands 3 East (S) (level 8)

Deepings RUFC
Ground Address: Deepings R.U.F.C. Linchfield Road Deeping St. James Peterborough PE6 8EP
Contact: 01778 345228
Email: club@deepingsrufc.co.uk
Website: www.deepingsrufc.co.uk
Directions: From the bypass enter Market Deeping at the round/about take the road towards Deeping St James, keep to the left through the town until sight footbridge, left at crossroads before bridge into Linchfield Road, turn immediate right through gates to ground.
Honorary Secretary: Mr Andrew Davis; 12 Chestnut Way Market Deeping Peterborough PE6 8LP
Tel: 01778 346972   Email: deepingdavis@aol.com
Fixtures Secretary: Mr Mick Pearce; 11 Stowgate Farm Deeping St James Peterborough PE6 8RW
Tel: 01778 341209
Email: mickpearce14@hotmail.co.uk
Club Colours: Black, Green & Gold Hoops
League: Midlands 3 East (S) (level 8)

Droitwich RFC
Ground Address: The Glyn Mitchell Memorial Ground Hanbury Road Droitwich Worcestershire WR9 8PR
Contact: 01905 771919
Email: robert.squire@uk.zurich.com
Website: www.droitwichrfc.co.uk
Directions: M5 J5, A38 towards Droitwich, turn towards town centre. At Traffic lights turn left into Hanbury Road, club 2 miles on left.
Honorary Secretary: Mr Robert Squire; 2 Showell Grove Droitwich Worcestershire WR9 8UD
Tel: 07801 135831
Email: robert.squire@uk.zurich.com
Fixtures Secretary: Mrs Carolyne Edwards; The Glyn Mitchell Memorial Ground Hanbury Road Droitwich Worcestershire WR9 8PR Tel: 01905 778699
Email: cazedwards@aol.com
Club Colours: Black & Gold Hoops
League: Midlands 2 West (S) (level 7)

Dronfield RUFC
Ground Address: Gosforth Fields, Stubley Drive, Dronfield Woodhouse. Dronfield Derbyshire S18 8QY
Email: david.tankard@eu.earthtech.com
Directions: To find Gosforth Fields Sports Association, Turn off the A61 and head for Dronfield. At the traffic lights near the Coach and Horses, turn off for Dronfield Woodhouse (B6056). Stay on this road until you go over the first speed bump, then turn left into Stubley Drive, follow down through the new house development and onto Gosforth Fields Car Park.
Honorary Secretary: Mr David Tankard; 192 Stubley Lane Dronfield Derbyshire S18 8YP Tel: 07986 240003
Email: david.tankard@aecom.com
Fixtures Secretary: Mr Verdun Mccauliffe; 56 Highfields Road Dronfield Derbyshire S18 1UW
Tel: 01246 415034   Email: verdtaf@googlemail.com
Club Colours: Red/Black shirts, Black shorts
League: Midlands 4 East (N) (level 9)

Dudley Wasps RFC
Ground Address: Dudley Wasps R.U.F.C. Heathbrook, Swindon Road, Wall Heath, Kingswinford. DY6 0AW
Contact: 01384 274469
Email: davep_robinson@yahoo.co.uk
Directions: See Dudley Kingswinford RFC
Fixtures Secretary: Mr Bill McLachlan; 32 Lynwood Avenue Wallheath Kingswinford DY6 9AJ
Tel: 01384 831279
Email: willmacdk@blueyonder.co.uk
Club Colours: Navy & sky blue hoops, Navy Shorts
League: Midlands 4 West (S) (level 9)

Dunlop RFC
Ground Address: Dunlop Sports and Social Club Burnaby Road, Radford Coventry CV6 4AX
Contact: 02476 662394
Email: Kim.challis@btinternet.com
Website: www.dunloprfc.co.uk
Directions: M6 J3, take A444 to Coventry, straight on at roundabout, past the Ricoh arena, over traffic lights, 2nd exit at next roundabout, move to middle lane at next roundabout, take 1st exit, move to right hand lane, at next roundabout take 2nd exit into Burnaby Road. Proceed for approx 1 mile, past the Pilot pub on your left. Ground entrance is 20 yards on the right before tall trees and green railings begin.
Honorary Secretary: Mrs Kim Challis; 29 James Dawson Drive Millisons Wood Coventry CV5 9QJ
Tel: 01676 522827
Email: kim.challis@btinternet.com
Fixtures Secretary: Mr Stuart Edwards; 250 Marston Lane Bedworth Nr Coventry West Midlands CV12 9AF
Tel: 07902 085579
Email: Stu.rugby@yahoo.co.uk
Club Colours: Black and Amber Hoops
League: Midlands 3 West (S) (level 8)

Earlsdon RFC
Ground Address: R. F. Brown Pavillion Mitchell Avenue, Canley Canley Coventry CV4 8DY
Contact: 024 76464467
Email: jimlorimer@tinyworld.co.uk
Website: www.earlsdonrfc.moonfruit.com
Directions: A45 to Police and Fire Stations, follow signs to Canley & Warwick University along Sir Henry Parkes Road. Take the third exit at the next roundabout and head down Charter Avenue. Then left onto Mitchell Ave we're at the bottom opposite the School. Nearest BR Station - Canley (0.68 miles)
Honorary Secretary: Mr James Lorimer; 245 Daventry Road Coventry West Midlands CV3 5HH
Tel: 07779 320965
Email: jimlorimer@tinyworld.co.uk
Fixtures Secretary: Mr Steve Meszar; 104 Beanfield Avenue Green Lane Coventry West Midlands CV3 6NX
Tel: 024 76416777
Email: S_M_Meszar@hotmail.com
Club Colours: Red and White Hoops , Black Shorts
League: Midlands 2 West (S) (level 7)

East Leake RFC
Ground Address: NOT POSTAL Costock Road Playing Fields Costock Road East Leake Loughborough LE12 6LY
Contact: 01509 856735
Email: secretary@eastleakerugby.org
Website: http://www.eastleakerugby.org
Directions: A60 N'gham towards L'boro, right at Costock towards E.Leake, ground on left M1 J24, A6 Towards L'boro, left onto A6006 towards Rempstone, left where signed for East Leake, through village, club on right For sat naigators LE12 6LY
Honorary Secretary: Mr Nigel Kendall; 35 Thistlebank East Leake Loughborough Leicestershire LE12 6RS
Tel: 01509 856735
Email: nigel.kendall@nottingham.ac.uk
Fixtures Secretary: Mr Graham Hey; 13 Cheviot Drive Shepshed Loughborough Leicestershire LE12 9ED
Tel: 01509 600204
Email: grahamh@O2email.co.uk
Club Colours: Maroon and White
League: Midlands 4 East (N) (level 9)

East Retford RUFC
Ground Address: Ordsall Road Retford Nottinghamshire DN22 7PW
Contact: 01777703243
Email: tedhenderson@retford510.freeserve.co.uk
Directions: From A1, join B620 from Worksop, past Ranby prison on left, through Babworth crossroads, right at mini roundabout, ground .5mile on right.
Honorary Secretary: Mr Edward Henderson; 51 Trent Street, Retford Nottinghamshire DN22 6NG Tel: 07753 397514
Email: edwardhenderson100@msn.com
Fixtures Secretary: Kevin Pattenden; 50 Waterfields, Retford Nottinghamshire DN22 6RE Tel: 07788 401866
Club Colours: Green & Amber shirts, Dark Blue shorts
League: Midlands 4 East (N) (level 9)

Eccleshall RUFC
Ground Address: Tacklers Baden Hall Farm Eccleshall ST21 6LG
Contact: 01785 817778
Email: admin@eccleshallrufc.co.uk
Website: www.eccleshallrufc.co.uk
Directions: From centre of Eccleshall follow A519 (Newcastle), take right fork after leaving town, past Drake Hall then follow signs to Baden Hall on right.
Honorary Secretary: Miss Vicki Slater; The George Inn Castle Street Eccleshall Stafford Staffordshire ST21 6DF
Tel: 07949 248638
Email: vicki@slatersales.co.uk
Fixtures Secretary: Mr Stuart Davies; 47 Badgers Croft Eccleshall Stafford Staffordshire ST21 6DS
Tel: 07921 646705
Email: sdavies@strongtie.com
Club Colours: Green/Black/Yellow (any combo)
League: Midlands 4 West (N) (level 9)

Edwardians FC
Ground Address: The Memorial Ground Streetsbrook Road Solihull B90 3PE
Contact: 0121 7039208
Email: bhewitson@hbj-gw.com
Directions: From the M42 junction 4 follow the A34 (Birmingham) for 3.5 miles. At Robin Hood island turn right onto the A4025 (Solihull) for 0.5 mile. The ground is on the left at the traffic lights.
Honorary Secretary: Mr Ben Hewitson; 25 Witley Avenue Solihull West Midlands B91 3JD
Tel: 07976 183552
Email: ben.hewitson@linpac.com
Fixtures Secretary: Mr Paul Clegg; c/o the club
Tel: 07985 415638
Email: pclegg@bellmicro.eu.com
Club Colours: Old Gold, Claret & Navy Irregular Hoops
League: Midlands 3 West (S) (level 8)

Essington RUFC
Ground Address: High Hill Centre High Hill Essington WV11 2DW
Contact: 01922 492795
Email: handmchandler@aol.com
Website: www.essingtonrugby.co.uk
Directions: M6 J11 A462 for 3 miles. Traffic lights turn right, Upper Sneyd Lane - 0.75 mile - club on left.opposite working mens club
Honorary Secretary: Mr Michael Chandler; 32 Coppice Road Walsall West Midlands WS9 9BL Tel: 01543 820611
Email: handmchandler@aol.com
Fixtures Secretary: Mr Graham Smith; 7 Oakwood Close Essington Wolverhampton West Midlands WV11 2DQ Tel: 01922 400222
Email: gandasmith@btopenworld.com
Club Colours: Black Shirts & Shorts, Red Socks
League: Midlands 4 West (N) (level 9)

Evesham RFC
Ground Address: Evesham Sports Club Albert Road Evesham WR11 4JX
Contact: 01386 446469
Website: www.eveshamrugbyclub.org.uk
Directions: A435 south into Evesham - over railway bridge, Albert Road is 2nd right off High Street, Evesham, go to end to Evesham Sports Club.
Honorary Secretary: Mrs Kate Icke; Evesham Rugby Football Club c/o Clement Rabjohns 111-113 High Street Evesham Worcestershire WR11 4XP Tel: 01386 712300
Email: kateicke@hotmail.co.uk
Fixtures Secretary: Mr Adam Huttlestone; 0 6, New Street Cheltenham Gloucestershire GL50 3LP
Tel: 01242 220237
Email: adam_huttlestone@hotmail.com
Club Colours: Navy & Maroon Hoops
League: Midlands 4 West (S) (level 9)

MIDLANDS LEVELS 7-10 & NON LEAGUE CLUBS

Five Ways Old Edwardians FC
Ground Address: Masshouse, Ash Lane Hopwood, Alvechurch Birmingham B48 7BD
Contact: 0 1214454909
Email: info@fwoe.co.uk
Website: www.fwoe.co.uk
Directions: M42 J2, signpost to Birmingham reach roundabout to Birmingham, 100yds before garage on right turn right into Ash Lane, club on right at end of lane.
Honorary Secretary: Mr Richard Lissiter; 138 Chatsworth Road Halesowen West Midlands B62 8TH
Tel: 0121 5596549
Email: rlisseter@aol.com
Fixtures Secretary: Mr Alex Nock; Masshouse, Ash Lane Hopwood, Alvechurch Birmingham West Midlands B31 2HZ Tel: 07736 051752
Email: nocalas@hotmail.com
Club Colours: Navy Blue & Amber
League: Midlands 5 West (N) (level 10)

Grimsby RUFC
Ground Address: The Pavilion Springfield Road Scartho Grimsby Lincolnshire DN33 3JF
Contact: 01472 878594
Email: grimsbyrufc@talktalkbusiness.net
Website: www.grimsby-rufc.co.uk
Directions: From M180/A180, take A1136, left at roundabout, right at Toothill roundabout, left at Bradley crossroads, right at Nuns corner, right fork, 1st right.
Honorary Secretary: Mr Lindsay Studd; 19 Chandlers Close, New Waltham Grimsby Lincolnshire DN36 4WH
Tel: 01472 825232
Email: lindsay.studd@ntlworld.com
Fixtures Secretary: Mr Keith Jones; 4 Mendip Avenue, Grimsby Lincolnshire DN33 3AA Tel: 07748 641680
Email: keithjones@gmx.co.uk
Club Colours: Royal Blue Shirts & Black Shorts
League: Midlands 2 East (N) (level 7)

Handsworth RUFC
Ground Address: Handsworth RUFC Charles Lewis Memorial Ground 450 Birmingham Road Walsall West Midlands WS5 3JP
Contact: 0121 3576427
Email: auriol2_bateman@hotmail.com
Website: www.handsworthrufc.com
Directions: M6 J7, take A34 towards Walsall, ground at bottom of hill at end of dual carriageway on left.
Honorary Secretary: Miss Auriol Bateman; 9 Harebell Close, Cannock Staffordshire WS12 3XA
Tel: 07919 411010
Email: auriol2_bateman@hotmail.com
Fixtures Secretary: Mr Kevin Harte; 12 Garman Close Great Barr, Birmingham West Midlands B43 6NB
Tel: 0121 3585390
Email: kevharte@btinternet.com
Club Colours: Red & White Hoops Black Shorts
League: Midlands 3 West (N) (level 8)

Hanford RFC
Ground Address: North Stafford Sports Club Whisper Lane Butterton Newcastle Staffordshire ST5 4EB
Contact: 01782 680734
Email: carltonhopley@hotmail.com
Website: www.rfu.com/Clubs/portals/HanfordRFC
Directions: M6 J15. 3rd exit off roundabout onto A519 (signed Ecceshall/Newport). Turn right at the lights by the transport depot onto Trentham Road (A5182). Carry on for 1.5 miles, Whisper Lane is the 2nd on the left. It is a tight turn so coaches may need to carry on past and turn round.
Honorary Secretary: Mr Carlton Hopley; 1 Seabridge Road Newcastle Staffordshire ST5 2HU
Tel: 01782 628021
Email: carltonhopley@hotmail.com
Fixtures Secretary: Mr Phil Goodall; 34 Wedgwood Road Stoke On Trent Staffordshire ST4 3LD
Tel: 01782 766562
Email: sandra.smith80@ntlworld.com
Club Colours: Red shirt with two black bands
League: Midlands 5 West (N) (level 10)

Harborne RFC
Ground Address: Club House Address: Harborne Cricket Club Old Church Avenue B17 0BE
Contact: 07800 700 343
Email: nick_d_jackson5@hotmail.com
Directions: We play our games at Metchley Park Lane behind the Queen Elizabeth Hospital. Our club house is based at Harborne Cricket Club located off Harborne Park Road.
Honorary Secretary: Mr Graham Hitchco; 81 Station Road, Harborne, Birmingham B17 9LR
Tel: 0121 4278290
Fixtures Secretary: Mr Stuart Cambridge; 69 White Road Quinton Birmingham West Midlands B32 2AG Tel: 07890 262460
Email: stuart.cambridge@barclayswealth.com
Club Colours: White and Red with Green Sleeves
League: Midlands 4 West (N) (level 9)

Harbury RFC
Ground Address: Harbury R.F.C. Waterloo Fields Middle Road, Harbury Middle Road, Harbury Leamington Spa Warwickshire CV33 9JN
Contact: 01926 613462
Website: http://www.harburyrfc.co.uk
Directions: 1 mile off Fosse Way, 2 miles north of Fosse Way with B4100 (Banbury-Warwick Road) between J.12 and J.13 M40.
Honorary Secretary: Mr David Jones; 20 Rupert Kettle Drive Bishops Itchington Southam Warks. CV47 2PU
Tel: 01926 614225
Email: dw.jones8@fsmail.net
Fixtures Secretary: Mr Jerry Birkbeck; 22 Campion Terrace Leamington Spa Warwickshire CV32 4SX
Tel: 01926 412640
Club Colours: Red & White Hoop Shirt, Black Shorts
League: Midlands 3 West (S) (level 8)

Harper Adams University College RFC
Ground Address: Harper Adams University College Edgmond Newport ShropshireTF10 8NB
Contact: 01952 815442
Email: bharper@harper-adams.ac.uk
Website: http://www.harper-adams.ac.uk/su/Rugby.htm
Directions: Maps to HAUC RUFC can be found @ www.harper-adams.ac.uk
Honorary Secretary: Ms Janet Fordham; Harper Adams University Coll Newport ShropshireTF10 8NB
Tel: 01952 815313
Email: jfordham@harper-adams.ac.uk
Club Colours: Navy Blue, Royal Blue and Yellow
League: Non League

Highley RFC
Ground Address: The Bache Arms High St Highley Nr. Bridgnorth WV166JU
Contact: 01746 861266
Email: robparr@highleyrfc.co.uk
Website: www.highleyrfc.co.uk
Honorary Secretary: Mr Rob Parr; 13 Witley Gardens Highley Nr Bridgnorth Shropshire WV16 6NH
Tel: 01746 862094   Email: robparr@highleyrfc.co.uk
Fixtures Secretary: Leon Aspin; Wyre Close 16 Nr Bridgnorth Highley Shropshire WV166DX
Tel: 07752 207823   Email: highleyrfc@hotmail.com
League: Midlands 5 East (S) (level 10)

Homerton College RFC
Ground Address: Homerton College Hills Road Cambridge CB2 2PH
Contact: 07968 701736
Email: jpbs2@cam.ac.uk
Honorary Secretary: Simon hill;
Fixtures Secretary: Mr Luke Aylward; 1 Collier Road Cambridge CB1 2AH
League: Non League

Hope Valley RUFC
Ground Address: Castleton Playing Fields Hollowford Road Hollowford Road Castleton S33 9HT
Contact: 07944 829503
Email: richard.spencer@replaymagazine.co.uk
Website: www.hopevalleyrufc.co.uk
Directions: From Sheffield A625 through Hathersage and Hope to Castleton, 100mtrs past Peak Hotel turn right into Back St, ground is 500mtrs on right.
Honorary Secretary: Mr Steve Richardson; Inglenook Market Place Castleton Hope Valley Derbyshire S33 8WQ Tel: 07973 709286
Email: remin@btconnect.com
Fixtures Secretary: Mr John Davies; Castleton Hope Valley South Yorks S33 8W Tel: 07973 305578
Email: john.davies10@btinternet.com
Club Colours: purple,green,white shirts and black shorts
League: Non League

Huntingdon & District RFC
Ground Address: The Racecourse Thrapston Road Brampton Huntingdon CambridgeshirePE28 4NL
Contact: 01480 869147
Email: frances_kent@tiscali.co.uk
Website: www.huntingdonrufc.co.uk
Directions: By Road From the East (Cambridge) and A14 At the A14 junction 23, take the A14 exit to M6/March/ Kettering/The Midlands/M1 (N)/A141/Corby. At the r'about, take the 1st exit onto A14 heading to M6/London/ Brampton/Kettering/M1 (N)/A1/Corby. Follow the A14 for approx 2 miles, then take the next slip road signposted, Brampton and Huntingdon, at the r'about take the 3rd exit (A1514)and follow the road for 800yds back over the AI4. At the mini r'about take the 2nd exit into Huntindon Racecourse, follow the access road for approx 800 yds,where the road splits bear right and then left, follow this road and the clubhouse will be in front of you. From the West and A14 (Northampton / Kettering) Follow the A14 to the A1 / A14 r'about, take the 2nd exit continuing on the A14 Thrapston road heading towards Huntingdon/ Harwich/ March/Brampton/ Felixstowe/ Cambridge/A141 . Keep in the left hand lane and after approx 800 yds take the slip road to Huntingdon racecourse and Brampton. At the mini roundabout take the 1st exit into Huntindon Racecourse, follow the access road for approx 800 yds,where the road splits bear right and then left, follow this road and the clubhouse will be in front of you. From the South (London A1) Follow the A1 North, taking the A14 exit toward M6/Huntingdon/Kettering/M1 (N)/Corby. At the r'about, take the 4nd exit continuing on the A14 Thrapston road heading towards Huntingdon/Harwich/ March/Brampton/ Felixstowe/Cambridge/A141 . Keep in the left hand lane and after approx 800 yds take the slip road to Huntingdon racecourse and Brampton. At the mini roundabout take the 1st exit into Huntindon Racecourse, follow the access road for approx 800 yds,where the road splits bear right and then left, follow this road and the clubhouse will be in front of you. From the North (London A1) Follow the A1 South, taking the A14 exit toward M6/Harwich/Felixstowe/M1 (N). At the r'about, take the 1st exit continuing on the A14 Thrapston road heading towards Huntingdon/Harwich/ March/ Brampton /Felixstowe/ Cambridge/A141 . Keep in the left hand lane and after approx 800 yds take the slip road to Huntingdon racecourse and Brampton. At the mini r'about take the 1st exit into Huntindon Racecourse, follow the access road for approx 800 yds,where the road splits bear right and then left, follow this road and the clubhouse will be in front of you. By Rail Huntingdon station is two miles from the club on the line from London King's Cross.
Honorary Secretary: Miss Frances Slowe; Dean Courtyard High Street Lower Dean Huntingdon CambridgeshirePE28 0LL Tel: 01480 869147
Email: frances_kent@tiscali.co.uk
Fixtures Secretary: Mr Timothy Furbank; Manor Farm Stirtloe St. Neots CambridgeshirePE19 5XW
Tel: 01480 810428   Email: tim@oakbankgc.co.uk
Club Colours: Green (Navy/Gold Hoop) Shirts, Green socks
League: Midlands 2 East (S) (level 7)

Kempston RFC
Ground Address: Sports Club 134 High Street Kempston Bedford MK42 7BN
Contact: 01234 853262
Email: kempstonrufc@btinternet.com
Website: http://www.kempstonrfc.org.uk
Directions: From jct.13 M1 - A421 Bedford, left at Azda roundabout, left at next roundabout, left at next roundabout, 1 mile to club on right just past Half Moon Pub. From A1 - exit at Black Cat roundabout A421 towards Bedford then Milton Keynes, at Azda roundabout
Honorary Secretary: Doctor Jim Bradley; 134 High Street Bell End Kempston Bedford MK42 7BN
Tel: 07910 595864
Email: jim_bradley15@hotmail.com
Fixtures Secretary: Doctor Chris Pitts; 57 Jowitt Avenue, Kempston Bedford MK42 8NW
Tel: 01234 840921
Email: pitts@family333.wanadoo.co.uk
Club Colours: Black with Red Arms
League: Midlands 4 East (S) (level 9)

Keresley RFC
Ground Address: The John E. Radford Fields Burrow Hill Lane, Corley Nr. Coventry Warwickshire CV7 8BE
Contact: 01676 540082
Email: keresleyrfc@btinternet.com
Website: www.keresleyrfc.co.uk
Directions: Situated off Bennetts Road North, just past Keresley Village.
Honorary Secretary: Mr Malcolm Jackson; 119 Bennetts Road South Coventry CV6 2FS
Tel: 02476 334589
Email: malcolm.jackson4@ntlworld.com
Fixtures Secretary: Mr Anthony Collins; 179 Broad Lane Coventry CV5 7AP Tel: 02476 712725
Email: antcollins7@yahoo.co.uk
Club Colours: Royal Blue,Scarlet,White
League: Midlands 4 West (S) (level 9)

Kesteven RUFC
Ground Address:
Woodnock Grantham Lincolnshire NG33 5AA
Contact: 01476 590561
Email: bill.berridge@btinternet.com
Website: www.kestevenrfc.co.uk
Directions: A52 South east out of Grantham towards Boston, past the TA. Camp then right at roundabout (B6403). Club on right after about 400 yards.
Honorary Secretary: Mr William Berridge; 60 Belton Grove, Grantham Lincolnshire NG31 9HH
Tel: 07743 335515
Email: bill.berridge@btinternet.com
Fixtures Secretary: Mr Walter Kirk; 11 Southlands Drive, Grantham Lincolnshire NG31 9DW
Tel: 01476 567042
Club Colours: Black Jerseys, White Shorts
League: Midlands 3 East (N) (level 8)

Keyworth RFC
Ground Address: The Clubhouse Willoughby Lane Widmerpool Nottingham Nottinghamshire NG12 5PU
Contact: 01509 889189
Email: kpkrfc@btinternet.com
Directions: From Nottingham 1. Take the A606 from Nottingham to Melton Mowbray. 2. Pass through Tollerton and Stanton on the Wolds. 3. Take right turn signposted Widmerpool immediately prior to A606/A46 interchange. 4. Follow road to T junction at end 5. Turn left and then take 2nd left to Willoughby, ground is on the right hand side. From A46/A606 interchange 1. Take A606 towards Nottingham 2. Take first turn left signposted Widmerpool 3. Then follow directions as 4 and 5 above
Honorary Secretary: Mr Mark King; 18 Victoria Road Bunny Nottingham NG11 6QF Tel: 07966 619690
Email: mark.king@footfall.com
Fixtures Secretary: Mrs [Elizabeth] Jill Stimpson; 3 New Row Cottages Willoughby On The Wolds Loughborough LE12 6TB Tel: 01509 880122
Club Colours: Black/Gold Hoops, Black Shorts
League: Midlands 5 East (N) (level 10)

Kidderminster Carolians RFC
Ground Address:
Marlpool Lane, Kidderminster, DY11 5HP
Contact: 01562 740043
Email: kcrfc@btconnect.com
Website: www.kcrfc.net
Directions: Follow signs from Kidderminster ringroad to Bridgnorth, at end Proud Cross Ringway is Jackson pub, Marlpool Lane is to one side, ground 400m from pub.
Honorary Secretary: Mr Keith Skirving; 43 Leawood Grove Kidderminster Worcestershire DY11 6JT Tel: 07810 321056
Email: kcrfc@btconnect.com
Fixtures Secretary: Mr Tim Carder; 1 Upper Birch Cottage Shatterford Bewdley Worcestershire DY12 1TR
Tel: 01299 861864
Email: Tim.Carder@towergate.co.uk
Club Colours: Black with gold hoops & black shorts
League: Midlands 2 West (S) (level 7)

Kings Norton RFC
Ground Address: Hopwood Park Ash Lane Hopwood Birmingham Worcestershire B48 7BB
Email: Contact@knrfc.com
Website: www.knrfc.co.uk
Directions: Leave the M42 at Junction 2.Take the A441 towards Birmingham.At the roundabout take the second exit and then turn second right, immediately in front of the petrol station, into Ash Lane. Follow the lane to Hopwood Park The home of Kings Norton Rugby Club (on the Left hand side). please note that there is another rugby/Cricket club on the right hand side of the lane.
Honorary Secretary: Mr Roger Adams; 2 Moorcroft Close Callow Hill Redditch Worcestershire B97 5WB
Tel: 07970 181139
Fixtures Secretary: Mr Stephen Miskin; 75 Rednal

Road Kings Norton Birmingham B38 8DT
Tel: 0121 4583918
Email: stephen.miskin@nhs.net
Club Colours: Red & Gold
League: Midlands 3 West (S) (level 8)

Ledbury RFC
Ground Address: Ross Road Playing Fields Ross Road, Ledbury Herefordshire HR8 2LP
Contact: 01531 631788
Email: bruce@lrfc.co.uk
Website: http://www.lrfc.co.uk/
Directions: Leave M50 at J 2. Take A417 to Ledbury for 4 miles. Take left turn at R/about and travel down by-pass. Next R/about take A449 to Ross-on-Wye, club can be found 100yds on right.
Honorary Secretary: Mr Jon Fenton; 12 Prince Rupert Road LEDBURY Herefordshire HR8 2FA
Tel: 07838118171
Email: jon.fenton@dairycrest.co.uk
Fixtures Secretary: Mr Trevor Humphrey; 8 Sunshine Close Ledbury Herefordshire HR8 2DZ
Tel: 07808 987846
Email: trevor.humphrey@xerox.com
Club Colours: Black & White Hoops
League: Midlands 3 West (S) (level 8)

Leek RUFC
Ground Address: F Ball Park Chestnut Walk St Edwards Cheddleton nr Leek Staffordshire ST13 7EB
Contact: 01538 361770
Email: john@collcap.co.uk
Website: www.leekrufc.co.uk
Directions: Leek's home ground, The F Ball Park, is located in the grounds of the old St Edwards hospital in Cheddleton. Having been redeveloped over the past few years, this area is known as St Edwards Park and is off the A520 Cheadle Road between Cheddleton and Leek. From the M6 south: Junction 14, A34 to Stone, A520 to Meir (passing over the A50) and towards Leek. After dropping down the hill through Cheddleton and past the Flint Mill on your left, take the first left into Wall Lane Terrace. Follow this road to a t-junction and turn left to The Post and Times Park. From Leek: A520 south towards Cheddleton. After passing the Travellers Rest pub on your left, turn right towards the top of the hill onto East Drive. Follow this road through to The F Ball Park.
Honorary Secretary: Mr Michael Whitehouse; 164 Chell Street Stoke On Trent Staffordshire ST1 6BD
Tel: 01782 261535
Email: michaelwhitehouse925@btinternet.com
Fixtures Secretary: Mr Gareth Jones; 2 Davenport Close Leek Staffordshire ST13 8NU Tel: 01538 382456
Email: gj46@sky.com
Club Colours: Royal blue & white hoops, royal blue shorts & socks
League: Midlands 3 West (N) (level 8)

Leesbrook RUFC
Ground Address: Asterdale Sports Centre Borrowash Road, Spondon Derby DE21 7PH
Email: steve.watt@falabs.com
Website: www.leesbrookrufc.com
Directions: M1 J25, take A52 towards Derby,3rd turn LEFT is Borrowash Road. From City Centre take A52, take turning marked Borrowash/Spondon (Ntm Old Road). Borrowash Road is on left opposite Clock Garage before Borrowash.
Honorary Secretary: Mr Stephen Watt; 28 Lawn Avenue Etwall Derby Derbyshire DE65 6JB
Tel: 07976 472890
Email: steve.watt@falabs.com
Fixtures Secretary: Mr Neil Johnson; 34 Horncastle Road Breadsall Derby DE21 4BW Tel: 07870 825680
Email: n.johnson433@ntlworld.com
Club Colours: Black with Green & Blue Band, Black Shorts & Socks
League: Midlands 4 East (N) (level 9)

Leicester Forest RFC
Ground Address: Leicester Forest R.F.C. Hinckley Road Leicester Forest East Leicester Leicestershire LE3 3PJ
Contact: 01162 387136
Email: lfrfc@aol.com
Website: www.leicesterforest.availablesports.com/
Directions: Ground is off the main A47 Leicester. Hinckley road 1.5miles from the Leicester Forest Services on the M1.
Honorary Secretary: Mr Micheal Beason; 43 Lindridge Lane Desford Leicester Leicestershire LE9 9GN
Tel: 07966 556210
Fixtures Secretary: Mr Tony Thraves; 5 Lynmouth Drive Wigston Leicester LE16 1BP Tel: 07976 259882
Email: tony_lfrfc@hotmail.co.uk
Club Colours: Royal & dark blue shirts, dark blue shorts.
League: Midlands 2 East (S) (level 7)

Lichfield RUFC
Ground Address: Lichfield RUFC Cooke Fields Tamworth Road Lichfield Staffordshire WS14 9JE
Contact: 01543 263020
Email: rkfathers@btinternet.com
Website: www.lichfieldrugby.co.uk
Directions: Take A51 from Lichfield to Tamworth for approx one mile. Ground behind Horse & Hockey public house.
Honorary Secretary: Mr Roger Fathers; 75 Spring Lane Whittington Lichfield Staffordshire WS14 9NA
Tel: 01543 433118
Email: rkfathers@btinternet.com
Fixtures Secretary: Mr David Preece; 75 Little Aston Lane Sutton Coldfield West Midlands B74 3UE
Tel: 0121 3533626
Email: davidwapreece@hotmail.co.uk
Club Colours: Myrtle green shirts, navy shorts, red socks
League: Midlands 2 West (N) (level 7)

Lincoln RFC
Ground Address: Lincoln R.F.C. Lindum Sports Ground St Giles Avenue Wragby Road Lincoln LN2 4PE
Contact: 01522 829354
Email: jackymcg@hotmail.com
Website: www.lincolnrugby.net
Directions: Head for Cathedral, club is located on Wragby Road in the 'Upill' area of Lincoln.
Honorary Secretary: Mrs Jacklynn Mcgrath; 8 Dunmore Close Lincoln LN5 8TN Tel: 01522 822477
Email: jackymcg@hotmail.com
Fixtures Secretary: Mr Tom Barton; 19 Southland Drive Lincoln LN6 8AU Tel: 07796 072498
Email: tom1_at_home@yahoo.co.uk
Club Colours: Red, Green & White Bands, Green Shorts
League: Midlands 2 East (N) (level 7)

Long Buckby RFC
Ground Address: Station Road Long Buckby Northampton NN6 7QA
Contact: 01327 842222
Directions: 0.25 mile from market square, along Station Road towards Daventry.
Honorary Secretary: Stuart Gilbert; 4 Orchard Close Hollowell Hollowell Northampton NN6 8RX
Tel: 01604 740466
Email: stuart.gilbert4@btinternet.com
Fixtures Secretary: as Hon. Sec.
Club Colours: Emerald shirts/navy sleeves, navy shorts
League: Midlands 3 East (S) (level 8)

Long Eaton RFC
Ground Address: For all Correspodence 0 Arbordee 6 Holland Meadow Long Eaton Nottingham NG10 1HL
Contact: 0115 9460907
Email: des.chapman@btinternet.com
Website: www.longeatonrfc.co.uk
Directions: M1 Jct 25. Follow signs to Long Eaton. Then West Park Leisure Centre. Club is based 150 mtrs from Leisure Centre Car Park.
Honorary Secretary: Mr Dean Fielder; 96 Petersham Rd Long Eaton Nottinghamshire NG10 4DG
Tel: 07515 886230   **Email:** dean.fielder@yahoo.co.uk
Fixtures Secretary: Mrs Lyn Ralfsy Tel: 07833 115026
Club Colours: Royal blue & white hoops, blue shorts
League: Midlands 5 East (N) (level 10)

Lordswood Dixonians RFC
Ground Address: Lordswood Boys School Hagley Road Edgbaston Birmingham West Midlands B17 8BJ
Contact: 07725 440264
Email: gregwatts@btopenworld.com
Website: www.ldrfc.com
Directions: From Five Ways Birmingham A456 direction Kidderminster in 2 miles turn left into Lordswood school shortly after Meadow Road.
Opposite the New Talbot pub.
Honorary Secretary: James Webb; 65 Cotton Lane Moseley Birmingham West Midlands B13 9SE
Tel: 07989 391322

Email: James.Webb@burges-salmon.com
Fixtures Secretary: as Hon. Sec.
Club Colours: Maroon green and black, black shorts
League: Midlands 2 West (N) (level 7)

Loughborough RFC
Ground Address: The Clubhouse Derby Road Playing Fields Loughborough LE11 5AD
Contact: 01509 216 093
Email: loughboroughrfc@hotmail.com
Directions: Turn onto Bishop Meadow Road. At Bishop Meadow R/about (A6) turn left at Pay Less DIY. First right then first left.
Honorary Secretary: Mr Adrian Ganderton; 33 Kingfisher Way Loughborough Leicestershire LE11 3NF
Tel: 0116 2045365   **Email:** apganderton@aol.com
Fixtures Secretary: Mr Nick Moore; 6 Maclean Avenue Loughborough Leicestershire LE11 5XX
Tel: 07931 903146
Club Colours: Navy Blue & Old Gold
League: Midlands 2 East (N) (level 7)

Ludlow RFC
Ground Address: Ludlow RFC The Linney Ludlow ShropshireSY8 1EE
Contact: 01584 875762
Email: david111roberts@gmail.com
Directions: Approaching Ludlow from north on A49 road, take first exit for Ludlow Town Centre take second turn right just after Honda Equipe into The Linney, follow road for .5 mile, club on right behind football pitch. Travel from south along Ludlow by pass and follow directions as per north.
Honorary Secretary: Mr David Roberts; Willowcroft Litmarsh Hereford HR1 3EZ Tel: 07974 647662
Email: david111roberts@googlemail.net
Fixtures Secretary: Mr Ian Townsend; 15 Watling Street South Church Stretton ShropshireSY6 7BG
Tel: 07717 690022   **Email:** ian.townsend@hsbc.com
Club Colours: Red Shirts, Black Shorts
League: Midlands 2 West (N) (level 7)

Lutterworth RFC
Ground Address: Lutterworth R.F.C. Ashby Lane Bittesswell Nr. Lutterworth LE17 4SQ
Contact: 01455 553115
Email: rugby@lutterworthrfc.com
Directions: Approx. 1.5 miles north off Lutterworth on A426 take left turn at small crossroads (sign posted to Lutterworth RFC).
Honorary Secretary: Mr Colin Hudson; 25 Maxwell Way Lutterworth Leicestershire LE17 4GS
Tel: 01788 534643
Email: colin.hudson6@btinternet.com
Fixtures Secretary: Mr Phil Duffin; 10 South Avenue Ullesthorpe Lutterworth Leicestershire LE17 5DG
Tel: 07850 610944
Email: phil@chechlacz.freeserve.co.uk
Club Colours: Red, White and Green Stripes
League: Midlands 2 East (S) (level 7)

Manor Park RFC
Ground Address: Griff & Coton Sports Club Heath End Road, Stockingford Nuneaton Warwickshire CV10 7HQ
Contact: 024 76389798
Email: chairman@mprfc.co.uk
Website: www.mprfc.co.uk
Directions: See location page on website M1-M6 J3, A444 Nuneaton, keep left at George Elliot Hospital, into Heath End Road, turn into Griff & Coton Sports Ground on right.
Honorary Secretary: Mr Bruce Jardine; 4 Astley Lane Bedworth Warwickshire CV12 0LS Tel: 07941 163985
Fixtures Secretary: Mr Jeffrey Badland; 32 Toler Road Abbey Green Nuneaton Warwickshire CV11 5EP
Tel: 024 7632904   Email: fixsec@mprfc.co.uk
Club Colours: Red & Black
League: Midlands 4 West (S) (level 9)

March Bears RUFC
Ground Address: March Bears RUFC Elm Road Sports Field Elm Road March CambridgeshirePE15 0BL
Contact: 01354 656937
Email: secretary@marchbearsrufc.org.uk
Website: www.marchbearsrufc.org.uk
Directions: Follow signs for HMP Whitemoor. The sportsfield is on the corner of Longhill Road, which leads to the prison.
Honorary Secretary: Ms Clairice Pepper; 73 Grounds Avenue March PE15 9BG Tel: 07739 512574
Email: secretary@marchbearsrufc.org.uk
Fixtures Secretary: Mr Colin Buck; 51 Ellingham Avenue March CambridgeshirePE15 9TE
Tel: 01353 4650074   Email: colin@colinbuck.co.uk
Club Colours: Maroon and White
League: Non League

Market Drayton RFC
Ground Address: NO CORRESPONDENCE TO THIS ADDRESS PLEASE Greenfields Sports Ground, Greenfields Lane Market Drayton ShropshireTF9 3SL
Contact: 01939 210321
Email: neilandrosie@hadnall.orangehome.co.uk
Directions: Turn into town centre from the Gingerbread Man pub. Greenfields is signposted 300m from the r/about on the righthand side of the bridge.
Honorary Secretary: Mr Neil Duxbury; 15 Old Farm Road Hadnall Shrewsbury ShropshireSY4 4BH
Tel: 07837 310957
Email: neilandrosie@hadnall.orangehome.co.uk
Fixtures Secretary: Mr David Cadwell; 5 Priors Lane Market Drayton ShropshireTF9 3UQ Tel: 01270 535150
Email: thecadwells@tiscali.co.uk
Club Colours: Black with Green Trim
League: Midlands 5 West (N) (level 10)

Market Harborough RUFC
Ground Address: Market Harborough R.U.F.C. Northampton Road Market Harborough Leicestershire LE16 9HF
Contact: 01858 469468
Directions: From the north head through Market Harborough town centre and follow signs for Northampton. At the edge of town turn right at the Leisure Centre and follow the road round to the clubhouse. From the south (A508) the club is on left coming in from the A14/M6
Honorary Secretary: John Curtis; Rose Cottage 11a Debdale Lane Westerby Leicestershire LE8 0QD
Tel: 0161 2793169   Email: ejcurtis@aol.com
Fixtures Secretary: Mr Barry Rolfe; 3 Hall Gardens Hall Gardens Green Lane North Kilworth Leicestershire LE17 6HQ Tel: 01858 880619
Email: rolfeandbazjen@btinternet.com
Club Colours: All Black
League: Midlands 2 East (S) (level 7)

Market Rasen & Louth RUFC
Ground Address: Willingham Road Market Rasen Lincolnshire LN8 3RE
Contact: 01673 843162
Email: clare@fenwickbros.co.uk
Website: www.rasenrugby.com
Directions: Situated 1 mile out of Market Rasen town centre heading east towards Louth on A631 on the right hand side, just passed De Aston Secondary School
Honorary Secretary: Mrs Clare Fenwick; Claxby House Farm Park Road Claxby Market Rasen Lincolnshire LN8 3YT Tel: 01673 828385
Email: clare@fenwickbros.co.uk
Fixtures Secretary: Mr Chris Miller; Jasmine Cottage Hill Rise Rothwell Market Rasen Lincolnshire LN7 6AZ
Tel: 07774 741525
Email: chris@miller25.plus.com
Club Colours: Red & Green Hoops, white shorts
League: Midlands 2 East (N) (level 7)

Meden Vale RFC
Ground Address: Welbeck Colliery Welfare Elkesley Road, Meden Vale Mansfield NG20 9PS
Contact: 01623 842267
Email: mikeheaton@flynn-associates.co.uk
Website: www.medenvalerugby.co.uk
Directions: From A60 turn towards Meden Vale, follow road until petrol station then turn left up the hill, signposted Welbeck Colliery Welfare, take 2nd left into car park. From A616, take the Meden Vale turning, approx 1.5 miles through Gleadthorpe, take 2nd right after railway bridge, signposted Welbeck Colliery Welfare, 2nd left into car park.
Honorary Secretary: Mr Michael Heaton; 17 Jackson Terrace Meden Vale Mansfield Notts. NG20 9PP
Tel: 01623 823573
Email: mikeheaton@flynn-associates.co.uk
Fixtures Secretary: Mr Nigel Baxter; 4 Butler Drive Blidworth Mansfield NG21 0QJ Tel: 07931 441841
Email: nigel_baxter@sky.com
Club Colours: Black with Red Sleeves
League: Midlands 5 East (N) (level 10)

Melbourne RFC
Ground Address: Melbourne R.F.C. Cockshutt Lane Melbourne DERBY Derbyshire DE73 8DJ
Contact: 01332 863529
Email: clubsecretary@melbourne-rfc.com
Website: http://www.melbourne-rfc.com
Directions: From M1, A453 to Melbourne. From Derby/Uttoxeter, A514 to Melbourne. Then B587 to Recreation Ground. Downloadable map on website.
Honorary Secretary: Ann-Marie Topliss; 11 Nettlefold Crescent Melbourne Derbyshire DE73 8DA
Tel: 07980 776835
Email: ann-marie.topliss@ramesys.com
Fixtures Secretary: Corinna West; 11 Church Lane Castle Donington Derbyshire DE74 2LG
Tel: 07773 680565
Email: Corinna.West@trinitas.org.uk
Club Colours: Bottle green and white
League: Midlands 3 East (N) (level 8)

Mellish RFC
Ground Address: Mellish RFC Ltd The Memorial Ground Mapperley Plains Arnold Nottingham NG3 5RX
Contact: 0115 9661313
Email: rbk570@yahoo.co.uk
Website: www.pitchero.com/clubs/mellishrfcltd
Directions: Ground situated on west side of the B684 road opposite The Travellers Rest Pub, 2 miles east of the turn off from the A614 Ollerton Road just north of the town of Arnold.
Honorary Secretary: Mr Bob Knowles; 7 Rannoch Rise Arnold Nottingham Nottinghamshire NG5 8FJ
Tel: 07753 850742
Email: rbk570@yahoo.co.uk
Fixtures Secretary: Mr Syd Harris; 18 Cirrus Drive, Watnall, Nottingham NG16 1FS Tel: 0115 9755222
Email: maisonharris@hotmail.com
Club Colours: green,gold & black
League: Midlands 3 East (N) (level 8)

Melton Mowbray RFC
Ground Address: King Edward VII Upper School Burton Rd Melton Mowbray Leicestershire LE13 1DR
Contact: 01664 563242
Email: john.hill@man.eu
Website: www.mmrfc.co.uk
Directions: Leave Melton Mowbray via the A606 to Oakham. Access is on the left past King Edward VII Upper School.
Honorary Secretary: Mr Hugh Middleton; 1 Dulverton Rd Melton Mowbray Leicestershire LE13 0SF
Tel: 079 33775486
Email: middleton_hugh@hotmail.com
Fixtures Secretary: Mr Steve Kerr; 30 Dorothy Avenue Melton Mowbray Leicestershire LE13 0LB
Tel: 01664 850954
Email: steve_mmrfc_fixtures@msn.com
League: Midlands 2 East (N) (level 7)

Moseley Oak RFC
Ground Address: Moseley Rugby Club Billesley Common Yardley Wood Road Billesley Birmingham B13 0ST
Contact: 07970 886815
Email: ben.jowett@kingsturge.com
Website: www.sellyoakrfc.co.uk
Directions: Moseley Oak RFC Ground share with Moseley Rugby Club, adjacent to Billesley Indoor Tennis Centre) - See Moseley FC for directions.
Honorary Secretary: Mr Ben Jowett; 33 Pitmaston Court Goodby Road Moseley Birmingham B13 8RL
Tel: 07528 446234
Email: benjowett@hotmail.com
Fixtures Secretary: Jon Underwood
Tel: 0121 4754026
Email: ellenu@blueyonder.co.uk
Club Colours: Red & White Hoops with Blue panelling, black shorts and red socks
League: Midlands 3 West (N) (level 8)

Newbold on Avon RFC
Ground Address: Newbold on Avon R.F.C. The Clubhouse Parkfield Road, Newbold On Avon Rugby Warwickshire CV21 1EZ
Contact: 01788 565811
Email: newboldrfc@btconnect.com
Website: www.newboldrfc.com
Directions: M6, J1 to Rugby. Continue towards Rugby and at end of duel carrageway turn right to Newbold (3/4 mile). At crossroads turn left at Crown Inn. Cross river bridge and Clubhouse is 50 yards on the right.
Honorary Secretary: Mr Roy Hall; 8 Belmont Road, Rugby Warwickshire CV22 5NZ Tel: 01788 334757
Email: r.t.hall@ntlworld.com
Fixtures Secretary: Mr Paul Bale; 135 Norman Road, Rugby Warwickshire CV21 1DW Tel: 01788 337470
Email: paulbalealg@hotmail.com
Club Colours: Red & Black
League: Midlands 2 West (S) (level 7)

Newcastle (Staffs) RUFC
Ground Address: Newcastle (Staffs) RUFC. The Pavillion Lilleshall Road Newcastle-under-Lyme Staffs. ST5 3BX
Contact: 01782 617042
Email: kevin.oneill@homecall.co.uk
Website: www.newcastlestaffsrufc.co.uk
Directions: M6 J15 to Newcastle, turn L. at 1st R/about, straight over next R/about, right at next R/about down Stafford Avenue, third Rd on left - Lilleshall Rd - past Cricket Ground on Right
Honorary Secretary: Mr Kevin O'Neill; 18 Ashbourne Drive Newcastle Staffordshire ST5 6RL
Tel: 07850 505401
Email: kevin.oneill@homecall.co.uk
Fixtures Secretary: Mr Michael Mulroy
Tel: 07521 716440
Email: mikemulroy@uwclub.net
Club Colours: Maroon & white hoops, black shorts & socks
League: Midlands 3 West (N) (level 8)

North Hykeham RUFC
Ground Address: NK RUFC, Hykeham PFA Club 319 Newark Road North Hykeham LN6 9RY
Contact: 01522 519905
Email: northkesteven.rufc@ntlworld.com
Directions: From A46 south of Lincoln, go towards Lincoln, look for Memorial Hall sign on left opposite North Kesteven School and Sports Centre.
Honorary Secretary: Malcolm Ross; 26 Lincoln Road Branston Lincoln Lincolnshire LN4 1PA
Tel: 01522 822618
Email: m.ross2008@btinternet.com
Fixtures Secretary: Mr Nigel Thomas; 192 Hykeham Road Lincoln LN6 8AR Tel: 07850 75601
Email: nigel.thomas8@btinternet.com
Club Colours: Black with Red,White & Green Hoops
League: Midlands 5 East (N) (level 10)

Northampton BBOB RFC
Ground Address: St. Andrews mill St. Andrews Road Northampton NN1 2PQ
Contact: 01604 632460
Email: jrf3170@aol.com
Website: www.bbobrfc.com
Directions: FROM NORTH Exit M1 J16. Take first exit (A45) off of roundabout. Stay on A45 for about 2 miles. Go straight across next 3 roundabouts. Turn LEFT at 2nd set of traffic lights (just past Northampton 'Saints' RFC). Straight across 3 sets of lights. LEFT into St Andrews Road, ground entrance on the left by Enterprise Car Hire, after the park. FROM SOUTH Exit M1 J15. Take 3rd exit at roundabout (A508 - Northampton). Stay on dual carriageway for about 2 miles. Take 2nd exit off roundabout (A508/Town Centre). Left at traffic lights at bottom of hill. 3rd exit at roundabout over bridge. Straight over next roundabout. 1st exit at next roundabout (Gasometer on left), take exit on right to traffic lights. Straight across these lights. Straight across next set of lights. Clubhouse and ground on left just pass the park behind Enterprise Car Rental.
Honorary Secretary: Mrs Joanna Foster; 46 Delapre Crescent Road Northampton NN4 8NH
Tel: 0779 5011723
Email: JRF3170@aol.com
Fixtures Secretary: Mr Fenton Goodes; 79 Queens Park Parade Northampton NN2 6LR Tel: 01604 710180
Club Colours: Light Blue, Dark Blue & Maroon
League: Midlands 2 East (S) (level 7)

Northampton Casuals RFC
Ground Address: Rush Mills House Old Bedford Road, Rush Mills Northampton Northamptonshire NN4 7AA
Contact: 01604 636716
Directions: Brief **Directions:** At M1 J15 take A508 to Northampton then the 4th slip road and take A428 to Bedford. At first roundabout go right and back towards Northampton, then take the first left.
Honorary Secretary: Mr Martyn Dimmock; 44a Park Drive Kings Heath Northampton NN5 7JU
Tel: 07779 411334

Email: mdimmock@photocorp.co.uk
Fixtures Secretary: Steffan Fowler; 21 West Paddock Court Lings Northampton NN3 8LQ Tel: 07800 635204
Email: stefanfowler24@hotmail.com
Club Colours: Black with Amber Band
League: Midlands 3 East (S) (level 8)

Northampton Heathens RFC
Ground Address:
The Artizan Artizan Road Northampton NN1 4HR
Contact: 01604 416442
Email: lon.dhodgkinson@cma-cgm.com
Website: http://www.northampton-heathens.co.uk/
Directions: From MI : leave at Junction 15, follow dual carriageway, leave at 2nd Northampton exit at Bedford Road roundabout (A428). Leave roundabout at 2nd exit into Rushmere Road. Proceed up hill [past Old Scouts RFC on left] then over traffic lights. Continue over second set of traffic lights [Abingdon Park on right] to a complex of three traffic lights. Turn left at the third set and past the County Ground on left to a mini roundabout where turn right. At next set of traffic lights [White Elephant public house diagonally opposite on right] turn left. The Raceourse is on the right and the entrance to the changing room carpark is on the right just before a further set of traffic lights. The changing rooms are to the left of the main pavilion [Jade Restaurant]. Changing room telephone = 01604 639250.
Honorary Secretary: Mr Derek Hodgkinson; 5 Pinetrees Weston Favell Northampton NN3 3ET
Tel: 07866 773871
Email: lon.dhodgkinson@cma-cgm.com
Fixtures Secretary: Mr Martin Robson; 8 Rockcroft East Hunsbury Northampton NN4 0UB
Tel: 01604 705987
Email: pat@microhosts.co.uk
Club Colours: Black with Amber Edging
League: Non League

Northampton Mens Own RFC
Ground Address: Northampton Mens Own RFC Stoke Road, Ashton. Northamptonshire NN72JA
Contact: 01604 862463
Directions: M1 J15, take A508 to Milton Keynes for 2.5 miles, through Roade Village, take next left turning at crossroads, after 1 mile, signed Ashton, ground 0.5mile on right.
Honorary Secretary: Mr Stephen Goryll; Westfield 18 Mill Lane Kislingbury Northampton NN7 4BD
Tel: 01604 830353
Email: slgoryll@tiscali.co.uk
Fixtures Secretary: Mr John Wilson; 11 Beech Avenue Northampton NN3 2HE
Tel: 07808 849375
Email: john.wilson823@o2.co.uk
Club Colours: White Shirts with Blue Hoops,
League: Midlands 3 East (S) (level 8)

Northampton Old Scouts RFC
Ground Address: Rushmere Road Northampton Northamptonshire NN1 5RY
Contact: 01604 633639
Website: www.nosrfc.com
Directions: From M1 - exit at Junction 15 and head towards Northampton on A508 dual carriageway. Take left exit sign posted to Northampton Town Centre and Bedford after crossing river Nene. The slip road takes you down to the Bedford Road roundabout, take 2nd exit into Rushmere Road and the club is situated approx. _ mile on left. From Bedford - enter roundabout as above from A428, take 3rd exit From Wellingborough - enter roundabout from A45, take 4th exit
Honorary Secretary: Mrs Anne Hodson; 292 Obelisk Rise Kingsthorpe Northampton NN2 8TW
Email: anne.hodson@urbandata.co.uk
Fixtures Secretary: Mr Keith Shurville; 41 Churchill Avenue Northampton NN3 6NY Tel: 07721 368477
Email: keith.shurville@emru.co.uk
Club Colours: Red, green, gold & navy hooped shirts, navy shorts
League: Midlands 2 East (S) (level 7)

Nottingham Boots Corsairs RFC
Ground Address: Holme Road, Lady Bay West Bridgford Nottinghamshire NG2 5BJ
Contact: 07710 083283
Email: rugbytom@tiscali.co.uk
Website: www.nbcrfc.orh.uk
Directions: Follow signs to either Trent Bridge Cricket or Nottingham Forest, the Athletic Grounds are at the junction of Lady Bay Bridge and Trent Boulevard.
Honorary Secretary: Mr Adrian Pritchard
Fixtures Secretary: Mr Peter Webb; 189 Measham Road Moira Swadlincote Derbyshire DE12 6AJ
Tel: 01509 554453
Email: pete_j_webb@yahoo.com
Club Colours: Green and white hoops
League: Midlands 5 East (N) (level 10)

Nottingham Casuals RFC
Ground Address: Canalside,Meadow Road Beeston Rylands Beeston Rylands Nottingham NG9 1JQ
Email: casuals@rugby-club.co.uk
Website: http://www.nottinghamcasuals.org.uk/
Directions: M1 J25, A52 to Nottingham, after 2nd roundabout, right at 2nd lights, straight across 2 crossroads, continue untill road makes sharp right, over bridge, turn left.
Honorary Secretary: Mr Andy Crowther; 18 Longleat Crescent Beeston Nottingham NG9 5EU
Tel: (0115)9 678390
Email: andyc@feedback.co.uk
Fixtures Secretary: Mr Lech Kluk; 46 Springfield Avenue Sandiacre Nottingham NG10 5LZ
Tel: 07713 149399
Email: lktrain@aol.com
Club Colours: Maroon, Black & White, Black Shorts
League: Midlands 3 East (N) (level 8)

Nottingham Medics RFC
Ground Address: 12 Hope Drive The Park Nottingham NG7 1DL
Contact: 07766 517513
Email: mzyyajh@nottingham.ac.uk
Website: www.nmrufc.co.uk
Directions: Home matches played at Nottingham Casuals Rugby Club
Honorary Secretary: David Rees; 66 Harlaxton Drive Lenton Nottingham Nottinghamshire NG7 1JB
Tel: 07870 104623
Email: mzyydmr@nottingham.ac.uk
Fixtures Secretary: Jonny Morris; Tel: 07738 010277
Club Colours: Green Blue and Gold
League: Non League

Nottingham Moderns RFC
Ground Address: Nottingham Moderns Rugby Club Main Road Willford Village Nottingham NG11 7AA
Contact: 0115 9811374
Email: info@nottinghammodernsrfc.org
Website: www.nottinghammodernsrfc.org
Directions: From M1 motorway Leave motorway at junction 24. Head East towards Nottingham along the A453.After passing Nottingham Trent University Campus (on left) proceed to next set of traffic lights. At traffic lights continue straight on and then bear left along slip road towards West Bridgford. At island take the first exit towards West Bridgford. Continue over mini-island to traffic lights. At traffic lights turn LEFT into Main Road. Clubhouse if located at the very end of Main Road on the left hand side adjacent to the Ferry Inn public house (please do not use the public house car park). From the East Proceed along the A52 and on to the junction with the A453. Bear left down slip-road to island. Take third exit towards West Bridgford. Continue over mini-island to traffic lights. At traffic lights turn LEFT into Main Road. Clubhouse if located at the very end of Main Road on the left hand side adjacent to the Ferry Inn public house (please do not use the public house car park).
Honorary Secretary: Mr Stu Newman; 5 Lambourne Gardens Woodthorpe Nottingham NG5 4PA
Tel: 07912 058269
Email: custandjo@ntlworld.com
Fixtures Secretary: Mark Green; Nethergate 10 Clifton Village Nottingham NG11 8NL Tel: 07912 519266
Email: mkgn2007@sky.com
Club Colours: Red, white & black irregular
League: Midlands 2 East (N) (level 7)

Nottingham Trent University RFC
Ground Address: The Point Bar Nottingham Trent University - Student Activities Clifton Campus Clifton Lane NG11 8NS
Contact: 07917 724149
Email: trentrugby@hotmail.com
Club Colours: Green and Blue
League: Non League

Nottinghamians RFC
Ground Address: Adbolton Lane West Bridgford Nottingham NG2 5AS
Contact: 0115 984 8722
Email: david.hampson@logicacmg.com
Directions: M1 jct 24, A453 to A52, the Nottingham ring road. Follow signs to Holme Pierrepont (National Water Sports Centre)
Honorary Secretary: Mr Phil Renshaw; 32 Florence Road West Bridgford Nottingham NG2 5HR
Tel: 0115 9142974
Email: philprenshaw302@hotmail.com
Fixtures Secretary: Mr Rod Exton; c/o the club
Tel: 0779 8523505
Email: rexton@btconnect.com
Club Colours: Purple Shirts, Black Shorts
League: Midlands 4 East (N) (level 9)

Oadby Wyggestonian RFC
Ground Address: Oadby Wyggestonian R.F.C. Oval Park Wigston Road, Oadby Leicestershire LE2 5JE
Contact: 0116 2714848
Email: info@owrfc.com
Website: www.owrfc.com
Directions: M1 J21, follow Leicester South & East for 4 miles to A50, turn right, left at roundabout, Ground 0.5 mile on left.
Honorary Secretary: Mr Luis Pazos-Alonso; 102 Haddenham Road Leicester LE3 2EG
Tel: 07710 718652
Email: ralonso@otmltd.com
Fixtures Secretary: Mr Malcolm Clarke; 2 Mablowe Field Wigston Leicester LE18 3UJ Tel: 07971 971126
Email: malcolm@malcolmclarke.orange.co.uk
Club Colours: BLACK, GOLD & WHITE SHIRTS
League: Midlands 4 East (S) (level 9)

Oakham RFC
Ground Address: The Showground Barleythorpe Road Barleythorpe Road Oakham LE15 6QH
Contact: 01572 724206
Email: steve@navitron.org.uk
Website: www.oakhamrfc.co.uk
Directions: Take the A606 Oakham to Melton Mowbray. Turn into Landsend Way at the Rutland VI form college and entrance to ground is on Left directly opposite Burley Fires Entrance.
Honorary Secretary: Yann Bomken; 17 Foxfield Way Oakham Leicestershire LE15 6PR Tel: 01572 770274
Email: yann.bomken@btinternet.com
Fixtures Secretary: Mr Stephen Knight; Manor House Cold Overton Road Cold Overton Oakham Leicestershire LE15 7QD Tel: 01664 454421
Email: steve@navitron.org.uk
Club Colours: Green & Yellow
League: Midlands 3 East (N) (level 8)

Old Coventrians RFC
Ground Address: Tile Hill Lane Tile Hill Coventry West Midlands CV4 9DE
Contact: 02476 715273
Email: michaeljowen39@gmail.com
Website: www.oldcoventriansrfc.co.uk
Directions: OCRFC is at junction of A45 (Fletchamstead Highway) / B4101 (Tile Hill Lane). On A45: from Birmingham turn left at Tile Hill Lane traffic lights, from South East filter right at Tile Hill Lane traffic lights - ground is 60 yards on left.
Honorary Secretary: Mr Bill Whetstone; 116 St. Martins Road Finham Coventry CV3 6ER
Tel: 02476 692460
Email: bill@Whetstone.plus.com
Fixtures Secretary: Mr Russ Brown; 36 Rothesay Avenue Tile Hill Coventry West Midlands CV4 9FJ
Tel: 02476 422369
Email: russbrown51@hotmail.com
Club Colours: Red, Black, Yellow
League: Midlands 2 West (S) (level 7)

Old Griffinians RFC
Ground Address: WM Travel Transport Stadium Wheelers Lane, Kings Heath Birmingham B13 0ST
Contact: 0121 687 2465
Email: andyrogers@oldgriffs.com
Directions: M42 J3, take A435 into B'ham, at Kings Heath turn right into Wheelers Lane and follow signs for Indoor Tennis Centre (B'ham A-Z page 106, grid ref C2).
Honorary Secretary: Mr Andy Rogers; 1 Prince Andrew Crescent Rubery Rednal Birmingham B45 0LZ
Tel: 07727 182321
Email: andyrogers@oldgriffs.com
Fixtures Secretary: Mr Adrian Johnson; 95 Green Meadow Road Selly Oak Birmingham B29 4DP
Tel: 07970 740742   Email: ade@oldgriffs.com
Club Colours: Black Shirts with multi red hoops black shorts
League: Midlands 4 West (N) (level 9)

Old Laurentians RFC
Ground Address:
Fenley Field Lime Tree Avenue Rugby CV22 7QT
Contact: 01788 810855
Website: www.oldlaurentianrfc.co.uk
Directions: From A45 take A4071 turn right into Alwyn Road, right again into Lime Tree Ave. Or, M6 onto Leicester Road, Bilton Road, Bilton Village, left into Alwyn Road and right into Lime Tree Ave.
Honorary Secretary: Mr Alan Willis; 45 Frobisher Road Rugby Warwickshire CV22 7HS Tel: 07849 615914
Email: awillis4@hotmail.co.uk
Fixtures Secretary: Mr Micheal Roberts; C/0 Club Address Fenley Field Lime Tree Avenue Rugby Warwickshire CV22 7QT   Tel: 07767 841348
Email: mike.roberts@cartersynergy.com
Club Colours: Maroon, gold & green Hoops, green shorts
League: Midlands 2 West (S) (level 7)

Old Leamingtonians RFC
Ground Address: The crofts Bericote Road Blackdown Leamington Spa Warwickshire CV32 6QP
Contact: 01926 424991
Email: lesgrafton@ntlworld.com
Website: www.olrfc.co.uk
Directions: From A46 take A452 towards Leamington Spa, after 600 yards take 1st exit at island towards Cubbington(signposted OLRFC), ground 0.75 mile on the right.
Honorary Secretary: Mrs Sally Hemming; 18 Kempton Crescent Leamington Spa Warwickshire CV32 7TS Tel: 07983 642477
Email: sally.hemming1@btinternet.com
Fixtures Secretary: Mr Martyn Rawbone; 20 Northumberland Road Leamington Spa Warwickshire CV32 6HA Tel: 0121 6984024
Club Colours: Blue and Gold hoops
League: Midlands 3 West (S) (level 8)

Old Newtonians RFC
Ground Address: Hinckley Road (A47) Leicester forest East Leicester LE3 3PJ
Contact: 0116 2392389
Email: gary.mills@oldnewtonians.co.uk
Website: www.oldnewtonians.co.uk
Directions: Follow main road A47 toward Hinckley from Leicester.At Leicester Forest East pass the Red Cow pub on right,continue along A47 for 1 mile, 200 metres past the cricket club and we are the rugby ground on right.
Honorary Secretary: Mr Gary Mills; Wood Lane 46 Wood Lane Quorn Leicestershire LE12 8DB
Tel: 01509 414823
Email: gary.mills@oldnewtonians.co.uk
Fixtures Secretary: Mr Peter Muggleton; 18 Roman Road Birstall Leicester LE4 4BA Tel: 0116 2676739
Email: peter.muggleton@yahoo.co.uk
Club Colours: Navy with white, green, red centre stripes
League: Midlands 2 East (S) (level 7)

Old Saltleians RFC
Ground Address: Old Saltleians R.F.C. Watton Lane Water Orton Warwickshire B46 1PH
Contact: 0121 7483380
Website: www.oldsaltleians.co.uk
Directions: Junction 2 of M6 signposted A446 Lichfield OR Junction 9 of M42 signposted A446 Coventry/Coleshill. Turn into Watton Lane at second set of traffic lights. Turn left before Motorway bridge. Entrance approximately 100m on left hand side.
Honorary Secretary: Mr Colin Gardner; 26 Julius Drive Coleshill Birmingham B46 1HL Tel: 01675 462193
Fixtures Secretary: Mr Len Berry; 40 Brooks Road Sutton Coldfield West Midlands B72 1HP
Tel: 07811 470378
Email: lenberry@onetel.com
Club Colours: Red & Gold Hoop Shirts, Navy Shorts
League: Midlands 2 West (N) (level 7)

Old Wheatleyans RFC
Ground Address: Norman Place Road Coundon Coventry CV6 2BU
Contact: 024 76334888
Directions: At J9 on Coventry ring road, take A4170 (Radford Rd), after 1.5 miles turn left into Norman Place Rd, entrance is at the far end of road, on left.
Honorary Secretary: Mr Andrew Hibberd; 59 Frilsham Way Coventry CV5 9LJ Tel: 02476 711955
Email: andy.hibberd@ntlworld.com
Fixtures Secretary: Mr Richard Hill; 89 Christchurch Road Coventry CV6 1JU Tel: 07900 003641
Email: katehill3@btconnect.com
Club Colours: Navy Blue, Maroon, Gold
League: Midlands 5 West (SE) (level 10)

Old Yardleians RFC
Ground Address: Tilehouse Lane Solihull B90 1PW
Contact: 0121 7443380
Email: mark.xc@blueyonder.co.uk
Website: www.oldyardsrugby.co.uk
Directions: From north M42 J4, Stratford Road, Dog Kennel Lane, Dickens Heath Road, Tythebarn Lane, Tilehouse Lane. From south, M42 J3 Alcester Lane, Station Lane, Lowbrook Lane, Tilehouse Lane.
Honorary Secretary: Mr Ray Tranter; 26 Clarendon Close, Brockhill, Redditch Worcestershire B97 6ST
Tel: 07976 243290
Email: ray.tranter@armstrongchase.co.uk
Club Colours: Old Gold, Maroon & Green
League: Midlands 3 West (N) (level 8)

Ollerton RFC
Ground Address: Boughton Sports Field Church Lane Boughton, Newark NG22 9JU
Contact: 01623 862527
Email: simonjhayward@btopenworld.com
Website: www.ollertonrugby.com
Directions: From A614 take A6075 thro' New Ollerton to Harrow Inn. On the APEX of the righthand bend turn left into Church Rd. In 200yds follow the road to the righthand side of the church into Church Lane.The ground is behind the Church. From the A1, from Tuxford take the A6075 towards ollerton turn right on the APEX of the lefthand bend at the Harrow Inn into Church Road.
Honorary Secretary: Mr David Harradine; 2 Petersmith Drive New Ollerton Newark Notts. NG22 9RU
Tel: 07989 323990   Email: d.harradine@tiscali.co.uk
Fixtures Secretary: Mr Clive Ford; 8 Linton Drive Boughton Newark Nottinghamshire NG22 9JH
Tel: 01623 862608
Email: cliveford320@btinternet.com
Club Colours: Yellow & Blue Hoops - Navy Shorts
League: Midlands 5 East (N) (level 10)

Oundle RFC
Ground Address: Occupation Road Oundle Peterborough PE8 4RU
Contact: 01832 273101
Email: duncan.hook@farming.co.uk

Directions: From Peterborough, cross bridge, turn right by garage, turn right then right again down single track road.
Honorary Secretary: Mr Duncan Smith; 39 Halford Street Thrapston Kettering Northamptonshire NN14 4LA Tel: 01832 733409
Fixtures Secretary: Mr Stephen Calnan; 7 Woodyard Close, Brigstock Kettering NN14 3LZ Tel: 01536 373151
Club Colours: Black with Red/White side flashes
League: Midlands 4 East (S) (level 9)

Pershore RFC
Ground Address: Piddle Park , Mill Lane Wyre Piddle Nr Pershore WR10 2JE
Contact: 01905 821444
Email: webmaster@prfc.co.uk
Directions: Between Worcester and Evesham on B4538, turn off main road in middle of village on the corner by the War Memorial club, .5mile down the lane.
Honorary Secretary: Mr David Griffiths; 83 Three Springs Road Pershore WR10 1HR Tel: 01386 561291
Email: charlieg83@myway.com
Club Colours: Black with red hoops
League: Midlands 3 West (S) (level 8)

Peterborough Lions RUFC
Ground Address: Peterborough Lions RUFC Flaxlands Bretton Woods Peterborough CambridgeshirePE3 8DF
Contact: 07736 895168
Email: mail@peterboroughlionsrugby.co.uk
Website: www.peterboroughlionsrugby.co.uk
Directions: From the North - Leave the A1 at the junction with the A47, Follow the A47 until you reach the exit for The Edith Cavell Hospital From the East - Follow the A47 until you reach the exit for The Edith Cavell Hospital From the West - Follow the A47 until you reach the exit for The Edith Cavell Hospital From the South - Leave the A1 at the Junction with the A1139, Follow the A1139 for approx 2 miles, exit A1139 onto the A1260 (Nene Parkway) and follow signs for Bretton centre, At Roundabout take 4th exit onto A47 (east) signed Wisbech, Follow the A47 until you reach the exit for The Edith Cavell Hospital ALL from The Edith Cavell Hospital Roundabout Follow signs to Bretton Centre (opposite side of carriageway to EC Hospital) At Roundabout take right turn (3rd Exit) onto Bretton Way Go straight ahead at lights (entrance to Sainsburys) At Next Roundabout turn right into Flaxland (Iceland & Sainsburys are on your right) Take 2nd Left, through gates and into car park.
Honorary Secretary: Mr Michael Marjoram; 57 Uplands Peterborough CambridgeshirePE4 5AF Tel: 07736 895168
Email: mike-marjoram@hotmail.com
Fixtures Secretary: Mr Mel Proud; 64 Ramsey Road Warboys CambridgeshirePE17 3RW
Email: mjproud@dsl.pipex.com
Club Colours: Bule shirts, White shorts
League: Midlands 2 East (S) (level 7)

Pinley RFC
Ground Address: Wyken Croft Wyken Wyken Coventry CV2 3EB
Contact: 02476 602059
Email: pinleyrfc@aol.com
Website: www.pinleyrfc.com
Honorary Secretary: Mr Michael Moore; 19 Angela Avenue Potters Green Coventry Warwickshire CV2 2GH Tel: 07877 499522
Email: pinleyrfcsecretary@hotmail.co.uk
Fixtures Secretary: Mr B Lester; Tel: 01203 443605
Club Colours: RED with BLACK trim
League: Midlands 4 West (S) (level 9)

Potton RFC
Ground Address: Potton RUFC Second Meadow Potton SG19 2QS
Contact: 01767 261693
Website: www.potton-rugby.org
Honorary Secretary: Katrina Ansell; 15 Sheffield Close Potton Bedfordshire SG19 2NY Tel: 07971 481550
Email: talk2trina@hotmail.com
Fixtures Secretary: Mr Geoff Corrin; 24 Mill Lane Potton Sandy Bedfordshire SG19 2PG
Tel: 07754 391023   Email: geoff@corrin.fsnet.co.uk
Club Colours: Blue & Gold
League: Non League

Queens RUFC
Ground Address: Putnoe Wood Wentworth Drive Bedford MK41 8QA
Contact: 01234 350874
Website: www.queensrufc.co.uk
Directions: From Bedford City Centre, take A428 Goldington Road towards Cambridge. Take B660 Kimbolton Road towards Kimbolton for 1.75 miles, turn right onto Wentworth Drive. Ground .5 mile on left.
Honorary Secretary: Mr Jason Cracknell; 64 Phillpotts Avenue Bedford MK40 3UD   Tel: 07976 559506
Email: jason.cracknell@cawleys.co.uk
Fixtures Secretary: Mr Rae Fisk; 119 Queens Drive Bedford Bedfordshire MK41 9JE Tel: 07545 545203
Email: fiskfamily@ntlworld.com
Club Colours: Maroon & white hoops.
League: Midlands 3 East (S) (level 8)

RAF Brampton RFC
Ground Address: Room W150 Swales Pavilion RAF Wyton PE29 2EP
Contact: 01480 452451 x5332
Email: tor-mechelec2a@esair.dlo.mod.uk
Directions: The Club plays at RAF Brampton which is on the edge of Brampton village, just off the A1 south of Huntingdon.
Honorary Secretary: Ian Greentree;
Email: jar-analyst87@jar.mod.uk
Club Colours: Blue & Black Quarters
League: Non League

MIDLANDS LEVELS 7-10 & NON LEAGUE CLUBS

RAF Coningsby RFC
Ground Address:
OIC Rugby RAF Coningsby LINCOLN LN4 4SY
Contact: 01526 347144
Email: rjackson@coningsby.raf.mod.uk
Directions: RAF Coningsby is situated close to the A153. Follow the A153 into Coningsby village and the station is signposted by the Lloyds Bank.
League: Non League

RAF Cosford RFC
Ground Address:
PWTS RAF Cosford Wolverhampton WV7 3EX
Contact: 01902 377 608
Honorary Secretary: G Harkhy
League: Non League

RAF Cottesmore Aces RFC
Ground Address: RAF Cottesmore Oakham Rutland Leicestershire LE15 7BL
Contact: 01572 812241 Ex 7954
Email: ctshiloc-logsso3@cottesmore.raf.mod.uk
Honorary Secretary: Andy Higgins; RNXO Room 105 Station HQ RAF Cottesmore Rutland Leicestershire LE15 7BL Tel: 01572 812241
Email: jfh-rnxo@cottesmore.raf.mod.uk
League: Non League

RAF Cranwell RFC
Ground Address: Cse Prop Offr DCAE Cranwell RAFC Cranwell NG34 8HB
League: Non League

RAF Waddington RFC
Ground Address: Officer IC Rugby RAF Waddington LINCOLN LN5 9NB
Contact: 01522 720271 ext 6681
Honorary Secretary: Mr Colin Whitham; SMS RAF Waddington Lincoln Lincolnshire LN5 9NB
Tel: 07748 140676
Email: colinwhitham@hotmail.com
Club Colours: Black and Gold
League: Non League

RAF Wittering RFC
Ground Address: OIC Rugby QCIT Royal Air Force Wittering PETERBOROUGH CambridgeshirePE8 6HB
Contact: 01780 783238
Email: witfhq-qcitqsc@wittering.raf.mod.uk
Directions: RAF Wittering is located a few miles north of Peterborough on the A1.
Honorary Secretary: Mr Jeremy Bryant; 18 Forth Close Oakham Leicestershire LE15 6JW Tel: 07944 067015
Email: jerry.bryant@talk21.com
Club Colours: Green shirts & yellow trim
League: Non League

Redditch RFC
Ground Address: Bromsgrove Road Redditch B97 4RN
Contact: 0152762207
Email: bcarr4@aol.com
Directions: Bromsgrove Highway - Birchfield Road - Bromsgrove Road.
Honorary Secretary: Mr Brian Carr; 60 Wychbury Road Brierley Hill West Midlands DY5 2XX
Tel: 01384 79092   Email: bcarr4@aol.com
Fixtures Secretary: Mr Paul Thurston; 18 Crendon Close Studley B80 7DB Tel: 01527 854802
Email: paul@indwash.co.uk
Club Colours: Navy and Light Blue shirts, Navy shorts
League: Midlands 3 West (S) (level 8)

Ripley Rhinos RFC
Ground Address:
Mill Hill School (no post) Peasehill Ripley DE5 3JQ
Contact: 01773 512719
Email: rugby@ripleyrhinos.com
Website: http://www.ripleyrhinos.com
Directions: From M1 J26 - take A610 into Ripley. At Codnor traffic lights, turn right. Go down hill, round bend, up hill, and turn left into Steam Mill Lane 100 yards after traffic lights. Mill Hill School 500 yards up on right hand side.
Honorary Secretary: Mr Dave Trubee; 42, Charnwood Drive RIPLEY Derbyshire DE5 3TB
Tel: (07816) 779018   Email: dtrubee@dircon.co.uk
Fixtures Secretary: Mr Stephen Cresswell; The Beehive 151 Peasehill Ripley Derbyshire DE5 3JN
Tel: 01773 749593
Email: stevecresswell@thebeehiveinn.fsnet.co.uk
Club Colours: Maroon shirts with white band
League: Non League

Rolls-Royce RFC
Ground Address: Gate 1 Victory Road Allenton Derby Derbyshire DE24 8BJ
Email: rollsroycerfc@hotmail.co.uk
Website: www.rollsroycerfc.co.uk
Directions: SatNav use DE24 9HX for the HSBC Bank at traffic lights near Gate 1entrance. Pick up A5111 Derby ring road and follow brown signs "Moorways Sports". Follow to end of Moor Lane, left at lights, first left into Gate 1. More details on club website.
Honorary Secretary: Mr Andrew Blackhurst; 34 Prestwick Way Chellaston Derby DE73 5AB
Tel: 07931 675212
Email: andy_blackhurst@hotmail.com
Fixtures Secretary: Seán Donohue; 10 Gower Street DERBY DE1 1SD Tel: 07504 060747
Club Colours: Maroon & Sky Blue Shirts, Blacks Shorts
League: Midlands 4 East (N) (level 9)

Rugby St Andrews RFC
Ground Address: 42 warren Road Rugby CV22 5LG
Contact: 01788 574722
Email: rwills@talktalk.net
Website: www.standrews.co.uk
Directions: Ashlawn Road runs between Dunchurch (A45) and Hillmorton (M1-Northampton)A428. Map on web site
Honorary Secretary: Mr Roger Wills; 42 Warren Road Rugby Warwickshire CV22 5LG Tel: 01788 574722

Email: rwills@talktalk.net
Fixtures Secretary: Mr Mick Coulson; 35 Eastwood Grove Rugby Warwickshire CV21 4DP
Tel: 01788 331051
Email: michael.coulson@sky.com
Club Colours: Light blue / dark blue
League: Midlands 3 East (S) (level 8)

Rugby Welsh RFC
Ground Address: RWRFC c/o 5A Slade Road Rugby Warwickshire CV21 3AD
Contact: 07872670309
Email: secretary@rugbywelsh.co.uk
Directions: Ground - Take A428 toward coventry from Rugby centre. Through Bilton village take 2nd left turning after the Black Horse pub. This is Alwyn Road and the ground is 1/2 mile or so on left.
Honorary Secretary: Mr Lee Cox; 5A Slade Road Rugby Warwickshire CV21 3AD Tel: 0787 2670309
Email: lee.2.cox@airwavesolutions.co.uk
Fixtures Secretary: Mr Mickey James; 17 Watson Road Chapelfields Coventry CV5 8EW Tel: 02476 712034
Email: michael_james@sky.com
Club Colours: Red Jerseys, Black Shorts
League: Midlands 4 West (S) (level 8)

Rugeley RUFC
Ground Address: 10 Upper Cross Roads Rugeley Staffordshire WS15 2JD
Contact: 077896 93006
Email: mderidder@ansonsllp.com
Website: www.rugeleyrugby.com
Directions: A460 towards Hednesford, just after the speed camera, take the first turning on your right marked Rugeley Lesisure Centre take first right to Rugeley Lesiure Centre postcode WS15 2HZ.
Honorary Secretary: Mr Martin de Ridder; 10 Upper Cross Road Rugeley Staffordshire WS15 2JD
Tel: 07789 693006
Email: mderidder@ansonsllp.com
Fixtures Secretary: as Hon. Sec.
Club Colours: Green & white hoop shirts, black shorts
League: Midlands 4 West (N) (level 9)

Rushden & Higham RUFC
Ground Address: Manor Park Bedford Road Rushden Northamptonshire NN10 0SA
Contact: 01933 312071
Email: fez@rhrufc.org
Website: www.rhrufc.org
Directions: Club situated at Bedford end of the A6 Rushden/Higham Ferrers Bypass. Approaching on A6 from Bedford take sliproad to Rushden, do not go onto by-pass. From Kettering turn right at roundabout at end of by-pass
Honorary Secretary: Mr Richard Fereday; 61 Spencer Road Rushden Northamptonshire NN10 6AD
Tel: 07721 646688
Email: richard@rfeinternational.com
Fixtures Secretary: Mr Tony Hughes; 102 Churchill Way Kettering Northamptonshire NN15 5BZ
Tel: 07804 805122
Email: tony.hughes20@talktalk.net
Club Colours: Black, White and Gold
League: Midlands 4 East (S) (level 9)

Sharnbrook & Colworth RFC
Ground Address: Sharnbrook Playing Fields Association Lodge Road Sharnbrook MK44 1JP
Contact: 01933386991
Email: bob.cowper@sky.com
Website: www.sharnbrookandcolworthrufc.com
Directions: Visit our website www.sharnbrookandcolworthrufc.com Go to www.streetmap.co.uk and enter MK44 1LQ
Honorary Secretary: Mrs Val Kester; 43 Loring Road, Sharnbrook Bedfordshire MK44 1JF Tel: 07786 996342
Email: Val_Kester2000@yahoo.co.uk
Fixtures Secretary: Mr Barry Beever; 19 High Street Kimbolton Huntingdon CambridgeshirePE28 0HB
Tel: 01480 861587
Club Colours: Emerald Green / Black
League: Non League

Shepshed RFC
Ground Address: 23a Chapel Street Shepshed Loughborough Leicestershire LE12 9AF
Contact: 01509 504858
Email: john.ryan2@btinternet.com
Directions: Follow signs to Hind Leys College. Chaniging rooms towards rear of college and pitch on main playing fields.
Honorary Secretary: Mr John Ryan; 23a Chapel Street Shepshed Loughborough Leicestershire LE12 9AF
Tel: 0116 2855620
Email: john.ryan2@btinternet.com
Fixtures Secretary: Mr Ray Short Tel: 01530 536861
League: Non League

Shipston on Stour RFC
Ground Address: Mayo Road Shipston on Stour Warwickshire CV36 4BH
Contact: 01608 662107
Email: secretary@shipstonrugbyclub.co.uk
Website: www.shipstonrugbyclub.co.uk
Directions: The club is signposted off the A3400 just north of the town centre. Turn opposite the Hospital into Badgers Crescent, left into Donnington Road, then right into Mayo Road. Shipston RFC is at the end.
Honorary Secretary: Mr Mark Ashworth; 14 Sandfield Lane Newbold On Stour Stratford Upon Avon Warwickshire CV37 8UN Tel: 07710 005705
Email: mark.ashworth@shipstonrugbyclub.co.uk
Fixtures Secretary: Mr Jim Meadows; Fox Holes, Alveston Hill Loxley Road Stratford upon Avon Warwickshire CV37 7RL Tel: 01789 269250
Email: cjimmeadows@yahoo.co.uk
Club Colours: All Black
League: Midlands 3 West (S) (level 8)

Shottery RFC
Ground Address: Pearcecroft Loxley Road Stratford Upon Avon CV37 7DP
Contact: 07989 321753
Email: dannyfox@o2email.co.uk
Website: www.shotteryrfc.com
Honorary Secretary: Mr Danny Farndon; 161 Cape Road Warwick Warwickshire CV34 5DT
Tel: 07989 3210753
Email: danny@valleygator.com
Fixtures Secretary: Mr Bill Austin; 21 Shelley Road Stratford Upon Avon CV37 7JR
Email: william.austin@airwavessolutions.co.uk
Club Colours: Royal blue
League: Non League

Shrewsbury RFC
Ground Address: Sundorne Castle Uffington Uffington Shrewsbury ShropshireSY4 4RR
Contact: 01743 353 380
Email: sec@shrewsburyrugbyclub.com
Website: http://www.shrewsburyrugbyclub.com
Directions: Follow M54/A5 to Shrewsbury by-pass where it meets the North/South A49. Follow A49 North (signed Whitchurch)until the roundabout marked B5062 Newport. Sundorne Castle ground 800mtrs on left.
Honorary Secretary: Garry Dean; C/0 Club Address Sundorne Castle Uffington Uffington Shrewsbury ShropshireSY4 4RR Tel: 07980819577
Email: 3RWELSH-D-PSAO@mod.uk
Fixtures Secretary: Mr Mark Turner; 28 Langley Drive Bayston Hill Shrewsbury Shropshire SY3 0PR
Tel: 07947 486015
Email: TURNERM@LIVE.CO.UK
Club Colours: Dark blue/light blue hoops.
League: Midlands 2 West (N) (level 7)

Silhillians RUFC
Ground Address: Warwick Road Copt Heath, Knowle Solihull West Midlands B93 9LW
Contact: 01564 777 680
Directions: J5 M42, then towards Knowle, ground 50yds on left hand side.
Honorary Secretary: Mr Graham Loader; 21 Bantock Gardens Finchfield Wolverhampton WV3 9LP
Tel: 01902 382731
Email: graham.loader@tarmac.co.uk
Fixtures Secretary: Mr Guy Pattinson; 8 Hartwell Close Solihull West Midlands B91 3YP Tel: 0121 7118753
Email: guy.pattinson@philips.com
Club Colours: Maroon, blue and white
League: Midlands 2 West (S) (level 7)

Skegness RUFC
Ground Address: Wainfleet Road Playing Fields Skegness PE25 2EL
Contact: 07919 648151
Email: Ahill135@aol.com
Website: http://skegness-rufc.co.uk/
Directions: A153 turn right for town centre, 0.5 mile turn right at Highwayman pub, ground across A52.
Honorary Secretary: Mr Andrew Hill; East Cottage Hanby Lane Welton-le-Marsh Spilsby Lincs. PE23 5TH
Tel: 01507 462774
Email: Ahill135@aol.com
Fixtures Secretary: Mr Darrell Crow; 3 Christopher Road Alford Lincolnshire LN13 0AB
Tel: 07903 661263
Email: dscrow@specialspeedltd.freeserve.co.uk
Club Colours:
Royal blue & white hooped shirts, navy shorts
League: Midlands 4 East (N) (level 9)

Sleaford RFC
Ground Address: The David Williams Pavilion Ruskington Road Sleaford NG34 8SP
Contact: 01529 303335
Email: contact@srfc.org.uk
Website: www.srfc.org.uk
Directions:
One mile north east of Sleaford on the A153 Skegness road, at the junction with the A17 Sleaford by-pass.
Honorary Secretary: Mr Peter Stokes; 5 Trevitt Close Sleaford Lincolnshire NG34 8BT Tel: 01529 307191
Email: pmsm5@btinternet.com
Fixtures Secretary: Liam kite Tel: 07817943530
Email: fixtures@srfc.org.uk
Club Colours: Scarlet Red and Black Hoops
League: Midlands 2 East (N) (level 7)

Southam RFC
Ground Address: Kineton Road Southam Southam Leamington Spa Warwickshire CV47 2DG
Contact: 01926 813674
Email: david@cooper8767.freeserve.co.uk
Directions: Take Leamington road (A425) off Southam by-pass (A423). Left at next roundabout, past Ind. Estate. Ground on right.
Honorary Secretary: Miss Gemma Else; 59 Hodnell Drive Southam Warwickshire CV47 1GQ
Tel: 077024 72938
Email: gemma.else@tiscali.co.uk
Fixtures Secretary: Mr Andy Else; 11 Spire Bank Southam Warwickshire CV47 1PB Tel: 07971 049098
Email: andy@southamservices.co.uk
Club Colours: Blue & White Hoops
League: Midlands 3 West (S) (level 8)

Southwell RFC
Ground Address: Southwell RUFC Park Lane Southwell NG25 0QN
Contact: 01636 812576
Email: gydna@msn.com
Website: www.southwellrfc.co.uk
Directions: On entering into Southwell follow signs to the recreation centre. The rugby club is behind the recreation centre.
Honorary Secretary: Mr Andrew Smith; Flat 8 Greet Lilly Mill Southwell Nottinghamshire NG25 0GL
Tel: 07780 956340
Email: andrew.smith@brc.ltd.uk
Fixtures Secretary: Mr Phil Gordon; Beggars Behind Main Street Morton Southwell Southwell Nottinghamshire NG25 0UT
Tel: 01636 830485 Email: pgrog1@aol.com
Club Colours: Maroon Shirts Navy Shorts
League: Midlands 3 East (N) (level 8)

Spalding RFC
Ground Address: Spalding RFC Memorial Field, St. Thomas Road Spalding PE11 2TT
Contact: 01775 714806
Email: geofnic@tinyworld.co.uk
Website: www.spaldingrfc.co.uk
Directions: From north, south & east, exit bypass at town centre sign, 1st left over river, immediate right, left into St. Thomas Road, from west, in town, 1st right after railway crossing.
Honorary Secretary: Mrs Catherine Duce; 1 Westhorpe Road Gosberton Spalding Lincolnshire PE11 4EW
Tel: 01775 841363
Email: catherineduce@hotmail.co.uk
Fixtures Secretary: Mr Martin Beecham; March Acre 0 Cowbit Road Spalding Lincolnshire PE11 2RH
Tel: 07887 821173
Email: martin.beecham@gistworld.com
Club Colours: Navy and Claret
League: Midlands 2 East (N) (level 7)

Spartans (Midlands) RUFC
Ground Address: Coppice Lane Middleton Nr. Tamworth Warwickshire B78 2BS
Contact: 07882 067746
Email: spartans2@btinternet.com
Website: www.spartansrugby.com
Directions: on the A446 approx 400 yards south of the Bassets Pole island, (junction of the A446/A38/A453)
Honorary Secretary: Mr Geoffrey Waterhouse; Jerrard Court 25 Flat 25 Pages Close Sutton Coldfield West Midlands B75 7SZ Tel: 07818 011090
Email: g.waterhouse101@btinternet.com
Fixtures Secretary: Mr Geoffrey Waterhouse; Jerrard Court 25 Flat 25 Pages Close Sutton Coldfield West Midlands B75 7SZ Tel: 07818 011090
Email: g.waterhouse101@btinternet.com
Club Colours: All Black
League: Midlands 2 West (S) (level 7)

St Ives (Midlands)
Ground Address: Somersham Road St. Ives CambridgeshirePE27 3LY
Contact: 01480 464 455
Email: info@stives-rfc.co.uk
Website: www.stivesrufc.co.uk
Directions: Exit A14 Junc 26 follow A1096 at fourth roundabout bear left then right at next signed B1040. Right at the next roundabout. Club _ mile on left.
Honorary Secretary: Mr Adam Scott; 3 Willow Green Needdingworth ST IVES Cambridgeshire
Tel: 07712 825686
Email: scotta@roadeschool.northants.sch.uk
Fixtures Secretary: Bryan Richardson; Woodside Way 31 St Ives Cambridgeshire PE27 3JQ
Tel: 01480 4667474
Club Colours: Blue and Black shirts
League: Midlands 5 East (S) (level 10)

St Leonards RFC
Ground Address: Stafford Cricket & Hockey Club Brian Westhead Pavilion Riverway Stafford ST16 3TH
Contact: 01785 251660
Email: richard.austin101@btinternet.com
Website: www.stleonardsrugby.com
Directions: From M6 junction - 13 Northbound - At the roundabout, take the 3rd exit onto A449 heading to Stafford - Go through 1 roundabout 3.0 mi - Continue on A34/Wolverhampton Rd 180 ft - Slight right to stay on A34/Wolverhampton Rd - Continue to follow A34 0.1 mi - Slight right at A34/Queensway 381 ft - Turn left at A34/Lichfield Rd 0.2 mi - Turn left at Riverway - Clubhouse is first turning on the right
Honorary Secretary: Mr Richard Austin; 42 Tithe Barn Road Stafford ST16 3PH Tel: 01785 245660
Email: richard.austin101@btinternet.com
Fixtures Secretary: Mr Paul Sargeant; 10 Levedale Close Stafford ST16 1JR Tel: 01785 254895
Email: sarge13@btinternet.com
Club Colours: Black with Amber hoop
League: Midlands 4 West (N) (level 9)

St Neots
Ground Address: The Pavillion The Common St Neots PE19 1RU
Contact: 07775762758
Email: jswanston@laingorourke.com
Directions: Follow signs to Little Paxton from town centre, ground on Right as you leave St. Neots (1 mile from Town Centre).
Honorary Secretary: Mr Jamie Swanston; 7 The Green Eltisley St. Neots CambridgeshirePE19 6TG
Tel: 07775 762758
Email: JSwanston@laingorourke.com
Fixtures Secretary: Mr Paul Tyler; 8 Gery Court Eaton Socon St. Neots PE19 8TA Tel: 07790 847615
Email: ptyler10@yahoo.co.uk
Club Colours: Light blue shirt with wide dark blue band
League: Midlands 5 East (S) (level 10)

Stafford RUFC
Ground Address: Stafford RUFC Castlefields Newport Road Stafford Staffordshire ST16 1BG
Contact: 01785 211241
Email: markc@custx.co.uk
Website: www.staffordrugbyclub.com
Directions: From the South take M6 to Junction 13 Follow A449 to Stafford for 1.5 miles and turn left marked Rowley Park Westway, continue to junction with Newport Rd, turn right, Club 500 yards on left. From North take M6 to Junction 14. Follow A34 to town centre then follow signs to A518 Newport or railway station. Go past station on your right. Cross over railway bridge and club is 200 yards on right
Honorary Secretary: Mr Mark Carter; Buxtons Teddesley Penkridge Stafford Staffordshire ST19 5RP
Tel: 07590 046476
Email: markc@custx.co.uk
Fixtures Secretary: Mr Richard Walklate; 19 Cooperative Street Stafford Staffordshire ST16 3BZ
Tel: 07968 095625
Email: r_walklate@hotmail.com
Club Colours: Black and Amber
League: Midlands 2 West (N) (level 7)

Staffordshire University (Stafford) RFC
Ground Address: Beaconside Sports Centre Staffordshire Universoty Weston Road Stafford ST18 0AD
Contact: 01785 353311
Email: ben@marksmail.org
Website: www.staffsunirugby.net
Honorary Secretary: Mr Caleb Kershaw
Email: caleb517@hotmail.co.uk
Fixtures Secretary: Mr Aaron Rogers
Club Colours: Navy, Red and White Shirts
League: Non League

Staffordshire University (Stoke) RFC
Ground Address: Staffordshire University Athletic Union College Road Stoke On Trent Staffordshire ST4 2DE
Contact: 01782 294628
Email: activities@staffs.ac.uk
Website: www.staffsunion.com
Directions: For directions log on to www.staffsunion.com
Club Colours: Blue/Red/White
League: Non League

Stamford College Old Boys RFC
Ground Address: Queen Eleanor Technology College Green Lane Stamford Lincolnshire PE9 1HE
Contact: 07515 415669
Directions: Follow signs for A6121 through town turning up Recreation Ground road and continue as far as possible, school on right.
Honorary Secretary: Mr Darren Crush; The Hurdler Pub 93 New Cross Road Stamford Lincolnshire PE9 1AL Tel: 07515 415669
Email: dmjc@crush-associates.com
Fixtures Secretary: Mr Raymond Bates; 55 Millfield Road Deeping St. James Peterborough PE6 8QX
Tel: 01780 767263
Email: ray.bates@tarmac.co.uk
Club Colours: Red & Green Hoops
League: Midlands 5 East (S) (level 10)

Stamford RUFC
Ground Address: Hambleton Road Stamford Lincolnshire PE9 2RZ
Contact: 07809 075733
Email: rolsengsl@hotmail.com
Website: http://clubs.rfu.com/Clubs/portals/stamfordrufc
Directions: Take Oakham/Melton Mowbray exit from A1, turn towards Stamford, approx 500 yds right turn into Lonsdale Rd, approx 200yds fork left into Hambleton Road.
Honorary Secretary: Ms Richard Olsen; 16 Lea View Ryhall Stamford Lincolnshire PE9 4HZ
Tel: 07976 642432
Email: rolsengsl@hotmail.com
Fixtures Secretary: Mr Christopher Mclaren; 111 Empingham Road Stamford Lincolnshire PE9 2SX
Tel: 07946 271682
Email: chrisneck@talktalk.net
Club Colours: Purple, black, white hoops, black shorts
League: Midlands 5 East (S) (level 10)

Stockwood Park RFC
Ground Address: Stockwood Park London Road Luton LU1 4BH
Contact: 01582 728 044
Directions: M1 J10, left at end of slip road, left at 1st set of traffic lights into Stockwood Park, club on right.
Honorary Secretary: Mrs Ann Budge; 45 Glenfield Road Luton Bedfordshire LU3 2JA Tel: 07879845854
Email: ann_budge@yahoo.co.uk
Fixtures Secretary: Mr Alan Casemore; 18 Victoria Street Dunstable Bedfordshire LU6 3BA
Tel: 07941 740999
Email: alan.casemore@ntlworld.com
Club Colours: Red with Yellow Hoop, Navy, Red
League: Midlands 3 East (S) (level 8)

Stockwood Park RFC
Ground Address: Stockwood Park London Road Luton LU1 4BH
Contact: 01582 728 044
Directions: M1 J10, left at end of slip road, left at 1st set of traffic lights into Stockwood Park, club on right.
Honorary Secretary: Mrs Ann Budge; 45 Glenfield Road Luton Bedfordshire LU3 2JA Tel: 07879845854
Email: ann_budge@yahoo.co.uk
Fixtures Secretary: Mr Alan Casemore; 18 Victoria Street Dunstable Bedfordshire LU6 3BA
Tel: 07941 740999
Email: alan.casemore@ntlworld.com
Club Colours: Red with Yellow Hoop, Navy, Red
League: Midlands 4 East (S) (level 9)

Stoke Old Boys RFC
Ground Address: Albert Gale Field Brookvale Avenue, Binley Brookvale Avenue, Binley Coventry CV3 2DG
Contact: 02476 453631
Email: adrian.rushton@btinternet.com
Website: www.stokeoldboys.co.uk
Directions: East off Binley Road, closest landmark is Binley Fire Station, 400 yards away.
Honorary Secretary: Mr Adrian Rushton; 82 Belgrave Road Wyken Coventry West Midlands CV2 5BH
Tel: 07791 685030
Email: adrian.rushton@btinternet.com
Fixtures Secretary: Mr David Henly; 104 Hermitage Road Coventry CV2 5GE Tel: 07884 315023
Email: dhenly7370@aol.com
Club Colours: Maroon & White Hoops
League: Midlands 4 West (S) (level 9)

Stone RUFC
Ground Address: Bibby's Sports & Social Club Tilling Drive Walton Stone ST15 0SJ
Contact: 07710 327492
Email: Fiona.m.foster@ntlworld.com
Website: www.stonerufc.co.uk
Directions: From A34 take B5026 to Eccleshall. Take first left 'Tilling Drive', Ground is at end of Tilling Drive.
Honorary Secretary: Mrs Fiona Foster; 28 Granville Terrace Stone Staffordshire ST15 8DF
Tel: 07710 327492
Email: fiona@compudal.com
Fixtures Secretary: Mr Simon Shiner; 2 Moorhouse Court Yarnfield Stone Staffordshire ST15 0TX
Tel: 07966610195
Email: sshiner@rac.co.uk
Club Colours: Maroon & Green Quarters, Black Shorts
League: Midlands 5 West (N) (level 10)

Stoneygate RFC
Ground Address: Stoneygate Rugby Club Covert Lane Scraptoft Leicester LE7 9SP
Contact: 0116 2419188
Website: www.stoneygate.uk.com
Directions: Stoneygate Rugby Club is five miles from the City centre. BY CAR, initially follow signs to Peterborough (A47) from the city centre. Approaching from the city centre or south, follow the ring road and signs for the A47. After four miles from the city centre leave the A7 by taking a left hand fork (into Scraptoft Lane) easily identified by the Shell petrol Station. Follow the signs for Scraptoft along Scraptoft Lane. At the top of the hill turn sharp right at the mini roundabout. You need to drive straight on down Covert Lane and the club is the first club, a third of a mile on the left hand side. FROM THE NORTH, the A607/A563 link road, which connects the A46 and the A47, is now open. When approaching from the (A46) north, travellers should turn left onto the A563 (sign posted A47 peterborough) and continue south before turning left into Scraptoft Lane by the Nuffield Hospital, the first junction with a set of traffic lights after the Tescos roundabout. Then as above. FROM THE EAST, again use the A47, but turn right off the A47 into Station Road, at the first set of traffic lights in the village of Bushby. At the top of the hill there is a roundabout, you want to take a right turn into Covert lane and the club is the first club, a third of a mile on the left hand side.
Honorary Secretary: Mr Steve Morris; 203 Evington Lane Leicester LE5 6DJ Tel: 0116 2628596
Email: steve.morris@dodds-partners.co.uk
Fixtures Secretary: Mr Roger Foxon; 33 Buddon Lane Quorn Leicestershire LE12 8AD Tel: 0116 2625564
Email: foxtayl@hotmail.com
Club Colours: Red & White Bands - Blue Shorts
League: Midlands 4 East (S) (level 9)

Stourbridge Lions RFC
Ground Address: Bridgnorth Road Stourton Stourbridge West Midlands DY7 6QZ
Contact: 01384 393889
Directions: Ground share with Stourbridge RFC From Stourbridge town centre ring road take the A458 (Bridgnorth). Stourton Park is about 1.5 miles on the left, less than half a mile into South Staffs. From the A449 Wolverhampton-Kidderminster road take the A458 (Stourbridge) at the Stewpony junction. Stourton Park is on the right after 1 mile. From the North leave the M5 at J3 and follow the A456 (Kidderminster) then the A491 (Stourbridge) to the town centre ring road, then as above. From the South West leave the M5 at J4 and follow the A491 (Stourbridge) to the town centre ring road, then as above. From the South East take either the M40 or M6 onto the M42 south/westbound, then onto the M5 northbound, exit J4 as above.
Honorary Secretary: Mr Justin Mansell; 8 Keir Place Stourbridge West Midlands DY8 4DT
Tel: 07974 927076
Email: justin.mansell@williamking.co.uk
Club Colours: Navy & White Hoops, Navy Shorts
League: Midlands 2 West (N) (level 7)

Stourport RFC
Ground Address: Walshes Meadow Harold Davies Drive Stourport-On-Severn DY13 0AA
Email: stourportrfc@hotmail.co.uk
Website: www.stourportrfc.co.uk
Directions: From Stourport Town Centre, cross river Severn bridge, turn immediate left towards Leisure Centre, follow the road to the end and turn off right through the gates, ground straight ahead, clubhouse in view.
Honorary Secretary: Miss Julia Deeley; 6 Mill Road Stourport-on-Severn Worcestershire DY13 9BG
Tel: 07985 438463
Email: stourportrfc@hotmail.co.uk
Fixtures Secretary: Mr Edwin Osborn; 4 The Paddock Burlish Farm Stourport-On-Severn Worcs. DY13 8PX
Tel: 01299 871439
Email: edandjayneosborn@btopenworld.com
Club Colours: Navy blue and yellow stripes
League: Midlands 5 West (SW) (level 10)

Tamworth RUFC
Ground Address: Wigginton Lodge Wigginton Park Tamworth Staffordshire B79 8ED
Contact: 01827 68794
Email: cathy.parker@btinternet.com
Website: http://clubs.rfu.com/Clubs/portals/TamworthRUFC
Directions: Head north out of town towards Burton, left turn into Thackeray Drive, just after Riftswood Pub, right at end of Thackerary Drive, next left onto Shelley Road, next left on Solway Close, end of drive.
Honorary Secretary: Mr Jeremy Tomson; 23 Falmouth Drive Amington Tamworth Staffordshire B77 3QJ
Tel: 07889 853958
Email: jtomson@talktalk.net
Fixtures Secretary: Mr Michael Krasnowski; C/o Tamworth Rugby Club Wigginton Lodge Wigginton Park Tamworth Staffordshire B79 8ED Tel: 07989 685322
Email: krash4897@fsmail.net
Club Colours: Maroon/White and Black hoops
League: Midlands 3 West (N) (level 8)

Telford Hornets RUFC
Ground Address: Town Park Hinkshay Road Dawley Telford TF4 3NZ
Contact: 01952418801
Email: lin@blueyonder.co.uk
Directions: M54, J4 for town centre, 2nd exit at roundabout, 1st exit next roundabout onto A442, continue to Castlefields roundabout, 4th exit at roundabout to Dawley, 4th right, club 0.75 mile on left.
Honorary Secretary: Mrs Linda Potts; 17 Ellesmere Court Newport ShropshireTF10 7SD Tel: 01952 418801
Email: lin@blueyonder.co.uk
Fixtures Secretary: Mr Michael Mcgrath; 37 Teawell Close The Rock Telford ShropshireTF3 5BL
Tel: 01952 506956
Email: mike.mcgrath@telford.gov.uk
Club Colours: Black & Gold Chest Band
League: Midlands 3 West (N) (level 8)

Tenbury RFC
Ground Address: Penlu Worcester Road Worcester Road Tenbury Wells WR15 8AP
Contact: 01584 891355
Email: Ajohnbradley@aol.com
Website: http://www.tenburyrfc.co.uk
Directions: Club House is located on the A456 next to Tenbury Hospital Pitches Palmers Meadow, Tenbury Wells some 3/4 mile from clubhouse - from clubhouse go through town, following signs to Swimming Pool. Pitches next to swimming pool.
Honorary Secretary: Mr John Bradley; 4 Belfry Close Clee Hill Ludlow ShropshireSY8 3RF
Tel: 01584 891355   Email: ajohnbradley@aol.com
Fixtures Secretary: Mr Dean Gervis; Treetops Apostles Oak Abberley Worcester Worcestershire WR6 6AD
Tel: 01299 896349
Club Colours: Green & Black Hoop shirts, black shorts
League: Midlands 5 West (SW) (level 10)

Thorney RUFC
Ground Address: Clubhouse Thorney Ex Servicemens Club Station Road PE6 0QE
Contact: 01733 810718
Email: christopher_s_crane@hotmail.com
Directions: The Ron Jacobs Playing Fields A47 from Peterborough towards WISBECH. Stay on the new by pass, just outside the village, keeping Thorney Village on the right hand side. Turn left at the roundabout signposted B1040 Crowland. The ground is 1 mile along this road away from the Village on the right hand side
Honorary Secretary: Mr C Crane; 8 Quorn Close Newborough Peterborough PE6 7RQ Tel: 07838 163087
Email: christopher_s_crane@hotmail.com
Fixtures Secretary: Mr Paul Smith; 2 The Maltings Thorney Peterborough CambridgeshirePE6 0QF
Tel: 01733 271049
Club Colours: Navy & Gold Quarters
League: Midlands 5 East (S) (level 10)

Towcestrians RFC
Ground Address: Greens Norton Road Towcester Northamptonshire NN12 8AW
Contact: 01327 350141
Email: richard.titmuss@towcestriansrfc.net
Directions: From the A43/A5 junction roundabout (Wayside VW) north of Towcester, take exit for Greens Norton and Blakesley, clubhouse and ground is situated approx 800 yards on right hand side.
Honorary Secretary: Mrs Jenny Osborne; 56 Barn Owl Close Grangewood Northampton NN4 0RQ
Tel: 07753 821921
Email: jennywrenn@btinternet.com
Fixtures Secretary: Mr Steve Burley; Thorstone Back Lane Chapel Brampton Northamptonshire NN6 8AJ
Tel: 01604 843424
Club Colours: Maroon with White Edged Amber Band, Black Shorts
League: Midlands 2 East (S) (level 7)

Trinity Guild RFC
Ground Address: Rowley Road Baginton Coventry Warwickshire CV8 3AL
Contact: 02476 693726
Email: info@tgrfc.com
Website: www.tgrfc.com
Directions: From north, follow A45 west of Coventry, follow airport signs. From south, follow A45 from M45. From west, Follow A46 to A45.
Honorary Secretary: Mr Steve Rawson; 2 wall hill road Coventry CV5 9dy Tel: 07920 592391
Email: secretary@tgrfc.co.uk
Fixtures Secretary: Mr K Lightowler; 37 Oakfield Road Coventry CV6 1ED Tel: 02476 598932
Club Colours: Maroon, Old Gold & Navy
League: Midlands 5 West (SE) (level 10)

Tupton RUFC
Ground Address: The Recreation Ground North Side Tupton Chesterfield Derbyshire S42 6DW
Contact: 01246 862059
Email: bubbleybob@tiscali.co.uk
Website: www.222.rfc.com
Directions: From Chesterfield south A61 to Tupton, left at roundabout into Queen Victoria Road, then 2nd left into North Side.
Honorary Secretary: Mr Robert Curry; 190 Queen Victoria Road Tupton Chesterfield S42 6DW
Tel: 07810 851158
Email: bubbleybob@tiscali.co.uk
Fixtures Secretary: Mr Ian Bulloch; 3 Nether Croft Road Brimington Chesterfield Derbyshire S43 1QD
Tel: 07791 400954
Email: bullyontheradio@ntlworld.com
Club Colours: Royal Blue with 3 Gold Hoops
League: Midlands 5 East (N) (level 10)

University of Aston RFC
Ground Address: Aston Students Guild Aston Triangle Birmingham B4 7ES
Contact: 0121 359 6531 / 4027
Email: Astoncobras@hotmail.com
Website: www.astonguild.org.uk/club_homepage.asp?clubid=71
Directions: Taking the M6 into Birmingham turn off at junction 6 to signposted (a38) aston expressway/ City centre. Continue on this route until you reach sgnposts for the bullring and indoor market, Take this turn off and follow the signs to aston university.
Honorary Secretary: Honorary Secretary; Athletic Union Aston Students Guild Aston Street Birmingham West Midlands B4 7ES Tel:
Fixtures Secretary: Charles Simpson; Aston Students Guild 60 Aston Street Birmingham B4 7ES
Tel: 07867 655315
Club Colours: Red, white and black
League: Non League

University of Derby RFC
Ground Address: University of Derby RFC c/o UDSU c/o UDSU Kedleston Road, Derby DE22 1GB
Contact: 01332 591507 (Mon - Fri)
Email: soj444@hotmail.com
Website: http://clubs.rfu.com/Clubs/portals/UniversityofDerbyRFC
Directions: Club is found on main University of Derby Campus and is sign posted from the city centre.
Honorary Secretary: Mr Simon Jones; 14 Honeycroft Close Belper Derbyshire DE56 1RL Tel: 07971951440
Email: soj444@hotmail.com
Fixtures Secretary: Mr Ian John Dennent; 9 Wood Common Grange Pelsell Walsall West Midlands
Club Colours: Forest, White and Black
League: Midlands 5 East (N) (level 10)

University of Leicester RFC
Ground Address:
40 Manor Road Oadby Leicester LE2 2LL
Contact: 0116 2719144
Email: mw80@le.ac.uk
Honorary Secretary: Helena Goodman; 33 Cornwall Close Warwick Warwickshire CV34 5HX
Tel: 07967 930858   Email: hg43@le.ac.uk
Club Colours: Black and Red
League: Non League

University of Lincoln RFC
Ground Address: Student Union Co-operative University of Lincoln Sports Centre Brayford Pool LN6 7TS
Contact: 01522 886434
Email: glwilson@lincoln.ac.uk
Website: www.lincolnsu.com
Hon. Secretary: Mr Edward Dalgleish; University of Lincoln Student Union Campus Way Lincoln LN6 7TS
Tel: 07786 686959
Email: lincolnrugby@hotmail.com
Fixtures Secretary: Andreas Zacharia; University of Lincoln Student Union Campus Way Lincoln LN6 7TS
Tel: 07925 494219
Email: andreas_zacharia@hotmail.co.uk
Club Colours: Royal Blue/ Yellow
League: Non League

University of Nottingham RFC
Ground Address: University of Nottingham University Playing Fields University Boulevard, Highfields Nottingham NG7 2RD
Contact: 0115 9515513
Fixtures Secretary: Mr Tom Broome
Tel: 07729 276534   Email: lpyatab@nottingham.ac.uk
League: Non League

University of Warwick RFC
Ground Address: The Students Union University of Warwick Coventry CV4 7AL
Contact: 07966023575
Email: su144@sunion.warwick.ac.uk
Honorary Secretary: Mr Ben Nolan
Fixtures Secretary: Mr Alex Petrides
Club Colours: Dark Blue
League: Non League

Upton-upon-Severn RFC
Ground Address: Sports Club (use secretary's address for correspondence) Old Street Upton-Upon-Severn Worcestershire WR8 0HW
Email: chris@c3-consulting.co.uk
Website: www.uptonrfc.org.uk
Directions: 10 miles south of Worcester and 7 miles north of Tewkesbury 2 miles off the A38 trunk road (A4104, signposted Upton-upon-Severn). Over river bridge, turn left through the town. The clubhouse and ground are on the right opposite the church.
Honorary Secretary: Mr Russell Price; 11 Sandpiper Crescent Malvern Worcestershire WR14 1UY
Tel: 01886 832975   Email: russy22@hotmail.com
Fixtures Secretary: Mr Nigel Banwell; 16 Riverside Close Upton-upon-Severn Worcester WR8 0JN
Tel: 07790 730688   Email: Nigel.Banwell@tesco.net
Club Colours: Black & White quarters
League: Midlands 3 West (S) (level 8)

Uttoxeter RFC
Ground Address: Uttoxeter RFC Oldfields Sports & Social Club Springfield Road Uttoxeter Staffs. ST14 7JX
Contact: 07813 933752
Email: lezannwilson@hotmail.com
Website: www.pitchero.com
Directions: From M1 take A50 to Uttoxeter boundary. Over 1st.R/about & turn left @ 2nd.(Ashbourne Rd)1/2 mile to Mini r/about(3 Tuns pub on right).Bear left & cont. down to Smithfield pub where the road bears right.Cont for 1/2 mile & Springfield Rd is 4th. on right
Honorary Secretary: Mr Glynne Wilson; 4 Chestnut Drive Ashbourne Derbyshire DE6 1HT
Tel: 01335 343153
Email: lezannwilson@hotmail.com
Fixtures Secretary: as Hon. Sec.
Club Colours: Orange & Black
League: Midlands 4 East (N) (level 9)

Vauxhall Motors RUFC
Ground Address: Vauxhall Recreation Club 20 Gypsy Lane Luton Bedfordshire LU1 3JH
Contact: 01582 418873
Email: nutterneate@hotmail.com
Website: www.vauxhallrugby.co.uk
Directions: Off M1 J10, follow signs to Luton Airport. Ground is on left as you approach 2nd roundabout.
Honorary Secretary: Mr Leo O'Neill; 10 Salton Link Emerson Valley Milton Keynes MK4 2JE
Tel: 07751 346200
Email: leo.oneill@beds.ac.uk
Fixtures Secretary: Mr Haydn Thomas; 15 Chiltern Rise Luton Bedfordshire LU1 5HF Tel: 01582 410489
Email: Haydn@synapse-creative.com
Club Colours: Royal Blue with Gold bands
League: Midlands 3 East (S) (level 8)

Veseyans RFC
Ground Address: Little Hardwick Road Streetly Sutton Coldfield West Midlands WS9 0SQ
Contact: 0121 3535388
Website: www.veseyansrfc.co.uk
Directions: A452 to Brownhills. Turn left at the Hardwick pub and the ground ia 1 mile further on the left.
Honorary Secretary: Mr Gavin Humphreys; 60 Grange Lane Sutton Coldfield West Midlands B75 5JX
Tel: 0121 3232458
Email: gavin.humphreys@blueyonder.co.uk
Fixtures Secretary: Mr Clive Burkin; 35 Impney Green Droitwich Worcestershire WR9 7EL Tel: 01905 774111
Email: clive_burkin@yahoo.co.uk
Club Colours: Black & White Hoops, Black Shorts
League: Midlands 3 West (N) (level 8)

Vipers RFC
Ground Address:
Blaby Bypass Whetstone Leicester LE8 6ND
Email: stephen.i.harris@bt.com
Directions: M1 J21, follow A46 to roundabout at Fosse Park, right onto B4114, straight over next roundabout, next roundabout left, next roundabout right, club on left at end of d/c.
Honorary Secretary: Mr Stephen Harris; 40 Wyndale Road Leicester LE2 3WR Tel: 0780 1759481
Email: stephen.i.harris@bt.com
Fixtures Secretary: Mr Christopher Hoult; 83 Main Street Markfield Leicester LE67 9UT
Tel: 01530 244656
Email: houltc1@longfield.leics.sch.uk
Club Colours: Green with Gold & Black Hoops
League: Midlands 2 East (S) (level 7)

Warley RFC
Ground Address: Warley Rugby Football Club Tatbank Road Oldbury West Midlands B69 4NH
Contact: 0121 5521048
Email: warley.attheclub@virgin.net
Website: www.warleyrfc.co.uk
Directions: From J2 on M5, follow A4123 to Birmingham. Turn left at traffic lights at Wing Wah restaurant, continue to traffic island at Merrivale pub, take 2nd exit(straight on), continue to traffic lights, left into Tatbank Rd, club is approximately 800m on the left.
Honorary Secretary: Mr Roger Jackson; Warley Rugby Football Club Tat Bank Road Oldbury West Midlands B69 4NH Tel: 0121 5521048
Email: warley.attheclub@virgin.net
Fixtures Secretary: Mr Peter Davies; 23 Holly Road Oldbury West Midlands B68 0AU Tel: 0121 4220166
Email: pdavies@anglesey.bham.sch.uk
Club Colours: Red & White Hoops, Black Shorts
League: Midlands 5 West (N) (level 10)

MIDLANDS

Warwickian RFC
Ground Address: Hampton Road Sports Ground Hampton Road Warwick CV34 6HX
Contact: 01926 496295
Email: patrickwing@yahoo.com
Directions: From the M40 J15 at Longbridge roundabout. Take the A429 to Warwick for about 1.5m. Turn left into Shakespeare Ave. At end of the road turn left at T-junction onto Hampton Rd. Warwickian RUFC is on the right a 100m after the bridge crossing the A46.
Honorary Secretary: Mr Patrick Wing; 57 Broadfern Road Knowle Solihull West Midlands B93 9DE
Tel: 07702 120977
Email: patrickwing@yahoo.com
Fixtures Secretary: Mr Deane Atkins; 17 Price Close West Warwick CV34 6NR Tel: 078061 832383
Email: datkins@citysprint.co.uk
Club Colours: Black, Maroon & Purple
League: Midlands 5 West (SE) (level 10)

Wednesbury RUFC
Ground Address: Wednesbury RUFC Woden Road North Old Park Wednesbury West Midlands WS10 9NP
Contact: 0121 5565005
Email: zorro.hughes@blueyonder.co.uk
Website: www.wednesbury-rufc.co.uk
Directions: Leave M6 at Junction 9 - take A461 to Wednesbury - turn right at 1st traffic lights into Myvod Rd - straight on over 2 roundabouts into Woden Road North - Club is 0.5 miles on right.
Honorary Secretary: Mr Neil Gadsby; Flat 4 St. Clements House Hallam Street West Bromwich West Midlands B71 4HB Tel: 0121 3575925
Fixtures Secretary: Mr Neil Wilson; 36 Turton Road Tipton DY4 9LH Tel: 0121 5301973
Email: neil@electric-fly.com
Club Colours: Green/Black and White Hoops
League: Midlands 3 West (N) (level 8)

Wellesbourne RFC
Ground Address: Wellesbourne Sports & Social Club, Loxley Close, Wellesbourne, Warwickshire, CV35 9NE
Email: samturner100@aol.com
Directions: The clubhouse is situated on the right hand side off Ettington Road, 0.2 miles from the centre of Wellesbourne.
Honorary Secretary: Ms Amanda Foster; 81 Elliott Drive Wellesbourne Warwickshire CV35 9RT
Tel: 07590 688946 Email: tweetie_pie18@hotmail.co.uk
Fixtures Secretary: Mr Andy Thomas; 4 Cherry Orchard Wellesbourne Warwickshire Tel: 07975 899867
Email: andydthomas@hotmail.co.uk
Club Colours: Light grey and yellow trimmings
League: Midlands 5 West (SE) (level 10)

Wellingborough O. G's RFC
Ground Address: W. O.G's HQ 46 Oxford Street Wellingborough NN8 4JH
Contact: 01933 353081
Email: bobosdiamond@aol.com

Directions: From Park Farm North go along Sywell road, ground is on right.
Honorary Secretary: Mr Stephen Gill; 222 Minerva Way Wellingborough Northamptonshire NN8 3TT
Tel: 0759 5023232
Email: steve.gill1985@btinternet.com
Fixtures Secretary: Mr Martin Kirby; 152 Northampton Road Wellingborough Northamptonshire NN8 3PJ
Tel: 07770 776396 Email: kirbsogs@aol.com
Club Colours: Claret and White
League: Midlands 4 East (S) (level 9)

West Bridgford RFC
Ground Address: The Memorial Ground Stamford Road, West Bridgford Nottinghamshire NG2 6GF
Contact: 0115 9232506
Email: ianm.wbrfc@sky.com
Website: http://www.wbrfc.co.uk
Directions: From the A52 carriageway, follow signs for West Bridgford at the roundabout (Travel Lodge). Take the first exit onto the A60 Loughborough Rd. After the cemetry turn right onto Boundary Rd, at the traffic lights turn left onto Melton Rd (A606). Take the second right onto Stamford Road. WBRFC is at the end of the road on your right.
Honorary Secretary: Mr Ian Marriott; 9 Lydney Park West Bridgford Nottingham NG2 7TJ
Tel: 0115 8784781 Email: ianm.wbrfc@sky.com
Fixtures Secretary: Mr Dan Sutton; 22 Vernon Avenue Wilford Nottingham NG11 7AE Tel: 0115 9818621
Email: davidsutton2003@aol.com
Club Colours: Black shirts with red & gold.
League: Midlands 2 East (N) (level 7)

Westwood RFC
Ground Address: Flaxlands Bretton Centre Bretton Peterborough Cambridgeshire PE3 8DF
Contact: 07738 005583
Email: timhumphreys_75@yahoo.co.uk
Website: www.westwoodrugbyclub.com
Directions: From the north - Leave A1 at jct for A47 East. Follow A47 Until turn off for Edith Cavell Hospital. Once at Edith Cavell hospital turn off, Follow signs for Bretton Centre. At Roundabout, turn Right (Bretton Way). Go through Lights, at next Roundabout, turn Right into Flaxland avenue. Take 2nd left in through gates and into ground. If any problems, please Phone Tim on 07738 005583. If using Sat Nav, use address first, i.e. Flaxland avenue, then try Postcode.
Honorary Secretary: Mr Tim Humphreys; evergreen view Northgate West Pinchbeck Spalding Lincolnshire PE11 3TB Tel: 07738 005583
Email: timhumphreys_75@yahoo.co.uk
Fixtures Secretary: Mr Duncan Davies; 36 Hedgelands Werrington Peterborough Cambridgeshire PE4 5AA
Tel: 07875 161462
Email: disorderly.davies@ntlworld.com
Club Colours: red shirts, local sposor logo,
League: Midlands 5 East (S) (level 10)

Wheaton Aston & Penkridge RUFC
Ground Address: Wheaton Aston Rugby Club The Monkton Recreation Centre Pinfold Lane Penkridge Stafford Staffordshire ST19 5QP
Contact: 07948 419778
Email: wap_rugby@mypostoffice.co.uk
Website: www.rfu.com/Clubs/portals/WheatonAstonPenkridgeRUFC
Directions: From the south:- M6 J12, A5 towards Telford, at 1st island take A449 towards Stafford. At mini island take 1st exit left (Bungham lane) over railway. Next junction turn right. Monkton recreation centre is approx 800yds on Right. From the North:- M6 Exit J13 At the roundabout, take the 3rd exit onto A449 heading towards Wolverhampton (approx 2.8 miles). In Penkridge town centre turn right at Pinfold Lane between Fox public house and ford dealership. Under Railway Bridge. Monkton Recreation Centre is approx 800 yards on left.
Honorary Secretary: Mr Jonathan Barclay; 6 Cinder Hill Lane Coven Wolverhampton WV9 5DT
Tel: 07715 479820
Email: wap_rugby@mypostoffice.co.uk
Fixtures Secretary: Mr Nick Hammond; 1 Primrose Close Wheaton Aston Stafford ST19 9PX
Tel: 01785 840907
Club Colours: Black and Gold Shirts, Black Shorts
League: Midlands 5 West (N) (level 10)

Whittington RFC
Ground Address: The Pavillion Lichfield Cricket & Hockey Club Collins Hill Eastern Avenue Lichfield WS13 7JG
Contact: 01543 263924
Email: robert@millsforgings.co.uk
Website: www.rfu.com/Clubs/portals/WhittingtonRFC
Directions: From Lichfield city centre : take the A51 signposted Stafford or Rugeley along Western Avenue as far as traffic lights at the Hedgehog pub (appx 1 mile). Turn right at lights onto Eastern Avenue, past Friary Grange Sports Centre and Grange Lane on the left. As Eastern Avenue descends the hill, at the end of the woods, the ground entrance is on the left. From A38 Southbound, leave A38 A5127 sign posted Lichfield, proceed through Streethay and over railway at Trent Valley. At first roundabout take fourth exit onto Eastern Ave. From A38 Northbound A5: ignore 1st exit to Lichfield and continue on A38 Northbound to A5192 second Lichfield exit. Turn left at end of slip road and go straight over next two roundabouts onto Eastern Ave. Ground is approx 1.5 miles on RHS of Eastern Ave.
Honorary Secretary: Mr Robert Allcott; 12 Burton Old Road Streethay Lichfield Staffordshire WS13 8LJ
Tel: 07812 901602
Email: robert@millsforgings.co.uk
Fixtures Secretary: Mr Martin Hughes; 0 Oakenfield Lichfield Staffordshire WS13 7HZ Tel: 07970 964724
Email: lennyhughes@yahoo.co.uk
Club Colours: Dark blue & White Hoops
League: Midlands 5 West (N) (level 10)

Willenhall RFC
Ground Address: Willenhall RFC Bognop Road Essington Nr Wolverhampton Staffordshire WV11 2BA
Contact: 01922 405694
Email: elfyn.pugh@talktalk.net
Website: www.rfu.com/Clubs/portals/WillenhallRFC
Directions: From the M6-M54 off at J1, take road towards Wolverhampton. At the second island turn left into Bognop Road. The club house is 1 mile towards Essington on right.
Honorary Secretary: Mr Elfyn Pugh; 9 Five Fields Road Willenhall West Midlands WV12 4NZ
Tel: 01902 607747
Email: elfyn.pugh@talktalk.net
Fixtures Secretary: Mr Paul Coyne; 180 Colman Avenue Wednesfield Wolverhampton WV11 3RU
Tel: 01902 560130
Email: coynie@email.com
Club Colours: Maroon & Black, Black shorts
League: Midlands 2 West (N) (level 7)

Wolverhampton RUFC
Ground Address: Rear of the RFU Castlecroft Castlecroft Road Wolverhampton WV3 8NA
Contact: 01902 763900
Email: iankendrick@btinternet.com
Website: www.wolverhamptonrugby.com
Directions: Wolverhampton ring road, take A454 Compton Road/Bridgnorth Road to traffic lights at Mermaid, turn left, 2nd right into castlecroft Avenue, ground straight ahead,past RFU.
Hon. Secretary: Mr Ian Kendrick; Cherry Tree Lodge 58 Sandy Lane Codsall Wolverhampton WV8 1EN
Tel: 07826 873544
Email: iankendrick@btinternet.com
Fixtures Secretary: Mr Mark Belcher; 19 Rochford Grove Wolverhampton West Midlands WV4 4JS
Tel: 07791 772850
Email: m.j.belcher@hotmail.com
Club Colours: All Black
League: Midlands 2 West (N) (level 7)

Woodrush RFC
Ground Address: Icknield Street Forhill Birmingham B38 0EL
Contact: 01564 822 878
Email: PJRS@leahyj99.freeserve.co.uk
Directions: M42 J3, take A435 to Birmingham, left to Weatheroak, over crossroads, past Kings Norton Golf Club, left at T junction, 1st right, ground on right.
Honorary Secretary: Mr Peter Leahy; 8 Burns Close Headless Cross Redditch Worcestershire B97 5BS
Tel: 01905 361869
Email: pjrs@leahyj99.freeserve.co.uk
Fixtures Secretary: Mr John Board; C/0 Club Address Icknield Street Forhill Birmingham B38 0EL
Tel: 07734 549403
Email: johnb@crownlabels.com
Club Colours: Emerald Green/White Hoops
League: Midlands 3 West (S) (level 8)

Worcester Wanderers RFC
Ground Address:
Sixways Pershore Lane Hindlip WR3 8ZE
Contact: 01905 454 183
Directions: Ground share with Worcester RFC Take Jst 6 off M5 towards Droitwich. Turn left after 400yds as signposted Worcester Rugby Centre.
Honorary Secretary: Mr Mike Clarke; 17 Himbleton Road St Johns Worcester WR2 6BA Tel: 01905 428767
Email: mjaclarke@f2s.com
Fixtures Secretary: Mr Roy Saunders; 37 Wivelden Avenue Wilden Top Stourport-on-Severn Worcestershire DY13 9JJ Tel: 07961 992307
Email: roysaunders37@aol.com
Club Colours: Navy and Old Gold
League: Midlands 2 West (S) (level 7)

Worksop RUFC
Ground Address: The Meadows Stubbing Lane Stubbing Lane Worksop S80 1NF
Contact: 01909 484247
Email: admin@worksoprufc.com
Website: www.worksoprufc.com
Directions: Get onto the Worksop bypass and at the roundabout with MillHouse Pub take the road to the town centre [Newcastle Avenue] take first left onto Stubbing Lane . The rugby club and grounds at the end of road
Honorary Secretary: Mr Ken Thompson; 35 Common Road Worksop S80 3JJ Tel: 01909 771761
Email: kenneththompson761@btinternet.com
Fixtures Secretary: Mr Liam Beard; 5 High Hoe Court Worksop S80 2PJ Tel: 07866 760751
Email: fixtures@worksoprufc.com
Club Colours: Black & White Hooped Shirts
League: Midlands 3 East (N) (level 8)

Yardley & District RFC
Ground Address: 1 Cole Hall Lane Stechford Birmingham B34 6HE
Contact: 0121 7898450
Email: info@ydrfc.co.uk
Website: www.ydrfc.co.uk
Directions: B'Ham outer ringroad A4040 to Stechford, at T/light Jcn of A4040/A47 take A47 Coleshill Rd, over 1st island, immediate right into H'way, 1st island right, over next island, ground left after bridge.
Honorary Secretary: Mr Roger Poultney; St Marys Park 77 Chapel Lane Wythall Birmingham B47 6JA
Tel: 01564 823894
Email: roger.poultney@sky.com
Fixtures Secretary: Mr John Shaw; 23 1 Cole Hall Lane Stechford Birmingham B34 6HE   Tel: 07767 404281
Email: FIXTURES@YDRFC.CO.UK
Club Colours: Royal Blue & Amber Hoops, Black Shorts
League: Midlands 4 West (N) (level 9)

Support the RFU Injured Players Foundation

RFU Injured Players Foundation

The Foundation helps and supports players from all levels of the game who suffer injuries whilst playing rugby which may cause permanent and severe disability.

Fundraising

We are incredibly grateful for every donation we receive. During the 08/09 season, we managed to support more grant applications than ever before thanks to the generosity of many people. Please do consider making a donation to the Injured Players Foundation as:

- **£50** - can buy an England Rugby shirt that we can have signed by the England squad and donated to a hospitalised player

- **£100** - can provide DVD or book vouchers to help keep an inpatient entertained during their hospital stay

- **£250** - can fund the carer costs on a short holiday for an injured player who wouldn't be able to have a break without the attendance of qualified support

- **£500** - can provide an injured player with basic internet-ready lap-top so they can keep in touch with friends and family whilst in hospital

Online donations can be made through www.JustGiving.co.uk by searching for "RFU IPF" and we currently have a number of people undertaking fundraising challenges to support the work of the Foundation. If you would like to undertake a fundraising activity for the RFU IPF, but are not sure how to go about it, or you think you would need assistance, please get in touch.

Visit www.rfuipf.org.uk to discover more and see how you can help

LONDON & SOUTH EAST DIVISION

LONDON & S.E.

STRUCTURE

Level

NATIONAL LEAGUE 3
LONDON & S.E.

5

6 — LONDON 1 NORTH

7 — London 2 North East · London 2 North West

8 — London 3 North East · London 3 North West

9 — Eastern Counties 1 · Essex 1 · Herts & Middlesex 1

10 — Eastern Counties 2 · Essex 2 · Herts & Middlesex 2

11 — Herts & Middlesex 3

12 — Herts & Middlesex 4

LONDON & SOUTH EAST

LONDON & SOUTH EAST DIVISION
CONTENTS

London & S.E.Division	Officials & League Secretaries	584
National League 3 London	08-09 League Table & 09-10 Fixture List	586
	Year by Year record - the last 10 years	587
	2009-10 Clubs	588
London 1 North	08-09 League table & 09-10 Fixture Grid	604
	2009-10 Clubs	605
London 1 South	08-09 League table & 09-10 Fixture Grid	610
	2009-10 Clubs	611
Other London & S.E.	2008-09 League Tables	616
	2009-10 Fixture Grids	622
	Level 7-10 Clubs	630

A complete club index appears at the back of the book,
showing which league each club is in for the 2009-10 season

DIVISION
2009-2010

	Level
NATIONAL LEAGUE 3 LONDON & S.E.	5
LONDON 1 SOUTH	6
London 2 South East / London 2 South West	7
London 3 South East / London 3 South West	8
Sussex 1 / Kent 1 / Hampshire 1 / Surrey 1	9
Remainder of Sussex Administered locally / Kent 2 / Hampshire 2 / Surrey 2	10
Surrey 3	11
Surrey 4	12

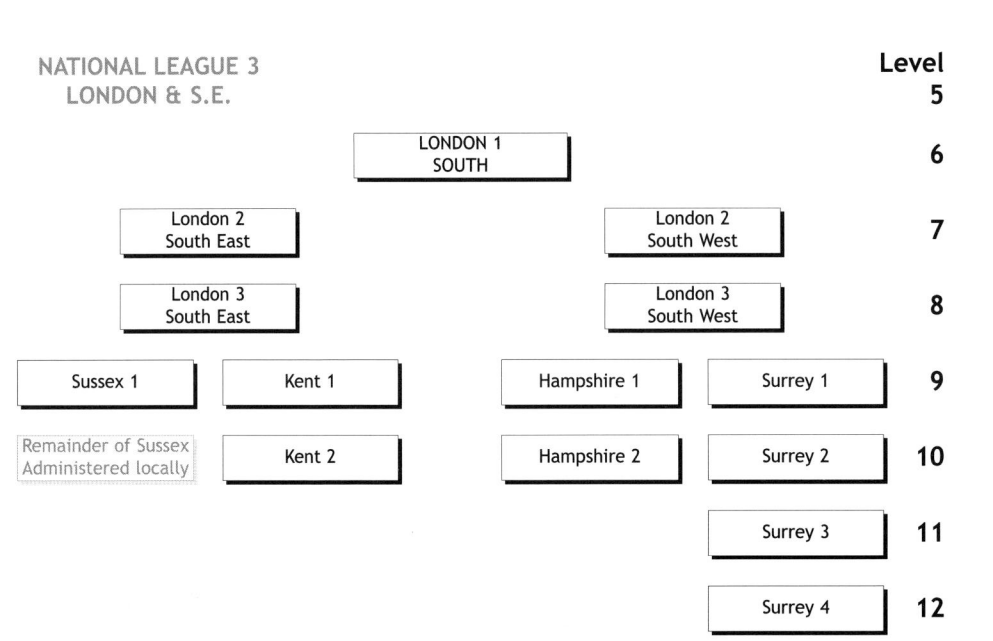

LONDON AND SOUTH EAST LEAGUES OFFICIALS 2009-10

COMMITTEE

	Position
David Williams 7, Sadlers Way, Hertford, Hertfordshire, SG14 2DZ Tel: 01992 586744 Fax: 01992 410552 email: david.williams280@ntlworld.com	Chairman
Mike Ward P.O. Box 140, Lowestoft, Suffolk, NR33 9XA Tel: 01502 539245 Fax: 01502 538670 email: londonrfu.competitions@btinternet.com	Divisional Administrator
Mike Stott Brick Kiln Farm, North Walsham, Norfolk, NR28 9LH Tel: 01692 409043 email: mikestott@tesco.net	Eastern Counties
Beiron Rees 45a, Eastwood Road, Goodmayes, Ilford, Essex, IG3 8UT Tel: 020 8597 1158 Fax: 020 8597 1158 email: beiron.rees@essexrugby.com	Essex
John Collins 4, Needlands Grove, Paulsgrove, Portsmouth, Hampshire, PO6 4QL Tel: 02392 380859 email: john.collins543@ntlworld.com	Hampshire
John Gregory 4 Caldecote, Stilton, Cambridgeshire, PE7 3SG Tel: 01733 246209 email: johngregory326@talktalk.net	Hertfordshire
Dennis Attwood 6, Somerset Gardens, Lewisham, London, SE13 7SY Tel: 020 8691 2820 Fax: 020 8355 9410 email: dennis.attwood@btinternet.com	Kent
Roger Willingale Fairmile Farm Cottage, Denby Road, Cobham, Surrey, KT11 1JY Tel: 01932 860849 Fax: 01932 860239 email: willingales@btinternet.com	Middlesex
Tony Price 32 Beverley Road, New Malden, Surrey, KT3 4AW Tel: 07801 837129 email: tp@lordprice.com	Surrey
John Thompson 1 Todhurst Cottages, Stane Street, North Heath, Pulborough, West Sussex, RH20 1DJ Tel: 01798 872744 Fax: 01798 872744 email: tommojollygood@hotmail.com	Sussex
Paul Astbury 32, Kneller Gardens, Isleworth, Middlesex, TW7 7NW Tel: 020 8898 5372 Fax: 020 8898 7977 email: paulastbury@uk2.net	Co-opted / RFU CSC
Paddy Ralston c/o Village Sports, 209, Worple Road, Raynes Park, London, SW20 8QY Tel: 020 8949 8912 email: paddy@kings.org.uk	Co-opted / Treasurer

LEAGUE SECRETARIES

Paul Astbury, 32, Kneller Gardens, Isleworth, Middlesex, TW7 7NW Tel: 020 8898 5372 Fax: 020 8898 7977 email: paulastbury@uk2.net	National 3 London
Roger Willingale, Fairmile Farm Cottage, Denby Road, Cobham, Surrey, KT11 1JY Tel: 01932 860849 Fax: 01932 860239 email: willingales@btinternet.com	London 1 North
John Thompson, 1 Todhurst Cottages, Stane St., North Heath, Pulborough, W. Sussex RH20 1DJ Tel: 01798 872744 Fax: 01798 872744 email: tommojollygood@hotmail.com	London 1 South

Mike Stott, Brick Kiln Farm, North Walsham, Norfolk, NR28 9LH Tel: 01692 409043 Fax: 01692 409043 email: mikestott@tesco.net	London 2 North East
Nick Alway, 20 Herndon Road, London, SW18 2DG Tel: 020 8870 6818 Fax: 020 8870 6818 email: nickalwaysrugby@hotmail.com	London 2 North West
Gerald Farrow, 84, Sedge Crescent, Weedswood, Chatham, Kent, ME5 0QD Tel: 01634 666255 email: Gerald.farrow@blueyonder.co.uk	London 2 South East
John Collins, 4, Neelands Grove, Paulsgrove, Portsmouth PO6 4QL Tel: 02392 380859 email: john.collins543@ntlworld.com	London 2 South West
Ron Hatch, 99, Ernest Road, Wivenhoe, Colchester, Essex, CO7 9LJ Tel: 01206 823548 Fax: 01206 823548 email: ron.hatch@virgin.net	London 3 North East
Subhash Kamath, 267 Uxbridge Rd, Hampton Hill, Hampton, Middx. TW12 1AR Tel: 020 8979 4339 email: subhashkhem2n@btinternet.com	London 3 North West
John Carley, 11, Vlissingen Drive, Deal, Kent, CT14 6TZ Tel: 01304 381273 Fax: 01304 381273	London 3 South East
Barry Myland, 36 Medina View, East Cowes, Isle of Wight, PO32 6LG Tel: 01983 280839 Fax: 01983 280839 email: barry.myland@btinternet.com	London 3 South West
Ian Forton, 183, Middletons Lane, Norwich, Norfolk, NR6 5SB Tel: 01603 400049 Fax: 01603 400049 email: iwf_5@talktalk.net	Eastern Counties 1
Marshall Self, Leylandi Cottage, Kings Head Terrace, Gt. Witchingham, Norfolk NR9 5QE Tel: 01603 872211 Fax: 01362 684280 email: bella872211@hotmail.com	Eastern Counties 2
Len Hymans, 32, Devon Way, Canvey Island, Essex, SS8 9YD Tel: 01268 693899 Fax: 01268 693899 email: l.hymans@blueyonder.co.uk	Essex 1
Beiron Rees, 45a, Eastwood Road, Goodmayes, Ilford, Essex, IG3 8UT Tel: 020 8597 1158 Fax: 020 8597 1158 email: beiron.rees@essexrugby.com	Essex 2
Rick Scott, 13 Masten Crescent, Rowner, Gosport, Hampshire PO13 9SX Tel: 023 9278 9778 email: Richard.scott987@ntlworld.com	Hampshire 1
John Sneezum, Bursledon Lodge, Salterns Lane, Old Bursledon, Southampton SO31 8DH Tel: 023 8040 2286 email: sneezumj@aol.com	Hampshire 2
John Carley, 11, Vlissingen Drive, Deal, Kent, CT14 6TZ Tel: 01304 381273 Fax: 01304 381273	Kent 1 & 2
Lucian Roberts, 40 Glenrosa Street, Fulham, London, SW6 2QZ Tel: 07971 917283 email: Lucian.roberts@catlin.com	Herts/Middlesex 1
John Gregory, 4 Caldecote, Nr Stilton, Cambridgeshire, PE7 3SG Tel: 01733 246209 email: johngregory326@talktalk.net	Herts/Middlesex 2
Andrew Smart, 169, Abbot's Road, Abbot's Langley, Hertfordshire, WD5 0BN Tel: 01923 330022 Fax: 01923 330022 email: Andrew-smart@ntlworld.com	Herts/Middlesex 3
Geoff Payne, 16, Brackenbridge Drive, South Ruislip, Middlesex, HA4 0NG Tel: 020 8845 0874 email: gpayne.rugby@virgin.net	Herts/Middlesex 4
Matthew Lunn, 60 Ember Farm Way, East Molesey, Surrey, KT8 2HX Tel: 07876 564 303 email: lunnmj@hotmail.com	Surrey 1
Paul Tanner, 1, Woodland Way, Morden, Surrey, SM4 4DS Tel: 020 8540 5784 Fax: 020 8540 5784 email: paul.tanner@swlstg-tr.nhs.uk	Surrey 2
Stephen Brierley, 1 Wallace Close, Fairlands, Guildford, Surrey, GU3 3NP Tel: 07836 794330 email: steve.brierley@btconnect.com	Surrey 3
Geoff Austin, 97, Clifton Road, Kingston, Surrey, KT2 6PL Tel: 020 8549 3757 email: Geoff.Austin@ukgateway.net	Surrey 4
Martin Doyle, 23 The Paddock, Maresfield, East Sussex, TN22 2HQ Tel: 07852 614130 email: martindoyley67@hotmail.com	Sussex 1

NATIONAL LEAGUE THREE
LONDON & S.E.

2008-09 LEAGUE TABLE (London 1)

		P	W	D	L	F	A	PD	Pts	
1	Shelford	22	19	1	2	576	281	295	39	
2	Barnes	22	19	1	2	616	349	267	39	
3	Jersey	22	15	2	5	559	336	223	32	
4	Hertford	22	13	0	9	562	409	153	26	
5	Old Albanians	22	12	0	10	496	387	109	24	
6	Bishop's Stortford	22	10	0	12	432	460	-28	20	
7	Luton	22	10	1	11	484	552	-68	19	-2
8	Tring	22	8	0	14	421	599	-178	16	
9	North Walsham	22	7	1	14	316	481	-165	15	
10	Portsmouth	22	7	0	15	341	583	-242	14	
11	Sutton & Epsom	22	6	0	16	482	626	-144	12	
12	Haywards Heath	22	3	0	19	333	555	-222	6	

2009-10 FIXTURES GRID

	Basingstoke	Bishop's S.	Bracknell	Diss	Dorking	Havant	Haywards H.	Hertford	Jersey	North Walsham	Old Albanians	Portsmouth	Sutton & E.	Tring
Basingstoke		05/12	17/10	06/03	19/09	09/01	20/03	03/10	31/10	13/02	14/11	10/04	12/12	23/01
Bishop's Stortford	27/03		03/10	13/02	05/09	12/12	06/03	19/09	17/10	23/01	31/10	28/11	14/11	09/01
Bracknell	30/01	16/01		12/09	24/10	20/02	26/09	07/11	05/09	05/12	19/12	10/10	20/03	13/03
Diss	07/11	24/10	12/12		13/03	28/11	30/01	27/03	09/01	19/09	10/10	20/02	03/10	05/09
Dorking	19/12	10/04	13/02	14/11		03/10	05/12	23/01	06/03	31/10	20/03	12/09	09/01	17/10
Havant	26/09	12/09	31/10	20/03	16/01		10/04	17/10	14/11	06/03	05/12	19/12	23/01	13/02
Haywards Heath	28/11	07/11	09/01	17/10	27/03	05/09		12/12	23/01	03/10	13/02	13/03	31/10	19/09
Hertford	16/01	19/12	06/03	05/12	10/10	30/01	12/09		20/03	14/11	10/04	26/09	13/02	31/10
Jersey	20/02	30/01	05/09	26/09	07/11	13/03	10/10	28/11		12/12	16/01	24/10	19/09	27/03
North Walsham	24/10	10/10	27/03	19/12	20/02	07/11	16/01	13/03	12/09		26/09	30/01	05/09	28/11
Old Albanians	13/03	20/02	19/09	23/01	28/11	27/03	24/10	05/09	03/10	09/01		07/11	17/10	12/12
Portsmouth	05/09	20/03	23/01	31/10	12/12	19/05	14/11	09/01	13/02	17/10	06/03		05/12	03/10
Sutton & Epsom	12/09	13/03	28/11	16/01	26/09	10/10	20/02	24/10	19/12	10/04	30/01	27/03		07/11
Tring	10/10	26/09	14/11	10/04	30/01	24/10	19/12	20/02	05/12	20/03	12/09	16/01	06/03	

YEAR BY YEAR RECORD
THE LAST 10 YEARS

Nos. of Clubs/Games	99-00 17/16	00-01 12/22	01-02 12/22	02-03 12/22	03-04 12/22	04-05 12/22	05-06 12/22	06-07 12/22	07-08 12/22	08-09 12/22
Barnes							5	6	4	2p/po
Basingstoke	1p		2			8	(SW1)	(SW1)	11r	
Bishop's Stortford					5	7	9	7	9	6
Camberley					11r					
Cambridge	4	8	12r			1p				
Canterbury				8	4	6	1p			
Cheshunt	17r		6	12r						
Civil Service									10r	
Ealing							4	2po		
Guildford & Godalming	11	11r						12r		
Harlow	6	6	11	9	12r					
Havant	8	2	1p		1p					
Haywards Heath			5	2			8	11r		12
Hertford				3	2				5	4
Jersey										3
London Nigerians			7	4	9	10r				
London Scottish						4	3	1p		
Luton										7
North Walsham										9
Norwich		4	4	11r						
Old Albanians					8	5	10	8	8	5
Old Colfeians	3	1p			9	11r				
Old Mid-Whitgiftian	15r									
Portsmouth								9	6	10
Richmond					3	2	4	1p		
Ruislip	13r									
Shelford								5	3	1p
Southend				1p						
Staines	2	3	8	7	10r		7	10r		
Sudbury	16r									
Sutton & Epsom	5	7	3	5	3	11r			7	11
Tabard							12r			
Thanet Wanderers	10	5	9	6	7	12r			12r	
Thurrock	9	10r								
Tring										8
Wimbledon	14r									
Winchester			9	10	10r					
Woodford	12r									
Worthing	7				6	2	6	3	2po	

BASINGSTOKE R.F.C.

President: John Evans, CBE, TD   **Chairman**: Dr Stephen Tristram   **Treasurer**: Adam Oliver

Club Secretary: David Crabbe, 126 Pack Lane, Kempshott, Basingstoke RG22 5HP
Tel: 01256 465085 (H)   Fax: 01256 814590   email:david.brfc@btinternet.com
Fixture Secretary: Mike Saunders   07929 031228   e-mail miksand@aol.com
Club Coach: Jim Kelly   0792 0091287   jimkelly@mobileemail.vodafone.net
Community Rugby Coach: Cliff Service   07766 554532   crc.brfc@btinternet.com

Address: Down Grange, Pack Lane, Basingstoke RG22 5HH   Tel: 01256 323308   Fax: 01256 814790
e-mail: basingstokerfc@btinternet.com   **Web** site: www.basingstokerfc.com   **Capacity**: 2,000 approx   Covered Seating: 250
Admission: Matchday - £3 members £5 non-members   **Nearest BR station**: Basingstoke (3 miles).
Directions: Directions and maps available on website, 'Contact Us' page, 'How to Find Us' button.
Car Parking: Some spaces available at club, but match day parking at the Athletic ground
Clubhouse: Open evenings and weekends, food available. Private and commercial functions can be catered for, day or evening.
Contact the Club on 01256 323308 or e-mail basingstokerfc@btinternet.com
Club Shop: Open training evenings and weekends or phone the club.
Founded: 1948   **Nickname**: Stoke   **Training Nights**: Tuesday and Thursday
Colours: Amber / blue shirts, blue shorts   **Change colours**: Sky blue shirts
Programme: Size: A5   Pages: 40+   Price: with admission   Advertising: Contact Sue Byett at the club
Editor: Colin Hibberd   email: microset@btclick.com

REVIEW OF THE SEASON 2008-09

After relegation from London 1 in 2007/08 the Club adopted 'the only way is up' approach for its Diamond Jubilee Season. The turbulence of pre-season was unforeseen but soon with a new coaching team in place and Neil Young continuing as skipper, preparations started to go well and we were confident of making our mark on London 2 South. So to Gravesend in the sun, where we dominated territory and possession for 90% of the game and still lost! Not quite what we had in mind, but as it turned out it was merely a glitch as the boys showed their class over the coming weeks and months.

Strengthened by our overseas players Andrew Fitchett and Paul Morris, the returning ever youthful, Steve Collins, and a settled back row of Simon Appleby, Dan Rees and Ross Stirling, we started playing to the patterns we had worked on in training and sides just didn't have an answer to our defensive system. We then encountered the monsoons of November, narrowly losing away to Cobham before drawing 5-5 in a 'classic' in the mud at Dorking. We bounced back by crushing Chobham 29-0 at home and eased our way to Christmas in the thick of the promotion race knowing that the key games would come at home against Cobham and Dorking. And so it proved.

We outclassed Cobham in a great all round team performance which set up the game of the season, at home to Dorking, what a day, what a game, what a finish! From there we showed great character to close out the double, Hampshire Cup winners and promoted back to London 1 as League Champions.

John Boyle and Christy White, both former players, sadly weren't there to see the final game, but we know they would be delighted with the victory and promotion.

LAST TEN SEASONS

	Division	P	W	D	L	F	A	P.D.	Pts	Pos
99-00	Lon 1	16	14	0	2	660	147	513	28	1p
00-01	N3S	26	7	1	18	333	686	-353	15	13r
01-02	Lon 1	22	16	2	4	648	342	306	34	2p/po
02-03	N3S	26	10	0	16	603	729	-126	20	12
03-04	N3S	26	6	0	20	456	940	-484	12	13r
04-05	Lon 1	22	8	0	14	443	638	-195	16	8
05-06	SW 1	22	15	1	6	705	328	377	31	4
06-07	SW1	22	12	0	10	491	505	-14	24	5
07-08	Lon 1	22	4	0	18	297	687	-390	8	11r
08-09	Lon 2S	22	18	1	3	641	216	425	37	1p

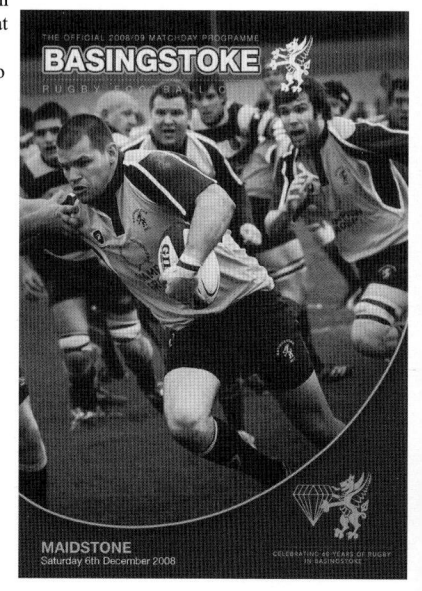

BISHOP'S STORTFORD R.F.C.

President: Chris Davies Tel: 07836 566860
Chairman: Perry Oliver Tel: 01279 814591
Club Secretary: Julia Rontree, 1 Barrington Cottages, Dunmow Rd, Hatfield Broad Oak, Bishop's Stortford CM22 7JH
Tel: 01279 718465 (H), 07806 621371 (M) email: julia.rontree@sky.com
Fixtures Secretary: Terry Ellis, Flat 2, 72 South Street, Bishop's Stortford, CM23 3AZ Tel: 01279 461186
1st XV Manager: Paul Woodford Tel: 07967 608237
Match Secretary / Referees Contact: Dermot Eustace
Tel: 01279 832065 (H), 07850 083871 (M) email: dermot.eustace@ntrlworld.com
Club Coach: Peter Engledow Tel: 07764 960407 (M) email: peterengledow@rfu.com
Ground Address: Silver Leys, Hadham Road, Bishop's Stortford, Herts, CM23 2QE
Tel: 01279 652092 email: julia.rontree@sky.com
Directions: From west A120 to roundabout at start of Bishop's Stortford by-pass.
Take A1250 to town centre. Ground is half a mile on the left
Capacity: 1,000 uncovered standing   **Car Parking**: approx 100   **Nearest BR Station**: Bishop's Stortford
Admission: Matchday £5 incl programme
Clubhouse: Open 7 days Food available matchdays & Sundays & by request.
Club function room available. Contact Chris Davies 01279 652092 or 07836 566860
Club Shop: Available throughout the week. Contact Bob Winnington on 07988 646384
Programme: Size A5   Pages 44   Price £5, includes admission
Founded: 1920   **Training Nights**: Tuesday & Thursday   **Website**: www.bsrfc.co.uk
Colours: Royal blue and white   **Change colours**: Predominantly Red

REVIEW OF THE SEASON 2007-08

Last season is widely regarded as one of the most successful ever for our 1st XV. A top six finish in London One and victory in the Herts Presidents Cup Final for the first time in 13 Years fulfilled all of the objectives asked of the squad by new coach Peter Engledow.

We are immensely proud of our status as a Community Amateur Sports Club (CASC) and our current success is undoubtedly founded on talent that we have nurtured through our vibrant Mini & Youth sections. No fewer than 14 of the victorious 18 man squad for that wonderful Cup final began playing their rugby as children at Bishops Stortford.

This year's crop of Colts continued to follow the trend set in recent years by their predecessors and advanced to the later stages of the National Colts cup as well as winning their County cup, County 7's cup and league competition.

The U17 age group took the plaudits within the Youth section winning their closely contested league and reaching the quarter final stage of the National Plate.

Our most pleasing accomplishment in Youth rugby last season was the significant improvement in the quality of rugby played by our B squads. All of our youth age groups run at least two squads and we continue to build upon a proven track record of encouraging from each player to perform to the very best of their ability.

As with the Youth every Mini age group from 6 to 12 are strong in numbers. The sight of several hundred Mini rugby players enjoying themselves each Sunday truly is a sight and indeed sound to behold. Our Mini's travel far and wide to Festivals galore and more often than not return with some sort of trophy.

We are all looking forward to Season 09/10 not least because it sees Chris 'Tubby' Davies take over from Charlie Dunsford as Club President. Our thanks go to Charlie for all he has achieved in his time at the helm and our best wishes to Tubby for what will I am sure, if nothing else will be an entertaining tenure.

LAST TEN SEASONS

	Division	P	W	D	L	F	A	P.D.	Pts	Pos
99-00	Lon 2N	16	13	1	2	575	229	346	27	2
00-01	Lon 2N	22	17	0	5	540	285	255	34	3
01-02	Lon 2N	22	18	1	3	521	260	261	37	3
02-03	Lon 2N	22	19	0	3	549	241	308	38	1p
03-04	Lon 1	22	12	1	9	389	342	47	23	5
04-05	Lon 1	22	8	1	13	383	540	-157	17	7
05-06	Lon 1	22	9	1	12	425	552	-127	*17	9
06-07	Lon 1	22	9	0	13	420	617	-197	18	7
07-08	Lon 1	22	7	0	15	342	528	-186	14	9
08-09	Lon 1	22	10	0	12	432	460	-28	20	6

BRACKNELL R.F.C.

President: Mr Jonathan Dance   **Chairman:** Mr Ian Hallam   **Treasurer:** Mr. Pat Casey
Club Secretary: Mr Peter Hickin, c/o Bracknell Rugby Club
Tel: 01344 424013   email: secretary@bracknellrugbyclub.com
Chairman of Rugby: Mr. Guy Young, c/o Bracknell Rugby Club
Tel: 01344 424013 or 07917 623441 (M) email: gcy61@btinternet.com
Head Coach: Ken Hopkins   **Commercial Secretary:** Mr Steven Ward
Address: Bracknell RFC, Lily Hill Park, Lily Hill Drive, Bracknell, Berks RG12 2UG
Tel: 01344 424013 email: Karen@bracknellrugbyclub.com
Capacity: 2240   Covered seating: 240 (Grandstand)
Directions: From M4 – J10 – A329(M) Bracknell B3408 Binfield follow to A329 Bracknell . Through town Towards Ascot turn left at the Running Horse Public House clubhouse and ground at rear. From M3 – J3-A322 Bracknell – A332 Ascot to Heatherwood Hospital roundabout A329 Bracknell at 2nd roundabout take third exit Running horse Public house on right Clubhouse and ground at rear.   **Nearest BR Station:** Martins Heron or Bracknell
Admission: Matchday: £5 incl. programme   **Car Parking:** 65 plus off site parking available
Clubhouse: Open Mon - Thur.11-11pm, Fri & Sat. 11am-1am, Sun 12-10.30. Snacks & bar meals available lunch times, early evenings & weekends.   Functions: Main Hall available to hire - contact email: barmanager@bracknellrugbyclub.com
Club Shop: Open Wed. 6.30-730pm, matchdays & Sun 9.30 to 12.30. Contact Mr. Ian Hallam
Programme: Size: A5   Pages: 52   Price: £2   Editor: Colin Watts
Founded: 1955   **Web site:** www.bracknellrugbyclub.com   **Training Nights:** Tues. & Thur. 7pm
Colours: Green with gold and black hoops   **Change colours:** Black with gold and green hoops

REVIEW OF THE SEASON 2008-09

The 2008-09 season proved to be another successful season for the Club, although we fell short of our primary objective which was for our 1st XV to gain promotion from SW1.

We played some excellent open rugby through the SW1 season, and defended strongly. This performance was reflected in the season's stats, in which we had both the best attacking and defending records in our league. Additionally, our captain (Ben Nowak) turned in yet another solid season and came out as top kicker in SW1. However, we were not consistent enough on the park, and failing to win both at home and away to Old Patesians and away to Chippenham were results which proved costly to our league campaign.

We reclaimed the Berkshire Cup, beating Redingensians in the final. It was particularly encouraging to see a number of our DHL Academy players contributing to this victory, and we look forward to their progression into the ranks of the 1st XV this season. Our strong 2nd team (led by Club stalwarts Greg Anstead and Alan Leishman) performed well in the Canterbury Shield and were unlucky (through match cancellations) not to win their league. This strength built a good 1st XV playing squad, helping us to cope with injuries in our SW1 league campaign. The 2nd team has also served as a sounding board for a number of Junior players emerging from the DHL Academy.

Our social sides (3rds, 4ths, and Ladies) have continued to provide enjoyable rugby for our local community, and have enjoyed their various triumphs (including their tour) during the season. Our Mini and Junior section has had yet another outstanding season, providing qualified coaches and rugby for over 300 local youngsters. Yet again, the section enjoyed a successful tour on and off the park to the Isle of Wight festival. Our DHL Academy produced more successes at U17 and U19 age groups, with the U17s reaching the final of the National Plate competition (our best performance ever). We were also pleased to provide a significant contribution to the Berkshire County teams at all age groups

LAST TEN SEASONS

	Division	P	W	D	L	F	A	P.D.	Pts	Pos
99-00	JN1	26	14	0	12	608	408	200	28	7
00-01	N2	26	22	0	4	752	310	442	44	1p
01-02	N1	26	4	0	22	418	823	-405	26	14r
02-03	N2	26	16	0	10	597	525	72	32	5
03-04	N2	26	12	1	13	494	605	-111	25	7
04-05	N2	26	8	1	17	503	666	-163	51	13r
05-06	N3S	26	2	0	24	364	903	-539	13	14r
06-07	SW1	22	10	0	12	450	430	20	20	8
07-08	SW1	22	19	0	3	640	292	348	38	2
08-09	SW1	22	14	1	6	569	292	277	29	2

The restructuring of the leagues and related promotions and demotions have all contributed to Bracknell's 1st XV transferring to the London & SE League this season for the first time. So, we say farewell to our colleagues in SW1, and we will miss our local derby matches; however, we look forward to the new challenges presented by playing different teams and to making new friends, and we are quivering with excitement at the prospect of our first "overseas" holiday (oops, fixture!) in Jersey.

Prudence off the park means that we continue to live within our financial means. This occasionally frustrates our playing ambitions in the short term, but is (we believe) the best way to long-term success for the Club and its members. We are expecting greater financial challenges in 2009-10, but expect to be challenging for promotion again this season!

DISS R.F.C.

President: David Ford   Tel: 01379 676385   email: dford@djfordcons.freeserve.co.uk
Chairman: Phillip Southgate   Tel: 01953 483209   email: nickiejane56@btinternet.com
Treasurer: Ian Webster   Tel:01379 651467   email: ian.webster@larking-gowen.co.uk
Hon Sec: Norman Potter   1 Mill Lane, Weybread, Diss, Norfolk IP21 5TP
Tel: 01379 586288   email: normanpotter@onestoppoultryshop.com
Fixtures Sec: Les Newman   Tel: 01379 640540   email les@newmans-online.co.uk
Director of Rugby: Henry Lind   Tel: 01379 652937
Ground Address: Diss R.F.C., Mackenders, Bellrope Lane, Roydon, Diss IP22 5RG
Tel: 01379 642891   email: dissrugbyclub@yahoo.co.uk
Correspondence Address: c/o Hartismere High School, Castleton Way, Eye, Suffolk IP23 7BL   Tel: 01379 872725
Directions: From Diss, head west out of town on the A1066 to Roydon. Drive through Roydon until you get to the White Hart Pub (on the left). Turn right opposite the pub into Bellrope Lane, Diss RFC is approx. 100m on the left. If travelling from Thetford on the A1066, turn left at the White Hart.
Club Shop: Open on matchdays 45mins before K.O. or see website.
Formed: 1958   **Training Nights:** Tuesday & Thursday 7pm   **Website:** www.dissrugby.com
Colours: Royal blue & white   **Programme** Editor: Andy Hales 01953 888897

London Two North Champions 2008-09

LAST TEN SEASONS

	Division	P	W	D	L	F	A	P.D.	Pts	Pos
99-00	Lon 2N	16	12	0	4	347	195	152	24	5
00-01	Lon 2N	22	9	1	12	323	500	-177	19	8
01-02	Lon 2N	22	6	0	16	298	463	-165	12	10
02-03	Lon 2N	22	10	0	12	335	568	-233	20	7
03-04	Lon 2N	22	5	1	16	228	693	-465	11	9
04-05	Lon 2N	22	3	0	19	235	707	-472	6	11r
05-06	Lon 3NE	22	16	0	6	448	244	204	32	2
06-07	Lon 3NE	20	5	2	13	299	390	-91	12	9
07-08	Lon 3NE	22	18	0	4	685	211	474	36	2p/po
08-09	Lon 2N	22	17	3	2	511	279	232	37	1p

591

DORKING R.F.C.

President: Ted Ivens Tel: 07803 616777 email: ted@ismsearch.com
Chairman: Shaun Grady Tel: 07802 467449 email: shaun.grady@astrazeneca.com
Club Secretary: Mark Thornberry, c/o Dorking RFC, The Pavilion, The Big Field, Brockham, Surrey RH3 7LZ
Tel: 07770 680799 email: mark@thornberry.co.uk
Fixtures Secretary: Ian McLean Tel: 07868 743820 email: ianjmclean@gmail.com
Club Captain: Michael Kornrumpf Tel: 07737 712189 email: michael@kornrumpf.co.uk
Director of Rugby: Richie Andrews Tel: 07872 377057 email: richieandrews@gmail.com
Playing & Coaching: Jim Evans Tel: 07789 480353 email: jimevans@vodafone.net
Youth Chairman: Kevin Beal Tel: 07768 600734 email: kbeal@btopenworld.com
Commercial Director: Roger Parkin email: roger.parkin@ntlworld.com
Press: Paul Mosley Tel: 07825 092408 email: mozza@mosley.org.uk
Ground Address: The Pavillion, The Big Field, Brockham, Surrey RH3 7LZ
Tel.: 01737 844282 email: drfc@thornberry.co.uk **Website**: www.dorkingrugbyclub.co.uk
Directions: From Dorking take A25 towards Reigate. After 2 miles turn right into Brockham Lane, then 1st left into Kiln Lane
Capacity: All uncovered standing. **Car Parking**: Ample **Nearest BR Station**: Dorking, Betchworth
Clubhouse: Open 7 days a week during the season. Available for private hire. Contact Dermot Pearce
Club Shop: Open Saturdays and Sundays or shop online. Contact Karen Thomas.
Formed: 1921 **Training Nights**: Tues & Thur (Seniors), Wed. (Girls, Youth & Touch) Guest Coach – 1 Tues every month
Colours: Red & white hoops, with blue flashes **Change colours**: Blue & white hoops, with red flashes.
Programme: Size: A5 Pages: 16 Price: £2.00 Editor: Paul Mosley

REVIEW OF THE SEASON 2008-09

The 2008-9 season saw the 1st XV achieve its third promotion in four years and will now be playing at a level not enjoyed since the heady days of the early '90s. A hard fought promotion play-off against a very good Staines side takes us, with a new competition format, into the National Leagues for the first time. For good measure we also reached the Surrey Cup Final and last 16 of the EDF Intermediate Cup, where we lost to the eventual winners.

Congratulations to Richie Andrews and his coaching team; Jason Hoad, Matt Hawks and Chris Deavin; all operating under the guiding hand of our Chairman of Playing, Jim Evans. Paul Hunt, Issy Heppenstall and the physiotherapy team all made a significant contribution.

The biggest thanks and congratulations go to the players for an incredible effort. We scored 118 league tries and 774 points and didn't lose a league game by more than a single score. The EBB Paper Player of the Year was Matt Noble who was top try scorer in the league and second highest point scorer. The winner of the Michael Case Memorial Most Improved Player Trophy was James Catton who played in every single game. Most pleasing is the continued movement of our youth players into the senior sides. 28 of the 45 players representing the 1st XV this season played youth rugby at the Club; a statistic we are immensely proud of. The A XV were second in the Surrey Premier League and the Extra A XV finished a creditable third in Surrey Combination 2.

Our Youth section continues to flourish with around 500 boys and girls turning out on Sundays. Elliot Daly was selected to play for England U16 whilst Ben Francis played for Scotland U17. From the crop of recent graduates, George Kruis continues to impress at Saracens whilst Chris York, now at Harlequins, was out in Japan with England for the U20 World Cup.

LAST TEN SEASONS

	Division	P	W	D	L	F	A	P.D.	Pts	Pos
99-00	Lon 2S	16	4	0	12	215	372	-157	8	15
00-01	Lon 3SW	16	6	0	10	243	348	-105	12	6
01-02	Lon 3SW	18	4	0	14	302	404	-102	8	9
02-03	Lon 3SW	18	5	0	13	298	581	-283	*4	10
03-04	Lon 4SW	18	12	0	6	440	253	187	254	3
04-05	Lon 4SW	18	15	0	3	526	198	328	*27	3
05-06	Lon 4SW	18	16	0	2	612	178	434	32	1p
06-07	Lon 3SW	22	17	1	4	605	273	332	35	2p/po
07-08	Lon 2S	22	11	1	10	392	447	-55	23	5
08-09	Lon 2S	22	16	3	3	772	266	506	35	2p/po

HAVANT R.F.C.

President: Ray Quinn   email: raypatquinn@hotmail.com
Chairman: Debbie Morgan   Tel: 02392 373894 (H)   07802 940931 (M)   email: debbiemorgan_1@hotmail.com
Director of Finance/Treasurer: Dave Roberts   email: drobbo14@aol.com   Tel: 01243 379499 B)   07879 627901 (M)
Club Secretary: Nigel Dade,   88 Loxwood Rd, Lovedean, Waterlooville, Hants, PO8 9TY
Tel: 02392 599659 (H)   07931 415099 (M)   email: n.dadehrfc@btinternet.com
Fixture Secretary: Mick Chalk Tel: 02392 472239 (H) 02392 542979 (B) email: sultan-esso2@nrta.mod.uk
Director of House & Ground Jon Mangnall   07860 780679 jonathan.mangnall@amxeurope.com
Director of Rugby: Simon Morgan   email: sfmorgan@hotmail.co.uk   Tel: 02392 373894 (H)   07714 447323 (M)
Commercial Manager: Bob Wilkinson   01243 371208 (H) robert.wilkinson1@btconnect.com
Head Coach: Tom Drewett   Tel: 078787 22123 (M)   email: tomdrewett@hotmail.com
Ground Address: Hooks Lane Ground, Fraser Rd, Bedhampton, Havant, Hants. PO9 3EJ
Tel: 02392 477843   Fax: 02392 470251   email: havantrfc@aol.com   Web site: www.havant-rfc.co.uk
Directions: From A3 & A3(M): At J 5 of A3(M), take slip road to B2177 and take first exit off r'about passing Rusty Cutter pub on your left. Over mini r'about and at next lights go straight on (right hand lane); bear left at level-crossing. Take 2nd left into James Road (Sign post for Havant RFC). Left at T-junction into Fraser Road - clubhouse is 200 metres on right, just beyond Hooks Lane **From M27 & A27**: M27 changes to A27 at Hilsea, Portsmouth and in 1 mile (after crossing intersection with A2030) keep to nearside lane. Take A3(M) for London, staying in nearside lane and after 150 yards take slip road to Bedhampton. Take 3rd exit off r'about on to B2177, passing the Rusty Cutter Inn on your left - then as above.
Capacity: 3,000   Covered Seating: 200   **Car Parking**: 200 at ground   **Nearest BR Station**: Havant
Admission: Matchdays £5 incl. programme
Clubhouse: Normal licensing hours, snacks available on matchdays. Functions: up to 150, contact Sarah Trevett 023 92 477843 (W) 07861 395404 (M).   **Club Shop**: Open Sat pm & Sun am during seaso
Founded: 1951   **Nickname**: Hav   **raining Nights**: Tues & Thur   **Colours**: Navy with red panels   **Change**: Red
Programme: Size: A5   Price: With entry   Pages: 36-40 (half ads, half content)
Editor: Roger Boydell, as above   Advertising: Bob Wilkinson

REVIEW OF THE SEASON 2008-09

After five seasons in National 3, we eventually had 'financial reality' catch up with us and found ourselves returning to Tier 5 for the 2009-10 season, hoping to regroup and bounce back as we have done before!

The season started disastrously, losing our first ten games which, unsurprisingly, saw us looking up at everyone else in the table at mid December.

At this point, a few other clubs hadn't been fairing much better, and it away at one of them, Chinnor, that a chink of light started to appear as we deservedly won our first victory. When this was followed by an excellent home win against Bridgwater and Albion the following week, which moved us out of the relegation places, the 'faithful' were beginning to believe that 'survival' was on the cards.

The following week we travelled away to Worthing, one of the two clubs below us, looking to cement the recovery and move further away from the' drop zone'. However, our local rivals had other ideas, and a good win for them set them on the road to recovery and dumped us back into the mire from which we never really managed to recover.

A good home win against Dings in mid-January gave false hope, but it was to be our only other victory, and, as other clubs in danger all started to show some sort of form, we became adrift and certain of relegation well before season end.

LAST TEN SEASONS

	Division	P	W	D	L	F	A	P.D.	Pts	Pos	Most Pts	Most Tries
99-00	Lon1	16	9	1	6	407	321	86	19	8		
00-01	Lon1	20	16	0	4	550	294	256	32	2		
01-02	Lon1	22	18	0	4	579	239	340	36	1		
02-03	N3 S	26	9	1	16	672	567	105	19	13	175 Sid Claffey	13 A Petzer
03-04	Lon 1	22	18	0	4	876	269	607	36	1p		
04-05	N3 S	26	12	1	13	664	609	55	66	7	175 Stephen Claffey	23 Cam Avery
05-06	N3 S	26	10	0	16	629	653	-24	*56	9	80 Cam Avery	16 Cam Avery
06-07	N3 S	26	17	0	9	736	433	303	86	3	155 Ngapaku Ngapaku	16 Cam Avery
07-08	N3 S	26	8	0	18	394	567	-173	41	10	92 Ngapaku Ngapaku	14 Dylan Raubenheimer
08-09	N3 S	26	3	0	23	347	882	-535	21	14r	41 Keith Molyneux	8 Greg Sullivan

593

HAYWARDS HEATH R.F.C.

President: The Hon. Nicholas Soames, MP   **Chairman:** Alan Jenkins   **Treasurer:** Ian Cunningham
Club Secretary: James Melody   c/o the club. email: honsec@hhrfc.co.uk
Fixture Secretary: James Melody (Senior Sides) c/o the club. Tel: 07795 551494 email: jamesmelody@gmail.com
Head Coach: Adam Vander   **PR & Press:** Paul Constantinou
Juniors/Minis: Mark Jenkins   **Club Captain:** Owen Ashton

Address: The Clubhouse, Whitemans Green, Cuckfield, W. Sussex RH17 5HX.
Tel: 01444 413950   email: club@hhrfc.co.uk   **Website:** www.hhrfc.co.uk.
Directions: Leave the A23 at its junction with the B2115 following the signs for Cuckfield.
The ground is about 2 miles from this junction just outside Cuckfield Village.
Nearest BR Station: Haywards Heath (3 miles)   **Car Parking:** 100 spaces
Capacity: 1,200, all uncovered standing.   **Admission:** Matchday - by programme £2.
Clubhouse: Open matchdays from 12.00. Burgers, sausages & snacks available.
Available for private hire, contact Graham Glenn.
Club Shop: Matchdays, Sundays and on-line contact Justin Graham.
Colours: Red & black graduated hoops   **Change colours:** Oxford & Cambridge blue graduated hoops
Founded: 1958   **Nickname:** 'Heath'   **Training Nights:** Tuesday & Thursday (Seniors)
Programme: Size: A5   Pages: 22   Price: £2   Advertising: Arthur Chopping

REVIEW OF THE SEASON 2008-09

The 1st XV were relegated from London 1 in an admirable battle that went to the last kick of the last game away at North Walsham.

League restructuring for 2009-10 meant that two clubs drawn from the bottom sides in each of London 1, North 1, Midlands 1 and South West 1 went down on the basis of their playing record. We had a significant advantage on points difference over Darlington (North 1) and Bedford Athletic (Midlands 1) but needed a win in our last game to be sure. In the event Bedford Athletic won their match and our loss meant that the points difference didn't come into play. It does however, illustrate just how close it really was.

So many games were keenly-contested affairs where we went down by a narrow margin. While we didn't win enough games, we certainly were worthy of our place in London 1 all season. The consensus amongst our rivals in the league was that we were not a relegation team. The basis of the reality in the numbers bore that not to be the case when it came to the crunch. We maintained our competitive focus right through to the end of the season, largely due to a coaching team led very ably by Paul Westgate and to the application of the players.

It's the confidence derived from the many positives referred to above that contributes to the clear wish of our 1st XV players to battle it out again following our reinstatement into the new National 3 London. We believe that there is certainly a job to be finished in the season ahead and believe we will show ourselves to be worthy of our berth.

LAST TEN SEASONS

	Division	P	W	D	L	F	A	P.D.	Pts	Pos
99-00	Lon 2S	22	21	0	1	613	188	425	42	1p
00-01	Lon 1	22	12	2	8	471	439	32	26	5
01-02	Lon 1	22	19	0	3	638	321	317	38	2p
02-03	N3S	26	10	0	16	491	578	-87	20	10
03-04	N3S	26	3	0	23	387	966	-579	20	14
04-05	Lon 1	22	9	1	12	444	533	-89	19	8
05-06	Lon 1	22	9	1	12	444	533	-89	19	8
06-07	Lon 1	22	6	0	16	409	650	-241	12	11r
07-08	Lon 2S	22	20	0	2	756	190	566	40	1p
08-09	Lon 1	22	3	0	19	333	555	-222	6	12r

HERTFORD R.F.C.

President: A C S (Ant) Irwin Tel: 01727 859553 (H) **Chairman:** Barry Young Tel: 01279 600768 (H)
Treasurer: Peter Finch Tel: 01920 465045 (H)
Club Secretary: Chris Learmonth, The White Cottage, 29 London Road, Sawbridgeworth, Herts. CM21 9EH.
Tel: 07977 204008   email: chris@learmonthandcoltd.uk
Fixture Secretary: John Atkinson, 86 Winterscroft Rd., Hoddesdon, Herts. EN11 8RJ
Tel: 01992 462206 (H)   Fax: 01920 460943 (Club) email: tony.edlin@btconnect.com
Director of Rugby: Clive Mann Tel: 01920 464718 (H) 07710 354782 (M)
Commercial Secretary: David Baseley Tel: 01763 241440 (B) 07831 884788 (M)
Ground Address: Highfields, Hoe Lane, Ware, Herts. SG12 9NZ
Tel: 01920 462975 Fax: 01920 460943 email tony.edlin@btconnect.com   **Website:** www.hertfordrfc.co.uk
Directions: Leave A10 at the A414 Hertford exit. Take B1502 to Great Amwell. After 300 yards, take 1st left into Hoe Lane.
The club is on the left after 400 yds.   **Nearest BR Station:** Ware (Hertford East/Liverpool St. line)
Admission: Matchday £5-00 (Non members) £3-00 (Members). Season Tickets N/A
Capacity: 1500   Seating: 150   Covered: 400   **Car Parking:** 300 spaces at club.
Clubhouse: Open every evening 6.30-11pm. Food available Thur & Sat. or by arrangement.
Functions contact Commercial Sec. David Baseley as above
Club Shop: Open Sat & Sun. during matches.
Programme: Size: A5   **Pages:** 52   **Price:** £3   **Editorial & Advertising:** Contact David Baseley, Commercial Secretary
Founded: 1932   **Training Nights:** Tuesday & Thursday
Club colours: Royal blue, black and gold, black shorts   **Change colours:** Gold.

REVIEW OF THE SEASON 2008-09

We were the second highest try scorers in the league with 79 - only Barnes with 84 scored more - and our backs scored more tries than any other set of backs. Yet we finished fourth and this underlines the problems we have with the lack of a consistent goal kicker.

Four teams did the double over us but each one had to work much harder in the second half of the season. There was certainly an improvement in the latter months but we tail off badly in april when a higher place in the league was unattainable.

Robbie Miller and David von Kotze our two Australian backs who both featured in the successful 2002-3 campaign are returning home and both made significant contributions, Miller in the 13 games he played and Von Kotze who was a regular from November onwards.

Several new players made a big impact , namely Ian Hardcastle, Matt Cross, utility back Alastair Fox and centre Jon Child. There was a welcome return from his travels for flanker Craig Wilson and we were delighted to have wing Adam Roberts back for the whole season after long-term injury. Two others in a similar situation were centre Steve Small and flanker Chris Rainbow and both returned at the end of the season. The latter with Graeme Walters did a fine coaching job and Rainbows one game for the club and three for the county were enough to convince the England counties selectors of his ability and he duly toured with the team to South Korea and Japan in June.

Second row James Weaver's first season as captain can be rated as a success and he can confidently look forward to his second campaign. Pride of place however , must go three teenagers full back Stuart Smart, centre Steve Ellis and prop Rob Schillaci who all graduated from the 1st XV to to the Under 20s and then to the full County championship side, a great achievement for three so young. In all eleven Hertford players represented the County in its successful journey to the Twickenham final where it lost narrowly to Cheshire.

LAST TEN SEASONS

	Division	P	W	D	L	F	A	P.D.	Pts	Pos
99-00	Lon 3NW	16	16	0	0	865	168	697	32	1
00-01	Lon 3NW	18	15	1	2	473	159	314	31	1p
01-02	Lon 2N	22	20	0	2	708	169	539	40	1p
02-03	Lon 1	22	16	0	6	593	370	223	32	3
03-04	Lon 1	22	18	0	4	625	276	349	36	2p*
04-05	N3S	26	14	1	11	588	505	83	70	5
05-06	N3S	26	11	0	15	523	764	-241	51	11
06-07	N3S	26	8	0	18	476	780	-304	44	12r
07-08	Lon 1	22	12	1	9	516	446	70	25	5
08-09	Lon 1	22	13	0	9	562	409	153	26	4

JERSEY R.F.C.

President:	David Lapidus	Tel: (H) 01534 481101 email: patjsy@jerseymail.co.uk
Chairman:	Bill Dempsey	Tel: (M) 07797 716321 email: BDempsey@mercurydistribution.com
Treasurer:	Brian Morris	Tel: (M) 07797 713590 email: bmorris@ifmjersey.com
Club Secretary:	Chris Lynch	3 Ville de L'Eglise, St. Peter, Jersey JE3 7AR
		Tel: (H) 01534 482 304 email: Ann_lynch69@hotmail.com
Fixture Secretary:	Kate. Adams	Tel: (H) 01534 484 509 (M) 07797 748 826 (W) 01534 613 072
Business Manager:	Adam Budworth	Tel: (M) 07797 712330. (H) 01534 744132. (W) 01534 835872.
Ground Address:	Rue des Landes, St. Peters, Jersey, C.I. JE4 5NQ	
	Tel: 01534 499929 Email: jerseyrugby.club@jerseymail.co.uk	

Directions: Opposite Airport on main road to St Helier.
Capacity: 250. Covered Seating: None.   **Admission:** No charge.   **Car Parking:** 80
Clubhouse: Open Training nights 6pm - 10pm. Weekends:During games.
Club Shop: Hours as above. Contact 01534 499929.
Programme: Size: A5   Pages: 8.   Price: £1.   Editor: Adam Budworth.
Advertising: Contact Club Manager Katie Arden on 01534 499929.
Founded: 1879.   **Website:** www.jerseyrugbyfootballclub.org   **Training Nights:** Tuesday & Thursday
Colours: Red Shirts, White Shorts.   **Change colours:** Blue Shirts, White shorts.

REVIEW OF THE SEASON 2008-09

In what was a first for JRFC With promotion to London division 1 it was the highest position that the club had achieved since league structure was put in place.

Jersey finished in 3rd place in this league behind Shelford and Barnes two very strong sides, it was more that we expected when we had our first away game against Tring last September of which we won it was very much going into the unknown.

We were very proud that we had eight or nine local Jersey born players involved in every game, which is not something that we had been able to do in the past, in 1970/1980 we might be able to have one or two, so this goes to show how far our Academy has come in the past 5 to 10 years and at the top of that list is Matt Bannahan plus lots of other age group boys representing Hampshire during the season.

We have had permission to put in two extra pitches which will be ready for the start of season 2010/11 which will bring our total to 5 pitches, which again is great for the future, with approx 400/430 boys and girls training each Sunday morning.

Jersey regained the Siam Cup which Guernsey had won for the past couple of years with a watching crowd of approx 5000, it was a great weekend of rugby with Jersey winning all but two of games played that weekend, won 12 lost 2.

We had a very successful vets tournament back in October with a total of 14 visiting teams, brings back memories of what rugby used to like, not sure if that is good or bad.

So all in all JRFC had a very good season with hopefully a lot more to come for the future.

Bill Dempsey , Chairman.

LAST TEN SEASONS

	Division	P	W	D	L	F	A	P.D.	Pts	Pos
99-00	Lon 3SW	16	14	0	2	504	140	364	28	2
00-01	Lon 3SW	16	8	1	7	396	341	55	17	4
01-02	Lon 3SW	18	10	0	8	370	402	-32	20	5
02-03	Lon 3SW	18	12	1	5	357	233	124	*23	3
03-04	Lon 3SW	18	11	1	6	398	222	176	23	3
04-05	Lon 3SW	20	20	0	0	771	293	478	40	1p
05-06	Lon 2S	22	13	1	8	610	487	123	*25	3
06-07	Lon 2S	22	16	0	6	554	641	213	32	3
07-08	Lon 2S	22	20	1	1	708	257	451	*39	2p/po
08-09	Lon 1	22	15	2	5	559	336	223	32	3

NORTH WALSHAM R.F.C.

President	Joe Hodges
Chairman	John H. Farrer, Darrow Wood Farm, Shelfanger Road, Diss, Norfolk IP22 4XY
	Tel (H) 01379 642153 (M) 07940 205362 e.mail jillandjohnfarrer@hotmail.com
Treasurer	David Gilbert email: vikingrugby@lineone.net
Club Secretary	Sue Yaxley, 14 Norwich Rd., North Walsham NR28 0DU
	Tel: 01692 404498 (H), 07717 127335 (M) email: sueyaxley@btopenworld.com
Fixtures Secretary	Tony Marcantonio, The White House, Southwood Rd., Beighton,Norwich. NR13 3AB.
Media Liaison	01493 751837 (H) 07944 690042 (M) email: tony.marcantonio@ukgateway.net
Youth Development Officer	Jon Perks c/o the club.

Address: Norwich Road, Scottow, Norwich, NR10 5BU Tel: 01692 538808
Capacity: 1,500   Covered Seating: 160   **Nearest BR Station**: North Walsham
Directions: From A11 or A140 head in towards Norwich turn left onto the ring road and take the B1150 (signposted North Walsham).. Keep on the B1150 through Horstead/Coltishall and the Ground is on left just past the Three Horseshoes PH.
Car Parking: Ample car parking within the grounds – Please DO NOT park on the roadside or in the lay-by close to the ground
Admission: Matchday £8 incl. programme. NB All matches kick off at 3pm.
Clubhouse: Open matchdays & training nights. Snacks & barmeals available, burger bar at pitchside.
Functions: Capacity 80, contact David Robinson 01692 538808
Club Shop: Open match days, Sunday Mornings and Thurs. eve. (training night) during season.
Founded: 1968   **Nickname**: Vikings   **Website**: www.nwrfc.co.uk
Colours: Black, green & white; black shorts   **Change colours**: White, green & black.   **Training Nights**: Tuesday & Thursday
Programme: Size: A5   Pages: 32   Price: with entry   Editor & Advertising: Office 01692 538808

REVIEW OF THE SEASON 2008-09

North Walsham Vikings ended, what has been for them, a difficult season with a couple of home wins on the final two Saturdays of the campaign but from day one it had been hard going.

With new coaching teams in place albeit all ex Walsham players of some experience there were lessons to be learned by all sides of the club. Having stayed in the National leagues for eighteen seasons there was probabaly a bit of a mind set that 'this is how we have always done it'.

However, there was to be a rude awakening. With the nucleus of the 'old side' still in place it was to be hoped that there would be some stability, but injuries and players moving away led to too many changes in the side from week to week and a lack of cohesion. Lee Sandberg clocked up his 50th appearance and gained his first International Cap, for Sweden against Holland. A great achievement and possibly the first Walsham player to gain full cap whilst playing at Scottow.

Walsham was not just about the first team. The Raiders suffered by having 50% of their games cancelled. On the positive side this season has seen the rebirth of the clubs third string: The Warriors who won all, bar three, of their games and topped the Woodfordes Norfolk Merit table. Also Alan Hepburn was able introduce some of the Under 19s to senior rugby and three or four who started their season with The Warriors made to into the first team.

A mixed season but the nucleus of the side will be here next season and with local derbies with promoted Diss to look forward to, we can settle down to enoy a well earned break.

LAST TEN SEASONS

	Division	P	W	D	L	F	A	P.D.	Pts	Pos	Most Points		Most Tries	
99-00	N2S	26	19	0	7	792	358	434	38	3	167	Tony Kingsmill	21	James Shanahan
00-01	N3S	26	12	1	13	550	461	89	25	6	149	Phil Friel	9	Kenny Dodds
01-02	N3S	26	18	1	7	631	396	235	37	3	125	Len Wilmot	16	Andy Thorpe
02-03	N3S	26	16	0	10	636	479	157	32	4	167	Len Wilmot	21	Andy Thorpe
03-04	N3S	26	19	0	7	674	435	239	38	3	160	Matthew Holmes	17	Andy Thorpe
04-05	N3S	26	18	0	8	548	362	186	87	3	114	Chris Borrett	12	Tim Malone
05-06	N3S	26	21	0	5	826	403	423	104	2	224	Andrew Dickson	18	Andy Thorpe
06-07	N3S	26	14	1	11	515	607	-92	*66	7	100	Andy Thorpe	20	Andy Thorpe
07-08	N3S	26	6	0	20	384	711	-327	33	13r	60	Andy Thorpe	12	Andy Thorpe
08-09	Lon 1	22	7	1	14	316	481	-165	15	9				

OLD ALBANIANS R.F.C.

President	Adrian Tominey	email: ajt@rudwickhall.fsnet.co.uk
Chairman	Rory Davis	Tel: 07748 146521 (M) 01727 843538 (H) email: rory.davis@oarugby.com
Treasurer	Bryan Short	Tel: 01582 715588 email: bcbshort@hotmail.com
Club Secretary	Peter Lipscomb	35 Gurney Court Rd., St Albans, Herts AL1 4QU
League Contact		01727 760466 (H) 020 8784 5924 (B) email: peter.lipscomb@oarugby.com
Sponsorship Secretary	Peter Kilborn	Tel: 07767 67648 e mail: peter.kilborn@oarugby.com
Fixtures Secretary	Darren Ead	1 Canberra Close, St Albans, Herts. AL3 6LW
		Tel: 07746 399 818 (M) 01727 763284 (H) email: darren.ead@oarugby.com
Club Captain	Paul Quinn	Tel: 07736 237 675 email: paul.quinn@apexcontracts.co.uk
Director of Rugby	Bruce Millar	60 Wick Ave., Wheathampstead, Herts. AL4 8QA
		Tel: 07980 389 128 email: bruce.millar@oarugby.com
Website & Communications	Peter Buttle	Tel: 07836 763 608 email: peter.buttle@buttle.co.uk
Press & Publicity	Robin Farrar	8 Palfrey Close, St. Albans AL3 5RE email: robin.farrar@oarugby.com
		Tel: 01727 832621 (H) 07866 445832 (M)
Membership Secretary	John Parkinson	Tel: 01582 821315 (H) 07971 750054 (M)
		email: john.parkinson@oarugby.com

OA Saints (Womens Rugby Team) Tasha Saint-Smith (Chair), email: tasha.saint-smith@oarugby.com
Ground Address: The Woollams Playing Fields, 160 Harpenden Rd., St Albans, Herts.AL3 6BB
               Tel: 01727 864 476 (Clubhouse) Fax: 01727 737644
Directions: North on A1081 out of St Albans, towards Harpenden, on the right.
Capacity: 2,000   Covered: 200   **Admission**: £5 incl. programme
Car Parking: 250 spaces in main club car park.   **Nearest BR Station**: St Albans (Thameslink)
Clubhouse: 7am -11pm each day. Food available. For functions contact Neil Dekker (General Manager) 01727 864476
Club Shop: Open Monday through Thursday eves, Sat pm.
Programme Size: A5   Pages: 32   Price: with admission   Editorial & Advertising: Peter Kilborn
Founded: 1924   **Nickname**: OAs   **Training Nights**: Tues & Thur.   **Website**: www.oarugby.com
Colours: Gold, maroon & navy hoops.   **Change colours**: Navy with gold and maroon side panels.

REVIEW OF THE SEASON 2008-09

OA's celebrated their sixth successive season in London One with a creditable 5th position which reflected home and away 'doubles' against all three of their Herts. rivals and two, incredibly close encounters with ultimate league champions Shelford.

Their success in the County would have been even sweeter but for Bishops Stortford's fight back 'from the brink' to snatch the Herts. Presidents Cup from their grasp during extra time in the final.

OAs' achievements were founded on a bigger, and better, squad blossoming from the fruits of the Mini and Junior section and consolidated by some astute signings by Head Coach Bruce Millar who was ably supported by Mark Langley throughout the campaign.

Tryfan Edwards and Terry Adams formed a new and effective partnership in the centre whilst Aussie recruits Nathan Byrne and James Kriukelis proved to be valuable assets both on and off the field.

Jo Vassie and Jamie Hearn led the welcome charge of OA Colts into the senior squad where their development gained momentum alongside experienced campaigners such as ex Saracens, Gregg Botterman and Paul Gustard.

Richard Gregg, characteristically, topped the scoring with 235 points to his name and together with Adam Gelman, Paul Gustard and Mark 'The Power' Evans, helped Herts. to reach the final of The County Championship Shield at Twickenham in May.

Awards for the season went to Simon Lye (Best Player), Tryfan Edwards (Players' Player), Mark Evans (Most Improved Player) and Peter Nelson (Most Commited).

Team of the Season, once again went to Rob Kennedy's Colts for their achievements in reaching the County Cup final and the National final at Franklins Gardens.

The new found strength in depth percolated down the Clubs' playing talent and all four remaining senior mens' teams enjoyed a high level of success in their respective leagues.

Robin Farrar

LAST TEN SEASONS

Division	P	W	D	L	F	A	P.D.	Pts	Pos
98-99	Lon 2N	16	10	1	5	346	266	80	19*	7
99-00	Lon 2N	22	10	1	11	425	394	31	21	6
00-01	Lon 2N	22	13	0	9	524	350	174	24*	5
01-02	Lon 2N	22	18	1	3	611	309	302	37	2
02-03	Lon 1	22	9	1	12	382	417	-35	19	8
03-04	Lon 1	22	13	0	9	478	535	-57	26	5
04-05	Lon 1	22	8	1	13	448	542	-94	*15	10
05-06	Lon 1	22	9	0	13	450	676	-226	18	8
07-08	Lon 1	22	9	0	13	403	563	-160	18	8
08-09	Lon 1	22	12	0	10	496	387	109	24	5

PORTSMOUTH R.F.C.
All email addresses @portsmouthrugbyclub.co.uk

President: Peter Golding Tel: 02392 484979 email: president@
Chairman: Pip Robson Tel: 02392 593555 email: chairman@
Treasurer: George Cook Tel: 02392 370567 email: treasurer@
House & Facilities: Jim Dixon Tel: 07946 411601 email: house@
Club Secretary: Cathy Whapham, 41 Stakes Hill Road, Waterlooville, Hants. PO7 7LA
Tel: 07808 912401 email: secretary@
Rugby Manager & Fixture Secretary: Nigel Morgan Tel: 02392 358766 email: rugby@
Commercial Administrator: Roger Wingrove email: commercial@
Social Administrator: Bryn Roberts email: social@
Playing Administrator: Gary Hemmings email: playing@
Mini & Juniors Chairman: Gary Hemmings Tel: 07766 076954   **Womens Rugby:** Fred French Tel: 07765 886911
Ground Address: Rugby Camp, Norway Road, Hilsea, Portsmouth, Hants. PO3 5EP
Tel: 02392 660610 or 02392 617255 (answerphone) email: secretary@portsmouthrugbyclub.co.uk
Directions: From the A27, take A2030 towards Southsea. At first set of traffic lights take right turn, and continue straight over 2 roundabouts and bridge. Entrance to Rugby Camp car park is on left immediately after bridge.
Nearest BR station: Hilsea   **Car Parking:** 200 spaces
Capacity: Ample, all uncovered standing   **Admission:** Free
Clubhouse: Open on training evenings from 6 pm, and on match days from 12 noon. Clubhouse is available for private hire, contact Glenda Green, Tel 023 9282 6894 or email: royalecaterers@aol.com
Club Shop: In Junior Clubhouse Michelle Upton 07769 866966   **Programme:** Size:A5 Pages:20 Price: £3
Editorial & Advertising: Peter Golding, Tel: 02392 484979   Roger Wingrove Tel: 01489 890273
Founded: 1886   **Website:** www.portsmouthrugbyclub.co.uk   **Training Nights:** Tuesday & Thursday
Colours: Black jersey with white and yellow hoops   **Change colours:** Gold jersey with white & black

REVIEW OF THE SEASON 2008-09

Portsmouth 1st XV had a mixed season - buoyed by their achievements in the EDF Intermediate Cup run and eventually reaching the semi-finals, and delighted in the performance and capability of their Colts fulfilling 1st XV selection – but disappointed to finish 10th in London One due to some near miss defeats.

Ultimately an exciting year, and yet again Portsmouth remains a dogged contender for the coming season with the added excitement of achieving National 3 status. Head coach, Ian Chandler, continues to develop strength in depth with home-grown Colts, returning players and thoughtful recruitment in key areas. Development and extension of the facilities at Portsmouth during the 08 and 09 seasons have been, and will remain, an important factor in player recruitment and retention.

The 2nd XV again faced a tough season in the Canterbury Shield, but had notable wins against Staines, Rosslyn Park Devt, Basingstoke and Bournemouth which reinforce their aims of a top six finish in the 09/10 season. The 1st and 2nd teams remain managed and coached as one squad, all players are given the same opportunities for selection, and the standard of rugby continues to be promising.

The 3rd XV, playing in Hampshire's Senior Merit League, provide an enviable mix of experience and youth, which develop and nurture player' skills. The 4th XV and Veterans offer social rugby at its best. Portsmouth Veterans were yet again runners up in the Veteran's Cup, toured to Belgium and hosted a touring team from Yorkshire.

LAST TEN SEASONS

	Division	P	W	D	L	F	A	P.D.	Pts	Pos
99-00	Lon 3SW	16	13	0	3	563	173	390	26	3
00-01	Lon 3SW	16	15	0	1	541	140	401	30	1p
01-02	Lon 2S	22	18	1	3	769	291	478	37	2
02-03	Lon 2S	22	17	0	5	627	313	314	34	2
03-04	Lon 2S	22	12	0	10	515	498	17	24	5
04-05	Lon 2S	22	17	1	4	541	281	260	35	2
05-06	Lon 2S	22	18	1	3	724	308	416	37	1p
06-07	Lon 1	22	8	0	14	392	723	-331	16	9
07-08	Lon 1	22	11	0	10	513	467	46	23	6
08-09	Lon 1	22	7	0	15	341	583	-242	14	10

Our Colts, Junior and Mini sections fuel our home grown player development, culture and Club camaraderie. Portsmouth embraces all levels of rugby, player development and enthusiastic volunteers.

The Ladies XV, the Valkyries, celebrated their 10th year at Portsmouth RFC and are delighted to secure the services of Syd Street as coach for the coming season.

We look forward to welcoming all visitors to Rugby Camp during the next season.

SUTTON & EPSOM R.F.C.

President: Peter Jenkins   **Chairman**: Gerald Classey   **Vice Chairman**: Mark Felstead
Chairman – Mini & Junior Sections: Dave Steel
Director of Rugby: Simon Shaylor   **Head coach**: Terry O'Connor
Club Secretary: Nick Harries Tel: 07887 628927 (M)   email: nickharriesrugby@btinternet.com
Fixture Secretary: Iain Frazer, 111 Benhill Road, Sutton, Surrey SM1 3RR
Tel: 020 8643 4835 (H); 020 7542 8549 (W)   email: iain.frazer@thomsonreuters.com
1st XV Manager: Ian Lovatt   Tel: 07801 433412   email: ian.lovatt@blueyonder.co.uk
Commercial Manager: Laura Caldwell Tel: 07789 113965 (M)   email: laura.serfc@googlEmail.com
Ground: Cuddington Court, Rugby Lane, Cheam Surrey SM2 7NF
Tel: 020 8642 0280 email: club@suttonrugby.co.uk   **Website**: www.suttonrugby.co.uk
Directions: M25, J8. Northbound on A217 towards Sutton. Left at Cheam traffic lights, straight on at cross-roads. 200 yards past Nonesuch High School on the left.   **Nearest BR Station**: Cheam   **Car Parking**: 300
Capacity: General ground plus 250 covered seating   **Admission**: Match day - by programme only- £3
Clubhouse: Open 11am-11pm. Food available.
Function room: Fully licensed. Available for hire. Contact Laura Caldwell, Commercial Manager
Club Shop: Fully stocked with club branded and non branded kit and equipment. Operated on club premises. For opening hours pleasec check the club website.
Programme Editor: John Ashton   Tel: 07703 189661 (M)   email: o jmashton@btinternet.com
Founded: 1881   **Training Nights**: Senior men - Tues & Thur, Senior ladies - Wed, Mini & Junior – weekends
Colours: Black & white broad hoops.   **Change colours**: Light blue

REVIEW OF THE SEASON 2008-09

This was a season of great expectation that didn't quite match up to the level of anticipation – although there were some notable successes.

The 1st XV had a mixed season and crucially didn't win the 50/50 games which they had won in previous years. Whilst we seemed to enjoy a reasonable amount of possession we didn't convert this into points and all too often, we allowed ourselves to concede points when playing on the back foot. Our defence was put under great stress on too many occasions – and having the worst defensive record in London 1 tells its own story. It is obvious where one of our key improvement areas lies for the coming season.

Once again, it was the Vets side that showed the club how to play rugby – playing attractive attacking rugby and succeeding in winning the Evergreen Cup for the fourth successive time and playing in the seventh consecutive final – with six wins out of these seven appearances! Our 1st XV wrapped up the season with further success by winning – and retaining - the Surrey Cup and our U21s also gave great hope for the future by also winning and retaining their Surrey Cup.

Our senior ladies side had an excellent season winning their league. The Mini and Junior sections of the club continued to develop and flourish with numbers continuing to increase and the standards on and off the field continuing to excel. The growth of the mini and junior sections is a real area of challenge for the club – because the administrative and organisational burden is increasing considerably. However, we are fortunate to have enormous numbers of willing volunteers and helpers who make all things possible! We continue to see great strides being made throughout the two sections and there were many successes throughout season in every age group – too many to mention.

LAST TEN SEASONS

	Division	P	W	D	L	F	A	P.D.	Pts	Pos
99-00	Lon 1	16	10	1	5	323	374	-51	21	5
00-01	Lon 1	20	9	1	10	433	471	-38	19	7
01-02	Lon 1	22	13	2	7	478	388	90	28	3
02-03	Lon 1	22	11	0	11	417	406	11	22	5
03-04	Lon 1	22	16	0	6	462	401	61	32	3
04-05	Lon 1	22	5	0	17	405	658	-253	10	11r
05-06	Lon 2S	22	11	0	11	501	462	39	22	6
06-07	Lon 2S	22	21	0	1	721	205	516	42	1p
07-08	Lon 1	22	11	0	11	549	568	-19	22	7
08-09	Lon 1	22	6	0	16	482	626	-144	12	11

The whole club is fiercely committed to maximising the development of all our young members in the coming season, as we fully expect our young players to one day contribute to the success of the senior rugby club.

For the season ahead we welcome our new head coach, Terry O'Connor, and his fellow coaches of Jimmy Joyce and Jeff Parsons. We are focusing on taking rugby back to basics in 2009/10 and developing the many youngsters that we have at the club. Playing in National 3 London & South East, our 1st XV needs to consolidate their position in the league. We are looking forward to an exciting season.

TRING R.U.F.C.

President: Niels Hvass   **Chairman:** Martyn Kirk   **Treasurer:** Lee Stewart
Club Secretary: Deric Newman, 54 Icknield Way, Tring, Herts. HP23 4HZ
Tel: 01442 827204 07768 056590 (M) Fax: 01442 890275 email: deric@dericnewman.co.uk
Fixtures Secretary: Malcolm Rose, 25 Grenadine Way, Tring, Herts HP23 5EA
Tel: (H) 01442 381110 (M) 07949 056 243 01923 208961(B) Email: malcolm.rose@galderma.com
Press Secretary: Deric Newman, as Club Secretary
Director of Rugby: Derek Truselle   **Commercial Secretary:** John Ball
Mini & Junior - Chairman: John Harrison **Treasurer:** Charles Lewis **Fixture Sec.:** Karen Harrison
Ground Address: Pendley Sports Ground, Cow Lane, Tring, Hertfordshire HP23 5NS
Directions: From M25 take junction 20, onto A41, leave A41 at Tring turn off, at roundabout turn right towards Berkhamsted, first left into Cow lane, rugby club 200m on the right. See website for map.
Capacity: All uncovered standing   **Admission:** No charge
Nearest BR Station: Tring - 1/2 mile.   **Car Parking:** Ample at the ground.
Clubhouse: Available for private hire.
For further information please contact the Bar Manager, Christine Coppcutt on 01442 822216 or 07763 371569
Club Shop: Clubhouse shop opening times - 1st Thur of the month 7pm - 8pm, Sat. 1.30pm - 2.30pm on matchdays and Sunday 9.30am - 1pm. Online shop at www.tringrugby.com
Founded: 1963   **Website:** www.tringrugby.com   **Training Nights:** Tues & Thur (Seniors)
Colours: Black shirts with gold trim.   **Change colours:** Black and gold hoops   **Programme:** N/A

REVIEW OF THE SEASON 2008-09

After four promotions in five seasons the young team from Hertfordshire were wary of this step up – their greatest yet. However Tring's inaugural season in London One was a success by any measure.

Under Head Coach Jon Lambden the club shifted sights from a finish inside the top two to a achieving a league position above the relegation zone.

Defeat in the opening fixtures against Jersey and Luton showed what they would be facing before a run of three victories built the teams belief. However the autumn proved a torrid time as the team lost four successive games by less than a score. Tring struggled to find another victory as 2008 came to a close and the loosing streak extended to nine games. It was not until the last day of January that the team secured any more points with a hard fought victory at home to Portsmouth.

With the league restructure reducing the chances of relegation, Tring knew that four victories from the final seven games of the season would keep them clear of the bottom spot, no matter how teams below performed. In the end it their place in the league for 2009/10 was secured with reversals of the defeats in those opening fixtures - wins at home to Luton and away to Jersey, undoubtedly the high point of the season, for the excellent hospitality as much as the two points; results that showed of how much the team had improved over the season.

The club rounded the season off with an excellent win against Hertford and finished the season in 8th place. Winger Tim Holgate was the leagues leading try scorer.

The playing squad has been retained for the coming season with depth added from a strong second team, champions of Canterbury Shield Division Four.

LAST TEN SEASONS

	Division	P	W	D	L	F	A	P.D.	Pts	Pos
99-00	L 3NW	16	4	0	12	188	603	-415	8	15
00-01	L 4NW	20	2	0	18	266	650	-384	*2	10r
01-02	H&M 1	18	8	0	10	291	312	-21	16	5
02-03	H&M 1	18	10	2	6	409	224	185	22	4
03-04	H&M 1	16	14	1	1	353	140	213	29	1p
04-05	L 4NW	16	15	0	1	370	131	239	*28	1p
05-06	L 3NW	22	18	0	4	559	252	307	36	2p/po
06-07	L 2N	22	17	0	5	499	358	141	34	2
07-08	L 2N	22	18	1	3	558	310	248	37	1p
08-09	Lon 1	22	8	0	14	421	599	-178	16	8

LONDON & SOUTH EAST

601

BISHOP'S STORTFORD 2008-09

DISS 2008-09

DORKING 2008-09

LONDON PHOTO CALL

NORTH WALSHAM 2008-09

Back Row: John Baines (Team Manager). Ian East (Fitness) Dave Smith(Coach) Tom Browes.Mike Rout. Chris Kent. Iain Beck.Richie Howlett.Leon Davies.Josh Reeves.Peter Clifford. Gideon Strydom.J.Burroughs.Nick Greenhall (Coach).Tim Malone Coach. Tony Marcantonio (Media Officer).
Front Row: Shane van Vuuren.Alan Turner.Adie Ball.Lee Sandberg.Stuart Loose(c).Will Farrer.Iain Young.Gareth Hoadley.

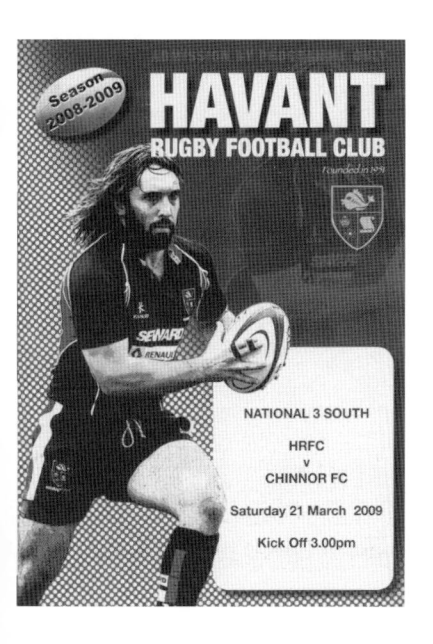

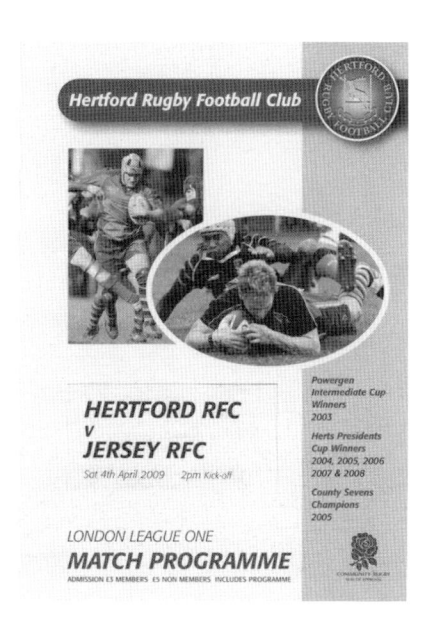

603

LONDON ONE NORTH

2008-09 LEAGUE TABLE London Two North

		P	W	D	L	F	A	PD	Pts	Adj
1	Diss	22	17	3	2	511	279	232	37	0
2	Staines	22	18	0	4	566	198	368	36	0
3	Bury St Edmunds	22	14	2	6	446	351	95	30	0
4	Civil Service	22	13	2	7	544	396	148	28	0
5	Chingford	22	12	1	9	450	269	181	25	0
6	Ruislip	22	12	0	10	399	426	-27	24	0
7	Eton Manor	22	8	3	11	354	395	-41	19	0
8	Woodford	22	9	1	12	489	548	-59	19	0
9	Letchworth Garden City	22	8	2	12	386	446	-60	18	0
10	Westcliff	22	6	1	15	300	484	-184	13	0
11	Stevenage Town	22	5	1	16	400	457	-57	11	0
12	Welwyn	22	2	0	20	188	784	-596	4	0

2009-10 FIXTURES GRID

	Brentwood	Bury St Edmunds	Chingford	Civil Service	Eton Manor	Harpenden	Letchworth G.C.	Rochford Hundred	Ruislip	Staines	Stevenage Town	Welwyn	Westcliff	Woodford
Brentwood		19/12	06/03	05/12	10/10	12/09	20/03	30/01	10/04	14/11	13/02	31/10	26/09	16/01
Bury St Edmunds	19/09		03/10	13/02	05/09	06/03	17/10	12/12	31/10	23/01	14/11	09/01	28/11	27/03
Chingford	07/11	16/01		12/09	24/10	26/09	10/04	20/02	19/12	05/12	20/03	13/03	10/10	30/01
Civil Service	27/03	24/10	12/12		13/03	30/01	09/01	28/11	10/10	19/09	03/10	05/09	20/02	07/11
Eton Manor	23/01	10/04	13/02	14/11		05/12	06/03	03/10	20/03	31/10	09/01	17/10	12/09	19/12
Harpenden	12/12	07/11	09/01	17/10	27/03		23/01	05/09	13/02	03/10	31/10	19/09	13/03	28/11
Letchworth Garden City	28/11	30/01	05/09	26/09	07/11	10/10		13/03	16/01	12/12	19/09	27/03	24/10	20/02
Rochford Hundred	17/10	12/09	31/10	20/03	16/01	10/04	14/11		05/12	06/03	23/01	13/02	19/12	26/09
Ruislip	05/09	20/02	19/09	23/01	28/11	24/10	03/10	27/03		09/01	17/10	12/12	07/11	13/03
Staines	13/03	10/10	27/03	19/12	20/02	16/01	12/09	07/11	26/09		05/09	28/11	30/01	24/10
Stevenage Town	24/10	13/03	28/11	16/01	26/09	20/02	19/12	10/10	30/01	10/04		07/11	27/03	12/09
Welwyn	20/02	26/09	14/11	10/04	30/01	19/12	05/12	24/10	12/09	20/03	06/03		16/01	10/10
Westcliff	09/01	20/03	23/01	31/10	12/12	14/11	13/02	19/09	06/03	17/10	05/12	03/10		05/09
Woodford	03/10	05/12	17/10	06/03	19/09	20/03	31/10	09/01	14/11	13/02	12/12	23/01	10/04	

BRENTWOOD R.F.C.

President: John Kerslake john.kerslake@brentwoodrugbyclub.com
Chairman: Kevin Ambrose **Treasurer:** Paul Kehoe **Clubhouse Manager:** Nigel Kirby
Club Secretary: John Smeaton, 16 Marston Beck Chelmsford Essex CM2 6RL
Tel: 07515 269674 email: jjej@btinternet.com
Fixtures Secretary: Paul Turner, 75 Victoria Road Brentwood CM14 5DR
Tel: 07890 8220663 email: paul.turner@brentwoodrugbyclub.com
Director of Rugby: Steve Killington Tel: 07771 926151 email: steve.killington@brentwoodrugbyclub.com
Youth Chairman: Bryn Williams email: bryn.Williams@brentwoodrugbyclub.com
Mini/Midi Chairman: John Tierney email: john.Tierney@brentwoodrugbyclub.com
Ground Address: King Georges Playing Fields, Ingrave Road, Brentwood CM13 2AQ Tel: 01277 210267 email: as Chairman
Directions: M25 Jct 28. Follow A1023 towards Brentwood town centre, along High Street to a double mini r'about. Right into Ingrave Road. Ground entrance is 0.75 mile on the right opposite" Masons Restaurant"
Capacity: All uncovered standing **Car Parking:** Ample **Nearest BR Station:** Brentwood
Clubhouse: Open training eves + Sat & Sun. Food available Sat & Sun in season. Available for private hire, contact Functions Coordinator Alison Jones 01277 229259 **Club Shop:** None.
Programme: Size: A5 Price: £2 incl. admission Advertising: Contact Elliot Shaw elliot.shaw@brentwoodrugbyclub.com
Founded: 1935 **Website:** www..brentwoodrugbyclub.co.uk
Colours: Claret, grey & white hoops, black shorts **Training Nights:** Tues & Thur. 7pm

BURY ST. EDMUNDS R.U.F.C.

President: Mr Michael Hemingway **Chairman:** Mr Phillip Torkington **Treasurer:** Anthony Mills
Hon Secretary: Simon Lord, Ashtrees, 32 Bury Road, Barrow IP29 5AB
Tel: (H) 01284 811 189 (W) 01394 613211 Email: Simon.Lord@defra.gsi.gov.uk
Fixtures Secretary: Mr Chris Wilbrahams, 3 Bear Meadow, Beyton, Bury St Edmunds. Suffolk. IP30 9HS
Tel: 01359 271592 email: Chris.wilbraham@tinyworld.co.uk
Team Secretary: Mr Mark Williams, 2 Mere Farm Cottages, Gt.Barton, Bury St Edmunds Tel: 01359 231021
Director of Rugby: Mr Terry Sands **Commercial Chairman:** Nigel Birrell 01284 763000 or 07860224425
Youth Chairman: Nigel Gossett. Copperfields Barn, Lawshall Road, Hawstead, nr Bury St Edmunds. IP29 5NR
Tel 01284 386764, 07791911282
Mini Chairman: Mr Andrew Spetch, 16 Tithe Close, Gazeley, Suffolk. CB8 8RS Tel: 01638 750134
Ground Address: The Haberden, Southgate Green, Bury St Edmunds, Suffolk IP33 2RN
Tel.: 01284 753120 email: enquiries@bserufc.org.uk **Website:** www.bserufc.co.uk/
Directions: Exit A14 at Bury East (A134 Sudbury Road) Ground 400m on right.
Capacity: 1,000 Seated: 200 **Car Parking:** 150 spaces at ground. **Nearest BR Station:** Bury St. Edmunds
Clubhouse: Open allday Sat & Sun & 5-10pm Mon-Fri. Food available. Available for private hire, contact Mark Eddison
Club Shop: Open Tues & Thur 7-8pm & Sun 10-1pm. Contact Kym Claridge c/o the club.
Colours: Green & gold banded shirst, black shorts & socks. **Change colours:** Various
Founded: 1925 **Nickname:** Wolves **Training Nights:** Tues & Thur 7pm (seniors); Wed 7pm (youth)
Programme: Size: A5 Pages: 6 Editorial & Advertising: Mr Martin Peacock Tel: 01284 761536 email: peacock@aol.com

CHINGFORD R.F.C.

President: John Garrett Tel: (H) 01992 307979 (M) 07855 025084 email: jpg59@hotmail.com
Director of Finance: Hayley Ford Tel: H) 020 8524 0904 (M) 07515051623 email: russ1001@btinternet.com
Club Secretary: Jeff Carratt, 24 Alpha Road, Chingford, E4 6TB
(H) 020 8524 2005 (M) 07793 956540 email: jeffrey.carratt@ntlworld.com
Fixture Secretary & Facilities: Ted Mills, 4 Laurel Gardens, Chingford, London E4 7PS
Tel: (H) 07930 882083 Email: TheMillsMob@ntlworld.com
Director of Rugby: Steve Slowik (H) 020 8529 6235 (M) 07775 678876
Junior Chairman: Aidan Little, 4 Poplar Shaw, Waltham Abbey, Essex, EN9 3NJ
Tel:(H) 01992 712734 (M) 07949038060 email: aidan.little@ntlworld.com
Ground Address: Lea Valley Playing Fields, Waltham Way, Chingford, London E4 8AQ
Tel: 020 8529 4879
Directions: M11 and then take A406 North Circular Road Westbound, after approx. 3 miles take A1009 exit signposted to Waltham Abbey/Chingford, last exit on r'about under A406 following A1009, Left at traffic lights following A1009, over mini r'about, Ground 1 mile on left. **Nearest BR station:** Chingford **Car Parking:** Yes.
Clubhouse: Contact: Ted Mills 07930 882 083 Email: Ted.Mills@chingfordrugby.co.uk **Club Shop:** Yes
Training Nights: Tuesday and Thursday; Juniors - Wednesday
Colours: Black, with Royal Blue and White hoops and socks. **Change colours:** Red.

CIVIL SERVICE F.C.

President: Mike Lee Tel: 07768 026472 **Chairman:** Stan Coats Tel: 07752 015143
Treasurer: Graham Clucas Tel:07850 750794 **Director of Rugby:** Nigel Rosser Tel: 07768 070503
Club Secretary: Nick Alway, 20, Herndon Road, London SW18 2DG
Tel: (H) 020 8870 6818 (M) 07831 142566 email: nickalwaysrugby@hotmail.com
Fixture Secretary: Ralph Hulme, 4 Beech Way, Blackmore End, Wheathampstead, Herts AL7 8LY
Tel: (H) 01438 832054 email: rlphhulme@aol.com
Team Secretary: Paul Tiller, 60, Dahomey Road, London SW16 6ND
Tel: (H) 020 8677 5284 (M) 07899 921903 email: paultiller@o2.co.uk
Ground Address: Duke's Meadows, Riverside Drive, Chiswick, London W4. Tel: 020 8994 1202
Directions: By Road: coming from the West, Staveley Gardens leads into Riverside Drive on the right off the A316 Chertsey Road before it meets the A4 at the Hogarth Roundabout: coming from Central London, or the East, take the A316 exit off the A4 at the Hogarth Roundabout, Staveley Gardens is on the left. **Nearest BR station:** Barnes Bridge
Capacity: 500 Covered: 20 **Admission:** £2 incl programme **Car Parking:** Ample
Programme: Size: A5 Pages: variable Price: with admission Editorial & Advertising: Contact Paul Tiller, as above
Founded: 1863 **Nickname:** 'Service' **Website:** www.civilservice-rugby.com
Colours: White **Change colours:** Blue **Training Nights:** Tuesday & Thursday

ETON MANOR R.F.C.

Chairman: Martin Pearl Tel: 07973 424139 email: mpearl@ntlworld.com
Treasurer: Paul Wilcocks
Club Secretary: Neil Taylor Tel: 07773 782608 (M) email: neil.taylor600@ntlworld.com
Fixtures Secretary: Ian Lovett Tel: 07720 414405
Director of Rugby: Ged White **Head Coaches:** Ian Edwards & Mark Cuschieri
Club Captain: Keith Munro Tel: 07881 82074
Youth Chairman: Terry Burton Tel: 07878 049571
Ground Address: The New Wilderness, Nutter Lane, Wanstead, London E11. Tel: 020-8532-2946 email: info@etonmanor.net
Directions: see website for map - www.etonmanor.net
Capacity: All uncovered standing **Car Parking:** Up to 150 cars **Nearest Station:** Wanstead (Underground Central Line)
Clubhouse: A modern building with 2 bars and extensive kitchen amenities. Open Tues, Wed & Thur 6.30-10.30pm, Sat 12-8pm & Sun 11am-3pm. Available for private hire catering for up to 300. Contact Joanne Connier Tel 07930 839151
Fully floodlit 1st team pitch available for evening hire.
Club Shop: Open Sundays 10.30am to 2pm or contact Steve Thompson 07786113202
Programme: £2 Editor and Advertising Terry Burton 07878 049571
Founded: 1928 **Website:** www.etonmanor.net **Training Nights:** Tues & Thur.
Colours: Navy blue with sky blue band **Change colours:** Yellow with navy blue

HARPENDEN R.F.C.

President: Peter Danby president@ **Chairman:** Jonathan Edwards chairman@ **Treasurer:** Rob Brown treasurer@
Club Secretary: Claire Mills, The Briars, 43 Ox Lane, Harpenden, Herts, AL5 4HF
Tel: 01582 462776 / 07940 535619 email: secretary@hrfc.com
Fixtures Secretary: Mark Lewis, 12 Holly Farm Close, Caddington, Beds, LU1 4ET
& Mini Chairman: Tel: 01582 410654 / 07939 824453 email: minis@hrfc.com
1st Team Manager: David Rapley, 19 Cowper Rd, Harpenden, Herts, AL5 5NF Tel: 07875 583373 email: Jdrapley19@aol.com
Head Coach: Alistair Barton email: director@hrfc.com
Director of Publicity: Simon Payne email: marketingandsponsorship@hrfc.com
Junior Chairman: Ian Cumming email: juniors@hrfc.com
Mini Fixtures Sec.: David Leigh email: david.leigh1@ntlworld.com
Ground Address: Redbourn Lane, Harpenden, Herts, AL5 2BA Tel: 01582 460711 email: secretary@hrfc.com
Directions: From M1 – Exit J9 take A5183 towards St Albans and Redbourn. Approx. 2 miles to roundabout. Take B487 left towards Harpenden. Club is 0.5 miles on the right. **From St Albans** – A1081 towards Harpenden. Approx 4 miles to roundabout. Take left turn for Redbourn. Club is about 1.5 miles on the left. **From Luton** – A1081 towards Harpenden. Approx 5 miles to major roundabout. Take right turn for Redbourn. Club is about 1.5 miles on the left.
Capacity: All uncovered standing. **Admission Free** **Car Parking:** Yes **Nearest Station:** Harpenden
Clubhouse: Available for private hire, contact John Hills 07785 960353 email: events@hrfc.com
Club Shop: Open Sun 9-1pm, Thur 7-8pm. Contact John Hills 07785 960353 **Training Nights:** Tues & Thur. 7.30pm
Founded: 1919 **Website:** www.hrfc.com **Colours:** Black with white stripes **Change colours:** Red

LETCHWORTH GARDEN CITY R.F.C.

President: Brian Burke **Chairman:** David Sharp **Treasurer:** Chris Marshall
Club Secretary: John Donegan, 24 Westholm, Letchworth Garden City, Herts. SG6 4JB
Tel: 01462 647721 email: john.donegan@ntlworld.com
Fixture Secretary: Peter Marsden, 23 Coppice Mead, Stotfold, Nr Hitchin, Beds. SG5 4JX Tel: 01462 835163
Director of Coaching: Mike Clements
Youth Chairman: Inder Johal
Ground Address: Legends Lane, Baldock Road, Letchworth Garden City, Hertfordshire SG6 2EN Tel: 01462 682554
Directions: Exit A1(M) at junction 9. Follow signs for Letchworth Garden City. At roundabout, take A505 towards Baldock. North Herts Leisure Centre is on right at next roundabout. **Nearest BR station:** Letchworth or Baldock.
Capacity: Unlimited uncovered standing **Admission:** By programme **Car Parking:** Ample
Clubhouse: open 12-12pm. food available on matchdays. Contact Peter Marsden.
Club Shop: Open Saturday & Sunday 12-6pm. Contact Mark Ellis. **Website:** www.letchworthrugby.com
Programme: Price; £2 incl. admission Editor: Chris Lunnon 07973 304747
Advertising: Contact Brian Burke Tel: 01462 422555, 07768 274037 (M)
Founded: 1924 **Nickname:** The Legends **Training Nights:** Tuesday & Thursday
Colours: Black & amber hoops, black shorts, black socks. **Change colours:** All black

ROCHFORD HUNDRED R.F.C.

President: Michael Drinkwater **Chairman:** Colin Wiseman **Treasurer:** Les Page
Club Secretary: Simon Wakefield, Meadowside, Tinnocks Lane, St. Lawrence bay, Southminster, Essex CM0 7NF
Tel: 01621 779900 email: simon@yellowadmiral.co.uk
Fixtures Secretary: Alan Gander, 7 Sovereign Heights, 17 Weir Pond Road, Rochford, Essex SS4 1AH
Tel: 07919 574668 email: alangander@btinternet.com
Team Secretary: Graham Pratt, 34 Appleyard Avenue, Hockley, Essex SS5 5AY
Tel: 01702 204348, 07751 455618 email: grahamgpratt@tiscali.co.uk
Director of Rugby: Dean Cutting **Youth Chairman:** Steve Cleare
Club Coaching Co-ordinator & Volunteer Co-ordinator: Davinia Sugden
Ground Address: Magnolia Road, Hawkwell, Essex SS4 3AD. Tel: 01702 544021 **Website:** www.rochfordrugby.com
Directions: From Rochford take Ashington Road to Rectory Road, then Magnolia Road by railway line
Car Parking: For 100 cars **Nearest BR Station:** Hockley
Capacity: 300 Seated: 50 **Matchday Admission:** £1.50
Clubhouse: Open Tues., Wed. & Thur 6-11pm; Sat/Fri 08.00-01.00.
Available for private hire, contact Keith Laver 07881 808224
Club Shop: Open Tues, Wed Thur 7-10pm, Sat & Sun 10-3pm. Contact Fred Webb 01702 207596
Founded: 1962 **Colours:** Black **Change colours:** White **Training Nights:** Tues & Thur.

RUISLIP R.F.C.

Chairman: Clive Parish Tel: 01895 852064 (M) 07769 748020
President: Adam Sharples Tel: 01895 475522; (M) 07973 654828
Treasurer: Bindi Sohi Tel: 07958 516162 (M) 01895 443828 (H)
Hon Secretary: Peter Osborne, 8 The Fairway, Ruislip, Middlesex HA4 0RT
Tel: 020 8582 3657 (H) 07860 759280 (M) email: peterosborne01@hotmail.com
Fixtures Secretary: Steve Hazell, 37 Wyteleaffe Close, Ruislip, Middlesex HA4 7SP Tel: (H) 01895 677779
(M) 07956 509980 (W) 0208 641 8710
Social Secretary: Denise Lacey Tel: 01895 678665 (M) 07904 605832
Rugby Manager: Neil Edwards Tel: 01895 813411 (M) 07881 511152
Ground Address: West End Rd, Ruislip, Middx HA4 6DR Tel.: 01895 633102 email: peterosborne01@hotmail.com
Directions: From the A40 turn off at the Polish War Memorial Junction - at Polish War Memorial roundabout take the 3rd exit onto West End Road - A4180 (signposted Ruislip) Entering South Ruislip. Go past R.A.F. Northolt Go past Ruislip Gardens Underground Station Continue until you come to a sharp double bend Before the mini-roundabout turn left into the Club Car Park **Nearest Station:** Ruislip Underground (Metropolitan & Picadilly lines)
Clubhouse: Available for private hire. Contact Chairman.
Formed: 1954 **Website:** www.ruisliprugbyclub.co.uk **Colours:** Maroon & white

STAINES R.F.C.

President: Tony Brightwell **Chairman:** Kevin Cloran **Treasurer:** Mike O'Reilly
Club Secretary: Kevin McMahon, 48 Ashley Park Avenue, Walton on Thames, Surrey KT12 1ES
Tel: 01932 244299, Mob: 07789 500752 email: kevinmcmahon249@btinternet .com
Fixture & Team Secretary: Jonathan Gibson, 24 South Road, Englefield Green, Egham, Surrey
Tel: 01784 477626, M 07764 580084 email: jonathangibson2@virgin.net
Director of Rugby: Bob Lawless **Commercial Secretary:** Kevin Cloran
Ground address: The Reeves, Snakey Lane (*formerly Feltham Hill Rd.*), Hanworth, Middlesex, TW13 7NB
Tel 0208 890 3051 0208 890 9885
Directions: Take Lower Feltham turnoff from A316. Towards Feltham, turn left into Snakey Lane. Ground is 1 mile on left. Full details & location map on the website.
Nearest BR Station: Feltham or Sunbury **Car Parking:** 250 spaces.
Capacity: Ample, all uncovered standing **Admission:** £5 incl. programme
Clubhouse: Open daily 12 noon-12 midnight. Food is available. Available for private hire contact Brett Schofield 07973 515341 brettcity@aol.com   **Club Shop:** Open matchdays. contact Brett Schofield.
Programme: Size: A5 Pages: 30 Price: with admission Editorial: Angie Channon 01793 787197 angietchannon@aol.com
Advertising: Contact Kevin Cloran 01753 642356
Founded: 1926 **Nickname:** Swans **Training Nights:** Tues & Thurs
Website: www.stainesrugby.co.uk **Club Colours:** Blue & red **Change colours:** light blue

STEVENAGE TOWN R.F.C.

Chairman: Steve Mudd **Treasurer:** Neil Wilson
Hon Sec: Tracy Dean, c/o the clubhouse
Tel: (M) 07738 833372 email: tracy.dean7@ntlworld.com
Fixtures Sec: Fred McCarthy 48 Fennel Drive, Biggleswade, Beds. SG18 8WD
Tel: 01767 221343, 07802 462913 (M) email: fred.mccarthy@ntlworld.com
Ground Address: The Clubhouse, North Road, Old Stevenage, Herts. SG1 4BB
Tel: 01438 359788 email: s.mudd@swifthorsman.co.uk
Directions: Leave A1(M) at Stevenage North, junction 8, take exit road towards Graveley, turn first right (after Garden Centre) towards Stevenage on B197. Ground 400yds on right, parking on access road by pitches. Ground is immediately behind Lister Hospital.
Nearest BR Station: Stevenage **Parking:** 60 cars
Admission: None - only special events.
Club Shop: Open Sunday 11.30-1pm - other times by appointment
Colours: Black shirts, with amber hoop edged with green, black shorts.
Change colours: Black, green & amber quarters
Founded: 1995 **Nickname:** Stags **Website:** www.stevenagerugby.com

WELWYN R.F.C.
President: Nick Waldock   **Chairman:** Bob Swindell Tel: 01707 324337   **Treasurer:** Roger Freeman Tel: 01707 882953
Hon Secretary: Malcolm Tucker, Leazes End, 2 Sandy Close, Hertford, Herts. SG14 2BB
Tel: (H) 01992 583369   email: malcolm.tucker@btinternet.com
Fixture & Team Secretary: Ian Atkinson, 35, Broomhills, Welwyn Garden City, Herts. AL7 1RE
Tel: (H) 01707 334130   email: isatkinson1@ntlworld.com
Club Coaches: Andy Riley, Tel: 07968 821805; Phil Waters, Tel: 07525 762810   **1st Team Captain:** Simon Banks
1st Team Manager: Ian Cousins 50, Chequers, Welwyn Garden City, Herts. AL7 4SJ Tel: 01707 897850
Ground Address: Hobbs Way, Colgrove, Welwyn Garden City, Herts AL8 6HX   Tel.: 01707 329116
Directions: A1(M) J4, Follow signs to Gosling Stadium, bear left into Parkway, left at next roundabout into Turmore Dale then first left into Colgrove and first right into Hobbs Way.   **Nearest BR station:** Welwyn Garden City
Capacity: Unlimited uncovered standing.   **Admission:** No charge   **Car Parking:** Ample
Clubhouse: Open Match days, Sundays and training nights. Food available Saturdays and Sundays after games. Available for private hire, contact Secretary.   **Club Shop:** Open Wed. 6-8 pm; Sat 12-2pm and Sun 9-12 am
Founded: 1931   **Training Nights:** Tues & Thur 7-9pm   **Website:** www.welwynrugby.co.uk   **Programme:** None
Colours: Maroon & white hoops, navy shorts, maroon & white socks   **Change colours:** Navy blue with maroon and white shirts.

WESTCLIFF R.F.C.
President: Chris Bard   Tel: 07879 622870   email: cbard@tolhurstfisher.com
Chairman: Rick Compton   Tel: 07875 168181   email: rick.compton@blueyonder.co.uk
Treasurer: Nigel Roskams   Tel: 07748 166533   email: Nigel.roskams@rbs.com
Bar and Facilities Manager: Len Radley   Tel: 07832 190245   email: len_radley@yahoo.co.uk
Director of Rugby & Club Coach: Bob Smith   Tel: 07887 833757   email: smithies5@btopenworld.com
Hon Secretary: Marcus Peters   Tel: 07966 369148   email: marcusstpeters@tiscali.co.uk
Ground Address: The Gables, Aviation Way, Southend-on-Sea, Essex SS2 6UN
Club House: 01702 541199   Fax: 01702 533917   Email: admin@westcliffrfc.co.uk
Directions: Approaching Southend on the A127, take the slip road off, following signs to Rochford, as you approach the Tesco superstore. At the r'about turn right (3rd exit). At the next r'about go straight on (2nd exit, care! Rochford is signposted left). At the next mini r'about take the first exit, left, into Aviation Way. The Gables is on your left after the sharp right bend.
Clubhouse: Available for private hire.   **Club Shop:** Contact Kay Duncombe
Formed: Formally Old Westcliffians RFC incorporated 1922   **Website:** www.westcliffrfc.co.uk
Training Nights: Seniors -Tuesday & Thursday
Colours: Maroon & old gold hoops/blue shorts/maroon socks

WOODFORD R.F.C.
President: Richard Berry   **Chairman:** Colin Granger   **Treasurer:** Joanne Coates
Club Secretary: Paul James, 46 Suffield Road London E4 9TA Tel: 020 8524 9658 email: paul.jwrfc@ntlworld.com
Fixtures Secretary: Graham Kane, 134 Wallwood Road, London, E11 1AN Tel: 020 8539 0390 email: kanegraham@aol.com
Director Of Rugby: Peter Christie   **Mini Chairman:** Ian Lillywhite   **Youth Chairman:** Charles Price
Chairman of Playing Committee: Andrew Whittaker   **Club Steward:** Susan Fox
Ground Address: "Highams", High Road, Woodford Green, Essex, IG8 9LB. Tel: 020 8504 6769
Directions- By Car: A406 north circular road to junction with the A104 (known locally as waterworks roundabout). Take A104 north signposted to Woodford Green and Epping. Go straight passing the Napier Arms to the triangle. The entrance to the ground is on the left opposite the Green before the traffic lights.   **By tube:** Victoria line to Walthamstow Central then a bus to the Castle, Woodford Green OR Central Line to Woodford. Turn left out of station into Snakes Lane West walk to Woodford High Road turn left at lights (opposite The Castle) the ground entrance is on the right
Capacity: All uncovered standing   **Car Parking:** 50 spaces   **Nearest BR Station:** Walthamstow Central
Clubhouse: Open training days, Sat. and Sun. in the playing season. Food is available.
Avaailable for private hire - contact Club Steward, Susan Fox. **Club Shop:** Open Saturday before matches & Sunday mornings
Programme: Size: A5   Price: £2   Editorial & Advertising: Colin Granger email: grangerc@hotmail.co.uk
Founded: 1924   **Website:** www.woodfordrfc.co.uk
Colours: Lavender, black & white.   **Change colours:** Red   **Training Nights:** Tuesday & Thursday

LONDON ONE SOUTH

2008-09 LEAGUE TABLE London Two South

		P	W	D	L	F	A	PD	Pts	Adj
1	Basingstoke	22	18	1	3	641	216	425	37	0
2	Dorking	22	16	3	3	772	266	506	35	0
3	Cobham	22	15	1	6	506	297	209	31	0
4	Gravesend	22	14	1	7	465	341	124	29	0
5	Dover	22	11	3	8	454	299	155	25	0
6	Chobham	22	11	1	10	443	379	64	23	0
7	Old Colfeians	22	9	2	11	345	377	-32	20	0
8	Sidcup	22	9	1	12	344	437	-93	19	0
9	Tunbridge Wells	22	7	2	13	355	528	-173	16	0
10	Thanet Wanderers	22	6	1	15	355	650	-295	13	0
11	Beckenham	22	6	0	16	314	594	-280	12	0
12	Maidstone	22	2	0	20	209	819	-610	4	0

2009-10 FIXTURES GRID

	Aylesford Bulls	Beckenham	Chichester	Chobham	Cobham	Dover	Gravesend	Maidstone	Old Colfeians	Old Elthamians	Sidcup	Thanet Wanderers	Tunbridge Wells	Wimbledon
Aylesford Bulls		10/10	19/09	09/01	03/10	28/11	30/01	24/10	07/11	13/03	05/09	20/02	27/03	12/12
Beckenham	23/01		09/01	03/10	17/10	27/03	24/10	20/02	13/03	28/11	12/12	07/11	05/09	19/09
Chichester	19/12	26/09		12/09	05/09	07/11	16/01	10/10	24/10	20/02	28/11	30/01	13/03	27/03
Chobham	26/09	16/01	12/12		19/09	13/03	10/10	30/01	20/02	07/11	27/03	24/10	28/11	05/09
Cobham	16/01	30/01	10/04	19/12		10/10	20/02	13/03	12/09	26/09	07/11	27/03	24/10	28/11
Dover	20/03	05/12	06/03	14/11	23/01		10/04	12/09	26/09	16/01	13/02	19/12	17/10	31/10
Gravesend	17/10	13/02	03/10	23/01	31/10	05/09		07/11	28/11	27/03	19/09	13/03	12/12	09/01
Maidstone	13/02	31/10	23/01	17/10	14/11	12/12	06/03		27/03	05/09	09/01	28/11	19/09	03/10
Old Colfeians	06/03	14/11	13/02	31/10	12/12	09/01	20/03	05/12		19/09	23/01	10/04	03/10	17/10
Old Elthamians	14/11	20/03	31/10	06/03	09/01	03/10	05/12	10/04	19/12		17/10	12/09	23/01	13/02
Sidcup	10/04	12/09	20/03	05/12	06/03	24/10	19/12	26/09	10/10	30/01		16/01	20/02	14/11
Thanet Wanderers	31/10	06/03	17/10	13/02	05/12	19/09	14/11	20/03	05/09	12/12	03/10		09/01	23/01
Tunbridge Wells	05/12	10/04	14/11	20/03	13/02	30/01	12/09	19/12	16/01	10/10	31/10	26/09		06/03
Wimbledon	12/09	19/12	05/12	10/04	20/03	20/02	26/09	16/01	30/01	24/10	13/03	10/10	07/11	

AYLESFORD BULLS R.F.C.

Hon. President: Andy Smith Tel: 07718 780060 email: hon.president@aylesfordbullsrugby.com
Chairman: Roger Williams   **Treasurer:** Clive Osborne
Hon. Secretary: Mrs Michele Mayhew; 113 Discovery Drive, Kings Hill, West Malling, Kent ME19 4DS
Tel: 01732 872339   07759385005 email: mdmayhew@btopenworld.com
Fixture Secretary: Dick Hooper Tel: 0711 491568   email: mensfixturesecretary@aylesfordbullsrugby.com
Director of Rugby: Neil Wiltshire
Commercial Secretary: Simon Williams
Ground Address: The Jack Williams Ground, Hall Road, Aylesford, ME20 7DS
Tel: 01622 790380 email: secretary@aylesfordbullsrugby.com
Directions: Leave M20 at J 5 and proceed to the next r'about (A20) approx. 500m. At the A20 r'about take 2nd exit (right) towards Aylesford. Go over the first set of traffic lights and move into right hand lane. At the next lights (Sainsbury's on left) turn right in to Hall Rd. Follow Hall Road until you pass under the M20, Aylesford RFC next right. **Please Note** - When entering the ground there is a strict 20mph speed limit along the drive.
Capacity: All uncovered standing   **Car Parking:** For 100 cars and 5 coaches
Nearest Station: Aylesford station in on the Maidstone West and Strood line
Clubhouse: Available for private hire. Contact Sue Robbins 01622 790380
Founded: 1975   **Website:** www.aylesfordbullsrugby.com
Colours: Red   **Change colours:** None   **Training Nights:** Mon & Thur (1st & 2nd XV).

BECKENHAM R.F.C.

President: William Sumner   **Chairman:** Paul Skelly   **Treasurer:** David Hepworth
Club Secretary: Tony Spong: 26 Glanfield Road, Beckenham, Kent, BR3 3JU
Tel (H): 020 8658 5189   (M) 07872 603771   email: tony.spong@ntlworld.com
Fixture Sec.: John Arger, 15 Thatcher Rd, Staplehurst, Kent TN12 0ND   Tel: (H) 01580 891550   email: Argerjm@aol.com
Team Secretary: Ken Hill Tel: (H) 020 8650 4101, (M) 07956 571606 email khill@phd.co.uk
Playing & Coaching: Paul Skelly, 45 Hayes Lane, Bromley BR2 9EE Tel: 07802 211779 email: skel@ntlworld.com
Ladies Section: Lorraine Hooton Tel (H) 020 8658 2963
Youth Chairman: Guy Landymore Tel (H) 020 8289 5178 (M) 07710 019040 email landymore@ntlworld.com
Marketing & advertising contact: Kevin O'Connell, 3 Howden Road, London SE25 4AS Tel: 020 8771 6804, 07850 009212 (M)
Ground Address: Balmoral Ave., Elmers End, Beckenham, Kent BR3 3RD Tel: 0208 650 7176 email: beckenhamrfc@hotmail.com
Directions: Entrance in Balmoral Avenue which runs between Eden Park Avenue & Upper Elmers End Rd. (A214). From bottom of Beckenham High Street take Croydon Rd. (A222), take the 6th turning on the left into Eden Park Av and then the 2nd on the right into Balmoral Avenue.   **Car Parking:** 100 on site   **Nearest BR & Croydon Tramlink station:** Elmers End & Beckenham Junction
Capacity: Uncovered standing   **Admission:** Free
Clubhouse: Open match days & Tues and Thurs pm (after training). Bar snacks available on match days. Clubhouse available for private hire; contact House and Grounds Manager, Brian Worboys (M) 07969 290530 email beckenhamrfc@hotmail.com
Club Shop: Open Sat all day & Sun am during playing season. Contact Desmond Walsh
Programme: Size: A5   Pages: 4   Price: £1   Editor: Kevin O'Connell   **Founded:** 1894   **Website:** www.beckenhamrfc.co.uk
Colours: Royal Blue & Old Gold   **Change colours:** Black and green   **Training Nights:** Tues & Thur 7.30–9.30pm

CHICHESTER R.F.C.

President: Alan Bradford **Chairman:** Keith Martin **Treasurer:** Paul Stanton
Club Secretary: Adam Davies, 33 Graydon Avenue, Chichester, West Sussex PO19 8RF
Tel: 01243 778406   email: adam.davies40@btinternet.com
Fixtures Secretary: Nigel Creasy, 2 Laburnham Grove, Chichester PO19 2EL
Tel: 07824 631623   email: nigel.creasy@cps.gsl.gov.uk
Team Secretary: Paul Colley Tel: 07940 950606   email: paul.colley@onearmymarketing.co.uk
Director of Rugby: Paul Colley, as above
Ground Address: Oaklands Park, Wellington Road, Chichester PO19 6BB   Tel: 01243 778406
Directions: Oaklands Park is near The Festival Theatre in Broyle Road to the north of Chichester centre. (Chichester to Midhurst Road). Turn right into Wellington Road and club entrance 100m on right
Capacity: 500, all uncovered standing   **Car Parking:** For 200 cars   **Nearest Station:** Chichester
Clubhouse: Open on matchdays only. Snacks available. Available for private hire, contact Mary Phillips 07957 886918
Club Shop: Open matchday, contact Mary Phillips, as above.
Programme: Size A5, Pages 4, free with admission.
Founded: 1926   **Nickname:** The Blues   **Website:** www.chichesterrfc.co.uk
Colours: Dark blue with light blue sash   **Change colours:** Light blue   **Training Nights:** Mon. & Thur.

CHOBHAM R.F.C.

President: Dick Fuller   **Chairman:** Vince Kerr   **Treasurer:** Peter Midson
Hon Secretary: Nigel Heslop, 98 Broad Street, Guildford, Surrey GU3 3BE
Tel: (H) 01483 535 840   (M) 07787 523 478   (Fax) 01483 850 345   Email: nigel@heslop6.demon.co.uk
Fixtures Secretary: Stephen Fisher
Tel: (M) 07817 571213   email: stephen.fisher@ntlworld.com
Director of Rugby: Harry Norman-Walker Tel: 07976 439 499 (M)
Commercial Manager: Mike Vandenberg Tel: 07774 120665
Communications Manager: Drew Davy Tel: 01344 873819
Ground Address: Fowlers Wells, Windsor Road, Chobham, Woking, Surrey GU24 8LD
Tel.: 01276-858616   email: admin@chobham-rugby.co.uk   **Website:** www.chobham-rugby.co.uk
Directions: From the M25, take J11 A320 Woking. At The Otter 3rd exit A319. 3.5 miles, past Fairoaks. At T-junction in Chobham, right into Windsor Road (B383). 0.2 mile, right opposite swimming pool shop.
From M3 J3 A322 Woking. Next roundabout, 1st exit A319 Chobham. -2.5 miles. Roundabout in Chobham, left (A319) High Street/Windsor Road. 0.5 miles- right opposite swimming pool shop.
Clubhouse: Open Tues & Thur eves., Sat & Sun.
For clubhouse hire please contact John Keywood on 01483 475495 or 07910 884237.
Founded: 1968   **Colours:** Dark blue with red & gold hoops   **Training Nights:** Tuesday & Thursday

COBHAM R.F.C.

Club Chairman: Tony Balkwill   **Treasurer:** Paul Cragg
Honorary Secretary: Richard Hornby; 23 Elm Tree Avenue, Esher, Surrey KT10 8JG
Tel: 0208 872 8801   email: richard.hornby@lynch-hall.co.uk
Fixture Secretary: Matt Lunn, 60 Ember Farm Way, East Molesey, Surrey KT8 0BL
Tel: 07876 546303 (M)   email: lunnmj@hotmail.com
Social Secretary: Claire McQuade
Ground Address: Cobham R.F.C., Old Surbitonians Memorial Sports Ground, Fairmile Lane, Cobham, Surrey KT11 2BU
Tel: 01932 863245   email: richard.hornby@lynch-hall.co.uk
Directions: The ground is a few minutes drive off the M25 Junction 10, north bound A3. See website for map.
Old Portsmouth road south from Esher approx 2.5 mls. Fairmile Lane is on left approx 400 mtrs after passing over the A3.
Clubhouse Manager: Bob Spavin Tel: 07740 825849
Club Shop: Open senior home matchdays and Sundays 10-12.30 during the season. Contact David Small
Colours: Blue, maroon & gold
Website: www.cobham-rugby.fsnet.co.uk
Formed: 1930 as Old Surbitonians, name changed 1989

DOVER R.F.C.

Chairman: Dick Catt Tel: 01304 852143   **Youth Chairman**: Paddy Mc Adam Tel: 07771 593619
Hon Secretary: Ray Biggs Biggs Opticians, 7 High Street, Dover, Kent CT16 1DP
Tel: (W) 01304 201000   email: raymond@biggsopticians.co.uk
Fixtures Secretary: Richard Dight, 15 Pauls Place, Dover, Kent CT16 2LD
Tel: 07734 605659 (M)   email: richard.dight@ntlworld.com
Ground Address: Crabble Athletic Ground, Crabble Road, River, Dover, Kent CT17 0JB
Contact Number: 01304 210296   email: rjc@doverrfc.co.uk
Directions: See website for detailed map, or briefly as below.
From M2/A2, at Esso garage take River exit, left at mini r/about, sharp right at lights, 300m on left.
From M20/A20 leave Dover on Canterbury Road, fork left at lights on Crabble Hill, 300m on left.
Clubhouse: Open Sat. matchdays from 2pm, Sunday lunch and Thur. early eve. Avilable for private hire, contact Howard Beardsell 01304 827784.

Club Shop: Open Sunday morning

Colours: Light & dark blue hoops

Website www.doverrfc.co.uk

GRAVESEND R.F.C.

President: Rodney Bardell   **Chairman**: Graham Haggar   **Treasurer**: Ms Gleny Johnston
Honorary Secretary: Rodney Baker, 25 The Downage, Gravesend, Kent DA11 7NB
Tel: (H) 01474 354076   email: abonnemalodge@btinternet.com
Fixtures Secretary: John Mather, 55 Lewis Road, Istead Rise, Gravesend, Kent DA13 9JQ
Tel: (M) 07841 671935   email: johnmather36@yahoo.com
Chairman of Grounds: Graham Russell
International Ticket Contact: John McKay, 28 Worcester Close, Istead Rise, Kent DA13 9JQ - Tel: 01474 833347
Ground Address: Rectory Field, Donald Biggs Drive, Milton Road, Gravesend, Kent DA12 2TL
Tel: 01474 534 840   email: as Secretary   **Website**: www.gravesendrfc.co.uk
Directions: M25 A2 intersection, head towards Dover, leave A2 at Gravesend East (Valley Drive), follow 1.75 mile to end, right at junction, proceed to roundabout, 1st exit - left, ground 0.75 mile on left, opposite G&M Motors.
Clubhouse: Open 7 days a week. The Clubhouse comprises 3 areas - the Main Hall, the Lounge Bar and the Players' Bar. The Main Hall and the Players' Bar are both available for hire, for further details and to make a booking, call 01474 534840 and ask for Steward, Mr Peter Ramsay. The Main Hall has a well-stocked bar, its own toilet facilities, a capacity of 250, seating area and a raised stage area.

Colours: Black and white broad horizontal bands   Change Colours: ????????

MAIDSTONE R.U.F.C.

President: Trevor Langley   **Chairman:** Wendy Pound 07801 545810   **Treasurer**: Dave Coleman
Club Secretary: Tom Challis, 72 Roseacre Lane, Bearsted, Maidstone, Kent ME14 4JG
Tel: (H) 01622 631 083 (M) 07990 891068 (W) 01322 297 000. Email: tjc@vizardswyeth.com
Fixture Secretary: Richard Ewence, Shalom, 71 Tonbridge Road, Maidstone, Kent ME16 8SA
Tel: (H) 01622 661346 07710 153463 (M) Email: richewence@supanet.com
Fixtures Secretary (Minis Section): Colin Denton Tel: 01622 726334 email: colin.denton.bt.com
Fixtures Secretary (Youth Section): Steve Vickers Tel: 01622 630552 (H), 07774 710041 (M)
Fist Team Coach: Tim McBennett 07956 295838.   **Director of Rugby**: Andy Golding 07950 337347
Ground Address: The William Day Mem. Ground, The Mote, Willow Way, Maidstone, Kent ME15 7RN
Tel: 01622 754 159 Fax: 01622 687378   Email: enquiries@maidstonerugby.org.uk
Directions: From M20 J7 Proceed 1-2 miles on A249 towards Maidstone at R/about keep left onto A20. 100yds to traffic lights turn right to Square Hill turn left at mini r/about into Mote Avenue.

Club Shop: Yes, see online

Founded: 1880.   **Website**: www.maidstonerugby.org.uk

Colours: Red, White & Black Hoops.   **Training Nights**: Tuesday and Thursday

OLD COLFEIANS RFC

President: John Nunn email: john@nunny.co.uk   **Chairman:** Dick Hussey email: dick.hussey@btinternet.com
Hon. Treasurer: Clive Corlett email: mccorlett@btinternet.com   **Sponsorship:** Clive Corlett
Hon. Secretary: Dave Baker, 4 The Chestnuts, St Pauls Cray Rd., Chislehurst BR7 6QD
Tel: 0208 467 0276   email: mrdavidbaker@hotmail.com
Hon. Fixture Sec.: David Nunn, 2 Springfield, Old Oxted, Surrey, RH8 9JL Tel: 07811 955478 email: david@nunny.co.uk
Team Secretary: Steve Hughes, 13 Perch Close, Leybourne Lakes, Larkfield, Kent, ME20 6TD
Tel: 07776 166161 email: steven.hughes@marksandspencer.com
Chairman Playing Committee: Brian Edwards Tel: 07802 804668 email: brianedwards1149@aol.com
Address: Horn Park, Eltham Road, Lee, London SE12 8UE   Tel: 0208 852 1181   **Website:** ocrfc.co.uk
Directions Ground is in Eltham Road opposite Weigall Road, on the A20, 600 metres in the direction of Lee, Lewisham and London from the intersection of the A20 / A205 / South Circular Road.   **Nearest BR Station:** Lee 10-15 min. walk.
Capacity: 1110   Covered Seating: 110   **Admission** £3 incl. prog. & parking Season: n/a   **Car Parking:** 100 at club
Clubhouse Mon-Fri 7-11pm, Sat 12-11 & Sun 12-3.   Food available matchdays only.   Functions: contact Julie McIntosh 07896 504112 email: juliemack68@btinternet.com   **Club Shop** Contact Christine Bailey email: sj.bailey1@btinternet.com
Founded: 1928   **Nickname:** O.Cs   **Colours:** Navy blue, burgundy, old gold & black bands
Change colours: Old gold with single narrow navy, burgundy & black bands   **Training Nights:** Tues & Thur, 7.30
Programme: A5, 40 pages, with admission Editor: Paul Wainman Tel: 01959 524351   email: wainmanpc22@yahoo.co.uk

OLD ELTHAMIANS R.F.C.

Chairman: Nick Burne
Club Secretary: David Clent, 64 Rochester Drive, Bexley, Kent DA5 1QA
Tel: 01322 529433   email: davidclent@hotmail.com
Fixtures Secretary: David Organ, 33 St. Marys Avenue, Shortlands, Bromley, Kent BR2 0PU
Tel: 020 84642542   email: dave.organ@sky.com
Director of Rugby: Alex Natera   **Club Captain:** Mike O'Connell
Commercial Director: Nick Warren
Minis Chairman: Alan Farmer Tel: 01689 872454 email: farmeram@aol.com
Youth Chairman: Stuart White Tel: 020 8851 1285 email: s_white_oe@yahoo.co.uk
Ground Address: Old Elthamians Sports Club, Foxbury Avenue, Perry Street, Chislehurst, Kent BR7 6HA   Tel: 0208 467 1296
Directions: From Junction 3 of the M25: At the roundabout take the 4th exit onto the A20, merge onto the A20 (signposted Lewisham). At Crittall's Corner continue forward (Warning: Speed Cameras along the A20). At Frognal Corner turn left off the A20, then at the roundabout take the 1st exit onto the A222 (signposted Bromley, Chislehurst). Turn right onto Foxbury Avenue and continue to the end to reach the club. See website for location map.
Capacity: All uncovered standing   **Car Parking:** Plenty at the ground   **Nearest Station:** Chislehurts
Founded: 1911   **Website:** www.oldelthamiansrfc.com
Colours: Royal blue and amber   **Training Nights:** Monday 7.30 and Wednesday 7.45pm

SIDCUP R.F.C.

President: Charles E R Prewer   Tel: (H) 020 8300 6088 email c.prewer@virgin.net
Chairman: Ian Anderson Tel: 0208 298 7753 email: ianderso@lehman.com
Treasurer: Dave Price, 13 Elmwood Drive, Bexley, Kent DA5 3PT.   Tel: (M) 07768 532034,   email dp@dpsplc.com
Hon Secretary: Paul Edwards, 14 Oak Apple, Gables Close, Lee, London SE12 0UB
Tel: 07949 548455   email: Paul.Edwards@ipitomi.com
Fixtures Secretary: Tom Lyons   Tel: (H) 020 8852 7342   email: t.lyons@btopenworld.com
Team Secretary: Tom Lyons as above
Director of Rugby: Phil West   Tel: (M) 07740 065089   email pj_west@hotmail.com
Ground Address: Crescent Farm, Sydney Road, Sidcup, Kent DA14 6RA
Tel.: 020 8300 2336   email: info@sidcuprfc.com   **Website:** www.sidcuprfc.co.uk
Directions: A20-A222 towards Sidcup (Chislehurst Rd), proceed to 1st set of traffic lights (Police Station), left into Main Road, left just past fire station into Sydney Road, ground 200 metres on left.
Nearest BR Station: New Eltham or Sidcup   **Car Parking:** 700
Capacity: 250.   Covered Seating: 100.   **Admission:** £2 by programme
Club Shop: Open Sat 12-2pm, Sun 10-12.30pm Contact Kathy Hill   07939 543888 email: juniorchair@sidcuprfc.com
Founded: 1883   **Nickname:** 'Cup'   **Training Nights:** Tuesday and Thursday
Colours: White shirts with navy blue & maroon trim, maroon shorts.   **Change colours:** Maroon.

THANET WANDERERS R.U.F.C.
President: Neil Armstrong   Chairman: Dave Whitehead   Treasurer: Andrew Watson
Club Secretary & Fixture Secretary: Peter Hawkins 51 Park Road, Ramsgate, Kent CT11 9TL
Tel: 01843 593142 (H & Fax)   07967 086232 (M)   e-mail: peterhawkins2000@yahoo.co.uk
Team Secretary: Michelle McLean, 5 St Lawrence Chase, Ramsgate, Kent CT11 0RD
Tel: 01843 599143 (H), 07890 663168 (M)   email: michelle.mclean@pfizer.com
Commercial Secretary: Alex Feeney Tel: 07816 492817   email: ajjf@hotmail.co.uk
Director of Rugby: Tom Carlier Tel: 01843 601126. 07734 602985(M)
Ground Address: St Peters Recreation Ground, Callis Court Road, Broadstairs, Kent CT10 3AE
Tel: 01843 866763   email: thanetwanderers@btinternet.com
Directions: A2 M2, A299, A256 A255 From Broadstairs Broadway turn left at traffic lights into St Peters Park Road.
Take the first right under the railway bridge and the ground is on the left after about 400 metres.
Nearest BR Station: Broadstairs   Car Parking: 50 spaces at the ground, others in the nearby streets.
Capacity: Unlimited uncovered standing   Admission: £3.50 with programme
Clubhouse: Open Tues & Thur evenings, Sat & Sun. Food available Thur, Sat & Sun.   For functions contact Gerry Doyle on 07811 732038   Club Shop: Open Thur evening & Sun morning. Contact Annette Whitehead 01843 581415
Programme: Size: A5   Pages: 24   Price: incl with admission   Editor: Alex Feeney   Advertising: Don Bullock
Colours: Blue black & gold hoops   Change colours: Black & white
Founded: 1886   Nickname: Wanderers   Training: Tuesday & Thursday   Website: www.thanetwanderers..co.uk

TUNBRIDGE WELLS R.F.C.
Chairman: Roger Clarke Tel: 07850 782 115   Email: roger.clarke@fdf.org.uk
Treasurer: Kathy Skinner Tel: 01892 549 235   Email: skinners205@tiscali.co.uk
Hon Secretary: Paul Hardwick Tel: 01892 531127 (H)   email: pd.hardwick@btinternet.com
Fixtures Secretary: Mike Harding, The Old Exchange, 14 Northfields, Speldhurst, Tunbridge Wells, Kent TN3 0PN
Tel: (H) 01892 861429   (W) 0208 289 2030   email: michael@chantlerkent.co.uk
Membership Secretary: Alan Skinner, Tel: 01892 549 235   Email: skinners205@tiscali.co.uk
Head Coach: Paul Hathaway   Tel: 07725 306 726   Email: Paulkathyhathaway@btinternet.com
1st XV Captain: Peter Binham   Tel: 07771 888 773   Email: peter.binham@fabermaunsell.com
Ground Address: St. Mark's Recreation Ground, Frant Road, Tunbridge Wells, Kent TN2 5LS
Directions: Approaching from North A21, A26. Travel through Southborough on A26. Follow through to Tunbridge Wells. Bear right at mini roundabout (A26) past Kent and Sussex Hospital on right. Down past the common through one set of lights. Bear left at mini roundabout (A267) and follow the road to the top of the hill. The club is on the left.
NB Please do not park outside the clubhouse along the main road. Parking is available in Forest Road (see map on website).
Capacity: All uncovered standing
Founded: 1931   Website: www.twrfc.com   Training Nights: Tuesday & Thursday 7.30pm
Colours: Navy blue and white quarters

WIMBLEDON R.F.C.
Chairman: James Boatman james@jamesboatman.co.uk
President: Mike Keane mike.keane@itv.com 07961 305081
Treasurer: Matthewe Bond mbond@mcr.uk.com
Club Secretary: Charlotte Willis, 11 Park Lane, Richmond, Surrey TW9 2RA
Tel: 07887 612364   email: charlotte.willis@btopenworld.com
Fixture Secretary: Mike Keane, 17 Auriol Park Road, Worcester Park, Surrey KT4 7DP
Tel: 07961 305081   email: mike.keane@mike.keane@itv.com
Head Coach: Chris Yates   email: yateschristian@hotmail.com
Club Captain: Andy Kerr   email: andykerr06@hotmail.com
Communications: Imo Hitchcock   email: imogenh@gmail.com
Sponsorship: Michael Simmonds   email: mjesimmonds@btconnect.com
Ground Address: Beverley Meads, Barham Road, Copse Hill, Wimbledon SW20 0ET
Tel: 020 89463156   email info@wimbledonrfc.co.uk   Website: www.wimbledonrfc.co.uk
Directions: From A3 take A238 towards Raynes Park, turn left at first roundabout to Copse Hill, then first left to Barham Road. Clubhouse is at the end.   Nearest Station: Raynes Park   Car Parking: 150 cars
Founded: 1865   Training Nights: Tuesday and Thursdays from 7:30 pm
Colours: Cambridge blue and claret hoops, white shorts

LONDON & S.E. DIVISION LEAGUE TABLES 2008-09

London 3 North East	P	W	D	L	PF	PA	PD	Pts	Adj
1 Rochford Hundred	22	18	0	4	565	277	288	36	0
2 Brentwood	22	17	0	5	490	244	246	34	0
3 Romford & Gidea Park	22	14	0	8	539	345	194	28	0
4 Thurrock	22	14	0	8	562	402	160	28	0
5 Sudbury	22	14	0	8	417	350	67	28	0
6 Braintree	22	12	0	10	473	347	126	24	0
7 Chelmsford	22	9	1	12	266	369	-103	19	0
8 Enfield Ignatians	22	7	3	12	347	392	-45	17	0
9 Saffron Walden	22	6	3	13	391	555	-164	15	0
10 Mersea Island	22	7	1	14	308	535	-227	15	0
11 Harlow	22	6	0	16	315	574	-259	12	0
12 Norwich	22	3	2	17	293	576	-283	6	-2

London 3 North West	P	W	D	L	PF	PA	PD	Pts	Adj
1 Harpenden	22	18	0	4	672	250	422	36	0
2 Hampstead	22	16	0	6	560	275	285	32	0
3 Tabard	22	15	0	7	530	339	191	30	0
4 St Albans	22	13	0	9	460	386	74	26	0
5 Imperial Medicals	22	11	0	11	519	487	32	22	0
6 Grasshoppers	22	10	0	12	443	466	-23	20	0
7 U.C.S. Old Boys	22	11	0	11	415	443	-28	20	-2
8 Hammersmith & Fulham	22	9	1	12	452	472	-20	19	0
9 Twickenham	22	9	0	13	314	506	-192	18	0
10 London New Zealand	22	7	1	14	311	467	-156	15	0
11 London Nigerian	22	7	0	15	366	615	-249	14	0
12 Finchley	22	5	0	17	333	669	-336	10	0

London 3 South East	P	W	D	L	PF	PA	PD	Pts	Ad
1 Old Elthamians	22	19	0	3	841	167	674	38	0
2 Aylesford Bulls	22	17	0	5	440	283	157	34	0
3 Hove	22	16	1	5	662	300	362	33	0
4 Old Reigatian	22	17	0	5	480	276	204	32	-2
5 Warlingham	22	14	0	8	543	341	202	28	0
6 Sevenoaks	22	9	2	11	395	457	-62	20	0
7 Deal & Betteshanger	22	9	2	11	358	467	-109	20	0
8 Purley John Fisher	22	8	0	14	370	540	-170	16	0
9 Lewes	22	6	0	16	317	476	-159	12	0
10 Old Dunstonians	22	5	0	17	276	643	-367	10	0
11 Eastbourne	22	6	1	15	280	723	-443	9	-4
12 Lordswood	22	3	0	19	142	431	-289	6	0

London 3 South West	P	W	D	L	PF	PA	PD	Pts	Adj
1 Chichester	22	18	0	4	598	231	367	36	0
2 Wimbledon	22	16	0	6	451	258	193	32	0
3 Guildford	22	15	1	6	491	321	170	31	0
4 Tottonians	22	14	0	8	488	321	167	28	0
5 London Cornish	22	12	3	7	387	345	42	27	0
6 Bognor	22	11	0	11	429	432	-3	22	0
7 Guernsey	22	10	0	12	463	385	78	20	0
8 London South Africa	22	8	1	13	411	555	-144	17	0
9 Effingham & Leatherhead	22	7	1	14	278	390	-112	15	0
10 KCS Old Boys	22	6	1	15	331	574	-243	13	0
11 London Irish Amateur	22	7	0	15	295	516	-221	10	-4
12 Winchester	22	4	1	17	265	559	-294	9	0

London 4 North East

		P	W	D	L	PF	PA	PD	Pts	Adj
1	Colchester	22	17	1	4	707	264	443	35	0
2	Ipswich	22	16	0	6	412	267	145	32	0
3	Beccles	22	13	1	8	410	309	101	27	0
4	South Woodham Ferrers	22	13	0	9	479	319	160	26	0
5	Canvey Island	22	13	0	9	354	312	42	26	0
6	Upminster	22	11	0	11	343	334	9	22	0
7	West Norfolk	22	10	2	10	404	456	-52	22	0
8	Dagenham	22	9	1	12	348	453	-105	19	0
9	Wymondham	22	9	0	13	402	378	24	18	0
10	Basildon	22	8	0	14	370	494	-124	16	0
11	Billericay	22	9	0	13	323	485	-162	16	-2
12	Crusaders	22	1	1	20	191	672	-481	1	-2

London 4 North West

		P	W	D	L	PF	PA	PD	Pts	Adj
1	Chiswick	20	17	1	2	649	196	453	35	0
2	Hemel Hempstead	20	16	1	3	735	293	442	33	0
3	Old Ashmoleans	20	15	2	3	648	277	371	32	0
4	Barnet Elizabethans	20	15	2	3	521	298	223	32	0
5	Haringey Rhinos	20	11	0	9	513	445	68	22	0
6	Datchworth	20	8	0	12	344	325	19	16	0
7	Old Hamptonians	20	9	0	11	432	543	-111	16	-2
8	Hitchin	20	7	0	13	281	406	-125	14	0
9	Bank Of England	20	5	0	15	315	556	-241	6	-4
10	Old Merchant Taylors'	20	4	0	16	217	687	-470	6	-2
11	Harrow	0	0	0	0	0	0	0	0	0
12	Fullerians	20	0	0	20	119	748	-629	0	0

London 4 South East

		P	W	D	L	PF	PA	PD	Pts	Adj
1	Tonbridge Juddian	22	22	0	0	1,085	163	922	44	0
2	Bromley	22	18	0	4	494	234	260	36	0
3	Heathfield & Wald'n	22	17	0	5	491	215	276	34	0
4	Folkestone	22	12	0	10	346	433	-87	24	0
5	Park House	22	11	0	11	338	462	-124	22	0
6	Charlton Park	22	10	1	11	411	421	-10	21	0
7	Crowborough	22	11	0	11	346	370	-24	20	-2
8	Horsham	22	10	0	12	405	448	-43	18	-2
9	East Grinstead	22	8	0	14	399	408	-9	16	0
10	Whitstable	22	7	1	14	251	501	-250	15	0
11	Hastings & Bexhill	22	3	0	19	204	676	-472	6	0
12	Beccehamian	22	2	0	20	219	658	-439	2	-2

London 4 South West

		P	W	D	L	PF	PA	PD	Pts	Adj
1	Weybridge Vandals	22	21	0	1	833	213	620	42	0
2	Trojans	22	21	0	1	665	185	480	42	0
3	Kingston	22	12	0	10	388	390	-2	24	0
4	Gosport and Fareham	22	11	1	10	408	436	-28	23	0
5	Old Wellingtonians	22	11	0	11	439	381	58	22	0
6	Old Mid-Whitgiftian	22	10	1	11	499	385	114	21	0
7	Old Alleynians	22	10	0	12	433	393	40	20	0
8	Camberley	22	9	0	13	442	482	-40	18	0
9	Ellingham & Ringwood	22	9	0	13	370	529	-159	18	0
10	Andover	22	6	0	16	338	618	-280	12	0
11	Old Wimbledonians	22	7	0	15	290	640	-350	12	-2
12	Petersfield	22	4	0	18	274	727	-453	8	0

LONDON & S.E. DIVISION LEAGUE TABLES 2008-09

LONDON & SOUTH EAST

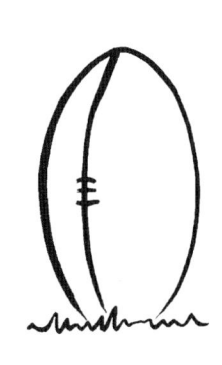

617

LONDON 3 NORTH EAST

E. Counties 1 ↑   ↑ Essex 1

Eastern Counties 1

		P	W	D	L	PF	PA	PD	Pts	Adj
1	Lowestoft & Yarmouth	18	16	0	2	609	171	438	32	0
2	Wisbech	18	15	0	3	634	136	498	28	-2
3	Newmarket	18	15	0	3	552	161	391	28	-2
4	Holt	18	9	0	9	329	296	33	18	0
5	Stowmarket	18	9	0	9	343	390	-47	18	0
6	Cantabrigian	18	7	1	10	276	311	-35	15	0
7	Thurston	18	6	0	12	283	583	-300	12	0
8	Woodbridge	18	5	1	12	202	366	-164	11	0
9	Fakenham	18	4	0	14	195	474	-279	8	0
10	Thetford	18	3	0	15	206	741	-535	6	0

Eastern Counties 2

		P	W	D	L	PF	PA	PD	Pts	Adj
1	Southwold	18	16	0	2	472	126	346	32	0
2	Ely	18	16	0	2	398	132	266	32	0
3	Ipswich Y.M.	18	15	0	3	527	150	377	30	0
4	Harwich & Dovercourt	18	11	0	7	443	214	229	20	-2
5	Swaffham	18	9	0	9	311	280	31	18	0
6	Haverhill & District	18	7	0	11	303	397	-94	14	0
7	Dereham	18	5	0	13	230	316	-86	10	0
8	Broadland	18	6	0	12	152	260	-108	10	-2
9	Hadleigh	18	4	0	14	218	339	-121	8	0
10	Lakenham Hewett	18	1	0	17	90	930	-840	2	0

Essex (Canterbury Jack) League 1

		P	W	D	L	PF	PA	PD	Pts	Adj
1	Wanstead	18	16	0	2	561	159	402	30	-2
2	Campion	18	14	0	4	533	239	294	28	0
3	Clacton	18	13	1	4	369	210	159	27	0
4	Bancroft	18	13	0	5	415	237	178	26	0
5	Old Brentwoods	18	9	0	9	383	315	68	18	0
6	Maldon	18	8	2	8	380	323	57	18	0
7	Thames	18	7	1	10	290	367	-77	13	-2
8	Ilford Wanderers	18	6	0	12	142	412	-270	12	0
9	Upper Clapton	18	1	0	17	206	561	-355	2	0
10	Writtle Wanderers	18	1	0	17	119	575	-456	2	0

Essex (Spitfire) League 2

		P	W	D	L	PF	PA	PD	Pts	Adj
1	Millwall	14	14	0	0	817	109	708	28	0
2	Old Cooperians	14	11	0	3	458	140	318	22	0
3	East London	14	10	0	4	470	200	270	20	0
4	May & Baker	14	7	0	7	277	316	-39	14	0
5	Loughton	14	5	0	9	227	566	-339	10	0
6	Runwell Wyverns	14	4	0	10	251	498	-247	8	0
7	Burnham-On-Crouch	14	3	1	10	197	498	-301	7	0
8	Kings Cross Steelers	14	1	1	12	168	538	-370	3	0

Essex (Oranjeboom) League 3

		P	W	D	L	PF	PA	PD	Pts	Adj
1	Pegasus Palmerians	12	12	0	0	412	51	361	24	0
2	Brightlingsea	12	9	0	3	447	114	333	18	0
3	Stanford Le Hope	12	9	0	3	238	130	108	18	0
4	Ongar	12	5	0	7	210	152	58	8	-2
5	Phantoms	12	4	0	8	106	318	-212	8	0
6	Ravens	12	2	0	10	118	399	-281	0	-4
7	Witham	12	1	0	11	132	499	-367	0	-

LONDON 3 NORTH WEST
↑ Herts & Middx. 1 ↑

Herts/Middlesex 1

		P	W	D	L	PF	PA	PD	Pts	Adjust
1	Cheshunt	18	15	1	2	504	135	369	31	0
2	Old Streetonians	18	14	0	4	535	195	340	28	0
3	West London	18	13	1	4	461	212	249	27	0
4	Harlequin Amateurs	18	11	0	7	332	301	31	22	0
5	Saracens Amateurs	18	9	3	6	409	227	182	21	0
6	Old Actonians	18	7	3	8	353	412	-59	17	0
7	Verulamians	18	7	1	10	295	357	-62	15	0
8	Kilburn Cosmos	18	5	1	12	403	370	33	11	0
9	Old Abbotstonians	18	4	0	14	260	540	-280	8	0
10	Old Millhillians	18	0	0	18	141	944	-803	0	0

Herts/Middlesex 2

		P	W	D	L	PF	PA	PD	Pts	Adjust
1	Hendon	16	14	0	2	430	159	271	28	0
2	Old Grammarians	16	12	2	2	290	155	135	26	0
3	Wasps	16	12	0	4	432	172	260	24	0
4	Old Haberdashers	16	9	2	5	279	182	97	20	0
5	H.A.C.	16	8	0	8	313	254	59	16	0
6	Uxbridge	16	3	1	12	193	427	-234	7	0
7	Mill Hill	16	6	0	10	228	359	-131	6	-6
8	Royston	16	3	0	13	156	424	-268	6	0
9	Belsize Park	16	2	1	13	120	309	-189	3	-2
	Thamesians	0	0	0	0	0	0	0	0	0

Herts/Middlesex 3

		P	W	D	L	PF	PA	PD	Pts	Adjust
1	Old Isleworthians	14	13	0	1	325	138	187	26	0
2	Hackney	14	11	1	2	340	141	199	23	0
3	Quintin	14	9	0	5	262	238	24	18	0
4	St Nicholas Old Boys	14	6	0	8	214	222	-8	12	0
5	London French	14	5	1	8	224	172	52	11	0
6	Cuffley	14	4	0	10	168	282	-114	8	0
7	Old Tottonians	14	4	0	10	126	295	-169	6	-2
8	Watford	14	3	0	11	169	340	-171	4	-2
	Borehamwood	0	0	0	0	0	0	0	0	0

Herts/Middlesex 4

		P	W	D	L	PF	PA	PD	Pts	Adjust
1	Hatfield	14	14	0	0	355	109	246	28	0
2	Pinner & Grammarians	14	11	0	3	346	95	251	22	0
3	Sudbury & London Springboks	14	7	0	7	442	265	177	14	0
4	Northolt	14	7	0	7	223	258	-35	14	0
5	British Airways	14	7	0	7	393	307	86	12	-2
6	G.W.R.	14	7	0	7	238	215	23	12	-2
7	Southgate	14	3	0	11	103	552	-449	6	0
8	Hayes	14	0	0	14	156	455	-299	-4	-4

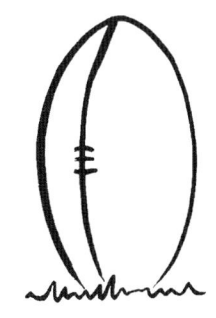

LONDON 3 SOUTH EAST

Sussex 1 ↑   ↑ Kent 1

Sussex 1		P	W	D	L	F	A	Pts	PD	Ad
1	Brighton	20	19	1	0	1,032	136	896	39	0
2	Uckfield	20	14	2	4	551	222	329	30	0
3	Hove II - Yeomen	20	13	0	7	541	287	254	26	0
4	Burgess Hill	20	12	0	8	413	468	-55	24	0
5	Crawley	20	11	1	8	376	328	48	23	0
6	Pulborough	20	8	1	11	433	437	-4	17	0
7	Seaford	20	8	1	11	320	432	-112	17	0
8	Holbrook	20	7	0	13	381	503	-122	14	0
9	Haywards Heath III	20	6	0	14	327	580	-253	12	0
10	Lewes II	20	6	0	14	246	680	-434	10	-2
11	Rye	20	3	0	17	136	683	-547	6	0

Kent 1		P	W	D	L	PF	PA	PD	Pts	Adj
1	Medway	22	18	0	4	530	276	254	36	0
2	Old Gravesendians	22	17	0	5	490	176	314	34	0
3	Sittingbourne	22	15	0	7	424	298	126	30	0
4	Old Olavians	22	16	0	6	505	273	232	26	-6
5	Dartfordians	22	12	0	10	371	322	49	24	0
6	Cranbrook	22	10	1	11	459	417	42	21	0
7	Vigo	22	10	1	11	382	347	35	21	0
8	Ashford	22	9	0	13	437	450	-13	18	0
9	Gillingham Anch.	22	10	0	12	346	384	-38	18	-2
10	Erith	22	9	1	12	389	412	-23	17	-2
11	Sheppey	22	4	1	17	272	560	-288	9	0
12	Askean	22	0	0	22	117	807	-690	0	0

Kent 2		P	W	D	L	PF	PA	PD	Pts	Adj
1	HSBC	18	17	0	1	598	185	413	34	0
2	Guys' Kings' & St Thomas' Hosp.	18	16	0	2	884	231	653	30	-2
3	Orpington	18	11	3	4	328	334	-6	25	0
4	Shooters Hill	18	11	2	5	383	302	81	22	-2
5	New Ash Green	18	10	1	7	286	275	11	21	0
6	Old Williamsonians	18	8	1	9	369	304	65	17	0
7	Brockleians	18	4	1	13	183	431	-248	9	0
8	Kings Coll. Hospital	18	4	0	14	231	449	-218	8	0
9	Foots Cray	18	3	0	15	142	414	-272	6	0
10	Bexley	18	2	0	16	156	635	-479	4	0

LONDON 3 SOUTH WEST

Hampshire 1 ↑   ↑ Surrey 1

Hampshire 1		P	W	D	L	PF	PA	PD	Pts	Adj
1	Fordingbridge	18	15	1	2	446	215	231	31	0
2	Sandown & Shanklin	18	12	2	4	372	179	193	26	0
3	United Services, Portsmouth	18	11	2	5	314	245	69	24	0
4	Farnborough	18	11	0	7	267	262	5	22	0
5	Alton	18	8	1	9	294	301	-7	17	0
6	Romsey	18	6	1	11	240	374	-134	13	0
7	Eastleigh	18	5	1	12	256	272	-16	11	0
8	East Dorset	18	6	0	12	213	296	-83	10	-2
9	New Milton & District	18	7	0	11	344	458	-114	10	-4
10	Southampton	18	5	0	13	226	370	-144	10	0

LONDON & S.E. DIVISION LEAGUE TABLES 2008-09

Hampshire 2

		P	W	D	L	PF	PA	PD	Pts	Adj
1	Aldershot & Fleet	14	12	0	2	529	107	422	24	0
2	Fareham Heathens	14	11	1	2	397	109	288	23	0
3	Millbrook	14	10	0	4	289	133	156	20	0
4	Overton	14	7	1	6	287	232	55	15	0
5	Isle Of Wight	14	7	0	7	297	291	6	14	0
6	Lytchett Minster	14	5	0	9	197	294	-97	10	0
7	Fawley	14	3	0	11	155	439	-284	6	0
8	Nomads	14	0	0	14	60	606	-546	-4	-4

Hampshire 3

		P	W	D	L	PF	PA	PD	Pts	Adj
1	Ventnor	12	10	0	2	294	113	181	20	0
2	Chineham	12	9	0	3	337	144	193	18	0
3	Alresford	12	6	1	5	226	230	-4	13	0
4	Kingsclere	12	6	0	6	213	256	-43	12	0
5	Paxton Pumas	12	6	0	6	198	221	-23	10	-2
6	Verwood	12	4	1	7	232	219	13	9	0
7	Stoneham	12	0	0	12	69	386	-317	-2	-2

Surrey 1

		P	W	D	L	PF	PA	PD	Pts	Adj
1	Old Paulines	18	13	0	5	281	222	59	26	0
2	Old Whitgiftians	18	12	1	5	379	191	188	25	0
3	Bec Old Boys	18	12	0	6	343	235	108	24	0
4	Old Freemens	18	9	1	8	285	260	25	19	0
5	Chipstead	18	9	0	9	282	238	44	18	0
6	Croydon	18	8	0	10	346	332	14	16	0
7	Farnham	18	8	0	10	199	327	-128	16	0
8	London Exiles	18	7	0	11	324	298	26	14	0
9	Battersea Ironsides	18	6	1	11	215	340	-125	13	0
10	Old Caterhamians	18	4	1	13	180	391	-211	9	0

Surrey 2

		P	W	D	L	PF	PA	PD	Pts	Adj
1	Teddington	16	15	0	1	471	116	355	30	0
2	Old Walcountians	16	14	0	2	508	177	331	28	0
3	Old Emanuel	16	9	1	6	394	293	101	19	0
4	Old Haileyburians	16	7	2	7	363	247	116	16	0
5	Cranleigh	16	8	0	8	268	349	-81	16	0
6	Old Cranleighans	16	7	0	9	242	327	-85	14	0
7	London Media	16	4	1	11	307	540	-233	9	0
8	Old Rutlishians	16	4	1	11	183	519	-336	9	0
9	Law Society	16	1	1	14	195	363	-168	1	-2

Surrey 3

		P	W	D	L	PF	PA	PD	Pts	Adj
1	Old Blues	18	17	0	1	684	133	551	34	0
2	Raynes Park	18	16	0	2	482	209	273	32	0
3	Mitcham	18	9	2	7	333	299	34	20	0
4	Worth Old Boys	18	9	0	9	392	332	60	18	0
5	Old Oundelians	18	9	0	9	365	380	-15	18	0
6	Streatham-Croydon	18	8	1	9	296	342	-46	17	0
7	Old Tiffinians	18	8	1	9	333	386	-53	17	0
8	Haslemere	18	5	0	13	176	419	-243	10	0
9	Merton	18	4	0	14	253	401	-148	8	0
10	Reigate	18	3	0	15	192	605	-413	6	0

Surrey 4

		P	W	D	L	PF	PA	PD	Pts	Adj
1	CL London	18	16	0	2	830	194	636	32	0
2	Old Radleian	18	15	0	3	619	131	488	30	0
3	Economicals	18	14	0	4	631	300	331	28	0
4	Old Glynonians	18	11	0	7	345	174	171	22	0
5	Guildfordians Bisons	18	7	1	10	264	495	-231	15	0
6	Woking	18	7	0	11	215	381	-166	14	0
7	Wandsworthians	18	7	0	11	229	427	-198	14	0
8	Lightwater	18	4	0	14	150	454	-304	6	-2
9	Egham Hollowegians	18	3	0	15	113	674	-561	6	0
10	Pelhamians	18	5	1	12	238	404	-166	5	-6

LONDON & S.E. DIVISION FIXTURE GRIDS 2009-2010

LONDON TWO NORTH EAST	Braintree	Chelmsford	Colchester	Enfield Ignatians	Harlow	Ipswich	Mersea Island	Norwich	Romford & Gidea Park	Saffron Walden	Sudbury	Thurrock
Braintree		26/09	19/12	27/03	06/03	17/10	30/01	16/01	05/12	12/09	14/11	07/11
Chelmsford	09/01		06/03	13/02	23/01	10/04	19/09	12/12	24/10	14/11	10/10	20/03
Colchester	19/09	28/11		24/10	10/10	12/12	10/04	20/03	23/01	13/02	09/01	20/02
Enfield Ignatians	12/12	07/11	30/01		19/09	28/11	20/03	20/02	09/01	17/10	10/04	16/01
Harlow	28/11	17/10	16/01	19/12		07/11	20/02	30/01	12/09	26/09	20/03	12/12
Ipswich	23/01	12/09	27/03	06/03	13/02		10/10	19/12	14/11	05/12	24/10	26/09
Mersea Island	24/10	19/12	12/09	05/12	14/11	16/01		26/09	06/03	27/03	13/02	17/10
Norwich	10/10	27/03	05/12	14/11	24/10	19/09	09/01		13/02	06/03	23/01	12/09
Romford & Gidea Park	20/03	30/01	17/10	26/09	10/04	20/02	28/11	07/11		16/01	12/12	19/12
Saffron Walden	10/04	20/02	07/11	23/01	09/01	20/03	12/12	28/11	10/10		19/09	30/01
Sudbury	20/02	16/01	26/09	12/09	05/12	30/01	07/11	17/10	27/03	19/12		28/11
Thurrock	13/02	05/12	14/11	10/10	27/03	09/01	23/01	10/04	19/09	24/10	06/03	

LONDON TWO NORTH WEST	Chiswick	Finchley	Grasshoppers	Hammersmith & F.	Hampstead	Hemel Hempstead	Imperial Medicals	London N. Z.	London Nigerian	St Albans	Tabard	U.C.S. Old Boys
Chiswick		12/09	20/03	19/12	17/10	30/01	12/12	26/09	16/01	07/11	20/02	28/11
Finchley	10/04		12/12	26/09	30/01	07/11	19/12	16/01	17/10	20/02	28/11	20/03
Grasshoppers	05/12	27/03		12/09	16/01	17/10	28/11	19/12	26/09	30/01	07/11	20/02
Hammersmith & Fulham	19/09	09/01	10/04		07/11	20/02	16/01	17/10	30/01	28/11	20/03	12/12
Hampstead	23/01	24/10	10/10	13/02		12/12	20/03	14/11	06/03	10/04	19/09	09/01
Hemel Hempstead	24/10	13/02	23/01	14/11	27/03		12/09	06/03	05/12	19/09	09/01	10/10
Imperial Medicals	27/03	19/09	06/03	10/10	05/12	10/04		24/10	14/11	09/01	23/01	13/02
London New Zealand	09/01	10/10	19/09	23/01	20/02	28/11	30/01		07/11	20/03	12/12	10/04
London Nigerian	10/10	23/01	09/01	24/10	28/11	20/03	20/02	13/02		12/12	10/04	19/09
St Albans	13/02	14/11	24/10	06/03	12/09	19/12	26/09	05/12	27/03		10/10	23/01
Tabard	14/11	06/03	13/02	05/12	19/12	26/09	17/10	27/03	12/09	16/01		24/10
U.C.S. Old Boys	06/03	05/12	14/11	27/03	26/09	16/01	07/11	12/09	19/12	17/10	30/01	

LEVEL SEVEN

LONDON TWO SOUTH EAST

	Bromley	Deal & Betteshanger	Eastbourne	Hove	KCS Old Boys	Lewes	Old Dunstonians	Old Reigatian	Purley John Fisher	Sevenoaks	Tonbridge Juddian	Warlingham
Bromley		13/02	05/12	24/10	09/01	23/01	19/09	10/04	10/10	06/03	14/11	27/03
Deal & Betteshanger	07/11		26/09	12/09	17/10	30/01	05/12	16/01	27/03	14/11	19/12	06/03
Eastbourne	20/03	09/01		14/11	10/04	19/09	24/10	12/12	13/02	10/10	06/03	23/01
Hove	30/01	10/04	20/02		20/03	12/12	10/10	28/11	23/01	19/09	07/11	09/01
KCS Old Boys	26/09	23/01	12/09	05/12		10/10	14/11	19/12	06/03	24/10	27/03	13/02
Lewes	17/10	24/10	19/12	27/03	16/01		06/03	26/09	05/12	13/02	12/09	14/11
Old Dunstonians	19/12	20/03	30/01	16/01	20/02	28/11		07/11	26/09	12/12	17/10	10/04
Old Reigatian	12/09	10/10	27/03	06/03	19/09	09/01	13/02		14/11	23/01	05/12	24/10
Purley John Fisher	16/01	12/12	07/11	17/10	28/11	20/03	09/01	20/02		10/04	30/01	19/09
Sevenoaks	28/11	20/02	16/01	19/12	30/01	07/11	27/03	17/10	12/09		26/09	05/12
Tonbridge Juddian	20/02	19/09	28/11	13/02	12/12	10/04	23/01	20/03	24/10	09/01		10/10
Warlingham	12/12	28/11	17/10	26/09	07/11	20/02	12/09	30/01	19/12	20/03	16/01	

LONDON TWO SOUTH WEST

	Bognor	Effingham & L'head	Guernsey	Guildford	London Cornish	Lon. Irish Amateur	Lon. South Africa	Tottonians	Trojans	Twickenham	Weybridge Vandals	Winchester
Bognor		28/11	13/02	20/02	20/03	10/10	10/04	09/01	19/09	12/12	24/10	23/01
Effingham & Leatherhead	06/03		14/11	20/03	12/12	23/01	19/09	10/10	09/01	10/04	13/02	24/10
Guernsey	07/11	20/02		30/01	28/11	09/01	12/12	19/09	10/04	20/03	23/01	10/10
Guildford	14/11	05/12	24/10		10/04	27/03	23/01	06/03	13/02	09/01	10/10	19/09
London Cornish	05/12	27/03	06/03	12/09		24/10	09/01	23/01	10/10	19/09	14/11	13/02
London Irish Amateur	16/01	17/10	26/09	12/12	30/01		20/02	20/03	28/11	07/11	19/12	12/09
London South Africa	12/09	19/12	27/03	17/10	26/09	14/11		13/02	24/10	16/01	05/12	06/03
Tottonians	26/09	16/01	19/12	28/11	17/10	05/12	07/11		20/02	30/01	12/09	27/03
Trojans	19/12	26/09	12/09	07/11	16/01	06/03	30/01	14/11		17/10	27/03	05/12
Twickenham	27/03	12/09	05/12	26/09	19/12	13/02	10/04	24/10	23/01		06/03	14/11
Weybridge Vandals	30/01	07/11	17/10	16/01	20/02	19/09	20/03	10/04	12/12	28/11		09/01
Winchester	17/10	30/01	16/01	19/12	07/11	10/04	28/11	12/12	20/03	20/02	26/09	

LONDON & S.E. DIVISION FIXTURE GRIDS 2009-2010

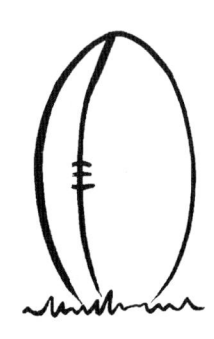

LONDON THREE

NORTH EAST		1	2	3	4	5	6	7	8	9	10	11	12
1	Basildon		30/01	07/11	16/01	10/04	12/12	09/01	19/09	17/10	20/02	28/11	20/03
2	Beccles	24/10		28/11	20/02	09/01	19/09	23/01	10/10	13/02	20/03	12/12	10/04
3	Billericay	13/02	06/03		20/03	10/10	09/01	24/10	23/01	14/11	12/12	10/04	19/09
4	Canvey Island	10/10	14/11	05/12		06/03	13/02	19/09	27/03	24/10	10/04	09/01	23/01
5	Dagenham	12/09	26/09	16/01	28/11		20/02	27/03	05/12	19/12	17/10	30/01	07/11
6	Lowestoft & Yarmouth	27/03	19/12	26/09	07/11	14/11		05/12	06/03	12/09	16/01	17/10	30/01
7	South Woodham Ferrers	26/09	17/10	30/01	19/12	12/12	20/03		10/04	16/01	07/11	20/02	28/11
8	Upminster	19/12	16/01	17/10	12/12	20/03	28/11	12/09		26/09	30/01	07/11	20/02
9	Wanstead	23/01	07/11	20/02	30/01	19/09	10/04	10/10	09/01		28/11	20/03	12/12
10	West Norfolk	14/11	05/12	27/03	12/09	23/01	10/10	13/02	24/10	06/03		19/09	09/01
11	Wisbech	06/03	27/03	12/09	26/09	24/10	23/01	14/11	13/02	05/12	19/12		10/10
12	Wymondham	05/12	12/09	19/12	17/10	13/02	24/10	06/03	14/11	27/03	26/09	16/01	

NORTH WEST		1	2	3	4	5	6	7	8	9	10	11	12
1	Bank Of England		17/10	20/03	07/11	28/11	26/09	20/02	12/12	19/12	30/01	10/04	16/01
2	Barnet Elizabethans	23/01		19/09	20/03	10/04	24/10	12/12	09/01	20/02	28/11	10/10	13/02
3	Cheshunt	05/12	19/12		16/01	30/01	27/03	17/10	14/11	07/11	26/09	06/03	12/09
4	Datchworth	13/02	05/12	10/10		09/01	14/11	19/09	23/01	12/09	27/03	24/10	06/03
5	Fullerians	06/03	12/09	24/10	26/09		05/12	16/01	13/02	17/10	19/12	14/11	27/03
6	Haringey Rhinos	09/01	30/01	12/12	20/02	20/03		28/11	10/04	16/01	07/11	19/09	17/10
7	Hitchin	14/11	27/03	23/01	19/12	10/10	06/03		24/10	26/09	12/09	13/02	05/12
8	Old Ashmoleans	27/03	26/09	20/02	17/10	07/11	12/09	30/01		28/11	16/01	05/12	19/12
9	Old Hamptonians	19/09	14/11	13/02	10/04	23/01	10/10	09/01	06/03		05/12	27/03	24/10
10	Old Merchant Taylors'	24/10	06/03	09/01	12/12	19/09	13/02	10/04	10/10	20/03		23/01	14/11
11	Old Streetonians	12/09	16/01	28/11	30/01	20/02	19/12	07/11	20/03	12/12	17/10		26/09
12	West London	10/10	07/11	10/04	28/11	12/12	23/01	20/03	19/09	30/01	20/02	09/01	

LONDON THREE

SOUTH EAST

		1	2	3	4	5	6	7	8	9	10	11	12
1	Brighton		09/01	24/10	10/10	20/03	20/02	23/01	19/09	10/04	28/11	13/02	12/12
2	Charlton Park	26/09		12/09	05/12	17/10	28/11	27/03	20/02	07/11	16/01	19/12	30/01
3	Crowborough	30/01	10/04		19/09	20/02	16/01	09/01	12/12	20/03	07/11	17/10	28/11
4	East Grinstead	16/01	20/03	19/12		30/01	12/12	12/09	28/11	20/02	17/10	26/09	07/11
5	Folkestone	05/12	23/01	14/11	24/10		12/09	13/02	10/10	09/01	27/03	06/03	19/09
6	Hastings & Bexhill	14/11	06/03	10/10	27/03	10/04		19/09	13/02	23/01	05/12	24/10	09/01
7	Heathfield & Wald'n	17/10	12/12	26/09	10/04	07/11	19/12		20/03	28/11	30/01	16/01	20/02
8	Horsham	19/12	14/11	27/03	06/03	16/01	07/11	05/12		30/01	26/09	12/09	17/10
9	Medway	12/09	13/02	05/12	14/11	26/09	17/10	06/03	24/10		19/12	27/03	16/01
10	Old Gravesendians	06/03	10/10	13/02	23/01	12/12	20/03	24/10	09/01	19/09		14/11	10/04
11	Park House	07/11	19/09	23/01	09/01	28/11	30/01	10/10	10/04	12/12	20/02		20/03
12	Whitstable	27/03	24/10	06/03	13/02	19/12	26/09	14/11	23/01	10/10	12/09	05/12	

SOUTH WEST

		1	2	3	4	5	6	7	8	9	10	11	12
1	Andover		19/12	07/11	20/02	20/03	28/11	10/04	16/01	30/01	12/12	26/09	17/10
2	Camberley	19/09		10/04	09/01	13/02	23/01	27/03	24/10	05/12	06/03	10/10	14/11
3	Ellingham & Ringwood	13/02	12/09		19/09	10/10	09/01	24/10	06/03	27/03	23/01	14/11	05/12
4	Fordingbridge	14/11	26/09	19/12		23/01	10/10	13/02	05/12	12/09	24/10	06/03	27/03
5	Gosport and Fareham	05/12	07/11	16/01	17/10		30/01	06/03	12/09	26/09	14/11	27/03	19/12
6	Kingston	06/03	17/10	26/09	16/01	24/10		14/11	27/03	19/12	13/02	05/12	12/09
7	Old Alleynians	12/09	12/12	30/01	07/11	28/11	20/02		26/09	17/10	20/03	19/12	16/01
8	Old Mid-Whitgiftian	10/10	30/01	28/11	20/03	10/04	12/12	09/01		20/02	19/09	23/01	07/11
9	Old Paulines	24/10	20/03	12/09	10/04	09/01	19/09	23/01	14/11		10/10	13/02	06/03
10	Old Wellingtonians	27/03	28/11	17/10	30/01	20/02	07/11	05/12	19/12	16/01		12/09	26/09
11	Old Wimbledonians	09/01	16/01	20/02	28/11	12/12	20/03	19/09	17/10	07/11	10/04		30/01
12	Sandown & Shanklin	23/01	20/02	20/03	12/12	19/09	10/04	10/10	13/02	28/11	09/01	24/10	

SUSSEX ONE

		1	2	3	4	5	6	7	8	9	10	11	12
1	Brighton 2nd XV		06/03	26/09	30/01	07/11	27/03	12/09	05/12	16/01	17/10	14/11	19/12
2	Burgess Hill	28/11		17/10	20/02	12/12	19/12	26/09	12/09	30/01	07/11	20/03	16/01
3	Crawley	09/01	23/01		19/09	20/03	13/02	14/11	24/10	12/12	10/04	10/10	06/03
4	Haywards Heath III	24/10	14/11	19/12		17/10	05/12	27/03	06/03	26/09	16/01	13/02	12/09
5	Holbrook	13/02	27/03	05/12	23/01		10/10	24/10	19/09	10/04	09/01	06/03	14/11
6	Hove II - Yeomen	12/12	19/09	07/11	20/03	16/01		17/10	09/01	20/02	28/11	10/04	30/01
7	Lewes II	10/04	09/01	20/02	12/12	30/01	23/01		10/10	28/11	20/03	19/09	07/11
8	Pulborough	20/03	10/04	30/01	28/11	19/12	26/09	16/01		07/11	20/02	12/12	17/10
9	Rye	10/10	24/10	27/03	09/01	12/09	14/11	06/03	13/02		19/09	23/01	05/12
10	Seaford	23/01	13/02	12/09	10/10	26/09	06/03	05/12	14/11	19/12		24/10	27/03
11	Uckfield	20/02	05/12	16/01	07/11	28/11	12/09	19/12	27/03	17/10	30/01		26/09
12	Worthing 3rd XV	19/09	10/10	28/11	10/04	20/02	24/10	13/02	23/01	20/03	12/12	09/01	

LONDON & S.E. DIVISION FIXTURE GRIDS 2009-2010

EASTERN COUNTIES ONE		1	2	3	4	5	6	7	8	9	10	11	12
1	Cantabrigian		09/01	17/10	28/11	16/01	20/02	19/09	07/11	30/01	10/04	12/12	20/03
2	Crusaders	26/09		16/01	20/02	19/12	07/11	10/04	30/01	17/10	12/12	20/03	28/11
3	Ely	23/01	10/10		20/03	30/01	28/11	09/01	20/02	07/11	19/09	10/04	12/12
4	Fakenham	06/03	14/11	05/12		26/09	19/12	13/02	12/09	27/03	24/10	23/01	10/10
5	Free Date	10/10	19/09	24/10	09/01		10/04	27/03	05/12	14/11	06/03	13/02	23/01
6	Holt	14/11	13/02	06/03	19/09	12/09		24/10	27/03	05/12	23/01	10/10	09/01
7	Newmarket	19/12	12/09	26/09	07/11	12/12	30/01		17/10	16/01	20/03	28/11	20/02
8	Southwold	13/02	24/10	14/11	10/04	20/03	12/12	23/01		06/03	10/10	09/01	19/09
9	Stowmarket	24/10	23/01	13/02	12/12	20/02	20/03	10/10	28/11		09/01	19/09	10/04
10	Thetford	12/09	27/03	19/12	30/01	28/11	17/10	05/12	16/01	26/09		20/02	07/11
11	Thurston	27/03	05/12	12/09	17/10	07/11	16/01	06/03	26/09	19/12	14/11		30/01
12	Woodbridge	05/12	06/03	27/03	16/01	17/10	26/09	14/11	19/12	12/09	13/02	24/10	

EASTERN COUNTIES TWO		1	2	3	4	5	6	7	8	9	10
1	Broadland		10/04	28/11	24/10	20/03	20/02	30/01	19/12	10/10	09/01
2	Dereham	19/09		20/02	30/01	28/11	24/10	10/10	20/03	09/01	19/12
3	Felixstowe	06/03	14/11		19/09	17/10	09/01	27/03	13/02	05/12	10/10
4	Hadleigh	13/02	17/10	10/04		26/09	19/12	06/03	16/01	14/11	20/03
5	Harwich & Dovercourt	05/12	06/03	30/01	09/01		10/10	19/09	14/11	27/03	24/10
6	Haverhill & District	14/11	13/02	26/09	27/03	16/01		05/12	17/10	06/03	19/09
7	Ipswich Y.M.	17/10	16/01	19/12	28/11	10/04	20/03		26/09	13/02	20/02
8	Lakenham Hewett	27/03	05/12	24/10	10/10	20/02	30/01	09/01		19/09	28/11
9	Mistley	16/01	26/09	20/03	20/02	19/12	28/11	24/10	10/04		30/01
10	Swaffham	26/09	27/03	16/01	05/12	13/02	10/04	14/11	06/03	17/10	

ESSEX ONE		1	2	3	4	5	6	7	8	9	10	11
1	Bancroft		12/09	30/01	27/03	05/12	17/10	28/11	07/11	20/02	26/09	19/12
2	Campion	10/04		28/11	09/01	19/09	20/02	16/01	20/03	12/12	30/01	17/10
3	Clacton	24/10	06/03		14/11	13/02	19/12	26/09	10/10	23/01	27/03	05/12
4	East London	12/12	26/09	20/02		10/04	07/11	19/12	28/11	20/03	17/10	16/01
5	Ilford Wanderers	20/03	19/12	07/11	12/09		30/01	12/12	20/02	28/11	16/01	26/09
6	Maldon	23/01	14/11	19/09	13/02	24/10		12/09	09/01	10/10	05/12	06/03
7	Millwall	06/03	10/10	09/01	19/09	27/03	10/04		23/01	13/02	14/11	24/10
8	Old Brentwoods	13/02	05/12	16/01	06/03	14/11	26/09	17/10		24/10	12/09	27/03
9	Old Cooperians	14/11	27/03	17/10	05/12	06/03	16/01	07/11	30/01		19/12	12/09
10	Thames	09/01	24/10	12/12	23/01	10/10	20/03	20/02	10/04	19/09		13/02
11	Upper Clapton	19/09	23/01	20/03	10/10	09/01	28/11	30/01	12/12	10/04	07/11	

ESSEX TWO		1	2	3	4	5	6	7	8	9	10	11	12
1	Brightlingsea		10/10	24/10	13/02	12/09	27/03	06/03	14/11	05/12	23/01	19/09	09/01
2	Burnham-On-Crouch	16/01		06/03	05/12	07/11	26/09	12/09	27/03	19/12	14/11	17/10	30/01
3	Kings Cross Steelers	30/01	28/11		12/09	12/12	17/10	26/09	19/12	16/01	20/03	07/11	20/02
4	Loughton	07/11	20/03	10/04		19/12	30/01	16/01	26/09	17/10	12/12	20/02	28/11
5	May & Baker	10/04	13/02	27/03	19/09		05/12	24/10	10/10	14/11	06/03	09/01	23/01
6	Ongar	12/12	09/01	23/01	24/10	20/03		14/11	13/02	06/03	10/10	10/04	19/09
7	Pegasus Palmerians	28/11	10/04	09/01	10/10	30/01	20/02		23/01	07/11	19/09	20/03	12/12
8	Phantoms	20/02	12/12	19/09	09/01	16/01	07/11	17/10		30/01	10/04	28/11	20/03
9	Runwell Wyverns	20/03	19/09	10/10	23/01	20/02	28/11	13/02	24/10		09/01	12/12	10/04
10	Stanford Le Hope	17/10	20/02	05/12	27/03	28/11	16/01	19/12	12/09	26/09		30/01	07/11
11	Witham	19/12	23/01	13/02	14/11	26/09	12/09	05/12	06/03	27/03	24/10		10/10
12	Writtle Wanderers	26/09	24/10	14/11	06/03	17/10	19/12	27/03	05/12	12/09	13/02	16/01	

HAMPSHIRE ONE

		1	2	3	4	5	6	7	8	9	10	11	12
1	Aldershot & Fleet		27/03	06/03	24/10	10/10	19/09	14/11	23/01	09/01	12/09	13/02	05/12
2	Alton	12/12		14/11	23/01	09/01	10/04	13/02	10/10	19/09	20/03	24/10	06/03
3	East Dorset	28/11	20/02		09/01	10/04	20/03	23/01	19/09	12/12	30/01	10/10	07/11
4	Eastleigh	30/01	17/10	26/09		28/11	07/11	19/12	20/03	20/02	12/12	12/09	16/01
5	Fareham Heathens	16/01	26/09	12/09	06/03		17/10	27/03	14/11	30/01	07/11	05/12	19/12
6	Farnborough	19/12	12/09	05/12	13/02	23/01		06/03	24/10	10/10	26/09	14/11	27/03
7	Millbrook	20/02	07/11	17/10	19/09	12/12	28/11		10/04	20/03	16/01	09/01	30/01
8	New Milton & District	17/10	16/01	19/12	05/12	20/02	30/01	12/09		07/11	28/11	27/03	26/09
9	Petersfield	26/09	19/12	27/03	14/11	24/10	16/01	05/12	13/02		17/10	06/03	12/09
10	Romsey	10/04	05/12	24/10	27/03	13/02	09/01	10/10	06/03	23/01		19/09	14/11
11	Southampton	07/11	30/01	16/01	10/04	20/03	20/02	26/09	12/12	28/11	19/12		17/10
12	United Services, Portsmouth	20/03	28/11	13/02	10/10	19/09	12/12	24/10	09/01	10/04	20/02	23/01	

HAMPSHIRE TWO

		1	2	3	4	5	6	7	8	9	10	11	12
1	Alresford		19/09	14/11	09/01	10/10	23/01	06/03	27/03	24/10	13/02	10/04	05/12
2	Chineham	19/12		17/10	20/02	26/09	28/11	12/12	10/04	16/01	20/03	07/11	30/01
3	Fawley	20/02	23/01		12/12	24/10	10/04	09/01	10/10	13/02	19/09	20/03	28/11
4	Isle Of Wight	26/09	14/11	27/03		06/03	10/10	24/10	13/02	05/12	23/01	19/12	12/09
5	Kingsclere	16/01	09/01	30/01	28/11		20/03	10/04	19/09	17/10	12/12	20/02	07/11
6	Lytchett Minster	17/10	06/03	12/09	16/01	05/12		13/02	14/11	27/03	24/10	26/09	19/12
7	Nomads	28/11	27/03	26/09	30/01	12/09	07/11		05/12	19/12	20/02	17/10	16/01
8	Overton	12/12	12/09	16/01	07/11	19/12	20/02	20/03		26/09	28/11	30/01	17/10
9	Paxton Pumas	30/01	10/10	07/11	20/03	23/01	12/12	19/09	09/01		10/04	28/11	20/02
10	Stoneham	07/11	05/12	19/12	17/10	27/03	30/01	14/11	06/03	12/09		16/01	26/09
11	Ventnor	12/09	13/02	05/12	19/09	14/11	09/01	23/01	24/10	06/03	10/10		27/03
12	Verwood	20/03	24/10	06/03	10/04	13/02	19/09	10/10	23/01	14/11	09/01	12/12	

KENT ONE

		1	2	3	4	5	6	7	8	9	10	11	12
1	Ashford		13/02	19/09	06/03	23/01	05/12	14/11	24/10	12/09	09/01	27/03	10/10
2	Beccehamian	07/11		20/02	16/01	12/12	17/10	26/09	10/04	19/12	28/11	30/01	20/03
3	Cranbrook	19/12	14/11		05/12	24/10	27/03	06/03	13/02	26/09	10/10	12/09	23/01
4	Dartfordians	28/11	10/10	20/03		19/09	07/11	23/01	09/01	30/01	12/12	20/02	10/04
5	Erith	17/10	27/03	30/01	19/12		26/09	12/09	05/12	28/11	07/11	16/01	20/02
6	Gillingham Anch.	20/03	23/01	12/12	13/02	09/01		24/10	10/10	20/02	10/04	28/11	19/09
7	Guys' Kings' & St Thomas' Hospital	20/02	09/01	28/11	17/10	10/04	30/01		19/09	16/01	20/03	07/11	12/12
8	HSBC	30/01	12/09	07/11	26/09	20/03	16/01	19/12		12/12	20/02	17/10	28/11
9	Old Olavians	10/04	19/09	09/01	24/10	06/03	14/11	10/10	27/03		23/01	05/12	13/02
10	Sheppey	26/09	06/03	16/01	27/03	13/02	12/09	05/12	14/11	17/10		19/12	24/10
11	Sittingbourne	12/12	24/10	10/04	14/11	10/10	06/03	13/02	23/01	20/03	19/09		09/01
12	Vigo	16/01	05/12	17/10	12/09	14/11	19/12	27/03	06/03	07/11	30/01	26/09	

KENT TWO

		1	2	3	4	5	6	7	8	9	10
1	Askean		26/09	06/03	14/11	10/04	20/03	13/02	17/10	16/01	19/12
2	Bexley	09/01		19/09	27/03	30/01	24/10	05/12	06/03	14/11	10/10
3	Brockleians	28/11	10/04		13/02	19/12	20/02	17/10	16/01	26/09	20/03
4	Foots Cray	20/02	19/12	24/10		20/03	30/01	16/01	26/09	10/04	28/11
5	Kings Coll. Hospital	19/09	17/10	27/03	05/12		10/10	06/03	14/11	13/02	09/01
6	Lordswood	05/12	13/02	14/11	17/10	16/01		26/09	27/03	06/03	10/04
7	New Ash Green	24/10	20/03	30/01	10/10	28/11	09/01		10/04	19/12	20/02
8	Old Williamsonians	30/01	28/11	10/10	09/01	20/02	19/12	19/09		20/03	24/10
9	Orpington	10/10	20/02	09/01	19/09	24/10	28/11	27/03	05/12		30/01
10	Shooters Hill	27/03	16/01	05/12	06/03	26/09	19/09	14/11	13/02	17/10	

LONDON & S.E. DIVISION FIXTURE GRIDS 2009-2010

HERTFORDSHIRE & MIDDLESEX feeding London 3 North West

ONE		1	2	3	4	5	6	7	8	9	10
1	Harlequin Amateurs		14/11	05/12	09/01	27/03	13/02	19/09	06/03	10/10	17/10
2	Hendon	20/02		09/01	24/10	10/10	20/03	30/01	19/09	19/12	28/11
3	Kilburn Cosmos	20/03	26/09		28/11	24/10	10/04	20/02	16/01	30/01	19/12
4	Old Abbotstonians	26/09	13/02	06/03		05/12	17/10	27/03	14/11	19/09	16/01
5	Old Actonians	19/12	16/01	13/02	20/03		26/09	28/11	17/10	20/02	10/04
6	Old Grammarians	24/10	05/12	19/09	30/01	09/01		10/10	27/03	28/11	20/02
7	Old Millhillians	10/04	17/10	14/11	19/12	06/03	16/01		13/02	20/03	26/09
8	Saracens Amateurs	28/11	10/04	10/10	20/02	30/01	19/12	24/10		09/01	20/03
9	Verulamians	16/01	27/03	17/10	10/04	14/11	06/03	05/12	26/09		13/02
10	Wasps	30/01	06/03	27/03	10/10	19/09	14/11	09/01	05/12	24/10	

TWO		1	2	3	4	5	6	7	8	9	10
1	Belsize Park		16/01	10/04	19/12	30/01	28/11	20/03	20/02	26/09	24/10
2	H.A.C.	10/10		19/12	20/03	09/01	20/02	28/11	24/10	10/04	30/01
3	Hackney	19/09	27/03		20/02	28/11	30/01	24/10	10/10	05/12	09/01
4	Mill Hill	27/03	05/12	14/11		24/10	10/10	30/01	09/01	06/03	19/09
5	Old Haberdashers	17/10	26/09	06/03	13/02		10/04	16/01	05/12	27/03	14/11
6	Old Isleworthians	06/03	14/11	17/10	16/01	19/09		26/09	27/03	13/02	05/12
7	Old Priorians	05/12	06/03	13/02	17/10	10/10	09/01		19/09	14/11	27/03
8	Quintin	14/11	13/02	16/01	26/09	20/03	19/12	10/04		17/10	06/03
9	Royston	09/01	19/09	20/03	28/11	19/12	24/10	20/02	30/01		10/10
10	Uxbridge	13/02	17/10	26/09	10/04	20/02	20/03	19/12	28/11	16/01	

THREE		1	2	3	4	5	6	7	8
1	Cuffley		05/12	30/01	09/01	27/03	19/09	10/10	14/11
2	Hatfield	06/03		14/11	10/10	19/09	09/01	30/01	19/12
3	Ickenham	24/10	20/02		19/09	05/12	27/03	09/01	10/10
4	London French	26/09	16/01	10/04		24/10	20/02	19/12	06/03
5	Old Tottonians	19/12	10/04	06/03	30/01		10/10	14/11	09/01
6	Pinner & Grammarians	10/04	26/09	19/12	14/11	16/01		06/03	30/01
7	Thamesians	16/01	24/10	26/09	27/03	20/02	05/12		19/09
8	Watford	20/02	27/03	16/01	05/12	26/09	24/10	10/04	

FOUR		1	2	3	4	5	6	7	8
1	British Airways		16/01	19/12	06/03	10/04	20/02	26/09	24/10
2	Chess Valley	10/10		30/01	19/12	14/11	09/01	06/03	19/09
3	G.W.R.	27/03	24/10		19/09	26/09	05/12	16/01	20/02
4	Harrow	05/12	27/03	10/04		16/01	24/10	20/02	26/09
5	Hayes	19/09	20/02	09/01	10/10		27/03	24/10	05/12
6	Northolt	14/11	26/09	06/03	30/01	19/12		10/04	16/01
7	Southgate	09/01	05/12	10/10	14/11	30/01	19/09		27/03
8	Sudbury & London Springboks	30/01	10/04	14/11	09/01	06/03	10/10	19/12	

SURREY feeding London 3 South West

ONE

		1	2	3	4	5	6	7	8	9	10
1	Battersea Ironsides		10/04	13/02	14/11	24/10	12/12	20/03	23/01	10/10	06/03
2	Bec Old Boys	26/09		06/03	05/12	14/11	16/01	17/10	13/02	24/10	27/03
3	Chipstead	07/11	28/11		17/10	10/04	20/02	16/01	12/12	20/03	30/01
4	Croydon	20/02	20/03	23/01		10/10	28/11	30/01	10/04	12/12	07/11
5	Farnham	30/01	20/02	26/09	16/01		07/11	12/12	20/03	28/11	17/10
6	London Exiles	27/03	10/10	14/11	06/03	13/02		26/09	24/10	23/01	05/12
7	Old Freemens	05/12	23/01	10/10	24/10	27/03	10/04		06/03	13/02	14/11
8	Old Walcountians	17/10	07/11	27/03	26/09	05/12	30/01	28/11		20/02	16/01
9	Old Whitgiftians	16/01	30/01	05/12	27/03	06/03	17/10	07/11	14/11		26/09
10	Teddington	28/11	12/12	24/10	13/02	23/01	20/03	20/02	10/10	10/04	

TWO

		1	2	3	4	5	6	7	8	9	10
1	Cranleigh		20/03	07/11	23/01	12/12	28/11	10/04	20/02	30/01	10/10
2	Law Society	05/12		27/03	06/03	24/10	16/01	13/02	26/09	17/10	14/10
3	London Media	13/02	12/12		24/10	10/04	20/03	10/10	28/11	20/02	23/01
4	Old Blues	17/10	28/11	30/01		20/03	20/02	12/12	07/11	16/01	10/04
5	Old Caterhamians	27/03	30/01	26/09	05/12		17/10	14/10	16/01	07/11	06/03
6	Old Cranleighans	06/03	10/10	05/12	14/10	23/01		24/10	27/03	26/09	13/02
7	Old Emanuel	26/09	07/11	16/01	27/03	20/02	30/01		17/10	28/11	05/12
8	Old Haileyburians	14/10	10/04	06/03	13/02	10/10	12/12	23/01		20/03	24/10
9	Old Rutlishians	24/10	23/01	14/10	10/10	13/02	10/04	06/03	05/12		27/03
10	Raynes Park	16/01	20/02	17/10	26/09	28/11	07/11	20/03	30/01	12/12	

THREE

		1	2	3	4	5	6	7	8	9	10
1	CL London		10/04	24/10	14/11	06/03	10/10	27/03	13/02	23/01	05/12
2	Haslemere	26/09		06/03	05/12	24/10	14/11	13/02	23/01	10/10	27/03
3	Merton	30/01	28/11		07/11	10/04	23/01	10/10	12/12	20/03	20/02
4	Mitcham	20/02	20/03	13/02		10/10	24/10	23/01	10/04	12/12	28/11
5	Old Amplefordians	28/11	30/01	26/09	16/01		27/03	05/12	20/02	07/11	17/10
6	Old Oundelians	16/01	20/02	17/10	30/01	12/12		10/04	20/03	28/11	07/11
7	Old Radleian	12/12	07/11	16/01	17/10	20/03	26/09		28/11	20/02	30/01
8	Old Tiffinians	07/11	17/10	27/03	26/09	14/11	05/12	06/03		30/01	16/01
9	Streatham-Croydon	17/10	16/01	05/12	27/03	13/02	06/03	14/11	24/10		26/09
10	Worth Old Boys	20/03	12/12	14/11	06/03	23/01	13/02	24/10	10/10	10/04	

FOUR

		1	2	3	4	5	6	7	8	9	10
1	Economicals		20/03	12/12	16/01	26/09	17/10	07/11	20/02	30/01	28/11
2	Egham Hollowegians	05/12		28/11	26/09	27/03	16/01	30/01	07/11	17/10	20/02
3	Free Date	27/03	06/03		24/10	10/10	14/11	10/04	23/01	05/12	13/02
4	Guildfordians Bisons	10/10	10/04	30/01		23/01	07/11	28/11	20/03	20/02	12/12
5	Lightwater	10/04	12/12	16/01	17/10		30/01	20/02	28/11	07/11	20/03
6	Old Glynonians	23/01	10/10	20/02	13/02	24/10		20/03	12/12	28/11	10/04
7	Pelhamians	13/02	24/10	26/09	06/03	14/11	05/12		10/10	27/03	23/01
8	Reigate	14/11	13/02	17/10	05/12	06/03	27/03	16/01		26/09	24/10
9	Wandsworthians	24/10	23/01	20/03	14/11	13/02	06/03	12/12	10/04		10/10
10	Woking	06/03	14/11	07/11	27/03	05/12	26/09	17/10	30/01	16/01	

LONDON & S.E. LEVEL 7-12 & NON LEAGUE CLUBS

Aldershot & Fleet RUFC
Ground Address: Aldershot & Fleet Rugby Club Aldershot Park Guildford Road GU12 4BP
Contact: 01252 654818
Email: info@fleetrugby.com
Directions: Leave the M3 at Junction 4, take the A331 to Aldershot Take Ash Road (A323) into Aldershot, following signs for Pools Complex, turn Left at the third set of traffic lights onto the Lower Farnham Road (B3208) Go straight over the mini roundabout, and turn left into Guildford Rd the entrance to ground is on the left at the end of Guildford road just before the cricket club. Under the barrier and follow the road round to the rugby pitches.
Honorary Secretary: Mr Merrik Knight; 7 Closeworth Road Farnborough HampshireGU14 6JH
Tel: 07801 883111   Email: merrikk@aol.com
Fixtures Secretary: Mr Sean Kavanagh; 89 Roberts Road Aldershot HampshireGU12 4RB
Tel: 01252 661324   Email: sean_telecad@hotmail.com
Club Colours: Red, White and Blue
League: Hampshire 1 (level 9)

Alresford RFC
Ground Address: Bighton Cricket Ground Nettlebed Lane Bighton Alresford HampshireSO24 9RB
Contact: 01962 774479
Email: secretary@alresfordrfc.org
Website: www.alresfordrfc.org
Directions: From the A31 Winchester - Alton Road take the B3047 off the by-pass into Alresford town. Arlebury Park is on the north side of the road opposite Perins School. The pitch is out of town, at Bighton.
Hon. Secretary: Mrs Sue Bell; Station Cottage Andover Road Micheldever Station Hampshire SO21 3AP
Tel: 01962 774479
Email: secretary@alresfordrfc.org
Fixtures Secretary: Mr Paul Rees; 2 Coniston Grove Alresford HampshireSO24 9NR Tel: 07739 699567
Email: fixtures@alresfordrfc.org
Club Colours: Gold, Green & Black
League: Hampshire 2 (level 10)

Alton RFC
Ground Address: Anstey Park Anstey Lane Alton HampshireGU34 2NB
Contact: 01420 82146
Email: info@alton-rfc.com
Website: www.alton-rfc.com
Directions: Follow A31 from Guildford or Winchester. At roundabout, north of Alton, take B3004 to Alton. Follow B3004 over railway and round to left. Entrance to Anstey Park on right beyond the Queens Head public house and at the end of the railings.
Honorary Secretary: Mr David Bugler; 27 Churchfields Kingsley Bordon HampshireGU35 9PJ
Tel: 01420 476789   Email: dai_b@hotmail.com

Fixtures Secretary: Mr Martin Simpson; 10 Gauvain Close Alton GU34 2SB Tel: 01420 86880
Email: roryandrew@simhacker.fsnet.co.uk
Club Colours: black body, red sleeves with white trim
League: Hampshire 1 (level 9)

Andover RFC Ltd
Ground Address: The Goodship Ground Foxcotte Park, Charlton Down Andover SP11 0TA
Contact: 01264 339518
Email: nick@andoverrfc.com
Website: www.nrwebsolutions.com/Arfc
Directions: From town centre take ring road to Portway Ind. Estate, turn into Goch Way, right onto Hatherden Rd, follow road for 0.75 mile to roundabout, turn into Sports Centre.
Honorary Secretary: Ivor Evans ; 29 Picton Road Andover SP10 2HQ   Tel: 01264 395320
Email: ivor.evans7@ntlworld.com
Fixtures Secretary: Mr Rod Smith; 17 Longstock Close Andover HampshireSP10 3UN Tel: 01264 359491
Email: carol.smith55@tiscali.co.uk
Club Colours: Black
League: London 3 South West (level 8)

Ash RFC
Ground Address: Pavilion The P Ash Recreation Ground Queens Road Queens Road Ash Kent CT3 2BG
Contact: 01304 813201
Email: noobeast@hotmail.com
Website: www.ashrugbyclub.co.uk
Directions: We are situated just off the A228 between Sandwich and Wingham. Take the second exit off the A228 into Ash, take the first left and we are 600 metres on the left hand side.
Honorary Secretary: Mr Paul Ralph; The Old Barn Ash Canterbury Kent CT3 2DL Tel: 01304 813201
Email: noobeast@hotmail.com
Fixtures Secretary: Mr Alan Warner Tel: 01304 812396
Email: djsandejs@tiscali.co.uk
Club Colours: Green Black White
Non League

Ashford RFC
Ground Address: Kinneys Field Canterbury Road, Bybrook Ashford Kent TN24 9QB
Contact: 01233 624 693
Email: jennyarfc@aol.com
Directions: M20 J9, follow signs for Canterbury. Turn right just after the Holiday Inn. Ashford Rugby Club sign at entrance.
Honorary Secretary: Mr Ian Nelson; 137 Lower Queens Road Ashford TN24 8HD Tel: 07808 557301
Email: ian.nelson@premierfoods.co.uk
Fixtures Secretary: Mr James Hall   Tel: 07955 220476
Club Colours: Red Amber & Black Hoops
League: Kent 1 (level 9)

Askean RFC
Ground Address: Askeans at WellHall Kidbrooke Lane Eltham London SE9 6TE
Contact: 0208 8500210
Email: Ianlunn@hotmail.com
Website: www.askeans.co.uk
Directions: A2 towards London. Turn right onto A205 - South Circular - towards Woolwich. Ground immediately on right by Fly Over. By Train to Eltham Station.Turn Right out of station. Kidbrooke Lane on Left. 5 Minutes.
Honorary Secretary: Ms Alison Gaze; 11a Old Road Lewisham London SE13 5SU Tel: 0208 8529943
Email: connon@supanet.com
Fixtures Secretary: Mr Nick Linklater; 9 Moordown Shooters Hill London SE18 4GB
Tel: 0794 1044866
Email: nick_linklater@hotmail.com
Club Colours: Blue, Black & White
League: Kent 2 (level 10)

Bancroft RFC
Ground Address: The Club House Buckhurst Way Buckhurst Hill Essex IG9 6JD
Contact: 020 85040429
Email: admin@bancroft-rfc.fsnet.co.uk
Website: www.bancroftrfc.co.uk
Directions: Club House, Buckhurst Way, Buckhurst Hill, Essex IG9 6JD Tel: 020 8504 0429 From M25 take M11/A406 to "Waterworks" junction with the A104, Marked A104 Epping, Woodford New Road to Woodford Green - Turn right into Broadmead Road at Castle Public House - left at 3rd lights into St. Barnabas Road - ground 1 mile on the right hand side, (before the railway bridge at Buckhurst Way).
Honorary Secretary: Mr Stephen Thirsk; 4 Bentley Way Woodford Green Essex IG8 0SE
Tel: 020 85082722   Email: ST@whiskers.co.uk
Fixtures Secretary: Mr David Patterson
Tel: 07968 817308   Email: david.patterson@rbos.com
Club Colours: Blue, Black, Claret & Light Blue
League: Essex 1 (level 9)

Bank of England RFC
Ground Address: Priory Lane Roehampton SW15 5JQ
Website: www.boerfc.com
Honorary Secretary: Mr Jonathan Anthony Hughes; 62 Shalstone Road London SW14 7HR
Fixtures Secretary: Mr Stephen Clow; 1 Oaklands Road London SW14 8NJ
Tel: 0208 8761472
Email: seclow@btinternet.com
Club Colours: Blue, White and Gold Hoops
League: London 3 North West (level 8)

Barnet Elizabethans RFC
Ground Address: Byng Road Barnet EN5 4NP
Contact: 020 84417534
Email: njlmoore007@yahoo.co.uk
Website: www.barnetrfc.com
Directions: From M25 (J23), take A1081 to Barnet. After 1.5 miles at pedestrian crossing, right into Alston Road, through width restriction, turn third right (Wentworth Road), then left (Byng Road) -ground at bottom end of road.
Honorary Secretary: Nigel Moore; 49 Garthland Drive Arkley Barnet Herts. EN5 3BD Tel: 020 84417534
Email: njlmoore007@yahoo.co.uk
Fixtures Secretary: Mr Peter Glenister; 47 Bury Lane Codicote Hitchin Herts. SG4 8XX Tel: 01438 820692
Email: pegmeg@btinternet.com
Club Colours: blue and red
League: London 3 North West (level 8)

Basildon RFC (Essex)
Ground Address: Gardiner's Close Basildon SS14 3AW
Contact: 01268 533136
Email: gsantry@ford.com
Website: www.basildonrugby.co.uk
Directions: From West: A127 London/S'thend arterial Rd., past 1st signs for B'don, right A132, right at 2nd r/about A1235, right at 1st lights (not Zebra) Gardiners Lane south is first left- ground at end.
Honorary Secretary: Mr Gary Santry; 4 Jefferson Avenue Laindon Basildon SS15 6JY
Tel: 07885 869446   Email: gsantry@ford.com
Fixtures Secretary: as Hon. Secretary
Club Colours: Bottle Green / White hooped Shirts
League: London 3 North East (level 8)

Battersea Ironsides RFC
Ground Address: Openview off Burntwood Lane off Burntwood Lane Wandsworth SW17 0AW
Contact: 020 8874 9913
Email: info@birfc.co.uk
Website: www.birfc.co.uk
Directions: From the south: A24 to Tooting Broadway, turn west on A217 towards Wandsworth, after 2nd r'about, Burntwood Lane is 2nd road on right. The pitches at Garratt Green are 500m on the right. The clubhouse and changing rooms are on the corner of Openview, a further 300m on the left. From the north: Wandsworth one-way system take A217 Garratt Lane to Burntwood Lane, 500m on the left after Earlsfield BR station.
Honorary Secretary: Mr Paul Tanner; 1 Woodland Way Morden Surrey SM4 4DS Tel: 020 85405784
Email: paul.tanner@swlstg-tr.nhs.uk
Fixtures Secretary: Mr Tony Szulc; Battersea Ironsides Rugby Football Club Burntwood Lane Earsfeild London sw17 0wa Tel: 07956 501794
Club Colours: Green Jerseys, White Band, White Shorts, Red Socks
League: Surrey 1 (level 9)

Bec Old Boys RFC
Ground Address: Spencer Sports Club Fieldview Fieldview Earlsfield SW18 3HF
Contact: 07765 860949
Email: daveklauber@dsktopp.fsnet.co.uk
Website: www.becrfc.co.uk
Directions: BY TRAIN Go to Earlsfield Station - 6 mins from club - 1 stop from Clapham Junction. Turn left out of station. Take first left - Magdalen Rd. Then take 3rd Right - Changing rooms 100 yds on Left (for Pitch & Changing Rooms) OR take 4th right - Spencer Club is 500 yds on Right (for Clubhouse & Bar - 2 mins further) BY ROAD Use A-Z or Tom-Tom Ground is in Earlsfield between Burntwood Lane (B229) and Magdalen Road. The entrance to the Changing Room & Pitches is on Openview Road 100 yds from Magdalen Road and the entrance to the Spencer Clubhouse & Bar is on Fieldview Road 200yds from Burntwood Lane
Honorary Secretary: Mr Dave Klauber; 40A Glencairn Road Streatham London SW16 5DF Tel: 07765 860 949
Email: daveklauber@dsktopp.fsnet.co.uk
Fixtures Secretary: Mr Gim Botting; 46 Summerley Street London SW18 4EU Tel: 020 72454000
Email: G.Botting@Olayangroup.com
Club Colours: Blue jerseys with gold hoop, white shorts
League: Surrey 1 (level 9)

Beccehamian RFC
Ground Address: Sparrows Den Corkscrew Hill West Wickham Kent BR4 9BB
Contact: 020 87778105
Email: secretary@beccehamians.co.uk
Website: www.beccehamians.co.uk
Directions: Corner of Corkscrew Hill and Addington Road (A2022)
Honorary Secretary: Mr Robert Keate; Sparrows Den Corkscrew Hill West Wickham Kent BR4 9BB Tel: 020 82895842
Email: Sharon.Keate@yahoo.com
Fixtures Secretary: Mr Clive Putner; 9 Druids Way Shortlands Bromley Kent BR2 0NQ Tel: 020 84607938
Email: clive@putner.fsnet.co.uk
Club Colours: Maroon, Black & White Hoops
League: Kent 1 (level 9)

Beccles RUFC
Ground Address: Beef Meadow Common Lane Common Lane Beccles NR34 9BX
Contact: 01502 712016
Website: www.becclesrufc.co.uk
Directions: Into Beccles from Morrisons r/about (A146), over mini r/about, follow rd left over crossing 1st left is Common Lane. From A12 take A145 to Beccles. Right at first lights then left at next. Right into Grove Rd then right over crossing. 1st left Common Lane
Honorary Secretary: Mr Keith Johnstone; 29 Pleasant Place Beccles SuffolkNR34 9YD Tel: 01502 710430
Email: keithjohnston@tiscali.co.uk

Fixtures Secretary: Mr Dick Grieve; Larch Cottage Walcott Road Bacton NorfolkNR12 0HB
Tel: 01692 651444
Email: dickiegrieve@fsmail.net
Club Colours: Black & Emerald
League: London 3 North East (level 8)

Belsize Park RFC
Ground Address: Club House The Chester Arms 87 Albany Street NW1 4BT
Contact: 07968 387203
Email: belsizerugby@googlemail.com
Website: www.belsizeparkrfc.com
Directions: The Chester Arms is in Albany Street, NW1 4BT which runs along the edge of Regents Park. The nearest tube is Great Portland Street on the Circle and Metropolitan lines. Park in the Outer Circle of Regents Part near Chester Gate.
Honorary Secretary: Mr Matthew Flynn; 20 Patrick Road Caversham Reading RG4 8DD
Tel: 0796 8387203   Email: flynn.matthew@gmail.com
Fixtures Secretary: Mr Adrian Price; 3 William Dyce Mews Streatham London SW16 6AW Tel:
Email: adrian.price@benfieldgroup.com
Club Colours: Black & Purple
League: Herts-Middlesex 2 (level 10)

Bexley RFC
Ground Address: Bexley R.F.C. Bexley Park Sports & Social Club Bexley Park, Calvert Drive Bexley Park, Calvert Drive Dartford Kent DA2 7GA
Contact: 01322 521093
Email: Paul_Herbert@bexleyrfc.co.uk
Website: www.bexleyrfc.co.uk
Honorary Secretary: Mr Alan Perry; 7 Pinewood Road Bostall Heath London SE2 0RY Tel: 0208 3119728
Email: perrya10@yahoo.co.uk
Fixtures Secretary: Mr Paul Herbert; 81 Marlborough Park Ave. Sidcup Kent DA16 9DY   Tel: 020 86943255
Email: herbert.paul@btinternet.com
Club Colours: Royal Blue and White Hoops
League: Kent 2 (level 10)

Billericay RFC
Ground Address: Willowbrook Sports & Social Club Stock Road Billericay Essex CM4 9PQ
Contact: 01277 622528
Email: billericayrfc@hotmail.co.uk
Website: http://www.billericay-rfc.co.uk/
Directions: From A12 Take exit for Billericay / Galleywood turn towards Stock. On exiting Stock you pass The Kings Head Public House on right. The club is 200 yards on the left, opposite the 2nd house after the pub (fourwinds).Look for the Stock Tennis Club sign. From A127 Take Billericay exit from A127. Follow A176 towards Billericay for approx 4 miles. Straight over at first two roundabouts , left at third. Right at roundabout in to high street. Through high street and straight over three roundabouts.Club on right after 400 yards. Opposite only house on left (fourwinds)

Honorary Secretary: Mr Geoff Maynard; 1 The Limes Galleywood Essex CM2 8RA Tel: 07836 298205
Email: geoffmaynard@ukonline.co.uk
Fixtures Secretary: Mr Andrew Collings; 6 Courtlands Billericay Essex CM12 9HX Tel: 07970 194995
Email: andycollings999@hotmail.com
Club Colours: Black Shirts with Gold Band ,
League: London 3 North East (level 8)

Black Baa Baas RFC

Ground Address: 47 Mordaunt Street London SW9 9RD
Contact: 07793 892978
Email: blackbaabaasrfc@gmail.com
Website: www.blackbaabaasrfc.com
Honorary Secretary: Mr Matt Wilcock; Gordon House Fullerton Road London SW18 1BX Tel: 07920 117457
Email: mwillcock@struttandparker.com
Fixtures Secretary: Andy Willcock Tel: 07870 999628
Club Colours: Black
Non League

Black Horse RFC

Ground Address: The Black Horse West Street Hertford Herts. SG13 8EZ
Contact: 01992 589612
Email: pauldouglass@hotmail.com
Website: www.blackhorserugby.co.uk
Directions: No regular home ground - Check which ground we're playing at!
Honorary Secretary: Mr Paul Douglass; 3c Balfour Street Hertford Herts. SG14 3AY Tel: 07789 400413
Email: pauldouglass@hotmail.com
Fixtures Secretary: Mr Neil Mcdonald; 29 Clarks Close Ware Herts. SG12 0QH Tel: 07903 969980
Email: neilmcd66@ntlworld.com
Club Colours: Black
Non League

Bognor RFC

Ground Address: Bognor R.F.C. Hampshire Avenue Bognor Regis West Sussex PO21 5JY
Contact: 01243 584197
Email: johnjennings4@aol.com
Website: www.bognor-rfc.com
Directions: Head west on A259 from the centre of Bognor. Turn left into Hampshire Avenue (marker for club on lamp post). Take 1st turn on left.
Hon. Secretary: John Jennings; 5 Church House Mews Felpham Road Bognor Regis W. Sussex PO22 7PH
Tel: 01243 864318 Email: johnjennings4@aol.com
Fixtures Secretary: Mr Bill Matthews; 100 Gravits Lane Bognor Regis West Sussex PO21 5LW
Tel: 07708 005700
Email: will-matthews@talktalk.net
Club Colours: Purple, Green and White hoops
League: London 2 South West (level 7)

Braintree RFC

Ground Address: Braintree R.F.C. The Clubhouse Robbswood, Beckers Green Rd Braintree Essex CM7 3PR
Contact: 01376 322282
Email: corinneaw@aol.com
Website: www.braintreerugbyclub.co.uk
Directions: From Braintree bypass A120 exit at Galleys Corner roundabout to Braintree East (B1018 Cressing Road), 300 metres turn right into Beckers GReen Road, Ground at end of road.
Honorary Secretary: Mr John Leech; 344 Cressing Road Braintree Essex CM7 3PE Tel: 01376 551778
Email: JLeech1336@aol.com
Fixtures Secretary: Mr David Salisbury-Higgs; 12 Grove Field Braintree Essex CM7 5NS
Tel: 07740 399043
Email: david@dashproperties.co.uk
Club Colours: Black and Amber
League: London 2 North East (level 7)

Brightlingsea RFC

Ground Address: Colne Community School Church Road Brightlingsea Essex CO7 0QL
Contact: 01206 241061
Email: jeff.dunn1@btinternet.com
Website: www.brfcuk.com
Directions: Colne School is on the main road as you enter the town.
Honorary Secretary: Mr Jeffrey Dunn; 21 Partridge Drive Fordham Colchester Essex CO6 3NH
Tel: 07736 978699
Email: jeff.dunn1@btinternet.com
Fixtures Secretary: Mr Graham Williams; 18 Hurst Green Brightlingsea Colchester CO7 0HG
Tel: 07762 208882
Email: williams562@btinternet.com
Club Colours: Red and Black with Black Shorts
League: Essex 2 (level 10)

Brighton RFC

Ground Address: Waterhall Playing Fields Mill Road, Patcham Brighton BN1 8YN
Contact: 01273 562729
Email: brightonrugby@btinternet.com
Website: www.brightonrugby.org.uk
Directions: From London A23 to Patcham roundabout, round r/about, turn into Mill Road, underneath Railway arch, 1st right, 1st left, straight up to club house.
Honorary Secretary: Mrs Melanie Richardson; 29 Nevill Road Rottingdean Brighton East Sussex BN2 7HH Tel: 01273 304343
Email: steve.s@brightonblues.co.uk
Fixtures Secretary: Mr Tudor Ellis; 47 Cuckfield Road Hurstpierpoint HASSOCKS West Sussex BN6 9RW Tel: 01273 831523
Email: ellis.tudor@gmail.com
Club Colours: Blue Shirts, Shorts, Blue Sock
League: London 3 South East (level 8)

British Airways RFC
Ground Address: Concorde Centre Crane Lodge Road High Street Cranford TW5 9RQ
Contact: 020 85132000
Email: david.wallin@mpsa.com
Website: www.britishairwaysrfc.co.uk
Directions: Take M4 J3 follow A312 to Feltham. At first lights turn left. Then left at first mini roundabout. Clubhouse is right at second mini roundabout.
Honorary Secretary: Mr David Wallin; 2 Caenshill House Chaucer Avenue Weybridge Surrey KT13 0PB
Tel: 01932 848467
Email: david.wallin@mpsa.com
Fixtures Secretary: Mr Brett Frische; The Meridian 11 Kenavon Drive Reading RG1 3DG   Tel: 07832 110648
Email: brettfrische@hotmail.com
Club Colours: Red, White & Blue Quarters
League: Herts-Middlesex 4 (level 12)

British Transport Police RFC
Ground Address: c/o East London Rugby Club Holland Road, West Ham, E15 3BP
Contact: 020 7474 6761
Email: nickbracken@hotmail.com
Honorary Secretary: Mr Alan Stobbs; 25 Camden Road London NW1 9LN Tel: 01992 610631
Email: alan.stobbs@essexrugby.com
Fixtures Secretary: Mr Nick Loader Tel: 07793 292488
Non League

Broadland - Gt. Yarmouth
Ground Address: Cobholm Playing Field Cobholm Great Yarmouth NorfolkNR31 0BA
Email: asabroadlandrfc@aol.com
Website: www.broadlandrfc.com
Directions: From Norwich A47. 1st r/about take 3rd exit over bridge, 400yds on right.
Honorary Secretary: Mr Russ Clarke; 162 Angel Road Norwich NR3 3JB Tel: 07836 208024
Email: Secretary@BroadlandRFC.com
Fixtures Secretary: Mr Adam Towfighi; 14 Alexandra Avenue Great Yarmouth NorfolkNR30 4ED
Tel: 07917 182010
Email: adam_towfighi@yahoo.co.uk
Club Colours: Red, White & Blue
League: East Counties 2 (level 10)

Brockleians RFC
Ground Address: Eltham Palace Road Eltham Eltham London SE9 5LX
Contact: 07792 204811
Email: alex.g.mills@btinternet.com
Website: www.brockleians.co.uk
Directions: A20 to junction with South Circular, turn into Eltham Palace Road at World of Leather.
Fixtures Secretary: Mr David Gearing Tel: 07811 931543
Email: DaveGearing@ukgateway.net
Club Colours: Chocolate brown, emerald green, old gold
League: Kent 2 (level 10)

Bromley RFC
Ground Address: Barnet Wood Road Hayes Kent BR2 7AA
Contact: 020 84623430
Website: www.bromleyrfc.co.uk
Directions: M25 J4 & A21 towards Bromley. At Locksbottom filter left at lights on A232. 0.5 mile to next lights then right & 1st left to Barnet Wood road.
Honorary Secretary: Mr Stephen Wardingley; Fourways 108 West Common Road Bromley BR2 7BY
Tel: 07710 582327
Email: steve.wardingley@yahoo.co.uk
Fixtures Secretary: Mr Roger Simpson; 24 Lakeside WIckham Road Bromley Kent BR3 6LX
Tel: 020 84025123   Email: rd.simpson@ntlworld.com
Club Colours: Black, Amber, Black
League: London 2 South East (level 7)

Brunel University (West London) RFC
Ground Address: Union of Brunel Students Brunel University Brunel University Uxbridge Middx.UB8 3PH
Contact: 01895 269269
Email: stuart.chatfield@brunel.ac.uk
Website: www.brunelstudents.com
Fixtures Secretary: Nick Taylor; UBS 0 The Hamilton Centre Brunel University Kingston Lane Uxbridge UB8 3PH Tel: 01895 267250
Email: nick.taylor@brunel.ac.uk
Club Colours: Chocolate with white and navy
Non League

Buckinghamshire New University
Ground Address: The Gawcott Fields Gawcott Road Gawcott
Contact: 01280 820342
Email: stefan.ridley@buckingham.ac.uk
Fixtures Secretary: Jill Kittle; High Wycombe Campus Queen Alexandra Road High Wycombe Bucks. HP11 2JZ
Tel: 01494 446330   Email: union@bcuc.ac.uk
Non League

Burgess Hill RFC
Ground Address: Southway Playing FIelds Poveys Close Burgess Hill RH15 9TA
Contact: 01444 232221
Email: neil@woodman.co.uk
Website: www.bhrfc.co.uk
Directions: From East - head into town on B2113 and follow until end. Turn right onto B2036 London Road, at junction with traffic lights, turn left. At Weald Inn, turn left into Weald Road then second right into Poveys Close and follow to end. From North, South or
Honorary Secretary: Mr Robin Roberts; 17 Cromwell Road Burgess Hill West Sussex RH15 8QH
Tel: 01444 257301   Email: robin_roberts@tiscali.co.uk
Fixtures Secretary: Mr Ross Hallifax; 0 Littlehampton Road Worthing BN13 1QZ   Tel: 07941 016836
Email: Ross.Hallifax@axa-insurance.co.uk
Club Colours: All Black
League: Sussex 1 (level 9)

Burnham-on-Crouch RUFC
Ground Address: Burnham-on-Crouch R.U.F.C. Dengie Hundred Sports Centre Millfields, Station Road Burnham On Crouch Essex CM0 8HS
Contact: 01621 784633
Email: info@burnhamrugby.co.uk
Website: www.burnhamrugby.co.uk
Directions: From all main routes contiue east (north of River Crouch), pick up B1010 into B-On-Crouch, right at T jctn, over rail bridge into town centre, library on right entrance to ground immediate right.
Honorary Secretary: Mr Bill Jones; 3 Maplins Garden Burnham-on-Crouch Essex CM0 8GE
Tel: 01621 785424
Email: billandsuejones@btinternet.com
Fixtures Secretary: Mr Ian Spurling; 2 Normandy Avenue Burnham-on-Crouch Essex CM0 8JJ
Tel: 07786 397815
Email: seniorfixtures@burnhamrugby.co.uk
Club Colours: Navy Blue and Amber Hoops
League: Essex 2 (level 10)

Camberley RFC
Ground Address: Watchetts Recreation Park Road Park Road Camberley Surrey GU15 2SR
Contact: 01276 25395
Email: president@camberleyrugby.org.uk
Website: www.camberleyrugby.org.uk
Directions: Ground is situated approximately one mile from junction 4 of the M3. On exiting the motorway initially follow signs for Farnborough and Frimley and Frimley Park Hospital. Take first slip road which is A325, follow to roundabout and take left turn (B3411)
Honorary Secretary: Derek Olsen; 19 Copse End Camberley Surrey GU15 2BP Tel: 01276 64791
Email: derek.olsen@btinternet.com
Fixtures Secretary: Ian Cardwell; Pine Cottage 1 Malborough Rise Camberley GU15 Tel: 07885 036 398
Email: iancardwell2044@btinternet.com
Club Colours: Black with amber collars
League: London 3 South West (level 8)

Campion
Ground Address: Cottons Park Cottons Approach Romford RM7 7AA
Email: info@campionrfc.com
Website: www.campionrfc.com
Honorary Secretary: Mr Peter O'Brien; 68 Lancaster Drive Elm Park Hornchurch Essex RM12 5ST
Tel: 01708 446980
Fixtures Secretary: Mr Pat Davis; 12 Highview Gardens Upminster Essex RM14 2YY
Tel: 07866 737793 Email: PatrickD@theipe.uk.com
Club Colours: Red & Black Hoops
League: Essex 1 (level 9)

Cantabrigian RFC
Ground Address: Sedley Taylor Road Cambridge Cambs.CB2 8PW
Contact: 01223 843830
Email: karl.grenz@aveva.com
Website: www.cantabs.co.uk
Directions: Leave M11 exit J11(A1309) to Cambridge. Head towards city centre for 1.5 miles. Right at traffic lights sign-posted Addenbrookes Hospital into Long Road. Left after railway bridge into Sedley Taylor Rd. Clubhouse is down a narrow entrance immediately on t
Honorary Secretary: Mr Karl Grenz; 23 Tunwells Lane Great Shelford Cambridge Cambs.CB22 5LJ
Tel: 01223 556652
Email: karl.grenz@aveva.com
Fixtures Secretary: Mr John Edmonds; 25 Granta Terrace Great Shelford Cumbria CA2 5DJ
Tel: 07764 268199
Email: johned40@hotmail.com
Club Colours: Navy Blue with White Hoops
League: East Counties 1 (level 9)

Canterbury Christ Church University RFC
Ground Address: Cante North Holmes Road Canterbury Kent CT1 1QU
Contact: 01227 782679
Website: www.canterbury.ac.uk/sport
Honorary Secretary: Mr Steve Bosel; Athletic Union Christ Church College RFC North Holmes Road Canterbury Kent CT1 1QU
Fixtures Secretary: Miss Claire Slater; Students Union Canterbury Christ Church University North Holmes Road Canterbury Kent CT1 1QU Tel: 01227 782271
Email: claire.slater@canterbury.ac.uk
Club Colours: Black & Claret
Non League

Canvey Island RFC
Ground Address: Tewkes Creek Dovervelt Road Canvey Island Essex SS8 8EY
Contact: 01268 681 881
Email: steveclarke_@hotmail.com
Directions: A130 to Sports Centre (Waterside Farm) Keep complex on right and Castle View School on left. Take 1st left after school. Ground 300yds on left.
Honorary Secretary: Gary Desmond; 387 Rayleigh Road Thundersley SS7 3ST Tel: 07846 443779
Email: geezer11@sky.com
Fixtures Secretary: Mr Kevin Hobart; 32 Tantelen Road Canvey Island Essex SS8 9QG
Email: kevin.hobart@blueyonder.co.uk
Club Colours: Red & Blue
League: London 3 North East (level 8)

Charlton Park RFC
Ground Address: Charlton Park R.F.C. 60a Broad Walk Kidbrooke London SE3 8NB
Contact: 0208 8561025
Email: andrew.potts57@ntlworld.com
Website: www.charltonpark.org.uk
Directions: The ground is located in Broad Walk, London SE3, which is found by leaving the A2 at the "Sun in the Sands" roundabout. If you are coming from Kent you have to "double back on yourself", so take the fourth exit. From central London it's the 3rd exit, follow "Local Traffic" and turn left onto the old A2 then take the first left, Broad Walk, four traffic bumps and your there, entrance on the right hand side.
Honorary Secretary: Mr Andy Potts; 37 Beechhill Road Eltham London SE9 1HJ   Tel: 07855 503306
Email: andrew.potts57@ntlworld.com
Fixtures Secretary: Mr Roe Belcher; 34 Green Lane London SE9 2AG   Tel: 07703 599452
Email: roe1.belcher@virgin.net
Club Colours: Red & White Hoops, Blue Shorts
League: London 3 South East (level 8)

Chelmsford RFC
Ground Address: Coronation Park Timsons Lane Springfield Chelmsford CM2 6AG
Contact: 01245 261159
Website: www.chelmsfordrugby.com
Directions: A12 to junction 19 - Follow signs to Springfield, over 2 roundabouts, at 3rd roundabout 3rd exit, under flyover, over r/about, 2nd turning left into Timsons Lane. Ground at end on right
Honorary Secretary: Mr Lawrence Crispin; 33 Jenner Mead Chelmsford CM2 6SJ   Tel: 020 76132047
Email: lcrispin@talk21.com
Fixtures Secretary: Ms Clare St John Coleman; 2 Meggy Tye Springfield Chelmsford CM2 6GA
Tel: 07885 344367
Email: claresjc@tiscali.co.uk
Club Colours: Navy Blue Shirts & Shorts
League: London 2 North East (level 7)

Cheshunt RFC
Ground Address: Rosedale Sports Club Andrews Lane Andrews Lane Cheshunt EN3 6TB
Contact: 01992 623983
Email: oldcestrians@btconnect.com
Website: www.cheshuntrugby.co.uk
Directions: M25 junction 25. A10 north to Cheshunt. First roundabout take first exit, straight over next three roundabouts, left into Andrews Lane. 100 yards on left.
Honorary Secretary: Mr Simon Embleton; 34 Bell Lane Broxbourne EN10 7HE   Tel: 01992 471514
Email: simon.embleton@ntlworld.com
Fixtures Secretary: Mr Gary Barton; 6 Spencer Avenue Cheshunt Waltham Cross Herts. EN7 6RR
Tel: 01992 636788
Email: garythedolphintrainer@hotmail.com
Club Colours: Green & White hooped shirts.
League: London 3 North West (level 8)

Chess Valley RFC
Ground Address: Rickmansworth Sports Club Park Road Rickmansworth Herts. WD3 1HU
Contact: 07815 960125
Website: www.chessvalleyrfc.co.uk
Directions: M25, J18, follow A404 to Rickmansworth. Club between town & Croxley Green & is signposted at bottom of Scots Bride Hill.
Honorary Secretary: Mr Craig Hocking; 15 Chesswood Court Bury Lane Rickmansworth Herts. WD3 1DF
Tel: 07815 960125
Email: craig.hocking@orange.co.uk
Fixtures Secretary: Mr Elliott Grace; 9 Epsom Court Bury Lane Mill End Rickmansworth Herts WD3 7HW
Tel: 0776 6724986
Email: elliot.grace@uk.gm.com
Club Colours: Black with green & white hoops
League: Herts-Middlesex 4 (level 12)

Chineham RFC
Ground Address: Basingstoke Sports & Social Club May's Bounty Cricket Ground Fairfields Road Basingstoke Hampshire RG21 3DR
Email: markgarner@chinehamrfc.org.uk
Website: www.chinehamrfc.org.uk
Directions: Directions from the M3 Leave M3 at Junction 6 Head towards Basingstoke At the first large roundabout (Black Dam), take a left turn A30/A339 Follow road (under bridge), towards next roundabout (Hackwood Road) and take the third exit towards 'Fairfields' Take the first turning on the left, round the Lamb Inn into Cliddesden Road Take the second turning on the right into Fairfields Road. Basingstoke and North Hants Cricket Club is at the end of Fairfields Road
Honorary Secretary: Mr Mark Garner; 93 Peggs Way Basingstoke Hampshire RG24 9FX   Tel: 01256 357807
Email: markcgarner@hotmail.com
Fixtures Secretary: Mr Mark Garner; 93 Peggs Way Basingstoke Hampshire RG24 9FX   Tel: 01256 357807
Email: markcgarner@hotmail.com
Club Colours: Black or Amber
League: Hampshire 2 (level 10)

Chipstead RFC
Ground Address: Chipstead Rugby Football Club The Meads The Meads Chipstead Surrey CR5 3SB
Contact: 07092 840705
Email: withchips@chipstead.co.uk
Website: www.chipstead.co.uk
Directions: Corner of Elmore Road, High Road Chipstead. Opp. the White Hart pub. Entrance to the ground is between the White Hart & the pond.
Honorary Secretary: Mr Graham Cox; 65 Nutfield Road Coulsdon Surrey CR5 3JP   Tel: 01903 825614
Email: graham1.cox@tiscali.co.uk
Fixtures Secretary: Mr Bob Adair   Tel: 07931 524671
Email: bobadair@whichers.com
Club Colours: Royal blue and gold
League: Surrey 1 (level 9)

Chiswick RFC
Ground Address: The Clubhouse Dukes Meadows Riverside Lands Chiswick, London Middx.W4 2SH
Contact: 07973 284637
Email: james@estaterun.com
Website: www.chiswickrugby.co.uk
Directions: Road: From London - Leave by A4 (cromwell Rd) cross Hammersmith Flyover. After one mile, keep left at Hogarth roundabout onto A316, signposted Richmond. Turn left immediately before Chiswick Bridge, signposted Riverside Lands School Playing Fields and fo
Honorary Secretary: Mr James Oliver; 15 Friars Place Lane London W3 7AG   Tel: 07973 284637
Email: james@estaterun.com
Fixtures Secretary: Mr Kelvin Campbell
Tel: 07706 356422
Club Colours: Maroon & Blue
League: London 2 North West (level 7)

Christ's College RFC
Ground Address: Christ's College St Andrew's Street St Andrew's Street Cambridge CB2 3BU
Contact: 07970 249136
Email: dk306@cam.ac.uk
Honorary Secretary: jonathan thompson
Email: jt357@cam.ac.uk
Fixtures Secretary: richard duncan Tel: 07985315034
Email: rd348@cam.ac.uk
Non League

CL London RFC
Contact: Alex Hacking
Email: hackinar@hotmail.com
Honorary Secretary: William Littlejohn
Hon Secretary Email: williamlittlejohns@dellmail.com
Fixtures Secretary: Alex Hacking Tel: 07810 350426
Email: hackinar@hotmail.com
League: Surrey 3 (level 11)

Clacton RFC
Ground Address: Rugby Clubhouse Recreation Ground Valley Road Clacton-on-Sea Essex CO15 6NA
Contact: 01255 673204
Email: susan.lee2711@btinternet.com
Website: www.rfu.com/clubs/clactonrugby
Directions: A133 to St Johns roundabout 2nd exit to St.Johns Rd Bear left at Ship PH to Valley Rd. Go under rail bridge. 50m. turn right past Bowls Club into car park.
Honorary Secretary: Mrs Susan Lee; Wakes Cottage Kirby Road Great Holland Frinton On Sea Essex CO13 0HS Tel: 01255 673204
Email: susan.lee2711@btinternet.com
Fixtures Secretary: Mr Colin Garrod; 24 Gainsford Avenue Clacton-on-Sea CO15 5AT Tel: 01255 434621
Email: colingarrod@tiscali.co.uk
Club Colours: Maroon shirts/navy shorts
League: Essex 1 (level 9)

Clare College RFC
Ground Address: Clare College Cambridge CB2 1TL
Contact: 07919 123284
Email: ac440@cam.ac.uk
Club Colours: Black and Yellow
Non League

Colchester RFC
Ground Address: Mill Road Playing Fields Mill Road Mile End Colchester CO4 5JF
Contact: 01206 851610
Email: tim@slaven5.freeserve.co.uk
Website: www.colchester-rugby.co.uk
Directions: Turn off A12 at Colchester North onto A1232 towards Colchester, right at traffic lights into Severalls Lane, over mini roundabout and left at next roundabout into Mill Road. Over another roundabout and club is 100 yards on right.
Honorary Secretary: Tim Slaven; 5 Barnardiston Road Colchester CO4 0DT Tel: 07795 211 693
Email: tim.slaven@amec.com
Fixtures Secretary: Mr Jon Roberts; 5 Spencer Close Maldon Essex CM9 6BX Tel: 01621 854043
Email: jonrobertsrugby@hotmail.com
Club Colours: Black
League: London 2 North East (level 7)

Corpus Christi College RFC
Ground Address: Corpus Christi College Trumpington Street Cambridge CB2 1RH
Contact: 07708 142401
Email: beh27@cam.ac.uk
Honorary Secretary: Ned Stuart-smith
Tel: 07950 093058
Email: ems57@cam.ac.uk
Fixtures Secretary: Ned Stuart-smith
Tel: 07950 093058
Email: ems57@cam.ac.uk
Non League

Cranbrook RFC
Ground Address: Tomlin Ground Angley Road Cranbrook Kent TN17 3LB
Contact: 01580 712777
Email: rugby@timfagg51.plus.com
Website: www.cranbrookrugby.com
Directions: Off A229 Hastings Roa, 14 miles south of Maidstone, 4 miles north of Hawkhurst at junction of Cranbrook bypass with Whitewell Lane.
Honorary Secretary: Mr Tim Fagg; Laurel Cottages 1 Vale Road Hawkhurst Kent TN18 4BU
Tel: 07799 118930
Email: rugby@timfagg51.plus.com
Fixtures Secretary: Simon Haydon; Church Cottages 1 Church Lane Beckley Rye East Sussex TN31 6UH
Tel: 01797 260345
Email: simonhaydon@btconnect.com
Club Colours: Magenta & White
League: Kent 1 (level 9)

Cranleigh RFC
Ground Address: Cranleigh RFC Wildwood Grounds Wildwood Lane Cranleigh Surrey GU6 8JR
Contact: 01483 272700
Email: nspong@msn.com
Website: www.cranleighrfc.co.uk
Directions: Signposted off A281 a couple of miles south of Cranleigh near the village of Alfold.
Hon. Secretary: Mr Kevin Maxted; Roseneath Station Road Rudgwick Horsham West Sussex RH12 3HB Tel: 01483 706104 Email: kkg01@fsmail.net
Fixtures Secretary: Mr Nigel Spong; Millook New Park Road Cranleigh Surrey GU6 7HJ Tel: 07836 560467
Email: nspong@msn.com
Club Colours: Navy Blue with Red Collar
League: Surrey 2 (level 10)

Crawley RFC
Ground Address: The Clubhouse Willoughby Fields, Ifield Avenue Crawley RH11 7LX
Contact: 01293 533 995
Email: home.chapman@btinternet.com
Directions: From M23 J10 Head towards Crawley, come to r-bout below flyover, take 3rd exit (sign Langley green) follow bypass to r-bout with lights, take second exit (sign A23/Horsham/superstore) follow A23 to r-bout, take 3rd exit (right)towards Charlwood, ground a
Honorary Secretary: Mr Paul Chapman; 19 Longwood View Crawley RH10 6PB   Tel: 01723 457788
Email: home.chapman@btinternet.com
Fixtures Secretary: Mr Martin Driver; 18 Casher Road Maiden Bower Crawley West Sussex RH10 7JG
Tel: 07840 358779   Email: barneybrit@msn.com
Club Colours: Claret with sky blue hoops
League: Sussex 1 (level 9)

Crowborough RFC
Ground Address: Steel Cross Crowborough TN6 2XB
Contact: 01892 665588
Email: info@crowboroughrugby.com
Website: www.crowboroughrugby.com
Directions: South on A26 from Tunbridge Wells, Club signposted at r/about after village of Boarshead.
Honorary Secretary: Mr Edwin Bridges; 6 Manor Way Crowborough East Sussex TN6 1LS Tel: 01892 662380
Email: eddiebridges20@hotmail.com
Fixtures Secretary: Mr Steve May; 5 Railway View Victoria Road Crowborough East Sussex TN6 2JQ
Tel: 01892 668102   Email: steve.may@cafebar.co.uk
Club Colours: Red with graduated white hoops, blue shorts
League: London 3 South East (level 8)

Croydon RFC
Ground Address: 135 Addington Road West Wickham Kent BR4 9BF
Contact: 0208 7775298
Email: croydonrfc@croydonrfc.com
Website: www.croydonrfc.com
Directions: From West Wickham go down Corkscrew Hill and turn right along the mad mile (Addington Road) at the roundabout by Beccehamians (Sparrows Den). We arc on the left just opposite the second lay by you will pass on your right. From East Croydon:New Addington trams run frequently to the Addington Village Terminus. Cross the road to the large pub. Turn right at the Church. Pass the Wrought Ironworks Forge, Cricket Club and Vicarage on your left with a row of houses on your right. A pathway, alongside the main road (A2022) on your right, will lead you to us in five minutes. From Charing Cross or London Bridge to Hayes, Kent:119 Croydon bus alight at Corkscrew Hill. Continue along path, Addington Road on your left, rugby and football pitches on your right. Cross road at end of second lay by. 314, 353 and 630 buses stop outside our Club. Ask for the Thames Water Pumping Station.
Honorary Secretary: Mrs Sue Randall; 72 Wydehurst Road Croydon Surrey CR0 6NG   Tel: 0208 6568299
Email: croydonrfc@croydonrfc.com
Fixtures Secretary: Mr Andy Smith; 7 Chesney Crescent New Addington Croydon Surrey CR0 0RN
Tel: 07908 742385 Email: andysmith620@hotmail.co.uk
League: Surrey 1 (level 9)

Crusaders RFC
Ground Address: Beckhythe Little Melton Nr Hethersett Norwich NorfolkNR9 3NP
Contact: 01603 416679
Email: mikeandlynda66@tiscali.co.uk
Website: www.crusadersrugbyclub.com
Directions: From southern bypass take Watton Road (B1108)heading away from Norwich, turn left past the garden centre to Little Melton. Go through village passing Village Inn pub on right. Turn left at phone box, then first right (to Hethersett), ground is 400 yards
Honorary Secretary: Mr Michael Dack; 66 Mansel Drive Old Catton Norwich NR6 7NB Tel: 01603 416679
Email: mikeandlynda66@tiscali.co.uk
Fixtures Secretary: Paul Dack; 3 Lodge Lane Norwich NorfolkNR6 7EA Tel: 01603 403883
Email: paul.dack@btopenworld.com
Club Colours: Black with yellow/green
League: East Counties 1 (level 9)

Cuffley RFC
Ground Address: Rosedale Sports Club Andrews Lane Cheshunt EN7 6TB
Contact: 07976 753699
Email: admin@cuffleyrugby.co.uk
Website: www.cuffleyrugby.co.uk
Directions: Junction 25 M25 take the A10 north to Cheshunt. At the first roundabout take the 1st exit (Lt Ellis Way). Straight over the next 2 roundabouts, then left into Andrews Lane. 100m on the left.
Honorary Secretary: Mr Chris Palmer; Centurion Crt 9 83 Camp Road St Albans Herts. AL1 5JN
Tel: 07929 005631   Email: chris@cuffleyrugby.co.uk
Fixtures Secretary: Mr Peter Cushing; 10 Lilac Drive Lutterworth Leics. LE17 4FP Tel: 07775 704130
Email: peter@cuffleyrugby.co.uk
Club Colours: Black Red Flash
League: Herts-Middlesex 3 (level 11)

Dagenham RUFC
Ground Address: The Pavillion, Central Park Rainham Road North Dagenham Essex RM10 7EJ
Contact: 0208 5938202
Email: mrandall305@aol.com
Website: www.drufc.co.uk
Directions: FRom A13 turn into Ballards Rd, jct of Princess Bowl/McDonalds. On to Bull r/about take 1st left. Pass Dagenham East R'stn. Over Eastbrook P.H. jct. Ground 300yds right through park gates.
Honorary Secretary: Mrs Julie Ketteringham; 55 Grasmere Avenue Hullbridge Hockley Essex SS5 6LB Tel: 0780 1337079
Email: juliek1961@fsmail.net
Fixtures Secretary: Mr Mark Randall; 305 Elm Road Shoeburyness Southend-on-Sea SS3 9RX
Tel: 07768 942387
Email: mrandall305@aol.com
Club Colours: Red & White Shirt/white shorts
League: London 3 North East (level 8)

Darenth Valley RFC
Ground Address: Leigh City Tech Green Street, Green Road Dartford Kent DA1 1QE
Contact: 07889 975823
Email: darenthvalley.rfc@btinternet.com
Directions: No clubhouse. Club plays at Leigh City Tech and moves on to local pub afterwards, The Irish Club Dartford. Changing/parking facilities at college where pitches are. Irish Club is opposite YMCA in Dartford town centre, 5 minutes from pitches.
Honorary Secretary: Mr Kenneth Parr; 95 Arethusa Road Rochester Kent ME1 2UN Tel: 07889 975823
Email: Darenthvalley.RFC@btinternet.com
Fixtures Secretary: Mrs Bella Blackston
Tel: 01322 272641   Email: bellabud26@yahoo.co.uk
Club Colours: Red Black shirts, black shorts
Non League

Dartfordians RFC
Ground Address: War Memorial Club House Bourne Road Bexley Kent DA5 1LW
Contact: 07956 324185
Email: jarrod.lawrence@btinternet.com
Website: www.dartfordiansrfc.co.uk
Directions: The ground is situated just off the A2 Black Prince- Post House Hotel turn off.
Honorary Secretary: Jo McDonald; 16 Glebelands off Iron Mill Lane Crayford Kent DA1 4RZ
Tel: 07748 965822   Email: jocmcd@ntlworld.com
Club Colours: Maroon & Old Gold
League: Kent 1 (level 9)

Datchworth RFC
Ground Address: Datchworth Green Datchworth SG3 6TL
Contact: 01438 812490
Email: ld_wyatt@hotmail.com
Website: www.datchworthrfc.co.uk
Directions: Leave the A1M (northbound) at junction 6 (Welwyn), head north towards Stevenage on B197. At Woolmer Green turn right towards Datchworth, pitches and clubhouse are behind the tennis courts.
Honorary Secretary: Mrs Diane Wyatt; 7 Hazeldell Watton at Stone Hertford SG14 3SL Tel: 01920 830407
Email: ld_wyatt@hotmail.com
Fixtures Secretary: Mr Robert Holgate; Sefton Road 198 Stevenage Herts. SG1 5RP Tel: 01438 587672
Club Colours: Green, Navy Blue & White
League: London 3 North West (level 8)

Deal & Betteshanger RFC
Ground Address: The Drill Field, Canada Road, Walmer, Kent CT14 7EJ
Contact: 01304 365892
Email: lions@dealandbettesrfc.org.uk
Website: www.dealandbettesrfc.org.uk
Directions: From Dover - follow the A258 into Deal, past Q8 garage, follow the Dover Rd. down to the junction with Walmer sea front (The Strand), take immediate left into Canada Rd. The entrance is 2nd left, half way along. Parking within the grounds is available.
Honorary Secretary: Mr David Rose; 27 Links Road Deal Kent CT14 6QF   Tel: 07713 052208
Email: davidrose@uk.bureauveritas.com
Fixtures Secretary: Mr Bob Sykes; Deal & Betteshanger Rugby Club The Drill Field Canada Road Walmer Deal Kent CT14 7EJ   Tel: 01227 374246
Club Colours: black
League: London 2 South East (level 7)

Dereham RFC
Ground Address: Moorgate Playing Fields Moorgate Road Dereham NR19 1JT
Contact: 07788 977618
Email: secretary@derehamrugby.org
Website: www.derehamrugby.org
Directions: See website
Honorary Secretary: Ms Karen Holmes; Twin Peaks Chapel Street Shipdham Thetford NorfolkIP25 7LB
Tel: 07788 977618   Email: secretary@derehamrugby.org
Fixtures Secretary: Mr Roy Head Tel: 01362 690649
Email: fixtures@derehamrugby.org
Club Colours: Maroon & black
League: East Counties 2 (level 10)

Downing College RFC
Ground Address: Downing College Regent Street Cambridge CB2 1DQ
Contact: 07730 613385
Email: jseg2@cam.ac.uk
Honorary Secretary: Mr James Moyle
Tel: 07912038183   Email: jm582@cam.ac.uk
Fixtures Secretary: as Hon. Sec.
Non League

LEVEL 7-12 AND NON LEAGUE CLUBS

East Dorset RFC
Ground Address: Iford Lane Playing Fields Iford Lane Bournemouth Dorset BH6 5NF
Contact: 01202 478711
Email: vicky_keating@yahoo.com
Website: www.eastdorsetrugby.com
Directions: From A338 road into Bournemouth. Take slip road just before fly-over - signpost Wimborne, Hospital, Southbourne. Follow road past Hospital & Tesco. At r'about - take 2nd exit, (straight over), Iford Lane. Follow road - go under railway bridge - fields
Honorary Secretary: Mr Gwyn Haigh; 46 Clingan Road Bournemouth Dorset BH6 5PZ   Tel: 07813 103660
Email: shagis12@hotmail.com
Fixtures Secretary: Ms Vicky Keating; 46 Clingan Road Bournemouth Dorset BH6 5PZ   Tel: 07949 113472
Email: vicky_keating@yahoo.com
Colours: Royal blue with gold & red sleeves & trim
League: Hampshire 1 (level 9)

East Grinstead RFC Ltd
Ground Address: Saint Hill Road East Grinstead West Sussex RH19 4JU
Contact: 01342 322338
Email: secretary@egrfc.com
Website: www.egrfc.com
Honorary Secretary: Mr Bob Russell; 1 Rose Cottages Plaistow Street Lingfield Surrey RH7 6AU
Tel: 01342 834648   Email: secretary@egrfc.com
Fixtures Secretary: Mrs Nikki Ward; 46 Hackenden Close East Grinstead West Sussex RH19 3DS
Tel: 01342 322701   Email: fixtures@egrfc.com
Club Colours: Blue with White Irregular Hoops
League: London 3 South East (level 8)

East London RFC
Ground Address:
71 Holland Road West Ham London E15 3BP
Contact: 020 74746761
Website: www.elrfc.co.uk
Directions: From Canning Town r/about proceed down Manor Road, turn right before West Ham tube station follow road round and turn right at Holland Road.
Honorary Secretary: Mr Michael Groombridge
Email: michael.groombridge@hsbc.com
Fixtures Secretary: Mr Matthew Radley
Club Colours: Maroon & Navy Hoops
League: Essex 1 (level 9)

East Peckham & Capel (The Villagers)
Ground Address: Mascalls Court Road Paddock Wood Kent TN12 6NZ
Contact: 01892 838290
Email: stuartdedman@tiscali.co.uk
Honorary Secretary: Mr Stuart Dedman; 27 Allington Road Paddock Wood Tonbridge Kent TN12 6AP
Tel: 07809 451223   Email: stuartdedman@tiscali.co.uk
Fixtures Secretary: Mr Nick Wickham
Tel: 07766 651071
Non League

Eastbourne RFC
Ground Address: Eastbourne R.F.C. Park Avenue Hampden Park Eastbourne East Sussex BN22 9QN
Contact: 01323 503076
Website: www.eastbournerugby.com
Directions: From the north take the A22 From the east and west take the A27 In all cases to Polegate where you take the A2270 to Eastbourne. Continue on this road till you come to the Willingdon roundabout. Take the first exit (Kings Drive) continue over the mini
Honorary Secretary: Mr Hugh Graham; 17a Pashley Road Eastbourne East Sussex BN20 8DU
Tel: 01323 419287   Email: hgcy@mistral.co.uk
Fixtures Secretary: Mr Charles Wise; 128 Wannock Lane Eastbourne East Sussex BN20 9SJ
Tel: 01323 482435
Email: charles@wise128.freeserve.co.uk
Club Colours: Navy Blue with Gold Hoops
League: London 2 South East (level 7)

Eastleigh RFC
Ground Address: The Hub Bishopstoke Playing Fields Eastleigh HampshireSO50 6LA
Contact: 02380 641312
Email: wayne.hayward@gmail.com
Website: www.eastleighrfc.co.uk
Directions: From Eastleigh Railway Station take turning over railway bridge to Fair Oak and ground is approx 600 yds on the left.
Honorary Secretary: Mr Wayne Hayward; 29c Upmill Close West End Southampton SO30 3HT
Tel: 02380 472611   Email: wayne.hayward@gmail.com
Fixtures Secretary: J Sneezham; Bursledon Lodge Salterns Lane Bursledon Southampton SO31 8DH
Tel: 02380 402286   Email: Sneezumj@aol.com
Club Colours: Black, Amber & Red
League: Hampshire 1 (level 9)

Economicals RFC
Ground Address: 60 South Eden Park Road Beckenham Kent BR3 3BG
Contact: 0208 776 2953
Email: steve.bowen@edenpark.fsworld.co.uk
Directions: To follow - the directions in the RFU handbook are excellent
Honorary Secretary: Mr Peter Drewienkiewicz; 60 South Eden Park Road Beckenham Kent BR3 3BG
Tel: 07790 908349   Email: mugley@hotmail.com
Fixtures Secretary: as Hon. Sec.
Tel: 07790 908349   Email: mugley@hotmail.com
Club Colours: Black, Gold & Bottle Green
League: Surrey 4 (level 12)

Effingham & Leatherhead RFC
Ground Address: Effingham & Leatherhead R.F.C. King George V Hall King George V Playing Fields Browns Lane Effingham Surrey KT24 5ND
Contact: 01372 458887
Email: info@eaglesrugby.co.uk
Website: www.eaglesrugby.co.uk

Directions: From M25, J10: Effingham signpost left on slip road south bound from M25 to A3, follow road until T junction. Turn right then immediately left and follow road through Effingham to traffic lights. Turn left and then first left into Browns Lane. Alternatively take the Guildford to Letherhead A246 road to Effingham. From Guildford, take first left after traffic lights; from Leatherhead, take second right after sign for Effingham and before traffic lights
Honorary Secretary: Mr Robin Page; 20 Southfields Road London SW18 1QN
Tel: 020 8871428   Email: rojopage@talktalk.net
Fixtures Secretary: Mr Edward Newton; 42 Milner Road Kingston upon Thames Surrey KT1 2AU
Tel: 020 76283700
Email: ed@42milnerrd.freeserve.co.uk
Club Colours: Amber, Green & Black
League: London 2 South West (level 7)

Egham Hollowegians RFC
Ground Address: Egham RFC Kings Lane, Englefield Green Egham Surrey TW20 0EU
Contact: 01784 47 4452
Directions: From Junction 13 on the M25 follow the A30 towards Camberly. Turn right after Royal Holloway College into Englefield Green, St. Judes Road, left after the second Mini roundabout to Bond Street which follows into Kings Lane. Club on the left hand side.
Honorary Secretary: Mr Edward O'Shea; 14 Ferndale Avenue Chertsey Surrey KT16 9RB
Tel: 01784 474415   Email: oshea.ep@pg.com
Fixtures Secretary: Mr Kimball Ingram; The Lathe Northbrook Estate Farnham Surrey GU10 5EU
Tel: 07595 081727
Email: kimball.ingram@mhseniorliving.co.uk
Club Colours: Black, Gold and Blue
League: Surrey 4 (level 12)

Ellingham & Ringwood RFC
Ground Address: Picket Post Near Ringwood New Forest Hampshire BH24 3HN
Contact: 01425 476668
Email: Steve.Benson@sha.co.uk
Website: www.errfc.com
Directions: On A31 eastbound after leaving Ringwood behind Shell garage next to Burley turning.
Honorary Secretary: Mr Howard Neale; Plas Bryn Carw Harthill Drove Redlynch Salisbury SP5 2HR
Tel: 01725 511621   Email: hjneale@aol.com
Fixtures Secretary: Mr Chris Finney; 5 Bickerley Terrace Ringwood BH24 1EQ
Club Colours: Navy Blue with Amber Hoop
League: London 3 South West (level 8)

Ely RFC
Ground Address: Ely R.U.F.C. The Playing Fields Downham Road Downham Road Ely CB6 2SH
Contact: 01353 664745
Email: secretary@elyrufc.co.uk
Website: www.elyrufc.co.uk/index.html

Directions: Just north of Ely. L.H.S. of A10 Ely bypass. Turn at roundabout sign-posted Little Downham. Turning immediately on left. (See www.elyrufc.co.uk)
Honorary Secretary: Mrs Debbie Marshall; 4 Langham Way Ely Cambs.CB6 1DZ   Tel: 01353 650485
Email: womens.rugby@elyrufc.co.uk
Fixtures Secretary: Mr Mark Mitzman; 4 Elmfield Ely Cambs.CB6 1BE   Tel: 01353 612094
Email: fixture.secretary@elyrufc.co.uk
Club Colours: Gold & Black Hoops, Black Shorts
League: East Counties 1 (level 9)

Emmanuel College RFC
Ground Address: Emmanuel College St Andrew's Street Cambridge CB2 3AP
Contact: 07773 873930
Email: cm403@cam.ac.uk
Honorary Secretary: Mr Robert Blythe
Email: rb487@cam.ac.uk
Fixtures Secretary: Mr Tom Jones
Tel: 07904482201   Email: tlj23@cam.ac.uk
Non League

Enfield Ignatians RFC
Ground Address: King George V Playing Fields Donkey Lane Carterhatch lane Donkey Lane Carterhatch lane Enfield Middx.EN1 3PL
Contact: 0208 363 2877
Email: mickcollins106@hotmail.com
Website: www.enfieldignatiansrfc.co.uk
Directions: From junction 25 of the M25 go south on the A10 towards London and turn right at the second set of traffic lights, immediately turn left into Donkey Lane.
Honorary Secretary: Mr Stephen Crofts; 5 Lynn Street Enfield Middx.EN2 0JY   Tel: 07957 130870
Email: steve.crofts@tubelines.com
Fixtures Secretary: Mr Simon Urquhart; 50 Brigadier Hill Enfield Middx.EN2 0NJ   Tel: 07595 271624
Email: simonurquhart@talktalk.net
Club Colours: Blue and Gold
League: London 2 North East (level 7)

Erith RFC
Ground Address: The Recreation Ground, Sussex Road Northumberland Heath Erith Kent DA8 1YA
Contact: 01322 432 295
Directions: From A2 Black Prince turn off follow signs for Bexleyheath. After going up Gravel Hill, head straight on at the Marriot Hotel and Albert pub traffic lights. Keep going straight on for approximately 1 mile, passing the bus garage on the right in the proc
Honorary Secretary: Mr Perry Francis; 12 Dickens Close Erith Kent DA8 1YF   Tel: 0207 6015356
Email: pelandang@sky.com
Fixtures Secretary: Mr Steve Cocks; 4 Hyde Road Bexleyheath Kent DA7 4NL   Tel: 07867 944755
Email: abchss@aol.com
Club Colours: Light blue and dark blue hoops
League: Kent 1 (level 9)

Essex Police RFC
Ground Address: Chelmsford RFC
Contact: 01245 261 159
Honorary Secretary: Mr Gerry Parker; Essex County Constabulary Force Headquarters Springfield Chelmsford
Email: gerry.parker@essex.pnn.police.uk
Non League

Fakenham RFC
Ground Address: Old Wells Road Fakenham NorfolkNR21 9QT
Contact: 01328 851007
Email: mark.house@fakenhamrugby.com
Website: www.fakenhamrugby.com
Directions: see our club site at www.fakenhamrugby.com
Honorary Secretary: Mr Chris Evans; 64 Boyd Avenue Dereham NorfolkNR19 1ND   Tel: 01362 694537
Email: chris.evans@fakenhamrugby.com
Fixtures Secretary: Mr Jonathon Strong; 17 Wells Road Fakenham NorfolkNR21 9EG   Tel: 07776 446270
Email: weetabixmaster@hotmail.com
Club Colours: Dark and light blue quarters
League: East Counties 1 (level 9)

Fareham Heathens RFC Ltd
Ground Address: Cams Alders Recreation Ground, Palmerston Bus. Pk Palmerston Drive Palmerston Drive Fareham PO14 1DJ
Contact: 01329 221793
Email: info@farehamheathens.co.uk
Website: www.farehamheathens.co.uk
Directions: From the centre of Fareham take the Gosport road, south, under the viaduct, get in the outside lane of the duel-carriage way, signposted Lee on Solent, over the Fly-over (Newgate Lane), take the first turning right into Palmerston Bus. Park, follow the ma
Honorary Secretary: Mr Rob Townsend; St. Francis House 186 Northern Parade Hilsea Portsmouth 9LU
Tel: 02392 662467
Email: dirobdaisy@aol.com
Fixtures Secretary: Mr Edward Monk; 10 Findon Road Gosport HampshirePO12 4EP
Tel: 07900 951771   Email: emonk@astrapooluk.com
Club Colours: Black
League: Hampshire 1 (level 9)

Farnborough RUFC
Ground Address: Tile Barn Close Cove Cove Farnborough GU14 8LS
Contact: 01252 542750
Email: contact@farnboroughrugby.co.uk
Website: www.farnboroughrugby.co.uk
Directions: From Junction 4 of the M3: on leaving the motorway follow signs for Farnborough. These lead to the A331 Blackwater Valley Relief Road - a major dual carriagway link between the M3 and A31. Within half a mile take the slip road signed A325 Farnborough. After two roundabouts serving the slip roads to the A311 pass the Farnborough retail park on the left - Macdonalds, Curry's etc. Take the first exit at the large roundabout and move to the outside lane to turn right at the traffic lights - half mile up the road. There is a signpost to Farnborough RUFC at this junction. Pass the Sixth Form College on the right and at the roundabout at the end of the road, turn left into Prospect Road.Tile Barn Close is the second turning on the right and is signposted FRUFC. From Farnborough Town: take the A325 towards the M3. turn left at the traffic lights sign posted to the club and follow the route above.
Honorary Secretary: Mr Cliff Huckle; Farnborough Rugby Club Tile Barn Close Cove Cove Farnborough HampshireGU14 8LS Tel: 07808 825732
Email: cliff.huckle@fujitsu-siemens.com
Fixtures Secretary: Mr A Mackay; 43 The Grove Farnborough HampshireGU14 6QS Tel: 01252 512363
Email: barrymackay1@aol.com
Club Colours: Dark / Light blue hoops
League: Hampshire 1 (level 9)

Farnham RUFC
Ground Address: Farnham RUFC off Riverdale Wrecclesham Farnham GU10 4QP
Contact: 01252 357845
Email: john.fairley@farnhamrugby.org
Website: www.farnhamrugby.org
Directions: Take A325 to Petersfield from A31 Farnham bypass, after 0.75mile pass Bear & Ragged Staff pub on right turn next right into Riverdale, 1st left onto recreation ground. DO NOT GO DOWN Westfield Lane.
Honorary Secretary: Mr Keith Daniels; 69 Badshot Park Farnham GU9 9NE   Tel: 01252 315979
Email: keithdaniels101@hotmail.com
Fixtures Secretary: Mr Bob Smith; 21 Riverside Close Farnborough HampshireGU14 8QT
Tel: 01252 650719   Email: smith.bob@ntlworld.com
Club Colours: Black & Yellow with one White Hoops
League: Surrey 1 (level 9)

Faversham RUFC
Ground Address: The Lodge, Recreation Ground Park Road Faversham Kent ME13 8HA
Contact: 01795 531718
Email: dave_suter_bs@hotmail.com
Website: www.favershamrugby.co.uk
Directions: From M2 J6 take A251 north to Favershamat T/Jct turn right onto A2. Take 4th turn left into Love Lane, just after shell petrol station. Follow Love Lane into Whitstable Road, take 2nd turn left Park Road (approx .75 mile from A2). Car park and changing ro
Honorary Secretary: Mr Simon Young; 2 Jacob's Yard Faversham Kent ME13 8NY   Tel: 01795 536638
Email: simonyoung1980@hotmail.com
Fixtures Secretary: Mr Ross Chipperton
Tel: 07963 891526
Club Colours: sky blue/white quarters
Non League

Fawley RFC
Ground Address: Waterside Sports and Social Club 179-181 Long Lane Holbury Southampton SO45 2PA
Contact: 023 80893750
Email: secretary@fawleyrfc.co.uk
Website: www.fawleyrfc.co.uk
Directions: From M27 J2 (271) follow A326 to Fawley for approx 8 miles. Ground is on the right after Hardley Roundabout.
Honorary Secretary: Mrs Julie Bisgrove; Adj Mousehole Southampton Road Hythe Southampton HampshireS045 5GQ Tel: 02380 841747
Email: secretary@fawleyrfc.co.uk
Fixtures Secretary: Mr Benjamin Maquire; Scottpaine Drive 9 Hythe Southampton SO45 6JY
Tel: 0787 6028427   Email: fixtures@fawleyrfc.co.uk
Club Colours: Scarlet Shirts & Socks, Blue Shorts
League: Hampshire 2 (level 10)

Felixstowe RFC
Ground Address: Coronation Sports Ground Mill Lane Mill Lane Felixstowe IP11 2LN
Contact: 01394 270150
Email: daniel.cain@hmcourts-service.gsi.gov.uk
Website: http://www.felixstowerugby.co.uk
Honorary Secretary: Mr Daniel Cain; 16 Berners Road Felixstowe SuffolkIP11 7LF Tel: 01394 278112
Email: daniel.cain@hmcourts-service.gsi.gov.uk
Fixtures Secretary: Mr Gareth Carr; 187 Grange Road Felixstowe SuffolkIP11 2QB Tel: 07920 095954
Email: gcarr81@yahoo.co.uk
Club Colours: Black and White hoops
League: East Counties 2 (level 10)

Finchley RFC
Ground Address: Summers Lane Finchley Finchley London N12 0PD
Contact: 0208 4453746
Email: colin.seabrook1@ntlworld.com
Website: www.finchleyrfc.co.uk
Directions: From North circular road (A406) take A1000 (High Road towards North Finchley), to Summers Lane.(2ns set of lights at top of hill.
Honorary Secretary: Mr Geoff Ottley; 125 Bells Hill Barnet Herts. EN5 2SY Tel: 020 84411623
Email: geoffreyottley125@btinternet.com
Fixtures Secretary: as Hon. Sec.
Club Colours: Scarlet and White 55mm Hoops
League: London 2 North West (level 7)

Fitzwilliam College RFC
Ground Address: Fitzwilliam College Huntingdon Road Cambridge CB3 0DG
Contact: 07763 815450
Email: ajla2@cam.ac.uk
Honorary Secretary: Mr Andrew Price; Fitzwilliam College Storey's Way Cambridge CB3 0DG Tel:
Email: ajpp2@cam.ac.uk
Fixtures Secretary: as Hon. Sec.
Non League

Folkestone RFC
Ground Address: New Burlington Field Bargrove Newington Folkestone Kent CT18 8BH
Contact: 01303 266887
Email: frccglane@aol.com
Website: http://www.folkestonerugbyclub.com
Directions: From M20 exit J12 (Cheriton) Follow A20 towards Lyminge for 1 mile, left at roundabout (old B2065 to Hythe.) Over M20 and Rail bridges, Club on right. From A259 in Hythe take the Blackhouse Hill (old B2065) to Lyminge and Elham, Club 2 mile on left.
Honorary Secretary: Colin Lane; The Garden Flat 8A Station Road Lyminge Folkestone CT18 8HP
Tel: 01303 864599   Email: frccglane@aol.com
Fixtures Secretary: Mr Alex Ruddock; 40 Langdon Road Folkestone CT19 4HY   Tel: 01303 276530
Email: alexruddock@f2s.com
Club Colours: Green /Navy/narrow White hoops
League: London 3 South East (level 8)

Footscray RUFC
Ground Address: 239a Footscray Road New Eltham New Eltham London SE9 2EL
Contact: 0208 8504698
Email: info@footscrayrufc.co.uk
Website: www.footscrayrufc.co.uk
Directions: From M25/M20 junction 3, Take A20 (Sidcup Road) West, towards London. At the first set of lights take the 2nd turning on the right into Green Lane. At the next junction, turn right into Footscray road. The club can be found on your left, after about three Nearest Station is New Eltham, Turn left out of station onto Footscray Road, Ground is approx 500 yards on left hand side of the road.
Honorary Secretary: Mr Simon Newark; 34 Faraday Avenue Sidcup Kent DA14 4JF   Tel: 07962 227016
Email: admin@footscrayrufc.co.uk
Fixtures Secretary: Mr Dan Kent; 3 Douglas Avenue New Malden Surrey KT3 6HT   Tel: 07968 511328
Email: daniel.kent@gmail.com
Club Colours: Royal Blue and gold hoops
League: Kent 2 (level 10)

Fordingbridge RFC
Ground Address: Recreation Ground Fordingbridge Hampshire SP6 3ER
Contact: 01425 654050
Email: goplay@fordingbridgerugby.co.uk
Website: www.fordingbridgerfc.co.uk
Directions: Off A338 (12 miles south of Salisbury and 8 miles north of ringwood) alongside bypass, western side adjacent to RIver Avon.
Honorary Secretary: Mr Russell Bird; 24 Pine Road Alderholt Fordingbridge SP6 3BJ   Tel: 01425 657633
Email: russelljbird@btinternet.com
Fixtures Secretary: Mr John Trim; Trees Fryern Court Road Burgate Fordingbridge HampshireSP6 1NG
Tel: 01425 652254   Email: johntrim49@yahoo.co.uk
Club Colours: Sky Blue with Black Shorts
League: London 3 South West (level 8)

Fullerians RFC
Ground Address: Fullerians RFC Coningesby Drive Coningesby Drive Watford Herts. WD17 3PB
Contact: 01923 224483
Email: Fullerians@supanet.com
Website: www.fullerians.co.uk
Directions: Watford Grammar School New Field, Coningesby Drive (end of Parkside Drive), Watford. WD1 3BD.
Honorary Secretary: Mr Mark Hardwidge; 65 Highland Drive Bushey Herts. WD23 4HH
Tel: 020 89500642   Email: Markh@blueydesign.com
Fixtures Secretary: Mr John Roberts; 33 Eastfield Avenue Watford WD24 4HH   Tel: 01923 254706
Email: john@robertsclan1.fsnet.co.uk
Club Colours: Red, green and black stripes.
League: London 3 North West (level 8)

G.W.R. RFC
Ground Address: Trailfinders Sports Club Vallis Way Ealing Middx.W13 0DD
Contact: 07976751299
Email: enquiries@gwrrugby.co.uk
Directions: By train to Ealing Broadway, then to Castle Bar Park Halt via E1, E2 or E9 buses.
Honorary Secretary: Howard Evans
Tel: 0208 8644533   Email: hevans@homecall.co.uk
Fixtures Secretary: Eamonn Dolan   Tel: 07904 314596
Club Colours: Cardinal & Black Jerseys
League: Herts-Middlesex 4 (level 12)

Gillingham Anchorians RFC
Ground Address: Anchorians Clubhouse Darland Avenue Gillingham Kent ME7 3AN
Contact: 07801 020180
Email: s.ferguson@hermes.co.uk
Website: www.anchoriansrfc.co.uk
Directions: Leave M2 by A278, turn left at terminal roundabout (signed A2 Gillingham). Across new roundabout. Left at 2nd traffic lights at Darland Avenue, ground 200yds on left.
Honorary Secretary: Mr Michael Niven; 62 Trevale Road Rochester Gillingham Kent ME1 3PA
Tel: 01634 313309   Email: niven_michael@hotmail.com
Fixtures Secretary: Mr Nigel Fray
Email: nigelfray@aol.com
Club Colours: Purple black & white hoops. black shorts
League: Kent 1 (level 9)

Girton College RFC
Ground Address: Girton College Huntingdon Road Cambridge CB3 0JG
Contact: 07792 745721
Email: je263@cam.ac.uk
Honorary Secretary: Andrew Russell; Girton College Huntingdon Road Cambridge CB£ 0JG
Tel: 07734 772817   Email: agr32@cam.ac.uk
Fixtures Secretary: Mr Andrew Badcock; Girton College Huntingdon Road Cambridge CB3 0JG
Tel: 07772 277337   Email: ajwb@cam.ac.uk
Non League

Goldsmiths College, University of London RFC
Address: Dixon Road New Cross London SE14 6NW
Contact: 020 8692 1406
Email: n.rogers@gold.ac.uk
Honorary Secretary: Kester Mollahan
Tel: 07742 077289
Fixtures Secretary: Miss Ruth Gibson; Goldsmiths S U Dixon Road New Cross London SE14 6NW
Tel: 0208 692 1406   Email: r.gibson@gold.ac.uk
Club Colours: Blue and Gold
Non League

Gonville & Caius College RFC
Ground Address: Gonville & Caius College Trinity Street Cambridge CB2 1TA
Contact: 07814 622972
Email: tcrb2@cam.ac.uk
Honorary Secretary: Jon Ridley   Tel: 07979 667365
Email: jdr34@cam.ac.uk
Fixtures Secretary: as Hon. Sec.
Non League

Gosport & Fareham RFC
Ground Address: Gosport Park Dolphin Crescent Gosport HampshirePO12 2HE
Contact: 02392 353235
Email: joe@cloke1.wanadoo.co.uk
Website: www.gosportandfarehamrfc.co.uk
Directions: Exit M27 at J11 to Fareham/Gosport A32. Follow A32 for approx 6 miles to Gosport Ferry/Bus Station. Continue past on South St over mini r/about (Pond left). 3rd lt into Kensington Rd, right at end. Lt over bridge, lt into Dolphin Crescent. Club at end.
Honorary Secretary: Mr Joe Cloke; 34 Richmond Road Gosport HampshirePO12 3QJ   Tel: 02392 510538
Email: joe@cloke1.wanadoo.co.uk
Fixtures Secretary: Mr Rick Miles; 4 Camden Terrace Camden Street Gosport HampshirePO12 3HY
Tel: 07886 812943
Email: rick.miles@fleet-support.co.uk
Club Colours: Royal Blue & Old Gold.
League: London 3 South West (level 8)

Grasshoppers RFC
Ground Address: Macfarlane Sports Ground MacFarlane Lane Off Syon Lane TW7 5PN
Contact: 07879 846002
Email: peter.baveystock@ntlworld.com
Website: http://www.grasshoppersrfc.com/
Directions: A4 Gillette, turn into Syon Lane, then just past Tescos on right.
Honorary Secretary: Mr Nick Dance; 12 Sydney Road Richmond Surrey TW9 1UB Tel: 0208 948 2589
Email: ndance@essentis.com
Fixtures Secretary: Mr Thomas Barber; 8 Kingsleigh Close Brentford Middx.TW8 0PA Tel: 07900 698058
Email: tom.barber@bhs.co.uk
Club Colours: Green, Gold & Black
League: London 2 North West (level 7)

Guernsey RUFC
Ground Address: Footes Lane St. Peter Port St. Peter Port Guernsey GY1 2UL
Contact: 01481 256463
Email: guernseyrugby@gtonline.net
Website: www.grufc.co.uk
Directions: Centre of the Island, 1/2 mile from airport.
Honorary Secretary: Mrs Natalie Davidson; Ariel Route de Cobo Castel Guernsey GY5 7UH Tel: 01481 256463
Email: natalie.davidson@cwgsy.net
Fixtures Secretary: Mr Carl Gardner; Pridelands Guelle Terrace Guelle Lane St Peter Port Guernsey GY1 2RA Tel: 07781 123148
Email: carl.gardner@gmail.com
Club Colours: Green & White
League: London 2 South West (level 7)

Guildford RFC
Ground Address: Guildford R.F.C. The Clubhouse Broadwater Guildford Road Godalming Surrey GU7 3BU
Contact: 01483 416199
Email: sue_m_gardner@yahoo.co.uk
Website: www.guildfordrugbyclub.co.uk
Directions: A3100 from Guildford to Godalming-beside Broadwater lake. Or From London, by-pass Guildford on A3. 1 mile past Guildford, fork left on to B3000 (towards Godalming) through Compton for 3 miles -right at roundabout -continue for about 300 yards, the clubhouse is situated on the right.
Honorary Secretary: Mrs Sue Gardner; 24 Warramill Road Godalming Surrey GU7 1LU   Tel: 07881 826000
Email: sue_m_gardner@yahoo.co.uk
Fixtures Secretary: Carrie Hayward; 31 Grange Close Godalming Surrey GU7 1XT   Tel: 07967 505093
Email: caroline.jane@ntlworld.com
Club Colours: Blue, White & Gold
League: London 2 South West (level 7)

Guildfordians RFC
Ground Address: The Pavilion London Road Guildford Surrey GU1 1TU
Contact: Clubhouse (01483) 300752
Email: antonymakepeace@yahoo.com
Website: http://www.guildfordiansrfc.co.uk
Directions: Travelling south on the A3, take the 2nd turn-off after the M25, signed to Guildford and Burpham, A3100 (the first turning is signed to Ockham and Ripley). Continue on this road, negotiating several mini r'abouts. At the fifth one (which is big and grassy) take the 2nd exit, which leads into London Road. Clubhouse is about 200 metres on the right. Travelling north on A3 pass under the Hog's Back road (A31), pass the exit to The Cathedral and University and take the next exit, signed Guildford Town Centre. At the end of the slip road there is a r'about, take the 2nd exit. Go straight on at the pedestrian lights, ignore town centre sign and continue straight over the next lights, (Ladymead Retail Park will be on your left hand side). Continue straight over the next lights (Stoke Crossroads), pass the Parkway pub and Travel Lodge on left, Stoke Park will then appear on your right, on your left will be Spectrum. At the r'about turn right (3rd exit) into London Road. Clubhouse is about 200 metres along on the right. From the east or west follow signs to Leisure Centre or Spectrum, it's the same place and eventually you will be guided to the Stoke Crossroads traffic lights, continue to follow the instructions to Spectrum. If you get hopelessly lost ask for directions to the Spectrum. (its just over the road from the park).
Honorary Secretary: Mr Ian Dodge; 6 Victoria Road Godalming Surrey GU7 1JR Tel: 07894 265499
Email: club.secretary@guildfordiansrfc.co.uk
Fixtures Secretary: Steve Brierley; 1 Wallace Close Fairlands Guildford GU3 3NP Tel: 07836 794 330
Email: senior.fixtures@guildfordiansrfc.co.uk
Club Colours: Green Shirt with White stripe
League: Surrey 4 (level 12)

Guys' Kings' & St Thomas' Hospital RFC
Ground Address: Renal Admin Department 6th Floor, Borough Wing Guys Hospital London SE1 9RT
Contact: 07831 809868
Email: geoff.koffman@gstt.nhs.uk
Website: www.guysrugby.com
Directions: From London A2 along Old Kent Road to New Cross. Follow directions to Brockley going down Brockley High Street, pass Crofton Park Station on your left, over mini-roundabout then on to traffic lights at top of hill. Turn sharp left at traffic lights onto B
Honorary Secretary: Mr Toby Welch
Email: toby.r.welch@gmail.com
Fixtures Secretary: Mr Oliver Howlett; B 314 East Street London SE17 ZSX   Tel: 07890 171024
Email: oliver.howlett@kcl.ac.uk
Club Colours: Navy Blue & Gold 4" Hoops
League: Kent 1 (level 9)

H.A.C. RFC
Address: Armoury House City Road London EC1Y 2BQ
Directions: Metropolitan/Northern & Circle Lines to Moorgate Station, proceed North, towards Finsbury Square on city Road, entrance to ground is 200m on the left.
Fixtures Secretary: Mr Justin Clark; CCD 18 Greek Street London W1D 4DS
Tel: 020 74344100   Email: justin@ccdpr.com
Club Colours: Navy and Maroon Hoops
League: Herts-Middlesex 2 (level 10)

Hackney RFC
Ground Address: Spring Hill Sports Ground Spring Hill Upper Clapton Hackney E5 9BL
Contact: 07795 394734
Email: hackneyrfc@hotmail.com
Website: www.hackneyrfc.co.uk
Honorary Secretary: Mr Simon Ferguson; 57 Albert st St Albans Herts. AL1 1 RT   Tel: 07795 394734
Email: simon.ferguson@rbi.co.uk
Fixtures Secretary: Mr Roy Irwin; Top Flat 49 Clapton Common London E5 9AA
Tel: 07905 372190   Email: roycanley@aol.com
Club Colours: Blue and green quarters
League: Herts-Middlesex 2 (level 10)

Hadleigh RFC
Ground Address: Layham Road Sports Ground Hadleigh, Ipswich Suffolk IP7 5NE
Contact: 01473 823231
Website: www.hadleighrufc.com
Directions: From Hadleigh High Street turn into Duke Street (marked to Lower Layham and flanked by library & chemist) over bridge and go on round bends, past millfield football grounds, club is on the left.
Honorary Secretary: Mrs Clare Wiltshire
Tel: 01473 280538   Email: clare@legacysearch.co.uk
Club Colours: Maroon & White
League: East Counties 2 (level 10)

Hammersmith & Fulham RFC
Ground Address: Hurlingham Park Hurlingham Road Fulham SW6 3RH
Email: Info@FulhamRugby.co.uk
Website: www.FulhamRugby.co.uk
Directions: From the North side of Putney Bridge turn into New Kings Road (A308). After 100 metres turn right under the railway bridge into Hurlingham Road. Ground is 300 metres on right.
Honorary Secretary: Mr Christopher Cuthbertson; 17 Wheatsheaf Lane London SW6 6LS Tel: 09732 712728
Email: Secretary@FulhamRugby.co.uk
Fixtures Secretary: Mr Lyndon Walters; Flat 6 Wilton Court Cavell Street London E1 2BN Tel: 07887 648875
Email: Fixtures@FulhamRugby.co.uk
Club Colours: Red with white and navy Bands
League: London 2 North West (level 7)

Hampstead RFC
Ground Address: Hampstead Heath Extension Hampstead Way Hampstead Way London NW11 7LH
Contact: 07967 154173
Email: mark.spilsbury@ukces.org
Website: www.hampsteadrugbyclub.co.uk
Directions: North Circular to Finchley Road, left into Millfield Way, cross Meadway, enter Hampstead Way. Look for posts and changing rooms on the left.
Honorary Secretary: Mr Mark Spilsbury; 39 Langbourne Avenue Highgate London N6 6PS
Tel: 07967 154173   Email: mark@spilsresearch.co.uk
Fixtures Secretary: Adrian D'Arcy; Flat 1, 1c Orleston Mews London N7 8LL   Tel: 07795 237038
Email: Adrian.DArcy@WSPGroup.com
Colours: Maroon & gold halves seperated by white band
League: London 2 North West (level 7)

Haringey Rhinos RFC
Ground Address: Haringey Rhinos Rugby Club White Hart Lane Community Sports Centre White Hart Lane Wood Green Middx. N22 5QW
Contact: 07871 109902
Email: haringeyrhinos@googlemail.com
Website: www.haringeyrhinos.co.uk
Directions: ROAD:White Hart Lane, N22, runs between Wood Green High Road (A105) and Great Cambridge Road(A10).WHLCSC is stadium complex on north side of road. Public Transport: Wood Green LTU Station (Piccadilly), turn left into Lordship Lane then W3 bus (eastwards) to White Hart Lane junction with Perth Rd.
Honorary Secretary: Mr Anthony Chadwick; 13 Redston Road Hornsey London N8 7HL
Tel: 07985 069800
Email: antony.chadwick@btinternet.com
Fixtures Secretary: Mr Nick Critchlow; 17 West Road Sawbridgeworth Herts. CM21 0BJ Tel: 07877 240448
Email: critchlow131@btinternet.com
Club Colours: Green,Scarlet & White Circlets
League: London 3 North West (level 8)

Harlequin Amateurs
Ground Address: ADMIN OFFICE Harlequin Amateurs Rugby Club c/o 29 Admiralty Way Teddington Middx.TW11 0NL
Contact: 07768 598896
Email: andybrampton@hotmail.com
Website: www.harlequinrugby.co.uk
Directions: Clubhouse is located on Ferry Road, Teddington - located right beside Teddington Lock - the large white construction has a chandlers shop downstairs, the Harlequin Amateurs clubhouse is upstairs! Opposite the Tide End Cottage Public house.
Honorary Secretary: Mr Andy Brampton; 29 Admiralty Way Teddington Middx.TW11 0NL Tel: 07768 598896
Email: andybrampton@hotmail.com
Fixtures Secretary: Mr Stephen Burgess; 65 Staunton Road Kingston Upon Thames KT2 5TN
Tel: 07768 994339   Email: stephen.burgess@hp.com
Club Colours: Harlequin
League: Herts-Middlesex 1 (level 9)

Harlow RFC
Ground Address: Ram Gorse Elizabeth Way Harlow Essex CM20 2JQ
Contact: 01279 860533
Email: secretary@harlow-rugby.co.uk
Website: www.harlow-rugby.co.uk
Directions: From M11 J7 follow the signs to Harlow A414, Follow Signs for Hertford / Harlow Town Railway Station (A414) then follow signs for Pinnicales Industrial Area Elizabeth Way Club on Right just past Burnt Mill Industrial Area
Honorary Secretary: Mr Christopher McFerran; 106 Carters Mead Harlow CM17 9ET   Tel: 01279 860533
Email: chris.mcferran@ntlworld.com
Fixtures Secretary: Mr Dave Sharp; 214 Waterhouse Moor Harlow Essex CM18 6BW
Tel: 01279 420154   Email: d.c.sharp@ntlworld.com
Club Colours: Red
League: London 2 North East (level 7)

Harrodians RFC
Ground Address: Barnes RFC Queen Elizabeths Walk Barnes London SW13 9SA
Contact: 0044 07799471085
Email: enquiries@barnesrfc.org
Website: www.barnesrfc.org

Directions: by CAR, TUBE, BUS or WALKING From Hammersmith Broadway (Tube / 33, 72 and 209 Bus) cross Hammersmith Bridge, proceed down Castlenau three-quarters mile turn left into Queen Elizabeth Walk at the Red Lion Pub, the Clubhouse is 50 yards on left. The Ground and changing rooms 800 yards further on at end of Queen Elizabeth Walk.at Barn Elms Sports Ground.There is a large car park at the ground. BY TRAIN Barnes Station (Not Barnes Bridge) Walk away from Rosslyn Park RFC along Rocks Lane, cross Barnes Common and turn right at the Red Lion Pub into Queen Elizabeth Walk (A 10 minute
Honorary Secretary: Mr David Doonan; 5 Elland Road Walton on Thames Surrey KT12 3JT Tel: 01932 242233 Email: daviddoonan@btinternet.com
Fixtures Secretary: Mr Ron Holley
Tel: 07775 785580   Email: ronholley@tiscali.co.uk
Non League

Harrow RFC
Ground Address: Grove Field Wood Lane Stanmore Hill Middx.HA7 4LF
Contact: 0208 9542615
Email: harrowrfc@hotmail.com
Website: www.harrowrfc.co.uk
Directions: From A41towards London at the Esso Garage roundabout, take the third exit across the MI up Brockley Hill. Take first right into Wood Lane. (past entrance to Royal National Orthopaedic Hopsital) Club 400 yards on the right at the junction with Warren Lane. From Stanmore go up Stanmore Hill turn into Wood Lane (at the speed camera). Club 200 yards on the left at the juction with Warren Lane
Honorary Secretary: Mr Andrew Smart; 169 Abbots Road Abbots Langley Herts. WD5 0BN
Tel: 07971 178633
Email: andrew-smart@ntlworld.com
Fixtures Secretary: as Hon. Sec.
Email: andrew-smart@ntlworld.com
Club Colours: Navy blue and white hoops
League: Herts-Middlesex 4 (level 12)

Harwich & Dovercourt RFC
Ground Address: Wick Lane Dovercourt Harwich CO12 3TA
Contact: 01255240255
Email: coyles5@tiscalli.co.uk
Directions: A120 from Colchester to Parkeston R'bout. 3rd exit, to top of hill. Turn left past hospital. Take 3rd right into Highfield Ave. Continue over crossroads into The Drive. Turn right at bottom. Turn immediately left, pass swimming pool. Clubhouse behind Pool
Honorary Secretary: Mr Trevor Armstrong; 7 Hazelville Close Harwich CO12 3TQ Tel: 01255 551162
Email: trevorarmstrong7@hotmail.co.uk
Fixtures Secretary: Mr Barry Male; 28 Mayes Lane Ramsey Harwich CO12 5EJ   Tel: 01255 886165
Email: barrymale10@hotmail.com
Club Colours: Black Shirts with one White Hoop
League: East Counties 2 (level 10)

Haslemere Community Rugby Club
Ground Address: Woolmer Hill Sports Ground Woolmer Hill Haslemere Surrey GU27 1QA
Contact: 01428 643072
Email: matthewmcgrory@hotmail.com
Website: www.haslemererugby.com
Directions: Off A3 turn down Sandy Lane at Bramshott Chase towards Hammer Vale, turn left to Woolmer Hill & then left to Woolmer Hill Sports Ground & school. If approaching from the north on A3, allow extra journey time until Hindhead tunnel is open in 2011. Nearest BR station is Haslemere on BR London to Portsmouth line
Honorary Secretary: Mr Malcolm Caird; Pear Tree Cottage Lurgashall Petworth West Sussex GU28 9ET
Tel: 01428 708120   Email: cairdkm@aol.com
Fixtures Secretary: Mr Matthew Mcgrory; 7 Avon Court Avon Road Farnham Surrey GU9 8PH
Tel: 07899 998067
Email: matthewmcgrory@hotmail.com
Club Colours: Blue and white hoops
League: Surrey 3 (level 11)

Hastings & Bexhill RFC
Ground Address: William Parker Lower School site Park Avenue Park Avenue Hastings TN34 2NT
Contact: 01424 444255
Email: hastings@hastingsrugby.org.uk
Website: www.hastingsrugby.org.uk
Directions: Take London road out of Hastings town centre and then into St. Helens Road adjacent to Alexander Park and follow signs to Rugby Club.
Honorary Secretary: Mr Len Bolton; 180 Harrow Lane St. Leonards-on-Sea East Sussex TN37 7JZ
Tel: 01424 755612   Email: elbow@macunlimited.net
Fixtures Secretary: Mr Paul Sandeman
Email: the.sandemans@virgin.net
Club Colours: Blue And White
League: London 3 South East (level 8)

Hatfield RFC
Ground Address:
96 Briars Lane Hatfield Herts. AL10 8EY
Contact: 01707 270772
Email: russell.doyle@ntlworld.com
Website: www.hatfieldrugby.co.uk
Directions: Exit J3 A1(M). Follow Comet Way (A1001) towards Hatfield town centre. At first roundabout turn right onto Cavendish Way. At roundabout straight over into Bishops Rise. Turn left into Woods Avenue, left again into Briars Lane.
Honorary Secretary: Miss Amy Nicholson; 27 Gladstone Road Ware Herts. SG12 0AG
Tel: 07968 976127   Email: rugby@amynicholson.com
Fixtures Secretary: Mr Toby Garrett; 13 Crossfield Road Hoddesdon Herts. EN11 0HL Tel: 07841 750999
Email: toby.garrett@smithsdetection.com
Club Colours: Black
League: Herts-Middlesex 3 (level 11)

LEVEL 7-12 AND NON LEAGUE CLUBS

Haverhill and District RFC
Ground Address: H.R.F.C Castle Playing Fields School Lane Haverhill Suffolk CB9 9DE
Contact: 01440 702871
Email: chris@crisalis.go-plus.net
Website: www.haverhillrfc.co.uk
Directions: From Haverhill bypass, take the roundabout exit signed Clements Estate. Take second left up School Lane. Map & details on website.
Honorary Secretary: Mr Ian Wade; H.R.F.C Castle Playing Fields School Lane Haverhill Kedington Suffolk CB9 9DE Tel: 01440 703668
Email: iandawade@sky.com
Fixtures Secretary: Mr Tony Hope; 2 Hart Close Haverhill CB9 9JR Tel: 07816 450932
Email: a-hope1@sky.com
Club Colours: Claret & Blue
League: East Counties 2 (level 10)

Hayes RFC
Ground Address: Grosvenor Playing Fields Kingshill Avenue Hayes Middx. UB4 8DB
Contact: 0208 723 9786
Email: admin@hayesrugby.com
Directions: From A40, off at "Target" roundabout head south, at next roundabout (White Hart) take Yeading Lane, at first major set of lights turn right into Kingshill Ave, Ground is 1 mile on right.
Honorary Secretary: Mr Neil Fretwell; Sandgate House Flat 15 Queens Walk Ealing London W5 1TN Tel: 07956 304909
Email: fretwellneil@aol.co.uk
Fixtures Secretary: Mr Neil Fretwell; Sandgate House Flat 15 Queens Walk Ealing London W5 1TN Tel: 07956 304909
Email: fretwellneil@aol.co.uk
Club Colours: Navy and Gold
League: Herts-Middlesex 4 (level 12)

Heathfield & Waldron RFC
Ground Address: Hardy Roberts Recreation Ground Cross in Hand Heathfield TN21 0TA
Contact: 01323 492309
Website: www.hwrfc.co.uk
Directions: Adjacent to Cross in Hand public house in centre of village opposite Esso garage.
Honorary Secretary: Mr Tim Ball; The Red House Rushlake Green East Sussex TN219QE Tel: 07802 932248
Email: tim_ball@shadboltlaw.com
Fixtures Secretary: Mr Will Hole TN210XX Tel: 01273 858858
Club Colours: Green & White Quarters, Green Shorts
League: London 3 South East (level 8)

Hemel Hempstead (Camelot) RFC
Ground Address: Club House Chaulden Lane Hemel Hempstead Herts. HP1 2BS
Contact: 01442 230353
Email: charles.teuma@ntlworld.com
Website: www.camelotrugby.co.uk
Directions: From roundabout on A4251 (old A41) outside train station, take Fishery Road. At roundabout turn left in to Northridge Way. Chaulden Lane and Club are 250 metres on the left.
Honorary Secretary: Mrs Debra Klyen; 2 Ryecroft Close Leverstock Green Hemel Hempstead HP2 4PL Tel: 01442 399092
Email: debbyk1@sky.com
Fixtures Secretary: Mr Robert Skinner; 137 Fern Drive Hemel Hempstead Herts. HP3 9ET Tel: 01442 246586
Club Colours: Royal Blue & White
League: London 2 North West (level 7)

Hendon RFC
Ground Address: Greenlands Lane Copthall Playing Fields Hendon NW4 1RL
Email: teb.rugby@googlemail.com
Website: www.hendonrfc.com
Directions: Directions From M1 southbound take Exit 2 onto A1 & Ground is on left approx 500 yards From A41 at 5 Ways Corner take A1 southbound & Ground is on left approx 500 yards
Honorary Secretary: Mr Tom Brownsell; 9 Winscombe Way Stanmore Middx. HA7 3AX Tel: 07771 860931
Email: teb.rugby@googlemail.com
Fixtures Secretary: Mr Craig Silver; 1 Gyles Park Stanmore Middx. HA7 1AN Tel: 07712 677400
Email: craig.silver@chesterton.co.uk
Club Colours: Green Black and White unequal hoops
League: Herts-Middlesex 1 (level 9)

Hitchin RFC
Ground Address: King George V Playing Fields Old Hale Way Hitchin Herts. SG5 1XL
Contact: 01603 615674
Email: ian@pyramidwindows.co.uk
Website: www.hitchinrfc.co.uk
Directions: At Angels Reply pub turn into Bearton Road, take second left into Old Hale Way, turn into ground by phone box.
Honorary Secretary: Mr Ian Cowling; 18 Willian Road Hitchin Herts. SG4 0LR Tel: 07769 686999
Email: ian@pyramidwindows.co.uk
Fixtures Secretary: Mr Steve Ward; 1 Tithe Close Codicote Hitchin Herts. SG4 8UX Tel: 01462 635857
Email: wardstephen@yahoo.co.uk
Club Colours: Maroon, Black & White Shirts, Black Shorts & Maroo
League: London 3 North West (level 8)

The following HM Ships share the same address, contact number, email and website.
They are all Non League.

Address: C/O Royal Navy Rugby Union HMS TEMERAIRE Portsmouth Hampshire PO1 2HB

Contact: 023 9272 5238

Email: cb-honsec-navy@therfu.com

Website: www.navyrugbyunion.co.uk

HMS Collingwood

HMS Gloucester

HMS Nelson

HMS Nottingham
Honorary Secretary: A Vercoe
Tel: 07802 356469
Email: 346-LPT@A.DII.MOD.UKe

HMS Richmond

HMS Southampton

HMS Sultan

HMS Westminster

Holbrook RFC
Ground Address: The Holbrook Club North Heath Lane Horsham RH12 5PJ
Contact: 01403 751150
Directions: From Crawley leave A264 at Rusper Roundabout towards Roffey, 3rd exit at next roundabout into Giblets Way. At mini roundabout turn left into North Heath Lane. As road starts to climb the Club is on left immediately after Drake Close.
Honorary Secretary: Mr Paul Bowen; 19 Pondtail Park Horsham RH12 5LD
Tel: 07930 981838
Email: pbowen@on-linepartnership.co.uk
Fixtures Secretary: Mr James Lowe; 187 St Leonards Road Horsham RH13 6BD
Tel: 07779 597040
Email: lowe_james@btconnect.com
Club Colours: Home: Dark Blue with White chevrons.
League: Sussex 1 (level 9)

Holt RFC
Ground Address: Bridge Road High Kelling Holt NR25 6QT
Contact: 01263 712191
Email: david.a.hitcham@barclayscorporate.com
Website: www.holfrfc.com
Directions: 1 1/2miles from Holt on the A148 road to Cromer - adequately signposted
Honorary Secretary: Mr David Hitcham; Kingsbridge House Burgh Norwich Norfolk NR11 6TW
Tel: 01603 279926
Email: david.a.hitcham@barclayscorporate.com
Fixtures Secretary: Mr Alan Gibbs; 6 Hill View Road Sheringham Norfolk NR26 8EP
Tel: 01263 820088   Email: alangill.gibbs@virgin.net
Club Colours: Black
League: East Counties 1 (level 9)

Horsham RUFC
Ground Address: PO Box 114 Horsham West Sussex RH13 6YE
Contact: 01403 265027
Website: www.horshamrufc.co.uk
Directions: From centre of Horsham take A281 to Brighton. At St. Leonards Arms pub turn left. Take 3rd right signposted Bucks Head and Ground is 600m on left.
Honorary Secretary: Mr Robert Fennelly; 25 The Pines Horsham West Sussex RH12 4UF
Tel: 07801 099034
Email: bob.fennelly@btinternet.com
Fixtures Secretary: Mr Marc Gumbrill; 51 St Leonards Road Horsham West Sussex RH13 6EH
Tel: 07718 779511   Email: mgumbrill@sky.com
Club Colours: Green/White
League: London 3 South East (level 8)

Hove RFC
Ground Address: Hove Recreation Ground Shirley Drive Hove East Sussex BN3 6QP
Contact: 01273 505 103
Email: clubhouse@hoverfc.com
Directions: From the north, travel down the A23 until you reach the A27. Go west on A27 and take first turn off A2038. Take second exit at roundabout (Dyke Road Avenue) and then first right (Woodland Drive). Take left into Shirley Drive (after a parade of shops) and then follow Shirley Drive until you reach the clubhouse on the right-hand side, slightly obscured by hedges.
Honorary Secretary: Mr Andrew Ward; 75 Hangleton Road Hove East Sussex BN3 7GH
Tel: 07789 777475
Email: andy@highlawn.co.uk
Fixtures Secretary: Mr Mike Richardson; 6 Wayside Westdene Brighton BN1 5HL
Tel: 07860 638092   Email: mr@railex.demon.co.uk
Club Colours: Sky Blue and Maroon
League: London 2 South East (level 7)

HSBC RFC
Ground Address: H.S.B.C. R.F.C. HSBC Group Sports & Social Club Lennard Road Beckenham Kent BR3 1QW
Contact: 020 89194366
Directions: Adjoining New Beckenham British Rail Station.
Honorary Secretary: Mr Mike Brooks; 54 Oaklands Avenue West Wickham Kent BR4 9LF
Tel: 07831 686629
Email: mikebrooks@hsbc.com
Fixtures Secretary: Mr Derek Smith; 2 Hurst Gardens Hurstpierpoint Hassocks West Sussex BN6 9ST
Tel: 07786 716936
Email: dereksmith1955@hotmail.co.uk
Club Colours: Black with red / white sleeves
League: Kent 1 (level 9)

Ickenham RFC
Ground Address: Ickenham Rugby Club Oak Avenue Ickenham Middx.UB10 8LP
Contact: 07740 584950
Email: info@ickenhamrugby.co.uk
Website: www.ickenhamrugby.co.uk
Directions: The club shares its ground with Ickenham Cricket Club and is situated at the end of: Oak Avenue Ickenham Middlesex UB10 8UT 01895 639 366 The club is within a 5 minute walking distance of both West Ruislip Station (Central Line) and Ickenham Station (Metropolitan Line & Piccadilly Line). By car it is easiest to leave the A40 atHilingdon Circus, follow signs to Ickenham, and then turn left into Oak Avenue (immediately adjacent to the Total Garage).
Honorary Secretary: Charlie Boden; 5 Rectory Way Ickenham Middx.UB10 8BP **Tel:** 07875 021 521
Email: charles.boden@scanstyle.com
Fixtures Secretary: Mr Roger Hickman; 87 Queens Road New Malden Surrey KT3 6BY Tel: 07866 582874
Club Colours: Black Shirts with Red & White
League: Herts-Middlesex 3 (level 11)

Ilford Wanderers RFC
Ground Address: IWRFC Sports Ground Forest Road Barkingside Ilford Essex IG6 3HJ
Contact: 020 85004622
Email: info@ilfordrfu.co.uk
Website: www.ilfordrfu.co.uk
Directions: By road A12 to Gants Hill R/bout. Follow Cranbrook Rd to Barkingside High Street, turn into Forest Rd at Fulwell Cross R/bout Fairlop Oak PH. Ground 1 mile left at signpost. By public transport, Central line to Hainault. Turn right from stn, 2nd right int
Honorary Secretary: Mr Steve Stuckey; 64 Meadow Rise Blackmore Ingatestone Essex CM4 0QY
Tel: 07860 430389
Email: steve.stuckey@btopenworld.com
Fixtures Secretary: Mr Beiron Rees; 0 Eastwood Road Ilford IG3 8UT **Tel:** 020 85971158
Email: beiron.rees@essexrugby.com
Club Colours: Green, White and Red hoops
League: Essex 1 (level 9)

Imperial Medicals RFC
Ground Address: Imperial Coll. School of Medicine Athletics Ground, Udney Park Road Teddington Middx.TW11 9BB
Contact: 07973 532986
Email: ben.wiles@imperial.ac.uk
Website: www.imperialmedicals.co.uk
Directions: Exit Teddington Station into Station Road, Turn right into Cromwell road. Udney Park Road is third on the left.
Honorary Secretary: Mr Timothy Rawson; Reynolds Building St. Dunstan's Road London W6 8RP
Tel: 07891 750151
Email: timothy.rawson07@imperial.ac.uk
Fixtures Secretary: Mr Timothy Rawson; Reynolds Building St. Dunstan's Road London W6 8RP
Tel: 07891 750151
Email: timothy.rawson07@imperial.ac.uk
Club Colours: Navy Blue + Red & Yellow Astid
League: London 2 North West (level 7)

Ipswich RFC
Ground Address: Humber Doucy Lane Ipswich IP4 3PZ
Contact: 01473 724072
Email: club@ipswich-rugby.co.uk
Website: www.ipswichrugby.com
Directions: A12 ToysRus roundabout straight over towards Ipswich at third traffic light garage on left & Right turn left go over two sets of lights & two roundabouts. Over bridge turn Left at end T junction.
Honorary Secretary: Mr Mark Greetham c/o the club.
Tel: 01473 724072 **Email:** club@ipswich-rugby.co.uk
Fixtures Secretary: Mr Roy Bouch c/o the club.
Tel: 01449 760250 **Email:** roy_boy45@hotmail.com
Club Colours: Black & Amber
League: London 2 North East (level 7)

Ipswich YM RFC
Ground Address: The Street Rushmere Rushmere St Andrew Ipswich SuffolkIP5 1DG
Contact: 01394 283907
Email: dickmdaniels@yahoo.co.uk
Website: www.ipswichymrugby.org.uk
Directions: From Colchester Road turn right?left into Rushmere Road. Straight across cross road past church on left. Club 50 meters on right.
Honorary Secretary: Mr Dick Daniels; 85 Western Avenue Felixstowe Suffolk IP11 9NT **Tel:** 07957 775951
Email: dickmdaniels@yahoo.co.uk
Fixtures Secretary: Mr Bob Hullis; 2 Godbold Close Kesgrave Ipswich IP5 2FE **Tel:** 07711 793815
Email: rhullis@jackson-civils.co.uk
Club Colours: Amber & Maroon Hoops
League: East Counties 2 (level 10)

Isle of Wight RFC
Ground Address: Wootton Recreation Ground Footways, Woottton Isle of Wight PO33 4NQ
Contact: 07739 100587
Email: info@iwrfc.co.uk
Website: www.iwrfc.co.uk

Directions: http://www.iwrfc.co.uk/directions_maps.htm
Honorary Secretary: Ms Louise Carrington; 110 Pelham Road Cowes Isle of Wight PO31 7DW
Tel: 07739 100587   Email: loucarrington@hotmail.co.uk
Fixtures Secretary: Mr Neil Brading; 88 Osborne Road East Cowes Isle of Wight PO32
Tel: 07717 531675   Email: n_brading@hotmail.com
Club Colours: Blue and Gold
League: Hampshire 2 (level 10)

ITC Catterick
Ground Address: Vimy Barracks Catterick Garrison North Yorkshire DL9 3PS
Contact: 07480 872723
Non League

JCU (NI)
Ground Address: HQ NI BFPO 825
Contact: 02982 263325
Non League

Jersey United Banks RFC
Ground Address: Grainville St. Saviour Jersey
Contact: 07797751781
Email: petehaw@dialstart.net
Honorary Secretary: Ms Cara Mackay; 6 Jardin De La Rai Springfield Road St Helier Jersey JE2 4LE
Tel: 0779 7741537
Email: Cara@cmackay36.freeserve.co.uk
Fixtures Secretary: Mr Julian De Gruchy; Dove Cottage St Blaize Rue De Fremont St John Jersey JE3 4DA
Tel: 0779 7827226   Email: julian.de-gruchy@ubs.com
Non League

Jesus College RFC
Ground Address: Jesus College Jesus Lane Cambridge Cambs.CB5 8BL
Contact: 079545 344249
Email: tg286@cam.ac.uk
Directions: Enter the College through the Chimney and walk into the porters the lodge. There enquire as to where the rugby pitches are.
Honorary Secretary: Ian Childs   Tel: 07912 523617
Fixtures Secretary: as Hon. Sec.
Club Colours: Black/Red
Non League

JHQ Rheindahlen
Ground Address: SO3 G4 Plans HQ ARRC BFPO 825
Contact: 02892 263325
Non League

KCS Old Boys RFC
Ground Address: Arthur Road Motspur Park Motspur Park New Malden Surrey KT3 6NA
Contact: 020 83362512
Email: paddy@kings.org.uk
Website: www.kings.org.uk
Directions: 5 mins walk from Motspur Park station, mainline BR from Waterloo. From A3, New Malden underpass, south on A2043, approx 400m left into Motspur Park (Rd) cto Arthur Road, 2nd right after level crossing.
Honorary Secretary: Mr Trevor Wingate; 22 Chilmark Gardens New Malden KT3 6RT   Tel: 020 82411903
Email: trwingate@blueyonder.co.uk
Fixtures Secretary: Mr Patrick Ralston; 209 Worple Road Raynes Park London SW20 8QY
Tel: 07958 232816   Email: paddy@kings.org.uk
League: London 2 South East (level 7)

Kew Occasionals RFC
Ground Address: Richmond Athletic Ground Kew Foot Road Kew Foot Road Richmond TW9 2SS
Contact: 0208 9400397
Email: kewoccasionals@googlemail.com
Honorary Secretary: Mr Reg Clark; 5 Maze Road Kew Richmond Surrey TW9 3DA
Tel: 020 72405024   mail: regclark@hotmail.co.uk
Fixtures Secretary: Camilla Campbell-Stanway; The Garden Flat 12 Stowe Road London W12 8BN
Tel: 07958 532899   Email: camillacstanway@yahoo.com
Non League

Kilburn Cosmos RFC
Ground Address: Gladstone Park Jct of Anson and Kendal Road Willesden Green London NW2 6BH
Email: rohan1.mcnaughtan@dsl.pipex.com
Website: www.kilburncosmos.co.uk
Directions: Nearest BR Station: Cricklewood Station Nearest Tube Station: Willesden Green / Dollis Hill
Honorary Secretary: Mr Jonathan Church; 151c Saltram Crescent Maida Hill London W9 3JT
Tel: 02071668526
Email: jonathan.church1@barclays.com
Fixtures Secretary: Mr Benjamin Zaug; 47 Gresham Road London NW10 9DA
Email: benjamin_zaug@yahoo.fr
Club Colours: Blue, Gold, Black and Green Quarters
League: Herts-Middlesex 1 (level 9)

Kings College Hospital
Ground Address: The Griffin Sports Club 12 Dulwich Village London SE21 7AL
Contact: 020 82992891
Email: secretary@kchrfc.co.uk
Website: www.kchrfc.co.uk
Directions: The Griffin Club About 150 yds south of North Dulwich BR Station, in the street named Dulwich Village. From the South Circular head north away from Dulwich College, go over the mini roundabout, across the lights and the entrance to the drive leading
Honorary Secretary: Mr Kevin Gutridge; 205 Camberwell New Road London SE5 0TJ
Tel: 07774 851458
Email: gutridge@btinternet.com
Fixtures Secretary: Mr Andrew Pearson; The Griffin Sports Club 12 Dulwich Village London SE21 7AL
Email: apearson@colfes.com
Club Colours: Navy, Maroon and Sky Hoops
League: Kent 2 (level 10)

Kings Cross Steelers RFC
Ground Address: Memorial Park Holland Road West Ham London E15 3BP
Contact: 07880 724097
Email: secretary@kxsrfc.com
Website: www.kxsrfc.com
Directions: Turn off A13 just before Canning Town flyover, turn north on A1011, (Manor Road), turn right just before West Ham tube station into Memorial Avenue, the road bends round into Holland Road. The Club is at the end of the road.
Honorary Secretary: Mr Christopher Fisher; 68a Broad Street Teddington Middx.TW11 8QY
Tel: 07880 724097   Email: fishec@gosh.nhs.uk
Fixtures Secretary: Mr Ian Chaplin; Ford Road Ford Arundel West Sussex BN18 0BX
Tel: 07890 949325   Email: ian.chaplin@btinternet.com
Club Colours: Royal Blue Body, Emerald Sides
League: Essex 2 (level 10)

Kingsclere RFC
Ground Address: Fieldgate Centre Fieldgate Drive Foxes Lane Kingsclere Newbury Berks. RG20 5SQ
Contact: 01635 299998
Email: info@kingsclererfc.co.uk
Website: www.kingsclererfc.co.uk
Directions: From Basingstoke Take the A339 head for Kingsclere until you reach the Kingsclere Industrial Estate r'about. Take the 1st exit and follow signs to the village. Follow the road until it starts to veer to the left, turn right into Foxes Lane. After approx. 200 meters turn right intoFieldgate Drive. From Newbury Take the A339 head for Kingsclere until you reach the Kingsclere Industrial Estate roundabou. Take the 3rd exit and follow the signs to the village. Then as above.
Honorary Secretary: Mr James Snelling; 11 Stevens Green St. Mary Bourne Andover HampshireSP11 6DF
Tel: 01264 738321   Email: jim.snelling@uk.delarue.com
Fixtures Secretary: Mr R Mckevitt; 12 Quilter Road Brighton Hill Basingstoke RG22 4HA Tel: 07717 187160
Club Colours: Red & White Hoops.
League: Hampshire 2 (level 10)

Kingston RFC
Ground Address: Rear of Clubhouse, King Edward Recreation Ground Hook Road Chessington Surrey KT9 1PL
Contact: 0208 3978385
Email: turnerscrum@blueyonder.co.uk
Website: www.kingstonrfc.com
Directions: Leave A3 at Hook r'about, follow sign for A243 Chessington, Entrance approx. 200 yds on right.
Honorary Secretary: Mrs Sandra Turner; 81 Douglas Road Surbiton Surrey KT6 7SD Tel: 020 882871218
Email: turnerscrum1@blueyonder.co.uk
Fixtures Secretary: Mr Ian Ockenden, Chandler Court 14 Tolworth Rise South Tolworth Surbiton Surrey KT5 9NN
Tel: 07967 589643   Email: i.ockenden@blueyonder.co.uk
Club Colours: Maroon and White Shirts, Blue Shorts
League: London 3 South West (level 8)

Kingston University RFC
Ground Address: Kingston University SU Penrhyn Road Kingston-upon-Thames Surrey KT1 2EE
Contact: 020 8547 8830
Email: I.Holmes@kingston.ac.uk
Website: www.kingstonsu.co.uk
Honorary Secretary: Honorary Secretary; Athletic Union Kingston University RFC Penrhyn Road Kingston Upon Thames Surrey KT1 2EE Tel:
Non League

Lakenham-Hewett RFC
Ground Address: Hilltop Sports Ground, Main Road Swardeston Norwich NorfolkNR14 8DU
Contact: 01508 578826
Email: info@lakenhamrugby.com
Website: www.rfu.com/clubs/lakenham
Directions: Approach Norwich on the Southern bypass, leave on the Norwich/Ipswich exit (A140), head towards Norwich, turn 1st left (B1113), Ground is on right about 1.25 miles
Honorary Secretary: Mr Edward Miles; 5 Karen Close Hethersett Norwich NorfolkNR9 3DG Tel: 01603 630012
Email: ed.miles@lakenhamhewettrfc.co.uk
Fixtures Secretary: Mr Oliver Harris
Tel: 07917 477687   Email: oliver.harris@gardline.co.uk
League: East Counties 2 (level 10)

Law Society RFC
Ground Address: Kings College Sportsground Windsor Avenue New Malden KT3 5HA
Contact: 02089498733
Email: p.watts606@btinternet.com
Website: www.lawsocietyrfc.co.uk
Directions: Take New Malden turn off the A3 .Then take the first available left from roundabout. Essentially wiggle straight on and you will come to Windsor Avenue.
Honorary Secretary: Mr Peter Watts; 29 Westmoreland Terrace London SW1V 4AQ
Tel: 07770 747457   Email: p.watts606@btinternet.com
Fixtures Secretary: Mr Martin Davidson; 32 Lavender Sweep london SW11 1HA
Tel: 07989 744832   Email: mjdcatz@hotmail.com
Club Colours: Purple & Black
League: Surrey 2 (level 10)

Lewes RFC
Ground Address: Stanley Turner Ground Kingston Road Lewes BN7 3NB
Contact: 01273 473732
Email: secretary@lewesrugby.com
Website: www.lewesrfc.org.uk
Directions: From the A23 take the A27 to Lewes past Sussex University to the 1st roundabout. Take the first exit to Lewes town centre then turn right at the traffic lights and right at the mini roundabout. The club is 200 yards on the left. See website - www.lewesrfc.org.uk
Honorary Secretary: Mr David Winsor; 26 Surrey Road Seaford East Sussex BN25 2NN   Tel: 07775 604912, 01323 891009   Email: secretary@lewesrugby.co.uk

Fixtures Secretary: Ms Ramelda Amir; 120 Wick Hall Fiurze Hill Hove East Sussex BN3 1NH
Tel: 01273 821058   Email: ramelda@aol.com
Club Colours: Blue & White Hoops
League: London 2 South East (level 7)

Lightwater RFC
Ground Address: Lightwater Sports Centre The Avenue The Avenue Lightwater Surrey GU18 5RG
Contact: 07985 806927
Email: lee.paine@virginmedia.co.uk
Website: www.lightwaterrfc.co.uk
Directions: Leave the M3 at Junction 3 and turn towards Guildford. Turn right about 100 yards down A322, across the dual carriageway into Lightwater Village. Take 2nd right The Avenue [Large Sign for Lightwater Country Park] and follow this road into the park. The club
Honorary Secretary: Mr Lee Paine; Priory Gardens Flat 3 53a Park Road Camberley GU15 2SP
Tel: 07985 806927   Email: lee.paine@virginmedia.co.uk
Fixtures Secretary: Mr David Forsaith; 87 Wordsworth Avenue Yateley Hampshire GU46 6YR
Tel: 07775 544904   Email: dforsaith@ntlworld.com
Club Colours: Emerald Green with black sides
League: Surrey 4 (level 12)

London Cornish RFC
Ground Address: Richardson-Evans Memorial Playing Fields Roehampton Vale Roehampton Vale SW15 3PQ
Contact: 07771 663591
Email: david@fletch.uk.com
Website: www.lcrfc.co.uk
Directions: Ground located 100 yards north of Robin Hood roundabout on A3 before Asda store
Honorary Secretary: Mr Jerry Rogers; 17 Chiltern Road Sandhurst Berkshire GU47 8NB   Tel: 07796 174339
Email: jerryrogers@francescos.org.uk
Fixtures Secretary: Mr Angus Milne; 13 Durand Gardens Stockwell London SW9 0PS
Tel: 07768 141101   Email: angus.m.milne@dnv.com
Club Colours: Black with narrow gold hoops
League: London 2 South West (level 7)

London Exiles RFC
Ground Address: Barn Elms Sports Fields Queen Elizabeth Walk (off Castelnau) Queen Elizabeth Walk (off Castelnau) Barnes SW13 9SA
Contact: 020 74936040
Email: paul.hubbard-brown@eu.jll.com
Website: www.londonexiles.co.uk
Directions: The club trains every wednesday evening during the season down at the Millenium Stadium in Battersea Park, London SW8. A map can be found on the Club's main website. Our home ground is Barn Elms Sports Fields in Barnes, south-west London.
Honorary Secretary: Mr Tim Edgehill; 11 Birchwood Road London SW17 9BQ Tel: 020 74936040
Email: Edge@londonexiles.co.uk
Club Colours: Claret White Blue
League: Surrey 1 (level 9)

London French RFC
Ground Address: Barn Elms Playing Fields Queen Elizabeth Walk, Rocks Lane Castelnau SW13 9WT
Contact: 07952 154794
Email: rugby@londonfrenchrfc.com
Website: www.londonfrenchrfc.com
Directions: From North over Hammersmith Bridge, down Castelnau to junction with Red Lion Pub. Ground is on the corner.
Honorary Secretary: Mr Greg Andrews; 48 Rosedene Avenue Streatham Hill SW16 2LT Tel: 07952 154794
Email: gregorylives@hotmail.com
Fixtures Secretary: Mr Jeremy Salsby; 52 Salcott Road London SW11 6DE Tel: 07711 664978
Email: jeremys@sotelevision.co.uk
Colours: French (royal) blue shirt, white shorts, red socks
League: Herts-Middlesex 3 (level 11)

London Irish Amateur RFC
Ground Address: London Irish Amateur RFC The Avenue Sunbury-On-Thames Middx. TW16 5EQ
Contact: 01932 787628
Email: liarfc@hotmail.com
Website: www.london-irish-amateur.co.uk
Directions: At J1 of M3 (joins A316) exit to roundabout (Sunbury Cross) onto the A308 towards Kempton Park. Go over the bridge and take the 2nd turning on the right
Honorary Secretary: Mr Terry Long; 9 Cypress Avenue Whitton Twickenham TW2 7JY Tel: 07989540809
Email: MTLong@aol.com
Fixtures Secretary: Mr Adrian Connor; 41 Old Lane Cobham Surrey KT11 1NW Tel: 07932 753037
Email: adrianconnor@f2s.com
Club Colours: Green Shirts & Socks, White Shorts.
League: London 2 South West (level 7)

London Media RFC
Ground Address: 2nd Floor Flat 328 Wandsworth Bridge Rd London SW6 2TZ
Contact: 0207 7231733
Email: will.johnston@londoncentralportfolio.com
Website: www.londonmediarfc.co.uk
Directions: Albert Bridge Road entrance to Battersea Park (Near Albert Bridge)
Honorary Secretary: Mr William Johnston; 40 Chandos Avenue London W5 4ER Tel: 07768 846860
Email: will.johnston@londoncentralportfolio.com
Club Colours: Black & White Quarters
League: Surrey 2 (level 10)

London Metropolitan University
Address: 166-220 Holloway Road London N7 8DB
Contact: 0207 753 5147
Fixtures Secretary: John McBennett; 166 Holloway Road London N7 8DB Tel: 07780 718038
Non League

London New Zealand RFC
Ground Address: Acton Sports Centre Park Place Acton W3 8JY
Contact: 020 8546 3647
Email: calum.maclean@dsl.pipex.com
Honorary Secretary: Miss Wendy Whitchurch; 25 Canbury Avenue Kingston upon Thames Surrey KT2 6JP
Tel: 020 76311311
Email: lnzsecretary@dsl.pipex.com
Club Colours: Black shirts, black shorts
League: London 2 North West (level 7)

London Nigerian RFC
Ground Address: Linford Christie Stadium Off Du Cane Road London W12 0DF
Contact: 07957 258 058
Email: tunde.adeniji@homeoffice.gsi.gov.uk
Directions: London Underground Take the central line to East Acton Station. Come out of exit and turn left up Erconwald Street Take the second right into Wulfstan Street Walk down to the T-Junction and take a left into Du Cane Road. Walk past the prison and
Honorary Secretary: Mr Gareth Howells; 35 Holcombe Road Tottenham Hale London N17 9AS
Tel: 07950 504284   Email: wkghowells@yahoo.co.uk
Fixtures Secretary: Mr Neal Fetterman
Club Colours: Green and White Shirts - Green Shorts
League: London 2 North West (level 7)

London School of Economics RFC
Ground Address: LSE Sports Ground Windsor Avenue New Malden Surrey KT3 5HB
Contact: 0207 955 7161
Honorary Secretary: Honorary Secretary; Athletic Union London School of Economics East Building Houghton Street London WC2A 2AE
Non League

London South Africa RFC
Ground Address: Imber Court Sports Club Ember Lane East Molesey KT8 0BT
Contact: 0208 7416060
Email: timwalsh@londonsouthafricarfc.co.uk
Website: www.londonsouthafricarfc.co.uk
Honorary Secretary: Trevor Johnson; Ducks Cottages 1 Nether Wallop Stockbridge HampshireSO20 8HE
Tel: 07967 736710
Email: tjrugby1@breathe.com
Fixtures Secretary: as Hon. Sec.
Club Colours: Green, Black, White & Yellow
League: London 2 South West (level 7)

London South Bank University RFC
Ground Address: Athletic Union Offices London South Bank University, 103 Borough Road SE1 0AA
Contact: 020 7815 7806
Email: auadmin@lsbu.ac.uk
Website: www.lsbu.ac.uk/sports
Directions: Directions: Tube/Rail: Elephant & Castle, on the Northern Line Buses: 12, 21, 35, 40, 42, 45, 53, 63, 68, 171, 172, 176, 343, 468, P3. Car/bike parking Car park is on Albany Road. There are disabled parking spaces and a bike parking area at Chumleigh Gardens off Albany Road.
Honorary Secretary: David Bull; AU Office London South Bank University 103 Borough Road London SE1 0AA Tel: 07817 601587
Email: bully1@hotmail.com
Fixtures Secretary: Layla Hawkins; LSBU AU Office 103 Borough Road London SE1 0AA Tel: 020 78157806
Email: auadmin@lsbu.ac.uk
Club Colours: Royal Blue & Yellow
Non League

Lordswood RFC
Ground Address: Lordswood R.F.C. Lordswood sports & social club Lordswood chatham Kent ME5 8YE
Contact: 0 1634861924
Email: s.wellings@btinternet.com
Website: www.lordswoodrfc.co.uk
Directions: Directions to Ground from M2 Leave M2 at junction A229 (Chatham). At roundabout take first exit (signed Chatham/Walderslade). At traffic lights turn right and stay in right hand lane. Go straight over first roundabout (signed Lordswood). Continue till next roundabout at end of road. Take 2nd exit into Lordswood Lane and continue to next roundabout. Take 3rd exit (Albermarle Road) and proceed to end of road. Turn left into North Dane Way and the ground (Lordswood sports and social club) is 500 yards on the right.
Honorary Secretary: Mr Allan Cannon; 64 Mayford Road Lordswood Kent ME5 8SZ Tel: 01634 300456
Email: al_cannon@blueyonder.co.uk
Fixtures Secretary: as Hon. Sec.
Club Colours: Black with Gold Collars, Black Shorts
League: Kent 2 (level 10)

Loughton RFC
Ground Address: Hornbeam Sports & Social Club Squirrels Lane Hornbeam Road IG9 6HH
Contact: 02085040065
Website: www.loughtonrfc.org.uk
Directions: A11 out of NE London to Woodford Green, turn right following police station into Monkhams Lane, follow to end & straight over crossroads into Chesnut Avenue, continue onto Squirrels Lane.
Honorary Secretary: Mr Duncan Kaye; 1 Collier Row Road Collier Row Romford, Essex RM5 3NP
Email: duncan.kaye@keysandlee.co.uk
Fixtures Secretary: Mr Scott Taylor; 179 Princes Road Buckhurst Hill Essex IG9 5DJ Tel: 01276 703303
Email: duncan.kaye@keysandlee.co.uk
Club Colours: White with one green & two black hoops
League: Essex 2 (level 10)

Lowestoft & Yarmouth RFC
Ground Address: Lowestoft & Yarmouth R.F.C. Gunton Park Old Lane Old Lane Corton Long Lane NR32 5HE
Contact: 01493 653095
Email: TheNel@aol.com
Website: www.lowestoftandyarmouthrfc.com

Directions: From Lowestoft follow A12 to Gt Yarmouth. Just before start of dual carriageway at Corton turn right. Travel 300 yards and turn right again. Drive to end of Old Lane and club is on your right. From Gt Yarmouth head towards Lowestoft on A12 and at end of
Honorary Secretary: Mr June Nelson; 70 Upper Cliff Road Gorleston Great Yarmouth NorfolkNR31 6AJ Tel: 01493 653095   Email: thenel@aol.com
Fixtures Secretary: Terence Colby Tel: 01502 585924
Club Colours: Blue & White
League: London 3 North East (level 8)

Lytchett Minster RFC
Ground Address: Lytchett Park Watery Lane Lytchett Minster Dorset BH16 6HZ
Contact: 01202 622877
Email: gregory.buxton@btinternet.com
Website: www.lmrfc.com
Directions: The pitches for Lytchett Minster Rugby Club can be found next to the St. Peters Finger Pub in Lytchett Minster. For detailed directions please visit are website at www.lmrfc.com
Honorary Secretary: Mr Gregory Buxton; 22 Barbers Gate Poole Dorset BH15 1ZA Tel: 07917 728564
Email: gregory.buxton@btinternet.com
Fixtures Secretary: Mr Mark Hobson; Broom Heyes Old Wareham Rd Beacon Hill Poole Dorset BH16 6AQ Tel: 07860 109009   Email: mark@dorsetland.co.uk
Club Colours: Red and Blue
League: Hampshire 2 (level 10)

Magdalene College RFC (Cambridge)
Address: Magdalene Street Cambridge Cambs.CB3 0AG
Contact: 079190 58154
Email: rcs31@cam.ac.uk
Honorary Secretary: Mr Bob Smith; Magdalene College Cambridge CB3 0AG Tel: 07919 058154
Email: rcs31@cam.ac.uk
Fixtures Secretary: Mr Alex Spain; Magdalene College Cambridge Cambs.CB3 0AG
Email: as926@cam.ac.uk
Club Colours: Purple / Navy
Non League

Maldon RFC
Ground Address: Drapers Farm Sports Club Drapers Chase Goldhanger Road Heybridge CM9 4QT
Contact: 01621 852152
Email: simon.maldonrfc@yahoo.co.uk
Website: www.maldonrfc.co.uk
Directions: Directions To Club: From A12 take A414 to Maldon, going through Danbury. At the roundabout with Morrisons, turn left and left again at the next roundabout onto the by-pass (B1018). At the end of the by-pass turn right at the roundabout then left at the next one onto the Causeway. Right at the next roundabout at the Anchor pub, past the Heybridge Inn pub on the right, over the bridge and right at the roundabout into Goldhanger Road. Take the fourth left into Draper's Chase just past the telephone box. The club is at the end of the chase.

Honorary Secretary: Mr Simon Peacock; 39 Writtle Road Chelmsford Essex CM1 3BS Tel: 07866 521087
Email: simon.peacock@gfk.com
Fixtures Secretary: Chris Murphy   Tel: 07926 279485
Email: chris.murphy@rjjfreight.co.uk
Club Colours: Royal Blue & White Hoops
League: Essex 1 (level 9)

May & Baker RFC
Ground Address: May & Baker Club Dagenham Road Dagenham Essex RM10 7UP
Contact: 0208 919 3156
Directions: A13,left at Macdonalds to roundabout. First exit past Dagenham East Station to traffic lights. Right & right again at mini roundabout.
Honorary Secretary: Mr Garry O'Sullivan; Songers Cottages 10 Dedham Road Boxted Colchester CO4 5SQ Tel: 01206 272293   Email: garryo@mbrfc.com
Fixtures Secretary: Mr Mike Parnell; Old Post Office The Street High Easter Chelmsford CM1 4QW
Tel: 01245 231302   Email: mikeparnell@msn.com
Club Colours: Black & red, white trim, black shorts
League: Essex 2 (level 10)

Medway RFC
Ground Address: Medway RFC Priestfields Rochester Kent ME1 3AD
Contact: 01634 847737
Email: medway.rugby@blueyonder.co.uk
Website: www.mrfc.net
Directions: M2 J3, follow A229 to Chatham, at Bridgewood roundabout take the B2097 (Maidstone Road) to Borstal, Approx 2 miles there is a church on the left,take the next left after the church in to Priestfield. At bottom of hill turn left into the car park.
Honorary Secretary: Martin O'Brien; 67 Herbert Road Rainham Gillingham ME8 9DA   Tel: 01634 305234
Email: mobrien1@blueyonder.co.uk
Fixtures Secretary: Mr Gerald Farrow; 84 Sedge Crescent Chatham Kent ME5 0QD   Tel: 01634 666255
Club Colours: Scarlet & Old Gold
League: London 3 South East (level 8)

Mersea Island RFC
Ground Address: East Mersea Activity Center East Road Colchester Essex CO5 8TQ
Contact: 01206 385218
Directions: Turn left over Causeway coming onto Island (check the tide is not over road). Centre is the 3rd road on the right, follow road to the centre.
Honorary Secretary: Mr Graham Marfleet; 10 Yorick Avenue West Mersea Colchester CO5 8HZ
Tel: 01206 385218
Email: graham@marfleetconstruction.co.uk
Fixtures Secretary: Mr Graham Marfleet; 10 Yorick Avenue West Mersea Colchester CO5 8HZ
Tel: 01206 385218
Email: graham@marfleetconstruction.co.uk
Club Colours: Light Blue
League: London 2 North East (level 7)

LEVEL 7-12 AND NON LEAGUE CLUBS

Merton RFC
Ground Address: Morden Recreation Ground Faversham Road Morden Surrey SM4 6RE
Contact: 0208 6435562
Email: mertonrfc@yahoo.com
Website: www.mertonrugby.org
Honorary Secretary: Mr Terry Clouter; 14 Park Crescent Twickenham Middx.TW2 6NT
Tel: 07966 824964   Email: Terry@Clouter.com
Fixtures Secretary: Mr Paul Webster; 39 Elthiron Road London SW6 4BW   Tel: 020 77360149
Club Colours: Black and gold diagonal halves
League: Surrey 3 (level 11)

Metropolitan Police (Hayes) RFC
Ground Address: The Warren Sports and Social Club Croydon Road Croydon Road Hayes Kent BR2 7AL
Contact: 020 8462 1266
Directions: From M25 take A21 N-> London. At Traffic Lights at Locksbottom turn left onto A232 Croydon Road. Continue on Croydon Road through two sets of traffic lights. MPHRFC is on the right as you pass through Hayes Common
Honorary Secretary: Mr Dominick KELLY; 39 Sherwood Way West Wickham Kent BR4 9PB
Tel: 07884 436247   Email: dkelly@fm-24.com
Fixtures Secretary: as Hon. Sec.
Club Colours: Black Shirts, Black Shorts
Non League

Metropolitan Police RFC
Ground Address: Imber Court Ember Lane E. Molesey Surrey KT8 0BT
Contact: 07747 764207
Email: info@imbercourt.com
Website: www.imbercourt.com
Directions: Follow signs to Hampton Court (Palace). From the south, take Ember Court Lane, the first exit off the roundabout on Hampton Court Way; from the north, cross the Thames keeping Hampton Court Palace on the left, at the first roundabout take the third exit,
Honorary Secretary: Ed Cudmore   Tel: 07595 360247
Email: edward.cudmore@met.police.uk
Fixtures Secretary: Mr Paul Brooks
Tel: 07970 840090   Email: paul.brooks@met.police.uk
Club Colours: Blue & Yellow
Non League

Middlesex University RFC
Ground Address: Competitive Sports Office Middx.University Enfield Campus EN3 4SA
Contact: 020 8411 4651
Email: S.SIPPLE@MDX.AC.UK
Honorary Secretary: Hon. Sec., Athletic Union Middlesex University Enfield Campus Queensway Enfield Middx.EN3 4SA
Fixtures Secretary: Mr Dai Cook; Sports Office Middlesex University Campus Way London NW4 4JF
Tel: 020 84114651   Email: D.Cook@mdx.ac.uk
Non League

Midhurst RFC
Ground Address: Midhurst R.F.C. The Pavilion Cowdray Park Cowdray Ruins Midhurst West Sussex GU29 9AL
Contact: 01730 816 465
Email: simon.flint@bbcel.co.uk
Directions: At mini r'about junction of A286 and A272 take entrance to Cowdray Park, turn left 200yds along drive.
Honorary Secretary: Mr Simon Flint; Broadoak Chichester Road Midhurst West Sussex GU29 9PF
Tel: 01225 478946   Email: simon.flint@bbcel.co.uk
Fixtures Secretary: Simon Jenkins; 40 Osborne Road Petersfield Hants GU32 2AE   Tel: 07831 422679
Club Colours: Gold with Royal Blue Hoop
Non League

Mill Hill RFC
Ground Address: Copthall Playing Fields Page Street Mill Hill NW7 2ED
Contact: 0208 2030685
Email: gazftopp@btopenworld.com
Website: www.millhillrugby.co.uk
Directions: Next to J2 of M1, follow signs for Barnet Copthall & Club is top of Page St at entrance road to Stadium.
Honorary Secretary: Gary Topp
Email: gazftopp@btopenworld.com
Fixtures Secretary: Alex Airey Tel: 07713 274862
Email: alex@redmaynedirey.co.uk
Club Colours: Chocolate & Old Gold Hoops
League: Herts-Middlesex 2 (level 10)

Millbrook RFC
Ground Address: Lordshill Recreation Ground Redbridge Lane, Lordshill Southampton SO16 9BP
Contact: 02380 733861
Email: chrisjackieings@tiscali.co.uk
Website: www.millbrookrfc.co.uk
Directions: M27 J3 to M271 to J1, A3051, 1st left into redbridge Lane, 1 mile on right.
Honorary Secretary: Mrs Jacqueline Ings; 4 Rufus Close Rownhams Southampton SO16 8LR
Tel: 07946 293853   Email: chris.ings@sky.com
Fixtures Secretary: Mr Christopher Ings; 4 Rufus Close Rownhams Southampton SO16 8LR Tel: 07505 094548
Email: chris.ings@sky.com
Club Colours: Emerald & Scarlet Hoops
League: Hampshire 1 (level 9)

Millwall RFC
Ground Address: 75 Manchester road Isle of dogs London E14 3DN
Contact: 07809 590731
Email: secretary@millwallrugby.com
Website: www.millwallrugby.com
Honorary Secretary: Victor Okpevba; 36 Glenforth Street LONDON SE10 0JQ Tel: 0208 3331592
Fixtures Secretary: Mr Mike Beech; 32 11 Caledonian Wharf London E14 3EN Tel: 07764 987141
Email: fixturesecretary@MillwallRugby.com
Club Colours: Red, Black and White
League: Essex 1 (level 9)

Mistley RFC
Ground Address: Furze Hill Playing Fields Shrublands Road Mistley Manningtree CO11 1HS
Email: sd_tate1@yahoo.co.uk
Directions: From A12 follow signs for Harwich A120 to Horsley Cross, turn left for Mistley, turn right at TV mast, take first left follow road through Mistley Heath, turn left at T - junction into Mistley. Left at first bend and immediate left again.
Honorary Secretary: Shelagh Tate; Amir Mill Lane Bradfield Manningtree Essex CO11 2UT
Tel: 01255 870596   Email: sd_tate1@yahoo.co.uk
Fixtures Secretary: Mr Stephen Betts; 44 Queensway Lawford Manningtree Essex CO11 1EW
Tel: 07768 805664   Email: in-visionglass@tiscali.co.uk
Club Colours: Red and purple qaurters
League: East Counties 2 (level 10)

Mitcham RFC
Ground Address: Dewsbury Cottage Poulter Park, Peterborough Road Carshalton Surrey SM5 1EE
Contact: 020 86483567
Email: mitchamrufc@googlemail.com
Website: www.mitchamrufc.co.uk
Directions: The Ground can only be entered from Peterborough Road.
Honorary Secretary: Laura Osbourne; 22 Greenhill Sutton Surrey SM1 3LG   Tel: 0787 5899365
Email: Laurao677@blueyonder.co.uk
Fixtures Secretary: Mr Tony Antoniou; 3 Penrith Road Thornton Heath Surrey CR7 8PN
Tel: 020 87718862   Email: tonymitcham3@aol.com
Club Colours: Green & Lavender Hoops
League: Surrey 3 (level 11)

New Ash Green RFC
Ground Address: The Sportsfield Punchcroft Road New Ash Green, Longfield Kent DA3 8HS
Contact: 01474 874660
Email: nagclub@btconnect.com
Website: www.newashgreenrfc.org
Directions: Leave A20 at Gorse Hill main Road and turn into Scratchers Lane Leave Scratchers Lane and turn into Fawkham Road. Take 1st right onto Brands Hatch Road At crossroads head straightforward onto Billet Hill At Tee junction turn left onto Ash Road Take 1st right onto Ash Road Leave Ash Road and turn right into Punch Croft Turn right into car park.
Honorary Secretary: Mr Mark Mcnamara; 93 Coltstead New Ash Green Longfield Kent DA3 8LW
Tel: 0796 2019360   Email: nagrfc@btinternet.com
Fixtures Secretary: Mr Paul Brookman; 6 Sullivan Close Dartford Kent DA1 2NJ   Tel: 0779 6897357
Email: paul.brookman@charrington.co.uk
Club Colours: Dark green & black quarters, black shorts.
League: Kent 2 (level 10)

New Milton & District RFC
Ground Address: Ashley Rugby Ground Ashley Road Ashley Road Ashley, New Milton Hampshire BH25 5BP
Contact: 01425 610401
Email: newmiltonrugby@btconnect.com
Website: www.newmiltonrugby.co.uk
Directions: From New Milton town centre, head towards Ashley. After about one mile, at the top of a small hill, there is a right turn marked New Milton & District Rugby Club. It is adjacent to Ashley Junior school.
Honorary Secretary: Mr Nick Hanmer; Walsingham Andrew Lane Ashley New Milton Hampshire BH25 5QD
Tel: 01425 616263
Email: nick.hanmer@tesco.net
Fixtures Secretary: Mr Phil Hoyle; 44 Grand Avenue Bournemouth BH6 3TA Tel: 07817 327554
Email: phil@preparedevents.co.uk
Club Colours: Green with blue and gold bands
League: Hampshire 1 (level 9)

Newmarket RFC
Ground Address: Sports Pavillion Scaltback Middle School Elizabeth Avenue CB8 0DJ
Contact: 01638 663082
Email: robert.voss@btinternet.com
Website: www.newmarketrugby.com
Directions: Leave A14 at A142. Head towards Newmarket. Turn right at Tesco's roundabout. Follow road to "T" junction. Turn Left. After Quarter mile, right at traffic lights into Elizabeth Avenue. 100 Yards, turn left into School
Honorary Secretary: Mr Robert Voss; 58 King Edward VII Road Newmarket Suffolk CB8 0EU
Tel: 01638 669596
Email: robert.voss@btinternet.com
Fixtures Secretary: Mr Paul Tapley; 0 Malting Lane Isleham Ely Cambs. CB7 5RZ   Tel: 01638 781201
Email: paultapley@btinternet.com
Club Colours: Black Shirts with Emerald Trim
League: East Counties 1 (level 9)

Nomads RFC
Ground Address: 58 Nomads Rugby Football Club Baffins Road Portsmouth PO3 6BG
Contact: 07971 966234
Email: secretary@nomadsrfc.com
Website: www.nomadsrfc.com
Directions: Training and playing facilities at Portsmouth University sports ground, Furze Lane, Milton, Portsmouth. Take Locksway Road, off Milton Road. Furze Lane on left hand side approx 1 mile from junction Milton Rd and Locksway Rd.
Honorary Secretary: Mr Martin Drum; 58 Baffins Road Portsmouth Hampshire PO3 6BG Tel: 07836 200654
Email: secretary@nomadsrfc.com
Fixtures Secretary: Roger Easey   Tel: 07762 580288
Club Colours: Red & Black Irregular Hoops
League: Hampshire 2 (level 10)

LEVEL 7-12 AND NON LEAGUE CLUBS

Northolt RFC
Ground Address: Cayton Sports & Social Club Cayton Green Park Cayton Road Cayton Road Greenford Middx.UB6 8BJ
Contact: 0208 8131701
Email: northolt.rugby@virgin.net
Website: www.northoltrfc.org.uk
Directions: Driving = take the A40 (Western Avenue) to Greenford (Bridge Hotel junction/A4127 Greenford Road), then go as if to rejoin the A40 towards London but stay in the left hand lane & join the slip road (by the petrol garage) that runs parallel with the A40 (Runneymede Gardens). Go to the end of this road and turn left into Cayton Rd. The ground is at the end of the road. by Tube = Central line to Greenford. Turn right out of the station and cross the road, then turn immediate left at the end of the shops into Uneeda Drive. Walk to the end of the road and cross Greenford Road by the zebra crossing, then continue straight in up Bennetts Avenue. The ground is at the end of the road. By Rail = Take the First Great Western line from Paddington towards Greenford and alight at South Greenford - this line can also be picked up at South Acton, Ealing Broadway or West Ealing. Turn left out of the South Greenford stop and use the footbridge to cross the A40 (Western Avenue). Turn left on the other side of the road then take the first right (40 metres away) into Cayton Road. The ground is at the end of the road
Honorary Secretary: Mr Clare Payne; 16 Brackenbridge Drive Ruislip HA4 0NG Tel: 0208 8450874
Email: northoltrugby.secretary@virgin.net
Fixtures Secretary: Mr Colin Chesson; 41 Barnham Road Greenford Middx.UB6 9LR Tel: 07729 390127
Email: colin.chesson@virgin.net
Club Colours: Sky/Navy Blue Hoops
League: Herts-Middlesex 4 (level 12)

Norwich Medics RFC
Ground Address: c/o School of Medicine, Health Policy and Practice University of East Anglia Norwich NorfolkNR4 7TJ
Email: medicsrugby@gmail.com
Website: http://www.nmsrfc.org.uk
Honorary Secretary: Duncan Watt; 86 Stafford Street Norwich Norfolk NR2 3BG
Tel: 07962 076282   Email: medicsrugby@gmail.com
Fixtures Secretary: Mr David McAroe; 86 Stafford Street Norwich Norfolk NR2 3BG
Tel: 07962 076282   Email: medicsrugby@gmail.com
Club Colours: sky blue / navy / white
Non League

Norwich RFC
Ground Address: Norwich RFC Ltd. Beeston Hyrne Beeston Hyrne Norwich NR12 7BW
Contact: 01603 426259
Email: a.pott@uea.ac.uk
Website: www.nurfc.com
Directions: From Norwich take B1150 toward North Walsham. After passing White Woman Lane and Redmayne Sports Field, ground on left.

Honorary Secretary: Mr Andy Pott; 34 Judges Walk Norwich NR4 7QF Tel: 01603 250144
Email: a.pott@uea.ac.uk
Fixtures Secretary: Mr Paul Spinks; 13 Snows Hill Chegrave Norwich NR14 6JR Tel:
Email: paul.spinks4@ntlworld.com
Club Colours: Maroon, Gold, Green
League: London 2 North East (level 7)

Old Abbotstonians RFC
Ground Address: Abbotstonians R.F.C. Old Pole Hill Open Spaces Gainsborough Road Gainsborough ROad Hayes UB4 8PS
Contact: 020 8845 1452
Email: abbots@abbotstonians.co.uk
Website: www.abbotstonians.co.uk
Directions: A40 exit for Hillingdon Long Lane towards Uxbridge Road, left at BP station, left onto Pole Hill Road (HSBC on corner), around bend, first left after bus stop, Club at end.
Honorary Secretary: Mr Vic Devers; 15 Fairfield Road West Drayton Middx.UB7 8EY Tel: 07917 611979
Email: v.devo1@homecall.co.uk
Fixtures Secretary: Mr Vic Devers; 15 Fairfield Road West Drayton Middx.UB7 8EY Tel: 07917 611979
Email: v.devo1@homecall.co.uk
Club Colours: Red & Blue
League: Herts-Middlesex 1 (level 9)

Old Actonians RFC
Ground Address: Old Actonians Sports Club Gunnersbury Drive Popes Lane W5 4LL
Contact: 07711 497745
Email: stuart.swb@googlemail.com
Website: www.oldactoniansrfc.com
Directions: Closest tube is Acton Town on the Piccadilly line. Turn left out of the tube. Walk down over the North Circular, cross the road to the BP station, turn left and carry on down Popes Lane, Gunnersbury Drive is the first on the right - 50 yards from the BP s
Honorary Secretary: Mr Lee Jones; 194 Meadvale Road Ealing Middx.W5 1LT Tel: 07703 194504
Email: joneslee@hotmail.co.uk
Fixtures Secretary: As Hon Sec
Club Colours: Blue and White Bar
League: Herts-Middlesex 1 (level 9)

Old Alleynians RFC
Ground Address: Old Alleynian Football Club Dulwich Common London SE21 7HA
Contact: 020 82990170
Email: mail@alleynian.org
Website: www.alleynian.org/rugby
Directions: Situated on the South Circular Road between college Road & Lorsdhip Lane. 10 minutes walk from West Dulwich Train Station.
Honorary Secretary: Mr Keith Munyama; 52 Finsen Road London SE5 9AW Tel: 07946 892187
Email: keith.munyama@wachovia.com

Fixtures Secretary: Mr Robin Tagart, c/o the club.
Tel: 020 77675503
Email: Robin.tagart@ingrealestate.co.uk
Club Colours: Navy Black & Sky Hoops
League: London 3 South West (level 8)

Old Amplefordians RFC
Ground Address: Reeds Weybridge RFC North Avenue North Avenue Whitley Village, Walton On Thames Surrey KT12 4EJ
Contact: 07939 551492
Email: pitty77@mac.com
Website: www.oarfc.com
Honorary Secretary: Mr Thomas Foster; 57A Archel Road London W14 9QJ
Tel: 07775 580685   Email: thomas.2.foster@bt.com
Fixtures Secretary: Tom de Lisle   Tel: 07813 216643
Email: Tom.deLisle@neptune-im.co.uk
Club Colours: Black
League: Surrey 3 (level 11)

Old Ashmoleans RFC
Ground Address: Bourneside Sports Ground The Bourne Southgate N14 6QY
Contact: 07970 828802
Email: geoff.bull@blueyonder.co.uk
Website: www.oarfc.co.uk
Directions: Pitches: Either (1) Broomfield School, Wilmer Way, London N14 7HY or (2) Firs Lane, Palmers Green, London N13 Directions to clubhouse: At Southgate roundabout turn into The Bourne, turn into entrance to Grovelands Priory Hospital, on junction of Queen Elizabeth Drive. Clubhouse 50 metres on right.
Honorary Secretary: Mr Geoffrey Bull; 60 Ladysmith Road Enfield Middx.EN1 3AA   Tel: 07970 828802
Email: geoff.bull@blueyonder.co.uk
Fixtures Secretary: Mr Simon Stamp; Leaf House 22 Flat 5 King Edward Road Barnet Herts. EN5 5AP
Tel: 07867 786045   Email: sstamp@hbgc.co.uk
Colours: Scarlet/emerald hoops, black shorts & socks
League: London 3 North West (level 8)

Old Blues RFC
Ground Address: Dornan Fields Arthur Road Motspur Park, nr New Malden Surrey KT3 6LX
Contact: 07768 373897
Email: gilessimons@firthrossmartin.com
Website: www.oldbluesrfc.com
Directions: Directions By Road: At New Malden underpass on the A3 take the Worcester Park exit. Take the second turning on the left (just by the pedestrian crossing lights), into Motspur Park (Road), continue along, over level-crossing at Motspur Park, past the B
Honorary Secretary: Mr Giles Simons; 105 Gaskarth Road London SW12 9NP   Tel: 07768373897
Email: gilessimons@firthrossmartin.com
Fixtures Secretary: Mr Chris Strathon; 6 York Mansions Earls Court London SW5 9AF Tel: 07870 626574
Club Colours: Navy blue, old gold & cardinal red stripe
League: Surrey 2 (level 10)

Old Brentwoods RFC
Ground Address: Old Brentwoods Club Ashwells Road Pilgrims Hatch Brentwood Essex CM15 9SE
Contact: 01277 374070
Email: contact@obrfc.org
Website: www.obrfc.org
Directions: Take the Ongar Road from Brentwood & after 2.5 miles turn right at the end of the "straight mile" into Ashwells Road. Ground is 1/4 mile on the left.
Honorary Secretary: Mr Tim Faiers; 1 Woodway Shenfield Brentwood Essex CM15 8LP
Tel: 020 82704545   Email: timfaiers@hotmail.com
Fixtures Secretary: Alastair Rigden; c/o Born & Rigden Ltd Kingfisher House 19 Springfield Lyons Approach Chelmsford Business Park Essex CM2 5LB
Tel: 01245 398706   Email: alastair.rigden@btinternet.com
Club Colours: Dark blue/light blue
League: Essex 1 (level 9)

Old Caterhamians RFC
Ground Address: Old Caterhamians RFC Park Avenue Caterham Surrey CR3 6AH   All Mail To: Hon Secretary
Contact: 07803 269252
Email: info@oldcats.co.uk
Website: www.oldcats.co.uk
Honorary Secretary: Mrs Karen Wimble; 10 Larch Close Warlingham CR6 9DD   Tel: 01883 381433
Email: oldcatsyouth@hotmail.co.uk
Fixtures Secretary: Mr Mark Rowland; 70 Reed Drive Redhill RH1 6TB   Tel: 01372 475299
Email: Mark.Rowland@gearbulk.com
Club Colours: Black, amber, silver, mauve, black shorts
League: Surrey 2 (level 10)

Old Cooperians RFC
Ground Address: Coopers Coborn School St Mary's Lane Upminster Essex RM14 3HS
Website: www.oldcooperiansrugbyclub.co.uk
Directions: From M25 J29, take slip road onto A127 westbound towards Romford. Take 3rd exit and turn left into Hall Lane towards Upminster. Follow road into Upminster town centre. Go past Railway Station on the left. Turn left at traffic lights into St Marys Lane. Go past The Masons pub on your left. School is on the right.
Honorary Secretary: Mr Rob Lancaster; 14 Broad Oaks Wickford Essex SS12 9BQ Tel: 07903 280879
Email: ocrfc@hotmail.com
Fixtures Secretary: as Hon. Sec.
Club Colours: Light blue with thin navy and gold hoops
League: Essex 1 (level 9)

Old Cranleighan RFC
Ground Address: Portsmouth Road Thames Ditton Thames Ditton Surrey KT7 0HB
Contact: 0 2083983092
Email: tp@lordprice.com
Website: www.ocrfc.com
Directions: On the Portsmouth Road in Thames Ditton, between the 'Scilliy Isles' roundabout and Giggs Hill Green, just by the long railway bridge.
Honorary Secretary: Mr Mark Lubbock; 51 Balham Park Road London SW12 8DX   Tel: 0207 638 1111
Email: mark.lubbock@ashurst.com
Fixtures Secretary: Mr Al Lawson; Rose Cottage Snowdenham Lane Bramley Hull Surrey HU5 0AS
Tel: 07780 705049   Email: al@aclawson.com
Club Colours: Blue, White & Gold Hoops
League: Surrey 2 (level 10)

Old Dunstonian RFC
Ground Address: St. Dunstan's Lane Langley Park Langley Park Beckenham Kent BR3 3SS
Contact: 0208 6501779
Email: Julian.Platford@aonbenfield.com
Website: www.odrfc.co.uk
Directions: From Bromley South station, right at lights Westmoreland Road, right at 2nd lights Hayes Lane, 2nd left Brabourne Rd, at the bottom entrance to St. Dunstans Lane is almost opp. between no's 114/6 Wickham Way.
Honorary Secretary: Mr Julian Platford; 34 Highfield Road Bromley BR1 2JW Tel: 07887 615488
Email: Julian.Platford@aon.co.uk
Fixtures Secretary: Mr Kavin Satchi; 49 Ravensbourne Park Crescent London SE6 4YG   Tel: 07904 069031
Club Colours: Navy blue with white hoop, white shorts
League: London 2 South East (level 7)

Old Emanuel RFC
Ground Address: Blagdons New Malden Surrey KT3 4PU
Contact: 020 83378778
Email: fergus@emanuelrugby.co.uk
Website: www.emanuelrugby.co.uk
Directions: Where Burlington Road crosses the A3 at New Malden. Using north bound slip road to London, Ground is 200yds on the left.
Honorary Secretary: Mr Ian Blair; 12 Moor Lane Chessington Surrey KT9 1BS Tel: 020 78486917
Email: ian.blair@kcl.ac.uk
Fixtures Secretary: Mr Joseph Knowles; Flat 1 176 Ewell Road Surbiton Surrey KT6 6HG
Tel: 07917 411440
Email: josephwknowles@hotmail.com
Club Colours: White shirts Blue & Gold trim
League: Surrey 2 (level 10)

Old Freemens RFC
Ground Address: Memorial Club House City of London Freemens School Ashtead Park KT21 1ET
Contact: 01372 274158
Email: james.tremaine@boiuk.com
Website: www.oldfreemens.co.uk
Directions: From the A24 Epsom to Leatherhead road in Ashtead turn into Park Lane (at the Epsom end of Ashtead), at the sign post to St Giles Church. Pass gates on the left and take the left fork continuing along Park Lane. The entrance to the school ground is 300 yards on the left.
Honorary Secretary: Mr James Tremaine; 8 Hurst Road East Molesey Surrey KT8 9AF Tel: 020 89414580
Email: james.tremaine@boiuk.com
Fixtures Secretary: Mr Malcolm Beech; 11 Nutcroft Grove Fetcham Leatherhead Surrey KT22 9LA
Tel: 07960 019129
Email: malcolm.beech@travisperkins.co.uk
Club Colours: Blue, Maroon & Gold Hoops
League: Surrey 1 (level 9)

Old Glynonians RFC
Ground Address: Priesthill Playing Field, Reigate Road
Contact: Chris Justham
Email: chrisjustham@hotmail.com
Website: www.oldglynonians.org.uk
Honorary Secretary: Mr Robin Davies
Email: robdavies127@hotmail.com
Fixtures Secretary: Chris Justham; 90 Pine Hill Epsom Surrey KT18 7BQ Tel: 07821 436860
Email: chrisjustham@hotmail.com
League: Surrey 4 (level 12)

Old Grammarians RFC
Ground Address: 180 Green Dragon Lane Winchmore Hill London N21 1EP
Contact: 0 2088821524
Email: OGRFC@aol.com
Website: www.oldgrammariansrfc.com
Directions: From M25 J24 (Potters Bar),take the A1005 towards Enfield, (pass Chase Farm Hospital and go over first mini roundabout) after about 3 miles, turn right at the next mini roundabout (there is a large church on the left) into Slades Hill, (watch for the speed camera) take the 4th left by a mini r'about into Bincote Road, this leads into to Worlds End Lane, after several further mini roundabouts, you will see the playing fields on your left, at the next mini r'about take the left fork into Green Dragon Lane,the entrance 80 yds on the left. (It is also signposted Middx University Sports Ground). If you are approaching from Green Lanes, and if heading towards Enfield Town, at Winchmore Hill, take a right into Green Dragon Lane, go up the hill and over two mini r'abouts the ground is on the right near the top of the Hill and just before another mini roundabout. If travelling from Enfield Town along Green Lanes, go over the traffic lights at Bush Hill Park, carry forward until you reach a sharp left turn in the road, on the right is Green Dragon Lane, turn right into Green Dragon Lane, and proceed as above. Address for Sat Nav : 180 Green Dragon Lane, Winchmore Hill, London N21 4EP
Honorary Secretary: Mrs Debbi Stockman-Rose; 140 Hedge Lane Palmers Green London N13 5ST
Tel: 07940 717574
Email: honsec@oldgrammariansrfc.com

Fixtures Secretary: Mr Dennis Morden; 415 Baker Street Enfield Middx.EN1 3QZ   Tel: 07719 887662
Email: dennis_morden@yahoo.co.uk
Club Colours: Navy Blue with Red & Light Blue
League: Herts-Middlesex 1 (level 9)

Old Gravesendians RFC
Ground Address: Old Gravesendians R.F.C. Fleetway Sports Ground Bronte View, Parrock Road Gravesend Kent DA12 1PX
Contact: 01474 365503
Email: rugby@ogrfc.freeserve.co.uk
Website: www.ogrfc.com
Directions: A2 to Gravesend (not Gravesend East), take A227 (Tollgate) towards town. Turn right at lights at 2nd jct. First turning at r/about into Parrock Rd. Ground second turning (Bronte View) on right.
Honorary Secretary: Mr Jeremy Strike; 33 Portland Road Gravesend Kent DA12 1DL
Tel: 07919 925551   Email: jstrike@blueyonder.co.uk
Fixtures Secretary: Mr Stuart Hodge; 61 Parrock Ave. Gravesend Kent DA12 1QG   Tel: 07850 498552
Email: stuart@shodge.freeserve.co.uk
Club Colours: Navy & Royal Blue hoops
League: London 3 South East (level 8)

Old Haberdashers RFC
Ground Address: Old Haberdashers Sports Ground Croxdale Road Theobald Street Theobald Street Borehamwood WD6 4PY
Contact: 01628 851496
Email: martin.s.baker@bt.com
Website: www.ohrfc.org
Directions: Borehamwood & Elstree Station at roundabout take Theobald Street towards Radlett. Croxdale Road on Right after.5mile. Ground on the left.
Honorary Secretary: Mr Martin Baker; Rookwood Hedsor Road Bourne End Bucks. SL8 5EE
Tel: 07710 070749   Email: martin.s.baker@bt.com
Fixtures Secretary: Nathan Williams; 2 Woodland Drive St Albans Herts. AL4 0EU Tel: 07956 528466
Email: nathanwilliams@michaelpage.com
Colours: Blue, white & magenta hoops, blue shorts
League: Herts-Middlesex 1 (level 9)

Old Haileyburians RFC
Ground Address: Old Haileyburians RFC Ruxley Lane Epsom Road, Ewell Surrey
Email: players@ohrfc.co.uk
Website: www.ohrfc.co.uk
Honorary Secretary: Mr Tom Hulme; Flat B8 Lloyds Wharf Mill Street London SE1 2BD
Tel: 07887 936485   Email: tom.hulme@teathers.com
Fixtures Secretary: Mr Edward Mitchell; Old Haileyburians RFC Ruxley Lane Epsom Road, Ewell Surrey SG8 9PX
Club Colours: Magenta & White Hoops
League: Surrey 2 (level 10)

Old Hamptonians RFC
Ground Address: Old Hamptonians R.F.C. Dean Road Hampton Hampton Hampton Middx.TW12 1AQ
Contact: 07980 616925
Email: mfox@bellmicro.eu
Website: www.oldhamptonians.co.uk
Directions: Leave A316 (London to M3)at signs for A316 Hampton proceed on to Uxbridge Road for half a mile right into Hanworth Road pass 3 schools on right before turning Right into Dean road.
Honorary Secretary: Mr Mark Fox; 154 Colne Road Twickenham Middx.TW2 6QS Tel: 07980 616925
Email: mfox@bellmicro.eu
Fixtures Secretary: Mr Simon Burman; 7 Station Road Hampton Wick Kingston-On-Thames Surrey KT1 4HG
Tel: 07766 656190
Email: simonburman@theschoolcentre.co.uk
Club Colours: Black, gold & silver hoops, black shorts
League: London 3 North West (level 8)

Old Isleworthians RFC
Ground Address: Memorial Ground 22a Wood Lane Isleworth Middx.TW7 5ED
Contact: 07771 655254
Email: antonye@its-ss.co.uk
Website: www.oirfc.co.uk
Directions: A4 (Great West Road) or London Road to Isleworth to Wood Lane.
Honorary Secretary: Mr John Davies; First Floor Flat 76 Schubert Road Putney SW15 2QS Tel: 07814 571244
Email: oirfc@hotmail.co.uk
Fixtures Secretary: Mr Antony Enright; 6 Magdala Road Isleworth Middx.TW7 7DD Tel: 07771 655254
Email: antonye@its-ss.co.uk
Colours: Blue jersey horizontal red band & grey stripe
League: Herts-Middlesex 2 (level 10)

Old Merchant Taylors' FC
Ground Address: Durrants Lincoln Way Croxley Green WD3 3ND
Contact: 07973 657412
Email: m.foster107@ntlworld.com
Website: www.omtrugby.co.uk
Directions: J18 M25, take the A404 to Rickmansworth station. Exit roundabout to Watford. Top of Scots Hill take 1st exit from mini roundabout with Sportsman on left. After Coach and Horses take right fork and then right to Baldwins Lane at the T-junction. At mini-roundabout left to Manor Way, then right to Kenilworth Drive, left to Rochester Way, then into Lincoln Way.
Honorary Secretary: Mr Mark Foster; 199 Uxbridge Road Mill End Rickmansworth Herts. WD3 8DP Tel: 07973 657412
Email: m.foster107@ntlworld.com
Fixtures Secretary: Mr Colin Wyatt; 14 Evelyn Avenue Ruislip Middx.HA4 8AS Tel: 07876 232407
Email: wyatt810@aol.com
Club Colours: Black shirts, black shorts
League: London 3 North West (level 8)

LEVEL 7-12 AND NON LEAGUE CLUBS

Old Mid-Whitgiftian RFC
Ground Address: Lime Meadow Avenue Sanderstead Surrey CR2 9AS
Contact: 0208 6572014
Email: theoldmids@yahoo.co.uk
Website: www.omwrfc.com
Directions: The club is based at the Old Mid Whitgiftian Association, Lime Meadow Avenue, Sanderstead, Surrey. The entrance is at the end of Lime Meadow Ave, or alternatively via Blacksmiths Hill. Tel:: 020-8657 2014.
Honorary Secretary: Mr Iain Munro; Burach 23 Purley Knoll Purley Surrey CR8 3AF Tel: 07736 648774
Email: iain.munro@babersmith.co.uk
Fixtures Secretary: Mr Andy Hillburn; 0 Foxearth Road South Croydon Surrey CR2 8EL Tel: 020 79178888
Email: Andy.Hillburn@landregistry.gsi.gov.uk
Club Colours: Black body with blue arms
League: London 3 South West (level 8)

Old Millhillians RFC
Ground Address: Millhillian Sports Club Headstone Lane Headstone Lane Harrow Middx.HA2 6NF
Contact: 0 2083493637
Website: www.omrfc.org.uk
Directions: Entrance to ground 20 yards to left of Headstone Lane Station, exit on opposite side, 5 minuits walk from the Station.
Honorary Secretary: Mrs Shalaka Karlekar
Tel: 07908 622473
Email: shalakakarlekar@hotmail.com
Fixtures Secretary: Mr Fred Ellis; 27 Meadowbank Rd Kingsbury London NW9 8LJ Tel: 020 8205 2922
Email: fred@freellis27.plus.com
Club Colours: Chocolate & White Hoops, Black Shorts.
League: Herts-Middlesex 2 (level 10)

Old Olavians RFC
Ground Address: St. Olave's School Goddington Lane Orpington Kent BR6 9SH
Contact: 07971 317811
Email: oorfc_info@yahoo.co.uk
Website: www.oorfc.co.uk
Directions: Leave the M25 at Junction 4. Follow the signs to Orpington. When you see the shops and the BP garage on your left, turn left into Goddington Lane after the Volvo Garage. St Olave's school is 300 yards on your right. Use the first entrance you come to.
Honorary Secretary: Mr Colin Matthews
Email: secretary@oorfc.co.uk
Fixtures Secretary: Mr Phillip Grayson
Email: depchair@oorfc.co.uk
Club Colours: Purple, Black and White Hoops
League: Kent 1 (level 9)

Old Oundelians RFC
Ground Address: Portsmouth Road, Thames Ditton, Surrey KT7 0HB Tel: 020 8398 3092
Contact: 07775 928505
Email: gsimmonds@lutron.com
Honorary Secretary: Mr Guy Simmonds; 69c Battersea Rise London Herts. SW11 1HN Tel: 07775 928505
Email: gsimmonds@lutron.com
Fixtures Secretary: as Hon. Sec.
League: Surrey 3 (level 11)

Old Paulines FC
Ground Address: Old Pauline Football Club St.Nicholas Road, off Speer Rd Thames Ditton Surrey KT7 0PW
Contact: 020 83981858
Email: johnahoward@bigfoot.com
Website: www.opfc.org.uk
Directions: BY TRAIN: 200m walk from Thames Ditton Station. BY ROAD: Turn EAST off Hampton Court Way (A309, midway between Hampton Court Bridge & 'Scilly Isles') at roundabout into Em
Honorary Secretary: Mr Richard Avery; 33 Shaftesbury Way Twickenham Middx.TW2 5RN Tel: 07887 573460
Email: honsec@opfc.org.uk
Fixtures Secretary: Mr Matthew Preece
Club Colours: Red, white and black hoops
League: London 3 South West (level 8)

Old Priorians RFC
Honorary Secretary: Mr Colin Stokes
Email: colin.stokes@harleymedical.com
Fixtures Secretary: Ed Conway
Club Colours: Green yellow
League: Herts-Middlesex 2 (level 10)

Old Radleian RFC
Ground Address: Old Deer Park, Kew Road, Richmond, TW9 2AZ
Honorary Secretary: Oliver Thompson; 229 Garden Flat, earlsfield Road, London SW18 3DE
Tel: 0797 3173016
Email: oliver.thompson@eu.sony.com
Fixtures Secretary: Charles Spelina; Flat 65 Aspect Court Lensbury Avenue London SW6 2TN
Tel: 0779 6397555
Email: cspelina@bluebayinvest.com
Club Colours: White
League: Surrey 3 (level 11)

Old Reigatian RFC
Ground Address: Geoffrey Knight Fields Park Lane Reigate Surrey RH2 8JX
Contact: 01737 247927
Website: www.reigatiansrufc.com
Directions: The ORRFC clubhouse and grounds are located in Park Lane, Reigate. Go west through Reigate High Street and turn left opposite the Red Cross pub. Grounds are half a mile on the right. The narrow lane and entrance is not suitable for large coaches.
Honorary Secretary: Mr David Forsyth; 76 Station Road Redhill Surrey RH1 1PL Tel: 01737 773533
Email: david.forsyth@goodhandandforsyth.co.uk
Fixtures Secretary: Mr David Payton; Babylon Lane Lower Kingswood Surrey KT20 6UU Tel: 01737 226701
Email: djpayton@tiscali.co.uk
Club Colours: Green and Blue
League: London 2 South East (level 7)

Old Rutlishians RFC
Ground Address: Old Rutlishians R.F.C. The Clubhouse Poplar road Merton park SW19 3JS ENGLAND
Contact: 0208 5423678
Email: oldrutsrugby@msn.com
Website: www.oldrutsrugby.com
Directions: Kingston Road Merton to Dorset Road by Merton Park level crossing, proceed along Dorset Road to Melrose Avenue, take left fork for Poplar Road. Nearest Railway stations: ``` Merton Park (Tramlink from Wimbledon Station) in Dorset Road Wimbledon Chase and South Merton
Honorary Secretary: Mr Peter Stokes; 50 Beeches Ave. Carshalton Surrey SM5 3LW   Tel: 07934 131343
Email: peter.stokes@blueyonder.co.uk
Fixtures Secretary: Mr Gary Forge; 0 Martin Way Morden, Surrey SM4 4AG Tel: 07973 226494
Email: gary.forge@fullers.co.uk
Club Colours: Gold, Silver, Azure & Black
League: Surrey 2 (level 10)

Old Streetonians RFC
Ground Address: Play at : East Marsh Hackney Marshes Homerton Road E9 5PF
Contact: 0208 3780312
Email: lynn@richardhay.demon.co.uk
Website: www.oldstreetrugby.com
Directions: We play at Hackney Marshes which is accessed from the B112 Homerton Road which is off the A12 four miles South of the junction between the A406 North Circular and the A12 or if coming from the South, four miles North of the Blackwall Tunnel. Exit the A12 onto A106/Eastway toward Stratford/Dalston/Hackney then onto Homerton Road. The entrance to the car park is 350 yards along Homerton Road on the right. Nearest tube station is Leyton which is just over a mile away.
Honorary Secretary: Mrs Lynn Hay; 73 Swallowfield Road Charlton London SE7 7NT Tel: 020 88581213
Email: lynn@richardhay.demon.co.uk
Fixtures Secretary: as Hon. Sec.
League: London 3 North West (level 8)

Old Suttonians RFC
Ground Address: Walch Pavilian Northey Avenue Cheam Sutton Surrey SM2 7HJ
Contact: 0208 6423423
Email: oldsutts.rfc@ntlworld.com
Directions: On A232 between Cheam & Ewell take exit on St Pauls church roundabout into Northey Avenue . Ground is 1/4 mile on the right.
Honorary Secretary: Mr Stuart Udall; 91 Beresford Road Sutton Surrey SM2 6ES   Tel: 020 86429892
Email: stuart.udall@aspect.com
Fixtures Secretary: Mr Barry O'Brian
Tel: 07803 158988   Email: barry.obrian@steria.co.uk
Club Colours: Red White & Black Hoops
Non League

Old Tiffinians RFC
Ground Address: Grist Memorial Ground Summer Road, off Hampton Court Way East Molesey Surrey KT8 9LS
Email: manstey@lsh.co.uk
Directions: Hampton Court roundabout along Hampton Court way (A309). To turn into Summer Road you have to go to roundabout and come back, it is then first left.
Honorary Secretary: Mr James Fentiman; 90 Cavendish Road Clapham SW12 0DF   Tel: 07947 546390
Email: fentiman11@yahoo.co.uk
Fixtures Secretary: Mr Greer Kirkwood; 28 Railton Road Guildford Surrey GU2 9LX   Tel: 01483 850705
Club Colours: Violet, White & Navy Blue Hoops
League: Surrey 3 (level 11)

Old Walcountians RFC
Ground Address: Carshalton Road Woodmansterne Surrey SM7 3HU
Contact: 0208 6474839
Email: nataliehicks@btinternet.com
Website: www.oldwalcountians.co.uk
Directions: Carshalton Road is approx 2 miles from A217 off Croydon Lane, the Club house is approx 0.5 mile along Carshalton Road on the left.
Honorary Secretary: Natalie Hicks; 15 Springfield Road Wallington Surrey SM6 0BD   Tel: 07704 769227
Email: nataliehicks@btinternet.com
Fixtures Secretary: As Hon Sec
Club Colours: Black with Blue & Gold Hoops
League: Surrey 1 (level 9)

Old Wellingtonians RFC
Ground Address: 27 Ruxley Lane Kingston Road Ewell Surrey KT19 0JB
Contact: 0208 393 3901
Directions: East off the A3 from Tolworth Roundabout
Honorary Secretary: Mr Steve Brownrigg; 125 Gassiot Road London SW17 8LD
Colours: Black with orange, light blue & yellow stripes
League: London 3 South West (level 8)

Old Whitgiftian RFC
Ground Address: Old Whitgiftian Clubhouse Croham Manor Road South Croydon Surrey CR2 7BG
Contact: 020 86862127
Email: rugby@owrfc.co.uk
Website: http://www.owrfc.co.uk/index.php
Directions: 1 mile south of central Croydon on A235, fork left at The Swan & Sugar Loaf pub, into Selsdon Road. Take the second exit at the next mini roundabout into Croham Road. The Club is half a mile on the right.
Honorary Secretary: Mr Ian Watson; 15 Searchwood Road Warlingham CR6 9BB   Tel: 01883 626273
Email: overspill.training@lineone.net
Fixtures Secretary: Mr Geoffrey Austin; 97 Clifton Road Kingston Upon Thames KT2 6PL
Tel: 07850 068409   Email: Geoff.Austin@ukgateway.net
Club Colours: Red, black, & blue hoops, white shorts
League: Surrey 1 (level 9)

Old Williamsonians RFC
Ground Address: Sir Joseph Williamsons Mathematical School Maidstone Road Rochester Kent ME1 3DT
Contact: 07768 363203
Email: rugby@oldwilliamsoniansrugby.com
Website: www.oldwilliamsoniansrugby.com
Honorary Secretary: Mr James Collins; 11 Warren Road Dartford DA1 1PS Tel: 07768 363203
Email: james@thecollinsmadhouse.com
Fixtures Secretary: Mr James Collins; 11 Warren Road Dartford DA1 1PS Tel: 07768 363203
Email: james@thecollinsmadhouse.com
Club Colours: Navy blue shirts with gold chest hoop
League: Kent 2 (level 10)

Old Wimbledonians RFC
Ground Address: 143 Coombe Lane London SW20 0BJ
Contact: 020 88790700
Email: m.parsons@talk21.com
Website: www.OWRUGBYCLUB.co.uk
Directions: From Raynes Park station follow Coombe Lane towards Kingston. Cross traffic lights at West Barnes Lane junction, ground approx 800yds on left.
Honorary Secretary: Mrs Margaret Parsons; Hawth Glaziers Lane Normandy Guildford Surrey GU3 2EA Tel: 01483 811103   Email: m.parsons@talk21.com
Fixtures Secretary: Mr Richard Brayne-Nicholls; 76 Camberley Avenue Raynes Park London SW20 0BQ Tel: 020 88488404
Email: richard.brayne-nicholls@aquapurge.com
Club Colours: Bottle Green, Maroon & Gold Hoops.
League: London 3 South West (level 8)

Ongar RFC
Ground Address: Love Lane High Street Ongar CM5 9BL
Contact: 01277 383636
Email: ndoubleday@btinternet.com
Website: www.ongarrugbyclub.co.uk
Directions: To Ongar from Brentwood A128, turn right into town, proceed along High Street, pass Tesco's on left then turn right into Love Lane, ground 300 meters on right. From Four Wanz roundabout to Town center, Love Lane on left before Tesco's
Honorary Secretary: Mr Nigel Doubleday; 31 Rochford Avenue Waltham Abbey Essex EN9 1SL
Tel: 07802 284346   Email: ndoubleday@btinternet.com
Fixtures Secretary: Peter Furness
Tel: 07843 583370   Email: peterfurness@gmail.com
Club Colours: Blue with Amber Band
League: Essex 2 (level 10)

Orpington RFC
Ground Address: Hoblingwell Wood, Recreation Ground Leesons Way, St. Paul's Cray Leesons Way, St. Paul's Cray Orpington Kent BR5 2QB
Contact: 020 83004592
Email: leigh_ann_compton@yahoo.co.uk
Website: www.orpingtonrfc.co.uk
Directions: From M25 J3, take A20 towards London. Take first exit, A224 Orpington, then first right, third left and third right into Leesons Way.
Honorary Secretary: Miss Leigh Compton; 51 Valley Road Orpington Kent BR2 8JB   Tel: 020 83004592
Email: l.a.compton@waterman-group.co.uk
Fixtures Secretary: Mr Jon Edwards; 51 Valley Road St Pauls Cray Orpington Kent BR5 3DG
Tel: 020 83004592   Email: jonedwards6@hotmail.com
Club Colours: Amber & Black
League: Kent 2 (level 10)

Overton RFC Ltd
Ground Address: The Old Cricket Ground Watch Lane Laverstoke, Nr. Overton. HampshireRG28 7NT
Contact: 07775 907579
Email: alancornell@btconnect.com
Website: http://www.overtonrugby.com/
Directions: At the traffic light in Overton, take the B3400 sign posted to Whitchurch, at Laverstoke pass the football pitches on left and cross a small bridge over the river Test. Immediately after the row of thatched cottages on the right, turn right by a telephnoe
Honorary Secretary: Mr Alan Cornell; 93 Downs Road South Wonston Winchester SO21 3EH
Tel: 02380 600088   Email: alancornell@btconnect.com
Fixtures Secretary: Mr Alex Cole; 15 Rochford Road Basingstoke HampshireRG21 7TQ Tel: 01256 410836
Club Colours: Royal Blue/Green piping
League: Hampshire 2 (level 10)

Park House FC
Ground Address: Barnet Wood Road Hayes Kent BR2 7AA
Contact: 07812 150732
Email: parkhouserfc@hotmail.com
Directions: A21 to Bromley (or from M25,J4), turn off on A233 (Oakleigh Rd) towards Biggin HIll, Barnet Wood Road is a turning on the right.
Hon. Secretary: Ms Sarah-Jane Rumble; Total Glass Solutions Ltd. 24 Hayes Street Bromley Kent BR2 7LD Tel: 020 84629988
Email: sarahjanerumble@hotmail.com
Fixtures Secretary: Greg Bunnage; 48 Southborough Road Bromley BR1 2EN   Tel: 07951 141627
Email: greg@gbunnage.freeserve.co.uk
Club Colours: Black Shirts with Red Circlet
League: London 3 South East (level 8)

Paxton Pumas RFC
Ground Address: Brookfield School Brook Lane Sarisbury Green SO31 7DU
Website: www.locksheathpumasrfc.org
Directions: M27 J 9 follow signs to Park Gate. At r'about with Chinese building on it continue across. At next r'about with Garage on it turn left onto Brook Lane. At next r'about take the 3rd exit and continue along Brook Lane. Brookfiled School is 400 metres on the right.
Honorary Secretary: Mike Parker; 1 Buttercup Close Hedge End Southampton HampshireSO30 4TU Tel: 07809 545321   Email: mighty_mike3@hotmail.co.uk
Fixtures Secretary: Gemma Curnow   Tel: 07590 896218
Email: gemmacurnow@hotmail.co.uk
Club Colours: Black & green
League: Hampshire 2 (level 10)

Pegasus-Palmerians RFC
Ground Address: Rugby Section Pegasus Club Pegasus Club Herd Lane, Corringham Essex SS17 9BJ
Contact: 01375 672205
Email: secretary@pegasuspalmerians.com
Website: www.pegasuspalmerians.com
Honorary Secretary: Mr John Baker; 1 Cresthill Avenue Essex RM17 5UJ Tel: 07963 614723
Email: Secretary@pegasuspalmerians.co.uk
Fixtures Secretary: Mr Ian Conway Tel: 07917 243380
Email: fixtures@pegasuspalmerians.co.uk
Club Colours: navy blue and gold hoops
League: Essex 2 (level 10)

Pelhamians RFC
Ground Address: Raynes Park Sports Ground Taunton Ave Raynes Park SW20 0BH
Contact: 07768311126
Email: johnnichols@frontlinemedia.com
Honorary Secretary: Mr John Nichols; 10 Cromford Way New Malden Surrey KT3 3AZ Tel: 077 68311126
Email: johnnichols@frontlinemedia.com
Fixtures Secretary: as Hon. Sec.
Club Colours: Black
League: Surrey 4 (level 12)

Pembroke College RFC
Ground Address: Pembroke College Trumpington Street Cambridge CB2 1RF
Contact: 07775 674622
Email: wejb2@cam.ac.uk
Honorary Secretary: Mr Sean Adams;
Email: sma47@cam.ac.uk
Fixtures Secretary: James Sharp;
Club Colours: Light and dark blue hoops
Non League

Peterhouse RFC
Ground Address: Peterhouse Trumpington Street Cambridge CB2 1RD
Contact: 07879 277606
Email: kmg32@cam.ac.uk
Honorary Secretary: Ian meikle Tel: 07806791269
Email: im293@cam.ac.uk
Fixtures Secretary: as Hon. Sec.
Non League

Petersfield RFC
Ground Address: The Clubhouse Penns Place Petersfield GU31 4EP
Contact: 01730 823908
Email: robert.mocatta@btinternet.com
Website: www.petersfieldrfc.com
Directions: East edge of town, co-located with East Hants District Council Offices and Taro Leisure Centre.
Honorary Secretary: Mr Robert Mocatta; Old Down Farm East Meon Petersfield HampshireGU32 1PL
Tel: 01730 823908
Email: robert.mocatta@btinternet.com
Fixtures Secretary: Mr Hadyn Smith; 44 Moggs Mead Petersfield HampshireGU31 4NX
Tel: 01730 261776   Email: hadyn.s@ntlworld.com
Club Colours: Red with White Hoop
League: Hampshire 1 (level 9)

Phantoms RFC
Address: c/o The Secretary 72 William Street Grays Essex RM17 6DZ
Contact: 01375 406019
Email: secretary@phantomsrfs.com
Website: www.phantomsrfc.com
Directions: From Canning Town E16 roundabout go north along Manor Road. Just before West Ham tube station turn right into Memorial avanue and follow the road to a T junction. Turn right into Holland Road and the Club House (East London RFC) is directly in front of you.
Honorary Secretary: Mrs Megan Harris-Mitchell; 72 William Street Grays Essex RM17 6DZ
Tel: 07785 311533   Email: megan_112a@hotmail.co.uk
Fixtures Secretary: Mr Christopher Tilson; 102 Springfield Gardens Upminster Essex RM14 3ET
Tel: 07751 440673
League: Essex 2 (level 10)

Phyllosans RFC
Ground Address: The New House Queens Street Hook Norton Oxfordshire OX15 5PJ
Contact: 01608 730381
Email: a.walsham@btinternet.com
Directions: No Club House
Honorary Secretary: Mr Albert Walsham; The New House, Queen Street Hook Norton Banbury Oxfordshire OX15 5PJ Tel: 01608 730381
Email: aw_phyllosans@btinternet.com
Fixtures Secretary: Mr Sam Samra; 7 Granton Avenue Upminster Essex RM14 2RX
Tel: 01708 446362   Email: ssamra1953@yahoo.co.uk
Non League

Pinner & Grammarians RFC Ltd.
Ground Address: Shaftesbury Playing Fields Grimsdyke Road Grimsdyke Road Hatch End HA5 4PW
Contact: 07885 466473
Email: andy@pinnerrfc.co.uk
Website: http://www.pinnerrfc.co.uk
Directions: By rail: Hatch End (NSG & B'loo) West A410 Uxbridge Road to Hatch End Broadway shops, right G'sdyke Road, second right H'view, first left into C'burn Avenue,Club is on the left.
Honorary Secretary: Mr Robin Greenwood; 4 South Drive Ruislip Middx.HA4 8EX   Tel: 07803 143137
Email: robin.greenwood@extraspaceselfstorage.co.uk
Fixtures Secretary: Mr Jon Blowers; Bix Design Studio 52 Pinner Green Pinner Middx.HA5 2AB
Tel: 020 886 86098
Email: mail@pinner-rugby-club.co.uk
Club Colours: Blue & Red Variated Hoops
League: Herts-Middlesex 3 (level 11)

Pulborough RFC
Ground Address: Freelands Pulborough Road Cootham, Pulborough West Sussex RH20 4HP
Contact: 01403 732239
Email: gkidner@promar-international.com
Website: www.pulboroughrfc.org.uk
Directions: The Ground is situated on the North side of the A283 Pulborough to Storrington road, 3 miles East of Pulborough and 1/4 mile West of The Crown Public House, Cootham.
Honorary Secretary: Mr Garry Kidner; 8 Arundel Close Southwater Horsham West Sussex RH13 9XD Tel: 07971 119129
Email: gkidner@promar-international.com
Fixtures Secretary: Mr Jez Michael-Beale; 21 Groomsland Drive Billingshurst West Sussex RH14 9HA Tel: 01403 786883
Email: j.michaelbeale@btinternet.com
Club Colours: Black & White Hoops
League: Sussex 1 (level 9)

Purley John Fisher RFC
Ground Address: Parsons Pightle Coulsdon Road Old Coulsdon Surrey CR5 1EE
Contact: 01737 553042
Email: pjfrfc@crippsy.com
Website: www.pjfrfc.co.uk
Directions: From M25 1.Turn off M25 at junction 7 onto M23 2.Continue onto A23 (Brighton Road) 3.After Coulsdon South train station take 1st Right into Marlpit Lane 4.Continue up into Old Coulsdon 5.Through Old Coulsdon until you reach a Petrol station on your Left 6.Purley John Fisher ground is next Right (100m) By Train Nearest station is Coulsdon South Taxi Tel: 0208 660 9000 By Bus Route no. 409 and 466 will take you from Croydon to the Ground via Purley on the Brighton Road, and Coulsdon South train station on Marlpit Lane
Honorary Secretary: Mr Steve Bruck; 20 Stanhope Avenue Hayes Kent BR2 7JR   Tel: 07740 319871
Email: steve.bruck@assocnews.co.uk
Fixtures Secretary: Mr Chris Doyle; 1 Hall Road Wallington Surrey SM6 0RT   Tel: 07966 793930
Email: cddoyle@blueyonder.co.uk
Club Colours: Blue, gold, black and white
League: London 2 South East (level 7)

Queen Mary, Univ of London, RFC
Ground Address: Queen Mary, University of London, Rugby Club 432 Bancroft Road London E1 4DH
Honorary Secretary: Toby Emmerson; The Blomely Centre Westfield Way London E1 4NP
Tel: 020 78828451   Email: toby.emmerson@qmsu.org
Fixtures Secretary: James Tuttiet   Tel: 07816 548495
Email: tuts10@hotmail.com
Club Colours: Royal blue with yellow chestba
Non League

Queens' College RFC (Cambridge)
Ground Address: Queens' College Silver Street Cambridge CB3 9ET
Contact: 07971 917452

Email: iac22@cam.ac.uk
Honorary Secretary: Mr James Thompson
Fixtures Secretary: Mr Brett Marshall
Non League

Quintin RFC
Ground Address: CSSC Sports Ground Dukes Meadows, Riverside Drive Chiswick W4 2SX
Contact: 01628 675899
Email: quintinrfc@hotmail.com
Website: www.quintinrfc.org.uk
Directions: From Hogarth / A4 roundabout A316 south towards Richmond. Follow for approx. 1 km. At traffic lights turn left in to Riverside Drive. Follow road (go past Fullers sports ground. Just before you get to river frontage, turn right in to entrance of CSSC Spor
Honorary Secretary: Mr Nigel Smith; 4 Australia Avenue Maidenhead Berks. SL6 7DJ Tel: 01628 675899
Email: nigelw.smith@btopenworld.com
Fixtures Secretary: Mr Adam Smith; 44 Berridge Mews West Hampstead London NW6 1RF Tel: 07795 023405
Club Colours: Scarlet & Green Shirts, Blue Shorts
League: Herts-Middlesex 2 (level 10)

RAC Bovingdon
Ground Address: c/o The Kings Royal Hussars Allwal Barracks Tidworth Wiltshire SP9 7BB
Contact: 01980 602569
Non League

RAC RFC
Honorary Secretary: M Rayner   Tel: 01980 90480
Non League

Racal Decca RFC
Ground Address: Deckers Sports and Social Club Kingston Road Tolworth Surrey KT5 9NT
Contact: 07980 802241
Email: rdrfcinfo@hotmail.com
Website: www.rdrfc.com
Directions: Situated just off A3. Turn off A3 at Tolworth roundabout (see Charrington Bowl and Tolworth Tower) onto the A240 towards Epsom. Take first left at traffic lights and immediately left again into the club car-park. Clubhouse is almost directly opposite the
Honorary Secretary: Mr Robert Holmes; 14 Elmshaw Road Putney London SW15 5EL   Tel: 07980 802241
Email: robertkholmes@btinternet.com
Fixtures Secretary: Mr Sean Phelan; 36 Ferndall Road West Ewell Epsom Surrey KT19 9NZ
Email: seanphelan32@hotmail.com
Club Colours: Royal Blue & White Hoops
Non League

RAF Henlow RFC
Ground Address: Major Mikkelson c/o Sgt Charnock DISC Chicksands Gym Shefford SG17 5PR
Contact: 01462 851515
Email: harrylotty@hotmail.com
Club Colours: Black and yellow. Or Plain Blue.
Non League

RAF High Wycombe/Halton RFC
Ground Address: Room 14, Building 1 1 Site RAF High Wycombe HP14 4UE
Contact: 01494 497751
Email: matt.murphy456@mod.uk
Hon. Secretary: Mr Darren Hedges; Hurricane Block 3N21 RAF High Wycombe High Wycombe HP14 4UE
Tel: 01494 496362   Email: Darren.Hedges186@mod.uk
Club Colours: Blue and Grey Quaters
Non League

RAF Honington RFC
Ground Address: RAF Honington RFC Bury St. Edmunds Bury St Edmunds SuffolkIP31 1EE
Contact: 01359 237320
Club Colours: Blue & Maroon
Non League

RAF Marham RFC
Ground Address: RAF Marham Bulls RFC RAF Marham Kings Lynn NorfolkPE33 9NP
Contact: 01760337261 Ext 4040
Email: madtomboy@btinternet.com
Honorary Secretary: M Leeming; OPS I.S. RAF Marham Marham Kings Lynn Norfolk PE33 9NP
Non League

RAF Odiham RFC
Ground Address: RAF Odiham Hook RG29 1QT
Contact: 01256 702 134 x 7537
Email: odiesw-sefoc@odiham.raf.mod.uk
Directions: RAF Odiham
Honorary Secretary: Mr David Widdison
Email: davidwiddison@btinternet.com
Club Colours: Red Black trim
Non League

Raynes Park RFC
Ground Address: Raynes Park Sports Ground Taunton Avenue Raynes Park SW20 0BH
Contact: 0208 9492448
Email: rprice07@harris.com
Website: www.raynesparkrfc.com
Directions: By road: Exit A3 Shannon Corner follow sign to Raynes Park. After 1.5 km turn left into Camberley Ave. and bear left into Taunton Ave.
Honorary Secretary: Mr Russell Price; 101 Belmont Avenue New Malden Surrey KT3 6QE
Tel: 020 89492448   Email: rprice07@harris.com
Fixtures Secretary: Mr James Martin
Tel: 07957 453698   Email: james.martin@nomura.com
Club Colours: Blue & Gold Shirts; Blue Short
League: Surrey 2 (level 10)

Reigate RFC
Ground Address: Reigate R.F.C. Eric Hodgkins Memorial Grond Colley Lane Reigate Surrey RH2 9JL
Contact: 07763 224585
Email: DarrenHALSTEAD@gatton-park.org.uk
Website: www.reigaterugby.com
Directions: M25 J8 south on Reigate Hill, before level crossing turn right into Somers Road, at the end of Somers Road turn right, then keep left into Colley Lane, Club 200m on right.
Honorary Secretary: Mr Norman Phillips; 28 Hurstleigh Drive Redhill Surrey RH1 2AA
Tel: 01737 212912
Email: wnorman.phillips@ntlworld.com
Fixtures Secretary: Mr Stephen Cope; 6 Holcon Court Redhill Surrey RH1 2JZ
Tel: 07855 425820
Email: stephen.cope@danisco.com
Club Colours: Royal / Sky Blue Hoops
League: Surrey 4 (level 12)

REME RFC
Ground Address: REME TDT, HQ DEME(A) Hazebrouck Bks Arborfield, Reading Berks. RG2 9NH
Contact: 0118 976 3607
Email: kwhite8514@aol.cm
Website: remerugby.co.uk
Honorary Secretary: Ms Teresa Gillespie; SEAE Box H015, Hazebrouck Bks Arborfield Reading RG2 9NJ
Tel: 0118 9763329
Club Colours: Red Shirts, Black Shorts, Yellow socks
Non League

Robinson College RFC
Ground Address: Robinson College Grange Road Cambridge CB3 9AN
Contact: 07759 421637
Email: gho21@cam.ac.uk
Honorary Secretary: Chris oulten   Tel: 07960087118
Email: cgo21@cam.ac.uk
Fixtures Secretary: as Hon. Sec.
Non League

Romford & Gidea Park RFC
Ground Address: Crowlands Crow Lane Romford Essex RM7 0EP
Contact: 01708 724870
Website: www.romfordrugby.org.uk
Directions: A12 to Moby Dick pub, from London right into Whalebone Lane North, at lights left into London Road, 0.5 mile onto Jutsums Lane, under bridge, (unsuitable for coaches) left into Crow Lane, Ground 100yds on right.
Honorary Secretary: Mr Dai Davies; 25 Stanley Avenue Gidea Park Romford RM2 5DL
Tel: 01708 724870
Email: dainamic50@hotmail.co.uk
Fixtures Secretary: Mr Tony Healey; 27 Lansbury Avenue Chadwell Heath Romford RM6 6SD
Tel: 07721 460411
Email: tony.healey@mundocomww.com
Club Colours: Black, Purple & White Jerseys with Black Shorts
League: London 2 North East (level 7)

LEVEL 7-12 AND NON LEAGUE CLUBS

Romsey RUFC
Ground Address: Romsey Sports Centre Lower Southampton Road Romsey SO51 8AF
Email: secretary@romseyrfc.co.uk
Website: www.romseyrfc.co.uk
Directions: On A27 into Romsey (follow signs for Rapids) from M27, Ground and Clubhouse is next to Romsey Rapids Swimming Centre off Southampton Rd
Honorary Secretary: Mr Daniel Simpson; Mountain Ash 6 Tilden Road Compton Winchester SO21 2DW
Tel: 07811 783695   Email: secretary@romseyrfc.co.uk
Fixtures Secretary: Mr Jamie Glanville; 3 Whitenap Close Romsey Hampshire SO51 5RT
Tel: 07787 152379   Email: jglanville@waitrose.com
Club Colours: Royal Blue + Gold Hoops, Blue Socks (Gold tops)
League: Hampshire 1 (level 9)

Royal Artillery RFC
Honorary Secretary: Mr K Blake
Non League

Royal Bank of Scotland RFC
Ground Address: Copers Cope Road Beckenham Kent BR3 1NZ
Contact: 020 86502307
Email: rugby@rbsrfc.com
Website: www.rbsrfc.com
Directions: Frequent trains from London Charing Cross and London Bridge to Lower Sydenham (30 min journey) From Lower Sydenham Station exit turning Right into Worsley Bridge Road, take the first turnung Right Ground is 250 yards on the Right. By car from London/Kent: Take the A21 to the junction with Beckenham Hill Road (A2015). Follow the A2015 for appox 1 mile, turn Right into Brackley Road. At end of Brackley Road, turn Right into Copers Cope Road, RBSRFC is about 500 yards on the Left.
Honorary Secretary: Mr Malcolm Munro; 7 Milton Close Sutton Surrey SM1 3BG   Tel: 07980 982617
Email: malcolm.munro@rbsrfc.com
Fixtures Secretary: Mr Les Giblin; 656 Davidson Road Croydon Surrey CR0 6DJ
Tel: 0845 3009262   Email: leslie.giblin@rbs.co.uk
Non League

Royal Engineers RFC
Honorary Secretary: Mr Mark (Chris) Fowke; 4 Gainsborough Close Farnborough GU14 6SW
Tel: 01634 822708
Non League

Royal Holloway, University of London RFC
Ground Address: RHUL Students Union Egham Hill Egham Surrey TW20 0EX
Contact: 01784 486 320
Honorary Secretary: Alex Bate; 31 Woodhaw Egham Surrey TW20 9AR Tel: 07742 360725
Email: a.bate@rhul.ac.uk
Club Colours: Green/White/Purple
Non League

Royal Military Academy Sandhurst
Ground Address: Camberely Surrey GU15 4PQ
Contact: 01276 41 2592
Non League

Royal Military College of Science
Ground Address: Shivernham Swindon Wilts. SN6 8LA
Contact: 01793 785501
Non League

Royal Regiment of Wales
Ground Address: Barker Barracks Paderborn British Forces Post Office 22 BFPO 805
Contact: 05251 101311
Non League

Royal Veterinary College RFC
Address: SU, Hawkshead Lane North Mimms Hatfield AL9 7TA   Contact: 01707 666310
Website: www.rvcsus.co.uk
Honorary Secretary: Jonathan Bryars; Royal Veterinary Collge RUFC Hawkshead Lane North Mymms Hatfield Herts. AL9 7TA   Email: jbryars@rvc.ac.uk
Fixtures Secretary: Jonathan Hughes; Royal Veterinary College RUFC Hawkshead Lane North Mymms Hatfield Herts. AL9 7TA
Tel: 07748 981134   Email: jhughes@rvc.ac.uk
Non League

Royston RFC
Ground Address: The Heath Sports Club Therfield Heath, Baldock Road Royston SG8 5BG
Contact: 01763 247522
Email: jamie@bluebridgefs.co.uk
Website: www.roystonrugby.co.uk
Directions: A10 North or South to r'about by cinema, turn west through town centre, past golf club on left, A505 from Baldock turn right at Little Chef, Club on right.
Honorary Secretary: Mr James Johnson; 29 Honey Way Royston Herts. SG8 7ES Tel: 01763 247522
Email: jamie@bluebridgefs.co.uk
Fixtures Secretary: Mr Godfrey Everett; 24 Clarkes Way Bassingbourn Royston Herts. SG8 5LT
Tel: 01525 219300
Email: godfreyeverett@hotmail.com
Club Colours: Black & White Hoops
League: Herts-Middlesex 2 (level 10)

Runwell Wyverns RFC
Ground Address: Runwell Hospital Sports and Social Club Runwel Chase Wickford SS11 7QA
Contact: 01268 414030
Email: runwellwyverns@sky.com
Website: www.runwellwyverns.co.uk
Honorary Secretary: Mr Roy Coombes; 1 Rye Mead Langdon Hills Basildon Essex SS16 6LJ
Tel: 07974 974397   Email: roy.coombes@sky.com
Fixtures Secretary: Mr Richard Mason; 3 Barrie Pavement Wickford Essex SS12 9DR
Tel: 07957 105108   Email: realm46@hotmail.com
Club Colours: Green with Red trim
League: Essex 2 (level 10)

Rye RFC
Ground Address: Rye R.F.C. New Road Rye Kent TN31 7LS
Contact: 01797 224867
Email: info@ryerugby.com
Website: www.ryerugby.com
Directions: Situated east of the main town on the A259 coast road.
Honorary Secretary: Mrs Helen Pierce; 1 Martello Place Tram Road Rye Harbour Rye E. Sussex TN31 7QZ
Tel: 01797 224753   Email: pierce20@btinternet.com
Fixtures Secretary: Mr David Ramus; Moat Farm Moat Lane Iden East Sussex TN31 7UU
Tel: 01797 280049   Email: daveram@cwcom.net
Club Colours: Red & White Quarters, Black Shorts
League: Sussex 1 (level 9)

Saffron Walden RFC
Ground Address: Springate Chickney Road Henham Herts. CM22 6BQ
Contact: 01279 850791
Email: info@swrfc.co.uk
Website: www.swrfc.co.uk
Directions: The club is situated in Henham village, 7 miles south of Saffron Walden. From Saffron Walden High Street, pass the war memorial & turn left at the mini roundabout onto Debden Road. Follow this road out of the town. Go over the cross roads heading through Debden village. After 2 miles turn right to Henham, follow this road for 3 miles to the club.
Hon. Secretary: Mr Malcolm Flood; Flat 15 Ingleside Court High St Saffron Walden Essex CB10 1EB
Tel: 01799 525574   Email: info@swrfc.co.uk
Fixtures Secretary: Mr Graham Marshall; 23 Newport Road Saffron Walden Essex CB11 4BS
Tel: 01799 501063
Email: graham.marshall2@ntlworld.com
Club Colours: Green shirts, white shorts
League: London 2 North East (level 7)

Sandown & Shanklin RFC
Ground Address: The Clubhouse Station Approach Sandown Sandown Isle of Wight HampshirePO36 9ES
Contact: 01983 404707
Email: webmaster@ssrfc.co.uk
Website: www.ssrfc.co.uk
Directions: By rail: Pitch is adjacent to Sandown Station. Use underpass to reach club. By road: Follow main Sandown Shanklin road to Lake, take 'The Fairway' - pitch on right opposite high school.
Honorary Secretary: Mr Geoff Giles; Sandown & Shanklin Rfc Station Approach Sandown Isle Of Wight HampshirePO36 9ES Tel: 01983 873235
Email: ggiow@aol.com
Fixtures Secretary: Mr Colin Bond; Sandown & Shanklin Rfc Station Approach Sandown Isle Of Wight HampshirePO36 9ES Tel: 01983 863621
Club Colours: Blue with red & white side band
League: London 3 South West (level 8)

Saracens Amateur RFC Ltd
Ground Address: Bramley Road Sports Ground Green Road Southgate London N14 4AB
Contact: 020 84499101
Email: charles.portsmouth@btinternet.com
Website: www.saracensamateurrugby.com
Honorary Secretary: Mr Charles Portsmouth; 71 Grange Park Avenue Grange Park London N21 2LN
Tel: 020 83643218
Email: charles.portsmouth@btinternet.com
Fixtures Secretary: Mr Sean Hughes; Bramley Road Sports Ground Green Road Southgate London N14 4AB
Tel: 01945 773089
Club Colours: Black
League: Herts-Middlesex 1 (level 9)

Sawston RFC
Address: Sawston Village College New Road New Road Sawston Cambs.CB22 3BP.   Contact: 01223 836615
Email: hazelcowan1@btinternet.com
Website: www.sawstonrugby.com
Directions: M11 J 10 (Duxford). Take A505 towards Newmarket. At large roundabout (BP garage/McDonalds) turn left. Follow road (Sawston bypass), and take 2nd right (crossroads). Take 2nd left into New Road. Continue along New Road - Sawston Villag
Honorary Secretary: Mrs Hazel Cowan; Sarsfield High Street West Wickham Cambs.CB21 4SB
Tel: 01223 290661
Email: hazelmcowan1@btinternet.com
Fixtures Secretary: Mr James Herbert c/o the club.
Tel: 07774 413884
Email: pippajames@herbie18.freeserve.co.uk
Club Colours: Black, Navy & White Quarters
Non League

SEAE Aborfield
Ground Address: HQ Coy, Hazebrouck Barracks Box No HO15 Arbofield RG2 9NH
Contact: 01189 769277
Honorary Secretary: Mr Steve O'Connor; HQ Coy, Hazebrouck Barracks Box No HO15 Arbofield RG2 9NH Tel: 0118 9763310
Non League

Seaford RFC
Ground Address: Salts Recreation Ground Richmond Road (off Dane Road) Seaford East Sussex BN25 1DR
Contact: 01323 892355
Email: info@seafordrfc.co.uk
Website: www.seafordrfc.com
Directions: Situated on the sea front just off the A259.
Honorary Secretary: Mrs Nicola Walker; Watermill House Mill Lane Hellingly East Sussex BN27 4EY
Tel: 01323 441629   Email: nicola.walker@cavcoms.com
Fixtures Secretary: Mr Paul Joy; Sandcliff Maurice Road Seaford East Sussex BN25 1BG
Tel: 01323 894019   Email: paulthejoys@aol.com
Club Colours: Scarlet Shirts with Navy Blue Shorts
League: Sussex 1 (level 9)

LEVEL 7-12 AND NON LEAGUE CLUBS

Selwyn College RFC
Ground Address: Selwyn College Grange Road Cambridge CB3 9DQ
Contact: 07801 945026
Email: jato2@cam.ac.uk
Honorary Secretary: Ali glass   Tel: 07950645374
Email: acdg2@cam.ac.uk
Fixtures Secretary: as Hon. Sec.
Non League

SEME Bordon
Ground Address: School of Electrical and Mechanical Engineering Re Prince Phillip Barracks Borden Hampshire GU35 0JE
Contact: 01420 482268
Honorary Secretary: Mr Keith White; 4 BN REME Prince Phillip Bks Budds Lane Bordon GU35 0JE
Email: kwhite8514@aol.com
Non League

Sevenoaks RFC
Ground Address: Knole Paddock Plymouth Drive Sevenoaks Kent TN13 3RP
Contact: 01732 452027
Email: nichollsandy@hotmail.com
Directions: J5 M25. Follow signs to Sevenoaks. At Riverhead r/about turn right up Amherst Hill. Left after BR station, right at top then left around Cricket Ground - Plymouth Drive on right.
Honorary Secretary: Mr Andy Nicholls; Brookers Cottage Back Lane Shipbourne Kent TN11 9PP
Tel: 07983 452671   Email: nichollsandy@hotmail.com
Fixtures Secretary: Mr Paul Vizard; 16 Tom Joyce Close Snodland Kent ME6 5BT   Tel: 01634 246479
Email: paul.vizard@btinternet.com
Club Colours: Navy & Gold
League: London 2 South East (level 7)

Sheppey Rugby Football Club Ltd
Ground Address: The Clubhouse, Scocles Field Lower Road, Minster Sherness Kent ME12 3RT
Contact: 01795 872082
Website: www.sheppeyrfc.co.uk
Directions: From M2 or M20 take A249 turnoff for Sheerness/Sittingbourne. Follow A249 onto Island. At first roundabout turn right. Club half a mile on the right, just past traffic lights.
Hon. Secretary: Mrs Joanna Bancroft; 2 The Lighthouse, Queens Rd, Minster Sherness Kent ME12 2HF
Tel: 07810198216   Email: tjbancroft@btinternet.com
Fixtures Secretary: Mr Andy Hosken; Westwood Augustine Road Minster Sherness Kent Me12 2NB
Tel: 07768 607519   Email: ajh@bsl.co.uk
Club Colours: White shirt with one red hoop.
League: Kent 1 (level 9)

Shooters Hill RFC
Ground Address: 123/1 Mayday Gardens Kidbrooke London SE3 8NP
Contact: 07974 791384
Email: neilsharp8@aol.com
Website: www.shootershillrfc.co.uk
Directions: From Well Hall r/about take signs for Woolwich & Ferry, over lights at top of hill, next left at Broadwalk, over 4 humps, left into Mayday Gdns, follow road to green on left, entrance to ground in corner.
Honorary Secretary: Mr Neil SHARP; 8 Monmouth Close Welling Kent DA16 2DX
Tel: 07974 791384   Email: neilsharp8@aol.com
Fixtures Secretary: Mr I Trevett; 76 Southwood Road London SE9 3QT   Tel: 020 88596693
Club Colours: Red, Blue, Yellow, Green
League: Kent 2 (level 10)

Shoreham RFC
Ground Address: 14 Southview Court Southview Close Southwick West Sussex BN42 4TX
Contact: 01273 592082   Email: srfcsecretary@live.co.uk
Website: www.shorehamrugby.com
Honorary Secretary: Mr Peter Gerry; Flat 14 Southview Court Southview Close Southwick Brighton BN42 4TX
Tel: 01273 592082   Email: srfcsecretary@live.co.uk
Fixtures Secretary: Mr James Garner
Tel: 07789 985513   Email: jgarner@wsgfl.org.uk
Club Colours: Bottle Green, Amber & Black Ho
Non League

Sidney Sussex College RFC
Ground Address: Sidney Sussex College RFC Sidney Sussex College CB2 3HU
Contact: 07708 818761   Email: ah448@cam.ac.uk
Honorary Secretary: Rupert Harrison
Tel: 07746851428   Email: rfmh3@cam.ac.uk
Fixtures Secretary: Rupert Harrison
Tel: 07746851428   Email: rfmh3@cam.ac.uk
Non League

Sittingbourne RFC
Ground Address: Gore Court Sports Club The Grove, Key Street Sittingbourne Kent ME10 1YT
Contact: 07710 425195
Email: srufc@swalenet.co.uk
Website: www.srufc.com
Directions: From M2 eastbound, A249 to Sittingbourne & Sheerness, after 2 miles take A2 towards Sittingbourne, after 0.5 mile turn left just after Sports ground, left again into club car park.
Honorary Secretary: Mr Steve Smith; Shenley Cottages 4 Shenley Road Headcorn Ashford Kent TN27 9HX
Tel: 07092 377726
Email: rfugeneratedspam@swalenet.co.uk
Fixtures Secretary: Mr Kevin Smith; 180 Park Road Sittingbourne Kent ME10 1E
Tel: 07984 079998   Email: kevinmsmith@sky.com
Club Colours: Navy & Amber
League: Kent 1 (level 9)

SOAS Warriors
Ground Address: Thornhaugh Street Russell Square
London WC1H 0XG
Contact: 020 7580 0916
Honorary Secretary: Honorary Secretary; Athletic
Union SOAS Warriors RFC School of Oriental and
African Studies Thornhaugh Street London WC1H 0XG
Fixtures Secretary: Miss Aileen Puhlmann; SOAS
Students Union Thornhaugh Street London WC1H 0XG
Tel: 0207 8984994   Email: sport.soc@soas.ac.uk
Non League

South Woodham Ferrers RFC
Ground Address: Saltcoats Playing Fields South
Woodham Ferrers Chelmsford Essex CM3 5WA
Contact: 01245 325987
Email: rugby@southwoodhamferrersrugby.co.uk
Website: www.southwoodhamferrersrugby.co.uk
Directions: From A127 take A130 to Chelms Road at
Rettenden Turnpike take A132 to South Woodham Ferrers.
On entering town follow signs to Saltcoats Ind. Estate.
Ground on left after 3rd r'about. From A12 Chelms Road
take A130 Southend at Rettenden Turnpike A132
Honorary Secretary: Mr Stefan Leszczuk; Great Oaks
Chelmsford Rd East Hanningfield Chelmsford CM3 8AL
Tel: 07817 918454   Email: stefanleszczuk@aol.com
Fixtures Secretary: Mr Harvey Witzer; Hainalt Cottage
Kitchener Road North Fambridge Chelmsford CM3 6NJ
Tel: 07703 340931   Email: hwitzer@tycoint.com
Club Colours: All Black
League: London 3 North East (level 8)

Southampton RFC
Ground Address: Test Playing Fields Lower Brownhill
Road Southampton SO16 9BP
Contact: 023 80737777
Email: niall_kc@hotmail.com
Website: www.southamptonrugby.co.uk
Directions: M27 onto M271, take 1st slip road, 1st exit
towards Lordshill, after 150 yds turn right into Lower
Brownhill Road. You will come to a sharp bend, this is
where the entrance is.
Honorary Secretary: Mr Steven Dewey; C/o Seastar
Survey Ocean Quay Marina Belvidere Road
Southampton SO14 5QY   Tel: 07977 571341
Email: steven@seastarsurvey.co.uk
Fixtures Secretary: Mr Rob Swain; P O Box 1215
Southampton HampshireSO16 9ZX   Tel: 07967 339932
Club Colours: Red & White Hoops
League: Hampshire 1 (level 9)

Southampton Solent University
Ground Address: 25 Redlands Drive Redlands Drive
Southampton SO19 7DA
Contact: 023 80319671
Email: matthew.bishop@solent.ac.uk
Website: http://www.solentrugby.co.uk/
Directions: See directions for Southampton RFC
Honorary Secretary: Mr Matt Bishop; Sport Solent
Solent University East Park Terrace Southampton
HampshireSO14 0YN   Tel: 02380 319125
Email: Matthew.Bishop@solent.ac.uk
Fixtures Secretary: Claire Taylor; Sport Solent East
Park Terrace Southampton HampshireSO14 0TY
Tel: 02380 319556   Email: claire.taylor@solent.ac.uk
Club Colours: Black
Non League

Southampton UOTC
Ground Address: Southampton University Officers
Training Corps 32 Carlton Place Southampton
HampshireSO15 2DX
Contact: 023 8033 2211/22 1581
Email: southampton.uotc@virgin.net
Non League

Southgate RFC
Ground Address: Green Road Southgate London N14 4AB
Contact: 0208 2455572
Website: www.southgaterfc.org
Directions: A406 from the East, exit for Arnos Grove
station to r'about, 2nd exit for Oakleigh Road South. A406
from the West, left for New Southgate Station, right at
Turrets pub, 1st exit r'about for Oakleigh Rd South.
Honorary Secretary: Mr Timothy Berg; 13 Barnard Hill
London N10 2HB
Tel: 07768 810040   Email: tb@tberg.freeserve.co.uk
Fixtures Secretary: Mr Thomas Lawrence; 1 Mardocks
Farm Cottages Wareside Ware Herts. SG12 7QN
Tel: 01920 444956   Email: stevelawrence3@mac.com
Club Colours: Dark Blue, Light Blue and Gold
League: Herts-Middlesex 4 (level 12)

Southwold RFC
Ground Address: The Pavillon The Common Southwold
IP18 6TB
Directions: From A12 take the A1095 towards
Southwold. Pass St. Felix School on your right, carry on
into Southwold. Over small bridge, over mini roundabout
(police & fire station on your right) turn right at Kings
Head. Rugby club is on your left 800m opposite water
Honorary Secretary: Mrs Sarah Doddington; 21
Woodfield Rd Shadingfield Beccles Suffolk NR34 8PD
Tel: 01502 575456
Email: s.doddington@prestige-nursing.co.uk
Fixtures Secretary: Mr Robert Scarle; 1 Millfields
Wangford Beccles NR34 8RG
Tel: 01502 578567   Email: rob.scarle@btopenworld.com
Club Colours: Black with Gold Hoop
League: East Counties 1 (level 9)

St Albans
Ground Address: The Clubhouse Oaklands Lane Smallford St. Albans Herts. AL4 0HR
Contact: 01727 869945
Email: monsmartin@aol.com
Website: www.stalbansrfc.com
Honorary Secretary: Mr Peter Clackson; 32 Chandlers Road Marshalswick St. Albans Herts. AL4 9RS
Tel: 07710 589074
Email: peter.clackson@ntlworld.com
Fixtures Secretary: Roly Everall; 49 Berners Drive St Albans Herts. AL1 2HZ   Tel: 07932591158
Email: roly.everall@ntlworld.com
Club Colours: Royal Blue & Gold Hoops, Navy
League: London 2 North West (level 7)

St Jacques RFC
Ground Address: King George V Playing Fields Rue Cohu Castel Guernsey
Contact: 01481 251807
Email: stefan.bampton@gov.gg
Website: www.stjacquesrfc.com
Honorary Secretary: Mr Jonathan Coyde; Kauri Rue Cohu Castel Guernsey GY5 7TG Tel: 07781 108399
Email: jonathan@normandie-group.com
Fixtures Secretary: Mr Richard Fyfe; Le Grand Fort Camp du Roi St Sampsons Guernsey GY2 4XD
Tel: 07781 421872   Email: rfyfe@cwgsy.net
Club Colours: Black / Gold
Non League

St John's College RFC
Ground Address: St John's College St John's Street Cambridge CB2 1TP
Contact: 07906 650411
Email: jmm68@cam.ac.uk
Honorary Secretary: Will Hall Tel: 07903 029839
Email: wjh33@cam.ac.uk
Fixtures Secretary: as Hon. Sec.
Non League

Stanford Le Hope RFC
Ground Address: SRGUG Clubhouse Stanford Rec. Ground Grove Road Stanford-le-Hope SS17 0ED
Contact: 01375 676000
Email: webmaster@stanfordrugby.co.uk
Website: www.stanfordrugby.co.uk
Directions: A13 to Stanford-Le-Hope then turn off at A1014. Right at roundabout into Corringham Road. left Rainbow Lane, First Right Billet Lane. Stanford recreation Ground at far end on left. Clubhouse at Top of Recreation Ground
Hon. Secretary: James Medlycott; 13 Stephens Cresent Horndon On The Hill Stanford-le-Hope Essex SS17 8LZ
Tel: 01375 677248 Email: jimmedlycott@btinternet.com
Fixtures Secretary: Mr Russell Jackson; 11 Fernside Close Corringham Essex SS179EJ Tel: 01375 644671
Email: russellrsvmille@yahoo.co.uk
Club Colours: Red and White and Black Hoops
League: Essex 2 (level 10)

Stoneham RUFC
Address: Suite XV 80 High Street Winchester SO23 9AT
Contact: 07815 055235
Email: mbe017@btconnect.com
Directions: The Wide Lane Pavilion University Of Southampton Sports Ground Wide Lane Eastleigh SO50 5PE Come off the M27 at Junction 5 Follow the signs to Eastleigh and take the first exit at the next roundabout. The entrance can be found on the left
Honorary Secretary: Mr John King; Suite XV 80 High Street Winchester SO23 9AT Tel: 07815 055235
Email: john.x.king@gmail.com
Fixtures Secretary: Mr Scott Evans; Suite XV 80 High Street Winchester HampshireSO23 9AT
Tel: 07917 853022
Club Colours: Blue and white quarters
League: Hampshire 2 (level 10)

Stowmarket RUFC
Ground Address: Stowmarket Rugby Club Chilton Fields Sports Club Chilton Way Stowmarket SuffolkIP14 1SZ
Contact: 01449 613181
Email: info@stowrugby.com
Website: www.stowrugby.com
Directions: From A14 Eastbound (From Bury St Edmunds, Cambridge and M11) and A14 Westbound (From Ipswich and A12) From A14 Eastbound and A14 Westbound, exit A14 at Junction 49 and follow the sign for A1308 Stowmarket to the roundabout at the bottom of the road. Take the second exit at the roundabout and follow the road into the Chilton Hall Estate (Chilton Way). Stowmarket RUFC is about half a mile up the road on the righthand side.
Honorary Secretary: Mrs Sue Kettle; 125 Spencer Way Stowmarket SuffolkIP14 1UQ Tel: 01449 612979
Email: sue@stowrugby.com
Fixtures Secretary: Mr Darryl Chapman; 19 West View Stowmarket SuffolkIP14 1SD Tel: 07834 259343
Email: darryl.chapman@dowcorning.com
Club Colours: Navy Blue
League: East Counties 1 (level 9)

Streatham-Croydon RFC
Ground Address: 159 Brigstock Road Thornton Heath Thornton Heath Surrey CR7 7JP
Contact: 0208 6841502
Email: info@scrfc.co.uk
Website: www.scrfc.co.uk
Directions: Buses: 60, 64, 109, 198, 250 or 289 to Thornton Heath Pond, thence three minute walk. 50 or 68 to Thornton Heath High Street, thence twelve minutes walk. Train (BR): to Thornton Heath (exit is on Brigstock Road), then either 10 minutes walk to right or
Honorary Secretary: Mr Owen Jones; 43 Abercairn Road Streatham Vale London SW16 5AE Tel: 0208 7644927
Email: owen3carrots@hotmail.com
Fixtures Secretary: Mr Steve Tillin Tel: 07701 070981
Club Colours: Maroon
League: Surrey 3 (level 11)

Sudbury & London Springboks RFC
Ground Address: C/o LPO Sports Club 136 Greenford Road Harrow Middx.HA1 3QL
Contact: 020 7284 0333
Email: johnconway@londonspringboks.com
Directions: Nearest station and tube is Sudbury Hill. Turn left out of the station and the club ground is situated behind the Rising Sun Pub
Honorary Secretary: Mr John Conway; 38 Courthope Road London NW3 2LD Tel: 07710 227376
Email: jcconway@supanet.com
Club Colours: Green Gold Red White & Blue Shirts, Black Shorts
League: Herts-Middlesex 4 (level 12)

Sudbury RFC
Ground Address: Moors Field Rugby Road Great Conard Sudbury CO10 0JR
Contact: 01787 377547
Email: admin@sudburyrfc.com
Website: www.sudburyrfc.com
Directions: Ground on B1508 Colchester, Bures, Sudbury Road, 1.5 miles from Sudbury Town Centre in Great Cornard. From town centre left after Kings Head, 1st right into Rugby Road.
Honorary Secretary: Mr Dan Connell; 10 Game Close Great Cornard Sudbury Suffolk CO10 0ZJ
Tel: 01787 464133
Email: dwconnell@btinternet.com
Fixtures Secretary: Mr Gregory Underwood; 11 Bures Road Great Cornard Sudbury Suffolk CO10 0EJ
Tel: 01787 373045
Email: gjulmu@btinternet.com
Club Colours: Navy with White Hoop
League: London 2 North East (level 7)

Swaffham Rugby Union Football Club
Ground Address: Swaffham RUFC North Pickenham Road Swaffham NorfolkPE37 7QX
Contact: 01760 724829
Email: fixtures@Swaffhamrugby.com
Website: www.swaffhamrugby.com
Directions: From East or West continue along A47 bypass and turn off at MacDonalds Drive Thru' into Swaffham. Just after 30 mph sign turn LEFT at Lydney House Hotel. Club is 200 yards on right. From A1065 South take first right AFTER junction with B1077 (South Pickenham).
Honorary Secretary: Mr Michael Fields; 112 Hills Road Saham Hills Thetford Norfolk IP257EZ
Tel: 01953 884962
Email: mfields@ridgeons.net
Fixtures Secretary: Mr Michael James; 39 King Street Swaffham NorfolkPE37 7BU
Tel: 07961 340373
Club Colours: Amber & Black Shirts
League: East Counties 2 (level 10)

Tabard RFC
Ground Address: King George V Playing fields Cobden Hill Radlett Nr. St Albans Herts. WD7 7JN
Contact: 020 82075564
Email: peter.cook@tabardrfc.com
Website: www.Tabardrfc.com
Directions: Directions - On A5183 Watling Street,from Elstree turn right after entering Radlett, blind entrance by high brick wall nearly opposite the "Cat and Fiddle" pub. Nearest Railway station Radlett (25 minutes from London St Pancras Thameslink).
Honorary Secretary: Mr Peter Cook; 32 Pinewood Close Borehamwood Herts. WD6 5NW
Tel: 07931 776928
Email: peter.cook@tabardrfc.com
Fixtures Secretary: Mr Ewen Webster; 0 Sandpit Lane St. Albans Herts. AL1 4BN Tel: 07881 444772
Email: ewen_webster@hotmail.com
Club Colours: Navy, Red and Gold
League: London 2 North West (level 7)

Teddington RFC
Ground Address: Teddington RFC Bushy Park Teddington TW11 0EA
Contact: 0208 9778765
Email: mark.jones@newstrademarketing.co.uk
Website: www.teddingtonrfc.co.uk
Directions: Ground is inside Bushy Park, next to the Coleshill Road pedestrian gate. We are adjacent to Teddington Cricket Club and, at the rear of The National Physical Laboratory (N.P.L.). Then nearest Train Station in Teddington, appox 10 minute walk away.
Honorary Secretary: Mr Mark Jones; 13 Conifers Close Teddington Middx.TW11 9JG Tel: 07831 292216
Fixtures Secretary: Mr Vince Harte; 47 Blandford Road Teddington Middx.TW11 0LG Tel: 07940 716690
Club Colours: Dark Blue
League: Surrey 1 (level 9)

Territorial Army
Honorary Secretary: Mr P Marsland; 31 Fairfax Road London W4 1EN Tel: 01753 686641
Non League

Thames RFC
Ground Address: Garron Lane South Ockendon RM15 5JQ
Contact: 07974 762959
Email: tony.smith@integra.co.uk
Website: www.thamesrfc.co.uk
Directions: Turn off Tunnel Junction, down Ship Lane, right at T junction, second off roundabout. First left, second left.
Honorary Secretary: Mr Tony Smith; 50 Love Lane Aveley South Ockendon Essex RM15 4HU
Tel: 020 73183033 Email: tony.smith@integral.co.uk
Fixtures Secretary: Mr Keith Greenwood; 4 The Green Wennington Rainham Essex RM13 9DX
Tel: 07775 974077 Email: kgreenw5@ford.com
Club Colours: Emerald Green & Black Hoops
League: Essex 1 (level 9)

Thames Valley University RFC
Ground Address: Thames Valley Uni Student Union Sports Dep, St Marys Road Ealing Middx.W5 5RF
Contact: 0797 369 3232
Email: sabatinoventre@hotmail.com
Website: www.tvu.ac.uk
Fixtures Secretary: Mr Sabatino Ventre; Thames Valley University St. Marys Road Ealing London W5 5RF
Tel: 07973 693232   Email: sabatino.ventre@tvu.ac.uk
Non League

Thamesians RFC
Ground Address: The Pavillion Twickenham Green Twickenham TW2 5AG
Contact: 020 83327274
Email: theclub@thamesians.com
Website: www.thamesians.co.uk
Honorary Secretary: Mr Alex Cook; 30C The Green Twickenham Middx.TW2 5AB   Tel: 07879 424424
Fixtures Secretary: Mr Andrew Philp; 17 Cumberland Close Twickenham Middx.TW1 1RS Tel: 07970 407 673
Email: andrew@itcontacts.com
Club Colours: Green and Red
League: Herts-Middlesex 3 (level 11)

The Mount RFC
Ground Address: HMP The Mount Molyneux Avenue Bovingdon HP3 0NZ
Contact: 01442 836430
Email: robin.woodgate@hmps.gsi.gov.uk
Directions: A41 to Hemel Hempstead, signposted Bovingdon and HMP The Mount.
Honorary Secretary: Robin Woodgate; The Mount Rfc Hmp The Mount Molyneux Avenue Bovingdon Hemel Hempstead Herts. HP3 0NZ Tel: 01442 836430
Email: robin.woodgate@hmps.gsi.gov.uk
Fixtures Secretary: Ms Helen Harding; The Mount Molyneux Avenue Bovingdon Hemel Hempstead Herts. HP3 0NZ Tel:
Email: helen-harding@hmps.gsi.gov.uk
Non League

Thetford RFC
Ground Address: Two Mile Bottom Munford Road Thetford IP24 1LW
Contact: 01842 755176
Email: juleswilkin@btinternet.com
Website: www.thetfordrugbyclub.com
Directions: From Thetford by-pass at top R/about take A134 King's Lynn Road. 1.5 miles down at bottom of hill on right hand side - concealed entrance.
Honorary Secretary: Mrs Lisa Tanner; 40 Sybil Wheeler Close Thetford NorfolkIP24 1TG Tel: 01842 766994
Email: lisa.tanner@tesco.net
Fixtures Secretary: Mr Terry Ellans; 32 Wagstaff Lane Jackdale Notts. NG16 5JJ   Tel: 01773 607913
Email: terence.ellans@ntlworld.com
Club Colours: Red & white hoop, white shorts
League: East Counties 1 (level 9)

Thurrock RFC
Ground Address: Oakfield Long Lane Grays Essex RM16 2QH
Contact: 01375 374877
Email: hermanboots@blueyonder.co.uk
Website: http://www.thurrockrfc.co.uk/
Directions: M25 from North, J31/A13 direction Southend, 2nd exit (Grays) 4th exit from 2nd roundabout off 1st left (Long Laner), 3 miles east to above address, right at flats.
Honorary Secretary: Mr Mike Stephenson; 45 Jesmond Road Grays Essex RM16 2QS Tel: 01375 409765
Email: hermanboots@blueyonder.co.uk
Fixtures Secretary: Mr Clive Banbury; Old School House High Rd North Stifford Grays Essex RM16 5UE
Tel: 01375 376370   Email: info@clivebanburg.com
Club Colours: Black with White Hoops
League: London 2 North East (level 7)

Thurston RUFC
Ground Address: Robinson Field Ixworth Road Thurston SuffolkIP31 3QE
Contact: 01359 232450
Email: Rugby@steds-fs.co.uk
Website: www.thurston-rufc.co.uk
Directions: Take the A14 East from Bury St Edmunds. Take the turning signposted Thurston. Follow the road to the T junction, and turn right under thr bridge and right again at mini roundabout. Continue out of the village and clubhouse on the right. (See Website – www.thurston-rufc.co.uk
Honorary Secretary: Lincoln Brown; 4 Cannon Street Bury St Edmunds Suffolk IP33 1JU
Email: lincoln@steds-fs.co.uk
Fixtures Secretary: Mr Jeremy Kendall; 1 Harrington Close Bury St. Edmunds Suffolk IP33 2AE
Tel: 01842 754151
Club Colours: Navy blue shirts + red collar & cuffs
League: East Counties 1 (level 9)

Tonbridge Juddians RFC
Ground Address: Tonbridge Juddians RFC The Clubhouse The Slade Tonbridge Kent TN9 1HR
Contact: 01732 358548
Email: TJRUFC@aol.com
Website: www.tjrfc.co.uk
Directions: From Tonbridge High Street, turn opposite Rose & Crown Hotel into Castle Street. Follow signs to swimming pool but turn right at bottom of Slade into club car park.
Honorary Secretary: Mr Peter Darbyshire; Capel Grange Farm Badsell Road Five Oak Green Tonbridge Kent TN12 6QX Tel: 01892 833608
Email: cdarbyshire@capelgrange.freeserve.co.uk
Fixtures Secretary: Mr David Carver; 50 Pennington Place Southborough Tunbridge Wells Kent TN4 0AQ
Tel: 07917 195224
Email: davidjcarver@tiscali.co.uk
Club Colours: Red, White and Blue Hoops
League: London 2 South East (level 7)

Tottonians RFC Ltd
Ground Address: Tottonians RFC Water Lane, Totton Water Lane, Totton Southampton HampshireSO40 3ZX
Contact: 023 80663810
Email: amy@tottonians.com
Website: www.tottonians.com
Directions: Full directions and maps are available on the website, www.tottonians.com/directions.htm
Honorary Secretary: Ms Amy Searle; 3 New Cottages Oxford Road Sutton Scotney Winchester HampshireSO21 3JH Tel: 01962 761368
Email: amy@tottonians.com
Fixtures Secretary: Mr Rob Angel; 30 Brackley Way Totton Southampton SO40 3HN Tel: 07870 855074
Email: arobrugby@aol.com
Club Colours: Green, white & black hoops
League: London 2 South West (level 7)

Trinity College RFC
Ground Address: Trinity College CB2 1TQ
Contact: 07981 739211
Email: eeh33@cam.ac.uk
Honorary Secretary: Jon Main
Fixtures Secretary: Tom Attenborough; 12 Burlington Gardens London W4 4LT
Tel: 07900 922699 Email: ta285@cam.ac.uk
Non League

Trinity Hall RFC
Ground Address: Trinity Hall RFC Trinity Hall Cambridge CB2 1TJ
Contact: 07765 518057
Email: rg28@cam.ac.uk
Website: http://www.curufc.cam.ac.uk
Honorary Secretary: Mr Tom Cheshire
Tel: 07970 253539 Email: tepc2@cam.ac.uk
Fixtures Secretary: as Hon. Sec.
Non League

Trojans FC
Ground Address: Trojans Club Stoneham Park, Stoneham Lane Eastleigh Eastleigh Southampton SO50 9HT
Contact: 023 80613068
Website: www.trojansrugby.co.uk
Directions: From Southampton, leave town on The Avenue. At the r'about at the end of the road, turn right into Bassett Green Road. Stay on this road for about 2 miles. You will pass the Stoneham Arms pub on your left. At the cross roads (traffic lights), turn left and, just past the Motorway bridge, turn left up the track to the Club. From the M3, at the r'about at the end of the M3, turn left into Bassett Green Road and continue as above.
Honorary Secretary: Mr John Mist; Westbury House 14 Bellevue Road Southampton SO15 2AY
Tel: 02380 339450 Email: john.mist@matthewsmist.co.uk
Fixtures Secretary: Mr Wyn Jones; The Flat Trojan Club Stoneham Lane Eastleigh HampshireSO50 9HT
Tel: 02380 643946 Email: w.jones@southampton.gov.uk
Club Colours: Blue with red hoops
League: London 2 South West (level 7)

Twickenham RFC
Ground Address: Parkfields South Road Hampton Middx.TW12 3PE
Website: www.twickenhamrugby.com
Email: sean_brereton@hotmail.com
Honorary Secretary: Mr Sean Brereton; 44 Steele Road Isleworth Middx.TW7 7HN   Tel: 07799 417410
Email: sean_brereton@hotmail.com
Fixtures Secretary: John Clissold; 3 Barlow Road Hampton Middx.TW12 2QP Tel: 07932 756643
Email: johnclissold@aol.com
Club Colours: Red and Black irregular hoops
League: London 2 South West (level 7)

U.C.S. Old Boys RFC
Address: Eve Pavilion UCS Playing Fields Ranulf Road /Farm Ave off Cricklewood Lane London NW2 2BH
Email: m.waterman@uhy-uk.com
Website: www.ucsobrfc.co.uk/rugby/
Directions: Call Fixtures Sec or www.multimap.com Car: - The pitches are located just off Finchley road and West End lane, with secure parking facilities available. (If the car park gates are locked park the car on hocroft gardens and use the footpath to access the club.) Tube: - The Jubilee Line Serves West Hampstead, from the tube it is a 15 minute walk up West End Lane to the ground Train:- West Hampstead is also served by the Thameslink (for you city Gents) and the Silverlink, giving easy access to all parts of London. Again the grounds are a 15 minute walk from the stations. Walking:- Follow West End Lane up the hill, past "La Brocca" on the left (a popular haunt), and continue past the fire station, and again past the police station. Continue to the Nautilus Chip shop and then take the path through Fortune Green, and the cemetery to reach the ground. The Club gates are on the left by the pitches
Honorary Secretary: Mr Daniel Chapman; Cholmley Gardens 103 West Hampstead London NW6 1UP
Tel: 020 74319982 Email: mary.daniel@blueyonder.co.uk
Fixtures Secretary: Mr Trevor Turton; 12 Thorverton Road London NW2 1RE   Tel: 07903 672273
Email: treverturton@hotmail.com
Club Colours: Hoops Maroon, Black & White
League: London 2 North West (level 7)

Uckfield RFC
Ground Address: Hempstead Playing Fields Nevill Road, Manor park Uckfield East Sussex TN221LX
Contact: 01825 768956
Website: www.uckfieldrugbyclub.co.uk
Directions: The Manor Park Estate is on northern outskirts of town, turn into Browns Lane entrance & tkae 2nd road on left, ground is at the end of the 3rd road on right.
Honorary Secretary: Mrs Alicia Nicholls; 7 Rock Hall Cottages High Street Uckfield East Sussex TN22 1HT
Tel: 01825 763957
Fixtures Secretary: Mr Martin Doyle; 23 The Paddock Maresfield East Sussex TN22 2HQ Tel: 07956 461289
Email: martindoyley67@hotmail.com
Club Colours: Amber with Purple & White Hoop
League: Sussex 1 (level 9)

United Services RFC
Ground Address: United Services Sports Club Burnaby Road Portsmouth PO1 2JE
Contact: 07958324504
Email: secretary@USPortsmouthRFC.co.uk
Directions: M275 into Portsmouth; across the first roundabout; right at the second roundabout; across third roundabout and through a set of traffic lights; at the next set of lights bear left then get into the right hand lane; after 300m you will come to another set of lights, turn right. The ground is on your left with the entrance after the next left (yet another set of lights!)
Club Colours: Royal & Scarlet Hoops
League: Hampshire 1 (level 9)

University College London RFC
Ground Address: UCLU Rugby Football Club UCL Union 25 Gordon Street WC1H 0AH
Contact: 07834210217
Email: rugby@ucl.ac.uk
Website: www.rfc.uclu.org
Honorary Secretary: Mr Johnny Glover; 25 Gordon Street London WC1H 0AY   Tel: 020 76797931
Email: uclu-csadmin@ucl.ac.uk
Club Colours: Purple & Blue
Non League

University of Brighton RFC
Ground Address: Falmer Field Village Way Falmer BN1 9SF
Fixtures Secretary: Ben Wyld; Dallington House 0 University of Brighton Falmer Brighton East Sussex BN1 9PH Tel: 01273 642871
Email: studentsports@brighton.ac.uk
Non League

University of Chichester
Ground Address: University College Chichester 3 Gladstone Cottages Water Lane, Angmering Village West Sussex BN16 4EL
Honorary Secretary: Lee Douglas; Bishop Otter Campus College Lane Chichester West Sussex PO19 6PE
Non League

University of East Anglia RFC
Ground Address: Sports Centre Norwich NR4 7TJ
Contact: 01603 592 507
Honorary Secretary: Mr Ian Welch; Union House University of East Anglia Earlham Rd Norwich NR4 7TJ Tel: 07779 702605   Email: i.welch@uea.ac.uk
Fixtures Secretary: Jacki Robinson; Union House University of East Anglia Earlham Rd Norwich NR4 7TJ Tel: 01603 592511 Email: jacki.robinson@uea.ac.uk
Non League

University of Greenwich RFC
Address: Avery Hill Road Eltham London SE9 2UG
Contact: 020 8331 9403 / 9599
Honorary Secretary: Miss Rachel Rogers; University of Greenwich students Union Southwood Site Avery Hill Road Eltham London SE9 2UG Tel: 020 83319403

Email: r.rogers@gre.ac.uk
Fixtures Secretary: as Hon. Sec.
Club Colours: Black with red trim
Non League

University of Hertfordshire RFC
Ground Address: c/o Student's Union College Lane Hatfield AL10 9AB
Contact: 01707 329 116
Fixtures Secretary: Ms K Hollands; Saracens Training Centre De Havilland Campus Mosquito Way Hatfield Herts. AL10 9EU   Tel: 01707 281180
Email: k.e.hollands@herts.ac.uk
Non League

University of Surrey RFC
Ground Address: Students' Union Union House Guildford Surrey GU2 7XH
Email: z.riding@surrey.ac.uk
Honorary Secretary: Andrew Grayland; 15 Lincoln Road Guildford Surrey GU2 9TJ   Tel: 07826 525820
Fixtures Secretary: as Hon. Sec.
Club Colours: blue and yellow
Non League

University of Sussex RFC
Address: Students' Union, Activities Centre Falmer House Falmer House Falmer, Brighton BN1 9QF
Email: rugby-men@ussu.sussex.ac.uk
Website: http://www.sussexrugby.co.uk
Directions: University of Sussex is located at Falmer, on the outskirts of Brighton, within easy reach of London and major international airports (Gatwick and Heathrow).
Fixtures Secretary: Naz Humphreys; Falmer House U S S U Falmer Brighton East Sussex BN1 9QF
Tel: 01273 877322   Email: n.humphreys@sussex.ac.uk
Club Colours: Black & White
Non League

University of Westminster RFC
Address: UWSU 32-38 Wells St London W1T 3UW
Contact: 0207 911 5000 ext 2340
Email: susports@westminster.ac.uk
Website: www.uwsu.com
Honorary Secretary: Mr Nas Said; 35 Marylebone Road London NW1 5LS Tel: 0207 911500
Fixtures Secretary: Miss Gemma Ferguson; 35 Marylebone Road London NW1 5LS
Tel: 07928 733541   Email: uowactivities@gmail.com
Club Colours: Maroon or Black
Non League

Upminster RFC
Ground Address: Hall Lane Playing Fields Hall Lane Upminster Essex RM14 3HL
Contact: 01277 821768
Email: martyn@farrow32.freeserve.co.uk
Website: www.urfc.com
Directions: Exit M25 at Junction 29(A127). Take A127 towards Romford and Upminster. Take the first Upminster exit on the A127. At top of slip road turn left

into Hall Lane. Playing fields and club entrance is approx 1km on left next to Upminster Golf club
Honorary Secretary: Mr Martyn Farrow; 7 Tipps Cross Mead Hook End Brentwood Essex CM15 0HS Tel: 01277 821768
Email: Martyn@Farrow32.freeserve.co.uk
Fixtures Secretary: Mr Craig Morgan; 12 Lankton Close Beckenham Kent BR3 5DZ Tel: 07971 886497
Colours: Royal blue/gold hoops with black trim & shorts
League: London 3 North East (level 8)

Upper Clapton FC
Ground Address: The Clubhouse Upland Road Thornwood Common Nr Epping Essex CM16 6NL
Contact: 01992 572588
Email: dwofclapton@aol.com
Website: www.upperclapton.com
Directions: Join M11,exit at J7, Follow signs to B1393 heading south to Epping. Uplands Road is on right about 500 yards after Rocky Garage and before Texaco garage. Sign posted 'Golf Range, Rugby Ground'
Honorary Secretary: Mr David Miller; 16 Wychford Drive Sawbridgeworth Herts. CM21 0HA
Tel: 01279 724849   Email: dwofclapton@aol.com
Fixtures Secretary: Mr Michael Doherty Loughton Essex IG10 3QE   Tel: 07801 045792
Email: mdoherty@kcc.com
Club Colours: Red & White 7" hoops
League: Essex 1 (level 9)

Uxbridge RFC
Ground Address: Uxbridge Cricket Club Park Road Uxbridge UB8 1NR
Email: rugby@uxbridgerfc.co.uk
Website: www.uxbridgerfc.co.uk
Directions: From M25 take J16 for A40, sign posted for Uxbrdige and London. Once on the A40 take the second turn off for Uxbridge, Uxbridge/Ickenham. The junction is called "Swakeley's Roundabout." Once at r'about, take right turn for Uxbridge on B483. After approx. 1/4 mile take the first left into "Gatting Way." At the bottom of "Gatting Way" left into Uxbridge Cricket & Rugby Club.
From M40: When travelling on M40 towards London, keep going until it becomes A40. Once on the A40 take the 2nd turn off for Uxbridge, Uxbridge/Ickenham. The junction is called "Swakeley's Roundabout." Then as above
From A40: When travelling from London on the A40 towards Uxbridge and the M40 & M25, take the first turn off for Uxbridge/Ickenham. The junction is called "Swakeley's Roundabout." Then as above
From Uxbridge Bus & Tube station: By bus: U1, direction Ruislip. By foot: Once at the Tube/Bus station, walk to the end of the Bus park. At the end turn right onto Belmont Road. When you get to a roundabout, continue over and carry on up Belmont Road. (Sainsbury's should be on your right as you climb the hill.) When you get to the next r'about turn left. Cross the road and take the first right into "Gatting Way." At the bottom of "Gatting Way" turn left into Uxbridge Rugby and Cricket Club.

Honorary Secretary: Miss Fiona Blaney; 19 Chestwood Grove Uxbridge Middx.UB10 0EL Tel: 01895 254041
Email: fifiblaney@hotmail.com
Fixtures Secretary: Mr Ralph Allen
Email: ralphallen@sky.com
Club Colours: Red, Black and white
League: Herts-Middlesex 2 (level 10)

Ventnor RFC
Ground Address: Watcombe Bottom Whitwell Road Ventnor Isle of Wight PO38 1LP
Contact: 07817 228885
Email: ventnorrfc@aol.com
Directions: Approach via Wroxall and take the Whitwell Road, ground next to end of speed limit.
Honorary Secretary: Mr David Martin; Fernleigh Apartments 10 Park Road Ventnor Isle of Wight PO38 1LE Tel: 07794 308103
Email: happymartins@hotmail.com
Fixtures Secretary: Mr Andy Walton; 15 Newcomen Road Lake Isle of Wight PO36 8NZ Tel: 01983 823263
Email: andrew.walton@iow.gov.uk
Club Colours: Navy Blue with White Hoop, Navy Blue Shorts & Sock
League: Hampshire 2 (level 10)

Verulamian RFC
Ground Address: Cotlandswick, North Orbital Road London Colney St. Albans Herts. AL2 1DW
Contact: 01727 822929
Email: verulamians@verulamians.co.uk
Website: www.verulamians.co.uk
Directions: Just off Orbital Road (A414) ground opposite nursery
Honorary Secretary: Mr JON WARD; 1 Garden Close St Albans AL1 4TX Tel: 07977 583956
Email: jonward@origincleaning.co.uk
Fixtures Secretary: Mr John White; 2 Foxes Lane Cuffley Potters Bar Herts. EN6 4JB Tel: 01707 875589
Email: john.white60@ntlworld.com
Club Colours: Royal Blue with Gold "V"
League: Herts-Middlesex 1 (level 9)

Verwood RUFC
Ground Address: Potterne Park Three Legged Cross Road Verwood Dorset BH31 6UQ
Contact: 01202 828656
Email: admin@verwoodrufc.org.uk
Website: www.verwoodrufc.org.uk
Honorary Secretary: Mr Niall Donnan; 199 Albion Way Verwood Dorset BH31 7LT Tel: 01202 828686
Email: niall.donnan@ipsen.com
Fixtures Secretary: Mr Kim Rex; 21 Sleepbrook Close Verwood Dorset BH31 6QE Tel: 07752 921601
Email: kimrex@verwoodrufc.org.uk
Club Colours: Red, White with a lttle Black
League: Hampshire 2 (level 10)

Vigo RFC
Ground Address: Swanswood Field Vigo Village, Harvel Road Vigo Kent DA13 0UA
Contact: 01732 823830
Email: oaklandsfarm@hotmail.com
Website: www.vigorfc.com
Directions: Directions; please phone fixtures secretary
Honorary Secretary: Mrs Helen Merchant; Oaklands Farm Leywood Road Harvel Gravesend Kent DA13 0UD
Tel: 01474 815825
Email: oaklandsfarm@hotmail.com
Fixtures Secretary: Mr John Taylor; Sandon Burnt House Lane Hawley Dartford DA2 7SP
Tel: 01322 227363   Email: johnedwintaylor@aol.com
Club Colours: Red & black shirts, black shorts & socks
League: Kent 1 (level 9)

Wandsworthians RFC
Ground Address: Kings College Sportsground. Windsor Avenue Windsor Avenue New Malden Surrey KT3 5HA
Contact: 07960 868392
Email: mark@mlucy.freeserve.co.uk
Website: www.wandsworthians.com
Directions: From A3 northbound take the junction with the A240 (Tolworth Tower) continue on the A3 for approx 1 mile, pass the speed camera (50mph!) and approx. 300m later turn hard left off the A3 into South Lane. Proceed straight on for 100 yards and turn left at the mini-r'about. Follow road around to the right (see KCL Pitch directions - signage on corner) and continue for 300 yards, clubhouse is on the left past the LSE ground.
Honorary Secretary: Rob Langham; 15 Sussex Place New Malden Surrey KT3 3PU   Tel: 07734 462848
Email: robert.langham@hays.com
Fixtures Secretary: Mr Paul Martin; 6 Heathcote Road Epsom Surrey KT18 5DX   Tel: 07900 224908
Email: p.martin@willmotts.com
Club Colours: Maroon, Gold & White stripes
League: Surrey 4 (level 12)

Wanstead RFC
Ground Address: Roding Lane North Woodford Green Essex IG8 8JY
Contact: 02085501561
Email: julian.greatrex@btinternet.com
Website: www.intheteam.com/wansteadrfc
Directions: From Charlie Brown roundabout (junction A113 & A1400) head East towards Gants Hill. After 800m turn Left at "Toby Carvery' into Roding Lane North. Club 800m on Left.
Honorary Secretary: Mr Julian Greatrex; 15 Grange Avenue Woodford Green Essex IG8 9JT
Tel: 020 85049866
Email: julian.greatrex@btinternet.com
Fixtures Secretary: Mr John Smith
Tel: 01708 748242   Email: kerloret@aol.com
Club Colours: Blue & White Hoops
League: London 3 North East (level 8)

Warlingham RFC
Ground Address: Limpsfield Road Warlingham Surrey CR6 9RB
Contact: 01883 622825
Email: clubhouse@warlingham-rfc.com
Website: www.warlingham-rfc.com
Directions: Exit M25 @ J 6 (Caterham / Godstone) and head northbound on the A22 towards Caterham At the first r'about (Anne Summers Roundabout) take the 4th exit -Succombs Hill. At the T junction turn right. At the T junction turn left onto Warlingham Green and go straight on. Clubhouse half mile on left (before Good Companions pub) From Croydon - follow A23 South, turn left at Red Deer PH up Sanderstead Hill; across r'about at top of hill, WRFC is @ 1 mile along Limpsfield Road on the right just after the Good Companions PH.
Hon. Secretary: Ms Debbie Lockwood; St. Matthews House 98 Flat 1 George Street Croydon CR0 1PJ
Tel: 020 77522131
Email: deborah.lockwood@edfenergy.com
Fixtures Secretary: Mrs Sally Powell; c/o the club.
Tel: 01883 622825
Email: warlingham.r.f.c@btconnect.com
Club Colours: Light Blue/ White hooped shirt
League: London 2 South East (level 7)

Wasps FC
Ground Address: Twyford Avenue Sports Ground Twyford Avenue Acton W3 9QA
Contact: 020 8993 8298
Email: genevieveglover@yahoo.co.uk
Directions: Twyford Avenue is on the North side of Uxbridge Road (A4020) about half a mile east of the junction with the North Circular Road (A406)at Ealing Common. Twyford Avenue is opposite the Tesco/Esso Garage on Uxbridge Road.
Honorary Secretary: Mr Joel Goodman; Wasps Football Club Twyford Avenue Acton W3 9QA Tel: 0208 9938384
Hon Secretary Email: joel.goodman@oracle.com
Fixtures Secretary: Phil Mannal Tel: 0208 9938384
League: Herts-Middlesex 1 (level 9)

Watford RFC
Ground Address: Knutsford Playing Fields Radlett Road Watford WD24 4LL
Contact: 01923 243 292
Email: mail@watfordrfc.co.uk
Directions: From the M1 junction 5 turnoff take the bypass towards Watford and Bushey at the next round a bout turn right over the bridge, car park on left clubhouse and pitches on right.
Honorary Secretary: Mr Brian De-Honri; 12 Stripling Way Watford Herts. WD18
Tel: 01923 801727   Email: bdehonri@hotmail.com
Fixtures Secretary: Mr B Cox; 10 Sherborne Way Croxley Green Rickmansworth Herts. WD3 3PF
Tel: 01923 497834
Club Colours: Red shirt with blue sleeve & white piping
League: Herts-Middlesex 3 (level 11)

678

West London RFC
Ground Address: London Marathon Playing Fields Birkbeck Avenue Greenford UB6 8LS
Email: westlondonrfc@aol.com
Website: www.westlondonrfc.com
Directions: From A40 Western Avenue, take A4127 (Greenford Road) North for 1/2 mile. Left into Ingram Way. Right into Oldfield Lane North. Left into Birkbeck Avenue, ground 400 yards on left.
Honorary Secretary: Mrs Annette Adams; 56 Chester Drive North Harrow Harrow Middx.HA2 7PU
Tel: 07803 712 158   Email: annetteadam56@sky.com
Fixtures Secretary: Mr Phil Noot; 20 Croft Road Chalfont St. Peter Gerrards Cross Bucks. SL9 9AF
Tel: 01753 888775   Email: noot.p@tiscali.co.uk
Club Colours: Red & Black Shirt with broad w
League: London 3 North West (level 8)

West Norfolk RUFC
Ground Address: Gatehouse Lane North Wootton King's Lynn NorfolkPE30 3RJ
Contact: 01553 631307
Email: j-langford@hotmail.co.uk
Website: www.westnorfolkrugby.com
Directions: A149 King's Lynn bypass towards Hunstanton. A148 towards King's Lynn at roundabout by Knight's Hill Hotel. Right at traffic lights T/right into Castle Rising Road. Left at T-junction s/p to North Wootton. Through village Green and turn left into Gatehouse Lane ground 200 mts on right
Honorary Secretary: Mr Matt Sackree; 9 Rosecroft South Wootton Kings Lynn Norfolk PE30 3WX
Tel: 07736 658373   Email: matt.sackree@interfaceflor.eu
Fixtures Secretary: Mr Roger Edwards; 0 Gaywood Road Kings Lynn Norfolk PE30 2PZ Tel: 01553 773784
Email: ransedwards@btinternet.com
Colours: French grey with broad cerise band, navy shorts
League: London 3 North East (level 8)

Weybridge Vandals RFC
Ground Address: Brownacres Walton Lane Walton on Thames Surrey KT12 1QP
Contact: 01932 227659
Email: info@weybridgevandals.co.uk
Website: www.weybridgevandals.co.uk
Directions: From M3 J1 take the A308 towards Staines. At first major junction turn left onto the A244. Enter Walton Lane to the right immediately after crossing the river at Walton Bridge. From Walton Bridge there are two bridges to the right on to Desborough Island, one for entry and one for exit. Go over the one nearest Walton Bridge. As you come down the bridge on the island side you will find the entrance to the Club in front of you as the road bears to the left.
Honorary Secretary: Mr John Sillwood; 21 Milton Drive Shepperton Middx. TW17 0JJ Tel: 01932 889798
Email: john.sillwood@ntlworld.com

Fixtures Secretary: Mr Paul Bryant; 3 Burcott Gardens Addlestone Surrey KT15 2DE Tel: 01932 846480
Email: rugbypaul1955@hotmail.com
Club Colours: Black, Green, Purple
League: London 2 South West (level 7)

Whitstable RFC
Ground Address: Reeves Way Chestfield Whitstable Kent CT5 3QS
Contact: 01227 794343
Email: info@whitstbalerugbyclub.co.uk
Website: www.whitstablerugbyclub.co.uk
Directions: A299 Thanet Way to Whitstable, by Chestfield roundabout. The ground is opposite Chestfield & Swalecliffe Railway Station.
Honorary Secretary: Mr Gary Edwards; 5 saxon shore Whitstable Kent CT5 1FB Tel: 07740 186082
Email: gary1edwards@yahoo.co.uk
Fixtures Secretary: Mr Roger Dengate; 16 Thornden Close Herne Bay Kent CT6 7RT Tel: 01227 365379
Email: ruthanrog@talktalk.net
Club Colours: Blue & White Hoops
League: London 3 South East (level 8)

Winchester RFC
Ground Address: Winchester RFC Ltd North Walls Park (Off Nuns Road) Winchester HampshireSO23 7EF
Contact: 01962 629768
Email: secretary@winchesterrugby.com
Website: http://www.winchesterrugby.com
Directions: M3 Leave at Junction 9. Head north on A34/A33. Keep to right hand lane marked A33 Basingstoke & Kingsworthy. Take the first left onto B3047 (Cart & Horses) for 1.2 miles. Turn Left into Russell Road. Turn right at end, then first left into Hillier Way. Our Grounds are 250 yds on right at end. Plenty of Car Parking behind and to the side of the Club House.
Honorary Secretary: Mr Brian Challis; 5 Manningford Close Winchester HampshireSO23 7EU
Tel: 01962 629752
Email: secretary@winchesterrugby.com
Fixtures Secretary: Mr Geoff Toogood; 31 Winslade Road Winchester HampshireSO22 6LN
Tel: 01962 881991   Email: geoff.jean@tiscali.co.uk
Club Colours: Black & Amber
League: London 2 South West (level 7)

Wisbech RFC
Ground Address: Chapel Road Wisbech PE13 1RF
Contact: 01945 463270
Directions: Along South Brink, (From A47) proceed to Old Market Place, turn left,ground aprox 200yds on right next to garage.
Honorary Secretary: Mrs Kate Bennett; Hillegom Back Road Fridaybridge Wisbech Cambs.PE14 0HU
Tel: 01945 861345   Email: katehbennett@btinternet.com
Fixtures Secretary: Mr Dave Dobson; 5 Buckingham Walk Wisbech Cambs.PE13 3HL   Tel: 01945 461223
Club Colours: Red Shirts, Blue Shorts
League: London 3 North East (level 8)

LEVEL 7-12 AND NON LEAGUE CLUBS

Witham RUFC
Ground Address: WRUFC Spa Road Witham Essex CM8 1UN
Contact: 07795 182679
Email: amdelec@btopenworld.com
Website: www.withamrugby.com
Directions: From A12 Chelmsford -Take first exit from A12 for Witham (B1389), stay on road for 2 miles - past Jack and Jenny pub on right.At traffic lights turn left into Spinks Lane. At T-Junction turn right into Highfield Road. Follow road round to left . Under rai
Honorary Secretary: Mr Tony Davis; 6 Gay Bowers Way Witham Essex CM8 1QP
Tel: 07795 182679   Email: amdelec@btinternet.com
Fixtures Secretary: Mr Grahaem Ball; 0 Church Street Witham Essex CM8 2JP Tel: 01376 503419
Email: grahaem@orange.net
Club Colours: Brown Shirts, Navy Shorts & Socks
League: Essex 2 (level 10)

Woking RFC
Ground Address: Woking RFC Camphill Road West Byfleet Surrey KT14 6EF
Contact: 01483 839230
Email: evan.marchant@btinternet.com
Honorary Secretary: Mr Neil Murphy; 70 Sandy Lane Woking Surrey GU22 8BH
Email: neil.murphy@molex.com
Fixtures Secretary: Mr Ian Vousden; 142 Blackmore Crescent Sheerwater Woking Surrey GU21 5NY
Tel: 01483 836217
Email: sec.wokingrugby@ntlworld.com
Club Colours: Black, Red and White Hoops, Black Shorts
League: Surrey 4 (level 12)

Woodbridge RFC
Ground Address: Hatchley Barn Orford Road Orford Road Woodbridge IP12 2PP
Contact: 01473 735715
Email: john.stanford@virgin.net
Website: www.woodbridgerugbyclub.co.uk
Directions: From North or South A12 take B1084 to Orford. Cross traffic lights, railway crossing to mini roundabout. Turn left then keep straight on past turning to Eyke. Entrance half mile on right before crossroads.
Honorary Secretary: Mr John Stanford; 41 Post Mill Gardens Grundisburgh Woodbridge SuffolkIP13 6UP
Tel: 01473 735715   Email: john.stanford@virgin.net
Fixtures Secretary: Mr Liam Kennedy; 129 Redwald Road Rendlesham Woodbridge SuffolkIP12 2TF
Tel: 01394 421760   Email: liam-kennedy@live.co.uk
Club Colours: Blue/Black Shirts, Black Shorts
League: East Counties 1 (level 9)

Worth Old Boys RFC
Ground Address: North Avenue Whiteley Village Walton on Thames
Directions: From A3 take A245 to Byfleet B365, right into Seven Hills Road. At roundabout take right onto Burnwood Road to Whiteley Village on the right.
Honorary Secretary: Mr Desmond Calnan; 41 The Mount Fetcham Surrey KT22 9EG
Fixtures Secretary: Mr Paul Kozary
Email: paul.kozary@drkw.com
Club Colours: Blue & Gold Quarters
League: Surrey 3 (level 11)

Writtle Wanderers
Ground Address: Fox Burrows Lane off Lordship Road off Lordship Road Chelmsford CM1 3RR
Contact: 07841 864727
Email: info@wwrufc.net
Website: www.wwrufc.net
Directions: Based at Writtle Agricultural College, signposted from the A414 two miles to the West of Chelmsford, Essex. Our ground can be found at the end of Fox Burrows Lane, which is immediately opposite the main entrance to Writtle College on Lordship Road, Wri
Honorary Secretary: Mr Jon Horne; 22 Whist Avenue Wickford Essex   SS11 8LN
Tel: 01245 351756   Email: bones@wwrufc.org
Fixtures Secretary: Mr Colm Coyle; 38 Stapleford Close Chelmsford CM2 0RB
Tel: 07729 976682   Email: colm@wwrufc.org
Club Colours: Orange with 3 black chest stripes
League: Essex 2 (level 10)

Wymondham RFC
Ground Address: Wymondham R.U.F.C. Foster Harrison Memorial Ground Tuttles Lane Wymondham Norfolk NR18 0EN
Contact: 01953 607332
Email: secretary@wymondhamrugby.com
Website: www.wymondhamrugby.com
Directions: Northern endexit A11 by-pass follow signs B1135 to Dereham - Tuttles Lane starts at second roundabout adjacent Waitrose, 200yds on right behind trees.
Hon. Secretary: Nic Sharp; Walnut Cottage 53, Church Lane Wicklewood Wymondham Norfolk NR18 9QH
Tel: 07885 475942
Email: secretary@wymondhamrugby.com
Fixtures Secretary: Mr Adrian Anema; 91 Hargham Road Attleborough Norfolk NR17 2HQ
Tel: 01953 887622
Email: adrian@panematrailers.co.uk
Club Colours: Black with red trim
League: London 3 North East (level 8)

SOUTH WEST DIVISION

CLIFTON RFC - SOUTH WEST ONE CHAMPIONS 2008-09

SOUTH WEST

STRUCTURE

Level					
5				NATIONAL LEAGUE 3 SOUTH WEST	
6			SOUTH WEST 1 EAST		
7		Southern Counties North		Southern Counties South	
8	BB & O Prem A	Berks, Bucks & Oxon Premier		Dorset & Wilts. 1 North	Dorset & Wilts. 1 South
9		Berks, Bucks & Oxon 1 North	Berks, Bucks & Oxon 1 South	Dorset & Wilts. 2 North	Dorset & Wilts. 2 South
10		Berks, Bucks & Oxon 2 North	Berks, Bucks & Oxon 2 South	Dor. & Wilts. 3 North	Dor. & Wilts. 3 South

SOUTH WEST

682

SOUTH WEST DIVISION
CONTENTS

South West Division	Officials & League Secretaries	684
National League 3 South West	08-09 League Table & 09-10 Fixture List	686
	Year by Year record - the last 10 years	687
	2009-10 Clubs	688
South West 1 East	08-09 League table & 09-10 Fixture Grid	704
	2009-10 Clubs	705
South West 1 West	08-09 League table & 09-10 Fixture Grid	710
	2009-10 Clubs	711
Other South West	2008-09 League Tables	716
	2009-10 Fixture Grids	724
	Level 7-12 Clubs	734

A complete club index appears at the back of the book, showing which league each club is in for the 2009-10 season

DIVISION
2009-2010

League	Level
NATIONAL LEAGUE 3 SOUTH WEST	5
SOUTH WEST 1 WEST	6
Western Counties West / Western Counties North	7
Cornwall & Devon / Gloucestershire Premier / Somerset Premier	8
Devon 1 North East / Devon 1 South West / Cornwall / Gloucestershire 1 / Somerset 1	9
Gloucestershire 2 / Som. 2 North / Som. 2 South	10
Gloucestershire 3 / Som. 3 North / Som. 3 South	11

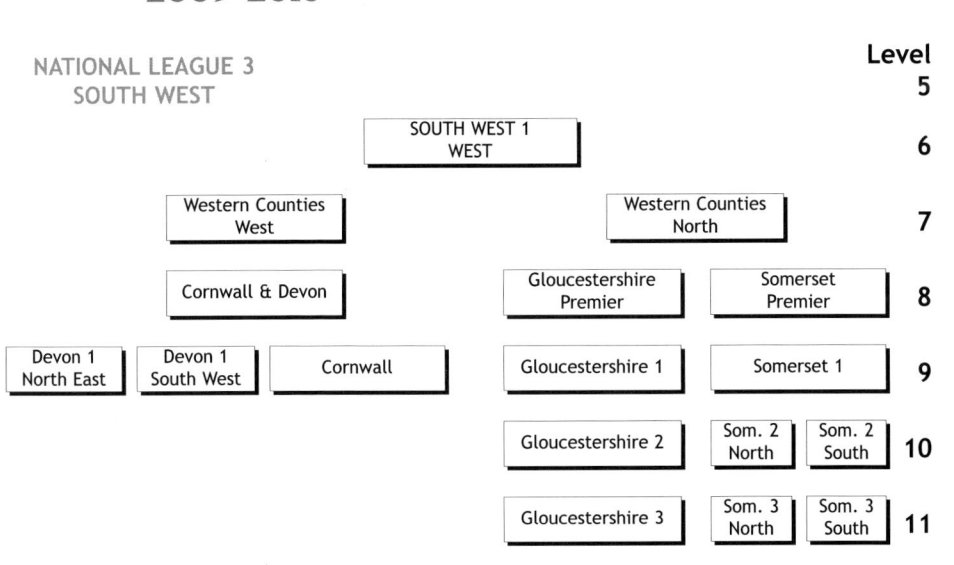

SOUTH WEST LEAGUES OFFICIALS 2009-10

N.J. Barber   **Chairman of Competition Sub-Committee**
2, The Crescent, Alexandra Road, ST IVES, Cornwall, TR26 1BY
H/F 01736 796861 B 01752 665951. EMAIL chairman@swrugby.co.uk

D. McAteer   **Deputy Chairman**
38 Silchester Road, Pamber Heath, TADLEY, Hants, RG26 3EF
H:0118 970 1245 B:0118 9303066 BF:0118 9303 411 M: 079 7667 0365
EMAIL: scn@swrugby.co.uk

M. Gee   **League Co-ordinating Secretary**
Foxglove Cottage, 70 Halsetown, ST IVES, Cornwall, TR26 3LZ
H/F 01736 797777 EMAIL secretary@swrugby.co.uk

B.L. Flanders   **Deputy League Co-ordinating Secretary & Treasurer**
Hillnest, Clanger Lane, Heywood, WESTBURY, BA13 4LL
H/F 01373 858798 EMAIL sw1e@swrugby.co.uk or treasurer@swrugby.co.uk

National 3 South West
A. Townsend, 2 Kencourt Close, GLOUCESTER, GL2 0QL
H/F 01452 522721 EMAIL n3sw@swrugby.co.uk   Deputy: N. J. Barber

South West 1 East
B. Flanders, Hillnest, Clanger Lane, Heywood, WESTBURY, BA13 4LL
H/F 01373.858798 EMAIL sw1e@swrugby.co.uk   Deputy: D. McAteer

South West 1 West
N.J. Barber, 2, The Crescent, Alexandra Road, ST IVES, Cornwall, TR26 1BY
H/F 01736 796861 B 01752 665951. EMAIL chairman@swrugby.co.uk   Deputy: A. Townsend

Berks/Bucks & Oxon Premier & Premier A
D. Bosley, 55 West Lockinge, WANTAGE Oxfordshire OX12 8QE
Tele. 01235 833688 (H), 07775 508818 (M). EMAIL bbop@swrugby.co.uk   Deputy: D. Stevens

Berks/Bucks & Oxon 1N & 2N
R. Hawkins, 21 Portway, Baughurst, TADLEY, Hants, RG26 5PD
H: 0118 9814615 M 0788 934 8415 EMAIL: bbonorth@swrugby.co.uk   Deputy: M Wild

Berks/Bucks & Oxon 1S & 2S
D. Stevens, 34 Gascoigne Way, Bloxham, BANBURY, Oxon, OX15 4TL
H 01295 721794 M: 0774 3948034 (M) EMAIL bbosouth@swrugby.co.uk   Deputy: D. McAteer

Cornwall/Devon League
T. O'Brien, 2 Rivulet Cottages, Church Street, Sidford, SIDMOUTH, Devon, EX10 9RD
H 01395 577403 M 07815 757057 EMAIL: cd@swrugby.co.uk   Deputy: G. Simpson

Cornwall League
D. Preece, 35 Higher Boskerris, Carbis Bay, ST IVES, Cornwall, TR26 2TL
H/F 01736 796694 M: 0776 975 7048 EMAIL: cornwall@swrugby.co.uk   Deputy: N. J. Barber

Devon 1 North & East
J. D Irvine, Great Rea Road, BRIXHAM, Devon, TQ5 9SW
H 01803 882219 EMAIL: dv1ne@swrugby.co.uk   Deputy: T. Clark

Devon 1 South & West
T. Clark, The Mill, Luppitt. HONITON, Devon, EX14 4UB
M 07812 449976 EMAIL: dv1sw@swrugby.co.uk   Deputy: J. D. Irvine

Dorset & Wilts 1N & 1S
N. Stafford, 5 Windsor Drive, TROWBRIDGE, Wilts, BA14 0JZ
H 01225 345305 EMAIL: dw1@swrugby.co.uk   Deputy: B. Flanders

Dorset & Wilts 2N & 3N
R. Jones, 36 Westbury Road, Yarnbrook, TROWBRIDGE, Wilts, BA14 6AG   Deputy: C. Drake
H: 01225 766647 B 01373 828447 M 077 1361 9535   EMAIL: dwnorth@swrugby.co.uk

Dorset & Wilts 2S & 3S
J. Constable, Grand View, Worgret, WAREHAM, Dorset, BH20 6AD
H: 01929 551468 M: 079 7050 0357 EMAIL dwsouth@swrugby.co.uk
Deputy: C. Drake. Folly's End, Wyke, Gillingham, Dorset SP8 4NA

Gloucester Premier & 1
M. Palmer, 56 Wiltshire Avenue, North Yate, BRISTOL, BS37 7UG
H:01454 315974   EMAIL glosp@swrugby.co.uk
Deputy: K. Plain, Foxhole Farm, Kinsham, TEWKESBURY, Gloucestershire, GL20 8HU
H/B/F 01684 772096.   EMAIL: keithplain@therfu.com

Gloucester 2 & 3
R. Ankerson, 4 Pipers Grove, Highnam, GLOUCESTER, GL2 4NJ
H 01452 302707 EMAIL glos2@swrugby.co.uk   Deputy: K. Plain

Southern Counties North
D. McAteer, 38 Silchester Road, Pamber Heath, TADLEY, Hants, RG26 3EF
H: 0118 970 1245 B: 0118 9303066 BF:0118 9303 411 M: 079 7667 0365
EMAIL: scn@swrugby.co.uk   Deputy: B. Flanders

Southern Counties South
M. Wild, 46 Castleview Road, Langley, SLOUGH, SL3 7NQ
H 01753 770870 B 01753 727007 M 078 5528 7523   EMAIL: scs@swrugby.co.uk   Deputy: N. Stafford

Somerset Premier
J. Whittock, Little Court, Winscombe Hill, WINSCOMBE, Avon, BS25 1DG
H 01934 844499 B 01278 722012 M 07919 406745 EMAIL sop@swrugby.co.uk   Deputy: S. Arnold

Somerset One
S. Arnold, 19 Millbank Close, Brislington, BRISTOL, BS4 4PY
H 0117 9090878 M 077 0331 9244   Email: so1@swrugby.co.uk   Deputy: D. Chalmers

Somerset Two N & S
P. Ham, 11 Wares Lane, Wemdon, BRIDGWATER, TA6 7RA
H: 01278 424 855 M: 078 8753 3074 F: 01278 376501 Email so2@swrugby.co.uk   Deputy: D. Chalmers

Somerset Three N & S
D. Chalmers, Battleborough Grange Hotel, Bristol Road, Brent Knoll, HIGHBRIDGE, TA9 4HJ
H: 01278 760208 M: 0788 793 1352 EMAIL: so3@swrugby.co.uk   Deputy: S. Arnold

Western Counties North
M. Thomas, 46 Treefield Road, CLEVEDON, Avon, BS21 6JB
H/F: 01275 875497   M: 07967041518   EMAIL wcn@swrugby.co.uk   Deputy: P. Ham

Western Counties West
D. Jenkins, 27 Tanwood View, BODMIN, Cornwall, PL31 2PN
H/F 01208 73160 EMAIL wcw@swrugby.co.uk   Deputy: D Preece

Other Committee Members

A. Boyer, 11 Christopher Court, Boundary Road, NEWBURY, Berks, RG14 7PQ   01635 40574

J. Dance, Birch Cottage, Padworth Common, READING, RG7 4QG
H 0118 970 0288/0118 970 1246 F 0118 970 1237. EMAIL JonathanDance@therfu.com

B. Morrison, First Eleven Sports Agency, P O BOX 3113, WOKINGHAM, RG41 4FB
B 0845 226 0311 F 0845 226 0511 EMAIL: rugby@firsteleven.co.uk

NATIONAL LEAGUE THREE SOUTH WEST

2008-09 LEAGUE TABLE (South West 1)

		P	W	D	L	F	A	PD	Pts	
1	Clifton	21	17	0	4	592	369	223	34	
2	Bracknell	21	14	1	6	569	292	277	29	
3	Bournemouth	22	14	1	7	539	392	147	29	
4	Old Patesians	22	14	1	7	503	372	131	29	
5	Redingensians	22	12	1	9	573	502	71	25	
6	Weston-Super-Mare	22	11	0	11	451	518	-67	22	
7	Barnstaple	22	10	0	12	437	538	-101	20	
8	Exmouth	22	10	0	12	454	588	-134	20	
9	Coney Hill	22	8	0	14	452	438	14	14	-2
10	Cleve	22	7	0	15	396	510	-114	12	-2
11	Oxford Harlequins	22	6	0	16	431	623	-192	12	
12	Chippenham	22	5	2	15	377	632	-255	12	

2009-10 FIXTURES GRID

	Barnstaple	Bournemouth	Chinnor	Chippenham	Cleve	Coney Hill	Exmouth	Maidenhead	Old Patesians	Oxford Quins	Reading	Redingensians	Taunton	Weston-s-Mare
Barnstaple		12/09	03/04	28/11	13/03	10/10	05/09	24/10	20/02	07/11	19/12	26/09	16/01	30/01
Bournemouth	12/12		05/09	03/04	28/11	30/01	19/09	20/02	07/11	13/03	26/09	16/01	10/10	24/10
Chinnor	05/12	10/04		13/03	07/11	16/01	20/03	30/01	24/10	20/02	12/09	19/12	26/09	10/10
Chippenham	20/03	05/12	14/11		20/02	26/09	06/03	10/10	30/01	24/10	10/04	12/09	19/12	16/01
Cleve	14/11	20/03	06/03	31/10		19/12	13/02	16/01	10/10	30/01	05/12	10/04	12/09	26/09
Coney Hill	23/01	17/10	03/10	09/01	19/09		14/11	03/04	05/09	12/12	13/02	31/10	06/03	28/11
Exmouth	10/04	19/12	28/11	07/11	24/10	13/03		12/09	26/09	10/10	16/01	30/01	20/02	03/04
Maidenhead	13/02	31/10	17/10	23/01	03/10	05/12	12/12		19/09	09/01	06/03	14/11	20/03	10/04
Old Patesians	31/10	06/03	13/02	17/10	23/01	10/04	09/01	19/12		03/10	14/11	20/03	05/12	12/09
Oxford Harlequins	06/03	14/11	31/10	13/02	17/10	12/09	23/01	26/09	16/01		20/03	05/12	10/04	19/12
Reading	19/09	09/01	12/12	05/09	03/04	24/10	03/10	07/11	13/03	28/11		10/10	30/01	20/02
Redingensians	09/01	03/10	19/09	12/12	05/09	20/02	17/10	13/03	28/11	03/04	23/01		24/10	07/11
Taunton	03/10	23/01	09/01	19/09	12/12	07/11	31/10	28/11	03/04	05/09	17/10	13/02		13/03
Weston-s-Mare	17/10	13/02	23/01	03/10	09/01	20/03	05/12	05/09	12/12	19/09	31/10	06/03	14/11	

YEAR BY YEAR RECORD
THE LAST 10 YEARS

Nos. of Clubs/Games	99-00 12/22	00-01 12/22	01-02 12/22	02-03 12/22	03-04 12/22	04-05 12/22	05-06 12/22	06-07 12/22	07-08 12/22	08-09 12/22
Barnstaple	3	4	3	4	11r					7
Basingstoke							4	5		
Berry Hill	10	9r		11r						
Bournemouth									5	3
Bracknell								8	2	2
Bridgwater & Albion			5	6	10	9	2			
Brixham										
Camborne										
Cheltenham				5	5	6	9	11r		
Chinnor				7	8	7	4	1p	1p	
Chippenham								6	10r	12
Cinderford	3	2		3	2	1p				
Cleve								2	4	10
Clevedon					3	8	9	11r		
Clifton				6	4	3	2p/po			1p
Coney Hill									9	9
Dings Crusaders			2	1p						
Dorchester	7	6	12r							
Exmouth										8
Gloucester O.B.	6	12r				11r				
Keynsham	2	8	8	9	8	12r				
Launceston	1p									
Maidenhead	5	3	10r			5	5	3	11r	
Marlow				12r						
Matson	11r									
Mounts Bay								1p		
Old Patesians	8	1p							6	4
Oxford Harlequins					10	6	8	9	7	11
Penryn						7	10r			
Reading			4	2	1p			6	10r	
Reading Abbey							7	12r		
Redingensians									8	5
St. Ives								7	12r	
St Marys O.B.					5	10r				
Spartans								12r		
Stroud	12r		9r							
Swanage & Wareham			7	11r						
Torquay Athletic	9	11r								
Truro		10r		7	12r					
Weston super Mare			1p				3	4	3	6

SOUTH WEST

687

BARNSTAPLE R.F.C.

All email addresses are - @barnstaplerfc.co.uk

President: John Courtney email: johncourtney@   **Chairman:** Martin Mogford email: martinmogford@

Treasurer: Karen Knill, Great Lilly Farm, Goodleigh, Barnstaple, EX32 7NQ
01271 328456 (H) 07974 348802 (M) email: karenknill@

Club Secretary: Trevor Edwards, 28 Charles Street, Barnstaple, North Devon, EX32 7BG
01271 344247 (H) 07971 929290 (M) email: trevoredwards@

Fixtures Secretary & Referee Liaison: Verity White-Quinn, 52 Vicarage Street, Barnstaple, Devon, EX32 7 BT
07951 343 683 email: veritywhite-quinn@

Director of Rugby: Kevin Squire email: kevinsquire@   **Commercial Secretary:** Mark Jenkins email: markjenkins@

Ground Address: Pottington Road, Barnstaple, Devon EX31 1JH Tel.: 01271 345627 email: team@barnstaplerfc.co.uk
Directions: On the approach to Barnstaple on the A361 North Devon Link, at the Roundabout, follow the signs to Ilfracombe After crossing the bridge turn right at the lights by the Barnstaple Hotel then turn first right into Pottington Road at the next set of lights. The Club is located at the bend at the end of the road.
Nearest BR Station: Barnstaple, about 1 mile away.   **Car Parking:** 130 spaces at the ground
Capacity: 2,000+ Covered Seating: 500   **Admission:** Matchday £5 (non members)
Clubhouse: Open matchdays & training nights. Hot snacks available on matchdays.
For function hire contact Bar Manager (Club answerer phone)   **Club Shop:** Open home 1st XV matchdays.
Founded: 1877   **Nickname:** Chiefs or Barum (pronounced bare-um)   **Training Nights:** Tuesday & Thursday 7.00pm
Colours: Scarlet shirt, white collar & shorts, red socks   **Change colours:** White   **Website:** www.barnstaplefc.co.uk

REVIEW OF THE SEASON 2008-09

Barnstaple returned to SW1 after a five year absence probably a year earlier than we had planned after a rebuilding process that had resulted in two consecutive promotions.

However, there was optimism as well as apprehension at the challenge that lay ahead from both players and coaches. The season kicked off with two great home victories against Weston super Mare and Bournemouth and then came a reality check. Not only did we suffer a right thrashing in our first away fixture at Coney Hill but the real disaster was that we picked up some long term injuries to key personnel at the same time.

We continued to pick up points at home but on the road it was a different story; as well as we played we were really struggling to win away from home. Thankfully, our home form eventually proved decisive in achieving our final mid-table position beating most of the top teams and finally winning our last two away games and hopefully the confidence we gained from these victories will prove decisive next season.

SW1 is a really competitive league and the level that this club aspires to. However, it has moved on a long way in the five years we were not competing in it and as a club we are going to have to work really hard both on and off the field to ensure we stay here.

LAST TEN SEASONS

	Division	P	W	D	L	F	A	P.D.	Pts	Pos
99-00	SW 1	22	15	0	7	492	232	260	30	3
00-01	SW 1	22	13	0	9	568	379	189	*24	4
01-02	SW 1	22	14	0	8	404	328	76	28	3
02-03	SW 1	22	12	1	9	362	359	3	25	4
03-04	SW 1	22	5	1	16	332	664	-332	11	11r
04-05	SW 2W	22	5	1	16	317	443	-126	11	12r
05-06	WC W	22	15	2	5	579	231	348	32	3
06-07	WC W	22	22	0	0	683	108	575	44	1p
07-08	SW 2W	22	18	0	4	567	203	364	36	2p/po
08-09	SW 1	22	10	0	12	437	538	-101	20	7

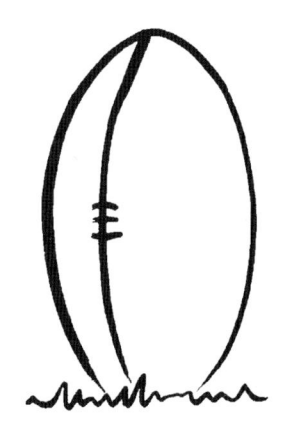

BOURNEMOUTH R.F.C.

President: Doug Warren   **Chairman:** Denis Eveleigh   **Treasurer:** Mark Valentine
Club Secretary: John Hardcastle, 31, Carbery Avenue, Southbourne, Bournemouth, Dorset, BH6 3LN
Tel: 01202 418251 (H)   e-mail: jhardc@tiscali.co.uk
Fixture Secretary: Mike Dedman, 9, Durlston Crescent, St Catherine's Hill, Christchurch, Dorset, BH23 2ST
Tel: 01202 470316 (H);   07840 558870 (M)   e-mail: mike.dedman@flour.com
Team Manager: Steve Buffery, 72 Namu Road, Winton, Bournemouth BH9 2QZ
Tel: 01202 529386, 07904 078529 email: buffery4@aol.com
Playing Committee Chairman: Denis Eveleigh, 9, East Ave, Talbot Woods, Bournemouth, BH3 7BS
Tel: 01202 298216, 07939 147810   email: denis.eveleigh@tiscali.co.uk
Commercial Manager: John Powell Tel: 01202 390955,   07831 351188   email: john.powell4040@ntlworld.com
Ground Address: Chapel Gate, West Parley, Christchurch, Dorset, BH23 6BG
Tel: 01202 843942   email: judy@bournemouthsportsclub.co.uk
Directions: Follow airport signs from A338. Keep airport on your right to roundabout. Turn right at roundabout and left into Club (Bournemouth Sports Club) grounds   **Nearest BR station:** Bournemouth or Christchurch
Capacity: 5000 Seated: 300 Covered: 200   **Admission:** £5 with prog.   **Car Parking:** 500 plus spaces
Clubhouse: Open 9am-11pm. Food available incl. hot food.. Functions contact Gavin Fisher 01202 581933
Club Shop: Open training nights, 1st XV home matchdays & Sun 9.30-1.30pm. Contact Joanna Warren 01202 709209
Programme: Size: A5 Pages: 36 Price: with admission   Advertising: Contact John Powell, Commercial Manager
Founded: 1893   **Nickname** (1st XV): Lions   **Website:** www.bournemouth-rugby.co.uk
Colours: Black and gold   **Change colours:** Blue and white   **Training Nights:** Tuesday & Thursday 7-9pm

REVIEW OF THE SEASON 2008-09

The season started much more positively than the previous one but for the first few weeks we seemed to alternate between winning and losing. However, at the Christmas break we had won 9 league games whilst losing only 3. We received a rude awakening when we played Ealing in the EDF Cup and realised that to compete in the higher leagues requires greater resources than currently available at Bournemouth. Like many other Clubs, we suffered with frozen grounds, after Christmas, and after a 5 week lay-off met bottom of the league, Oxford Harlequins, on a very wet and soggy pitch. It was no surprise to the many spectators when Oxford turned out to be the worthy winners. Thus started another results sequence when we lost games we should have won and won some we wouldn't have been surprised to lose. At the end of a very long and disjointed season we found ourselves 3rd in the league, the highest we have ever achieved.

We again had a good run in the county cup scoring a total of 157 points to 6 against us to win the final against our old adversaries, Swanage and Wareham. After numerous late season injuries a much-weakened side defended their Bournemouth 7s title in May only to lose by 2 points to an unrecognisable local side.

All in all, it has been a good season and we were happy to have ended it so high in the table. We look forward to competing in the newly vamped and enlarged National 3 South West league next season.

LAST TEN SEASONS

	Division	P	W	D	L	F	A	P.D.	Pts	Pos
99-00	SC S	18	5	1	12	260	462	-202	11	8
00-01	SC S	16	5	0	11	232	248	-16	*8	7
01-02	SC S	18	12	0	6	555	277	278	24	3
02-03	SC S	18	9	1	8	451	344	107	19	5
03-04	SC S	16	8	1	7	280	391	-111	17	4
04-05	SC S	22	18	1	3	646	246	400	37	1p
05-06	SW 2E	22	18	0	4	734	295	439	36	3
06-07	SW 2E	22	17	1	4	678	269	409	35	2p/po
07-08	SW 1	22	11	1	10	520	405	115	*21	5
08-09	SW 1	22	14	1	7	539	392	147	29	3

CHINNOR R.F.C.

President: Simon Vickers Tel: 01844 295100 (B) email: president@chinnor-rfc.co.uk
Chairman: Geoff Corpe Tel: 07770 646484 email: chairman@chinnor-rfc.co.uk
Secretary: Carol Bradbrook-Taylor, 71 Clifden Road, Wormingham, Buckinghamshire HP18 9JR
  01844 339948 (H) 07947 073838 email: secretary@chinnor-rfc.co.uk
Treasurer: Malcolm Clamp Tel: 01844 215113 (H) 07988 643997email: treasurer@chinnor-rfc.co.uk
Fixture Secretary: Peter Matthews, 5, Sevenacres, Thame, Oxon. OX9 3JQ
  Tel: 01844 217947 (H) 07736 716458 (M) email: fixtures@chinnor-rfc.co.uk
Junior Chairmen: Andy Seaton Tel: 07768 517452 (M) email: juniorchairman@chinnor-rfc.co.uk
Address: The Pavilion, Kingsey Road, Thame, Oxon. OX9 3JL
  Tel: 01844 213735 Fax: 01844 213907 email: info@chinnor-rfc.com
Directions: Situated on the Thame Western bypass at the junction with the A4129 Thame-Princes Risborough road Map: www.chinnor-rfc.com/images/Directions.pdf
Nearest BR Station: Thame / Haddenham Parkway **Car Parking:** 100 plus
Capacity: Ample - all uncovered **Admission:** Matchday £5 No season tickets available
Clubhouse: Open 12noon-11pm every day. Clubhouse Manager: Brian Taylor
Club Shop: Matchdays & Sun am. Contact Sue O'Donnell email: shop@chinnor-rfc.com
Founded: 1963 **Training Nights:** Tuesday & Thursday (Seniors) **Website:** www.chinnor-rfc.com
Colours: Black with narrow white hoops, black shorts and socks **Change colours:** Gold
Size: A5 Pages: 40 Price: with entry Editorial/Advertising: Contact: Bill O'Donnell email: enews@chinnor-rfc.com

REVIEW OF THE SEASON 2008-09

Chinnor's return to the national leagues for 2008-09 was, initially, a happy event. After a one season stay at national level in 2007-08, Chinnor had battled well in South West 1 to be promoted straight back to National 3 South. They were determined to stay longer this time but their dream was dashed towards the end of the season.

Of the 28 games played in National 3 South, Chinnor won 7, drew 2 but lost 17. Their downfall was the number of matches lost narrowly. 7 of the 17 matches lost were by 8 points or less.

The first and last matches of the season were against London Scottish and were heavy defeats. The best results of the season were the home match against Ealing and the away match against Rugby Lions. In both matches, Chinnor showed the level of rugby that could be attained when everything clicked.

Chinnor used 45 players to complete all their fixtures. Darren Oxley and Matt Hutchings started all matches. There were many long term injuries and Australian flanker Angus Neilson was only able to play half a season because of injuries. Several players were unavailable for representational reasons. Prop Bob Baker and hooker Arthur Ellis were frequently off for England u20s for both training camps and 6 Nations matches. Bob Baker also played three times in the Guinness Premiership for Wasps and also for England u20s in the World Championship.

James Cathcart led the points scorers with 99 and Ben Hewitt, James Serrano and Richie Williams all scored 6 tries each. Newcomers Toby Prescott and Arthur Ellis had fine seasons and young Adam Hastings at 6 has improved considerably.

Behind the scenes, the coaching and medical support continued to be influential.

Spirits remain high and the goal is again to gain promotion.

LAST TEN SEASONS

	Division	P	W	D	L	F	A	P.D.	Pts	Pos
99-00	SW2E	22	12	0	10	408	386	22	24	3
00-01	SW2E	22	18	0	4	640	226	414	36	1p
01-02	SW1	22	11	0	11	421	372	49	22	7
02-03	SW1	22	9	0	13	412	401	11	18	8
03-04	SW1	22	10	0	12	492	540	-48	20	7
04-05	SW1	22	12	1	9	566	466	100	25	4
05-06	SW1	22	20	0	2	723	242	481	40	1p
06-07	N3 S	26	4	1	21	362	949	-587	23	12r
07-08	SW 1	22	19	2	1	665	317	348	40	1p
08-09	N3 S	26	7	2	17	455	703	-248	40	13r

CHINNOR
RFC
THAME

CHIPPENHAM R.F.C.

President: Rod Turvey   **Treasurer:** Steve Regan email: treasurer@chippenhamrfc.co.uk
Chairman: Mark Parry Tel: 01249 446454 (H) 07791 960552 (M) email: mike.parry@sky.com
Clubhouse Manager: Peter Livesey 01249 446997 email: mike.parry@sky.com
PR & Marketing Officer: Frances North Tel: 01249 465410 (H) 07917 190904 (M) email: fm_north@hotmail.com
Club Secretary & Fixture Secretary: Darren McMillian, 13, Loyalty Street, Chippenham, Wilts. SN14 0EG
Tel: 01249 460677 07740 192199 (M) email: secretary@chippenhamrfc.co.uk
Senior Section Chairman: Ian Banister, c/o the club. email: ianbanister@orange.net
Membership Secretary: Michael K Mohan Tel: 01249 460509 (H) 07968 961552 (M) email: michael69m@hotmail.com
Junior Rugby Chairman: Tim Dunford   **Mini Rugby Chairman:** tba
Head Coach: Hentie Martens   **Club Captain:** James Gaiger
League Contact: Ian Banister, c/o the club. email: ianbanister@orange.net
Ground Address: Allington Field, Sheldon Corner, Frogwell, Chippenham, Wilts. SN14 0YZ
Tel: 01249 446997 Fax 01249 656390 email: Club.chiprfc@btconnect.com
Directions: A420 towards Bristol. Turn left by Allington Farm shop for Corsham & Sheldon Manor. After 600yds turn sharp left, entrance on left. (Now no entrance from Frogwell Lane)
Nearest BR station: Chippenham   **Car Parking:** 100 spaces
Capacity: 1,000   **Admission:** By programme £4 non-members, £2 members. Season n/a.
Clubhouse: Open 11am–11pm Mon-Sat. Sun 10am–10.30pm. Food available match days. Available for private hire, contact Peter Livesey Tel: 01249 446997   **Club Shop:** Open matchdays & Sun morning. Contact Peter Livesey
Programme: Size: A5 Pages: 18 Price: with entry Editor: Rod Turvey Advertising: Frances North
Founded: 1898 **Nickname:** 'Chipp'   **Website:** www.chippenhanrfc.co.uk   **Training Nights:** Tuesday & Thursday
Colours: Black & white irregular hoops   **Change colours:** Black & red irregular hoops

REVIEW OF THE SEASON 2008-09

The response of all the players who played in the first team was magnificent this season always playing with a great spirit. It was always going to be difficult back in SW1 where many clubs operate at a semi pro level however we continue with our limited finances to look at the best coaching and playing structure to support the players.

The 2nd XV had a very good season finishing second in D&W division 1 (North) with 34 pts and winning the County 2nd team final against a strong Bournemouth team. The team consists of many young players which reflects the development the club does in the mini and junior sections and through their attendance at training this season.

The scale of injuries particularly in the first team squad showed in our results, we continued to use a large number of players in the first team. The club will continue developing our youngsters and will be aligning the development squad with the rest of the senior section with their training and coaching support.

LAST TEN SEASONS

	Division	P	W	D	L	F	A	P.D.	Pts	Pos
99-00	SW2E	22	15	0	7	473	307	166	30	2
00-01	SW2E	22	17	0	5	686	233	453	34	3
01-02	SW2E	22	19	0	3	610	245	365	38	2
02-03	SW2E	22	12	0	10	447	367	80	24	5
03-04	SW2E	22	13	0	9	470	356	114	24*	4
04-05	SW2E	20	17	0	3	491	259	232	34	2p
05-06	SW1	22	11	0	11	489	411	78	22	6
06-07	SW1	22	10	0	12	447	450	-3	20	10r
07-08	SW2E	22	19	1	2	664	242	422	39	1p
08-09	SW1	22	5	2	15	377	632	-255	12	12

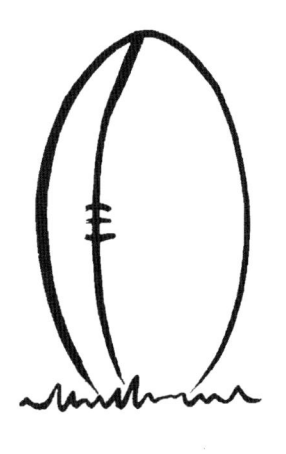

CLEVE R.F.C.

President: Roy Price   **Chairman:** Chris George   **Treasurer:** John Tasker

Club Secretary: Roy Price, 6 Ham Farm Lane, Emersons Green, Bristol BS16 7BW
Tel: (H) 01179 567430 (M) 07816 452886 email: cp007d6304@blueyonder.co.uk

Fixture Secretary: Steve Williams, 15 Lincombe Road, Downend, Bristol BS16 5UB
Tel: (H) 01179 402159 (M) 07949 287118 e mail: wilf69@blueyonder.co.uk

Commercial and Event Manager: Karen Perrott

Ground Address: The Hayfields, Cossham Street, Mangotsfield, Bristol BS16 9EN
Tel: 0117 957 5775 email: admin@cleverugby.co.uk

Directions: From M4: Leave M4 at J19 for M32. Leave M32 at J1 (very near after leaving M4).Turn left at end of slip road onto A4174.Continue along A4174 until you turn left at DRAMWAY Roundabout onto B4465, signposted Pucklechurch and Shortwood. At top of hill turn right to Shortwood. Cleve RFC is on left after passing The Bridge public house.   **Nearest BR station:** Bristol Parkway   **Car Parking:** 250 spaces

Capacity: 1200 (150 covered standing)   **Admission:** £5 incl programme (non Members), £3 (social members)
Clubhouse: Tues. to Saturday 12 noon to 11.00pm. Sunday 11.00 am to 6.00pm. Food available training nights and Saturdays.   Functions: Bookable through Event and Commercial Managers
Club Shop: Open matchdays, Sunday mornings 10-12pm and training nights.
Programme: Size: A5   Pages: 22.   Price: Included in admission
Founded: 1922   **Website:** www.cleverugby.co.uk
Colours: Maroon and white.   **Change colours:** Sky blue.   **Training Nights:** Tuesday and Thursday.

REVIEW OF THE SEASON 2008-09

Cleve finished in 9th place in the league and but for restructuring would have been relegated. This was an extremely disappointing situation from a results point of view but there were several plus points to the season. Eight games were lost by fewer than 6 points and if there had been bonus points, the league position would have been much improved. The side was very inexperienced and young but at the same time talented. This was borne out by the club having 5 players in the Gloucestershire u-20 team that won the County Championship. The task now is to keep these players and let them benefit from the experience gained.

The season also started with a new coaching team in place – Head Coach Aaron James, a New Zealander with premiership experience with Wasps, and Chris Lilley, the former Bath prop. Both had worked together for the past 5 years as Academy coaches at Bath. South West 1 was a steep learning curve and the anticipation is that the experience will benefit the club in season 09/10. Highlights of the season were the home games against eventual league winners Clifton (lost 13-18) and runners-up, Bracknell (lost 19-21). These games showed that league position counted for nothing in what was a very competitive league.

Based in Mangotsfield on the eastern fringe of Bristol (10 minutes from either Junction 18 or 19 of the M4), the club boasts excellent facilities both on and off the pitch, having moved to The Hayfields in October 1997.

There is a thriving mini and junior section that has consistently produced players not only for the first team but also for both Bristol and Bath.

LAST TEN SEASONS

	Division	P	W	D	L	F	A	P.D.	Pts	Pos
99-00	WC N	16	8	0	8	332	280	52	16	8
00-01	WC N	22	20	0	2	575	197	378	40	1p
01-02	SW 2W	22	14	1	7	527	312	215	29	4
02-03	SW 2W	22	7	0	15	382	511	-129	14	9
03-04	SW 2W	22	11	0	11	432	377	55	22	6
04-05	SW 2W	22	14	1	7	587	409	178	29	3
05-06	SW 2E	22	21	0	1	809	171	638	42	1p
06-07	SW 1	22	17	0	5	835	340	495	34	2
07-08	SW 1	22	13	0	9	469	417	52	26	4
08-09	SW 1	22	7	0	15	396	510	-114	12	10

CONEY HILL R.F.C.

President: Eddie Rooney, 2 Fairford Way, Saintbridge, Gloucester. GL4 4AY
Tel: 01452 532946   email: eddie.rooney@coneyhillrfc.com
Treasurer: Sandra Berry   Tel: 07799 767179 (M)   email sandra.berry@coneyhillrfc.com
Chairman: Wes Hall, 30 Quaill Close, Barnwood, Gloucester GL4 3EY
Tel: 01452 612325,   07769 668534 (M)   email: wes.hall@coneyhillrfc.com
Club Secretary: Ken Stokes, 1 Stanway Road, Gloucester GL4 4RE
Tel: 01452 539279,   07974 184583 (M)   email: honorarysecretary@coneyhillrfc.com
Fixtures Secretary: Paul Firth, 13 Birch Avenue, Coney Hill, Gloucester GL4 4NJ
Tel: 07936 788513   email: rugby@coneyhillrfc.com

Ground Address: Metz Way, Coney Hill, Gloucester GL4 7NT Contact Tel: 01452 306 239
Directions: Take the Gloucester ring road A38 (Eastern Ave) to the junction with the A4302 (Homesbase DIY Store & Currys) turn into Metz Way away from City centre towards KFC, club is .25 mile on left.
Nearest BR Station: Gloucester   **Car Parking**: Ample at ground
Capacity: 300, all uncovered standing   **Admission**: £2
Clubhouse: Both the main function room and the skittle alley are available for private hire. Contact club.
Club Shop: see website for online shopping.
Founded: 1947   **Nickname**: Yellow Hammers
Colours: Amber & black   **Change colours**: Red   **Website**: www.coneyhillrfc.com

REVIEW OF THE SEASON 2008-09

After a meeting at the Walnut Tree Pub in 1947 and playing their home games on land off Birch Avenue, The Coney Hill Rugby Football Club was formed. The original club badge earnt them the nick-name 'Yellow Hammers', this will only be remembered by stalwarts of the club as the badge was changed during the 1960's and so the nick-name disappeared. One tradition that is still obvious today is the club's motto 'Numquam Mori - Never Die' displayed by the players positive attitude and abrasive style of play.

Enjoying an envious record in the NGC competition was enforced again last season with the First XV being reigning champions since 2001, Second XV champions since 2004 & not forgetting the Third XV winning 3 out of the last 4 season's titles.

The First XV were finalists in the County Cup & currently play league rugby in division South West One. The results were 8 wins & 13 losses – (5 of those losses by 5 points or fewer) Scoring 452 points and conceding 438.

The outgoing season has been one to build from & with the appointment of next seasons club coach Paul Morris, formerly the GRFU's Under 20's team coach who won last seasons championship at Twickenham, & the fine appointment of the influential Mark Rimmer as club captain the 'Hill' is hopeful of another successful season.

The committees have also been working hard to match the efforts of their players. They are improving the clubs off the field activities with the development of their website, www.coneyhillrfc.com which contains all the latest news and information & gaining the RFU's 'Seal of Approval' accreditation.

The club is also looking to grow its stars of the future. The thriving Junior sections Under 13's are being bolstered by Under 10's & 16's age groups next season - things are very positive looking forward.

LAST TEN SEASONS

	Division	P	W	D	L	F	A	P.D.	Pts	Pos
99-00	WC N	16	15	0	1	423	193	230	30	1
00-01	WC N	22	11	0	11	285	298	-13	*20	7
01-02	WC N	22	15	0	7	603	398	205	30	3
02-03	WC W	22	20	1	1	856	233	623	41	1p
03-04	SW 2W	22	15	0	7	566	403	163	30	3
04-05	SW 2W	22	16	0	6	560	354	206	32	2
05-06	SW 2W	22	13	0	9	529	399	130	24	5
06-07	SW 2W	22	18	1	3	800	302	498	37	1p
07-08	SW 1	22	9	0	13	411	534	-123	18	9
08-09	SW 1	22	8	0	14	452	438	14	*14	9

EXMOUTH R.F.C.

President: Keith Pyne
Chairman: Chris Parks email: chairman@exmouthrugby.co.uk
Club Secretary: Norman Forte JP, 26 Madeira Villas, Exmouth, Devon EX8 1QP
Tel: (H) 01395 277300   email: secretary@exmouthrugby.co.uk
Fixture Secretary: Gerry Williams, 40 Bapton Close, Exmouth, EX8 3LQ
Tel: 01395 271373 email: fixture-secretary@exmouthrugby.co.uk
Team Secretary: David Radford, 72 Salterton Road, Exmouth, EX8 2NF
Tel: 01395 263343 email: match-secretary@exmouthrugby.co.uk
Director of Rugby: Chris Wright email: rugby-manager@exmouthrugby.co.uk
Commercial Secretary: Janet McCarthy email: admin-secretary@exmouthrugby.co.uk
Ground Address: Imperial Recreation Ground, Royal Avenue, Exmouth EX8 1DG
Tel: 01395 263665 or 01395 264925 email: enquiries@exmouthrugby.co.uk
Directions: M5 to Sandy Gate Exeter, exit here, follow signs to Exmouth for 8 miles, enter Exmouth on town bypass from which ground can be seen by River Exe.   **Nearest BR Station:** Exmouth. (Mainline: Exeter)
Capacity: Unlimited uncovered standing   **Admission:** By programme   **Car Parking:** 100 spaces at club
Clubhouse: Open weekends & upon request. The club's facilities are available to hire and can accommodate 120 seated.
Contact Nigel Harris, 07815 883345, email: facilities-manager@exmouthrugby.co.uk
Club Shop: To place an order see Maureen Wright or Dawn Witkiss in the rugby club on most Saturdays or Sundays, or alternatively email shop@exmouthrugby.co.uk
Founded: 1873.   **Nickname:** Cockles   **Website:** www.exmouthrugby.co.uk
Colours: Heliotrope, black & white   **Change colours:** Yellow and black   **Training Nights:** Tuesdays and Thursdays
Programme: Size: A5   Pages: 30   Price: £5   Editorial / Advertising: Janet McCarthy (see above)

REVIEW OF THE SEASON 2008-09

Exmouth had a solid first season in South West One after their slow climb up the RFU league pyramid with three promotions in the last 10 years which included a six year stay in South West Two West before winning promotion last season as Champions.

We ended their first season of rugby at this level in eight place level on points with Barnstaple and some six points clear of ninth placed Coney Hill. They collected 10 wins in 22 matches.

We started the season with just one win in the opening five league matches with a home success over Old Patesians. Then thinks picked up and we put together a run of three wins in four matches including an away win in the EDF Cup away at Bromley. Two successive away defeats followed before we returned to winning ways in the league with a home win over Barnstaple.

A narrow 15-14 win at Cleve was our first away win of the season in the league and this was followed with another narrow away win at Redingensians 17-15. Next was a win at home against the eventual Champions Clifton 16-10 which was followed with an away win at Old Patesians whom we did the double over and we also did the double over Cleve.

We can now look forward to a second season of rugby at this level in the newly named National Three South West.

LAST TEN SEASONS

	Division	P	W	D	L	F	A	P.D.	Pts	Pos
99-00	C & D	18	15	0	3	482	220	262	30	1p
00-01	WCW	22	16	0	6	618	273	345	32	3
01-02	WCW	22	20	0	2	869	213	656	40	1p
02-03	SW2W	22	13	2	7	551	401	150	28	4
03-04	SW2W	22	9	0	13	417	498	-81	18	9
04-05	SW2W	22	8	1	13	378	476	-98	17	9
05-06	SW2W	22	8	0	14	370	528	-158	16	7
06-07	SW2W	22	11	0	11	634	438	196	22	7
07-08	SW2W	22	20	0	2	539	280	259	40	1p
08-09	SW 1	22	10	0	12	454	588	-134	20	8

SOUTH WEST

694

MAIDENHEAD R.U.F.C.

President: K J Lawton 3 Manor Lane Maidenhead SL6 2QN Tel:01628 629688
Chief Executive: J. Wanklyn, Cherry Trees, Canon Hill Way, Bray, SL6 2EX
Secretary: G. Cowen, 31, Furze Platt Road, Maidenhead SL6 7NE Tel: 01628 629237
Treasurer: S M Egan
Fixture & Match Secretary: David Perry, 8, Langworthy End, Holyport, SL6 2HJ Tel: 07894 961746
Director of Rugby: G.Macdonald, `Gildoran`, Bakers Lane, Pinkneys Green, Maidenhead, SL6 6QQ
Press Liaison: Maidenhead Advertiser
Club Captain: Steve Prince Tel: 07886 249195
Ground Address: Braywick Park, Braywick Road, Maidenhad SL6 1BN Tel: 01628 629663
Directions: Junction8/9 of the M4 follow signs for Maidenhead centre. As you drive down Braywick road you will see the opportunity to cross the dual carriage way straight into the entrance of the ground.
Capacity: 1750   **Covered Seating:** 250   **Nearest BR Station:** Maidenhead
Clubhouse: Open during normal licensing hours. Food is available. For Private functions contact Lyn Armstrong.
Club Shop: Open on match days.
Founded: 1921   **Nickname:** Maids   **Website:** www.maidenheadrfc.com
Colours: Magenta, violet and black.   **Change:** Green, violet & black   **Training Nights:** Tuesday & Thursday

REVIEW OF THE SEASON 2008-09

After a disappointing season, in May 2008 the players and committee at Maidenhead acted together to rectify matters. The appointment of Chairman, John Wanklyn, and Head Coach, Ricky Khan, combined effectively to create a positive spirit throughout the Club for 2008-2009, from the U-7s to the Senior XVs. A new Elite Squad was formed, ably led by lock Mark Mueller, and joined by several ex-Colts and new young players from the Wasps Academy.

As a result the 1st XV bounced straight back into N3SW, winning 21 out of 22 games and scoring 112 tries, with 21 each coming for Alex Cannon and Andre Botha, who jointly led the league try table. Cannon even broke the Club`s individual scoring record in a league game with 34 in the game at Swanage. The team had the best defensive record in their league as well, leaking a mere 206 points, and young players such as Ryan Long, Will Page, Ed Keohane, James Emmanuel and Freddie Stockwell all had outstanding seasons.

In mid-January Mark Mueller broke a leg and Aussie No 8 Greg Riley took over the Captain`s mantle, steering his side through a rocky February, before they finished in triumph with some outstanding displays of running rugby in March and April, which brought large crowds to Braywick as the possibility of promotion beckoned.

Meanwhile the Elite Squad 2nd XV were enjoying a mid-table position in the Canterbury Shield at their first attempt, and the 3rd XV were on their way to win BBO1S, scoring over 1000 points in the process and gaining promotion to BBO Premier A, whilst the reformed 4th XV finished second in the TVIL. Amongst the Junior teams, the U-14s and U-15s won their leagues, and the whole Youth Section contributed to an exciting and thoroughly enjoyable season for everyone.

For 2009-2010, Khan looks forward to further developing his squad and will be supported by the appointment of ex-Scottish International, Gordon Macdonald, to the post of Director of Senior Rugby. Everyone is looking forward to another great season and to welcoming all new and old friends to Braywick.

LAST TEN SEASONS

	Division	P	W	D	L	F	A	P.D.	Pts	Pos
99-00	SW1	22	14	0	8	652	421	231	28	5
00-01	SW1	22	12	1	9	444	376	68	25	3
01-02	SW1	22	9	0	13	463	511	-48	18	10r
02-03	SW2E	22	17	0	5	567	333	234	34	3
03-04	SW2E	22	21	0	1	825	298	527	42	1p
04-05	SW1	22	12	0	10	497	501	-4	24	5
05-06	SW1	22	14	1	7	682	488	194	29	5
06-07	SW1	22	15	0	7	682	379	303	30	3
07-08	SW1	22	7	1	14	416	584	-168	15	11r
08-09	SW2E	22	21	0	1	773	206	567	42	1p

OLD PATESIANS R.F.C.

President: Dick Tyler   **Chairman:** Michael Angell   **Treasurer:** Mark Schofield
Club Secretary   Steve Cohen, Rosslyn, Moorend Grove, Cheltenham, Glos, GL53 0EX
   Tel: 01242 520873 (H)   07986 969214 (M)   email: cohens@cohenfamily.plus.com
Fixture & Team   Mark Knight, 14B Canterbury Walk, Warden Hill, Cheltenham, Glos, GL51 5HG
   Secretary   Tel: 01242 698756 (H)   01242 271583 (W)   0771 9857761 (M)   email: glad99@knights97.freeserve.co.uk
Registration Secretary   John Smith   details as Commercial Sec.
Director of Rugby   Matthew Cape, 10 Pinetrees, Charlton Kings, Cheltenham, Glos. GL53 0NB
   email: Matthew.cape@thechelsea.co.uk or capefamilyhome@aol.com
   Tel 01242 579657 (H)   01242 271193 (W)   07836 558567 (M)
Commercial Secretary   John Smith, 24 Wisteria Court, Up Hatherley, Cheltenham, Glos, GL51 3WG
   Tel: 01242 863646 (H)   07770 634949 (M)   email: John.smith@accetts.com
Address: Old Patesians Clubhouse, Everest Road, Cheltenham. GL53 9LG
Tel: 01242 524633   email: cohens@cohenfamily.plus.com
Directions: Not Easy – recommend see website or use Internet.   Everest Road is off the Old Bath road, on the south side of Cheltenham. The turning for Everest Rd is opposite the Wheatsheaf Inn, with the ground at the end of the road.
Nearest BR Station: Cheltenham, 3 miles. NB No near bus service, so taxi or walk.   **Car Parking:** 50 spaces at ground
Capacity: 500 all uncovered standing   **Admission:** Matchday: £4 incl. programme. Season tickets: £40
Clubhouse: Open eves 6-11pm, matchdays 12-11pm. & Sun. 7-11pm. Food available at all times except Saturday afternoon. Available for hire, contact Terry or Pauline Higgs.
Club Shop: Open Sunday am 10.00-12.00 Contact Tracy Gardner 01242 573624
Programme: **Size:** A5   **Pages:** 40   **Price:** With admission   **Editorial & Advertising:** John Smith
Founded: 1913   **Nickname:** Old Pats   **Training Nights:** Tuesday & Thursday
Colours: Magenta, navy & white hoops   **Change colours:** White   **Website:** www.oldpats.co.uk

REVIEW OF THE SEASON 2008-09

The aim for the 2008 – 09 season was to improve on the performance from the previous season and to finish in the top half of the league. This was achieved with a top four finish with the 2nd, 3rd and 4th placed teams equal on points separated only by points difference. A fantastic achievement with some outstanding victories against the top placed teams running in some fine tries and setting new standards for ourselves.

Pats yet again faced injuries to key players however the strength of the squad and the emergence of key younger players coming to the fore maintained the momentum and kept the pressure on the other sides pushing for promotion. Managing to lose 4 games with scores in the last 5 minutes demonstrated the work still to be done and maintained the focus.

The coaching of Dave Pointon and Lee Fortey continues to stretch the players and see the squad achieve things which they would have not believed possible. With significant changes to the playing style stretching the ball across the full width of the pitch and bringing the outside backs into play with regularity as demonstrated by Henry Bird scoring 13 league tries! He and the rest of the backs tested every defence.

The Pats continue to build for the 2009 – 10 season and set themselves new standards and increased expectations. The core of the squad remains in place with a number of new players identified to join for the new season together with a number of players who missed the majority of last season aiming to return. We will continue to play open attacking rugby and hope to focus on increased consistency on the pitch and ground developments off the pitch.

LAST TEN SEASONS

	Division	P	W	D	L	F	A	P.D.	Pts	Pos	Most Points	Most Tries
99-00	SW1	22	8	1	13	386	583	-197	17	8		
00-01	SW1	22	21	0	1	593	209	384	42	1p	197 Tony Robinson	20 Will Morgan
01-02	N3S	26	15	0	11	596	683	-87	30	5	107 Russell Nunn	13 Will Morgan
02-03	N3S	26	14	0	12	644	544	100	28	5	152 S Pollock	9 B Matthews & S Pollock
03-04	N3S	26	13	0	13	614	659	-45	26	7	133 Robert Nock	13 James O'Brien
04-05	N3S	26	9	1	16	527	622	-95	48	11	114 Russell Nunn	10 James Pettigrew
05-06	N3S	26	8	0	18	479	686	-207	42	12	103 Robert Nock	9 Ben Parker
06-07	N3S	26	4	0	22	447	751	-304	28	13r	94 Russell Nunn	7 James Pettigrew & Chris Mellon
07-08	SW 1	22	9	2	11	477	362	115	20	6		
08-09	SW 1	22	14	1	7	503	372	131	29	4		

OXFORD HARLEQUINS R.F.C.

President: Steve Cottrell **Treasurer:** John Waters
Chairman: Kevin Johnson Tel: 07887 557585 email: badgerno8@btopenworld.com
Club Secretary: Keith Latham, 29 Churchill Way, Long Hanborough, Witney Oxon. OX29 8JJ
Tel/Fax: 01993 881985 (H) 07967 206098 (M) email: keith.latham@tinyworld.co.uk
Fixture Sec. & League Contact as Club Secretary **Director Of Rugby:** Matthew Maudsley
Ground Address: Horspath Road, Marston Ferry Road, Oxford OX4 2RR
Tel.: 01865 775765 email: info@oxfordharlequins.com

Directions: From the junction of the London bound A40 and the Oxford ring road, travel 1.5 miles south on the ring road to the traffic lights signed Hudspeth. Turn left, and the ground is about 500 yards on the left, immediately after the industrial estate.

Capacity: 2000 - all uncovered. Seating: 30 **Car Parking:** 300 cars
Nearest BR Station: Oxford **Admission:** Matchday: £3
Clubhouse: Open match days from mid day, Training nights from 7pm. Food is availabe when club is open
Clubhouse available for private hire. Contact Clare Johnson 01993 882207
Club Shop: Open Match days and training nights.
Programme: Size: A5 Pages: 16 Price: Included with admission
Editorial & Advertising: Keith Latham 01993 881985
Formed: 1996 **Nickname:** The Quins **Website:** www.oxfordharlequins.com
Colours: Red and blue with thin white and yellow strips **Training Nights:** Tuesday and Thurdays

REVIEW OF THE SEASON 2008-09

Season 2008-2009 proved the most difficult in Oxford Harlequins short history. At the end of season 2007 – 2008 nine of the first team squad left, five returned to their native countries and the others moved on.

Whilst very strong below the first team, the club fielding another 3 / 4 teams weren't able to recruit or have players available at the begining of the season.

The club struggled. In October 2009 Director of rugby Matthew Maudsley resigned and unfortunately for rugby in general decided to take time away from the game.

Whilst this was a massive blow for the club, Harlequins were very lucky to have a proven successful candidate already working in the wings in the form of ex Chinnor coach John Brodley.

Within a very short time John started working minor miracles turning the club around and putting it on a positive /winning track. Bringing players in from local schools, colleges and universities, including players such as current US Eagle Will Johnson. John also blooded a number of players from Oxford Rugby academy (Under 21) successfully into the squad.

As a result of this turn around, Oxford Harlequins managed to remain a level 5 club and will complete in the new Nation 3 South West league next year.

In the new year Oxford Harlequins retained the County Cup in April beating Banbury by a record score at Iffley Road for the fourth year in succession.

The highly successful colt side also beat Banbury in the County Colt final at Banbury.

This success has acted as a stimulus, already Martin Nutt has returned from Newbury as a player/coach and Craig Burrows has joined us from Chinnor. Both players were regulars in the national leagues.

As this articles is being written, other players with national experience have indicated their desire to join the setup for the new season.

Coupled with players stepping up from the academy the future looks a lot brighter than it did last year.

LEAGUE HISTORY

	Division	P	W	D	L	F	A	P.D.	Pts	Pos
99-00	SCN	18	12	1	5	485	248	237	25	25
00-01	SCN	20	10	1	9	434	341	93	21	5
01-02	SCN	18	17	0	1	933	163	770	34	1p
02-03	SW2E	22	19	0	3	679	292	387	38	1p
03-04	SW1	22	8	2	12	456	510	-54	18	10
04-05	SW1	22	11	0	11	494	523	-29	22	6
05-06	SW1	22	7	0	15	341	552	-211	14	8
06-07	SW1	22	9	2	11	512	496	16	20	9
07-08	SW 1	22	9	2	11	472	452	20	*18	7
08-09	SW 1	22	6	0	16	431	623	-192	12	11

READING R.F.C.

President:	Mike Reynolds	0118 969 6592		email: president@
Chairman:	Craig Hunter	0118 969 6592	07798 844202 (M)	email: chairman@
Treasurer:	Julie Blakey	0118 969 6592		email: julieblakey66@hotmail.com
Hon. Secretary:	Heather Allen	0118 969 6592	07901 555052 (M)	email: allah59@yahoo.co.uk
Membership Secretary:	Matt Healey	0118 969 6592	07528 200679 (M)	email: membershipsecretary@
Rugby Administrator:	Alan Bright	0118 961 6595	07815 744756 (M)	email: awbright@msn.com
Chairman of Rugby:	Kevin Rackley	0118 933 8977	07720 883827 (M)	email: rackleys@dsl.pipex.com

All correspondence c/o the club. Incomplete email addresses are @ 'readingrfc.co.uk'

Address: Reading RFC, Holme Park, Sonning Lane, Reading RG4 6ST
Tel: 0118 969 6592   **Fax:** 0118 969 6593   **e-mail:** enquiries@readingrfc.co.uk   **Website:** www.readingrfc.co.uk
Directions: M4 J10 (A329M). Head towards Reading, continue on A329M until you see the signs for Reading A4, as you leave A329M, right towards Woodley/Sonning/Maidenhead on the A4. Continue along A4, over railway bridge, take the first left into Sonning Lane, (signs for Reading RFC on junction). After 250m turn left into Holme Park Farm Lane then immediately right into the club.
Nearest BR Station: Reading, by short taxi journey (10 mins).   **Car Parking:** 350 at ground, 200 nearby
Capacity: 2500   Covered Seating: 200
Admission: Matchday: Non members £5, members £4, including programme.   Season tickets available.
Clubhouse: Open Tuesday & Thursday 6-11 and at weekends. Snacks & bar meals available. Functions capacity to 200.
Contact Mel Short 0118 969 6592.
Club Shop: Open Training nights and matchdays.
Contact Mark Everett Tel: 0118 969 6592 email: facilitieschairman@readingrfc.co.uk

Programme: Size: A5   Pages: 8   Price: with admission   Editor: Craig Hunter   **Training Nights:** Tues & Thur
Founded: 1898   **Nickname:** Green Machine   **Colours:** Myrtle & white   **Change colours:** Yellow

REVIEW OF THE SEASON 2008-09

Reading 1st XV had an excellent season finishing as runners up in South West 2 East and gaining promotion to National South West 3 by beating Newton Abbot in the play-off.

This success also continued further as the Reading U18 Girls won their National Cup whilst they have also gained two international caps at England U21.

Other Youth teams performed well and across the board all teams have moved forward. Other senior sides, the Wanderers and the Rhinos have also had fantastic seasons and have contributed to the new vibrancy that permeates all levels in the club.

Our best season for many years!

LAST TEN SEASONS

	Division	P	W	D	L	F	A	P.D.	Pts	Pos
99-00	JN1	26	6	0	20	442	626	-184	12	13r
00-01	3S	22	9	1	16	462	643	-181	19	11r
01-02	SW1	22	12	2	8	480	345	135	26	4
02-03	SW1	22	18	1	3	542	297	245	37	2
03-04	SW1	22	19	0	3	742	314	428	38	1p
04-05	N3S	26	13	0	13	674	743	-69	67	6
05-06	N3S	26	6	0	20	526	868	-342	34	13r
06-07	SW1	22	11	1	10	595	542	53	23	6
07-08	SW1	22	7	2	13	483	587	-104	16	10r
08-09	SW 2E	22	19	0	3	946	252	694	38	2p/po

REDINGENSIANS R.F.C.

President: Ian Duncan **Chairman**: Andrew Lynch **Treasurer**: Robin Davies
Club Secretary: John Cook, 95 Century Court, Grove End Road, London NW8 9LD
Tel: 0207 289 1887 (H) 0207 149 6280 (B)
Fixtures Secretary: George Nattriss, 64 Broadwater Road, Twyford, Reading RG10 0EU
Tel: 0118 934 0685 (H) email: george@natts.com
Match Secretary: John Taylor Tel: 0118 941 1444 (H) john.m.taylor@maple-comms.co.uk
Membership Secretary: Chris Hodgson Tel: 01628 821 058 email: chris@tythebarn.fslife.co.uk
Fundraising Secretary: Julian Lidstone, Bays Platt, Skirmett, Henley on Thames RG9 6TD
01491 638 322 (H) 07850 879 201 (M) email: email: lidstone@skirmett-washrooms.co.uk
Youth Chairman: Alan Jones, 1 Dunnock Way, Wargrave, Reading RG10 8LR
Tel: 0118 9404 303 (H) email: enquiries@wokinghamsport.co.uk
Youth Fixtures: Roger Batchelor, Clevedon, 62 New Road, Twyford, Reading RG10 9PT
Tel: 0118 934 1794 (H) 07761 192 501 (M) email: roger.batchelor@reading.gov.uk
Director Of Rugby: Gary Reynolds Tel: 0118 962 7485 (H) 07799 695 640 (M) 01491 570 301
email: gary.reynolds@courtiers.co.uk
Coach: Alun Rise Tel: 07827 829 349 (M)
Ground Address: Old Redingensians Sports Ground, Old Bath Road, Sonning, Berks RG4 6TQ
Tel: 0118 969 5259   email: info@redingensians.info
Directions: From M4 Exit J 10 and follow the signs for Reading onto the A329(M). At the 2nd exit, signposts to Reading exit the A329(M) and take the 3rd exit (turn right) off the r'about signed to Maidenhead, Woodley etc. Again at the 2nd r'about take the 3rd exit (almost straight over) and follow the road up the hill towards a large oval shaped r'about with a large BP petrol station in the centre and follow the signs to Maidenhead on the A4. Go straight over the last r'about for 50 yds, again signs for Maidenhead and in the centre of the dual carriageway there is a signpost for Redingensians RFC & CC. Turn right at this signpost onto the Old Bath Road and then immediately Left. Redingensians RFC can be found approx 100 yds down - on the right, at the end. **Capacity**: All uncovered standing **Nearest BR Station**: Twyford **Car Parking**: Ample.
Formed: 1924 **Nickname**: ORs **Colours**: Dark blue, light blue and white hoops.
Training Nights: Tues & Thur 7pm. **Website**: www.redingensians.info **Change colours**: Red shirts, white shorts
Clubhouse: Open Sat & Sun 12-22.30, Tue & Thur from 19.00.
Available for functions - contact Ian Clarke 0118 942 5705 (day) 0118 969 5259 (eve).
Club Shop: Open Sun am. Carol Clark 0118 945 3960 (H) email: carol_clark@hotmail.com

REVIEW OF THE SEASON 2008-09

By a quirk of the computer the side's first seven games were against the league's seven weakest sides as defined by the final league table. When they were all won the treasurer started developing a nervous twitch, but eight defeats in the next nine games saw the twitch disappear as reality set in.

A final position of fifth left everyone happy and victory at Clifton on 2nd May provided a fitting farewell to young coach, Tom Hoines. A flurry of yellow cards greeted Lofty Milne's 42nd birthday that day. Rather surprisingly Lofty did not receive one himself. The second-row has "previous" when it comes to cards.

LAST TEN SEASONS

	Division	P	W	D	L	F	A	P.D.	Pts	Pos
99-00	SC S	18	13	0	5	433	244	189	26	3
00-01	SC S	16	14	1	1	389	162	227	29	1p
01-02	SW 2E	22	6	0	16	334	517	-183	12	11r
02-03	SC S	18	7	0	11	282	445	-163	14	7
03-04	SC S	16	5	0	11	227	335	-108	10	7
04-05	SC S	22	10	0	12	335	410	-75	20	9
05-06	SC N	22	20	0	2	671	295	376	40	1p
06-07	SW 2E	22	19	0	3	700	404	296	38	1p
07-08	SW 1	22	9	0	13	403	459	-56	18	8
08-09	SW 1	22	12	1	9	573	502	71	25	5

Although the Berkshire Cup was surrendered to Bracknell, revenge came ten days later in the final of the Berkshire Floodlit Sevens. The Seven then flew to Amsterdam, winning their first five games before coming up against the International Marauders.

The seconds moved into the Canterbury leagues and did really well; the thirds held their own in a higher league, the fourths came second in their league and the fifths won theirs. The Colts won in Antwerp, beating Nottingham in the final of that tournament, the Under 17's made the last sixteen of the National Cup and the Academy side won the National U18 Touch Rugby Championship.

If it was not the best season in the club's history it certainly felt like it.

TAUNTON R.F.C.

President: Keith Cooling   **Chairman:** Linda Harris   **Treasurer:** Jerry Winter

Club Secretary: Oli Massingham, c/o the club
Tel: 01823 336363 (Club)   07866 680351 (M)   email: onmass01@hotmail.com
Fixture / Team Secretary: Rod Reed, 22 Barrow Drive, Taunton Tel: 01823 276354
Director of Rugby: Lee Waddon , 01823 272247, e-mail: lee.waddon@tauntonrfc.co.uk
Commercial Manager: Steve Sanger-Davies, c/o the club. Tel 01823 336363 e-mail: general manager@tauntonrfc.co.uk
Ground Address: Hyde Park, Hyde Lane, Taunton, Somerset TA2 8BU   Tel: 01823 336363   Fax: 01823 336767
email: rugby@tauntonrfc.co.uk   **Website:** www.tauntonrfc.co.uk
Directions: J 25 of M5 head towards Taunton. At first set of lights (Taunton RFC signposted before the lights) turn right onto A38 towards Bridgwater. 1/2 mile over railway bridge (again signposted) turn right at Bathpool Inn into Hyde Lane. Follow road around for further 1/2 mile - club entrance appears on right hand side.   **Car Parking:** 200
Capacity: 2,000   **Seated:** 200   **Covered:** 300   **Admission:** Matchday £4   **Nearest BR station:** Taunton
Clubhouse: Open 9am-11pm, with food available.   **Functions:** The club has modern facilities (see web site) and is able to hold many types of function. Contact Steve Sanger-Davies   email : functions@tauntonrfc.co.uk
Programme: **Size:** A5   **Pages:** 16   **Price:** £2   **Editorial & Advertising:** Steve Sanger-Davies
Founded: 1875   **Colours:** Crimson, black & white   **Change colours:** Black   **Training Nights:** Tuesday & Thursday

REVIEW OF THE SEASON 2008-09

Taunton Rugby Football Club has enjoyed a most successful season both on and off the field of play.

The 1st XV gained promotion win as league champions of Tribute South West two west by completing an unbeaten season winning all twenty two league fixtures, scoring 820 points for and conceeding 217 points.

The 1st XV under the guidance of player coach Dave Sims, the former England and Gloucester second row forward and Simon Martin, the former Bristol, Bedford and Per-Temp Bees centre, three quarter moved the club forward in achieving the rugby levels set out in the clubs mission statement. The team including some very experienced senior players along with many home grown local players that have progressed through from the clubs junior and colts sides really impressed. The squad and the club now looks forward to playing next season in the newly named National League Three South West League following the league restructuring and will be looking to continue to build on their season success.

The clubs 2nd XV, the United, had a very successful season and gained promotion as runners up in the Somerset 1 League and will play next season in the Somerset Premier League.

The Thirds XV, the Wanderers, had a disappointing season playing in Somerset 2 South but have continued to improve during the season.

The Colts XV, have had a most successful season and have continued to produce some really fine players for the future. The Colts also made it to the last eight of the National Cup this season.

The clubs Junior sections have again been most successful this season with many honours being achieved at many tournaments and festivals.

The clubs Under 16 team were County Cup winners after a fine display at Bath's Recreational Ground. The team's hooker, Will Tanner, achieved international recognition during the season and the club was very honoured to receive from Will, an England 16 group international shirt.

LAST TEN SEASONS

	Division	P	W	D	L	F	A	P.D.	Pts	Pos
99-00	SW2 W	22	6	1	15	403	590	-187	*11	11r
00-01	WC N	22	17	1	4	706	364	342	35	2
01-02	SW2 W	22	10	0	12	497	543	-46	*18	8
02-03	SW2 W	22	6	1	15	408	559	-151	13	10
03-04	SW2 W	22	6	0	16	344	608	-264	12	11r
04-05	WC N	22	16	2	4	601	289	312	34	1p
05-06	SW2 W	22	7	0	15	382	630	-248	14	9
06-07	SW2 W	22	10	1	11	571	516	55	21	9
07-08	SW2 W	22	15	1	6	523	253	270	31	3
08-09	SW2 W	22	22	0	0	820	217	603	44	1p

Ladies rugby within the club regretfully, has had a bit of a difficult season, however, the Fillies section continues to attract players and much success has been achieved by them this season

WESTON-SUPER-MARE R.F.C.

President: John Brentnall   **Chairman:** Ray Monelle   **Treasurer:** Barry Sparks
Club Secretary: Jack Russell, 22 Cecil Road, Weston-s-Mare BS23 2NT
01934 631690 (T/F)   07747 867788 (M) email: tonyrussell2@aol.com
Fixture Secretary: Dave Simpson 01934 413011 (H)   07929 833856 (M)
Coaching Co-ordinator: Peter Sloman 07949 349067 (M)
Commercial Secretary: Adele Tincknell 07764 691851 (M)

Ground Address: The Recreation Ground, Drove Road, Weston super Mare BS23 3PA Office 01934 625643 Clubhouse 01934 623118
Directions: From North: M5, J21 and follow dual carriageway "Town centre and station". You'll pass new housing, Hornets rfc, Sports center and Industrial estates.and then at 5th. r'about take 2nd exit. Ground visible on lhs. From **South** M5, J22. Follow road to WSM for 4-5 miles You will reach a r'about at bottom of hill (hospital on lhs) .Stay on main road and take 2nd right into Devonshire Rd. (keep school on your left). Stay on road until you reach r'about (Playing fields on lhs). First left at this r'about. Ground visible on lhs. Spectators car park in front of ground, players and officials use back gates behind main stand.
Nearest BR Station: Weston-s-Mare, 100 yds from ground   **Car Parking:** 200+
Capacity: 2,000   Covered Seating: 400   **Admission:** Season £72   Matchday £5
Clubhouse: Tues to Fri 7-11pm, Sat & Sun 12-11pm. Snacks available on matchdays only.
Functions: 1 large function room & 2 meeting rooms. Contact Louise Abraham 07799 664812 (M) or 01934 623118 (am)
Founded: 1875   **Nickname:** Seasiders   **Training Nights:** Tues & Thur 7pm   **Website:** www.westonrugby.co.uk
Colours: Predominantly blue with red & white   **Change colours:** Predominantly red with blue & white
Programme: Size: A5   Price: £1   Pages: 20/22   Advertising Contact: Adele Tincknell 07764 691851(M)

REVIEW OF THE SEASON 2008-09

The pre-season portents were not good. Player defections, departures and retirements left the squad severely depleted. New coach Dave Healy must have thought he'd made a wrong decision as he wondered where his first team was going to come from, but things improved. A hard core of veterans and experience combined with several exciting, and very young players turned things around. Team spirit improved, as did the on field performance although a temporary post-Christmas dip in form resulted in lost points following abject showings against Barnstaple, where the home side lost to the worst away record in the League, and sub standard away efforts against Bracknells' semi- professionals, Oxford Harlequins, Redingensians and Bournemouth. However all were beaten at Weston with outstanding team efforts against Bracknell and Bournemouth denting the play- off aspirations of both sides, showing what might have been with a little more consistency and a stronger squad but following early misgivings, the coach would doubtless have gladly settled for 6th position at the outset. The County Cup was also won for the fifth year in eight.

Following a pleasant respite, the increased number of teams and the location of the promoted sides will now mean a return to the fortnightly crawl up the M4. Why Berkshire comes into the South West remains a total mystery!

The second team romped to promotion in their League, scoring 1200 points and conceding 74, and.

the third team also won promotion almost as convincingly, doing it the hard way by winning all bar two of their away games, and having to suffer numerous no-shows by opposition who had received the courtesy of a reciprocal visit. One never hears of a team crying off at home through a lack of front row players but it's become the standard Thursday night phone call from embarassed Fixtures Secretaries of away teams!

The Vets continue to perform admirably with many playing regularly for the third xv and providing admirable and valuable guidance for the younger players. Their touring tradition was upheld with a well supported trip to Scotland.

The Colts maintained their high standards, winning the County Cup for the sixth year running. Three of last seasons' team became first team regulars and similar progress is expected from some players this year.

The Junior section continues to thrive, well organised with teams at every age group.

Club morale remains high and vibrant. After one season and a nervous start, coach Healy feels that he has joined a "rugby club".

LAST TEN SEASONS

	Division	P	W	D	L	F	A	P.D.	Pts	Pos
99-00	N2S	26	11	0	15	512	598	-86	20	11
00-01	N2S	26	7	1	18	370	691	-321	15	12r
01-02	SW1	22	19	0	3	479	259	220	38	1
02-03	N3S	26	13	0	13	496	522	-26	26	6
03-04	N3S	26	12	0	14	555	570	-15	24	8
04-05	N3S	26	7	1	18	449	727	-278	41	12r
05-06	SW1	22	16	1	5	702	248	454	33	3
06-07	SW1	22	13	1	8	525	445	80	27	4
07-08	SW1	22	13	1	8	496	413	83	27	3
08-09	SW1	22	11	0	11	451	518	-67	22	6

BARNSTAPLE 2008-09

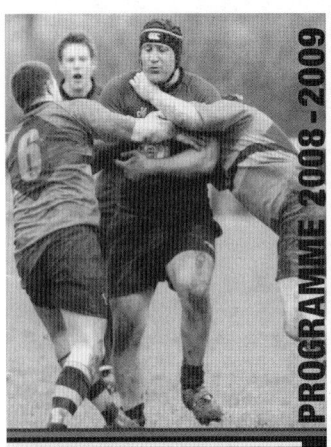

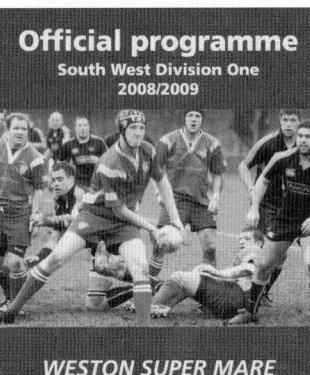

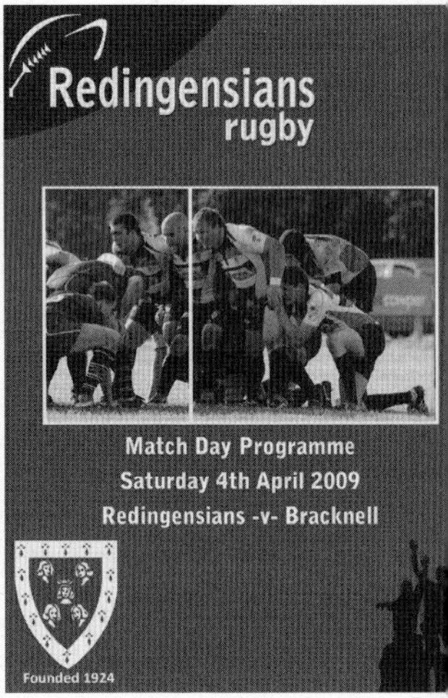

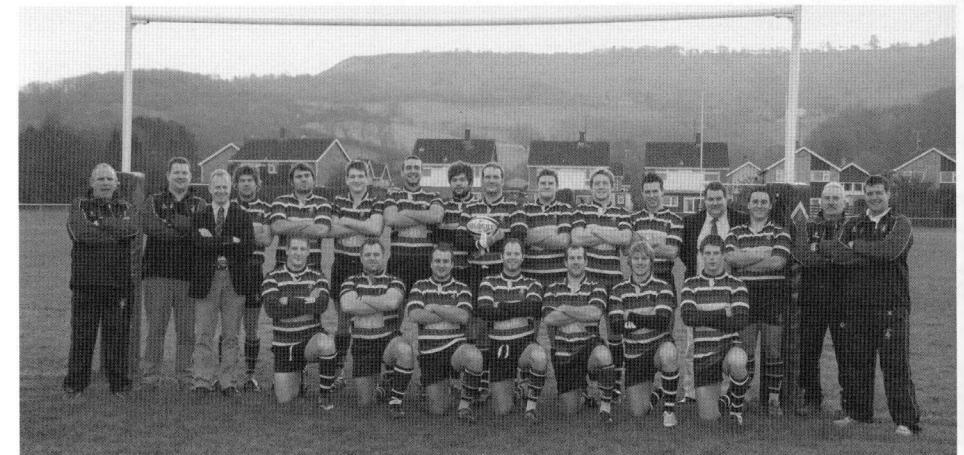

OLD PATESIANS 2008-09

SOUTH WEST PHOTO CALL

TAUNTON - South West Two West Champions 2008-09

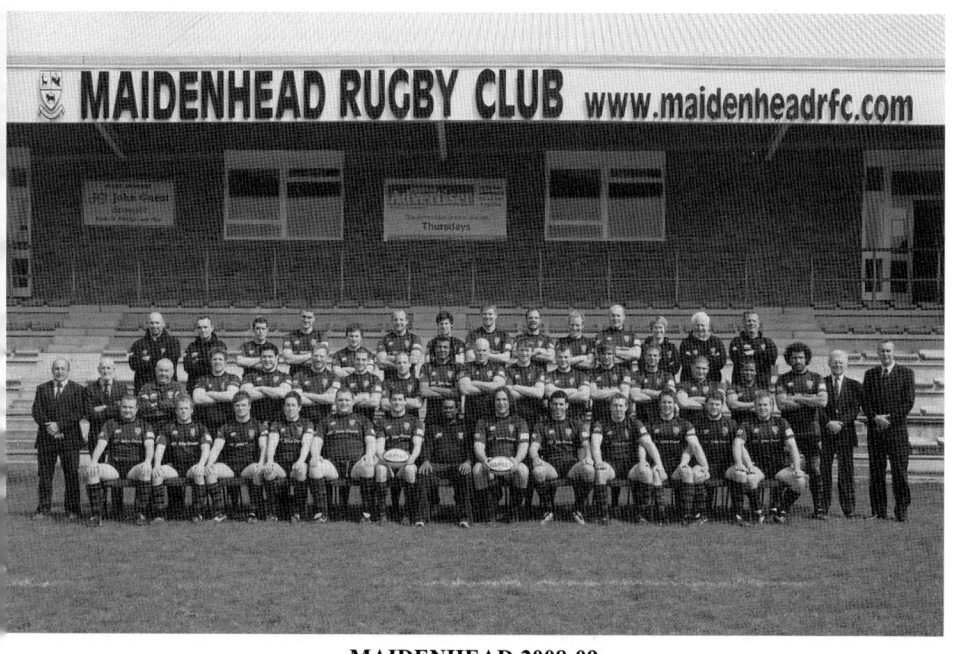

MAIDENHEAD 2008-09

SOUTH WEST ONE EAST

2008-09 LEAGUE TABLE SouthWest Two East

		P	W	D	L	F	A	PD	Pts	Adj
1	Maidenhead	22	21	0	1	773	206	567	42	0
2	Reading	22	19	0	3	946	252	694	38	0
3	Cheltenham	22	19	0	3	816	269	547	38	0
4	Swanage & Wareham	22	13	0	9	422	421	1	26	0
5	Salisbury	22	10	1	11	508	630	-122	21	0
6	Wallingford	22	11	0	11	431	424	7	20	-2
7	High Wycombe	22	10	0	12	328	498	-170	20	0
8	Trowbridge	22	9	0	13	498	538	-40	18	0
9	Olney	22	7	0	15	310	623	-313	14	0
10	Reading Abbey	22	5	0	17	294	567	-273	8	-2
11	Bletchley	22	4	0	18	254	690	-436	6	-2
12	Henley Wanderers	22	3	1	18	231	693	-462	5	-2

2009-10 FIXTURES GRID

	Bletchley	Buckingham	Cheltenham	High Wycombe	Marlow	Oakmeadians	Olney	Reading Abbey	Salisbury	Swanage & Wareham	Trowbridge	Walcot	Wallingford	Wootton Bassett
Bletchley		31/10	06/03	03/10	20/03	05/12	10/04	13/02	19/09	09/01	23/01	14/11	12/12	17/10
Buckingham	20/02		26/09	28/11	10/10	30/01	24/10	12/12	07/11	13/03	27/03	16/01	19/09	05/09
Cheltenham	07/11	09/01		27/03	30/01	24/10	20/02	19/09	13/03	28/11	05/09	10/10	03/10	12/12
High Wycombe	16/01	20/03	05/12		12/09	19/12	26/09	14/11	10/10	30/01	31/10	10/04	13/02	06/03
Marlow	28/11	23/01	17/10	12/12		07/11	13/03	03/10	27/03	05/09	19/09	13/02	31/10	09/01
Oakmeadians	27/03	17/10	13/02	19/09	06/03		28/11	23/01	05/09	12/12	09/01	31/10	14/11	03/10
Olney	05/09	13/02	31/10	09/01	14/11	20/03		17/10	12/12	19/09	03/10	06/03	05/12	23/01
Reading Abbey	24/10	12/09	19/12	13/03	16/01	10/10	30/01		20/02	07/11	28/11	26/09	05/09	27/03
Salisbury	19/12	06/03	14/11	23/01	05/12	10/04	12/09	31/10		03/10	17/10	20/03	09/01	13/02
Swanage & Wareham	26/09	14/11	20/03	17/10	10/04	12/09	19/12	06/03	16/01		13/02	05/12	23/01	31/10
Trowbridge	10/10	05/12	10/04	20/02	19/12	26/09	16/01	20/03	30/01	24/10		12/09	06/03	14/11
Walcot	13/03	03/10	23/01	05/09	24/10	20/02	07/11	09/01	28/11	27/03	12/12		17/10	19/09
Wallingford	12/09	19/12	16/01	24/10	20/02	13/03	27/03	10/04	26/09	10/10	07/11	30/01		28/11
Wootton Bassett	30/01	10/04	12/09	07/11	26/09	16/01	10/10	05/12	24/10	20/02	13/03	19/12	20/03	

BLETCHLEY R.U.F.C.

President: Paul Warren email: Paul.Warren@JacksonColes.co.uk 07802 468957
Chairman: Chris Goodman email: CJGatAGS@aol.com   Tel: 07831 622179
Secretary: Darren Davies   email: Darren.Davies@wirthresearch.com   Tel: 07917 114956
Treasurer: Mark Smith   email: mark.a.smith@bnymellon.com   Tel: 07765 253357
Fixtures Sec: Richard Jackaman   email: rj1221@sky.com   Tel: 07921 367436
Referees Contact: Paul Goffin   email: paul.goffin@dsl.pipex.com   Tel: 07966 455093
County Representative: David Parker   email: Bletchleyvps@aol.com   Tel: 07971 519156
Chair/Director of Rugby: Richard Jackaman   email: rj1221@sky.com   Tel: 07921 367436
Junior & Mini representative: Ken Rowe   email: klr@pt.com   Tel: 07921 367436
Ladies rugby contact: Louise Goffin,   email: ljgoffin@gmail.com,   Tel: 07973 797599
Ground Address: Bletchley RUFC, Manor Fields, Bletchley, Milton Keynes, Bucks MK2 2HX   Tel.: 01908 372298
Directions: Located on the southern edge of Milton Keynes access for cars is off Watling Street/V4 (the old A5). The turn-off is to the right when heading south from Fenny Stratford, after the bridges over the Grand Union Canal and the Great Ouse River, opposite Dobbies Garden Centre.
Clubhouse: open training eves, Sat pm & Sun am.Available for private hire.   **Club Shop:** Online via club website.
Founded: 1947   **Colours:** Maroon and white hoops   **Website:**   www.bletchleyrugby.com

BUCKINGHAM R.U.F.C.

President: Eric Curtis
Treasurer: Alan Leach   Tel: 01327 858778,   07957 551165   email: alan@leach.me.uk
Chairman: Mark Blackwell   Tel 01327 860719,   07767 870520   email: mark@blackwellprojects.co.uk
Club Secretary: Finlay Gemmell, 22 Elmfields Gate, Winslow, Bucks, MK18 3JG
Tel: 01296 714640,   07881 988380   email: finlay.gemmell@xerox.com
Fixtures Secretary: Paul Carr, Churchill Farmhouse, Church Hill Whaddon , Bucks, MK17 0LZ
Tel: 01908 502654,   07825 931046   email: paulcarr59@tiscali.co.uk
Team Secretary: Eric Curtis, 1 Queen St, Stony Stratford, MK11 1EG
Tel: 01908 562026, 07881 578614   email: happyhooker2@talktalk.net
Senior Coaches: Adam Izzard Tel: 07764 412539   &   Ben Wilson Tel: 07786 243130
Youth Chairman: Ed Gurney   Tel: 07778 673359   **Mini Rugby Coordinator:** James Weir   Tel: 07710 126660
Ground Address: The Floyd Field, Maids Moreton, Nr Buckingham MK18 1RF
Tel: 01280 815474   email: clubcaptain@buckinghamrugby.com   **Website:** www.buckinghamrugby.co.uk
Directions: From Buckingham town centre take the A413 towards Towcester
After approx 0.5 miles, the ground is on the right as you approach Maids Moreton village.
Capacity: Unlimited uncovered standing   **Car Parking:** for150 cars.   **Matchday Admission:** £2 with programme
Clubhouse: Open Saturday and Sunday match days.   Available for hire, contact   Julie Nichols on 07921 002353
Club Shop: Match days and on line shop, contact Simon Smith   07748 180809
Programme: Size: A5   Pages: 8   Price: with admission   Contact: Tony Hinton   07788 410684
Founded: 1933   **Colours:** Green with white hoops   **Training Nights:** Tues & Thur.

CHELTENHAM R.F.C.

President: Keith Plain **Chairman:** Steve Ratcliffe **Vice Chairman:** Dave Mason
Secretary: David Evans, Cliff Cottage, Leckhampton Hill, Cheltenham, GL53 9QG
Tel: 01242 514519 (M) 07970 713585 email: davidevans@cliffcottage.demon.co.uk
Fixtures Secretary: Mike Edwards, 1 The Old Bakery, Well Lane, Guiting Power, GL54 5UP Tel: 01451 850232
Business Manager: Mal Place Tel: 01242 672725
Director of Rugby: Liam Middleton 07769 722731 (M) **Rugby Manager:** Jeff McMahon Tel: 07722 019185 (M)
Ground Address: Prince of Wales Stadium, Tommy Taylors Lane, Cheltenham, Glos GL50 4NJ
Tel: Clubhouse: 01242 525393 Office / Fax: 01242 522085 email: info@cheltenhamtigers.com
Directions: From **North**: M5 J10, follow signs to Cheltenham Recreation Centre, St Pauls. From **South**: Off at J11 of M5, Turn left at GCHQ traveling to the end of Princess Elizabeth Way. Follow signs to Cheltenham Recreation Centre, St Pauls.
Nearest BR Station: Cheltenham Spa **Car Parking:** 300 on ground
Capacity: 3000 Covered Seating: 500 **Admission:** Matchday - Adults £4, Concessions £2 Season £45
Clubhouse: Mon – Thurs 6.30-10pm, Sat 11am-11pm & Sun 10am-2pm. The clubhouse is always available for private hire, contact Clubhouse manager Rod Hands 01242 525393 **Club Shop:** Newlands Park 10-1pm
Programme: Size: A5 Price: £1 Pages: 6 Editor: Dave Banyard
Advertising: From £200 per page/per season, contact Dave Banyard
Founded: 1889 **Nickname:** Town or Tigers **Website:** www.cheltenhamtigers.com
Colours: Red & black **Change colours:** Light blue **Training Nights:** Tuesday & Thursday

HIGH WYCOMBE R.U.F.C.

President: Bill Page 01494 868114 (H) email:wlpage@btinternet.com
Treasurer: Dave Peasley 01494 447549 (H) email:dave_peasley@yahoo.co.uk
Chairman: Ross MacKerron 01844 354011 email:rbmackerron@aol.com
Club Secretary: Don Dickerson, 3 Talbot Avenue, High Wycombe, Bucks. HP13 5HZ
01494 532024 (H) email: d.dickerson@sky.com
Fixture Secretary: Terry Brown, Deerleap, Primrose Hill, Widmer End, High Wycombe, Bucks. HP15 6HU
01494 716390 (H) email: terry.brown715@talktalk.net
Team Secretary: Mike Baud, 2 Littleworth Road, Downley, High Wycombe, Bucks. HP15 7AN
01494 528084 (H) email: michael.baud@btinternet.com
Chairman of Rugby: Mike Cussell 01494 569456 (H) email:mike@b-loony.co.uk
Youth Section Chairman: Glenn Gavin 01494 521528 (H) email:glenn.gavin@btinternet.com
Juniors Manager: Mike Banton 01494 521528 (H) email:mike.banton@hwrufc.com
Minis Manager: Mrs Mary Auton 01442 266898 (H) email:paul.auton@btinternet.com
Ground Address: Kingsmead Road, High Wycombe, Bucks HP11 1JB Tel: 01494 524407 **Website:** www.hwrufc.com
Directions: M40 J4 to A404 (Amersham) into town centre. Right on r'about onto A40 (Beaconsfield). After 3rd mini roundabout turn right into Abbey Barn Road. After 800 metres sharp left into Kingsmead road. Club on 800 metres on left. **Nearest BR Station:** High Wycombe
Capacity: Unlimited uncovered standing. **Admission:** Matchday - £2 incl. programme. **Car Parking:** 40 cars on site
Clubhouse: Variable opening hours. Food available Sat afternoons & Sun lunch. Functions contact Don Dickerson, Club Sec.
Club Shop: Open Sat afternoons & Sun lunchtime. **Colours:** Narrow black, green & white hoops **Change colours:** Black & green
Formed: 12.01.1929 (Present club) originally 1891 **Nickname:** 'Wycs' **Training Nights:** Tuesday & Thursday
Programme: Size: A5 Pages: 32 Price: £2 Editor: Don Dickerson Advertising: Page £150, 1/2 Page £80, both + VAT

MARLOW R.F.C.

President: Peter Bradley email: president@ **Chairman:** Gwyn Stone email: chairman@
Vice Chairman: Rob Thompson **Director of Finance:** Clifford Perkins
Club Secretary: Paul Kuiken, 45B Totteridge Lane, High Wycombe, Bucks. HP13 7QD Tel: 07967 701811 email: secretary@
Fixtures Secretary: Leighton Jones Tel: 07810 636962 email: fixtures@
Director of Marketing & Evenst: Linda Gillespie Refer enquiries to club office number email: office@
Club Captain: Chris Brooke-Carter email: clubcaptain@
Director of Mini Rugby: Tim Platt email: minis@
Director of Communications & PR: Edward Pringle-Stacey Tel: 07775 537714 email: communications@
Director Administration: Alan Sivers email: admin@
All unfinished email addresses are @marlowrfc.com, also cc the office as a second port of call
Ground Address: Marlow RFC, Riverwoods, Marlow, Buckinghamshire SL7 1QU
Tel: Main clubhouse: 01628-477054 Club Office Tel/Fax: 01628 483971 email: office@marlowrfc.com
Directions: For detailed map please see website. **Admission:** Matchday £3, Season not available.
Capacity: Unlimited uncovered standing **Car Parking:** Ample parking at ground **Nearest Station:** Marlow
Clubhouse: 7 days per week. Food & drink available 1st XV matches. Available to hire for private functions. Contact Office.
Club Shop: Open Sat & Sun, also on-line. **Programme:** A5, 18 pages, Price with admission, Editor: Ed Pringle-Stacey see above.
Founded: 1947 (3rd Feb.) **Website:** www.marlowrfc.com
Colours: Black, white & gold hoops **Change colours:** White, black & gold hoops **Training Nights:** Tues & Thur. (Seniors)

OAKMEDIANS R.F.C.

President: Peter Feltham Tel. 01202 766075 **Chairman**: Contact President
Treasurer: Duncan Stone Tel. 01202 706240
Club Secretary: Rebecca Davies, 79 Everest Road, Christchurch, BH23 3AZ
Tel: 07758 991777 email: r.davies79@btinternet.com
Fixtures Secretary: Steve Warrington, 48 Gordon Road, Poole, Dorset, BH12 1EB
Tel: 01202 763709 (H) 01258 830300 (B) email: steven.warrington@virgin.net
League Secretary: George Jones Tel: 01305 771284 (works fax. 01305 838600) email: mr.taff@gejones.f2s.com
Director of Rugby: James Croker Tel: 07727 095810 email: jamesthecoach@hotmail.com
Club House Manager: Dave Hart Tel: 01202 770602 email: janehart1962@aol.com
Ground Address: Oakmeadians RFC, The Clubhouse, Central Drive, Meyrick Park, Bournemouth, BH2 6LJ
Tel: 01202 789497 email: info@oakmeadians-rfc.com
Directions: From junction of A35 Wessex Way and A347 Wimborne Road turn onto A347 Wimborne Road. Take 1st left into Braidley Road. At the r'about at the end of Braidley Road turn right. At the T junction turn right. Car park on the left and ground on right.
Capacity: All uncovered standing   **Admission**: By programme   **Car Parking**: Off Central Drive   **Nearest Station**:
Clubhouse: Open 7 days a week. Hot meals, snacks & confectionary available. Available for private hire.
Contact Dave Hart 07813 718668   **Club Shop**: 7 days a week contact manager Jane Hart 07813 718668
Programme: Size: A5   Pages: Vary   Price: £3   Editorial & Advertising : James Minney 07706 139743
Founded: 1963   **Nickname**: The Bears   **Website**: www.oakmeadians-rfc.com
Colours: Blue, white horizontal bands   **Change colours**: Green   **Training Nights**: Tues & Thur. eves.

OLNEY R.F.C.

President: Mannie Howkins   Tel: 01908 551411   email: mannie.howkins@btinternet.com
Hon. Chairman: Stuart Parkin   Tel: 01234 711792   email: stuart@stuartparkin.freeserve.co.uk
Hon. Treasurer: Chris Talbot   Tel: 01234 305765   email: christalbot@ntlworld.com
Hon. Secretary: Mike Bebbington, 51 Elmlea Drive, Olney, Bucks MK46 5HU
Tel: 01234 714640   07733 216027   email: mikebebbington@btinternet.com
Fixture Secretary: David Middleditch; 6 Mayfield Road, Spinney Hill, Northampton NN3 2RE Tel: 07916 302701
Chairman of Mini & Junior Section: Dave Combes
Tel: (H) 01908 615359 (M) 07841 047464 email: dave.combes@talktalk.net
Ground Address: The Recreation Ground, East Street Olney Bucks. MK46 4DW
Tel.: 01234 712780   email: info@olneyrfc.co.uk
Directions: From Newport Pagnell M1 J14 take A509 north.
On entering Olney, pass church and right at Market place, left into East Street. Ground 300 yards on right.
Club Shop: Contact Alec Tebby, or visit our on-line shop
Founded: 1877   **Training Nights**: Tuesday & Thursday 7pm   **Website**: www.olneyrfc.co.uk
Colours: Cerise and French Grey Hoops

READING ABBEY R.F.C.

President: Ray Hocking   **Chairman**: Colin Northey   **Treasurer**: Rod Ward
Club & Team Secretary: Scott Mansfield, 92 Wayside Green, Woodcote RG8 0QJ
Tel: 01491 680386 (H) 07815 496088 (M) email:secretary@readingabbeyrfc.co.uk
Fixture Secretary: Mrs Lynne Lee, Cotswold, Behoes Lane, Woodcote, Reading RG8 0PP
Tel: 01491 680102 (H)   email: fixtures@readingabbeyrfc.org
Director of Rugby: Peter Lucek
Ground Address: Rosehill, Peppard Road, Emmer Green, Reading, RG4 8XA   Tel: 0118 972 2881
Directions: North of Reading on B481 Caversham to Sonning Common road, 1 mile on the left after leaving the built up area. Full directions on web site.
Nearest BR station: Reading   **Car Parking**: 100 hard standing + overflow for 500+
Capacity: Ample uncovered standing   Covered: 40   **Admission**: Matchday £3 .   Season not available
Clubhouse: Open Tues, Thur & Fri 8-11pm, Sat 12-11pm, Sun 12-2pm.. Functions: Seat up to 120; buffet for 250; hall capacity 300. Contact Rod Ward, Tel: 0118 941 9163 (H) 0118 945 5511 (B) 07801 318553(M)
Club Shop: Thur, Sat & Sun when club is open. Contact Ian / Paula Machin.
Programme: Size: A5   Pages: 16   Price: £2   Editor: Brian Rennell
Founded: 1956   **Nickname**: Abbey   **Website**: www.abbeyrfc.org
Colours: Navy blue, green and white   **Change colours**: Red   **Training Nights**: Tuesday & Thursday 7pm

SALISBURY R.F.C.
President: Bob Baker
Chairman: David Murley Tel: 01722 327728 email: david.murley@sotonct.co.uk
Club Secretary: Dr G W Jack, 14 Windlesham Road, Salisbury, Wilts SP1 3PY
Tel: (H) 01722 335542 email: g.w.jack@talk21.com
Fixture Secretary / Team Secretary: Neil Bowditch, 8, Swaynes House, 64, Winchester Street, Salisbury.
Tel: 01722 504575 email: .bowditch@ntlworld.com
Director of Rugby: Mark Rogers   **Sponsorship:** Ronnie Mussell 01722 339779
Match officials contact: Adrian Wood 01722 325051
Ground Address: Castle Road, Salisbury, Wiltshire SP1 3SA   Tel: 01722 325717   email: enq@salisburyrfc.org
Directions: On A345 on north side of Salisbury just south of Old Sarum   **Nearest BR station:** Salisbury
Capacity: 450, all uncovered standing: **Admission:** £3   **Car Parking:** 150
Clubhouse: Open 19:00-23:00 Mon-Fri, 12:00-23:00 Sat 12:00-02:00 Sun. 12noon-11.30pm.
For food availablity and functions contact Terry Taylor at the clubhouse.
Club Shop: Open Sunday 10am - 1pm. Contact Nicki Cooper
Programme: Size: A5   Pages: 48   Price: with admission   Advertising: Ronnie Mussell
Founded: 1923   **Website:** www.salisburyrfc.org
Colours: Green & white   **Change colours:** Blue and gold   **Training Nights:** Tuesdays and Thursdays

SWANAGE & WAREHAM R.F.C.
President: John Burgess   **Chairman:** Steve Orchard CBE   **Treasurer:** Paul Thomas
Club Secretary: Kevin Large, 20 Gannets Park, Swanage. Tel 01929 426523 / 426716 email centaur-fs@btconnect.com
Fixture Secretary: John Constable, Grand View, Puddletown Road, Worgret, Wareham, Dorset.
Tel: 01929-551468 email: j.constable@swansrugby.freeserve.co.uk
League Contact: Ray Graves Tel: 01929 554290
Chairman Coaching Committee: Bob Croom
Chair Mini and Youth Section: Lee Cockwell   01929554894   e-mail   leecockwell@hotmail.com
Ground Address: Bestwall, Wareham, Dorset BH20 4HY   Tel: 01929 552224
Directions: Signposted from crossroads in Wareham town centre. See website for maps.   **Nearest BR Station**: Wareham
Capacity: All uncovered standing.   **Admission:** Matchday £3   **Car Parking:** Plenty at ground.
Clubhouse: Open Sat from 1.30pm (closed during match) & Sun from 11.30am.   Contact Anna Jones   07944248633 e-mail annajones@talktalk.net
Kit Sales: Contact Donna Jaques Tel: 01202 669788, 07931 290506 (M)
Formed: 1953   **Nickname**: The Swans   **Website**: www.swansrugby.co.uk
Colours: Maroon and white   **Change colours:** n/a   **Training Nights**: Tuesday & Thursday

TROWBRIDGE R.F.C.
Hon. President: John Elliott   **Hon. Finance Manager**: Christopher Lamb
Honorary Secretary: Christopher Lamb; 3 Coppice Wood, West Ashton Road, Trowbridge Wilts BA14 6DN
Tel: 01225 751119   email: chrisf.lamb@btopenworld.com
Fixtures Secretary: Alistair Morrison 22 Campion Drive Trowbridge Wilts. BA14 0XZ
Tel: (H) 01225 755135 (M) 07963 640890   Email: alistair.morrison@blueyonder.co.uk
Head Coach: Mac McHugh   Tel: 07976 848927 (M)
Ground Address: Trowbridge RFC, Ashton Park, Green Lane, Trowbridge, Wilts. BA14 7DJ
Tel.: 01225 761389   email: info@trowbridgerfc.co.uk
Directions: 1. From Devizes (A361) - at 2nd roundabout turn left and after 200 yards turn left into Green Lane.
2. From Frome/Bath - follow signs into Trowbridge then towards Devizes - on dual carriageway go under pedestrian bridge by Tescos. Turn right
Founded: 18th Dec. 1931   **Training Nights:** Seniors - Tues & Thur 7.30
Website: www.trowbridgerfc.co.uk
Colours: Light blue, dark blue and gold hoops

WALCOT R.F.C.

President: John Gifford   **Chairman:** Simon Chambers   **Treasurer:** Simon Chambers
Hon Secretary: Simon Morgan, 125 Lymore Avenue, Bath BA2 1AX
Tel. 01225 335426   email shmorgan@tiscali.co.uk
Fixtures Secretary: Gerry Wheeler, 28 Priddy Close, Frome, Somerset BA11 2XZ
Tel: (H) 01373 469688   email: geraldwheeler@btinternet.com
Youth Organiser: Gary Dagger, 65 Marsden Road, Kingsway, Bath, BA2 2LQ
Tel: 01225 330497 (H)   07909 983127 (M)   email gary.dagger@yahoo.com
Club Captain: James Gay
Ground Address: Albert Field, Lansdown, Bath, Somerset BA1 9BJ   Tel.: 01225 330199
Directions: Follow the signs from City centre to Lansdown, proceed along top towards racecourse/golf club halfway on right is ground opposite the bus park and ride site. Map available on the website.
Nearest BR station: Bath Spa   **Car Parking:** Space for 80 cars, plus additional parking opposite ground.
Capacity: 500, all uncovered standing   **Admission:** Matchday £3
Clubhouse: Open training nights and matchdays.   Snacks available.
Clubhouse available for private function hire contact 07733 404307.
Programme: Size: A5   Price: with admission.   Advertising: Contact Matt Hall email: matt@ripedigital.co.uk
Colours: Black & white hoops.   **Change colours:** Light blue.
Founded: 1882   **Website:** www.walcotrugby.co.uk   **Training Nights:** Tuesday & Thursday.

WALLINGFORD R.F.C.

President: Nick Castle Tel: 01491 641669, 07802 305540 (M)   email: nick@ncastle.fs.net.co.uk
Chairman: Jerry Walters Tel: 01491 833194, 07765 091359 (M)   email: jerrywalters@btopenworld.com
Hon. Treasurer: Rae Young Tel: 07792 166792 (M)   email: raeyoung1977@yahoo.co.uk
Hon. Secretary: Bill Strang, 4 Aston Close, Wallingford, Oxon, OX10 9AY.
Tel: 07780 991408   email bill.strang@hotmail.co.uk
Hon. Fixtures Secretary: Martin Hoare
Tel: 01491 834485,   Mobile: 07747 800633 or 07918 646581   email: martin.hoare3@btinternet.com
Club Captain & Club Coach: Chris Norrington   Tel: 01491 834427,   07050 041464 (M)   email: nozz@btinternet.com
Ground Address: Hithercroft Sports Park, Hithercroft Road, Wallingford OX10 9ES
Tel.: 01491 833194   email: rugby@wallingfordrfc.com
Directions: From Didcot on the A4130 go past Brightwell-cum-Sotwell on right and come to r'bout and turn right on to Wallingford by-pass. First r'bout on bypass turn left and ground on left after 100 yards. From Reading/Oxford direction then go on to bypass from A4074 and go straight over two r-abouts one after each other and over railway crossing and then next r-about turn right and ground entrance 100 yards on the left.
Club Shop: see website for merchandise
Website: www.wallingfordrfc.com
Colours: Amber & Black   **Training Nights:** Tuesday & Thursday 7pm

WOOTTON BASSETT R.F.C.

President: Mark Wightman   **Chairman:** Chris Elias   **Treasurer:** Terry Aylett
Club Secretary: Roger Harries, 7 Homefield, Wootton Bassett SN48 DE
Tel: 01793 852358 Fax: 01793 855234   email: Roger.harries@ineos-nova.com
Fixtures Secretary: Jim Brierley, 25 Broad Town Rd, Broad Town, SN4 7RB
Tel: 01793 731810   email: laurajim@brierleybroadtown.freeserve.co.uk
Team Secretary & Senior Playing Manager: Ted Edwards, 11 Middle Ground, Woodshaw, Wootton Bassett SN4 8LJ
Tel: 07919 533899   email: Frosty.ted@btinternet.com
Marketing and Sponsorship Manager: Jon Spillane email: Jon.spillane@infor.com
Mini/Junior Playing Manager: Steve Cameron   Tel: 07876 147487   email: rugby.balls@btopenworld.com
Youth Playing Manager: Steve Pinniger, stevepinniger@aol.com
Ground Address: Rylands Field, Stonover Lane , Wootton Bassett SN4 8QX   Tel: 01793 851745
Directions: J16 M4, towards Wootton Bassett, straight over roundabout, next left, 300m on left
Capacity: All uncovered standing   **Car Parking:** For 50 cars   **Nearest Station:** Swindon
Clubhouse: Open Tues-Fri 19.30-23.00, Sat 11.30-23.30, Sun 12.00- 22.30. Food available.
Available for private hire, contact Les Birch, 01793 851425   **Club Shop:** Open Sat & Sun, contact Mark Roshier.
Programme: A5, 8 pages, £2   Editor & Advertising: Jim Brierley, as above
Founded: 1971   **Nickname:** Wiltshire All Blacks   **Website:** www.bassettrfc.com
Colours: All black   **Change colours:** Red shirts, black shorts   **Training Nights:** Tues & Thur.

SOUTH WEST ONE WEST

2008-09 LEAGUE TABLE SouthWest Two West

		P	W	D	L	F	A	PD	Pts	Adj
1	Taunton	22	22	0	0	820	217	603	44	0
2	Newton Abbot	22	18	0	4	630	224	406	36	0
3	Avonmouth Old Boys	22	17	0	5	534	322	212	34	0
4	St Ives (SW)	22	12	2	8	424	320	104	26	0
5	Sidmouth	22	11	0	11	406	441	-35	22	0
6	Paignton	22	10	1	11	408	467	-59	21	0
7	Brixham	22	9	1	12	364	473	-109	19	0
8	Torquay Athletic	22	8	1	13	405	410	-5	17	0
9	Clevedon	22	7	1	14	368	534	-166	15	0
10	Yatton	22	6	1	15	285	545	-260	13	0
11	St Mary's Old Boys (SW)	22	6	0	16	334	635	-301	10	-2
12	Walcot	22	2	1	19	221	611	-390	3	-2

2009-10 FIXTURES GRID

	Avonmouth O.B.	Brixham	Chosen Hill F.P.	Clevedon	Cullompton	Hartpury College	Ivybridge	Newton Abbot	Paignton	Sidmouth	St Ives (SW)	St Mary's O.B. (SW)	Torquay Athletic	Yatton
Avonmouth Old Boys		12/09	19/12	26/09	16/01	10/10	30/01	24/10	20/02	07/11	13/03	28/11	27/03	05/09
Brixham	12/12		26/09	16/01	10/10	30/01	24/10	20/02	07/11	13/03	28/11	27/03	05/09	19/12
Chosen Hill F. P.	19/09	09/01		10/10	30/01	24/10	20/02	07/11	13/03	28/11	27/03	05/09	12/12	03/10
Clevedon	09/01	03/10	23/01		24/10	20/02	07/11	13/03	28/11	27/03	05/09	12/12	19/09	17/10
Cullompton	03/10	23/01	17/10	13/02		07/11	13/03	28/11	27/03	05/09	12/12	19/09	09/01	31/10
Hartpury College	23/01	17/10	13/02	31/10	06/03		28/11	27/03	05/09	12/12	19/09	09/01	03/10	14/11
Ivybridge	17/10	13/02	31/10	06/03	14/11	20/03		05/09	12/12	19/09	09/01	03/10	23/01	05/12
Newton Abbot	13/02	31/10	06/03	14/11	20/03	05/12	10/04		19/09	09/01	03/10	23/01	17/10	12/12
Paignton	31/10	06/03	14/11	20/03	05/12	10/04	12/09	19/12		03/10	23/01	17/10	13/02	09/01
Sidmouth	06/03	14/11	20/03	05/12	10/04	12/09	19/12	26/09	16/01		17/10	13/02	31/10	23/01
St Ives (SW)	14/11	20/03	05/12	10/04	12/09	19/12	26/09	16/01	10/10	30/01		31/10	06/03	13/02
St Mary's O.B. (SW)	20/03	05/12	10/04	12/09	19/12	26/09	16/01	10/10	30/01	24/10	20/02		14/11	06/03
Torquay Athletic	05/12	10/04	12/09	19/12	26/09	16/01	10/10	30/01	24/10	20/02	07/11	13/03		20/03
Yatton	10/04	19/12	16/01	30/01	20/02	13/03	27/03	12/09	26/09	10/10	24/10	07/11	28/11	

AVONMOUTH OLD BOYS R.F.C.
President: Rodney Kennett   **Chairman**: Steve Leyshon   **Treasurer**: Steve Leyshon
Hon. Secretary: Rodney Kennett, 41 Woodland Grove, Bristol BS9 2BD
Tel: (H) 0117 968 3598   email: chris.rodkennett@btinternet.com
Fixtures Secretary: Andy Woodruff, 69 Priory Road, Shirehampton, Bristol BS11 9TF
Tel: (H) 0117 9833066   (W) 0117 936 3066   (M) 07793 904926   email: andy.woodruff@airbus.com
Chairman of Rugby: Ted Britton   **Head Coach**: Wayne Hone   **Club Captain**: Grant Britton
Ground Address: Barracks Lane, Avonmouth, Bristol BS11 9NG   Tel.: 0117 982 9093
Directions: Exit the M5 at J 18 and follow signs for Shirehampton. At the Avonmouth Roundabout take the first exit onto the B4054. Drive back under the M5 Avonmouth Bridge. Take the first left into Barracks Lane. Mind the speed ramps and the Clubhouse is at the end of the lane - and the bar is probably open!
Nearest BR Station: Avonmouth via Bristol Temple Meads.   **Car Parking**: Adequate at ground.
Capacity: All uncovered standing   **Admission**: Free
Clubhouse: Available for private hire, contact Club Steward Paul Sollars
Colours: Red / Black   **Change colours**: White   **Training Nights**: Seniors - Tues & Thur 7.30; Juniors - Wed 6pm
Founded: 1897   **Nickname**: 'The Mouth'   **Website**: www.avonmouthrfc.co.uk

BRIXHAM R.F.C.
President: J D Irvine Esq BEM   **Chairman**: Chris Forster   **Treasurer**: Steve Shipway
Secretary: Bob Houston, St Cloud. Cliff Park. Road. Paignton .TQ4 5NB Tel: 01803 550427 email: bobhouston@fclnet.com
Fixture & Match Secretary: Andrew Forster, 33 Wishings Road. Brixham.TQ 5 9 SG
Tel: 01803 851657 (H)   07717045552 (M)   email: andrew.d.forster@btinternet.com
Director of Rugby: Steve Shipway 01803 855138
Youth Chairman & Secretary: Brian Pitman Tel: 01803 859202 (H) 0780310401 (M) email:bryan@pitman33.freeserve.co.uk
Press Officer: Phillip Wills Tel: 01803 882162 (b) 01803 855425 (h) 07979784091 (m) email phil@brixhamrugby.org
Club Registrar & League Contact: Glyn Jenkins Tel: 01803 859424, 07879 040836, email: gm.jenkins@virgin.net
Ground Address: Astley Park, Rea Barn Road, Brixham, Devon TQ5 9EA Tel: 01803 882162 (Bar) 01803 855511 (O) email: as Press Off.
Directions: Follow signs for Torbay. Pick up A 3022. Follow signs for Brixham. On entering Brixham follow signs for Berry Head Country Park or marina car park. Club is on route to either.t.   **Car Parking**: 200   **Nearest BR station**: Paignton
Capacity: 4,000 Covered Seating: 150   **Admission**: Matchday £4 incl programme. Season: £60
Clubhouse: Open 11-11.30pm daily. Food available matchdays only. Function contact Mrs Karen Harvey 01803 882162
Club Shop: Match days only. Contact Steve McKee 01803 853542 (H)   0788 796770 email: Mckeestev@aol.com
Programme: **Size**: A5   **Pages**: 32   **Price**: with admission   **Editor**: Phil Wills 01803 882162 (B) 01803 855425 (H)
Advertising: Page: £150, 1/2 page: £80, 1/4 page £40. contact Mike Walker 01803 856735
Founded: 1874   **Nickname**: The Fishermen   **Website**: www.brixhamrugby.com
Colours: Black with white band   **Change colours**: Red or royal blue   **Training Nights**: Tuesday & Thursday 7-9pm.

CHOSEN HILL F.P. R.F.C.

President: Mrs Sue Turner   **Chairman:** Bob Savory   **Treasurer:** Julian Herbert
Hon. Secretary: Mr Dave Morris; 20 Moselle Drive Churchdown Gloucester GL3 2RY Tel: 01452 856955
Fixtures Secretary & Rugby Manager: Bill King Tel: 07733 154133
Ground Address: The Clubhouse, Brookfield Road, Chuchdown, Gloucestershire GL3 2PF
Tel: 01452 712384 email: chair@chosenhillrfc.co.uk
Directions: From the M5 Junction 11 take the exit for Cheltenham. Drive until the first roundabout and take the first exit. (Gloucester road). Take the first left turning. (for Churchdown). Drive for approx 1 mile over the humped railway bridge, until you reach the right turn for Churchdown. Turn toward Churchdown we are on the right just over the motorway bridge. Visit our web site for directions www.chosenhillrfc.co.uk
Capacity: All uncovered standing   **Car Parking:**   **Nearest Station:**
Clubhouse: Open Tues 6 - 10.30pm, Thur 6 - 11.30pm, Sat (Sep-May) 12.30 - 10pm, Sat (Jun-Aug) 1pm - 9pm, Sun 12 - 4.30pm. Available for private hire, contact The Clubhouse or Karen Masters - Clubhouse Manager Tel: 079178 70311
Club Shop: see website.   **Programme:** None
Founded: 1970   **Website:** www.chosenhillrfc.co.uk
Colours: Myrtle green & white   **Change colours:**   **Training Nights:** Tues & Thur.

CLEVEDON R.F.C.

President: Michael Thomas   **Chairman:** Dave Russell   **Hon. Treasurer:** James Hayward
Hon. Secretary: Paul Squires, Manesty, Duck Lane, Kenn, North Somerset BS21 6TP.
Tel 01275 877271. email: paulsquires@atworkappointments.co.uk
Fixture Secretary: Sue Davis 2 Newlands Green, Clevedon, North Somerset BS21 5BU Tel: 01275 877687
Team Secretary: Mike Thomas, 46 Treefield Road, Clevedon, BS21 6JB
Tel: 01275 875497 email: mikesthomas@tesco.net
Rugby Chairman: Tony Dauncey 07903 440717   **Club Coach:** Mike Rafter   **1st XV Captain:** James Shopland
Commercial Manager: Chris Knowles, 25 Dart Road, Clevedon, BS21 6LS Tel: 01275 875715
Youth Chairman: Russell Davis, 18, Porlock Road, Clevedon, BS216JN
Ground Address: Coleridge Vale Playing Fields, Southey Road, Clevedon, N Somerset BS21 6PF
Tel: 01275 877772   **Website:** www.clevedonrfc.co.uk
Directions: From M5 head towards town centre. Ground is opposite Safeway car park.   **Nearest BR Station:** Yatton
Capacity: Unlimited uncovered standing   **Admission:** £2   **Car Parking:** Limited spaces
Clubhouse & Club Shop: Opening hours vary, contact Commercial Secretary
Matchday programme: Pages: 12 Price: £2 Advertising; contact Commercial Secretary
Founded: 1921   **Nickname:** Cs   **Training Nights:** Tuesday & Thursday 6.30pm
Colours: Royal blue & old gold hooped shirts, navy shorts & socks   **Change colours:** Navy blue or black

CULLOMPTON R.F.C.

President: Maurice Gwynne   **Treasurer:** Helen Gwynne
Chairman: Viv Pring, 32 Bilbie Close, Cullompton, Devon EX15
Tel: 07794 572 420 email: vrpring@yahoo.com
Club Secretary: Helen Whitton; Brooklands, Brook Road, Cullompton, Devon EX15 1DS
Tel: 01884 33076 email: helenwhitton@btinternet.com
Fixtures Secretary: Derek Keeling, 7 Andrewallen Road, Rockwell Green, Wellington, Somerset TA21 9DY
Tel: 01823 660199 email: del2sal@btinternet.com
Coach: Charlie Mahon Tel: 0777 802 1643
Playing Chairman: Andy Knowles Tel: 07760 178 8658
Club Captain: Robbie Hammett Tel: 07894 725 752
Ground Address: Stafford Park, Knowle Lane, Cullompton, Devon EX15 1PZ Tel: 01884 32480
Directions: Leave M5 at J28 and go towards town centre. Turn right by Manor Hotel, past fire station, turn left to Langlands Rd, turn right at end of road, club at top of lane.
Founded: 1892   **Website:** www.cullomptonrugby.com
Colours: Red and black   **Change colours:**   **Training Nights:** Tues & Thur.

HARTPURY COLLEGE R.F.C.

Chairman: Malcolm Wharton, Principal of Hartpury college.
Club Secretary: Joanna Cawthorn, Hartpury College, Hartpury, Gloucester, GL19 3BE
Tel: 01452 702389   email: Joanna.cawthorn@hartpury.ac.uk
Fixtures Secretary: as Club Secretary
Director of Rugby: Allan Lewis   07967 384922
Coach: Chris Dewsnap   07545 171704
Ground Address: Hartpury College, Hartpury, Gloucester, GL19 3BE
Tel: 01452 702389   email: joanna.cawthorn@hartpury.ac.uk
Directions: Hartpury College is on the A417, 4 miles north of Gloucester. There may be heavy traffic around Gloucester, so you are advised to approach from the M5 or M50 motorways.
For detailed maps and directions please see website - www.hartpury.ac.uk/contact/directions.asp
Capacity: Ample standing plus 330 seat grandstand.   **Admission:** Free
Car Parking: Ample at college   **Nearest BR Station:** Gloucester
Clubhouse: None   **Club Shop:** None.   **Programme:** None
Founded: 2004   **Website:** www.hartpury.ac.uk
Colours: Red & black   **Change colours:** Predominantly black with red band

IVYBRIDGE R.F.C.

President: Alan Knight   **Chairman:** John Belcher   **Treasurer:** Treve Mitchell
Club Secretary: Will Willden, 8 Buddle Close, Ivybridge, Devon PL21 0JU
Tel: 07776 785552   email: willwillden@yahoo.com
Fixtures Secretary: Stephanie Newman, 10 Erme Mews, Park Street, Ivybridge, Devon PL21 9DP
Tel: 01752 896403,   07767 418385   email: wennam@aol.com
Director of Rugby: Spenser Owen   Tel: 07977 422305
Team Secretary: Robin Lumley, 6 Woolms Meadow, Ivybridge, Devon. PL21 9UF
Tel: 0783 333369   email: r.lumley@btinternet.com
Mini/Junior Chairman: Paul Setter 57 Pykes Down, Ivybridge Devon. PL21 0BY
Ground Address: Ivybridge RFC, Cross-in-Hand, Exeter Road, Ivybridge, Devon PL21 0JP   Tel: 01752 894352
Directions: From the A38, the main Exeter/Plymouth road, follow the Park & Ride signs. The Ground is almost opposite the station exit.   **Car Parking:** 100+ at ground.   **Nearest BR Station:** 400metres
Capacity: 1000 -all uncovered standing   Matchday admission: £2
Clubhouse: Open Tues-Fri 7-11pm, Sat 12-12, Sun 12-3pm. Available for private hire, contact club.
Club Shop: Open Fri 7-9pm and on matchdays. Also see website.   **Programme:** A5, 20 pages, Price with entry
Founded: Nov. 1975   **Nickname:** Bridgers   **Website:** www.ivybridgerugby.co.uk
Colours: Green and black   **Change colours:** Blue   **Training Nights:** Tues & Thur. (Seniors)

NEWTON ABBOT R.F.C.

President: Mr. Ian Glendinning   **Chairman:** Mr. Graham Rooke F.C.A email: grahamr@peplows.co.uk
Secretary: c/o Chairman - Graham Rooke   email: as above.
Tel: 01626 334701 (eves) 01626 208802 (daytime)   07710 522230 (M)
Fixtures Secretary: Mr. Roy Bryant, 26 Kiln Orchard Newton Abbot TQ12 1AN
Tel: (W). 01803 616180   (Eve) 01626 363014   email: Lorraine.Tate@stagecoachbus.com
Rugby Manager: Mr. Keith MacLean, 121 Exeter Rd Kingsteignton Newton Abbot TQ12 3NA
Tel: 01626 351493 (H) 01626 367620 (O)   email: keithmaclean@btconnect.com
Ground Address: Rackerhayes, Newton Rd, Kingsteignton,   Newton Abbot TQ12 3AD
Tel: 01626 354150   email: grahamr@peplows.co.uk
Directions: Leave A380 at Ware Barton Jct. Follow Sign to Racecourse turn Left at Fairway Roundabout then first Right. Ground is behind the Industrial Units.   **Nearest BR Station:** Newton Abbot   **Car Parking:** 50 Cars
Capacity: 1,000 Covered Seating: 120   **Admission** Prices: 1st XV Match day £5.00.   Season £30
Clubhouse: Open training evenings 6.30-10pm, matchdays 12-12pm & Sun 12-3pm.   Food available match days & Sunday. Functions contact Mrs. Sue MacLean Tel: Club 01626 354150, Home 01626 351493 email suecmac@fsmail.net.
Club shop: Open as clubhouse. Contact Mr. Phil Burford at Ground email: pburford@epwin.co.uk
Founded: 1883   **Nickname:** All Whites   **Training Nights:** Tuesday, Wednesday, Thursday
Colours: All white   **Change Colours:** Green or blue shirts   **Website:** www.allwhitesrugby.com
Programme: Size: A5   Pages: 40   Price: with admission   Editor: Russ Baker email russbaker_uk@yahoo.com
Advertising Contact: Richard Carus   email richard.carus@sky.com

SOUTH WEST

713

PAIGNTON R.F.C.

President: Norman Harries   **Chairman**: Steve Lambswood   **Treasurer**: Mick Claire
Honorary Secretary: Mrs Sue Hunt; 4 Lower Polsham Road, Paignton, Devon TQ3 2AF
Tel: 01803 524444,   08974 148241   email: sue.hunt@devon.gov.uk
Fixture Secretary: Mr Neil Stoddard; 1 Kingsway Court, Paignton Devon TQ4 7AR
Tel: 07963 370952   email: stoddsandturvs@talktalk.net
Ground Address: Queens Park, Queens Road, Paignton, Devon TQ4 6AT
Tel: 01803 559382   email: information@paigntonrugby.net
Directions: From M5/A38 follow signs to Torbay then Paignton. After Kingskerswell turn right at r'about to Paignton. Turn left at third r'about (town centre & seafront). Traffic lights at bottom of hill turn right. Get into one way system. just before station turn left over railway track. Take 3rd right (Queens Road) clubhouse / grounds on the right
Capacity: Unlimited uncovered standing
Nearest BR Station: Paignton   **Parking**: None at ground
Admission: £4
Club Shop: Open matchdays 12-6pm, Sundays 10.30-2pm
Founded: 1883   **Nickname**: Cherries   **Website**: www.rfu.com/clubs/paignton
Colours: Red & white hoops   **Change colours**: Blue and black

SIDMOUTH R.F.C.

Chairman: Terry O'Brien (see Fixtures Sec.)
Hon. Secretary: Colin Chesterton, Everys, 104 High Street, Sidmouth, Devon Ex10 8EF
Tel 01395 577983   email: colin.chesterton@everys.co.uk
Fixtures Sec.: Terry O'Brien, Rivulet Cottages, 2 Church Street, Sidford, Sidmouth, Devon EX10 9RD
Tel: 01395 577403   email: tobrien@sidmouthrfc.co.uk
Hon. Treasurer: Paul Whitehouse, Little Gables, Redwood Road, Sidmouth EX10 9AB
Tel 01395 579818   email: pwhitehouse@sidmouthrfc.co.uk
Match / Referee Liaison: Robert Baugh Tel 01392 252016
Ground Address: The Blackmore Field Heydon's Lane Sidmouth Devon EX10 8NJ
Contact Tel.: 01395 516786   email: cdunford@sidmouthrfc.co.uk   Website: www.sidmouthrfc.co.uk
Directions: PLEASE NOTE THERE IS NO PARKING AT THE GROUND. From M5 Junction 30 take A3052 to Sidmouth/Lyme Regis. After about 10 miles take right turn to Sidmouth opposite The Bowd Inn. After 2 miles go straight across mini roundabout (Woodlands Hotel on right). After 200 metres stop at junction with zebra crossing. This is drop off point for coaches (coaches turn right to coach park). Walk down Coburg Road on left and turn first left into Heydon's Lane, 50 metres to the ground. Supporters travelling by car can park free and walk at East Devon Council Offices 1/4 mile before Woodlands Hotel.
Formed: 1884   **Training Nights**: Tuesday & Thursday 7pm   **Colours**: Green shirts, black shorts

ST. IVES R.F.C.

President: Charles Guppy   **Chairman**: Andrew Baragwanath   **Vice Chairman**: Denis Preece
Club Secretary: Julie Rowe, 'Tally Ho', St Anta Road, Carbis Bay, St Ives, Cornwall, TR26 2LE.
Tel: 01736 798155 (H), 01736 795346   email: julie.rowe@btinternet.com
Fixture Secretary: Mike Gee, 'Fox Glove Cottage', 70 Halsetown, St. Ives, Cornwall TR26 3LZ
Tel: (H) 01736 797777   email: secretary@swrugby.co.uk
Director of Rugby: Ian Morgan   **First XV Manager**: Ian Deacon
President Mini/Junior Section: Brian Prisk Tel.: 01736 793420, Mob: 07759 343 153
Ground Address: The Clubhouse, Alexandra Road, St Ives, Cornwall TR27 1ER
Tel: 01736 795346 / 794166   email: info@stives-rfc.co.uk   Website: www.stives-rfc.co.uk
Directions:: From Lelant, follow holiday route into St Ives, turn left after garage. Map available on the website.
Admission: Matchday £5.   **Nearest BR station**: St Ives.   **Car Parking**: 300 cars.
Clubhouse: Evenings 7 - 11pm.; Sat: Noon - 1am. Food avaiable on match days. The clubhouse is available for private hire, contact Club Steward on 01736 795346.
Founded: 1887.   **Nickname**: The Hakes   **Training Nights**: Tuesdays and Thursdays.
Colours: Blue and white shirts, navy shorts & socks   **Change colours**: White and blue shirts.
Programme: Size: A5   Pages: 56   Price: with admission   Editor:

ST. MARY'S O.B. R.F.C.

President: Mr Robert Irving   **Chairman:** Dr John Redmond   **Treasurer:** Mr Kenneth Squires
Club Secretary: Mrs Gay Brewer, 19 Burchells Green Road, Kingswood, Bristol BS15 1DT
Tel: (H) 0117 961 4104 (M) 0777 305 8256   email: gbru4smob@yahoo.co.uk
Fixtures Secretary: Mr Alen O'Keeffe, 18 Lawford Avanue, Little Stoke, Bristol BS34 6JR   Tel: 0117 9698681
Team Secretary: Mr I Rawlings, 272 Juniper Way Bristol BS32 2DR   Tel: 01454 201953
Coach: Mr Shane Claridge
Ground Address: Northwood Park, Trench Lane, Bristol BS32 4JZ
Tel: 01454 250489   email: clubhouse@smorugby.co.uk
Brief Directions: Leave the M5 at J16 and head towards Bristol. Turn left at 1st roundabout and then left again onto Woodlands Lane, Bradley Stoke ground 1 mile on left   **Nearest BR Station:** Bristol Parkway
Admission: Matchday: £4   Season: £50
Clubhouse: Open most nights 7-10.30pm. Food available Sat. & Sun. Function facilities for 100. Contact Andy Weare (Billy) on 07970 575377.   **Club Shop:** Contact: Andy Weare (as above)
Programme Size: A5   Price: with admission   Editor: Jim Cooke   Advertising: Contact club
Founded: 1900   **Training Nights:** Tuesday & Thursday   **Website:** www.smobrugby.co.uk
Colours: Emerald green & black   **Change colours:** Yellow

TORQUAY ATHLETIC R.U.F.C.

President: Allan Forsyth   **Chairman:** Peter Gratton-Davey   **Treasurer:** Colin Whitford
Club Secretary: John Ian Clayden, 17 Sutton Close, Barton, Torquay TQ2 8LL
Tel: 01803 324288   email: jandkclayden1@tiscali.co.uk
Fixture Secretary: Bill Thomas, 112 Westhill Torquay TQ1 4NT   Tel: 01803 315325   email: pandedwards@eurobell.co.uk
Match Secretary: Paul Edwards, 20 Barnfield Road, Livermead, Torquay TQ2 6TN
Tel: 01803 408670   email: pandedwards@eurobell.co.uk
Director Of Rugby: Colin Rylance Tel: 01803 311729   **Commercial Secretary:** Terry Hannaford Tel: 07980 798080
Ground Address: The Recreation Ground, Rathmore Road, Seafront, Torquay TQ2 6NX   Tel./Fax: 01803 293842
Directions: The A380 takes you from the end of the M5 into Torquay, stay on the A380 right up to the Torquay seafront lights, turn right along seafront towards Paignton, (right hand lane) & turn right again (Grand Hotel in front of you) after 75 yards where on your right is the entrance to the Rec (marked Torquay Cricket Club & Torquay Rugby Club).
Capacity: 5,000   Seated: 500   Covered: 350   **Admission:** Matchday £5   Season: £60. Concessions available
Car Parking: 90 cars + several coaches.   **Nearest BR Station:** Torquay (1 minute)
Clubhouse: Open all day at weekends plus weekday eves. Food available matchday only. Functions: Very wide range of hirings available all year, contact Mrs.Karen Webber at the club or 07791 520575 (M)   **Website:** www.torquayrugby.co.uk
Club Shop: Open matchdays & most weekday evenings. Contact Colin Hill at. the Club
Programme: All enquiries to Brian Chammings (Vice-Chairman) Tel: 01 803 406524 & email: chamtics@blueyonder.co.uk
Formed: 1875   **Nickname:** 'Tics'   **Colours:** Black & white. **Change:** Red & white   **Training Nights:** Tues & Thur 6pm.

YATTON R.F.C.

Chairman: Paul Griffin, 3, The Old School, 6, Church Road, Yatton, North Somerset BS49 4HH
Tel: 01934 838780 (H)   07831269763 (M)   e-mail: lesleyspilgrim@aol.com
Club Secretary: Mrs Leslie Griffin   as above except   07920 268354 (M)
Treasurer: Paul Edwards, Greenacre, Sandmead Road, Sandford, Winscombe, North Somerset BS25 5QG
Tel/Fax: 01934 822425 (H);   Mob: 07717 363213   email: pauledwards@greenacre.fslife.co.uk
Fixtures Secretary: Alan Walters, 86, Hawthorn Crescent, Yatton, North Somerset BS49 4BF
Tel: 01934 835118 (H)   email: millyvanillychillywilly@hotmail.com
Team Secretary: Ian John   Tel: 01275 852934 (H) 0792212 4364 (M)   email: ianjohn@hotmail.com
Director of Rugby: Des Chalmers   Tel: 01278 760208 (H) 07887 931352 (M
Commercial Secretary: Jason Clarke   email: jasonandsuzy@btinternet.com
Junior Chairman: Pete Williams   Tel: 01934 834582   email: pete@zappa01.demon.co.uk
Ground Address: The Park, North End, Yatton, North Somerset BS49 4AR   Tel:. 01934 832085   **Website:** www.yattonrugby.co.uk
Directions: East of Clevedon, M5 motorway junction 20 on B3133, clubhouse on outskirts of village of Yatton
Nearest BR station: Yatton   **Car Parking:** approx 150   **Founded:** 1968
Capacity: 1,000+   **Covered standing:** 400+   **Admission:** Matchday donations; V.P. membership £50
Clubhouse: Open Tue & Thur Evenings, Saturday & Sunday. Meals & pitch side café. Available for private hire, contact Paul Edwards. Club Shop: Open training evenings & matchdys. Contact Pat & John Crew.
Programme: Size: A5 Pages: 20   Editors: Keith Duthie/Paul Edwards   Advertising: Jason Clarke or Chris Haynes
Colours: Amber and black hoops.   **Change colours:** Green   **Training Nights:** Tuesday & Thursday

SOUTH WEST DIVISION LEAGUE TABLES 2008-09

WESTERN COUNTIES NORTH

Gloucestershire Premier ↑   ↑ Somerset Premier

High Bridge Jewellers Gloucester Premier

		P	W	D	L	PF	PA	PD	Pts	Adj
1	Drybrook	22	21	0	1	677	187	490	42	
2	Southmead	22	18	0	4	629	252	377	36	
3	Cirencester	22	15	0	7	642	273	369	30	
4	Matson	22	13	1	8	498	320	178	27	
5	Bristol Saracens	22	12	1	9	671	297	374	25	
6	Old Richians	22	12	0	10	507	388	119	24	
7	Whitehall	22	12	0	10	395	457	-62	24	
8	Old Colstonians	22	9	0	13	451	416	35	18	
9	Gloucester Old Boys	22	8	0	14	301	448	-147	16	
10	Spartans (Gloucester)	22	8	0	14	267	653	-386	14	-2
11	Frampton Cotterell	22	3	0	19	226	788	-562	6	
12	Hucclecote	22	0	0	22	120	905	-785	0	

High Bridge Jewellers Gloucester 1

		P	W	D	L	PF	PA	PD	Pts	Adj
1	Tewkesbury	22	20	1	1	669	186	483	41	
2	Ross On Wye	22	16	2	4	426	254	172	34	
3	Cheltenham Civil Service	22	15	2	5	474	369	105	32	
4	Old Bristolians	22	13	0	9	465	369	96	26	
5	Brockworth	22	12	0	10	364	372	-8	24	
6	Chipping Sodbury	22	10	3	9	323	277	46	21	-2
7	Longlevens	22	10	1	11	386	361	25	21	
8	Dursley	22	9	0	13	460	445	15	18	
9	Bishopston	22	8	1	13	364	495	-131	17	
10	Ashley Down Old Boys	22	6	0	16	434	731	-297	12	
11	Aretians	22	4	0	18	248	507	-259	8	
12	Painswick	22	4	0	18	326	573	-247	6	-2

High Bridge Jewellers Gloucester 2

		P	W	D	L	PF	PA	PD	Pts	Adj
1	Bream	20	20	0	0	906	68	838	40	
2	Old Cryptians	20	18	0	2	648	144	504	36	
3	Kingswood	20	15	0	5	525	183	342	30	
4	Old Elizabethans	20	10	0	10	400	352	48	20	
5	Greyhound	20	10	0	10	272	469	-197	20	
6	Tetbury	20	8	1	11	354	461	-107	15	-2
7	Westbury-on-Severn	20	7	0	13	170	421	-251	14	
8	Bristol Aeroplane Co	20	6	0	14	234	424	-190	12	
9	Cheltenham Saracens	20	6	2	12	239	440	-201	12	-2
10	Cainscross	20	3	1	16	218	737	-519	7	
11	Tredworth	20	5	0	15	172	439	-267	0	-10

High Bridge Jewellers Gloucester 3

		P	W	D	L	PF	PA	PD	Pts	Adj
1	St Brendan's Old Boys	16	16	0	0	557	66	491	32	
2	Cotham Park	16	14	0	2	522	146	376	28	
3	Smiths (Industries)	16	10	0	6	310	174	136	20	
4	Minchinhampton	16	7	0	9	339	314	25	14	
5	Newent	16	7	0	9	268	289	-21	14	
6	Bristol Telephone Area	16	7	0	9	213	326	-113	14	
7	Wotton	16	6	1	9	160	365	-205	13	
8	Gloucester Civil Service	16	3	0	13	211	471	-260	6	
9	Gloucester All Blues	16	1	1	14	92	521	-429	3	0

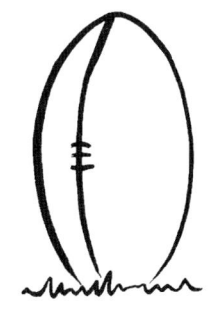

SOUTH WEST DIVISION LEAGUE TABLES 2008-09

Tribute Somerset Premier	P	W	D	L	PF	PA	PD	Pts	Adj
1 Burnham on Sea	22	17	1	4	594	396	198	35	
2 North Petherton	22	17	0	5	422	325	97	34	
3 Tor	22	14	2	6	566	317	249	30	
4 Bristol Harlequins	22	14	0	8	627	378	249	28	
5 Stothert & Pitt	22	13	0	9	487	494	-7	26	
6 Chew Valley	22	10	0	12	401	424	-23	20	
7 Chard	22	9	1	12	454	515	-61	19	
8 Midsomer Norton	22	9	0	13	376	364	12	18	
9 Winscombe	22	9	0	13	345	437	-92	18	
10 Wells	22	8	1	13	397	389	8	17	
11 Avon	22	7	1	14	377	505	-128	15	
12 Old Sulians	22	2	0	20	278	780	-502	4	

Tribute Somerset 1	P	W	D	L	PF	PA	PD	Pts	Adj
1 St Bernadettes Old Boys	22	21	0	1	729	135	594	42	
2 Taunton II	22	19	0	3	837	185	652	38	
3 Gordano	22	17	0	5	705	304	401	34	
4 Nailsea & Backwell	22	14	0	8	517	331	186	28	
5 Combe Down	21	12	0	9	410	308	102	24	
6 Old Redcliffians II	21	11	1	9	306	435	-129	23	
7 Wiveliscombe	22	8	1	13	424	493	-69	17	
8 Imperial	22	8	0	14	411	455	-44	16	
9 Old Culverhaysians	22	6	3	13	276	593	-317	15	
10 Broad Plain	22	5	2	15	283	598	-315	12	
11 Keynsham II	22	4	0	18	160	679	-519	4	-4
12 Bristol Barbarians	22	2	1	19	168	710	-542	3	-2

Tribute Somerset 2 North	P	W	D	L	PF	PA	PD	Pts	Adj
1 St Mary's Old Boys II	22	21	1	0	644	153	491	43	
2 Midsomer Nort II	22	19	0	3	651	236	415	38	
3 Yatton II	22	15	1	6	520	292	228	31	
4 Hornets II	22	13	2	7	527	295	232	28	
5 Winscombe II	22	11	1	10	460	451	9	23	
6 Walcot II	22	11	0	11	467	361	106	20	-2
7 Bristol Harlequins II	22	11	0	11	373	377	-4	18	-4
8 Clevedon II	22	8	0	14	332	525	-193	14	-2
9 Bath Old Edwardians	22	7	0	15	407	662	-255	12	-2
10 Oldfield Old Boys II	22	7	1	14	384	333	51	11	-4
11 Gordano II	22	3	0	19	217	742	-525	6	
12 Stothert & Pitt II	22	3	0	19	193	748	-555	0	-6

Tribute Somerset 2 South	P	W	D	L	PF	PA	PD	Pts	Adj
1 Weston-s-Mare II	20	20	0	0	1,255	76	1,179	40	
2 Bridgwater & Albion III	20	16	0	4	712	176	536	30	-2
3 Minehead Barbarians II	20	14	1	5	645	195	450	27	-2
4 Tor II	20	13	0	7	611	314	297	26	
5 Wells II	20	11	0	9	323	429	-106	22	
6 Wellington II	19	10	0	9	360	402	-42	18	-2
7 Crewkerne	20	9	0	11	265	504	-239	18	
8 Somerton	20	4	1	15	265	714	-449	9	
9 Taunton III	19	5	0	14	303	671	-368	8	-2
10 Martock	20	4	0	16	200	888	-688	4	-4
11 Ivel Barbarians II	20	2	0	18	152	722	-570	-2	-6

Tribute Somerset 3 North

	P	W	D	L	PF	PA	PD	Pts	Adj
1 Old Redcliffians III	22	20	0	2	590	146	444	40	
2 Clevedon III	22	17	0	5	447	259	188	34	
3 Avon II	22	15	1	6	643	266	377	31	
4 Keynsham III	21	16	0	5	664	216	448	28	-4
5 Nailsea & Backwell II	22	13	1	8	451	396	55	27	
6 Walcot III	21	13	0	8	617	381	236	20	-6
7 Midsomer Nort III	22	5	1	16	240	632	-392	11	
8 Yatton III	22	5	1	16	280	568	-288	9	-2
9 Chew Valley II	22	8	0	14	352	356	-4	8	-8
10 Old Sulians II	22	5	0	17	307	624	-317	6	-4
11 Oldfield Old Boys III	22	6	1	15	235	482	-247	5	-8
12 Old Culver II	22	5	1	16	182	682	-500	5	-6

Tribute Somerset 3 South

	P	W	D	L	PF	PA	PD	Pts	Adj
1 Weston-s-Mare III	20	17	0	3	734	143	591	34	
2 Castle Cary	20	17	0	3	513	161	352	34	
3 Chard III	20	15	0	5	665	227	438	30	
4 North Petherton II	20	11	0	9	433	345	88	22	
5 Burnham on S II	20	10	1	9	376	486	-110	21	
6 Morganians	20	8	1	11	277	439	-162	17	
7 Minehead Barbarians III	20	8	1	11	309	614	-305	17	
8 Wiveliscombe II	20	10	0	10	472	269	203	16	-4
9 Tor III	20	7	1	12	240	421	-181	9	-6
10 Wellington III	20	3	0	17	255	439	-184	0	-6
11 Winscombe III	20	2	0	18	112	842	-730	-2	-6

SOUTHERN COUNTIES SOUTH

Dorset & Wilts 1 North ↑   ↑ Dorset & Wilts 1 South

Dorset & Wilts 1 North

	P	W	D	L	PF	PA	PD	Pts	Adj
1 Devizes	22	20	0	2	925	106	819	40	
2 Chippenham II	22	18	0	4	818	237	581	34	-2
3 Marlborough	22	17	0	5	720	244	476	34	
4 Melksham	22	17	0	5	725	293	432	34	
5 Corsham II	22	14	0	8	407	347	60	28	
6 Sutton Benger	22	9	0	13	342	445	-103	16	-2
7 Cricklade	22	7	1	14	315	633	-318	15	
8 Calne	21	7	0	14	324	474	-150	14	
9 Wootton Bassett II	22	8	0	14	350	624	-274	14	-2
10 Swindon II	22	5	1	16	318	852	-534	11	
11 Supermarine	22	5	0	17	185	728	-543	10	
12 Fairford	21	3	0	18	186	632	-446	-4	-10

Dorset & Wilts 1 South

	P	W	D	L	PF	PA	PD	Pts	Adj
1 Dorchester	20	16	1	3	607	157	450	33	
2 Bridport	20	15	2	3	865	201	664	32	
3 Weymouth	20	15	1	4	615	238	377	31	
4 Frome II	20	12	1	7	278	346	-68	25	
5 Swanage & W II	20	12	0	8	558	300	258	24	
6 North Dorset II	20	10	1	9	493	362	131	21	
7 Salisbury II	20	10	0	10	365	495	-130	20	
8 Warminster	20	9	0	11	401	668	-267	18	
9 Puddletown	20	4	0	16	190	531	-341	8	
10 Westbury	20	3	0	17	202	602	-400	6	
11 Wimborne II	20	1	0	19	123	797	-674	0	-2

SOUTHERN COUNTIES SOUTH
Dorset & Wilts 1 North ▲   ▲ Dorset & Wilts 1 South

Dorset & Wilts 2 North

		P	W	D	L	PF	PA	PD	Pts	Adj
1	Trowbridge II	20	19	0	1	910	178	732	38	
2	Avonvale	20	18	0	2	811	194	617	36	
3	Pewsey Vale	20	14	1	5	397	320	77	29	
4	Devizes II	20	12	1	7	446	299	147	25	
5	Colerne	20	12	1	7	492	246	246	23	-2
6	Combe Down II	20	10	0	10	373	382	-9	20	
7	Melksham II	20	7	1	12	350	548	-198	15	
8	Bath Saracens	20	5	0	15	216	814	-598	10	
9	Chippenham III	20	5	0	15	340	529	-189	4	-6
10	Wootton Bassett III	20	4	0	16	268	604	-336	2	-6
11	Calne II	20	2	0	18	198	687	-489	-2	-6

Dorset & Wilts 2 South

		P	W	D	L	PF	PA	PD	Pts	Adj
1	Oakmeadians II	18	14	0	4	732	202	530	28	
2	Bridport II	18	14	0	4	579	252	327	28	
3	Blandford	18	14	0	4	506	263	243	28	
4	Bournemouth III	18	13	0	5	465	301	164	26	
5	North Dorset III	18	9	0	9	308	301	7	18	
6	Dorchester II	18	8	0	10	424	279	145	12	-4
7	Swanage & W III	18	5	0	13	262	515	-253	8	-2
8	Lytchett Minster II	18	3	1	14	189	594	-405	5	-2
9	Wheatsheaf Cabin Crew	18	4	1	13	204	656	-452	5	-4
10	Wimborne III	18	5	0	13	217	523	-306	4	-6

Dorset & Wilts 3 North

		P	W	D	L	PF	PA	PD	Pts	Adj
1	Minety II	12	10	0	2	259	115	144	20	
2	Swindon College Old Boys II	12	10	0	2	282	142	140	20	
3	Supermarine II	12	6	1	5	284	241	43	13	
4	Aldbourne/Hungerford	12	5	0	7	241	253	-12	10	
5	Swindon III	12	5	1	6	379	192	187	9	-2
6	Melksham III	12	4	0	8	96	371	-275	8	
7	Pewsey Vale II	12	1	0	11	98	325	-227	0	-2

Dorset & Wilts 3 South

		P	W	D	L	PF	PA	PD	Pts	Adj
1	Fordingbridge II	16	15	0	1	644	121	523	30	
2	Ellingham & Ringwood II	16	14	0	2	567	165	402	28	
3	Oakmeadians III	16	11	0	5	471	288	183	22	
4	Poole	16	10	0	6	470	188	282	20	
5	Weymouth II	16	7	0	9	300	293	7	14	
6	North Dorset IV	16	7	0	9	379	395	-16	14	
7	Swan & Ware IV	16	4	0	12	197	511	-314	6	-2
8	Blandford II	16	3	0	13	100	496	-396	4	-2
9	Puddletown	16	1	0	15	108	779	-671	0	-2

Dorset & Wilts 3 West

		P	W	D	L	PF	PA	PD	Pts	Adj
1	Bradford-on-Avon II	14	11	0	3	409	166	243	22	
2	South Wilts	14	11	0	3	340	216	124	22	
3	Wincanton	14	9	0	5	321	213	108	18	
4	Frome III	14	9	0	5	218	167	51	18	
5	Trowbridge III	14	5	0	9	194	260	-66	8	-2
6	Midsomer Norton IV	14	4	0	10	201	380	-179	8	
7	Castle Cary II	14	4	0	10	153	358	-205	8	
8	Westbury II	14	3	0	11	184	260	-76	0	-6

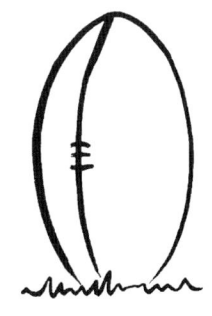

SOUTH WEST DIVISION LEAGUE TABLES 2008-09

SOUTHERN COUNTIES NORTH
↑ Berks, Bucks & Oxon Prem. ↑

Berks/Bucks & Oxon Premier	P	W	D	L	PF	PA	PD	Pts	Adj
1 Newbury Stags	20	19	0	1	895	128	767	38	
2 Amersham & Chiltern	20	17	0	3	734	259	475	34	
3 Broadmoor Staff	20	15	0	5	676	347	329	30	
4 Oxford	20	12	0	8	460	459	1	24	
5 Drifters	20	8	2	10	310	416	-106	18	
6 Phoenix	20	6	2	12	350	502	-152	14	
7 Stow-on-the-Wold	20	7	0	13	247	423	-176	14	
8 Swindon College Old Boys	20	7	0	13	384	587	-203	12	-2
9 Gosford All Blacks	20	6	1	13	327	613	-286	11	-2
10 Abingdon	20	6	0	14	243	600	-357	10	-2
11 Harwell	20	4	1	15	346	638	-292	9	

Berks/Bucks & Oxon Prem A	P	W	D	L	PF	PA	PD	Pts	Adj
1 Wallingford II	22	15	1	6	481	267	214	31	
2 Witney II	22	14	1	7	419	317	102	29	
3 Marlow II	22	13	3	6	410	309	101	29	
4 Oxford Harlequins II	22	13	1	8	625	531	94	27	
5 Amersham & Chiltern II	22	12	2	8	469	388	81	26	
6 Chinnor III	22	13	1	8	402	251	151	25	-2
7 Reading Abbey II	22	8	4	10	359	428	-69	20	
8 Redingensians II	22	9	1	12	434	433	1	19	
9 Windsor II	22	9	1	12	337	376	-39	19	
10 Buckingham II	22	8	1	13	420	481	-61	13	-4
11 Henley Wanderers II	22	5	2	15	402	534	-132	8	-4
12 Bracknell III	22	4	0	18	288	731	-443	8	

Berks/Bucks & Oxon 1 North	P	W	D	L	PF	PA	PD	Pts	Adj
1 Bicester II	18	16	0	2	676	286	390	32	
2 Aylesbury Athletic	18	12	0	6	465	323	142	24	
3 High Wycombe II	18	9	1	8	323	441	-118	19	
4 Chesham	18	8	1	9	309	300	9	17	
5 Witney III	18	8	0	10	321	304	17	16	
6 Beaconsfield II	18	9	0	9	316	311	5	16	-2
7 Banbury II	18	9	0	9	297	323	-26	12	
8 Bletchley II	18	8	0	10	268	226	42	10	-6
9 Aylesbury II	18	5	0	13	241	396	-155	8	-2
10 Buckingham III	18	5	0	13	176	482	-306	6	-4

Berks/Bucks & Oxon 1 South	P	W	D	L	PF	PA	PD	Pts	Adj
1 Maidenhead III	18	18	0	0	922	100	822	36	
2 Thatcham	18	15	0	3	659	173	486	30	
3 Oxford Harlequins III	18	14	0	4	464	216	248	28	
4 Tadley II	18	10	1	7	449	442	7	21	
5 Littlemore	18	12	0	6	427	294	133	20	-4
6 Hungerford	18	8	0	10	297	295	2	14	-2
7 Aldermaston	18	5	0	13	228	674	-446	8	-2
8 Grove II	18	2	0	16	204	713	-509	4	
9 Berkshire Shire Hall	18	3	1	14	174	549	-375	3	-4
10 Didcot	18	2	0	16	212	580	-368	0	-4

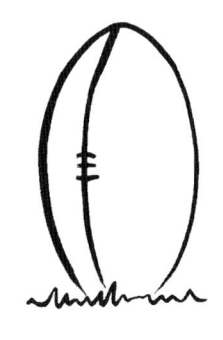

SOUTH WEST DIVISION LEAGUE TABLES 2008-09

Berks/Bucks & Oxon 2 North	P	W	D	L	PF	PA	PD	Pts	Adj
1 Amersham & Chiltern III	16	15	1	0	757	106	651	31	
2 Chinnor IV	16	12	1	3	278	189	89	25	
3 Chipping Norton II	16	10	1	5	345	232	113	21	
4 Winslow	16	8	0	8	249	314	-65	16	
5 Witney IV	16	6	1	9	172	419	-247	11	-2
6 Bicester III	16	6	2	8	260	207	53	8	-6
7 High Wycombe III	16	4	0	12	118	306	-188	4	-4
8 Aylesbury III	16	5	0	11	185	395	-210	2	-8
9 Banbury III	16	3	0	13	217	413	-196	-2	-8

Berks/Bucks & Oxon 2 South	P	W	D	L	PF	PA	PD	Pts	Adj
1 Reading II	16	16	0	0	675	71	604	32	
2 Redingensians III	16	13	0	3	362	220	142	26	
3 Farnham Royal	16	11	0	5	330	209	121	22	
4 Windsor III	16	10	0	6	468	216	252	18	-2
5 Phoenix II	16	9	0	7	276	309	-33	18	
6 Newbury IV	16	4	0	12	222	336	-114	2	-6
7 Abingdon II	16	3	1	12	201	366	-165	1	-6
8 Harwell II	16	2	1	13	139	648	-509	1	-4
9 Grove III	16	3	0	13	154	452	-298	0	-6

SOUTH WEST DIVISION FIXTURE GRIDS 2009-2010

SOUTHERN COUNTIES NORTH	Amersham & Chiltern	Aylesbury	Beaconsfield	Bicester	Chipping Norton	Grove	Milton Keynes	Newbury Stags	Slough	Swindon	Windsor	Witney
Amersham & Chiltern		26/09	09/01	06/03	23/01	31/10	13/02	14/11	10/10	05/12	10/04	12/09
Aylesbury	19/12		10/10	05/12	31/10	13/02	14/11	06/03	23/01	10/04	12/09	03/10
Beaconsfield	03/10	16/01		10/04	13/02	14/11	06/03	05/12	31/10	12/09	19/12	17/10
Bicester	28/11	20/03	12/12		26/09	09/01	10/10	23/01	17/04	07/11	20/02	30/01
Chipping Norton	17/10	30/01	07/11	19/12		05/12	10/04	12/09	20/02	03/10	16/01	28/11
Grove	30/01	07/11	20/02	03/10	20/03		12/09	19/12	28/11	16/01	17/10	12/12
Milton Keynes	07/11	20/02	28/11	16/01	12/12	17/04		03/10	20/03	17/10	30/01	19/12
Newbury Stags	20/02	28/11	20/03	17/10	17/04	26/09	09/01		12/12	30/01	07/11	16/01
Slough	16/01	17/10	30/01	12/09	14/11	06/03	05/12	10/04		19/12	03/10	07/11
Swindon	20/03	12/12	17/04	13/02	09/01	10/10	23/01	31/10	26/09		28/11	20/02
Windsor	12/12	17/04	26/09	14/11	10/10	23/01	31/10	13/02	09/01	06/03		20/03
Witney	17/04	09/01	23/01	31/10	06/03	10/04	26/09	10/10	13/02	14/11	05/12	

SOUTHERN COUNTIES SOUTH	Bradford-on-Avon	Corsham	Devizes	Dorchester	Frome	Ivel Barbarians	Minety	North Dorset	Oldfield Old Boys	Sherborne	Tadley	Wimborne
Bradford-on-Avon		26/09	06/03	10/04	05/12	10/10	13/02	14/11	09/01	23/01	31/10	12/09
Corsham	19/12		05/12	12/09	10/04	23/01	14/11	06/03	10/10	31/10	13/02	03/10
Devizes	28/11	20/03		20/02	07/11	17/04	10/10	23/01	12/12	26/09	09/01	30/01
Dorchester	12/12	17/04	14/11		06/03	09/01	31/10	13/02	26/09	10/10	23/01	20/03
Frome	20/03	12/12	13/02	28/11		26/09	23/01	31/10	17/04	09/01	10/10	20/02
Ivel Barbarians	16/01	17/10	12/09	03/10	19/12		05/12	10/04	30/01	14/11	06/03	07/11
Minety	07/11	20/02	16/01	30/01	17/10	20/03		03/10	28/11	12/12	17/04	19/12
North Dorset	20/02	28/11	17/10	07/11	30/01	12/12	09/01		20/03	17/04	26/09	16/01
Oldfield Old Boys	03/10	16/01	10/04	19/12	12/09	31/10	06/03	05/12		13/02	14/11	17/10
Sherborne	17/10	30/01	19/12	16/01	03/10	20/02	10/04	12/09	07/11		05/12	28/11
Tadley	30/01	07/11	03/10	17/10	16/01	28/11	12/09	19/12	20/02	20/03		12/12
Wimborne	17/04	09/01	31/10	05/12	14/11	13/02	26/09	10/10	23/01	06/03	10/04	

LEVEL SEVEN

WESTERN COUNTIES NORTH

	Barton Hill	Berry Hill	Burnham on Sea	Drybrook	Gordon League	Hornets	Keynsham	North Bristol	Old Centralians	Old Redcliffians	Southmead	Stroud	Thornbury	Widden Old Boys
Barton Hill		12/09	19/12	26/09	16/01	10/10	28/11	24/10	20/02	07/11	13/03	30/01	27/03	05/09
Berry Hill	12/12		26/09	16/01	10/10	30/01	27/03	20/02	07/11	13/03	28/11	24/10	05/09	19/09
Burnham on Sea	19/09	09/01		10/10	30/01	24/10	05/09	07/11	13/03	28/11	27/03	20/02	12/12	03/10
Drybrook	09/01	03/10	23/01		24/10	20/02	12/12	13/03	28/11	27/03	05/09	07/11	19/09	17/10
Gordon League	03/10	23/01	17/10	13/02		07/11	19/09	28/11	27/03	05/09	12/12	13/03	09/01	31/10
Hornets	23/01	17/10	13/02	31/10	06/03		09/01	27/03	05/09	12/12	19/09	28/11	03/10	14/11
Keynsham	20/03	05/12	10/04	12/09	19/12	26/09		10/10	30/01	24/10	20/02	16/01	14/11	06/03
North Bristol	13/02	31/10	06/03	14/11	20/03	05/12	23/01		19/09	09/01	03/10	10/04	17/10	12/12
Old Centralians	31/10	06/03	14/11	20/03	05/12	10/04	17/10	19/12		03/10	23/01	12/09	13/02	09/01
Old Redcliffians	06/03	14/11	20/03	05/12	10/04	12/09	13/02	26/09	16/01		17/10	19/12	31/10	23/01
Southmead	14/11	20/03	05/12	10/04	12/09	19/12	31/10	16/01	10/10	30/01		26/09	06/03	13/02
Stroud	17/10	13/02	31/10	06/03	14/11	20/03	03/10	05/09	12/12	19/09	09/01		23/01	05/12
Thornbury	05/12	10/04	12/09	19/12	26/09	16/01	13/03	30/01	24/10	20/02	07/11	10/10		20/03
Widden Old Boys	10/04	19/12	16/01	30/01	20/02	13/03	07/11	12/09	26/09	10/10	24/10	27/03	28/11	

WESTERN COUNTIES WEST

	Bude	Camborne	Devonport Services	Kingsbridge	Minehead Barbarians	Newquay Hornets	North Petherton	Okehampton	Penryn	Tavistock	Tiverton	Truro	Wadebridge Camels	Withycombe
Bude		12/09	19/12	26/09	16/01	10/10	30/01	24/10	20/02	07/11	13/03	28/11	27/03	05/09
Camborne	12/12		26/09	16/01	10/10	30/01	24/10	20/02	07/11	13/03	28/11	27/03	05/09	19/09
Devonport Services	19/09	09/01		10/10	30/01	24/10	20/02	07/11	13/03	28/11	27/03	05/09	12/12	03/10
Kingsbridge	09/01	03/10	23/01		24/10	20/02	07/11	13/03	28/11	27/03	05/09	12/12	19/09	17/10
Minehead Barbarians	03/10	23/01	17/10	13/02		07/11	13/03	28/11	27/03	05/09	12/12	19/09	09/01	31/10
Newquay Hornets	23/01	17/10	13/02	31/10	06/03		28/11	27/03	05/09	12/12	19/09	09/01	03/10	14/11
North Petherton	17/10	13/02	31/10	06/03	14/11	20/03		05/09	12/12	19/09	09/01	03/10	23/01	05/12
Okehampton	13/02	31/10	06/03	14/11	20/03	05/12	10/04		19/09	09/01	03/10	23/01	17/10	12/12
Penryn	31/10	06/03	14/11	20/03	05/12	10/04	12/09	19/12		03/10	23/01	17/10	13/02	09/01
Tavistock	06/03	14/11	20/03	05/12	10/04	12/09	19/12	26/09	16/01		17/10	13/02	31/10	23/01
Tiverton	14/11	20/03	05/12	10/04	12/09	19/12	26/09	16/01	10/10	30/01		31/10	06/03	13/02
Truro	20/03	05/12	10/04	12/09	19/12	26/09	16/01	10/10	30/01	24/10	20/02		14/11	06/03
Wadebridge Camels	05/12	10/04	12/09	19/12	26/09	16/01	10/10	30/01	24/10	20/02	07/11	13/03		20/03
Withycombe	10/04	19/12	16/01	30/01	20/02	13/03	27/03	12/09	26/09	10/10	24/10	07/11	28/11	

SOUTH WEST

SOUTH WEST DIVISION FIXTURE GRIDS 2009-2010

BERKSHIRE, BUCKINGHAMSHIRE & OXFORDSHIRE

	PREMIER	1	2	3	4	5	6	7	8	9	10	11	12
1	Abingdon		26/09	10/04	10/10	12/09	31/10	13/02	14/11	05/12	06/03	23/01	09/01
2	Alchester	19/12		12/09	23/01	03/10	13/02	14/11	06/03	10/04	05/12	31/10	10/10
3	Broadmoor Staff	12/12	17/04		09/01	20/03	23/01	31/10	13/02	06/03	14/11	10/10	26/09
4	Drifters	16/01	17/10	03/10		07/11	06/03	05/12	10/04	19/12	12/09	14/11	30/01
5	Gosford All Blacks	17/04	09/01	05/12	13/02		10/04	26/09	10/10	14/11	31/10	06/03	23/01
6	Harwell	30/01	07/11	17/10	28/11	12/12		12/09	19/12	16/01	03/10	20/03	20/02
7	Oxford	07/11	20/02	30/01	20/03	19/12	17/04		03/10	17/10	16/01	12/12	28/11
8	Phoenix	20/02	28/11	07/11	12/12	16/01	26/09	09/01		30/01	17/10	17/04	20/03
9	Spare Week	20/03	12/12	28/11	26/09	20/02	10/10	23/01	31/10		13/02	09/01	17/04
10	Stow-on-the-Wold	28/11	20/03	20/02	17/04	30/01	09/01	10/10	23/01	07/11		26/09	12/12
11	Swindon College O.B.	17/10	30/01	16/01	20/02	28/11	05/12	10/04	12/09	03/10	19/12		07/11
12	Thatcham	03/10	16/01	19/12	31/10	17/10	14/11	06/03	05/12	12/09	10/04	13/02	

	PREMIER A	1	2	3	4	5	6	7	8	9	10	11	12	13	14
1	Amersham & Chil II		09/01	28/11	20/02	24/10	03/10	12/12	23/01	13/03	27/03	05/09	07/11	19/09	17/10
2	Bicester II	26/09		20/02	10/10	16/01	12/09	28/11	19/12	24/10	07/11	13/03	30/01	27/03	05/09
3	Buckingham II	20/03	31/10		10/04	05/12	06/03	17/10	14/11	19/12	03/10	23/01	12/09	13/02	09/01
4	Chinnor III	31/10	23/01	05/09		06/03	17/10	09/01	13/02	27/03	12/12	19/09	28/11	03/10	14/11
5	High Wycombe II	13/02	03/10	27/03	07/11		23/01	19/09	17/10	28/11	05/09	12/12	13/03	09/01	31/10
6	Maidenhead III	16/01	12/12	07/11	30/01	10/10		27/03	26/09	20/02	13/03	28/11	24/10	05/09	19/09
7	Marlow II	12/09	20/03	30/01	26/09	19/12	05/12		10/04	10/10	24/10	20/02	16/01	14/11	06/03
8	Oxford Harlequins II	10/10	19/09	13/03	24/10	30/01	09/01	05/09		07/11	28/11	27/03	20/02	12/12	03/10
9	Reading Abbey II	14/11	13/02	19/09	05/12	20/03	31/10	23/01	06/03		09/01	03/10	10/04	17/10	12/12
10	Reading II	05/12	06/03	16/01	12/09	10/04	14/11	13/02	20/03	26/09		17/10	19/12	31/10	23/01
11	Redingensians III	10/04	14/11	10/10	19/12	12/09	20/03	31/10	05/12	16/01	30/01		26/09	06/03	13/02
12	Wallingford II	06/03	17/10	12/12	20/03	14/11	13/02	03/10	31/10	05/09	19/09	09/01		23/01	05/12
13	Windsor II	19/12	05/12	24/10	16/01	26/09	10/04	13/03	12/09	30/01	20/02	07/11	10/10		20/03
14	Witney II	30/01	10/04	26/09	13/03	20/02	19/12	07/11	16/01	12/09	10/10	24/10	27/03	28/11	

	ONE NORTH	1	2	3	4	5	6	7	8	9	10	11
1	Amersham & Chil III		20/02	03/10	20/03	16/01	30/01	07/11	28/11	12/12	17/10	17/04
2	Aylesbury Athletic	14/11		06/03	23/01	05/12	12/09	19/12	10/10	31/10	10/04	13/02
3	Aylesbury II	09/01	28/11		12/12	17/10	07/11	20/02	20/03	17/04	30/01	26/09
4	Banbury II	05/12	17/10	10/04		12/09	03/10	16/01	30/01	14/11	19/12	06/03
5	Beaconsfield II	10/10	20/03	23/01	17/04		20/02	28/11	12/12	26/09	07/11	09/01
6	Bletchley II	31/10	17/04	13/02	09/01	14/11		12/12	26/09	10/10	06/03	23/01
7	Chesham	13/02	26/09	14/11	10/10	06/03	10/04		09/01	23/01	05/12	31/10
8	Chinnor IV	06/03	16/01	05/12	31/10	10/04	19/12	03/10		13/02	12/09	14/11
9	Oxford Harlequins III	10/04	30/01	12/09	20/02	19/12	16/01	17/10	07/11		03/10	05/12
10	Wheatley	23/01	12/12	31/10	26/09	13/02	28/11	20/03	17/04	09/01		10/10
11	Witney III	12/09	07/11	19/12	28/11	03/10	17/10	30/01	20/02	20/03	16/01	

BERKSHIRE, BUCKINGHAMSHIRE & OXFORDSHIRE

	ONE SOUTH	1	2	3	4	5	6	7	8	9	10	11
1	Aldermaston		26/09	09/01	10/10	05/12	31/10	13/02	14/11	06/03	12/09	10/04
2	Berkshire Shire Hall	19/12		10/10	23/01	10/04	13/02	14/11	06/03	05/12	03/10	12/09
3	Bracknell III	03/10	16/01		31/10	12/09	14/11	06/03	05/12	10/04	17/10	19/12
4	Farnham Royal	16/01	17/10	30/01		19/12	06/03	05/12	10/04	12/09	07/11	03/10
5	Grove II	20/03	12/12	17/04	26/09		10/10	23/01	31/10	13/02	20/02	28/11
6	Henley Hawks III	30/01	07/11	20/02	28/11	16/01		12/09	19/12	03/10	12/12	17/10
7	Hungerford	07/11	20/02	28/11	20/03	17/10	17/04		03/10	16/01	19/12	30/01
8	Littlemore	20/02	28/11	20/03	12/12	30/01	26/09	09/01		17/10	16/01	07/11
9	Redingensians IV	28/11	20/03	12/12	17/04	07/11	09/01	10/10	23/01		30/01	20/02
10	Tadley II	17/04	09/01	23/01	13/02	14/11	10/04	26/09	10/10	31/10		05/12
11	Windsor III	12/12	17/04	26/09	09/01	06/03	23/01	31/10	13/02	14/11	20/03	

	TWO NORTH	1	2	3	4	5	6	7	8	9	10	11
1	Aylesbury III		05/12	09/01	10/10	10/04	31/10	13/02	14/11	06/03	26/09	12/09
2	Banbury III	20/03		17/04	26/09	28/11	10/10	23/01	31/10	13/02	12/12	20/02
3	Bicester III	03/10	12/09		31/10	19/12	14/11	06/03	05/12	10/04	16/01	17/10
4	Buckingham III	16/01	19/12	30/01		03/10	06/03	05/12	10/04	12/09	17/10	07/11
5	Chipping Norton II	12/12	06/03	26/09	09/01		23/01	31/10	13/02	14/11	17/04	20/03
6	Gosford All Blacks II	30/01	16/01	20/02	28/11	17/10		12/09	19/12	03/10	07/11	12/12
7	High Wycombe III	07/11	17/10	28/11	20/03	30/01	17/04		03/10	16/01	20/02	19/12
8	Marlow III	20/02	30/01	20/03	12/12	07/11	26/09	09/01		17/10	28/11	16/01
9	Princes Risborough	28/11	07/11	12/12	17/04	20/02	09/01	10/10	23/01		20/03	30/01
10	Winslow	19/12	10/04	10/10	23/01	12/09	13/02	14/11	06/03	05/12		03/10
11	Witney IV	17/04	14/11	23/01	13/02	05/12	10/04	26/09	10/10	31/10	09/01	

	TWO SOUTH	1	2	3	4	5	6	7	8	9	10	11
1	Abingdon II		14/11	10/10	12/09	23/01	31/10	13/02	26/09	05/12	06/03	10/04
2	Didcot	20/02		12/12	16/01	17/04	26/09	09/01	28/11	30/01	17/10	07/11
3	Grove III	16/01	10/04		07/11	14/11	06/03	05/12	17/10	19/12	12/09	03/10
4	Harwell II	17/04	10/10	13/02		06/03	10/04	26/09	09/01	14/11	31/10	05/12
5	Kingsclere II	17/10	12/09	20/02	28/11		05/12	10/04	30/01	03/10	19/12	16/01
6	Maidenhead IV	30/01	19/12	28/11	12/12	20/03		12/09	07/11	16/01	03/10	17/10
7	Newbury IV	07/11	03/10	20/03	19/12	12/12	17/04		20/02	17/10	16/01	30/01
8	Phoenix II	19/12	06/03	23/01	03/10	31/10	13/02	14/11		10/04	05/12	12/09
9	Slough II	20/03	31/10	26/09	20/02	09/01	10/10	23/01	12/12		13/02	28/11
10	Thatcham II	28/11	23/01	17/04	30/01	26/09	09/01	10/10	20/03	07/11		20/02
11	Wallingford III	12/12	13/02	09/01	20/03	10/10	23/01	31/10	17/04	06/03	14/11	

SOUTH WEST DIVISION FIXTURE GRIDS 2009-2010

DORSET & WILTSHIRE

ONE NORTH	1	2	3	4	5	6	7	8	9	10	11	12
1 Avonvale		14/11	09/01	10/10	23/01	31/10	13/02	26/09	06/03	05/12	10/04	12/09
2 Calne	20/02		20/03	12/12	17/04	26/09	09/01	28/11	17/10	30/01	07/11	16/01
3 Chippenham II	03/10	05/12		31/10	13/02	14/11	06/03	16/01	10/04	12/09	19/12	17/10
4 Corsham II	16/01	10/04	30/01		14/11	06/03	05/12	17/10	12/09	19/12	03/10	07/11
5 Cricklade	17/10	12/09	07/11	20/02		05/12	10/04	30/01	19/12	03/10	16/01	28/11
6 Marlborough	30/01	19/12	20/02	28/11	20/03		12/09	07/11	03/10	16/01	17/10	12/12
7 Melksham	07/11	03/10	28/11	20/03	12/12	17/04		20/02	16/01	17/10	30/01	19/12
8 Supermarine	19/12	06/03	10/10	23/01	31/10	13/02	14/11		05/12	10/04	12/09	03/10
9 Sutton Benger	28/11	23/01	12/12	17/04	26/09	09/01	10/10	20/03		07/11	20/02	30/01
10 Swindon II	20/03	31/10	17/04	26/09	09/01	10/10	23/01	12/12	13/02		28/11	20/02
11 Trowbridge II	12/12	13/02	26/09	09/01	10/10	23/01	31/10	17/04	14/11	06/03		20/03
12 Wootton Bassett II	17/04	10/10	23/01	13/02	06/03	10/04	26/09	09/01	31/10	14/11	05/12	

ONE SOUTH	1	2	3	4	5	6	7	8	9	10	11	12
1 Blandford		14/11	09/01	10/10	23/01	12/09	13/02	26/09	06/03	05/12	10/04	31/10
2 Bridport	20/02		20/03	12/12	17/04	16/01	09/01	28/11	17/10	30/01	07/11	26/09
3 Frome II	03/10	05/12		31/10	13/02	17/10	06/03	16/01	10/04	12/09	19/12	14/11
4 North Dorset II	16/01	10/04	30/01		14/11	07/11	05/12	17/10	12/09	19/12	03/10	06/03
5 Oakmeadians II	17/10	12/09	07/11	20/02		28/11	10/04	30/01	19/12	03/10	16/01	05/12
6 Puddletown	17/04	10/10	23/01	13/02	06/03		26/09	09/01	31/10	14/11	05/12	10/04
7 Salisbury II	07/11	03/10	28/11	20/03	12/12	19/12		20/02	16/01	17/10	30/01	17/04
8 Swanage & W II	19/12	06/03	10/10	23/01	31/10	03/10	14/11		05/12	10/04	12/09	13/02
9 Warminster	28/11	23/01	12/12	17/04	26/09	30/01	10/10	20/03		07/11	20/02	09/01
10 Westbury	20/03	31/10	17/04	26/09	09/01	20/02	23/01	12/12	13/02		28/11	10/10
11 Weymouth	12/12	13/02	26/09	09/01	10/10	20/03	31/10	17/04	14/11	06/03		23/01
12 Wimborne II	30/01	19/12	20/02	28/11	20/03	12/12	12/09	07/11	03/10	16/01	17/10	

TWO NORTH	1	2	3	4	5	6	7	8	9	10	11	12
1 Bath Saracens		09/01	17/10	17/04	12/12	16/01	30/01	20/03	20/02	28/11	07/11	26/09
2 Bradford-on-Avon II	03/10		16/01	12/12	20/03	19/12	17/10	28/11	07/11	20/02	30/01	17/04
3 Chippenham III	23/01	10/10		26/09	17/04	30/01	07/11	12/12	28/11	20/03	20/02	09/01
4 Colerne	12/09	10/04	19/12		20/02	28/11	03/10	07/11	17/10	30/01	16/01	05/12
5 Combe Down II	10/04	05/12	12/09	14/11		07/11	19/12	30/01	16/01	17/10	03/10	06/03
6 Devizes II	10/10	26/09	31/10	06/03	13/02		14/11	23/01	17/04	09/01	05/12	10/04
7 Fairford	31/10	23/01	13/02	09/01	26/09	20/02		17/04	20/03	12/12	28/11	10/10
8 Melksham II	05/12	06/03	10/04	13/02	31/10	17/10	12/09		03/10	16/01	19/12	14/11
9 Minety	14/11	13/02	06/03	23/01	10/10	12/09	05/12	09/01		26/09	10/04	31/10
10 Pewsey Vale	06/03	14/11	05/12	31/10	23/01	03/10	10/04	10/10	19/12		12/09	13/02
11 Swindon Coll. O.B. II	13/02	31/10	14/11	10/10	09/01	20/03	06/03	26/09	12/12	17/04		23/01
12 Wootton Bassett III	19/12	12/09	03/10	20/03	28/11	12/12	16/01	20/02	30/01	07/11	17/10	

728

DORSET & WILTSHIRE

TWO SOUTH	1	2	3	4	5	6	7	8	9	10	11	12
1 Bournemouth III		28/11	17/04	17/10	20/03	26/09	30/01	20/02	12/12	09/01	07/11	16/01
2 Bridport II	06/03		31/10	05/12	10/10	13/02	10/04	19/12	23/01	14/11	12/09	03/10
3 Dorchester II	12/09	30/01		19/12	07/11	05/12	03/10	17/10	20/02	10/04	16/01	28/11
4 Ellingham & Ringwood II	23/01	20/03	26/09		12/12	09/01	07/11	28/11	17/04	10/10	20/02	30/01
5 Fordingbridge II	05/12	16/01	13/02	10/04		14/11	12/09	03/10	31/10	06/03	19/12	17/10
6 Lytchett Minster II	19/12	07/11	20/03	03/10	20/02		16/01	30/01	28/11	12/09	17/10	12/12
7 North Dorset III	31/10	12/12	09/01	13/02	17/04	10/10		20/03	26/09	23/01	28/11	20/02
8 Salisbury III	14/11	26/09	23/01	06/03	09/01	31/10	05/12		10/10	13/02	10/04	12/09
9 Sherborne II	10/04	17/10	14/11	12/09	30/01	06/03	19/12	16/01		05/12	03/10	07/11
10 South Wilts	03/10	20/02	12/12	16/01	28/11	17/04	17/10	07/11	20/03		30/01	19/12
11 Swanage & W III	13/02	17/04	10/10	14/11	26/09	23/01	06/03	12/12	09/01	31/10		20/03
12 Wheatsheaf Cabin Crew	10/10	09/01	06/03	31/10	23/01	10/04	14/11	17/04	13/02	26/09	05/12	

THREE NORTH	1	2	3	4	5	6	7	8	9	10	11	12
1 Aldbourne/Hungerford		20/02	17/10	28/11	19/12	16/01	30/01	03/10	07/11	20/03	12/12	17/04
2 Calne II	14/11		10/04	10/10	03/10	05/12	12/09	06/03	19/12	23/01	31/10	13/02
3 Corsham III	23/01	12/12		17/04	20/02	13/02	28/11	31/10	20/03	26/09	09/01	10/10
4 Devizes III	06/03	16/01	12/09		17/10	10/04	19/12	05/12	03/10	31/10	13/02	14/11
5 Marlborough II	26/09	09/01	14/11	23/01		31/10	05/12	10/10	17/04	13/02	06/03	10/04
6 Melksham III	10/10	20/03	07/11	12/12	30/01		20/02	23/01	28/11	17/04	26/09	09/01
7 Midsomer Norton IV	31/10	17/04	06/03	26/09	20/03	14/11		13/02	12/12	09/01	10/10	23/01
8 Pewsey Vale II	09/01	28/11	30/01	20/03	16/01	17/10	07/11		20/02	12/12	17/04	26/09
9 Supermarine II	13/02	26/09	05/12	09/01	12/09	06/03	10/04	14/11		10/10	23/01	31/10
10 Swindon III	05/12	17/10	19/12	30/01	07/11	12/09	03/10	10/04	16/01		14/11	06/03
11 Trowbridge II	10/04	30/01	03/10	07/11	28/11	19/12	16/01	12/09	17/10	20/02		05/12
12 Westbury II	12/09	07/11	16/01	20/02	12/12	03/10	17/10	19/12	30/01	28/11	20/03	

THREE SOUTH	1	2	3	4	5	6	7	8	9	10	11
1 Blandford II		20/02	28/11	19/12	30/01	07/11	17/04	03/10	12/12	17/10	16/01
2 Bournemouth IV	14/11		10/10	03/10	12/09	19/12	13/02	06/03	31/10	10/04	05/12
3 East Dorset II	06/03	16/01		17/10	19/12	03/10	14/11	05/12	13/02	12/09	10/04
4 North Dorset IV	26/09	09/01	23/01		05/12	17/04	10/04	10/10	06/03	14/11	31/10
5 Oakmeadians III	31/10	17/04	26/09	20/03		12/12	23/01	13/02	10/10	06/03	14/11
6 Poole	13/02	26/09	09/01	12/09	10/04		31/10	14/11	23/01	05/12	06/03
7 Puddletown II	12/09	07/11	20/02	12/12	17/10	30/01		19/12	20/03	16/01	03/10
8 Swan & Ware IV	09/01	28/11	20/03	16/01	07/11	20/02	26/09		17/04	30/01	17/10
9 Weymouth II	10/04	30/01	07/11	28/11	16/01	17/10	05/12	12/09		03/10	19/12
10 Wimborne III	23/01	12/12	17/04	20/02	28/11	20/03	10/10	31/10	09/01		13/02
11 Wincanton	10/10	20/03	12/12	30/01	20/02	28/11	09/01	23/01	26/09	07/11	

SOUTH WEST DIVISION FIXTURE GRIDS 2009-2010

TRIBUTE CORNWALL AND DEVON

		1	2	3	4	5	6	7	8	9	10	11	12	13	14
1	Bideford		12/09	19/12	05/09	16/01	10/10	30/01	24/10	20/02	07/11	13/03	27/03	28/11	26/09
2	Crediton	12/12		26/09	19/09	10/10	30/01	24/10	20/02	07/11	13/03	28/11	05/09	27/03	16/01
3	Exeter Saracens	19/09	09/01		03/10	30/01	24/10	20/02	07/11	13/03	28/11	27/03	12/12	05/09	10/10
4	Falmouth	10/04	19/12	16/01		20/02	13/03	27/03	12/09	26/09	10/10	24/10	28/11	07/11	30/01
5	Hayle	03/10	23/01	17/10	31/10		07/11	13/03	28/11	27/03	05/09	12/12	09/01	19/09	13/02
6	Liskeard-Looe	23/01	17/10	13/02	14/11	06/03		28/11	27/03	05/09	12/12	19/09	03/10	09/01	31/10
7	Old Plymothian & M.	17/10	13/02	31/10	05/12	14/11	20/03		05/09	12/12	19/09	09/01	23/01	03/10	06/03
8	Plymstock Albion Oaks	13/02	31/10	06/03	12/12	20/03	05/12	10/04		19/09	09/01	03/10	17/10	23/01	14/11
9	Saltash	31/10	06/03	14/11	09/01	05/12	10/04	12/09	19/12		03/10	23/01	13/02	17/10	20/03
10	St Austell	06/03	14/11	20/03	23/01	10/04	12/09	19/12	26/09	16/01		17/10	31/10	13/02	05/12
11	Stithians	14/11	20/03	05/12	13/02	12/09	19/12	26/09	16/01	10/10	30/01		06/03	31/10	10/04
12	Teignmouth	05/12	10/04	12/09	20/03	26/09	16/01	10/10	30/01	24/10	20/02	07/11		13/03	19/12
13	Torrington	20/03	05/12	10/04	06/03	19/12	26/09	16/01	10/10	30/01	24/10	20/02	14/11		12/09
14	Wellington	09/01	03/10	23/01	17/10	24/10	20/02	07/11	13/03	28/11	27/03	05/09	19/09	12/12	

TRIBUTE CORNWALL

		1	2	3	4	5	6	7	8	9	10	11	12
1	Bodmin		26/09	09/01	10/10	23/01	31/10	13/02	14/11	06/03	05/12	10/04	12/09
2	Camborne S o M	19/12		10/10	23/01	31/10	13/02	14/11	06/03	05/12	10/04	12/09	03/10
3	Helston	03/10	16/01		31/10	13/02	14/11	06/03	05/12	10/04	12/09	19/12	17/10
4	Illogan Park	16/01	17/10	30/01		14/11	06/03	05/12	10/04	12/09	19/12	03/10	07/11
5	Lankelly-Fowey	17/10	30/01	07/11	20/02		05/12	10/04	12/09	19/12	03/10	16/01	28/11
6	Perranporth	30/01	07/11	20/02	28/11	20/03		12/09	19/12	03/10	16/01	17/10	12/12
7	Redruth Albany	07/11	20/02	28/11	20/03	12/12	17/04		03/10	16/01	17/10	30/01	19/12
8	Roseland	20/02	28/11	20/03	12/12	17/04	26/09	09/01		17/10	30/01	07/11	16/01
9	St Agnes	28/11	20/03	12/12	17/04	26/09	09/01	10/10	23/01		07/11	20/02	30/01
10	St Day	20/03	12/12	17/04	26/09	09/01	10/10	23/01	31/10	13/02		28/11	20/02
11	St Just	12/12	17/04	26/09	09/01	10/10	23/01	31/10	13/02	14/11	06/03		20/03
12	Veor	17/04	09/01	23/01	13/02	06/03	10/04	26/09	10/10	31/10	14/11	05/12	

DEVON 1 NORTH EAST

		1	2	3	4	5	6	7	8	9
1	Buckfastleigh Ramblers		12/09	14/11	26/09	05/12	10/10	19/12	24/10	09/01
2	Honiton	07/11		26/09	05/12	10/10	19/12	24/10	09/01	05/09
3	Ilfracombe	19/09	28/11		10/10	19/12	24/10	09/01	05/09	07/11
4	New Cross	28/11	03/10	12/12		24/10	09/01	05/09	07/11	19/09
5	North Tawton	03/10	12/12	17/10	02/01		05/09	07/11	19/09	28/11
6	South Molton	12/12	17/10	02/01	31/10	16/01		19/09	28/11	03/10
7	Topsham	17/10	02/01	31/10	16/01	12/09	14/11		03/10	12/12
8	Totnes	02/01	31/10	16/01	12/09	14/11	26/09	05/12		17/10
9	Wessex	31/10	16/01	12/09	14/11	26/09	05/12	10/10	19/12	

DEVON 1 SOUTH WEST

		1	2	3	4	5	6	7	8	9
1	Dartmouth		02/01	12/09	12/12	26/09	28/11	10/10	07/11	24/10
2	Devonport HSOB	05/09		10/10	12/09	07/11	12/12	24/10	26/09	09/01
3	Old Technicians	19/12	14/11		17/10	19/09	16/01	05/12	31/10	03/10
4	Plymouth Argaum	19/09	19/12	07/11		24/10	26/09	09/01	28/11	05/09
5	Plymouth Barbarians	05/12	17/10	12/12	16/01		31/10	03/10	02/01	14/11
6	Plympton Victoria	03/10	19/09	24/10	05/12	09/01		05/09	10/10	19/12
7	Salcombe	14/11	16/01	26/09	31/10	28/11	02/01		12/09	17/10
8	St Columba & Torpoint	17/10	05/12	09/01	03/10	05/09	14/11	19/12		19/09
9	Tamar Saracens	16/01	31/10	28/11	02/01	10/10	12/09	07/11	12/12	

GLOUCESTERSHIRE

PREMIER	1	2	3	4	5	6	7	8	9	10	11	12
1 Bristol Saracens		26/09	09/01	10/10	23/01	31/10	13/02	14/11	06/03	05/12	10/04	12/09
2 Cirencester	19/12		10/10	23/01	31/10	13/02	14/11	06/03	05/12	10/04	12/09	03/10
3 Frampton Cotterell	03/10	16/01		31/10	13/02	14/11	06/03	05/12	10/04	12/09	19/12	17/10
4 Gloucester Old Boys	16/01	17/10	30/01		14/11	06/03	05/12	10/04	12/09	19/12	03/10	07/11
5 Hucclecote	17/10	30/01	07/11	20/02		05/12	10/04	12/09	19/12	03/10	16/01	28/11
6 Matson	30/01	07/11	20/02	28/11	20/03		12/09	19/12	03/10	16/01	17/10	12/12
7 Old Colstonians	07/11	20/02	28/11	20/03	12/12	17/04		03/10	16/01	17/10	30/01	19/12
8 Old Richians	20/02	28/11	20/03	12/12	17/04	26/09	09/01		17/10	30/01	07/11	16/01
9 Ross On Wye	28/11	20/03	12/12	17/04	26/09	09/01	10/10	23/01		07/11	20/02	30/01
10 Spartans (Gloucester)	20/03	12/12	17/04	26/09	09/01	10/10	23/01	31/10	13/02		28/11	20/02
11 Tewkesbury	12/12	17/04	26/09	09/01	10/10	23/01	31/10	13/02	14/11	06/03		20/03
12 Whitehall	17/04	09/01	23/01	13/02	06/03	10/04	26/09	10/10	31/10	14/11	05/12	

ONE	1	2	3	4	5	6	7	8	9	10	11	12
1 Aretians		26/09	09/01	10/10	23/01	31/10	13/02	14/11	06/03	05/12	10/04	12/09
2 Ashley Down Old Boys	19/12		10/10	23/01	31/10	13/02	14/11	06/03	05/12	10/04	12/09	03/10
3 Bishopston	03/10	16/01		31/10	13/02	14/11	06/03	05/12	10/04	12/09	19/12	17/10
4 Bream	16/01	17/10	30/01		14/11	06/03	05/12	10/04	12/09	19/12	03/10	07/11
5 Brockworth	17/10	30/01	07/11	20/02		05/12	10/04	12/09	19/12	03/10	16/01	28/11
6 Cheltenham Civil Service	30/01	07/11	20/02	28/11	20/03		12/09	19/12	03/10	16/01	17/10	12/12
7 Chipping Sodbury	07/11	20/02	28/11	20/03	12/12	17/04		03/10	16/01	17/10	30/01	19/12
8 Dursley	20/02	28/11	20/03	12/12	17/04	26/09	09/01		17/10	30/01	07/11	16/01
9 Longlevens	28/11	20/03	12/12	17/04	26/09	09/01	10/10	23/01		07/11	20/02	30/01
10 Old Bristolians	20/03	12/12	17/04	26/09	09/01	10/10	23/01	31/10	13/02		28/11	20/02
11 Old Cryptians	12/12	17/04	26/09	09/01	10/10	23/01	31/10	13/02	14/11	06/03		20/03
12 Painswick	17/04	09/01	23/01	13/02	06/03	10/04	26/09	10/10	31/10	14/11	05/12	

TWO	1	2	3	4	5	6	7	8	9	10	11
1 Bristol Aeroplane Co		26/09	09/01	10/10	23/01	31/10	13/02	14/11	06/03	05/12	10/04
2 Cainscross	19/12		10/10	23/01	31/10	13/02	14/11	06/03	05/12	10/04	12/09
3 Cheltenham Saracens	03/10	16/01		31/10	13/02	14/11	06/03	05/12	10/04	12/09	19/12
4 Cotham Park	16/01	17/10	30/01		14/11	06/03	05/12	10/04	12/09	19/12	03/10
5 Greyhound	17/10	30/01	07/11	20/02		05/12	10/04	12/09	19/12	03/10	16/01
6 Kingswood	30/01	07/11	20/02	28/11	20/03		12/09	19/12	03/10	16/01	17/10
7 Old Elizabethans	07/11	20/02	28/11	20/03	12/12	17/04		03/10	16/01	17/10	30/01
8 St Brendan's Old Boys	20/02	28/11	20/03	12/12	17/04	26/09	09/01		17/10	30/01	07/11
9 Tetbury	28/11	20/03	12/12	17/04	26/09	09/01	10/10	23/01		07/11	20/02
10 Tredworth	20/03	12/12	17/04	26/09	09/01	10/10	23/01	31/10	13/02		28/11
11 Westbury-on-Severn	12/12	17/04	26/09	09/01	10/10	23/01	31/10	13/02	14/11	06/03	

THREE	1	2	3	4	5	6	7	8
1 Bristol Telephone Area		10/04	23/01	31/10	20/02	28/11	20/03	26/09
2 Dowty	09/01		31/10	20/02	28/11	20/03	26/09	17/10
3 Gloucester All Blues	17/10	30/01		28/11	20/03	26/09	09/01	14/11
4 Gloucester Civil Service	30/01	14/11	06/03		26/09	09/01	17/10	12/12
5 Minchinhampton	14/11	06/03	12/12	10/04		17/10	30/01	09/01
6 Newent	06/03	12/12	10/04	10/10	23/01		14/11	30/01
7 Smiths (Industries)	12/12	10/04	10/10	23/01	31/10	20/02		06/03
8 Wotton	10/04	23/01	20/02	20/03	10/10	31/10	28/11	

SOUTH WEST DIVISION FIXTURE GRIDS 2009-2010

SOMERSET

PREMIER	1	2	3	4	5	6	7	8	9	10	11	12
1 Avon		26/09	09/01	10/10	23/01	31/10	13/02	14/11	06/03	05/12	10/04	12/09
2 Bristol Harlequins	19/12		10/10	23/01	31/10	13/02	14/11	06/03	05/12	10/04	12/09	03/10
3 Chard	03/10	16/01		31/10	13/02	14/11	06/03	05/12	10/04	12/09	19/12	17/10
4 Chew Valley	16/01	17/10	30/01		14/11	06/03	05/12	10/04	12/09	19/12	03/10	07/11
5 Midsomer Norton	17/10	30/01	07/11	20/02		05/12	10/04	12/09	19/12	03/10	16/01	28/11
6 Old Sulians	30/01	07/11	20/02	28/11	20/03		12/09	19/12	03/10	16/01	17/10	12/12
7 St Bernadettes O.B.	07/11	20/02	28/11	20/03	12/12	17/04		03/10	16/01	17/10	30/01	19/12
8 Stothert & Pitt	20/02	28/11	20/03	12/12	17/04	26/09	09/01		17/10	30/01	07/11	16/01
9 Taunton II	28/11	20/03	12/12	17/04	26/09	09/01	10/10	23/01		07/11	20/02	30/01
10 Tor	20/03	12/12	17/04	26/09	09/01	10/10	23/01	31/10	13/02		28/11	20/02
11 Wells	12/12	17/04	26/09	09/01	10/10	23/01	31/10	13/02	14/11	06/03		20/03
12 Winscombe	17/04	09/01	23/01	13/02	06/03	10/04	26/09	10/10	31/10	14/11	05/12	

ONE	1	2	3	4	5	6	7	8	9	10	11	12
1 Bristol Barbarians		26/09	05/12	10/10	23/01	31/10	13/02	14/11	06/03	09/01	10/04	12/09
2 Broad Plain	19/12		10/04	23/01	31/10	13/02	14/11	06/03	05/12	10/10	12/09	03/10
3 Combe Down	20/03	12/12		26/09	09/01	10/10	23/01	31/10	13/02	17/04	28/11	20/02
4 Gordano	16/01	17/10	19/12		14/11	06/03	05/12	10/04	12/09	30/01	03/10	07/11
5 Imperial	17/10	30/01	03/10	20/02		05/12	10/04	12/09	19/12	07/11	16/01	28/11
6 Keynsham II	30/01	07/11	16/01	28/11	20/03		12/09	19/12	03/10	20/02	17/10	12/12
7 Nailsea & Backwell	07/11	20/02	17/10	20/03	12/12	17/04		03/10	16/01	28/11	30/01	19/12
8 Old Culverhaysians	20/02	28/11	30/01	12/12	17/04	26/09	09/01		17/10	20/03	07/11	16/01
9 Old Redcliffians II	28/11	20/03	07/11	17/04	26/09	09/01	10/10	23/01		12/12	20/02	30/01
10 St Mary's Old Boys II	03/10	16/01	12/09	31/10	13/02	14/11	06/03	05/12	10/04		19/12	17/10
11 Weston-s-Mare II	12/12	17/04	06/03	09/01	10/10	23/01	31/10	13/02	14/11	26/09		20/03
12 Wiveliscombe	17/04	09/01	14/11	13/02	06/03	10/04	26/09	10/10	31/10	23/01	05/12	

TWO NORTH	1	2	3	4	5	6	7	8	9	10	11	12	13
1 Bath Old Edwardians		12/09	19/12	28/11	16/01	10/10	30/01	20/02	24/10	07/11	13/03	26/09	27/03
2 Bristol Harlequins II	12/12		26/09	27/03	10/10	30/01	24/10	07/11	20/02	13/03	28/11	16/01	05/09
3 Clevedon II	19/09	09/01		05/09	30/01	24/10	20/02	13/03	07/11	28/11	27/03	10/10	12/12
4 Gordano II	20/03	05/12	10/04		19/12	26/09	16/01	30/01	10/10	24/10	20/02	12/09	14/11
5 Hornets II	03/10	23/01	17/10	19/09		07/11	13/03	27/03	28/11	05/09	12/12	13/02	09/01
6 Midsomer Nort II	23/01	17/10	13/02	09/01	06/03		28/11	05/09	27/03	12/12	19/09	31/10	03/10
7 Old Redcliffians III	17/10	13/02	31/10	03/10	14/11	20/03		12/12	05/09	19/09	09/01	06/03	23/01
8 Oldfield Old Boys II	31/10	06/03	14/11	17/10	05/12	10/04	12/09		19/12	03/10	23/01	20/03	13/02
9 St Bernadettes II	13/02	31/10	06/03	23/01	20/03	05/12	10/04	19/09		09/01	03/10	14/11	17/10
10 Tor II	06/03	14/11	20/03	13/02	10/04	12/09	19/12	16/01	26/09		17/10	05/12	31/10
11 Walcot II	14/11	20/03	05/12	31/10	12/09	19/12	26/09	10/10	16/01	30/01		10/04	06/03
12 Winscombe II	09/01	03/10	23/01	12/12	24/10	20/02	07/11	28/11	13/03	27/03	05/09		19/09
13 Yatton II	05/12	10/04	12/09	13/03	26/09	16/01	10/10	24/10	30/01	20/02	07/11	19/12	

SOMERSET

TWO SOUTH

		1	2	3	4	5	6	7	8	9	10	11	12	13
1	Bridgwater & A. III		10/10	20/02	26/09	16/01	12/09	30/01	24/10	19/12	28/11	13/03	27/03	05/09
2	Castle Cary	23/01		05/09	31/10	06/03	17/10	28/11	27/03	13/02	09/01	19/09	03/10	14/11
3	Chard II	31/10	10/04		20/03	05/12	06/03	12/09	19/12	14/11	17/10	23/01	13/02	09/01
4	Crewkerne	09/01	20/02	28/11		24/10	03/10	07/11	13/03	23/01	12/12	05/09	19/09	17/10
5	Ivel Barbarians II	03/10	07/11	27/03	13/02		23/01	13/03	28/11	17/10	19/09	12/12	09/01	31/10
6	Martock	12/12	30/01	07/11	16/01	10/10		24/10	20/02	26/09	27/03	28/11	05/09	19/09
7	Minehead Babas II	17/10	20/03	12/12	06/03	14/11	13/02		05/09	31/10	03/10	09/01	23/01	05/12
8	North Petherton II	13/02	05/12	19/09	14/11	20/03	31/10	10/04		06/03	23/01	03/10	17/10	12/12
9	Somerton	19/09	24/10	13/03	10/10	30/01	09/01	20/02	07/11		05/09	27/03	12/12	03/10
10	Taunton III	20/03	26/09	30/01	12/09	19/12	05/12	16/01	10/10	10/04		20/02	14/11	06/03
11	Wellington II	14/11	19/12	10/10	10/04	12/09	20/03	26/09	16/01	05/12	31/10		06/03	13/02
12	Wells II	05/12	16/01	24/10	19/12	26/09	10/04	10/10	30/01	12/09	13/03	07/11		20/03
13	Weston-s-Mare III	10/04	13/03	26/09	30/01	20/02	19/12	27/03	12/09	16/01	07/11	24/10	28/11	

THREE NORTH

		1	2	3	4	5	6	7	8	9	10	11	12	13
1	Avon II		30/01	05/12	31/10	12/09	06/03	26/09	16/01	10/10	20/03	14/11	10/04	19/12
2	Clevedon III	17/10		20/03	13/02	10/04	31/10	19/12	26/09	16/01	14/11	06/03	05/12	12/09
3	Frome III	27/03	28/11		05/09	30/01	12/12	20/02	07/11	13/03	09/01	19/09	10/10	24/10
4	Imperial II	20/02	24/10	10/04		19/12	14/11	16/01	10/10	30/01	05/12	20/03	12/09	26/09
5	Keynsham III	12/12	05/09	17/10	19/09		09/01	13/03	28/11	27/03	23/01	03/10	13/02	07/11
6	Midsomer Nort III	07/11	20/02	12/09	13/03	26/09		10/10	30/01	24/10	10/04	05/12	19/12	16/01
7	Nailsea & Backwell II	09/01	19/09	31/10	03/10	14/11	23/01		05/09	12/12	13/02	17/10	06/03	20/03
8	Old Culver II	03/10	09/01	06/03	23/01	20/03	17/10	10/04		19/09	31/10	13/02	14/11	05/12
9	Old Sulians II	23/01	03/10	14/11	17/10	05/12	13/02	12/09	19/12		06/03	31/10	20/03	10/04
10	Oldfield Old Boys III	28/11	13/03	26/09	27/03	10/10	05/09	24/10	20/02	07/11		12/12	16/01	30/01
11	Stothert & Pitt II	13/03	07/11	19/12	28/11	16/01	27/03	30/01	24/10	20/02	12/09		26/09	10/10
12	Walcot III	05/09	27/03	23/01	12/12	24/10	19/09	07/11	13/03	28/11	03/10	09/01		20/02
13	Yatton III	19/09	12/12	13/02	09/01	06/03	03/10	28/11	27/03	05/09	17/10	23/01	31/10	

THREE SOUTH

		1	2	3	4	5	6	7	8	9	10	11	12	13
1	Burnham on S II		27/03	12/09	20/02	28/11	05/09	30/01	19/12	26/09	10/10	13/03	16/01	24/10
2	Castle Cary II	05/12		10/04	24/10	13/03	20/03	10/10	12/09	19/12	16/01	07/11	26/09	30/01
3	Chard III	12/12	05/09		07/11	27/03	19/09	24/10	26/09	16/01	30/01	28/11	10/10	20/02
4	Chew Valley II	31/10	13/02	06/03		17/10	09/01	12/09	14/11	20/03	10/04	23/01	05/12	19/12
5	Hornets III	20/03	14/11	05/12	30/01		06/03	16/01	10/04	12/09	26/09	20/02	19/12	10/10
6	Minehead Babas III	10/04	28/11	19/12	26/09	07/11		27/03	16/01	30/01	13/03	24/10	20/02	12/12
7	Morganians	17/10	23/01	13/02	12/12	03/10	05/12		31/10	06/03	20/03	09/01	14/11	05/09
8	Tor III	19/09	12/12	09/01	13/03	05/09	03/10	20/02		10/10	24/10	27/03	30/01	07/11
9	Wellington III	09/01	19/09	03/10	28/11	12/12	17/10	07/11	23/01		20/02	05/09	24/10	13/03
10	Wells III	23/01	03/10	17/10	05/09	09/01	14/11	28/11	13/02	31/10		19/09	06/03	27/03
11	Winscombe II	14/11	06/03	20/03	10/10	31/10	13/02	26/09	05/12	10/04	19/12		12/09	16/01
12	Wiveliscombe II	03/10	09/01	23/01	27/03	19/09	31/10	13/03	17/10	13/02	07/11	12/12		28/11
13	Wyvern	13/02	17/10	31/10	19/09	23/01	12/12	10/04	06/03	14/11	05/12	03/10	20/03	

SOUTH WEST LEVEL 7-11 & NON LEAGUE CLUBS

Abingdon RFC
Ground Address: Southern Sports Park Lambrick Way Abingdon OX14 5TJ
Contact: 01235 553810
Email: help@abingdonrufc.com
Website: www.abingdonrufc.co.uk
Directions: Exit Abington on the B4017, Drayton Road. Just prior to leaving the town limits, take left into Preston Road. Lambrick Way is 3rd turning on the right.
Honorary Secretary: Mr Simon North, The Gate House Faringdon Road Abingdon Oxfordshire OX14 1BG
Tel: 01235 206254
Email: simon@masonsneedlecraft.co.uk
Fixtures Secretary: Mr Andrew Abbey, 35 Masefield Crescent Abingdon Oxfordshire OX14 5PH
Tel: 01235 202957 Email: AndrewABBS@aol.com
Club Colours: Black with green / gold chest hoops
League: Berks-Bucks & Oxon Premier (level 8)

Alchester RFC
Honorary Secretary: Mr Keith Nash, 20 Blencowe Drive Brackley NN13 6HH
Tel: 07989 582645 Email: bgg1989@hotmail.co.uk
Fixtures Secretary: Steven Coogan, 8 Ewart Close Bicester Oxfordshire Tel: 01869 253736
Club Colours: Blue
League: Berks-Bucks & Oxon Premier (level 8)

Aldbourne Dabchicks RFC
Ground Address: The Crown Hotel The Square Aldbourne SN8 2DU
Contact: 01672 540075
Email: ewan.hayward@btinternet.com
Directions: Travelling on the B4192 from Swindon, when you reach Aldbourne the road turns sharply right and then sharply left. The Crown can be seen on the left hand side, behind the pond. Changing rooms are in the courtyard of the pub. To get to the pitch, continue on the B4192 over a mini roundabout and take the next right (Farm Lane). Take the second left, and the car park is on the right, behind a chain link fence. To get to the field, follow the chain link fence down the side of the football pitch and turn left at the end. Enjoy !
Honorary Secretary: Mr Ewan Hayward, Aldbourne Marlborough Wilts. SN8 2EH Tel: 01672 540475
Email: ewan.hayward@btinternet.com
Fixtures Secretary: Mr Paul Beresford, The Crown Hotel, The Square, Aldbourne, Malborough, Wilts. SN8 1XX   Tel: 01672 540620
Email: beresford.pbhome@btinternet.com
Club Colours: Sky Blue & Navy hoops
League: Dorset & Wilts 3 North (level 10)

Aldermaston RFC
Ground Address: Aldermaston Rugby Club AWE Aldermaston Berks. RG7 4PR
Contact: 0118 9814615
Email: Enquiries@aldermastonrugby.com
Website: www.aldermastonrugby.com
Directions: From Basingstoke follow direction to Tadley on A340 then for AWE, then for Recreational Society.
Honorary Secretary: Mr R Hawkins, 21 Portway Baughurst Tadley Hampshire RG26 5PD
Tel: 07889 348415 Email: randthawkins@hotmail.com
Fixtures Secretary: Mr Ian Martin, 16 Brackenwood Drive Tadley Hampshire RG26 4YB
Tel: 07791 370511 Email: ian.g.martin@awe.co.uk
Club Colours: Scarlet Shirts, Black Shorts
League: Berks-Bucks & Oxon 1 S (level 9)

Amersham & Chiltern RFC
Ground Address: Amersham & Chilten R.F.C. Ash Grove Weedon Lane, Chesham Bois Amersham Bucks. HP6 5QU
Contact: 01494 725 161
Email: mail@chilternrugby.com
Directions: From Amersham/Chesham road take Cooperkins Lane (signed for Hyde Heath), Weedon Lane is 2nd left.
Honorary Secretary: Mr Ralph Hayward, 62 Clifton Road Chesham Bois Amersham Bucks. HP6 5PN
Tel: 01494 431787
Email: jane@assonline.co.uk
Club Colours: Claret & White
League: Southern Counties North (level 7)

Aretians
Ground Address: Station Road Little Stoke Bristol BS34 6HW
Contact: 01454 888069
Email: webmaster@aretians.org.uk
Website: www.aretians.org.uk
Directions: M5 J16, A38 into Bristol, at flyover turn left signed Yate (gypsy patch lane), along road to railway bridge, directly left past bridge, ground approx 600 yards on right on Station Road.
Honorary Secretary: Mr John Jacques, 22 Olympus Close Little Stoke Bristol BS34 6HZ
Tel: 07867 905205 Email: aretianssec@aol.com
Fixtures Secretary: Mr John Lewis, 60 Arlington Road St. Annes Brislington Bristol BS4 4AJ
Tel: 077860 61804 Email: john.lewis@priorityexpress.co.uk
Club Colours: Black
League: Gloucester 1 (level 9)

Ashley Down Old Boys RFC
Ground Address: Lockleaze Combination Ground Bonnington Walk Lockleaze BS7 9YU
Contact: 07970171139
Email: Chris.S.Brown@axa-sunlife.co.uk
Website: www.ashleydownrfc.org.uk
Directions: From Filton Avenue, into Bonnington Walk, left at railway bridge, 0.25 mile along lane.
Honorary Secretary: Mr Chris Brown, 18 Mackie Avenue Filton Bristol BS34 7ND
Tel: 07970 171139
Email: Chris.S.Brown@axa-sunlife.co.uk
Fixtures Secretary: Mr Pat Donovan, 38 Memorial Road Hanham Bristol BS15 3JQ
Tel: 0117 9679649
Club Colours: Purple & White
League: Gloucester 1 (level 7)

Avon RFC
Ground Address: Hicks Field, London Road East Batheaston Bath Somerset BA1 6BD
Contact: 01225 852446
Email: Enquiries@AvonRFC.co.uk
Website: www.avonrfc.co.uk
Directions: From the A46 take the exit for Bath. At the r-a-b the club is signposted (heading for Batheaston) approx a quarter mile fromtthe r-a-b on the right hand side just at the end of the rank of houses.
Honorary Secretary: Mr Steve Mead, 10 Ludlow Close Willsbridge Bristol BS30 6EA
Tel: 01179 328616
Email: stevemead@bristolhome.fsnet.co.uk
Fixtures Secretary: Mr Paul Kirby,
Club Colours: Black & Amber
League: Somerset Premier (level 8)

Avonvale RFC
Ground Address: The Clubhouse, Bathford Playing FIelds Bathford Bath BA1 7SW
Contact: 01225 858195
Email: avonvalerfc@blueyonder.co.uk
Website: www.avonvalerfc.org.uk
Directions: A4 out of Bath, through Batheaston, right at next roundabout, under railway bridge and next left, club house is along a track next to phone box 200yds up Bathford Hill. See web site for map.
Honorary Secretary: Mr Stephen Ball, 59 Catherine Way Batheaston Bath BA1 7NY
Tel: 01225 859497   Email: baller43@fsmail.net
Fixtures Secretary: Mr Stephen Vowles, 72 Locksbrook Road Bath BA1 3ES   Tel: 01225 333852
Club Colours: Navy Blue and White
League: Dorset & Wilts 1 North (level 8)

Aylesbury Athletic RFC
Ground Address: H. M. Prison Bierton Road Aylesbury Bucks. HP20 1EH
Contact: 01246444318
Honorary Secretary: R Hemming, H M Prison Bierton Road Aylesbury Bucks. HP20 1EH
Tel: 01296 444000   Email: nolpeo@aol.com
Fixtures Secretary: R Hemming, H M Prison Bierton Road Aylesbury Bucks. HP20 1EH
Tel: 01296 444000   Email: nolpeo@aol.com
League: Berks-Bucks & Oxon 1 N (level 9)

Aylesbury RFC
Ground Address: Ostlers Field Brook End, Weston Turville Aylesbury Bucks. HP22 5RN
Contact: +44 (0)1296 427404
Email: john@fraser8020.fsworld.co.uk
Directions: Head West from Aston Clinton Bypass. At Aston Clinton Road, take the first exit onto Aston Clinton Road. Continue on Aylesbury Road. At the roundabout, take the second exit onto Western Road, continue on Brook End. Turn Right. Arrive at Aylesbury RFC. Take A413 towards Wendover, Turn at roundabout on B454 towards Weston Turville & Aston Clinton. Over 2 roundabouts, club 250 mt on left.
Honorary Secretary: Mr Daniel O'Donnell, 19 Water Lily Aylesbury Bucks. HP19 0FJ
Tel: 07976 914828
Email: daniel.odonnell@blackberry.orange.co.uk
Fixtures Secretary: Mr Stewart Frost, 18 Byron Road Aylesbury Bucks. HP21 7LU
Club Colours: Magenta and Black Hoops (Shirt)
League: Southern Counties North (level 7)

Balliol RFC
Ground Address: c/o Balliol College Broad Street Oxford OX1 3BJ
Contact: 07949557117
Email: samuel.brown@balliol.ox.ac.uk
Non League

Barton Hill RFC
Ground Address: Duncombe Lane Speedwell Bristol BS15 1NR
Contact: 07867 834864
Email: peor@blueyonder.co.uk
Directions: Follow roads to Lodge Causeway,(B4048) Fishponds. At lights half way up Causeway turn right into Berkeley road(B4465). which then goes into whitfields road after a about 400meters there is a left hand turning in to duncombe lane
Honorary Secretary: Mr Peter O' Regan, 20 Winscombe Close Keynsham Bristol BS31 2HR
Tel: 01179 832684   Email: peor@blueyonder.co.uk
Fixtures Secretary: Mr John Rigby, 171 Whitefield Road Speedwell Bristol BS5 7TF
Tel: 07754 743515   Email: riggers171@hotmail.com
Club Colours: White with Cherry Band
League: Western Counties North (level 7)

LEVEL 7-11 & NON LEAGUE CLUBS

Basildon (Berks) RFC
Ground Address: Recreation Ground (Not for correspondence) Bethesda Street Upper Basildon Berks.
Email: drones@deadbugs.co.uk
Website: www.drones-rfc.org.uk
Honorary Secretary: Mr Duncan Butler, 3 Ash Grove Bradfield Reading Berks. RG7 6HZ
Tel: 07799 478873   Email: duncan.butler@dhl.com
Fixtures Secretary: Jon Ridley, Hollycroft Hill Bottom Whitchurch Hill Reading Berks. Rg8 7PT
Tel: 07802 445179
Club Colours: Yellow & Black Hoops
Non League

Bath Old Edwardians
Ground Address:
King Edwards School Field Bathampton BA2 6TR
Contact: 01225316026
Email: buzz@batholdedwardians.org
Directions: M4 J18, A46 to Bath, London road towards Bathampton village. Ground is opp church. From Bath take A36
Honorary Secretary: Mr Andrew Charlton, 2 Royal Crescent Bath BA1 2LR   Tel: 07812 956970
Email: onethejuggler@yahoo.co.uk
Fixtures Secretary: Mr Richard Shipp, 4 Worcester Court Larkhall Bath BA1 6QT
Tel: 01793 555055   Email: rshipp@ssg-security.co.uk
Club Colours: Maroon, Gold, Blue
League: Somerset 2 North (level 10)

Bath Saracens RFC
Ground Address: Sulis Sports Ground Claverton Down Bath BA2 7AU
Contact: 01225424613
Email: kathmikeyork@hotmail.co.uk
Website: www.bathsaracens.co.uk
Directions: please see www.bathsaracens.co.uk.
Fixtures Secretary: Mr R Lawrence, 91 Englishcombe Lane Bath BA2 2EH   Tel: 07802 797756
Email: robbie.lawrence21@btinternet.com
Club Colours: Navy Blue,Cardinal Red,Gold
League: Dorset & Wilts 2 North (level 9)

Beaconsfield RFC
Ground Address: Oak Lodge Meadow Windsor End Beaconsfield Bucks. HP9 2SQ
Contact: 01494 673783
Email: steve.dymond@bt.com
Website: www.brfc.org.uk
Directions: Exit M40 at Junction 2 and follow signs to Beaconsfield. At the centre of the Old Town (roundabout at Parish Church) turn left,signposted local traffic only, and the club is 800metres and on your left.
Fixtures Secretary: Mr Mike Wood, 23 Chilton Close Tylers Green Penn High Wycombe Bucks. HP10 8AQ
Tel: 01494 607767
Club Colours: Green and Gold Hooped Jerseys
League: Southern Counties North (level 7)

Berkshire Shire Hall RFC
Ground Address: Berkshire Sports and Social Club Sonning Lane, Sonning Reading Berks. RG4 6ST
Contact: 0118 9691340
Email: paul.chandler@pantheongroup.co.uk
Website: www.shirehallrugby.co.uk
Directions: From Reading head towards A4 up Shepherds House Hill, pass BP garage on right , take left Sonning Lane , second turning on the right.
Honorary Secretary: Mr Brian Cooper,
Fixtures Secretary: Mr Brian Cooper,
Club Colours: Yellow and Blue Hoops
League: Berks-Bucks & Oxon 1 S (level 9)

Berry Hill RFC
Ground Address:
Lakers Road. Berry Hill. Coleford. GL16 8QT
Contact: 01594 833800
Email: Lee.Osborne@Xerox.Com
Website: www.berryhillrfc.co.uk
Directions: From M4 Severn Bridge M48 to Chepstow B4428 to Coleford follow signs for Berry Hill. From M50 A40 to Monmouth then A4136 to Berry Hill. From Gloucester A40 then Follow A4136 from Huntley to Berry Hill.
Honorary Secretary: Mr Lee Osborne, 30 Prospect Close Bells Place Coleford Coleford GL16 7LA
Tel: 01594 833800   Email: lee.osborne@xerox.com
Fixtures Secretary: Mr Keith Horrobin
Tel: 01594 822490
Club Colours: Black and Amber
League: Western Counties North (level 7)

Bicester RFC
Ground Address: Bicester Rugby Club Oxford Road Bicester OX26 2AB
Contact: 01869 241993
Email: BRUFC@rtfmsoftware.com
Website: www.bicesterrufc.org.uk
Directions: From the centre of the town, take the road toward Oxford. The Clubhouse is on the left when leaving the town. From Junction 9 M40 take the A41 towards town. The club is on the right next to Tesco's.
Honorary Secretary: Mr Trevor Bethell, 63 Partridge Chase Bicester Oxfordshire OX26 6XF
Tel: 01869 244760
Email: tmb@forcefield.fslife.co.uk
Fixtures Secretary: Mr George Davies, 166 Barry Avenue Bicester Oxfordshire OX26 2HB
Tel: 01869 241993
Club Colours: Red, amber & brown shirts, navy shorts
League: Southern Counties North (level 7)

Bideford RFC
Ground Address: Bideford R.F.C. King George's Field Riverside, Bank End Bideford Devon EX39 2QS
Contact: 01237 474049
Email: derekstaddon@dsl.pipex.com
Directions: N.D. link road (A39), left end of Bideford New Bridge into town until reach river, immediate left at Charles Kingsley statue, proceed River Bank Road to Bideford RFC car park.
Honorary Secretary: Ms Carol Norman, 3 Chudleigh Terrace Torrington Lane Bideford Devon EX39 4BG
Tel: 01237 424033
Fixtures Secretary: Mr Colin Balsdon, 15 Middleton Road Bideford Devon EX39 3LU
Tel: 01237 472166
Club Colours: Cherry and White Hoops
League: Cornwall-Devon (level 8)

Bishopston RFC
Ground Address: Bonnington Walk Lockleaze Bristol BS7 9XH
Contact: 0117 969 1916
Honorary Secretary: Mr Dave Martin, 17 Queens Drive Bishopston Bristol BS7 8JR
Tel: 0117 9240747 Email: rhino1950@yahoo.co.uk
Fixtures Secretary: Mr Stuart Brain, 46 Clarence Avenue Staple Hill Bristol BS16 5SX
Tel: 07989 366664
Club Colours: Black with red hoop edged with gold
League: Gloucester 1 (level 9)

Blagdon
Ground Address: The Mead Blagdon Bristol
Email: blagdonrfc@yahoo.co.uk
Directions: Turn left off the A38 at Churchhill traffic lights and follow road for approx. 3 miles into Blagdon.
Honorary Secretary: Mr Henry King, 12 Lewmond Avenue Wells BA5 2TS
Tel: 01749 673721
Email: blagdonrfc@googlemail.com
Fixtures Secretary: Mr Richard Probert, 26 Longcross Felton Bristol BS40 9YH
Tel: 07900 643660
Email: raprobert@hotmail.com
Club Colours: Green & Black hoops
Non League

Blandford RFC
Ground Address: Club House 53a East Street Blandford Forum Dorset DT11 7DX
Contact: 07917 768897
Email: leanivan@gmail.com
Website: www.blandfordrfc.com
Directions: Ground address - Blandford School, take the Shaftstbury Road from Town Centre and the ground is behind the sports centre.
Honorary Secretary: Mrs Leani Haim, 31 Old Farm Gardens Blandford Forum Dorset DT11 7UU
Tel: 07917 768897   Email: leanivan@gmail.com
Fixtures Secretary: Mr Dave Stringer, Valley View Dorchester Hill Blandford St. Mary Blandford Forum Dorset DT11 9AB
Tel: 01258 456954   Email: dave.stringer2@btinternet.com
Club Colours: Brown, Gold, Red & White Hoops
League: Dorset & Wilts 1 South (level 8)

Bodmin RFC
Ground Address: Bodmin R.F.C. Clifden Park Carmminow Cross Bodmin Cornwall PL30 4AW
Contact: 01208 74629
Email: andyrichards1961@hotmail.co.uk
Website: http://clubs.rfu.com/Clubs/portals/BodminRFC/Default.aspx
Directions: Directions: Off A38 before flyover at A30. Take B road signed posted to Lanhydrock 400yds turn right down private lane.
Honorary Secretary: Mrs Susan Whittington, Icarus Fore Street Hessenford Torpoint Cornwall PL11 3HP
Tel: 01503 240635
Email: susan-_whittington@tiscali.co.uk
Fixtures Secretary: Mr Ray Hunt, Trebodwyn Launceston Road Bodmin Cornwall PL31 2AR
Tel: 01208 72705
Club Colours: Light Blue with Dark Blue Band
League: Cornwall League (level 9)

Bournemouth University RFC
Ground Address: Slades Farm Ensbury Park Bournemouth Dorset
Contact: 01202 595012
Email: lreeve@bournemouth.ac.uk
Website: www.bournemouth.ac.uk/sports
Honorary Secretary: Honorary Secretary, Department of Sport and Recreation Bournemouth University Poole House Fern Barrow Poole Dorset BH12 5BB
Fixtures Secretary: Miss Amanda Kevern,
Email: akevern@bournemouth.ac.uk
Club Colours: Royal Blue/Navy & Two White Hoops
Non League

Bradford-on-Avon RFC
Ground Address: Broom Ground, Ashley Lane Winsley Bradford-on-Avon Wilts. BA15 2HR
Contact: 01225 309003
Email: marmizen@aol.com
Directions: Two miles from Bradford town centre, just north of the B3108 Winsley by-pass.
Honorary Secretary: Mr Peter Macgregor, 24 Bearfield Buildings Bradford On Avon Wilts. BA15 1RP
Tel: 01225 865107
Email: peter@bearfld.demon.co.uk
Fixtures Secretary: Mrs Karen Wilson, 23 Kingsfield Bradford On Avon Wilts. BA15 1AN
Tel: 07791 446610
Email: karenwilsonboa@aol.com
Club Colours: Red & Black
League: Southern Counties South (level 7)

LEVEL 7-11 & NON LEAGUE CLUBS

Brasenose RFC
Ground Address: c/o Brasenose College Radcliffe Square Oxford OX1 4AJ
Email: colum.elliett-kelly@bnc.ox.ac.uk
Non League

Bream RFC
Ground Address: High St. Bream Nr. Lydney GL15 6JE
Contact: 01594 562320
Directions: Approx. 3 miles off main A48 Gloucester to Chepstow road, turn right after Westbury Homes site on right hand side.
Honorary Secretary: Mr Graham Moxey, Homestead New Road Bream Lydney Gloucestershire GL15 6HJ
Tel: 01594 562345
Email: joelmoxey@gmail.com
Fixtures Secretary: as Hon. Sec.
Email: joelmoxey@gmail.com
League: Gloucester 1 (level 9)

Bridport RFC
Ground Address: Bridport R.F.C. Bridport Leisure Centre Brewery Fields Brewery Fields Bridport Dorset DT6 5LN
Contact: 01308 423338
Email: adrianbutler@hstead.eclipse.co.uk
Website: www.bridportrfc.co.uk
Directions: Take A35 Bridport By Pass , at R'about south of town turn R. (North). After 300yrds turn L. at Traffic Lightsopp. Safeway Store.
Fixtures Secretary: Jason Blackmore, Fox Ridge North Allington Bridport Dorset BT6 5EQ
Tel: 07765 255922
Email: brfc.fixtures@googlemail.com
Club Colours: Blue, White & Red
League: Dorset & Wilts 1 South (level 8)

Bristol Aeroplane Co. RFC
Ground Address: BAWA Sports Field 589, Southmead Road Filton BS34 7RG
Contact: 01179 768066
Directions: From M4/M5 motorway junction at Almonsbury take A38 south to Bristol, at roundabout at Filton turn right. Ground down Southmead road on the right
Honorary Secretary: Mr Andrew Macleod, 28 Fourth Avenue Bristol AVON BS7 0RW
Tel: 07968 124250
Email: bacrfcsecretary@yahoo.co.uk
Fixtures Secretary: Mr Mike Rogers, Bawa Sportsfield 589 Southmead Road Filton Bristol AVON BS12 7DG
Tel: 07746 879954
Club Colours: Red, white and blue hoops
League: Gloucester 2 (level 10)

Bristol Barbarians (Formerly British Gas Bristol)
Ground Address:
Norton Lane Whitchurch Bristol BS14 0BT
Contact: 01275 833514
Email: ma@bristolbarbarians.co.uk
Website: www.bristolbarbarians.co.uk

Directions: On A37 from Bristol, past Black Lion pub,over bridge, right by playground. 1st gate on right.
Honorary Secretary: Mr Brendan Murphy, 59 Berkeley Road Bishopston Bristol AVON BS7 8HQ
Tel: 07876 735153
Email: brendan@guide2bristol.com
Fixtures Secretary: Mr Ian Hiller
Club Colours: Black & white hoops
League: Somerset 1 (level 9)

Bristol Harlequins RFC
Ground Address: Valhalla, Broomhill Road Brislington Brislington Bristol BS4 5RG
Contact: 0117 9721650
Email: info@bristolharlequins.com
Website: www.bristolharlequins.com
Directions: The Ground is situated behind St.Brendans College on the A4 between Bath and Bristol.
Honorary Secretary: Mr Ian Nunnerley, 17 Warmington Road Bristol BS14 9HG
Tel: 0117 9711597
Email: ian@nunnerley.wanadoo.co.uk
Club Colours: Blue, Black & White Hoops
League: Somerset Premier (level 8)

Bristol Saracens RFC
Ground Address: Bakewell Memorial Ground Station Road Cribbs Causeway Henbury BS10 7TT
Contact: 0117 9500037
Email: catherine.miles@blueyonder.co.uk
Website: www.bristolsaracensrfc.co.uk
Directions: M5 J17 towards Bristol city centre, approx. 1000 meters at 2nd roundabout on right.
Honorary Secretary: Mr Chris Matthews, 6 Wellington Drive Henleaze Bristol BS9 4SR
Tel: 07768 990980
Email: c.j.matthews49@btinternet.com
Fixtures Secretary: Mark Parkman, 26 Cransley Crescent Henleaze Bristol BS9 4PG
Tel: 01179 621441   Email: mark.parkman@sky.com
Club Colours: Myrtle green & white shirts
League: Gloucester Premier (level 8)

Bristol Telephone Area RFC
Ground Address: BT Sports Ground Stockwood Lane Stockwood Whitchurch BS14 8SJ
Contact: 01275 891776
Website: www.btarfc.org
Directions: Take A37 (Wells road) for approx. 4 miles from city centre, left at Black Lion pub at Whitchurch, ground approx 1 mile on right.
Honorary Secretary: Mr David Button, 20 Kingshill Road Knowle Park Bristol AVON BS4 2SG
Tel: 01179 719774
Email: dave.button@premierfoods.co.uk
Fixtures Secretary: Mr Chris Watts
Club Colours: Blue with Red & White V-neck
League: Gloucester 3 (level 11)

BRNC Dartmouth
Ground Address: C/O Royal Navy Rugby Union HMS TEMERAIRE Portsmouth Hampshire PO1 2HB
Contact: 023 9272 4193
Email: cb-honsec-navy@therfu.com
Website: www.navyrugbyunion.co.uk
Honorary Secretary: C Edwards
Tel: 01803 677035
Email: brnc-11t@a.dii.mod.uk
Non League

Broad Plain RFC
Ground Address: Broad Plain R.F.C. St Johns park St Johns lane Bedminster Bristol AVON BS3 5AZ
Contact: 01179 638531
Email: broadplainrugbyclub@btconnect.com
Website: www.broadplainrfc.co.uk
Honorary Secretary: Miss Kelly Daveridge, 125 Bristol South End Bedminster Bristol AVON BS3 5BT
Tel: 07775 692334
Email: kellydaveridge@hotmail.com
Fixtures Secretary: Mr John Daveridge, 115 Ravenhill Road Bedminster Bristol BS3 4LS
Tel: 07866 410954
Email: daveridgejohn@yahoo.co.uk
Club Colours: Blue maroon & gold hoops
League: Somerset 1 (level 9)

Broadmoor Staff RFC
Ground Address: Cricket Field Grove Broadmoor Estate Crowthorne Berks. RG45 7EG
Website: http://www.broadmoorrugby.com
Directions: From M4 junction 10 towards Bracknell on A329M At the end of the A329M (large roundabout) take the 2nd exit towards Southern Industrial Estate (Waitrose) Next mini roundabout take 2nd exit to next roundabout where you should take the 3rd exit (Peacock Lane) Currently, a new estate is being built, follow the directions for Wokingham & Crowthorne, takes you over three new roundabouts. The road after this is a little twisty and windy but stay on this road until you reach the next roundabout take the 2nd exit (straight over) Follow to the next roundabout (Chequered) take 3rd exit towards Crowthorne After 20 yards turn left into Brookers Corner which follows into Upper Broadmoor Road Follow to the top of the hill (there are traffic calming chicanes on this road) at the junction the Hospital wall is directly in front of you look to the right and you will see the pitch the changing facilities and parking are on the right (Cricket Field Grove).
Honorary Secretary: Mr Alan Fenton, 8 Russell Close Bracknell Berks. RG12 7FE
Tel: 077 67850127
Email: honsec@broadmoorrugby.com
Fixtures Secretary: Mr Chris Bennett, 71 Ringwood Bracknell Berks. RG12 8YQ
Tel: 078 7519 2706
Email: fixsec@broadmoorrugby.com
Club Colours: Black w/- Gold
League: Berks-Bucks & Oxon Premier (level 8)

Brockworth RFC
Ground Address: Mill Lane Brockworth Gloucester GL3 4HQ
Contact: 01452 862 556
Email: gazzerhammond@hotmail.com
Directions: Leave M5 at junction 11A follow A417 towards Cirencester , leave A417 at first junction turning onto A46 Cheltenham - Stroud Road , turn right at roundabout towards Stroud , take first turning right into Mill Lane , pass school on left, Rugby Club is 200
Honorary Secretary: Mr Dave Alden, 37 Boverton Avenue Brockworth Gloucester GL3 4ER
Tel: 07747 125779 Email: dabr23668@blueyonder.co.uk
Fixtures Secretary: Mr Pete Hickey, 63 Falfield Road Tuffley Gloucester GL4 0ND
Tel: 01452 308819 Email: peterhickey@blueyonder.co.uk
Club Colours: Black with White 'V'
League: Gloucester 1 (level 9)

Buckfastleigh Ramblers RFC
Ground Address: The Cricket Ground Buckfastleigh Devon TQ11 0BE
Contact: 01364 642768
Email: sue.farley@millwood.uk.com
Honorary Secretary: Mrs Nicky Leibrick, 11 Orchard Close Kingsteignton Devon TQ12 3DF
Tel: 07813 538378 Email: steveleibrick@aol.com
Fixtures Secretary: Mr T Major, 3 Duckspond Close Buckfastleigh Tel: 07740 805858
Club Colours: Black & Gold
League: Devon 1 North & East (level 9)

Bude RFC
Ground Address: Bencoolen Meadows, Bude, Cornwall EX23 8QG
Contact: 01288 359566
Email: jane@jpettit.freeserve.co.uk
Directions: Turn into Stratton Rd off A39 and turn left at the bottom of hill into kings hill (by the petrol station) then take the 1st right and then the 2nd right into Bude rugby club.
Honorary Secretary: Mrs Jane Pettit, Manor Barn Poughill Bude Cornwall EX23 9HA
Tel: 01288 359566 Email: janepettit@hotmail.com
Club Colours: Maroon & sky blue hoops
League: Western Counties West (level 7)

Burnham-on-Sea
Ground Address: Burnham Association of Sports Clubs Stoddens Road Burnham-on-Sea Somerset TA8 2NZ
Contact: 01934 751009/750245
Email: secretary@burnhamonsearfc.org.uk
Directions: From M5 J22 take second exit towards Burnham on Sea. After 2-3 miles turn right at Tescos r'about onto Stoddens Rd. Ground is 1 mile on right.
Hon. Secretary: Katie Ede Email: katie.ede@sky.com
Fixtures Secretary: Mr Christopher Jones, 32 Chapel Road Pawlett Bridgwater Somerset TA6 4SH
Tel: 01278 684194
Club Colours: Blue/white jersey
League: Western Counties North (level 7)

LEVEL 7-11 & NON LEAGUE CLUBS

Cainscross RFC
Ground Address: Victory Park, Cainscross, Stroud, Glos. GL5 4JE
Contact: 01453 757181
Email: David.Roberts7@tesco.net
Directions: Take 2nd exit from Horse Trough R'about. Westward Road Ebley into Church road (on left just before Imo carwash). When travelling from M5.
Honorary Secretary: Mr Dave Roberts, 24 Upper Church Road Cainscross Stroud Gloucestershire GL5 4JF
Tel: 01453 757181   Email: david.roberts7@tesco.net
Fixtures Secretary: Mr Keith Elliott, 136 The Old Common Chalford Stroud Gloucestershire GL6 8JT
Email: bodge.elliott@virgin.net
Club Colours: Amber & blue
League: Gloucester 2 (level 10)

Calne RFC
Ground Address: Recreation Ground Anchor Road Calne SN11 8DX
Email: play4calne@btopenworld.com
Website: www.calnerfc.co.uk
Directions: Heading East along the A4: At the traffic light in the centre of Calne turn left. 50 metres take left fork for Anchor Road. Proceed up to the top of the incline. At the top find the Recreation Ground and Club house on the left a further 100 metre along t
Honorary Secretary: Mr Matthew Snell, 0 Magnolia Rise Calne Wilts. SN11 0QP
Tel: 07816 686764
Email: play4calne@btopenworld.com
Fixtures Secretary: Mr Jonathan Hope-Smith, 55 Anchor Road Calne Wilts. SN11 8EA
Tel: 01249 817483
Email: johnnyhs@atacuk.demon.co.uk
Club Colours: Blue with Red & White Hoops
League: Dorset & Wilts 1 North (level 8)

Camborne RFC
Ground Address: Crane Park Clubhouse (Camborne Recreation Ground) Cranberry Rd Camborne TR14 7PW
Contact: 01209 712684
Email: wnorthbywest@aol.com
Directions: Leave the A30 Westbound at the 'Camborne West' junction, take the first left, and left again at the roundabout into Camborne, carry straight on for approx half a mile and follow signs for Camborne RFC on right hand side.
Honorary Secretary: Mr Stephen West, Shorebase Killivose Road Camborne Cornwall TR14 7RN
Tel: 01736 795618
Email: wnorthbywest@aol.com
Fixtures Secretary: Ewart White
Tel: 01209 713745
Club Colours: Cherry and White
League: Western Counties West (level 7)

Camborne School of Mines RFC
Ground Address: Camborne School of Mines Tremough Campus Penryn Cornwall TR10 9EZ
Contact: 01326 371828
Email: P.J.Foster@csm.ex.ac.uk
Directions: Share Ground with Penryn RFC, Penryn, Cornwall.
Honorary Secretary: Mr Patrick Foster, 22 Gwarth an Drae Helston Cornwall TR13 0BS
Tel: 01326 560310
Email: p.j.foster@csm.ex.ac.uk
Club Colours: Navy, Gold & Silver Hoops
League: Cornwall League (level 9)

Castle Cary RFC
Ground Address: Brookhouse Field Nr. Alhampton, Ditcheat Castle Cary BA7 7AF
Contact: 01963 370642
Email: Vivarmson@hsbc.com
Directions: The ground is located off the A371, approximately two miles from Castle Cary town centre, in the direction of Bristol/Bath near the train station.
Honorary Secretary: Ms Viv Armson, Sweet Apple Barn Rodgrove Wincanton Somerset BA9 9QU
Tel: 07836 275437
Email: vivarmson@hsbc.com
Fixtures Secretary: Mr Gareth Watts, 15 Woodforde Green Ansford Castle Cary BA7 7LD
Tel: 01963 350162
Club Colours: Black & Red Hoops
League: Somerset 2 South (level 10)

CDO LOGS REGT
Ground Address: C/O Royal Navy Rugby Union HMS TEMERAIRE Portsmouth Hampshire PO1 2HB
Contact: 023 9272 5238
Email: cb-honsec-navy@therfu.com
Non League

Chard RFC
Ground Address: The Park Essex Close Chard Somerset TA20 1RH
Contact: 01460 62495
Email: secretary@chardrfc.co.uk
Directions: Bottom of Chard High Street (by Cerdic), 100 yards up Essex Close.
Honorary Secretary: Mr Brian Twigg, Stepps House Broadway Ilminster Somerset TA19 9RG
Tel: 01460 57700
Email: briantwigg@globalinteriors-southwest.co.uk
Fixtures Secretary: Mr Richard Adams, 43 Crimchard Chard Somerset TA20 1jt
Tel: 077 38643204
Email: rpadams@btinternet.com
Club Colours: Black red & gold
League: Somerset Premier (level 8)

Cheltenham Civil Service RFC
Ground Address: Civil Service Sports Ground Tewkesbury Road, Uckington Cheltenham GL51 9SL
Contact: 01242 680424
Email: rugby@cacssa.org.uk
Website: www.ccsrfc.ndo.co.uk
Directions: In Uckington, west of Cheltenham on A4019 to Tewkesbury. Maps, directions, and satellite picture can be found on the club website
Honorary Secretary: Mr Peter Shortell, 81 Hales Road Cheltenham Gloucestershire GL52 6SR
Tel: 01242 510849   Email: pshortell@bigfoot.com
Fixtures Secretary: Mr Kaz Dabrowski, 2 Genista Way Up Hatherley Cheltenham Gloucestershire GL51 3XZ
Tel: 01242 863040   Email: kazdee@talktalk.net
Club Colours: Navy Blue shirts and shorts, Red socks
League: Gloucester 1 (level 9)

Cheltenham Saracens RFC
Ground Address: Cheltenham Saracens Sports Club 16-20 Swindon Road Cheltenham GL50 4AL
Contact: 07789903380
Website: www.csrfc.co.uk
Directions: 1st & 2nd Team Games 'King George V Playing Fields' - GL51 8DT Exit Junction 11 M5 Follow A40 towards Cheltenham pass GCHQ, take left at next roundabout (Princess Elizabeth Way) Follow P.E. Way through Coronation Square (Second Exit), at end take right at roundabout.
Honorary Secretary: Mr John Bradley, 347 Innsworth Lane Churchdown Gloucester GL3 1EY
Tel: 01452 855545
Email: cheltsaracensrugby@hotmail.com
Fixtures Secretary: Mr Jimmy O'Shea, Cheltenham Saracens Sports Club 16-20 Swindon Road Cheltenham Gloucestershire GL50 4AL
Tel: 07876 195884   Email: corkicjim@aol.com
Club Colours: Royal Blue with Gold Circle
League: Gloucester 2 (level 10)

Chesham RUFC
Ground Address: Chesham Park Community College Chartridge Lane Chesham HP5 2RG
Contact: 01494 784951
Email: cheshamrufc@btconnect.com
Website: www.cheshamrugbyclub.co.uk
Directions: Location: Follow dual carriage way (St Marys Way) to the centre of Chesham. At roundabout take exit onto Park Road/Chartridge Lane with the park on the left. At the top of the hill on the left is Chesham Park Community College. Take the furthest (secon
Honorary Secretary: Mr Steven Morris, Chartridge Hill House 109 Flat 2 Chartridge Lane Chesham Bucks. HP5 2RG   Tel: 07887 632704
Email: secretary@cheshamrugbyclub.co.uk
Fixtures Secretary: Mr Richard King, 75 Darvell Drive Chesham Bucks. HP5 2QN   Tel: 07710 011633
Email: fixtures@cheshamrugbyclub.co.uk
Club Colours: Blue and Claret hoops
League: Berks-Bucks & Oxon 2 1 N (level 9)

Chew Valley RFC
Ground Address: Lobbingtons Chew Lane Chew Stoke BS40 8UE
Contact: 07768 773825
Email: mjb-jlb@supanet.com
Directions: Between Chew Stoke and Chew Magna, next to Chew Valley School.
Honorary Secretary: Matt Burke, Maple Lodge Sutton Yard Sutton Hill Road Bishop Sutton Avon BS39 5UR
Tel: 07768 773825   Email: mjb-jlb@supanet.com
Fixtures Secretary: Mr Ian Hall, 2 Chalk Farm Close Norton Malreward Pensford Bristol BS39 4HQ
Tel: 01275 837987   Email: consettonian@aol.com
League: Somerset Premier (level 8)

Chipping Norton RFC
Ground Address: Greystones Burford Road Chipping Norton Oxfordshire OX7 5UY
Contact: 01608 643968
Email: cnrufc@btconnect.com
Website: www.cnrufc.co.uk
Directions: 1 mile from the centre of Chipping Norton on the A361 heading towards Burford, left side of road. Goal posts identifying the site can be clearly seen from the road. Grid Ref: SP 31657 25840
Honorary Secretary: Glenn Chapman, 26 Hanover close charlbury Oxfordshire ox73td
Tel: 01608 811077
Email: glennchapman@btinternet.com
Fixtures Secretary: Mr Jason Gillett, Ashmy Cottage Main Rd Oddington Moreton-in-Marsh Glos. GL56 0XW
Tel: 07879 897303
Email: sprogdie@moogie.fslife.co.uk
Club Colours: Red and Black hoops
League: Southern Counties North (level 7)

Chipping Sodbury RFC
Ground Address: The Ridings Wickwar Road Chipping Sodbury BS37 6BQ
Contact: 01454 853633
Email: csrfc@uk2.net
Directions: Take Wickwar Rd out of Chipping Sodbury. The ground is .5 mile on the right hand side.
Honorary Secretary: Mr Mark Barker, The Apartment 44 The High Street Chipping Sodbury Avon BS37 6AH
Tel: 01454 853308
Email: mark.barker@rolls-royce.com
Fixtures Secretary: Mr Gary Fry
Tel: 07771 530252   Email: garypfry@hotmail.com
Club Colours: Black
League: Gloucester 1 (level 9)

Christchurch RFC
Ground Address: c/o Christ Church College St. Aldate's Oxford OX1 1DP
Contact: 07789814499
Email: duncan.chiah@chch.ox.ac.uk
Non League

LEVEL 7-11 & NON LEAGUE CLUBS

Cirencester RFC
Ground Address: The Whiteway Cirencester Gloucestershire GL7 2ER
Contact: 0 1285654434
Email: chairman@crfc.co.uk
Website: www.crfc.co.uk
Directions: Positioned at traffic lights on main Gloucester to Swindon A419 road, approx 1 mile from town centre.
Honorary Secretary: Mrs Lisa Priestner, 47 Tarlton Cirencester Gloucestershire GL7 6PA
Tel: 01285 770906
Email: lisapriestner-crfc@hotmail.com
Fixtures Secretary: Mrs Sharon Scrivens, The Bees Knees Watermoor Cirencester Gloucestershire GL7 1LF
Tel: 01285 652215
Club Colours: Red & black hoops, Black shorts
League: Gloucester Premier (level 8)

Colerne RFC
Ground Address: Higgins Field Bath Road Colerne SN14 8QP
Contact: 01225 742328
Email: ben.harraway@dial.pipex.com
Honorary Secretary: Mr Ben Harraway, Northwood Farm Colerne Chippenham Wilts. SN14 8QP
Tel: 07762 823844
Email: ben.harraway@dial.pipex.com
Fixtures Secretary: Mr John Hutchinson, 7 Grocyn Close Colerne Chippenham Wilts. SN14 8DZ
Tel: 01225 744336
Email: dianeandjohnhutchinson@talktalk.net
Club Colours: Black
League: Dorset & Wilts 1 North (level 8)

Combe Down RFC
Ground Address: Holly's Corner North Road Combe Down BA2 5DE
Contact: 01225832075
Email: combedownrfc@aol.com
Website: www.combedownrfc.com
Directions: Follow A3062 from Bath to Combe Down. Club situated 100 yards from MOD Foxhill site.
Honorary Secretary: Mr Warren Miller, 60 Hansford Square Combe Down Bath BA2 5LJ
Tel: 01225 837750
Email: combedownrfc@aol.com
Fixtures Secretary: Mr Steve White, 48 Blackmore Drive Southdown Bath Somerset BA2 1JN
Tel: 07801 456270
Club Colours: Black & amber
League: Somerset 1 (level 9)

Corpus Christie/Somerville RFC
Ground Address: c/o Somerville College Woodstock Road Oxford OX2 6HD
Contact: 07717803711
Email: thomas.charlick@some.ox.ac.uk
Non League

Corsham RFC
Ground Address: Corsham RFC Lacock Road Corsham Wilts. SN13 9QG
Contact: 01249 782733
Email: craig.avent@virgin.net
Directions: From centre of town follow signs for Melksham and at mini roundabout by War memorial go straight on sign posted Lacock (this is Lacock road). After approximatley half a mile the ground is on the right, 100 hundred yards after football club.
Honorary Secretary: Mr Pete Coombs, 18 Glebe Way Corsham Wilts. SN13 9UL
Tel: 07968 385646
Email: pete@coombs18.co.uk
Fixtures Secretary: Mr Richard Slade, 46 Paul Street Corsham Wilts. SN13 9DG
Tel: 01249 712683
Email: richard.slade4@tiscali.co.uk
Club Colours: Red,White,Black hoops
League: Southern Counties South (level 7)

Cotham Park RFC
Ground Address: Cotham Park RFC Upper Farm, Beggar Bush Lane Failand, Bristol Somerset BS8 3TF
Contact: 01275 392501
Email: meechans@btinternet.com
Website: www.cothamparkrfc.co.uk
Directions: M5 J19 , A369 towards Bristol, left on A3129(Beggar Bush Lane)
Honorary Secretary: Mr Christopher Meechan, 13 Hillside Road Long Ashton Bristol BS41 9LG
Tel: 01275 393697
Email: meechans@btinternet.com
Fixtures Secretary: Mr Nick Mortell, 5 Orchard Road Shirehampton Bristol BS119RW
Tel: 07787170265
Email: nick.mortell@waht.swest.nhs.uk
Club Colours: Black & White
League: Gloucester 2 (level 10)

Crediton RFC
Ground Address: Crediton R.F.C. Blagdon Exhibition Road Crediton Devon EX17 1BY
Contact: 01363 772784
Email: paul@blagdon15.eclipse.co.uk
Website: www.creditonrugby.com
Directions: M5 to Exter , A377 to Crediton then A3072 towards Tiverton, club on left hand side of road.
Honorary Secretary: Mrs Lynn Andrews, Mount Penny Hookway Crediton Devon EX17 3PU
Tel: 01363 773298
Email: lynn.andrews4@btopenworld.com
Fixtures Secretary: Mr M Leyman, Pepperlake New Buildings Sandford Crediton Devon EX17 4PZ
Tel: 07736 878356
Club Colours: Black and Amber
League: Cornwall-Devon (level 8)

Crewkerne
Ground Address:
Henhayes Crewkerne Somerset TA18 7JJ
Contact: 01460 74105
Email: racheljmorris@aol.com
Directions: Head for Crewkerne town centre. Follow signs to the Aqua Centre or Henhayes, situated besides car park. Park in main car park. Clubhouse/ field are visible from car park.
Honorary Secretary: Mrs Rachel Morris, 9 Middle Path Crewkerne Somerset TA18 8BG
Tel: 07971 855282
Email: racheljmorris@aol.com
Fixtures Secretary: Mr Trevor Boyer, 55 St. James Beaminster Dorset DT8 3PW
Tel: 01308 863169
Club Colours: Scarlet & Black Hoops
League: Somerset 2 South (level 10)

Cricklade RFC
Ground Address: Cricklade RFC Fairview Field Cricklade Wilts. SN6 6BA
Contact: 01793 750749
Email: john.a88ott@lineone.net
Website: www.crickladerfc.co.uk
Directions: From the M4 junction 15 take the A419 Swindon continuing on the A419 towards Cirencester take the left turn off the A419 signposted Cricklade, Malmesbury. At your first roundabout go straight on look to your left and you will see the pitch. Changing facilities are currently at the Cricklade Leisure Centre which is signposted from the centre of Cricklade.
Honorary Secretary: Mr John Abbott, 4 North Wall Cricklade Swindon Wilts. SN6 6DU
Tel: 01793 750749   Email: john.a88ott@lineone.net
Fixtures Secretary: Miss Nicola Mcknight, 47 Stockham Close Cricklade Swindon Wilts. SN6 6EF
Tel: 07769 736904
Email: nicolamcknight@hotmail.com
Club Colours: Red/Green Quarters Black Shorts
League: Dorset & Wilts 1 North (level 8)

CTCRM Lympstone
Ground Address: C/O Royal Navy Rugby Union HMS TEMERAIRE Portsmouth Hampshire PO1 2HB
Contact: 023 9272 4193
Email: cb-honsec-navy@therfu.com
Website: www.navyrugbyunion.co.uk
Non League

Dartmouth RFC
Ground Address: Roseville Pavilion Roseville Street Dartmouth Devon TQ6 9QH
Contact: 01803 833994
Directions: Milton Lane : Enter Dartmouth from Totnes. First right , past Park & ride, Dartmouth School & Community College.
Honorary Secretary: Mr Nick Shillabeer, 82 Above Town Dartmouth Devon TQ6 9RQ
Email: nshillabeer@mac.com

Fixtures Secretary: Mr Steve Atkins, 125 Victoria Road Dartmouth Devon TQ6 9DY
Tel: 07790 261986   Email: ackey@btinternet.co.uk
Club Colours: red with green flash black shorts
League: Devon 1 South & West (level 9)

Devizes RFC
Ground Address: Chivers Ground, The Sports Club London Road Devizes Wilts. SN10 2DL
Contact: 01380 723763
Email: secretary@devizesrfc.org.uk
Website: http://www.devizesrfc.org.uk
Directions: From the East, we're just after the Police HQ before the canal bridge. From the West, we're immediately after the canal bridge and before Police HQ.
Honorary Secretary: Mr Clive Meaney, 10 Park Road Market Lavington Devizes Wilts. SN10 4ED
Tel: 07976 610547   Email: secretary@devizesrfc.org.uk
Fixtures Secretary: Mr James Plank, 36 Roundway Park Devizes Wilts. SN10 2ED
Tel: 07815 796962   Email: milkoplank@aol.com
Club Colours: Black with White Hoops
League: Southern Counties South (level 7)

Devonport HSOB
Ground Address: Stonehouse Creek Leisure & Social Club Kings Road Stonehouse Plymouth Devon PL1 3SF
Contact: 01752 606722
Email: mail@dhsobrfc.com
Website: www.dhsobrfc.com
Directions: Leave A38 head at Marsh Mills roundabout (Sainsburys). Follow signs to City Centre (A374). At Charles Church r'about (Staples) take 1st. exit. At next r'bout take 3rd. exit (Royal Parade). At next r'about 2nd. exit then straight on through lights onto Union
Honorary Secretary: Mrs Andrea Buckley, 14 South View Terrace St Judes Plymouth Devon PL4 9DQ
Tel: 07795 822737
Email: acbuckley@blueyonder.co.uk
Fixtures Secretary: Mr Darren Rosevear, Clarendon House 1-3 Albert Road Stoke Plymouth Devon PL2 1AP
Tel: 07967 301263
Email: darren.rosevear@daiichi-sankyo.co.uk
League: Devon 1 South & West (level 9)

Devonport Services RFC
Ground Address: The Rectory Field 2nd Avenue 2nd Avenue Plymouth Devon PL1 5QE
Contact: 01752 501559
Email: devonportservices@yahoo.com
Website: www.dsrfc-youth.org.uk
Directions: Maps are issued to visiting clubs
Honorary Secretary: Lt Col Allan Berry, RM (rtd), 36 Beechwood Avenue Mutley Plymouth PL4 6PW
Tel: 01752 662443   Email: berrya@a.dii.mod.uk
Fixtures Secretary: Mr Steve Lomax, 243 Fort Austin Ave Plymouth Devon PL6 5ST
Tel: 0774 278534   Email: stevedeanchloe@aol.com
Club Colours: Navy shirts & blue shorts
League: Western Counties West (level 7)

LEVEL 7-11 & NON LEAGUE CLUBS   743

Didcot RFC
Ground Address: Edmonds Park c/o 8 Colborne Rd Didcot Oxfordshire OX11 0AB
Contact: 01235 510669
Email: contact@didcotrufc.com
Website: www.didcotrfc.com
Directions: From the Broadway turn into Mereland Road at Barclays Bank. Straight ahead passing St. Birinus School on your right. Take second left in to Green Close. Take second left into a private road. Follow the road over a bridge to the pitches.
Honorary Secretary: Mr Paul Costello, 16 North Bush Furlong Didcot Oxfordshire OX11 9DY
Tel: 01235 510669
Email: paul.costello@sanofi-aventis.com
Fixtures Secretary: Mr John Stephens
Tel: 07917 791416
Email: johnstephens@3663.co.uk
Club Colours: Red, White & Black Hoops
League: Berks-Bucks & Oxon 2 S (level 10)

Dorchester RFC
Ground Address: Dorchester RFC Coburg Road Dorchester Dorset DT1 2HX
Contact: 01305 265692
Email: webmaster@dorchester-rfc.co.uk
Website: www.dorchester-rfc.co.uk
Directions: From the by-pass follow signsto "West Dorset Leisure Centre".
Honorary Secretary: Mr Graham Aspley, 5 Nappers Court Charles Street Dorchester Dorset DT1 1EE
Tel: 01305 269944
Email: aspley.mail@btconnect.com
Fixtures Secretary: Mr David Harris, 56 Mount Skippet Way Crossways Dorchester DT2 8TP
Tel: 01305 854237
Email: daveandkaran@rosie76.fsnet.co.uk
Club Colours: Green & White Hoops
League: Southern Counties South (level 7)

Dowty RFC
Ground Address: Dowty RFC Tennis Centre Plock Court Longford GL9 2ED
Contact: 0 1452859388
Email: gillblackwell@tesco.net
Honorary Secretary: Mrs Gill Blackwell, 6 Kaybourne Crescent Churchdown Gloucester GL3 2HL
Tel: 07759 864042
Email: gillblackwell@tesco.net
Fixtures Secretary: Mr Nick Hodges, 21 Orchard Road Longlevens Gloucester GL2 0HX
Tel: 07980 863883
Club Colours: Blue, White & Grey Hoops
League: Gloucester 3 (level 11)

Drifters RFC
Ground Address: Farnham Common Sports CLub One Pin Lane Farnham Common SL2 3QY
Contact: 01753 644190
Email: rogerellis@hotmail.com
Website: www.fcsc.org.uk/drifters
Directions: M4 J6 head north on A355, or M40 J2 head south on A355 One Pin Lane half mile north of Farnham Common village
Honorary Secretary: Mr Roger Ellis, 59 Knox Green Binfield Bracknell Berks. RG42 4NZ
Tel: 01344 459902
Email: rogerellis@hotmail.com
Fixtures Secretary: Mr Stanley Bannister, White Cottage Beaconsfield Road Farnham Common Slough SL2 3HU
Tel: 01753 539840
Email: stan@bannisterhome.fsnet.co.uk
Club Colours: Black, with gold & magenta central hoops
League: Berks-Bucks & Oxon Premier (level 8)

Drybrook RFC
Ground Address: Mannings Ground High Street Drybrook GL17 9EU
Contact: 01594 543948
Email: roger.hale@talk21.com
Website: www.drybrookrfc.com
Directions: Clubhouse & ground is situated at top of High Street, Drybrook which is close to the A4136, Gloucester/Monmouth Road. Post Code for Sat/Nav - GL17 9EU
Honorary Secretary: Mr Glyn Tingle, 16 Woodland Road Drybrook Gloucestershire GL17 9HE
Tel: 01594 544334
Fixtures Secretary: Mr Dereck Trigg, Back Lane 4 Hawthorns Road Drybrook Gloucestershire GL17 9BU
Tel: 01594 542258
Club Colours: Green, Black & White
League: Western Counties North (level 7)

Dursley RFC Limited
Ground Address: Stinchcombe Stragglers The Avenue, Stinchcombe Dursley GL11 6AJ
Contact: 01453 543693
Email: simon.bilous@ukgateway.net
Website: www.dursleyrfc.co.uk
Directions: Directions: located on Dursley to Wotton-under-Edge road (B4060), on the right just before entering Stinchcombe village if travelling from Dursley
Honorary Secretary: Mr Phil Case, 0 Parkview Road Berkeley Gloucestershire GL13 9TD
Tel: 01453 819221
Email: philip_case@hotmail.com
Fixtures Secretary: Mr Tony Powell, 55 Oakfield Way Sharpness Berkeley Gloucestershire GL13 9UT
Tel: 01453 811484
Club Colours: Maroon with amber hoop (change: green)
League: Gloucester 1 (level 9)

Exeter RFC (Oxford University)
Ground Address: c/o Exeter College Turl Street Oxford OX1 3DP
Contact: 07960137603
Email: charles.morris@exeter.ox.ac.uk
Honorary Secretary: Mr Mark Heywood, Lincoln Court 5 226 Willesden Lane London NW2 5RG
Tel: 00750 0038954
Email: mark.heywood@ocado.com
Non League

Exeter Saracens RFC
Ground Address: Exhibition Field Summer Lane, Whipton Summer Lane, Whipton Exeter EX4 8NN
Contact: 01392 462651
Email: rugby@exetersaracens.co.uk
Directions: From M5 follow signs for Exeter Arena or from other direction follow Whipton signs then Exeter signs.
Honorary Secretary: Mr Hugh Dorliac, 36 Beacon Heath Exeter Devon EX4 8NR
Tel: 01392 677820
Email: hdor51@blueyonder.co.uk
Fixtures Secretary: Mr Kevin Ricketts, 6 Gloucester Road Exeter Devon EX4 2EF
Tel: 01392 211166
Club Colours: Red shirts with white collar, black shorts
League: Cornwall-Devon (level 8)

Fairford RFC
Ground Address: Fairford R.F.C. The Marlborough Arms Cirencester Road Fairford GL7 4BS
Contact: 07764 999 110
Email: secretary@fairfordrfc.com
Honorary Secretary: Christopher Jackson, 21 Beauchamp Close Fairford Gloucestershire GL7 4LP
Tel: 01285 713234
Email: csjackson@tiscali.co.uk
Club Colours: Emerald & Black Hoops
League: Dorset & Wilts 2 North (level 9)

Falmouth RFC
Ground Address: The Recreation Ground Dracaena Avenue Falmouth TR11 2EU
Contact: 01326 311304
Email: theobservatory@talktalk.net
Website: www.falrfc.com
Directions: Right at the traffic lights on A39 (by SAAB Garage) and left into and along Dracaena Ave, visable from main road. Ground at junction of Trengenver and Killigrew roads.
Honorary Secretary: Mr John Body, 4 Carrick Road Falmouth Cornwall TR11 4PQ
Email: Jbody@ABERFAL.FREESERVE.CO.UK
Fixtures Secretary: Mr Michael Tregidgo, 78 Trefusis Road Redruth Cornwall TR15 2JL
Tel: 01209 210263
Email: mike_tregidgo@europe.pall.com
Club Colours: Black with white hoops
League: Cornwall-Devon (level 8)

Farnham Royal RFC
Ground Address: THE CLUB HOUSE Farnham Sports Field Beaconsfield Road Beaconsfield Road Farnham Royal Bucks. SL2 3BP
Contact: 01753 646252
Website: www.frrufc.com
Directions: Directions from the M4: - Exit the M4 at Junction 6. Take the A355 (Farnham Road) Northbound towards Beaconsfield. Go through four sets of lights and at the roundabout take the second exit towards Beaconsfield. At the first mini-roundabout take second
Honorary Secretary: Mrs Margaret Moffat, 16 Balmoral Close Cippenham Slough SL1 6JP
Tel: 01753 646252
Email: moffatstgeorges@aol.com
Fixtures Secretary: Mr Christopher Norman, 63 St. Davids Close Iver Heath Iver Bucks. SL0 0RS
Tel: 07947 271837
Email: chrisnorman100@hotmail.com
Club Colours: Black & White Hoops
League: Berks-Bucks & Oxon 1 S (level 9)

Frampton Cotterell RFC
Ground Address: Crossbow House Frampton Cotterell Bristol BS36 2DA
Contact: 07812 202760
Email: stevebucks@supanet.com
Directions: see www.fcrfc.com for full directions and location maps etc.
Honorary Secretary: Mr Steve Buckley, 125 Ratcliffe Drive Stoke Gifford Bristol BS34 8TZ
Tel: 07812 202760
Fixtures Secretary: Mr Nathan Cole, Flat 4 444 Church Road Frampton Cotterell Bristol BS36 2AQ
Tel: 07971 616287
Email: nathan_cole_ee@hotmail.com
Club Colours: Green Black & Gold shirts
League: Gloucester Premier (level 8)

Frome RFC
Ground Address: The Clubhouse Gypsy Lane Frome BA11 2NA
Contact: 01373 462506
Email: secretary@fromerfc.org
Website: www.fromerfc.org
Directions: Follow signs for Leisure Centre, Frome RFC is signposted from the Bath road/Princess Ann road traffic lights.
Honorary Secretary: Mr Paul Holdaway, 4 4 Market Place, Nunney, Frome Somerset BA11 4LY
Tel: 07720 448454
Email: secretary@fromerfc.org
Fixtures Secretary: Mr Trevor Osborne, 85 Nightingale Avenue Frome Somerset BA11 2UW
Tel: 01373 300889
Email: fixtures@fromerfc.org
Club Colours: Red, white and black hoops
League: Southern Counties South (level 7)

SOUTH WEST

LEVEL 7-11 & NON LEAGUE CLUBS 745

Gloucester Civil Service RFC
Ground Address: Estcourt Road Gloucester GL1 3LG
Contact: 01452 532802
Directions: M5 J11 , A40 to Gloucester, continue on A40 to Longford roundabout, left at Longford Inn (Beefeater) left at next roundabout, Ground is on immediate right.
Honorary Secretary: Mr Richard Sheppard, 95 Lavington Drive Longlevens Gloucester GL2 0HR
Tel: 01452 532802
Email: rsheppard@dis-ltd.co.uk
Fixtures Secretary: Ian Yeates, 22 Humber Place Brockworth Gloucester GL3 4LZ
Tel: 01452 863059
Club Colours: Blue,White,Red Varying Hoops
League: Gloucester 3 (level 11)

Gloucester Old Boys RFC
Ground Address: Armscroft Park off Horton Road Gloucester GL1 3QA
Contact: 01452 302390
Email: gloucesteroldboysrfc@yahoo.co.uk
Website: www.gloucesteroldboysrfc.co.uk
Honorary Secretary: Mr Ray Ellis
Tel: 01452 525375
Fixtures Secretary: Mr T Galvin, 15 Armscroft Way Gloucester GL2 0ST
Tel: 07971 055055 Email: steveno9@msn.com
Club Colours: Claret , Gold & Navy
League: Gloucester Premier (level 8)

Gordano RFC
Ground Address: Gordano RFC, Caswell lane Portbury Bristol BS20 7UF
Contact: 01275373486
Email: info@gordanorfc.co.uk
Directions: J19 on M5 , take A396, head into village of Portbury and bear left at the village green.
Honorary Secretary: Mr Daniel Martin, 23 Falcon Close Portishead Bristol BS20 6UT
Tel: 07866 259408
Email: dan.martin@heritagebathrooms.com
Fixtures Secretary: Mr Alan Stanton, 7 Halswell Road Clevedon AVON BS21 6LD
Tel: 01633 637482
Email: stan_the_man@blueyonder.co.uk
Club Colours: Red and Black
League: Somerset 1 (level 9)

Gordon League RFC
Ground Address: Hempsted Lane Gloucester GL2 5JN
Contact: 01452 303434
Email: gordonleague@yahoo.co.uk
Website: www.gordonleague.com
Directions: From the West: Approaching on the A48/A40 towards Gloucester City Centre, you will pass Over Farm Shop and the Dog at Over Public House, at the next r'about head right toward the City Centre (Over Causeway). Get into the right hand lane ready to turn right at the traffic lights, follow the road straight over the next set of lights (you should see the Colin Campbell Pub down on the left) you are now on Hempsted Lane, head up the road until you reach another r'about. Branch off right and carry straight on up Hempsted Lane, the Gordon League is a little further on to your left. From the North: From the North Gloucester is best reached via the M5 motorway. Exit at junction 11 and head for Gloucester City centre. At the first r'about you come to take the third major exit towards Ross (be careful, there is an entrance to Government buildings immediately to your left - do not count this). At the end of this dual-carriageway is a r'about, go straight over this (again signposted Ross) at the next r'about bear left signposted City Centre (Over Causeway). Get into the right hand lane ready to turn right at the traffic lights, follow the road straight over the next set of lights (past the Colin Campbell Pub) you are now on Hempsted Lane, head up the road until you reach another r'about. Branch off right and carry straight on up Hempsted Lane, the Gordon League is a little further on to your left. From the South (West): Approach Gloucester along the M5 and leave the motorway at junction 12. Follow the signs for Gloucester. As you approach the outskirts of the city you will encounter a large traffic light complex. Follow the signs for Hempstead (left hand/centre lanes), you will go through 2 further sets of lights, the road start to climb to another set of light go straight again, after about 300 yards you will be able to see the Club Grounds on your left, at the next r'about turn left up Hempsted Lane and the Club is on the left. From the East: Leave the M4 motorway at junction 15 and head for Cirencester/Gloucester along the A419/A417. This road is dual carriage-way most of the way and should be followed along it's full length. The dual-carriageway ends at a small r'about and is reduced to two-way traffic, eventually running downhill to a r'about located next to a pub called 'The Air Balloon'. Turn left there and head down the steep hill towards Gloucester. This road opens back out into dual-carriageway which should be followed until it reaches a junction with another by-pass (do not take the M5 motorway turn-off). Follow signs for Gloucester and continue until you reach a large r'about with several large office buildings surrounding it. Take the third exit (towards Longlevens/Ross). At the end of this road is another large r'about. From here take the second exit towards Ross. At the end of this dual-carriageway is a r'about, go straight over this (again signposted Ross) at the next r'about bear left signposted City Centre (Over Causeway). Get into the right hand lane ready to turn right at the traffic lights, follow the road straight over the next set of lights (past the Colin Campbell Pub) you are now on Hempsted Lane, head up the road until you reach another r'about. Branch off right and carry straight on up Hempsted Lane and the Gordon League is a little further on to your left.
Honorary Secretary: Mr David Bucknell c/o the club
Tel: 07789 383030 Email: david@buckers.net
Fixtures Secretary: Mr Gareth Williams, Otter Road 6 Abbeymead Gloucester GL4 5TF Tel: 0778 9903455
Club Colours: White Shirt with Red Sash, White Shorts
League: Western Counties North (level 7)

Gosford All Blacks RFC
Ground Address: Stratfield Brake Sports Ground Frieze Way Kidlington Oxfordshire OX5 1UP
Contact: 01865 373994
Email: davideustice@gosfordrugby.com
Website: www.gosfordrugby.com
Directions: Directions: From Oxford or A34, follow signs to A44 towards Woodstock. Turn right onto Frieze Way dual-carriageway at roundabout after A34. Follow signs to Stratfield Brake.Or take A4260 to Kidlington roundabout (Sainsbury's)& follow signs.
Honorary Secretary: Mr David Eustice, 196 Oxford Road Kidlington Oxfordshire OX5 1EB
Tel: 07854 077608
Email: david.eustice@btinternet.com
Fixtures Secretary: Mr Murray Stewart, Flat 1 32 Victoria Road Abingdon Oxfordshire OX14 1DQ
Tel: 07832 049804
Email: murraystewart@hotmail.com
Club Colours: Black
League: Berks-Bucks & Oxon Premier (level 8)

Greyhound RFC Limited
Ground Address: Hereford City Sports Club Grandstand Road Hereford HR4 9NG
Contact: 01432 354221
Email: braither@hotmail.co.uk
Website: www.freewebs.com/greyhoundrugbyclub
Directions: Turn off A49 Leominster Road. Keeping the Leisure Centre on your right follow the road to the mini roundabout. Take 2nd left and the club is on the right hand side approx 250 yds.
Honorary Secretary: Mr Allan Braithwaite, 31 Manor Fields Burghill Hereford HR4 7RR
Tel: 07775 724365
Email: braither@hotmail.co.uk
Fixtures Secretary: Mr Kevin Bufton, 7 Ripon Walk Hereford HR4 9UF Tel: 07875 296191
Club Colours: Pale blue/navy/red
League: Gloucester 2 (level 10)

Grove RFC
Ground Address: Cane Lane Grove Grove Wantage Oxfordshire OX12 0AA
Contact: 01235 762750
Website: www.groverfc.co.uk
Directions: From Oxford (A338) turn right into village, right at roundabout left at roundabout (Brereton Dv), left at end to Cane Lane. From the South enter village at lights . Left at the roundabout into D'worth Road, follow as above.
Honorary Secretary: Mr Earl Ashford, 6 Milton Lane Steventon Abingdon Oxfordshire OX13 6SA
Tel: 01252 831315
Email: e.ashford@tiscali.co.uk
Fixtures Secretary: Mr Adrian Amies, 50 Mably Grove Wantage Oxfordshire OX12 9XW
Tel: 07970 455627
Club Colours: Red & blue shirts, blue shorts, red socks
League: Southern Counties North (level 7)

Harwell RFC
Contact: 01235 833688
Email: dougbosley@btinternet.com
Directions: Situated at the Harwell IBC From the south, A34 from Newbury, come off at the Chilton Interchange. Follow the road to the left, (A4185) you will see the Main Gate and Rugby posts a few yards down the road. Park in Carpark, changing rooms are to the right of main gate. From the north, come off the A34 at the Milton Interchange and take the A4130 towards Wantage, at Rowstock r'about go straight over and take the A4185 towards Chilton, you will come to the Main Gate of Harwell IBC on your right.
Honorary Secretary: Mr Douglas Bosley, 55 West Lockinge Wantage Oxfordshire OX12 8QE
Tel: 01235 833688   Mobile 07775 508818
Fixtures Secretary: Mrs Jenny Bosley, 55 West Lockinge Wantage Oxfordshire OX11
Tel: 01235 833688
Email: dougbosley@btinternet.com
Club Colours: Dark Blue Sky Blue and White
League: Berks-Bucks & Oxon Premier (level 8)

Hayle RFC
Ground Address: Hayle R.F.C. Memorial Park Marsh Lane Hayle TR27 4PS
Contact: 01736 753320
Email: hayle@rfc3587.fsnet.co.uk
Directions: Take A30 to first roundabout, ground immediately in front.
Honorary Secretary: Ms Kathryn Hobson, 14 Lelant Meadows Lelant St. Ives Cornwall TR26 3JS
Fixtures Secretary: Mr Mike Gee, 70 Halsetown St. Ives Cornwall TR26 3LZ
Tel: 01736 797777 Email: swrfu@lineone.net
Club Colours: Green, Black & White
League: Cornwall-Devon (level 8)

Helston RFC
Ground Address: Helston RFC King George V Playing Fields Clodgey Lane Helston TR13 8PJ
Contact: 01326 569195
Directions: A39 into north of town past Tesco, 0.25 mile on right, before Flambards Theme Park.
Honorary Secretary: Mrs Phina Mcstein, Granite Cottage Porkellis Boswin Cornwall TR13 0HR
Tel: 01209 860443   Email: phinamcstein@tiscali.co.uk
Club Colours: Blue and White
League: Cornwall League (level 9)

Hertford RFC (Oxford)
Ground Address: c/o Hertford College Catte Street Oxford OX1 3BW
Contact: 07725817186
Email: gareth.lond@hertford.ox.ac.uk
Honorary Secretary: Mr Tim Dean, Hertford College Catte Street Oxford OX1 3BW
Tel: 07749 664284
Email: tim.dean@hertford.oxford.ac.uk
Non League

LEVEL 7-11 & NON LEAGUE CLUBS

The following HM Ships share the same address, email and website. They are all Non League.

Address: C/O Royal Navy Rugby Union HMS TEMERAIRE Portsmouth Hampshire PO1 2HB

Email: cb-honsec-navy@therfu.com

Website: www.navyrugbyunion.co.uk

HMS Albion
Contact: 023 9272 4193

HMS Bulwark
Contact: 023 9272 4193

HMS Cambeltown
Contact: 023 9272 5238

HMS Cornwall
Contact: 023 9272 4193

HMS Cumberland
Contact: 023 9272 4193

HMS Drake
Contact: 023 9272 5238
Email: sinclairsinc@aol.com

HMS Heron
Contact: 023 9272 5238

HMS Lancaster
Contact: 023 9272 5238
Hon. Secretary: Mr Shaun Turl

HMS Monmouth
Contact: 023 9272 4193

HMS Montrose
Contact: 023 9272 4193

HMS Ocean
Contact: 023 9272 4193

HMS Portland
Contact: 023 9272 4193

HMS Raleigh
Contact: 023 9272 4193

HMS Seahawk
Contact: 023 9272 4193

HMS Somerset
Contact: 023 9272 4193

Honiton RFC
Ground Address: Allhallows Playing Fields Northcote Lane Honiton Devon EX14 1NH
Contact: 01404 46820
Email: honitonrugbyclub@hotmail.co.uk
Directions: Allhallows playing field is right next to the towns only sports centre which is situated on the West side of the High Street.
Honorary Secretary: Mr Jeremy Rice, 184 High Street Honiton Devon EX14 1LA
Tel: 01404 46820
Email: jeremy.rice@btinternet.com
Fixtures Secretary: Mr Andy Canniford, 20 Rosemount Close Honiton Devon EX14 2RP
Tel: 01404 43714
Email: andycanni@hotmail.com
Club Colours: Red Black & Amber Hoops
League: Devon 1 North & East (level 9)

Hornets RFC
Ground Address: Hutton Moor Park Hutton Moor Road Weston-super-Mare Somerset BS22 8LY
Contact: 01934 621433
Email: steve.hanney@yahoo.co.uk
Website: www.hornetsrugby.net
Directions: J21 on the M5 dual carriage way to Weston-super-mare. Straight across two roundabouts, turn right at filter light - The Ground is on your right.
Honorary Secretary: Mr Steve Hanney, 3 Portishead Road Worle Weston-super-Mare Somerset BS22 7UX
Tel: 07736 858885
Email: steve.hanney@yahoo.co.uk
Fixtures Secretary: Dave Pollard, 216 Locking Road Weston-s-Mare Somerset BS23 3LU
Tel: 07903467177
Email: dave.pollard60@tesco.net
Club Colours: Black & Amber
League: Western Counties North (level 7)

Hucclecote RFC
Ground Address: The Old School Field Charlies Way Churchdown Lane Gloucester Gloucestershire GL3 3QH
Contact: 0 1452621281
Email: hucclecoterfc@btinternet.com
Directions: Exit M5 (north) J11a. To Gloucester take left at Zoons Ct roundabout to next lights. Turn right to Hucclecote, right at second set of lights in to Churchdown Lane. The club is on the right past the school.
Honorary Secretary: Mr Mark Howkins, 15 Insley Gardens Hucclecote Gloucester GL3 3AN
Tel: 01452 611864   Email: mhowkins@btinternet.com
Fixtures Secretary: Mr Steve Hanslow, 22 Hillview Road Hucclecote Gloucester GL3 3LG
Tel: 07808 822713
Email: steve.hanslow@blueyonder.co.uk
Club Colours: Amber
League: Gloucester Premier (level 8)

Hungerford RFC
Ground Address: Triangle Field Priory Road Hungerford Berks. RG170AN
Contact: 01635 30760
Email: andrew.spaak@btinternet.com
Website: www.hungerford-rfc.co.uk
Directions: From the South approach Hungerford via A338. 200 yards after new roundabout, turn right into Priory Road. Half mile on right is John O'Guant School, pass this school and turn left through gate after 100 yards. From North, West or East - Go into Hungerford High Street and up over 2 mini roundabouts and after the last mini roundabout 100yds on the rights is Priory Road
Honorary Secretary: Mr Martin Digweed, 2 Homefield way Hungerford Berks. RG17 0JY
Tel: 01488 682187   Email: mdigweed@harris.com
Fixtures Secretary: Mr Andy Spaak, 19 Salcombe Road Newbury Berks. RG14 6EB   Tel: 07815 290587
Email: Andrew.Spaak@btinternet.com
Club Colours: Porter Shirt with Hungerford R
League: Berks-Bucks & Oxon 1 S (level 9)

Ilfracombe RFC
Ground Address:
4 Langleigh Terrace Ilfracombe Devon EX34 8EB
Email: jane@cj-nautical-imaging.co.uk
Directions: From town centre take road to east signed Combe Martin, look out for swimming pool, club on the left close by.
Honorary Secretary: Jane Perrin, Langleigh Terrace 4 Ilfracombe Devon EX34 8EB   Tel: 07980 707515
Email: jane@cj-nautical-imaging.co.uk
Fixtures Secretary: Mr R Crabb, 43 Oak Tree Gardens Ilfracombe Devon EX34 9LU   Tel: 01271 863011
Club Colours: Blue & White Hoops
League: Devon 1 North & East (level 9)

Illogan Park RFC
Ground Address: Paynters Lane End, Sports Field 2 Sparnon Terrace Redruth TR15 2RF
Contact: 01209210208
Email: annecollingsnicholls8@hotmail.com
Directions: Turn off A30 at Portreath and head for Pool. Turn right down Cheriot Road for 1 mile. Ground is on the left.
Honorary Secretary: Mr Tony Nicholls, 2 Sparnon Terrace Redruth Cornwall TR15 2RF
Tel: 01209 210208   Email: tonynic@hotmail.com
Fixtures Secretary: Mr Martin Bray, 70 Raymond Road Redruth Cornwall TR15 2HF
Tel: 01209 714463
Club Colours: Gold & Black
League: Cornwall League (level 9)

Imperial
Ground Address: South Bristol Sports Centre Imperial RFC West Town Lane Knowle Bristol BS4 5BN
Contact: 0117 9038681
Email: info@imperialrfc.org.uk
Website: www.imperialrfc.org.uk
Directions: From Wells Road (A37) turn by Happy Landings pub into West Town Lane. From Bath Road(A4), at traffic lights by Lidl turn into West Town Lane.
Honorary Secretary: Mr Craig Pullinger, Imperial Fire & Security 369 Bath Road Arnos Vale Bristol BS4 3EW
Tel: 07970 782060
Email: craigpullinger@btopenworld.com
Fixtures Secretary: Mr Aaron Binns, 59 Rookery Way Whitchurch Bristol BS14 0DZ   Tel: 07968 788596
Email: aaron@airtekscaffoldingltd.com
Club Colours: Myrtle and Amber Shirts, Blue Shorts
League: Somerset 1 (level 9)

Ivel Barbarians RFC
Ground Address: Yeovil Showground Dorchester Road Yeovil Somerset BA22 9RA
Contact: 01935 474591
Website: www.ivelrugby.com
Honorary Secretary: Mrs Alison Bennett, 36 The Glebe Queen Camel Yeovil Somerset BA22 7PR
Tel: 01935 850004
Email: Alison.Bennett@yeovil.ac.uk
Fixtures Secretary: Mr Richard Gaston
Tel: 01935 472371
Club Colours: Black and White Quarters - Black Shorts
League: Southern Counties South (level 7)

Jesus RFC
Address: c/o Jesus College Turl Street Oxford OX1 3DW
Contact: 07773483185
Email: stephen.jenkins@jesus.ox.ac.uk
Non League

Keble RFC
Address: c/o Keble College Parks Rd Oxford OX1 3PG
Contact: 07732769438
Email: peter.bolton@keb.ox.ac.uk
Non League

Keynsham RFC
Ground Address: Crown Fields Bristol Road Keynsham BS31 2BE
Contact: 0117 9872520
Email: info@keynshamrugby.co.uk
Website: www.keynshamrugby.co.uk
Honorary Secretary: Mrs Christine Wetton, High Trees The Glen Saltford Bath BS31 3JP
Tel: 01225 874604
Email: wettoncccj@aol.com
Fixtures Secretary: Mr Ashton Broad
Tel: 01275 831605   Email: ashtonbroad@tiscali.co.uk
Club Colours: Black and amber
League: Western Counties North (level 7)

LEVEL 7-11 & NON LEAGUE CLUBS

Kingsbridge RFC
Ground Address: High House Derby Road Kingsbridge Devon TQ7 1JL
Contact: 01548 852051
Email: martin@krfc.fsnet.co.uk
Website: www.kingsbridgerugby.co.uk
Directions: From centre of Kingsbridge take Dartmouth road alongside estuary, take first left and first right to the top of the hill.
Honorary Secretary: Mr Martin Newman, 5 The Sidings Old Station Road Kingsbridge TQ7 1FB
Tel: 01548 853976   Email: martin@krfc.fsnet.co.uk
Fixtures Secretary: Mr Mike Jones, 6 Washabrook Way Kingsbridge Devon TQ7 1RJ
Tel: 01548 857130   Email: ebjmike@btinternet.com
Club Colours: Blue and White
League: Western Counties West (level 7)

Kingswood RFC
Ground Address: Deanery Road Playing Field Grimsbury Road Kingswood BS15 9SE   Contact: 0117 9675001
Email: markphillips@tinyworld.co.uk
Website: www.kingswoodrfc.co.uk
Directions: From Bristol on the A420, turn right into Grimsbury Rd immediately before the Tennis Court pub (if you get to the A4174 Avon Ring Road you've gone too far). Ground is first left.
Honorary Secretary: Mr James Stacey, 1 Empire Crescent Hanham Bristol BS15 3GG
Tel: 0117 9603248   Email: jimstacey81@hotmail.com
Fixtures Secretary: Mr Steve Wood Tel: 0777 99605122
Email: fixtures@kingswoodrfc.co.uk
Club Colours: Sky Blue and Chocolate Brown
League: Gloucester 2 (level 10)

Lady Margaret Hall / Trinity RFC
Ground Address: c/o Lady Margaret Hall College Norham Gardens Oxford OX2 6QA
Email: benjamin.murray@lmh.ox.ac.uk
Honorary Secretary: Mr William Mackintosh, Lady Margaret Hall Norham Gardens Oxford OX2 6QA
Email: william.mackintosh@lmh.ox.ac.uk
Non League

Lankelly-Fowey RFC
Ground Address: Lankelly-Fowey RFC Lankelly Farm Lankelly Lane Fowey PL23 1HN
Contact: 01726 832966
Email: enquiries@lankellyfoweyrfc.com
Website: www.lankellyfoweyrfc.com
Directions: On entering Fowey, turn right into Lankelly Lane, follow road until T junction, turn left, Ground is 100yds on right.
Hon. Secretary: Mr Rob Bell, 33 Pentreath Close Long Meadow Fowey Cornwall PL23 1EP Tel: 07812 022354
Email: ROB@WAYOUTWEST03.FREESERVE.CO.UK
Fixtures Secretary: Mr Nigel Dennis, 32 Allenvale Gypsy Lane Liskeard Cornwall PL14 5HL
Tel: 01579 347678
Club Colours: Navy Blue and White
League: Cornwall League (level 7)

Leyhill RFC
Address: H. M. P. Prison Leyhill Wotton-under-Edge
Contact: 01454 260 681
Honorary Secretary: Mr Nigel Burfitt, H M Prison Leyhill Wotton-under-Edge Gloucestershire GL12 8BT
Tel: 01454 264083
Email: nigel.burfitt@HMPS.gsi.gov.uk
Non League

Liskeard-Looe RFC
Ground Address: Lux Park Coldstyle Road Liskeard Cornwall PL14 3HZ
Contact: 01752 814612
Email: barry.mumford69@live.co.uk
Directions: Ask for Leisure Centre, near the town center.
Honorary Secretary: Mr Barry Mumford, 51 Hamoaze Road Torpoint PL11 2EF
Tel: 07896 603062 Email: barry.mumford69@live.co.uk
Fixtures Secretary: Mr Andrew George, 8 Westwood Liskeard Cornwall PL14 6DG
Tel: 07974 674721   Email: info@cesurveys.com
Club Colours: Red and Black Hoops
League: Cornwall-Devon (level 8)

Littlemore RFC
Ground Address: Peers School Sandy Lane Sandy Lane Oxford OX4 6JY
Contact: 01865 715776
Email: lrfc@littlemorerfc.org.uk
Website: www.littlemorerfc.org.uk
Directions: Oxon ring road to Cowley (eastern bypass A4142), past the Rover plant on left, left turn and sign post to Peers School.
Honorary Secretary: Mr Marc West, 47 Envlode Drive Berinsfield Wallingford Oxfordshire OX10 7NZ
Tel: 07976 318077 Email: west25189675@hotmail.com
Fixtures Secretary: Mr Russell Hixon, The Cottage 10 Bishopstone Bishopstone Aylesbury Bucks. HP17 8SE
Tel: 07795 185170 Email: russell.hixon@eu.thewg.com
Club Colours: Royal Blue and White
League: Berks-Bucks & Oxon 1 S (level 9)

Longlevens RFC
Ground Address: Longlevens R.F.C. Longford Lane Longlevens Glos Gloucestershire GL2 9EU
Contact: 01452 306880
Email: spanlrfc@blueyonder.co.uk
Website: www.longlevensrfc.co.uk
Directions: M5 exit J 11 head towards Gloucester, straight over first roundabout, second set of lights, turn right into old cheltenham road straight over cross roads and take the second right into Longlevens RFC.
Honorary Secretary: Mr Philip Lane, 11 Cotswold Gardens Longlevens Gloucester GL2 0DR
Tel: 07831 775208   Email: philip.lane@hp.com
Fixtures Secretary: Mr Colin Rose Tel: 07860 433004
Email: colinroselonglevensrfc@blueyonder.co.uk
Club Colours: Red and White
League: Gloucester 1 (level 9)

Magdalen College RFC (Oxford)
Address: Magdalen College High St., Oxford OX1 4AU
Contact: 01865 276000
Website: www.magd.ox.ac.uk
Directions: Ground - Marston Road, Oxford OX3 0EQ
Honorary Secretary: Mr Mark Blandford-Baker, Magdalen College High Street Oxford OX1 4AU
Tel: 01865 276050
Email: mark.blandford-baker@magd.ox.ac.uk
Club Colours: Black, White, Red
Non League

Marlborough RFC
Ground Address: The Common Free's Avenue Free's Avenue Marlborough Wilts. SN8 1DL
Contact: 01672 810718
Email: rodneyandjoyce@supanet.com
Website: www.marlboroughrugbyclub.co.uk
Directions: Take Swindon road out of Marlborough then left at Common and right into Frees Ave.
Honorary Secretary: Mrs Joyce Adams, 10 Ailesbury Way Burbage Marlborough Wilts. SN8 3TD
Tel: 01672 810718
Email: rodneyandjoyce@supanet.com
Fixtures Secretary: Mr Darren Greening, 12 St. Martins Marlborough Wilts. SN8 1AR   Tel: 07962 213403
Email: darrengreening32@hotmail.com
Club Colours: Black & Amber
League: Dorset & Wilts 1 North (level 8)

Martock RFC
Ground Address: Registered Office is 3A North Street 3A North Street Martock Somerset TA12 6DH
Contact: 01935 823514
Email: m.crouch844@btinternet.com
Directions: Martock Recreation Ground: Take Martock exit from A303 at Percombe Hill. Turn left at T-junction to join Stoke Road. Ground is on left hand side after about a mile.
Honorary Secretary: Mr Philip Jackson, Church Lodge Cottage Church Street Martock Somerset TA12 6JL
Tel: 07714 244049   Email: pbj@captpbj.com
Fixtures Secretary: Mr John Hole, 13 Hollies Close Bower Hinton Martock Somerset TA12 6LB
Tel: 07718 317932
Email: john.hole@britishcollegessport.org
Club Colours: Green & Black quarters
League: Somerset 2 South (level 10)

Matson RFC
Ground Address: Redwell Road Matson Rugby Club House Matson Gloucestershire GL4 6JG
Contact: 01452 528963
Email: c.ravers@hotmail.co.uk
Website: www.matsonrugby.co.uk
Directions: Three miles south of city centre on B4073, adjacent to dry ski slope.
Honorary Secretary: Mr Christopher Ravenhill, 92 Matson ave,Matson, Gloucester Gloucestershire gl4 6hs
Tel: 01452 543922

Email: c.ravers@hotmail.co.uk
Fixtures Secretary: Mr Daniel Herd, 15 Beacon Road Matson Gloucester GL4 6JN
Club Colours: Black Shirts and White Shorts
League: Gloucester Premier (level 8)

Melksham (C.A.T's) RFC
Ground Address: Melksham Rugby Club Melksham House Market Place Melksham Wilts. SN12 6ES
Contact: 07926 929858
Email: andycadwallader@wiltshire.gov.uk
Website: www.melkshamrfc.co.uk
Directions: Follow signs to Melksham town centre until you reach the Market Place Roundabout, the Navy Tavern is on one side and Town Hall on other side. Turn into the Market Place Car Park which is on the Town Hall side and follow signs to the football club.
Honorary Secretary: Mr Andrew Cadwallader, 2 Chalfield Crescent Melksham Wilts. SN12 7BU
Tel: 01225 707428
Email: andycadwallader@wiltshire.gov.uk
Fixtures Secretary: Mr Marc Bound, 27 Sarum Avenue Melksham Wilts. SN12 6BN
Tel: 01225 700889   Email: bigbounder@hotmail.co.uk
Club Colours: Navy Blue & Sky Blue Hoops
League: Dorset & Wilts 1 North (level 8)

Midsomer Norton RFC
Ground Address: Midsomer Norton R.F.C. Norton Down Playing Fields Silver Street Midsomer Norton Radstock BA3 2UE
Contact: 01761 412827
Website: www.midsomernortonrfc.co.uk
Directions: From town centre follow Shepton Mallet road (B3355) for approx 800m.Ground on right.
Honorary Secretary: Mr Ian Tiley, 9 May Tree Road Radstock AVON BA3 3TU   Tel: 01761 437670
Email: ian.tiley@ruh-bath.swest.nhs.uk
Fixtures Secretary: Mr Rob Porter, Upper Lentney Farm Kilmersdon Radstock BA3 5SL
Tel: 01225 448832   Email: lentneyfarm@ukonline.co.uk
Club Colours: Cherry and White Hoops , Black Shorts
League: Somerset Premier (level 8)

Milton Keynes RUFC
Ground Address: Milton Keynes R.F.C. Field Lane Greenleys Wolverton Milton Keynes Beds. MK12 6AZ
Contact: 01908 312858
Email: info@miltonkeynesrugby.com
Website: www.mkrufc.com
Directions: Travel from Stoney Stratford town centre towards Wolverton, right at double roundabout into Gt Monics ST (V5), proceed across roundabout right into Field Lane, right at T junction, next left into club house.
Honorary Secretary: Mrs Jo Slater, 9 Haithwaite Two Mile Ash MK8 8LJ
Tel: 07941 076008   Email: jolslater@aol.com
Fixtures Secretary: Mr David Eales
Tel: 01296 714422
League: Southern Counties North (level 7)

LEVEL 7-11 & NON LEAGUE CLUBS

Minchinhampton RFC
Ground Address: Downfield Cottage Bulls Cross Sheepscombe Stroud Gloucestershire GL6 7HU
Contact: 01452 810970
Email: mrfc@minchinhamptonrfc.com
Website: www.minchinhamptonrfc.com
Directions: Ground Situated on A417 from Stroud towards Stonekouse & M5- Approx 1mile from centre of Stroud.
Honorary Secretary: Mr Robert Edmonds, Downfield Cottage Bulls Cross Sheepscombe Stroud Gloucestershire GL6 7HU
Tel: 01452 872430
Email: mrfc@minchinhamptonrfc.com
Fixtures Secretary: Mr Clive Eagles, C/0 Club Address Downfield Cottage Bulls Cross Sheepscombe Stroud Gloucestershire GL6 7HU
Tel: 01452 882742
Club Colours: Green, Black and White Hoops
League: Gloucester 3 (level 11)

Minehead Barbarians RFC
Ground Address: The Tom Stewart Field Ellicombe Lane, Ellicombe Minehead Somerset TA24 6TR
Contact: 01643707155
Email: mbarbarian.rfc@virgin.net
Website: www.mineheadbarbariansrfc.co.uk
Directions: Minehead Barbarians RFC Ltd is located just off the A39 on the eastern outskirts of Minehead. Turn off at Roundabout signed Ellicombe, entrance 400 metres from main road, ample parking
Honorary Secretary: Mr Colin Howells, 46 Lower Park Minehead Somerset TA24 8AY
Tel: 01643 702487
Email: candj@audley46.fsnet.co.uk
Fixtures Secretary: Mr Grahame Symes, 51 Hill View Road Carhampton Minehead TA24 6LS
Tel: 01643 821367
Email: fayeandgrahame@aol.com
Club Colours: Black & White Hoops
League: Western Counties West (level 7)

Minety RFC
Ground Address: Minety RFC The Playing Fields Sawyers Hill Minety SN16 9QL
Contact: 01666 822839
Email: gareth.dyer@btinternet.com
Directions: M4 Jn 16: Wootton Bassett exit then 2nd exit at next mini-rndbt then straight on at next rndbt (signed Malmesbury). Under Mway then 1st right after 200 yds. On 2 miles to crossroads where turn left for Minety. Follow road, which swings 90 deg to right after
Honorary Secretary: Mr Kevin Holdaway
Fixtures Secretary: Mr Ken Judd, 32 Langstone Way Westlea Swindon Wilts. SN5 7BU
Tel: 07802 661109
Email: kenjudd@tiscali.co.uk
Club Colours: Green and Purple Hoops
League: Southern Counties South (level 7)

Morganians RFC
Ground Address: The Clubhouse Chedzoy Lane Bridgwater TA7 8QW
Contact: 01278 423434
Email: pete@donnachie63.fsnet.co.uk
Directions: Bath Road from Bridgwater, A39 Bridgwater to Glastonbury road, over Motorway bridge, turn left opposite Mole Valley Farmers, then left into Club.
Honorary Secretary: Mr Peter Donnachie, Cullyhana Church Road Redhill Bristol BS40 5SG
Tel: 07974 235071
Fixtures Secretary: Paul Grimstead Tel: 07939 696585
Club Colours: Navy shirts with gold and red
League: Somerset 3 South (level 11)

Nailsea & Backwell
Ground Address: West End Park West End Lane Nailsea BS48 4SY
Contact: 01275 810 818
Email: paul.julia@blueyonder.co.uk
Directions: M5 J 20 follow signs to Nailsea. At traffic lights in Nailsea, club signposted to the right. Follow this road to edge of built up area and club on the left hand side. From Bristol, follow A370 towards Weston SM and take B3130 into Nailsea. In the town, go straight over at the lights and continue as above. Map on website.
Honorary Secretary: Mr Jeffrey Morris, 1 Broom Farm Close Nailsea Bristol BS48 4YJ   Tel: 01275 852807
Email: jeffsue.morris@blueyonder.co.uk
Fixtures Secretary: Stephen Gillard Tel: 0780 9720243
Club Colours: Black & White
League: Somerset 1 (level 9)

New / Templeton RFC
Ground Address: c/o New College Holywell Street Oxford OX1 3BN
Contact: 07749455089
Email: tom.newton@new.ox.ac.uk
Non League

New Cross RFC
Ground Address: Abbrook Park Sports Strap Lane Kingsteignton Newton Abbot Devon TQ12 3PS
Email: admin@newcrossrfc.co.uk
Website: www.newcrossrfc.co.uk
Directions: From Exeter, join A380 towards Torbay, take first exit for Kingsteignton, then take 2nd right just after the Ten Tors pub into Five Lanes. Right into Abbrook Park Sports & Social Club. From Torquay, join A380 and take the 2nd exit to Kingsteignton, turn left at the junction, then take 2nd right just after Ten Tors pub into Five Lanes. Then as above. From Plymouth, A38 towards Exeter, take exit for Chudleigh, left for Kingsteignton 3 miles, turn left at New Cross roundabout, just after clay pits, left again _ of a mile into Abbrook Park
Honorary Secretary: Mr Clinton Mill, 14 Whiteway Road Kingsteignton TQ12 3HL
Tel: 01626 207502 Email: clint-new-cross-rfc@live.com
Fixtures Secretary: as Hon. Sec.
Club Colours: White with a green purple & black Stripe
League: Devon 1 North & East (level 9)

Newbury Stags RFC
Ground Address: Monks Lane Newbury RG14 7RW
Contact: 07774 203162
Email: nbeal@nbeal.wanadoo.co.uk
Website: www.newburystags-rfc.co.uk
Directions: see www.newburystags-rfc.co.uk or newburyrfc.co.uk Ground address Newbury RFC Monks Lane Newbury RG14 7RW
Honorary Secretary: Mrs Carol Hawkins, 8 Balfour Crescent Newbury Berks. RG14 6SN
Tel: 01635 524043
Fixtures Secretary: Brian Lee,
Club Colours: Light & Dark Blue
League: Southern Counties North (level 7)

Newent RFC
Ground Address: Recreation Ground Watery Lane Newent GL18 1PX
Website: www.newentrugby.co.uk
Directions: Drive into centre of town, turn right into Watery Lane by the library/health centre, Ground is on the right about 400 meters along Watery Lane.
Honorary Secretary: Mrs Carrol Gough, Overton Farm Cold Harbour Lane Oxenhall Newent Glos. GL18 1DJ
Tel: 01531 820191
Email: secretary-newentrfc@hotmail.com
Fixtures Secretary: Chris Steward
Tel: 01452 790608
Club Colours: Green & Gold
League: Gloucester 3 (level 11)

Newquay Hornets RFC
Ground Address: Newquay Sports Centre Yeoman Way Yeoman Way Newquay Cornwall TR7 2SL
Contact: 01637 875533
Email: jg.broadstone@btconnect.com
Directions: From Bodmin/St Austell Newquay via A3058, left at Chester Road, 2nd left Whitegate Road, left at T junction. The Club is 50 yards on the left. From Redruth Newquay via A3075 and A392. Right at Mellanvrane Roundabout, across mini roundabouts into Edgcumbe Avenue. Across mini-roundabout into Hilgrove Road. Bear right and signposted first on right. Follow Tretherras Road to the end. Newquay Sports Centre entrance on left.
Honorary Secretary: Mr Russell Edwards, 17 St Thomas Road Newquay Cornwall TR7 1RS
Tel: 01637 871479
Email: russ@macnetdesign.co.uk
Fixtures Secretary: Mr Reg Roberts, 18 St. Annes Road Newquay Cornwall TR7 2SA
Tel: 01637 874568
Email: r.roberts16@ntlworld.com
Club Colours: Green &White Hoops
League: Western Counties West (level 7)

North Bristol RFC
Ground Address: Oaklands Gloucester Road Gloucester Road Almondsbury BS32 4AG
Contact: 01454 612740
Email: info@northbristolrfc.co.uk
Website: www.northbristolrfc.co.uk
Directions: Leave the M5 at Junction 16 and head towards Almondsbury / Thornbury. The club is fifty metres from the motorway on the left. It is sign posted.
Honorary Secretary: Mr Steven Bold, Oaklands Gloucester Road Almondsbury Bristol BS32 4AG
Tel: 0117 9798516
Email: boldys@blueyonder.co.uk
Fixtures Secretary: Mr Mike Cottle, 33 Clavell Road Henbury Bristol BS10 7EJ
Tel: 0117 9506182
Email: chepstowcharlie1947@msn.com
Club Colours: Royal & Scarlet Hoops
League: Western Counties North (level 7)

North Dorset RFC
Ground Address: North Dorset R.F.C. Slaughtergate Longbury Hill Lane Gillingham Dorset SP8 5SY
Contact: 01747 822748
Email: rugby@ndrfc.co.uk
Website: www.ndrfc.co.uk
Directions: Take Wincanton Road (B3081) from town centre, Longbury Hill Lane is on the right about 1 mile from the town, 300yds after the end of 30mph zone. Nearest train station is Gillingham (Dorset).
Honorary Secretary: Mr Nigel Mattravers, 4 West Court Templecombe Somerset BA8 0JT
Tel: 01963 370071
Email: nigel.mattravers@gtuk.com
Fixtures Secretary: Mr Steve Donald, 63 Marlott Road Gillingham Dorset SP8 4FA
Tel: 07974 923819
Club Colours: Green & Navy
League: Southern Counties South (level 7)

North Petherton
Ground Address: North Petherton RFC Beggars Brook North Petherton TA6 6NW
Contact: 01278 663028
Email: prince15@btinternet.com
Website: www.north-petherton-rfc.co.uk
Directions: through North Petherton towards Taunton, club is on left hand side (through lay-by) as you leave the town
Honorary Secretary: Mr Clive Pearn, 48 Broadland Avenue North Petherton Somerset TA6 6QT
Tel: 01278 663032
Fixtures Secretary: Mr Russell Williams, Lowenva, Newton Road, North Petherton Somerset TA6 6SN
Tel: 07525 636283
Email: cidermanruss@yahoo.co.uk
Club Colours: Black & White Hoops
League: Western Counties West (level 7)

North Tawton RFC
Ground Address: Taw Meadow fore st North Tawton Devon EX20 2ED
Contact: 01837 82516
Email: peter.hoggins@talk21.com
Directions: Directions to Club;- If coming into town from Exeter or Okehampton direction enter town and keep to left hand side of clock tower in square, follow road until just before bridge - Club is on right hand side. If entering town from Cheese Factory side go over the bridge and turn left into the Club
Honorary Secretary: Mrs Sarah Short, Briarmead Slade Hill North Tawton Devon EX20 2DR Tel: 01837 82706
Email: sarah@short4933.freeserve.co.uk
Fixtures Secretary: Mrs Sarah Quick, Victoria Cottages 7 North Tawton Devon EX20 2DF Tel: 01837 82704
Email: sarahquick104@btinternet.com
Club Colours: Black & Amber
League: Devon 1 North & East (level 9)

Okehampton RFC
Ground Address: Showfield Oaklands Okehampton Devon EX20 1LG
Contact: 07768614950
Website: www.okerugby.com
Directions: From the town centre follow signs for Hatherleigh (A386). Continue up hill from mini-roundabout (by Waitrose Supermarket) approx 200m. Turn right into Glendale Road, Clubhouse is approximately 100m on right
Honorary Secretary: Martin Grant, 8 Barton Road Okehampton Devon EX20 1NW
Tel: 01837 53831 Email: martin@gtiprint.co.uk
Fixtures Secretary: Mr Colin Ewen, C/O Club Address Showfield Showfield Okehampton Devon EX20 1LG
Tel: 01837 53762 Email: lynnewen@aol.com
Club Colours: maroon and amber hoops
League: Western Counties West (level 7)

Old Ashtonians RFC
Ground Address: Ashton Park School Blackmoors Lane, Bower Ashton Bristol BS3 2JJ
Contact: c/o 0117 987 7796
Directions: From city follow signs for Portishead, Ashton Park School is indicated at first r'about (turn left).
Honorary Secretary: Mr Stewart Gudge, Ashton Park School Blackmoors Lane, Bower Ashton Bristol BS3 2JJ
Tel: 01275 830083 Email: stewartjgudge@aol.com
Club Colours: Blue Shirt, Yellow band
Non League

Old Bristolians RFC
Ground Address: Memorial Playing Field Longwell Lane, Failand Bristol BS8 3TQ
Contact: 01275 392137
Website: www.obsrc.com
Directions: Off B3129 Beggar Bush Lane, Failand, behind Corus Hotel Bristol (formerly called Redwood Lodge Country Club).
Honorary Secretary: Mr Charles Vanderlande, 74 Berkeley Road Bishopston Bristol BS7 8HG
Tel: 07891 693944
Email: charles.vdl@roxburghmilkins.com
Fixtures Secretary: Mr Lyndon Davies, 21 Ashgrove Road Bedminster Bristol BS3 3JP
Tel: 07748 928546
Email: lyndonfd@hotmail.com
Club Colours: green, gold and maroon
League: Gloucester 1 (level 9)

Old Centralians RFC
Ground Address: Saintbridge Sports Centre Painswick Road Gloucester GL4 4QX
Contact: 01452 527992
Email: stan005b8609@blueyonder.co.uk
Website: www.oldcentralians.co.uk
Directions: Follow B4073 from Gloucester Ring Road. The Ground is approx 400m on the right just before the traffic lights.
Fixtures Secretary: Mr Mark Fritchley, 44 Fieldfare Abbeydale Gloucester GL4 4WF
Tel: 01452 532900
Club Colours: Navy blue & Royal blue Quarters with Gold Trimming
League: Western Counties North (level 7)

Old Colstonians RFC
Ground Address: Colstons School Bell Hill, Stapleton Bristol BS16 1BJ
Contact: 0117 965 5207
Directions: M32 Eastville roundabout up hill towards Stapleton. Enter school gates at top of hill.
Honorary Secretary: Mr Andrew Pritchard, 31 Brook Road Fishponds Bristol BS16 3SQ
Tel: 07985 192962
Email: andy.orange@blueyonder.co.uk
Fixtures Secretary: Mr Simon Wilkins, 13 Florence Park Westbury Park Bristol BS6 7LS
Tel: 07776 180013
Email: simon@unitedbuilders.fslife.co.uk
Club Colours: Blue, Black & Gold
League: Gloucester Premier (level 8)

Old Cryptians RFC
Ground Address: Memorial Ground Tuffley Avenue Tuffley Avenue Gloucester GL1 5NS
Contact: 01452 532002
Email: adrianhenleydavies@yahoo.co.uk
Website: www.oldcrptiansrfc.com
Directions: Off Bristol Road to Tuffley Ave. The Ground is 1 mile on the right before Stroud Road.
Honorary Secretary: Mr Adrian Henley-Davies, 2 Brooksdie Cottage 81 Larkhay Road Hucclecote Gloucester Gloucestershire GL3 3NQ
Tel: 07931 535806
Email: adrianhenleydavies@yahoo.co.uk
Fixtures Secretary: Mr Derek Howell
Email: howzatglos@hotmail.com
Club Colours: Maroon, Blue and Gold Stripes
League: Gloucester 1 (level 9)

Old Culverhaysians
Ground Address: Clubhouse Old Fosse Road, Odd Down
Old Fosse Road, Odd Down Bath BA2 2SS
Contact: 01225 832081
Email: waynemiller1@blueyonder.co.uk
Directions: Take Wells road out of Bath approx. 1 mile. At Harverster Red Lion pub roundabout go staight on. Turn right in to Old Fosse Road. The clubhouse is approximately 1/2 mile on left hand side
Honorary Secretary: Mr Wayne Miller, 19 Chantry Mead Road Bath BA2 2DE   Tel: 01225 340717
Email: waynemiller1@blueyonder.co.uk
Fixtures Secretary: Mr Nigel Frankcom, 58 Haycombe Drive Bath BA2 1PG
Tel: 01225 400691   Email: nigelfranky@hotmail.co.uk
Club Colours: Black
League: Somerset 1 (level 9)

Old Elizabethans RFC
Ground Address: Severn Road Hallen Bristol BS10 7RZ
Contact: 0117959 1071
Directions: M5 J17 turn towards Pelning at roundabout then 1st left, continue for 2-3 miles until junction with King William IV pub on right, turn right, The Club is 200yards on the left.
Honorary Secretary: Mr David Perkins, 855 Filton Avenue Filton Bristol BS34 7HJ   Tel: 0117 9692545
Fixtures Secretary: Mr P Abel, 2 Dublin Crescent Bristol BS9 4NA
Tel: 07973 194508   Email: pabel@ceravision.net
Club Colours: Blue, White & Old Gold Hoops
League: Gloucester 2 (level 10)

Old Plymothian & Mannamedian RFC
Ground Address: OPM RFC (OPM SUITE) Plymouth College Ford Park Road, PL4 6RN
Contact: 01752 296327
Email: info@opmrugby.com
Website: www.opmrugby.com
Directions: How to find us- leave the A38 at Marsh Mills and Plympton direction, Turn right towards Plymstock, after 1/2 mile. Right again at top of hill and continue for 1.5 miles, our gound is on left.
Honorary Secretary: Mr David Glastonbury, 49 Compton Avenue Plymouth Devon PL3 5DA
Tel: 01752 669037
Email: d.glastonbury@jenkinspotter.co.uk
Fixtures Secretary: Mrs Sue Mathias, 2 Selkirk Place Crownhill Plymouth PL5 3BY
Tel: 01752 310890
Club Colours: Claret and Blue Quarters
League: Cornwall-Devon (level 2)

Old Redcliffians
Ground Address: Scotland Lane Brislington Bristol AVON BS4 5LU
Contact: 0117 9778501
Directions: From A34 from Bristol, turn right at Macdonalds/Park & Ride, trevel for 0.25 mile. The Ground is on the right hand side.
Honorary Secretary: Mr Richard Yandell, 11 Imperial Walk Knowle Bristol BS14 9AD
Tel: 0117 9030395   Email: richardyandell@hotmail.com
Fixtures Secretary: Mr Russell Yandell
Tel: 01275 373444
Club Colours: Red & Black Hoops
League: Western Counties North (level 7)

Old Richians RFC
Ground Address: Sandyleaze Longlevens Gloucestershire GL2 0PX
Contact: 01452 524649
Email: gripsky@richians.freeserve.co.uk
Website: http://orrfc.gripsky.co.uk
Directions: Turn into Nine Elms Road from Cheltenham Road & follow to Sir Thomas Rich's School.
Honorary Secretary: Ms Josie Collier, 5 Foxleigh Crescent Gloucester GL2 0XW
Tel: 01452 416138   Email: sccolliers@blueyonder.co.uk
Fixtures Secretary: Mr Steve Collier, 5 Foxleigh Crescent Gloucester GL2 0XW
Tel: 07941 365473   Email: sccollies@blueyonder.co.uk
Club Colours: Royal Blue & Gold
League: Gloucester Premier (level 8)

Old Sulians RFC Ltd
Ground Address: Lansdown Road Bath BA1 9BH
Contact: 01225 310201
Email: terry.haines@virgin.net
Website: www.oldsulians.co.uk
Directions: Follow Lansdown Road from city centre, ground is on left 400m past MOD site.
Honorary Secretary: Mr Terry Haines, 0 Rockliffe Avenue Bath BA2 6QP
Tel: 0117 9797540   Email: terry.haines@virgin.net
Fixtures Secretary: Mr Tony Slee, 8 Godwins Close Atworth Melksham Wilts. SN12 8LD
Tel: 01225 703812
Club Colours: Blue and Red
League: Somerset Premier (level 8)

Old Technicians RFC
Ground Address: Weston Mill Oak Villa Ferndale Road, Weston Mill Plymouth Devon PL2 2EL
Contact: 01752 308217
Directions: From the A38 take the Weston mill turn off. Turn left at the traffic lights next to the fire station, then next left into the carpark behind the fire station.
Honorary Secretary: Mr Bill Bryan, 74 Durham Avenue St Judes Plymouth PL4 8SR   Tel: 01752 224124
Email: mollyandbillybryan@yahoo.co.uk
Club Colours: Black shirts with white circlet, black shorts
League: Devon 1 South & West (level 9)

LEVEL 7-11 & NON LEAGUE CLUBS

Oldfield Old Boys
Ground Address: Shaft Road Combe Down Combe Down Bath BA2 7HP
Contact: 01225 834135
Email: pb@lcplc.co.uk
Website: www.oldfieldrfc.com
Directions: From Bath follow signs to the University, continue past towards Combe Down, take left turn down Shaft Road to ground.
Honorary Secretary: Mr Steve Godwin, 12 Lime Grove Gardens Bath BA2 4HE
Tel: 01225 318612   Email: stevegodwin36@hotmail.com
Fixtures Secretary: Mr Chris Shaw, 214a Black Berry Lane Conkwell Bradford Upon Avon Wilts. BA15 2JF
Tel: 07968 703430   Email: cshaw8@btinternet.com
Club Colours: Maroon & Gold
League: Southern Counties South (level 7)

Oriel RFC
Address: Oriel College Oriel Square Oxford OX1 4EW
Contact: 077895117301
Email: dougal.meston@oriel.ox.ac.uk
Non League

Oxford Brookes University RFC
Ground Address: Centre for Sport Gipsy Lane, Headington Oxford OX3 0BP
Contact: 01865 483 166
Honorary Secretary: Mr Will Dallimore, OBU Centre for Sport Cheney Student Village Cheney Lane Oxford Oxfordshire OX3 0BD
Tel: 07701 052886   Email: Wdallimore86@hotmail.com
Fixtures Secretary: as Hon. Sec.
Club Colours: Pink with yellow spots
Non League

Oxford RFC
Ground Address: Southern Bypass Ground North Hinksey Village off Southern Bypass Oxford OX2 0NA
Contact: 01865 243984
Website: www.oxfordrfc.co.uk
Directions: Ground can only be approached from A34 going south, turn left off A34, sign posted .
Honorary Secretary: Mrs Kay Honner, 361 Woodstock Road Oxford OX2 8AA
Tel: 01865 438655   Email: honnerk@yahoo.co.uk
Fixtures Secretary: Mr Keith Latham, 29 Churchill Way Long Hanborough Witney Oxfordshire OX29 8JJ
Tel: 07967 206098
Email: keith.latham@tinyworld.co.uk
Club Colours: Green, Black & Silver Hoops, red socks
League: Berks-Bucks & Oxon Premier (level 8)

Oxford University Greyhounds RFC
Ground Address: c/o University Sports Centre Jackdaw Lane Off Iffley Road OX4 1SR
Contact: 01865 432000
Email: tim.stevens@sport.ox.ac.uk
Honorary Secretary: Mr Tim Stevens, OURFC Jackdaw Lane Iffley Road Oxford Oxfordshire OX4 1SR
Tel: 01865 432000   Email: tim.stevens@sport.ox.ac.uk

Fixtures Secretary: as Hon. Sec.
Club Colours: Navy blue & grey hoops, blue shorts
Non League

Oxford University RFC
Ground Address: OURFC Jackdaw Lane Iffley Road Oxford OX4 1SR
Contact: 01865 432000
Email: tim.stevens@sport.ox.ac.uk
Website: www.ourfc.org
Honorary Secretary: Mr Tim Stevens, OURFC Jackdaw Lane Iffley Road Oxford Oxfordshire OX4 1SR
Tel: 01865 432000   Email: tim.stevens@sport.ox.ac.uk
Fixtures Secretary: as Hon. Sec.
Club Colours: Navy blue shirts, shorts & socks
Non League

Painswick RFC
Ground Address: The Clubhouse Broadham Fields Stroud Road Painswick GL6 6QL
Contact: 01452 813735
Email: julian@westrip84.freeserve.co.uk
Website: www.painswickrugby.co.uk
Directions: Painswick RFC is located just south of Painswick village on the main A46 between Cheltenham and Stroud.
Honorary Secretary: Mr Julian Mitchell, 18 The Wordens Stroud Gloucestershire GL5 4RX
Tel: 07747 600764
Email: julian@westrip84.freeserve.co.uk
Fixtures Secretary: Mr Martin Hayward, 4 Coldwell Close Middleyard Stroud Gloucestershire GL10 3QN
Tel: 07792 911292
Club Colours: Cherry & White Hoops, Navy Shorts
League: Gloucester 1 (level 9)

Pembroke RFC
Ground Address: c/o Pembroke College St. Aldate's Oxford OX1 1DW
Email: robert.white@pmb.ox.ac.uk
Non League

Penryn RFC
Ground Address: The Memorial Ground Kernick Road Kernick Road Penryn TR10 8NT
Contact: 01326 372239
Email: mdove87@tiscali.co.uk
Website: www.penrynrugby.com
Directions: From ExeterA30 to Launceston, head towards Bodmin, then follow signs for Truro. From Truro A39 to Falmouth, continue on the to the distributer road,at Asda roundabout turn to Penryn,ground 500 meters on left industrial estate ground second left.
Honorary Secretary: Mr Peter Le Patourel, 3 The Square Penryn Cornwall TR10 8JQ
Tel: 01326 372672   Email: peterlepat@onetel.com
Fixtures Secretary: Doctor Michael Dove, Fourways Treworthal Rd Perranwell Station Truro Cornwall TR3 7QB
Tel: 01872 864058   Email: mdove87@talktalk.net
Club Colours: Red and Black Hoops
League: Western Counties West (level 7)

Perranporth RFC
Ground Address: The Droop Ponsmere Valley
Perranporth Perranporth Truro Cornwall TR6 0BW
Contact: 01872 572968
Email: mowen@carrickhousing.org.uk
Website: www.perranporthrfc.co.uk
Directions: From Newquay turn right at Goonhavern roundabouts, continue for approx 2 miles, past the Golf club on right, down steep Hill 1st turning on the left.
Honorary Secretary: Mr Daniel Wallis, 7 Polvella Close Newquay Cornwall TR7 1QG
Email: dansoogle@googlemail.com
Fixtures Secretary: Mr Steven Arthur, Chalcotts Farm Rose Truro Cornwall TR4 9PL
Club Colours: Green & Gold
League: Cornwall League (level 9)

Pewsey Vale RFC
Ground Address: The Angela Yeates Memorial Community Sports Ground, Wilcot Rd Pewsey SN9 5NL
Contact: 07976 882103
Email: daroskin@aol.com
Website: www.clubs.rfu.com/clubs/portals/pvrfc
Directions: A345 from Marlborough, Turn R into Wilcot Road (After Railway Bridge), carry on for approx 1 Mile set of lights on the bridge. Stay Right (signposted Wilcot) carry on for 500 Metres. Ground on Left. WARNING SAT-NAV INNACURATE ON THIS POSTCODE.
Honorary Secretary: Mr David Aroskin, 47 Swan Meadow Pewsey Wilts. SN9 5HP
Tel: 07976 882103   Email: daroskin@aol.com
Fixtures Secretary: as Hon. Sec.
Club Colours: Black,Red,Royal Blue,and White
League: Dorset & Wilts 2 North (level 9)

Phoenix RFC
Ground Address: Institute Road Taplow SL6 0NS
Contact: 01628 664 319
Directions: M4 J7, take A4 towards Maidenhead, after Sainsburys superstore take next right (0.5 mile) then first left after the bridge is Institute Road.
Honorary Secretary: Mr Neil Bennett, 18 Hag Hill Rise Taplow Maidenhead Berks. SL6 0LS
Tel: 01628 605611   Email: phoenixnumber2@aol.com
Fixtures Secretary: Mr Steve Rafferty, 86 Chalklands Bourne End Bucks. SL8 5TJ
Tel: 01628 523164   Email: rafferty90@aol.com
Club Colours: Red/black quarters, black shorts & socks.
League: Berks-Bucks & Oxon Premier (level 8)

Plymouth Argaum RFC
Ground Address: Bickleigh Down Road Roborough Roborough Plymouth Devon PL6 7AD
Contact: 01752 772156
Email: juniors@argaum.org.uk
Website: http://www.argaum.org.uk
Directions: To find us from the A38 Devon Expressway, take the Manadon turn-off and head North on the A386 towards Tavistock. Travel past the Derriford Hospital r'about, past Plymouth Airport, take 1st exit at the Woolwell (tescos) r'about continue along the Roborough Bypass towards tavistock(Dual Carriageway) until the Belliver Industrial Estate r'about. Go right around the r'about and travel back down the bypass on the Southbound side, take the first exit (Roborough) and at the cross roads, go straight on into Bickleigh Down Road. Follow the road for about 400m and Plymouth Argaum is on the right hand side.
Honorary Secretary: Mr Geoffrey Kelly, 90 Plymouth Road Plympton Plymouth PL7 4NB   Tel: 07971 051109
Fixtures Secretary: Mr Stuart Quarterman, 28 Almond Drive Chaddlewood Plymouth Devon PL7 2WY
Tel: 01752 550743   Email: stuwieq@argaum.org.uk
Club Colours: Bottle Green, Black, White
League: Devon 1 South & West (level 9)

Plymouth Barbarians RFC
Ground Address: C/O 87 Blackstone Close 87 Blackstone Close Plymouth Devon PL9 8UW
Contact: 07808 286017
Email: pete_derry@plymouthbarbariansrfc.co.uk
Website: www.plymouthbarbariansrfc.co.uk
Honorary Secretary: Mr Peter Derry, 87 Blackstone Close Elburton Plymouth PL9 8UW   Tel: 07808 286017
Email: pte.derry@plymouthbarbariansrfc.co.uk
Fixtures Secretary: Mr Paul Routley, C S S A Recreation Road Plymouth Devon PL3 3NA
Tel: 07813 656943   Email: proutley_uk@yahoo.co.uk
Club Colours: Black and White Shirts - Black
League: Devon 1 South & West (level 9)

Plympton Victoria RFC
Ground Address: 37 Tovey Crescent Manadon Park Plymouth Devon PL5 3US
Contact: 01752 766228
Email: plymptonvictoria@yahoo.co.uk
Honorary Secretary: Mrs Rebecca Witts, 37 Tovey Crescent Manadon Park Plymouth Devon PL5 3US
Tel: 07837 651770
Email: plymptonvictoria@yahoo.co.uk
Fixtures Secretary: Mr Kevin Jefferies, 0 Neal Close Plymouth Devon PL7 1YY
Tel: 07958 767027   Email: kevjefferies@yahoo.co.uk
Club Colours: Red Gold & Black
League: Devon 1 South & West (level 9)

Plymstock Albion Oaks RFC
Address:129 Holmwood Avenue Plymouth PL9 9EZ
Contact: 01752 770140
Email: secretary@paorfc.co.uk
Website: www.paorfc.co.uk
Directions: Leave A38 at Marsh Mills roundabout, take A374 towards city, turn left onto A379 Billacombe Rd, left at 3rd roundabout into Haye Road. King George V Playing Fields are on the right.
Honorary Secretary: Mr Christopher Jane, 129 Holmwood Avenue Plymstock Plymouth PL9 9EZ
Tel: 01752 310886   Email: secretary@paorfc.co.uk
Fixtures Secretary: Mr Dave Osborne, 161 Billacombe Road Plymstock PL9 7HB   Tel: 01752 318492
Email: marktheozman@googlemail.co.uk
Club Colours: Green & Gold
League: Cornwall-Devon (level 8)

LEVEL 7-11 & NON LEAGUE CLUBS

Poole RFC
Ground Address: Hamworthy Recreation Ground Turlin Moor, Blandford Rd Hamworthy, Poole Dorset BH16 5BW
Contact: 07906 966175
Email: barryross33@ntlworld.com
Directions: From Poole quay, follow directions to Hamworthy, over the lifting bridge & continue for 2 miles, turn left opposite Texaco petrol station on right. From A35 follow signs for Rockley Park (B3068 Blandford Road)and turn right before Texaco petrol station on left.
Honorary Secretary: Mr John Spriggs, 75 Fitzworth Avenue Hamworthy Poole Dorset BH16 5AZ
Tel: 07886 673121   Email: johnspriggs@fsmail.com
Fixtures Secretary: Mr Peter Lambert, 12 Goldfinch Road Poole Dorset BH17 7TD
Tel: 07733 942610   Email: petelambert@talktalk.net
Club Colours: Blue & Amber
League: Dorset & Wilts 3 South (level 10)

Princes Risborough RFC
Contact: 07976 253044
Email: swansonplans@aol.com
Honorary Secretary: Mr Spencer Swanson,
Tel: 07976 253044 or 01844 346834
Email: swansonplans@aol.com
Fixtures Secretary: Tom Audley   Tel: 07855 758657
Club Colours: Black, White & Red
League: Berks-Bucks & Oxon 2 N (level 10)

Puddletown RFC
Ground Address: The Clubhouse Enterprise Park Piddlehinton Dorchester Dorset DT2 7UA
Contact: 01305 848808
Email: puddletownrfc@hotmail.com
Directions: Leave Dorchester on the A35 east, after 1/4 mile turn left on B3143, 3 miles on the right hand side is the Enterprise Park, an old army camp club.
Honorary Secretary: Mr Ray Stephens, 7 Athelhampton Road Puddletown Dorchester Dorset DT2 8SR
Tel: 07966 412467
Email: puddletownrfc@hotmail.com
Fixtures Secretary: Mr Geoff Puryer, 0 North Street Charminster Dorchester Dorset DT2 9QZ
Tel: 01305 259223
Email: geoff.puryer@tiscali.co.uk
Club Colours: Red Shirts, Black Shorts
League: Dorset & Wilts 1 South (level 8)

Queen's College (Oxford) RUFC
Ground Address: The Queen's College High Street Oxford OX1 4AW
Contact: 01865 279182
Email: martin.edwards@queens.ox.ac.uk
Honorary Secretary: Mr Martin Edwards
Email: martin.edwards@queens.ox.ac.uk
Fixtures Secretary: Mr Tom Davies
Email: TomDavies@queens.ox.ac.uk
Non League

RAF Benson RFC
Address: UMO 28 (AC) Sqn RAF Benson OX10 6AA
Contact: 01491 837766 ext7652
Email: 28sqnumo@benson.raf.mod.uk
Club Colours: Blue/White, Black/Yellow
Non League

RAF Brize Norton RUFC
Ground Address: Gymnasium RAF Brize Norton Carterton Oxfordshire OX18 3LX
Contact: 01993 897220
Email: rattenm341@brizenorton.raf.mod.uk
Club Colours: Red / Black
Non League

RAF Lyneham RFC
Ground Address: Cpl Chris King Eng Plans Terminal Building RAF Lyneham SN15 4PZ
Contact: 07825660817
Email: chrisking1234@hotmail.com
Honorary Secretary: Mr Ged Burgwyn, The Officers Mess RAF Lyneham Chippenham Wilts. SN15 4PZ
Tel: 01249 896414   Email: gedburgwyn@hotmail.com
Club Colours: Black with Gold Trim
Non League

RAF St Mawgan RFC
Address: RAF St Mawgan Newquay Cornwall TR8 4HP
Contact: 01637 853614
Email: chairman@stmawganrfc.com
Honorary Secretary: Mr Russ Milsom, 1
Tel: 07931 555149   Email: secretary@stmawganrfc.com
Club Colours: Red, White, Green, Black Hoops
Non League

Redruth Albany RFC
Ground Address: Redruth Albany RFC Station Hill Redruth Cornwall TR15 2PP
Contact: 01209 216745
Directions: Ajacent to Redruth Cricket Club behind Trewirgie School, Falmouth Rd, Redruth, 0.5 mile from the Train station
Honorary Secretary: Mr Stephen Barnes, 2 Station Road Pool Redruth Cornwall TR15 3DX
Tel: 01209 212558   Email: rbarnes@cornwall.gov.uk
Fixtures Secretary: Clive Williams, 122 Trefysis Road Redruth Cornwall TR15 2JN   Tel: 01209 210256
Club Colours: Royal Blue Shirts,Black Shorts
League: Cornwall League (level 9)

Roseland RFC
Ground Address: Philleigh. Truro Cornwall TR2 5NB
Contact: 01872 580001
Email: mail@roselandrfc.co.uk
Website: www.roselandrfc.co.uk
Directions: 15 miles from Truro on the Roseland peninsular, signed Tregony & Towary, St Mawes.
Honorary Secretary: Miss Alison Sutton, Church View Road 4 Probus Truro Cornwall TR2 4JH
Tel: 07834 231865
Email: ASutton@nalders.co.uk
Fixtures Secretary: Bud Rosewall
Tel: 01326 270397
Club Colours: Navy & Scarlet
League: Cornwall League (level 9)

Ross-On-Wye
Ground Address: C/O The Drop Inn Station Street Ross-On-Wye Herefordshire HR9 7AG
Contact: 01989 563256(club)
Email: BRIAN.A.COOKE@BTINTERNET.COM
Directions: play at Ross Sports Centre wilton road ross-on-wye
Honorary Secretary: Mr Dave Cooke, 4 Old Nursery Close Wilton Ross-on-Wye Herefordshire HR9 6BG
Tel: 01989 564626
Email: brian.a.cooke@btinternet.com
Fixtures Secretary: Mr Dave Cooke, 4 Old Nursery Close Wilton Ross-on-Wye Herefordshire HR9 6BG
Tel: 01989 564626
Email: brian.a.cooke@btinternet.com
Club Colours: Royal Blue & White Hoops
League: Gloucester Premier (level 8)

Royal Agricultural College RFC
Ground Address: SU Stroud Road Cirencester GL7 6JS
Contact: 01285 652 187
Honorary Secretary: Honorary Secretary, Sports Office Royal Agricultural RFC Stroud Road Cirencester Gloucestershire GL7 6JS
Non League

Royal Signals Corp RUFC
Ground Address: c/o ACISG Basil Hill Barracks Corsham Wilts. SN13 9NR
Contact: 01225 814376
Non League

Salcombe RFC
Ground Address: Twomeads Camperdown Road Salcombe Devon TQ8 8AX
Contact: 01548 842639
Website: www.rfu.com/clubs/salcombe
Directions: From Exeter A38 follow Kingsbridge signs. From Kingsbridge follow Salcombe A381 signs. On approaching Salcombe pass petrol station on the right, turn left at crossroads onto Onslow Road. Take 1st right, St Dunstan's Rd, 2nd left, Camperdown Road.
Honorary Secretary: Phil Lowe, Beacon House Bonfire Hill Salcombe Devon TQ8 8EF
Tel: 01548 844135

Email: phlowe@aol.com
Fixtures Secretary: John Sprague, Hideaway Knowle Road Salcombe Devon TQ8 8EH
Tel: 01548 843044
Email: hideaway9@btinternet.com
Club Colours: Red/white jerseys, white shorts
League: Devon 1 South & West (level 9)

Saltash RFC
Ground Address: Saltash RFC Moorlands Lane Moorlands Lane Saltash PL12 4HJ
Contact: 01752 847227
Email: info@saltashrugby.com
Website: www.saltashrugby.com
Directions: From A38 westwards over Tamar Bridge, through tunnel, left at 1st t'about, right at lights, then 2nd right into Moorlands Lane , Clubhouse at end of lane.
Honorary Secretary: Mr Ian Ruse, 18 Glebe Avenue Saltash Cornwall PL12 6EU   Tel: 01752 843368
Fixtures Secretary: Mr Bill Ryan, 7 Clear View Saltash Cornwall PL12 6HB   Tel: 07766 357740
Club Colours: Black,Gold & Red panels
League: Cornwall-Devon (level 8)

Sherborne RFC
Ground Address: The Terrace Playing Fields Gainsborough Park Sherborne Dorset DT9 5NS
Contact: 07775 590477
Email: contact@sherbornerugby.co.uk
Website: www.sherbornerugby.co.uk
Directions: From A30 take A352 towards Dorchester. The Terrace playing fields are halfway up the hill on the left hand side.
Honorary Secretary: Mr Paul Jacobs, 1 The Furlongs Sherborne Dorset DT9 4DQ
Tel: 01935 813673   Email: PJ.1TF@Tiscali.co.uk
Fixtures Secretary: Mr Nigel O'Grady, Wescot Westbury Sherborne Dorset DT9 3RA
Tel: 07971 111893   Email: nog_007@hotmail.com
Club Colours: Black
League: Southern Counties South (level 7)

Slough RFC
Ground Address: Tamblyn Fields, Upton Court Park Upton Court Road Slough Berks. SL3 7LT
Contact: 01753 522107
Directions: Exit M4 junction 5 towards Slough. At 2nd lights (fire station to left) turn left into Upton Court Road. Club entrance drive approx 700 metres on left, signposted. Club at end of drive. IF ARRIVING BY COACH OR HIGH VEHICLE 'PHONE CLUB
Honorary Secretary: Mr Ian Wright, 13 Castle Street Slough SL1 2AX
Tel: 01753 821645   Email: ian.wright1@ge.com
Fixtures Secretary: Mr Clive Blackman, 11 Coleridge Crescent Colnbrook Slough SL3 0PY
Tel: 07720 439441
Email: clive.blackman@btinternet.com
Club Colours: Sage Green & White, Black Shorts
League: Southern Counties North (level 7)

LEVEL 7-11 & NON LEAGUE CLUBS   759

Smiths (Industries) RFC
Ground Address: Newlands Park Sports & Social Venue Southam Lane Evesham Road Bishops Cleeve Cheltenham Gloucestershire GL52 3PE
Contact: 01242 672752
Email: smithsrugby@googlemail.com
Website: www.smiths-rfc.co.uk
Directions: 2 miles north of Cheltenham on A435.
Honorary Secretary: Mr Michael Wakeman, Gardeners Arms Beckford Road Alderton Tewkesbury Gloucestershire GL20 8NL
Tel: 01242 620250
Fixtures Secretary: Mr David Cole
Email: dcole@laneshealth.com
Club Colours: Black, White and Blue
League: Gloucester 3 (level 11)

Somerton RFC
Ground Address: Somerton Sports club Gassons Lane Somerton Somerset TA11 6HS
Contact: 07870 861731
Email: somerton@somertonrfc.co.uk
Directions: see website
Honorary Secretary: Mr Mike Fullegar, 16 May Pole Knap Somerton Somerset TA11 6HR
Tel: 01458 272122
Email: pat.fullegar@tiscalli.co.uk
Fixtures Secretary: Jerry Phillips, 23 Glenville Road Yeovil Somerset BA21 5AN
Tel: 07870 861731
Email: jerry.phillips@friary.co.uk
Club Colours: blue & yellow
League: Somerset 2 South (level 10)

South Molton RFC
Ground Address: Unicorn Park Station Road South Molton Devon EX36
Email: the.frosties@btinternet.com
Directions: Taking Pathfields exit on the North Devon link road when reading signs for South Molton, take first right then first left.
Honorary Secretary: Ms Kate Rowe, 2 Kingdon Avenue South Molton Devon EX36 4GJ
Tel: 01769 574650
Email: kate.rowe@molevalleyfarmers.com
Fixtures Secretary: Mr Denis Cronk
Club Colours: Black jersey, white collar, black shorts, b&w socks
League: Devon 1 North & East (level 9)

South Wilts Rugby Club
Ground Address: 50 Warwick Close Salisbury Wilts. SP1 3LS
Contact: 07793 139754
Email: taffyprop@hotmail.co.uk
Honorary Secretary: Mr William Roper, 90 Bouverie Avenue Salisbury Wilts. SP2 8DX
Tel: 01722 329250
Email: fortyfooter@hotmail.com
League: Dorset & Wilts 2 South (level 9)

Southmead RFC
Ground Address: The Greenway Centre Doncaster Road Bristol AVON BS10 5PY
Contact: 0117 9593060
Email: southmeadrfc@blueyonder.co.uk
Honorary Secretary: Mr Phillip Clark, 33 Marmion Crescent Henbury Bristol BS10 7PA
Tel: 0785 3375127
Email: southmeadrfc@blueyonder.co.uk
Fixtures Secretary: Mr Ian "Muddy" Waters
Tel: 07748703221
Email: muddy.waters@blueyonder.co.uk
Club Colours: Navy blue shirt with emerald green sides
League: Western Counties North (level 7)

Spartans (Gloucester) RFC
Ground Address: St. Catherines Meadow Cattlemarket Gloucester GL1 2ST
Contact: 01452410552
Honorary Secretary: Mr Phil Minns, 39 Swan Road Gloucester GL1 3BJ
Tel: 01452 547128   Email: phil.minns@hotmail.co.uk
Fixtures Secretary: Mr Tony Toney, St. Catherines Meadow Cattlemarket Gloucester GL1 2ST
Email: hiltontoney@btinternet.com
Club Colours: Red & Black
League: Gloucester Premier (level 8)

St Agnes RFC
Ground Address: Enys Park West Polberro St. Agnes Cornwall TR5 0ST
Contact: 01872 553673
Directions: Turn left opp. church , turn right after 800 yards, Enys Park is 200 yards on right.
Honorary Secretary: Miss Emma Davidge, Bolster Cottage Wheal Kitty St. Agnes Cornwall TR5 0RE
Tel: 0796 7108998   Email: edavidge@hotmail.com
Fixtures Secretary: Mr Tim Bawden, 1 Tap House Peterville St. Agnes Cornwall TR5 0QU
Tel: 01872 553095
Club Colours: Black & Red Hoops
League: Cornwall League (level 9)

St Austell RFC
Ground Address: St. Austell R.F.C. Tregorrick Park, Tregorrick Lane, St. Austell Cornwall PL26 7AG
Contact: 01726 76430
Email: tregorrickpark@hotmail.co.uk
Website: www.saintsrugby.net
Directions: Located on the road behind Asda superstore and next to Mount Edgecombe Hospice. From StAustell By-Pass take turning to Penrice Hospital. First right before Hospital.
Honorary Secretary: Mr Graham Walker, 28 Tremena Gardens St. Austell Cornwall PL25 5QH
Tel: 01726 63707   Email: gew04@hotmail.com
Fixtures Secretary: Mr Bernie Shepherd, 128 Landreath Place St. Blazey Par PL24 2LA Tel: 07799 876920
Club Colours: Red & White Hoops
League: Cornwall-Devon (level 8)

St Bernadettes Old Boys
Ground Address: Hengrove Park Bamfield Road
Whitchurch BS14 0XD
Contact: 01275 891 500
Email: sbobrfc@btconnect.com
Website: www.stbernadettesrfc.co.uk
Directions: From A37 - Follow sign for Bristol Airport at traffic lights in a large dip on junction with Airport Rd, turn left 0.5 mile at traffic lights, signed Action Indoor Sports, club is 0.25 mile right, before sports centre running track. From Bristol Airport on A38 turn right at the Kings Head pub. At bottom of this road turn right towards Bishopsworth. At mini roundabout turn left and stay on this road untill you reach a very large round about and follow the signs for "Action Indoor Sports" . The club is 200m on the left past this building.
Honorary Secretary: Mr Oliver James, 26 Haycombe Bristol BS14 0AJ
Tel: 01275 545784
Email: ollejames@hotmail.co.uk
Fixtures Secretary: Mr Mark Hanson, C/0 Club Secretary 39 Woodleigh Gardens Bristol BS14 9JA
Tel: 01275 832803
Club Colours: Green and Blue Hoops
League: Somerset Premier (level 8)

St Brendan's O.B. RFC
Ground Address: c/o Coombe Dingle Sports Complex Coombe Lane Stoke Bishop BS9 2BJ
Contact: 0117 9241390
Website: sbobrfc.co.uk
Honorary Secretary: Mr Richard Kolanko, 91 Church Road Horfield Bristol BS7 8SD
Tel: 0772 0988613
Email: richard.kolanko@btopenworld.com
Fixtures Secretary: Mr Larry Brien, 18 Westfield Road Banwell AVON BS29 6BA
Tel: 07788 744112
Email: larry.brien@orange.co.uk
Club Colours: Maroon & Old Gold Hoops
League: Gloucester 2 (level 10)

St Catherines RFC
Ground Address: c/o St. Catherine's College Manor Road Oxford OX1 3UJ
Email: james.demellow@stcatz.ox.ac.uk
Non League

St Columba & Torpoint
Ground Address: Defiance Field Torpoint PL11 2JW
Contact: 01752 816894
Email: spike@grandslam.orangehome.co.uk
Directions: From Torpoint ferry follow the A374 towards Antony for approx.1 mile the club is situated on the left hand side of the road with a hidden entrance. Opposite fuel tanks.
Honorary Secretary: Mr Barry Davies, 38 Wavish Park Torpoint Cornwall PL11 2HJ
Tel: 01752 813850

Fixtures Secretary: Mr Barry Davies, 38 Wavish Park Torpoint Cornwall PL11 2HJ
Tel: 01752 813850
Club Colours: Scarlet With Thin Royal Blue Hoops
League: Devon 1 South & West (level 9)

St Day
Ground Address: The Playing Field, St. Day 28, Scorrier Street, St. Day Redruth TR16 5LH
Contact: 0 1209821522
Email: cookster999@hotmail.com
Directions: Leave A30 at Scorrier exit, left past Cross Roads Hotel, at crossroads go straight across ground hust less than 1 mile.
Honorary Secretary: Mr Ryan Cook, 28 Scorrier Street St. Day Redruth Cornwall TR16 5LH
Tel: 01209 821522   Email: cookster999@hotmail.com
Club Colours: White with Cherry Hoops
League: Cornwall League (level 9)

St Edmund Hall RFC
Ground Address: c/o St. Edmund Hall Queens Lane Oxford OX1 4AR
Contact: 07738007003
Email: ryan.buckingham@seh.ox.ac.uk
Non League

St Hughs RFC
Ground Address: c/o St. Hughs College St. Margaret's Road Oxford OX2 6LE
Contact: 07709572393
Email: joseph.thornton@st-hughs.ox.ac.uk
Non League

St Just RFC
Ground Address: St. Just RFC Tregeseal St Just in Penwith Penzance Cornwall TR19 7PN
Contact: 01736 788593
Email: racheltrembath@btinternet.com
Website: www.stjustrfc.co.uk
Directions: Follow the A30 down Cornwall to Penzance then take the A3071 to St.Just.The club can be found in Tregeseal Valley bellow the town of St.Just (6 miles from Lands End). See also the find us page at www.stjustrfc.co.uk
Honorary Secretary: Mrs Rachel Trembath, 22 Nancherrow St. Just Penzance TR19 7PW
Tel: 07977 607870
Email: racheltrembath@btinternet.com
Fixtures Secretary: Mr Edward Bolitho, Trevorgans Farm St. Buryan Penzance Cornwall TR19 6HP
Tel: 07980 826613
Club Colours: All Black
League: Cornwall League (level 9)

St Peters RFC
Ground Address: c/o St. Peter's College New Inn Hall Street Oxford OX1 2DL
Contact: 07791179956
Email: david.conway@spc.ox.ac.uk
Non League

Stithians RFC
Ground Address: Playing Field Stithians
Contact: 0 1209860155
Email: norman@npdassociates.com
Website: www.stithiansrfc.com
Directions: Opposite the Church in the centre of the village. The village lies in the centre of the triangle formed by Redruth, Falmouth & Helston.
Hon. Secretary: Mr Norman Garlick, Treskewes Cottage Trewithen Moor Stithians Truro Cornwall TR3 7DU
Tel: 07779 654586   Email: norman@npdassociates.com
Fixtures Secretary: Mr Nigel Vague, Trewince Farm Stithians Truro Cornwall TR3 7BZ
Tel: 01209 860155
Club Colours: Black/Pink Shoulders
League: Cornwall-Devon (level 8)

Stothert and Pitt RFC
Ground Address: Adamsfield Bristol Road Corston Bath Somerset BA2 9DJ
Contact: 01225 874802
Email: info@stothertandpittrfc.co.uk
Website: www.stotherandpittrfc.co.uk
Directions: M4,Junction 18(Tormarton)take the Bath(A46)exit on roundabout.At end of A46 turn right onto the A4(west)continue through the city centre heading towards Bristol(A4) and the clubhouse is on the righthand side just before the village of Saltford.
Honorary Secretary: Mr Roger Garraway, 2 Westfield Park South Lower Weston Bath BA1 3HT
Tel: 01225 328396
Fixtures Secretary: Mr Carlos Orzabal de la Quintana, 0 Clarence Street Walcot Bath BA1 5NS
Tel: 01225 314805   Email: clorzabal@yahoo.com
Club Colours: Blue, Black & Amber
League: Somerset Premier (level 8)

Stow-on-the-Wold & District RFC
Ground Address: Stow-on-the-Wold & District R.F.C. Oddington Road Stow-on-the-Wold Glos. GL54 1JJ
Contact: 01451 830887
Email: stowrfc@googlemail.com
Website: www.stowrfc.co.uk
Directions: From Stow take the A436 Chipping Norton Road for c. 1.5 miles. Stow RFC is sign posted to the right up a tarmac drive to the right.
Honorary Secretary: Mr Stuart Cherry, Brown Edge Cottage Salperton Cheltenham Glos. GL54 4EF
Tel: 07703 355278   Email: stowrfc@gmail.com
Fixtures Secretary: Mr Phil Lane, 24 Tinkers Close Moreton-in-Marsh Gloucestershire GL56 0NE
Tel: 07786 650380
Club Colours: Black & White Hoops
League: Berks-Bucks & Oxon Premier (level 8)

Stroud RFC
Ground Address: Fromehall Park Dudbridge Hill Stroud GL5 3HS
Email: Roger.Hughes@Softlogic.co.uk
Directions: M5-Junction 13 and then A419 to roundabout at Sainsburys supermarket. 1st left at roundabout and then 2nd left at next roundabout. Ground then on left opposite Focus DIY store.
Alternatively if coming via A46 ground on left at traffic lights at Golden Cr
Honorary Secretary: Mr Roger Hughes, Berryfields House, Bristol Road, Stonehouse, Gloucestershire GL10 2BQ
Tel: 01453 791345
Email: roger.hughes@softlogic.co.uk
Fixtures Secretary: Mr Peter Cook, 13 Mill Farm Drive Paganhill Stroud Gloucestershire GL5 4JZ
Tel: 07787 582137   Email: peter.cook35@btinternet.com
Club Colours: Blue & white hoops, dark blue shorts
League: Western Counties North (level 7)

Supermarine RFC
Ground Address: Supermarine Road South Marston nr Swindon Wilts. SN3 4SY
Contact: 01793 824828
Email: geebee5@ukonline.co.uk
Website: www.supermarinerugby.co.uk
Directions: From South, East & West take J15 off M4 onto A419(N). Turn onto A361 (marked Highworth / Honda) and follow road past industrial estate. Turn Right at next roundabout. Club is 100 yds on Left.
From North take J11A off M5 onto A417/A419 to Swindon, then as above.
Honorary Secretary: Mr Geoff Bath, 2 Folly Drive Highworth Swindon Wilts. SN6 7JR
Tel: 07768 731 126
Email: geebee5@ukonline.co.uk
Fixtures Secretary: Mr Matthew Smith, Supermarine Rfc Highworth Road South Marston Wilts. SN3 4SY
Tel: 07904 455497
Email: matthew.smith@uk.zurich.com
Club Colours: Dark Blue & Sky Blue Quarters
League: Dorset & Wilts 1 North (level 8)

Sutton Benger RFC
Ground Address: The Village Hall Chestnut Road Sutton Benger Wilts. SN15 4SL
Contact: 01249 720081
Email: info@suttonbengerrfc.com
Directions: From J17 M4 take the B4122 exit and follow the signs to Sutton Benger. Continue through the village past the church on the left, and turn next right into Sutton Lane. Turn first right again into Chestnut Road, and the ground is the first turning on the le
Honorary Secretary: Mr Richard Waddington, 11 Bell Piece Sutton Benger Chippenham Wilts. SN15 4SL
Tel: 07768 474981   Email: rjwadd@aol.com
Fixtures Secretary: As Hon. Sec.
Club Colours: Navy blue and pink
League: Dorset & Wilts 1 North (level 8)

Swindon College Old Boys RFC
Ground Address: Nationwide Pavilion Pipers Way Pipers Way Swindon Wilts. SN1 3HJ
Contact: 07786 937244
Email: lynnwaters66@hotmail.com
Website: www.scobrfc.org
Directions: 1st XV Nationwide pavilion pipers way: M4 J15 Take A419 & turn left at first roundabout signposted Swindon follow dual carriageway at next roundabout take 1st exit onto Marlborough Road signposted Old Town. After one mile turn left into Pipers Way signposted golf complex & Ground is on left after the entranc to the golf club. 2nd XV Croft sports ground Marlborough Lane: As above untill the roundabout at Pipers way at which take the 2nd exit to the Marriott hotel, turn right at the hotel then first left
Honorary Secretary: Mrs Lynn Waters, 5 Little Avenue Swindon Wilts. SN2 1NL
Tel: 01793 522768
Email: lynnwaters66@hotmail.com
Fixtures Secretary: Mr Philip Tyler, 13 Orchard Hill Faringdon Oxfordshire SN7 7EH
Tel: 07725 068625
Email: Phill.Tyler@lloydstsb.co.uk
Club Colours: Black/Red
League: Berks-Bucks & Oxon Premier (level 8)

Swindon RFC
Ground Address: Swindon R.F.C. The New Pavillion Greenbridge Road Swindon Wilts. SN3 3LA
Contact: 01793 521148
Email: chair@swindonrfc.co.uk
Website: www.swindonrfc.co.uk
Directions: From J15 M4 turn North on A419(Cirencester) until junction of A419 with A420(Oxford). Follow signs for Swindon Town Centre. At big roundabout, turn left into Dorcan Way. Right at mini roundabout into Greenbridge Rd. We are 50m down on the left.
Honorary Secretary: Mr Vince Badminton, 37 Merton Avenue Swindon SN2 7PY
Email: vbadminton@batten-allen.co.uk
Fixtures Secretary: Mr Dai Kalynka, 12 Baskerville Road Covingham Swindon SN3 5DD
Tel: 01793 521148
Email: d_kalynka@hotmail.com
Club Colours: Navy Blue & Amber
League: Southern Counties North (level 7)

Tadley RFC
Ground Address:
Red Lane Aldermaston Reading Berks. RG7 4PA
Contact: 044 1189700072
Email: secretary@tadleyrfc.co.uk
Website: www.tadleyrfc.co.uk
Directions: M4 Junction 12 - follow A4 towards Newbury - left onto A340 - Aldermaston Village turn left follow road for approx I mile ground on left M3 Junction 6 - follow signs for A340 to Tadley - through Tadley Follow signs for Burghfield and Reading - Red Lane o

Honorary Secretary: Mr Richard Barnes, Cherry Tree Cottage 14 14, Newtown Tadley Hampshire RG26 4BP
Tel: 07774 623642
Email: richard.j.barnes@hp.com
Fixtures Secretary: Mr Stephen Murphy, 151 Stephens Road Tadley Hampshire RG26 3RT
Tel: 0118 9814952
Email: sjmurphy@onetel.com
Club Colours: Black and amber
League: Southern Counties South (level 7)

Tamar Saracens RFC
Ground Address: Parkway Sports Club Ernesettle Lane Ernesettle Plymouth Devon PL5 2EY
Contact: 01752 363080
Email: andy.jameson@xfab.com
Website: www.tamarsaracensrfc.co.uk
Directions: A38 to St Budeaux, turn off then follow the sign for Ernesettle Lane Club on the right hand side.
Honorary Secretary: Mr Ken Gianasi, 74 Kathlaven Street St Budeaux Plymouth PL5 1PY
Tel: 01752 367466
Email: kengiannasi@yahoo.co.uk
Fixtures Secretary: Mr John Miller, 24 Byard Close Plymouth Devon PL5 2AQ
Tel: 01252 363595
Email: j.miller846@btinternet.com
Club Colours: Green & Black. Change: Red & White
League: Devon 1 South & West (level 9)

Tavistock RFC
Ground Address: Tavistock R.F.C. Sandy Park Trelawny Road Tavistock Devon PL19 0JL
Contact: 01822 618275
Email: jlawson2@toucansurf.com
Website: http://www.tavistockrugbyclub.co.uk
Directions: From centre of Tavistock (the square) go north uphill at mini roundabout between banks then under the viaduct. Take 2nd right (Trelawny road, very sharp right turn through 180 degrees) and drive for approximately half a mile. For coaches -- Please inform TRFC prior to visit to allow policing to club as very narrow turning in Trelawny Road
Honorary Secretary: Mr Jeff Lawson, 4 Mount Ford Tavistock Devon PL19 8EB
Tel: 01822 616588
Email: jlawson2@toucansurf.com
Fixtures Secretary: Mr Bob Boreham, Pinemere St Anns Chapel Gunnislake, Cornwall Devon PL18 9HP
Tel: 01822 833492
Email: bboreham@btconnect.com
Club Colours: Black & Red
League: Western Counties West (level 7)

Teignmouth RFC
Ground Address: Bitton Sports Ground, Bitton Park Road, Teignmouth Devon TQ14 9DQ
Contact: 01626 774714
Email: teignmouthrfc@hotmail.com
Website: www.rfu.com/clubs/portal/teignmouth
Directions: We are situated opposite County Garage. The main route from Cornwall is to get to Shaldon bridge and just carry on as if going to Teignmouth town. The alternative is to go down the Exeter Hill and turn right and follow road as if going to Newton Abbot.
Honorary Secretary: Ms Maureen Powell, 131 Bitton Park Road TEIGNMOUTH TQ14 9DQ
Tel: 01626 774950
Email: maureen.powell1@tesco.net
Fixtures Secretary: Mr Craig Adamson, 131 Bitton Park Road Teignmouth Devon TQ14 9DQ
Tel: 01626 774534
Email: craig.adamson@coastalwaste.com
Club Colours: Red, White and Black Hoops
League: Cornwall-Devon (level 8)

Tetbury RFC
Ground Address: The Recreation Ground Hampton Street Hampton Street Tetbury GL8 8JN
Contact: 0 1666500365
Email: philmorris@tetburyrfc.co.uk
Website: www.tetburyrfc.co.uk
Directions: On the B4014 (Hampton Street) out of Tetbury towards Avening, the Ground is situated on the left between the railings opposite Court Field. Club colours are black and amber
Honorary Secretary: Mr Martin Holloway, 6 Northfield Road Tetbury Gloucestershire GL8 8HB
Tel: 07918 900334
Email: martin.holloway@ukonline.co.uk
Fixtures Secretary: Mr Matt Smith, 42 Longtree Close Tetbury Gloucestershire GL8 8LW   Tel: 07824 829571
Club Colours: Black & Gold
League: Gloucester 2 (level 10)

Tewkesbury RFC
Ground Address: The Moats Lankett Lane Lankett Lane Tewkesbury Gloucestershire GL20 5PG
Contact: 01684 298829
Email: tewkesbury_rfc@yahoo.co.uk
Directions: Junction 9/M5. Go Tewkesbury Town Centre. At roundabout in centre go 1st left to Gloucester. After 100m go 1st left - Gander Lane. Cross stream, ignore 3T limit, Cricket Club on left then carpark. Take entrance to small carpark to right of entrance to Car
Honorary Secretary: Mr Geoff Sallis, 9 Rope Walk Tewkesbury Gloucestershire GL20 5DS
Tel: 01684 297397   Email: GS140955@aol.com
Fixtures Secretary: Mr Kevin Cromwell, 38 East Street Tewkesbury Gloucestershire GL20 5NR
Tel: 07860 230711   Email: kevin.cromwell@talktalk.net
Club Colours: Black and Amber
League: Gloucester Premier (level 8)

Thatcham RFC
Ground Address: Henwick Worthy Sports Fields Henwick Lane Thatcham Berks. RG18 3BN
Directions: Directions to Thatcham's ground: Henwick Worthy Sports Field is situated mid way between Thatcham and Newbury directly adjacent to the A4. Turn off the A4 (Bath Road) into Henwick Lane and after 100m turn left into the ground.
Honorary Secretary: Mrs Chris Rance, 21 Ilkley Way Thatcham Berks. RG19 3LG
Tel: 01635 866739
Email: christinebrance@hotmail.com
Fixtures Secretary: Mr Paul Clutton, Buttercup Place Thatcham Berks. RG18 4BT
Tel: 07766 222327
Club Colours: Navy blue & red quarters, blue shorts
League: Berks-Bucks & Oxon Premier (level 8)

The Tor RFC
Ground Address: Lowerside Park Lowerside Lane Glastonbury BA6 9BH
Contact: 01458 832236
Email: jamie.payne@uwe.ac.uk
Website: www.torrfc.co.uk
Directions: Ajacent to & signposted off A39 at Glastonbury.
Honorary Secretary: Mrs Carol Mountain, 16 Badgers Green Road Street Somerset BA16 0PT
Tel: 01458 446582
Email: carolmountain@talktalk.net
Fixtures Secretary: Mr Keith Elver, 18 Hurmans Close Ashcott Bridgwater TA7 9PT
Tel: 07974 567851
Email: keithelver@btinternet.com
Club Colours: Maroon Shirts, Navy Blue Shorts
League: Somerset Premier (level 8)

Thornbury RFC
Ground Address: Rockhampton Road Newton Thornbury BS35 1LG
Contact: 01454 412096
Email: euan.forsythe@talktalk.net
Website: www.thornburyrfc.com
Directions: From the North, leave the M5 at J14 and follow A38 to wards Bristol. Turn right onto B4061 (Thornbury) and after 3.6 kms, turn right towards Rockhampton. From the South, follow B4061 north from town centre to Upper Morton. Turn left towards Rockhampton. Club is on the edge of Rockhampton village.
Honorary Secretary: Mr Euan Forsythe, 9 Jubilee Drive Thornbury Bristol BS35 2YG
Tel: 07717 832737
Email: euan.forsythe@talktalk.net
Fixtures Secretary: Mr Paul Dack, 10 Rosslyn Way Thornbury Bristol BS35 1SF
Tel: 01454 416068
Email: paul_dack@flygt.com
Club Colours: Amber and Black with a Red Stripe
League: Western Counties North (level 7)

Tiverton RFC
Ground Address: Coronation Field Bolham Road Tiverton Devon EX16 6SG
Contact: 01884 252271
Email: marg-sampson@dsl.pipex.com
Directions: M5 J27 north towards Tiverton, 7 miles roundabout at end of dual carriageway left to Tiverton, Ground is 250meters on the right just before footbridge over road.
Honorary Secretary: Mrs Margaret Sampson, 5 Shillands Tiverton Devon EX16 5AA
Tel: 07811 069059
Email: marg-sampson@dsl.pipex.com
Fixtures Secretary: Mr D Sanders, 11 Chinon Place Tiverton Devon EX16 5QE   Tel: 01884 243395
Club Colours: Light & Dark Blue
League: Western Counties West (level 7)

Topsham RFC
Ground Address: Bonfire Field Topsham Exeter Devon EX3 0LY
Contact: 01392 873 651
Email: keethsmeeth@aol.com
Directions: Approaching Topsham from Exeter it is the last field on the left before the built up area.
Honorary Secretary: Mr Keith Smith, The Old Warehouse 2 Denver Road Topsham Exeter EX3 0BS
Tel: 01392 678943
Fixtures Secretary: Mr Dave Tanner
Tel: 01392 256145   Email: Dskatann1@aol.com
Club Colours: Light & Dark Blue Hoops
League: Devon 1 North & East (level 9)

Torrington RFC
Ground Address: Donnacroft Torrington EX38 7HT
Contact: 07791250545
Email: gina@westgina.wanadoo.co.uk
Directions: Situated on B3227 south Molton Road.
Honorary Secretary: Keely Father, C/0 Club Address Donnacroft Torrington Devon EX38 7HT
Tel: 01805 622746   Email: andy.keely@virgin.net
Club Colours: Green, Black & White Hoops
League: Cornwall-Devon (level 8)

Totnes RFC
Ground Address: The Clubhouse Borough Park Totnes Devon TQ9 5XW
Contact: 01803 867796
Email: darren.berry@taylorwimpey.com
Website: www.totnesrfc.co.uk
Directions: Pitch and Clubhouse on public park adjacent to railway station.
Honorary Secretary: Mich Keen, 31 Higher Polsham Road Paignton Devon TQ3 2SZ
Email: mishkeen08@hotmail.co.uk
Fixtures Secretary: Mr John Massey
Tel: 07768 340 520
Email: John.Massey@carlsberg.co.uk
Club Colours: Royal Blue Shirts & White Shorts
League: Devon 1 North & East (level 9)

Tredworth RFC
Ground Address: The Lannet King Edwards Avenue Gloucester Gloucestershire
Contact: 01452 308939
Email: tredworth.rfc@blueyonder.co.uk
Website: www.thetred.com
Directions: Bristol Road towards City, turn right at lights into Tuffley Avenue, take 5th turning on left into The Oval, straight through to King Edwards Avenue
Honorary Secretary: Mr Neil Edkins, 7 San Remo Stroud Road Gloucester GL1 5LW
Tel: 01452 530525
Email: tredworth.rfc@blueyonder.co.uk
Fixtures Secretary: Mr Steven Wall, 8 Selwyn Road Gloucester GL4 6UQ
Tel: 07883 784885
Email: stevewalll@hotmail.co.uk
Club Colours: Green & Black Hoops
League: Gloucester 2 (level 10)

Truro RFC
Ground Address: Truro R.F.C. St. Clements Hill Truro Cornwall TR1 1NY
Contact: 01872 274750
Email: admin@trurorfc.co.uk
Website: www.trurorfc.co.uk
Directions: A30 leave at sign post for Trispen A39 to Truro at large roundabout, enter left St. Clements Hill next to Police Station. Ground on right at the top of the hill.
Honorary Secretary: Mr Stuart Nicholls, 0 Creekside View Tresillian Truro Cornwall TR2 4BS
Tel: 01872 247765
Email: stuart.nicholls@Openreach.co.uk
Fixtures Secretary: Mr Mandy Champion, Roserrow Tregye Road Carnon Downs Truro TR3 6JQ
Tel: 01872 863538
Club Colours: Blue & Amber
League: Western Counties West (level 7)

University of Bath RFC
Ground Address: University of Bath Students' Union Sports Association University of Bath BA2 7AY
Contact: 07968 718168
Email: ma2bar@bath.ac.uk
Directions: found at www.bath.ac.uk/getting-here/
Non League

University of Bath Spa
Ground Address: Students Union, Newton Park St. Loe Bath BA2 9BN
Contact: 01225 826 007
Honorary Secretary: Mr Roger Wedell, Bath Spa University College Newton St. Loe Bath BA2 9BN
Tel: 01225 826007
Fixtures Secretary: Mr James Coll, Bath Spa University Newton Park Newton St. Loe Bath AVON BA2 9BN
Tel: 07796 187345
Email: bathsparugby@hotmail.com
Non League

LEVEL 7-11 & NON LEAGUE CLUBS

University of Bristol RFC
Ground Address: University Playing Fields Coombe Dingle Coombe Lane Stoke Bishop BS9 2BJ
Contact: 0117 9686628
Email: peter.johnson49@btopenworld.com
Directions: Directions to Coombe Dingle Sports Complex It is easiest to enter Bristol by the M5 then A4018 rather than going down the M32 and trying to navigate through the city. Entering Bristol on the M5: - Exit M5 at Junction 17 and follow the A4018 signed Bristol (West)/Clifton. - Remain on this road and at the end of Westbury Road. - Turn right at the roundabout onto Parry's Lane. - Turn right onto Coombe Lane and the entrance to Coombe Dingle is 1/4 mile down on the right hand side. Entering Bristol from Severn Bridge (M4 West): - Exit M4 at junction 20, onto the M5 south, then follow the above. Entering Bristol on M4 from the East: - From the M4 go past the M32 and continue to the M5 South bound. Then follow the above.
Honorary Secretary: James Cumberland
Tel: 07763 860575   Email: jc7113@bristol.ac.uk
Fixtures Secretary: Andrew Coury
Tel: 07817 284040   Email: ac8336@bris.ac.uk
Club Colours: Maroon, White and Black
Non League

University of Exeter RFC
Ground Address: University of Exeter Sports Park Stocker Road EX4 4QN
Contact: 01392 263 595
Email: n.e.beasant@ex.ac.uk
Directions: Directions to Duckes Meadow Playing Fields (All Rugby matches) MAP 1 - Exit the M5 at Junction 30 and take the A379 to the Countess Wear roundabout, Take the third exit onto the Topsham Road and continue along this road, Turn left into Salmonpool Lane aft
Honorary Secretary: Ms Charlotte Edwards, University of Exeter Sports Hall Stocker Road Exeter EX4 4QN
Tel: 01392 263505
Email: c.c.edwards@ex.ac.uk
Fixtures Secretary: Fixtures Secretary EURFC, University of Exeter Sports Hall Stocker Road Exeter Devon EX4 4QN
Tel: 01392 263599
Club Colours: Green White & Black, Black
Non League

University of Plymouth RFC
Ground Address: SU Drake CIrcus Plymouth PL4 8AA
Contact: 01752 232 283
Honorary Secretary: Honorary Secretary, Athletic Union University of Plymouth RFC Drake Circus Plymouth Devon PL4 8AA
Fixtures Secretary: Ms Julie Kinchin, Athletic Union University of Plymouth RFC Drake Circus Plymouth Devon PL4 8AA
Tel: 01752 238520
Email: vpsports@upsu.com
Non League

University of Portsmouth RFC
Ground Address: University of Portsmouth SU Student Centre Cambridge Road Portsmouth PO1 2EF
Contact: 023 92843671
Honorary Secretary: Mr Nick Parker, 27 Napier Road Southsea Hampshire PO5 2RA
Tel: 07984 343518
Email: Nicholas.parker@port.ac.uk
Fixtures Secretary: Wayne Gardiner, Sport & Societies Co-ordinator UPSU The Student Centre Cambridge Road Portsmouth Hampshire PO1 2EF
Tel: 02392 843671
Email: wayne.gardiner@port.ac.uk
Club Colours: Purple, Black & White
Non League

University of Reading RFC
Ground Address: RUSU Clubs Office PO Box 230, Whiteknights Reading Berks. RG6 6AZ
Contact: 0118 986 5111
Non League

University of the West of England RFC
Ground Address: Sports Administrator, UWESU Activities Centre Frenchay Campus, Coldharbour Lane Frenchay, Bristol BS16 1QY
Contact: 0117 344 2719
Honorary Secretary: Honorary Secretary, Athletic Union University of The West of England RFC Frenchay Campus Coldharbour Lane Bristol BS16 1QY
Fixtures Secretary: James Polson, UWESU Sports Centre Frenchay Campus Coldharbour Lane Bristol Avon BS16 1QY
Tel: 07779 221771
Non League

Veor RFC
Ground Address: Wheal Gerry Cliff View Road Camborne Cornwall
Contact: 01209 710974
Email: j-c@tesco.net
Directions: Turn off A30 signed Cambourne & Pool, right at traffic lights down hill, right again before pedestrian crossing, 0.5 mile right again after TA centre, Ground is 100yds on the right.
Honorary Secretary: Mrs Karen Gilbert, 86 Sunnyside Parc Illogan Redruth Cornwall TR15 3LY
Tel: 01209 211676
Fixtures Secretary: Mr Mike Hollyoake, 38 Park Road Camborne Cornwall TR14 8Q
Tel: 01209 616300
Email: thehollyoakes38@talktalk.net
Club Colours: Yellow and Black
League: Cornwall League (level 9)

Wadebridge Camels RFC
Ground Address: Boscarne Trenant Vale Wadebridge Cornwall PL27 6AJ
Contact: 07754 586779
Email: mattbailey24@hotmail.co.uk
Website: www.wadebridgecamelsrfc.co.uk
Directions: Opposite Egloshayle Church
Honorary Secretary: Mr Matt Bailey, Boscarne Trenant Vale Wadebridge Cornwall PL27 6AJ
Tel: 07754 586779
Email: mattbailey24@hotmail.co.uk
Fixtures Secretary: Mr Matt Bailey, Boscarne Trenant Vale Wadebridge Cornwall PL27 6AJ
Tel: 07754 586779
Email: mattbailey24@hotmail.co.uk
Club Colours: Chocolate & Gold
League: Western Counties West (level 7)

Wadham RFC
Ground Address: c/o Wadham College Parks Road Oxford OX1 3PN
Contact: 07763015569
Email: matthew.sumner@wadh.ox.ac.uk
Non League

Warminster RFC
Ground Address: Folly Lane Sports Ground Folly Lane Warminster Wilts. BA12 7RG
Contact: 01985 301788
Email: eve.jenkins@blueyonder.co.uk
Directions: From A350 roundabout on by pass head onto Warminster. Past "Bell & Crown" on left, next left into Fore Street. At next roundabout 2nd left onto Thornhill Road, then left onto Folly Lane. Ground 200yrds on right.
Honorary Secretary: Mrs Eve Jenkins, 15 Were Close Warminster Wilts. BA12 8TB
Tel: 01985 212261
Email: eve.jenkins@blueyonder.co.uk
Fixtures Secretary: Mr Steve Evans, 3 The Maltings Market Place Warminster Wilts. BA12 9AW
Tel: 01985 212750
Club Colours: Royal Blue & Amber Hoops
League: Dorset & Wilts 1 South (level 8)

Wellington RFC
Ground Address: The Athletic Ground Corams Lane Wellington Somerset TA21 8LL
Contact: 01823 663758
Email: keeble_ted@yahoo.co.uk
Website: www.wellingtonrugby.co.uk
Directions: Leave M5 at junction 26 or from A38 from Taunton at the Chelston Roundabout, carry on into Wellington and turn right at the central traffic lights into North St, turn left at the Sportsman Pub. Enter via the Sports Centre Car Park.
Honorary Secretary: Mr Nick Robins, 37 Bircham Road Taunton Somerset TA2 8EX
Tel: 01823 323350
Email: nicholas.r@waitrose.com
Fixtures Secretary: Mr Ashley Colman, 101 Galmington Road Taunton Somerset TA1 5NP
Tel: 07775544949
Email: Ashley.Colman1@barclays.com
Club Colours: Red and Black staggered hoops
League: Cornwall-Devon (level 8)

Wells RFC
Ground Address: Charter Way Wells Somerset BA5 2FB
Contact: 01749 672823
Email: contact@wellsrugbyclub.co.uk
Website: www.wellsrugbyrfc.co.uk
Directions: Off the Portway A371 or follow signs to the Leisure Centre (which is next door).
Hon. Secretary: Mrs Dawn Hickman, Sunset Mount Pleasant Pilton Shepton Mallet Somerset BA4 4BL
Tel: 01749 890746
Email: contact@wellsrugbyclub.co.uk
Fixtures Secretary: Mrs Dawn Hickman, Sunset Mount Pleasant Pilton Shepton Mallet Somerset BA4 4BL
Tel: 01749 890746
Email: contact@wellsrugbyclub.co.uk
Club Colours: black and white hoops
League: Somerset Premier (level 8)

Wessex RFC
Ground Address: c/o Honorary Secretary 75 Wardrew Road St. Thomas Exeter Devon EX4 1HA
Contact: 01392 427144
Email: mail@wessexrfc.co.uk
Website: www.wessexrfc.co.uk
Directions: To Flowerpot Field, Exwick Playing Fields, Exeter. From J31 M5 to A30 follow signs to Exeter then Exwick, along Buddle Lane turn right into Oakhampton Road, turn left onto Western Road.
Honorary Secretary: Mr Simon Farmer, 75 Wardrew Road St. Thomas Exeter Devon EX4 1HA
Tel: 01392 427144
Email: hon.secretary@wessexrfc.co.uk
Fixtures Secretary: Mr Paul Andrews, 21 Salisbury Road Exeter EX4 6LU   Tel: 07739 893904
Email: fixtures.secretary@wessexrfc.co.uk
Club Colours: Bottle green jersey amber collars
League: Devon 1 North & East (level 9)

Westbury RFC
Ground Address: Leighton Sport Ground Wellhead Lane Wellhead Lane Westbury Wilts. BA13 3PW
Contact: 01225 766647
Email: jrugbymaster@aol.com
Website: www.westburyrfc.org.uk
Directions: Warminster Road (A350) opposite Cedar Hotel turn into Wellhead Lane, Ground is 300 meters on the left.
Honorary Secretary: Mr Allex Turner, 115 Eden Vale Road Westbury Wilts. BA13 3QG
Tel: 07952 230799
Email: allexturner@yahoo.com
Fixtures Secretary: Mr Gareth Vaughan
Tel: 07528 643192
Club Colours: Emerald & Black
League: Dorset & Wilts 1 South (level 8)

Westbury-on-Severn RFC
Ground Address: The Village Hall Westbury on Severn GL14 1RD
Contact: 07931 738945
Email: gladref@yahoo.co.uk
Directions: Parish Gounds Westbury-on-Severn A48 from Gloucester to Chepstow. Ground on left hand side before entering Westbury 0n Severn.
Honorary Secretary: Miss Samantha Boulton, Jade Cottage Bullo Pill Newnham Gloucestershire GL14 1DZ
Tel: 07931 738945   Email: gladref@yahoo.co.uk
Fixtures Secretary: Mr Mark Cinderey, 5 Ellerslie Ryefield Rd Ross on Wye Herefordshire HR9 5LS
Tel: 01989 565583
Email: mcinderey@tiscali.co.uk
Club Colours: Royal Blue & White Hoops
League: Gloucester 2 (level 10)

Weymouth RFC
Ground Address: Weymouth RFC Ltd Monmouth Avenue Weymouth Dorset DT3 5HZ
Contact: 01305 778889
Email: enquiries@weymouthrfc.org.uk
Website: www.weymouthrfc.org.uk
Directions: Traveling from Dorchester, straight over first roundabout (Manor Road) pass entrance to Morrison's Supermarket on left, take third turning left (sign Weymouth RFC at pavement level) into Monmouth Avenue. Traveling from Wool/Wareham to first roundabout (Chalbury Corner), turn right, continue to traffic lights. Turn left continue to Manor Road roundabout above.
Honorary Secretary: Mr Christopher Davis, 3 Hawthorn Close Weymouth DT4 9UG
Tel: 07736 599021   Email: chris.davis35@virgin.net
Fixtures Secretary: Mr Gary Heald, Flat 12 Belle Vue Court Belle Vue Road Weymouth Dorset DT4 8SA
Tel: 07815 877529
Email: gheald@btinternet.com
Club Colours: Light blue with Dark Blue circles
League: Dorset & Wilts 1 South (level 8)

Wheatley RUFC
Ground Address: Holton Playing Fields Holton Oxford OX33 1QL
Contact: 01865 873476
Website: www.wheatleyrfc.com
Directions: GROUND: Playing Fields, Holton, Wheatley, Oxford OX33 1QL Tel: (01865) 873476 From Oxford , leave the A40 at the "Wheatley" signs. Turn left at the T-junction and the ground will be found on the left about 500 yards from the turn. From London, take the turning from the A40 or A418 to Wheatley and follow the signs to Oxford. Turn right at the mini-roundabout, pass over the A40 and the ground will be found about 800 yards to the left.
Honorary Secretary: Mr Ewan Mckenzie, Dionach Greenford House London Rd Wheatley Oxford OX33 1JH
Tel: 01865 877830
Fixtures Secretary: Mr Peter Ramsdale, 41 Windmill Lane Wheatley Oxford OX33 1TA   Tel: 07768 300314
Club Colours: Purple, Black and White
League: Berks-Bucks & Oxon 1 N (level 9)

Wheatsheaf Cabin Crew RFC
Ground Address: Salisbury Agricultural Centre Salisbury Road, Netherhampton Salisbury Road, Netherhampton Salisbury Wilts. SP2 8RH
Contact: 01722 782446
Email: goodhopecottage@hotmail.co.uk
Website: www.wheatsheafrugby.co.uk
Directions: SP2 8RH for ground SP4 6NQ for our Pub in Lower Woodford
Honorary Secretary: Mr Daniel Randall, Good Hope Cottage Lower Woodford Salisbury Wilts. SP4 6NQ
Tel: 01722 782446
Email: goodhopecottage@hotmail.co.uk
Fixtures Secretary: Mr Simon Gollop, 0 Ramleaze Drive Salisbury Wilts. SP2 9PA
Tel: 01722 421755   Email: gollops@hotmail.com
Club Colours: Green shirts, Black shorts
League: Dorset & Wilts 2 South (level 9)

Whitehall RFC
Ground Address: Speedwell Recreation Ground Foundry Lane, Speedwell Bristol BS5 7UE
Contact: 0117 9659736
Email: Iain.pring@speedyhire.com
Website: www.whitehallrfc.org
Directions: Off B4465 Whitehall Road at Crofts End, turn right into Deep Pit Road, take 2nd left. From M32 J2 follow sign post up Muller Road, left at roundabout.
Honorary Secretary: Ms Stacey Watkins, 176 Kingsway St George Bristol BS5 8NX
Tel: 07870435876
Email: staceywatkins@blueyonder.co.uk
Fixtures Secretary: Mr Wayne Millard, 13 Abbey Road Wellingborough Northants. NN8 2JW
Tel: 0117 9400778   Email: wpmillard@blueyonder.co.uk
Club Colours: Myrtle Green & Gold
League: Gloucester Premier (level 8)

Widden Old Boys RFC
Ground Address: Memorial Ground Tuffley Avenue
Tuffley Avenue Gloucester Gloucestershire GL1 5NS
Contact: 01452 304392
Email: info@widdenrugby.co.uk
Website: www.widdenrugby.co.uk
Directions: See official website
Honorary Secretary: Mrs Glenda Mcwalter, 52 The
Causeway Quedgeley Gloucester GL2 4LD
Tel: 07894 866372
Email: glendamcwalter@widdenrugby.co.uk
Fixtures Secretary: Mr Mike Charnock, North Point, 12
Severn Road Gloucester Docks Gloucester
Gloucestershire GL1 2LE
Tel: 07843 618639
Email: mikecharnock@mtconline.co.uk
Club Colours: Bottle Green Shirts
League: Western Counties North (level 7)

Wiltshire Police RFC
Ground Address: Police Headquarters London Road
Devizes Wilts. SN10 2DN
Contact: 07968 514355
Email: dave.williams@wiltshire.pnn.police.uk
Honorary Secretary: Mr Dave Williams, Police H/Q
London Road Devizes Wilts. SN10 2DN
Tel: 07968 514355
Email: Dave.Willams@wiltshire.pnn.police.uk
Fixtures Secretary: Neil Le-Maire, Police Headquarters
London Road Devizes Wilts. SN10 2DN
Tel: 07877720775
Email: Neil.Le-Maire@wiltshire.pnn.police.uk
Club Colours: Royal blue/Navy blue hoops
Non League

Wimborne RFC
Ground Address: Leigh Park Gordon Road Gordon Road
Wimborne Dorset BH21 2AP
Contact: 01202 882602
Email: jud@wimbornerugbyclub.co.uk
Website: www.wimbornerugbyclub.co.uk
Directions: From A31 take B3073(approx 2 miles east of
Wimborne)follow road towards town centre for about 1.5
miles and turn left in to Gordon Road. Wimborne RFC
Leigh Park 250 yards ahead.
Honorary Secretary: Mr Pete Thompson, 119 Lower
Blandford Road Broadstone Dorset BH18 8NT
Tel: 01305 202784
Email: peter.thompson@wmt.co.uk
Fixtures Secretary: Mr Dennis Fry, 4 Hillside Gardens
Corfe Mullen Wimborne Dorset BH21 3UL
Tel: 01202 695116
Email: family.fry@talktalk.net
Club Colours: All Black
League: Southern Counties South (level 7)

Wincanton RFC
Ground Address: Wincanton Sports Ground Moor lane
Wincanton Somerset BA9 9EJ
Contact: 07976 390291
Email: oldiescottage@hotmail.co.uk
Directions: Approaching Wincanton from the A303, past
Safeway and take the first right hand turning AFTER the
Fire Station into Moor Lane. Continue for approx. half a
mile down Moor Lane under the bridge and the ground is
on the left hand side.
Honorary Secretary: Mr Luke Thorne, 62 Sweetmans
Road Shaftesbury Dorset SP7 8EH
Tel: 07796 990141
Email: luket_horne@yahoo.com
Club Colours: Black & Amber or for a change Yellow
League: Dorset & Wilts 3 South (level 10)

Windsor RFC
Ground Address: Home Park Datchet Road Windsor
Berks. SL4 6HX
Contact: 01753 860807
Email: info@windsorrugby.info
Website: www.windsorrugby.info
Directions: M4 Jct 6 towards Windsor. Take 1st exit off
dual carriage way then 1st left to Town Centre. Straight
on over 3 sets of Traffic Lights. At roundabt take 1st exit
then under railway bridge, road then bends right, right
then left. Over Traffic Lights past Royal Oak Pub on
right. At mini roundabout turn left into Romney Lock
Road through car park. Windsor RFC is the second
building on the right.
Honorary Secretary: Mr Graham Sandilands, 1
Harcourt Road Windsor Berks. SL4 5NA
Tel: 07740 945537
Email: graham.sandilands@tiscali.co.uk
Fixtures Secretary: Mr John Laing, 41 Clewer Park
Windsor Berks. SL4 5HE
Tel: 01753 862169   Email: w.laing234@btinternet.com
Club Colours: Black, Maroon, Bottle & Gold Quarters
League: Southern Counties North (level 7)

Winscombe RFC
Ground Address: Eastfield The Lynch Winscombe
Somerset BS25 1AR
Contact: 01934 842002
Email: paul.lund4@btinternet.com
Website: www.winscombe-rugby.co.uk
Directions: Turn off A38 into Winscombe, turn left into
The Lynch. The Recreation Ground is on the 1st right
hand bend.
Honorary Secretary: Mr Paul Lund, 0 The Lynch
Winscombe AVON BS25 1AR
Tel: 01934 842002
Email: paul.lund4@btinternet.com
Fixtures Secretary: Mr Ted Sands, 7 Belmont Road
Winscombe AVON BS25 1LE
Tel: 07807 309837   Email: tedsands7@aol.com
Club Colours: Black with White Hoops
League: Somerset Premier (level 8)

Winslow RFC
Ground Address: The Nags Head 39, Sheep Street Winslow Bucks. MK18 3HL
Contact: 01296 713036
Email: winslowrfc.sec@btconnect.com
Website: www.winslowrufc.co.uk
Directions: A413 through Winslow, 0.5 mile towards Buckingham from town centre Turn left into Avenue Road, 1st right into Park Road and through gates into Winslow Centre. Changing rooms are at rear near the Gym, away & referee changing is upstairs. Club House is at the Nags Head - Return to the A413 main road through Winslow, turning right towards Aylesbury, pub is approx 3/4 mile on left
Honorary Secretary: Mr James Walker, 15 McLernon Way Winslow Buckingham MK18 3FE
Tel: 01296 713036
Email: winslowrfc.sec@btconnect.com
Fixtures Secretary: Mr Jim Williams
Club Colours: Blue, Gold, Black and White Squares
League: Berks-Bucks & Oxon 2 N (level 10)

Withycombe RFC
Ground Address: Raleigh Park 36, Hulham Road Exmouth Devon EX8 3HS
Contact: 01395 266762
Website: www.withycomberugby.co.uk
Directions: M5 South J30, take A376 to Exmouth, at Box Junction before traffic lights turn left into Hulham Road, Ground is 200 yards on the right.
Honorary Secretary: Mr David Josey, 2 Larch Close Exmouth EX8 5NQ
Tel: 01395 275038
Email: dave@josey.fsnet.co.uk
Fixtures Secretary: Mr John Passmore, Christer House Ebford Lane Edford Exeter EX3 0QX
Tel: 01392 873094
Club Colours: Green & Black
League: Western Counties West (level 7)

Witney RFC
Ground Address: Witney Road Hailey Witney OX29 9UH
Contact: 0780 252 0 252
Email: wrfc@fsmail.net
Directions: Leave Witney centre by Bridge Street, towards Oxford & Bicester, left at mini roundabout, keep along main road passsing garage on right, Ground on left after about 1 mile.
Honorary Secretary: Mr Paul Copperwheat, East End Northleigh Witney Oxford OX29 6PZ
Fixtures Secretary: Mr Pete Holiday, 88 Blakin Avenue Witney OX8 6SX
Tel: 01993 201301
Email: wrfc@fsmail.net
Club Colours: Black Hoops on Sky Blue
League: Southern Counties North (level 7)

Wiveliscombe
Ground Address: West Road Taunton Somerset TA4 2TB
Directions: Take B3227 from Taunton to Barnstable, ground is on left towards end of town.
Honorary Secretary: Mr Authur Moore, West Road Wiveliscombe Taunton Somerset TA4 2TB
Tel: 01823 442642
Email: wendy@hookings.fslife.co.uk
Fixtures Secretary: Mr Robert Bulfield, 11 The Malthouse Hauling Way Wiveliscombe Taunton Somerset TA4 2PP
Tel: 01984 624509
League: Somerset 1 (level 9)

Worcester College RFC
Ground Address: c/o Worcester College Walton Street Oxford OX1 2HB
Contact: 01865-278300
Email: david.bradshaw@worc.ox.ac.uk
Honorary Secretary: Doctor David Bradshaw, Worcester College Oxford OX1 2HB
Tel: 01865 27388
Email: david.bradshaw@worc.ox.ac.uk
Non League

Wotton RFC
Ground Address: KLB School Wotton Road Kingswood Wotton Under Edge Gloucestershire GL12 8RB
Contact: 07793 267069
Email: jason.cropper@tiscali.co.uk
Website: www.wottonrugby.com
Directions: Take B4058 towards M5 out of Wotton, Ground is on the left at the foot of the hill.Parking at KLB School GL12 8RB
Honorary Secretary: Mr Jason Cropper, Woodview Locombe Place Wotton Under Edge Glos. GL12 7HZ
Tel: 07793 267069
Email: jason.cropper@tiscali.co.uk
Fixtures Secretary: Ed Holcombe, Blanchworth House Blanchworth Stinchcombe Dursley Glos. GL11 6BB
Tel: 07786 541453
Club Colours: Black & Amber Hoops
League: Gloucester 3 (level 11)

Wyvern
Ground Address: Wyvern Club Mountfields Road Taunton TA1 3BJ
Contact: 01823 284 591
Email: secretary@wyvernrfc.co.uk
Website: www.wyvernrfc.co.uk
Honorary Secretary: Mr Dean Tindal, 4 Bartlett Close Taunton Somerset TA1 4NZ
Tel: 01823 254137   Email: t1nny@lineone.net
Fixtures Secretary: Mr Martin Howe, 11 Bluebell Close Taunton Somerset TA1 3XQ
Tel: 0870 0637694   Email: martin@thehowes.co.uk
Club Colours: Scarlet
League: Somerset 3 South (level 11)

PLAYERS
PREMIERSHIP

This section covers all League matches, National Cup matches and European matches played by players who qualify. To qualify a player will have appeared in 10 or more games last season for clubs playing in the Premiership this coming season 2009-10, plus Bristol who were relegated.

						Comp	Apps	Pts	T	P	C	DG
Nick	**Abendanon**	27.08.86	England	178cm	83 kg							
			Bath	Right Wing		NL	45(8)	35	7	-	-	-
						NC	3(1)	-	-	-	-	-
						ES	12(4)	45	9	-	-	-
						HC	7	5	1	-	-	-
Luke	**Abraham**	26.09.83	England	188cm	104 kg							
			Sale	Openside Flanker		NL	9 (3)	-	-	-	-	-
						HC	4	-	-	-	-	-
			Leicester Tigers	Openside Flanker		NL	19(25)	10	2	-	-	-
						NC	3(2)	5	1	-	-	-
						HC	2(9)	-	-	-	-	-
			Nuneaton	Openside Flanker								
Anthony	**Allen**	01.09.86	England	180cm	92 kg							
			Gloucester	Centre		NL	54(5)	65	13	-	-	-
						NC	5(1)	-	-	-	-	-
						ES	5(2)	10	2	-	-	-
						HC	12(2)	30	6	-	-	-
Delon	**Armitage**	15.12.83	England									
			London Irish	Left Wing		NL	78(6)	195	23	10	20	-
						NC	6(0)	3	-	-	1	-
						ES	19(0)	84	13	2	5	-
						HC	10(2)	42	8	1	-	-
Steffon	**Armitage**	20.09.85	England									
			London Irish	Openside Flanker		NL	46(12)	50	10	-	-	-
						NC	6(1)	5	1	-	-	-
						HC	5(6)	5	1	-	-	-
						ES	5 (1)	10	2	-	-	-
			Saracens	Openside Flanker		NL	2(5)	15	3	-	-	-
			Hertford	Openside Flanker		NL	3(3)	5	1	-	-	-
John	**Arr**	29.11.88	England									
			Worcester	Scrum Half		NL	1(10)	-	-	-	-	-
						NC	0(2)	-	-	-	-	-
						ES	0(7)	-	-	-	-	-
Luke	**Arscott**	07.07.84	England	185cm	100 kg							
			Bristol	Full Back		NL	36(1)	18	3	-	1	-
						NC	3(1)	-	-	-	-	-
						ES	3(2)	10	2	-	-	-
						HC	6(0)	10	2	-	-	-
			Exeter	Right Wing		NL	0(5)	5	1	-	-	-
						NC	0(1)	-	-	-	-	-
			Plymouth Albion	Right Wing		NL	36(13)	57	11	1	-	-
						NC	6(0)	20	4	-	-	-
Tom	**Arscott**	25.07.87	England									
			Bristol	Left Wing		NL	28(1)	49	8	3	-	1
						NC	3(0)	-	-	-	-	-
						HC	3(0)	5	1	-	-	-
						ES	5 (1)	-	-	-	-	-
			Plymouth Albion	Left Wing		NL	19(5)	45	9	-	-	-
						NC	1(1)	-	-	-	-	-

771

PLAYERS - PREMIERSHIP

						Comp	Apps	Pts	T	P	C	DG
Chris	Ashton	29.03.87	England Northampton	Winger		NL	29(5)	202	40	1	-	-
						NC	3	10	2	-	-	-
						ES	6	35	7	-	-	-
Marcos	Ayerza	12.01.83	Argentina Leicester Tigers	Hooker		NL	35(8)	20	4	-	-	-
						NC	5(2)	5	1	-	-	-
						HC	17(2)	-	-	-	-	-
Olivier	Azam	21.10.74	France Gloucester	185cm Hooker	115 kg	NL	96(39)	100	20	-	-	-
						NC	7(3)	5	1	-	-	-
						ES	3(2)	5	1	-	-	-
						HC	25(6)	15	3	-	-	-
			ASM Clermont Auvergne	Hooker		ES	4(1)	10	2	-	-	-
						HC	4(2)	5	1	-	-	-
James	Bailey	05.08.83	England London Irish	180cm Left Wing	84 kg	NL	1(1)	-	-	-	-	-
						NC	2	5	1	-	-	-
						ES	2(1)	5	1	-	-	-
			Bristol	Left Wing		NL	18(1)	45	9	-	-	-
						NC	4(0)	25	5	-	-	-
			Gloucester	Left Wing		NL	38(18)	55	11	-	-	-
						NC	3(3)	5	1	-	-	-
						ES	0(3)	-	-	-	-	-
						HC	5(3)	5	1	-	-	-
Adam	Balding	07.12.79	England Newcastle	191cm No. 8	104 kg	NL	17	5	1	-	-	-
						NC	1	-	-	-	-	-
						ES	6	-	-	-	-	-
			Gloucester	No. 8		NL	29(13)	5	1	-	-	-
						NC	6(0)	5	1	-	-	-
						ES	2(0)	5	1	-	-	-
						HC	5(6)	5	1	-	-	-
		Loan	Leeds	No. 8		NL	7(4)	-	-	-	-	-
			Leicester Tigers	No. 8		NL	31(38)	10	2	-	-	-
						NC	6(6)	15	3	-	-	-
						HC	6(11)	-	-	-	-	-
			Moseley	No. 8		NL	2(0)	-	-	-	-	-
Iain	Balshaw	18.04.79	England Gloucester	186cm Full Back	83 kg	NL	35(2)	65	13	-	-	-
						NC	5(0)	15	3	-	-	-
						HC	15(1)	30	6	-	-	-
			Leeds	Right Wing		NL	14(3)	15	2	1	-	1
						NC	3(0)	-	-	-	-	-
						ES	4(1)	10	2	-	-	-
			Bath	Right Wing		NL	80(9)	191	36	1	-	3
						NC	6(2)	10	2	-	-	-
						ES	10(0)	27	5	1	-	-
						HC	18(1)	22	4	1	-	-
Matt	Banahan	30.12.86	England Bath	201cm Right Wing	110 kg	NL	33(2)	70	14	-	-	-
						NC	1(1)	-	-	-	-	-
						ES	5(2)	30	6	-	-	-
						HC	7	10	2	-	-	-
Olly	Barkley	28.11.81	England Gloucester	178cm Outside Half	83 kg	NL	13(6)	127	1	7	36	-
						NC	2(2)	13	-	2	3	-
						HC	5(1)	50	-	10	10	-
			Bath	Outside Half		NL	111(11)	1108	15	122	261	2
						NC	9(1)	85	-	11	21	-
						ES	28(3)	397	14	87	51	-
						HC	19(2)	167	-	25	39	-

PLAYERS - PREMIERSHIP

							Comp	Apps	Pts	T	P	C	DG
David	Barnes	12.07.76	England	183cm	112 kg								
			Bath	Prop			NL	120(34)	5	1	-	-	-
							NC	7(4)	5	1	-	-	-
							ES	23(4)	-	-	-	-	-
							HC	18(7)	10	2	-	-	-
			Harlequins	Prop			NL	22(9)	5	1	-	-	-
							NC	4(0)	-	-	-	-	-
							HC	3(0)	-	-	-	-	-
			Newcastle	Prop			NL	0(1)	-	-	-	-	-
							NC	1(0)	-	-	-	-	-
							ES	0(1)	-	-	-	-	-
			West Hartlepool	Prop			NL	9(1)	5	1	-	-	-
Ed	Barnes	14.01.81	England										
			Bristol	Outside Half			NL	27(5)	151	-	26	33	-
							NC	0(2)	-	-	-	-	-
							ES	4	38	-	7	8	-
			Plymouth Albion	Outside Half			NL	67(10)	118	7	25	8	3
							NC	6(3)	20	1	6	1	-
			Bath	Outside Half			NL	0(1)	-	-	-	-	-
			Bedford	Outside Half			NL	33(12)	174	4	35	23	5
Dan	Barrell	03.02.86	England										
			Saracens	No. 8			NL	5(14)	5	1	-	-	-
							NC	3(1)	-	-	-	-	-
							EC	1(3)	5	1	-	-	-
			Esher	No. 8			NL	13(5)	15	3	-	-	-
							NC	1(0)	-	-	-	-	-
			Hertford	No. 8			NL	3(2)	5	1	-	-	-
De Wet	Barry	24.06.78	South Africa	187cm	90 kg								
			Harlequins	Centre			NL	13(14)	5	1	-	-	-
							NC	4(2)	10	2	-	-	-
							HC	4(1)	5	1	-	-	-
			Western Stormers	Centre									
Mike	Baxter	16.12.84	England	178cm	94 kg								
			Bath	Scrum Half			NL	0(12)	-	-	-	-	-
							NC	1(3)	-	-	-	-	-
							ES	1(1)	-	-	-	-	-
							HC	1(4)	-	-	-	-	-
			Pertemps Bees	Scrum Half			NL	6(17)	-	-	-	-	-
							NC	0(3)	-	-	-	-	-
			Gloucester	Scrum Half									
			Newbury	Scrum Half			NL	4(6)	-	-	-	-	-
							NC	1(0)	-	-	-	-	-
Andy	Beattie	06.09.78	England	196cm	108 kg								
			Bath	Blindside Flanker			NL	117(15)	40	8	-	-	-
							NC	7(3)	-	-	-	-	-
							ES	25(3)	35	7	-	-	-
							HC	18(1)	20	4	-	-	-
			Exeter	No. 8			NL	38(11)	80	16	-	-	-
							NC	2(1)	-	-	-	-	-
Joe	Bedford	16.07.84	England										
			Leeds	Scrum Half			NL	39(10)	15	3	-	-	-
							NC	3(2)	-	-	-	-	-
							ES	4(2)	10	2	-	-	-
			Rotherham	Scrum Half			NL	45(9)	75	15	-	-	-
							NC	1(1)	-	-	-	-	-
			Bracknell	Scrum Half			NL	6(1)	-	-	-	-	-
			Saracens	Scrum Half			NL	0(1)	-	-	-	-	-

PLAYERS - PREMIERSHIP

							Comp	Apps	Pts	T	P	C	DG
Duncan	Bell	01.10.74	England	188cm	125 kg								
			Bath	Prop			NL	83(17)	20	4	-	-	-
							NC	10(0)	5	1	-	-	-
							ES	5(2)	-	-	-	-	-
							HC	12(6)	5	1	-	-	-
			Fylde	Prop			NL	1(0)	-	-	-	-	-
			Pontypridd	Prop			NL	10(0)	5	1	-	-	-
							ES	15(0)	-	-	-	-	-
			Sale Sharks	Prop			NL	54(22)	20	4	-	-	-
							NC	8(3)	5	1	-	-	-
							ES	6(5)	-	-	-	-	-
Chris	Bell	07.07.83	England	188cm	95 kg								
			Sale Sharks	Centre			NL	38(8)	55	11	-	-	-
							NC	5(0)	25	5	-	-	-
							ES	4(0)	10	2	-	-	-
							HC	4(3)	13	2	-	-	1
			Harlequins	Centre			NL	22(12)	15	3	-	-	-
							NC	3(2)	-	-	-	-	-
							ES	6(2)	15	3	-	-	-
							HC	2(0)	5	1	-	-	-
			Leeds	Centre			NL	29(4)	40	8	-	-	-
							NC	3(0)	10	2	-	-	-
							ES	7(0)	20	4	-	-	-
							HC	1(2)	-	-	-	-	-
			Plymouth Albion	Centre			NL	6(0)	5	1	-	-	-
Miles	Benjamin	11.05.88	England										
			Worcester	Right Wing			NL	26(6)	50	10	-	-	-
							NC	2(1)	15	3	-	-	-
							ES	9(2)	30	6	-	-	-
Shaun	Berne	08.01.79	Australia	173cm	84 kg								
			Bath	Outside Half			NL	50(33)	197	19	18	18	4
							NC	5(2)	9	-	3	1	-
							ES	10(6)	54	8	7	-	-
							HC	8(4)	30	6	-	-	-
			New South Wales	Outside Half									
Tom	Biggs	22.08.84	England										
			Leeds	Left Wing			NL	73(10)	195	39	-	-	-
							NC	6(0)	35	7	-	-	-
							ES	11(1)	20	4	-	-	-
							HC	4(1)	5	1	-	-	-
Richard	Birkett	01.10.79	England	193cm	104 kg								
			London Wasps	No. 8			NL	112(25)	20	4	-	-	-
							NC	10(4)	-	-	-	-	-
							ES	9(0)	-	-	-	-	-
							HC	18(8)	-	-	-	-	-
Lee	Blackett	21.11.82	England										
			Leeds	Centre			NL	28(6)	60	12	-	-	-
							NC	6(1)	-	-	-	-	-
							ES	4(1)	10	2	-	-	-
			Rotherham	Centre			NL	42(8)	60	11	1	-	1
							NC	3(1)	-	-	-	-	-
Dave	Blaney	03.03.79	Ireland										
			Bristol	Hooker			NL	3(13)	-	-	-	-	-
							NC	6(3)	15	3	-	-	-
							ES	6(4)	-	-	-	-	-
							HC	0(4)	5	1	-	-	-
			Leinster	Hooker			NC	0(1)	-	-	-	-	-
							HC	1(9)	-	-	-	-	-

PLAYERS - PREMIERSHIP

						Comp	Apps	Pts	T	P	C	DG
Richard	Blaze	19.04.85	England	201cm	115 kg							
			Leicester Tigers	Lock		NL	4(8)	-	-	-	-	-
						NC	3(0)	-	-	-	-	-
						EC	0(2)	-	-	-	-	-
			Worcester	Lock		NL	6(13)	-	-	-	-	-
						NC	2(0)	-	-	-	-	-
						ES	4(2)	-	-	-	-	-
Steve	Borthwick	12.10.79	England	199cm	101 kg							
			Saracens	Lock		NL	11	5	1	-	-	-
						NC	1	-	-	-	-	-
						ES	8	-	-	-	-	-
			Bath	Lock		NL	159(3)	15	3	-	-	-
						NC	14(0)	-	-	-	-	-
						ES	24(0)	5	1	-	-	-
						HC	29(2)	10	2	-	-	-
Marco	Bortolami	12.06.80	Italy									
			Gloucester	Lock		NL	33(9)	10	2	-	-	-
						NC	4(2)	-	-	-	-	-
						HC	15(2)	5	1	-	-	-
			Padova	Lock		ES	12(0)	-	-	-	-	-
			Narbonne	Lock		ES	5(0)	-	-	-	-	-
Gary	Botha	12.10.81	South Africa	181cm	100 kg							
			Harlequins	Prop		NL	18(6)	20	4	-	-	-
						NC	1(1)	-	-	-	-	-
						HC	5(2)	-	-	-	-	-
			Northern Bulls	Prop								
			Natal Sharks	Hooker								
Will	Bowley	05.03.84	England									
			Worcester	Lock		NL	17(5)	5	1	-	-	-
						NC	1(2)	10	2	-	-	-
						ES	8(11)	10	2	-	-	-
			London Welsh	Lock		NL	7(0)	5	1	-	-	-
			Nottingham	Lock		NL	5(3)	5	1	-	-	-
						NC	2(0)	-	-	-	-	-
			Stourbridge	Lock		NL	14(1)	20	4	-	-	-
Neil	Brew	09.03.79	South Africa									
			Bristol	Centre		NL	38(4)	20	4	-	-	-
						NC	2(0)	-	-	-	-	-
						ES	5(1)	-	-	-	-	-
						HC	5(0)	5	1	-	-	-
Neil	Briggs	01.06.85	England									
			Sale Sharks	Hooker		NL	26(18)	20	4	-	-	-
						NC	1(1)	-	-	-	-	-
						ES	3(3)	-	-	-	-	-
						HC	5(2)	-	-	-	-	-
			Rotherham	Hooker		NL	13(8)	15	3	-	-	-
						NC	1(0)	-	-	-	-	-
			Sheffield	Hooker		NL	2(0)	-	-	-	-	-
Chris	Brooker	31.05.86	England	178cm	108 kg							
			Harlequins	Hooker		NL	2(8)	5	1	-	-	-
						NC	3(0)	-	-	-	-	-
						HC	1(1)	-	-	-	-	-
			Cleve	Hooker		NC	2(1)	10	2	-	-	-
			Bath	Hooker		NL	0(1)	-	-	-	-	-
						NC	0(2)	-	-	-	-	-

PLAYERS - PREMIERSHIP

						Comp	Apps	Pts	T	P	C	DG
John	Brooks	11.11.77	England	178cm	108 kg							
			Harlequins	Prop		NL	1(6)	-	-	-	-	-
						NC	1(0)	-	-	-	-	-
						HC	0(1)	-	-	-	-	-
			Northampton	Prop		NL	5(1)	-	-	-	-	-
						HC	2(0)	-	-	-	-	-
			Bedford	Prop		NL	78(43)	15	3	-	-	-
						NC	6(5)	10	2	-	-	-
James	Brooks	06.04.80	England	178cm	84 kg							
			Leeds	Outside Half		NL	10(15)	80	7-	21	1	-
						NC	3(1)	15	1	2	2	-
						ES	0(3)	-	-	-	-	-
			Blackheath	Outside Half		NL	2(1)	10	2	-	-	-
			London Wasps	Outside Half		NL	7(28)	8	-	1	-	2
						NC	2(1)	5	1	-	-	-
						HC	2(6)	8	-	4	-	-
			Northampton	Outside Half		NL	22(37)	33	6	-	-	1
						NC	4(4)	5	1	-	-	-
						HC	4(7)	5	1	-	-	-
Alex	Brown	17.05.79	England	201cm	111 kg							
			Gloucester	Lock		NL	107(3)	25	5	-	-	-
						NC	9(2)	5	1	-	-	-
						ES	6(1)	5	1	-	-	-
						HC	24(1)	-	-	-	-	-
			Bristol	Lock		NL	60(4)	15	3	-	-	-
						NC	4(0)	-	-	-	-	-
						ES	11(1)	5	1	-	-	-
						HC	6(0)	-	-	-	-	-
Mike	Brown	04.09.85	England	193cm	117 kg							
			Harlequins	Full Back		NL	69(6)	142	28	1	-	-
						NC	5(3)	10	2	-	-	-
						ES	4(0)	24	4	2	-	-
						HC	11(0)	15	3	-	-	-
Daniel	Browne	13.04.79	Ireland									
			Bath	No. 8		NL	26(7)	40	8	-	-	-
						NC	4(0)	-	-	-	-	-
						ES	2(4)	5	1	-	-	-
						HC	4	-	-	-	-	-
			Northampton	No. 8		NL	27(3)	15	3	-	-	-
						NC	3(0)	-	-	-	-	-
						ES	5(0)	5	1	-	-	-
						HC	6(0)	5	1	-	-	-
			Grenoble	No. 8		ES	1(0)	-	-	-	-	-
Sebastien	Bruno	26.08.74	France									
			Sale Sharks	Hooker		NL	52(21)	30	6	-	-	-
						NC	4(3)	-	-	-	-	-
						ES	8(3)	5	1	-	-	-
						HC	11(1)	-	-	-	-	-
			Pau	Hooker		ES	2(0)	-	-	-	-	-
			Beziers	Hooker		ES	5(3)	5	1	-	-	-
						HC	2(0)	-	-	-	-	-
Nathan	Budgett	02.11.75	Wales									
			Bristol	Lock		NL	35(14)	-	-	-	-	-
						NC	5(0)	-	-	-	-	-
						ES	5(2)	5	1	-	-	-
						HC	1(0)	-	-	-	-	-
			Cardiff	Blindside Flanker		HC	0(6)	-	-	-	-	-
			Neath	Openside Flanker								
			Ebbw Vale	Openside Flanker		ES	2(1)	-	-	-	-	-
						HC	4(1)	-	-	-	-	-
			Bridgend	Openside Flanker		ES	2(0)	-	-	-	-	-
						HC	3(3)	-	-	-	-	-
			Celtic Warriors	Openside Flanker		HC	0(2)	-	-	-	-	-

PLAYERS - PREMIERSHIP

					Comp	Apps	Pts	T	P	C	DG
Peter	**Buxton**	21.08.78	England								
			Gloucester	Blindside Flanker	NL	89(33)	20	4	-	-	-
					NC	7(4)	5	1	-	-	-
					ES	7(1)	-	-	-	-	-
					HC	29(6)	5	1	-	-	-
			Moseley	Blindside Flanker	NL	56(4)	80	16	-	-	-
					NC	2(0)	-	-	-	-	-
			Newport	Blindside Flanker	HC	8(1)	5	1	-	-	-
Matthew	**Cairns**	31.03.79	England	178cm 95 kg							
			Saracens	Hooker	NL	81(69)	40	8	-	-	-
					NC	9(4)	5	1	-	-	-
					ES	13(11)	72	14	1	-	-
					HC	6(8)	-	-	-	-	-
			Sale Sharks	Hooker	NL	10(9)	20	4	-	-	-
					NC	3(1)	-	-	-	-	-
					HC	3(3)	-	-	-	-	-
Danny	**Care**	02.01.87	England								
			Harlequins	Scrum Half	NL	27(6)	48	9	-	-	1
					NC	4(1)	-	-	-	-	-
					ES	2(2)	5	1	-	-	-
					HC	10( )	13	2	-	-	1
			Leeds	Scrum Half	NL	2(12)	10	2	-	-	-
					ES	2(0)	11	1	3	-	-
					HC	0(4)	-	-	-	-	-
Joe	**Carlisle**	04.12.87	England								
			Pertemps Bees	Outside Half	NL	2(1)	21	1	5	2	-
			Worcester	Outside Half	NL	6(4)	23	-	7	3	-
					NC	1(2)	2	-	1	-	-
					ES	4(6)	63	2	16	7	-
Bob	**Casey**	18.07.78	Ireland								
			London Irish	Lock	NL	123(6)	20	4	-	-	-
					NC	12(1)	-	-	-	-	-
					ES	17(2)	10	2	-	-	-
					HC	14(0)	5	1	-	-	-
			Leinster	Lock	HC	13(5)	10	2	-	-	-
Martin	**Castrogiovanni**	21.10.81	Italy	188cm 122 kg							
			Leicester Tigers	Prop	NL	20(13)	10	2	-	-	-
					NC	4(1)	5	1	-	-	-
					HC	13(2)	-	-	-	-	-
			Calvisano	Prop	HC	14(6)	-	-	-	-	-
Mike	**Catt**	17.09.71	England	178cm 86 kg							
			London Irish	Centre	NL	59(8)	58	6	5	3	3
					NC	3(1)	3	-	-	-	1
					ES	8(0)	10	1	1	1	-
					HC	9(0)	10	2	-	-	-
			Bath	Outside Half	NL	121(5)	526	32	78	64	6
					NC	8(0)	30	1	2	6	1
					ES	1(3)	5	1	-	-	-
					HC	28(0)	78	9	6	6	1
Sebastian	**Chabel**	08.12.77	France								
			Sale Sharks	No. 8	NL	74(5)	40	8	-	-	-
					NC	7(0)	5	1	-	-	-
					ES	11(0)	20	4	-	-	-
					HC	15(1)	25	5	-	-	-
			Bourgoin	Blindside Flanker	HC	12(1)	20	4	-	-	-
Hall	**Charlton**	25.10.79	England	180cm 89 kg							
			Newcastle	Scrum Half	NL	80(49)	40	8	-	-	-
					NC	9(3)	-	-	-	-	-
					ES	18(11)	15	3	-	-	-
					HC	7(5)	-	-	-	-	-
			Blaydon	Scrum Half	NL	4(0)	-	-	-	-	-
					NC	1(0)	-	-	-	-	-

PLAYERS - PREMIERSHIP

						Comp	Apps	Pts	T	P	C	DG
Tom	**Cheeseman**	22.03.86	Wales Bath	183cm Centre	90 kg	NL NC ES HC	26(13) 8(2) 6(5) 6(3)	20 20 10 10	4 4 2 2	- - - -	- - - -	- - - -
Kris	**Chesney**	02.03.74	England Saracens Bristol	198cm Lock Lock	114 kg	NL NC ES HC NL	170(50) 14(10) 24(8) 18(4) 4(0)	80 10 25 - 5	16 2 5 - 1	- - - - -	- - - - -	- - - - -
George	**Chuter**	09.07.76	England Leicester Tigers Saracens	178cm Hooker Hooker	103 kg	NL NC HC NL NC ES HC	79(34) 7(3) 30(11) 60(7) 8(0) 2(1) 6(0)	40 5 30 35 10 - -	8 1 6 7 2 - -	- - - - - - -	- - - - - - -	- - - - - - -
Danny	**Cipriani**	02.11.87	England London Wasps	183cm Outside Half	90 kg	NL NC HC	36(9) 7(1) 16(3)	356 51 132	11 2 5	50 10 19	66 7 23	1 - -
Michael	**Claassens**	29.01.82	South Africa Bath	178cm Scrum Half	87 kg	NL NC ES HC	34(2) 2(0) 5(3) 7	45 - 5 5	9 - 1 1	- - - -	- - - -	- - - -

Prev. Clubs: Cats, Scrum Half; Cheetahs, Scrum Half

Alex	**Clarke**	09.01.81	England Bristol Bath Moseley	180cm Prop Prop Prop	108 kg	NL NC ES HC NL NL NC	57(33) 5(7) 7(6) 3(2) 0(1) 22(4) 1(0)	30 - - - - 5 5	6 - - - - 1 1	- - - - - - -	- - - - - - -	- - - - - - -
Callum	**Clarke**	10.06.89	England Leeds	Openside Flanker		NL NC ES	26(7) 2(0) 4(3)	15 - 5	3 - 1	- - -	- - -	- - -
Jon	**Clarke**	22.10.83	England Northampton	190cm Centre	90kg	NL NC ES HC	60(5) 5 11 3	65 15 15 -	13 3 3 -	- - - -	- - - -	- - - -
William	**Cliff**	17.10.88 (Loan)	England Manchester Sale Sharks Macclesfield	Scrum Half Scrum Half Scrum Half	78 kg	NL NC NL NC ES NL NC	2(12) 2(0) 1(11) 0(2) 0(2) 2(6) 1(0)	5 - 5 - 5 - -	1 - 1 - 1 - -	- - - - - - -	- - - - - - -	- - - - - - -

PLAYERS - PREMIERSHIP

							Comp	Apps	Pts	T	P	C	DG
Brent	**Cockbain**	15.11.74	Wales	202cm	122 kg								
			London Irish	Lock			NL	2(6)	-	-	-	-	-
							ES	4(1)	-	-	-	-	-
			Sale Sharks	Lock			NL	16(7)	-	-	-	-	-
							NC	2	-	-	-	-	-
							ES	0(1)	-	-	-	-	-
							HC	2 (3)	-	-	-	-	-
			Cardiff	Lock									
			Pontypridd	Lock			ES	15(1)	-	-	-	-	-
							HC	6(0)	5	1	-	-	-
			Celtic Warriors	Lock			HC	3(1)	-	-	-	-	-
			Ospreys	Lock			NC	3(1)	-	-	-	-	-
							HC	8 (3)	-	-	-	-	-
Danie	**Coetzee**	02.09.77	South Africa	185cm	103 kg								
			London Irish	Prop			NL	30(22)	-	-	-	-	-
							NC	3(1)	-	-	-	-	-
							HC	2(7)	-	-	-	-	-
							ES	2 (2)	-	-	-	-	-
			Northern Bulls	Prop									
Gareth	**Cooper**	07.05.79	Wales	171cm	76 kg								
			Gloucester	Scrum Half			NL	12(11)	-	-	-	-	-
							NC	1(4)	-	-	-	-	-
							HC	6(4)	-	-	-	-	-
			Bath	Scrum Half			NL	56(12)	75	15	-	-	-
							NC	3(0)	5	1	-	-	-
							ES	8(1)	-	-	-	-	-
							HC	7(6)	15	3	-	-	-
			Gwent Dragons	Scrum Half			NC	2(2)	-	-	-	-	-
							ES	5(2)	10	2	-	-	-
							HC	7(2)	10	2	-	-	-
			Celtic Warriors	Scrum Half			HC	3(1)	5	1	-	-	-
Matt	**Cornwell**	16.01.85	England	186cm	90 kg								
			Leicester Tigers	Centre			NL	13(21)	20	4	-	-	-
							NC	2(1)	-	-	-	-	-
							HC	2(5)	-	-	-	-	-
Martin	**Corry**	12.10.73	England	196cm	111 kg								
			Leicester Tigers	No. 8			NL	159(15)	75	15	-	-	-
							NC	18(2)	10	2	-	-	-
							HC	66(3)	35	7	-	-	-
			Bristol	Blindside Flanker			NL	29(0)	35	7	-	-	-
							NC	1(0)	-	-	-	-	-
							ES	2(0)	-	-	-	-	-
Sean	**Cox**	16.01.85	England										
			Orrell	Lock			NL	1(1)	-	-	-	-	-
			Sale Sharks	Lock			NL	22(18)	-	-	-	-	-
							NC	2(4)	5	1	-	-	-
							ES	5(1)	-	-	-	-	-
							HC	1(1)	-	-	-	-	-
			Sedgley Park	Lock			NL	2(1)	5	1	-	-	-
			Vale of Lune	Lock			NL	12(0)	20	4	-	-	-
Jordan	**Crane**	03.06.86	England	191cm	103 kg								
			Leicester Tigers	No. 8			NL	41(6)	55	11	-	-	-
							NC	8(2)	5	1	-	-	-
							HC	13(3)	15	3	-	-	-
			Leeds	No 8			NL	11(6)	5	1	-	-	-
							ES	3(4)	20	4	-	-	-
							HC	2(1)	-	-	-	-	-
Loki	**Crichton**	14.03.76	Samoa										
			Newcastle	Full Back			NL	7(9)	34	1	7	5	-
							NC	1(0)	-	-	-	-	-
							ES	0(4)	10	2	-	-	-
			Worcester	Full Back			NL	12(7)	73	3	11	11	1
							NC	2(1)	10	1	1	1	-
							ES	5(1)	19	-	5	3	-
			Waikato Chiefs	Full Back									

779

PLAYERS - PREMIERSHIP

							Comp	Apps	Pts	T	P	C	DG
Alex	**Crockett**	20.11.81	England		180cm	93 kg							
			Bath		Centre		NL	73(17)	65	13	-	-	-
							NC	4(0)	5	1	-	-	-
							ES	17(1)	35	7	-	-	-
							HC	11(2)	5	1	-	-	-
Tom	**Croft**	07.11.85	England		196cm	104 kg							
			Leicester Tigers		Blindside Flanker		NL	34(10)	40	8	-	-	-
							NC	4(2)	5	1	-	-	-
							HC	10(1)	5	1	-	-	-
Darren	**Crompton**	12.09.72	England		188cm	114 kg							
			Bath		Prop		NL	2(1)	-	-	-	-	-
			Bristol		Prop		NL	139(17)	40	8	-	-	-
							NC	9(2)	-	-	-	-	-
							ES	18(7)	-	-	-	-	-
							HC	7(5)	-	-	-	-	-
			Richmond		Prop		NL	53(7)	5	1	-	-	-
							NC	4(1)	-	-	-	-	-
							ES	2(1)	-	-	-	-	-
			Cardiff		Prop		HC	2(4)	-	-	-	-	-
Mark	**Cueto**	26.12.79	England		182cm	93 kg							
			Sale Sharks		Right Wing		NL	124(4)	320	64	-	-	-
							NC	12(0)	15	3	-	-	-
							ES	18(0)	70	14	-	-	-
							HC	25(0)	35	7	-	-	-
Declan	**Danagher**	11.01.80	England		190cm	102 kg							
			London Irish		No. 8		NL	100(42)	65	13	-	-	-
							NC	12(2)	-	-	-	-	-
							ES	24(10)	35	7	-	-	-
							HC	14(2)	5	1	-	-	-
Mefin	**Davies**	02.09.72	Wales										
			Gloucester		Hooker		NL	27(14)	-	-	-	-	-
							NC	4(0)	-	-	-	-	-
							ES	8(1)	-	-	-	-	-
							HC	4(0)	-	-	-	-	-
			Leicester Tigers		Hooker		NL	10(12)	5	1	-	-	-
							NC	2(3)	-	-	-	-	-
							HC	0(2)	-	-	-	-	-
			Pontypridd		Hooker		ES	15(1)	10	2	-	-	-
			Neath		Hooker		ES	1(0)	-	-	-	-	-
							HC	11(1)	10	2	-	-	-
			Celtic Warriors		Hooker		HC	5(0)	-	-	-	-	-
			Ospreys		Hooker		HC	0(4)	-	-	-	-	-
Christian	**Day**	24.06.83	England										
			Northampton		Lock		NL	9 (5)	-	-	-	-	-
							NC	1 (1)	-	-	-	-	-
							ES	3 (2)	-	-	-	-	-
			Sale Sharks		Lock		NL	33(29)	-	-	-	-	-
							NC	5(4)	-	-	-	-	-
							ES	6(4)	5	1	-	-	-
Prev. Club: Stade Francais, Lock							HC	3(5)	-	-	-	-	-
Neil	**de Koch**	20.11.78	South Africa		178cm	80 kg							
			Saracens		Scrum Half		NL	35(0)	25	5	-	-	-
							NC	2(0)	-	-	-	-	-
							ES	6(0)	10	2	-	-	-
Prev. Club: Western Stormers, Scrum Half							HC	8(0)	-	-	-	-	-

PLAYERS - PREMIERSHIP

					Comp	Apps	Pts	T	P	C	DG
Tomas	**De Vedia**	31.05.82	Argentina								
			London Irish	Left Wing	NL	7(2)	20	4	-	-	-
					NC	3(0)	5	1	-	-	-
					HC	5(1)	20	4	-	-	-
					ES	(1)	-	-	-	-	-
			Saracens	Left Wing	NL	4(8)	10	2	-	-	-
					NC	2(1)	5	1	-	-	-
					ES	1(3)	20	4	-	-	-
Louis	**Deacon**	07.10.80	England	196cm	111 kg						
			Leicester Tigers	Lock	NL	109(14)	30	6	-	-	-
					NC	10(3)	-	-	-	-	-
					EC	38(4)	15	3	-	-	-
Brett	**Deacon**	07.03.82	England	193cm	108 kg						
			Leicester Tigers	Lock	NL	52(19)	15	3	-	-	-
					NC	4(1)	-	-	-	-	-
					EC	6(9)	10	2	-	-	-
Gareth	**Delve**	30.12.82	Wales	191cm	102 kg						
			Bath	Blindside Flanker	NL	15(28)	20	4	-	-	-
					NC	0(2)	-	-	-	-	-
					ES	2(3)	-	-	-	-	-
					HC	5(6)	-	-	-	-	-
			Gloucester	Blindside Flanker	NL	15(4)	-	-	-	-	-
					NC	3(1)	5	1	-	-	-
					HC	4(3)	5	1	-	-	-
Clarke	**Dermody**	22.04.80	New Zealand								
			London Irish	Prop	NL	24(2)	5	1	-	-	-
					NC	4(1)	-	-	-	-	-
					HC	3(0)	-	-	-	-	-
					ES	1 (6)	-	-	-	-	-
Prev. Club: Otago Highlanders, Hooker											
Alberto	**Di Bernardo**	04.11.80	Italy								
			Leeds	Outside Half	NL	31(6)	338	4	78	49	5
					NC	5(2)	48	-	18	4	-
					ES	6(0)	67	-	11	14	1
			Cornish Pirates	Outside Half	NL	26(1)	293	2	56	56	1
					NC	3(1)	36	-	6	6	2
			L'Aquila	Outside Half	ES	4(1)	31	1	7	3	1
Alan	**Dickens**	04.02.76	England								
			Northampton	Scrum Half	NL	(3)	-	-	-	-	-
					NC	(2)	-	-	-	-	-
					ES	(4)	-	-	-	-	-
			Leeds	Scrum Half	NL	42(16)	25	5	-	-	-
					NC	3(4)	-	-	-	-	-
					ES	5(5)	20	4	-	-	-
					HC	1(0)	-	-	-	-	-
			Manchester	Scrum Half	NL	25(0)	20	4	-	-	-
					NC	2(0)	5	1	-	-	-
			Sale Sharks	Scrum Half	NL	3(15)	-	-	-	-	-
					NC	0(1)	-	-	-	-	-
					ES	4(2)	-	-	-	-	-
			Saracens	Scrum Half	NL	16(26)	-	-	-	-	-
					NC	2(2)	-	-	-	-	-
					ES	1(5)	-	-	-	-	-
					HC	2(7)	-	-	-	-	-
			Stourbridge	Scrum Half	NL	15(0)	35	7	-	-	-
Alasdair	**Dickinson**	11.09.83	Scotland								
			Gloucester	Prop	NL	7(10)	-	-	-	-	-
					NC	5(1)	-	-	-	-	-
					HC	6(1)	-	-	-	-	-
			Moseley	Prop	NL	2(0)	5	1	-	-	-
			Edinburgh Reivers	Prop	NC	2(0)	-	-	-	-	-
					HC	5(8)	5	1	-	-	-

PLAYERS - PREMIERSHIP

Name		DOB	Country/Club	Details		Comp	Apps	Pts	T	P	C	DG
Lee	Dickson	29.03.85	England	180cm	76 kg							
			Northampton	Scrum Half		NL	18(4)	5	1	-	-	-
						NC	3(1)	5	1	-	-	-
						ES	4(4)	5	1	-	-	-
			Newcastle	Scrum Half		NL	21(22)	-	-	-	-	-
						NC	2(3)	-	-	-	-	-
						ES	5(9)	10	2	-	-	-
Paul	Diggin	23.01.85	England	173cm	84kg							
			Northampton	Winger		NL	51(10)	140	28	-	-	-
						NC	7(3)	10	2	-	-	-
						ES	5(1)	20	4	-	-	-
						HC	5(1)	20	4	-	-	-
Pieter	Dixon	17.10.77	Zimbabwe									
			Bath	Hooker		NL	29(25)	20	4	-	-	-
						NC	2(1)	-	-	-	-	-
						ES	3(7)	-	-	-	-	-
						HC	4(6)	-	-	-	-	-
			Western Stormers	Hooker								
David	Doherty	28.01.87	England									
			Sale Sharks	Scrum Half		NL	14(0)	5	1	-	-	-
						NC	1(0)	-	-	-	-	-
						HC	5(0)	5	1	-	-	-
			Henley Hawks	Left Wing		NL	1(0)	-	-	-	-	-
			Leeds	Right Wing		NL	13(5)	10	1	1	1	-
						NC	1(1)	10	2	-	-	-
						ES	1(0)	5	1	-	-	-
						HC	2(3)	10	2	-	-	-
			London Wasps	Right Wing		NL	9(5)	10	2	-	-	-
						NC	3(0)	-	-	-	-	-
						HC	2(0)	7	1	1	-	-
			London Welsh	Right Wing		NL	1(0)	-	-	-	-	-
James	Downey	23.03.81	Ireland									
			Northampton	Centre		NL	41	30	6	-	-	-
						NC	7	5	1	-	-	-
						ES	7	-	-	-	-	-
			Connacht			ES	4	5	1	-	-	-
			Calvisano			HC	4	5	1	-	-	-
Phil	Dowson	01.10.81	England	190cm	106 kg							
			Newcastle	No. 8		NL	77(17)	45	9	-	-	-
						NC	7(3)	15	3	-	-	-
						ES	15(2)	35	7	-	-	-
						HC	7(2)	-	-	-	-	-
			Darlington MP	No. 8		NL	2(0)	-	-	-	-	-
Jon	Dunbar	04.04.80	England									
			Leeds	Blindside Flanker		NL	67(19)	75	15	-	-	-
						NC	5(4)	5	1	-	-	-
						ES	7(2)	10	2	-	-	-
						HC	2(2)	-	-	-	-	-
			Newcastle	Blindside Flanker		NL	43(12)	20	4	-	-	-
						NC	5(1)	-	-	-	-	-
						ES	10(0)	-	-	-	-	-
						HC	4(1)	-	-	-	-	-
Mark	Easter	19.10.82	England	191cm	102kg							
			Northampton	Back row		NL	40(14)	50	10	-	-	-
						NC	6(3)	5	1	-	-	-
						ES	6 (1)	20	4	-	-	-
						HC	1(4)	-	-	-	-	-

PLAYERS - PREMIERSHIP

						Comp	Apps	Pts	T	P	C	DG
Nick	**Easter**	15.08.78	England	194cm	115 kg							
			Harlequins	No. 8		NL	74(7)	130	261	-	-	-
						NC	7(0)	15	3	-	-	-
						ES	5(0)	-	-	-	-	-
						HC	14(2)	5	1	-	-	-
			Orrell	No. 8		NL	62(5)	135	27	-	-	-
						NC	6(0)	20	4	-	-	-
			Rosslyn Park	No. 8		NL	4(0)	-	-	-	-	-
						NC	1(1)	5	1	-	-	-
Joe	**El Abd**	23.02.80	England	188cm	102 kg							
			Bath	Openside Flanker		NL	3(5)	-	-	-	-	-
						EC	0(1)	-	-	-	-	-
			Bristol	Openside Flanker		NL	93(5)	40	8	-	-	-
						NC	6(1)	-	-	-	-	-
						ES	8(1)	15	3	-	-	-
						HC	4(2)	-	-	-	-	-
			Caerphilly	Openside Flanker		ES	5(0)	5	1	-	-	-
Anthony	**Elliott**	02.02.81	England									
			Bristol	Right Wing		NL	7(1)	15	3	-	-	-
						HC	2(0)	-	-	-	-	-
						ES	1	-	-	-	-	-
						NC	1	-	-	-	-	-
			Newcastle	Left Wing		NL	17(3)	57	11	1	-	-
						NC	3(0)	-	-	-	-	-
						ES	5(0)	5	1	-	-	-
			Rotherham	Right Wing		NL	34(1)	42	8	1	-	-
						ES	2(0)	-	-	-	-	-
			Sale Sharks	Right Wing		NL	8(6)	20	4	-	-	-
						ES	4(3)	30	6	-	-	-
						HC	0(1)	-	-	-	-	-
			West Hartlepool	Right Wing		NL	9(1)	-	-	-	-	-
Ayoola	**Erinle**	20.02.80	England	191cm	110 kg							
			Leicester Tigers	Centre		NL	10(10)	25	5	-	-	-
						NC	2(1)	-	-	-	-	-
						HC	3(0)	-	-	-	-	-
			Nottingham	Centre	Loan	NL	4	5	1	-	-	-
			London Wasps	Centre		NL	45(30)	90	18	-	-	-
						NC	3(1)	5	1	-	-	-
						ES	3(5)	5	1	-	-	-
						HC	6(14)	20	4	-	-	-
			Henley Hawks	Centre		NL	7(3)	20	4	-	-	-
						NC	0(1)	-	-	-	-	-
			Reading	Right Wing		NL	16(0)	30	6	-	-	-
Jim	**Evans**	02.08.80	England	201cm	107 kg							
			Harlequins	Lock		NL	79(43)	60	12	-	-	-
						NC	6(3)	-	-	-	-	-
						ES	12(3)	10	2	-	-	-
						EC	7(3)	-	-	-	-	-
Nick	**Evans**	14.08.80	New Zealand	178 cm	84 kg							
			Harlequins	Lock		NL	13(0)	130	2	12	31	1
						NC	(1)	2	-	1	-	-
						EC	5(0)	33	-	6	6	1
Barry	**Everitt**	09.03.76	Ireland	175cm	80kg							
			Northampton	Fly half		NL	12(6)	120	2	25	20	-
						NC	1 (1)	10	-	2	2	-
						ES	(5)	11	-	4	1	-
			London Irish	Fly half		NL	91(26)	1236	7	95	312	25
						NC	13(4)	136	-	23	27	3
						ES	14(4)	267	3	39	55	3
						HC	8(4)	111	1	11	25	3
			Munster			HC	6	11	-	1	3	-

PLAYERS - PREMIERSHIP

							Comp	Apps	Pts	T	P	C	DG
Jonathan	**Faamatuainu**	29.12.83	Samoa										
			Bath	Blindside Flanker			NL	27(25)	40	8	-	-	-
							NC	4(3)	-	-	-	-	-
							HC	3 (3)	-	-	-	-	-
							ES	4(7)	15	3	-	-	-
Andy	**Farrell**	30.05.75	England	190cm	102 kg								
			Saracens	Centre			NL	22(5)	12	1	2	1	-
							NC	5(2)	8	-	1	2	-
							ES	7(0)	5	1	-	-	-
							HC	7(0)	5	1	-	-	-
Prev. Clubs: Wigan (RL)													
Lionel	**Faure**	26.11.77	France										
			Sale Sharks	Prop			NL	31(9)	-	-	-	-	-
							NC	4(0)	-	-	-	-	-
							ES	4(2)	5	1	-	-	-
							HC	5(4)	-	-	-	-	-
			ASM Clermont Auvergne	Prop									
			Pau	Prop			ES	2(1)	-	-	-	-	-
			La Rochelle	Prop			ES	4(1)	-	-	-	-	-
Ignacio	**Fernandez Lobbe**	20.11.74	Argentina	195cm	113 kg								
			Northampton	Lock			NL	15 (4)	-	-	-	-	-
							ES	7 (1)	-	-	-	-	-
							NC	2 (1)	-	-	-	-	-
			Sale Sharks	Lock			NL	21(10)	15	3	-	-	-
							NC	2(2)	5	1	-	-	-
							ES	7(2)	-	-	-	-	-
							HC	5(4)	10	2	-	-	-
			Begles-Bordeaux	No. 8			ES	1(0)	-	-	-	-	-
Juan Martin Fernandez Lobbe		19.11.81	Argentina										
			Sale Sharks	Openside Flanker			NL	42(4)	45	9	-	-	-
							NC	5(1)	-	-	-	-	-
							ES	5(2)	10	2	-	-	-
							HC	8(1)	20	4	-	-	-
David	**Flatman**	21.01.80	England	183cm	111 kg								
			Bath	Prop			NL	51(10)	-	-	-	-	-
							NC	6(1)	-	-	-	-	-
							ES	7(1)	-	-	-	-	-
							HC	7(2)	-	-	-	-	-
			Newbury	Prop			NL	1(0)	-	-	-	-	-
			Saracens	Prop			NL	58(15)	25	5	-	-	-
							NC	8(0)	10	2	-	-	-
							ES	5(1)	10	2	-	-	-
							HC	11(1)	-	-	-	-	-
Toby	**Flood**	08.08.85	England	188cm	95 kg								
			Leicester	Fly Half			NL	11	126	4	14	26	-
							NC	1	-	-	-	-	-
							HC	7	76	3	14	11	-
			Newcastle	Centre			NL	38(10)	127	8	15	17	2
							NC	5(0)	28	-	8	3	1
							ES	16(3)	106	7	28	5	-
							HC	0(1)	-	-	-	-	-
			Darlington MP	Full Back			NL	1(0)	-	-	-	-	-
Riki	**Flutey**	10.02.80	New Zealand										
			London Irish	Outside Half			NL	31(0)	175	10	19	26	3
							NC	2(0)	13	2	-	1	-
							ES	7(0)	75	3	21	4	2
							EC	1(1)	-	-	-	-	-
			London Wasps	Outside Half			NL	29(0)	38	7	-	-	1
							NC	4(0)	-	-	-	-	-
							EC	10(0)	10	2	-	-	-
			Wellington Hurricanes	Outside Half									

PLAYERS - PREMIERSHIP

						Comp	Apps	Pts	T	P	C	DG
Ben	**Foden**	22.07.85	England									
			Northampton	Full Back		NL	14 (6)	20	4	-	-	-
						NC	3 (0)	5	1	-	-	-
						ES	8	15	3	-	-	-
			Sale Sharks	Full Back		NL	31 (14)	50	10	-	-	-
						NC	3 (1)	-	-	-	-	-
						ES	6 (3)	-	-	-	-	-
						HC	5 (1)	20	4	-	-	-
			Chester	Centre		NL	18 (2)	70	14	-	-	-
						NC	3 (2)	5	1	-	-	-
Chris	**Fortey**	25.08.75	England	180cm	103 kg							
			Gloucester	Hooker		NL	76 (53)	20	4	-	-	-
						NC	7 (6)	5	1	-	-	-
						ES	6 (3)	10	2	-	-	-
						HC	8 (5)	-	-	-	-	-
			Worcester	Hooker		NL	41 (24)	10	2	-	-	-
						NC	3 (2)	-	-	-	-	-
						ES	12 (10)	-	-	-	-	-
Mark	**Foster**	02.09.83	England	183cm	95 kg							
			Gloucester	Right Wing		NL	45 (11)	55	11	-	-	-
						NC	9 (0)	10	2	-	-	-
						ES	7 (1)	25	5	-	-	-
						HC	6 (1)	25	5	-	-	-
			Moseley	Right Wing		NL	5 (0)	15	3	-	-	-
			Pertemps Bees	Right Wing		NL	1 (1)	-	-	-	-	-
			Newbury	Right Wing		NL	8 (0)	40	8	-	-	-
Hendre	**Fourie**	19.09.79	South Africa									
			Leeds	Blindside Flanker		NL	24 (4)	55	11	-	-	-
			Rotherham	Blindside Flanker		NL	47 (5)	75	15	-	-	-
						NC	3 (1)	10	2	-	-	-
Tom	**French**	27.11.83	England	182cm	106 kg							
			Henley Hawks	Prop	Loan	NL	23 (0)	10	2	-	-	-
			London Wasps	Prop		NL	14 (13)	-	-	-	-	-
						NC	2 (2)	-	-	-	-	-
						HC	1 (3)	-	-	-	-	-
Tani	**Fuga**	14.07.73	Samoa	180cm	98 kg							
			Harlequins	Hooker		NL	101 (33)	80	16	-	-	-
						NC	11 (2)	10	2	-	-	-
						ES	16 (8)	20	4	-	-	-
						HC	11 (3)	-	-	-	-	-
Eliota Fuimaono Sapolu		31.10.80	Samoa									
			Bath	Centre		NL	30 (13)	15	3	-	-	-
						ES	11 (0)	5	1	-	-	-
						HC	3 (1)	-	-	-	-	-
						NC	2	-	-	-	-	-
Warren	**Fury**	10.12.85	Wales									
			London Irish	Scrum Half		NL	3 (8)	-	-	-	-	-
						NC	1 (2)	5	1	-	-	-
						ES	(3)	5	1	-	-	-
			London Wasps	Scrum Half		NL	2 (5)	-	-	-	-	-
			London Welsh	Scrum Half		NL	6 (8)	5	1	-	-	-
						NC	1 (0)	-	-	-	-	-
Marcel	**Garvey**	21.04.83	England	173cm	88 kg							
			Gloucester	Right Wing		NL	56 (5)	90	18	-	-	-
						NC	6 (3)	15	3	-	-	-
						ES	4 (1)	15	3	-	-	-
						HC	17 (0)	50	10	-	-	-
			Worcester	Left Wing		NL	36 (4)	35	7	-	-	-
						NC	3 (0)	5	1	-	-	-
						ES	11 (0)	30	6	-	-	-

PLAYERS - PREMIERSHIP

							Comp	Apps	Pts	T	P	C	DG
Rico	**Gear**	20.02.78	New Zealand		179cm	88 kg							
			Worcester		Right Wing		NL	24(3)	25	5	-	-	-
							ES	13(2)	60	12	-	-	-
							NC	1	-	-	-	-	-
			Auckland Blues		Wing								
			Canterbury Crusaders		Wing								
Shane	**Geraghty**	12.08.86	England		180cm	86 kg							
			London Irish		Outside Half		NL	31(9)	129	6	15	22	1
							NC	4(1)	5	-	1	1	-
							ES	3(8)	40	2	12	2	-
							HC	6(3)	39	4	5	3	-
Craig	**Gillies**	06.05.76	England										
			Gloucester		Lock		NL	0(1)	-	-	-	-	-
			Richmond		Lock		NL	46(0)	5	1	-	-	-
							NC	7(0)	-	-	-	-	-
							ES	3(0)	-	-	-	-	-
			Worcester		Lock		NL	132(8)	5	1	-	-	-
							NC	11(1)	5	1	-	-	-
							ES	26(5)	15	3	-	-	-
			Llanelli		Lock		HC	10(3)	5	1	-	-	-
Jon	**Golding**	06.05.82	England		183cm	115 kg							
			Newcastle		Prop		NL	24(18)	15	3	-	-	-
							NC	3(3)	5	1	-	-	-
							ES	6(10)	10	2	-	-	-
			Northampton		Prop		NL	0(4)	-	-	-	-	-
							HC	0(1)	-	-	-	-	-
Andy	**Gomersall**	24.07.74	England		178cm	86 kg							
			Harlequins		Scrum Half		NL	20(6)	10	2	-	-	-
							NC	4(1)	-	-	-	-	-
							ES	3(1)	-	-	-	-	-
							HC	2(2)	-	-	-	-	-
			Worcester		Scrum Half		NL	13(6)	5	1	-	-	-
							ES	3(4)	10	2	-	-	-
			Bath		Scrum Half		NL	0(2)	-	-	-	-	-
			Bedford		Scrum Half		NL	20(0)	70	3	11	11	-
							NC	1(0)	-	-	-	-	-
							ES	3(0)	8	-	1	2	-
			Gloucester		Scrum Half		NL	73(15)	73	10	1	6	1
							NC	8(2)	15	3	-	-	-
							ES	3(3)	4	-	2	-	-
							HC	22(3)	2	-	1	-	-
			London Wasps		Scrum Half		NL	53(9)	55	11	-	-	-
							NC	3(4)	-	-	-	-	-
							HC	8(1)	10	2	-	-	-
Chris	**Goodman**	06.07.85	England		188cm	104 kg							
			Bath		No. 8		NL	7(17)	-	-	-	-	-
							NC	3(2)	-	-	-	-	-
							ES	6(4)	-	-	-	-	-
John	**Goodridge**	26.02.81	England		186cm	90 kg							
			Leeds		Full Back		NL	16(14)	55	11	-	-	-
							NC	7(0)	10	2	-	-	-
							ES	1(1)	-	-	-	-	-
			Pertemps Bees		Full Back		NL	21(0)	50	10	-	-	-
			Gloucester		Full Back		NL	48(11)	35	7	-	-	-
							NC	6(0)	10	2	-	-	-
							ES	5(4)	5	1	-	-	-
							HC	10(1)	20	4	-	-	-

PLAYERS - PREMIERSHIP

							Comp	Apps	Pts	T	P	C	DG
Danny	Grewcock	07.11.72	England	198cm	111 kg								
			Bath	Lock			NL	110(5)	25	5	-	-	-
							NC	9(1)	-	-	-	-	-
							ES	26(2)	15	3	-	-	-
							HC	18(0)	15	3	-	-	-
			Saracens	Lock			NL	60(3)	25	5	-	-	-
							NC	11(0)	10	2	-	-	-
							ES	4(1)	-	-	-	-	-
							HC	11(0)	-	-	-	-	-
			Coventry	Lock			NL	19(0)	15	3	-	-	-
James	Grindal	18.08.80	England	175cm	84 kg								
			Newcastle	Scrum Half			NL	68(46)	25	5	-	-	-
							NC	5(4)	-	-	-	-	-
							ES	18(10)	20	4	-	-	-
							HC	3(4)	-	-	-	-	-
			Leicester Tigers	Scrum Half			NL	11(12)	20	4	-	-	-
							NC	1(1)	-	-	-	-	-
							HC	2(1)	-	-	-	-	-
Tom	Guest	05.07.84	England	193cm	117 kg								
			Harlequins	Blindside Flanker			NL	33(29)	55	11	-	-	-
							NC	2(6)	-	-	-	-	-
							ES	1(4)	5	1	-	-	-
							HC	3(2)	-	-	-	-	-
			London Welsh	Blindside Flanker			NL	2(0)	10	2	-	-	-
			Esher	Blindside Flanker			NL	5(0)	5	1	-	-	-
Christopher Hala'ufia		24.10.78	Tonga										
			London Irish	No 8			NL	24 (0)	15	3	-	-	-
							NC	1 (1)	-	-	-	-	-
							ES	4 (1)	10	2	-	-	-
			Harlequins	No. 8			NL	12(14)	-	-	-	-	-
							NC	4(1)	5	1	-	-	-
							ES	2(0)	5	1	-	-	-
							HC	4(2)	-	-	-	-	-
			Rotherham	No. 8			NL	10(6)	40	8	-	-	-
							NC	1(0)	10	2	-	-	-
			Gran Parma Rugby	No. 8									
			Bradford Bingley	No. 8			NL	18(0)	135	27	-	-	-
John	Hart	20.03.82	England	195cm	113 kg								
			London Wasps	No. 8			NL	57(25)	20	4	-	-	-
							NC	7(2)	5	1	-	-	-
							HC	8(4)	-	-	-	-	-
Dylan	Hartley	24.05.86	England	185cm	113kg								
			Northampton	Hooker			NL	41(18)	35	7	-	-	-
							NC	6(4)	-	-	-	-	-
							ES	8(3)	-	-	-	-	-
							HC	1(5)	-	-	-	-	-
James	Haskell	02.04.85	England	193cm	111 kg								
			London Wasps	Blindside Flanker			NL	34(20)	30	6	-	-	-
							NC	8(3)	15	3	-	-	-
							HC	13(7)	25	5	-	-	-
Richard	Haughton	08.11.80	England	188cm	82 kg								
			Saracens	Right Wing			NL	96(11)	160	32	-	-	-
							NC	9(3)	10	2	-	-	-
							ES	18(2)	75	15	-	-	-
							HC	8(0)	25	5	-	-	-
Rob	Hawkins	14.04.83	England	183cm	97 kg								
			Bath	Hooker			NL	8(27)	15	3	-	-	-
							NC	5(1)	-	-	-	-	-
							ES	2(6)	5	1	-	-	-
							HC	0(1)	-	-	-	-	-

PLAYERS - PREMIERSHIP

Name		DOB	Country/Club	Position			Comp	Apps	Pts	T	P	C	DG
Carl	Hayman	14.11.79	New Zealand	193cm	120 kg								
			Newcastle	Prop			NL	27(2)	5	1	-	-	-
							NC	1(1)	-	-	-	-	-
							ES	9(0)	5	1	-	-	-
Prev. Clubs: Otago Highlanders, Prop													
Andrew	Hazell	25.04.78	England	183cm	92 kg								
			Gloucester	Openside Flanker			NL	104(36)	50	10	-	-	-
							NC	15(4)	-	-	-	-	-
							ES	10(1)	25	5	-	-	-
							HC	15(8)	5	1	-	-	-
John	Hepworth	25.12.82	Ireland										
			Leeds	Outside Half			NL	56(7)	120	24	-	-	-
							NC	5(3)	15	3	-	-	-
							ES	3(3)	5	1	-	-	-
			Leinster	Centre			NC	2(0)	5	1	-	-	-
							HC	0(4)	-	-	-	-	-
Ben	Herring	14.03.80	New Zealand										
			Leicester Tigers	Openside Flanker			NL	13(4)	20	4	-	-	-
							NC	2(1)	-	-	-	-	-
							HC	1(0)	5	1	-	-	-
Prev. Clubs: Otago Highlanders, Wellington Hurricanes													
Peter	Hewat	17.03.78	Australia										
			London Irish	Full Back			NL	30(2)	232	5	24	50	3
							HC	8(0)	95	4	15	15	-
							ES	6(0)	80	6	22	2	-
							NC	2(0)	25	2	3	3	-
			New South Wales	Full Back									
Eoghan	Hickey	29.10.81	Ireland										
			London Irish	Outside Half			NL	13(6)	76	-	5	22	-
							NC	3(2)	26	-	7	4	-
							HC	1(2)	7	1	1	-	-
			Worcester	Outside Half			NL	2(0)	21	-	3	5	-
							ES	2(0)	4	-	2	-	-
			Leinster	Outside Half			HC	0(2)	-	-	-	-	-
Andrew	Higgins	13.07.81	England	180cm	85 kg								
			Bath	Centre			NL	65(11)	90	18	-	-	-
							NC	8(0)	20	4	-	-	-
							ES	10(0)	20	4	-	-	-
							HC	7(4)	10	2	-	-	-
			Bristol	Centre			NL	23(4)	25	5	-	-	-
							NC	0(2)	5	1	-	-	-
							ES	6(1)	10	2	-	-	-
							HC	5(1)	5	1	-	-	-
			Worcester	Centre			NL	23(0)	50	10	-	-	-
							NC	2(0)	-	-	-	-	-
Leigh	Hinton	21.02.79	England	182cm	88 kg								
			Leeds	Full Back			NL	64(7)	426	24	78	50	-
							NC	5(4)	14	2	2	-	-
							ES	6(1)	15	3	-	-	-
			Pertemps Bees	Full Back			NL	22(1)	109	6	17	15	-
							NC	1(1)	24	2	4	2	-
			Bedford	Full Back			NL	25(0)	347	10	45	69	-
							NC	3(0)	26	-	7	4	-
			Moseley	Left Wing			NL	32(5)	227	9	31	40	-
							NC	1(1)	8	1	-	1	-
			Orrell	Full Back			NL	26(0)	313	23	69	20	-
							NC	2(1)	9	1	2	-	-
			Worcester	Centre			NL	0(1)	-	-	-	-	-
			Gwent Dragons	Full Back			NC	1(0)	-	-	-	-	-
							HC	0(1)	-	-	-	-	-

PLAYERS - PREMIERSHIP

							Comp	Apps	Pts	T	P	C	DG
Dan	**Hipkiss**	04.06.82	England	178cm	90 kg								
			Leicester Tigers	Centre			NL	54(11)	70	14	-	-	-
							NC	8(2)	20	4	-	-	-
							HC	21(4)	20	4	-	-	-
Robert	**Hoadley**	28.03.80	Ireland	185cm	87 kg								
			London Wasps	Centre			NL	22(18)	20	4	-	-	-
							NC	5(1)	-	-	-	-	-
							HC	3(4)	5	1	-	-	-
			London Irish	Centre			NL	24(11)	10	2	-	-	-
							NC	2(3)	-	-	-	-	-
							ES	10(0)	25	5	-	-	-
Jason	**Hobson**	10.02.83	England	180cm	114 kg								
			Bristol	Prop			NL	31(16)	25	5	-	-	-
							NC	8(0)	5	1	-	-	-
							ES	2(0)	-	-	-	-	-
							HC	6(0)	-	-	-	-	-
			Pertemps Bees	Prop			NL	5(3)	-	-	-	-	-
			Dings Crusaders	Prop			NL	2(1)	-	-	-	-	-
			Exeter	Prop			NL	17(22)	25	5	-	-	-
							NC	2(5)	-	-	-	-	-
Charlie	**Hodgson**	12.11.80	England	178cm	81 kg								
			Sale Sharks	Outside Half			NL	124(4)	1510	27	203	295	28
							NC	11(1)	118	2	18	21	3
							ES	20(7)	288	9	48	48	1
							HC	18(2)	201	4	35	34	3
Paul	**Hodgson**	25.04.82	England	173cm	77 kg								
			London Irish	Scrum Half			NL	85(15)	45	9	-	-	-
							NC	3(4)	-	-	-	-	-
							ES	15(2)	10	2	-	-	-
							HC	7(6)	-	-	-	-	-
			Bristol	Scrum Half			NL	21(15)	15	3	-	-	-
							NC	4(1)	5	1	-	-	-
Michael	**Holford**	11.08.82	England	180cm	105 kg								
			London Wasps	Prop			NL	4(9)	-	-	-	-	-
							NC	1(1)	-	-	-	-	-
							EC	0(2)	-	-	-	-	-
			Leicester Tigers	Prop			NL	23(22)	20	4	-	-	-
							NC	3(1)	-	-	-	-	-
							EC	0(6)	-	-	-	-	-
			Bedford	Prop			NL	1(1)	-	-	-	-	-
			London Welsh	Prop			NL	2(1)	-	-	-	-	-
Stuart	**Hooper**	18.11.81	England	195cm	105 kg								
			Bath	Lock			NL	18 (4)	15	3	-	-	-
							NC	1 (2)	5	1	-	-	-
							HC	5 (2)	5	1	-	-	-
			Leeds	Lock			NL	78(11)	25	5	-	-	-
							NC	7(1)	-	-	-	-	-
							ES	7(2)	15	3	-	-	-
							HC	5(2)	-	-	-	-	-
			Saracens	Lock			NL	17(14)	5	1	-	-	-
							NC	2(2)	-	-	-	-	-
							ES	8(4)	-	-	-	-	-
Adam	**Hopcroft**	03.08.79	England	181cm	110 kg								
			Leeds	Prop			NL	3(11)	-	-	-	-	-
							NC	2(2)	5	1	-	-	-
							ES	0(2)	-	-	-	-	-
			Otley	Prop			NL	4 (0)	-	-	-	-	-
			Rotherham	Prop			NL	36(17)	10	2	-	-	-
							NC	1(1)	-	-	-	-	-
			Bath	Prop			NL	0(4)	-	-	-	-	-
							HC	0(5)	-	-	-	-	-
			Henley Hawks	Prop			NL	67(9)	15	3	-	-	-
							NC	4(2)	-	-	-	-	-

PLAYERS - PREMIERSHIP

							Comp	Apps	Pts	T	P	C	DG
Kai	**Horstmann**	21.09.81	England	196cm	106 kg								
			Worcester	Blindside Flanker			NL	68(9)	35	7	-	-	-
							NC	4(1)	5	1	-	-	-
							ES	25(1)	25	5	-	-	-
			Harlequins	Blindside Flanker			NL	3(6)	-	-	-	-	-
							ES	2(2)	10	2	-	-	-
							HC	1(0)	-	-	-	-	-
James	**Hudson**	28.10.81	England										
			London Irish	Lock			NL	28(20)	10	2	-	-	-
							NC	6(1)	-	-	-	-	-
							HC	3(10)	-	-	-	-	-
							ES	4 (1)	10	2	-	-	-
			Bath	Lock			NL	16(9)	10	2	-	-	-
							NC	0(1)	-	-	-	-	-
							ES	2(0)	5	1	-	-	-
							HC	3(6)	5	1	-	-	-
Raphael	**Ibanez**	17.02.73	France										
			London Wasps	Hooker			NL	29(11)	45	9	-	-	-
							NC	1(2)	-	-	-	-	-
							EC	21(0)	20	4	-	-	-
			Saracens	Hooker			NL	12(12)	5	1	-	-	-
							NC	1(0)	-	-	-	-	-
							ES	6(1)	10	2	-	-	-
			Castres	Hooker			NL	4(0)	-	-	-	-	-
							ES	2(1)	-	-	-	-	-
							HC	6(0)	-	-	-	-	-
			Dax	Hooker			HC	4(1)	-	-	-	-	-
			Perpignan	Hooker			HC	7(0)	15	3	-	-	-
Paulica	**Ion**	10.01.83	Romania										
			Bath	Prop			NL	2(9)	-	-	-	-	-
							NC	2(2)	-	-	-	-	-
							ES	5(2)	-	-	-	-	-
			Bucuresti	Prop			ES	1(0)	-	-	-	-	-
Chris	**Jack**	05.09.78	New Zealand	202cm	112 kg								
			Saracens	Lock			NL	23(0)	-	-	-	-	-
							NC	1(0)	-	-	-	-	-
							HC	3(0)	10	2	-	-	-
							ES	7 (0)	5	1	-	-	-
			Canterbury Crusaders	Lock									
Glen	**Jackson**	23.10.75	New Zealand	180cm	84 kg								
			Saracens	Outside Half			NL	87(6)	1005	12	123	223	10
							NC	6(1)	68	-	10	16	-
							ES	14(1)	217	4	40	37	2
Prev. Club: Waikato Chiefs, Outside Half							EC	14(0)	193	3	32	36	2
William	**James**	22.12.76	Wales										
			Gloucester	Lock			NL	29(11)	10	2	-	-	-
							NC	7(1)	-	-	-	-	-
							HC	2(5)	-	-	-	-	-
			Moseley	Lock			NL	1(0)	-	-	-	-	-
			Cornish Pirates	Lock			NL	33(9)	5	1	-	-	-
							NC	4(0)	-	-	-	-	-
			Plymouth Albion	Lock			NL	67(5)	80	16	-	-	-
							NC	4(0)	-	-	-	-	-
			Pontypridd	Lock			HC	6(3)	-	-	-	-	-
Butch	**James**	08.07.79	South Africa	184cm	97 kg								
			Bath	Outside Half			NL	28(0)	233	4	36	47	-
							NC	1(0)	-	-	-	-	-
							HC	7(0)	47	-	7	11	-
Prev. Club: Natal Sharks, Outside Half							ES	7(0)	44	3	7	5	-

PLAYERS - PREMIERSHIP

							Comp	Apps	Pts	T	P	C	DG
Adrian	Jarvis	12.12.83	England	188cm	83 kg								
			Bristol	Outside Half			NL	9 (2)	41	-	7	9	-
							NC	1	6	-	-	2	-
							ES	3 (2)	30	-	3	8	-
			Harlequins	Outside Half			NL	38(27)	436	4	85	82	-
							NC	6(2)	47	1	12	5	1
							ES	6(0)	77	1	12	16	-
							HC	4(3)	23	-	4	5	-
Gary	Johnson	24.04.84	England	193cm	106 kg								
			London Irish	Lock			NL	9(17)	-	-	-	-	-
							NC	3(3)	-	-	-	-	-
							HC	1(5)	-	-	-	-	-
			London Welsh	Lock			NC	0(1)	-	-	-	-	-
			Esher	Lock			NL	4(1)	5	1	-	-	-
							NC	1(0)	-	-	-	-	-
Census	Johnson	01.01.82	Samoa										
			Saracens	Prop			NL	33(11)	20	4	-	-	-
							NC	4(2)	5	1	-	-	-
							ES	9(1)	5	1	-	-	-
							HC	4(2)	5	1	-	-	-
			Biarritz	Prop			HC	3(0)	-	-	-	-	-
Ceri	Jones	19.06.77	Wales										
			Harlequins	Prop			NL	116(16)	100	20	-	-	-
							NC	8(1)	10	2	-	-	-
							ES	8(4)	15	3	-	-	-
							HC	17(1)	-	-	-	-	-
			Newport	Prop			ES	1(0)	-	-	-	-	-
							HC	3(7)	-	-	-	-	-
Chris	Jones	24.08.80	England	201cm	111 kg								
			Sale Sharks	Lock			NL	124(12)	90	18	-	-	-
							NC	11(1)	10	2	-	-	-
							ES	8(6)	-	-	-	-	-
							HC	25(4)	5	1	-	-	-
Steve J	Jones	01.09.79	Scotland	183cm	83 kg								
			Newcastle	Outside Half			NL	17(9)	15	-	3	2	1
							NC	5(0)	7	1	1	-	-
							ES	7(1)	38	1	9	5	-
			Scottish Borders	Outside Half			HC	3(3)	4	-	2	-	-
Ben	Kay	14.12.75	England	198cm	112 kg								
			Leicester Tigers	Lock			NL	131(23)	35	7	-	-	-
							NC	19(1)	5	1	-	-	-
							HC	54(9)	10	2	-	-	-
			Waterloo	Lock			NL	44(1)	-	-	-	-	-
Benjamin	Kayser	26.07.84	France										
			Leicester Tigers	Hooker			NL	17(16)	5	1	-	-	-
							NC	3(2)	-	-	-	-	-
							HC	9(4)	-	-	-	-	-
			Stade Francais	Hooker			HC	3(10)	10	2	-	-	-
Rudi	Keil	08.12.77	South Africa										
			Sale Sharks	Centre			NL	11(7)	5	1	-	-	-
							NC	4(2)	5	1	-	-	-
							HC	1 (3)	5	1	-	-	-
							ES	3(2)	-	-	-	-	-
			Gloucester	Centre			NL	11(5)	10	2	-	-	-
							NC	1(0)	-	-	-	-	-
							HC	0(3)	-	-	-	-	-
			Natal Sharks	Centre									

PLAYERS - PREMIERSHIP

						Comp	Apps	Pts	T	P	C	DG
Nick	**Kennedy**	19.08.81	England	203cm	119 kg							
			London Irish	Lock		NL	83(18)	10	2	-	-	-
						NC	9(2)	-	-	-	-	-
						ES	10(3)	-	-	-	-	-
						HC	11(1)	5	1	-	-	-
Olly	**Kohn**	19.05.81	England	201cm	123 kg							
			Harlequins	Lock		NL	44(2)	5	1	-	-	-
						NC	4(0)	-	-	-	-	-
						ES	4(1)	5	1	-	-	-
						HC	5(2)	-	-	-	-	-
			Bristol	Lock		NL	21(9)	10	2	-	-	-
						NC	5(1)	-	-	-	-	-
						ES	0(2)	-	-	-	-	-
			Plymouth Albion	Lock		NL	12(14)	25	5	-	-	-
						NC	1(2)	-	-	-	-	-
Andy	**Kyriacou**	04.01.83	England	180cm	105 kg							
			Saracens	Hooker		NL	2(18)	-	-	-	-	-
						NC	0(5)	5	1	-	-	-
						ES	1(4)	-	-	-	-	-
						HC	0(3)	-	-	-	-	-
			Munster	Hooker		HC	0(4)	5	1	-	-	-
			Leeds	Hooker		NL	0(2)	-	-	-	-	-
			Sale Sharks	Hooker		HC	0(1)	-	-	-	-	-
Tonga	**Laa'aetoa**	04.03.80	Tonga									
			London Irish	Prop		NL	39(23)	5	1	-	-	-
						NC	4(2)	-	-	-	-	-
						HC	9(5)	-	-	-	-	-
						ES	5 (1)	-	-	-	-	-
			Nottingham	Prop		NL	29(10)	15	3	-	-	-
						NC	1(2)	-	-	-	-	-
			Orrell	Prop		NL	17(1)	-	-	-	-	-
						NC	4(0)	-	-	-	-	-
Ryan	**Lamb**	18.05.86	England	175cm	86 kg							
			Gloucester	Outside Half		NL	43(12)	351	8	52	65	4
						NC	5(1)	26	1	3	3	2
						ES	3(0)	32	-	7	6	-
						HC	15(3)	141	5	25	22	-
			Pertemps Bees	Outside Half		NL	3(13)	36	1	8	5	-
						NC	2(0)	10	1	1	1	-
Rory	**Lamont**	10.10.82	Scotland									
			Sale Sharks	Right Wing		NL	11(0)	20	4	-	-	-
						NC	2(1)	5	1	-	-	-
						ES	3(0)	20	4	-	-	-
						HC	3 (0)	-	-	-	-	-
			Glasgow Cal.	Full Back		NC	4(0)	5	1	-	-	-
						ES	7(0)	25	5	-	-	-
						HC	5(0)	10	2	-	-	-
Sean	**Lamont**	15.01.81	Scotland									
			Northampton	Right Wing		NL	38(6)	80	16	-	-	-
						NC	4(0)	5	1	-	-	-
						ES	8(1)	10	2	-	-	-
						HC	3 (0)	-	-	-	-	-
			Glasgow Cal.	Full Back		ES	4(0)	15	3	-	-	-
						HC	5(0)	15	3	-	-	-
Rory	**Lawson**	12.03.81	Scotland									
			Gloucester	Scrum Half		NL	33(19)	30	6	-	-	-
						NC	7(2)	10	2	-	-	-
						HC	9(9)	5	1	-	-	-
			Edinburgh Reivers	Scrum Half		HC	5(7)	5	1	-	-	-

PLAYERS - PREMIERSHIP

					Comp	Apps	Pts	T	P	C	DG
Scott	**Lawson**	28.09.81	Scotland								
			Gloucester	Hooker	NL	4 (2)	-	-	-	-	-
					NC	1 (2)	5	1	-	-	-
					HC	1 (3)	-	-	-	-	-
			Sale Sharks	Hooker	NL	1(4)	-	-	-	-	-
					NC	2(0)	-	-	-	-	-
					ES	1(3)	-	-	-	-	-
			Glasgow Cal.	Hooker	ES	3(5)	-	-	-	-	-
					HC	6(6)	5	1	-	-	-
David	**Lemi**	10.02.82	Samoa								
			Bristol	Right Wing	NL	64(3)	168	33	-	-	1
					NC	2(0)	10	2-	-	-	-
					ES	9(1)	50	8	2	2	-
					HC	4(0)	10	2	-	-	-
Daniel	**Leo**	02.10.82	Samoa								
			London Wasps	Lock	NL	28(21)	15	3	-	-	-
					NC	3(4)	-	-	-	-	-
					HC	2(9)	-	-	-	-	-
Francisco	**Leonelli Morey**	03.05.78	Argentina								
			Saracens	Left Wing	NL	12(2)	40	8	-	-	-
					NC	4(0)	5	1	-	-	-
					HC	2(1)	5	1	-	-	-
					ES	1 (1)	-	-	-	-	-
			Edinburgh Reivers	Left Wing	HC	3(1)	5	1	-	-	-
			Glasgow Cal.	Left Wing	ES	1(0)	5	1	-	-	-
Ben	**Lewitt**	23.10.79	England	191cm	97kg						
			Northampton	Back row	NL	20(20)	20	4	-	-	-
					NC	6 (2)	5	1	-	-	-
					ES	3	-	-	-	-	-
					HC	2(2)	-	-	-	-	-
			Bedford Blues	Back row	NL	20	20	4	-	-	-
					NC	4	10	2	-	-	-
			Orrell	Back row	NL	44(6)	40	8	-	-	-
					NC	6	5	1	-	-	-
			Rugby Lions	Back row	NL	13(5)	-	-	-	-	-
			Leicester Tigers	Back row	NL	(1)	-	-	-	-	-
					NC	(1)	-	-	-	-	-
Josh	**Lewsey**	30.11.76	England	180cm	85 kg						
			London Wasps	Full Back	NL	163(11)	230	46	-	-	-
					NC	16(1)	25	5	-	-	-
					ES	4(1)	10	2	-	-	-
					HC	46(3)	80	16	-	-	-
			Bristol	Full Back	NL	22(3)	46	7	1	3	-
					NC	1(0)	-	-	-	-	-
					ES	5(0)	2	-	1	-	-
Scott	**Linklater**	25.02.79	New Zealand								
			Bristol	Prop	NL	29(12)	30	6	-	-	-
					NC	1(3)	-	-	-	-	-
					ES	2(1)	-	-	-	-	-
					HC	0(2)	-	-	-	-	-
			Waikato Chiefs	Prop							
Michael	**Lipman**	16.01.80	England	185cm	99 kg						
			Bath	Openside Flanker	NL	76(6)	50	10	-	-	-
					NC	6(0)	-	-	-	-	-
					ES	15(1)	15	3	-	-	-
					HC	8(3)	20	4	-	-	-
			Bristol	Openside Flanker	NL	21(5)	5	1	-	-	-
					NC	0(1)	-	-	-	-	-
					ES	1(3)	-	-	-	-	-
					HC	2(2)	-	-	-	-	-

793

PLAYERS - PREMIERSHIP

						Comp	Apps	Pts	T	P	C	DG
Leon	**Lloyd**	22.09.77	England	193cm	93 kg							
			Gloucester	Centre		NL	6(2)	25	5	-	-	-
						NC	1(0)	-	-	-	-	-
						HC	1(2)	-	-	-	-	-
			Leicester Tigers	Centre		NL	146(16)	175	35	-	-	-
						NC	18(2)	55	11	-	-	-
						HC	44(5)	95	19	-	-	-
Nick	**Lloyd**	12.10.76	England									
			Saracens	Prop		NL	29(31)	10	2	-	-	-
						NC	8(2)	-	-	-	-	-
						ES	8(5)	5	1	-	-	-
						HC	7(1)	-	-	-	-	-
			Rotherham	Prop		NL	41(4)	20	4	-	-	-
						NC	3(3)	10	2	-	-	-
						ES	4(1)	5	1	-	-	-
			Wakefield	Prop		NL	82(7)	60	12	-	-	-
						NC	6(0)	5	1	-	-	-
Andy	**Long**	02.09.77	England	181cm	99 kg							
			Newcastle	Hooker		NL	53(30)	15	3	-	-	-
						NC	2(8)	-	-	-	-	-
						ES	9(11)	10	2	-	-	-
						HC	5(0)	-	-	-	-	-
			Bath	Hooker		NL	36(45)	20	4	-	-	-
						NC	1(4)	-	-	-	-	-
						ES	4(3)	-	-	-	-	-
						HC	9(11)	5	1	-	-	-
			Rotherham	Hooker		NL	6(4)	5	1	-	-	-
			Munster	Hooker								
Erik	**Lund**	03.07.79	Norway									
			Leeds	Lock		NL	25(7)	10	2	-	-	-
						NC	7(1)	10	2	-	-	-
						ES	6(0)	-	-	-	-	-
			Rotherham	Lock		NL	18(7)	20	4	-	-	-
			Sedgley Park	Lock		NL	58(1)	5	1	-	-	-
						NC	1(0)	-	-	-	-	-
			Fylde	Lock		NL	25(2)	15	3	-	-	-
						NC	1(0)	-	-	-	-	-
			Manchester	Lock		NL	4(5)	-	-	-	-	-
						NC	0(1)	-	-	-	-	-
Hal	**Luscombe**	23.02.81	Wales									
			Worcester	Centre		NL	4 (2)	-	-	-	-	-
						ES	2 (1)	-	-	-	-	-
			Harlequins	Centre		NL	22(2)	25	5	-	-	-
						NC	2(0)	-	-	-	-	-
						ES	4(1)	5	1	-	-	-
						HC	4(0)	5	1	-	-	-
			Newport	Centre		HC	3(1)	-	-	-	-	-
			Gwent Dragons	Centre		NC	1(0)	-	-	-	-	-
						HC	13(0)	15	3	-	-	-
Aleki	**Lutui**	01.07.78	Tonga									
			Worcester	Hooker		NL	36(15)	30	6	-	-	-
						NC	5(1)	5	1	-	-	-
						ES	16(4)	15	3	-	-	-
			Waikato Chiefs	Hooker								
Viliami	**Ma'asi**	31.07.78	Tonga									
			Leeds	Hooker		NL	20(10)	20	4	-	-	-
						NC	1(7)	-	-	-	-	-
						ES	3(1)	15	3	-	-	-
			Cornish Pirates	Hooker		NL	86(29)	115	23	-	-	-
						NC	8(0)	15	3	-	-	-

PLAYERS - PREMIERSHIP

						Comp	Apps	Pts	T	P	C	DG
Joe	**Maddock**	20.12.78	New Zealand	173cm	86 kg							
			Bath	Right Wing		NL	69(10)	115	23	-	-	-
						NC	5(1)	13	2	-	1	-
						ES	12(1)	25	5	-	-	-
						HC	7(0)	15	3	-	-	-
			Canterbury Crusaders	Right Wing								
Chris	**Malone**	08.01.78	Australia	182cm	89 kg							
			Harlequins	Outside Half		NL	18(10)	182	3	34	30	32
						NC	2(2)	17	-	4	3	-
						HC	6(2)	46	-	8	10	-
			Bath	Outside Half		NL	72(13)	479	8	38	99	22
						NC	6(2)	40	1	4	9	-
						ES	7(12)	49	1	7	10	-
						HC	11(3)	37	-	2	8	3
			Bristol	Outside Half		NL	1(0)	14	-	4	2	-
			Exeter	Outside Half		NL	21(1)	247	5	45	37	7
						NC	4(0)	32	-	7	6	-
Seilala	**Mapusua**	27.02.80	Samoa									
			London Irish	Centre		NL	52(0)	55	11	-	-	-
						NC	2(1)	5	1	-	-	-
						ES	5	15	3	-	-	-
						HC	12(0)	5	1	-	-	-
			Otago Highlanders	Centre								
Justin	**Marshall**	05.08.73	New Zealand	179cm	94 kg							
			Saracens	Scrum Half		NL	7 (2)	3	-	-	-	1
			Leeds	Scrum Half		NL	19(0)	10	2	-	-	-
						HC	5(0)	11	1	-	-	2
			Ospreys	Scrum Half		NC	6(2)	10	2	-	-	-
						HC	12(1)	20	4	-	-	-
			Canterbury Crusaders	Scrum Half								
Tajiv	**Masson**	27.02.85	England	180cm	94 kg							
			Harlequins	Centre		NL	21(5)	25	5	-	-	-
						NC	5(2)	5	1	-	-	-
						HC	1(4)	-	-	-	-	-
			London Welsh	Centre		NL	1(0)	5	1	-	-	-
Aaron	**Mauger**	29.11.80	New Zealand	181cm	93 kg							
			Leicester Tigers	Centre		NL	27(1)	20	4	-	-	-
						NC	1(0)	-	-	-	-	-
						HC	7(2)	15	3	-	-	-
			Canterbury Crusaders	Centre								
Tom	**May**	05.02.79	England	177cm	92 kg							
			Newcastle	Centre		NL	189(4)	383	49	21	26	6
						NC	23(0)	33	6	-	-	1
						ES	38(4)	80	11	2	4	3
						HC	12(0)	15	3	-	-	-
Chris	**Mayor**	19.05.82	England									
			Northampton	Winger		NL	3 (10)	-	-	-	-	-
						NC	3 (0)	5	1	-	-	-
						ES	3 (2)	15	3	-	-	-
			Sale Sharks	Right Wing		NL	41(37)	50	10	-	-	-
						NC	5(6)	15	3	-	-	-
						ES	7(4)	55	11	-	-	-
						HC	9(5)	5	1	-	-	-
Mike	**MacDonald**	27.11.80	United States									
			Leeds	Prop		NL	59(8)	100	20	-	-	-
						NC	3(1)	15	3	-	-	-
						ES	6(0)	-	-	-	-	-
			Worcester	Prop		NL	1(7)	-	-	-	-	-
						ES	0(6)	-	-	-	-	-

PLAYERS - PREMIERSHIP

						Comp	Apps	Pts	T	P	C	DG
Luke	**McAlister**	28.08.83	New Zealand	180cm	95 kg							
			Sale Sharks	Centre		NL	23(2)	110	2	8	28	-
						NC	1(0)	8	1	-	1	-
						HC	6	45	1	5	9	1
Prev. Club: Auckland Blues, Outside Half						ES	4(0)	41	2	5	7	-
Joe	**McDonnell**	01.03.73	New Zealand	180cm	110 kg							
			Newcastle	Prop		NL	24(5)	5	1	-	-	-
						NC	4(2)	-	-	-	-	-
						ES	8(0)	5	1	-	-	-
Prev. Clubs: Otago Highlanders, Prop; Wellington Hurricanes, Prop												
Tom	**McGee**	07.09.79	Scotland									
			Leeds	Prop		NL	36(17)	10	2	-	-	-
						NC	5(2)	5-	1-	-	-	-
Prev. Club: Edinburgh Reivers						ES	2(3)	-	-	-	-	-
Lee	**Mears**	05.03.79	England	176cm	90 kg							
			Bath	Hooker		NL	61(53)	35	7	-	-	-
						NC	2(8)	5	1	-	-	-
						ES	15(12)	-	-	-	-	-
						HC	15(4)	-	-	-	-	-
Tom	**Mercey**	15.06.87	England									
			Saracens	Prop		NL	9(14)	-	-	-	-	-
						NC	3(4)	-	-	-	-	-
						ES	2(5)	-	-	-	-	-
						HC	0(3)	-	-	-	-	-
Ugo	**Monye**	13.04.83	England	186cm	84 kg							
			Harlequins	Left Wing		NL	81(14)	235	47	-	-	-
						NC	8(0)	30	6	-	-	-
						ES	9(1)	15	3	-	-	-
						HC	10(0)	15	3	-	-	-
Nils	**Mordt**	05.12.83	England	185cm	94 kg							
			Northampton	Centre		NL	(1)	-	-	-	-	-
						NC	2(0)	-	-	-	-	-
			London Irish	Centre		NL	33(25)	18	1	5	1	-
						NC	3(2)	5	1	-	-	-
						ES	6(3)	2	-	1	-	-
						EC	0(1)	-	-	-	-	-
Alejandro	**Moreno**	26.04.73	Italy									
			Leicester Tigers	Prop		NL	19(12)	-	-	-	-	-
						NC	0(5)	-	-	-	-	-
						HC	6(3)	-	-	-	-	-
			Worcester	Prop		NL	13(9)	-	-	-	-	-
						NC	1(2)	-	-	-	-	-
			Agen	Prop		ES	1(0)	-	-	-	-	-
			Brive	Prop		ES	0(5)	-	-	-	-	-
			Perpignan	Prop		HC	2(2)	-	-	-	-	-
Olly	**Morgan**	03.11.85	England	188cm	91 kg							
			Gloucester	Full Back		NL	44(9)	75	15	-	-	-
						NC	6(1)	5	1	-	-	-
						ES	6(0)	5	1	-	-	-
						HC	10(2)	10	2	-	-	-
			Bracknell	Full Back		NL	1(0)	5	1	-	-	-
			Gloucester O.B.	Full Back		NL	2(2)	-	-	-	-	-
Darren	**Morris**	24.09.74	Wales									
			Worcester	Prop		NL	26(18)	-	-	-	-	-
						NC	5(2)	-	-	-	-	-
						ES	11(2)	5	1	-	-	-
			Leicester Tigers	Prop		NL	37(20)	5	1	-	-	-
						NC	2(0)	-	-	-	-	-
						HC	12(7)	-	-	-	-	-
			Swansea	Prop		HC	18(2)	-	-	-	-	-
			Neath	Prop								

PLAYERS - PREMIERSHIP

						Comp	Apps	Pts	T	P	C	DG
Matt	**Mullan**	15.03.86	England	183cm	105 kg							
			Worcester	Prop		NL	21(10)	10	2	-	-	-
						NC	3(0)	-	-	-	-	-
						ES	7(6)	15	3	-	-	-
			Pertemps Bees	Prop		NL	0(5)	-	-	-	-	-
Geordan	**Murphy**	19.04.78	Ireland	183cm	79 kg							
			Leicester Tigers	Full Back		NL	134(12)	393	52	26	23	4
						NC	11(3)	8	1	-	-	1
						HC	62(1)	142	22	10	4	-
Dan	**Murphy**	27.10.85	England									
			London Irish	Prop		NL	7(16)	-	-	-	-	-
						NC	2(2)	-	-	-	-	-
						HC	4(3)	5	1	-	-	-
						ES	2 (2)	-	-	-	-	-
			Bracknell	Prop		NL	12(6)	10	2	-	-	-
						NC	0(1)	-	-	-	-	-
			Sutton	Prop		NL	3(2)	-	-	-	-	-
Johne	**Murphy**	10.11.84	Ireland	185cm	92 kg							
			Leicester Tigers	Right Wing		NL	43(7)	76	13	1	3	-
						NC	8(2)	25	5	-	-	-
						HC	6(5)	20	4	-	-	-
Phil	**Murphy**	01.04.80	England		112 kg							
			Worcester	Lock		NL	43(22)	10	2	-	-	-
						NC	3(2)	-	-	-	-	-
						ES	14(4)	-	-	-	-	-
			Leeds	Lock		NL	50(26)	10	2	-	-	-
						NC	1(4)	-	-	-	-	-
						ES	7(2)	-	-	-	-	-
						HC	5(1)	-	-	-	-	-
			Orrell	Lock		NL	6(1)	-	-	-	-	-
			Wakefield	Lock		NL	3(0)	-	-	-	-	-
Euan	**Murray**	07.08.80	Scotland									
			Northampton	Prop		NL	23(5)	10	2	-	-	-
						NC	3(2)	-	-	-	-	-
						ES	7 (0)	-	-	-	-	-
			Glasgow	Prop		ES	9	-	-	-	-	-
						HC	6(2)	-	-	-	-	-
Kearnan	**Myall**	15.12.86	England									
			Leeds	Lock		NL	49(16)	40	8	-	-	-
						NC	6(1)	5	1	-	-	-
						ES	1(0)	-	-	-	-	-
Stephen	**Myler**	21.07.84	England									
			Northampton	Fly half		NL	35(17)	363	9	75	53	3
						NC	5(4)	30	-	3	8	-
						ES	9	135	-	25	24	1
						HC	1(1)	2	-	1	-	-
Luke	**Narraway**	07.09.83	England	190cm	100 kg							
			Gloucester	Openside Flanker		NL	46(16)	20	4	-	-	-
						NC	4(3)	-	-	-	-	-
						ES	3(4)	5	1	-	-	-
						HC	13(3)	20	4	-	-	-
			Pertemps Bees	Openside Flanker		NL	1(3)	10	2	-	-	-
			Cheltenham	Openside Flanker		NL	9(0)	5	1	-	-	-
Carlos	**Nieto**	28.04.76	Italy									
			Gloucester	Prop		NL	34(4)	-	-	-	-	-
						NC	4(2)	-	-	-	-	-
						HC	19(0)	-	-	-	-	-
			Viadana	Prop		ES	5(2)	-	-	-	-	-
			Gran Parma Rugby	Prop		ES	8(3)	-	-	-	-	-

PLAYERS - PREMIERSHIP

							Comp	Apps	Pts	T	P	C	DG
Jamie	Noon	09.05.79	England Newcastle		177cm Centre	86 kg	NL NC ES HC	157(10) 19(0) 47(2) 11(0)	178 25 80 5	35 5 16 1	- - - -	- - - -	1 - - -
Rhys	Oakley	16.09.80	Wales Leeds		Openside Flanker		NL NC ES	69(5) 7(0) 4(1)	50 5 -	10 1 -	- - -	- - -	- - -
			Bristol		Openside Flanker		NL NC HC	13(4) 1(0) 5(1)	- - -	- - -	- - -	- - -	- - -
			Gwent Dragons		No. 8		NC HC	0(2) 4(8)	- -	- -	- -	- -	- -
Topsy	Ojo	28.07.85	England London Irish		183cm Right Wing	85 kg	NL NC ES HC	63(7) 4(0) 11(1) 8(1)	115 - 55 5	23 - 11 1	- - - -	- - - -	- - - -
Fabio	Ongaro	23.09.77	Italy Saracens		Hooker		NL NC ES HC	27(5) 3(1) 11(1) 3(5)	5 - - -	1 - - -	- - - -	- - - -	- - - -
			Benetton Treviso		Hooker		ES HC	5(3) 17(6)	- -	- -	- -	- -	- -
David	Paice	24.11.83	England London Irish		185cm Hooker	101 kg	NL NC ES HC	40(26) 3(3) 3(10) 11(2)	25 - 5 -	5 - 1 -	- - - -	- - - -	- - - -
Fosi	Palaamo	23.08.76	Samoa Leeds		Prop		NL NC ES	14(12) 3(2) 2(1)	10 - 5	2 - 1	- - -	- - -	- - -
Tom	Palmer	27.03.79	England London Wasps		Lock	105 kg	NL NC HC	32(6) 2(0) 11(2)	15 - -	3 - -	- - -	- - -	- - -
			Leeds		Lock		NL NC ES HC	142(12) 13(1) 7(6) 9(0)	85 10 5 10	17 2 1 2	- - - -	- - - -	- - - -
Geoffrey	Parling	28.10.83	England Newcastle		195cm Lock	105 kg	NL NC ES HC	60(25) 3(1) 13(9) 1(0)	30 - 10 -	6 - 2 -	- - - -	- - - -	- - - -
Jeremy	Paul	14.03.77	Australia Gloucester		183cm Hooker	117 kg	NL NC HC	1(5) 2(0) 0(1)	- - -	- - -	- - -	- - -	- - -
Prev. Club: ACT, Hooker													
Danny	Paul	15.12.86	England Leeds		Prop		NL NC ES	11(34) 2(2) 5(3)	40 - -	8 - -	- - -	- - -	- - -
			Otley		Prop		NL	0(1)	-	-	-	-	-

PLAYERS - PREMIERSHIP

							Comp	Apps	Pts	T	P	C	DG
Tim	Payne	29.04.79	England	185cm	117 kg								
			London Wasps	Prop			NL	97(14)	15	3	-	-	-
							NC	10(1)	5	1	-	-	-
							HC	31(4)	15	3	-	-	-
			Bristol	Prop			NL	2(6)	-	-	-	-	-
							NC	0(1)	-	-	-	-	-
			Coventry	Prop			NL	12(11)	5	1	-	-	-
							NC	2(2)	-	-	-	-	-
			Cardiff	Prop			HC	3(2)	-	-	-	-	-
Jonathan	Pendlebury	15.01.83	England										
			Leeds Carnegie	Lock			NL	23(5)	15	3	-	-	-
							NC	2(1)	-	-	-	-	-
			Moseley	Lock			NL	0(2)	-	-	-	-	-
			Gloucester	Lock			NL	9(20)	-	-	-	-	-
							NC	1(1)	-	-	-	-	-
							EC	1(1)	-	-	-	-	-
							ES	4(3)	-	-	-	-	-
			Rotherham	Lock			NL	11(14)	10	2	-	-	-
							NC	2(0)	-	-	-	-	-
							ES	5(1)	5	1	-	-	-
			Bath	Lock			NL	0(1)	-	-	-	-	-
Chris	Pennell	26.04.87	England										
			Worcester	Full Back			NL	13(6)	17	1	-	4	-
							NC	3(0)	-	-	-	-	-
							ES	5(2)	15	3	-	-	-
Rod	Penney	22.07.78	England										
			Saracens	Centre			NL	34(19)	55	11	-	-	-
							NC	4(1)	10	2	-	-	-
							ES	6(3)	20	4	-	-	-
							HC	4(1)	15	3	-	-	-
			London Irish	Centre			NL	16(2)	10	2	-	-	-
							NC	1(0)	-	-	-	-	-
							ES	5(2)	5	1	-	-	-
			Orrell	Centre			NL	22(1)	45	9	-	-	-
							NC	3(0)	10	2	-	-	-
			Dudley Kingwinsford	Centre			NL	5(1)	30	6	-	-	-
James	Percival	09.02.83	England										
			Harlequins	Lock			NL	18(4)	-	-	-	-	-
							NC	3(0)	-	-	-	-	-
							HC	8(0)	5	1	-	-	-
			Bedford	Lock			NL	12(0)	5	1	-	-	-
							NC	2(0)	5	1	-	-	-
			Coventry	Lock			NL	14(2)	5	1	-	-	-
							NC	0(1)	-	-	-	-	-
			Worcester	Lock			NL	0(2)	-	-	-	-	-
							NC	1(1)	-	-	-	-	-
Andy	Perry	28.12.74	England	196cm	117 kg								
			Newcastle	Lock			NL	47(11)	5	1	-	-	-
							NC	5(1)	-	-	-	-	-
							ES	17(6)	-	-	-	-	-
			Plymouth Albion	Lock			NL	74(3)	60	12	-	-	-
							NC	6(2)	10	2	-	-	-
			Exeter	Lock			NL	13(17)	5	1	-	-	-
							NC	1(2)	-	-	-	-	-
Shaun	Perry	04.05.78	England										
			Bristol	Scrum Half			NL	53(3)	50	10	-	-	-
							NC	1(0)	-	-	-	-	-
							ES	8(0)	20	4	-	-	-
							HC	4(0)	-	-	-	-	-
			Coventry	Scrum Half			NL	31(7)	35	7	-	-	-
							NC	2(0)	5	1	-	-	-
			Dudley Kingwinsford	Scrum Half			NL	70(0)	266	50	5	2	-
							NC	3(0)	20	4	-	-	-

PLAYERS - PREMIERSHIP

							Comp	Apps	Pts	T	P	C	DG
Ollie	**Phillips**	08.09.82	England	180cm		92 kg							
			Newcastle	Right Wing			NL	20(12)	45	9	-	-	-
							NC	4(0)	15	3	-	-	-
							ES	4(4)	60	12	-	-	-
			Otley	Right Wing			NL	6(0)	-	-	-	-	-
Matt	**Powell**	08.05.78	Wales	178cm		89 kg							
			Worcester	Scrum Half			NL	74(33)	40	8	-	-	-
							NC	9(3)	2	-	1	-	-
							ES	23(6)	15	3	-	-	-
			Harlequins	Scrum Half			NL	26(20)	5	1	-	-	-
							NC	6(2)	-	-	-	-	-
							ES	9(2)	5	1	-	-	-
							HC	1(4)	-	-	-	-	-
			Saracens	Scrum Half			NL	5(12)	10	2	-	-	-
							NC	1(0)	5	1	-	-	-
							HC	1(0)	5	1	-	-	-
Ryan	**Powell**	01.07.80	Wales										
			Worcester	Scrum Half			NL	26(15)	5	1	-	-	-
							NC	3(2)	-	-	-	-	-
							ES	9(6)	15	3	-	-	-
			Cardiff	Scrum Half			NC	3(2)	5	1	-	-	-
							HC	12(7)	5	1	-	-	-
			Ebbw Vale	Scrum Half			HC	1(0)	-	-	-	-	-
Adam	**Powell**	01.01.87	England										
			Saracens	Centre			NL	38(15)	55	11	-	-	-
							NC	4(1)	5	1	-	-	-
							ES	6(2)	10	2	-	-	-
							HC	1(3)	-	-	-	-	-
Akapusi	**Qera**	24.04.84	Fiji										
			Gloucester	Openside Flanker			NL	14(3)	30	6	-	-	-
							NC	3(1)	-	-	-	-	-
							HC	6(0)	15	3	-	-	-
			Pertemps Bees	Openside Flanker			NL	25(2)	80	16	-	-	-
							NC	3(1)	5	1	-	-	-
Seru	**Rabeni**	27.12.78	Fiji	188cm		95 kg							
			Leicester Tigers	Centre			NL	29(8)	60	12	-	-	-
							NC	3(1)	5	1	-	-	-
Prev. Club: Otago Highlanders							EC	11(7)	25	5	-	-	-
Alex	**Rae**	02.06.86	England	196cm		99kg							
			Northampton	Back row			NL	28(10)	5	1	-	-	-
							NC	6	-	-	-	-	-
Dale	**Rasmussen**	06.07.77	Samoa										
			Worcester	Centre			NL	93(2)	45	9	-	-	-
							NC	4(1)	-	-	-	-	-
							ES	20(1)	30	6	-	-	-
			Exeter	Centre			NL	14(0)	15	3	-	-	-
Kameli	**Ratuvou**	06.11.82	Fiji										
			Saracens	Left Wing			NL	40(2)	70	14	-	-	-
							NC	4(1)	20	4	-	-	-
							ES	11(1)	30	6	-	-	-
							HC	6(2)	25	5	-	-	-
Mosese	**Raulini**	27.06.75	Fiji										
			Saracens	Scrum Half			NL	7(48)	15	3	-	-	-
							NC	6(4)	10	2	-	-	-
							ES	5(7)	10	2	-	-	-
							HC	1(5)	-	-	-	-	-
Faan	**Rautenbach**	22.02.76	South Africa	190cm		128 kg							
			London Irish	Prop			NL	42(3)	10	2	-	-	-
							NC	3(0)	-	-	-	-	-
							ES	3(1)	-	-	-	-	-
Prev. Clubs: Western Stormers, Cats							HC	4(2)	-	-	-	-	-

PLAYERS - PREMIERSHIP

						Comp	Apps	Pts	T	P	C	DG
Rob	**Rawlinson**	23.08.76	England		90 kg							
			Leeds	Hooker		NL	101(58)	25	5	-	-	-
						NC	4(4)	5	1	-	-	-
						ES	9(6)	10	2	-	-	-
						HC	3(5)	5	1	-	-	-
			Orrell	Hooker		NL	22(13)	-	-	-	-	-
						ES	1(0)	-	-	-	-	-
Greg	**Rawlinson**	14.08.78	New Zealand									
			Worcester	Lock		NL	31(3)	15	3	-	-	-
						NC	3(0)	-	-	-	-	-
Prev. Club: Auckland Blues						ES	12(1)	5	1	-	-	-
Eion	**Redden**	20.11.80	Ireland									
			London Wasps	Scrum Half		NL	47(15)	40	8	-	-	-
						NC	6(3)	5	1	-	-	-
						HC	23(1)	25	5	-	-	-
			Munster	Scrum Half		HC	0(8)	-	-	-	-	-
			Connacht	Scrum Half		ES	11(0)	10	2	-	-	-
Tom	**Rees**	11.09.84	England	182cm	98 kg							
			London Wasps	Openside Flanker		NL	48(12)	50	10	-	-	-
						NC	8(1)	10	2	-	-	-
						EC	18(3)	20	4	-	-	-
Mark	**Regan**	28.01.72	England	178cm	95 kg							
			Bristol	Hooker		NL	79(7)	30	6	-	-	-
						NC	3(0)	-	-	-	-	-
						ES	9(0)	-	-	-	-	-
						HC	6(0)	-	-	-	-	-
			Leeds	Hooker		NL	40(9)	15	3	-	-	-
						NC	7(0)	5	1	-	-	-
						ES	4(3)	5	1	-	-	-
						HC	6(0)	5	1	-	-	-
			Bath	Hooker		NL	75(21)	35	7	-	-	-
						NC	4(0)	-	-	-	-	-
						HC	19(7)	-	-	-	-	-
Bruce	**Reihana**	06.04.76	New Zealand	184cm	93kg							
			Northampton	FB/Winger		NL	135(4)	730	55	106	81	-
						NC	13	71	4	6	13	-
						HC	14	33	5	1	2	-
						ES	14	89	6	16	9	-
Peter	**Richards**	10.03.78	England	178cm	83 kg							
			London Irish	Scrum Half		NL	28(16)	25	5	-	-	-
						NC	4(2)	5	1	-	-	-
						ES	7(2)	20	4	-	-	-
						HC	7(1)	10	2	-	-	-
			Gloucester	Scrum Half		NL	25(11)	40	8	-	-	-
						NC	1(1)	10	2	-	-	-
						ES	6(2)	30	6	-	-	-
						HC	4(2)	5	1	-	-	-
			Harlequins	Scrum Half		NL	23(7)	13	2	-	-	1
						NC	2(3)	5	1	-	-	-
						ES	0(2)	-	-	-	-	-
						HC	2(0)	-	-	-	-	-
			London Wasps	Scrum Half		NL	19(15)	30	6	-	-	-
						NC	2(1)	5	1	-	-	-
						HC	3(6)	-	-	-	-	-
			Bristol	Scrum Half		NL	3(15)	5	1	-	-	-
						NC	1(0)	-	-	-	-	-
						HC	0(4)	-	-	-	-	-
			Benetton Treviso	Scrum Half		HC	2 (1)	5	1	-	-	-

PLAYERS - PREMIERSHIP

						Comp	Apps	Pts	T	P	C	DG
Oriol	**Ripol**	06.09.75	Spain									
			Sale Sharks	Right Wing		NL	50(5)	65	13	-	-	-
						NC	5(0)	15	3	-	-	-
						ES	6(1)	15	3	-	-	-
						HC	5(2)	15	3	-	-	-
			Northampton	Right Wing		NL	21(8)	30	6	-	-	-
						NC	1(0)	-	-	-	-	-
						HC	6(3)	5	1	-	-	-
			Rotherham	Right Wing		NL	15(6)	75	15	-	-	-
						NC	1(0)	-	-	-	-	-
Eifion	**Roberts**	13.02.81	Wales									
			Sale Sharks	Prop		NL	34(17)	10	2	-	-	-
						NC	3(0)	-	-	-	-	-
						ES	4(3)	-	-	-	-	-
						HC	8(2)	5	1	-	-	-
Lee	**Robinson**	30.12.80	England									
			Bristol	Right Wing		NL	55(4)	85	17	-	-	-
						NC	5(0)	5	1	-	-	-
						ES	13(3)	70	14	-	-	-
						HC	2(0)	-	-	-	-	-
			Plymouth Albion	Right Wing		NL	49(5)	170	34	-	-	-
						NC	5(0)	30	6	-	-	-
Mark	**Robinson**	21.08.75	New Zealand	179cm	90kg							
			London Wasps	Scrum Half		NL	7 (5)	-	-	-	-	-
						NC	3 (0)	5	1	-	-	-
						HC	(2)	-	-	-	-	-
			Northampton	Scrum Half		NL	72(19)	95	19	-	-	-
						NC	3(6)	10	2	-	-	-
						ES	4	5	1	-	-	-
						HC	16(1)	15	3	-	-	-
Chris	**Robshaw**	04.06.86	England	188cm	92 kg							
			Harlequins	Blindside Flanker		NL	48(5)	35	7	-	-	-
						NC	5(1)	5	1	-	-	-
						HC	9(0)	5	1	-	-	-
George	**Robson**	04.11.85	England	196cm	109 kg							
			Harlequins	Lock		NL	22(15)	15	3	-	-	-
						NC	2(3)	5	1	-	-	-
						HC	3 (4)	5	1	-	-	-
					ES	0(1)	-	-	-	-	-	
			London Welsh	Lock		NL	9(0)	10	2	-	-	-
			Esher	Lock		NL	12(1)	-	-	-	-	-
Kieran	**Roche**	03.05.79	England	198cm	107 kg							
			London Irish	Lock		NL	56(26)	15	3	-	-	-
						NC	3(2)	-	-	-	-	-
						ES	13(6)	10	2	-	-	-
						HC	10(0)	5	1	-	-	-
			Rugby Lions	Lock		NL	1(0)	-	-	-	-	-
			Saracens	No. 8		NL	16(24)	-	-	-	-	-
						NC	1(3)	-	-	-	-	-
						ES	3(4)	15	3	-	-	-
						HC	0(1)	5	1	-	-	-
Gordon	**Ross**	08.03.78	Scotland									
			Saracens	Outside Half		NL	7(10)	79	1	10	17	1
						NC	5(0)	64	-	11	13	1
						HC	0(3)	-	-	-	-	-
						ES	2 (2)	29	-	7	5	-
			Leeds	Outside Half		NL	61(6)	442	7	49	93	10
						NC	7(1)	72	-	15	12	2
						ES	9(2)	91	-	32	9	-
						HC	9(2)	69	-	12	14	1
			Edinburgh Reivers	Outside Half		HC	4(2)	46	-	2	12	2
			Castres	Outside Half		HC	2(4)	23	-	7	3	-

PLAYERS - PREMIERSHIP

						Comp	Apps	Pts	T	P	C	DG
Mike	**Ross**	21.12.79	England									
			Harlequins	Prop		NL	58(4)	-	-	-	-	-
						NC	6(0)	-	-	-	-	-
						ES	5(0)	-	-	-	-	-
						HC	11(0)	-	-	-	-	-
John	**Rudd**	26.05.81	England	188cm	108 kg							
			Newcastle	Left Wing		NL	50(2)	25	5	-	-	-
						NC	7(1)	15	3	-	-	-
						ES	13(2)	20	4	-	-	-
			Northampton	Left Wing		NL	25(10)	20	4	-	-	-
						NC	1(0)	5	1	-	-	-
						ES	2(4)	15	3	-	-	-
						HC	6(0)	-	-	-	-	-
			Bedford	Left Wing		NL	11(5)	20	4	-	-	-
						NC	1(1)	5	1	-	-	-
			Harlequins	Left Wing		NL	0(1)	-	-	-	-	-
			London Wasps	Left Wing		NL	23(7)	27	5	1	-	-
						NC	2(0)	5	1	-	-	-
						ES	7(0)	25	5	-	-	-
						HC	3(3)	15	3	-	-	-
Brent	**Russell**	05.03.80	South Africa	174cm	78 kg							
			Saracens	Full Back		NL	8(2)	25	5	-	-	-
						NC	1(0)	-	-	-	-	-
						EC	5(0)	2	-	1	-	-
Prev. Clubs: Western Stormers, Natal Sharks												
Shaun	**Ruwers**	12.10.82	Other									
			Worcester	Prop		NL	1(6)	5	1	-	-	-
						NC	(1)	-	-	-	-	-
						ES	0(6)	-	-	-	-	-
			Waterloo	Prop		NL	36(8)	-	-	-	-	-
						NC	2(0)	-	-	-	-	-
Tom	**Ryder**	21.02.85	England	196cm	105 kg							
			Saracens	Lock		NL	30(21)	5	1	-	-	-
						NC	6(2)	-	-	-	-	-
						ES	3(3)	-	-	-	-	-
						HC	1(6)	-	-	-	-	-
			Leicester Tigers	Lock		NL	1(5)	-	-	-	-	-
			Bedford	Lock		NL	1(0)	-	-	-	-	-
			Orrell	Lock		NL	2(2)	-	-	-	-	-
Paul	**Sackey**	08.11.79	England	186cm	86 kg							
			London Wasps	Right Wing		NL	57(0)	140	28	-	-	-
						NC	5(0)	15	3	-	-	-
						HC	24(0)	55	11	-	-	-
			London Irish	Right Wing		NL	88(1)	150	30	-	-	-
						NC	12(0)	25	5	-	-	-
						ES	13(0)	30	6	-	-	-
						HC	6(0)	10	2	-	-	-
			Bedford	Right Wing		NL	14(3)	45	9	-	-	-
						NC	1(0)	-	-	-	-	-
						ES	3(0)	5	1	-	-	-
Matthew	**Salter**	02.12.76	England	194cm	100 kg							
			Bristol	Blindside Flanker		NL	115(13)	30	6	-	-	-
						NC	6(4)	10	2	-	-	-
						ES	16(4)	-	-	-	-	-
						HC	9(1)	-	-	-	-	-
			Leeds	Blindside Flanker		NL	16(3)	5	1	-	-	-
						NC	1(1)	-	-	-	-	-
						HC	1(1)	-	-	-	-	-
			West Hartlepool	Blindside Flanker		NL	5(2)	-	-	-	-	-

PLAYERS - PREMIERSHIP

							Comp	Apps	Pts	T	P	C	DG
Pat	**Sanderson**	06.09.77	England		191cm	104 kg							
			Worcester		Openside Flanker		NL	84(0)	50	10	-	-	-
							NC	3(1)	10	2	-	-	-
							ES	24(1)	50	10	-	-	-
			Harlequins		Openside Flanker		NL	58(7)	50	10	-	-	-
							NC	5(1)	-	-	-	-	-
							ES	12(2)	25	5	-	-	-
							HC	8(2)	5	1	-	-	-
			Sale Sharks		Openside Flanker		NL	31(6)	35	7	-	-	-
							NC	2(1)	-	-	-	-	-
							ES	6(1)	5	1	-	-	-
Apolosi	**Satala**	14.08.78	Fiji										
			Gloucester		Lock		NL	10 (5)	5	1	-	-	-
							NC	1 (2)	5	1	-	-	-
							HC	3 (2)	-	-	-	-	-
			Leeds		Lock		NL	8(1)	10	2	-	-	-
							NC	3(0)	5	1	-	-	-
							ES	3(2)	-	-	-	-	-r
			Edinburgh Reivers										
Dan	**Scarbrough**	16.02.78	England			84 kg							
		Loan	London Welsh		Right Wing		NL	1(0)	-	-	-	-	-
			Saracens		Right Wing		NL	53(5)	63	12	-	-	1
							NC	3(0)	-	-	-	-	-
							ES	7(1)	20	4	-	-	-
							HC	4(2)	5	1	-	-	-
			Leeds		Right Wing		NL	55(4)	135	27	-	-	-
							NC	6(0)	20	4	-	-	-
							ES	9(0)	20	4	-	-	-
							HC	3(1)	5	1	-	-	-
			Wakefield		Right Wing		NL	43(2)	85	17	-	-	-
							NC	3(0)	-	-	-	-	-
James	**Scayesbrook**	01.01.82	England		191cm	89 kg							
			Bath		Openside Flanker		NL	56(63)	25	5	-	-	-
							NC	10(7)	5	1	-	-	-
							ES	15(10)	25	5	-	-	-
							HC	7(6)	-	-	-	-	-
Dean	**Schofield**	19.01.79	England		198cm	114 kg							
			Sale Sharks		Lock		NL	121(18)	75	15	-	-	-
							NC	7(2)	-	-	-	-	-
							ES	13(5)	5	1	-	-	-
							HC	23(4)	10	2	-	-	-
			Wakefield		Lock		NL	16(1)	15	3	-	-	-
							NC	2(0)	-	-	-	-	-
Elvis	**Seveali'i**	20.06.78	Samoa										
			London Irish		Centre		NL	15 (5)	5	1	-	-	-
							NC	1 (0)	-	-	-	-	-
							ES	5 (1)	25	5	-	-	-
			Sale Sharks		Centre		NL	26(3)	15	3	-	-	-
							NC	2(0)	-	-	-	-	-
							ES	1(0)	-	-	-	-	-
							HC	8(0)	5	1	-	-	-
			Bath		Centre		NL	4(2)	10	2	-	-	-
							ES	3(0)	15	3	-	-	-
			Ospreys		Centre		HC	5(5)	5	1	-	-	-
David	**Seymour**	27.09.84	England		180cm	89 kg							
			Saracens		Openside Flanker		NL	45(27)	-	-	-	-	-
							NC	5(3)	5	1	-	-	-
							ES	11(2)	5	1	-	-	-
							HC	2(8)	5	1	-	-	-
			Chinnor		Openside Flanker		NL	38(0)	55	11	-	-	-

PLAYERS - PREMIERSHIP

							Comp	Apps	Pts	T	P	C	DG
Joe	Shaw	20.02.80	England	183cm	89 kg								
			Newcastle	Full Back			NL	44(19)	35	7	-	-	-
							NC	6(1)	5	1	-	-	-
							ES	9(2)	7	1	1	-	-
							HC	1(2)	-	-	-	-	-
			Blaydon	Full Back			NL	2(0)	3	-	-	1	-
			Northampton	Full Back			NL	13(6)	20	4	-	-	-
							NC	2(1)	-	-	-	-	-
							HC	1(1)	5	1	-	-	-
			Sale Sharks	Full Back			NL	5(3)	18	-	3	4	-
							NC	0(1)	-	-	-	-	-
							ES	2(0)	-	-	-	-	-
Simon	Shaw	01.09.72	England	203cm	127 kg								
			London Wasps	Lock			NL	186(22)	93	18	-	-	1
							NC	14(2)	-	-	-	-	-
							ES	7(1)	10	2	-	-	-
							HC	55(3)	20	4	-	-	-
			Bristol	Lock			NL	25(0)	15	3	-	-	-
							NC	1(0)	-	-	-	-	-
							ES	4(0)	-	-	-	-	-
Andrew	Sheridan	01.11.79	England	196cm	130 kg								
			Sale Sharks	Prop			NL	59(14)	25	5	-	-	-
							NC	5(0)	5	1	-	-	-
							ES	11(1)	5	1	-	-	-
							HC	13(2)	5	1	-	-	-
			Bristol	Lock			NL	33(30)	25	5	-	-	-
							NC	1(3)	5	1	-	-	-
							ES	6(2)	-	-	-	-	-
							HC	3(3)	-	-	-	-	-
			Richmond	Lock			NL	3(2)	-	-	-	-	-
							NC	2(0)	5	1	-	-	-
Paul	Shields	25.09.78	Ireland										
			Northampton	Hooker			NL	14(14)	30	6	-	-	-
							NC	4(2)	-	-	-	-	-
							ES	1 (5)	-	-	-	-	-
			Ulster	Hooker			HC	10(12)	5	1	-	-	-
Peter	Short	20.06.79	England	194cm	114 kg								
			Bath	Lock			NL	56(21)	20	4	-	-	-
							NC	3(1)	-	-	-	-	-
							ES	11(5)	-	-	-	-	-
							HC	6(2)	-	-	-	-	-
			Leicester Tigers	Blindside Flanker			NL	17(23)	-	-	-	-	-
							NC	2(2)	10	2	-	-	-
							HC	2(6)	-	-	-	-	-
			Moseley	Blindside Flanker			NL	8(9)	-	-	-	-	-
			Newbury	Lock			NC	1(0)	-	-	-	-	-
			Narbonne	Blindside Flanker			ES	8(1)	10	2	-	-	-
James	Simpson-Daniel	30.05.82	England	182cm	85 kg								
			Gloucester	Right Wing			NL	104(14)	220	44	-	-	-
							NC	11(2)	20	4	-	-	-
							ES	12(0)	70	14	-	-	-
							HC	28(2)	95	19	-	-	-
Will	Skinner	08.02.84	England										
			Harlequins	Openside Flanker			NL	40(11)	15	3	-	-	-
							NC	7(0)	-	-	-	-	-
							ES	2(0)	5	1	-	-	-
							HC	8(2)	-	-	-	-	-
			Leicester Tigers	Openside Flanker			NL	10(22)	20	4	-	-	-
							NC	0(2)	-	-	-	-	-
							HC	0(5)	-	-	-	-	-

PLAYERS - PREMIERSHIP

						Comp	Apps	Pts	T	P	C	DG
Ben	Skirving	09.10.83	England Saracens	No. 8		NL NC ES HC	69(27) 8(2) 20(5) 13(0)	50 - 5 10	10 - 1 2	- - - -	- - - -	- - - -
George	Skivington	03.12.82	England London Wasps	198cm Lock	95 kg	NL NC HC	53(16) 9(1) 12(8)	15 5 15	3 1 3	- - -	- - -	- - -
Richard	Skuse	11.09.80	England London Irish	180cm Prop	117 kg	NL NC ES HC	20(18) 3(1) 7(3) 4(4)	5 - - -	1 - - -	- - - -	- - - -	- - - -
			Bristol Caerphilly	Prop Prop		NL ES	4(9) 2(1)	- -	- -	- -	- -	- -
Tom	Smith	31.10.71	Scotland Northampton	178cm Prop	105kg	NL NC ES HC	113(20) 13(2) 6(8) 24(3)	45 - - 5	9 - - 1	- - - -	- - - -	- - - -
			Brive Glasgow	Prop Prop		ES HC	4(1) 8	- 5	- 1	- -	- -	- -
Steve	So'oialo	11.05.77	Samoa Harlequins	Scrum Half		NL NC ES HC	46(24) 3(2) 1(3) 7(5)	60 - - -	12 - - -	- - - -	- - - -	- - - -
			Orrell	Scrum Half		NL NC	36(7) 4(0)	60 10	12 2	- -	- -	- -
Mark	Sorenson	12.02.87	New Zealand Newcastle	Lock		NL NC ES	48(3) 6(0) 15(0)	- - -	- - -	- - -	- - -	- - -
Kevin	Sorrell	06.03.77	England Saracens	183cm Centre	80 kg	NL NC ES HC	182(17) 10(8) 30(5) 22(2)	203 5 39 15	21 1 7 3	10 - 2 -	26 - - -	- - - -
Carlos	Spencer	14.10.75	New Zealand Gloucester Northampton	184cm Fly half Fly half	95kg	NL NL NC ES HC	8 (1) 74(3) 6 5 7	10 163 - 15 51	- 15 - 3 1	2 11 - - 17	2 19 - - 4	- 3 - - -
Boris	Stankovich	01.09.80	New Zealand Leicester Tigers	Prop		NL NC HC	20(2) 5(0) 1 (1)	5 - -	1 - -	- - -	- - -	- - -
			Albi	Prop		ES	0(1)	-	-	-	-	-
Jeremy	Staunton	07.05.80	Ireland London Wasps	Outside Half		NL NC HC	18(12) 4(1) 5(2)	91 16 25	3 - 1	11 2 1	16 3 6	2 1 -
			London Irish Harlequins	Outside Half Outside Half		NL NL NC HC NC	3(2) 18(3) 1(0) 3(2) 1(1)	21 186 7 24 -	- 2 1 - -	3 25 1 3 -	5 41 - 6 -	- 1 - - -
			Munster	Outside Half		HC	16(11)	20	4	-	-	-

806

PLAYERS - PREMIERSHIP

						Comp	Apps	Pts	T	P	C	DG
Michael	**Stephenson**	20.09.80	England	182cm	83 kg							
			Bath	Left Wing		NL	33(17)	33	6	-	-	1
						NC	7(1)	10	2	-	-	-
						ES	9(4)	25	5	-	-	-
						HC	6(2)	25	5	-	-	-
			Newcastle	Left Wing		NL	92(4)	160	32	-	-	-
						NC	12(2)	25	5	-	-	-
						ES	14(0)	50	10	-	-	-
						HC	10(3)	15	3	-	-	-
Matthew	**Stevens**	01.10.82	England	183cm	115 kg							
			Bath	Prop		NL	40(31)	20	3	-	-	-
						NC	3(3)	5	1	-	-	-
						ES	13(8)	20	4	-	-	-
						HC	12(5)	15	3	-	-	-
Barry	**Stewart**	03.06.75	Scotland									
			Northampton	Prop		NL	27(7)	-	-	-	-	-
						NC	6(1)	-	-	-	-	-
						ES	2 (1)	-	-	-	-	-
			Sale Sharks	Prop		NL	66(38)	5	1	-	-	-
						NC	7(3)	-	-	-	-	-
						ES	2(5)	-	-	-	-	-
						HC	11(8)	-	-	-	-	-
			Edinburgh	Prop		HC	22	-	-	-	-	-
Jason	**Strange**	08.10.73	Wales									
			Leds Carnegie	Outside Half		NL	10 (1)	118	1	40	11	-
						NC	2 (0)	8	-	1	2	-
			Bristol	Outside Half		NL	63(20)	706	4	115	149	3
						NC	7(2)	52	-	14	8	-
						ES	3(6)	40	-	17	2	-
						HC	3(3)	16	-	2	4	-
			Pertemps Bees	Outside Half		NL	1(2)	14	-	4	2	-
			Rotherham	Outside Half		NL	6(1)	38	1	6	7	-
						NC	1(0)	5	-	1	1	-
						ES	1(1)	8	-	1	2	-
			Newport	Outside Half		HC	8(4)	98	1	15	21	-
			Ebbw Vale	Outside Half		ES	1(2)	10	-	2	2	-
						HC	6(0)	32	-	1	10	-
David	**Strettle**	23.07.83	England	183cm	78 kg							
			Harlequins	Left Wing		NL	35(3)	55	11	-	-	-
						NC	4(0)	5	1	-	-	-
						ES	3(1)	5	1	-	-	-
						HC	6(0)	-	-	-	-	-
			Rotherham	Left Wing		NL	39(2)	135	27	-	-	-
						NC	3(0)	-	-	-	-	-
Alasdair	**Strokosch**	21.02.83	Scotland									
			Gloucester	Lock		NL	24(8)	5	1	-	-	-
						NC	7(0)	-	-	-	-	-
						HC	9(2)	5	1	-	-	-
			Edinburgh Reivers	Lock		HC	12(9)	10	2	-	-	-
Sailosi	**Tagicakibau**	14.11.82	Samoa									
			London Irish	Left Wing		NL	58(2)	105	21	-	-	-
						NC	5(0)	10	2	-	-	-
						ES	7(0)	20	4	-	-	-
						HC	10(1)	10	2	-	-	-
Prev. Club: Waikato Chiefs												
Matthew	**Tait**	06.02.86	England	180cm	80 kg							
			Sale Sharks	Centre		NL	14 (2)	5	1	-	-	-
						HC	2 (3)	-	-	-	-	-
			Newcastle	Centre		NL	51(5)	65	13	-	-	-
						NC	3(1)	5	1	-	-	-
						ES	20(0)	37	7	1	-	-
						HC	4(1)	5	1	-	-	-

PLAYERS - PREMIERSHIP

						Comp	Apps	Pts	T	P	C	DG
Alex	**Tait**	18.03.88	England									
			Newcastle	Full Back		NL	17(2)	-	-	-	-	-
						NC	0(2)	-	-	-	-	-
						ES	3(2)	20	4	-	-	-
		Loan	Darlington MP	Full Back		NL	3(0)	5	1	-	-	-
		Loan	Westoe	Full Back		NL	4(0)	14	2	2	-	-
Netani	**Talei**	19.03.83	Fiji									
			Worcester	No. 8		NL	18(9)	15	3	-	-	-
						NC	5(0)	5	1	-	-	-
						ES	9(3)	5	1	-	-	-
			Doncaster	No. 8		NL	10(5)	25	5	-	-	-
						NC	0(2)	5	1	-	-	-
Tevita	**Taumoepeau**	16.05.74	Tonga									
			Worcester	Prop		NL	56(16)	10	2	-	-	-
						NC	7(0)	-	-	-	-	-
						ES	25(1)	5	1	-	-	-
			Northampton	Prop		NL	7(1)	-	-	-	-	-
			Bourgoin	Prop		HC	1(1)	-	-	-	-	-
			Auckland Blues	Prop								
			Waikato Chiefs	Prop								
Hayden	**Thomas**	18.10.78	England	173cm	80 kg							
			Bristol	Scrum Half		NL	4(15)	5	1	-	-	-
						NC	2(1)	-	-	-	-	-
						ES	1 (1)	-	-	-	-	-
			Gloucester	Scrum Half		NL	8(18)	5	1	-	-	-
						NC	1(0)	-	-	-	-	-
						ES	3(6)	10	2	-	-	-
			Exeter	Scrum Half		NL	45(4)	95	19	-	-	-
						NC	4(0)	20	4	-	-	-
Lee	**Thomas**	02.06.84	Wales									
			Sale Sharks	Centre		NL	31(10)	121	6	11	21	2
						NC	2(3)	29	1	3	6	-
						ES	4(0)	22	1	7	1	-
						HC	4(0)	17	-	1	5	-
			Cardiff	Centre		NC	2(2)	20	-	1	6	-
						HC	4(7)	43	-	5	9	2
			Celtic Warriors	Centre								
Matt	**Thompson**	12.12.82	England	187cm	115 kg							
			Newcastle	Hooker		NL	58(62)	25	5	-	-	-
						NC	9(3)	5	1	-	-	-
						ES	21(13)	40	8	-	-	-
						HC	1(6)	-	-	-	-	-
Richard	**Thorpe**	01.11.84	England	185cm	98 kg							
			London Irish	Openside Flanker		NL	30(17)	35	7	-	-	-
						NC	4(3)	15	3	-	-	-
						ES	6 (0)	-	-	-	-	-
						HC	2(5)	15	3	-	-	-
			Newbury	Blindside Flanker		NL	2(0)	-	-	-	-	-
			Esher	Blindside Flanker		NL	3(1)	-	-	-	-	-
Ed	**Thrower**	01.09.82	England	184cm	86 kg							
			London Irish	Full Back		NL	1(7)	10	2	-	-	-
						NC	0(3)	-	-	-	-	-
						ES	5(2)	27	5	1	-	-
			London Wasps	Full Back		NL	10(6)	72	6	6	10	-
						NC	1(0)	-	-	-	-	-
			London Welsh	Full Back		NL	1(0)	-	-	-	-	-
			Saracens	Right Wing		NL	4(6)	5	1	-	-	-
						NC	4(6)	5	1	-	-	-
						HC	0(3)	-	-	-	-	-
						ES	(1)	-	-	-	-	-

PLAYERS - PREMIERSHIP

							Comp	Apps	Pts	T	P	C	DG
Gonzalo	Tiesi	25.04.85	Argentina										
			Harlequins	Full Back			NL	16(0)	10	2	-	-	-
							HC	6(0)	-	-	-	-	-
			London Irish	Full Back			NL	8(8)	15	3	-	-	-
							NC	3(0)	5	1	-	-	-
							ES	2(1)	10	2	-	-	-
							HC	3(6)	5	1	-	-	-
Mike	Tindall	18.10.78	England	188cm	92 kg								
			Gloucester	Centre			NL	47(3)	43	7	1	2	-
							NC	5(0)	-	-	-	-	-
							ES	8(0)	15	3	-	-	-
							HC	13(2)	20	4	-	-	-
			Bath	Centre			NL	80(5)	133	26	-	1	-
							NC	5(0)	-	-	-	-	-
							ES	4(1)	15	3	-	-	-
							HC	18(0)	12	2	1	-	-
Andrew	Titterell	10.01.81	England	176cm	93 kg								
			Gloucester	Hooker			NL	14(13)	5	1	-	-	-
							NC	1(3)	-	-	-	-	-
							HC	3(7)	5	1	-	-	-
			Sale Sharks	Hooker			NL	80(41)	35	7	-	-	-
							NC	3(5)	5	1	-	-	-
							ES	14(5)	15	3	-	-	-
							HC	7(12)	5	1	-	-	-
			Waterloo	Hooker			NL	0(1)	-	-	-	-	-
Alfie	Tooala	30.01.81	Samoa										
			Bristol	Blindside Flanker			NL	33(15)	10	2	-	-	-
							NC	2(0)	-	-	-	-	-
							ES	4(1)	5	1	-	-	-
							HC	2(3)	5	1	-	-	-
			Orrell	Blindside Flanker			NL	19(3)	50	10	-	-	-
							NC	3(0)	10	2	-	-	-
			Plymouth Albion	Blindside Flanker			NL	41(2)	75	15	-	-	-
							NC	5(0)	15	3	-	-	-
			Rotherham	Blindside Flanker			NL	29(14)	90	18	-	-	-
							NC	4(3)	5	1	-	-	-
Alesana	Tuilagi	24.02.81	Samoa	185cm	110 kg								
			Leicester Tigers	Left Wing			NL	36(17)	90	18	-	-	-
							NC	9(0)	10	2	-	-	-
							HC	11(8)	20	4	-	-	-
			Parma	Left Wing			ES	6(1)	20	4	-	-	-
Anitele'a	Tuilagi	06.05.86	Samoa										
			Sale Sharks	Centre			NL	5(3)	-	-	-	-	-
							NC	2(0)	-	-	-	-	-
							HC	3(0)	5	1	-	-	-
			Leeds	Centre			NL	13(20)	35	7	-	-	-
							NC	3(0)	-	-	-	-	-
							ES	3(1)	5	1	-	-	-
Sam	Tuitupou	01.02.82	New Zealand										
			Worcester	Centre			NL	23(0)	25	5	-	-	-
							NC	3(0)	5	1	-	-	-
							ES	9(0)	30	6	-	-	-
-Stuart	Turner	22.04.72	England	183cm	108 kg								
			Sale Sharks	Prop			NL	83(64)	20	4	-	-	-
							NC	6(6)	-	-	-	-	-
							ES	16(3)	-	-	-	-	-
							HC	13(14)	-	-	-	-	-
			Orrell	Prop			NL	53(1)	5	1	-	-	-
							NC	1(0)	-	-	-	-	-
							ES	1(0)	-	-	-	-	-
			Rotherham	Prop			NL	38(3)	20	4	-	-	-
							NC	3(0)	-	-	-	-	-
							ES	4(2)	-	-	-	-	-
			Worcester	Prop			NL	5(3)	5	1	-	-	-

PLAYERS - PREMIERSHIP

							Comp	Apps	Pts	T	P	C	DG
Jordan	Turner-Hall	05.01.88	England	183cm	102 kg								
			Harlequins	Centre			NL	39(7)	25	5	-	-	-
							NC	3(2)	-	-	-	-	-
							ES	3(0)	-	-	-	-	-
							HC	8(0)	15	3	-	-	-
Lesley	Vainikolo	04.05.79	England	188cm	112 kg								
			Gloucester	Left Wing			NL	20(1)	60	12	-	-	-
							NC	3(1)	15	3	-	-	-
							EC	7(2)	20	4	-	-	-
Mark	van Gisbergen	30.06.77	England	180cm	89 kg								
			London Wasps	Outside Half			NL	109(14)	744	18	105	148	-
							NC	6(4)	37	1	7	6	-
							ES	7(2)	24	2	4	2	-
							HC	29(6)	208	7	34	35	-
Tom	Varndell	16.08.85	England	191cm	96 kg								
			Leicester Tigers	Left Wing			NL	58(17)	220	44	-	-	-
							NC	9(2)	25	5	-	-	-
							HC	13(4)	60	12	-	-	-
			Bedford	Left Wing			NL	2(0)	10	2	-	-	-
Sam	Vesty	26.11.81	England	183cm	80 kg								
			Leicester Tigers	Outside Half			NL	83(17)	150	10	23	16	2
							NC	8(4)	24	2	4	2	-
							HC	21(9)	54	2	4	11	1
Rob	Vickerman	25.09.85	England										
			Leeds	Right Wing			NL	25(9)	40	8	-	-	-
							NC	3(1)	15	3	-	-	-
							ES	6(1)	5	1	-	-	-
							HC	5(0)	-	-	-	-	-
Rob	Vickers	02.12.81	England										
			Newcastle	Hooker			NL	13(8)	-	-	-	-	-
							ES	2(7)	10	2	-	-	-
							NC	2 (1)	5	1	-	-	-
			Tynedale	Hooker			NL	16(10)	25	5	-	-	-
							NC	2(1)	-	-	-	-	-
			Harrogate	Hooker			NL	8(16)	-	-	-	-	-
							NC	1(1)	-	-	-	-	-
Philip	Vickery	14.03.76	England	191cm	121 kg								
			Gloucester	Prop			NL	74(19)	15	3	-	-	-
							NC	6(2)	-	-	-	-	-
							ES	16(2)	-	-	-	-	-
							HC	21(2)	-	-	-	-	-
			London Wasps	Prop			NL	20(3)	-	-	-	-	-
							NC	3(0)	-	-	-	-	-
							HC	18(0)	5	1	-	-	-
Cobus	Visagie	31.10.73	South Africa	185cm	118 kg								
			Saracens	Prop			NL	62(22)	-	-	-	-	-
							NC	7(2)	-	-	-	-	-
							ES	11(3)	-	-	-	-	-
							HC	8(0)	-	-	-	-	-
			Western Stormers	Prop									
Tim	Visser	29.05.87	England										
			Newcastle	Centre			NL	20(13)	35	7	-	-	-
							NC	2(3)	5	1	-	-	-
							ES	11(7)	25	5	-	-	-
			Tynedale	Centre			NL	4 (0)	25	4	-	-	-
			Northampton	Centre			NL	3(0)	10	2	-	-	-
			Darlington MP	Centre			NL	7(2)	15	3	-	-	-

PLAYERS - PREMIERSHIP

							Comp	Apps	Pts	T	P	C	DG
Tom	Voyce	05.01.81	England	185cm	82 kg								
			London Wasps	Left Wing			NL	116(2)	200	40	-	-	-
							NC	12(0)	45	9	-	-	-
							HC	36(2)	75	15	-	-	-
			Bath	Left Wing			NL	46(11)	70	14	-	-	-
							NC	1(1)	-	-	-	-	-
							ES	4(3)	10	2	-	-	-
							HC	6(3)	35	7	-	-	-
Hugh	Vyvyan	08.09.76	England	198cm	102 kg								
			Saracens	No. 8			NL	86(9)	40	8	-	-	-
							NC	6(0)	5	1	-	-	-
							ES	11(4)	-	-	-	-	-
							HC	14(0)	23	4	-	-	1
			Newcastle	Lock			NL	84(23)	60	12	-	-	-
							NC	13(3)	10	2	-	-	-
							ES	19(4)	20	4	-	-	-
							HC	4(2)	5	1	-	-	-
David	Walder	07.05.78	England	178cm	83 kg								
			London Wasps	Outside Half			NL	19(14)	226	-	23	57	3
							NC	2(4)	16	-	2	4	-
							HC	1(2)	22	1	1	5	-
			Newcastle	Outside Half			NL	74(24)	499	12	56	94	15
							NC	10(2)	88	4	16	11	1
							ES	17(6)	201	8	58	15	-
							HC	11(1)	26	1	3	3	2
Dominic	Waldouck	26.09.87	England	180cm	86 kg								
		Loan	Blackheath	Centre			NL	0(1)	5	1	-	-	-
			London Wasps	Centre			NL	35(2)	30	6	-	-	-
							NC	3(1)	-	-	-	-	-
							HC	12(1)	15	3	-	-	-
Willie	Walker	19.05.78	New Zealand										
			Worcester	Outside Half			NL	8 (1)	74	1	6	17	2
			Gloucester	Outside Half			NL	27(16)	266	3	34	57	4
							NC	5(1)	39	2	4	7	-
							HC	4(8)	25	1	7	1	1
			Otago Highlanders	Full Back									
Joe	Ward	03.06.80	New Zealand	183cm	108 kg								
			London Wasps	Hooker			NL	39(22)	20	4	-	-	-
							NC	5(1)	5	1	-	-	-
							HC	1(13)	-	-	-	-	-
			Wellington Hurricanes	Hooker									
Micky	Ward	09.01.79	England	180cm	108 kg								
			Newcastle	Prop			NL	114(66)	15	3	-	-	-
							NC	15(3)	-	-	-	-	-
							ES	32(16)	25	5	-	-	-
							HC	8(4)	-	-	-	-	-
Dan	Ward-Smith	02.01.78	England										
			Bristol	No. 8			NL	55(10)	30	6	-	-	-
							ES	11(1)	30	6	-	-	-
							HC	2(1)	-	-	-	-	-
			Plymouth Albion	No. 8			NL	128(0)	460	92	-	-	-
							NC	11(2)	40	8	-	-	-
Rob	Webber	01.08.86	England										
			London Wasps	Hooker			NL	17(6)	5	1	-	-	-
							NC	3(2)	-	-	-	-	-
							HC	4(3)	-	-	-	-	-
			Blackheath	Hooker			NL	17(6)	35	7	-	-	-
							NC	2(0)	-	-	-	-	-
			Leeds	Hooker			ES	0(2)	-	-	-	-	-

PLAYERS - PREMIERSHIP

						Comp	Apps	Pts	T	P	C	DG
Marco	Wentzel	06.05.79	South Africa	200cm	103 kg							
			Leicester Tigers	Lock		NL	18(9)	-	-	-	-	-
						NC	2(1)	-	-	-	-	-
						HC	6(4)	-	-	-	-	-
			Benetton Treviso	Lock		HC	12(1)	5	1	-	-	-
Prev. Clubs: Northern Bulls, Lock; Cats, Lock												
Julian	White	14.05.73	England	186cm	114 kg							
			Leicester Tigers	Prop		NL	60(12)	5	1	-	-	-
						NC	5(3)	-	-	-	-	-
						HC	25(7)	5	1	-	-	-
			Bristol	Prop		NL	26(1)	5	1	-	-	-
						NC	1(0)	-	-	-	-	-
						ES	7(0)	-	-	-	-	-
						HC	3(0)	-	-	-	-	-
			Saracens	Prop		NL	32(5)	15	3	-	-	-
						NC	5(0)	-	-	-	-	-
						HC	6(1)	-	-	-	-	-
Jason	White	17.04.78	Scotland									
			Sale Sharks	Blindside Flanker		NL	62(9)	10	2	-	-	-
						NC	9(1)	-	-	-	-	-
						ES	10(1)	5	1	-	-	-
						HC	13(2)	10	2	-	-	-
			Glasgow Cal.	Lock		HC	28(0)	15	3	-	-	-
			Caledonia	Lock		HC	4(1)	5	1	-	-	-
Richard	Wigglesworth	09.06.83	England	175cm	84 kg							
			Sale Sharks	Scrum Half		NL	55(38)	43	4	4	5	-
						NC	8(3)	-	-	-	-	-
						ES	9(5)	29	3	7	-	-
						HC	11(7)	11	-	4	1	-
Jonny	Wilkinson	25.05.79	England	178cm	84 kg							
			Newcastle	Outside Half		NL	129(9)	1484	24	196	302	22
						NC	16(1)	201	1	23	49	1
						ES	22(2)	315	4	47	66	1
						HC	5(1)	79	-	5	22	1
Tom	Williams	12.10.83	England	180cm	83 kg							
			Harlequins	Right Wing		NL	61(15)	120	24	-	-	-
						NC	9(1)	14	2	2	-	-
						ES	5(0)	15	3	-	-	-
						HC	12(1)	30	6	-	-	-
Edward	Williamson	31.03.84	England	187cm	95 kg							
			Newcastle	Blindside Flanker		NL	14(8)	5	1	-	-	-
						NC	1(2)	-	-	-	-	-
						ES	4(1)	5	1	-	-	-
			Tynedale	Blindside Flanker		NL	1(0)	-	-	-	-	-
			Darlington MP	Blindside Flanker		NL	2(1)	5	1	-	-	-
Dave	Wilson	09.04.85	England	184cm	117 kg							
			Newcastle	Prop		NL	22(32)	5	1	-	-	-
						NC	3(3)	-	-	-	-	-
						ES	8(4)	-	-	-	-	-
						HC	0(1)	-	-	-	-	-
Brent	Wilson	09.09.81	New Zealand	196cm	108 kg							
			Newcastle	Blindside Flanker		NL	30(25)	25	5	-	-	-
						NC	5(3)	5	1	-	-	-
						ES	15(3)	25	5	-	-	-
Russell	Winter	17.08.75	South Africa									
			Newcastle	No. 8		NL	20(13)	10	2	-	-	-
						NC	5(1)	-	-	-	-	-
						ES	3(7)	5	1	-	-	-
			Natal Sharks	No. 8								
			Cats	No. 8								

PLAYERS - PREMIERSHIP

						Comp	Apps	Pts	T	P	C	DG
Roy	**Winters**	13.12.75	England	194cm	102 kg							
			Bristol	Blindside Flanker		NL	56(14)	15	3	-	-	-
						ES	12(0)	-	-	-	-	-
						NC	2 (0)	-	-	-	-	-
						HC	5(1)	5	1	-	-	-
			Bedford	Blindside Flanker		NL	66(8)	40	8	-	-	-
						NC	2(0)	5	1	-	-	-
						ES	5(1)	-	-	-	-	-
			Harlequins	Blindside Flanker		NL	45(28)	5	1	-	-	-
						NC	5(1)	-	-	-	-	-
						ES	13(2)	10	2	-	-	-
						HC	7(2)	-	-	-	-	-
Nick	**Wood**	09.01.83	England	186cm	109 kg							
			Gloucester	Prop		NL	63(24)	20	4	-	-	-
						NC	4(3)	-	-	-	-	-
						ES	3(1)	10	2	-	-	-
						HC	8(4)	-	-	-	-	-
Tom	**Wood**	03.11.86	England									
			Worcester	Lock		NL	25(3)	-	-	-	-	-
						NC	1(1)	-	-	-	-	-
						ES	8(1)	5	1	-	-	-
Ben	**Woods**	09.06.82	England	188cm	101 kg							
			Leicester	Blindside Flanker		NL	12 (5)	5	1	-	-	-
						HC	6 (0)	5	1	-	-	-
			Newcastle	Blindside Flanker		NL	43(10)	20	4	-	-	-
						NC	3(1)	-	-	-	-	-
						ES	15(5)	15	3	-	-	-
Joe	**Worsley**	14.06.77	England	196cm	108 kg							
			London Wasps	Openside Flanker		NL	167(16)	140	28	-	-	-
						NC	13(1)	-	-	-	-	-
						ES	5(1)	5	1	-	-	-
						HC	45(4)	50	10	-	-	-
Dave	**Young**	18.12.85	Scotland	185cm	117 kg							
			Gloucester	Prop		NL	1 (4)	-	-	-	-	-
						NC	1 (0)	-	-	-	-	-
						HC	(0)	-	-	-	-	-
			Leicester Tigers	Prop		NL	1(8)	-	-	-	-	-
						NC	2(0)	-	-	-	-	-
						HC	0(1)	-	-	-	-	-
			Doncaster	Prop		NL	1(3)	-	-	-	-	-
Ben	**Youngs**	05.09.89	England									
			Leicester Tigers	Scrum Half		NL	2(18)	5	1	-	-	-
						NC	1(1)	5	1	-	-	-
						HC	1(4)	-	-	-	-	-

CLUB INDEX

Club	Page Ref	League	Level
Abingdon	734-770	Berks/Bucks & Oxon Premier	8
Acklam	462-495	Durham/Northumberland Division Two	8
Adwick Le Street	462-495	Yorkshire Division Five	11
Aireborough	462-495	Yorkshire Division Three	9
Alcester	544-579	Midlands 4 West (South)	9
Alchester	734-770	Berks/Bucks & Oxon Premier	8
Aldbourne/Hungerford	734-770	Dorset & Wilts 3 North	10
Aldermaston	734-770	Berks/Bucks & Oxon 1 South	9
Aldershot & Fleet	630-680	Hampshire 1	9
Aldridge	544-579	Midlands 5 West (North)	10
Aldwinians	462-495	North Lancs/Cumbria	7
All Spartans OB	544-579	Midlands 5 East (North)	10
Alnwick	462-495	Durham/Northumberland Division One	7
Alresford	630-680	Hampshire 2	10
Alton	630-680	Hampshire 1	9
Altrincham Kersal	447	North One West	6
Amber Valley	544-579	Midlands 3 East (North)	8
Amersham & Chiltern	734-770	Southern Counties North	7
Ampthill	504	National Division Three Midlands	5
Andover	630-680	London 3 South West	8
Anselmians	462-495	South Lancs/Cheshire Division One	7
Anstey	544-579	Midlands 5 East (South)	10
Aretians	734-770	Gloucester 1	9
Ashbourne	544-579	Midlands 2 West (North)	7
Ashby	544-579	Midlands 3 East (North)	8
Ashfield	544-579	Midlands 3 East (North)	8
Ashford	630-680	Kent 1	9
Ashington	462-495	Durham/Northumberland Division One	7
Ashley Down Old Boys	734-770	Gloucester 1	9
Ashton-on-Mersey	462-495	South Lancs/Cheshire Division Two	8
Ashton-Under-Lyne	462-495	North Lancashire Division One	8
Askean	630-680	Kent 2	10
Aspatria	447	North One West	6
Aspatria Eagles	462-495	Cumbria	8
Aston Old Edwardians	544-579	Midlands 2 West (North)	7
Atherstone	544-579	Midlands 5 West (South East)	10
Avon	734-770	Tribute Somerset Premier	8
Avonmouth Old Boys	711	Tribute South West 1 West	6
Avonvale	734-770	Dorset & Wilts 1 North	8
Aylesbury	734-770	Southern Counties North	7
Aylesbury Athletic	734-770	Berks/Bucks & Oxon 1 North	9
Aylesford Bulls	611	London 1 South	6
Aylestone Athletic	544-579	Midlands East (South) B	9
Aylestone St James	544-579	Midlands 2 East (South)	7
Aylestonians	544-579	Midlands 5 East (South)	10
Baildon	462-495	Yorkshire Division Three	9
Bakewell Mannerians	544-579	Midlands 2 East (North)	7
Banbury	544-579	Midlands 2 East (South)	7
Bancroft	630-680	Essex (Canterbury Jack) League 1	7
Bank Of England	630-680	London 3 North West	8
Barkers Butts	544-579	Midlands 2 West (South)	7
Barking	378	National League 2 South	4
Barnes	380	National League 2 South	4
Barnet Elizabethans	630-680	London 3 North West	8
Barnsley	462-495	Yorkshire Division Two	8
Barnstaple	688	National League 3 South West	5
Barton & District	544-579	Midlands 3 East (North)	8
Barton Hill	734-770	Tribute Western Counties North	7

814

Club	Page Ref	League	Level
Barton-Under-Needwood	544-579	Midlands 4 West (North)	9
Basildon	630-680	London 3 North East	8
Basingstoke	588	National 3 London & SE	5
Bath	44	The Guinness Premiership	1
Bath Old Edwardians	734-770	Tribute Somerset 2 North	10
Bath Saracens	734-770	Dorset & Wilts 2 North	9
Battersea Ironsides	630-680	Surrey 1	9
Beaconsfield	734-770	Southern Counties North	7
Bec Old Boys	630-680	Surrey 1	9
Beccehamian	630-680	Kent 1	9
Beccles	630-680	London 3 North East	8
Beckenham	611	London 1 South	6
Bedford	138	The Championship	2
Bedford Athletic	505	National Division Three Midlands	5
Bedford Swifts	544-579	Midlands 3 East (South)	8
Bedworth	544-579	Midlands 2 West (South)	7
Belgrave	544-579	Midlands 2 East (North)	7
Belper	544-579	Midlands 4 East (North)	9
Belsize Park	630-680	Herts/Middlesex 2	10
Berkshire Shire Hall	734-770	Berks/Bucks & Oxon 1 South	9
Berkswell & Balsall	544-579	Midlands 2 West (South)	7
Berry Hill	734-770	Tribute Western Counties North	7
Beverley	424	National League 3 North	5
Bexley	630-680	Kent 2	10
Bicester	734-770	Southern Counties North	7
Bideford	734-770	Tribute Cornwall/Devon	8
Biggleswade	544-579	Midlands East (South) A	9
Billericay	630-680	London 3 North East	8
Billingham	441	North One East	6
Birchfield (Lancs)	462-495	North Lancashire Division One	8
Birkenhead Park	425	National League 3 North	5
Birmingham C.S.	544-579	Midlands 5 West (South West)	10
Birmingham Exiles	544-579	Midlands 4 West (South)	9
Birmingham & Solihull	144	The Championship	2
Bishop Auckland	462-495	Durham/Northumberland Division Two	8
Bishops Castle & Onny Valley	544-579	Midlands 3 West (North)	8
Bishop's Stortford	589	National 3 London & SE	5
Bishopston	734-770	Gloucester 1	9
Blackburn	448	North One West	6
Blackheath	232	National League 1	3
Blackpool	462-495	North Lancashire Division Two	9
Blandford	734-770	Dorset & Wilts 1 South	8
Blaydon	236	National League 1	3
Bletchley	705	South West 1 East	6
Bloxwich	544-579	Midlands 3 West (North)	8
Blyth	462-495	Durham/Northumberland Division Two	8
Bodmin	734-770	Tribute Cornwall League	9
Bognor	630-680	London 2 South West	7
Bolton	462-495	North Lancashire Division One	8
Boston	544-579	Midlands 3 East (North)	8
Bournemouth	689	National League 3 South West	5
Bournville	529	Midlands 1 West	6
Bowdon	462-495	South Lancs/Cheshire Division One	7
Brackley	544-579	Midlands 3 East (South)	8
Bracknell	590	National 3 London & SE	5
Bradford & Bingley	330	National League 2 North	4
Bradford Salem	462-495	Yorkshire Division One	7
Bradford-on-Avon	734-770	Southern Counties South	7

CLUB INDEX

Club	Page Ref	League	Level
Braintree	630-680	London 2 North East	7
Bramley Phoenix	462-495	Yorkshire Division Three	9
Bream	734-770	Gloucester 1	9
Bredon Star	544-579	Midlands 5 West (South West)	10
Brentwood	605	London 1 North	6
Bridgnorth	544-579	Midlands 2 West (North)	7
Bridgwater & Albion	382	National League 2 South	4
Bridlington	462-495	Yorkshire Division One	8
Bridport	734-770	Dorset & Wilts 1 South	8
Brightlingsea	630-680	Essex (Spitfire) League 2	10
Brighton	630-680	London 3 South East	8
Bristol	150	The Championship	2
Bristol Aeroplane Co	734-770	Gloucester 2	10
Bristol Barbarians	734-770	Tribute Somerset 1	9
Bristol Harlequins	734-770	Tribute Somerset Premier	8
Bristol Saracens	734-770	Gloucester Premier	8
Bristol Telephone Area	734-770	Gloucester 3	11
British Airways	630-680	Herts/Middlesex 4	12
Brixham	711	Tribute South West 1 West	6
Broad Plain	734-770	Tribute Somerset 1	9
Broadland	630-680	Eastern Counties 2	10
Broadmoor Staff	734-770	Berks/Bucks & Oxon Premier	8
Broadstreet	332	National League 2 North	4
Brockleians	630-680	Kent 2	10
Brockworth	734-770	Gloucester 1	9
Bromley	630-680	London 2 South East	7
Bromsgrove	506	National Division Three Midlands	5
Bromyard	544-579	Midlands 5 West (South West)	10
Broughton Park	448	North One West	6
Buckfastleigh Ramblers	734-770	Tribute Devon One North & East	9
Buckingham	705	South West 1 East	6
Bude	734-770	Tribute Western Counties West	7
Bugbrooke	544-579	Midlands 3 East (South)	8
Burgess Hill	630-680	Sussex 1	9
Burley	462-495	Yorkshire Division Four	10
Burnage	448	North One West	6
Burnham on Sea	734-770	Tribute Western Counties North	7
Burnham-On-Crouch	630-680	Essex (Spitfire) League 2	10
Burnley	462-495	North Lancs/Cumbria	7
Burntwood	544-579	Midlands 3 West (North)	8
Burton	529	Midlands 1 West	6
Bury	462-495	North Lancashire Division One	8
Bury St Edmunds	605	London 1 North	6
Buxton	462-495	South Lancs/Cheshire Division Two	8
Cainscross	734-770	Gloucester 2	10
Caldy	334	National League 2 North	4
Calne	734-770	Dorset & Wilts 1 North	8
Camberley	630-680	London 3 South West	8
Camborne	734-770	Tribute Western Counties West	7
Camborne S o M	734-770	Tribute Cornwall League	9
Cambridge	240	National League 1	3
Camp Hill	530	Midlands 1 West	6
Campion	630-680	Essex (Canterbury Jack) League 1	9
Cannock	544-579	Midlands 4 West (North)	9
Cantabrigian	630-680	Eastern Counties 1	9
Canterbury	384	National League 2 South	4
Canvey Island	630-680	London 3 North East	8
Capenhurst	462-495	South Lancs/Cheshire Division Three	9

Club	Page Ref	League	Level
Carlisle	441	North One East	6
Carnforth	462-495	North Lancashire Division Two	9
Castle Cary	734-770	Tribute Somerset 2 South	10
Castle Donington	544-579	Midlands 4 East (North)	9
Castleford	462-495	Yorkshire Division One	7
Chaddesley Corbett	544-579	Midlands 5 West (South West)	10
Chard	734-770	Tribute Somerset Premier	8
Charlton Park	630-680	London 3 South East	8
Chelmsford	630-680	London 2 North East	7
Cheltenham	706	South West 1 East	6
Cheltenham Civil Service	734-770	Gloucester 1	9
Cheltenham North	530	Midlands 1 West	6
Cheltenham Saracens	734-770	Gloucester 2	10
Chesham	734-770	Berks/Bucks & Oxon 1 North	9
Cheshunt	630-680	London 3 North West	8
Chess Valley	630-680	Herts/Middlesex 4	12
Chester	426	National League 3 North	5
Chesterfield Panthers	544-579	Midlands 4 East (North)	9
Chester-Le-Street	462-495	Durham/Northumberland Division Three	9
Chew Valley	734-770	Tribute Somerset Premier	8
Chichester	612	London 1 South	6
Chineham	630-680	Hampshire 2	10
Chingford	606	London 1 North	6
Chinnor	690	National League 3 South West	5
Chippenham	691	National League 3 South West	5
Chipping Norton	734-770	Southern Counties North	7
Chipping Sodbury	734-770	Gloucester 1	9
Chipstead	630-680	Surrey 1	9
Chiswick	630-680	London 2 North West	7
Chobham	612	London 1 South	6
Chorley	462-495	North Lancashire Division Two	9
Chosen Hill Former Pupils	712	Tribute South West 1 West	6
Cinderford	244	National League 1	3
Cirencester	734-770	Gloucester Premier	8
Civil Service	606	London 1 North	6
CL London	630-680	Surrey 3	11
Clacton	630-680	Essex (Canterbury Jack) League 1	9
Claverdon	544-579	Midlands 5 West (South West)	10
Cleckheaton	427	National League 3 North	5
Clee Hill	544-579	Midlands 5 West (South West)	10
Cleethorpes	544-579	Midlands 4 East (North)	9
Cleobury Mortimer	544-579	Midlands 4 West (North)	9
Cleve	692	National League 3 South West	5
Clevedon	712	Tribute South West 1 West	6
Clifton	386	National League 2 South	4
Coalville	544-579	Midlands 2 East (North)	7
Cobham	612	London 1 South	6
Cockermouth	462-495	Cumbria	8
Colchester	630-680	London 2 North East	7
Colerne	734-770	Dorset & Wilts 2 North	9
Colne & Nelson	462-495	North Lancashire Division Two	9
Combe Down	734-770	Tribute Somerset 1	9
Coney Hill	693	National League 3 South West	5
Congleton	462-495	South Lancs/Cheshire Division Three	9
Consett	462-495	Durham/Northumberland Division One	7
Copsewood	544-579	Midlands 5 West (South East)	10
Corsham	734-770	Southern Counties South	7
Cotham Park	734-770	Gloucester 2	10

CLUB INDEX

Club	Page Ref	League	Level
Coventrians	544-579	Midlands 5 West (South East)	10
Coventry	156	The Championship	2
Coventry Saracens	544-579	Midlands 5 West (South East)	10
Coventry Technical	544-579	Midlands 5 West (South East)	10
Coventry Welsh	544-579	Midlands 4 West (South)	9
Cranbrook	630-680	Kent 1	9
Cranleigh	630-680	Surrey 2	10
Crawley	630-680	Sussex 1	9
Crediton	734-770	Tribute Cornwall/Devon	8
Creighton	462-495	Cumbria	8
Crewe and Nantwich	462-495	South Lancs/Cheshire Division Two	8
Crewkerne	734-770	Tribute Somerset 2 South	10
Cricklade	734-770	Dorset & Wilts 1 North	8
Crowborough	630-680	London 3 South East	8
Croydon	630-680	Surrey 1	9
Crusaders	630-680	Eastern Counties 1	9
Cuffley	630-680	Herts/Middlesex 3	11
Cullompton	712	Tribute South West 1 West	6
Dagenham	630-680	London 3 North East	8
Darlington	442	North One East	6
Darlington Mowden Park	428	National League 3 North	5
Dartfordians	630-680	Kent 1	9
Dartmouth	734-770	Tribute Devon One South & West	9
Datchworth	630-680	London 3 North West	8
Daventry	544-579	Midlands 3 East (South)	8
De La Salle (Salford)	462-495	North Lancashire Division One	8
Deal & Betteshanger	630-680	London 2 South East	7
Deepings	544-579	Midlands 3 East (South)	8
Derby	523	Midlands 1 East	6
Dereham	630-680	Eastern Counties 2	10
Devizes	734-770	Southern Counties South	7
Devonport HSOB	734-770	Tribute Devon One South & West	9
Devonport Services	734-770	Tribute Western Counties West	7
Didcot	734-770	Berks/Bucks & Oxon 2 South	10
Didsbury Toc H	462-495	North Lancashire Division One	8
Dings Crusaders	388	National League 2 South	4
Dinnington	462-495	Yorkshire Division One	7
Diss	591	National 3 London & SE	5
Doncaster	162	The Championship	2
Doncaster Phoenix	462-495	Yorkshire Division Two	8
Dorchester	734-770	Southern Counties South	7
Dorking	592	National 3 London & SE	5
Douglas (I.O.M.)	462-495	South Lancs/Cheshire Division Two	8
Dover	613	London 1 South	6
Dowty	734-770	Gloucester 3	11
Driffield	442	North One East	6
Drifters	734-770	Berks/Bucks & Oxon Premier	8
Droitwich	544-579	Midlands 2 West (South)	7
Dronfield	544-579	Midlands 4 East (North)	9
Drybrook	734-770	Tribute Western Counties North	7
Dudley Kingswinford	530	Midlands 1 West	6
Dudley Wasps	544-579	Midlands 4 West (South)	9
Dukinfield	462-495	South Lancs/Cheshire Division One	7
Dunlop	544-579	Midlands 3 West (South)	8
Dunstablians	523	Midlands 1 East	6
Durham City	442	North One East	6
Dursley	734-770	Gloucester 1	9
Eagle	462-495	North Lancashire Division Two	9

Club	Page Ref	League	Level
Ealing	390	National League 2 South	4
Earlsdon	544-579	Midlands 2 West (South)	7
East Dorset	630-680	Hampshire 1	9
East Grinstead	630-680	London 3 South East	8
East Leake	544-579	Midlands 4 East (North)	9
East London	630-680	Essex (Canterbury Jack) League 1	9
East Retford	544-579	Midlands 4 East (North)	9
Eastbourne	630-680	London 2 South East	7
Eastleigh	630-680	Hampshire 1	9
Eccles	462-495	North Lancs/Cumbria	7
Eccleshall	544-579	Midlands 4 West (North)	9
Economicals	630-680	Surrey 4	12
Edwardians	544-579	Midlands 3 West (South)	8
Effingham & Leatherhead	630-680	London 2 South West	7
Egham Hollowegians	630-680	Surrey 4	12
Egremont	462-495	Cumbria	8
Ellesmere Port	462-495	South Lancs/Cheshire Division Three	9
Ellingham & Ringwood	630-680	London 3 South West	8
Ely	630-680	Eastern Counties 1	9
Enfield Ignatians	630-680	London 2 North East	7
Erith	630-680	Kent 1	9
Esher	248	National League 1	3
Essington	544-579	Midlands 4 West (North)	9
Eton Manor	606	London 1 North	6
Evesham	544-579	Midlands 4 West (South)	9
Exeter	168	The Championship	2
Exeter Saracens	734-770	Tribute Cornwall/Devon	8
Exmouth	694	National League 3 South West	5
Fairford	734-770	Dorset & Wilts 2 North	9
Fakenham	630-680	Eastern Counties 1	9
Falmouth	734-770	Tribute Cornwall/Devon	8
Fareham Heathens	630-680	Hampshire 1	9
Farnborough	630-680	Hampshire 1	9
Farnham	630-680	Surrey 1	9
Farnham Royal	734-770	Berks/Bucks & Oxon 1 South	9
Fawley	630-680	Hampshire 2	10
Felixstowe	630-680	Eastern Counties 2	10
Finchley	630-680	London 2 North West	7
Five Ways O.E.	544-579	Midlands 5 West (North)	10
Fleetwood	462-495	North Lancs/Cumbria	7
Folkestone	630-680	London 3 South East	8
Foots Cray	630-680	Kent 2	10
Fordingbridge	630-680	London 3 South West	8
Frampton Cotterell	734-770	Gloucester Premier	8
Frome	734-770	Southern Counties South	7
Fullerians	630-680	London 3 North West	8
Furness	462-495	North Lancs/Cumbria	7
Fylde	336	National League 2 North	4
G.W.R.	630-680	Herts/Middlesex 4	12
Garforth	462-495	Yorkshire Division Three	9
Garstang	462-495	North Lancashire Division One	8
Gateshead	443	North One East	6
Gillingham Anch.	630-680	Kent 1	9
Glossop	462-495	South Lancs/Cheshire Division One	7
Gloucester	50	The Guinness Premiership	1
Gloucester All Blues	734-770	Gloucester 3	11
Gloucester Civil Service	734-770	Gloucester 3	11
Gloucester Old Boys	734-770	Gloucester Premier	8

CLUB INDEX

Club	Page Ref	League	Level
Goole	462-495	Yorkshire Division Two	8
Gordano	734-770	Tribute Somerset 1	9
Gordon League	734-770	Tribute Western Counties North	7
Gosford All Blacks	734-770	Berks/Bucks & Oxon Premier	8
Gosforth	462-495	Durham/Northumberland Division One	7
Gosforth Greengarth	462-495	Cumbria	8
Gosport and Fareham	630-680	London 3 South West	8
Grasshoppers	630-680	London 2 North West	7
Gravesend	613	London 1 South	6
Greyhound	734-770	Gloucester 2	10
Grimsby	544-579	Midlands 2 East (North)	7
Grove	734-770	Southern Counties North	7
Guernsey	630-680	London 2 South West	7
Guildford	630-680	London 2 South West	7
Guildfordians Bisons	630-680	Surrey 4	12
Guisborough	462-495	Durham/Northumberland Division Three	9
Guys' Kings' & St Thomas' Hospital	630-680	Kent 1	9
H.A.C.	630-680	Herts/Middlesex 2	10
Hackney	630-680	Herts/Middlesex 2	10
Hadleigh	630-680	Eastern Counties 2	10
Halifax Vandals	462-495	Yorkshire Division Three	9
Halifax Vikings	462-495	Yorkshire Division Six	12
Hammersmith & Fulham	630-680	London 2 North West	7
Hampstead	630-680	London 2 North West	7
Handsworth	544-579	Midlands 3 West (North)	8
Hanford	544-579	Midlands 5 West (North)	10
Harborne	544-579	Midlands 4 West (North)	9
Harbury	544-579	Midlands 3 West (South)	8
Haringey Rhinos	630-680	London 3 North West	8
Harlequin Amateurs	630-680	Herts/Middlesex 1	9
Harlequins	56	The Guinness Premiership	1
Harlow	630-680	London 2 North East	7
Harpenden	607	London 1 North	6
Harrogate	338	National League 2 North	4
Harrogate Pythons	462-495	Yorkshire Division Four	10
Harrow	630-680	Herts/Middlesex 4	12
Hartlepool	462-495	Durham/Northumberland Division One	7
Hartlepool Athletic	462-495	Durham/Northumberland Division Three	9
Hartlepool B.B.O.B.	462-495	Durham/Northumberland Division Three	9
Hartlepool Rovers	443	North One East	6
Hartpury College	713	Tribute South West 1 West	6
Harwell	734-770	Berks/Bucks & Oxon Premier	8
Harwich & Dovercourt	630-680	Eastern Counties 2	10
Haslemere	630-680	Surrey 3	11
Hastings & Bexhill	630-680	London 3 South East	8
Hatfield	630-680	Herts/Middlesex 3	11
Havant	593	National 3 London & SE	5
Haverhill & District	630-680	Eastern Counties 2	10
Hawcoat Park	462-495	North Lancashire Division One	8
Hayes	630-680	Herts/Middlesex 4	12
Hayle	734-770	Tribute Cornwall/Devon	8
Haywards Heath	594	National 3 London & SE	5
Heath	462-495	Yorkshire Division One	7
Heathfield & Wald'n	630-680	London 3 South East	8
Heaton Moor	462-495	North Lancs/Cumbria	7
Helsby	462-495	South Lancs/Cheshire Division Three	9
Helston	734-770	Tribute Cornwall League	9
Hemel Hempstead	630-680	London 2 North West	7

820

Club	Page Ref	League	Level
Hemsworth	462-495	Yorkshire Division Four	10
Hendon	630-680	Herts/Middlesex 1	9
Henley	392	National League 2 South	4
Hereford	507	National Division Three Midlands	5
Hertford	595	National 3 London & SE	5
Hessle	462-495	Yorkshire Division Two	8
High Wycombe	706	South West 1 East	6
Highley	544-579	Midlands 5 West (South West)	10
Hinckley	508	National Division Three Midlands	5
Hitchin	630-680	London 3 North West	8
Holbrook	630-680	Sussex 1	9
Holmes Chapel	462-495	South Lancs/Cheshire Division Three	9
Holt	630-680	Eastern Counties 1	9
Honiton	734-770	Tribute Devon One North & East	9
Horden	462-495	Durham/Northumberland Division One	7
Hornets	734-770	Tribute Western Counties North	7
Hornsea	462-495	Yorkshire Division Four	10
Horsham	630-680	London 3 South East	8
Houghton	462-495	Durham/Northumberland Division Two	8
Hove	630-680	London 2 South East	7
Hoylake	462-495	South Lancs/Cheshire Division One	7
HSBC	630-680	Kent 1	9
Hucclecote	734-770	Gloucester Premier	8
Huddersfield	340	National League 2 North	4
Huddersfield Y.M.C.A.	462-495	Yorkshire Division Two	8
Hull	342	National League 2 North	4
Hull Ionians	344	National League 2 North	4
Hullensians	462-495	Yorkshire Division Two	8
Hungerford	734-770	Berks/Bucks & Oxon 1 South	9
Huntingdon & District	544-579	Midlands 2 East (South)	7
Hutton	462-495	North Lancashire Division One	8
Ickenham	630-680	Herts/Middlesex 3	11
Ilford Wanderers	630-680	Essex (Canterbury Jack) League 1	9
Ilfracombe	734-770	Tribute Devon One North & East	9
Ilkeston	523	Midlands 1 East	6
Ilkley	443	North One East	6
Illogan Park	734-770	Tribute Cornwall League	9
Imperial	734-770	Tribute Somerset 1	9
Imperial Medicals	630-680	London 2 North West	7
Ipswich	630-680	London 2 North East	7
Ipswich Y.M.	630-680	Eastern Counties 2	10
Isle Of Wight	630-680	Hampshire 2	10
Ivel Barbarians	734-770	Southern Counties South	7
Ivybridge	713	Tribute South West 1 West	6
Jersey	596	National 3 London & SE	5
KCS Old Boys	630-680	London 2 South East	7
Keighley	462-495	Yorkshire Division One	7
Kempston	544-579	Midlands East (South) B	9
Kendal	346	National League 2 North	4
Kenilworth	509	National Division Three Midlands	5
Keresley	544-579	Midlands 4 West (South)	9
Kesteven	544-579	Midlands 3 East (North)	8
Keswick	462-495	North Lancs/Cumbria	7
Kettering	510	National Division Three Midlands	5
Keynsham	734-770	Tribute Western Counties North	7
Keyworth	544-579	Midlands 5 East (North)	10
Kidderminster	544-579	Midlands 2 West (South)	7
Kilburn Cosmos	630-680	Herts/Middlesex 1	9

CLUB INDEX

821

CLUB INDEX

Club	Page Ref	League	Level
Kings Coll. Hospital	630-680	Kent 2	10
Kings Cross Steelers	630-680	Essex (Spitfire) League 2	10
Kings Norton	544-579	Midlands 3 West (South)	8
Kingsbridge	734-770	Tribute Western Counties West	7
Kingsclere	630-680	Hampshire 2	10
Kingston	630-680	London 3 South West	8
Kingswood	734-770	Gloucester 2	10
Kirkby Lonsdale	462-495	North Lancs/Cumbria	7
Knaresborough	462-495	Yorkshire Division Five	11
Knottingley	462-495	Yorkshire Division Two	8
Knutsford	462-495	South Lancs/Cheshire Division Three	9
Lakenham Hewett	630-680	Eastern Counties 2	10
Lankelly-Fowey	734-770	Tribute Cornwall League	9
Launceston	254	National League 1	3
Law Society	630-680	Surrey 2	10
Leamington	531	Midlands 1 West	6
Ledbury	544-579	Midlands 3 West (South)	8
Leeds	62	The Guinness Premiership	1
Leeds Corinthians	462-495	Yorkshire Division Four	10
Leeds Medics	462-495	Yorkshire Division Four	10
Leeds Metropolitan University	462-495	Yorkshire Division Four	10
Leek	544-579	Midlands 3 West (North)	8
Leesbrook	544-579	Midlands 4 East (North)	9
Leicester Forest	544-579	Midlands 2 East (South)	7
Leicester Lions	348	National League 2 North	4
Leicester Tigers	68	The Guinness Premiership	1
Leigh	449	North One West	6
Leighton Buzzard	524	Midlands 1 East	6
Leodiensian	462-495	Yorkshire Division Two	8
Letchworth Garden City	607	London 1 North	6
Lewes	630-680	London 2 South East	7
Lichfield	544-579	Midlands 2 West (North)	7
Lightwater	630-680	Surrey 4	12
Lincoln	544-579	Midlands 2 East (North)	7
Linley	462-495	South Lancs/Cheshire Division Three	9
Liskeard-Looe	734-770	Tribute Cornwall/Devon	8
Littleborough	462-495	North Lancashire Division One	8
Littlemore	734-770	Berks/Bucks & Oxon 1 South	9
Liverpool Collegiate	462-495	South Lancs/Cheshire Division Two	8
Liverpool St Helens	449	North One West	6
London Cornish	630-680	London 2 South West	7
London Exiles	630-680	Surrey 1	9
London French	630-680	Herts/Middlesex 3	11
London Irish Amateur	630-680	London 2 South West	7
London Media	630-680	Surrey 2	10
London New Zealand	630-680	London 2 North West	7
London Nigerian	630-680	London 2 North West	7
London Scottish	258	National League 1	3
London South Africa	630-680	London 2 South West	7
London Irish	74	The Guinness Premiership	1
London Wasps	80	The Guinness Premiership	1
London Welsh	174	The Championship	2
Long Buckby	544-579	Midlands 3 East (South)	8
Long Eaton	544-579	Midlands 5 East (North)	10
Longlevens	734-770	Gloucester 1	9
Longton	511	National Division Three Midlands	5
Lordswood	630-680	Kent 2	10
Lordswood Dixonians	544-579	Midlands 2 West (North)	7

Club	Page Ref	League	Level
Loughborough	544-579	Midlands 2 East (North)	7
Loughborough Students	350	National League 2 North	4
Loughton	630-680	Essex (Spitfire) League 2	10
Lowestoft & Yarmouth	630-680	London 3 North East	8
Luctonians	512	National Division Three Midlands	5
Ludlow	544-579	Midlands 2 West (North)	7
Luton	513	National Division Three Midlands	5
Lutterworth	544-579	Midlands 2 East (South)	7
Lydney	394	National League 2 South	4
Lymm	449	North One West	6
Lytchett Minster	630-680	Hampshire 2	10
Macclesfield	352	National League 2 North	4
Maidenhead	695	National League 3 South West	5
Maidstone	613	London 1 South	6
Maldon	630-680	Essex (Canterbury Jack) League 1	9
Malton and Norton	462-495	Yorkshire Division One	7
Malvern	514	National Division Three Midlands	5
Manchester	264	National League 1	3
Manor Park	544-579	Midlands 4 West (South)	9
Mansfield	524	Midlands 1 East	6
Marist	462-495	Yorkshire Division Five	11
Market Bosworth	524	Midlands 1 East	6
Market Drayton	544-579	Midlands 5 West (North)	10
Market Harborough	544-579	Midlands 2 East (South)	7
Market Rasen & Louth	544-579	Midlands 2 East (North)	7
Marlborough	734-770	Dorset & Wilts 1 North	8
Marlow	706	South West 1 East	6
Marple	462-495	South Lancs/Cheshire Division Two	8
Martock	734-770	Tribute Somerset 2 South	10
Matlock	525	Midlands 1 East	6
Matson	734-770	Gloucester Premier	8
May & Baker	630-680	Essex (Spitfire) League 2	10
Meden Vale	544-579	Midlands 5 East (North)	10
Medicals	462-495	Durham/Northumberland Division Two	8
Medway	630-680	London 3 South East	8
Melbourne	544-579	Midlands 3 East (North)	8
Melksham	734-770	Dorset & Wilts 1 North	8
Mellish	544-579	Midlands 3 East (North)	8
Melton Mowbray	544-579	Midlands 2 East (North)	7
Mersea Island	630-680	London 2 North East	7
Merton	630-680	Surrey 3	11
Middlesbrough	429	National League 3 North	5
Midsomer Norton	734-770	Tribute Somerset Premier	8
Mill Hill	630-680	Herts/Middlesex 2	10
Millbrook	630-680	Hampshire 1	9
Millom	462-495	Cumbria	8
Millwall	630-680	Essex (Canterbury Jack) League 1	9
Milton Keynes	734-770	Southern Counties North	7
Minchinhampton	734-770	Gloucester 3	11
Minehead Barbarians	734-770	Tribute Western Counties West	7
Minety	734-770	Southern Counties South	7
Mistley	630-680	Eastern Counties 2	10
Mitcham	630-680	Surrey 3	11
Moore	462-495	South Lancs/Cheshire Division Two	8
Moortown	462-495	Yorkshire Division Two	8
Moresby	462-495	Cumbria	8
Morganians	734-770	Tribute Somerset 3 South	11
Morley	430	National League 3 North	5

CLUB INDEX

823

CLUB INDEX

Club	Page Ref	League	Level
Morpeth	444	North One East	6
Mosborough	462-495	Yorkshire Division Five	11
Moseley	180	The Championship	2
Moseley Oak	544-579	Midlands 3 West (North)	8
Mossley Hill	462-495	North Lancashire Division Two	9
Mounts Bay	396	National League 2 South	4
Nailsea & Backwell	734-770	Tribute Somerset 1	9
Netherhall	462-495	North Lancs/Cumbria	7
New Ash Green	630-680	Kent 2	10
New Brighton	450	North One West	6
New Cross	734-770	Tribute Devon One North & East	9
New Milton & District	630-680	Hampshire 1	9
Newark	525	Midlands 1 East	6
Newbold on Avon	544-579	Midlands 2 West (South)	7
Newbury Blues	270	National League 1	3
Newbury Stags	734-770	Southern Counties North	7
Newcastle (Staffs)	544-579	Midlands 3 West (North)	8
Newcastle Falcons	86	The Guinness Premiership	1
Newent	734-770	Gloucester 3	11
Newmarket	630-680	Eastern Counties 1	9
Newport (Salop)	515	National Division Three Midlands	5
Newquay Hornets	734-770	Tribute Western Counties West	7
Newton Abbot	713	Tribute South West 1 West	6
Newton Aycliffe	462-495	Durham/Northumberland Division Three	9
Newton-le-Willows	462-495	North Lancashire Division Two	9
Nomads	630-680	Hampshire 2	10
North Bristol	734-770	Tribute Western Counties North	7
North Dorset	734-770	Southern Counties South	7
North Hykeham	544-579	Midlands 5 East (North)	10
North Manchester	462-495	North Lancashire Division Two	9
North Petherton	734-770	Tribute Western Counties West	7
North Ribblesdale	462-495	Yorkshire Division Two	8
North Shields	462-495	Durham/Northumberland Division Two	8
North Tawton	734-770	Tribute Devon One North & East	9
North Walsham	597	National 3 London & SE	5
Northallerton	462-495	Yorkshire Division Three	9
Northampton	92	The Guinness Premiership	1
Northampton BBOB	544-579	Midlands 2 East (South)	7
Northampton Casuals	544-579	Midlands 3 East (South)	8
Northampton Mens Own	544-579	Midlands 3 East (South)	8
Northampton Old Scouts	544-579	Midlands 2 East (South)	7
Northern	462-495	Durham/Northumberland Division One	7
Northolt	630-680	Herts/Middlesex 4	12
Northwich	450	North One West	6
Norwich	630-680	London 2 North East	7
Nottingham	186	The Championship	2
Nottingham Boots Corsairs	544-579	Midlands 5 East (North)	10
Nottingham Casuals	544-579	Midlands 3 East (North)	8
Nottingham Moderns	544-579	Midlands 2 East (North)	7
Nottinghamians	544-579	Midlands 4 East (North)	9
Nuneaton	276	National League 1	3
Nuneaton Old Edwardians	531	Midlands 1 West	6
Oadby Wyggestonians	544-579	Midlands East (South) B	9
Oakham	544-579	Midlands 3 East (North)	8
Oakmedians	707	South West 1 East	6
Okehampton	734-770	Tribute Western Counties West	7
Old Abbotstonians	630-680	Herts/Middlesex 1	9
Old Actonians	630-680	Herts/Middlesex 1	9

Club	Page Ref	League	Level
Old Albanians	598	National 3 London & SE	5
Old Alleynians	630-680	London 3 South West	8
Old Amplefordians	630-680	Surrey 3	11
Old Ashmoleans	630-680	London 3 North West	8
Old Bedians	462-495	North Lancashire Division One	8
Old Blues	630-680	Surrey 2	10
Old Brentwoods	630-680	Essex (Canterbury Jack) League 1	9
Old Bristolians	734-770	Gloucester 1	9
Old Brodleians	444	North One East	6
Old Caterhamians	630-680	Surrey 2	10
Old Centralians	734-770	Tribute Western Counties North	7
Old Colfeians	614	London 1 South	6
Old Colstonians	734-770	Gloucester Premier	8
Old Cooperians	630-680	Essex (Canterbury Jack) League 1	9
Old Coventrians	544-579	Midlands 2 West (South)	7
Old Cranleighans	630-680	Surrey 2	10
Old Crossleyans	444	North One East	6
Old Cryptians	734-770	Gloucester 1	9
Old Culverhaysians	734-770	Tribute Somerset 1	9
Old Dunstonians	630-680	London 2 South East	7
Old Elizabethans	734-770	Gloucester 2	10
Old Elthamians	614	London 1 South	6
Old Emanuel	630-680	Surrey 2	10
Old Freemens	630-680	Surrey 1	9
Old Glynonians	630-680	Surrey 4	12
Old Grammarians	630-680	Herts/Middlesex 1	9
Old Gravesendians	630-680	London 3 South East	8
Old Griffinians	544-579	Midlands 4 West (North)	9
Old Grovians	462-495	Yorkshire Division Four	10
Old Haberdashers	630-680	Herts/Middlesex 1	9
Old Haileyburians	630-680	Surrey 2	10
Old Halesonians	531	Midlands 1 West	6
Old Hamptonians	630-680	London 3 North West	8
Old Isleworthians	630-680	Herts/Middlesex 2	10
Old Laurentians	544-579	Midlands 2 West (South)	7
Old Leamingtonians	544-579	Midlands 3 West (South)	8
Old Merchant Taylors'	630-680	London 3 North West	8
Old Mid-Whitgiftian	630-680	London 3 South West	8
Old Millhillians	630-680	Herts/Middlesex 2	10
Old Modernians	462-495	Yorkshire Division Three	9
Old Newtonians	544-579	Midlands 2 East (South)	7
Old Northamptonians	526	Midlands 1 East	6
Old Olavians	630-680	Kent 1	9
Old Otliensians	462-495	Yorkshire Division Three	9
Old Oundelians	630-680	Surrey 3	11
Old Patesians	696	National League 3 South West	5
Old Paulines	630-680	London 3 South West	8
Old Plymothian & Mannamedian	734-770	Tribute Cornwall/Devon	8
Old Priorians	630-680	Herts/Middlesex 2	10
Old Radleian	630-680	Surrey 3	11
Old Redcliffians	734-770	Tribute Western Counties North	7
Old Reigatian	630-680	London 2 South East	7
Old Richians	734-770	Gloucester Premier	8
Old Rishworthian	462-495	Yorkshire Division Three	9
Old Rutlishians	630-680	Surrey 2	10
Old Saltleians	544-579	Midlands 2 West (North)	7
Old Streetonians	630-680	London 3 North West	8
Old Sulians	734-770	Tribute Somerset Premier	8

CLUB INDEX

825

CLUB INDEX

Club	Page Ref	League	Level
Old Technicians	734-770	Tribute Devon One South & West	9
Old Tiffinians	630-680	Surrey 3	11
Old Tottonians	630-680	Herts/Middlesex 3	11
Old Walcountians	630-680	Surrey 1	9
Old Wellingtonians	630-680	London 3 South West	8
Old Wheatleyans	544-579	Midlands 5 West (South East)	10
Old Whitgiftians	630-680	Surrey 1	9
Old Williamsonians	630-680	Kent 2	10
Old Wimbledonians	630-680	London 3 South West	8
Old Yardleians	544-579	Midlands 3 West (North)	8
Oldershaw	462-495	South Lancs/Cheshire Division Two	8
Oldfield Old Boys	734-770	Southern Counties South	7
Oldham	462-495	North Lancs/Cumbria	7
Ollerton	544-579	Midlands 5 East (North)	10
Olney	707	South West 1 East	6
Ongar	630-680	Essex (Spitfire) League 2	10
Ormskirk	462-495	South Lancs/Cheshire Division One	7
Orpington	630-680	Kent 2	10
Orrell Anvils	462-495	South Lancs/Cheshire Division Two	8
Ossett	462-495	Yorkshire Division Four	10
Oswestry	462-495	South Lancs/Cheshire Division One	7
Otley	282	National League 1	3
Otley Knights	462-495	Yorkshire Division Six	12
Oundle	544-579	Midlands East (South) A	9
Overton	630-680	Hampshire 2	10
Oxford	734-770	Berks/Bucks & Oxon Premier	8
Oxford Harlequins	697	National League 3 South West	5
Paignton	714	Tribute South West 1 West	6
Painswick	734-770	Gloucester 1	9
Park House	630-680	London 3 South East	8
Parkonians	462-495	South Lancs/Cheshire Division Three	9
Paviors	526	Midlands 1 East	6
Paxton Pumas	630-680	Hampshire 2	10
Pegasus Palmerians	630-680	Essex (Spitfire) League 2	10
Pelhamians	630-680	Surrey 4	12
Penrith	431	National League 3 North	5
Penryn	734-770	Tribute Western Counties West	7
Penzance/Newlyn	192	The Championship	2
Percy Park	445	North One East	6
Perranporth	734-770	Tribute Cornwall League	9
Pershore	544-579	Midlands 3 West (South)	8
Peterborough	516	National Division Three Midlands	5
Peterborough Lions	544-579	Midlands 2 East (South)	7
Petersfield	630-680	Hampshire 1	9
Pewsey Vale	734-770	Dorset & Wilts 2 North	9
Phantoms	630-680	Essex (Spitfire) League 2	10
Phoenix	734-770	Berks/Bucks & Oxon Premier	8
Pinley	544-579	Midlands 4 West (South)	9
Pinner & Grammarians	630-680	Herts/Middlesex 3	11
Plymouth Argaum	734-770	Tribute Devon One South & West	9
Plymouth Barbarians	734-770	Tribute Devon One South & West	9
Plymouth Albion	198	The Championship	2
Plympton Victoria	734-770	Tribute Devon One South & West	9
Plymstock Albion Oaks	734-770	Tribute Cornwall/Devon	8
Pocklington	462-495	Yorkshire Division Two	8
Pontefract	445	North One East	6
Pontefract Pythons	462-495	Yorkshire Division Five	11
Ponteland	462-495	Durham/Northumberland Division Two	8

Club	Page Ref	League	Level
Poole	734-770	Dorset & Wilts 3 South	10
Port Sunlight	462-495	South Lancs/Cheshire Division Three	9
Portsmouth	599	National 3 London & SE	5
Prenton	462-495	South Lancs/Cheshire Division Three	9
Preston Grasshoppers	354	National League 2 North	4
Princes Risborough	734-770	Berks/Bucks & Oxon 2 North	10
Prudhoe & Stocksfield	462-495	Durham/Northumberland Division Three	9
Puddletown	734-770	Dorset & Wilts 1 South	8
Pulborough	630-680	Sussex 1	9
Purley John Fisher	630-680	London 2 South East	7
Queens	544-579	Midlands 3 East (South)	8
Quintin	630-680	Herts/Middlesex 2	10
Ramsey (IoM)	462-495	South Lancs/Cheshire Division Three	9
Rawmarsh	462-495	Yorkshire Division Six	12
Raynes Park	630-680	Surrey 2	10
Reading	698	National League 3 South West	5
Reading Abbey	707	South West 1 East	6
Redcar	462-495	Durham/Northumberland Division One	7
Redditch	544-579	Midlands 3 West (South)	8
Redingensians	699	National League 3 South West	5
Redruth	288	National League 1	3
Redruth Albany	734-770	Tribute Cornwall League	9
Reigate	630-680	Surrey 4	12
Richmond	398	National League 2 South	4
Ripon	462-495	Yorkshire Division Two	8
Rochdale	432	National League 3 North	5
Rochford Hundred	607	London 1 North	6
Rolls Royce	544-579	Midlands 4 East (North)	9
Romford & Gidea Park	630-680	London 2 North East	7
Romsey	630-680	Hampshire 1	9
Roseland	734-770	Tribute Cornwall League	9
Ross On Wye	734-770	Gloucester Premier	8
Rossendale	433	National League 3 North	5
Rossington Hornets	462-495	Yorkshire Division Six	12
Rosslyn Park	400	National League 2 South	4
Rotherham	204	The Championship	2
Rotherham Phoenix	462-495	Yorkshire Division Four	10
Roundhegians	462-495	Yorkshire Division Three	9
Royston	630-680	Herts/Middlesex 2	10
Rugby Lions	356	National League 2 North	4
Rugby St Andrews	544-579	Midlands 3 East (South)	8
Rugby Welsh	544-579	Midlands 4 West (South)	9
Rugeley	544-579	Midlands 4 West (North)	9
Ruislip	608	London 1 North	6
Runwell Wyverns	630-680	Essex (Spitfire) League 2	10
Rushden & Higham	544-579	Midlands East (South) A	9
Ruskin Park	462-495	South Lancs/Cheshire Division Two	8
Rye	630-680	Sussex 1	9
Ryton	462-495	Durham/Northumberland Division One	7
Saffron Walden	630-680	London 2 North East	7
Salcombe	734-770	Tribute Devon One South & West	9
Sale	462-495	South Lancs/Cheshire Division One	7
Sale Sharks	98	The Guinness Premiership	1
Salisbury	708	South West 1 East	6
Saltash	734-770	Tribute Cornwall/Devon	8
Sandal	445	North One East	6
Sandbach	450	North One West	6
Sandown & Shanklin	630-680	London 3 South West	8

CLUB INDEX

827

CLUB INDEX

Club	Page Ref	League	Level
Saracens	104	The Guinness Premiership	1
Saracens Amateurs	630-680	Herts/Middlesex 1	9
Scarborough	462-495	Yorkshire Division One	7
Scunthorpe	526	Midlands 1 East	6
Seaford	630-680	Sussex 1	9
Seaham	462-495	Durham/Northumberland Division Three	9
Seaton Carew	462-495	Durham/Northumberland Division Two	8
Sedgefield	462-495	Durham/Northumberland Division Three	9
Sedgley Park	292	National League 1	3
Sefton	462-495	South Lancs/Cheshire Division Two	8
Selby	462-495	Yorkshire Division One	7
Sevenoaks	630-680	London 2 South East	7
Sheffield	462-495	Yorkshire Division One	7
Sheffield Medicals	462-495	Yorkshire Division Four	10
Sheffield Oaks	462-495	Yorkshire Division Six	12
Sheffield Tigers	434	National League 3 North	5
Shelford	402	National League 2 South	4
Sheppey	630-680	Kent 1	9
Sherborne	734-770	Southern Counties South	7
Shipston on Stour	544-579	Midlands 3 West (South)	8
Shooters Hill	630-680	Kent 2	10
Shrewsbury	544-579	Midlands 2 West (North)	7
Sidcup	614	London 1 South	6
Sidmouth	714	Tribute South West 1 West	6
Silhillians	544-579	Midlands 2 West (South)	7
Sittingbourne	630-680	Kent 1	9
Skegness	544-579	Midlands 4 East (North)	9
Skipton	462-495	Yorkshire Division One	7
Sleaford	544-579	Midlands 2 East (North)	7
Slough	734-770	Southern Counties North	7
Smiths (Industries)	734-770	Gloucester 3	11
Solihull	532	Midlands 1 West	6
Somerton	734-770	Tribute Somerset 2 South	10
South Leicester	517	National Division Three Midlands	5
South Molton	734-770	Tribute Devon One North & East	9
South Park Rangers	462-495	Durham/Northumberland Division Three	9
South Tyneside College	462-495	Durham/Northumberland Division Three	9
South Wilts	734-770	Dorset & Wilts 2 South	9
South Woodham Ferrers	630-680	London 3 North East	8
Southam	544-579	Midlands 3 West (South)	8
Southampton	630-680	Hampshire 1	9
Southend	404	National League 2 South	4
Southgate	630-680	Herts/Middlesex 4	12
Southmead	734-770	Tribute Western Counties North	7
Southport	462-495	South Lancs/Cheshire Division Two	8
Southwell	544-579	Midlands 3 East (North)	8
Southwold	630-680	Eastern Counties 1	9
Spalding	544-579	Midlands 2 East (North)	7
Spartans (Gloucester)	734-770	Gloucester Premier	8
Spartans (Midlands)	544-579	Midlands 2 West (South)	7
St Agnes	734-770	Tribute Cornwall League	9
St Albans	630-680	London 2 North West	7
St Austell	734-770	Tribute Cornwall/Devon	8
St Benedicts	462-495	North Lancs/Cumbria	7
St Bernadettes Old Boys	734-770	Tribute Somerset Premier	8
St Brendan's Old Boys	734-770	Gloucester 2	10
St Columba & Torpoint	734-770	Tribute Devon One South & West	9
St Day	734-770	Tribute Cornwall League	9

828

Club	Page Ref	League	Level
St Edward's O.B.	462-495	North Lancashire Division Two	9
St Ives (Midlands)	544-579	Midlands East (South) A	9
St Ives (SW)	714	Tribute South West 1 West	6
St Just	734-770	Tribute Cornwall League	9
St Leonards	544-579	Midlands 4 West (North)	9
St Mary's O.B. (Lancs)	462-495	North Lancashire Division Two	9
St Mary's Old Boys (SW)	715	Tribute South West 1 West	6
St Neots	544-579	Midlands East (South) A	9
Stafford	544-579	Midlands 2 West (North)	7
Staines	608	London 1 North	6
Stamford	544-579	Midlands East (South) B	9
Stamford College Old Boys	544-579	Midlands East (South) B	9
Stanford Le Hope	630-680	Essex (Spitfire) League 2	10
Stanley Rodillians	462-495	Yorkshire Division Five	11
Stevenage Town	608	London 1 North	6
Stewarts & Lloyds	527	Midlands 1 East	6
Stithians	734-770	Tribute Cornwall/Devon	8
Stockport	435	National League 3 North	5
Stocksbridge	462-495	Yorkshire Division Five	11
Stockton	462-495	Durham/Northumberland Division One	7
Stockwood Park	544-579	Midlands 3 East (South)	8
Stoke Old Boys	544-579	Midlands 4 West (South)	9
Stoke on Trent	532	Midlands 1 West	6
Stone	544-579	Midlands 5 West (North)	10
Stoneham	630-680	Hampshire 2	10
Stoneygate	544-579	Midlands East (South) B	9
Stothert & Pitt	734-770	Tribute Somerset Premier	8
Stourbridge	298	National League 1	3
Stourbridge Lions	544-579	Midlands 2 West (North)	7
Stourport	544-579	Midlands 5 West (South West)	10
Stowmarket	630-680	Eastern Counties 1	9
Stow-on-the-Wold	734-770	Berks/Bucks & Oxon Premier	8
Stratford Upon Avon	532	Midlands 1 West	6
Streatham-Croydon	630-680	Surrey 3	11
Stroud	734-770	Tribute Western Counties North	7
Sudbury	630-680	London 2 North East	7
Sudbury & London Springboks	630-680	Herts/Middlesex 4	12
Sunderland	462-495	Durham/Northumberland Division One	7
Supermarine	734-770	Dorset & Wilts 1 North	8
Sutton & Epsom	600	National 3 London & SE	5
Sutton Benger	734-770	Dorset & Wilts 1 North	8
Sutton Coldfield	533	Midlands 1 West	6
Swaffham	630-680	Eastern Counties 2	10
Swanage & Wareham	708	South West 1 East	6
Swindon	734-770	Southern Counties North	7
Swindon College Old Boys	734-770	Berks/Bucks & Oxon Premier	8
Syston	527	Midlands 1 East	6
Tabard	630-680	London 2 North West	7
Tadley	734-770	Southern Counties South	7
Tamar Saracens	734-770	Tribute Devon One South & West	9
Tamworth	544-579	Midlands 3 West (North)	8
Tarleton	462-495	North Lancashire Division One	8
Taunton	700	National League 3 South West	5
Tavistock	734-770	Tribute Western Counties West	7
Team Northumbria	462-495	Durham/Northumberland Division One	7
Teddington	630-680	Surrey 1	9
Teignmouth	734-770	Tribute Cornwall/Devon	8
Telford Hornets	544-579	Midlands 3 West (North)	8

CLUB INDEX

Club	Page Ref	League	Level
Tenbury	544-579	Midlands 5 West (South West)	10
Tetbury	734-770	Gloucester 2	10
Tewkesbury	734-770	Gloucester Premier	8
Thames	630-680	Essex (Canterbury Jack) League 1	9
Thamesians	630-680	Herts/Middlesex 3	11
Thanet Wanderers	614	London 1 South	6
Thatcham	734-770	Berks/Bucks & Oxon Premier	8
Thetford	630-680	Eastern Counties 1	9
Thornbury	734-770	Tribute Western Counties North	7
Thornensians	462-495	Yorkshire Division Three	9
Thorney	544-579	Midlands East (South) B	9
Thurrock	630-680	London 2 North East	7
Thurston	630-680	Eastern Counties 1	9
Tiverton	734-770	Tribute Western Counties West	7
To be arranged 1	462-495	Durham/Northumberland Division One	7
Tonbridge Juddian	630-680	London 2 South East	7
Topsham	734-770	Tribute Devon One North & East	9
Tor	734-770	Tribute Somerset Premier	8
Torquay Athletic	715	Tribute South West 1 West	6
Torrington	734-770	Tribute Cornwall/Devon	8
Totnes	734-770	Tribute Devon One North & East	9
Tottonians	630-680	London 2 South West	7
Towcestrians	544-579	Midlands 2 East (South)	7
Trafford MV	462-495	North Lancashire Division One	8
Tredworth	734-770	Gloucester 2	10
Trentham	462-495	South Lancs/Cheshire Division Two	8
Tring	601	National 3 London & SE	5
Trinity Guild	544-579	Midlands 5 West (South East)	10
Trojans	630-680	London 2 South West	7
Trowbridge	708	South West 1 East	6
Truro	734-770	Tribute Western Counties West	7
Tunbridge Wells	615	London 1 South	6
Tupton	544-579	Midlands 5 East (North)	10
Twickenham	630-680	London 2 South West	7
Tyldesley	451	North One West	6
Tynedale	302	National League 1	3
U.C.S. Old Boys	630-680	London 2 North West	7
Uckfield	630-680	Sussex 1	9
United Services, Portsmouth	630-680	Hampshire 1	9
University Of Derby	544-579	Midlands 5 East (North)	10
University of Leeds	462-495	Yorkshire Division Six	12
Upminster	630-680	London 3 North East	8
Upper Clapton	630-680	Essex (Canterbury Jack) League 1	9
Upper Eden	462-495	North Lancs/Cumbria	7
Upton-on-Severn	544-579	Midlands 3 West (South)	8
Uttoxeter	544-579	Midlands 4 East (North)	9
Uxbridge	630-680	Herts/Middlesex 2	10
Vagabonds (I.O.M.)	462-495	South Lancs/Cheshire Division One	7
Vale of Lune	451	North One West	6
Vauxhall Motors	544-579	Midlands 3 East (South)	8
Ventnor	630-680	Hampshire 2	10
Veor	734-770	Tribute Cornwall League	9
Verulamians	630-680	Herts/Middlesex 1	9
Verwood	630-680	Hampshire 2	10
Veseyans	544-579	Midlands 3 West (North)	8
Vigo	630-680	Kent 1	9
Vipers	544-579	Midlands 2 East (South)	7
Wadebridge Camels	734-770	Tribute Western Counties West	7

Club	Page Ref	League	Level
Walcot	709	South West 1 East	6
Wallasey	462-495	South Lancs/Cheshire Division Two	8
Wallingford	709	South West 1 East	6
Wallsend	462-495	Durham/Northumberland Division One	7
Walsall	533	Midlands 1 West	6
Wandsworthians	630-680	Surrey 4	12
Wanstead	630-680	London 3 North East	8
Warley	544-579	Midlands 5 West (North)	10
Warlingham	630-680	London 2 South East	7
Warminster	734-770	Dorset & Wilts 1 South	8
Warrington	462-495	South Lancs/Cheshire Division One	7
Warwickian	544-579	Midlands 5 West (South East)	10
Washington	462-495	Durham/Northumberland Division Three	9
Wasps	630-680	Herts/Middlesex 1	9
Waterloo	358	National League 2 North	4
Watford	630-680	Herts/Middlesex 3	11
Wath Upon Dearne	462-495	Yorkshire Division Three	9
Wednesbury	544-579	Midlands 3 West (North)	8
Wellesbourne	544-579	Midlands 5 West (South East)	10
Wellingborough	527	Midlands 1 East	6
Wellingborough O.G.	544-579	Midlands East (South) A	9
Wellington	734-770	Tribute Cornwall/Devon	8
Wells	734-770	Tribute Somerset Premier	8
Welwyn	609	London 1 North	6
Wessex	734-770	Tribute Devon One North & East	9
West Bridgford	544-579	Midlands 2 East (North)	7
West Hartlepool	436	National League 3 North	5
West Leeds	462-495	Yorkshire Division Two	8
West London	630-680	London 3 North West	8
West Norfolk	630-680	London 3 North East	8
West Park (St Helens)	437	National League 3 North	5
West Park Leeds	462-495	Yorkshire Division Two	8
West Park Warriors	462-495	North Lancashire Division Two	9
Westbury	734-770	Dorset & Wilts 1 South	8
Westbury-on-Severn	734-770	Gloucester 2	10
Westcliff	609	London 1 North	6
Westcombe Park	406	National League 2 South	4
Westoe	360	National League 2 North	4
Weston-Super-Mare	701	National League 3 South West	5
Westwood	544-579	Midlands East (South) A	9
Wetherby	462-495	Yorkshire Division Six	12
Weybridge Vandals	630-680	London 2 South West	7
Weymouth	734-770	Dorset & Wilts 1 South	8
Wharfedale	306	National League 1	3
Wheatley	734-770	Berks/Bucks & Oxon 1 North	9
Wheatley Hills	462-495	Yorkshire Division One	7
Wheaton Aston	544-579	Midlands 5 West (North)	10
Wheatsheaf Cabin Crew	734-770	Dorset & Wilts 2 South	9
Whitby	462-495	Durham/Northumberland Division Three	9
Whitchurch	533	Midlands 1 West	6
Whitehall	734-770	Gloucester Premier	8
Whitehaven	462-495	Cumbria	8
Whitley Bay Rockcliff	462-495	Durham/Northumberland Division Two	8
Whitstable	630-680	London 3 South East	8
Whittington	544-579	Midlands 5 West (North)	10
Wibsey	462-495	Yorkshire Division Five	11
Widden Old Boys	734-770	Tribute Western Counties North	7
Widnes	462-495	South Lancs/Cheshire Division One	7

CLUB INDEX

Club	Page Ref	League	Level
Wigan	462-495	South Lancs/Cheshire Division One	7
Wigton	462-495	North Lancs/Cumbria	7
Wigton Wanderers	462-495	Cumbria	8
Willenhall	544-579	Midlands 2 West (North)	7
Wilmslow	451	North One West	6
Wimbledon	615	London 1 South	6
Wimborne	734-770	Southern Counties South	7
Wincanton	734-770	Dorset & Wilts 3 South	10
Winchester	630-680	London 2 South West	7
Windermere	462-495	North Lancashire Division One	8
Windsor	734-770	Southern Counties North	7
Winlaton Vulcans	462-495	Durham/Northumberland Division Two	8
Winnington Park	462-495	South Lancs/Cheshire Division One	7
Winscombe	734-770	Tribute Somerset Premier	8
Winslow	734-770	Berks/Bucks & Oxon 2 North	10
Wirral	462-495	South Lancs/Cheshire Division One	7
Wisbech	630-680	London 3 North East	8
Witham	630-680	Essex (Spitfire) League 2	10
Withycombe	734-770	Tribute Western Counties West	7
Witney	734-770	Southern Counties North	7
Wiveliscombe	734-770	Tribute Somerset 1	9
Woking	630-680	Surrey 4	12
Wolverhampton	544-579	Midlands 2 West (North)	7
Woodbridge	630-680	Eastern Counties 1	9
Woodford	609	London 1 North	6
Woodrush	544-579	Midlands 3 West (South)	8
Wootton Bassett	709	South West 1 East	6
Worcester	110	The Guinness Premiership	1
Worcester Wanderers	544-579	Midlands 2 West (South)	7
Workington	462-495	North Lancs/Cumbria	7
Workington Steelers	462-495	Cumbria	8
Worksop	544-579	Midlands 3 East (North)	8
Worth Old Boys	630-680	Surrey 3	11
Worthing	408	National League 2 South	4
Wotton	734-770	Gloucester 3	11
Writtle Wanderers	630-680	Essex (Spitfire) League 2	10
Wymondham	630-680	London 3 North East	8
Wyvern	734-770	Tribute Somerset 3 South	11
Yardley & District	544-579	Midlands 4 West (North)	9
Yarm	462-495	Durham/Northumberland Division Two	8
Yarnbury	462-495	Yorkshire Division One	7
Yatton	504	Tribute South West 1 West	6
York	462-495	Yorkshire Division One	7
York Railway Institute	462-495	Yorkshire Division Four	10

832